Gleim Publications, Inc., offers five university-level study systems:

*Auditing & Systems Exam Questions and Explanations with Exam Prep CD-Rom*
*Business Law/Legal Studies Exam Questions and Explanations with Exam Prep CD-Rom*
*Federal Tax Exam Questions and Explanations with Exam Prep CD-Rom*
*Financial Accounting Exam Questions and Explanations with Exam Prep CD-Rom*
*Cost/Managerial Accounting Exam Questions and Explanations with Exam Prep CD-Rom*

The following is a list of Gleim examination review systems:

*CIA Review: Part I, Internal Audit Role in Governance, Risk, and Control*
*CIA Review: Part II, Conducting the Internal Audit Engagement*
*CIA Review: Part III, Business Analysis and Information Technology*
*CIA Review: Part IV, Business Management Skills*

*CMA Review: Part 1, Business Analysis*
*CMA Review: Part 2, Management Accounting and Reporting*
*CMA Review: Part 3, Strategic Management*
*CMA Review: Part 4, Business Applications*

*CPA Review: Financial*
*CPA Review: Auditing*
*CPA Review: Business*
*CPA Review: Regulation*

*EA Review: Part 1, Individuals*
*EA Review: Part 2, Businesses*
*EA Review: Part 3, Representation, Practice, and Procedures*

An order form is provided at the back of this book or contact us at www.gleim.com or (800) 87-GLEIM.

**Groundwood Paper and Highlighters** — All Gleim books are printed on high quality groundwood paper. We recommend you use a non-bleed-through (dry) highlighter (e.g., the Avery *Glidestick*™ -- ask for it at your local office supply store) when highlighting page items within these books.

D1361749

# REVIEWERS AND CONTRIBUTORS

Garrett Gleim, B.S., University of Pennsylvania, is one of our vice presidents. Mr. Gleim coordinated the production staff, reviewed the manuscript, and provided production assistance throughout the project.

Grady M. Irwin, J.D., is a graduate of the University of Florida College of Law, and he has taught in the University of Florida College of Business. Mr. Irwin provided substantial editorial assistance throughout the project.

John F. Rebstock, CIA, B.S., Fisher School of Accounting, University of Florida, specializes in ensuring that our answer explanations and Knowledge Transfer Outlines are user-friendly. Mr. Rebstock reviewed portions of the manuscript.

Stewart B. White, B.M., *Cum Laude*, University of Richmond, B.S., Virginia Commonwealth University, has passed the CPA and CISA exams and has worked in the fields of retail management, financial audit, IT audit, COBOL programming, and data warehouse management. He extensively revised portions of this manuscript.

# A PERSONAL THANKS

This manual would not have been possible without the extraordinary effort and dedication of Julie Cutlip, Megan Ford, Mumbi Ngugi, Eileen Nickl, and Teresa Soard, who typed the entire manuscript and all revisions and drafted and laid out the diagrams and illustrations in this book.

The authors appreciate the proofreading and production assistance of Daniel Bonilla, Katherine Goodrich, Emily Gorovsky, James Harvin, Jean Marzullo, Shane Rapp, and Martha Willis.

The authors also appreciate the critical reading assistance of Lance Cottle, Seth Kaye, Maggie Lee, Patrick Osborn, and Danielle Sheets.

Finally, we appreciate the encouragement, support, and tolerance of our families throughout this project.

# NONDISCLOSED EXAM

The CMA is a nondisclosed exam, and you will encounter questions that may be totally unfamiliar to you. That is the nature of nondisclosed exams. Please follow the study suggestions on pages 12 through 14. We have the best and most efficient CMA exam prep system for success.

**THIRTEENTH EDITION**

# GLEIM's

# CMA Review

## Part 2
## Management Accounting and Reporting

by

Irvin N. Gleim, Ph.D., CPA, CIA, CMA, CFM

and

Dale L. Flesher, Ph.D., CPA, CIA, CMA, CFM

### ABOUT THE AUTHORS

Irvin N. Gleim is Professor Emeritus in the Fisher School of Accounting at the University of Florida and is a member of the American Accounting Association, Academy of Legal Studies in Business, American Institute of Certified Public Accountants, Association of Government Accountants, Florida Institute of Certified Public Accountants, The Institute of Internal Auditors, and the Institute of Management Accountants. He has had articles published in the *Journal of Accountancy, The Accounting Review,* and *The American Business Law Journal* and is author/coauthor of numerous accounting and aviation books and CPE courses.

Dale L. Flesher is the Arthur Andersen Alumni Professor in the School of Accountancy at the University of Mississippi and has written over 300 articles for business and professional journals, including *Management Accounting, Journal of Accountancy,* and *The Accounting Review,* as well as numerous books. He is a member of the Institute of Management Accountants, American Institute of Certified Public Accountants, The Institute of Internal Auditors, American Accounting Association, and American Taxation Association. He is a past editor of *The Accounting Historians' Journal* and is a trustee and past president of the Academy of Accounting Historians.

**Gleim Publications, Inc.**
P.O. Box 12848
University Station
Gainesville, Florida 32604
(800) 87-GLEIM or (800) 874-5346
(352) 375-0772
FAX: (352) 375-6940
Internet: www.gleim.com
E-mail: admin@gleim.com

This is the first printing of the thirteenth edition of *CMA Review: Part 2*. Please e-mail update@gleim.com with **CMA 2 13-1** included in the subject or text. You will receive our current update as a reply. Updates are available until the next edition is published.

EXAMPLE:

To:        update@gleim.com
From:      your e-mail address
Subject:   **CMA 2 13-1**

ISSN: 1093-2550

ISBN: 1-58194-506-X

## ACKNOWLEDGMENTS

The authors are indebted to the Institute of Certified Management Accountants for permission to use problem materials from past CMA examinations. Questions and unofficial answers from the Certified Management Accountant Examinations, copyright © 1982 through 1997 by the Institute of Management Accountants, are reprinted and/or adapted with permission.

The authors are also indebted to The Institute of Internal Auditors, Inc. for permission to use Certified Internal Auditor Examination Questions and Suggested Solutions, copyright © 1985 through 1996 by The Institute of Internal Auditors, Inc.

The authors also appreciate and thank the American Institute of Certified Public Accountants, Inc. Material from Uniform Certified Public Accountant Examination questions and unofficial answers, Copyright © 1981-2003 by the American Institute of Certified Public Accountants, Inc., is reprinted and/or adapted with permission.

This publication was printed and bound by Corley Printing Company, St. Louis, MO, a registered ISO-9002 company. More information about Corley Printing Company is available at www.corleyprinting.com or by calling (314) 739-3777.

Visit our website (www.gleim.com) for the latest updates and information on all of our products.

*This publication is designed to provide accurate and authoritative information with regard to the subject matter covered. It is sold with the understanding that the publisher is not engaged in rendering legal, accounting, or other professional service.*

*If legal advice or other expert assistance is required, the services of a competent professional person should be sought.*

(From a declaration of principles jointly adopted by a Committee of the American Bar Association and a Committee of Publishers.)

# TABLE OF CONTENTS

# PREFACE FOR CMA PART 2 CANDIDATES

The purpose of this book is to help **you** prepare **yourself** to pass Part 2 of the CMA examination under the CMA exam guidelines effective July 1, 2004. The overriding consideration is to provide an inexpensive, effective, and easy-to-use study program. This manual

1. Defines topics tested on Part 2 of the CMA exam.

2. Explains how to optimize your exam score by analyzing how the CMA exam is constructed, administered, and graded.

3. Outlines the new subject matter tested on Part 2 of the CMA exam in 20 easy-to-use study units.

4. Presents questions to prepare you to answer questions on Part 2 of the CMA exam. The answer explanations are presented to the immediate right of the questions for your convenience. You MUST cover these answers until you commit to the correct answer. Use the bookmark provided at the back of this book.

5. Illustrates individual question answering techniques to minimize selecting incorrect answers and to maximize your exam score.

6. Suggests exam-taking techniques to help you maintain control and achieve success.

This is the Thirteenth Edition of *CMA Review* for Part 2, which covers only Part 2 of the CMA exam. This new edition includes the following features and benefits:

1. Gleim's content and structure are organized to closely follow the IMA's Learning Outcome Statements, thus ensuring your study time is spent preparing to Pass the Exam!

2. Core Concepts at the end of each Knowledge Transfer Outline allow CMA candidates to obtain an overview of each study unit, as well as ensure that they understand the basic concepts.

3. Many examples throughout the Knowledge Transfer Outlines clarify harder-to-understand concepts.

4. Comprehensive coverage of all topics including Statement of Financial Accounting Standards 154, the IMA's new *Statement of Ethical Professional Practice*, and information technology.

To maximize the efficiency of your review program, begin by **studying** (not reading) the introduction in this book. "Preparing for and Taking the CMA Exam" is very short but very important. It has been carefully organized and written to provide you with important information to assist you in successfully completing Part 2 of the CMA examination.

Thank you for your interest in our review materials. We very much appreciate the thousands of letters and suggestions we have received from CIA, CMA, and CPA candidates since 1974. Please give us feedback concerning this book. Do NOT disclose information about individual questions beyond subject matter not covered in our books. Tell us which part and which topics were NOT covered or were inadequately covered. The last page has been designed to help you note corrections and suggestions throughout your study process. Please tear it out and mail or fax it to us with your comments.

Finally, THANK YOU for recommending our products to others.

Good Luck on the Exam,

*Irvin N. Gleim*
*Dale L. Flesher*
September 2006

# PREPARING FOR AND TAKING THE CMA EXAM

## ABOUT THE CMA EXAM

### Introduction

CMA is the acronym for Certified Management Accountant.

The CMA examination has been and will continue to be developed and offered by the Institute of Certified Management Accountants (ICMA) in approximately 200 locations in the U.S. and an additional 200 international locations.

Please note that as of July 1, 2004, the IMA made substantial changes to the CMA exam. Gleim/Flesher Thirteenth Edition *CMA Review* is intended for the newly revised exam. If you have registered for the unchanged exam, which will be available through December 2007, you will need to study using Gleim/Flesher Eleventh Edition *CMA Review*, which will be available as long as the exam is administered. Note: In order to take the unchanged exam, you must have registered with the ICMA prior to June 30, 2004.

All material in this introduction is related to the REVISED CMA EXAM.

*CMA Review: Part 2 contains this 19-page Introduction and 20 study units of outlines and multiple-choice questions that cover all of the material tested on Part 2 of the CMA exam. This Introduction discusses exam content, pass rates, administration, organization, background information, preparing for the CMA exam, and taking the CMA exam. We urge you to read the next 18 pages carefully because they will help you dramatically improve your study and test-taking procedures.*

### Corporate Management Accounting

1. Objective: Maximize the value of the firm by optimizing

   a. Long-term investment strategies
   b. The capital structure, i.e., how these long-term investments are funded
   c. Short-term cash flow management

2. Corporate financial management involves a financial manager, usually a vice-president/chief financial officer, who is assisted by the

   a. Treasurer -- cash, credit, capital outlay management
   b. Controller -- financial, cost, tax accounting

3. All accounting and finance personnel are beneficiaries of CMA participation.

4. The body of knowledge necessary for proficiency in management accounting is set forth in the ICMA's Content Specification Outlines and Learning Outcome Statements for the CMA exam.

5. The diagram below illustrates an entity combining the factors of production into finished goods (arrows to the right) with money flowing to the left.

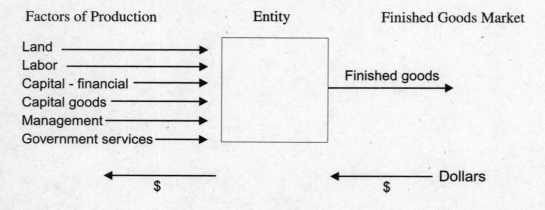

6. Put CMA in perspective when considering the production of goods or services in our capitalistic society. An entity combines the factors of production into finished goods.

    a. Note that the CMA program focuses on financial capital and the other factors of production as well as the finished goods market, while the CEO (chief executive officer) has overall responsibility for the entity's operations.

## Objectives and Content of the CMA Examination

The CMA certification program has four objectives:

1. "To establish management accounting and financial management as recognized professions by identifying the role of the professional, the underlying body of knowledge, and a course of study by which such knowledge is acquired"

2. "To encourage higher educational standards in the management accounting and financial management fields"

3. "To establish an objective measure of an individual's knowledge and competence in the fields of management accounting and financial management"

4. "To encourage continued professional development"

The exam tests the candidates' knowledge and ability with respect to the current state of the fields of management accounting and financial management.

We have arranged the subject matter tested on the CMA examination into 20 study units for each part. Each part is presented in a separate book. All of these books contain review outlines and prior CMA exam questions and answers.

## LISTING OF GLEIM STUDY UNITS*

**Part 1: Business Analysis**

1. Factors Affecting the Firm
2. Consumption and Production
3. Market Structures
4. Macroeconomic Issues, Measures, and Cycles
5. Government Participation in the Economy
6. Comparative Advantage and Free Trade
7. Trade Barriers and Agreements
8. Foreign Exchange
9. Other Global Business Topics
10. Risk Assessment and Controls
11. Internal Auditing
12. Systems Controls and Security Measures
13. Forecasting
14. Linear Programming and Network Analysis
15. Probability, Decision Trees, and Other Techniques
16. The Development of Accounting Standards
17. Financial Statement Assurance
18. Liquidity, Capital Structure, and Solvency
19. Return on Investment, Profitability, and Earnings
20. Other Analytical Issues

**Part 2: Management Accounting and Reporting**

1. Budgeting
2. Cost Management Terminology and Concepts
3. Job-Order Costing, Overhead Costs, and Service Department Allocation
4. Process Costing and Other Cost Accumulation Systems
5. Overview of Information Systems and Systems Development and Design
6. Technology of Information Systems
7. Electronic Commerce and Other Topics
8. Cost and Variance Measures
9. Responsibility Accounting and Financial Measures
10. The Balanced Scorecard and Quality Considerations
11. Overview of External Financial Reporting
12. Overview of Financial Statements
13. Cash and Receivables
14. Inventories and Investments
15. Long-Lived Assets
16. Liabilities
17. Equity and Revenue Recognition
18. Other Income Statement Items
19. Business Combinations and Derivatives
20. SEC Requirements and the Annual Report

**Part 3: Strategic Management**

1. Strategic and Tactical Planning
2. Manufacturing Paradigms
3. Business Process Performance
4. Marketing's Strategic Role within the Firm
5. Marketing Information and Market Segmentation
6. Other Marketing Topics
7. Risk and Return
8. Financial Instruments
9. Cost of Capital
10. Managing Current Assets
11. Financing Current Assets
12. The Decision Process
13. Data Concepts Relevant to Decision Making
14. Cost-Volume-Profit Analysis
15. Marginal Analysis
16. Cost-Based Pricing
17. The Capital Budgeting Process
18. Discounted Cash Flow and Payback
19. Ranking Investment Projects
20. Risk Analysis and Real Options

**Part 4: Business Applications**

1. Organization Structures
2. Jobs and Teams
3. Leadership Styles and Sources of Power
4. Motivational Theories and Diversity Issues
5. Organization Communication
6. Behavior – Alignment of Organizational Goals
7. Behavior – Budgeting and Standard Setting
8. Behavior – Reporting and Performance Evaluation
9. Ethics as Tested on the CMA Exam
10. Part 1 Review – Business Economics and Global Business
11. Part 1 Review – Internal Controls and Quantitative Methods
12. Part 1 Review – Financial Statement Analysis
13. Part 2 Review – Budget Preparation and Cost Management
14. Part 2 Review – Information Management and Performance Measurement
15. Part 2 Review – External Financial Reporting I
16. Part 2 Review – External Financial Reporting II
17. Part 3 Review – Strategic Planning and Strategic Marketing
18. Part 3 Review – Corporate Finance
19. Part 3 Review – Decision Analysis
20. Part 3 Review – Investment Decisions

### *WARNING!!!

About 30% of CMA test questions will require mathematical calculations. Practice computational questions to prepare for exam success!

Each study unit begins with the Learning Outcome Statements from the Institute of Management Accountants, followed by our Knowledge Transfer Outline, then our Core Concepts, and finally multiple-choice questions.

The *CMA Review* study unit titles and organization differ somewhat from the subtopic titles used by the ICMA in its content specification outlines (see the next page) for the CMA exam. The selection of study units for *CMA Review: Part 2* is based on the types and number of questions that have appeared on past CMA exams, as well as the extensiveness of past and expected future exam coverage as defined in both the ICMA Content Specification Outlines and Learning Outcome Statements (LOSs).

## Content Specification Outlines

The ICMA has developed content specification outlines and has committed to follow them on each examination. A complete CSO for Part 2 is presented in Appendix C beginning on page 829. Each examination will cover the major topics specified below; e.g., Budget Preparation will constitute 15% of each Part 2 examination.

Candidates for the CMA designation are expected to have a minimum level of business knowledge that transcends all examination parts. This minimum level includes knowledge of basic financial statements, time value of money concepts, and elementary statistics. Specific discussion of the ICMA's Levels of Performance (A, B, and C) is provided below.

---

### ICMA'S CMA CONTENT SPECIFICATION OVERVIEW

**Part 1: Business Analysis**
(3 hours – 110 questions)

| | | |
|---|---|---|
| Business Economics | 25% | Level B |
| Global Business | 20% | Level B |
| Internal Controls | 15% | Level A |
| Quantitative Methods | 15% | Level B |
| Financial Statement Analysis | 25% | Level B |

**Part 2: Management Accounting and Reporting**
(4 hours – 140 questions)

| | | |
|---|---|---|
| Budget Preparation | 15% | Level C |
| Cost Management | 25% | Level C |
| Information Management | 15% | Level A |
| Performance Measurement | 20% | Level C |
| External Financial Reporting | 25% | Level B |

**Part 3: Strategic Management**
(3 hours – 110 questions)

| | | |
|---|---|---|
| Strategic Planning | 15% | Level B |
| Strategic Marketing | 15% | Level A |
| Corporate Finance | 25% | Level B |
| Decision Analysis | 25% | Level C |
| Investment Decisions | 20% | Level C |

**Part 4: Business Applications (Level C)**
(3 hours – 3-7 essays)

All topics from Parts 1, 2, and 3 plus:

Organization Management
Organization Communication
Behavioral Issues
Ethical Considerations

---

## Learning Outcome Statements

In addition to the Content Specification Outlines, the ICMA has published Learning Outcome Statements (LOSs) that specify what you should be able to do. Before you study our knowledge transfer outline, read the LOS at the beginning of each study unit. This will alert you to what is expected and required of you.

## Level of Performance Required

All parts of the exam appear to be tested at the skill level of a final examination for the appropriate course at a good school of business. The ICMA has specified three levels of coverage as reproduced below and indicated in its content specification outlines. You will evaluate and compare the difficulty of each part of the CMA exam as you work the questions in this book.

**Authors' Note:** Rely on the questions at the end of each study unit in each *CMA Review* book and *CMA Test Prep* CD-Rom.

**Level A:** Requiring the skill levels of knowledge and comprehension.

**Level B:** Requiring the skill levels of knowledge, comprehension, application, and analysis.

**Level C:** Requiring all six skill levels: knowledge, comprehension, application, analysis, synthesis, and evaluation.

See Appendix E for a reprint of the ICMA's discussion of "Types and Levels of Exam Questions."

## Conceptual vs. Calculation Questions

About 30% of CMA Part 2 test questions will be calculations in contrast to conceptual questions. When you take the test, it may appear that more than 40% of the questions are calculation-type because they take longer and are "more difficult."

## How Ethics and Taxes Are Tested

Ethical issues and considerations will be tested on Part 4, Business Applications. At least one question in this part will be devoted to an ethical situation presented in a business-oriented context. Candidates will be expected to evaluate the issues involved and make recommendations for the resolution of the situation.

With regard to federal income taxation issues, candidates will be expected to understand the impact of income taxes when reporting and analyzing financial results. In addition, the tax code provisions that impact decisions (e.g., depreciation, interest, etc.) will be tested. See Appendix A.

## Requirements to Attain the CMA Designation

The CMA designation is granted only by the ICMA. Candidates must complete the following steps to become a CMA:

1.  Become a member of the Institute of Management Accountants. You can submit an application for IMA membership with your application for certification.

2.  Complete the certification information section on the IMA application and register for the CMA examination.

3.  Pass all four parts of the CMA examination. "Continuous candidacy" is required to retain credit after successful completion of one or more parts. "Continuous candidacy" includes IMA membership and, since July 1, 2001, candidates must pass all four parts of the exam within 4 years. The 4-year period begins with the first part passed.

4.  Fulfill or expect to fulfill the education requirements (see below).

5.  Be employed or expect to be employed in a position that meets the experience requirement (see below and next page).

6.  Provide two character references proving you are of good moral character.

7.  Comply with the IMA's Statement of Ethical Professional Practice.

Credit can be retained indefinitely as long as these requirements are fulfilled. Once a designation is earned, the CMA is a member of the Institute of Certified Management Accountants and must comply with the program's CPE requirement and maintain IMA membership in good standing.

## Education and Experience Requirements

Candidates seeking admission to the CMA program must meet one of the following educational credentials:

1.  Hold a baccalaureate degree, in any area, from an accredited college or university. Degrees from foreign institutions must be evaluated by an independent agency approved by the ICMA (visit the IMA website at www.imanet.org for a list of foreign universities that are acceptable without an evaluation); or

2.  Pass the U.S. CPA examination or hold another professional qualification issued in a foreign country that is comparable to the CPA, CMA, etc.; or

3.  Achieve a score in the 50th percentile or higher on either the Graduate Management Admissions Test (GMAT) or the Graduate Record Examination (GRE).

NOTE: Educational credentials may be submitted when applying or at a later date. The educational credentials must qualify in order to be certified.

Two continuous years of **professional experience** in financial management and/or management accounting are required any time prior to or within 7 years of passing the examination.

1. Professional experience shall be defined as full-time continuous experience at a level where judgments are regularly made that employ the principles of financial management and/or management accounting, e.g.,

   a. Financial analysis
   b. Budget preparation
   c. Management information systems analysis
   d. Financial management
   e. Management accounting
   f. Auditing in government, finance, or industry
   g. Management consulting
   h. Auditing in public accounting
   i. Research, teaching, or consulting related to management accounting (for teaching, a significant portion required to be above the principles level)

2. Employment in functions that require the occasional application of financial management or management accounting principles, but are not essentially management accounting oriented, will not satisfy the requirement, e.g.,

   a. Computer operations
   b. Sales and marketing
   c. Manufacturing
   d. Engineering
   e. Personnel
   f. Employment in internships, trainee, clerical, or nontechnical positions

3. Continuous part-time positions of 20 hours per week meeting the definition of qualified experience will count toward the experience requirement at a rate of one year of experience for every two years of part-time employment.

If you have any questions about the acceptability of your work experience or baccalaureate degree, please write or call the ICMA. Include a complete description of your situation. You will receive a response from the ICMA as soon as your request is evaluated.

Institute of Certified Management Accountants
10 Paragon Drive
Montvale, NJ 07645-1718
(201) 573-9000
(800) 638-4427

NOTE: The ICMA Board of Regents has compiled a list of U.S. and international certifications for which they will grant a waiver of Part 1. To be granted the waiver, acceptable proof must be supplied to the ICMA along with the appropriate waiver fee. For example, you can waive Part 1 of the CMA exam if you have passed the U.S. CPA exam. To receive the waiver, you must request that a letter from your state board be sent directly to the ICMA confirming your licensure or passing of the U.S. CPA exam; copies are not acceptable. Visit www.imanet.org for the complete listing of accepted certifications.

## The Institute of Management Accountants (IMA)

Conceived as an educational organization to develop the individual management accountant professionally and to provide business management with the most advanced techniques and procedures, the IMA was founded as the National Association of Cost Accountants in 1919 with 37 charter members. It grew rapidly, with 2,000 applications for membership in the first year, and today it is the largest management accounting association in the world, with approximately 67,000 members and more than 230 chapters in the U.S. and 10 abroad.

The IMA has made major contributions to business management through its continuing education program, with courses and seminars conducted in numerous locations across the country; its two magazines, *Strategic Finance*, which is a monthly publication, and *Management Accounting Quarterly*, which is a new online journal; other literature, including research reports, monographs, and books; a technical inquiry service; a library; the annual international conference; and frequent meetings at chapter levels.

Membership in the IMA is open to all persons interested in advancing their knowledge of accounting or financial management. It is required for CMA candidates and CMAs.

### IMA Dues in the USA, Canada, and Mexico

1.  **Regular:** 1 year, $185
2.  **Associate:** 1st year, $61
3.  **Associate:** 2nd year, $122
4.  **Academic member:** $93; must be a full-time faculty member and reside in the U.S., Canada, or Mexico
5.  **Student:** $37; must have 6 or more equivalent hours per semester and reside in the U.S., Canada, or Mexico

Membership application forms may be obtained by writing the Institute of Management Accountants, 10 Paragon Drive, Montvale, NJ 07645-1718, or calling (201) 573-9000 or (800) 638-4427. A sample of the two-page form appears in Appendix B on pages 825 and 826. Or, visit the IMA's website and complete the form online.

## The Institute of Certified Management Accountants (ICMA)

The ICMA is located at the IMA headquarters in Montvale, New Jersey. The only function of the ICMA is to offer and administer the CMA designations. The staff consists of the managing director, the director of examinations, and support staff. The ICMA occupies about 2,000 square feet of office space in the IMA headquarters. This office is where new examination questions are prepared and where all records are kept.

### ICMA Board of Regents Staff

The ICMA Board of Regents is a special committee of the IMA established to direct the CMA programs for financial managers and management accountants through the ICMA.

The Board of Regents consists of 16 regents, one of whom is designated as chair by the president of the IMA. The regents are appointed by the president of the IMA to serve 3-year terms. Membership on the Board of Regents rotates, with one-third of the regents being appointed each year. The regents usually meet twice a year for 1 or 2 days.

The managing director of the ICMA, the director of examinations, and the ICMA staff are located at the ICMA office in Montvale, NJ. They undertake all of the day-to-day work with respect to the CMA programs.

## How to (1) Apply and (2) Register for the CMA Exam

First, you are required to **apply both for membership** in the IMA **and for admission** into the Certification Program (see sample application form in Appendix B on pages 827 and 828).

Apply to join the IMA and the Certification Program **today** -- it takes only a few minutes. Application to the certification program requires education, employment, and reference data. The educational and experience requirements are discussed on pages 6 and 7. You must provide two references: one from your employer and the second from someone other than a family member or fellow employee. An official transcript providing proof of graduation is also required after you have completed the exams. There is a $125 credentialing fee (waived for students). Once a person has become a candidate, there is no participant's fee other than IMA membership dues.

Second, it is necessary to **register** each time you wish to sit for the exams. The exam registration form (see pages 825 and 826) is very simple (it takes about 2 minutes to complete). The registration fee for each part of the exam is $130. There is an additional $35 processing fee per part for candidates taking the examination at an international site, making the fee $165 per part. Graduating seniors, full-time graduate students, and full-time faculty are charged special rates as discussed below.

Order a registration booklet and IMA membership application form from the ICMA at (800) 638-4427, extension 510. The IMA encourages candidates to view information and complete an IMA application and exam registration forms online. Visit the IMA's website at www.imanet.org for more information.

### Special Student Examination Fee

U.S., Canadian, and Mexican college students may take five examination parts at $65 per part (versus the normal $130). These discounts must be used within the year following application or they will be forfeited. To be eligible for this discount, students must

1. Provide the name of someone who can verify student status.
2. Apply to the ICMA while enrolled in school.
3. Upon graduation, arrange for an official copy of your transcript to be sent to the ICMA.

### Fees for Full-Time Professors

Full-time faculty members are permitted to take five examination parts once at no charge. The fee for any parts that must be retaken is 50% of the normal fee. To qualify, a faculty member must submit a letter on school stationery affirming his/her full-time status. Faculty should sit for the CMA examinations because a professor's status as a CMA encourages students to enter the program. Full-time doctoral students who plan to pursue a teaching career are treated as faculty members for purposes of qualifying for the free examination.

### ICMA Refund Policy

In general, the fees paid to the ICMA previously discussed are nonrefundable. However, a candidate withdrawing from the examination within 30 days of registration may receive a credit for the examination fee less a $25 processing charge. Failure to take the examination within the assigned 120-day authorization period will result in the loss of examination fees; there will be no refund or credit available.

## Pass/Fail and Grade Reports

"Candidates are given different 'forms' of the exam and it is therefore necessary to establish a passing score for each form, taking into consideration the relative difficulty of the items contained in each form.  In order to equate all scores for all forms of the exam, the scores for each part are placed along a scale from 200 to 700.  On this scale, a score of 500 represents the minimum passing scaled score.  One form of the exam might require a passing percentage of 70% and another a passing percentage of 65%; both of these passing percentages would represent a scaled score of 500.  The scaled score allows candidates to know how they performed in relation to the passing standard of 500."  If you fail the exam, you may register to take it again as soon as you like.  However, you may not sit for any part more than three times in a one-year period.

## Maintaining Your CMA Designation

Membership in the IMA is required to maintain your CMA certificates.  The general membership fee is $185.  There is no additional participant fee.

Continuing professional education is required of CMAs to maintain their proficiency in the fields of managerial accounting and financial management.  Beginning the calendar year after successful completion of the CMA exams, 30 hours of CPE must be completed, which is about 4 days per year.  Qualifying topics include all aspects of accounting, business applications of mathematics and statistics, computer science, economics, finance, management, production, marketing, business law, and behavioral science.

Credit for hours of study will be given for participation in programs sponsored by businesses, educational institutions, or professional and trade associations at either the national or local level.

Programs conducted by an individual's employer must provide for an instructor or course leader.  There must be formal instructional training material.  On-the-job training does not qualify.  An affidavit from the employer is required to attest to the hours of instruction.  The programs may be seminars, workshops, technical meetings, or college courses under the direction of an instructor.  The method of instruction may include lecture, discussion, case studies, and teaching aids such as training films and cassettes.

Credit for hours of study may be given for technical articles published in business, professional, or trade journals, and for major technical talks given for the first time before business, professional, or trade organizations.  The specific hours of credit in each case will be determined by the Institute.

## CMA Test Administration

After registering for an exam part, the ICMA will send you authorization to take the exam, which will have a 120-day window.  The authorization will instruct you to call the Thomson Prometric registration office at (800) 479-6370 and register for your test at a local Thomson Prometric testing center.  You may also register online at www.prometric.com.  Call your testing center a day or two before your test to confirm your time and obtain directions to the testing center, or visit www.prometric.com.

## INSTRUCTIONS TO DOMESTIC CANDIDATES

The letter accompanying these instructions is your authorization to schedule the taking of your examination part(s) with Thomson Prometric. Please note that you have a separate authorization number for each part that you registered to take. Questions regarding your registration with ICMA should be directed to 800-638-4427, ext. 1521.

You should contact Thomson Prometric for your appointment(s) **at your earliest convenience**, as ICMA is not responsible if you delay scheduling and there are no longer appointments available within your authorization period.

### Scheduling with Thomson Prometric

The interval dates shown on your authorization letter represent the time/authorization period during which you are authorized to take CMA examination part(s).

- Before contacting Thomson Prometric, select two or three dates during your authorization period that are convenient for you to take the examination in case your first choice is not available. Please be aware that Saturdays fill quickly and you may not be able to get a Saturday appointment.
- Choose a Thomson Prometric Center by checking the list of sites at www.prometric.com or ask the Thomson Prometric Call Center representative to suggest a center close to your home or office.
- Be sure you have your authorization number(s) from the accompanying letter handy, as you will be required to provide this information.
- To schedule your examination, you can log onto the Internet 24 hours, 7 days a week by visiting www.prometric.com. You can also call Thomson Prometric's Candidate Service Call Center at 800-479-6370 or the local Thomson Prometric Testing Center of your choice. Online is the recommended choice to schedule your test.
- Once you have scheduled your appointment, it is strongly suggested that you confirm the date and time of your appointment by visiting www.prometric.com and selecting the View/Print Appointment option.

### Reschedule or Cancellation of a Scheduled Appointment

If you find that you are unable to keep a scheduled appointment at Thomson Prometric or wish to move your appointment to another date, **you must do so three business days** before the appointment. To cancel or reschedule your appointment, please have your confirmation number ready and visit www.prometric.com or call 800-479-6370 and select option 1 to be directed to the automated system. Both options are available 24 hours, 7 days a week. If you cancel an appointment, you must wait 72 hours before calling to make a new appointment. If you do not comply with this **reschedule/cancellation policy**, you will be considered a "no-show" and you will need to reregister with the ICMA and REPAY the examination fee.

### Cancellation Examples

- If your exam date is on Friday at 3 p.m., you must cancel by noon, on the Tuesday before your scheduled appointment date.
- If your exam date is on Thursday at 8 a.m., you must cancel by 8 a.m., on the Monday before your scheduled appointment date.
- If your exam date is on Saturday at 10 a.m., you must cancel by 10 a.m., on the Wednesday before your scheduled appointment date.
- Upon written request, ICMA will consider limited time period extensions of the authorization period. For a processing fee of $30, ICMA can grant a one-time 60-day extension for parts 1, 2, 3, and 4 of the previous version of the CMA exams, and parts 1, 2, and 3 of the revised CMA exam. For a processing fee of $50, ICMA can grant a one-time extension to the following monthly testing window for part 4 of the revised exam.

### ICMA Credit Policy

If you do not take an examination within the authorized time period (and did not miss a scheduled appointment with Thomson Prometric), you will receive a nonrefundable credit for 50% of your exam fees that is good for six months and can be applied to future registrations. Students and faculty, who registered at a discounted fee, will receive no credit; however, the discounts will be restored for future use.

### General Instructions

- You should arrive at the Thomson Prometric Testing Center **30 minutes** before the time of your appointment. If you are more than 15 minutes late for your scheduled appointment, you may lose your scheduled sitting and be required to reschedule at a later date at an additional cost.
- You will be required to sign the Thomson Prometric Log Book when you enter the center.
- For admission to the examination, you will be required to present **two** forms of identification, one with a photograph, both with your signature. Approved photo IDs are a passport, driver's license, military ID, credit card with photo, or company ID. Student IDs are **not** acceptable. You **will not be** permitted into the examination without proper identification.
- Small lockers are available at the test centers for personal belongings. Items such as purses, briefcases, and jackets will not be allowed in the testing room.
- Small battery or solar powered electronic calculators restricted to a maximum of six functions - addition, subtraction, multiplication, division, square root, and percent - are allowed. The calculator must be non-programmable and must not use any type of tape. Candidates **will not** be allowed to use calculators that do not comply with these restrictions.
- Candidates will receive ONE scratch paper booklet initially during their examination. However, if you require more sheets during the exam in order to complete calculations, you should raise your hand and ask the test center personnel for ONE additional booklet. Candidates are able to keep one used booklet in case they need to refer back to previous calculations. Candidates will be permitted to trade in ONE or TWO used booklets for ONE or TWO new booklets. Candidates are only permitted to have TWO booklets at any given time. The test center personnel will then collect and destroy ALL booklets from each candidate at the end of their testing session.
- The test center will provide pencils for use in making calculations, etc., on the provided scratch paper booklet(s).
- The staff at the Thomson Prometric Testing Center is not involved in the development of the examination or the procedures governing the evaluation of your performance. Questions or comments on the examination content or performance evaluation should be directed only to the ICMA, as this is a nondisclosed examination.
- At the beginning of your test administration, you will be given the opportunity to take a tutorial that introduces the testing screens; the tutorial is not part of your testing time and may be repeated if the candidate wishes; however, total tutorial time is limited.
- Upon completion of each examination part, your performance results will be displayed on the screen, and you will also receive a printed and embossed copy of your results before leaving the testing center. (Part 4 "Revised" - Business Applications is graded offline and there is no immediate performance feedback. Grades are mailed to candidates approximately 30 days after each testing period.)

### Computer Testing Procedures

When you arrive at the computer testing center, you will be required to check in. Be sure to bring your authorization letter and two forms of identification, one with a photograph, both with your signature. If you have any questions, please call the IMA at (800) 638-4427.

Next, you will be taken into the testing room and seated at a computer terminal. You will be provided with pencils and scrap paper. You are permitted to use a 6-function, non-programmable calculator. A person from the testing center will assist you in logging on the system, and you will be asked to confirm your personal data. Then you will be prompted and given an online introduction to the computer testing system and you will view a tutorial.

If you have used our *CMA Test Prep* CD-Rom, you will be conversant with the computer testing methodology and environment and you will probably want to skip the tutorial and begin the actual test immediately. Once you begin your test, you will be allowed 3 hours to complete the actual test. This is just over 1.6 minutes per question. You may take a break during the exam, BUT the clock continues to run during your break. Before you leave the testing center, you will be required to check out of the testing center.

## PREPARING FOR THE CMA EXAM

### How Many Parts to Take

We suggest that you take one part at a time. For a list of the Gleim/Flesher study units in each part, see page 4. See page 5 for the ICMA Content Specification Overview for all parts.

CMA Part 1:    Business Analysis
CMA Part 2:    Management Accounting and Reporting
CMA Part 3:    Strategic Management
CMA Part 4:    Business Applications

Candidates can maintain credit for passed parts as long as they maintain continuous candidacy. "Continuous candidacy" includes IMA membership and, since July 1, 2001, candidates must pass all four parts of the exam within 4 years. Note that a candidate receives 12 hours of continuing professional education for each exam part passed.

### How to Study a Study Unit (Books and CD-Rom)

Twenty-question tests in the *CMA Test Prep* CD-Rom will help you to focus on your weaker areas. Make it a game: How much can you improve?

Our *CMA Test Prep* forces you to commit to your answer choice before looking at answer explanations; thus, you are preparing under true exam conditions. It also keeps track of your time and performance history for each study unit, which is available in either a table or graphical format.

Simplify the exam preparation process by following our suggested steps listed below. DO NOT omit the step in which you diagnose the reasons for answering questions incorrectly; i.e., learn from your mistakes while studying so you avoid making similar mistakes on the CMA exam.

1.    In test mode, answer a 20-question diagnostic test from each study unit before studying any other information.

2.    Study the Knowledge Transfer Outline for the corresponding study unit in your Gleim/Flesher book. Place special emphasis on the weaker areas that you identified with the initial diagnostic quiz in Step 1.

3.    Take two or three 20-question tests in test mode after you have studied the Knowledge Transfer Outline.

4. After EACH test session, immediately switch to study mode and select "questions missed from last session." It is imperative that you analyze why you answered each question incorrectly.

5. Continue this process until you approach a predetermined proficiency level, e.g., 75%+.

6. Modify this process to suit your individual learning process.

    a. Learning from questions you answer incorrectly is very important. Each question you answer incorrectly is an **opportunity** to avoid missing actual test questions on your CMA exam. Thus, you should carefully study the answer explanations provided until you understand why the original answer you chose is wrong, as well as why the correct answer indicated is correct. This study technique is clearly the difference between passing and failing for many CMA candidates.

    b. Also, you **must** determine why you answered questions incorrectly and learn how to avoid the same error in the future. Reasons for missing questions include:

        1) Misreading the requirement (stem)
        2) Not understanding what is required
        3) Making a math error
        4) Applying the wrong rule or concept
        5) Being distracted by one or more of the answers
        6) Incorrectly eliminating answers from consideration
        7) Not having any knowledge of the topic tested
        8) Employing bad intuition (WHY?) when guessing

    c. It is also important to verify that you answered correctly for the right reasons. Otherwise, if the material is tested on the CMA exam in a different manner, you may not answer it correctly.

    d. It is imperative that you complete your predetermined number of study units per week so you can review your progress and realize how attainable a comprehensive CMA review program is when using Gleim/Flesher books and CD-Rom. Remember to meet or beat your schedule to give yourself confidence.

## Gleim/Flesher Audio Reviews

Gleim/Flesher *CMA Review* Audios provide a 15- to 40-minute introductory review for each study unit. Each review provides a comprehensive overview of the outline in the *CMA Review* book. The purpose is to get candidates "started" so they can relate to the questions they will answer before reading the study outlines in each study unit.

The audios are short and to the point, as is the entire Gleim System for Success. We are working to get you through the CMA exam with the minimum time, cost, and frustration. You can listen to an informative discussion about the CMA exam and hear a sample of an audio review (CVP Applications) on our website at www.gleim.com/accounting/demos/.

## *CMA Gleim Online*

*CMA Gleim Online* is a versatile, interactive, self-study review program delivered via the Internet. With *CMA Gleim Online*, Gleim guarantees that you will pass the CMA exam on your first sitting. It is divided into four courses (one for each part of the CMA exam).

Each course is broken down into 20 individual, manageable study units. Completion time per study unit will vary from 1-5 hours. Each study unit in the course contains an audiovisual presentation, 30 true/false study questions, 10-20 pages of Knowledge Transfer Outlines, and two 20-question multiple-choice quizzes.

*CMA Gleim Online* provides you with a Personal Counselor, who will provide support to ensure your competitive edge. *CMA Gleim Online* is a great way to get confidence as you prepare with Gleim. This confidence will continue during and after the exam.

### How to Study a Study Unit Using Gleim's Complete System

To ensure that you are using your time effectively, we recommend that you follow the steps listed below when using all of the materials together (books, CD-Rom, audios, and *Gleim Online*):

1.   (25-30 minutes) In the *Gleim Online* course, complete Multiple-Choice Quiz #1 in 20-25 minutes (excluding the review session).  It is expected that your scores will be low on the first quiz.

     a.   Immediately following the quiz, review both the correct and incorrect answer explanations for each question.

2.   (15-30 minutes) Use the audiovisual presentation for an overview of the study unit.  The Gleim *CMA Review Audios* can be substituted for audiovisual presentations and can be used while driving to work, exercising, etc.

3.   (30-45 minutes) Complete the 30-question True/False quiz.  It is interactive and most effective if used prior to studying the Knowledge Transfer Outline.

4.   (60 minutes) Study the Knowledge Transfer Outline, specifically the troublesome areas identified from the multiple-choice questions in the *Gleim Online* course.  The Knowledge Transfer Outlines can be studied either online or from the books.

5.   (25-30 minutes) Complete Multiple-Choice Quiz #2 in the *Gleim Online* course.

     a.   Immediately following the quiz, review both the correct and incorrect answer explanations for each question.

6.   (40-50 minutes) Complete two 20-question quizzes while in Test Mode from the *CMA Test Prep* CD-Rom.

When using our complete system as described above and on the previous pages, you will complete all 20 units in about 70-80 hours.  Then spend about 10-20 hours using the *CMA Test Prep* CD-Rom to create customized tests for the problem areas that you identified.  To review the entire section before the exam, use the *CMA Test Prep* CD-Rom to create 20-question quizzes that draw questions from all twenty study units.  Continue taking 20-question quizzes until you approach a 75%+ proficiency level.

---

Avoid studying Gleim questions to learn the correct answers.  Use questions to help you <u>learn</u> how to answer CMA questions <u>under exam conditions</u>.  Expect the unexpected and be prepared to deal with the unexpected.  Always take one 20-question test in test mode *before* studying the material in each study unit.  These test sessions will allow you to practice answering questions you have not seen before.  Become an educated guesser when you encounter questions in doubt; you will outperform the inexperienced exam taker.

---

After you complete each 20-question test, ALWAYS do a study session of questions you missed.  FOCUS on why you selected the incorrect answer, NOT the correct answer.  You want to learn from your mistakes during study so you avoid mistakes on the exam.

## Study Plan and Time Budget

Complete one study unit at a time. Initially, budget 3 to 4 hours per study unit (1 to 2 hours studying the outline and 1 to 2 minutes each on all the multiple-choice questions). Depending on your background, you may need more or less time to prepare.

| | |
|---|---:|
| This Introduction | 2 |
| 20 study units at 4 hours each | 80 |
| General review | 8 |
| Total Hours | 90 |

Each week you should evaluate your progress and review your preparation plans for the time remaining prior to the exam. Use a calendar to note the exam dates and the weeks to go before the exam. Marking a calendar will facilitate your planning. Review your commitments, e.g., out-of-town assignments, personal responsibilities, etc., and note them on your calendar to assist you in keeping to your schedule.

## Control: How To Be in

You have to be in control to be successful during exam preparation and execution. Control can also contribute greatly to your personal and other professional goals. The objective is to be confident that the best possible performance is being generated. Control is a process whereby you

1. Develop expectations, standards, budgets, and plans.
2. Undertake activity, production, study, and learning.
3. Measure the activity, production, output, and knowledge.
4. Compare actual activity with expected and budgeted activity.
5. Modify the activity, behavior, or study to better achieve the desired outcome.
6. Revise expectations and standards in light of actual experience.
7. Continue the process or restart the process in the future.

The objective is to be confident that the best possible performance is being generated. Most accountants study this process in relation to standard costs, i.e., establish cost standards and compute cost variances.

Every day you rely on control systems implicitly. For example, when you groom your hair, you use a control system. You have expectations about the desired appearance of your hair and the time required to style it. You monitor your progress and make adjustments as appropriate. The control process, therefore, is applicable to all of your endeavors, both professional and personal. You should refine your personal control processes specifically toward passing the CMA exam.

Develop and enforce standards in all of your endeavors. Exercise control, implicitly or explicitly. Most endeavors will improve with explicit control. This is particularly true with certification examinations and other academic tests.

1. Practice your question-answering techniques (and develop control) as you prepare answers/solutions to practice questions/problems during your study program.

2. Develop explicit control over your study programs based on the control process discussed previously.

3. Think about using more explicit control systems over any and all of your endeavors.

4. Seek continuous improvement to meet your needs given a particular situation or constraint. Additional practice will result in further efficiencies.

## Multiple-Choice Question-Answering Technique

The following suggestions are to assist you in maximizing your score on each part of the CMA exam. Remember, knowing how to take the exam and how to answer individual questions is as important as studying/reviewing the subject matter tested on the exam.

1.  **Budget your time.**

    a.  We make this point with emphasis. Just as you would fill up your gas tank prior to reaching empty, so too should you finish your exam before time expires.

    b.  You have 180 minutes to answer 110 questions, i.e., 1.6 minutes per question. We suggest you attempt to answer eight questions every 10 minutes, which is 1.25 minutes per question. This would result in completing 110 questions in 137 minutes to give you almost 45 minutes to review questions that you have marked. See 3.c.2) below for a brief discussion on marking questions at Prometric.

    c.  On your Prometric computer screen, the time remaining (starting with 180 minutes) appears at the upper right corner of your screen.

2.  **Answer the items in numerical order.**

    a.  Do **not** agonize over any one item. Stay within your time budget.

    b.  It is not necessary to "mark" unanswered questions. Prometric provides options to review both unanswered questions and marked questions.

3.  **For each item**

    a.  **Read the question** stem carefully (the part of the question that precedes the answer choices) to determine the precise requirement.

        1)  Focusing on what is required enables you to ignore extraneous information and to proceed directly to determining the correct answer.

            a)  Be especially careful to note when the requirement is an **exception**; e.g., "All of the following statements regarding a company's internal rate of return are true except:."

    b.  **Determine the correct answer** before reading the answer choices. The objective is to avoid allowing the answer choices to affect your reading of the question.

        1)  When four answer choices are presented, three of them are incorrect. They are called distractors for a very good reason.

        2)  Read each answer choice with close attention.

            a)  Even if answer (A) appears to be the correct choice, do not skip the remaining answer choices. Answer (B), (C), or (D) may be better.

            b)  Treat each answer choice as a true-false question.

    c.  **Select the best answer.** The answer is selected by either pressing the answer letter on your keyboard or by using your mouse. Select the most likely or best answer choice. If you are uncertain, make an educated guess.

        1)  The CMA does not penalize guessing because your score is determined by the number of correct responses. Thus, you should answer every question.

        2)  As you answer a question, you can mark it by pressing "M" or unmark a marked question by pressing "M." After you have answered, marked, or looked at and not answered all 110 questions, you will be presented with a summary screen that shows how many questions you did not answer and how many you marked. You then have the option of revisiting all of the unanswered questions and "marked" questions.

4. **Prometric Computer Screen Layout**

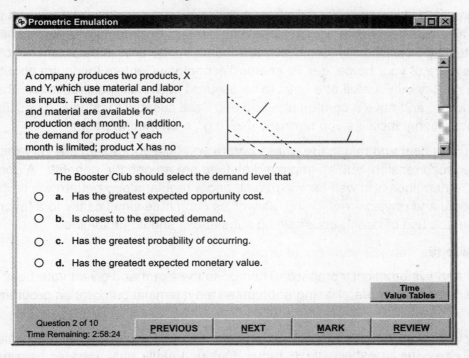

NOTE:  A menu offering a number of options is displayed at the bottom of the question screen.  The options enable you to view the previous question or the next question, mark a question to be revisited, or request help.  You may select an option by pressing the appropriate symbol key or highlighted letter on your keyboard or by clicking on the symbol or letter with your mouse.

1) View the previous question by indicating the letter **P** or the left arrow key.
2) View the next question by indicating the letter **N** or the right arrow key.
3) Mark a question by indicating the letter **M**.
4) Request help by indicating the question mark.

USE GLEIM/FLESHER *CMA TEST PREP* CD-Rom.  It emulates the Prometric testing procedures and environment including computer screen layout, software operation, etc.

## TAKING THE CMA EXAM

### CMA Examination Checklist

1. Acquire your study materials.  Rely on this book, *CMA Test Prep* CD-Rom, and *CMA Gleim Online*.  Consider our audios as a supplement, which can be used while you commute, exercise, etc.

2. **Apply** for membership in the IMA (see pages 825 and 826).  **Register** to take the desired part of the exam using the examination registration form (pages 827 and 828) and send it with your applications to the ICMA.  Take one part at a time.  When you register and pay $130 for a part ($165 for exams at international sites), you have 120 days to take the part.  Upon receipt of authorization to take the exam, call Prometric to schedule your test.

3. Plan your preparation process.  It's easy.  You have 20 study units to complete.

4. Orderly, controlled preparation builds confidence, reduces anxiety, and produces success!

5. PASS THE EXAMINATION (study this Introduction)!

## Logistical and Health Concerns

As soon as the ICMA sends you a computer-based test authorization, call and schedule your test at a convenient time and convenient Prometric testing center. In almost all cases, you should be able to drive to your testing site, take the test, and return home in one day. If the exam is not being given within driving distance of your home, call Prometric Technology Centers to inquire about accommodations. Stay by yourself at a hotel to be assured of avoiding distractions. The hotel room should be soundproof and have a comfortable bed and desk suitable for study. If possible, stay at a hotel with the recreational facilities you normally use, e.g., a swimming pool.

Proper exercise, diet, and rest in the weeks before you take your exam are very important. High energy levels, reduced tension, and an improved attitude are among the benefits. A good aerobic fitness program, a nutritious and well-balanced diet, and a regular sleep pattern will promote your long-term emotional and physical well-being, as well as contribute significantly to a favorable exam result. Of course, the use of health-undermining substances should be avoided.

## Exam Psychology

Plan ahead and systematically prepare. Then go to the exam and give it your best: neither you nor anyone else can expect more. Having undertaken a systematic preparation program, you will do fine.

Maintain a positive attitude and do not become depressed if you encounter difficulties before or during the exam. An optimist will usually do better than an equally well-prepared pessimist. Remember, you have reason to be optimistic because you will be competing with many less-qualified persons who have not prepared as well as you have.

## Calculators

Only simple six-function calculators are permitted (i.e., addition, subtraction, multiplication, division, square root, percent). Candidates are responsible for providing their own calculators. You should be thoroughly experienced in the operations of your calculator. Make sure it has fresh batteries just prior to the examination.

1. Consider bringing a backup calculator with you.
2. The calculator must be small, quiet, and battery- or solar-powered so it will not be distracting to other candidates.
3. The calculator may have a memory. However, the memory must be temporary and erase when the memory is cleared or the calculator is turned off.
4. The calculator must not use any type of tape.
5. The calculator must be nonprogrammable.
6. Nonconforming calculators and calculator instruction books are not permitted.
7. We suggest that you study using the calculator that you will be bringing to the exam so that you are completely comfortable using it.

## Examination Tactics

1. Remember to bring your authorization and appropriate identification to the exam site. The photo ID requirement is strictly enforced.
2. Arrive at the test center at least 30 minutes prior to the scheduled exam time to allow for orientation and check-in procedures. Your appointment may be canceled if you are more than 15 minutes late.

3. Dressing for exam success means emphasizing comfort, not appearance. Be prepared to adjust for changes in temperature, e.g., to remove or put on a sweater.

4. Do not bring notes, this text, other books, etc., into the Prometric testing center. You will only make yourself nervous and confused by trying to cram the last 5 minutes before the exam. Books are not allowed in the testing room, anyway. You should, however, bring an appropriate calculator.

5. Adequate scratch paper and pencils are provided. You must turn in your scratch paper as you leave the exam site. Any breath mints, gum, etc., should be in your pocket as they may distract other persons taking the test.

6. As soon as you complete the exam, we would like you to e-mail, fax, or write to us with your comments on our books and software. We are particularly interested in which topics need to be added or expanded in our books and software. We are NOT asking about specific CMA questions; rather, we are asking for feedback on our books and software.

### Recap of CMA Part 2 Exam Coverage

**ICMA Major Topics and Percent Coverage**

A. Budget Preparation--15% (Level C)

B. Cost Management--25% (Level C)

C. Information Management--15% (Level A)

D. Performance Measurement--20% (Level C)

E. External Financial Reporting--25% (Level B)

**Gleim/Flesher Study Units**

1. Budgeting

2. Cost Management Terminology and Concepts
3. Job-Order Costing, Overhead Costs, and Service Department Allocation
4. Process Costing and Other Cost Accumulation Systems

5. Overview of Information Systems and Systems Development and Design
6. Technology of Information Systems
7. Electronic Commerce and Other Topics

8. Cost and Variance Measures
9. Responsibility Accounting and Financial Measures
10. The Balance Scorecard and Quality Considerations

11. Overview of External Financial Reporting
12. Overview of Financial Statements
13. Cash and Receivables
14. Inventories and Investments
15. Long-Lived Assets
16. Liabilities
17. Equity and Revenue Recognition
18. Other Income Statement Items
19. Business Combinations and Derivatives
20. SEC Requirements and the Annual Report

---

### WARNING!!!

About 30% of CMA test questions will require mathematical calculations. Practice computational questions to prepare for exam success!

---

# GO FOR IT!
# IT'S YOURS TO PASS!

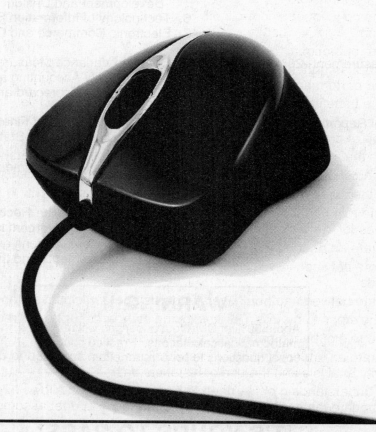

# STUDY UNIT ONE
# BUDGETING

(21 pages of outline)

This study unit covers **budget preparation**. The relative weight assigned to this major topic in Part 2 of the exam is **15%** at **skill level C** (all six skill types required).

After studying the outlines and answering the multiple-choice questions in this study unit, you will have the skills necessary to address the following topics listed in the IMA's Learning Outcome Statements:

Part 2 – Section A.1. Budgeting concepts

The candidate should be able to:

a. demonstrate an understanding of the role that budgeting plays in formulating short-term objectives and planning and controlling operations to meet those objectives

b. identify the characteristics that define successful budgeting

c. demonstrate an understanding of the role that budgets play in measuring performance against established goals

d. show how the budgeting process facilitates communication among organizational units and enhances coordination of organizational activities

e. explain the concept of a controllable cost as it relates to both budgeting and performance evaluation

f. prepare an operational budget

g. demonstrate an understanding of the concept of management-by-objective and how it relates to performance evaluation

h. identify the benefits and limitations of management-by-objective

i. demonstrate an understanding of how the planning process coordinates the efficient allocation of organizational resources

j. recognize the appropriate time frame for various types of budgets

k. identify who should participate in the budgeting process for optimum success

l. describe the role of top management in successful budgeting

m. identify the role of top management or the budget committee in providing appropriate guidelines for the budget and identify items that should be included in these guidelines

n. demonstrate an understanding of the use of cost standards in budgeting

o. differentiate between ideal (theoretical) standards and currently attainable (practical) standards

p. differentiate between authoritative standards and participative standards

q. identify the steps to be taken in developing standards for both direct material and direct labor

r. define the role of benchmarking in standard setting

s. demonstrate an understanding of the techniques that are used to develop standards, such as activity analysis and the use of historical data

t. show an understanding of the need to have a policy that allows budget revisions that accommodate the impact of significant changes in budget assumptions

## Part 2 – Section A.2.  Budget systems

For each of the budget systems identified (annual/master budgets, project budgeting, activity-based budgeting, zero-based budgeting, continuous budgeting, kaizen budgeting, and flexible budgeting), the candidate should be able to:

a.   define its purpose, appropriate use, and time frame
b.   identify the budget components and explain the interrelationships among the components
c.   demonstrate an understanding of how the budget is developed
d.   compare and contrast the benefits and limitations of the budget system
e.   calculate budget components on the basis of information presented
f.   evaluate a business situation and recommend the appropriate budget solution

## Part 2 – Section A.3.  Annual profit plan and supporting schedules

The candidate should be able to:

a.   demonstrate an understanding of the role the sales budget plays in the development of an annual profit plan
b.   identify the factors that should be considered when preparing a sales forecast and evaluate the feasibility of the sales forecast based on business information provided
c.   identify the components of a sales budget and prepare a sales budget based on relevant information provided
d.   demonstrate an understanding of the relationship between the sales budget and the production budget
e.   identify the role that inventory levels play in the preparation of a production budget and define other factors that should be considered when preparing a production budget
f.   prepare a production budget based on relevant information provided and evaluate the feasibility of achieving sales goals on the basis of production plans
g.   demonstrate an understanding of the relationship between the direct materials budget, the direct labor budget, and the production budget
h.   define the use of inventory levels and purchasing policies in developing a direct materials budget and the role that labor skills, union contracts, and hiring policies play in the development of a direct labor budget
i.   prepare direct materials and direct labor budgets based on relevant information provided and evaluate the feasibility of achieving production goals on the basis of these budgets
j.   identify the components of an employee benefit statement, e.g., employer contributions to Social Security, health and life insurance, and pension contributions
k.   demonstrate an understanding of alternative ways of allocating employee benefit expense, e.g., as a portion of direct labor expense or as overhead, and the effect that allocation has on the financial statements
l.   demonstrate an understanding of the relationship between the overhead budget and the production budget
m.   demonstrate an understanding that a portion of the overhead budget may vary directly with production quantities, while a portion of the overhead budget may consist of fixed expenses
n.   define the components of overhead expense and prepare an overhead budget based on relevant information provided
o.   identify the components of the cost of goods sold budget and demonstrate an understanding of the relationship between the cost of goods sold budget, the pro forma income statement, and the pro forma statement of financial position
p.   demonstrate an understanding of contribution margin per unit and total contribution margin, identify the appropriate use of these concepts, and calculate both unit and total contribution margin
q.   prepare a cost of goods sold budget based on relevant information provided

r.   identify the components of the selling and administrative budget and demonstrate an understanding of the nature of these expenses

s.   describe the relationship between the selling and administrative budget, the·pro forma income statement, and the pro forma statement of financial position

t.   understand how some components of the selling and administrative budget may affect the contribution margin

u.   demonstrate an understanding of the relationship between the budget for acquisition of capital assets, the cash budget, and the pro forma financial statements

v.   define the purposes of the cash budget and understand the relationship between the cash budget and all other budgets

w.   identify the elements of a cash budget and demonstrate an understanding of the relationship between credit policies and purchasing (payables) policies and the cash budget

x.   prepare a cash budget from information given and recommend the optimal investment/financing strategy

y.   define the purpose of a pro forma income statement, a pro forma statement of financial position, and a pro forma cash flow statement and understand the relationship among these statements and all other budgets

z.   prepare a pro forma income statement, a pro forma statement of financial position, and a pro forma cash flow statement from relevant information provided

## 1.1 BUDGETING CONCEPTS

1.   A **budget** is the formal quantification of management's plans.  It is a tool for

   a.   **Planning** for achieving the organization's objectives
   b.   **Controlling** spending and revenue-generating processes
   c.   **Communicating** with personnel at all levels of the organization
   d.   **Motivating** employees toward achieving the objectives
   e.   **Evaluating** performance

2.   The budget is a **planning** tool.

   a.   Companies that prepare budgets **anticipate problems** before they occur.

      1)   EXAMPLE:  If a company runs out of a critical raw material, it may have to shut down.  At best, it will incur extremely high freight costs to have the needed materials rushed in.  The company with a budget will have anticipated the shortage and planned to avoid it.

      2)   A firm that has no objectives may not always make the best decisions.  A firm with an objective, in the form of a budget, will be able to plan.

   b.   No organization can prepare an effective budget until the board and senior management formulate the **mission statement**.

      1)   The mission statement embodies the organization's reason for being, e.g., increase shareholder value through providing global telecommunications services to consumers.

      2)   Next, the organization draws up its **long-term objectives**, which are the means through which the mission will be fulfilled, e.g., hold a 40% market share of U.S. cell phone users within five years.

      3)   Once the long-term objectives are in place, the **priorities** of the organization will be clear.  Awareness of priorities is crucial for the **allocation of limited resources**, e.g., how many cell towers, each of which require the outlay of construction and maintenance costs, will provide the optimum amount of coverage.

      4)   **Short-term objectives** flow directly from the priorities, e.g., determine how many cell towers are needed and where they can feasibly be placed in the Metro Atlanta region.

c.   **Strategic budgeting** is a form of long-range planning based on identifying and specifying organizational goals and objectives.

1)   The organization begins by evaluating its strengths, weaknesses, opportunities, and threats (a **SWOT analysis**) and assessing risk levels.  The influences of internal and external factors are then forecasted to derive the best strategy for reaching the organization's objectives.

2)   Among the external or environmental factors to be considered are general economic conditions and their expected trends, governmental regulatory measures, the labor market in the company's locale, and the activities of competitors.

3)   Strategic budgets and other plans are translated into measurable and achievable intermediate and operational plans.  Thus, these plans must be considered with, and contribute to achieving, the strategic objectives.

   a)   **Strategic** plans – budgets developed by senior managers have time frames of up to 10 years (or more).

   b)   **Intermediate** plans – budgets developed by middle managers have time frames of up to 2 years.

   c)   **Operational** plans – budgets developed by lower-level managers have time frames of 1 week to 1 year.

3.   The budget is a **control** tool.

a.   Budgets provide a basis for **controlling (monitoring and revising) activities** of an organization.

1)   The initial budget is a planning tool.  To monitor how actual performance compares with the budget, budget reports are produced periodically during the year.

   a)   The difference between actual performance and a budgeted amount is called a **variance**.  Analysis of variances reveals the efficient or inefficient use of company resources (see Study Unit 8, "Cost and Variance Measures").

b.   A budget helps a firm control costs by setting cost **standards** or guidelines.  Budgets and other standards, including standard costs, are formal estimates of future performance.

1)   A **standard-cost system** is designed to alert management when the actual costs of production differ significantly from target or standard costs.

   a)   Standard costs are budgeted unit costs established to motivate optimal productivity and efficiency.  They are monetary measures with which actual costs are compared.

2)   A standard cost is not just an average of past costs, but an objectively determined estimate of what a cost should be.

   a)   For example, it may be based on accounting, engineering, or statistical quality control studies.

   b)   Because of the impact of fixed costs in most businesses, a standard costing system is usually not effective unless the company also has a **flexible budgeting** system.

      i)   Flexible budgeting uses standard costs to prepare budgets for multiple activity levels (see item 7.b. under subunit 1.2).

3) **Ideal (perfection, theoretical, or maximum efficiency) standards** are standard costs that are set for production under optimal conditions.

    a) They are based on the work of the most skilled workers with no allowance for waste, spoilage, machine breakdowns, or other downtime.

    b) Tight standards can have positive behavioral implications if workers are motivated to strive for excellence. However, they are not in wide use because they can have negative behavioral effects if the standards are impossible to attain.

    c) Ideal, or tight, standards are ordinarily replaced by currently attainable standards for cash budgeting, product costing, and budgeting departmental performance. Otherwise, accurate financial planning will be impossible.

    d) Ideal standards have been adopted by some companies that apply continuous improvement and other total quality management principles.

4) **Practical (currently attainable) standards** may be defined as the performance that is reasonably expected to be achieved with an allowance for normal spoilage, waste, and downtime.

    a) An alternative interpretation is that practical standards represent possible but difficult-to-attain results.

5) **Benchmarking** is one means of setting performance standards.

    a) It is a continuous process of quantitative and qualitative measurement of the difference between the organization's performance of an activity and the performance by the best-in-class organization.

    b) Benchmarking also analyzes the key actions and root causes that contribute to the performance gap.

6) **Activity analysis** identifies, describes, and evaluates activities to determine what they accomplish, who performs them, the resources they use, and their value to the organization.

    a) Value-adding activities should continue to be performed and provide the basis for performance standards.

    b) Activity analysis also is defined as the determination of the optimal or standard methods and inputs required to accomplish a given task.

    c) Inputs include the amounts and kinds of equipment, facilities, materials, and labor. Engineering analysis, cost accounting, time-and-motion study, and other approaches may be useful.

7) **Historical information** may be helpful in setting standards, provided that circumstances have not changed materially.

8) **Target costing standards** may be set when a product must be sold at a target price. The assumption is that continuous improvement practices will succeed in driving costs down to the targeted levels.

  c. For the budgetary process to serve effectively as a control and evaluative function, it must be **integrated** with the **accounting system** and the **organizational structure**. Such integration is one of the characteristics of a successful budget program.

    1) Integration enhances control by transmitting data and assigning the responsibility for explaining variances to the proper organizational subunits.

  d. Often an organization will find that the **assumptions** under which the budget was prepared undergo **significant change** during the year. A policy must be in place to accommodate revisions to the budget resulting from these changes. Accommodation of change is a key characteristic of successful budgeting.

    1) If such a policy is not in place, managers can come to believe they are being held to a budget that is no longer possible to achieve, and morale can suffer.

e.    Information gained during the year as actual results and variances are reported can be used to help the company take corrective action.

1)    These steps make up a **control loop**:

a)    Establishing standards of performance (the budget)
b)    Measuring actual performance
c)    Analyzing and comparing performance with standards (budget reports)
d)    Devising and implementing corrective actions
e)    Reviewing and revising the standards

4.    The budget is a **communication** tool.

a.    A budget can help tell employees what objectives the firm is attempting to accomplish.

1)    If the firm does not have an overall budget, each department tends to pursue its own objectives without regard to what is good for the firm as a whole.  Thus, a budget promotes **goal congruence**.  The planning process coordinates the efficient allocation of organizational resources.

2)    For example, the sales department may want to keep as much inventory as possible so that no sales will be lost, but the treasurer may want to keep the inventory as low as possible so that cash need not be spent any sooner than necessary.  If the budget specifies the level of inventory, all employees can work toward the same goals.

b.    Budgets facilitate **coordination** of the activities of a firm.  The overall budget, often called the **master** or **comprehensive budget**, encompasses both the **operating and financial** budget processes.

c.    An example of a coordination activity is the purchasing of raw materials.

1)    Materials are needed prior to production, but the proper quantity to buy cannot be determined until it is determined how many units of product are to be manufactured.

2)    Thus, a production budget (in units) is a prerequisite to the preparation of a materials purchases budget.

3)    Similarly, a direct labor budget is based on how many units are to be produced and how fast the workers are.

a)    Labor standards are also complex in that they must consider the impact of the learning curve on productivity.

5.    The budget is a **motivational** tool.

a.    A budget helps to motivate employees to pursue the organization's objectives.

1)    A budget must be seen as realistic by employees before it can become a good motivational tool.

2)    Employees are particularly motivated if they help prepare the budget.  Thus, the budgeting and standard-setting processes are considered better if they are participative.

3)    A manager who is asked to prepare a budget for his/her department will work hard to stay within the budget.

4)    Achievement of challenging goals has positive effects on employee performance and self-esteem.

b.    Budgets also may reveal the progress of highly effective managers.

1)    Consequently, managers should not view budgets negatively.  A budget is just as likely to help as to hinder a manager's career.

2)    A manager also may use a budget as a personal self-evaluation tool.

    c.    Unfortunately, the budget is not always viewed in a positive manner. Some managers view a budget as a restriction.

    d.    Employees are more apt to have a positive feeling toward a budget if some degree of flexibility is allowed.

6.    The budget is an **evaluative** tool.

    a.    Comparing actual results to the budget allows managers at all levels to evaluate their own performance, as well as evaluate the performance of subordinate managers.

    b.    **Controllability** is a key concept in the use of budgets and other standards to evaluate performance.

        1)    Controllability is the extent to which a manager can influence activities and related revenues, costs, or other items.

            a)    In principle, it is proportionate to, but not coextensive with, responsibility.

        2)    Controllability is difficult to isolate because few costs, revenues, etc., are under the sole influence of one manager.

            a)    Also, separating the effects of current management's decisions from those of former management is difficult.

        3)    If responsibility exceeds the extent to which a manager can influence an activity, the result may be reduced morale, a decline in managerial effort, and poor performance.

            a)    Such a manager encounters greater risk because his/her success depends on uncontrollable factors. Thus, a manager in these circumstances should be compensated for the incremental risk assumed.

        4)    However, if a manager is accountable solely for activities over which (s)he has extensive influence, the manager may develop too narrow a focus.

            a)    For example, the manager of a cost center may make decisions based only on cost efficiency and ignore the overall effectiveness goals of the organization. By extending the manager's responsibility to profits as well as costs, the organization may encourage desirable behavior congruent with overall goals, such as improved coordination with marketing personnel, even though the manager still does not control revenues.

            b)    Furthermore, a manager who does not control an activity may nevertheless be the individual who is best informed about it. Thus, a purchasing agent may be in the best position to explain price variances even though (s)he cannot control them.

7.    A **budget manual** describes how a budget is to be prepared and provides appropriate guidelines for the budgeting process. Items usually appearing in a budget manual include a budget planning calendar and distribution instructions for all budget schedules.

    a.    The **budget planning calendar** is the schedule of activities for the development and adoption of the budget.

        1)    It should include a list of dates indicating when specific information is to be provided to others by each information source.

        2)    The preparation of a master budget usually takes **several months**. A firm with a calendar year-end may start the budget process in September, anticipating its completion by the first of December.

        3)    Because all of the individual departmental budgets are based on forecasts prepared by others and the budgets of other departments, it is essential to have a planning calendar to integrate the entire process.

    b.   Distribution instructions are important because of the interdependencies of a master budget.

       1)   Once a schedule is prepared, other departments in the organization use the schedule to prepare their own budgets.

       2)   Without distribution instructions, someone who needs a particular schedule might be overlooked, and the whole budget process will be set back.

8.   **Participative budgeting** (grass-roots budgeting) and standard setting use input from lower-level and middle-level employees.

    a.   Participation encourages employees to have a sense of ownership of the output of the process.

       1)   The result is an acceptance of, and commitment to, the goals expressed in the budget.

       2)   A purely **top-down approach** (an imposed budget that sets **authoritative** rather than participative standards) is much less likely to foster this sense of commitment. Thus, participative standard-setting is considered superior to authoritative standard-setting.

    b.   Participation also enables employees to relate performance to rewards or penalties.

       1)   The actual impact of budgetary participation depends on cultural, organizational, interpersonal, and individual variables, such as personality.

    c.   A further advantage of participation is that it provides a broader information base.

       1)   Lower- and middle-level managers have knowledge that senior managers and staff may lack.

       2)   Thus, a key decision in the budget and standard-setting process is to identify who in the organization can provide useful input. For example, top management is better at establishing strategic budgets because these individuals possess the necessary input.

    d.   Disadvantages of participative budgeting and standard setting include its cost in terms of time and money.

       1)   Furthermore, the quality of participation is affected by the goals, values, beliefs, and expectations of those involved.

           a)   A manager who expects his/her request to be reduced may inflate the amount.

           b)   If a budget is to be used as a performance evaluator, a manager asked for an estimate may provide one that is easily attained.

    e.   Participation in developing a budget may result in **padding** of the budget, also known as budgetary slack.

       1)   **Budgetary slack** is the excess of resources budgeted over the resources necessary to achieve organizational goals.

           a)   The natural tendency of a manager is to negotiate for a less stringent measure of performance so as to avoid unfavorable variances from expectations.

       2)   Management may create slack by overestimating costs and underestimating revenues.

           a)   A firm may decrease slack by emphasizing the consideration of all variables, holding in-depth reviews during budget development, and allowing for flexibility in making additional budget changes.

      f.    A **budget committee**, composed of top management, reviews and approves the master budget submitted by operating managers. The budget committee also may make adjustments to the budget submitted by the operating managers.

            1)    The budget committee approves and circulates the budget manual, which provides guidelines for budget preparation.

9.    **Management-by-objectives (MBO)** is a behavioral, communications-oriented, responsibility-focused, and participative approach to management and employee self direction. Accordingly, MBO stresses the need to involve all affected parties in the budgeting process.

      a.    MBO is a top-down process because the organization's objectives are restated for each lower level.

            1)    For example, the budgets (quantitative statements of objectives) at each successive level of the organization have a **means-end relationship**. One level's ends provide the next higher level's means for achieving its objectives.

            2)    Ideally, the means-end chain ties together the parts of the organization so that the various means all focus on the same ultimate ends (objectives).

      b.    MBO is based on the philosophy that employees want to work hard if they know what is expected, like to understand what their jobs actually entail, and are capable of self-direction and self-motivation.

            1)    Thus, MBO is also a **bottom-up process** because of the participation of subordinates.

      c.    The following are the four **common elements** of MBO programs:

            1)    Establishment of objectives jointly by the superior and subordinate.

            2)    Specificity of objectives. Multiple performance measures are agreed upon so that the subordinate will not neglect other facets of his/her job to concentrate on a single objective.

            3)    Specificity of the time within which objectives are to be achieved.

            4)    Ongoing feedback that permits an individual to monitor and adjust his/her performance.

      d.    The following are **benefits** of MBO:

            1)    Opens up communication between manager and subordinate
            2)    Allows subordinate to participate in setting job objectives
            3)    Forces specification of organizational objectives throughout the organization
            4)    Allows subordinates to be measured on what they do, not on personality traits
            5)    Facilitates employee development

      e.    The following are **limitations** of MBO:

            1)    Failure of managers to accept the philosophy behind MBO
            2)    Failure to give objectives-setters adequate guidelines
            3)    Difficulty in setting truly verifiable objectives
            4)    Tendency for objectives to be short-term only
            5)    Tendency for plans under MBO to become inflexible, making it difficult to adapt to change
            6)    Lack of precise management knowledge of a task, resulting in a supervisor's allowing a subordinate to set inappropriate objectives
            7)    Emphasis on quantitative factors, causing employees to focus on the ends rather than the means, thus possibly jeopardizing the quality of the output

10.   Stop and review! You have completed the outline for this subunit. Study multiple-choice questions 1 through 18 beginning on page 42.

## 1.2 BUDGET SYSTEMS

1.  The **master, or comprehensive, budget** encompasses the organization's operating and financial plans for a specified period, ordinarily a year (see subunit 1.3).

2.  A **project budget** consists of all the costs expected to attach to a particular project, such as the design of a new airliner or the building of a single ship.

    a.  While the project is obviously part of the company's overall line of business, the costs and profits associated with it are significant enough to be tracked separately.

    b.  A project will typically use resources from many parts of the organization, e.g., design, engineering, production, marketing, accounting, human resources.

        1)  All of these aspects of the project budget must align with those of the firm's master budget.

3.  **Activity-based budgeting** applies activity-based costing principles (see subunit 4.2) to budgeting.

    a.  It focuses on the numerous activities necessary to produce and market goods and services and requires analysis of cost drivers. Budget line items are related to activities performed.

        1)  This approach contrasts with the traditional emphasis on functions or spending categories.

        2)  The costs of non-value-added activities are quantified.

    b.  Activity-based budgeting provides greater detail than traditional functional or spending-category budgeting, especially regarding indirect costs, because it permits the isolation of numerous cost drivers.

        1)  A **cost pool** is established for each activity, and a cost driver is identified for each pool.

        2)  The budgeted cost for each pool is determined by multiplying the demand for the activity by the estimated cost of a unit of the activity.

4.  **Zero-based budgeting (ZBB)** is a budget and planning process in which each manager must justify his/her department's entire budget every budget cycle.

    a.  The concept originated in the U.S. Department of Agriculture in the early 1960s but was abandoned. Texas Instruments Corporation began using it in the late 1960s and early 1970s, as did the state of Georgia under Governor Jimmy Carter. Carter also tried to introduce the concept into the federal budget system when he served as president (1977–1980).

    b.  ZBB differs from the traditional concept of **incremental budgeting**, in which the current year's budget is simply adjusted to allow for changes planned for the coming year.

        1)  The managerial advantage of incremental budgeting is that the manager has to put forth less effort to justify changes in the budget.

    c.  Under ZBB, a manager must build the budget every year from a base of zero. All expenditures must be justified regardless of variance from previous years.

        1)  The objective is to encourage periodic reexamination of all costs in the hope that some can be reduced or eliminated.

    d.  ZBB begins with the deepest budgetary units of the entity.

        1)  It requires determination of objectives, operations, and costs for each activity and the alternative means of carrying out that activity.

        2)  Different levels of service (work effort) are evaluated for each activity, measures of work and performance are established, and activities are ranked according to their importance to the entity.

3) For each budgetary unit, a decision package is prepared that describes various levels of service that may be provided, including at least one level of service lower than the current one.

    a) Accordingly, ZBB requires managers to justify each expenditure for each budget period and to review each cost component from a cost-benefit perspective.

  e. The major limitation of ZBB is that it requires more time and effort to prepare than a traditional budget.

5. A **continuous (rolling) budget** is one that is revised on a regular (continuous) basis.

  a. Typically, a company continuously extends such a budget for an additional month or quarter in accordance with new data as the current month or quarter ends.

    1) For example, if the budget cycle is one year, a budget for the next 12 months will be available continuously as each month ends.

  b. The principal advantage of a rolling budget is that it requires managers always to be thinking ahead.

    1) The disadvantage is the amount of time managers must constantly spend on budget preparation.

6. The Japanese term **kaizen** means continuous improvement, and **kaizen budgeting** assumes the continuous improvement of products and processes.

  a. It requires estimates of the effects of improvements and the costs of their implementation.

  b. Accordingly, kaizen budgeting is based not on the existing system but on changes yet to be made.

  c. Budget targets, for example, **target costs**, cannot be reached unless those improvements occur.

7. A **static budget** is based on only one level of sales or production.

  a. The level of production and the containment of costs are, though related, two separate managerial tasks.

    1) EXAMPLE: A company has the following information for the period:

|  | Actual | Static Budget | Static Variance |
|---|---|---|---|
| Production in units | 1,000 | 1,200 | 200 U |
| Direct materials (units × $6) | $ 6,000 | $ 7,200 | $1,200 F |
| Direct labor (units × $10) | 10,000 | 12,000 | 2,000 F |
| Variable overhead (units × $5) | 5,000 | 6,000 | 1,000 F |
| Total variable costs | $21,000 | $25,200 | $4,200 F |

From these results, it appears that, although the production manager failed to achieve his/her production quota, (s)he did a good job of cost control.

  b. Contrast this with a **flexible budget**, which is a series of budgets prepared for many levels of activity.

    1) At the end of the period, management can compare actual performance with the appropriate budgeted level in the flexible budget.

2)  EXAMPLE: This is the flexible budget comparison for the company at the 1,000 unit level of production:

|  | Actual | Flexible Budget | Flexible Variance |
|---|---|---|---|
| Production in units | 1,000 | 1,000 | -- |
| Direct materials (units × $6) | $ 6,000 | $ 6,000 | $    -- |
| Direct labor (units × $10) | 10,000 | 10,000 | -- |
| Variable overhead (units × $5) | 5,000 | 5,000 | -- |
| Total variable costs | $21,000 | $21,000 | $    -- |

It is clear that the production manager merely incurred the expected costs for the production level that was actually achieved.

8.  A **life-cycle budget** estimates a product's revenues and expenses over its entire life cycle beginning with research and development and ending with the withdrawal of customer support.

   a.  Life-cycle budgeting is intended to account for the costs at all stages of the **value chain** (R&D, design, production, marketing, distribution, and customer service). This information is important for pricing decisions because revenues must cover costs incurred in each stage of the value chain, not just production.

   b.  Life-cycle budgeting emphasizes the relationships among costs incurred at different value-chain stages, e.g., the effect of reduced design costs on future customer-service costs.

   c.  Life-cycle budgeting also highlights the distinction between **incurring costs** (actually using resources) and **locking in (designing in) future costs**.

   d.  Life-cycle concepts are also helpful in **target costing** and **target pricing**.

   e.  See also subunit 4.3.

9.  Stop and review! You have completed the outline for this subunit. Study multiple-choice questions 19 through 38 beginning on page 47.

## 1.3 ANNUAL PROFIT PLAN AND SUPPORTING SCHEDULES

1.  The **master budget**, also called the comprehensive budget or **annual profit plan**, encompasses the organization's **operating** and **financial plans** for a specified period (ordinarily a year or single operating cycle).

   a.  In the **operating budget**, the emphasis is on obtaining and using current resources. It contains the

   1)  Sales budget
   2)  Production budget
   3)  Direct materials budget
   4)  Direct labor budget
   5)  Manufacturing overhead budget
   6)  Cost of goods sold budget
   7)  Ending finished goods inventory budget
   8)  Research and development budget
   9)  Design budget
   10) Marketing budget
   11) Distribution budget
   12) Customer service budget
   13) Administrative budget
   14) Pro forma income statement

    b.    In the **financial budget**, the emphasis is on obtaining the funds needed to purchase operating assets. It contains the

        1)    Capital budget (completed before operating budget is begun)
        2)    Cash budget
        3)    Pro forma balance sheet
        4)    Pro forma statement of cash flows

    c.    The two areas of the master budget interrelate when the pro forma income statement (from the operating budget) is used to prepare the cash budget (from the financial budget).

2.    Before the operating budget cycle begins, the parameters are set by the board-approved **capital budget**.

    a.    The capital budget must have a a multi-year perspective to allow sufficient time to

        1)    Plan financing of major expenditures for long-term assets such as equipment, buildings, and land.
        2)    Receive custom orders of specialized equipment, buildings, etc.

    b.    Several techniques are used as a part of the capital budgeting process to determine how to rank potential capital projects.

        1)    A procedure for ranking projects according to their risk and return characteristics is necessary because every organization has finite resources. These procedures include

            a)    Net present value method (NPV)
            b)    Internal rate of return method (IRR)
            c)    Payback method

        2)    These procedures are described in Gleim's *CMA Review, Part 3*, Study Unit 17, "The Capital Budgeting Process."

    c.    One aspect of capital budgeting is the development of **project budgets** for the management and control of long-term projects.

        1)    These budgets may address the financial activity, actual versus planned costs of completing the project, and post-investment audits of the actual results of a project compared with the forecasted costs and benefits.

3.    The **sales (revenue) budget** presents sales in units at their projected selling prices.

    a.    The sales budget is usually the first part of the operating budget prepared.

        1)    Sales volume affects production and purchasing levels, operating expenses, and cash flow. Accordingly, accurate **sales forecasts** are crucial.
        2)    A forecast considers such factors as trends in sales, conditions in the economy and industry, activities of competitors, credit and pricing policies, marketing methods, and the existence of back orders.

    b.    Sales are usually budgeted by product or department.

    c.    The sales budget establishes targets for sales personnel.

    d.    EXAMPLE of a sales budget. Note the price cut in the third month, which is **expected** to boost sales.

| | April | May | June | 2nd Quarter Totals | Ref. |
|---|---|---|---|---|---|
| Projected sales in units | 1,000 | 1,200 | 1,800 | 4,000 | SB1 |
| Selling price | × $400 | × $400 | × $380 | | |
| Projected total sales | $400,000 | $480,000 | $684,000 | $1,564,000 | SB2 |

4.  The **production budget** (for a manufacturing firm) is based on the sales forecast, in units, plus or minus the desired inventory change.

    a.  A production budget is

        1)  Prepared for each department.
        2)  Used to plan when items will be produced.
        3)  Usually stated in units instead of dollars.

    b.  EXAMPLE of a production budget.

| | Source | April | May | June | 2nd Quarter Totals | Ref. |
|---|---|---|---|---|---|---|
| Projected sales in units | SB1 | 1,000 | 1,200 | 1,800 | 4,000 | |
| Add: desired ending inventory | | | | | | |
| (10% of next month's sales) | | 120 | 180 | 200 | | |
| Total needed | | 1,120 | 1,380 | 2,000 | 4,500 | |
| Less: beginning inventory | | (100) | (120) | (180) | | |
| Units to be produced | | 1,020 | 1,260 | 1,820 | 4,100 | PB |

5.  When the production budget has been completed, it is used to prepare three additional budgets. The first of these is the **direct materials budget**.

    a.  EXAMPLES of two direct materials budgets. Note that the process is expected to experience improved efficiency with regard to raw material A in the third month.

| Raw Material A | Source | April | May | June | 2nd Quarter Totals | Ref. |
|---|---|---|---|---|---|---|
| Units to be produced | PB | 1,020 | 1,260 | 1,820 | 4,100 | |
| Raw material per finished product | | × 4 | × 4 | × 3 | | DMB1 |
| Total needed for production | | 4,080 | 5,040 | 5,460 | 14,580 | |
| Add: desired ending inventory | | | | | | |
| (20% of next month's need) | | 1,008 | 1,092 | 1,600 | | |
| Total needs | | 5,088 | 6,132 | 7,060 | 18,280 | |
| Less: beginning inventory | | (400) | (1,008) | (1,092) | | |
| Raw material to be purchased | | 4,688 | 5,124 | 5,968 | 15,780 | |
| Raw material cost per unit | | × $12 | × $12 | × $12 | | DMB2 |
| Cost of raw material to be purchased | | $56,256 | $61,488 | $71,616 | $189,360 | DMB3 |

Note that a price break on raw material B is expected in the third month.

| Raw Material B | Source | April | May | June | 2nd Quarter Totals | Ref. |
|---|---|---|---|---|---|---|
| Units to be produced | PB | 1,020 | 1,260 | 1,820 | 4,100 | |
| Raw material per finished product | | × 2 | × 2 | × 2 | | DMB4 |
| Total needed for production | | 2,040 | 2,520 | 3,640 | 8,200 | |
| Add: desired ending inventory | | | | | | |
| (20% of next month's need) | | 504 | 728 | 900 | | |
| Total needs | | 2,544 | 3,248 | 4,540 | 10,332 | |
| Less: beginning inventory | | (200) | (504) | (728) | | |
| Raw material to be purchased | | 2,344 | 2,744 | 3,812 | 8,900 | |
| Raw material cost per unit | | × $10 | × $10 | × $8 | | DMB5 |
| Cost of raw material to be purchased | | $23,440 | $27,440 | $30,496 | $81,376 | DMB6 |

6.  The **direct labor budget** depends on wage rates, amounts and types of production, numbers and skill levels of employees to be hired, etc. It may also depend on employee benefits, such as employer contributions to Social Security, insurance, and pensions.

a. **EXAMPLE** of a direct labor budget. No new efficiencies are expected, and the wage rate is set by contract with the union.

| | Source | April | May | June | 2nd Quarter Totals | Ref. |
|---|---|---|---|---|---|---|
| Units to be produced | PB | 1,020 | 1,260 | 1,820 | 4,100 | |
| Direct labor hours per unit | | × 2 | × 2 | × 2 | | DLB1 |
| Projected total direct labor hours | | 2,040 | 2,520 | 3,640 | 8,200 | |
| Direct labor cost per hour | | × $24 | × $24 | × $24 | | DLB2 |
| Total projected direct labor cost | | $48,960 | $60,480 | $87,360 | $196,800 | DLB3 |

b. Direct labor costs usually include not just wages but employee benefits as well.

   1) This full-costing approach is desirable because the amounts paid for employee benefits are inextricably linked with the production of the company's product.

      a) Some manufacturers treat employee benefits as a part of overhead rather than direct labor. Whichever approach is chosen, the external financial statements show the same impact on net income. Note that the financial statements may be impacted by how the costs are allocated.

   2) An **employee benefit statement** shows how much of an employee's pay for a period is made up of wages and how much is made up of fringe benefits, e.g., contributions to Social Security, health and life insurance, and pension contributions.

c. Once the material and labor budgets are completed, they must be evaluated for reasonableness. For example, can the company hire the number of employees anticipated in the budget, are materials sufficiently available, and are facilities available to store the desired ending inventories?

7. The **manufacturing overhead budget** is a function of how overhead varies with particular cost drivers.

   a. **Fixed** and **variable** components of overhead should be treated separately.

   b. EXAMPLE of a manufacturing overhead budget. Note that variable overhead is applied based on direct labor hours.

| | Source | April | May | June | 2nd Quarter Totals | Ref. |
|---|---|---|---|---|---|---|
| Projected total direct labor hours | DLB1 | 2,040 | 2,520 | 3,640 | 8,200 | |
| Variable OH rate per direct labor hour | | × $2 | × $2 | × $2 | | |
| Projected variable overhead | | $4,080 | $5,040 | $7,280 | $16,400 | |
| Projected fixed overhead | | 9,000 | 9,000 | 9,000 | 27,000 | |
| Total projected manufacturing OH | | $13,080 | $14,040 | $16,280 | $43,400 | MOB1 |
| Average OH dollars per direct labor hour | | $6.41 | $5.57 | $4.47 | $5.29 | MOB2 |

8. The **ending finished goods inventory budget** can be prepared now that the components of finished goods cost have been projected.

   a. EXAMPLE of an ending finished goods inventory budget. FIFO is assumed for all inventories. Note that the financial statements would be different if another inventory valuation method, such as LIFO or weighted average, were used.

| | Source | Qty | Input cost | Cost per finished unit | Cost in 200 units at June 30 | Ref. |
|---|---|---|---|---|---|---|
| Production costs in ending inventory: | | | | | | |
| Direct materials – raw material A | DMB1, 2 | 3 | $12.00 | $36.00 | $7,200 | |
| Direct materials – raw material B | DMB4, 5 | 2 | $8.00 | 16.00 | 3,200 | |
| Direct labor | DLB1, 2 | 2 | $24.00 | 48.00 | 9,600 | |
| Manufacturing overhead | MOB2 | 2 | $4.47 | 8.94 | 1,788 | |
| Finished goods cost | | | | $108.94 | $21,788 | EFGIB |

9. The **cost of goods sold budget** reflects direct materials usage, direct labor, overhead, and the change in finished goods inventory.

a. EXAMPLE of a cost of goods sold budget for the quarter.

| | Source | | | Ref. |
|---|---|---|---|---|
| Beginning finished goods inventory | | | $ 16,200 | |
| Manufacturing costs: | | | | |
| Direct materials used – A | DMB3 | $189,360 | | |
| Direct materials used – B | DMB6 | 81,376 | | |
| Direct labor employed | DLB3 | 196,800 | | |
| Manufacturing overhead | MOB1 | 43,400 | | |
| Cost of goods manufactured | | | $510,936 | |
| Cost of goods available for sale | | | $527,136 | |
| Ending finished goods inventory | EFGIB | | (21,788) | |
| Cost of goods sold | | | $505,348 | CGSB |

10. Other budgets prepared during the operating budget process are those for **R&D**, **design**, **marketing**, **distribution**, **customer service**, and **administrative costs**.

a. As in the case of overhead, these budgets should distinguish between fixed and variable costs. These budgets, the sales budget, and the cost of goods sold budget are used to prepare the **pro forma operating income statement**.

b. The development of separate R&D, design, marketing, distribution, customer service, and administrative budgets reflects a **value chain** approach. An alternative is to prepare a single **selling and administrative budget** for nonproduction costs.

c. The variable and fixed portions of selling and administrative costs must be treated separately.

1) Some S&A costs vary directly and proportionately with the level of sales. As more product is sold, sales representatives must travel more miles and serve more customers.

2) Other S&A expenses, such as sales support staff, are fixed; they must be paid no matter the level of sales.

3) As the variable portion of S&A costs increases, **contribution margin**, i.e., the amount available for covering fixed costs, is decreased. Contribution margin is the excess of sales over variable costs.

d. EXAMPLE of a nonmanufacturing costs budget. Note the separate treatment of the variable and fixed portions of cost.

| | Source | April | May | June | 2nd Quarter Totals | Ref. |
|---|---|---|---|---|---|---|
| Variable nonmanufacturing costs: | | | | | | |
| Projected sales in units | SB1 | 1,000 | 1,200 | 1,800 | 4,000 | |
| Variable S&A expenses ($3 per unit sold) | | × $3 | × $3 | × $3 | | |
| Total variable nonmanufacturing costs | | $3,000 | $3,600 | $5,400 | $12,000 | |
| | | | | | | |
| Fixed nonmanufacturing costs: | | | | | | |
| Research and development | | $8,000 | $8,000 | $8,000 | $24,000 | |
| Design | | 4,000 | 4,000 | 4,000 | 12,000 | |
| Marketing | | 7,000 | 7,000 | 7,000 | 21,000 | |
| Distribution | | 10,000 | 10,000 | 10,000 | 30,000 | |
| Customer service | | 11,000 | 11,000 | 11,000 | 33,000 | |
| Administrative | | 50,000 | 50,000 | 50,000 | 150,000 | |
| Total fixed nonmanufacturing costs | | $90,000 | $90,000 | $90,000 | $270,000 | |
| | | | | | | |
| Total nonmanufacturing costs | | $93,000 | $93,600 | $95,400 | $282,000 | NMB |

e. Note that there can be tradeoffs among elements of selling expense that can affect contribution margin. For example, use of fixed advertising expense will increase contribution margin, while the same sales level might be reached using variable sales commissions, a method that would reduce contribution margin.

11. The **pro forma income statement** is the culmination of the operating budget process.

a. **Pro forma** is a Latin phrase that can be loosely translated "as if." Financial statements are referred to as pro forma when they reflect projected, rather than actual, results.

b. It is used to decide whether the budgeted activities will result in an acceptable level of income. If the initial pro forma income statement shows a loss or an unacceptable level of income, the entire budgeting process must begin again.

| | Source | |
|---|---|---|
| Sales | SB2 | $1,564,000 |
| Cost of goods sold | CGSB | (505,348) |
| Gross margin | | $1,058,652 |
| Nonmanufacturing costs | NMB | (282,000) |
| Operating income | | $ 776,652 |

12. The **cash budget** is part of the financial budget cycle and ties together all the schedules from the operating budget.

a. A cash budget is vital because an organization must have adequate cash at all times. Almost all organizations, regardless of size, prepare a cash budget.

1) Even with plenty of other assets, an organization with a temporary shortage of cash can be driven into bankruptcy.

2) Proper planning can keep an entity from financial embarrassment. Thus, cash budgets are prepared not only for annual and quarterly periods but also for monthly and weekly periods.

3) It is particularly important for organizations operating in seasonal industries.

4) A cash budget projects cash receipts and disbursements for planning and control purposes. Hence, it helps prevent not only cash emergencies but also excessive idle cash.

5) Cash budgeting facilitates planning for loans and other financing.

a) A bank is more likely to lend money to a firm if the money will not be needed immediately.

6) Credit granting and purchasing policies (working capital finance) affect cash balances. Firms attempt to expedite cash receipts and delay cash payments.

b. First, a **cash collection schedule** must be prepared. It projects the inflows of cash from customer payments.

1) EXAMPLE of a cash collection schedule. Note the assumption that 5% of sales will prove to be uncollectible.

| | Source | April | May | June | Ref. |
|---|---|---|---|---|---|
| Projected sales | SB2 | $400,000 | $480,000 | $684,000 | |
| Cash collections from sales: | | | | | |
| From 2nd prior month sales (30%) | | 54,000 | 66,000 | 120,000 | |
| From prior month sales (50%) | | 110,000 | 200,000 | 240,000 | |
| From current month sales (15%) | | 60,000 | 72,000 | 102,600 | |
| Total cash collections from sales | | $224,000 | $338,000 | $462,600 | PCCS |
| | | | | | |
| Projected February sales | | $180,000 | | | |
| Projected March sales | | $220,000 | | | |

c.   Next, a **projected cash disbursements** schedule for raw materials is prepared.

1)   EXAMPLE of a raw materials cash disbursements schedule.

| | Source | April | May | June | Ref. |
|---|---|---|---|---|---|
| Projected raw materials cost – A | DMB3 | $56,256 | $61,488 | $71,616 | |
| Cash payments for purchases of A: | | | | | |
| For prior month purchases (40%) | | 18,000 | 22,502 | 24,595 | |
| For current month purchases (60%) | | 33,754 | 36,893 | 42,970 | |
| Total cash disbursements for A | | $51,754 | $59,395 | $67,565 | PCDS1 |
| | | | | | |
| Projected raw materials cost – B | DMB6 | $23,440 | $27,440 | $30,496 | |
| Cash payments for purchases of B: | | | | | |
| For prior month purchases (40%) | | 6,800 | 9,376 | 10,976 | |
| For current month purchases (60%) | | 10,200 | 16,464 | 18,298 | |
| Total cash disbursements for B | | $17,000 | $25,840 | $29,274 | PCDS2 |
| | | | | | |
| Projected March raw materials cost – A | | $45,000 | | | |
| Projected March raw materials cost – B | | $17,000 | | | |

d.   The **cash budget** is part of the financial budget.  It combines source data from the operating budget and produces a comprehensive picture of where the company's cash flows are expected to come from and where they are expected to go.

1)   EXAMPLE of a cash budget.

| | Source | April | May | June |
|---|---|---|---|---|
| Beginning cash balance | | $ 50,000 | $ 50,206 | $100,851 |
| Cash collections from sales | PCCS | 224,000 | 338,000 | 462,600 |
| Cash available for disbursement | | $274,000 | $388,206 | $563,451 |
| Cash disbursements: | | | | |
| For raw material A | PCDS1 | $ 51,754 | $ 59,395 | $ 67,565 |
| For raw material B | PCDS2 | 17,000 | 25,840 | 29,274 |
| For direct labor | DLB3 | 48,960 | 60,480 | 87,360 |
| For manufacturing overhead | MOB1 | 13,080 | 14,040 | 16,280 |
| For nonmanufacturing costs | NMB | 93,000 | 93,600 | 95,400 |
| For equipment purchases | Cap. Budg. | 0 | 0 | 30,000 |
| Total disbursements | | $223,794 | $253,355 | $325,878 |
| Surplus of cash available over disbursements | | $ 50,206 | $184,851 | $171,573 |
| Desired ending cash balance | | 100,000 | 100,000 | 100,000 |
| Surplus (deficiency) of cash | | $ (49,794) | $ 84,851 | $ 71,573 |
| | | | | |
| Financing: | | | | |
| Borrowings | | $ 50,000 | $        0 | $        0 |
| Repayments | | 0 | (50,000) | 0 |
| Net financing | | $ 50,000 | $ (50,000) | $        0 |
| | | | | |
| Ending cash balance | | $100,206 | $ 34,851 | $ 71,573 |

2)   The bottom section of the cash budget deals with the investment or financing strategy when too much or too little cash is anticipated.

13. The final two budgeted financial statements can be prepared at this point.

    a. The **pro forma balance sheet** is prepared using the cash and capital budgets and the pro forma income statement.

        1) The pro forma balance sheet is the beginning-of-the-period balance sheet updated for projected changes in cash, receivables, payables, inventory, etc.

        2) If the balance sheet indicates that a contractual agreement may be violated, the budgeting process must be repeated.

            a) For example, some loan agreements require that owners' equity be maintained at some percentage of total debt or that current assets be maintained at a given multiple of current liabilities.

    b. The **pro forma statement of cash flows** classifies cash receipts and disbursements depending on whether they are from operating, investing, or financing activities.

        1) The direct presentation reports the major classes of gross cash operating receipts and payments and the difference between them.

        2) The indirect presentation reconciles net income with net operating cash flow. Under GAAP, this reconciliation must be disclosed whichever presentation is chosen.

            a) The reconciliation requires balance sheet data, such as the changes in accounts receivable, accounts payable, and inventory, as well as net income.

    c. All the pro forma statements are interrelated (articulated), e.g., the pro forma cash flow statement will include anticipated borrowing. The interest on this borrowing will appear in the pro forma income statement.

14.   This diagram depicts the **budget cycle** for a manufacturing firm that includes all elements of the value chain:

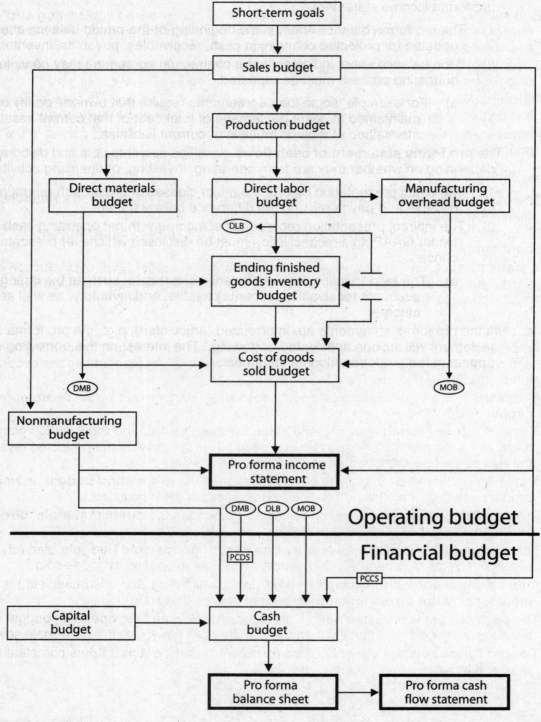

15.   Stop and review!  You have completed the outline for this subunit.  Study multiple-choice questions 39 through 101 beginning on page 53.

## 1.4 CORE CONCEPTS

Budgeting Concepts

- Budgeting is vital to any modern organization. It serves as an aid in **planning and controlling** operations, **communicating with and motivating** employees at all levels, and **evaluating** both organizational and personal performance.
- The budget process usually takes several months and must be **thoroughly planned**. A **budget manual** is distributed to all managers involved.
- **Participative budgeting** involves receiving input from middle- and lower-level employees. It is generally more realistic and more successful than **top-down budgeting**.
- **Management-by-objectives** stresses the need to involve all affected parties in the budgeting process.

Budget Systems

- The **master, or comprehensive, budget** encompasses an organization's **financial and operating plans** for a full year (or operating cycle).
- Budgeting techniques includes **activity-based** budgeting, **zero-based** budgeting, **continuous** budgeting, and **kaizen** budgeting.
- A **static budget** reflects all revenue and cost items at a **single level** of production and sales. A **flexible budget** reflects what revenues and costs should be at **various levels** of production and sales.

Annual Profit Plan and Supporting Schedules

- An organization's **master budget** consists of an **operating budget**, concerning revenues and costs from ongoing operations, and a **financial budget**, concerning the obtaining of funds needed to purchase operating assets.
- Before the operating budget cycle begins, the parameters are set by the board-approved **capital budget**.
- The next step is the preparation of the **sales budget**, in which the organization plans how many units it intends to sell and for what price. This will provide the projected revenue for the rest of the operating budget.
- The sales budget leads directly to the preparation of the **production budget**, in which units produced and desired finished goods inventory levels are calculated.
- Projected production expenses are planned by means of the **direct materials**, **direct labor**, and **manufacturing overhead budgets**.
- The **ending finished goods inventory** and **cost of goods sold budgets** plan for, respectively, costs capitalized in inventory and costs expensed in goods sold.
- After the **nonmanufacturing cost budget** (R&D, marketing, administrative, etc.) is prepared, the **pro forma income statement** can be drawn up.
- The **cash budget** is prepared next. This is the glue between the operating budget and financial budget. The organization must plan its cash flows carefully to remain solvent.
- The **pro forma balance sheet** and **pro forma statement of cash flows** complete the master budget.

## QUESTIONS

### 1.1 Budgeting Concepts

**1.** Which one of the following best describes the role of top management in the budgeting process? Top management

A. Should be involved only in the approval process.

B. Lacks the detailed knowledge of the daily operations and should limit their involvement.

C. Needs to be involved, including using the budget process to communicate goals.

D. Needs to separate the budgeting process and the business planning process into two separate processes.

**Answer (C) is correct.** *(CMA, adapted)*

**REQUIRED:** The best description of top management's role in the budgeting process.

**DISCUSSION:** Among other things, the budget is a tool by which management can communicate goals to lower-level employees. It is also a tool for motivating employees to reach those goals. For the budget to function in these communication and motivating roles, top management must be involved in the process. This involvement does not extend to dictating the exact numerical contents of the budget since top management lacks a detailed knowledge of daily operations.

Answer (A) is incorrect because top managers can use the budget for motivational and communication purposes; they should do more than merely sign off on the finished document. Answer (B) is incorrect because top managers should be involved in the budget process even though they lack detailed knowledge of daily operations; the budget can still communicate company objectives and goals. Answer (D) is incorrect because the budget process is a part of the overall planning process.

**2.** Kallert Manufacturing currently uses the company's budget only as a planning tool. Management has decided that it would be beneficial also to use budgets for control purposes. In order to implement this change, the management accountant must

A. Appoint a budget director.

B. Organize a budget committee.

C. Develop forecasting procedures.

D. Synchronize the budgeting and accounting system with the organizational structure.

**Answer (D) is correct.** *(CMA, adapted)*

**REQUIRED:** The action the management accountant must take to use the budget as a control tool.

**DISCUSSION:** A budget can be many tools in one. It can be used for planning, controlling, communication, motivation, and evaluation. The accounting system contains a great deal of the data that feeds the budget process, as well as the data that will be compared with the budget for control and evaluation purposes. For the budget to serve effectively in these multiple roles, it must be integrated with the accounting system and the organizational structure. Relating the budgeting and accounting systems to the organizational structure will therefore enhance planning, control, and evaluation by transmitting data and assigning variances to the proper organizational subunits.

Answer (A) is incorrect because a budget director should already exist under the current budget system. Answer (B) is incorrect because a budget committee should already exist under the current budget system. Answer (C) is incorrect because forecasting procedures should already exist under the current budget system.

**3.** When developing a budget, an external factor to consider in the planning process is

A. A change to a decentralized management system.

B. The implementation of a new bonus program.

C. New product development.

D. The merger of two competitors.

**Answer (D) is correct.** *(CMA, adapted)*

**REQUIRED:** The external factor that should be considered during the budget planning process.

**DISCUSSION:** Several planning assumptions should be made at the beginning of the budget process. Some of these assumptions are internal factors; others are external to the company. External factors include general economic conditions and their expected trend, governmental regulatory measures, the labor market in the locale of the company's facilities, and activities of competitors, including the effects of mergers.

Answer (A) is incorrect because changes in management is an internal factor. Answer (B) is incorrect because employee compensation is an internal factor. Answer (C) is incorrect because a new product line is an internal factor.

**4.** While an operating budget is a key element in planning and control, it is not likely to

- A. Establish a commitment of company resources.
- B. Set out long-range, strategic concepts.
- C. Integrate organizational activities.
- D. Provide subsidiary planning information.

Answer (B) is correct. *(CIA, adapted)*
REQUIRED: What a budget is not likely to do.
DISCUSSION: Budgets seldom set out long-range strategic concepts because they usually deal with the quantitative allocation of people and resources. Strategic concepts are overall goals for the organization and are almost always stated in words.
Answer (A) is incorrect because budgets do commit company resources in that the allotment of scarce resources is the primary purpose of a budget. Answer (C) is incorrect because budgets do integrate organizational activities. Failure of a budget to integrate activities will result in the budgeting of more or less materials and resources than are available to the organization. Answer (D) is incorrect because subsidiary plans can be made directly from overall budgets.

**5.** Planning is receiving increased attention by many organizations. Which of the following is true?

- A. Long-range planning is usually performed by lower-level personnel.
- B. The time devoted to planning is inversely related to the organizational level.
- C. Planning requires historical and projected data.
- D. The extent of detail in planning information varies directly with the organizational level.

Answer (C) is correct. *(CIA, adapted)*
REQUIRED: The true statement about planning.
DISCUSSION: All planning requires the use of historical and projected data. Without estimates of future conditions, no planning can take place.
Answer (A) is incorrect because long-range planning is almost always performed by high-level personnel. Answer (B) is incorrect because the time devoted to planning is directly, not inversely, proportional to the organizational level. The higher the executive, the more time is spent on planning. Answer (D) is incorrect because the extent of detail in planning information varies inversely with organizational level. Thus, the lower the level on which plans are being made, the more details are available for planning purposes.

**6.** When budgets are used to evaluate performance and to set limits on spending, the process will often result in departments adding something "extra" to ensure the budgets will be met. This "extra" is

- A. Management by objectives.
- B. Strategic planning.
- C. Continuous budgeting.
- D. Budgetary slack.

Answer (D) is correct. *(CMA, adapted)*
REQUIRED: The term for the extra padding that is sometimes put into budgets to make them easier to achieve.
DISCUSSION: Budgetary slack is the term referring to the underestimation of probable performance in a budget. With slack in a budget, a manager can achieve the budget more easily. Slack must be avoided if a budget is to have its desired effects.
Answer (A) is incorrect because management by objectives (MBO) is a behavioral, communications-oriented responsibility approach to employee self-direction. Answer (B) is incorrect because strategic planning is a method of long-term planning. Answer (C) is incorrect because continuous (or rolling) budgeting is a method of extending each budget by an additional period as each period passes.

**7.** In a well-run organization, a manager may have responsibility for activities that (s)he cannot significantly influence. This arrangement may be justified because of the

- A. Manager's knowledge about the activities and the potential for behavioral change.
- B. Manager's knowledge about the activities but not the potential for behavioral change.
- C. Improvement in managerial morale, effort, and performance.
- D. Improvement in managerial morale and the potential for behavioral change.

Answer (A) is correct. *(Publisher)*
REQUIRED: The reason(s) for assigning responsibility without control.
DISCUSSION: A manager who does not control an activity may nevertheless be the individual who is best informed about it. Thus, a purchasing agent may be in the best position to explain price variances even though (s)he cannot control them. Moreover, if a manager is accountable solely for activities over which (s)he has extensive influence, the manager may develop too narrow a focus. For example, the manager of a cost center may make decisions based only on cost efficiency and ignore the overall effectiveness goals of the organization. By extending the manager's responsibility to profits as well as costs without changing his/her level of control, the organization may encourage desirable behavior congruent with overall goals, such as improved coordination with marketing personnel.
Answer (B) is incorrect because the potential for favorable behavioral change may justify assigning responsibility without control. Answer (C) is incorrect because, if responsibility exceeds the extent to which a manager can influence an activity, the result may be reduced morale, a decline in managerial effort, and poor performance. Answer (D) is incorrect because, if responsibility exceeds the extent to which a manager can influence an activity, the result may be reduced morale.

**8.** An advantage of participative budgeting is that it

A. Minimizes the cost of developing budgets.

B. Reduces the effect on the budgetary process of employee biases.

C. Yields information known to management but not to employees.

D. Encourages acceptance of the budget by employees.

Answer (D) is correct.  *(Publisher)*
**REQUIRED:** The advantage of participative budgeting.
**DISCUSSION:** Participative budgeting (grass-roots budgeting) and standard-setting use input from lower-level and middle-level employees. Participation encourages employees to have a sense of ownership of the output of the process. The result is an acceptance of and commitment to the goals expressed in the budget.
Answer (A) is incorrect because disadvantages of participative budgeting and standard-setting include the cost in terms of time and money. Answer (B) is incorrect because the quality of participation is affected by the goals, values, beliefs, and expectations of those involved. Answer (C) is incorrect because an advantage of participative budgeting is that it yields information known to employees but not to management.

**9.** The budgeting process should be one that motivates managers and employees to work toward organizational objectives. Which one of the following is least likely to motivate managers?

A. Participation by subordinates in the budgetary process.

B. Having top management set budget levels.

C. Use of management by exception.

D. Holding subordinates accountable for the items they control.

Answer (B) is correct.  *(CMA, adapted)*
**REQUIRED:** The aspect of the budgeting process least likely to motivate managers.
**DISCUSSION:** One of the roles of a budget is to motivate employees to achieve organizational objectives. Before a budget can be an effective motivational tool, it must be viewed as realistic by employees, so targets should be attainable. Thus, employees will be more committed to the budget if they participate in its preparation. A manager who helps to prepare a budget is more likely to work hard to achieve the budgeted figures. Thus, the least effective way of producing a budget for motivational purposes is for top management to impose it on the lower levels of management.
Answer (A) is incorrect because participation fosters a sense of ownership. Answer (C) is incorrect because use of management by exception devotes managerial effort to matters of significance. Answer (D) is incorrect because accountability provides an incentive for good performance.

**10.** In an organization that plans by using comprehensive budgeting, the master budget is

A. A compilation of all the separate operational and financial budget schedules of the organization.

B. The booklet containing budget guidelines, policies, and forms to use in the budgeting process.

C. The current budget updated for operations for part of the current year.

D. A budget of a not-for-profit organization after it is approved by the appropriate authoritative body.

Answer (A) is correct.  *(CMA, adapted)*
**REQUIRED:** The nature of the master budget.
**DISCUSSION:** Budgets coordinate the various activities of a firm. A company's overall budget, often called the master or comprehensive budget, encompasses the organization's operating and financial plans for a specified period, ordinarily a year. Thus, all other budgets are subsets of the master budget. The operating budget is the part of the master budget that consists of the pro forma income statement and related budgets. Its emphasis is on obtaining and using resources. The financial budget is the part of the master budget that includes the cash budget, capital budget, pro forma balance sheet, and pro forma statement of cash flows. Its emphasis is on obtaining the funds needed to purchase operating assets.
Answer (B) is incorrect because the booklet containing budget guidelines, policies, and forms to use in the budgeting process is the budget manual. Answer (C) is incorrect because the current budget updated for operations for part of the current year is a continuous budget. Answer (D) is incorrect because a master budget may be prepared by a for-profit entity.

**11.** A budget manual, which enhances the operation of a budget system, is most likely to include

    A. A chart of accounts.

    B. Distribution instructions for budget schedules.

    C. Employee hiring policies.

    D. Documentation of the accounting system software.

Answer (B) is correct. *(CMA, adapted)*
    **REQUIRED:** The item normally included in a budget manual.
    **DISCUSSION:** A budget manual describes how a budget is to be prepared. Items usually included in a budget manual are a planning calendar and distribution instructions for all budget schedules. Distribution instructions are important because, once a schedule is prepared, other departments within the organization will use the schedule to prepare their own budgets. Without distribution instructions, someone who needs a particular schedule may be overlooked.
    Answer (A) is incorrect because the chart of accounts is normally located in the accounting manual. Answer (C) is incorrect because employee hiring policies are not needed for budget preparation. Answer (D) is incorrect because software documentation is not needed in the budget preparation process.

**12.** A planning calendar in budgeting is the

    A. Calendar period covered by the budget.

    B. Schedule of activities for the development and adoption of the budget.

    C. Calendar period covered by the annual budget and the long-range plan.

    D. Sales forecast by months in the annual budget period.

Answer (B) is correct. *(CMA, adapted)*
    **REQUIRED:** The definition of a budget planning calendar.
    **DISCUSSION:** The budget planning calendar is the schedule of activities for the development and adoption of the budget. It should include a list of dates indicating when specific information is to be provided by each information source to others. The preparation of a master budget usually takes several months. For instance, many firms start the budget for the next calendar year some time in September in hopes of having it completed by December 1. Because all of the individual departmental budgets are based on forecasts prepared by others and the budgets of other departments, it is essential to have a planning calendar to ensure the proper integration of the entire process.
    Answer (A) is incorrect because the period covered by the budget precedes the events in the planning calendar.
    Answer (C) is incorrect because the period covered by the budget precedes the events in the planning calendar.
    Answer (D) is incorrect because the planning calendar is not associated with sales.

**13.** Which one of the following is not considered to be a benefit of participative budgeting?

    A. Individuals at all organizational levels are recognized as being part of the team; this results in greater support of the organization.

    B. The budget estimates are prepared by those in direct contact with various activities.

    C. Managers are more motivated to reach the budget objectives since they participated in setting them.

    D. When managers set the final targets for the budget, senior management need not be concerned with the overall profitability of current operations.

Answer (D) is correct. *(CMA, adapted)*
    **REQUIRED:** The item that is not considered to be a benefit of participative budgeting.
    **DISCUSSION:** One of the behavioral considerations of budgeting is the extent of participation in the process by managers at all levels within the organization. Managers are more motivated to achieve budgeted goals when they are involved in budget preparation. A broad level of participation usually leads to greater support for the budget and the entity as a whole, as well as a greater understanding of what is to be accomplished. Advantages of a participative budget include greater accuracy of budget estimates. Managers with immediate operational responsibility for activities have a better understanding of what results can be achieved and at what costs. Also, managers cannot blame unrealistic objectives as an excuse for not achieving budget expectations when they have helped to establish those objectives. Despite the involvement of lower level managers, senior management must still participate in the budget process to ensure that the combined objectives of the various departments are consistent with profitability objectives of the company.
    Answer (A) is incorrect because participative budgeting promotes teamwork. Answer (B) is incorrect because a participative budget involves those most directly affected. Answer (C) is incorrect because a participative budget is a powerful motivator.

**14.** Which one of the following organizational policies is most likely to result in undesirable managerial behavior?

    A. Patel Chemicals sponsors television coverage of cricket matches between national teams representing India and Pakistan. The expenses of such media sponsorship are not allocated to its various divisions.

    B. Joe Walk, the chief executive officer of Eagle Rock Brewery, wrote a memorandum to his executives stating, "Operating plans are contracts, and they should be met without fail."

    C. The budgeting process at Madsen Manufacturing starts with operating managers providing goals for their respective departments.

    D. Fullbright Lighting holds quarterly meetings of departmental managers to consider possible changes in the budgeted targets due to changing conditions.

Answer (B) is correct.  *(CMA, adapted)*
    **REQUIRED:** The organizational policy most likely to result in undesirable managerial behavior.
    **DISCUSSION:** Control is the process of making certain that plans are achieving the desired objectives. A budget is one of the most common control devices. It is a plan for the future; it is not a contract. To interpret a budget or other plan to be as inflexible as a contract may encourage a manager to act in ways contrary to the company's best interests in a misguided effort to meet the criteria set forth.
    Answer (A) is incorrect because, if the costs are not allocated to individual managers, they have no reason to object to the allocation. Answer (C) is incorrect because participative budgeting obtains the support of those involved and is likely to foster desirable behavior. Answer (D) is incorrect because changing budget targets as conditions change results in setting fairer performance objectives.

**15.** MBO managers are most likely to believe that employees

    A. Dislike their work.

    B. Avoid responsibility whenever possible.

    C. Work best when threatened with punishment.

    D. Are self-motivated.

Answer (D) is correct.  *(Publisher)*
    **REQUIRED:** The characteristic an MBO manager attributes to employees.
    **DISCUSSION:** MBO managers believe that employees are committed to achieving objectives, working hard to receive the rewards of achievement, and striving for self-actualization. The MBO view is that employees enjoy work, need little supervision, seek responsibility, and are imaginative problem solvers.
    Answer (A) is incorrect because disliking their work is a characteristic that authoritarian managers attribute to their employees. Answer (B) is incorrect because avoiding responsibility whenever possible is a characteristic that authoritarian managers attribute to their employees. Answer (C) is incorrect because working best when threatened with punishment is a characteristic that authoritarian managers attribute to their employees.

**16.** A budget is often the result of a management-by-objectives (MBO) program. A characteristic of MBO is

    A. Development of a single measure of employee performance.

    B. Statement of objectives in general terms.

    C. Establishment of objectives through both top-down and bottom-up processes.

    D. A flexible time frame for achievement of objectives.

Answer (C) is correct.  *(Publisher)*
    **REQUIRED:** The characteristic of MBO.
    **DISCUSSION:** Budgets and standards are often the result of a formal management-by-objectives program. MBO is a top-down process because the organization's objectives are successively restated into objectives for each lower level. However, it is also a bottom-up process because of the participation of subordinates.
    Answer (A) is incorrect because multiple measures of employee performance are preferable. Answer (B) is incorrect because objectives should be specific. Answer (D) is incorrect because a specific time period is established.

**17.** A company has a compensation system for its managers based on an MBO approach. The essential premise of MBO is that

A. Compensation should be based on qualitative factors.

B. Employees should be concerned with routine matters, and managers should attend to exceptions.

C. Employees should participate in setting goals.

D. Managers should establish objectives for their employees.

Answer (C) is correct. *(Publisher)*
  **REQUIRED:** The essential premise of MBO.
  **DISCUSSION:** The hallmark of MBO is the mutual setting of goals by the superior and the subordinate as a basis for performance evaluation. Based on the philosophy that employees want to work hard if they know what is expected, MBO requires senior management participation and commitment to the program, integration of the objectives for all subunits into a compatible system directed toward accomplishment of overall objectives, provision for regular reporting of performance, and free and honest communication between superior and subordinates. Subordinates must make careful assessments of their abilities and their interests, and managers must "coach" subordinates rather than dictate their proper goals. Flexibility must be maintained up and down the organizational hierarchy to accommodate unforeseen changes, and the review and analysis of results before setting the next round of goals is a vital part of the process.
  Answer (A) is incorrect because objectives may be set in terms of both quantitative measures (such as sales dollars) and qualitative ones (such as improved service). Answer (B) is incorrect because it describes management by exception. Answer (D) is incorrect because setting objectives should be participative.

**18.** The primary role of the budget director and the budgeting department is to

A. Settle disputes among operating executives during the development of the annual operating plan.

B. Develop the annual profit plan by selecting the alternatives to be adopted from the suggestions submitted by the various operating segments.

C. Justify the budget to the executive committee of the board of directors.

D. Compile the budget and manage the budget process.

Answer (D) is correct. *(CMA, adapted)*
  **REQUIRED:** The primary role of the budget director and the budgeting department.
  **DISCUSSION:** The budget department is responsible for compiling the budget and managing the budget process. The budget director and department are not responsible for actually developing the estimates on which the budget is based. This role is performed by those to whom the resulting budget will be applicable. The budget director has staff, not line, authority. (S)he has a technical and advisory role. The final decision-making responsibility rests with line management.

## 1.2 Budget Systems

**19.** A continuous profit plan

A. Is a plan that is revised monthly or quarterly.

B. Is an annual plan that is part of a 5-year plan.

C. Is a plan devised by a full-time planning staff.

D. Works best for a company that can reliably forecast events a year or more into the future.

Answer (A) is correct. *(CMA, adapted)*
  **REQUIRED:** The definition of a continuous profit plan.
  **DISCUSSION:** A continuous, or rolling, budget (profit plan) is one that is revised on a regular or continuous basis. Typically, a company that uses continuous budgeting extends the budget for another month or quarter in accordance with new data as the current month or quarter ends. For example, if the budget is for 12 months, a budget for the next year will always be available at the end of each interim period. Continuous budgeting encourages a longer-term perspective regardless of how little time remains in the company's current fiscal year.
  Answer (B) is incorrect because a continuous profit plan is one that is revised and extended as available information changes. Answer (C) is incorrect because a continuous plan can be prepared by either a full-time or part-time staff. Answer (D) is incorrect because it is the lack of reliable long-range information that makes the continuous profit plan so worthwhile.

**20.** A continuous (rolling) budget

A. Presents planned activities for a period but does not present a firm commitment.

B. Presents the plan for only one level of activity and does not adjust to changes in the level of activity.

C. Presents the plan for a range of activity so that the plan can be adjusted for changes in activity.

D. Drops the current month or quarter and adds a future month or quarter as the current month or quarter is completed.

Answer (D) is correct.  *(CMA, adapted)*
    **REQUIRED:** The true statement about a continuous budget.
    **DISCUSSION:** A continuous, or rolling, budget is one that is revised on a regular (continuous) basis. Typically, a company extends such a budget for another month or quarter in accordance with new data as the current month or quarter ends. For example, if the budget is for 12 months, a budget for the next 12 months will be available continuously as each month ends.
    Answer (A) is incorrect because a continuous budget does present a firm commitment. Answer (B) is incorrect because a continuous budget can be for various levels of activity; a budget prepared for only one level of activity is a static budget. Answer (C) is incorrect because a budget that presents a range of activity so that the plan can be adjusted for changes in activity is a flexible budget.

**21.** Flexible budgets

A. Provide for external factors affecting company profitability.

B. Are used to evaluate capacity use.

C. Are budgets that project costs based on anticipated future improvements.

D. Accommodate changes in activity levels.

Answer (D) is correct.  *(CMA, adapted)*
    **REQUIRED:** The true statement about flexible budgets.
    **DISCUSSION:** A flexible budget is actually a series of budgets prepared for various levels of activity. A flexible budget adjusts the master budget for changes in activity so that actual results can be compared with meaningful budget amounts. The assumptions are that total fixed costs and unit variable costs are constant within the relevant range.
    Answer (A) is incorrect because flexible budgets address external factors only to the extent that activity is affected. Answer (B) is incorrect because a flexible budget essentially restates variable costs for different activity levels within the relevant range. Hence, a flexible budget variance does not address capacity use. An output level (production volume) variance is a fixed cost variance. Answer (C) is incorrect because, by definition, flexible budgets address differences in activity levels only within the relevant range.

**22.** A static budget

A. Drops the current month or quarter and adds a future month or a future quarter as the current month or quarter is completed.

B. Presents a statement of expectations for a period but does not present a firm commitment.

C. Presents the plan for only one level of activity and does not adjust to changes in the level of activity.

D. Presents the plan for a range of activity so that the plan can be adjusted for changes in activity.

Answer (C) is correct.  *(CMA, adapted)*
    **REQUIRED:** The definition of a static budget.
    **DISCUSSION:** A static budget plans for only one level of activity and does not provide for changed levels of activity.
    Answer (A) is incorrect because budgets dropping the current month or quarter and adding a future month or quarter as the current month or quarter is completed are known as continuous budgets. Answer (B) is incorrect because a statement of expectations for a period without a firm commitment is a forecast. Answer (D) is incorrect because a budget planning for a range of activities so the plan can be adjusted for a change in activity level is known as a flexible budget.

**23.** A flexible budget

A. Classifies budget requests by activity and estimates the benefits arising from each activity.

B. Presents a statement of expectations for a period but does not present a firm commitment.

C. Presents the plan for only one level of activity and does not adjust to changes in the level of activity.

D. Presents the plan for a range of activity so that the plan can be adjusted for changes in activity.

Answer (D) is correct.  *(CMA, adapted)*
    **REQUIRED:** The definition of a flexible budget.
    **DISCUSSION:** A flexible budget provides plans for a range of activity so that the budget can be adapted to the actual level of activity.
    Answer (A) is incorrect because budgets classifying requests by activity and estimating the benefits of each activity are "program planning and budgeting systems (PPBS)." Answer (B) is incorrect because a statement of expectations for a period without a firm commitment is a forecast. Answer (C) is incorrect because a budget prepared for only one level of activity is a static budget.

**24.** Butteco has the following cost components for 100,000 units of product for the year:

| | |
|---|---|
| Direct materials | $200,000 |
| Direct labor | 100,000 |
| Manufacturing overhead | 200,000 |
| Selling and administrative expense | 150,000 |

All costs are variable except for $100,000 of manufacturing overhead and $100,000 of selling and administrative expenses. The total costs to produce and sell 110,000 units for the year are

A. $650,000

B. $715,000

C. $695,000

D. $540,000

Answer (C) is correct. *(CMA, adapted)*
**REQUIRED:** The flexible budget costs for producing and selling a given quantity.
**DISCUSSION:** Direct materials unit costs are strictly variable at $2 ($200,000 ÷ 100,000 units). Similarly, direct labor has a variable unit cost of $1 ($100,000 ÷ 100,000 units). The $200,000 of manufacturing overhead for 100,000 units is 50%. The variable unit cost is $1. Selling costs are $100,000 fixed and $50,000 variable for production of 100,000 units, and the variable unit selling expenses is $.50 ($50,000 ÷ 100,000 units). The total unit variable cost is therefore $4.50 ($2 + $1 + $1 + $.50). Fixed costs are $200,000. At a production level of 110,000 units, variable costs are $495,000 (110,000 units × $4.50). Hence, total costs are $695,000 ($495,000 + $200,000).
Answer (A) is incorrect because $650,000 is the cost at a production level of 100,000 units. Answer (B) is incorrect because $715,000 assumes a variable unit cost of $6.50 with no fixed costs. Answer (D) is incorrect because total costs are $695,000 based on a unit variable cost of $4.50 each.

**25.** Comparing actual results with a budget based on achieved volume is possible with the use of a

A. Monthly budget.

B. Master budget.

C. Rolling budget.

D. Flexible budget.

Answer (D) is correct. *(CMA, adapted)*
**REQUIRED:** The budget that permits easy comparison of actual results with a budget based on achieved volume.
**DISCUSSION:** A flexible budget is essentially a series of several budgets prepared for many levels of sales or production. At the end of the period, management can compare actual costs or performance with the appropriate budgeted level in the flexible budget. A flexible budget is designed to allow adjustment of the budget to the actual level of activity before comparing the budgeted activity with actual results.
Answer (A) is incorrect because comparing results using a monthly budget is no easier than using a budget of any other duration. Answer (B) is incorrect because a master budget is the overall budget. It will not facilitate comparisons unless it is also a flexible budget. Answer (C) is incorrect because a rolling (or continuous) budget is revised on a regular (continuous) basis. It will not facilitate comparisons unless it is also a flexible budget.

**26.** Which one of the following budgeting methodologies would be most appropriate for a firm facing a significant level of uncertainty in unit sales volumes for next year?

A. Top-down budgeting.

B. Life-cycle budgeting.

C. Static budgeting.

D. Flexible budgeting.

Answer (D) is correct. *(CMA, adapted)*
**REQUIRED:** The budgeting methodology most appropriate for a firm facing significant uncertainty about unit sales volumes.
**DISCUSSION:** Flexible budgeting prepares a series of budgets for many levels of sales. At the end of the period, management can compare actual sales performance with the appropriate budgeted level in the flexible budget. A flexible budget is designed to allow adjustment of the budget to the actual level of activity before comparing the budgeted activity with actual results.
Answer (A) is incorrect because top-down budgeting entails imposition of a budget by top management on lower-level employees. It is the antithesis of participatory budgeting. Answer (B) is incorrect because life-cycle budgeting estimates a product's revenues and costs for each link in the value chain from R&D and design to production, marketing, distribution, and customer service. The product life cycle ends when customer service is withdrawn. Answer (C) is incorrect because a static budget is for only one level of activity.

**27.** Barnes Corporation expected to sell 150,000 board games during the month of November, and the company's master budget contained the following data related to the sale and production of these games:

| | |
|---|---:|
| Revenue | $2,400,000 |
| Cost of goods sold: | |
|   Direct materials | 675,000 |
|   Direct labor | 300,000 |
|   Variable overhead | 450,000 |
|   Contribution | $ 975,000 |
| Fixed overhead | 250,000 |
| Fixed selling and administration | 500,000 |
|   Operating income | $ 225,000 |

Actual sales during November were 180,000 games. Using a flexible budget, the company expects the operating income for the month of November to be

A. $225,000

B. $270,000

C. $420,000

D. $510,000

Answer (C) is correct. *(CMA, adapted)*
**REQUIRED:** The expected operating income based on a flexible budget at a given production level.
**DISCUSSION:** Revenue of $2,400,000 reflects a unit selling price of $16 ($2,400,000 ÷ 150,000 games). The contribution margin is $975,000, or $6.50 per game ($975,000 ÷ 150,000 games). Increasing sales will result in an increased contribution margin of $195,000 (30,000 games × $6.50). Assuming no additional fixed costs, net income will increase to $420,000 ($225,000 originally reported + $195,000).
Answer (A) is incorrect because $225,000 is the net income before the increase in sales. Answer (B) is incorrect because net income was originally $1.50 per game. The $270,000 figure simply extrapolates that amount to sales of 180,000 games. Answer (D) is incorrect because $510,000 treats variable overhead as a fixed cost. Variable overhead is a $3 component ($450,000 ÷ 150,000 units) of unit variable cost.

**28.** A company has the following budget formula for annual electricity expense in its shop:

Expense = $7,200 + (Units produced × $0.60)

If management expects to produce 20,000 units during February, the appropriate monthly flexible budget allowance for the purpose of performance evaluation should be

A. $7,200

B. $12,000

C. $12,600

D. $19,200

Answer (C) is correct. *(Publisher)*
**REQUIRED:** The monthly flexible budget allowance.
**DISCUSSION:** The formula is for an annual period. Thus, the first step is to divide the $7,200 of fixed costs by 12 months to arrive at monthly fixed costs of $600. Variable costs will be $.60 per unit, or $12,000 for 20,000 units. The total flexible budget amount is therefore $12,600 ($600 + $12,000).
Answer (A) is incorrect because $7,200 is the annual fixed cost. Answer (B) is incorrect because $12,000 is the variable cost. Answer (D) is incorrect because $19,200 is based on fixed costs of $7,200.

**29.** National Telephone has been forced by competition to drastically cut operating costs which has resulted in a change from static budgeting to flexible budgeting. Which one of the following steps will not help National Telephone gain maximum acceptance of the proposed budgeting system?

A. Implementing the change quickly.

B. Focusing departmental reports only on items that are under managers' control.

C. Demonstrating top management support for the change.

D. Ensuring that variances highlight good performances as well as pinpoint weaknesses.

Answer (A) is correct. *(CMA, adapted)*
**REQUIRED:** The step that will not help a firm gain maximum acceptance of a flexible budgeting system.
**DISCUSSION:** Any changes in a budget system should, like any organizational change, be properly communicated to all affected employees to reduce fear of personal, social, or economic adjustments. A participative management approach to effecting change should avoid arbitrary, capricious, or prejudicial actions; provide ample notice, including information about the reasons for the change, its precise nature, and the expected results; allow maximum participation in the implementation of the change; and anticipate and, to the extent possible, accommodate the needs of those involved. Accordingly, a rapid change in a budget system is not recommended because employees may not be able to understand the need for, or benefits of, the new system.
Answer (B) is incorrect because a flexible budget better enables managers to control their operations. The budget figures within their control are emphasized. Answer (C) is incorrect because any budgeting change must have the support of top management to ensure acceptance at lower levels. Answer (D) is incorrect because employee morale benefits from recognizing good performance.

**30.** When preparing a performance report for a cost center using flexible budgeting techniques, the planned cost column should be based on the

A. Budgeted amount in the original budget prepared before the beginning of the year.

B. Actual amount for the same period in the preceding year.

C. Budget adjusted to the actual level of activity for the period being reported.

D. Budget adjusted to the planned level of activity for the period being reported.

Answer (C) is correct. *(CMA, adapted)*
**REQUIRED:** The basis for the planned cost column in a flexible budget performance report.
**DISCUSSION:** If a report is to be used for performance evaluation, the planned cost column should be based on the actual level of activity for the period. The ability to adjust amounts for varying activity levels is the primary advantage of flexible budgeting.
Answer (A) is incorrect because the static budget amount is not useful for comparison purposes. The budget for the actual activity level achieved is more important. Answer (B) is incorrect because prior-year figures are not useful if activity levels are different. Answer (D) is incorrect because a budget based on planned activity level is not as meaningful as one based on actual activity level.

**31.** The use of standard costs in the budgeting process signifies that an organization has most likely implemented a

A. Flexible budget.

B. Capital budget.

C. Zero-based budget.

D. Static budget.

Answer (A) is correct. *(CMA, adapted)*
**REQUIRED:** The budget most likely implemented by a company that uses standard costs.
**DISCUSSION:** A flexible budget is a series of budgets prepared for many levels of sales or production. Another view is that it is based on cost formulas, or standard costs. Thus, the cost formulas are fed into the computerized budget program along with the actual level of sales or production. The result is a budget created for the actual level of activity.
Answer (B) is incorrect because a capital budget is a means of evaluating long-term investments and has nothing to do with standard costs. Answer (C) is incorrect because a zero-based budget is a planning process in which each manager must justify a department's entire budget each year. The budget is built from the base of zero each year. Answer (D) is incorrect because a static budget is for one level of activity. It can be based on expected actual or standard costs.

**32.** A plan that is created using budgeted revenue and costs but is based on the actual units of output is known as a

A. Continuous budget.

B. Flexible budget.

C. Strategic plan.

D. Static budget.

Answer (B) is correct. *(CMA, adapted)*
**REQUIRED:** The plan based on budgeted revenue and costs and actual output.
**DISCUSSION:** A flexible budget is a series of several budgets prepared for many levels of sales or output. Given a flexible budget, management can compare actual costs or performance with the appropriate budgeted level in the flexible budget. A flexible budget is designed to allow adjustment of the budget to the actual level of activity before comparing the budgeted activity with actual results.
Answer (A) is incorrect because a continuous budget is revised on a regular (continuous) basis by extending it for another month or quarter in accordance with new data as the current month or quarter ends. Answer (C) is incorrect because a strategic plan is a long-term planning device. Answer (D) is incorrect because a static (fixed) budget is prepared for only one level of output. That level will probably not be the level of actual operations.

**33.** The difference between the actual amounts and the flexible budget amounts for the actual output achieved is the

A. Production volume variance.

B. Flexible budget variance.

C. Sales volume variance.

D. Standard cost variance.

Answer (B) is correct. *(CMA, adapted)*
**REQUIRED:** The term meaning the difference between the actual amounts and the flexible budget amounts.
**DISCUSSION:** A flexible budget is a series of several budgets prepared for many levels of activity. A flexible budget allows adjustment of the budget to the actual level before comparing the budgeted and actual results. The difference between the flexible budget and actual figures is known as the flexible budget variance.
Answer (A) is incorrect because production volume variance (or the idle capacity variance) is based on the difference between actual and budgeted levels of production in terms of quantities. Answer (C) is incorrect because sales volume variance is based on the difference between actual and budgeted sales volume without regard to cost. Answer (D) is incorrect because a standard cost variance is not necessarily based on a flexible budget.

**34.** Which one of the following statements regarding the difference between a flexible budget and a static budget is true?

- A. A flexible budget primarily is prepared for planning purposes, while a static budget is prepared for performance evaluation.

- B. A flexible budget provides cost allowances for different levels of activity, whereas a static budget provides costs for one level of activity.

- C. A flexible budget includes only variable costs, whereas a static budget includes only fixed costs.

- D. A flexible budget is established by operating management, while a static budget is determined by top management.

Answer (B) is correct.  *(CMA, adapted)*
**REQUIRED:** The difference between a flexible and a fixed budget.
**DISCUSSION:** A flexible budget provides cost allowances for different levels of activity, but a static budget provides costs for only one level of activity. Both budgets show the same types of costs. In a sense, a flexible budget is a series of budgets prepared for many different levels of activity. A flexible budget allows adjustment of the budget to the actual level of activity before comparing the budgeted activity with actual results.
Answer (A) is incorrect because both budgets are prepared for both planning and performance evaluation purposes. Answer (C) is incorrect because both budgets include both fixed and variable costs. Answer (D) is incorrect because either budget can be established by any level of management.

**35.** A systemized approach known as ZBB

- A. Presents planned activities for a period of time but does not present a firm commitment.

- B. Divides the activities of individual responsibility centers into a series of packages that are prioritized.

- C. Classifies the budget by the prior year's activity and estimates the benefits arising from each activity.

- D. Commences with the current level of spending.

Answer (B) is correct.  *(CMA, adapted)*
**REQUIRED:** The true statement about zero-based budgeting (ZBB).
**DISCUSSION:** ZBB is a budgeting process in which each manager must justify a department's entire budget every year. ZBB differs from the traditional concept of budgeting in which a budget is largely based on the expenditures of the previous year. For each budgetary unit, ZBB prepares a decision package describing various levels of service that may be provided, including at least one level lower than the current one. Each component is evaluated from a cost-benefit perspective and then prioritized.
Answer (A) is incorrect because ZBB does represent a firm commitment. Answer (C) is incorrect because ZBB is not based on prior year's activities. Answer (D) is incorrect because ZBB starts from a base of zero.

**36.** An advantage of incremental budgeting when compared with zero-based budgeting is that incremental budgeting

- A. Encourages adopting new projects quickly.

- B. Accepts the existing base as being satisfactory.

- C. Eliminates functions and duties that have outlived their usefulness.

- D. Eliminates the need to review all functions periodically to obtain optimum use of resources.

Answer (B) is correct.  *(CMA, adapted)*
**REQUIRED:** The advantage of incremental budgeting compared with zero-based budgeting (ZBB).
**DISCUSSION:** Incremental budgeting simply adjusts the current year's budget to allow for changes planned for the coming year; a manager is not asked to justify the base portion of the budget. ZBB, however, requires a manager to justify the entire budget for each year. Incremental budgeting offers to managers the advantage of requiring less managerial effort to justify changes in the budget.
Answer (A) is incorrect because both types of budgets treat new projects in the same manner. Answer (C) is incorrect because reexamining functions and duties that may have outlived their usefulness is an advantage of ZBB. Answer (D) is incorrect because periodic review of functions is essential regardless of the budgetary system used.

**37.** The major appeal of zero-based budgeting is that it

- A. Solves the problem of measuring program effectiveness.

- B. Relates performance to resource inputs by an integrated planning and resource-allocation process.

- C. Reduces significantly the time required to review a budget.

- D. Deals with some of the problems of the incremental approach to budgeting.

Answer (D) is correct.  *(CIA, adapted)*
**REQUIRED:** The major appeal of zero-based budgeting.
**DISCUSSION:** The traditional approach to budgeting is to merely increase last year's figures by a given percentage or increment. Zero-based budgeting divides programs into packages of goals, activities, and required resources. The cost of each package is then calculated afresh, without regard to previous performance.
Answer (A) is incorrect because zero-based budgeting is not primarily a measurement tool for program effectiveness. Answer (B) is incorrect because the relationship of performance to resource inputs by integrated planning and resource allocation is part of the PPBS, or planning-programming-budgeting system. Answer (C) is incorrect because zero-based budgeting generally increases the time required to review a budget rather than reduces it; i.e., it consists of a determination of resources needed rather than an extrapolation of resources used in prior periods.

**38.** The budgeting tool or process in which estimates of revenues and expenses are prepared for each product beginning with the product's research and development phase and traced through to its customer support phase is a(n)

    A. Master budget.

    B. Activity-based budget.

    C. Zero-based budget.

    D. Life-cycle budget.

Answer (D) is correct. *(CMA, adapted)*
    **REQUIRED:** The budget tool that involves estimating a product's revenues and expenses from R&D through customer support.
    **DISCUSSION:** A life-cycle budget estimates a product's revenues and expenses over its expected life cycle. This approach is especially useful when revenues and related costs do not occur in the same periods. It emphasizes the need to budget revenues to cover all costs, not just those for production. Hence, costs are determined for all value-chain categories: upstream (R&D, design), manufacturing, and downstream (marketing, distribution, and customer service). The result is to highlight upstream and downstream costs that often receive insufficient attention.
    Answer (A) is incorrect because a master budget summarizes all of a company's budgets and plans. Answer (B) is incorrect because an activity-based budget emphasizes the costs of activities, which are the basic cost objects in activity-based costing. Answer (C) is incorrect because a zero-based budget requires each manager to justify his/her subunit's entire budget each year.

## 1.3 Annual Profit Plan and Supporting Schedules

**39.** The objectives upon which an annual profit plan is most effectively based are

    A. Financial measures, such as net income, return on investment, and earnings per share.

    B. Quantitative measures, such as growth in unit sales, number of employees, and manufacturing capacity.

    C. Qualitative measures of organizational activity, such as product innovation leadership, product quality levels, and product safety.

    D. A combination of financial, quantitative, and qualitative measures.

Answer (D) is correct. *(CMA, adapted)*
    **REQUIRED:** The objectives upon which an annual profit plan is most effectively based.
    **DISCUSSION:** An annual profit plan should be based upon an organization's objectives. Objectives vary with the organization's type and stage of development. Broad objectives should be established at the top and retranslated in more specific terms as they are communicated downward in a means-end hierarchy. Each subunit may have its own specific goals. A conflict sometimes exists in determining organizational objectives. For example, customer service may be one objective, but profitability or return on investment may be a conflicting objective. Thus, the annual profit plan is usually based on a combination of financial, quantitative, and qualitative measures. Objectives change over time. A century ago, profits were the most important corporate objective. Today, social responsibility also plays a role.
    Answer (A) is incorrect because more than financial measures are needed to prepare a profit plan. Long-term quality measures must also be considered. Answer (B) is incorrect because quantitative measures are insufficient if financial measures are not also considered. Answer (C) is incorrect because qualitative measures are insufficient if financial measures are not also considered.

**40.** The budget that describes the long-term position, goals, and objectives of an entity within its environment is the

    A. Capital budget.

    B. Operating budget.

    C. Cash management budget.

    D. Strategic budget.

Answer (D) is correct. *(CMA, adapted)*
    **REQUIRED:** The budget that describes the long-term position, goals, and objectives of an entity.
    **DISCUSSION:** Strategic budgeting is a form of long-range planning based on identifying and specifying organizational goals and objectives. The strengths and weaknesses of the organization are evaluated and risk levels are assessed. The influences of environmental factors are forecast to derive the best strategy for reaching the organization's objectives.
    Answer (A) is incorrect because capital budgeting involves evaluating specific long-term investment decisions. Answer (B) is incorrect because the operating budget is a short-range management tool. Answer (C) is incorrect because cash management is a short-range consideration related to liquidity.

**41.** The production budget process usually begins with the

A. Direct labor budget.

B. Direct materials budget.

C. Manufacturing overhead budget.

D. Sales budget.

Answer (D) is correct.   *(CMA, adapted)*
**REQUIRED:** The first step in the preparation of a production budget.
**DISCUSSION:** Neither a master budget nor a production budget can be prepared until after the sales budget has been completed. Once a firm knows its expected sales, production can be estimated. The production budget is based on assumptions appearing in the sales budget; thus, the sales budget is the first step in the preparation of a production budget.
Answer (A) is incorrect because the direct labor budget cannot be prepared until after unit production figures have been compiled. Answer (B) is incorrect because the direct materials budget cannot be prepared until after the unit production figures have been compiled. Answer (C) is incorrect because the manufacturing overhead budget cannot be prepared until after the unit production figures have been compiled.

**42.** The master budget process usually begins with the

A. Production budget.

B. Operating budget.

C. Financial budget.

D. Sales budget.

Answer (D) is correct.   *(CMA, adapted)*
**REQUIRED:** The type of budget that usually begins the master budget process.
**DISCUSSION:** A master or comprehensive budget consolidates all budgets into an overall planning and control document for the organization. The preparation of a master budget usually takes several months. The sales budget is the first budget prepared because it is the basis for all subsequent budgets. Once a firm can estimate sales, the next step is to decide how much to produce or purchase.
Answer (A) is incorrect because the production budget normally cannot be prepared until the expected sales are known. Answer (B) is incorrect because the operating budget is another term for the budget used on a day-to-day basis for managing operations. It cannot be prepared until after the sales budget is prepared. Answer (C) is incorrect because preparation of the sales budget is the first step in the overall budgeting process.

**43.** Individual budget schedules are prepared to develop an annual comprehensive or master budget. The budget schedule that would provide the necessary input data for the direct labor budget would be the

A. Sales forecast.

B. Raw materials purchases budget.

C. Schedule of cash receipts and disbursements.

D. Production budget.

Answer (D) is correct.   *(CMA, adapted)*
**REQUIRED:** The budget schedule that would provide the input data for the direct labor budget.
**DISCUSSION:** A master budget typically begins with the preparation of a sales budget. The next step is to prepare a production budget. Once the production budget has been completed, the next step is to prepare the direct labor, raw material, and overhead budgets. Thus, the production budget provides the data for the completion of the direct labor budget.
Answer (A) is incorrect because the sales forecast is insufficient for completion of the direct labor budget. Answer (B) is incorrect because the raw material purchases budget is not needed to prepare a direct labor budget. Answer (C) is incorrect because the schedule of cash receipts and disbursements cannot be prepared until after the direct labor budget has been completed.

**44.** Which one of the following is the best characteristic concerning the capital budget? The capital budget is a(n)

A. Plan to insure that there are sufficient funds available for the operating needs of the company.

B. Exercise that sets the long-range goals of the company including the consideration of external influences caused by others in the market.

C. Plan that results in the cash requirements during the operating cycle.

D. Plan that assesses the long-term needs of the company for plant and equipment purchases.

Answer (D) is correct.   *(CMA, adapted)*
**REQUIRED:** The true statement about the capital budget.
**DISCUSSION:** Capital budgeting is the process of planning expenditures for long-lived assets. It involves choosing among investment proposals using a ranking procedure. Evaluations are based on various measures involving the rate of ROI.
Answer (A) is incorrect because capital budgeting involves long-term investment needs, not immediate operating needs. Answer (B) is incorrect because strategic planning establishes long-term goals in the context of relevant factors in the firm's environment. Answer (C) is incorrect because cash budgeting determines operating cash flows. Capital budgeting evaluates the rate of return on specific investment alternatives.

**45.** The information contained in a cost of goods manufactured budget most directly relates to the

- A. Materials used, direct labor, overhead applied, and ending work-in-process budgets.
- B. Materials used, direct labor, overhead applied, and work-in-process inventories budgets.
- C. Materials used, direct labor, overhead applied, work-in-process inventories, and finished goods inventories budgets.
- D. Materials used, direct labor, overhead applied, and finished goods inventories budgets.

Answer (B) is correct. *(CMA, adapted)*
**REQUIRED:** The items contained in a cost of goods manufactured budget.
**DISCUSSION:** Cost of goods manufactured is equivalent to a retailer's purchases. It equals all manufacturing costs incurred during the period, plus beginning work-in-process, minus ending work-in-process. A cost of goods manufactured budget is therefore based on materials, direct labor, factory overhead, and work-in-process.
Answer (A) is incorrect because both beginning and ending work-in-process must be included. Answer (C) is incorrect because finished goods are excluded. They are the end product of the manufacturing process. Answer (D) is incorrect because finished goods are excluded. They are the end product of the manufacturing process.

**46.** All of the following are considered operating budgets except the

- A. Sales budget.
- B. Materials budget.
- C. Production budget.
- D. Capital budget.

Answer (D) is correct. *(CMA, adapted)*
**REQUIRED:** The budget that is not considered a part of the operating budget.
**DISCUSSION:** The operating budget consists of all budgets that concern normal operating activities, including the sales budget, production budget, materials budget, direct labor budget, and factory overhead budget. The capital expenditures budget, which outlines needs for new capital investment, is not a part of normal operations. The capital expenditures budget is sometimes prepared more than a year in advance to allow sufficient time to secure financing for these major expenditures. The long lead time is also necessary to allow sufficient time for custom orders of specialized equipment and buildings.

**47.** Which one of the following items should be done first when developing a comprehensive budget for a manufacturing company?

- A. Determination of the advertising budget.
- B. Development of a sales budget.
- C. Development of the capital budget.
- D. Preparation of a pro forma income statement.

Answer (B) is correct. *(CMA, adapted)*
**REQUIRED:** The first step in developing a comprehensive budget for a manufacturing company.
**DISCUSSION:** The sales budget is usually the first to be prepared because all other elements of a comprehensive budget depend on projected sales. For example, the production budget is based on an estimate of unit sales and desired inventory levels. Thus, sales volume affects purchasing levels, operating expenses, and cash flow.
Answer (A) is incorrect because the amount of advertising cost depends on the desired level of sales. Answer (C) is incorrect because expenditures for productive capacity are a function of long-term estimates of demand for the firm's products. Answer (D) is incorrect because preparation of a pro forma income statement is one of the final steps in the budgetary process. It cannot be prepared until after all sales, production, and expense budgets are finished.

**48.** Which one of the following statements regarding selling and administrative budgets is most accurate?

- A. Selling and administrative budgets are usually optional.
- B. Selling and administrative budgets are fixed in nature.
- C. Selling and administrative budgets are difficult to allocate by month and are best presented as one number for the entire year.
- D. Selling and administrative budgets need to be detailed in order that the key assumptions can be better understood.

Answer (D) is correct. *(CMA, adapted)*
**REQUIRED:** The most accurate statement about selling and administrative budgets.
**DISCUSSION:** Sales and administrative budgets are prepared after the sales budget. They are among the components of the operating budget process, which culminates in a budgeted (pro forma) income statement. Like the other budgets, they constitute prospective information based on the preparer's assumptions about conditions expected to exist and actions expected to be taken.
Answer (A) is incorrect because selling and administrative budgets are no more optional than any other component of the master budget. Answer (B) is incorrect because selling and administrative budgets have both variable and fixed components. Answer (C) is incorrect because selling and administrative budgets should be prepared on the same basis as the remainder of the budget, typically on at least a monthly basis.

**49.** The cash receipts budget includes

A. Funded depreciation.

B. Operating supplies.

C. Extinguishment of debt.

D. Loan proceeds.

**Answer (D) is correct.**  *(CMA, adapted)*
**REQUIRED:** The item included in a cash receipts budget.
**DISCUSSION:** A cash budget may be prepared monthly or even weekly to facilitate cash planning and control. The purpose is to anticipate cash needs while minimizing the amount of idle cash. The cash receipts section of the budget includes all sources of cash. One such source is the proceeds of loans.
Answer (A) is incorrect because funded depreciation involves cash outlays. Answer (B) is incorrect because purchases of supplies involves cash outlays. Answer (C) is incorrect because the extinguishment of debt involves cash outlays.

**50.** Which one of the following items is the last schedule to be prepared in the normal budget preparation process?

A. Cash budget.

B. Cost of goods sold budget.

C. Manufacturing overhead budget.

D. Selling expense budget.

**Answer (A) is correct.**  *(CMA, adapted)*
**REQUIRED:** The last schedule prepared.
**DISCUSSION:** The budget preparation process normally begins with the sales budget and continues through the preparation of pro forma financial statements. The last schedule prepared before the financial statements is the cash budget. The cash budget is a schedule of estimated cash collections and payments. The various operating budgets and the capital budget are inputs to the cash budgeting process.
Answer (B) is incorrect because the cost of goods sold budget provides information necessary to prepare the cash budget. Answer (C) is incorrect because the manufacturing overhead budget provides information necessary to prepare the cash budget. Answer (D) is incorrect because the selling expense budget provides information necessary to prepare the cash budget.

**51.** Which one of the following items would have to be included for a company preparing a schedule of cash receipts and disbursements for the calendar year 20X1?

A. A purchase order issued in December 20X1 for items to be delivered in February 20X2.

B. Dividends declared in November 20X1 to be paid in January 20X2 to shareholders of record as of December 20X1.

C. The amount of uncollectible customer accounts for 20X1.

D. The borrowing of funds from a bank on a note payable taken out in June 20X1 with an agreement to pay the principal and interest in June 20X2.

**Answer (D) is correct.**  *(CMA, adapted)*
**REQUIRED:** The item included in a cash budget for 20X1.
**DISCUSSION:** A schedule of cash receipts and disbursements (cash budget) should include all cash inflows and outflows during the period without regard to the accrual accounting treatment of the transactions. Hence, it should include all checks written and all sources of cash, including borrowings. A borrowing from a bank in June 20X1 should appear as a cash receipt for 20X1.
Answer (A) is incorrect because the cash disbursement presumably will not occur until 20X2. Answer (B) is incorrect because the cash flow will not occur until dividends are paid in 20X2. Answer (C) is incorrect because bad debt expense is a noncash item.

**52.** Which one of the following may be considered an independent item in the preparation of the master budget?

A. Ending inventory budget.

B. Capital investment budget.

C. Pro forma income statement.

D. Pro forma statement of financial position.

**Answer (B) is correct.**  *(CMA, adapted)*
**REQUIRED:** The independent item in the preparation of the master budget.
**DISCUSSION:** The capital investment budget may be prepared more than a year in advance, unlike the other elements of the master budget. Because of the long-term commitments that must be made for some types of capital investments, planning must be done far in advance and is based on needs in future years as opposed to the current year's needs.
Answer (A) is incorrect because the ending inventory budget is based on the current production budget. Answer (C) is incorrect because the pro forma income statement is based on the sales budget, expense budgets, and all other elements of the current master budget. Answer (D) is incorrect because the pro forma balance sheet is based on the other elements of the current master budget.

**53.** Of the following items, the one item that would not be considered in evaluating the adequacy of the budgeted annual operating income for a company is

A. Earnings per share.

B. Industry average for earnings on sales.

C. Internal rate of return.

D. Price-earnings ratio.

Answer (C) is correct.  *(CMA, adapted)*
**REQUIRED:** The item not considered in evaluating the adequacy of the budgeted annual operating income.
**DISCUSSION:** When a company prepares the first draft of its pro forma income statement, management must evaluate whether earnings meet company objectives. This evaluation is based on such factors as desired earnings per share, average earnings for other firms in the industry, a desired price-earnings ratio, and needed return on investment. The internal rate of return (IRR) is not a means of evaluating a budget because IRR is used to evaluate long-term investments. It is the discount rate at which a project's net present value is zero.
Answer (A) is incorrect because EPS is a measure of financial performance. Answer (B) is incorrect because the industry average for earnings on sales is a measure of financial performance. Answer (D) is incorrect because the P-E ratio is a measure of financial performance.

**54.** For the month of December, Crystal Clear Bottling expects to sell 12,500 cases of Cranberry Sparkling Water at $24.80 per case and 33,100 cases of Lemon Dream Cola at $32.00 per case. Sales personnel receive 6% commission on each case of Cranberry Sparkling Water and 8% commission on each case of Lemon Dream Cola. In order to receive a commission on a product, the sales personnel team must meet the individual product revenue quota. The sales quota for Cranberry Sparkling Water is $500,000, and the sales quota for Lemon Dream Cola is $1,000,000. The sales commission that should be budgeted for December is

A. $4,736

B. $82,152

C. $84,736

D. $103,336

Answer (C) is correct.  *(CMA, adapted)*
**REQUIRED:** The budgeted sales commissions for the month.
**DISCUSSION:** The sale of 12,500 cases of Cranberry at $24.80 per case produces revenue of $310,000, an amount that does not qualify for commissions. The sale of 33,100 cases of Lemon at $32 per case produces revenue of $1,059,200. This amount is greater than the minimum and therefore qualifies for a commission of $84,736 ($1,059,200 × 8%). This calculation assumes that commissions are paid on all sales if the revenue quota is met.
Answer (A) is incorrect because $4,736 is the commission on $59,200 of Lemon sales. Answer (B) is incorrect because $82,152 equals 6% of all sales. Answer (D) is incorrect because $103,336 assumes that a commission of $18,600 is paid on Cranberry.

**55.** Karmel, Inc. pays out sales commissions to its sales team in the month the company receives cash for payment. These commissions equal 5% of total (monthly) cash inflows as a result of sales. Karmel has budgeted sales of $300,000 for August, $400,000 for September, and $200,000 for October. Approximately half of all sales are on credit, and the other half are all cash sales. Experience indicates that 70% of the budgeted credit sales will be collected in the month following the sale, 20% the month after that, and 10% of the sales will be uncollectible. Based on this information, what should be the total amount of sales commissions paid out by Karmel in the month of October?

A. $8,500

B. $13,500

C. $17,000

D. $22,000

Answer (B) is correct.  *(Publisher)*
**REQUIRED:** The sales commissions paid during October.
**DISCUSSION:** Cash sales for the month of October are budgeted at $100,000 (half of $200,000 overall sales). Projections for collections of credit sales in August indicate that 20% will be cash inflows for Karmel, Inc. in October, or ($150,000 × 20%) = $30,000. Projections for collections of credit sales in September indicate that 70% will be cash inflows for Karmel, Inc. in October, or ($200,000 × 70%) = $140,000. Therefore, total cash inflows projected for the month of October equal $100,000 + $30,000 + $140,000 = $270,000. Because sales commissions are set at 5% of monthly cash inflows, the sales commissions for October equal ($270,000 × 5%) = $13,500.
Answer (A) is incorrect because $8,500 results from failure to consider the cash sales made during October. Answer (C) is incorrect because $17,000 is based on total sales for August and September rather than credit sales. Answer (D) is incorrect because $22,000 results from using total sales rather than credit sales.

**56.** Nick Klaus is a divisional manager for Tot Toys. He has been assigned the task of creating a production budget for his division, which produces the company's most popular stuffed animal. Budgeted sales for this toy for the next year have been set at 650,000 units, desired ending finished goods inventory is 200,000 units, and Klaus would like there to be 100,000 equivalent units in ending work-in-process inventory. The starting finished goods inventory for the next year will be 300,000 units, with 75,000 equivalent units in beginning work-in-process inventory. How many equivalent units should Klaus plan for his division to produce?

    A.  550,000

    B.  575,000

    C.  725,000

    D.  925,000

Answer (B) is correct.  *(Publisher)*
    **REQUIRED:** The number of equivalent units to be produced.
    **DISCUSSION:** Using production-related budgets, units to produce equals budgeted sales + desired ending finished goods inventory + desired equivalent units in ending work-in-process inventory – beginning finished goods inventory – equivalent units in beginning work-in-process inventory. Therefore, in this case, units to produce is equal to 650,000 + 200,000 + 100,000 – 300,000 – 75,000 = 575,000.
    Answer (A) is incorrect because 550,000 results from ignoring the change in work-in-process inventory. Answer (C) is incorrect because 725,000 results from reversing the treatment of beginning and ending inventories. Answer (D) is incorrect because 925,000 results from a failure to consider beginning inventories.

**57.** Flesher Farms is preparing its cash budget for the next year. Sales are expected to be $100,000 in January, $200,000 in February, $300,000 in March, and $100,000 in April. Approximately half of all sales are cash sales, and the other half are on credit. Experience indicates that 70% of the credit sales will be collected in the month following the sale, 20% the month after that, and 10% in the third month after the sale. What are the budgeted collections for April?

    A.  $130,000

    B.  $180,000

    C.  $260,000

    D.  $360,000

Answer (B) is correct.  *(Publisher)*
    **REQUIRED:** The budgeted collections for April.
    **DISCUSSION:** Collections from April cash sales will be half of total sales, or $50,000. From January's $50,000 of credit sales, collections should be 10%, or $5,000. From February's $100,000 of credit sales, collections should be 20%, or $20,000. From March's $150,000 of credit sales, collections will be 70%, or $105,000. Thus, total collections will amount to $180,000.
    Answer (A) is incorrect because $130,000 results from a failure to include the cash sales for April. Answer (C) is incorrect because half of total sales is used to calculate collections from credit sales, and April's cash sales must be included. Answer (D) is incorrect because $360,000 results from using total sales for the first 3 months instead of credit sales.

**58.** Trumbull Company budgeted sales on account of $120,000 for July, $211,000 for August, and $198,000 for September. Collection experience indicates that 60% of the budgeted sales will be collected the month after the sale, 36% will be collected the second month, and 4% will be uncollectible. The cash receipts from accounts receivable that should be budgeted for September would be

    A.  $169,800

    B.  $147,960

    C.  $197,880

    D.  $194,760

Answer (A) is correct.  *(CMA, adapted)*
    **REQUIRED:** The budgeted cash receipts for September.
    **DISCUSSION:** The budgeted cash collections for September are $169,800 [($120,000 July sales × 36%) + ($211,000 August sales × 60%)].
    Answer (B) is incorrect because $147,960 results from reversing the percentages for July and August. Answer (C) is incorrect because $197,880 results from using the wrong months (August and September) and reversing the percentages. Answer (D) is incorrect because $194,760 assumes collections were for August and September.

**59.** Whopper, Inc. budgeted sales on account of $150,000 for July, $210,000 for August, and $198,000 for September. Collection experience indicates that 60% of the budgeted sales will be collected the month after the sale, 36% the second month, and 4% will be uncollectible. The cash receipts from accounts receivable that should be budgeted for September equal

A. $180,000

B. $165,600

C. $194,400

D. $198,000

Answer (A) is correct. *(Publisher)*
**REQUIRED:** The budgeted cash receipts from sales on account for September.
**DISCUSSION:** The budgeted cash collections for September equal $180,000.

| | | |
|---|---|---|
| July: | $150,000 × .36 = | $ 54,000 |
| Aug.: | 210,000 × .60 = | 126,000 |
| | | $180,000 |

Answer (B) is incorrect because $165,600 results from reversing the percentages for July and August. Answer (C) is incorrect because $194,400 equals budgeted collections for October. Answer (D) is incorrect because $198,000 equals September sales.

---

Questions 60 and 61 are based on the following information.

Daffy Tunes manufactures a toy rabbit with moving parts and a built-in voice box. Projected sales in units for the next 5 months are as follows:

| Month | Projected Sales in Units |
|---|---|
| January | 30,000 |
| February | 36,000 |
| March | 33,000 |
| April | 40,000 |
| May | 29,000 |

Each rabbit requires basic materials that Daffy purchases from a single supplier at $3.50 per rabbit. Voice boxes are purchased from another supplier at $1.00 each. Assembly labor cost is $2.00 per rabbit, and variable overhead cost is $.50 per rabbit. Fixed manufacturing overhead applicable to rabbit production is $12,000 per month. Daffy's policy is to manufacture 1.5 times the coming month's projected sales every other month, starting with January (i.e., odd-numbered months) for February sales, and to manufacture 0.5 times the coming month's projected sales in alternate months (i.e., even-numbered months). This allows Daffy to allocate limited manufacturing resources to other products as needed during the even-numbered months.

---

**60.** The unit production budget for toy rabbits for January is

A. 45,000 units.

B. 16,500 units.

C. 54,000 units.

D. 14,500 units.

Answer (C) is correct. *(CMA, adapted)*
**REQUIRED:** The unit production budget for January.
**DISCUSSION:** January's production should be 1.5 times February's sales. Thus, the production budget for January should be 54,000 units (36,000 units of February sales × 1.5).
Answer (A) is incorrect because 45,000 is based on January sales. Answer (B) is incorrect because 16,500 is budgeted production for February. Answer (D) is incorrect because 14,500 is budgeted production for April.

**61.** The dollar production budget for toy rabbits for February is

A. $327,000

B. $390,000

C. $113,500

D. $127,500

Answer (D) is correct. *(CMA, adapted)*
**REQUIRED:** The dollar production budget for February.
**DISCUSSION:** The units to be produced in February equal 50% of March sales, or 16,500 units (33,000 × .5). The unit variable cost is $7.00 ($3.50 + $1.00 + $2.00 + $.50), so total variable costs are $115,500 (16,500 × $7). Thus, the dollar production budget for February is $127,500 ($115,500 VUC + $12,000 FC).
Answer (A) is incorrect because $327,000 is based on January sales. Answer (B) is incorrect because $390,000 is the production budget for January. Answer (C) is incorrect because $113,500 is the production budget for April.

**62.** For the month of June, Wilder Cherry Company expects to sell 12,500 cases of small cherries at $25 per case and 33,000 cases of large cherries at $32 per case. Sales personnel receive a 6% commission on each case of small cherries and an 8% commission on each case of large cherries. To receive a commission on a product, the sales personnel team must meet the individual product revenue quota. The sales quotas for small cherries and large cherries are $500,000 and $1 million, respectively. What are the sales commissions budgeted for June?

    A.  $109,440

    B.  $84,480

    C.  $82,110

    D.  $4,480

Answer (B) is correct.  *(Publisher)*
**REQUIRED:** The budgeted sales commissions.
**DISCUSSION:** The sale of 12,500 cases of small cherries at $25 per case produces revenue of $312,500. Because this amount is below the $500,000 minimum, no commissions should be budgeted for small cherries. The sale of 33,000 cases of large cherries at $32 per case produces revenue of $1,056,000. This amount is greater than the $1 million minimum and therefore qualifies for a commission of $84,480 ($1,056,000 × 8%). The problem did not state that a commission would be paid only on amounts exceeding the minimum. Hence, all sales qualify once the minimum is reached.
Answer (A) is incorrect because $109,440 assumes that an 8% commission was paid on all sales. Answer (C) is incorrect because $82,110 is based on a 6% commission on all sales. Answer (D) is incorrect because $4,480 is the commission on the $56,000 of large cherries sales in excess of the minimum.

**63.** The Matthew Nichols Company budgeted sales of $200,000 for July, $280,000 for August, $198,000 for September and $200,000 for October. Approximately 75% of sales are on credit; the remainder are cash sales. Collection experience indicates that 60% of the budgeted credit sales will be collected the month after the sale, 36% will be collected the second month, and 4% will be uncollectible. The cash receipts budgeted for October equal

    A.  $164,700

    B.  $200,000

    C.  $214,700

    D.  $244,400

Answer (C) is correct.  *(Publisher)*
**REQUIRED:** The budgeted cash receipts for October.
**DISCUSSION:** Credit sales for August and September are $210,000 ($280,000 × 75%) and $148,500 ($198,000 × 75%), respectively. Cash sales for October are $50,000 [$200,000 × (1.00 − .75)]. The cash collections during October should therefore be $214,700.

| | | | |
|---|---|---|---|
| August: | $210,000 × .36 = | $ 75,600 |
| September: | 148,500 × .60 = | 89,100 |
| October: | 50,000 × 1.00 = | 50,000 |
| | | $214,700 |

Answer (A) is incorrect because $164,700 fails to include October cash sales. Answer (B) is incorrect because $200,000 equals total sales for October. Answer (D) is incorrect because $244,400 assumes September credit sales were $198,000.

**64.** A company has developed the budget formula below for estimating its shipping expenses. Shipments have historically averaged 12 pounds per shipment.

*Shipping costs* = $18,000 + (*Pounds shipped* × $.60)

The planned activity and actual activity regarding orders and shipments for the current month are given in the following schedule:

| | Plan | Actual |
|---|---|---|
| Sales orders | 800 | 780 |
| Shipments | 800 | 820 |
| Units shipped | 8,000 | 9,000 |
| Sales | $120,000 | $144,000 |
| Total pounds shipped | 9,600 | 12,500 |

The actual shipping costs for the month amounted to $21,000. The appropriate monthly flexible budget allowance for shipping costs for the purpose of performance evaluation should be

    A.  $18,000

    B.  $18,492

    C.  $23,760

    D.  $25,500

Answer (D) is correct.  *(Publisher)*
**REQUIRED:** The appropriate budgeted amount for shipping costs.
**DISCUSSION:** According to the flexible budget formula, total fixed costs and unit variable cost are expected to be $18,000 and $.60, respectively. Thus, budgeted variable costs for the actual output should be $7,500 (12,500 lbs. × $.60). Adding the variable costs to the $18,000 of fixed costs produces a budget total of $25,500.
Answer (A) is incorrect because $18,000 equals the fixed costs. Answer (B) is incorrect because $18,492 is based on the number of shipments. Answer (C) is incorrect because $23,760 is based on planned pounds shipped of 9,600.

Questions 65 and 66 are based on the following information.

The Raymar Company is preparing its cash budget for the months of April and May. The firm has established a $200,000 line of credit with its bank at a 12% annual rate of interest on which borrowings for cash deficits must be made in $10,000 increments. There is no outstanding balance on the line of credit loan on April 1. Principal repayments are to be made in any month in which there is a surplus of cash. Interest is to be paid monthly. If there are no outstanding balances on the loans, Raymar will invest any cash in excess of its desired end-of-month cash balance in U.S. Treasury bills. Raymar intends to maintain a minimum balance of $100,000 at the end of each month by either borrowing for deficits below the minimum balance or investing any excess cash. Expected monthly collection and disbursement patterns are shown in the column to the right.

- Collections. 50% of the current month's sales budget and 50% of the previous month's sales budget.
- Accounts payable disbursements. 75% of the current month's accounts payable budget and 25% of the previous month's accounts payable budget.
- All other disbursements occur in the month in which they are budgeted.

### Budget Information

|                    | March    | April    | May       |
|--------------------|----------|----------|-----------|
| Sales              | $40,000  | $50,000  | $100,000  |
| Accounts payable   | 30,000   | 40,000   | 40,000    |
| Payroll            | 60,000   | 70,000   | 50,000    |
| Other disbursements| 25,000   | 30,000   | 10,000    |

**65.** In April, Raymar's budget will result in

A. $45,000 in excess cash.

B. A need to borrow $50,000 on its line of credit for the cash deficit.

C. A need to borrow $100,000 on its line of credit for the cash deficit.

D. A need to borrow $90,000 on its line of credit for the cash deficit.

Answer (C) is correct. *(CMA, adapted)*
**REQUIRED:** The effect on cash by the end of April.
**DISCUSSION:** Assuming Raymar maintained a $100,000 cash balance at the end of March, the amount to be borrowed or invested in April is the difference between cash receipts and disbursements. April's cash collections are $45,000 [($50,000 April sales × 50%) + ($40,000 March sales × 50%)]. Disbursements for accounts payable are $37,500 [($40,000 April payables × 75%) + ($30,000 March payables × 25%)]. In addition to the accounts payable disbursements, payroll and other disbursements will require an additional $100,000. Hence, total disbursements are estimated to be $137,500. The net negative cash flow (amount to be borrowed to reach the required minimum cash balance of $100,000) is $92,500 ($137,500 − $45,000). Because the line of credit must be drawn upon in $10,000 increments, the loan must be for $100,000.
Answer (A) is incorrect because $45,000 equals cash receipts. Answer (B) is incorrect because the cash deficit will be $92,500 without borrowing. Answer (D) is incorrect because a loan of only $90,000 would still leave a negative cash balance of $2,500.

**66.** In May, Raymar will be required to

A. Repay $20,000 principal and pay $1,000 interest.

B. Repay $90,000 principal and pay $100 interest.

C. Pay $900 interest.

D. Borrow an additional $20,000 and pay $1,000 interest.

Answer (D) is correct. *(CMA, adapted)*
**REQUIRED:** The transaction required in May.
**DISCUSSION:** The company will have to borrow $100,000 in April, which means that interest will have to be paid in May at the rate of 1% per month (12% annual rate). Consequently, interest expense is $1,000 ($100,000 × 1%). May receipts are $75,000 [($100,000 May sales × 50%) + ($50,000 April sales × 50%)]. Disbursements in May are $40,000 [($40,000 May payables × 75%) + ($40,000 April payables × 25%)]. In addition to the May accounts payable disbursements, payroll and other disbursements are $60,000, bringing total disbursements to $101,000 ($60,000 + $40,000 + $1,000). Thus, disbursements exceed receipts by $26,000 ($101,000 − $75,000). However, cash has a beginning surplus balance of $7,500 ($100,000 April loan − $92,500 negative cash flow for April calculated using the collections and disbursements information given). As a result, the company needs to borrow an additional $18,500 to eliminate its cash deficit. Given the requirement that loans be in $10,000 increments, the May loan must be for $20,000.
Answer (A) is incorrect because no funds are available to repay the loan. May receipts are less than May disbursements. Answer (B) is incorrect because no funds are available to repay the loan. May receipts are less than May disbursements. Answer (C) is incorrect because the 1% interest is calculated on a $100,000 loan, not a $90,000 loan.

Questions 67 through 69 are based on the following information.

Mountain Corporation manufactures cabinets but outsources the handles. Eight handles are needed for a cabinet, with assembly requiring 30 minutes of direct labor per unit. Ending finished goods inventory is planned to consist of 50% of projected unit sales for the next month, and ending handles inventory is planned to be 80% of the requirement for the next month's projected unit output of finished goods.

Mountain's projected unit sales:

| | |
|---|---|
| October | 4,600 |
| November | 5,000 |
| December | 4,200 |
| January | 6,000 |

Mountain's ending inventories in units at September 30:

| | |
|---|---|
| Finished goods | 3,800 |
| Handles | 16,000 |

**67.** The number of units finished during December is

A. 3,000

B. 5,100

C. 4,200

D. 5,000

Answer (B) is correct.  *(Publisher)*
**REQUIRED:** The finished units for December.
**DISCUSSION:** The company will need 4,200 finished units to meet the sales estimate for December. In addition, 3,000 finished units (6,000 unit sales in January × 50%) should be in inventory at the end of December. The total requirement is therefore 7,200 units (4,200 + 3,000). Of these units, 2,100 (4,200 unit sales in December × 50%) should be available from November's ending inventory. Consequently, production in December should be 5,100 units (7,200 – 2,100).
Answer (A) is incorrect because 3,000 units equals the ending inventory for December. Answer (C) is incorrect because 4,200 units equals December's projected sales. Answer (D) is incorrect because 5,000 equals November's sales.

**68.** The number of handles to be purchased in October is

A. 39,840

B. 76,800

C. 40,000

D. 36,800

Answer (A) is correct.  *(Publisher)*
**REQUIRED:** The handles to be purchased in October.
**DISCUSSION:** To determine the correct number of handles purchased for October, the projected unit output of finished goods for October and November must be calculated.

| | |
|---|---|
| Projected sales of cabinets in October | 4,600 |
| Plus: Required ending inventory | |
| (50% of projected November sales) | 2,500 |
| Minus: Beginning inventory | (3,800) |
| Total cabinet production for October | 3,300 |

| | |
|---|---|
| Projected sales of cabinets in November | 5,000 |
| Plus: Required ending inventory | |
| (50% of projected December sales) | 2,100 |
| Minus: Beginning inventory | |
| (Ending inventory from October) | (2,500) |
| Total cabinet production for November | 4,600 |

The calculation to determine the number of handles to be purchased is as follows:

| | |
|---|---|
| Handles for October production | |
| (3,300 × 8 handles per cabinet) | 26,400 |
| Handles for November production | |
| required in October ending inventory | |
| (4,600 × 8 × 80%) | 29,440 |
| Minus: Beginning inventory | (16,000) |
| Total handles to be purchased in October | 39,840 |

Answer (B) is incorrect because 76,800 equals the total required for October and November sales. Answer (C) is incorrect because 40,000 equals the total required for November's sales. Answer (D) is incorrect because 36,800 equals the total required for October's sales.

**69.** Given that a full-time employee works 160 hours per month, no overtime is allowed, and part-time employees may be used, how many full-time equivalent employees are needed to assemble the output of finished units in November?

A. 14.375

B. 28.75

C. 15.625

D. 31.25

Answer (A) is correct. *(Publisher)*

**REQUIRED:** The full-time equivalent employees needed to assemble the output of finished units in November.

**DISCUSSION:** Projected unit sales for November equal 5,000, of which 2,500 (5,000 × 50%) should come from October's ending inventory. Ending inventory for November should be 2,100 units (4,200 unit sales projected for December × 50%). Accordingly, output for November should be 4,600 units (5,000 – 2,500 + 2,100), and these units will require 2,300 direct labor hours for assembly [4,600 units × (30 minutes ÷ 60 minutes per hour)]. The full-time equivalent number of employees needed to assemble 4,600 units is therefore 14.375 (2,300 hours ÷ 160 hours per full-time employee).

Answer (B) is incorrect because 28.75 assumes 4,600 hours of assembly. Answer (C) is incorrect because 15.625 assumes 2,500 hours of assembly. Answer (D) is incorrect because 31.25 assumes 5,000 hours of assembly.

**70.** Zohar Company's budget contains the following information:

Zohar Company

| | Units |
|---|---|
| Beginning finished goods inventory | 85 |
| Beginning work-in-process in equivalent units | 10 |
| Desired ending finished goods inventory | 100 |
| Desired ending work-in-process in equivalent units | 40 |
| Projected sales | 1,800 |

How many equivalent units should Zohar plan to produce?

A. 1,800

B. 1,565

C. 1,815

D. 1,845

Answer (D) is correct. *(CMA, adapted)*

**REQUIRED:** The equivalent units to produce in the coming year.

**DISCUSSION:** The finished units needed equal 1,815:

| | |
|---|---|
| Needed for sales | 1,800 |
| Needed for ending inventory | 100 |
| Total finished units needed | 1,900 |
| Minus: Beginning inventory | 85 |
| Finished units needed | 1,815 |

The units to be produced equal 1,845:

| | |
|---|---|
| Finished units needed | 1,815 |
| Needed for ending inventory | 40 |
| Total units in process | 1,855 |
| Minus: Beginning WIP inventory | 10 |
| Units to be produced | 1,845 |

Answer (A) is incorrect because 1,800 equals projected unit sales. Answer (B) is incorrect because 1,565 equals units needed for sales minus all inventory amounts. Answer (C) is incorrect because 1,815 equals finished units needed.

**71.** When sales volume is seasonal in nature, certain items in the budget must be coordinated. The three most significant items to coordinate in budgeting seasonal sales volume are

A. Production volume, finished goods inventory, and sales volume.

B. Direct labor hours, work-in-process inventory, and sales volume.

C. Raw material inventory, direct labor hours, and manufacturing overhead costs.

D. Raw material inventory, work-in-process inventory, and production volume.

Answer (A) is correct. *(CMA, adapted)*

**REQUIRED:** The three most significant items to coordinate in budgeting seasonal sales volume.

**DISCUSSION:** The most difficult items to coordinate in any budget, particularly for a seasonal business, are production volume, finished goods inventory, and sales. Budgets usually begin with sales volume and proceed to production volume, but the reverse is sometimes used when production is more of an issue than generation of sales. Inventory levels are also important because sales cannot occur without inventory, and the maintenance of high inventory levels is costly.

Answer (B) is incorrect because direct labor hours and work-in-process are only two components of a production budget. Answer (C) is incorrect because sales is usually the most important aspect of any budget. Answer (D) is incorrect because sales is usually the most important aspect of any budget.

Questions 72 through 76 are based on the following information.

Karmee Company has been accumulating operating data in order to prepare an annual profit plan. Details regarding Karmee's sales for the first 6 months of the coming year are as follows:

| Estimated Monthly Sales | | Type of Monthly Sale | |
|---|---|---|---|
| January | $600,000 | Cash sales | 20% |
| February | 650,000 | Credit sales | 80% |
| March | 700,000 | | |
| April | 625,000 | | |
| May | 720,000 | | |
| June | 800,000 | | |

| Collection Pattern for Credit Sales | |
|---|---|
| Month of sale | 30% |
| One month following sale | 40% |
| Second month following sale | 25% |

Karmee's cost of goods sold averages 40% of the sales value. Karmee's objective is to maintain a target inventory equal to 30% of the next month's sales in units. Purchases of merchandise for resale are paid for in the month following the sale.

The variable operating expenses (other than cost of goods sold) for Karmee are 10% of sales and are paid for in the month following the sale. The annual fixed operating expenses are presented below. All of these are incurred uniformly throughout the year and paid monthly except for insurance and property taxes. Insurance is paid quarterly in January, April, July, and October. Property taxes are paid twice a year in April and October.

| Annual Fixed Operating Costs | |
|---|---|
| Advertising | $ 720,000 |
| Depreciation | 420,000 |
| Insurance | 180,000 |
| Property taxes | 240,000 |
| Salaries | 1,080,000 |

**72.** The amount of cash collected in March for Karmee Company from the sales made during March will be

A. $140,000

B. $308,000

C. $350,000

D. $636,000

Answer (B) is correct. *(CMA, adapted)*
**REQUIRED:** The cash collected in March on March sales.
**DISCUSSION:** Cash sales are 20% of monthly sales, credit sales are 80% of monthly sales, and collections on credit sales are 30% in the month of sale. Consequently, cash collected during a month equals 44% [20% + (30% × 80%)] of sales for that month. Cash collections in March on March sales were therefore $308,000 ($700,000 × 44%).
Answer (A) is incorrect because $140,000 excludes collections on March credit sales. Answer (C) is incorrect because $350,000 assumes 20% of sales are for cash and that collections on credit sales equal 30% of total sales. Answer (D) is incorrect because $636,000 equals total cash collections during March on first quarter sales.

**73.** Karmee Company's total cash receipts for the month of April will be

A. $504,000

B. $629,000

C. $653,000

D. $707,400

Answer (B) is correct. *(CMA, adapted)*
**REQUIRED:** The total cash receipts for April.
**DISCUSSION:** Cash collected during a month on sales for that month equals 44% of total sales. Hence, cash receipts in April on April's sales are $275,000 ($625,000 × 44%). April collections on March credit sales equal $224,000 ($700,000 × 40% × 80%). April collections on February credit sales equal $130,000 ($650,000 × 25% × 80%). Thus, total cash receipts for April were $629,000 ($275,000 + $224,000 + $130,000).
Answer (A) is incorrect because $504,000 ignores $125,000 of April cash sales. Answer (C) is incorrect because $653,000 includes $24,000 of bad debts from January sales. Answer (D) is incorrect because $707,400 represents June collections.

**74.** The purchase of merchandise that Karmee Company will need to make during February will be

A. $254,000

B. $260,000

C. $266,000

D. $338,000

Answer (C) is correct. *(CMA, adapted)*
**REQUIRED:** The purchase of merchandise for February.
**DISCUSSION:** Purchases equal cost of goods sold, plus ending inventory, minus beginning inventory. Estimated cost of goods sold for February equals $260,000 ($650,000 sales × 40%). Ending inventory is given as 30% of sales in units. Stated at cost, this amount equals $84,000 ($700,000 March sales × 30% × 40%). Furthermore, beginning inventory is $78,000 ($260,000 CGS for February × 30%). Thus, purchases equal $266,000 ($260,000 + $84,000 − $78,000).
Answer (A) is incorrect because $254,000 reverses the treatment of the change in inventory. Answer (B) is incorrect because $260,000 is February CGS. Answer (D) is incorrect because $338,000 equals the sum of CGS and beginning inventory.

**75.** The amount for cost of goods sold that will appear on Karmee Company's pro forma income statement for the month of February will be

A.  $195,000

B.  $254,000

C.  $260,000

D.  $272,000

Answer (C) is correct.  *(CMA, adapted)*
    **REQUIRED:** The cost of goods sold for February.
    **DISCUSSION:** Cost of goods sold is expected to be 40% of sales. Thus, cost of goods sold is $260,000 ($650,000 February sales × 40%).
    Answer (A) is incorrect because $195,000 is based on 30% of sales. Answer (B) is incorrect because $254,000 equals cost of goods sold, minus ending inventory, plus beginning inventory. Answer (D) is incorrect because $272,000 equals purchases, plus ending inventory, minus beginning inventory.

**76.** The total cash disbursements that Karmee Company will make for the operating expenses (expenses other than the cost of goods sold) during the month of April will be

A.  $255,000

B.  $290,000

C.  $385,000

D.  $420,000

Answer (C) is correct.  *(CMA, adapted)*
    **REQUIRED:** The total cash disbursements for operating expenses during April.
    **DISCUSSION:** Cash disbursements for variable operating expenses in April (excluding cost of goods sold) equal $70,000 ($700,000 March sales × 10%). Cash disbursements for fixed operating expenses (excluding depreciation, a noncash expense) include advertising ($720,000 ÷ 12 = $60,000), salaries ($1,080,000 ÷ 12 = $90,000), insurance ($180,000 ÷ 4 = $45,000), and property taxes ($240,000 ÷ 2 = $120,000). Hence, cash payments for April operating expenses are $385,000 ($70,000 + $60,000 + $90,000 + $45,000 + $120,000).
    Answer (A) is incorrect because $255,000 excludes variable selling expenses and advertising. Answer (B) is incorrect because $290,000 includes depreciation but excludes variable selling expenses and advertising. Answer (D) is incorrect because $420,000 includes depreciation.

---

Questions 77 and 78 are based on the following information.

Historically, Pine Hill Wood Products has had no significant bad debt experience with its customers. Cash sales have accounted for 10% of total sales, and payments for credit sales have been received as follows:

40% of credit sales in the month of the sale
30% of credit sales in the first subsequent month
25% of credit sales in the second subsequent month
5% of credit sales in the third subsequent month

The forecast for both cash and credit sales is as follows:

| Month | Sales |
|---|---|
| January | $95,000 |
| February | 65,000 |
| March | 70,000 |
| April | 80,000 |
| May | 85,000 |

---

**77.** What is the forecasted cash inflow for Pine Hill Wood Products for May?

A.  $70,875

B.  $76,500

C.  $79,375

D.  $83,650

Answer (C) is correct.  *(CMA, adapted)*
    **REQUIRED:** The forecasted cash inflow for May.
    **DISCUSSION:** The cash inflows for May will come from May cash sales of $8,500 ($85,000 × 10%), May credit sales of $30,600 ($85,000 × 90% × 40%), April sales of $21,600 ($80,000 × 30% × 90%), March sales of $15,750 ($70,000 × 25% × 90%), and February sales of $2,925 ($65,000 × 5% × 90%). The total is $79,375.
    Answer (A) is incorrect because $70,875 omits May cash sales. Answer (B) is incorrect because $76,500 equals May credit sales. Answer (D) is incorrect because $83,650 includes 5% of January's credit sales.

**78.** Due to deteriorating economic conditions, Pine Hill Wood Products has now decided that its cash forecast should include a bad debt adjustment of 2% of credit sales, beginning with sales for the month of April. The 5% collection in the fourth month should be reduced to reflect the bad debt. Because of this policy change, the total expected cash inflow related to sales made in April will

A.  Be unchanged.

B.  Decrease by $1,260.00.

C.  Decrease by $1,440.00.

D.  Decrease by $1,530.00.

Answer (A) is correct.  *(CMA, adapted)*
    **REQUIRED:** The cash inflows related to April sales given a bad debt adjustment.
    **DISCUSSION:** The collections in the 4th month will be affected by $1,440, but the month of the sale will be unchanged.
    Answer (B) is incorrect because $1,260 is 2% of March credit sales. Answer (C) is incorrect because the collections in the 4th month will be affected by $1,440, but the month of the sale will be unchanged. Answer (D) is incorrect because $1,530 is 2% of May credit sales.

Questions 79 through 83 are based on the following information.

The information was adapted from a question on Part 4 of the December 1990 CMA examination that concerned preparation of a pro forma statement of cost of goods sold. The following is Watson Corporation's pro forma statement of cost of goods sold for the year ended August 31, year 2.

### Watson Corporation
### Pro Forma Statement of Cost of Goods Sold
### For the Year Ending August 31, Year 2
### ($000 omitted)

| | | |
|---|---:|---:|
| Direct materials: | | |
| Materials inventory, 9/1/year 1 | $ 1,200 | |
| Materials purchased | 11,400 | |
| Materials available for use | 12,600 | |
| Materials inventory, 8/31/year 2 | 1,480 | |
|   Direct materials consumed | | $11,120 |
| Direct labor | | 980 |
| Manufacturing overhead: | | |
| Indirect materials | 1,112 | |
| General overhead | 2,800 | 3,912 |
| Cost of goods manufactured | | 16,012 |
| Finished goods inventory, 9/1/year 1 | | 930 |
| Cost of goods available for sale | | 16,942 |
| Finished goods inventory, 8/31/year 2 | | 377 |
| Cost of goods sold | | $16,565 |

The results for the first quarter required the following changes in the budget assumptions:

- The estimated production in units for the fiscal year should be revised from 140,000 to 145,000 units with the balance of production being scheduled in equal segments over the last 9 months of the year. The actual first quarter's production was 25,000 units.

- The planned inventory for finished goods of 3,300 units at the end of the fiscal year remains unchanged and will be valued at the average manufacturing cost for the year. The finished goods inventory of 9,300 units on September 1, year 1 had dropped to 9,000 units by November 30, year 1.

- Due to a new labor agreement, the labor rate will increase 8% effective June 1, year 2, the beginning of the fourth quarter, instead of the previously anticipated effective date of September 1, year 2, the beginning of the next fiscal year.

- The assumptions remain unchanged for direct materials inventory at 16,000 units for the beginning inventory and 18,500 units for the ending inventory. Direct materials inventory is valued on a FIFO basis. During the first quarter, direct materials for 27,500 units of output were purchased for $2,200,000. Although direct materials will be purchased evenly for the last 9 months, the cost of the direct materials will increase by 5% on March 1, year 2, the beginning of the third quarter.

- Indirect materials costs will continue to be projected at 10% of the cost of direct materials consumed.

- One-half of general manufacturing overhead is considered fixed.

**79.** Watson's revised pro forma cost of goods sold statement will report direct materials purchased of

- A. $11,400,000
- B. $11,600,000
- C. $11,800,000
- D. $12,120,000

Answer (D) is correct. *(Publisher)*
**REQUIRED:** The revised direct materials purchased.
**DISCUSSION:** During the first quarter, direct materials for 27,500 units of output were purchased for $2,200,000, or $80 per output unit ($2,200,000 ÷ 27,500). Given that 145,000 units are to be produced and that inventory will increase by 2,500 units (18,500 ending inventory – 16,000 beginning inventory), units to be purchased evenly over the last 9 months equal 120,000 ($145,000 units produced + 2,500 inventory increase – 27,500 units purchased in the first quarter). Accordingly, 40,000 units (120,000 ÷ 3 quarters) will be purchased in the second quarter for $80 per unit, a total of $3,200,000. Moreover, 80,000 units (120,000 – 40,000) will be purchased in the third and fourth quarters for $84 per unit ($80 × 1.05), a total of $6,720,000. The revised pro forma total of direct materials purchased equals $12,120,000 ($2,200,000 + $3,200,000 + $6,720,000).

Answer (A) is incorrect because $11,400,000 is the original pro forma amount. Answer (B) is incorrect because $11,600,000 equals $80 times 145,000 units. Answer (C) is incorrect because $11,800,000 assumes that the final 80,000 units will be purchased at $80 per unit.

**80.** The revised pro forma ending direct materials inventory is

    A. $1,280,000

    B. $1,480,000

    C. $1,520,136

    D. $1,554,000

Answer (D) is correct. *(Publisher)*
    **REQUIRED:** The revised pro forma ending direct materials inventory.
    **DISCUSSION:** Given a FIFO inventory flow assumption, the revised pro forma ending direct materials inventory consists of 18,500 units from the final materials purchase. During the first quarter, direct materials for 27,500 units of output were purchased for $2,200,000, or $80 per output unit ($2,200,000 ÷ 27,500). The cost of direct materials increased by 5% on March 1; thus, the unit price of the final direct materials purchase is $84. Thus, the revised pro forma ending direct materials inventory is $1,554,000 (18,500 units × $84).
    Answer (A) is incorrect because $1,280,000 equals 16,000 units times $80 per unit. Answer (B) is incorrect because $1,480,000 equals 18,500 units times $80 per unit. Answer (C) is incorrect because $1,520,136 is calculated at the average cost of units to be purchased.

**81.** The revised pro forma amount of direct labor cost is

    A. $980,000

    B. $1,037,400

    C. $1,058,400

    D. $1,096,200

Answer (B) is correct. *(Publisher)*
    **REQUIRED:** The revised pro forma amount of direct labor cost.
    **DISCUSSION:** Given that 25,000 units were produced in the first quarter, 145,000 total units are to be produced, and production is scheduled in equal segments over the last 9 months (3 quarters); 120,000 units at 40,000 units per quarter are projected to be produced during the last 9 months. Furthermore, the labor rate will increase by 8% in the fourth quarter. Consequently, given a labor rate of $7 per unit during the first 3 quarters ($980,000 original pro forma labor cost ÷ 140,000 original estimated unit output), the fourth quarter labor rate will be $7.56 per unit ($7 × 1.08). The revised pro forma amount of direct labor cost is therefore $1,037,400 {[(25,000 units in the first quarter + 80,000 units in the second and third quarters) × $7] + (40,000 units in the fourth quarter × $7.56)}.
    Answer (A) is incorrect because $980,000 is the original direct pro forma labor cost. Answer (C) is incorrect because $1,058,400 equals $7.56 times 140,000 units. Answer (D) is incorrect because $1,096,200 equals $7.56 times 145,000 units.

**82.** The revised pro forma cost of goods manufactured is

    A. $15,430,000

    B. $16,012,000

    C. $16,830,000

    D. $17,760,000

Answer (C) is correct. *(Publisher)*
    **REQUIRED:** The revised pro forma cost of goods manufactured.
    **DISCUSSION:** The revised pro forma direct labor cost was determined to be $1,037,400. The beginning materials inventory was given as $1,200,000. Revised pro forma direct materials purchases and ending inventory were determined to be $12,120,000 and $1,554,000, respectively. Accordingly, revised pro forma direct materials consumed equals $11,766,000 ($1,200,000 + $12,120,000 – $1,554,000). Indirect materials continue to be projected at 10% of direct materials consumed, or $1,176,600 (10% × $11,766,000). Given original pro forma general manufacturing overhead of $2,800,000 and that 50% of this amount, or $1,400,000, is fixed, the variable overhead applied is $1,450,000 {[($2,800,000 – $1,400,000) ÷ 140,000 original estimated unit production] × 145,000 revised estimated unit production}. The revised pro forma cost of goods manufactured is therefore $16,830,000 ($11,766,000 DM + $1,037,400 DL + $1,176,600 indirect materials + $1,400,000 FOH + $1,450,000 VOH).
    Answer (A) is incorrect because $15,430,000 omits fixed general overhead. Answer (B) is incorrect because $16,012,000 is the original pro forma cost of goods manufactured. Answer (D) is incorrect because $17,760,000 is the cost of goods available for sale.

**83.** Refer to the information on the preceding page(s). The revised pro forma cost of goods sold is

A. $16,565,000

B. $16,942,000

C. $17,376,972

D. $17,760,000

Answer (C) is correct.    *(Publisher)*
**REQUIRED:** The revised pro forma cost of goods sold.
**DISCUSSION:** The revised pro forma cost of goods manufactured was determined in the preceding question to be $16,830,000. The beginning pro forma finished goods inventory is given as $930,000. The pro forma ending finished goods inventory continues to be 3,300 units, but it will be valued at the pro forma average annual manufacturing cost ($16,830,000 CGM ÷ 145,000 revised unit output). Thus, pro forma ending finished goods equals $383,028 [3,300 units × ($16,830,000 ÷ 145,000)]. The revised pro forma cost of goods sold (CGM + beginning FG – ending FG) is therefore equal to $17,376,972 ($16,830,000 CGM + $930,000 – $383,028).
Answer (A) is incorrect because $16,565,000 equals the original pro forma cost of goods sold. Answer (B) is incorrect because $16,942,000 equals the original pro forma cost of goods available for sale. Answer (D) is incorrect because $17,760,000 equals the revised pro forma cost of goods available for sale.

---

Questions 84 through 86 are based on the following information.

This information was adapted from a question on Part 4 of the June 1990 CMA examination that concerned preparation of a pro forma income statement. Easecom manufactures products for networking video-conferencing equipment. Production of specialized units is, to a large extent, performed under contract, with standard units manufactured to marketing projections. Maintenance of customer equipment is an important area of customer satisfaction. Easecom's income statement for the fiscal year ended October 31, year 1 is presented below.

Easecom
Income Statement
For the Year Ended October 31, Year 1
($000 omitted)

| | |
|---|---:|
| Net sales | |
| Equipment | $6,000 |
| Maintenance contracts | 1,800 |
| Total net sales | 7,800 |
| | |
| Expenses: | |
| Cost of goods sold | 4,600 |
| Customer maintenance | 1,000 |
| Selling expense | 600 |
| Administrative expense | 900 |
| Interest expense | 150 |
| Total expenses | 7,250 |
| Income before income taxes | 550 |
| Income taxes | 220 |
| Net income | $ 330 |

Easecom's management considered the growing video-conferencing market when it proposed the following actions for fiscal year 2:

- Increase equipment sales prices by 10%.
- Increase the cost of each unit sold by 3% for needed technology and quality improvements, and increased variable costs.
- Increase maintenance inventory by $250,000 at the beginning of the year and add two maintenance technicians at a total cost of $130,000 to cover wages and related travel expenses. These revisions are intended to improve customer service and response time. The increased inventory will be financed at an annual interest rate of 12%; no other borrowings or loan reductions are contemplated during fiscal year 2. All other assets will be held to fiscal year 1 levels.
- Increase selling expenses by $250,000 but hold administrative expenses at year levels.
- The effective rate for year 2 federal and state taxes is expected to be 40%, the same as year 1.

These actions are expected to increase equipment unit sales by 6%, with a corresponding 6% growth in maintenance contracts.

---

**84.** In its pro forma income statement for the fiscal year ending October 31, year 2, Easecom estimated that total net sales will be

A. $8,904,000

B. $7,800,000

C. $6,996,000

D. $6,000,000

Answer (A) is correct.    *(Publisher)*
**REQUIRED:** The pro forma total net sales.
**DISCUSSION:** Equipment unit sales and price will increase by 6% and 10%, respectively. Hence, equipment sales will be $6,996,000 ($6,000,000 for the year ended 10/31/year 1 × 1.06 × 1.10). Maintenance contracts will be increased by 6%. Hence, maintenance sales will be $1,908,000 ($1,800,000 for the year ended 10/31/year 1 × 1.06). The pro forma total net sales will therefore be $8,904,000 ($6,996,000 + $1,908,000).
Answer (B) is incorrect because $7,800,000 equals total net sales for the year ended October 31, year 1. Answer (C) is incorrect because $6,996,000 omits sales of maintenance contracts. Answer (D) is incorrect because $6,000,000 equals equipment sales for the year ended October 31, year 1.

**85.** In its pro forma income statement for the year ended October 31, year 2, Easecom estimated that cost of goods sold will be

A. $8,082,280

B. $7,250,000

C. $5,022,280

D. $4,600,000

Answer (C) is correct. *(Publisher)*
REQUIRED: The pro forma cost of goods sold.
DISCUSSION: The cost and unit sales of equipment are expected to increase by 3% and 6%, respectively. Accordingly, pro forma cost of goods sold will be $5,022,280 ($4,600,000 for the year ended 10/31/year 1 × 1.03 × 1.06).
Answer (A) is incorrect because $8,082,280 equals pro forma total expenses. Answer (B) is incorrect because $7,250,000 equals total expenses for the year ended October 31, year 1. Answer (D) is incorrect because $4,600,000 equals cost of goods sold for the year ended October 31, year 1.

**86.** In its pro forma income statement for the year ended October 31, year 2, Easecom estimated that its net income will be

A. $493,032

B. $330,000

C. $328,688

D. $220,000

Answer (A) is correct. *(Publisher)*
REQUIRED: The pro forma net income.
DISCUSSION: As calculated in previous questions, pro forma total sales equals $8,904,000, and pro forma cost of goods sold equals $5,022,280. Customer maintenance expense will increase to $1,130,000 ($1,000,000 for the year ended 10/31/year 1 + $130,000 wages and travel expenses increase for year 2), and selling expenses will increase to $850,000 ($600,000 for the year ended 10/31/year 1 + $250,000 increase for year 2). Administrative expense is unchanged at $900,000, but interest is projected to increase from $150,000 to $180,000 [$150,000 + ($250,000 × 12% inventory financing rate)]. Consequently, total pro forma expenses are $8,082,280 ($5,022,280 + $1,130,000 + $850,000 + $900,000 + $180,000). Pro forma pretax income is therefore $821,720 ($8,904,000 total net sales − $8,082,032 total expenses), and pro forma net income is $493,032 [$821,720 × (1.0 − .40 tax rate)].
Answer (B) is incorrect because $330,000 equals net income for the year ended October 31, year 1. Answer (C) is incorrect because $328,688 equals pro forma income taxes. Answer (D) is incorrect because $220,000 equals income taxes for the year ended October 31, year 1.

**87.** The Yummy Dog Bone Company is anticipating that a major supplier might experience a strike this year. Because of the nature of the product and emphasis on quality, extra production cannot be stored as finished goods inventory. When developing a contingency budget that would anticipate a direct materials buildup, the two most significant items that will be affected are

A. Production volume and direct material.

B. Sales and ending inventory.

C. Production and cash flow.

D. Direct materials and cash flow.

Answer (D) is correct. *(CMA, adapted)*
REQUIRED: The two most significant items in a contingency budget anticipating a direct materials buildup.
DISCUSSION: The most significant items are those that will vary between the contingency budget and the regular budget. The company cannot increase its finished goods inventory, but it can increase its inventory of the direct materials provided by the supplier. Thus, the items most affected will be direct materials and cash. The cash budget will be affected because of the need to pay for direct materials prior to their usage.
Answer (A) is incorrect because the nature of the product prevents an increase in production volume to augment finished goods inventory. Answer (B) is incorrect because sales are dependent on demand, a factor not affected by the strike. Sales may decrease, however, if the company suffers a stockout. Furthermore, ending finished goods inventory cannot increase because of the nature of the product. Answer (C) is incorrect because the nature of the product prevents an increase in production volume to augment finished goods inventory.

Questions 88 through 96 are based on the following information.

This information was adapted from a question on Part 4 of the December 1988 CMA examination that concerned preparation of a pro forma statement of financial position. Jefferson Binders, Inc. is a manufacturer of notebooks with a comprehensive annual budgeting process that ends with the preparation of pro forma financial statements. All underlying budget schedules have been completed for the year ending December 31, year 2 and selected data from these schedules are presented below. Also shown are the pro forma statement of cash receipts and disbursements for the year ending December 31, year 2 and the pro forma statement of financial position as of December 31, year 1. Jefferson uses the accrual basis of accounting.

To facilitate the budgeting process, Jefferson accumulates all raw materials, direct labor, manufacturing overhead (with the exception of depreciation), selling, and administrative costs in an account called expenses payable. The company's income tax rate is 40%, and income tax expense is classified as current income taxes payable.

### Selected data from year 2 budget schedules:

- The majority of sales are on account.

| Unit Sales | Unit Price | Total Revenue |
|---|---|---|
| 9,500,000 | $5.50 | $52,250,000 |

- Production

| Production Units | Unit Cost | Total Manufacturing Cost |
|---|---|---|
| 9,640,000 | $4.75 | $45,790,000 |

- Raw Materials Purchases

| Item | Quantity | Unit Cost | Total Purchases |
|---|---|---|---|
| Ring Assembly | 9,600,000 | $.80 | 7,680,000 |
| Cover (2 per unit) | 18,800,000 | $.30 | 5,640,000 |

- Raw Materials Purchases

| Production Hours | Cost per Hour | Total Cost |
|---|---|---|
| 2,410,000 | $9.00 | $21,690,000 |

Each unit requires 15 minutes of direct labor time.

- The manufacturing overhead rate is $4.40 per direct labor hour ($10,604,000 ÷ 2,410,000 hours).

| | |
|---|---|
| Variable overhead | $ 5,790,000 |
| Supervisory salaries | 1,250,000 |
| Depreciation | 724,000 |
| Other fixed costs | 2,840,000 |
| Total manufacturing overhead | $10,604,000 |

- Selling and Administrative Expenses

| | |
|---|---|
| Selling expense | $1,875,000 |
| Administrative expense | 3,080,000 |
| Total expense | $4,955,000 |

- Each semi-annual mortgage payment consists of interest plus an even principal reduction of $100,000. Interest payments for year 2 are $250,000.

### Jefferson Binders, Inc.
### Pro Forma Statement of Cash Receipts and Disbursements
### For the Year Ending December 31, Year 2
### ($000 omitted)

| | |
|---|---|
| Cash balance 1/1/year 2 (estimated) | $    565 |
| **Cash receipts** | |
| Cash sales | 5,300 |
| Collection of accounts receivable | 46,600 |
| Proceeds from sale of additional common stock (20,000 shares) | 420 |
| Total cash available | $52,885 |
| **Cash disbursements** | |
| Raw materials | $13,380 |
| Direct labor | 21,640 |
| Manufacturing overhead | 9,650 |
| Selling and administrative expense | 4,980 |
| Income taxes | 860 |
| Purchase of equipment | 1,200 |
| Cash dividends | 320 |
| Mortgage payment | 450 |
| Total disbursements | $52,480 |
| Projected cash balance 12/31/year 2 | $    405 |

### Jefferson Binders, Inc.
### Pro Forma Statement of Financial Position
### as of December 31, Year 1
### ($000 omitted)

#### Assets

| | |
|---|---|
| Cash | $     565 |
| Accounts receivable | 825 |
| Raw materials inventory* | 301 |
| Finished goods inventory** | 608 |
| Total current assets | $ 2,299 |
| Land | $ 1,757 |
| Property, plant, and equipment | 12,400 |
| Minus: Accumulated depreciation | 2,960 |
| Total long-term assets | $11,197 |
| Total assets | $13,496 |

#### Liabilities and Equity

| | |
|---|---|
| Expenses payable | $     690 |
| Mortgage payable | 200 |
| Income taxes payable | 356 |
| Total current liabilities | $ 1,246 |
| Long-term mortgage payable | $ 2,700 |
| Total liabilities | $ 3,946 |
| Common stock (500,000 shares authorized, 300,000 shares outstanding, $10 par value) | $ 3,000 |
| Paid-in capital in excess of par | 5,400 |
| Retained earnings | 1,150 |
| Total equity | $ 9,550 |
| Total liabilities and equity | $13,496 |

*65,000 ring assemblies at $.80 each
830,000 covers at $.30 each
**128,000 units at $4.75 each

**88.** Pro forma net income for the year ending December 31, year 2 is

    A. $1,152,000

    B. $1,302,000

    C. $1,920,000

    D. $2,170,000

Answer (A) is correct. *(Publisher)*
    **REQUIRED:** The pro forma net income.
    **DISCUSSION:** The following is the pro forma income statement for the year ending December 31, year 2:

| | |
|---|---:|
| Sales revenue | $ 52,250,000 |
| Cost of goods sold (9,500,000 units × $4.75) | (45,125,000) |
| Selling expense | (1,875,000) |
| Administrative expense | (3,080,000) |
| Operating income | $ 2,170,000 |
| Interest expense | (250,000) |
| Income before tax | $ 1,920,000 |
| Taxes ($1,920,000 × 40%) | (768,000) |
| Net income | $ 1,152,000 |

    Answer (B) is incorrect because $1,302,000 omits interest expense. Answer (C) is incorrect because $1,920,000 is pretax income. Answer (D) is incorrect because $2,170,000 is operating income.

**89.** The pro forma accounts receivable balance at December 31, year 2 is

    A. $350,000

    B. $405,000

    C. $825,000

    D. $1,175,000

Answer (D) is correct. *(Publisher)*
    **REQUIRED:** The pro forma accounts receivable balance.
    **DISCUSSION:** The pro forma accounts receivable balance at December 31, year 2 is determined as follows:

| | | |
|---|---:|---:|
| Beginning balance | | $ 825,000 |
| Total sales | $52,250,000 | |
| Minus: cash sales | (5,300,000) | 46,950,000 |
| | | $ 47,775,000 |
| Minus: collections | | (46,600,000) |
| Ending balance | | $ 1,175,000 |

    Answer (A) is incorrect because $350,000 is the excess of credit sales over collections. Answer (B) is incorrect because $405,000 is the cash balance. Answer (C) is incorrect because $825,000 is the beginning balance.

**90.** The pro forma finished goods balance at December 31, year 2 is

    A. $608,000

    B. $665,000

    C. $1,273,000

    D. $1,378,000

Answer (C) is correct. *(Publisher)*
    **REQUIRED:** The pro forma finished goods balance.
    **DISCUSSION:** Given that the unit cost of items in the beginning inventory equals the unit cost of current production (or that a LIFO flow assumption is used), the pro forma finished goods balance at December 31, year 2 is determined as follows:

| | |
|---|---:|
| Beginning balance | $ 608,000 |
| Completed (9,640,000 units × $4.75) | 45,790,000 |
| | $ 46,398,000 |
| Cost of goods sold (9,500,000 units × $4.75) | (45,125,000) |
| Ending balance | $ 1,273,000 |

    Answer (A) is incorrect because $608,000 is the beginning balance. Answer (B) is incorrect because $665,000 omits the beginning balance. Answer (D) is incorrect because $1,378,000 is based on the unit sales price of $5.50.

**91.** The pro forma total current assets balance at December 31, year 2 is

    A. $2,299,000

    B. $2,978,000

    C. $2,573,000

    D. $2,448,000

Answer (B) is correct. *(Publisher)*
    **REQUIRED:** The pro forma total current assets balance.
    **DISCUSSION:** The projected cash balance at year-end is given as $405,000. The ending balances of accounts receivable, raw materials, and finished goods were determined in preceding questions to be $1,175,000, $125,000, and $1,273,000, respectively. Thus, the pro forma total current assets balance equals $2,978,000 ($405,000 + $1,175,000 + $125,000 + $1,273,000).
    Answer (A) is incorrect because $2,299,000 equals the pro forma total current assets balance as of December 31, year 1. Answer (C) is incorrect because $2,573,000 omits cash. Answer (D) is incorrect because $2,448,000 omits cash and raw materials.

**92.** Refer to the information on the preceding page(s). The pro forma direct materials balance at December 31, year 2 is

A. $125,000

B. $157,000

C. $269,000

D. $301,000

**Answer (A) is correct.** *(Publisher)*
**REQUIRED:** The pro forma direct materials balance.
**DISCUSSION:** Given that the unit costs of ring assemblies and covers in the beginning inventory are the same as their current purchase prices, the pro forma direct materials balance at December 31, year 2 is determined as follows:

| | | |
|---|---|---|
| Beginning balance | | $ 301,000 |
| Purchases - ring assembly | | 7,680,000 |
| Purchases - covers | | 5,640,000 |
| | | $ 13,621,000 |
| Minus: Amounts used | | |
| Ring assemblies | | |
| (9,640,000 × $.80) | $7,712,000 | |
| Covers (9,640,000 × 2 × $.30) | 5,784,000 | (13,496,000) |
| Ending balance | | $ 125,000 |

Answer (B) is incorrect because $157,000 omits the purchases and usage of ring assemblies. Answer (C) is incorrect because $269,000 omits the purchases and usage of covers. Answer (D) is incorrect because $301,000 is the beginning balance.

**93.** Refer to the information on the preceding page(s). The pro forma total assets balance at December 31, year 2 is

A. $11,673,000

B. $14,651,000

C. $18,335,000

D. $22,019,000

**Answer (B) is correct.** *(Publisher)*
**REQUIRED:** The pro forma total assets balance.
**DISCUSSION:** As determined in the preceding question, the total current assets balance is $2,978,000. Land has a $1,757,000 balance that apparently has not been projected to change since preparation of the December 31, year 1 pro forma statement of financial position. The property, plant, and equipment balance is $13,600,000 ($12,400,000 beginning balance + $1,200,000 purchase of equipment), and accumulated depreciation is $3,684,000 ($2,960,000 beginning balance + $724,000 current period depreciation). Hence, total assets equal $14,651,000 ($2,978,000 + $1,757,000 + $13,600,000 − $3,684,000).

Answer (A) is incorrect because $11,673,000 equals total long-term assets. Answer (C) is incorrect because $18,335,000 omits depreciation. Answer (D) is incorrect because $22,019,000 adds depreciation.

**94.** Refer to the information on the preceding page(s). The pro forma expenses payable balance at December 31, year 2 is

A. $195,000

B. $609,000

C. $885,000

D. $1,609,000

**Answer (C) is correct.** *(Publisher)*
**REQUIRED:** The pro forma expenses payable balance.
**DISCUSSION:** Jefferson accumulates direct materials, direct labor, manufacturing overhead (exclusive of depreciation), and selling and administrative costs in expenses payable. The pro forma expenses payable balance at December 31, year 2 is determined as follows:

| | | |
|---|---|---|
| Beginning balance | | $ 690,000 |
| Additions: | | |
| Direct materials | | |
| ($7,680,000 + $5,640,000) | $13,320,000 | |
| Labor | 21,690,000 | |
| Overhead | | |
| ($10,604,000 − $724,000) | 9,880,000 | |
| Selling & administrative | 4,955,000 | 49,845,000 |
| | | $ 50,535,000 |
| Minus payments: | | |
| Direct materials | $13,380,000 | |
| Labor | 21,640,000 | |
| Overhead | 9,650,000 | |
| Selling & administrative | 4,980,000 | (49,650,000) |
| Ending balance | | $ 885,000 |

Answer (A) is incorrect because $195,000 is the difference between total additions to the account and total payments. Answer (B) is incorrect because $609,000 is the beginning balance. Answer (D) is incorrect because $1,609,000 results from not subtracting depreciation.

**95.** Refer to the information on the preceding page(s). The pro forma total liabilities balance at December 31, year 2 is

A. $1,349,000

B. $3,849,000

C. $3,946,000

D. $14,651,000

Answer (B) is correct. *(Publisher)*
**REQUIRED:** The pro forma total liabilities balance.
**DISCUSSION:** The expenses payable balance was determined in the preceding question to be $885,000. The beginning balances of the current and long-term portions of the mortgage payable were $200,000 and $2,700,000, respectively. Given semi-annual payments of $100,000, the current portion at December 31, year 2 remains $200,000 (2 principal payments due in year 3 × $100,000), and the long-term portion is reduced to $2,500,000 ($2,700,000 − $200,000 of principal transferred to current). Income tax expense was determined in a preceding question to be $768,000. Hence, income tax payable equals $264,000 ($356,000 beginning balance + $768,000 current expense − $860,000 paid). The pro forma total liabilities balance was therefore $3,849,000 ($885,000 expenses payable + $200,000 current mortgage payable + $264,000 income tax payable + $2,500,000 long-term mortgage payable).
Answer (A) is incorrect because $1,349,000 equals total current liabilities. Answer (C) is incorrect because $3,946,000 equals the beginning balance. Answer (D) is incorrect because $14,651,000 equals the sum of total liabilities and equity.

**96.** Refer to the information on the preceding page(s). The pro forma total equity balance at December 31, year 2 is

A. $10,802,000

B. $11,122,000

C. $13,496,000

D. $14,651,000

Answer (A) is correct. *(Publisher)*
**REQUIRED:** The pro forma total equity balance.
**DISCUSSION:** The proceeds of the issuance of 20,000 common shares ($10 par value) equaled $420,000, and cash dividends paid equaled $320,000. Moreover, net income was determined to be $1,152,000. Accordingly, total equity at December 31, year 2 is determined as follows:

| | | |
|---|---|---|
| Common stock | | |
|   Beginning balance | $3,000,000 | |
|   Issue of stock | | |
|     (20,000 shares × $10 par) | 200,000 | |
|   Ending balance | | $3,200,000 |
| | | |
| Paid-in capital in excess of par | | |
|   Beginning balance | $5,400,000 | |
|   Issue of stock | | |
|     ($420,000 − $200,000) | 220,000 | |
|   Ending balance | | $5,620,000 |
| | | |
| Retained earnings | | |
|   Beginning balance | $1,150,000 | |
|   Net income | 1,152,000 | |
| | $2,302,000 | |
|   Dividends | (320,000) | |
|   Ending balance | | 1,982,000 |
| Total equity | | $10,802,000 |

Answer (B) is incorrect because $11,122,000 does not consider the dividends paid. Answer (C) is incorrect because $13,496,000 is the beginning balance of total liabilities and equity. Answer (D) is incorrect because $14,651,000 is the ending balance of total liabilities and equity.

Questions 97 through 99 are based on the following information.

Rokat Corporation is a manufacturer of tables sold to schools, restaurants, hotels, and other institutions. The table tops are manufactured by Rokat, but the table legs are purchased from an outside supplier. The Assembly Department takes a manufactured table top and attaches the four purchased table legs. It takes 20 minutes of labor to assemble a table. The company follows a policy of producing enough tables to ensure that 40% of next month's sales are in the finished goods inventory. Rokat also purchases sufficient raw materials to ensure that direct materials inventory is 60% of the following month's scheduled production.

Rokat's sales budget in units for the next quarter is as follows:

| | |
|---|---|
| July | 2,300 |
| August | 2,500 |
| September | 2,100 |

Rokat's ending inventories in units for June 30 are

| | |
|---|---|
| Finished goods | 1,900 |
| Direct materials (legs) | 4,000 |

**97.** The number of tables to be produced during August is

A. 1,400 tables.

B. 2,340 tables.

C. 1,440 tables.

D. 1,900 tables.

Answer (B) is correct. *(CMA, adapted)*
**REQUIRED:** The number of tables to be produced.
**DISCUSSION:** The company will need 2,500 finished units for August sales. In addition, 840 units (2,100 September unit sales × 40%) should be in inventory at the end of August. August sales plus the desired ending inventory equals 3,340 units. Of these units, 40% of August's sales, or 1,000 units, should be available from beginning inventory. Consequently, production in August should be 2,340 units.
Answer (A) is incorrect because 1,400 tables is the number to be produced in July. Answer (C) is incorrect because 4,440 tables is based on July's beginning inventory. Answer (D) is incorrect because 1,900 tables equals July's beginning inventory.

**98.** Assume the required production for August and September is 1,600 and 1,800 units, respectively, and the July 31 direct materials inventory is 4,200 units. The number of table legs to be purchased in August is

A. 6,520 legs.

B. 9,400 legs.

C. 2,200 legs.

D. 6,400 legs.

Answer (A) is correct. *(CMA, adapted)*
**REQUIRED:** The number of table legs to be purchased.
**DISCUSSION:** The August production of 1,600 units will require 6,400 table legs. September's production of 1,800 units will require 7,200 table legs. Thus, inventory at the end of August should be 4,320 legs (7,200 legs × 60%). The total of legs needed during August is 10,720 (6,400 + 4,320), of which 4,200 are available from the July 31 ending inventory. The remaining 6,520 legs must be purchased during August.
Answer (B) is incorrect because 9,400 legs is based on an ending inventory of 100% of September's production. Answer (C) is incorrect because 2,200 legs fails to consider the legs needed for the ending inventory. Answer (D) is incorrect because 6,400 legs is the amount needed for August production.

**99.** Assume that Rokat Corporation will produce 1,800 units in the month of September. How many employees will be required for the Assembly Department? (Fractional employees are acceptable since employees can be hired on a part-time basis. Assume a 40-hour week and a 4-week month.)

A. 15 employees.

B. 3.75 employees.

C. 60 employees.

D. 600 employees.

Answer (B) is correct. *(CMA, adapted)*
**REQUIRED:** The number of employees required.
**DISCUSSION:** Each unit requires 20 minutes of assembly time, or 1/3 of an hour. The assembly of 1,800 units will therefore require 600 hours of labor (1,800 × 1/3). At 40 hours per week for 4 weeks, each employee will work 160 hours during the month. Thus, 3.75 employees (600 ÷ 160) are needed.
Answer (A) is incorrect because 15 employees assumes production occurs in a single 40-hour week. Answer (C) is incorrect because 60 employees assumes that each leg requires 20 minutes to assemble and that production occurs in a single 40-hour week. Answer (D) is incorrect because 600 is the number of hours needed, not the number of employees.

Questions 100 and 101 are based on the following information.

Jordan Auto has developed the following production plan:

| Month | Units |
|---|---|
| January | 10,000 |
| February | 8,000 |
| March | 9,000 |
| April | 12,000 |

Each unit contains 3 pounds of direct materials. The desired direct materials ending inventory each month is 120% of the next month's production, plus 500 pounds. (The beginning inventory meets this requirement.) Jordan has developed the following direct labor standards for production of these units:

| | Department 1 | Department 2 |
|---|---|---|
| Hours per unit | 2.0 | 0.5 |
| Hourly rate | $6.75 | $12.00 |

**100.** How much direct materials should Jordan Auto purchase in March?

A. 27,000 pounds.

B. 32,900 pounds.

C. 36,000 pounds.

D. 37,800 pounds.

Answer (D) is correct. *(CMA, adapted)*
**REQUIRED:** The direct materials to purchase in March.
**DISCUSSION:** Jordan needs 27,000 pounds (3 × 9,000 units) of materials for March production. It also needs 43,700 pounds {[(3 × 12,000 units to be produced in April) × 120%] + 500} for ending inventory. Given a beginning inventory of 32,900 pounds {[(3 × 9,000 units to be produced in March) × 120%] + 500}, required purchases equal 37,800 pounds (27,000 pounds + 43,700 pounds – 32,900 pounds).
Answer (A) is incorrect because 27,000 pounds is the usage for March. Answer (B) is incorrect because 32,900 pounds is the beginning inventory. Answer (C) is incorrect because 36,000 pounds is the usage for April.

**101.** Jordan Auto's total budgeted direct labor dollars for February usage should be

A. $156,000

B. $165,750

C. $175,500

D. $210,600

Answer (A) is correct. *(CMA, adapted)*
**REQUIRED:** The total budgeted direct labor dollars for February.
**DISCUSSION:** The standard unit labor cost is $19.50 [($6.75 × 2 hours in Department 1) + ($12 × .5 hour in Department 2)], so the total budgeted direct labor dollars for February equal $156,000 (8,000 units × $19.50).
Answer (B) is incorrect because $165,750 is for 500 more units than budgeted usage. Answer (C) is incorrect because $175,500 is the amount for March. Answer (D) is incorrect because $210,600 is for 120% of budgeted March production.

Use Gleim's *CMA Test Prep* for interactive testing with **over 2,000 additional multiple-choice questions!**

# STUDY UNIT TWO
# COST MANAGEMENT TERMINOLOGY AND CONCEPTS

(21 pages of outline)

This study unit is the **first of three** on **cost management**. The relative weight assigned to this major topic in Part 2 of the exam is **25%** at **skill level C** (all six skill types required). The three study units are

Study Unit 2: Cost Management Terminology and Concepts
Study Unit 3: Job-Order Costing, Overhead Costs, and Service Department Allocation
Study Unit 4: Process Costing and Other Cost Accumulation Systems

This study unit consists of numerous definitions. These definitions occupy relatively few pages, but they require your careful analysis and deliberation. Please think about each definition after reading it. How would you explain the concept to a nonaccountant? Try to achieve a working knowledge of each definition. Thus, you should be able to apply a definition in the context of a quantitative problem. For example, you may never see a question asking for a definition of absorption costing, but you will be given a set of numbers and asked to compute inventory or cost of goods sold using absorption costing. Most of the terms will appear again in a later study unit where you will be exposed to more detail about the subject. Actually, you may want to return to this study unit again later and use it as a review once you have completed all of the study units in the book.

After studying the outlines and answering the multiple-choice questions in this study unit, you will have the skills necessary to address the following topics listed in the IMA's Learning Outcome Statements:

Part 2 – Section B.1. Terminology

The candidate should be able to:

a. identify and differentiate all cost items reported on the income statement
b. identify and calculate those costs incurred to complete a product and reported as cost of goods sold
c. identify and calculate those costs incurred for current operations but not included in cost of goods sold
d. identify and calculate the components of cost concepts such as prime cost, conversion cost, overhead cost, carrying cost, sunk cost, discretionary cost, and opportunity cost
e. demonstrate an understanding of the characteristics that differentiate fixed costs, variable costs, and mixed costs and evaluate the effect that changes in production volume have on these costs
f. describe the importance of timely and accurate costing information as a tool for strategic planning and management decision making

Part 2 – Section B.2.  Measurement concepts

The candidate should be able to:

a.   demonstrate an understanding of the behavior of fixed and variable costs in the long and short terms and how a change in assumptions regarding cost type or relevant range affects these costs

b.   recognize cost objects and cost pools and assign costs to appropriate activities

c.   demonstrate an understanding of the nature and types of cost drivers and the causal relationship that exists between cost drivers and costs incurred

d.   demonstrate a thorough understanding of the various methods for measuring costs and accumulating work-in-process and finished goods inventories and a basic understanding of how inventories are relieved

e.   identify and calculate the components of cost measurement techniques such as actual costing, normal costing, and standard costing; recognize the appropriate use of each technique; and describe the benefits and limitations of each technique

f.   demonstrate an understanding of the characteristics of variable costing and absorption costing and the benefits and limitations of these measurement concepts

g.   calculate inventory costs using both variable costing and absorption costing

h.   demonstrate an understanding of how the use of variable costing or absorption costing affects the value of inventory, cost of goods sold, and operating income

i.   recognize the appropriate use of joint product and by-product costing and demonstrate an understanding of concepts such as split-off point and separable costs

j.   determine the allocation of joint product and by-product costs using the physical measure method, the sales value at split-off method, gross profit (gross margin) method, and the net realizable value method; and describe the benefits and limitations of each method

## 2.1 BROAD CATEGORIES OF COSTS

1.   **Manufacturing vs. Nonmanufacturing**

a.   The **costs of manufacturing** a product can be classified as one of three types:

1)   **Direct materials** are those tangible inputs to the manufacturing process that can practicably be traced to the product, e.g., sheet metal welded together for a piece of heavy equipment.

a)   All costs of bringing raw materials to the production line, e.g., transportation-in, are included in the cost of direct materials.

2)   **Direct labor** is the cost of human labor that can practicably be traced to the product, e.g., the wages of the welder.

3)   **Manufacturing overhead** consists of all costs of manufacturing that are not direct materials or direct labor.

a)   **Indirect materials** are tangible inputs to the manufacturing process that cannot practicably be traced to the product, e.g., the welding compound used to put together a piece of heavy equipment.

b)   **Indirect labor** is the cost of human labor connected with the manufacturing process that cannot practicably be traced to the product, e.g., the wages of assembly line supervisors and janitorial staff.

c)   **Factory operating costs** such as utilities, real estate taxes, insurance, depreciation on factory equipment, etc.

    b.   Manufacturing costs are often grouped into the following classifications:

        1)  **Prime cost** equals direct materials plus direct labor, i.e., those costs directly attributable to a product.

        2)  **Conversion cost** equals direct labor plus manufacturing overhead, i.e., the costs of converting raw materials into the finished product.

    c.   Operating a manufacturing concern requires the incurrence of **nonmanufacturing costs**:

        1)  **Selling (marketing) costs** are those costs incurred in getting the product from the factory to the consumer, e.g., sales personnel salaries and product transportation.

        2)  **Administrative expenses** are those costs incurred by a company not directly related to producing or marketing the product, e.g., executive salaries and depreciation on the headquarters building.

2.   **Product vs. Period**

    a.   One of the most important classifications a managerial accountant can make is whether to capitalize costs in finished goods inventory or to expense them as incurred.

        1)  Whichever costs are capitalized as part of finished goods inventory are referred to as **product, or inventoriable, costs**. They eventually become a **component of cost of goods sold**.

        2)  Those costs not capitalized in finished goods inventory are termed **period costs** and are **excluded from cost of goods sold**.

    b.   This distinction is crucial because of the required treatment of manufacturing costs for external financial reporting purposes.

        1)  **Under GAAP**, all manufacturing costs (direct materials, direct labor, variable overhead, and fixed overhead), must be treated as product costs, i.e., not recognized as expenses until the inventory is sold. At the same time, no portion of selling and administrative costs may be treated as product costs.

        2)  For **internal reporting**, a manufacturer has other options. For example, a manufacturer may choose to treat the fixed portion of manufacturing overhead as a period cost (see subunit 2.7).

3.   **Direct vs. Indirect**

    a.   Costs can be classified by how they are assigned to cost objects.

        1)  A **direct cost** is one that can be associated with a particular cost object in an economically feasible way, i.e., **traced** to that object.

        2)  An **indirect cost** is one that cannot be associated with a cost object in an economically feasible way and thus must be **allocated** to that cost object.

           a)  For example, depreciation on the headquarters building is a direct cost when treating the building as a whole, but it is an indirect cost of each department located in the building.

           b)  To simplify the allocation process, cost pools are established to collect costs prior to allocation. Manufacturing overhead is an example of an indirect cost pool.

4.    **Fixed vs. Variable**

    a.    Costs are also classified by their behavior.

        1)    **Fixed costs in total** remain unchanged in the short run regardless of production level, e.g., the amount paid for an assembly line is the same even if production is halted entirely.

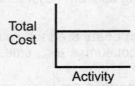

            a)    **Fixed cost per unit**, however, varies indirectly with the activity level.

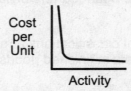

        2)    **Variable costs in total** vary directly and proportionally with changes in volume, e.g., direct materials.

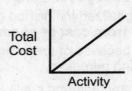

            a)    **Variable cost per unit**, however, remains constant in the short run regardless of changes in activity.

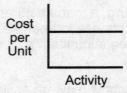

        3)    **Mixed (semivariable) costs** combine fixed and variable elements, e.g., rental on a car that carries a flat fee per month plus an additional fee for each mile driven.

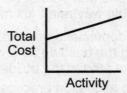

    b.    Four of the above costs are **linear-cost functions**, i.e., they change at a constant rate (or remain unchanged) over the short run.

        1)    Fixed cost per unit, however, is an example of a **nonlinear-cost function**.

            a)    Fixed cost per unit has an asymptotic character, approaching both axes closely while never intersecting them, and shows a high degree of variability over its range taken as a whole.

   2)   Another type of nonlinear-cost function is a **step-cost function**, one that is constant over small ranges of output but increases by steps (discrete amounts) as levels of activity increase.

   a)   Both fixed and variable costs can display step-cost characteristics.

   b)   If the steps are relatively narrow, these costs are usually treated as variable.  If the steps are wide, they are more akin to fixed costs.

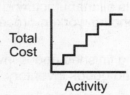

   c.   The cost behaviors described in this item all pertain to the **relevant range**, which encompasses the range of activity (production volume) within which variable costs per unit and fixed costs in total are both constant.

   1)   Within the relevant range, the **marginal/incremental cost** of one additional unit of production **is the same**.

   2)   Management accountants capture the concept of relevant range when they say that "All costs are variable in the long run."

   d.   See also subunit 2.5.

5.   Stop and review!  You have completed the outline for this subunit.  Study multiple-choice questions 1 through 17 beginning on page 98.

## 2.2 TYPES OF COSTS

**Avoidable costs** are those that may be eliminated by not engaging in an activity or by performing it more efficiently.  Contrast with committed costs.

**Carrying cost** is the cost of storing or holding inventory.  Examples include the cost of capital, insurance, warehousing, breakage, and obsolescence.

**Committed costs** arise from holding property, plant, and equipment.  Examples are insurance, real estate taxes, lease payments, and depreciation.  They are by nature long-term and cannot be reduced by lowering the short-term level of production.  Contrast with avoidable costs.

**Common cost** is the shared operating cost of a cost object (plant, facility, activity, etc.) used by two or more entities.

**Controllable costs** are directly regulated by management at a given level of production within a given time span.  Contrast with fixed costs, which are not controllable in the short run.

**Conversion costs** are the costs of converting raw materials into finished goods, i.e., direct labor and factory overhead.

A **cost** is defined by the IMA as follows:  "(1) In management accounting, a measurement in monetary terms of the amount of resources used for some purpose.  The term by itself is not operational.  It becomes operational when modified by a term that defines the purpose, such as acquisition cost, incremental cost, or fixed cost.  (2) In financial accounting, the sacrifice measured by the price paid or required to be paid to acquire goods or services.  The term 'cost' is often used when referring to the valuation of a good or service acquired.  When 'cost' is used in this sense, a cost is an asset.  When the benefits of the acquisition (the goods or services) expire, the cost becomes an expense or loss."

**Cost behavior** is the relationship between costs and activities.  It is the amount of change in a cost related to the activity level.  See item 4. under subunit 2.1.

A **cost driver** is defined by the IMA as "a measure of activity, such as direct labor hours, machine hours, beds occupied, computer time used, flight hours, miles driven, or contracts, that is a causal factor in the incurrence of cost to an entity." It is a basis used to assign costs to cost objects.

A **cost object** is anything (e.g., a department, a product, a process) to which costs can be attached.

**Cost of goods manufactured** equals all manufacturing costs incurred during the period, plus beginning work-in-process, minus ending work-in-process. It is equivalent to a retailer's purchases.

**Cost of goods sold** equals beginning finished goods inventory, plus cost of goods manufactured (or purchases), minus ending finished goods inventory.

**Cost pools** are accounts in which a variety of similar cost elements with a common cause are accumulated prior to allocation to cost objects on some common basis. The overhead account is a cost pool into which various types of overhead are accumulated prior to their allocation. In activity-based accounting, a cost pool is established for each activity.

**Differential (incremental) cost** is the difference in total cost between two decisions.

**Direct costs**. See items 1.a.1) and 2) under subunit 2.1.

**Direct labor costs**. See item 1.a.2) under subunit 2.1.

**Direct materials costs**. See item 1.a.1) under subunit 2.1.

**Discretionary costs** are characterized by uncertainty about the relationship between input (the costs) and the value of the related output. They also tend to be the subject of a periodic (e.g., annual) outlay decision. Advertising and research costs are examples.

**Engineered costs** are costs having a clear relationship to output. Direct materials cost is an example.

**Executional cost drivers** capture a firm's operational decisions on how best to employ its resources to achieve its objectives. Executional drivers are determined by management policy, style, and culture. Examples are workforce involvement, existence of a quality assurance program, capacity utilization, relations with suppliers, etc. Together with structural cost drivers, executional cost drivers are an integral part of activity-based costing.

**Fixed costs**. See item 4.a.1) under subunit 2.1.

**Full product cost** is the long-term total cost of making and selling a product. It includes the costs of all business functions.

**Gross margin (gross profit)** is the difference between sales and the absorption cost of goods sold. It should be contrasted with contribution margin (sales − variable costs) and profit margin (income ÷ revenue).

**Imputed costs** are properly attributable to a cost object even though no transaction has occurred that would be routinely recognized in the accounts. They may be outlay costs or opportunity costs, but in either case they should be considered in decision making. An example of an imputed cost is the profit lost as a result of being unable to fill orders because the inventory level is too low.

**Incremental (differential) cost** is the difference in total cost between two decisions.

**Indirect costs**. See item 1.a.3)a) under subunit 2.1.

**Joint costs** are incurred in the production of two or more products by a common process from a common input up to the point at which the products become separable (the split-off point). Hence, they are irrelevant to the timing of sales. Contrast with separable costs.

**Linear-cost functions**. See item 4.b. under subunit 2.1.

**Marginal cost** is the sum of the costs necessary to effect a one-unit increase in the activity level.

**Mixed (semivariable) costs**.  See item 4.a.3) under subunit 2.1.

**Opportunity cost** is the maximum benefit forgone by using a scarce resource for a given purpose and not for the next-best alternative.

**Out-of-pocket (outlay) costs** require cash outflows (expenditures) currently or in the future.

**Period costs**.  See item 2.a.2) under subunit 2.1.

**Prime costs**.  See item 1.b.1) under subunit 2.1.

**Product (inventoriable) costs**.  See item 2.a.1) under subunit 2.1.

**Quality costs** are costs of conformance (prevention and appraisal) and nonconformance (internal failure and external failure) with quality standards.

**Relevant costs** are those expected future costs that vary with the action taken.  All other costs are assumed to be constant and thus have no effect on (are irrelevant to) the decision.  Contrast with sunk costs.

**Relevant range**.  See item 4.c under subunit 2.1.

**Resource drivers** are the cost drivers that reflect use of resources by an activity.

**Separable costs** are those incurred for a joint product beyond the split-off point.  Thus, they are identifiable with specific products and are relevant to the decision when to sell.  Contrast with joint costs.

**Standard costs** are predetermined, attainable unit costs.  Standard cost systems isolate deviations (variances) of actual from expected costs.  Standard costs can be used with both job-order and process-costing systems.

**Step-cost functions**.  See item 4.b.2) under subunit 2.1.

**Structural cost drivers** are organizational factors that determine the economic structure driving the cost of a firm's products.  They reflect a firm's long-term decisions, which position the firm in its industry and marketplace.  They are:  the firm's scale of operations; the experience level of the firm; the level of technology used within the firm; and the complexity of the firm's operations.  Together with executional cost drivers, structural cost drivers are an integral part of activity-based costing.

**Sunk costs** are past costs or costs that the entity has irrevocably committed to incur.  Because they are unavoidable and will therefore not vary with the option chosen, they are not relevant to future decisions.  Contrast with relevant costs.

**Transferred-in costs** are those incurred in a preceding department and received in a subsequent department in a multi-departmental production setting.

**Value-adding costs** are the costs of activities that cannot be eliminated without reducing the quality, responsiveness, or quantity of the output required by a customer or the organization.

**Variable cost**.  See item 4.a.2) under subunit 2.1.

1.  Stop and review!  You have completed the outline for this subunit.  Study multiple-choice questions 18 through 28 beginning on page 102.

## 2.3 COSTING TECHNIQUES

**Absorption costing** (sometimes called full or full absorption costing) treats all manufacturing costs as product costs.  These costs include variable and fixed manufacturing costs whether direct or indirect.  Thus, fixed manufacturing overhead is inventoried.  Contrast with variable (direct) costing.

**Activity-based costing** is defined by the IMA as "identifies the causal relationship between the incurrence of cost and activities, determines the underlying driver of the activities, establishes cost pools related to individual drivers, develops costing rates, and applies cost to product on the basis of resources consumed (drivers)."  ABC makes extensive use of cost drivers.

**Activity drivers** are cost drivers that measure the demands on activities by next-stage cost objects.

**Actual costing** charges all product costs (direct materials, direct labor, and manufacturing overhead) based on actual rates.  Contrast with normal costing and extended normal costing.

**Backflush costing** is often used with a just-in-time (JIT) inventory system when manufacturing cells are used.  It delays costing until goods are finished.  Standard costs are then flushed backward through the system to assign costs to products.  The result is that detailed tracking of costs is eliminated.  The system is best suited to companies that maintain low inventories because costs then flow directly to cost of goods sold.

The **constant gross-margin percentage NRV method** for allocating joint costs is based on using the same gross margin percentage for all of the products.

**Cost accounting** includes (1) managerial accounting in the sense that its purpose can be to provide internal reports for use in planning and control and in making nonroutine decisions, and (2) financial accounting because its product costing function satisfies requirements for reporting externally to shareholders, government, and various outside parties.  A cost accounting system has numerous objectives, including product costing, assessing department efficiency, inventory valuation, income determination, and planning, evaluating, and controlling operations.

**Cost allocation** is performed when associating a cost with a specific cost object (i.e., cost tracing) is not economically feasible.  Because the cost is not directly traceable to the cost object, a systematic and rational basis for allocation must be used.

**Direct costing**.  *See variable costing.*

The **direct method** for allocating service department cost apportions service department costs directly to production departments.  It makes no allocation of costs of the services rendered to other service departments and is thus less accurate than the step-down and reciprocal methods.

The **estimated net realizable value method** for allocating joint costs is a variation of the relative sales value method.  The significant difference is that under the estimated NRV method all separable costs necessary to make the product salable are added in before the allocation is made.

**Extended normal costing** charges all product costs (direct materials, direct labor, and manufacturing overhead) based on normalized (budgeted) rates.  Contrast with actual costing and normal costing.

**Full costing**. *See absorption costing.*

The **high-low method** of estimating a cost function uses only the highest and lowest observed values of the cost driver within the relevant range.  Contrast with the regression (scattergraph) method.

**Job-order costing** is appropriate when producing products with individual characteristics or when identifiable groupings are possible, e.g., batches of certain styles or types of furniture.  The unique aspect of job-order costing is the identification of costs to specific units or a particular job.  Contrast with process costing.

**Life-cycle costing** estimates a product's revenues and expenses over its expected life cycle.  The result is to highlight upstream and downstream costs in the cost planning process that often receive insufficient attention.  Emphasis is on the need to price products to cover all costs, not just production costs.

**Normal costing** charges product costs based on actual direct labor and materials but applies overhead on the basis of budgeted (normalized) rates.  Contrast with actual costing and extended normal costing.

**Operation costing** is a hybrid of job-order and process costing systems. It is used by companies that manufacture goods that undergo some similar and some dissimilar processes. Operation costing accumulates total conversion costs and determines a unit conversion cost for each operation. However, direct materials costs are charged specifically to products as in job-order systems.

The **physical unit method** for allocating joint costs employs a physical measure such as volume, weight, or a linear measure.

**Process costing** is used to assign costs to similar products that are mass produced on a continuous basis. Process costing is an averaging process that calculates the average cost of all units. Contrast with job-order costing.

The **reciprocal method** for allocating service department cost uses simultaneous equations to allocate each service department's costs among the departments providing mutual services before reallocation to other users and is thus more accurate than the direct and step-down methods.

The **regression (scattergraph) method** of estimating a cost function is quite complex and determines the average rate of variability of a mixed cost. Contrast with the high-low method.

The **sales-value at split-off method** for allocating joint costs is based upon each of the joint products' relative proportion of total sales value ultimately attributable to the period's production.

**Standard costing** is a system designed to alert management when the actual costs of production different significantly from target costs. A standard cost involves objectively determining what cost should be, not simply estimating it based on experience.

The **step-down method** for allocating service department cost allocation is a sequential, not a reciprocal, process. These costs are allocated to other service departments as well as to users. The starting point may be the service department that rendered the greatest percentage of its services to other service departments or that incurred the greatest dollar amount of services to other service departments. It is more accurate than the direct method but less accurate than the reciprocal method.

**Target costing** is the practice of calculating the price for a product by adding the desired unit profit margin to the total unit cost. It is an adjunct concept of target pricing.

**Variable costing** (also called direct costing) considers only variable manufacturing costs to be product costs, i.e., inventoriable. Fixed manufacturing costs are considered period costs and are expensed as incurred. Direct costing is not a satisfactory description because it implies traceability. Contrast with absorption (full) costing.

1.  Stop and review! You have completed the outline for this subunit. Study multiple-choice questions 29 through 38 beginning on page 106.

## 2.4 MANUFACTURING TERMINOLOGY

**Abnormal spoilage** is spoilage that is not expected to occur under normal, efficient operating conditions. The cost of abnormal spoilage should be separately identified and reported to management. Abnormal spoilage is typically treated as a period cost (a loss) because of its unusual nature.

**By-products** are products of relatively small total value that are produced simultaneously from a common manufacturing process with products of greater value and quantity (joint products).

**Joint products** are two or more separate products produced by a common manufacturing process from a common input. The joint costs of two or more joint products with significant values may be allocated to the joint products based upon their sales value, net realizable value, or a physical measure at the point they become separate.

In **just-in-time (JIT)** manufacturing systems, each operation produces only what is required by the next operation, and components and materials arrive just in time to be used. Thus, JIT purchasing and inventory control systems arrange for supplier deliveries just in time for use. JIT systems are demand-pull systems.

**Kaizen** is a Japanese word that refers to continuous improvement. Kaizen often entails making improvements through the accumulation of small betterment activities rather than major innovations. Thus, a Kaizen budget assumes the continuous improvement of products and processes.

A **manufacturing cell** is a group of all of the machines and workers needed to produce a certain product.

**Normal capacity** is the long-term average level of activity that will approximate demand over a period that includes seasonal, cyclical, and trend variations. Deviations in a given year will be offset in subsequent years.

**Normal spoilage** is the spoilage that occurs under normal operating conditions. It is essentially uncontrollable in the short run. Normal spoilage arises under efficient operations and is treated as a product cost.

**Practical capacity** is the maximum level at which output is produced efficiently. It allows for unavoidable delays in production for maintenance, holidays, etc. Use of practical capacity as a denominator value usually results in underapplied overhead because it always exceeds the actual level of use.

**Rework** consists of units that do not meet standards of salability but can be brought to salable condition with additional effort. The decision to rework or discard is based on whether the marginal revenue to be gained from selling the reworked units exceeds the marginal cost of performing the rework.

**Scrap** consists of raw materials left over from the production cycle but still usable for purposes other than those for which it was originally intended. Scrap may be sold to outside customers, usually for a nominal amount, or may be used for a different production process.

**Split-off point** is the stage of production at which joint products and by-products are separable.

**Theoretical (ideal) capacity** is the maximum capacity assuming continuous operations with no holidays, downtime, etc.

**Waste** is the amount of raw materials left over from a production process or production cycle for which there is no further use. Waste is usually not salable at any price and must be discarded.

1.    Stop and review! You have completed the outline for this subunit. Study multiple-choice questions 39 through 44 beginning on page 109.

## 2.5 COST BEHAVIOR, COST OBJECTS, AND COST DRIVERS

1.    Costs can be classified by their **behavior**, i.e., how they are affected by changes in production volume.

   a.    The **relevant range** defines the limits within which the cost and revenue relationships remain linear and fixed costs are not changeable. The relevant range is established by the efficiency of a company's current manufacturing plant, its agreements with labor unions and suppliers, etc.

   b.    **Variable costs in total** vary directly and proportionally with changes in volume. However, **variable costs per unit** remain constant over the relevant range.

1) EXAMPLE: A company requires a unit of direct material to be used in each finished good it produces. Within the relevant range, each unit costs the same, but the total spent on them increases as production increases.

| Number of Units Produced | Cost per Unit | Total Cost of Units |
|---|---|---|
| 0 | $10 | $0 |
| 100 | $10 | $1,000 |
| 1,000 | $10 | $10,000 |
| 5,000 | $10 | $50,000 |
| 10,000 | $10 | $100,000 |

c. **Fixed costs in total** remain unchanged over the short run regardless of production level. However, **fixed costs per unit** vary indirectly with the activity level.

1) EXAMPLE: The historical cost of the assembly line is settled, but its cost per unit decreases as production increases.

| Number of Units Produced | Cost of Assembly Line | Per Unit Cost of Assembly Line |
|---|---|---|
| 0 | $1,000,000 | $1,000,000 |
| 100 | $1,000,000 | $10,000 |
| 1,000 | $1,000,000 | $1,000 |
| 5,000 | $1,000,000 | $200 |
| 10,000 | $1,000,000 | $100 |

d. **Mixed (semivariable) costs** vary over the relevant range. The fixed portion remains constant, and the variable portion changes directly and proportionally with the level of production.

1) EXAMPLE: The company rents a piece of machinery to make its production line more efficient. The rental is $150,000 per year plus $1 for every unit produced.

| Number of Units Produced | Fixed Cost of Extra Machine | Variable Cost of Extra Machine | Total Cost of Extra Machine |
|---|---|---|---|
| 0 | $150,000 | $0 | $150,000 |
| 100 | $150,000 | $100 | $150,100 |
| 1,000 | $150,000 | $1,000 | $151,000 |
| 5,000 | $150,000 | $5,000 | $155,000 |
| 10,000 | $150,000 | $10,000 | $160,000 |

2) Sometimes the fixed and variable portions of a mixed cost are not set by contract as in the above example and thus must be estimated.

3) Two methods of estimating the behavior of mixed costs are in general use:

a) The **high-low method** is the less accurate but quicker of the two methods.

   i) The difference in cost between the highest and lowest levels of activity is divided by the difference in the activity level to arrive at the variable portion of the cost.

   ii) EXAMPLE: A company has the following data:

| Month | Machine Hours | Maintenance Costs |
|---|---|---|
| April | 1,000 | $2,275 |
| May | 1,600 | $3,400 |
| June | 1,200 | $2,650 |
| July | 800 | $1,900 |
| August | 1,200 | $2,650 |
| September | 1,000 | $2,275 |

        iii)   The numerator can be derived by subtracting the cost at the lowest level (July) from the cost at the highest level (May) [$3,400 − $1,900 = $1,500].

        iv)   The denominator can be derived by subtracting the lowest level of activity (July) from the highest level (May) [1,600 − 800 = 800].

        v)   The variable portion of the cost is therefore $1.875 per machine hour ($1,500 ÷ 800).

        vi)   The fixed portion can be calculated by inserting the appropriate values for either the high or low month in the range:

$$\text{Fixed portion} = \text{Total cost} - \text{Variable portion}$$
$$= \$1,900 - (800 \text{ hours} \times \$1.875)$$
$$= \$1,900 - \$1,500$$
$$= \$400$$

    b)   The **regression (scattergraph) method** is considerably more complex and determines the average rate of variability of a mixed cost rather than the variability between the high and low points in the range.

  e.   All costs are changeable in the **long run**. Investment in new, more productive equipment results in higher total fixed costs, but may result in lower total and per unit variable costs.

2.   A **cost object** is anything for which an organization wishes to perform cost tracking.

  a.   Examples include:

    1)   A **product**, such as a carbonated beverage.
    2)   A **service**, such as an audit engagement.
    3)   A **project**, such as the design of a new airliner.

  b.   **Intermediate cost objects** receive temporary accumulations of costs as the cost pools move from their originating points to the final cost objects. **Final cost objects**, such as a job, product, or process, should be logically linked with the cost pool based on a cause-and-effect relationship.

3.   A **cost driver** is any factor that attaches cost to production.

  a.   To be effective, a cost driver must have a **direct cause-and-effect** relationship with production. To extend the above examples:

| Output | Cost Drivers |
|---|---|
| Carbonated Beverage | - Gallons of syrup<br>- Tons of aluminum<br>- Worker hours |
| Audit engagement | - Staff hours<br>- Manager hours<br>- Partner hours<br>- IT staff hours |
| New airliner | - New CAD software<br>- Designer hours<br>- Modeler hours<br>- Modeling materials<br>- Wind tunnel hours |

  b.   See also items 5. and 6. under subunit 4.2.

4.   Stop and review! You have completed the outline for this subunit. Study multiple-choice questions 45 through 49 beginning on page 111.

## 2.6 ACTUAL/NORMAL/STANDARD COSTS

1. **Actual costing** is the most accurate method of accumulating costs. However, it is also the least timely and most volatile method.

   a. After the end of the production period, all actual costs incurred for a cost object are totaled; indirect costs are allocated.

   b. Because per unit costs depend on the level of production in a period, large fluctuations arise from period to period. This volatility can lead to the reporting of misleading financial information.

2. **Normal costing** charges actual direct materials and direct labor to a cost object, but applies overhead on the basis of budgeted (normalized) rates.

   a. This compensates for the fluctuations in unit cost inherent in actual costing (see item 3. under subunit 3.2).

3. **Standard costing** is a system designed to alert management when the actual costs of production differ significantly from target ("standard") costs. See item 3.b. under subunit 1.1.

4. Stop and review! You have completed the outline for this subunit. Study multiple-choice questions 50 through 55 beginning on page 112.

## 2.7 ABSORPTION (FULL) VS. VARIABLE (DIRECT) COSTING

1. Under **absorption costing** (sometimes called full or full absorption costing), the fixed portion of manufacturing overhead is "absorbed" into the cost of each product.

   a. **Product cost** thus includes **all manufacturing costs, both fixed and variable**.

   b. Absorption-basis cost of goods sold is subtracted from sales to arrive at gross margin.

   c. Total selling and administrative expenses (i.e., fixed and variable) are then subtracted from gross margin to arrive at operating income.

   d. This method is **required under GAAP** for external reporting purposes **and under the Internal Revenue Code** for tax purposes. The justification is that, for external reporting, product cost should include all manufacturing costs.

2. **Variable costing** (sometimes called direct costing) is more appropriate for internal reporting.

   a. The term "direct costing" is somewhat misleading because it suggests traceability, which is not what is meant in this context. "Variable costing" is more suitable.

   b. **Product cost** includes **only variable manufacturing costs**.

   c. Variable cost of goods sold and the variable portion of selling and administrative expenses are subtracted from gross margin to arrive at **contribution margin**.

      1) This figure (sales – total variable costs) is an important element of the variable costing income statement because it is the amount available for **covering fixed costs** (fixed manufacturing and fixed selling and administrative).

      2) For this reason, some accountants call the method **contribution margin reporting**.

      3) This is an important metric internally but is generally irrelevant to outside financial statement users.

3.    EXAMPLE:  A firm, during its first month in business, produced 100 units and sold 80 while incurring the following costs:

| | |
|---|---:|
| Direct materials | $1,000 |
| Direct labor | 2,000 |
| Variable overhead | 1,500 |
| Manufacturing costs used in variable costing | $4,500 |
| Fixed overhead | 3,000 |
| Manufacturing costs used in absorption costing | $7,500 |

a.    The impact on the financial statements from using one method over the other can be seen in these calculations:

Cost per unit:
Absorption ($7,500 ÷ 100 units)          $75
Variable ($4,500 ÷ 100 units)            45

Ending inventory:
Absorption ($75 × 20 units)          $1,500
Variable ($45 × 20 units)            900

b.    Assume also that the 80 units were sold at a price of $100 each, and the company incurred $200 of variable selling and administrative expenses and $600 of fixed selling and administrative expenses.  The following are the income statements prepared using the two methods:

| Absorption Costing (Required under GAAP) | | | Variable Costing (For Internal Reporting Only) | | |
|---|---:|---:|---|---:|---:|
| **Sales** | | **$8,000** | **Sales** | | **$8,000** |
| Beginning inventory | $     0 | | Beginning inventory | $     0 | |
| Mfg. costs -- variable and fixed | 7,500 | | Variable manufacturing costs | 4,500 | |
| Goods available for sale | $7,500 | | Goods available for sale | $4,500 | |
| Less:  ending inventory | (1,500) | | Less:  ending inventory | (900) | |
| **Absorption cost of goods sold** | | **(6,000)** | **Variable cost of goods sold** | | **(3,600)** |
| | | | Variable S&A expenses | | (200) |
| **Gross margin** | | **$2,000** | **Contribution margin** | | **$4,200** |
| | | | Fixed overhead | | (3,000) |
| S&A exp. -- variable and fixed | | (800) | Fixed S&A expenses | | (600) |
| **Operating income** | | **$1,200** | **Operating income** | | **$   600** |

c.    The $600 difference in operating income ($1,200 – $600) is the difference between the two ending inventory values ($1,500 – $900).

1)    In essence, the absorption method treats 20% of the fixed overhead costs ($3,000 × 20% = $600) as an asset because 20% of the month's production (100 available – 80 sold = 20 on hand) is still in inventory.

4.    As production and sales levels change, the two methods have varying impacts on **operating income**.

a.    When **production and sales are equal** for a period, the two methods report the **same** operating income.

1)    Total fixed costs budgeted for the period are charged to sales revenue in the period under both methods.

b.   When **production and sales are not equal** for a period, the two methods report **different** operating income.

1)   ILLUSTRATION:

| **When production** | **When production** |
|---|---|
| △ △ △ △ △ △ △ △ | △ △ △ |
| **exceeds sales,** | **is less than sales,** |
| △ △ △ | △ △ △ △ △ △ △ △ |
| **ending inventory expands.** | **ending inventory contracts.** |
| ↑↑↑↑↑↑↑↑↑↑↑↑↑↑↑ | ↓↓↓↓↓↓ |
| **Under absorption costing,** some fixed costs are still embedded in ending inventory. | **Under absorption costing,** fixed costs embedded in beginning inventory have been expensed. |
| **Under variable costing,** all fixed costs have been expensed. | **Under variable costing,** only the current period's fixed costs are expensed. |
| Therefore, | Therefore, |
| **operating income is higher under <u>absorption</u> costing.** | **operating income is higher under <u>variable</u> costing.** |

c.   Under **absorption** costing, operating income **behaves erratically** and sometimes moves in the opposite direction from sales.

1)   Under **variable** costing, operating income always moves in the **same direction as sales volume**.

2)   Operating income differences tend to be larger when calculations are made for short periods. In the long run, the two methods will report the same total operating income if sales equal production.

a)   The inequalities between production and sales are usually minor over an extended period.

b)   Production cannot continually exceed sales because an enterprise cannot produce more than it can sell in the long run.

3)   EXTENDED EXAMPLE: A company has the following sales and cost data:

|  | Year 1 | Year 2 | Year 3 |
|---|---|---|---|
| Production in units | 40,000 | 50,000 | 0 |
| Sales in units | 30,000 | 30,000 | 30,000 |
| Ending inventory in units (FIFO) | 10,000 | 30,000 | 0 |
| Unit sales price | $1.00 | | |
| Unit variable cost | $0.50 | | |
| Fixed manufacturing costs | $4,000 | per year | |
| Variable S&A expenses | $0.03333 | per unit | |
| Fixed S&A expenses | $1,000 | per year | |

Compare the three-year income statements prepared under the two methods:

| Absorption Costing (Required under GAAP) | | | | Variable Costing (For Internal Reporting Only) | | | |
|---|---|---|---|---|---|---|---|
| | Year 1 | Year 2 | Year 3 | | Year 1 | Year 2 | Year 3 |
| Sales | $30,000 | $30,000 | $30,000 | Sales | $30,000 | $30,000 | $30,000 |
| Beginning inventory | $    0 | $ 6,000 | $17,400 | Beginning inventory | $    0 | $ 5,000 | $15,000 |
| Mfg. costs -- var. and fixed | 24,000 | 29,000 | 4,000 | Variable mfg. costs | 20,000 | 25,000 | 0 |
| Goods available for sale | $24,000 | $35,000 | $21,400 | Goods avail. for sale | $20,000 | $30,000 | $15,000 |
| Less: ending inventory | (6,000) | (17,400) | 0 | Less: ending inventory | (5,000) | (15,000) | 0 |
| Absorption CGS | $18,000 | $17,600 | $21,400 | Variable CGS | $15,000 | $15,000 | $15,000 |
| | | | | Variable S&A exps. | (1,000) | (1,000) | (1,000) |
| Gross margin | $12,000 | $12,000 | $ 8,600 | Contribution margin | $14,000 | $14,000 | $14,000 |
| | | | | Fixed mfg. costs | (4,000) | (4,000) | (4,000) |
| S&A exps. -- var. and fixed | (2,000) | (2,000) | (2,000) | Fixed S&A expenses | (1,000) | (1,000) | (1,000) |
| Operating income | $10,000 | $10,400 | $ 6,600 | Operating income | $ 9,000 | $ 9,000 | $ 9,000 |

a)   Note that, assuming zero inventory at the beginning of year 1 and at the end of year 3, the total operating income for the 3-year period is the same under either costing method.

b)   Absorption costing shows a higher operating income than variable costing in years 1 and 2 because fixed overhead has been capitalized and does not get expensed until year 3.

   i)   Variable costing, on the other hand, treats fixed overhead as an expense of the period in which the cost is incurred.

   ii)   In year 2, despite the same cash flow, there is a $1,400 difference between the final operating income figures and an even greater difference in year 3.

c)   If fixed costs increase relative to variable costs, the differences become more dramatic (here, 50% of the selling price is variable manufacturing cost, and fixed overhead is no more than 20% of the variable manufacturing cost).

5.   Stop and review! You have completed the outline for this subunit. Study multiple-choice questions 56 through 77 beginning on page 114.

## 2.8 JOINT PRODUCT AND BY-PRODUCT COSTING

1.   When two or more separate products are produced by a common manufacturing process from a common input, the outputs from the process are **joint products**.

   a.   **Joint (common) costs** are those costs incurred up to the point where the products become separately identifiable, called the split-off point.

      1)   Joint costs include direct materials, direct labor, and manufacturing overhead. Because they are not separately identifiable, they must be allocated to the individual joint products.

      2)   EXAMPLE: Crude oil can be refined into multiple salable products. All costs incurred in getting the crude oil to the distilling tower are joint costs.

   b.   At the **split-off point**, the joint products acquire separate identities. Costs incurred after split-off are separable costs.

      1)   **Separable costs** can be identified with a particular joint product and allocated to a specific unit of output.

   2) EXAMPLE: Once crude oil has been distilled into asphalt, fuel oil, diesel fuel, kerosene, and gasoline, costs incurred in further refining and distributing these individual products are separable costs.

2. Several methods are available to **allocate joint costs**. These can be grouped into two approaches.

  a. A **physical measure-based approach** employs a physical measure such as volume, weight, or a linear measure.

   1) The **physical-unit method** allocates joint production costs to each product based on their relative proportions of the measure selected.

   2) EXAMPLE: A refinery processes 1,000 barrels of crude oil and incurs $100,000 of processing costs. The process results in the following outputs. Under the physical-unit method, the joint costs up to split-off are allocated as follows:

| | | |
|---|---|---|
| Asphalt | $100,000 × (300 barrels ÷ 1,000 barrels) = | $ 30,000 |
| Fuel oil | $100,000 × (300 barrels ÷ 1,000 barrels) = | $ 30,000 |
| Diesel fuel | $100,000 × (200 barrels ÷ 1,000 barrels) = | $ 20,000 |
| Kerosene | $100,000 × (100 barrels ÷ 1,000 barrels) = | $ 10,000 |
| Gasoline | $100,000 × (100 barrels ÷ 1,000 barrels) = | $ 10,000 |
| | | $100,000 |

   3) The physical-unit method's simplicity makes it appealing, but it does not match costs with the individual products' revenue-generating potential.

  b. A **market-based approach** assigns a proportionate amount of the total cost to each product on a quantitative basis.

   1) These allocations are performed using the entire production run for an accounting period, not units sold. This is because the joint costs were incurred on all the units produced, not just those sold.

   2) Three major methods of allocation are available under this approach.

   3) The **sales-value at split-off method** is based on the relative sales values of the separate products at split-off.

    a) EXAMPLE: The refinery estimates that the five outputs can sell for the following prices at split-off:

| | | |
|---|---|---|
| Asphalt | 300 barrels @ $ 60/barrel = | $ 18,000 |
| Fuel oil | 300 barrels @ $180/barrel = | $ 54,000 |
| Diesel fuel | 200 barrels @ $160/barrel = | $ 32,000 |
| Kerosene | 200 barrels @ $ 80/barrel = | $ 8,000 |
| Gasoline | 100 barrels @ $180/barrel = | $ 18,000 |
| | | $130,000 |

    The total expected sales value for the entire production run at split-off is thus $130,000. Multiply the total joint costs to be allocated by the proportion of the total expected sales of each product:

| | | |
|---|---|---|
| Asphalt | $100,000 × ($18,000 ÷ $130,000) = | $ 13,846 |
| Fuel oil | $100,000 × ($54,000 ÷ $130,000) = | $ 41,538 |
| Diesel fuel | $100,000 × ($32,000 ÷ $130,000) = | $ 24,616 |
| Kerosene | $100,000 × ($ 8,000 ÷ $130,000) = | $ 6,154 |
| Gasoline | $100,000 × ($18,000 ÷ $130,000) = | $ 13,846 |
| | | $100,000 |

4) The **estimated net realizable value (NRV)** method also allocates joint costs based on the relative market values of the products.

    a) The significant difference is that, under the estimated NRV method, all separable costs necessary to make the product salable are added in before the allocation is made.

    b) EXAMPLE: The refinery estimates final sales prices as follows:

| | | |
|---|---|---|
| Asphalt | 300 barrels @ $ 70/barrel = | $ 21,000 |
| Fuel oil | 300 barrels @ $200/barrel = | $ 60,000 |
| Diesel fuel | 200 barrels @ $180/barrel = | $ 36,000 |
| Kerosene | 100 barrels @ $ 90/barrel = | $ 9,000 |
| Gasoline | 100 barrels @ $190/barrel = | $ 19,000 |
| | | $145,000 |

From these amounts, separable costs are deducted:

| | | |
|---|---|---|
| Asphalt | $21,000 – $1,000 = | $ 20,000 |
| Fuel oil | $60,000 – $1,000 = | $ 59,000 |
| Diesel fuel | $36,000 – $1,000 = | $ 35,000 |
| Kerosene | $ 9,000 – $2,000 = | $ 7,000 |
| Gasoline | $19,000 – $2,000 = | $ 17,000 |
| | | $138,000 |

The total final sales value for the entire production run is thus $138,000. Multiply the total joint costs to be allocated by the proportion of the final expected sales of each product:

| | | |
|---|---|---|
| Asphalt | $100,000 × ($20,000 ÷ $138,000) = | $ 14,493 |
| Fuel oil | $100,000 × ($59,000 ÷ $138,000) = | $ 42,754 |
| Diesel fuel | $100,000 × ($35,000 ÷ $138,000) = | $ 25,362 |
| Kerosene | $100,000 × ($ 7,000 ÷ $138,000) = | $ 5,072 |
| Gasoline | $100,000 × ($17,000 ÷ $138,000) = | $ 12,319 |
| | | $100,000 |

5) The **constant gross-margin percentage NRV** method is based on allocating joint costs so that the gross-margin percentage is the same for every product.

    a) There are three steps under this method:

        i) Determine the overall gross-margin percentage.

        ii) Subtract the appropriate gross margin from the final sales value of each product to calculate total costs for that product.

        iii) Subtract the separable costs to arrive at the joint cost amount.

    b) EXAMPLE: The refinery uses the same calculation of expected final sales price as under the estimated NRV method:

| | | |
|---|---|---|
| Asphalt | 300 barrels @ $ 70/barrel = | $ 21,000 |
| Fuel oil | 300 barrels @ $200/barrel = | $ 60,000 |
| Diesel fuel | 200 barrels @ $180/barrel = | $ 36,000 |
| Kerosene | 100 barrels @ $ 90/barrel = | $ 9,000 |
| Gasoline | 100 barrels @ $190/barrel = | $ 19,000 |
| | | $145,000 |

The final sales value for the entire production run is thus $145,000. From this total the joint costs and total separable costs are deducted to arrive at a total gross margin for all products:

$145,000 – $100,000 – $7,000 = $38,000

The gross margin percentage can then be derived:

$38,000 ÷ $145,000 = 26.21%

Deduct the gross margin from each product to arrive at a cost of goods sold:

| | | |
|---|---|---|
| Asphalt | $21,000 – ($21,000 × 26.21%) = | $ 15,497 |
| Fuel oil | $60,000 – ($60,000 × 26.21%) = | $ 44,276 |
| Diesel fuel | $36,000 – ($36,000 × 26.21%) = | $ 26,565 |
| Kerosene | $ 9,000 – ($ 9,000 × 26.21%) = | $ 6,641 |
| Gasoline | $19,000 – ($19,000 × 26.21%) = | $ 14,021 |
| | | $107,000 |

Deduct the separable costs from each product to arrive at the allocated joint costs:

| | | |
|---|---|---|
| Asphalt | $15,497 – $1,000 = | $ 14,497 |
| Fuel oil | $44,276 – $1,000 = | $ 43,276 |
| Diesel fuel | $26,566 – $1,000 = | $ 25,565 |
| Kerosene | $ 6,641 – $2,000 = | $ 4,641 |
| Gasoline | $14,021 – $2,000 = | $ 12,021 |
| | | $100,000 |

3.  **By-products** are one or more products of relatively small total value that are produced simultaneously from a common manufacturing process with products of greater value and quantity.

    a.  EXAMPLE: Certain gases may be generated during petroleum refining. They are of much less value than the main outputs of the process and may simply be burned away as waste or processed further for possible sale (see item 4.).

    b.  If by-products are to be sold, the most cost-effective method for the initial recognition is to account for their value at the **time of sale** as a reduction in the cost of goods sold or as a revenue.

        1)  There is thus no cost of sales for by-products under this method.

    c.  The alternative is to recognize their value at the **time of production**, a method that results in the recording of by-product inventory.

        1)  Under this method, the value of the by-product may be treated as a reduction in cost of goods sold or as a separate revenue item.

        2)  The value to be reported for by-products may be sales revenue, sales revenue minus a normal profit, or estimated net realizable value.

    d.  Regardless of the timing of their recognition in the accounts, by-products usually do not receive an allocation of joint costs because the cost of this accounting treatment ordinarily exceeds the benefit.

        1)  However, allocating joint costs to by-products is acceptable despite their small relative values.

    e.  Although **scrap** is similar to a by-product, joint costs are almost never allocated to scrap.

4.  The decision to **sell or process further** is made on the basis of the incremental revenue to be gained by further processing exceeding the incremental cost thereof.

    a.  The joint cost of the product is irrelevant because it is a sunk (already expended) cost.

5.  Stop and review! You have completed the outline for this subunit. Study multiple-choice questions 78 through 93 beginning on page 122.

## 2.9 CORE CONCEPTS

### Broad Categories of Costs

- The most important distinction for a management accountant in the classification of costs is between **manufacturing** and **nonmanufacturing costs**.
- Different costing techniques report manufacturing and nonmanufacturing costs differently. Those included in cost of goods sold are called **product costs**, and those not included in cost of goods sold are referred to as **period costs**.
- Costs must be classified by their **behavior**, i.e., fixed vs. variable vs. mixed. **Fixed costs** in total remain constant over the short-run, but total **variable costs** fluctuate. In the long run, all costs are variable.
- The **relevant range** is roughly equivalent to the **short run**, i.e., it is the period during which variable costs per unit and fixed costs in total are both constant.

### Types of Costs

- Costs can be classified in **contrasting groups** , e.g., avoidable vs. committed, prime vs. conversion, relevant vs. sunk.
- A **cost object** is anything (e.g., a department, a product, or a process) to which costs can be attached.
- A **cost driver** is the basis used to assign costs to cost objects, e.g., direct materials used.

### Costing Techniques

- Costs can be **applied** to cost objects and **reported** in various ways.
- The two fundamental techniques for tracking manufacturing costs are **job-order costing** (for unique or distinctive products) and **process costing** (for mass quantities of homogeneous products).
- **Activity-based costing** makes extensive use of cost drivers to accurately attach costs to the most appropriate objects.
- **Actual costing** is the most accurate method, but it leads to large fluctuations in net income even when sales are relatively stable. **Normal** and **extended normal costing** are techniques for smoothing costs and net income.
- **Standard costing** sets expected costs as guideposts so that management can easily tell when prices of inputs, production levels, etc., are not within predicted ranges.

### Manufacturing Terminology

- **Spoilage**, those finished goods which do not meet quality standards, can be experienced at either a **normal** level or an **abnormal** level.
- **Joint products** are two or more separate products produced by a common manufacturing process from a common input. The point at which the products become distinguishable, and thus can have **separable costs** traced to them, is the **split-off point**. Up to that point, all costs incurred, being untraceable to a particular product, are considered **joint costs**.
- **Just-in-time** manufacturing systems attempt to reduce the costs of carrying inventory by keeping on hand only what is needed for immediate production.
- **Kaizen** is a Japanese word that refers to continuous improvement. Kaizen often entails making improvements through the accumulation of small betterment activities rather than major innovations.

## Cost Behavior, Cost Objects, and Cost Drivers

- **Variable costs in total** vary directly and proportionally with changes in volume. However, **variable costs per unit** remain constant over the relevant range.
- **Fixed costs in total** remain unchanged over the short run regardless of production level. However, **fixed costs per unit** vary indirectly with the activity level.
- **Mixed (semivariable) costs** vary over the relevant range. The fixed portion remains constant and the variable portion changes directly and proportionally with the level of production.
- A **cost object** is anything (e.g., a department, a product, or a process) to which costs can be attached.
- To be effective, a **cost driver** must have a direct cause-and-effect relationship with production.

## Actual/Normal/Standard Costs

- **Actual costing** is the most accurate method of accumulating costs. However, it is also the least timely and most volatile method.
- **Normal costing** charges actual direct materials and direct labor to a cost object but applies overhead on the basis of budgeted (normalized) rates.
- **Standard costing** is a system designed to alert management when the actual costs of production differ significantly from target ("standard") costs.

## Absorption (Full) vs. Variable (Direct) Costing

- **Full (absorption) costing** treats all manufacturing costs, fixed and variable alike, as product costs. A portion of the current period's manufacturing cost is thus deferred until the period when the product is sold. This treatment is required under GAAP.
- **Variable (direct) costing**, on the other hand, treats the fixed portion of manufacturing overhead as a period cost. Those costs are recognized every period, regardless of the level of sales. This treatment can only be used for internal reporting purposes.
- Due to **the effects of absorbing fixed overhead**, operating income is higher under absorption costing when production exceeds sales. When sales exceed production, operating income is higher under variable costing.

## Joint-Product and By-Product Costing

- Two families of approaches are used in applying joint costs, a **physical measure-based approach** and a **market-based approach**.
- A physical measure-based approach employs the **physical-unit method** to allocate joint costs, e.g., costs associated with raw lumber can be applied to 2 x 4s, 4 x 4s, etc. based on what percentage of the final goods produced each type represents.
- A market-based approach can employ **one of three methods**:
  - The **sales-value at split-off method** is based on the relative sales values of the separate products at split-off.
  - The **estimated net realizable value (NRV) method** also employs sales-value at split-off, but it includes all subsequent separable costs necessary to make the product salable.
  - The **constant gross-margin percentage NRV method** is based on allocating joint costs so that the gross-margin percentage is the same for every product.
- **By-products** are one or more products of relatively small total value that are produced simultaneously from a common manufacturing process with products of greater value and quantity.

## QUESTIONS

### 2.1 Broad Categories of Costs

**1.** The terms direct cost and indirect cost are commonly used in accounting. A particular cost might be considered a direct cost of a manufacturing department but an indirect cost of the product produced in the manufacturing department. Classifying a cost as either direct or indirect depends upon

    A. The behavior of the cost in response to volume changes.

    B. Whether the cost is expensed in the period in which it is incurred.

    C. The cost objective to which the cost is being related.

    D. Whether an expenditure is unavoidable because it cannot be changed regardless of any action taken.

Answer (C) is correct. *(CMA, adapted)*
    **REQUIRED:** The factor that influences whether a cost is classified as direct or indirect.
    **DISCUSSION:** A direct cost can be specifically associated with a single cost object in an economically feasible way. An indirect cost cannot be specifically associated with a single cost object. Thus, the specific cost object influences whether a cost is direct or indirect. For example, a cost might be directly associated with a single plant. The same cost, however, might not be directly associated with a particular department in the plant.
    Answer (A) is incorrect because behavior in response to volume changes is a factor only if the cost object is a product. Answer (B) is incorrect because the timing of an expense is not a means of classifying a cost as direct or indirect. Answer (D) is incorrect because both direct and indirect costs can be either avoidable or unavoidable, depending upon the cost object.

**2.** Which one of the following best describes direct labor?

    A. A prime cost.

    B. A period cost.

    C. A product cost.

    D. Both a product cost and a prime cost.

Answer (D) is correct. *(CMA, adapted)*
    **REQUIRED:** The best description of direct labor.
    **DISCUSSION:** Direct labor is both a product cost and a prime cost. Product costs are incurred to produce units of output and are deferred to future periods to the extent that output is not sold. Prime costs are defined as direct materials and direct labor.
    Answer (A) is incorrect because direct labor is also a product cost. Answer (B) is incorrect because a period cost is expensed when incurred. Direct labor cost is inventoriable. Answer (C) is incorrect because direct labor is also a prime cost.

**3.** Inventoriable costs

    A. Include only the prime costs of manufacturing a product.

    B. Include only the conversion costs of manufacturing a product.

    C. Are expensed when products become part of finished goods inventory.

    D. Are regarded as assets before the products are sold.

Answer (D) is correct. *(CMA, adapted)*
    **REQUIRED:** The true statement about inventoriable costs.
    **DISCUSSION:** Under an absorption costing system, inventoriable (product) costs include all costs necessary for good production. These include direct materials and conversion costs (direct labor and overhead). Both fixed and variable overhead is included in inventory under an absorption costing system. Inventoriable costs are treated as assets until the products are sold because they represent future economic benefits. These costs are expensed at the time of sale.
    Answer (A) is incorrect because overhead costs as well as prime costs (direct materials and labor) are included in inventory. Answer (B) is incorrect because materials costs are also included. Answer (C) is incorrect because inventory costs are expensed when the goods are sold, not when they are transferred to finished goods.

**4.** In cost terminology, conversion costs consist of

    A. Direct and indirect labor.

    B. Direct labor and direct materials.

    C. Direct labor and factory overhead.

    D. Indirect labor and variable factory overhead.

Answer (C) is correct. *(CMA, adapted)*
    **REQUIRED:** The components of conversion costs.
    **DISCUSSION:** Conversion costs consist of direct labor and factory overhead. These are the costs of converting raw materials into a finished product.
    Answer (A) is incorrect because all factory overhead is included in conversion costs, not just indirect labor. Answer (B) is incorrect because direct materials are not an element of conversion costs; they are a prime cost. Answer (D) is incorrect because direct labor is also an element of conversion costs.

**5.** An assembly plant accumulates its variable and fixed manufacturing overhead costs in a single cost pool, which is then applied to work in process using a single application base. The assembly plant management wants to estimate the magnitude of the total manufacturing overhead costs for different volume levels of the application activity base using a flexible budget formula. If there is an increase in the application activity base that is within the relevant range of activity for the assembly plant, which one of the following relationships regarding variable and fixed costs is true?

A. The variable cost per unit is constant, and the total fixed costs decrease.

B. The variable cost per unit is constant, and the total fixed costs increase.

C. The variable cost per unit and the total fixed costs remain constant.

D. The variable cost per unit increases, and the total fixed costs remain constant.

Answer (C) is correct. *(CIA, adapted)*
**REQUIRED:** The effect on variable and fixed costs of a change in activity within the relevant range.
**DISCUSSION:** Total variable cost changes when changes in the activity level occur within the relevant range. The cost per unit for a variable cost is constant for all activity levels within the relevant range. Thus, if the activity volume increases within the relevant range, total variable costs will increase. A fixed cost does not change when volume changes occur in the activity level within the relevant range. If the activity volume increases within the relevant range, total fixed costs will remain unchanged.

**6.** A company is attempting to determine if there is a cause-and-effect relationship between scrap value and output produced. The following exhibit presents the company's scrap data for the last fiscal year:

Scrap as a Percent of Standard Dollar
Value of Output Produced

| Month | Standard Dollar Value of Output | Percent Scrap (%) |
|---|---|---|
| Nov 20X7 | $1,500,000 | 4.5 |
| Dec 20X7 | $1,650,000 | 2.5 |
| Jan 20X8 | $1,600,000 | 3.0 |
| Feb 20X8 | $1,550,000 | 2.5 |
| Mar 20X8 | $1,650,000 | 1.5 |
| Apr 20X8 | $1,500,000 | 4.0 |
| May 20X8 | $1,400,000 | 2.5 |
| Jun 20X8 | $1,300,000 | 3.5 |
| Jul 20X8 | $1,650,000 | 5.5 |
| Aug 20X8 | $1,000,000 | 4.5 |
| Sep 20X8 | $1,400,000 | 3.5 |
| Oct 20X8 | $1,600,000 | 2.5 |

The company's scrap value in relation to the standard dollar value of output produced appears to be

A. A variable cost.

B. A fixed cost.

C. A semi-fixed cost.

D. Unrelated to the standard dollar value of output.

Answer (D) is correct. *(CIA, adapted)*
**REQUIRED:** The scrap value in relation to the standard dollar value of output.
**DISCUSSION:** There is no systematic relationship between standard dollars shipped and the percentage of scrap.
Answer (A) is incorrect because a variable cost would remain a constant percentage of standard dollars shipped. Answer (B) is incorrect because a fixed cost would be a lower percentage when standard dollars shipped were high than when they were low. Answer (C) is incorrect because a semi-fixed cost as a percentage would move up and down with standard dollars shipped, with a base level higher than zero percent.

**7.** Conversion costs do not include

A. Depreciation.

B. Direct materials.

C. Indirect labor.

D. Indirect materials.

Answer (B) is correct.  *(CMA, adapted)*
**REQUIRED:** The item not included in conversion costs.
**DISCUSSION:** Conversion costs are necessary to convert raw materials into finished products. They include all manufacturing costs, for example, direct labor and factory overhead, other than direct materials.
Answer (A) is incorrect because depreciation is a factory overhead cost and therefore is a conversion cost. Answer (C) is incorrect because indirect labor is a factory overhead cost and therefore is a conversion cost. Answer (D) is incorrect because indirect materials are factory overhead costs and therefore are conversion costs.

**8.** Conversion cost pricing

A. Places minimal emphasis on the cost of materials used in manufacturing a product.

B. Could be used when the customer furnishes the material used in manufacturing a product.

C. Places heavy emphasis on indirect costs and disregards consideration of direct costs.

D. Places heavy emphasis on direct costs and disregards consideration of indirect costs.

Answer (B) is correct.  *(CMA, adapted)*
**REQUIRED:** The true statement about conversion cost pricing.
**DISCUSSION:** Conversion costs consist of direct labor and factory overhead, the costs of converting raw materials into finished goods. Normally, a company does not consider only conversion costs in making pricing decisions, but if the customer were to furnish the raw materials, conversion cost pricing would be appropriate.
Answer (A) is incorrect because conversion cost pricing does not place any emphasis on raw materials cost. Answer (C) is incorrect because direct labor is an element of conversion costs. Answer (D) is incorrect because factory overhead is an indirect cost that is an element of conversion costs.

**9.** The difference between variable costs and fixed costs is

A. Variable costs per unit fluctuate and fixed costs per unit remain constant.

B. Variable costs per unit are fixed over the relevant range and fixed costs per unit are variable.

C. Total variable costs are variable over the relevant range and fixed in the long term, while fixed costs never change.

D. Variable costs per unit change in varying increments, while fixed costs per unit change in equal increments.

Answer (B) is correct.  *(CMA, adapted)*
**REQUIRED:** The difference between variable and fixed costs.
**DISCUSSION:** Fixed costs remain unchanged within the relevant range for a given period despite fluctuations in activity, but per unit fixed costs do change as the level of activity changes. Thus, fixed costs are fixed in total but vary per unit as activity changes. Total variable costs vary directly with activity. They are fixed per unit, but vary in total.
Answer (A) is incorrect because variable costs are fixed per unit; they do not fluctuate. Fixed costs per unit change as production changes. Answer (C) is incorrect because all costs are variable in the long term. Answer (D) is incorrect because unit variable costs are fixed in the short term.

**10.** Which one of the following categories of cost is most likely not considered a component of fixed factory overhead?

A. Rent.

B. Property taxes.

C. Depreciation.

D. Power.

Answer (D) is correct.  *(CMA, adapted)*
**REQUIRED:** The item of cost most likely not considered a component of fixed factory overhead.
**DISCUSSION:** A fixed cost is one that remains unchanged within the relevant range for a given period despite fluctuations in activity. Such items as rent, property taxes, depreciation, and supervisory salaries are normally fixed costs because they do not vary with changes in production. Power costs, however, are at least partially variable because they increase as usage increases.
Answer (A) is incorrect because rent is an example of fixed factory overhead. Answer (B) is incorrect because property taxes are an example of fixed factory overhead. Answer (C) is incorrect because depreciation is an example of fixed factory overhead.

**11.** The term "prime costs" refers to

A. Manufacturing costs incurred to produce units of output.

B. All costs associated with manufacturing other than direct labor costs and raw material costs.

C. The sum of direct labor costs and all factory overhead costs.

D. The sum of raw material costs and direct labor costs.

Answer (D) is correct.  *(CMA, adapted)*
**REQUIRED:** The definition of prime costs.
**DISCUSSION:** Prime costs are raw material costs and direct labor costs.
Answer (A) is incorrect because manufacturing costs incurred to produce output are inventoriable costs. Answer (B) is incorrect because all costs associated with manufacturing other than direct labor costs and raw material costs are overhead costs. Answer (C) is incorrect because the sum of direct labor and overhead is conversion cost.

**12.** "Committed costs" are

A. Costs which management decides to incur in the current period to enable the company to achieve objectives other than the filling of orders placed by customers.

B. Costs which are likely to respond to the amount of attention devoted to them by a specified manager.

C. Costs which are governed mainly by past decisions that established the present levels of operating and organizational capacity and which only change slowly in response to small changes in capacity.

D. Amortization of costs which were capitalized in previous periods.

Answer (C) is correct.  *(CMA, adapted)*
**REQUIRED:** The definition of committed costs.
**DISCUSSION:** Committed costs are those which are required as a result of past decisions.
Answer (A) is incorrect because costs incurred in a current period to achieve objectives other than the filling of orders by customers are known as discretionary costs. Answer (B) is incorrect because costs which are likely to respond to the amount of attention devoted to them by a specified manager are controllable costs. Answer (D) is incorrect because amortization of costs capitalized in previous periods is depreciation.

**13.** "Discretionary costs" are

A. Costs which management decides to incur in the current period to enable the company to achieve objectives other than the filling of orders placed by customers.

B. Costs which are likely to respond to the amount of attention devoted to them by a specified manger.

C. Costs which are governed mainly by past decisions that established the present levels of operating and organizational capacity and which only change slowly in response to small changes in capacity.

D. Costs which will be unaffected by current managerial decisions.

Answer (A) is correct.  *(CMA, adapted)*
**REQUIRED:** The definition of discretionary costs.
**DISCUSSION:** Discretionary costs are those that are incurred in the current period at the "discretion" of management, and are not required to fill orders by customers.
Answer (B) is incorrect because costs which are likely to respond to the amount of attention devoted to them by a specified manager are controllable costs. Answer (C) is incorrect because costs required as a result of past decisions are committed costs. Answer (D) is incorrect because costs unaffected by managerial decisions are costs such as committed costs and depreciation that were determined by decisions of previous periods.

**14.** "Controllable costs" are

A. Costs which management decides to incur in the current period to enable the company to achieve objectives other than the filling of orders placed by customers.

B. Costs which are likely to respond to the amount of attention devoted to them by a specified manger.

C. Costs which fluctuate in total in response to small changes in the rate of utilization of capacity.

D. Costs which will be unaffected by current managerial decisions.

Answer (B) is correct.  *(CMA, adapted)*
**REQUIRED:** The definition of controllable costs.
**DISCUSSION:** Controllable costs can be affected by the efforts of a manager.
Answer (A) is incorrect because costs incurred in a current period to achieve objectives other than the filling of orders by customers are known as discretionary costs. Answer (C) is incorrect because costs that fluctuate with small changes in volume are variable costs. Answer (D) is incorrect because costs that are unaffected by managerial decisions are costs such as committed costs and depreciation that was determined by decisions of previous periods.

**15.** Which of the following is the best example of a variable cost?

   A. The corporate president's salary.

   B. Cost of raw material.

   C. Interest charges.

   D. Property taxes.

**Answer (B) is correct.** *(CMA, adapted)*
   **REQUIRED:** The item that is a variable cost.
   **DISCUSSION:** Variable costs vary directly with the level of production. As production increases or decreases, material cost increases or decreases, usually in a direct relationship.
   Answer (A) is incorrect because the president's salary usually does not vary with production levels. Answer (C) is incorrect because interest charges are independent of production levels. They are called "fixed" costs and are elements of overhead. Answer (D) is incorrect because property taxes are independent of production levels. They are called "fixed" costs and are elements of overhead.

---

Questions 16 and 17 are based on the following information.

Estimated unit costs for a company using full absorption costing and operating at a production level of 12,000 units per month:

| Cost Item | Estimated Unit Cost |
| --- | --- |
| Direct material | $32 |
| Direct labor | 20 |
| Variable manufacturing overhead | 15 |
| Fixed manufacturing overhead | 6 |
| Variable selling | 3 |
| Fixed selling | 4 |

---

**16.** Estimated conversion costs per unit are

   A. $35

   B. $41

   C. $44

   D. $48

**Answer (B) is correct.** *(CMA, adapted)*
   **REQUIRED:** Amount of estimated conversion costs per unit.
   **DISCUSSION:** Conversion costs consist of labor plus fixed and variable manufacturing overhead. The total is $41 ($20 + $15 + $6).
   Answer (A) is incorrect because $35 properly includes direct labor but improperly includes only the variable portion of manufacturing overhead. Answer (C) is incorrect because $44 properly includes direct labor and both components of manufacturing overhead but improperly includes a portion of selling expenses. Answer (D) is incorrect because $48 properly includes direct labor and both components of manufacturing overhead but improperly includes selling expenses.

**17.** Estimated prime costs per unit are

   A. $73

   B. $32

   C. $67

   D. $52

**Answer (D) is correct.** *(CMA, adapted)*
   **REQUIRED:** Estimated prime costs per unit for the month.
   **DISCUSSION:** Prime costs consist of direct materials and direct labor. The total is $52 ($32 + $20).
   Answer (A) is incorrect because $73 properly includes direct materials and direct labor but improperly includes manufacturing overhead. Answer (B) is incorrect because $32 properly includes direct materials but improperly excludes direct labor. Answer (C) is incorrect because $67 properly includes direct materials and direct labor but improperly includes a portion of manufacturing overhead.

---

## 2.2 Types of Costs

**18.** The sum of the costs necessary to effect a one-unit increase in the activity level is a(n)

   A. Differential cost.

   B. Opportunity cost.

   C. Marginal cost.

   D. Incremental cost.

**Answer (C) is correct.** *(Publisher)*
   **REQUIRED:** The cost accounting term.
   **DISCUSSION:** A marginal cost is the sum of the costs necessary to effect a one-unit increase in the activity level.
   Answer (A) is incorrect because differential (or incremental) cost is the difference in total cost between two decisions. Answer (B) is incorrect because opportunity cost is the maximum benefit forgone by using a scarce resource for a given purpose. It is the benefit, for example, the contribution to income, provided by the best alternative use of that resource. Answer (D) is incorrect because differential (or incremental) cost is the difference in total cost between two decisions.

**19.** Cost drivers are

A. Activities that cause costs to increase as the activity increases.

B. Accounting techniques used to control costs.

C. Accounting measurements used to evaluate whether or not performance is proceeding according to plan.

D. A mechanical basis, such as machine hours, computer time, size of equipment, or square footage of factory, used to assign costs to activities.

Answer (A) is correct. *(CMA, adapted)*
**REQUIRED:** The definition of a cost driver.
**DISCUSSION:** A cost driver is "a measure of activity, such as direct labor hours, machine hours, beds occupied, computer time used, flight hours, miles driven, or contracts, that is a causal factor in the incurrence of cost to an entity" (IMA). It is a basis used to assign costs to cost objects.
Answer (B) is incorrect because cost drivers are measures of activities that cause the incurrence of costs. Answer (C) is incorrect because cost drivers are not accounting measurements but measures of activities that cause costs. Answer (D) is incorrect because, although cost drivers may be used to assign costs, they are not necessarily mechanical. For example, a cost driver for pension benefits is employee salaries.

**20.** A cost that may be eliminated by performing an activity more efficiently is a(n)

A. Opportunity cost.

B. Avoidable cost.

C. Cost driver.

D. Indirect cost.

Answer (B) is correct. *(Publisher)*
**REQUIRED:** The cost eliminated by performing an activity more efficiently.
**DISCUSSION:** Avoidable costs are those that may be eliminated by not engaging in an activity or by performing it more efficiently.
Answer (A) is incorrect because opportunity cost is the maximum benefit forgone by using a scarce resource for a given purpose. It is the benefit, for example, the contribution to income, provided by the best alternative use of that resource. Answer (C) is incorrect because a cost driver "is a measure of activity, such as direct labor hours, machine hours, beds occupied, computer time used, flight hours, miles driven, or contracts, that is a causal factor in the incurrence of cost to an entity" (SMA 2A). Answer (D) is incorrect because indirect costs cannot be specifically associated with a given cost object in an economically feasible way. They are also defined as costs that are not directly identified with one final cost object but that are identified with two or more final cost objects or with at least one intermediate cost object.

**21.** In joint-product costing and analysis, which one of the following costs is relevant when deciding the point at which a product should be sold to maximize profits?

A. Separable costs after the split-off point.

B. Joint costs to the split-off point.

C. Sales salaries for the period when the units were produced.

D. Purchase costs of the materials required for the joint products.

Answer (A) is correct. *(CMA, adapted)*
**REQUIRED:** The cost relevant to deciding when a joint product should be sold.
**DISCUSSION:** Joint products are created from processing a common input. Joint costs are incurred prior to the split-off point and cannot be identified with a particular joint product. As a result, joint costs are irrelevant to the timing of sale. However, separable costs incurred after the split-off point are relevant because, if incremental revenues exceed the separable costs, products should be processed further, not sold at the split-off point.
Answer (B) is incorrect because joint costs have no effect on the decision as to when to sell a product. Answer (C) is incorrect because sales salaries for the production period do not affect the decision. Answer (D) is incorrect because purchase costs are joint costs.

**22.** The assignment of raw material costs to the major end products resulting from refining a barrel of crude oil is best described as

A. Indirect costing.

B. Joint costing.

C. Differential costing.

D. Incremental costing.

Answer (B) is correct. *(CIA, adapted)*
**REQUIRED:** The type of costing that assigns raw material costs to the major end products in oil refining.
**DISCUSSION:** Joint products are common products created from processing a single input (e.g., gasoline, diesel fuel, and kerosene). Joint products have common costs until they reach the split-off point. Joint costing assigns common costs to joint products.
Answer (A) is incorrect because indirect costing is a nonsense term. Direct costing charges products only with variable costs. Answer (C) is incorrect because differential costing is not a commonly used term, but it could mean costing common products at a fixed differential. Answer (D) is incorrect because incremental costing is not a common term either, but it could mean costing in increments.

Questions 23 through 28 are based on the following information.

Huron Industries has recently developed two new products, a cleaning unit for video discs and a disc duplicator for reproducing movies taken with a video camera. However, Huron has only enough plant capacity to introduce one of these products during the current year. The company controller has gathered the following data to assist management in deciding which product should be selected for production.

Huron's fixed overhead includes rent and utilities, equipment depreciation, and supervisory salaries. Selling and administrative expenses are not allocated to products.

|  | Disc Duplicator | Cleaning Unit |
|---|---|---|
| Raw materials | $ 44.00 | $ 36.00 |
| Machining at $12 per hr. | 18.00 | 15.00 |
| Assembly at $10 per hr. | 30.00 | 10.00 |
| Variable overhead at $8 per hr. | 36.00 | 18.00 |
| Fixed overhead at $4 per hr. | 18.00 | 9.00 |
| Total cost | $ 146.00 | $ 88.00 |
| Suggested selling price | $ 169.95 | $ 99.98 |
| Actual research and development costs | $240,000 | $175,000 |
| Proposed advertising and promotion costs | $500,000 | $350,000 |

**23.** For Huron's disc duplicator, the unit costs for raw materials, machining, and assembly represent

A. Conversion costs.

B. Separable costs.

C. Committed costs.

D. Prime costs.

Answer (D) is correct. *(CMA, adapted)*
REQUIRED: The type of cost represented by raw materials, machining, and assembly.
DISCUSSION: Raw materials and direct labor (such as machining and assembly) are a manufacturer's prime costs.
Answer (A) is incorrect because conversion costs consist of direct labor and overhead. Answer (B) is incorrect because separable costs are incurred beyond the point at which jointly produced items become separately identifiable. Answer (C) is incorrect because committed costs result when an entity holds fixed assets; examples include long-term lease payments and depreciation.

**24.** The difference between the $99.98 suggested selling price for Huron's video disc cleaning unit and its total unit cost of $88.00 represents the unit's

A. Contribution margin ratio.

B. Gross profit.

C. Contribution.

D. Gross profit margin ratio.

Answer (B) is correct. *(CMA, adapted)*
REQUIRED: The difference between selling price and unit cost.
DISCUSSION: Gross profit is the difference between sales price and the full absorption cost of goods sold.
Answer (A) is incorrect because contribution margin ratio is the ratio of contribution margin (sales – variable costs) to sales. Answer (C) is incorrect because contribution (margin) is the difference between unit selling price and unit variable costs. Fixed costs are not considered. Answer (D) is incorrect because the gross profit margin ratio equals gross profit divided by sales.

**25.** The total overhead cost of $27.00 for Huron's video disc cleaning unit is a

A. Carrying cost.

B. Discretionary cost.

C. Sunk cost.

D. Mixed cost.

Answer (D) is correct. *(CMA, adapted)*
REQUIRED: The nature of total overhead.
DISCUSSION: A mixed cost is a combination of fixed and variable elements. Consequently, the $27 of total overhead cost is mixed because it contains both fixed overhead and variable overhead.
Answer (A) is incorrect because a carrying cost is the cost of carrying inventory; examples are insurance and rent on warehouse facilities. Answer (B) is incorrect because a discretionary cost (a managed or program cost) results from a periodic decision about the total amount to be spent. It is also characterized by uncertainty about the relationship between input and the value of the related output. Examples are advertising and R&D costs. Answer (C) is incorrect because a sunk cost is a past cost or a cost that the entity has irrevocably committed to incur. Because it is unavoidable, it is not relevant to future decisions.

**26.** Research and development costs for Huron's two new products are

    A.  Conversion costs.

    B.  Sunk costs.

    C.  Relevant costs.

    D.  Avoidable costs.

**Answer (B) is correct.**  *(CMA, adapted)*
    **REQUIRED:** The nature of R&D costs.
    **DISCUSSION:** Before they are incurred, R&D costs are often considered to be discretionary. However, Huron's R&D costs have already been incurred. Thus, they are sunk costs. A sunk cost is a past cost or a cost that the entity has irrevocably committed to incur. Because it is unavoidable, it is not relevant to future decisions.
    Answer (A) is incorrect because conversion costs are composed of direct labor and factory overhead, that is, costs incurred to convert materials into a finished product. Answer (C) is incorrect because relevant costs are expected future costs that vary with the action taken. A cost that has already been incurred is not relevant to future decisions. Answer (D) is incorrect because avoidable costs may be eliminated by not engaging in an activity or by performing it more efficiently.

**27.** The advertising and promotion costs for the product selected by Huron will be

    A.  Discretionary costs.

    B.  Opportunity costs.

    C.  Committed costs.

    D.  Incremental costs.

**Answer (A) is correct.**  *(CMA, adapted)*
    **REQUIRED:** The nature of advertising and promotion costs.
    **DISCUSSION:** A discretionary cost (a managed or program cost) results from a periodic decision about the total amount to be spent. It is also characterized by uncertainty about the relationship between input and the value of the related output. Examples are advertising and R&D costs.
    Answer (B) is incorrect because an opportunity cost is the maximum benefit forgone by using a scarce resource for a given purpose. It is the benefit provided by the next best use of a particular resource. Answer (C) is incorrect because committed costs are those for which management has made a long-term commitment. They typically result when a firm holds fixed assets. Examples include long-term lease payments and depreciation. Answer (D) is incorrect because incremental costs are the differences in costs between two decision choices.

**28.** The costs included in Huron's fixed overhead are

    A.  Joint costs.

    B.  Committed costs.

    C.  Opportunity costs.

    D.  Prime costs.

**Answer (B) is correct.**  *(CMA, adapted)*
    **REQUIRED:** The nature of fixed overhead.
    **DISCUSSION:** Committed costs are those for which management has made a long-term commitment. They typically result when a firm holds fixed assets. Examples include long-term lease payments and depreciation. Committed costs are typically fixed costs.
    Answer (A) is incorrect because joint (common) costs are incurred in the production of two or more inseparable products up to the point at which the products become separable. Answer (C) is incorrect because an opportunity cost is the maximum benefit forgone by using a scarce resource for a given purpose; it is the benefit provided by the next best use of a particular resource. Answer (D) is incorrect because prime costs are composed of raw material and direct labor costs.

## 2.3 Costing Techniques

**29.** Which of the following is a type of costing that refers to the continuous accumulations of small betterment activities rather than innovative improvements?

A. Target costing.

B. Kaizen costing.

C. Variable costing.

D. Process costing.

Answer (B) is correct.   *(Publisher)*
**REQUIRED:** The cost accounting term.
**DISCUSSION:** Kaizen costing supports the cost reduction process in the manufacturing phase of existing products. Kaizen is a Japanese word that refers to continuous improvement. Kaizen makes improvements through the accumulations of small betterment activities rather than innovative improvements.
Answer (A) is incorrect because target costing (pricing) begins with a target price, which is the expected market price given the company's knowledge of its customers and competitors. Subtracting the unit target profit margin determines the long-term target cost. Answer (C) is incorrect because variable (direct) costing considers only variable manufacturing costs to be product costs, i.e., inventoriable. Fixed manufacturing costs are considered period costs and are expensed as incurred. Answer (D) is incorrect because process costing is used to assign costs to similar products that are mass produced on a continuous basis. Costs are accumulated by departments or cost centers rather than by jobs, work-in-process is stated in terms of equivalent units, and unit costs are established on a departmental basis. Process costing is an averaging process that calculates the average cost of all units.

**30.** Which one of the following considers the impact of fixed overhead costs?

A. Full absorption costing.

B. Marginal costing.

C. Direct costing.

D. Variable costing.

Answer (A) is correct.   *(CMA, adapted)*
**REQUIRED:** The method of costing that considers the impact of fixed overhead costs.
**DISCUSSION:** Full absorption costing treats fixed factory overhead costs as product costs. Thus, inventory and cost of goods sold include (absorb) fixed factory overhead.
Answer (B) is incorrect because marginal costing considers only the incremental costs of producing an additional unit of product. In most cases marginal costs are variable costs. Answer (C) is incorrect because direct (variable) costing treats only variable costs as product costs. Answer (D) is incorrect because direct (variable) costing treats only variable costs as product costs.

**31.** Costs are allocated to cost objects in many ways and for many reasons. Which one of the following is a purpose of cost allocation?

A. Evaluating revenue center performance.

B. Measuring income and assets for external reporting.

C. Budgeting cash and controlling expenditures.

D. Aiding in variable costing for internal reporting.

Answer (B) is correct.   *(CMA, adapted)*
**REQUIRED:** The purpose of cost allocation.
**DISCUSSION:** Cost allocation is the process of assigning and reassigning costs to cost objects. It is used for those costs that cannot be directly associated with a specific cost object. Cost allocation is often used for purposes of measuring income and assets for external reporting purposes. Cost allocation is less meaningful for internal purposes because responsibility accounting systems emphasize controllability, a process often ignored in cost allocation.
Answer (A) is incorrect because a revenue center is evaluated on the basis of revenue generated, without regard to costs. Answer (C) is incorrect because cost allocation is not necessary for cash budgeting and controlling expenditures. Answer (D) is incorrect because allocations are not needed for variable costing, which concerns direct, not indirect, costs.

**32.** Which one of the following is least likely to be an objective of a cost accounting system?

A. Product costing.

B. Department efficiency.

C. Inventory valuation.

D. Sales commission determination.

Answer (D) is correct. *(CMA, adapted)*
**REQUIRED:** The item that is the least likely to be an objective of a cost accounting system.
**DISCUSSION:** A cost accounting system has numerous objectives, including product costing, assessing departmental efficiency, inventory valuation, income determination, and planning, evaluating, and controlling operations. Determining sales commissions is not an objective of a cost accounting system because such commissions are based on sales, not costs.
Answer (A) is incorrect because product costing is an objective of a cost accounting system. Answer (B) is incorrect because department efficiency is an objective of a cost accounting system. Answer (C) is incorrect because inventory valuation is an objective of a cost accounting system.

**33.** In a broad sense, cost accounting can best be defined within the accounting system as

A. Internal and external reporting that may be used in making nonroutine decisions and in developing plans and policies.

B. External reporting to government, various outside parties, and shareholders.

C. Internal reporting for use in management planning and control, and external reporting to the extent its product-costing function satisfies external reporting requirements.

D. Internal reporting for use in planning and controlling routine operations.

Answer (C) is correct. *(Publisher)*
**REQUIRED:** The definition of cost accounting within the accounting system.
**DISCUSSION:** Cost accounting is a combination of (1) managerial accounting in the sense that its purpose can be to provide internal reports for use in planning and control and in making nonroutine decisions, and (2) financial accounting because its product-costing function satisfies external reporting requirements for reporting to shareholders, government, and various outside parties.
Answer (A) is incorrect because cost accounting is concerned with more than just reporting to be used in making nonroutine decisions. Answer (B) is incorrect because cost accounting also provides information for internal reporting. Answer (D) is incorrect because managerial accounting entails internal reporting for use in planning and controlling routine operations.

**34.** An accounting system that collects financial and operating data on the basis of the underlying nature and extent of the cost drivers is

A. Direct costing.

B. Activity-based costing.

C. Cycle-time costing.

D. Variable costing.

Answer (B) is correct. *(CMA, adapted)*
**REQUIRED:** The accounting system that collects data on the basis of cost drivers.
**DISCUSSION:** An activity-based costing (ABC) system identifies the causal relationship between the incurrence of cost and the underlying activities that cause those costs. Under an ABC system, costs are applied to products on the basis of resources consumed (drivers).
Answer (A) is incorrect because direct costing is a system that treats fixed costs as period costs; in other words, production costs consist only of variable costs, while fixed costs are expensed as incurred. Answer (C) is incorrect because cycle time is the period from the time a customer places an order to the time that product is delivered. Answer (D) is incorrect because variable costing is the same as direct costing, which expenses fixed costs as incurred.

**35.** Because this allocation method recognizes that service departments often provide each other with interdepartmental service, it is theoretically considered to be the most accurate method for allocating service department costs to production departments. This method is the

A. Direct method.

B. Variable method.

C. Reciprocal method.

D. Linear method.

Answer (C) is correct. *(CMA, adapted)*
**REQUIRED:** The most accurate method for allocating service department costs to production departments.
**DISCUSSION:** The three most common methods of allocating service department costs are the direct method, the step method, and the reciprocal method (also called the simultaneous equations method). The reciprocal method is theoretically the preferred method because it recognizes reciprocal services among service departments.
Answer (A) is incorrect because the direct method does not recognize the fact that service departments might provide services to each other; all costs are assigned directly to production departments. Answer (B) is incorrect because the variable method is a nonsense term as used here. Answer (D) is incorrect because the linear method is not one of the methods used to allocate departmental costs.

**36.** In target costing,

   A.  The market price of the product is taken as a given.

   B.  Only raw materials, labor, and variable overhead cannot exceed a threshold target.

   C.  Only raw materials cannot exceed a threshold target.

   D.  Raw materials are recorded directly to cost of goods sold.

Answer (A) is correct. *(CMA, adapted)*
   **REQUIRED:** The true statement about target costing.
   **DISCUSSION:** Target costing begins with a target price, which is the expected market price given the company's knowledge of its customers and competitors. Subtracting the unit target profit margin determines the long-term target cost. If this cost is lower than the full cost, the company may need to adopt comprehensive cost-cutting measures. For example, in the furniture industry, certain price points are popular with buyers: a couch might sell better at $400 than at $200 because consumers question the quality of a $200 couch and thus will not buy the lower-priced item. The result is that furniture manufacturers view $400 as the target price of a couch, and the cost must be lower.
   Answer (B) is incorrect because all product cost categories are addressed by target costing. Answer (C) is incorrect because all product cost categories are addressed by target costing. Answer (D) is incorrect because the manner in which raw materials costs are accounted for is irrelevant.

**37.** An operation costing system is

   A.  Identical to a process costing system except that actual cost is used for manufacturing overhead.

   B.  The same as a process costing system except that materials are allocated on the basis of batches of production.

   C.  The same as a job order costing system except that materials are accounted for in the same way as they are in a process costing system.

   D.  The same as a job order costing system except that no overhead allocations are made since actual costs are used throughout.

Answer (B) is correct. *(CMA, adapted)*
   **REQUIRED:** The definition of an operation costing system.
   **DISCUSSION:** Operation costing is a hybrid of job-order and process costing systems wherein materials are allocated on the basis of batches of production. It is used by companies that manufacture goods that undergo some similar and some dissimilar processes. Operation costing accumulates total conversion costs and determines a unit conversion cost for each operation. However, direct materials costs are charged specifically to products or batches as in job-order systems.
   Answer (A) is incorrect because operation costing differs from process costing in the treatment of materials. Answer (C) is incorrect because operation costing differs from process costing in the treatment of materials. Answer (D) is incorrect because overhead allocations are made in operation costing.

**38.** Life-cycle costing

   A.  Is sometimes used as a basis for cost planning and product pricing.

   B.  Includes only manufacturing costs incurred over the life of the product.

   C.  Includes only manufacturing cost, selling expense, and distribution expense.

   D.  Emphasizes cost savings opportunities during the manufacturing cycle.

Answer (A) is correct. *(CMA, adapted)*
   **REQUIRED:** The true statement about life-cycle costing.
   **DISCUSSION:** Life-cycle costing estimates a product's revenues and expenses over its expected life cycle. This approach is especially useful when revenues and related costs do not occur in the same periods. It emphasizes the need to price products to cover all costs, not just those for production. Hence, costs are determined for all value-chain categories: upstream (R&D, design), manufacturing, and downstream (marketing, distribution, and customer service). The result is to highlight upstream and downstream costs in the cost planning process that often receive insufficient attention.
   Answer (B) is incorrect because the life-cycle model includes the upstream (R&D and design) and downstream (marketing, distribution, and customer service) elements of the value chain as well as manufacturing costs. Answer (C) is incorrect because the life-cycle model includes the upstream (R&D and design) and downstream (marketing, distribution, and customer service) elements of the value chain as well as manufacturing costs. Answer (D) is incorrect because life-cycle costing emphasizes the significance of locked-in costs, target costing, and value engineering for pricing and cost control. Thus, cost savings at all stages of the life cycle are important.

## 2.4 Manufacturing Terminology

**39.** Spoilage that is not expected to occur under normal, efficient operating conditions is considered

- A. Abnormal spoilage.
- B. Actual spoilage.
- C. Normal spoilage.
- D. Residual spoilage.

**Answer (A) is correct.** *(Publisher)*
**REQUIRED:** The cost accounting term.
**DISCUSSION:** Abnormal spoilage is spoilage that is not expected to occur under normal, efficient operation conditions.
Answer (B) is incorrect because actual spoilage is the spoilage that occurred. Answer (C) is incorrect because normal spoilage is expected to occur. Answer (D) is incorrect because residual spoilage is a nonsense term.

**40.** The amount of raw materials left over from a production process or production cycle for which there is no further use is

- A. Scrap.
- B. Abnormal spoilage.
- C. Waste.
- D. Normal spoilage.

**Answer (C) is correct.** *(Publisher)*
**REQUIRED:** The raw materials left over from a production process or production cycle for which there is no further use.
**DISCUSSION:** Waste is the amount of raw materials left over from a production process or production cycle for which there is no further use. Waste is usually not salable at any price and must be discarded.
Answer (A) is incorrect because scrap consists of raw materials left over from the production cycle but still usable for purposes other than those for which it was originally intended. Scrap may be sold to outside customers, usually for a nominal amount, or may be used for a different production process. Answer (B) is incorrect because abnormal spoilage is spoilage that is not expected to occur under normal, efficient operating conditions. The cost of abnormal spoilage should be separately identified and reported to management. Abnormal spoilage is typically treated as a period cost (a loss) because of its unusual nature. Answer (D) is incorrect because normal spoilage is the spoilage that occurs under normal operating conditions. It is essentially uncontrollable in the short run. Normal spoilage arises under efficient operations and is treated as a product cost.

**41.** When compared with normal spoilage, abnormal spoilage

- A. Arises more frequently from factors that are inherent in the manufacturing process.
- B. Is given the same accounting treatment as normal spoilage.
- C. Is generally thought to be more controllable by production management than normal spoilage.
- D. Is not typically influenced by the "tightness" of production standards.

**Answer (C) is correct.** *(CMA, adapted)*
**REQUIRED:** The nature of abnormal spoilage.
**DISCUSSION:** Spoiled goods are defective items that cannot be feasibly reworked. Traditional cost accounting systems distinguish between normal and abnormal spoilage because, in some operations, a degree of spoilage is viewed as inevitable. However, organizations that have adopted rigorous approaches to quality regard normal spoilage as minimal or even nonexistent. Thus, all spoilage may be identified as abnormal. Normal spoilage occurs under normal, efficient operating conditions. It is spoilage that is uncontrollable in the short run and therefore should be expressed as a function of good output (treated as a product cost). Accordingly, normal spoilage is assigned to all good units in process costing systems, that is, all units that have passed the inspection point at which the spoilage was detected. If normal spoilage is attributable to a specific job, only the disposal value of the normally spoiled goods is removed from work-in-process, thereby assigning the cost of normal spoilage to the good units remaining in the specific job. Abnormal spoilage is not expected to occur under normal, efficient operating conditions. The cost of abnormal spoilage should be separately identified and reported. Abnormal spoilage is typically treated as a period cost (a loss) because it is unusual.
Answer (A) is incorrect because normal spoilage arises more frequently from factors that are inherent in the manufacturing process. Answer (B) is incorrect because abnormal spoilage costs are treated as a loss, and normal spoilage costs are inventoried. Answer (D) is incorrect because the tighter the standards, the more likely that any spoilage will be deemed to be abnormal.

**42.** The upper limit of a company's productive output capacity given its existing resources is called

A. Excess capacity.

B. Cycle-time capacity.

C. Practical capacity.

D. Theoretical capacity.

Answer (C) is correct.   *(CMA, adapted)*
REQUIRED:  The upper limit of a company's productive output capacity given its existing resources.
DISCUSSION:  Practical capacity is the maximum level at which output is produced efficiently, with an allowance for unavoidable interruptions, for example, for holidays and scheduled maintenance.  Because this level will be higher than expected capacity, its use will ordinarily result in underapplied fixed factory overhead.
Answer (A) is incorrect because excess capacity is unused capacity.  Answer (B) is incorrect because manufacturing lead (cycle) time is the sum of setup time and manufacturing time for a customer order.  It is a component of customer response time. Answer (D) is incorrect because theoretical capacity makes no allowance for unavoidable interruptions.

**43.** Products of relatively small total value that are produced simultaneously from a common manufacturing process with products of greater value and quantity are

A. Scrap.

B. By-products.

C. Waste.

D. Abnormal spoilage.

Answer (B) is correct.   *(Publisher)*
REQUIRED:  The cost accounting term.
DISCUSSION:  By-products are products of relatively small total value that are produced simultaneously from a common manufacturing process with products of greater value and quantity (joint products).
Answer (A) is incorrect because scrap consists of raw materials left over from the production cycle but still usable for purposes other than those for which they were originally intended.  Scrap may be sold to outside customers, usually for a nominal amount, or may be used for a different production process.  Answer (C) is incorrect because waste is the amount of raw materials left over from a production process or production cycle for which there is no further use.  Waste is usually not salable at any price and must be discarded.  Answer (D) is incorrect because abnormal spoilage is spoilage that is not expected to occur under normal, efficient operating conditions.  The cost of abnormal spoilage should be separately identified and reported to management.  Abnormal spoilage is typically treated as a period cost (a loss) because of its unusual nature.

**44.** Practical capacity as a plant capacity concept

A. Assumes all personnel and equipment will operate at peak efficiency and total plant capacity will be used.

B. Does not consider idle time caused by inadequate sales demand.

C. Includes consideration of idle time caused by both limited sales orders and human and equipment inefficiencies.

D. Is the production volume that is necessary to meet sales demand for the next year.

Answer (B) is correct.   *(CMA, adapted)*
REQUIRED:  The true statement about practical capacity.
DISCUSSION:  Practical capacity is the maximum level at which output is produced efficiently.  It includes consideration of idle time caused by human and equipment inefficiencies but not by inadequate sales demand.  Practical capacity exceeds the other commonly used denominator levels included in the calculation of the fixed factory overhead rate.  Because practical capacity will almost always exceed the actual use of capacity, it will result in an unfavorable production volume variance. Moreover, this variance (the difference between budgeted fixed overhead and the fixed overhead applied based on standard input allowed for the actual output) will be greatest given a practical capacity measure.  The unfavorable production volume variance is charged to income summary, so the effect of using a larger denominator volume is the more rapid write-off of fixed overhead (practical capacity may be used for federal income tax purposes).
Answer (A) is incorrect because theoretical capacity assumes all personnel and equipment will operate at peak efficiency and total plant capacity will be used.  Answer (C) is incorrect because practical capacity ignores demand. Answer (D) is incorrect because the production volume to meet a given production level may be more or less than practical capacity.  Horngren, Foster, and Datar call this volume the master-budget volume.

## 2.5 Cost Behavior, Cost Objects, and Cost Drivers

**45.** The difference between variable costs and fixed costs is

A. Variable costs per unit fluctuate and fixed costs per unit remain constant.

B. Variable costs per unit are fixed over the relevant range and fixed costs per unit are variable.

C. Total variable costs are variable over the relevant range and fixed in the long term, while fixed costs never change.

D. Variable costs per unit change in varying increments, while fixed costs per unit change in equal increments.

Answer (B) is correct. *(CMA, adapted)*
**REQUIRED:** The difference between variable and fixed costs.
**DISCUSSION:** Fixed costs remain unchanged within the relevant range for a given period despite fluctuations in activity, but per unit fixed costs do change as the level of activity changes. Thus, fixed costs are fixed in total but vary per unit as activity changes. Total variable costs vary directly with activity. They are fixed per unit, but vary in total.
Answer (A) is incorrect because variable costs are fixed per unit; they do not fluctuate. Fixed costs per unit change as production changes. Answer (C) is incorrect because all costs are variable in the long term. Answer (D) is incorrect because unit variable costs are fixed in the short term.

**46.** The controller of JoyCo has requested a quick estimate of the manufacturing supplies needed for the Morton Plant for the month of July when production is expected to be 470,000 units to meet the ending inventory requirements and sales of 475,000 units. JoyCo's budget analyst has the following actual data for the last 3 months:

| Month | Production in Units | Manufacturing Supplies |
|-------|---------------------|------------------------|
| March | 450,000 | $723,060 |
| April | 540,000 | 853,560 |
| May | 480,000 | 766,560 |

Using these data and the high-low method to develop a cost estimating equation, the estimate of needed manufacturing supplies for July would be

A. $652,500

B. $681,500

C. $749,180

D. $752,060

Answer (D) is correct. *(CMA, adapted)*
**REQUIRED:** The estimate of needed manufacturing supplies using the high-low method.
**DISCUSSION:** The fixed and variable portions of mixed costs may be estimated by identifying the highest and the lowest costs within the relevant range. The difference in cost divided by the difference in activity is the variable rate. Once the variable rate is found, the fixed portion is determinable. April and March provide the highest and lowest amounts. The difference in production was 90,000 units (540,000 April – 450,000 March), and the difference in the cost of supplies was $130,500 ($853,560 – $723,060). Hence, the unit variable cost was $1.45 ($130,500 ÷ 90,000 units). The total variable costs for March must have been $652,500 (450,000 units × $1.45 VC per unit), and the fixed cost must therefore have been $70,560 ($723,060 – $652,500). The probable costs for July equal $681,500 (470,000 units × $1.45 VC per unit), plus $70,560 of fixed costs, a total of $752,060.
Answer (A) is incorrect because $652,500 equals the total variable costs for March. Answer (B) is incorrect because $681,500 is the variable portion of the total costs. Answer (C) is incorrect because $749,180 is a nonsense answer.

**47.** Which one of the following categories of cost is most likely not considered a component of fixed factory overhead?

A. Rent.

B. Property taxes.

C. Depreciation.

D. Power.

Answer (D) is correct. *(CMA, adapted)*
**REQUIRED:** The item of cost most likely not considered a component of fixed factory overhead.
**DISCUSSION:** A fixed cost is one that remains unchanged within the relevant range for a given period despite fluctuations in activity. Such items as rent, property taxes, depreciation, and supervisory salaries are normally fixed costs because they do not vary with changes in production. Power costs, however, are at least partially variable because they increase as usage increases.
Answer (A) is incorrect because rent is an example of fixed factory overhead. Answer (B) is incorrect because property taxes are an example of fixed factory overhead. Answer (C) is incorrect because depreciation is an example of fixed factory overhead.

Questions 48 and 49 are based on the following information. A company wants to determine its marketing costs for budgeting purposes. Activity measures and costs incurred for 4 months of the current year are presented in the table below. Advertising is considered to be a discretionary cost. Salespersons are paid monthly salaries plus commissions. The sales force was increased from 20 to 21 individuals during the month of May.

|  | March | April | May | June |
|---|---|---|---|---|
| **Activity measures:** | | | | |
| Sales orders | 2,000 | 1,800 | 2,400 | 2,300 |
| Units sold | 55,000 | 60,000 | 70,000 | 65,000 |
| Dollar sales | $1,150,000 | $1,200,000 | $1,330,000 | $1,275,000 |
| **Marketing costs:** | | | | |
| Advertising | $ 190,000 | $ 200,000 | $ 190,000 | $ 190,000 |
| Sales salaries | 20,000 | 20,000 | 21,000 | 21,000 |
| Commissions | 23,000 | 24,000 | 26,600 | 25,500 |
| Shipping costs | 93,000 | 100,000 | 114,000 | 107,000 |
| Total costs | $ 326,000 | $ 344,000 | $ 351,600 | $ 343,500 |

**48.** Which of the following most appropriately describes the classification and behavior of shipping costs?

|  | Classification | Behavior |
|---|---|---|
| A. | Variable cost | $1.66 per unit sold |
| B. | Mixed cost | $16,000 per month plus $1.40 per unit sold |
| C. | Mixed cost | $30,000 per month plus $35.00 per sales order |
| D. | Mixed cost | $58,000 per month plus $23.33 per sales order |

Answer (B) is correct. *(CIA, adapted)*
**REQUIRED:** The item that describes the classification and behavior of shipping costs.
**DISCUSSION:** Using the high-low method, the variable and fixed costs for shipping can be calculated. The difference in cost levels divided by the difference in unit volume equals the variable cost per unit of $1.40 [($114,000 – $93,000) ÷ (70,000 – 55,000)]. The variable cost for 70,000 units is $98,000 (70,000 × $1.40). Subtracting the variable cost from total shipping cost results in the fixed cost of $16,000 ($114,000 – $98,000).
Answer (A) is incorrect because $1.66 is the average cost over 4 months. Answer (C) is incorrect because $30,000 per month plus $35.00 per sales order is based on orders instead of sales, and the March shipping costs are incorrectly matched with the April orders. Answer (D) is incorrect because $58,000 per month plus $23.33 per sales order is based on orders.

**49.** In relation to the dollar amount of sales, which of the following cost classifications is appropriate for advertising and sales salaries costs?

|  | Advertising | Sales Salaries |
|---|---|---|
| A. | Variable cost | Fixed cost |
| B. | Fixed cost | Variable cost |
| C. | Mixed cost | Mixed cost |
| D. | Fixed cost | Fixed cost |

Answer (D) is correct. *(CIA, adapted)*
**REQUIRED:** The cost classifications for advertising and sales salaries costs.
**DISCUSSION:** Both advertising and sales salaries should be classified as fixed costs. The advertising was constant for 3 of the 4 months and would be considered fixed in terms of dollar sales. Sales salaries also did not vary with dollar sales.
Answer (A) is incorrect because advertising cost is considered fixed. Answer (B) is incorrect because sales salaries are considered fixed in terms of dollar sales. Answer (C) is incorrect because advertising and sales salaries are considered fixed costs in terms of dollar sales.

## 2.6 Actual/Normal/Standard Costs

**50.** Which one of the following is least likely to be involved in establishing standard costs for evaluation purposes?

A. Budgetary accountants.

B. Industrial engineers.

C. Top management.

D. Quality control personnel.

Answer (C) is correct. *(CMA, adapted)*
**REQUIRED:** The persons least likely to be involved in the establishment of standard costs.
**DISCUSSION:** A standard cost is an estimate of what a cost should be under normal operating conditions based on studies by accountants and engineers. In addition, line management is usually involved in the setting of standard costs as are quality control personnel. Top management would not be involved because cost estimation is a lower level operating activity. Participation by affected employees in all control systems permits all concerned to understand both performance levels desired and the measurement criteria being applied.
Answer (A) is incorrect because budgetary accountants are involved in the setting of standard costs. Answer (B) is incorrect because industrial engineers are involved in the setting of standard costs. Answer (D) is incorrect because quality control personnel are involved in the setting of standard costs.

**51.** A difference between standard costs used for cost control and budgeted costs

- A. Can exist because standard costs must be determined after the budget is completed.
- B. Can exist because standard costs represent what costs should be, whereas budgeted costs represent expected actual costs.
- C. Can exist because budgeted costs are historical costs, whereas standard costs are based on engineering studies.
- D. Cannot exist because they should be the same amounts.

Answer (B) is correct. *(CMA, adapted)*
**REQUIRED:** The true statement about the difference between standard costs and budgeted costs.
**DISCUSSION:** Standard costs are predetermined, attainable unit costs. Standard cost systems isolate deviations (variances) of actual from expected costs. One advantage of standard costs is that they facilitate flexible budgeting. Accordingly, standard and budgeted costs should not differ when standards are currently attainable. However, in practice, budgeted (estimated actual) costs may differ from standard costs when operating conditions are not expected to reflect those anticipated when the standards were developed.
Answer (A) is incorrect because standard costs are determined independently of the budget. Answer (C) is incorrect because budgeted costs are expected future costs, not historical costs. Answer (D) is incorrect because budgeted and standard costs should in principle be the same, but in practice they will differ when standard costs are not expected to be currently attainable.

**52.** A standard costing system is most often used by a firm in conjunction with

- A. Management by objectives.
- B. Target (hurdle) rates of return.
- C. Participative management programs.
- D. Flexible budgets.

Answer (D) is correct. *(CMA, adapted)*
**REQUIRED:** The manner in which a standard costing system is most often used.
**DISCUSSION:** A standard cost is an estimate of what a cost should be under normal operating conditions based on accounting and engineering studies. Comparing actual and standard costs permits an evaluation of the effectiveness of managerial performance. Because of the impact of fixed costs in most businesses, a standard costing system is usually not effective unless the company also has a flexible budgeting system. Flexible budgeting uses standard costs to prepare budgets for multiple activity levels.
Answer (A) is incorrect because MBO is a behavioral, communication-oriented, responsibility approach to employee self-direction. Although MBO can be used with standard costs, the two are not necessarily related. Answer (B) is incorrect because rates of return relate to revenues as well as costs, but a standard costing system concerns costs only. Answer (C) is incorrect because participative management stresses multidirectional communication. It has no relationship to standard costs.

**53.** The best basis upon which cost standards should be set to measure controllable production inefficiencies is

- A. Engineering standards based on ideal performance.
- B. Normal capacity.
- C. Recent average historical performance.
- D. Engineering standards based on attainable performance.

Answer (D) is correct. *(CMA, adapted)*
**REQUIRED:** The best basis upon which cost standards should be set.
**DISCUSSION:** Standards must be accepted by those who will carry them out if they are to have maximum effectiveness. Subordinates should believe that standards are both fair and achievable. Otherwise, they may tend to sabotage, ignore, or circumvent them. Standard costs are often based on the results of time and motion studies, or other types of engineering standards.
Answer (A) is incorrect because employees may not cooperate with standards based on ideal performance. Attainable standards are usually better for motivational purposes. Answer (B) is incorrect because normal capacity may not be sufficient to control production inefficiencies. Answer (C) is incorrect because historical performance may not always be a guide to future performance, and standards should be based on anticipated future conditions.

**54.** Which one of the following statements about ideal standards is false?

A. Ideal standards are also called theoretical or maximum-efficiency standards.

B. Ideal standards do not make provisions for workers with different degrees of experience and skill levels.

C. Ideal standards make no allowance for waste, spoilage, and machine breakdowns.

D. Ideal standards can be used for cash budgeting or product costing.

Answer (D) is correct.  *(CMA, adapted)*
**REQUIRED:** The false statement about ideal standards.
**DISCUSSION:** Ideal (perfect, theoretical, or maximum-efficiency) standards are standard costs that are set for production under optimal conditions. They are based on the work of the most skilled workers with no allowance for waste, spoilage, machine breakdowns, or other downtime. Tight standards can have positive behavioral implications if workers are motivated to strive for excellence. However, they are not in wide use because they can have negative behavioral effects if the standards are impossible to attain. Ideal, or tight, standards are ordinarily replaced by currently attainable standards for cash budgeting, product costing, and budgeting departmental performance. Otherwise, accurate financial planning will be impossible.
Answer (A) is incorrect because ideal standards are perfection standards. Answer (B) is incorrect because ideal standards are based solely on the most efficient workers. Answer (C) is incorrect because ideal standards assume optimal conditions.

**55.** Which one of the following statements pertaining to practical standards is false?

A. Practical standards can be used for product costing and cash budgeting.

B. The use of practical standards usually encourages desirable employee behavior.

C. A firm using practical standards has no reason to make any midyear adjustments to the production standards if an old machine is replaced by a newer, faster machine.

D. Under practical standards, exceptions from standards are less likely; consequently, managers will be better able to practice management by exception.

Answer (C) is correct.  *(CMA, adapted)*
**REQUIRED:** The false statement about practical standards.
**DISCUSSION:** Practical or currently attainable standards may be defined as the performance that is reasonably expected to be achieved with an allowance for normal spoilage, waste, and downtime. An alternative interpretation is that practical standards represent possible but difficult-to-attain results. The use of practical standards does not, however, negate the need to adjust standards if working conditions change.
Answer (A) is incorrect because practical standards are more appropriate than ideal standards for purposes of cash budgeting, product costing, and departmental performance budgeting. Under one interpretation of the term, practical standards are the expected results. Answer (B) is incorrect because practical standards encourage employees to work diligently but do not require perfect efficiency. Thus, employees are less likely to be frustrated by an inability to reach objectives than if ideal standards were set. Answer (D) is incorrect because practical standards reflect expectations or at least standards that are more likely to be attainable than ideal standards. Consequently, unfavorable variances indicate that operations have not been normally efficient and effective.

## 2.7 Absorption (Full) vs. Variable (Direct) Costing

**56.** Which of the following statements is true for a firm that uses variable costing?

A. The cost of a unit of product changes because of changes in number of units manufactured.

B. Profits fluctuate with sales.

C. An idle facility variation is calculated.

D. Product costs include variable administrative costs.

Answer (B) is correct.  *(CMA, adapted)*
**REQUIRED:** The true statement about variable costing.
**DISCUSSION:** In a variable costing system, only the variable costs are recorded as product costs. All fixed costs are expensed in the period incurred. Because changes in the relationship between production levels and sales levels do not cause changes in the amount of fixed manufacturing cost expensed, profits more directly follow the trends in sales.
Answer (A) is incorrect because the cost of a unit of product changing owing to a change in the number of units manufactured is a characteristic of absorption costing systems. Answer (C) is incorrect because idle facility variation is a characteristic of absorption costing systems. Answer (D) is incorrect because neither variable nor absorption costing includes administrative costs in inventory.

**57.** When a firm prepares financial reports by using absorption costing,

    A. Profits will always increase with increases in sales.

    B. Profits will always decrease with decreases in sales.

    C. Profits may decrease with increased sales even if there is no change in selling prices and costs.

    D. Decreased output and constant sales result in increased profits.

Answer (C) is correct. *(CMA, adapted)*
    **REQUIRED:** The profit relationship between output and sales under absorption costing.
    **DISCUSSION:** In an absorption costing system, fixed overhead costs are included in inventory. When sales exceed production, more overhead is expensed under absorption costing due to fixed overhead carried over from the prior inventory. If sales increase over production, more than one period's overhead is recognized as expense. Accordingly, if the increase in overhead expensed is greater than the contribution margin of the increased units sold, profit may be lower with an increased level of sales.
    Answer (A) is incorrect because profit is a function of both sales and production, so it will not always move in the same direction as sales. Answer (B) is incorrect because profit is a function of both sales and production, so it will not always move in the same direction as sales. Answer (D) is incorrect because decreased output will increase the unit cost of items sold. Fixed overhead per unit will increase.

**58.** Which method of inventory costing treats direct manufacturing costs and manufacturing overhead costs, both variable and fixed, as inventoriable costs?

    A. Direct costing.

    B. Variable costing.

    C. Absorption costing.

    D. Conversion costing.

Answer (C) is correct. *(CMA, adapted)*
    **REQUIRED:** The method of inventory costing that treats direct manufacturing costs and all manufacturing overhead as inventoriable.
    **DISCUSSION:** Absorption (full) costing considers all manufacturing costs to be inventoriable as product costs. These costs include variable and fixed manufacturing costs, whether direct or indirect. The alternative to absorption is known as variable (direct) costing.
    Answer (A) is incorrect because variable (direct) costing does not inventory fixed overhead. Answer (B) is incorrect because variable (direct) costing does not inventory fixed overhead. Answer (D) is incorrect because conversion costs include direct labor and overhead but not direct materials.

**59.** The difference between the sales price and total variable costs is

    A. Gross operating profit.

    B. Net profit.

    C. The breakeven point.

    D. The contribution margin.

Answer (D) is correct. *(CMA, adapted)*
    **REQUIRED:** The difference between sales price and total variable costs.
    **DISCUSSION:** The contribution margin is calculated by subtracting all variable costs from sales revenue. It represents the portion of sales that is available for covering fixed costs and profit.
    Answer (A) is incorrect because gross operating profit is the net result after deducting all manufacturing costs from sales, including both fixed and variable costs. Answer (B) is incorrect because net profit is the remainder after deducting from revenue all costs, both fixed and variable. Answer (C) is incorrect because the breakeven point is the level of sales that equals the sum of fixed and variable costs.

**60.** Which one of the following statements is true regarding absorption costing and variable costing?

    A. Overhead costs are treated in the same manner under both costing methods.

    B. If finished goods inventory increases, absorption costing results in higher income.

    C. Variable manufacturing costs are lower under variable costing.

    D. Gross margins are the same under both costing methods.

Answer (B) is correct. *(CMA, adapted)*
    **REQUIRED:** The true statement regarding absorption costing and variable costing.
    **DISCUSSION:** Under variable costing, inventories are charged only with the variable costs of production. Fixed manufacturing costs are expensed as period costs. Absorption costing charges to inventory all costs of production. If finished goods inventory increases, absorption costing results in higher income because it capitalizes some fixed costs that would have been expensed under variable costing. When inventory declines, variable costing results in higher income because some fixed costs capitalized under the absorption method in prior periods are expensed in the current period.
    Answer (A) is incorrect because fixed overhead is treated differently under the two methods. Answer (C) is incorrect because variable costs are the same under either method. Answer (D) is incorrect because gross margins will be different. Fixed factory overhead is expensed under variable costing and capitalized under the absorption method.

**61.** The contribution margin is the excess of revenues over

- A. Cost of goods sold.
- B. Manufacturing cost.
- C. Direct cost.
- D. All variable costs.

Answer (D) is correct.  *(CMA, adapted)*
   **REQUIRED:** The definition of the contribution margin.
   **DISCUSSION:** Contribution margin is the excess of revenues over all variable costs (including both manufacturing and nonmanufacturing variable costs) that vary with an output-related cost driver. The contribution margin equals the revenues that contribute toward covering the fixed costs and providing a net income.
   Answer (A) is incorrect because revenues minus cost of goods sold is gross profit (margin). Answer (B) is incorrect because nonmanufacturing variable costs are also part of the calculation. Answer (C) is incorrect because a direct cost is a cost that can be feasibly associated with a single cost object.

**62.** The costing method that is properly classified for both external and internal reporting purposes is

|   | External Reporting | Internal Reporting |
|---|---|---|
| A. Activity-based costing | No | Yes |
| B. Job-order costing | No | Yes |
| C. Variable costing | No | Yes |
| D. Process costing | No | No |

Answer (C) is correct.  *(CMA, adapted)*
   **REQUIRED:** The costing method that is properly classified for both internal and external reporting purposes.
   **DISCUSSION:** Activity-based costing, job-order costing, process costing, and standard costing can all be used for both internal and external purposes. Variable costing is not acceptable under GAAP for external reporting purposes.
   Answer (A) is incorrect because ABC is appropriate for external as well as internal purposes. Answer (B) is incorrect because job-order costing is acceptable for external reporting purposes. Answer (D) is incorrect because process costing is acceptable for external reporting purposes.

**63.** Absorption costing and variable costing are two different methods of assigning costs to units produced. Of the 4 cost items listed below, identify the one that is not correctly accounted for as a product cost.

|   | Part of Product Cost Under | |
|---|---|---|
|   | Absorption Costing | Variable Costing |
| A. Manufacturing supplies | Yes | Yes |
| B. Insurance on factory | Yes | No |
| C. Direct labor cost | Yes | Yes |
| D. Packaging and shipping costs | Yes | Yes |

Answer (D) is correct.  *(CMA, adapted)*
   **REQUIRED:** The cost not correctly accounted for.
   **DISCUSSION:** Under absorption costing, all manufacturing costs, both fixed and variable, are treated as product costs. Under variable costing, only variable costs of manufacturing are inventoried as product costs. Fixed manufacturing costs are expensed as period costs. Packaging and shipping costs are not product costs under either method because they are incurred after the goods have been manufactured. Instead, they are included in selling and administrative expenses for the period.
   Answer (A) is incorrect because manufacturing supplies are variable costs inventoried under both methods. Answer (B) is incorrect because factory insurance is a fixed manufacturing cost inventoried under absorption costing but written off as a period cost under variable costing. Answer (C) is incorrect because direct labor cost is a product cost under both methods.

**64.** Jansen, Inc. pays bonuses to its managers based on operating income. The company uses absorption costing, and overhead is applied on the basis of direct labor hours. To increase bonuses, Jansen's managers may do all of the following except

- A. Produce those products requiring the most direct labor.
- B. Defer expenses such as maintenance to a future period.
- C. Increase production schedules independent of customer demands.
- D. Decrease production of those items requiring the most direct labor.

Answer (D) is correct.  *(CMA, adapted)*
   **REQUIRED:** The action that will not increase bonuses based on operating income.
   **DISCUSSION:** Under an absorption costing system, income can be manipulated by producing more products than are sold because more fixed manufacturing overhead will be allocated to the ending inventory. When inventory increases, some fixed costs are capitalized rather than expensed. Decreasing production, however, will result in lower income because more of the fixed manufacturing overhead will be expensed.
   Answer (A) is incorrect because producing more of the products requiring the most direct labor will permit more fixed overhead to be capitalized in the inventory account. Answer (B) is incorrect because deferring expenses such as maintenance will increase income in the current period (but may result in long-range losses caused by excessive down-time). Answer (C) is incorrect because increasing production without a concurrent increase in demand applies more fixed costs to inventory.

Questions 65 and 66 are based on the following information. A manufacturer at the end of its fiscal year recorded the data below:

| | |
|---|---|
| Prime cost | $800,000 |
| Variable manufacturing overhead | 100,000 |
| Fixed manufacturing overhead | 160,000 |
| Variable selling and other expenses | 80,000 |
| Fixed selling and other expenses | 40,000 |

**65.** If the manufacturer uses variable costing, the inventoriable costs for the fiscal year are

A. $800,000

B. $900,000

C. $980,000

D. $1,060,000

Answer (B) is correct. *(CMA, adapted)*
   **REQUIRED:** The inventoriable costs using the variable costing method.
   **DISCUSSION:** The only costs capitalized are the variable costs of manufacturing. Prime costs (direct materials and direct labor) are variable.

| | |
|---|---|
| Prime costs (direct materials and direct labor) | $800,000 |
| Variable manufacturing overhead | 100,000 |
| Total inventoriable costs | $900,000 |

   Answer (A) is incorrect because $800,000 equals only the prime costs. Answer (C) is incorrect because $980,000 includes the variable selling and other expenses. Answer (D) is incorrect because $1,060,000 equals inventoriable costs under absorption costing.

**66.** Using absorption (full) costing, inventoriable costs are

A. $800,000

B. $900,000

C. $1,060,000

D. $1,180,000

Answer (C) is correct. *(CMA, adapted)*
   **REQUIRED:** The inventoriable costs using the absorption costing method.
   **DISCUSSION:** The absorption method is required for financial statements prepared according to GAAP. It charges all costs of production to inventories. The prime costs of $800,000, variable manufacturing overhead of $100,000, and the fixed manufacturing overhead of $160,000 are included. They total $1,060,000.
   Answer (A) is incorrect because $800,000 equals only prime costs. Answer (B) is incorrect because $900,000 equals inventoriable costs under variable costing. Answer (D) is incorrect because $1,180,000 includes the fixed and variable selling and other expenses.

Questions 67 through 73 are based on the following information.

Valyn Corporation employs an absorption costing system for internal reporting purposes; however, the company is considering using variable costing. Data regarding Valyn's planned and actual operations for the calendar year are presented below.

|  | Planned Activity | Actual Activity |
|---|---|---|
| Beginning finished goods inventory in units | 35,000 | 35,000 |
| Sales in units | 140,000 | 125,000 |
| Production in units | 140,000 | 130,000 |

The planned per-unit cost figures shown in the next schedule were based on the estimated production and sale of 140,000 units for the year. Valyn uses a predetermined manufacturing overhead rate for applying manufacturing overhead to its product; thus, a combined manufacturing overhead rate of $9.00 per unit was employed for absorption costing purposes. Any over- or underapplied manufacturing overhead is closed to the cost of goods sold account at the end of the reporting year.

| | | Planned Costs | | Incurred |
|---|---|---|---|---|
| | | Per Unit | Total | Costs |
| Direct materials | | $12.00 | $1,680,000 | $1,560,000 |
| Direct labor | | 9.00 | 1,260,000 | 1,170,000 |
| Variable manufacturing overhead | | 4.00 | 560,000 | 520,000 |
| Fixed manufacturing overhead | | 5.00 | 700,000 | 715,000 |
| Variable selling expenses | | 8.00 | 1,120,000 | 1,000,000 |
| Fixed selling expenses | | 7.00 | 980,000 | 980,000 |
| Variable administrative expenses | | 2.00 | 280,000 | 250,000 |
| Fixed administrative expenses | | 3.00 | 420,000 | 425,000 |
| Total | | $50.00 | $7,000,000 | $6,620,000 |

The beginning finished goods inventory for absorption costing purposes was valued at the previous year's planned unit manufacturing cost, which was the same as the current year's planned unit manufacturing cost. There are no work-in-process inventories at either the beginning or the end of the year. The planned and actual unit selling price for the current year was $70.00 per unit.

**67.** The value of Valyn Corporation's actual ending finished goods inventory on the absorption costing basis was

A. $900,000

B. $1,200,000

C. $1,220,000

D. $1,350,000

Answer (B) is correct. *(CMA, adapted)*
**REQUIRED:** The actual finished goods ending inventory using absorption costing.
**DISCUSSION:** Under the absorption method, unit cost is $30 ($12 direct materials + $9 direct labor + $4 variable overhead + $5 fixed overhead). Given beginning inventory of 35,000 units, the ending inventory equals 40,000 units (35,000 BI + 130,000 produced – 125,000 sold). Hence, ending inventory was $1,200,000 (40,000 units × $30).

**68.** Valyn Corporation's total fixed costs expensed this year on the absorption costing basis were

A. $2,095,000

B. $2,120,000

C. $2,055,000

D. $2,030,000

Answer (A) is correct. *(CMA, adapted)*
**REQUIRED:** The total fixed costs on the absorption costing basis.
**DISCUSSION:** Under the absorption method, all selling and administrative fixed costs are charged to the current period. Accordingly, $980,000 of selling expenses and $425,000 of actual fixed administrative expenses were expensed during the year. The fixed manufacturing costs must be calculated after giving consideration to the increase in inventory during the period (some fixed costs were capitalized) and to the underapplied overhead. The beginning finished goods inventory included 35,000 units, each of which had absorbed $5 of fixed manufacturing overhead. Each unit produced during the year also absorbed $5 of fixed manufacturing overhead. Given that 125,000 of those units were sold, cost of goods sold was debited for $625,000 of fixed overhead (125,000 units × $5). At year-end, the underapplied overhead was also added to cost of goods sold. Because production was expected to be 140,000 units, the overhead application rate for the $700,000 of planned fixed manufacturing overhead was $5 per unit. Only 130,000 units were manufactured. Hence, $650,000 (130,000 units × $5) of overhead was applied to units in process. Because inventory increased from 35,000 to 40,000 units (see question 67), $25,000 (5,000-unit increase × $5) of the applied fixed manufacturing overhead for the period was inventoried, not expensed. Actual overhead was $715,000, so the underapplied overhead was $65,000 ($715,000 – $650,000). This amount was charged to cost of goods sold at year-end. The total of the fixed costs expensed was therefore $2,095,000 ($980,000 selling expenses + $425,000 administrative expenses + $625,000 standard manufacturing overhead costs of units sold + $65,000 underapplied overhead).

**69.** The value of Valyn Corporation's actual ending finished goods inventory on the variable costing basis was

- A. $1,400,000
- B. $1,125,000
- C. $1,000,000
- D. $750,000

Answer (C) is correct. *(CMA, adapted)*
  **REQUIRED:** The actual finished goods ending inventory using variable costing.
  **DISCUSSION:** Using variable costing, the unit cost of ending inventory is $25 ($12 direct materials + $9 direct labor + $4 variable overhead). Given beginning inventory of 35,000 units, the ending inventory equals 40,000 units (35,000 BI + 130,000 produced – 125,000 sold). Thus, ending inventory was $1,000,000 (40,000 units × $25).

**70.** Valyn Corporation's absorption costing operating income was

- A. Higher than variable costing operating income because actual production exceeded actual sales.
- B. Lower than variable costing operating income because actual production exceeded actual sales.
- C. Lower than variable costing operating income because actual production was less than planned production.
- D. Lower than variable costing operating income because actual sales were less than planned sales.

Answer (A) is correct. *(CMA, adapted)*
  **REQUIRED:** The true statement comparing absorption costing and variable costing income.
  **DISCUSSION:** Absorption costing results in a higher income figure than variable costing whenever production exceeds sales because absorption costing capitalizes some fixed factory overhead as part of inventory. These costs are expensed during the period incurred under variable costing. Consequently, variable costing recognizes greater expenses and lower income when production exceeds sales. The reverse is true when sales exceed production. In that case, the absorption method results in a lower income because some fixed costs of previous periods absorbed by the beginning inventory are expensed in the current period as cost of goods sold. Variable costing income is never burdened with fixed costs of previous periods.
  Answer (B) is incorrect because an increase in inventory results in a higher income under absorption costing. Answer (C) is incorrect because the important relationship is between actual production and actual sales, not between actual and planned production. Answer (D) is incorrect because planned sales do not determine actual income.

**71.** Valyn Corporation's actual manufacturing contribution margin calculated on the variable costing basis was

- A. $4,375,000
- B. $4,935,000
- C. $4,910,000
- D. $5,625,000

Answer (D) is correct. *(CMA, adapted)*
  **REQUIRED:** The actual contribution margin on the variable costing basis.
  **DISCUSSION:** At $70 per unit, actual sales revenue was $8,750,000 for 125,000 units. Actual variable costs of manufacturing were $25 per unit ($12 + $9 + $4). The unit costs incurred for the actual production level of 130,000 units were the same as the unit costs for a planned production level of 140,000 units. These unit costs were the same for units manufactured in both the current and previous year. For example, total planned direct materials cost for 140,000 units was $1,680,000, or $12 per unit. The incurred unit cost was also $12 ($1,560,000 ÷ 130,000 units). Thus, total variable manufacturing cost was $3,125,000 (125,000 units × $25). Consequently, manufacturing contribution margin was $5,625,000 ($8,750,000 – $3,125,000).

**72.** The difference between Valyn Corporation's operating income calculated on the absorption costing basis and calculated on the variable costing basis was

- A. $65,000
- B. $25,000
- C. $40,000
- D. $90,000

Answer (B) is correct. *(CMA, adapted)*
  **REQUIRED:** The difference between absorption costing and variable costing income.
  **DISCUSSION:** The difference is caused by the capitalization of some of the fixed manufacturing overhead. When inventories increase during the period, the absorption method capitalizes that overhead and transfers it to future periods. The variable costing method expenses it in the current period. Inventories increased by 5,000 units during the period, and each of those units would have included $5 of fixed manufacturing overhead under absorption costing. Accordingly, $25,000 of fixed manufacturing overhead would have been capitalized. Recognizing $25,000 of fixed costs in the balance sheet instead of the income statement results in a $25,000 difference in income between the two costing methods.

**73.** Refer to the information on the preceding page(s). The total variable cost currently expensed by Valyn Corporation on the variable costing basis was

A. $4,375,000

B. $4,500,000

C. $4,325,000

D. $4,550,000

Answer (A) is correct.  *(CMA, adapted)*
  **REQUIRED:** The total variable cost expensed under the variable costing method.
  **DISCUSSION:** The unit variable manufacturing cost was $25 ($12 direct materials + $9 direct labor + $4 variable overhead).  Other variable costs included selling expenses ($8 per unit) and administrative expenses ($2 per unit).  The unit selling and administrative costs actually incurred for sales of 125,000 units were the same as the planned unit costs.  For example, actual unit variable selling expense was $8 ($1,000,000 ÷ 125,000 units sold), which equaled the planned unit cost.  Thus, total unit variable cost was $35 ($25 + $8 + $2).  The total expensed was $4,375,000 (125,000 units sold × $35).

---

Questions 74 and 75 are based on the following information.  Osawa, Inc. planned and actually manufactured 200,000 units of its single product in its first year of operations.  Variable manufacturing costs were $30 per unit of product.  Planned and actual fixed manufacturing costs were $600,000, and selling and administrative costs totaled $400,000.  Osawa sold 120,000 units of product at a selling price of $40 per unit.

---

**74.** Osawa's operating income using absorption (full) costing is

A. $200,000

B. $440,000

C. $600,000

D. $840,000

Answer (B) is correct.  *(CMA, adapted)*
  **REQUIRED:** Operating income under absorption costing.
  **DISCUSSION:** Absorption costing net income is computed as follows:

| | | |
|---|---:|---:|
| Sales (120,000 units × $40) | | $4,800,000 |
| Variable production costs | | |
| (200,000 units × $30) | $6,000,000 | |
| Fixed production costs | 600,000 | |
| Total production costs (200,000 units) | $6,600,000 | |
| Ending inventory (80,000 units × $33) | (2,640,000) | |
| | | |
| Cost of goods sold | | (3,960,000) |
| Gross profit | | $ 840,000 |
| Selling and administrative expenses | | (400,000) |
| Operating income | | $ 440,000 |

  Answer (A) is incorrect because $200,000 is the operating income under variable costing.  Answer (C) is incorrect because $600,000 is the operating income that results from capitalizing $240,000 fixed manufacturing costs and $160,000 of selling and administrative costs (the $160,000 is incorrect as all selling and administrative costs should be expensed).  Answer (D) is incorrect because $840,000 is the gross profit under absorption costing, i.e., before selling and administrative expenses.

**75.** Osawa's operating income for the year using variable costing is

A. $200,000

B. $440,000

C. $800,000

D. $600,000

Answer (A) is correct.  *(CMA, adapted)*
  **REQUIRED:** The operating income under variable costing.
  **DISCUSSION:** The contribution margin from manufacturing (sales – variable costs) is $10 ($40 – $30) per unit sold, or $1,200,000 (120,000 units × $10).  The fixed costs of manufacturing ($600,000) and selling and administrative costs ($400,000) are deducted from the contribution margin to arrive at an operating income of $200,000.  The difference between the absorption income of $440,000 and the $200,000 of variable costing income is attributable to capitalization of the fixed manufacturing costs under the absorption method.  Because 40% of the goods produced are still in inventory (80,000 ÷ 200,000), 40% of the $600,000 in fixed costs, or $240,000, was capitalized under the absorption method.  That amount was expensed under the variable costing method.
  Answer (B) is incorrect because $440,000 is the operating income under absorption costing.  Answer (C) is incorrect because $800,000 is the operating income if fixed costs of manufacturing are not deducted.  Answer (D) is incorrect because $600,000 is the operating income that results from capitalizing 40% of both fixed manufacturing costs and selling and administrative costs.

Questions 76 and 77 are based on the following information. The following is taken from Fortech Company's records for the current fiscal year ended November 30:

| | |
|---|---|
| Direct materials used | $300,000 |
| Direct labor | 100,000 |
| Variable manufacturing overhead | 50,000 |
| Fixed manufacturing overhead | 80,000 |
| Selling and admin. costs--variable | 40,000 |
| Selling and admin. costs--fixed | 20,000 |

**76.** If Fortech Company uses variable costing, the inventoriable costs for the fiscal year are

A. $400,000

B. $450,000

C. $490,000

D. $530,000

Answer (B) is correct. *(CMA, adapted)*
**REQUIRED:** The inventoriable costs using the variable costing method.
**DISCUSSION:** Under variable costing, the only costs that are capitalized are the variable costs of manufacturing. These include

| | |
|---|---|
| Direct materials used | $300,000 |
| Direct labor | 100,000 |
| Variable manufacturing overhead | 50,000 |
| Total inventoriable costs | $450,000 |

Answer (A) is incorrect because $400,000 does not include $50,000 of variable manufacturing overhead. Answer (C) is incorrect because the $40,000 of variable selling and administrative costs should not be included in the inventoriable costs. Answer (D) is incorrect because $530,000 is the inventoriable cost under absorption (full) costing.

**77.** Using absorption (full) costing, inventoriable costs are

A. $400,000

B. $450,000

C. $530,000

D. $590,000

Answer (C) is correct. *(CMA, adapted)*
**REQUIRED:** The inventoriable costs using the absorption costing method.
**DISCUSSION:** The absorption method is required for financial statements prepared according to GAAP. It charges all costs of production to inventories. The variable cost of materials of $300,000, direct labor of $100,000, variable manufacturing overhead of $50,000, and the fixed manufacturing overhead of $80,000 are included. They total $530,000.
Answer (A) is incorrect because $400,000 does not include $80,000 of fixed manufacturing overhead and $50,000 of variable manufacturing overhead. Answer (B) is incorrect because $450,000 is the inventoriable cost under variable costing. Answer (D) is incorrect because $590,000 includes the fixed and variable selling and administrative costs.

## 2.8 Joint Product and By-Product Costing

**78.** Joint costs are useful for

A. Setting the selling price of a product.

B. Determining whether to continue producing an item.

C. Evaluating management by means of a responsibility reporting system.

D. Determining inventory cost for accounting purposes.

**Answer (D) is correct.** *(CIA, adapted)*
**REQUIRED:** The usefulness of joint costs in cost accounting.
**DISCUSSION:** Joint costs are useful for inventory costing when two or more identifiable products emerge from a common production process. The joint costs of production must be allocated on some basis, such as relative sales value.
Answer (A) is incorrect because items such as additional processing costs, competitive conditions in sales markets, and the relative contribution margins of all products derived from the common process must be considered in setting selling prices. Answer (B) is incorrect because items such as additional processing costs, competitive conditions in sales markets, and the relative contribution margins of all products derived from the common process must be considered in determining whether to continue producing an item. Answer (C) is incorrect because management of one department may have no control over joint costs.

**79.** In joint-product costing and analysis, which one of the following costs is relevant when deciding the point at which a product should be sold to maximize profits?

A. Separable costs after the split-off point.

B. Joint costs to the split-off point.

C. Sales salaries for the period when the units were produced.

D. Purchase costs of the materials required for the joint products.

**Answer (A) is correct.** *(CMA, adapted)*
**REQUIRED:** The cost relevant to deciding when a joint product should be sold.
**DISCUSSION:** Joint products are created from processing a common input. Joint costs are incurred prior to the split-off point and cannot be identified with a particular joint product. As a result, joint costs are irrelevant to the timing of sale. However, separable costs incurred after the split-off point are relevant because, if incremental revenues exceed the separable costs, products should be processed further, not sold at the split-off point.
Answer (B) is incorrect because joint costs have no effect on the decision as to when to sell a product. Answer (C) is incorrect because sales salaries for the production period do not affect the decision. Answer (D) is incorrect because purchase costs are joint costs.

Questions 80 and 81 are based on the following information.

Petro-Chem, Inc. is a small company that acquires high-grade crude oil from low-volume production wells owned by individuals and small partnerships. The crude oil is processed in a single refinery into Two Oil, Six Oil, and impure distillates. Petro-Chem does not have the technology or capacity to process these products further and sells most of its output each month to major refineries. There were no beginning inventories of finished goods or work-in-process on November 1. The production costs and output of Petro-Chem for November are in the right column.

| | |
|---|---|
| Crude oil acquired and placed in production | $5,000,000 |
| Direct labor and related costs | 2,000,000 |
| Manufacturing overhead | 3,000,000 |
| Production and sales | |

- Two Oil, 300,000 barrels produced; 80,000 barrels sold at $20 each.
- Six Oil, 240,000 barrels produced; 120,000 barrels sold at $30 each.
- Distillates, 120,000 barrels produced and sold at $15 per barrel.

**80.** The portion of the joint production costs assigned to Six Oil based upon physical output would be

A. $3,636,000

B. $3,750,000

C. $1,818,000

D. $7,500,000

Answer (A) is correct. *(CMA, adapted)*

**REQUIRED:** The joint production costs assigned to Six Oil based on physical output.

**DISCUSSION:** The total production costs incurred are $10,000,000, consisting of crude oil of $5,000,000, direct labor of $2,000,000, and manufacturing overhead of $3,000,000. The total physical output was 660,000 barrels, consisting of 300,000 barrels of Two Oil, 240,000 barrels of Six Oil, and 120,000 barrels of distillates. Thus, the allocation (rounded) is $3,636,000 {[240,000 ÷ (300,000 + 240,000 + 120,000)] × $10,000,000}.

Answer (B) is incorrect because $3,750,000 is based on the physical quantity of units sold, not units produced. Answer (C) is incorrect because $1,818,000 is the amount that would be assigned to distillates. Answer (D) is incorrect because Six Oil does not compose 75% of the total output in barrels.

**81.** The portion of the joint production costs assigned to Two Oil based upon the relative sales value of output would be

A. $4,800,000

B. $4,000,000

C. $2,286,000

D. $2,500,000

Answer (B) is correct. *(CMA, adapted)*

**REQUIRED:** The joint production costs assigned to Two Oil based on relative sales value.

**DISCUSSION:** The total production costs incurred are $10,000,000, consisting of crude oil of $5,000,000, direct labor of $2,000,000, and manufacturing overhead of $3,000,000. The total value of the output is as follows:

| | |
|---|---|
| Two Oil (300,000 barrels × $20) | $ 6,000,000 |
| Six Oil (240,000 barrels × $30) | 7,200,000 |
| Distillates (120,000 barrels × $15) | 1,800,000 |
| Total sales value | $15,000,000 |

Because Two Oil composes 40% of the total sales value ($6,000,000 ÷ $15,000,000), it will be assigned 40% of the $10,000,000 of joint costs, or $4,000,000.

Answer (A) is incorrect because $4,800,000 is the amount that would be assigned to Six Oil. Answer (C) is incorrect because $2,286,000 is based on the relative sales value of units sold. Answer (D) is incorrect because $2,500,000 is based on the physical quantity of barrels sold.

**82.** The principal disadvantage of using the physical quantity method of allocating joint costs is that

A. Costs assigned to inventories may have no relationship to value.

B. Physical quantities may be difficult to measure.

C. Additional processing costs affect the allocation base.

D. Joint costs, by definition, should not be separated on a unit basis.

Answer (A) is correct.  *(CMA, adapted)*
**REQUIRED:**  The principal disadvantage of using the physical quantity method of allocating joint costs.
**DISCUSSION:**  Joint costs are most often assigned on the basis of relative sales values or net realizable values.  Basing allocations on physical quantities, such as pounds, gallons, etc., is usually not desirable because the costs assigned may have no relationship to value.  When large items have low selling prices and small items have high selling prices, the large items might always sell at a loss when physical quantities are used to allocate joint costs.
Answer (B) is incorrect because physical quantities are usually easy to measure.  Answer (C) is incorrect because additional processing costs will have no more effect on the allocation of joint costs based on physical quantities than any other base.  Answer (D) is incorrect because the purpose of allocating joint costs, under any method, is to separate such costs on a unit basis.

Questions 83 through 85 are based on the following information.

Travis Petroleum is a small company that acquires crude oil and manufactures it into three intermediate products, differing only in grade.  The products are Grade One, Grade Two, and Grade Three.  No beginning inventories of finished goods or work-in-process existed on November 1.  The production costs for November were as follows (assume separable costs were negligible):

| Crude oil acquired and put | |
|---|---|
| into production | $4,000,000 |
| Direct labor and related costs | 2,000,000 |
| Manufacturing overhead | 3,000,000 |

The output and sales for November were as follows:

| | Grade One | Grade Two | Grade Three |
|---|---|---|---|
| Barrels produced | 300,000 | 240,000 | 120,000 |
| Barrels sold | 80,000 | 120,000 | 120,000 |
| Prices per barrel sold | $30 | $40 | $50 |

**83.** The portion of the joint production costs assigned to Grade Two based upon physical output is (rounded to the nearest thousand dollars)

A. $3,273,000

B. $3,375,000

C. $1,636,000

D. $3,512,000

Answer (A) is correct.  *(Publisher)*
**REQUIRED:**  The joint production costs assigned.
**DISCUSSION:**  Total joint production costs incurred were $9,000,000 ($4,000,000 + $2,000,000 + $3,000,000).  The total physical output was 660,000 barrels (300,000 barrels of Grade One + 240,000 barrels of Grade Two + 120,000 barrels of Grade Three).  Thus, on a physical output basis, Grade Two should be allocated $3,273,000 [(240,000 ÷ 660,000) × $9,000,000].
Answer (B) is incorrect because $3,375,000 is based on the physical quantity of units sold, not units produced.  Answer (C) is incorrect because $1,636,000 is the amount assigned to Grade Three.  Answer (D) is incorrect because $3,512,000 is the amount assigned to Grade Two if the relative sales value method is used.

**84.** The portion of the joint production costs assigned to Grade One based upon the relative sales value of output is (rounded to the nearest thousand dollars)

A. $3,512,000

B. $3,293,000

C. $1,636,000

D. $4,091,000

Answer (B) is correct.  *(Publisher)*
**REQUIRED:**  The joint production costs assigned.
**DISCUSSION:**  Total joint production costs incurred were $9,000,000, ($4,000,000 + $2,000,000 + $3,000,000).  The sales values of the three products are as follows:

| | |
|---|---|
| Grade One (300,000 barrels × $30) | $  9,000,000 |
| Grade Two (240,000 barrels × $40) | 9,600,000 |
| Grade Three (120,000 barrels × $50) | 6,000,000 |
| Total sales value | $24,600,000 |

Consequently, Grade One should be assigned joint costs of $3,293,000 [($9,000,000 ÷ $24,600,000) × $9,000,000].
Answer (A) is incorrect because $3,512,000 is the amount assigned to Grade Two.  Answer (C) is incorrect because $1,636,000 is based on the relative sales values of units sold, not units produced.  Answer (D) is incorrect because $4,091,000 is based on the physical quantity of barrels produced.

**85.** Based on the relative sales values of output, cost of the ending inventory of Grade Two is

A. $3,512,000

B. $1,756,000

C. $1,636,000

D. $3,375,000

Answer (B) is correct. *(Publisher)*
**REQUIRED:** The value of the ending inventory.
**DISCUSSION:** The total sales value of the oil produced was determined in the preceding question to be $24,600,000. The total sales value of Grade Two was determined to be $9,600,000. Accordingly, costs assigned to Grade Two on a relative sales value basis (rounded) equal $3,512,000 [($4,000,000 + $3,000,000 + $2,000,000) × ($9,600,000 ÷ $24,600,000)]. Thus, the value of the ending inventory of Grade Two should be $1,756,000 [120,000 barrels in EI × ($3,512,000 ÷ 240,000 barrels produced)].
Answer (A) is incorrect because $3,512,000 is the total joint cost assigned to the output of Grade Two. Answer (C) is incorrect because $1,636,000 is based on the relative sales values of units sold. Answer (D) is incorrect because $3,375,000 is the total joint cost assigned to the output of Grade Two based on the relative physical volume of units sold.

Questions 86 and 87 are based on the following information. A manufacturing company uses a joint production process that produces three products at the split-off point. Joint production costs during April were $720,000. The company uses the sales value method for allocating joint costs. Product information for April was as follows:

| | Product | | |
| --- | --- | --- | --- |
| | R | S | T |
| Units produced | 2,500 | 5,000 | 7,500 |
| Units sold | 2,000 | 6,000 | 7,000 |
| Sales prices: | | | |
| At split-off | $100 | $80 | $20 |
| After further processing | $150 | $115 | $30 |
| Costs to process after split-off | $150,000 | $150,000 | $100,000 |

**86.** Assume that all three products are main products and that they can be sold at the split-off point or processed further, whichever is economically beneficial to the company. What is the total cost of Product S in April if joint cost allocation is based on sales value at split-off?

A. $375,000

B. $390,000

C. $510,000

D. $571,463

Answer (C) is correct. *(CIA, adapted)*
**REQUIRED:** The total cost of Product S in April.
**DISCUSSION:** Total sales value at split-off is $800,000 [(2,500 × $100) + (5,000 × $80) + (7,500 × $20)]. Product S accounts for 50% (5,000 × $80 = $400,000) of the sales value and therefore $360,000 ($720,000 × 50%) of the joint costs. The total cost of Product S is $510,000 ($360,000 allocated costs + $150,000 differential costs).
Answer (A) is incorrect because $375,000 is the total cost of R. Answer (B) is incorrect because $390,000 is based on the physical units method of allocating the joint costs. Answer (D) is incorrect because $571,463 uses the sales value at split-off based on actual sales.

**87.** Assume that Product T is treated as a by-product and that the company accounts for the by-product at net realizable value as a reduction of joint cost. Assume also that Products S and T must be processed further before they can be sold. What is the total cost of Product R in April if joint cost allocation is based on net realizable values?

A. $220,370

B. $370,370

C. $374,630

D. $595,000

Answer (A) is correct. *(CIA, adapted)*
**REQUIRED:** The total cost of Product R for April.
**DISCUSSION:** The net realizable value (NRV) method is an appropriate method of allocation when products cannot be sold at split-off. Further processing of R, which is salable at split-off, is not economical because the cost of $150,000 exceeds the benefit [2,500 units × ($150 – $100) = $125,000]. Thus, R's NRV is $250,000 (2,500 units × $100 price at split-off). However, S and T must be processed further. S's NRV is $425,000 [(5,000 units × $115) – $150,000], and T's NRV is $125,000 [(7,500 units × $30) – $100,000]. Given that the NRV of T is a reduction of joint cost, the total joint cost to be allocated is therefore $595,000 ($720,000 – $125,000 NRV of T). Accordingly, based on the NRV method, the joint cost allocated to R is $220,370 {[$250,000 R's NRV ÷ ($250,000 R's NRV + $425,000 S's NRV)] × $595,000 allocable joint cost}. Because further processing of R is uneconomical, the total cost of R is $220,370.
Answer (B) is incorrect because $370,370 includes additional processing costs. Answer (C) is incorrect because $374,630 is the joint cost allocated to S. Answer (D) is incorrect because $595,000 is the allocable joint cost.

Questions 88 through 92 are based on the following information.

| | | |
|---|---|---|
| Atlas Foods produces the following three supplemental food products simultaneously through a refining process costing $93,000. | Alfa | 10,000 pounds of Alfa, a popular but relatively rare grain supplement having a caloric value of 4,400 calories per pound. |
| The joint products, Alfa and Betters, have a final selling price of $4 per pound and $10 per pound, respectively, after additional processing costs of $2 per pound of each product are incurred after the split-off point. Morefeed, a by-product, is sold at the split-off point for $3 per pound. | Betters | 5,000 pounds of Betters, a flavoring material high in carbohydrates with a caloric value of 11,200 calories per pound. |
| | Morefeed | 1,000 pounds of Morefeed, used as a cattle feed supplement with a caloric value of 1,000 calories per pound. |

**88.** Assuming Atlas Foods inventories Morefeed, the by-product, the joint cost to be allocated to Alfa using the net realizable value method is

A. $3,000

B. $30,000

C. $31,000

D. $60,000

Answer (B) is correct. *(CMA, adapted)*
**REQUIRED:** The joint cost allocated to Alfa based on net realizable values if the by-product is inventoried.
**DISCUSSION:** The NRV at split-off for each of the joint products must be determined. Given that Alfa has a $4 selling price and an additional $2 of processing costs, the value at the split-off is $2 per pound. The total value at split-off for 10,000 pounds is $20,000. Betters has a $10 selling price and an additional $2 of processing costs. Thus, the value at split-off is $8 per pound. The total value of 5,000 pounds of Betters is therefore $40,000. The 1,000 pounds of Morefeed has a split-off value of $3 per pound, or $3,000. Assuming that Morefeed (a by-product) is inventoried (recognized in the accounts when produced) and treated as a reduction of joint costs, the allocable joint cost is $90,000 ($93,000 – $3,000). (NOTE: Several other methods of accounting for by-products are possible.) The total net realizable value of the main products is $60,000 ($20,000 Alfa + $40,000 Betters). The allocation to Alfa is $30,000 [($20,000 ÷ $60,000) × $90,000].
Answer (A) is incorrect because $3,000 is the value of the by-product. Answer (C) is incorrect because $31,000 fails to adjust the joint processing cost for the value of the by-product. Answer (D) is incorrect because $60,000 is the amount allocated to Betters.

**89.** Assuming Atlas Foods inventories Morefeed, the by-product, the joint cost to be allocated to Alfa, using the physical quantity method is

A. $3,000

B. $30,000

C. $31,000

D. $60,000

Answer (D) is correct. *(CMA, adapted)*
**REQUIRED:** The joint cost allocated to Alfa based on the physical quantity method if the by-product is inventoried.
**DISCUSSION:** Joint cost is $93,000 and Morefeed has a split-off value of $3,000 (1,000 pounds × $3 split-off value per pound). Assuming the latter amount is treated as a reduction in joint cost, the allocable joint cost is $90,000. The total physical quantity (volume) of the two joint products is 15,000 pounds (10,000 Alfa + 5,000 Betters). Hence, $60,000 of the net joint costs [(10,000 ÷ 15,000) × $90,000] should be allocated to Alfa.
Answer (A) is incorrect because $3,000 is the value of the by-product. Answer (B) is incorrect because $30,000 is based on the net realizable value method. Answer (C) is incorrect because $31,000 is based on the net realizable value method and fails to adjust the joint processing cost for the value of the by-product.

**90.** Assuming Atlas Foods inventories Morefeed, the by-product, the joint cost to be allocated to Betters using the weighted-quantity method based on caloric value per pound is

A. $39,208

B. $39,600

C. $40,920

D. $50,400

Answer (D) is correct. *(CMA, adapted)*
**REQUIRED:** The joint cost allocated to Betters based on weighted quantities if the by-product is inventoried.
**DISCUSSION:** The net allocable joint cost is $90,000, assuming the value of Morefeed is inventoried and treated as a reduction in joint costs. The caloric value of Alfa is 44,000,000 (4,400 × 10,000 pounds), the caloric value of Betters is 56,000,000 (11,200 × 5,000 pounds), and the total is 100,000,000. Of this total volume, Alfa makes up 44% and Betters 56%. Thus, $50,400 ($90,000 × 56%) should be allocated to Betters.
Answer (A) is incorrect because $39,208 is the amount allocated to Alfa if the 1,000,000 calories attributable to Morefeed is included in the computation. Answer (B) is incorrect because $39,600 is the allocation to Alfa. Answer (C) is incorrect because $40,920 is the allocation to Alfa if the sales value of the by-product is not treated as a reduction of joint cost.

**91.** Assuming Atlas Foods inventories Morefeed, the by-product, and that it incurs no additional processing costs for Alfa and Betters, the joint cost to be allocated to Alfa using the gross market value method is

A. $36,000

B. $40,000

C. $41,333

D. $50,000

Answer (B) is correct. *(CMA, adapted)*
**REQUIRED:** The joint cost allocated to Alfa using the gross market value method if the by-product is inventoried.
**DISCUSSION:** The gross market value of Alfa is $40,000 (10,000 pounds × $4), Betters has a total gross value of $50,000 (5,000 pounds × $10), and Morefeed has a split-off value of $3,000. If the value of Morefeed is inventoried and treated as a reduction in joint cost, the allocable joint cost is $90,000 ($93,000 – $3,000). The total gross value of the two main products is $90,000 ($40,000 + $50,000). Of this total value, $40,000 should be allocated to Alfa [($40,000 ÷ $90,000) × $90,000].
Answer (A) is incorrect because $36,000 is based on 40%, not 4/9. Answer (C) is incorrect because $41,333 fails to adjust the joint cost by the value of the by-product. Answer (D) is incorrect because $50,000 is the joint cost allocated to Betters.

**92.** Assuming Atlas Foods does not inventory Morefeed, the by-product, the joint cost to be allocated to Betters using the net realizable value method is

A. $30,000

B. $31,000

C. $52,080

D. $62,000

Answer (D) is correct. *(CMA, adapted)*
**REQUIRED:** The joint cost allocated to Betters based on net realizable values if the by-product is not inventoried.
**DISCUSSION:** The NRV of Alfa is $20,000 [10,000 pounds × ($4 selling price – $2 additional processing costs)], and the NRV of Betters is $40,000 [5,000 pounds × ($10 selling price – $2 additional processing costs)]. If the joint cost is not adjusted for the value of the by-production, the amount allocated to Betters is $62,000 {[$40,000 ÷ ($20,000 + $40,000)] × $93,000}.
Answer (A) is incorrect because $30,000 is the amount allocated to Alfa when the by-product is inventoried. Answer (B) is incorrect because $31,000 is the amount allocated to Alfa when the by-product is not inventoried. Answer (C) is incorrect because $52,080 assumes that a weighting method using caloric value is used.

**93.** Lankip Company produces two main products and a by-product out of a joint process. The ratio of output quantities to input quantities of direct material used in the joint process remains consistent from month to month. Lankip has employed the physical-volume method to allocate joint production costs to the two main products. The net realizable value of the by-product is used to reduce the joint production costs before the joint costs are allocated to the main products. Data regarding Lankip's operations for the current month are presented in the chart below. During the month, Lankip incurred joint production costs of $2,520,000. The main products are not marketable at the split-off point and, thus, have to be processed further.

|  | First Main Product | Second Main Product | By-product |
|---|---|---|---|
| Monthly output in pounds | 90,000 | 150,000 | 60,000 |
| Selling price per pound | $30 | $14 | $2 |
| Separable process costs | $540,000 | $660,000 | |

The amount of joint production cost that Lankip would allocate to the Second Main Product by using the physical-volume method to allocate joint production costs would be

- A. $1,200,000
- B. $1,260,000
- C. $1,500,000
- D. $1,575,000

Answer (C) is correct. *(CMA, adapted)*
**REQUIRED:** The joint cost allocated to the Second Main Product based on physical volume.
**DISCUSSION:** The joint cost to be allocated is $2,400,000 [$2,520,000 total joint cost – (60,000 pounds of the by-product) × $2]. Accordingly, the joint cost to be allocated to the Second Main Product on a physical-volume basis is $1,500,000 {[150,000 pounds ÷ (90,000 pounds + 150,000 pounds) × $2,400,000]}.
Answer (A) is incorrect because $1,200,000 assumes that the by-product is charged with a portion of the net joint cost. Answer (B) is incorrect because $1,260,000 assumes that the by-product is charged with a portion of the gross joint cost. Answer (D) is incorrect because $1,575,000 does not deduct by-product NRV from the joint cost.

---

Use Gleim's *CMA Test Prep* for interactive testing with **over 2,000 additional multiple-choice questions!**

# STUDY UNIT THREE
# JOB-ORDER COSTING, OVERHEAD COSTS, AND SERVICE DEPARTMENT ALLOCATION

(12 pages of outline)

This study unit is the **second of three** on **cost management**. The relative weight assigned to this major topic in Part 2 of the exam is **25%** at **skill level C** (all six skill types required). The three study units are

Study Unit 2: Cost Management Terminology and Concepts
Study Unit 3: Job-Order Costing, Overhead Costs, and Service Department Allocation
Study Unit 4: Process Costing and Other Cost Accumulation Systems

The materials in this and the next study unit are heavily tested on the exam. Be prepared for many rigorous computational questions.

After studying the outlines and answering the multiple-choice questions in this study unit, you will have the skills necessary to address the following topics listed in the IMA's Learning Outcome Statements:

Part 2 – Section B.3. Accumulation systems

For the cost accumulation system identified (job-order costing), the candidate should be able to:

a. define the nature of the system, understand the cost flows of the system, and recognize its appropriate use
b. calculate inventory values and cost of goods sold
c. understand how to account for normal and abnormal spoilage
d. understand the strategic value of cost information regarding products and services, pricing, overhead allocations, and other issues
e. understand the benefits and limitations of each cost accumulation system

NOTE: Statements f. through k. are covered in Study Unit 4.

Part 2 – Section B.4. Overhead costs

The candidate should be able to:

a. demonstrate an understanding of the fixed and variable nature of overhead expenses
b. determine the appropriate time frame for both variable and fixed overhead expenses
c. demonstrate an understanding that overhead rates can be determined in a variety of ways, e.g., plant-wide rates, departmental rates, and individual cost driver rates and describe the benefits and limitations of each of these methods
d. identify the components of variable overhead expense
e. determine the appropriate allocation base for variable overhead expenses
f. calculate the per unit variable overhead expense
g. identify the components of fixed overhead expense
h. identify the appropriate allocation base for fixed overhead expense and demonstrate an understanding that because the allocation base is generally variable (e.g., direct labor hours), fixed overhead is often over- or under-applied

i.    calculate the fixed overhead application rate

j.    demonstrate an understanding of overhead control accounts, overhead allocation accounts, and the expensing of over- or under-applied overhead expenses

NOTE:  Statements k. and l. are covered in Study Unit 4.

m.    demonstrate an understanding of the need to allocate the cost of service departments such as Human Resources or Information Technology to production departments

n.    understand and use the direct method, the reciprocal method, and the step-down method to allocate service department costs

## 3.1 JOB-ORDER COSTING

1.    Job-order costing is concerned with **accumulating costs by specific job**.

    a.    This method is appropriate when producing products with individual characteristics or when identifiable groupings are possible, e.g., batches of certain styles or types of furniture.

    b.    Units (jobs) should be dissimilar enough to warrant the special record keeping required by job-order costing.

2.    The accumulation of costs in a job-order system follows the document flow, whether printed or electronic.

    a.    A **sales order** is received from a customer requesting a product or special group of products.

    b.    The sales order is approved and a **production order** is issued.

    c.    The physical inputs required for the production process are obtained from suppliers.

| | | |
|---|---|---|
| Raw materials | $XXX | |
|     Accounts payable | | $XXX |

    d.    Production commences and three documents feed cost amounts into the costing system:

        1)    **Materials requisition forms** request **direct materials** to be pulled from the warehouse and sent to the production line.

| | | |
|---|---|---|
| Work-in-process -- Job 1015 | $XXX | |
|     Raw materials | | $XXX |

        2)    **Time tickets** track the **direct labor** that workers expend on various jobs.

| | | |
|---|---|---|
| Work-in-process -- Job 1015 | $XXX | |
|     Wages payable | | $XXX |

        3)    These two of the three major components of product cost (direct materials and direct labor) are charged to work-in-process using the **actual amounts** incurred.

    e.    Under job-order costing, the third component, **manufacturing overhead**, is charged using an **estimated rate**.

        1)    The application of an estimated overhead rate is necessary under job-order costing because the outputs are customized and the processes vary from period to period

            a)    Contrast this with the treatment of overhead under process costing in which actual overhead costs incurred are charged to work-in-process at the end of the period (see subunit 4.1).

        2)    As indirect costs are paid throughout the year, they are collected in the **manufacturing overhead control account**.

            a)    Note that work-in-process is not affected when actual overhead costs are incurred.

| | | |
|---|---|---|
| Manufacturing overhead control | $XXX | |
|     Property taxes payable | | $XXX |
| Manufacturing overhead control | $XXX | |
|     Prepaid insurance | | $XXX |
| Manufacturing overhead control | $XXX | |
|     Accumulated depreciation -- factory equipment | | $XXX |

        3)    Overhead costs are applied to ("absorbed" by) each job based on a **predetermined overhead application rate** for the year (see item 2. under subunit 3.2).

            a)    At the beginning of the year, an estimate is made of the total amount that will be spent for manufacturing overhead during that year.

            b)    This total is divided by the allocation base, such as direct labor hours or machine hours, to arrive at the application rate.

            c)    The amount applied equals the number of units of the allocation base used during the period times the application rate.

                i)    The credit is to manufacturing overhead applied, a contra-account for manufacturing overhead control.

| | | |
|---|---|---|
| Work-in-process -- Job 1015 | $XXX | |
|     Manufacturing overhead applied | | $XXX |

                ii)    By tracking applied overhead in a contra-account, the actual costs incurred during the period can always be determined by querying the balance in the manufacturing overhead control account.

            d)    At the end of each period, it can be determined whether overhead was over- or underapplied (see item 2.b. under subunit 3.2).

    f.    The amounts from the input documents are accumulated on **job-cost sheets**. These serve as a subsidiary ledger page for each job.

        1)    The total of all job-cost sheets will equal the balance in the general ledger work-in-process account.

3.    Output that does not meet the quality standards for salability is considered spoilage.

    a.    If the spoilage is the amount expected in the ordinary course of production, it is considered **normal spoilage.**

        1)    The accounting treatment is to include normal spoilage as a product cost.

        2)    This is accomplished by allowing the net cost of the spoilage to remain in the work-in-process account of the job that generated it.

            a)    If the normal spoilage is worthless and must be discarded, no entry is made.

            b)    If the normal spoilage can be sold, the entry is:

| | | |
|---|---|---|
| Spoiled inventory (at fair market value) | $XX | |
|     Work-in-process -- Job 1015 | | $XX |

b. If the spoilage is over and above the amount expected in the ordinary course of production, it is considered **abnormal spoilage**.

1) The accounting treatment is to highlight abnormal spoilage as a period cost so that management can address the deficiency that caused it.

2) This is accomplished by charging a loss account for the net cost of the spoilage.

a) If the abnormal spoilage is worthless and must be discarded, the entry is:

| | | |
|---|---|---|
| Loss from abnormal spoilage | | |
| (costs up to point of inspection) | $XX | |
| Work-in-process -- Job 1015 | | $XX |

b) If the abnormal spoilage can be sold, the entry is:

| | | |
|---|---|---|
| Spoiled inventory | $XX | |
| Loss from abnormal spoilage (difference) | XX | |
| Work-in-process -- Job 1015 | | |
| (costs up to point of inspection) | | $XX |

4. When a job order is completed, all the costs are transferred to finished goods.

| | | |
|---|---|---|
| Finished goods | $X,XXX | |
| Work-in-process -- Job 1015 | | $X,XXX |

5. When the output is sold, the appropriate portion of the cost is transferred to cost of goods sold.

| | | |
|---|---|---|
| Cost of goods sold | $X,XXX | |
| Finished goods | | $X,XXX |

6. The following diagram depicts the flow of cost accumulation in a job-order costing system:

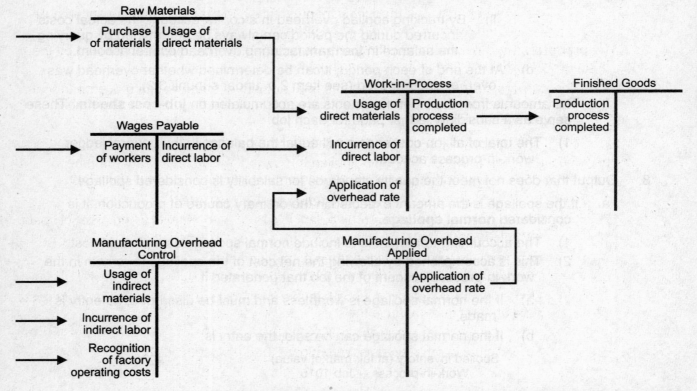

7. Stop and review! You have completed the outline for this subunit. Study multiple-choice questions 1 through 5 beginning on page 140.

## 3.2 OVERHEAD COSTS AND NORMAL COSTING

1. Whenever overhead is to be allocated, as in job-order costing and activity-based costing (see subunit 4.2), an appropriate **allocation base** must be chosen.

   a. In traditional cost accounting, allocation bases include direct labor hours, direct labor cost, machine hours, materials cost, and units of production.

   b. The crucial quality of an allocation base is that it be a **cost driver** of the costs in the pool to be allocated.

      1) Recall that a cost driver must capture a **cause-and-effect relationship** between the cost being allocated and the cost object to which the costs are being attached.

      2) Overhead is usually allocated to products based upon the **level of activity**.

         a) For example, if overhead is largely made up of machine maintenance, the activity base may be machine hours.

         b) In capital-intensive industries, the amount of overhead will probably be related more to machine hours than to either direct labor hours or direct labor cost.

         c) In labor-intensive industries, overhead is usually allocated on a labor activity base.

            i) If more overhead is incurred by the more highly skilled and paid employees, the overhead rate should be based upon direct labor cost rather than direct labor hours.

      3) Overhead is usually not allocated on the basis of units produced because of the lack of a cause-and-effect relationship.

         a) When only one product is manufactured, this method may be acceptable because all costs are to be charged to the single product.

2. The **predetermined overhead application rate** equals budgeted overhead divided by the budgeted activity level (measure of capacity).

   a. The **numerator** of the calculation is the total amount of manufacturing overhead that must be allocated for the period, i.e., the sum of indirect materials, indirect labor, depreciation, factory insurance, etc.

      1) The **denominator** is the allocation base.

   b. Inevitably, the overhead amounts applied throughout the year will vary from the amount actually incurred, which is only determinable once the job is complete.

      1) This variance is called **over- or underapplied overhead**.

      2) Overapplied overhead (a credit balance in overhead) results when product costs are overstated because the

         a) Activity level was higher than expected, or
         b) Actual overhead costs were lower than expected.

      3) Underapplied overhead (a debit balance in overhead) results when product costs are understated because the

         a) Activity level was lower than expected, or
         b) Actual overhead costs were higher than expected.

4) Over- and underapplied overhead is subject to one of two treatments:

a) If the variance is **immaterial**, it can be closed directly to cost of goods sold.

If overapplied:

| | |
|---|---|
| Manufacturing overhead applied | $XXX |
|     Cost of goods sold | $XXX |

If underapplied:

| | |
|---|---|
| Cost of goods sold | $XXX |
|     Manufacturing overhead applied | $XXX |

b) If the variance is **material**, it should be allocated based on the relative values of work-in-process, finished goods, and cost of goods sold.

If overapplied:

| | |
|---|---|
| Manufacturing overhead applied (balance) | $XXX |
|     Work-in-process (overapplied amount × allocation %) | $XXX |
|     Finished goods (overapplied amount × allocation %) | XXX |
|     Cost of goods sold (overapplied amount × allocation %) | XXX |
|     Manufacturing overhead control (balance) | XXX |

If underapplied:

| | |
|---|---|
| Manufacturing overhead applied (balance) | $XXX |
| Work-in-process (underapplied amount × allocation %) | XXX |
| Finished goods (underapplied amount × allocation %) | XXX |
| Cost of goods sold (underapplied amount × allocation %) | XXX |
|     Manufacturing overhead control (balance) | $XXX |

3. During times of low production, per-unit overhead charges will skyrocket. This leads to higher product costs during years of lower production and to distortions in the financial statements.

a. EXAMPLE: A manufacturing firm is expecting the following units of production and sales over a three-year period. Note that production is expected to fluctuate but sales are expected to be even:

| | Year 1 | Year 2 | Year 3 | Totals |
|---|---|---|---|---|
| Production | 10,000 | 6,000 | 8,000 | 24,000 |
| Sales | 7,000 | 7,000 | 7,000 | 21,000 |

Variable overhead costs are calculated at $1 per unit, and fixed overhead is projected to remain constant over the period:

| | Year 1 | Year 2 | Year 3 | Totals |
|---|---|---|---|---|
| Variable overhead cost | $10,000 | $6,000 | $8,000 | $24,000 |
| Fixed overhead cost | 20,000 | 20,000 | 20,000 | 60,000 |
| Total overhead cost | $30,000 | $26,000 | $28,000 | $84,000 |

Next, the overhead application rate for each year is calculated.

| | Year 1 | Year 2 | Year 3 |
|---|---|---|---|
| Estimated total overhead | $30,000 | $26,000 | $28,000 |
| Estimated production | $\dfrac{\$30,000}{10,000} = \$3.00$ | $\dfrac{\$26,000}{6,000} = \$4.33$ | $\dfrac{\$28,000}{8,000} = \$3.50$ |

These fluctuations in the applied overhead rate will lead to fluctuations in unit cost:

| | Year 1 | Year 2 | Year 3 |
|---|---|---|---|
| Direct materials | $ 3.00 | $ 3.00 | $ 3.00 |
| Direct labor | 4.00 | 4.00 | 4.00 |
| Manufacturing overhead | 3.00 | 4.33 | 3.50 |
| Total overhead cost | $10.00 | $11.33 | $10.50 |

The comparative income statements make clear the distorting effect:

| | Year 1 | Year 2 | Year 3 | Totals |
|---|---|---|---|---|
| Production: | | | | |
| From Year 1 | 7,000 | 3,000 | | |
| From Year 2 | | 4,000 | 2,000 | |
| From Year 3 | | | 5,000 | |
| Expected unit sales | 7,000 | 7,000 | 7,000 | |
| Expected selling price | × $12 | × $12 | × $12 | |
| Total expected sales | $84,000 | $84,000 | $84,000 | $252,000 |
| Cost of goods sold: | | | | |
| From Year 1 | $70,000 | $30,000 | | |
| From Year 2 | | 45,333 | $22,667 | |
| From Year 3 | | | 52,500 | |
| Total expected CGS | $70,000 | $75,333 | $75,167 | $220,500 |
| Gross margin | $14,000 | $ 8,667 | $ 8,833 | $ 31,500 |

Large fluctuations in gross margin are reported during a period when there was no fluctuation at all in the company's underlying cost structure.

b. To prevent these distortions in the financial statements, **normal costing** derives the overhead application rate by looking at several years at a time, not just one.

    1) EXAMPLE: Instead of using a different overhead application rate for each year, the company uses a single average figure for the period.

        a) The company expects to produce 24,000 units over three years.

        b) Dividing the fixed overhead for each year of $20,000 by an average of 8,000 units per year yields a fixed overhead application rate of $2.50.

        c) The new total overhead application rate per unit is $3.50 ($1.00 variable cost + $2.50 fixed cost).

        d) The new per-unit cost for all three years is thus $10.50 ($3.00 direct materials + $4.00 direct labor + $3.50 overhead application rate).

        e) The revised income statements prepared using a normalized overhead rate reveal the smoothing effect on gross margin:

| | Year 1 | Year 2 | Year 3 | Totals |
|---|---|---|---|---|
| Production: | | | | |
| From Year 1 | 7,000 | 3,000 | | |
| From Year 2 | | 4,000 | 2,000 | |
| From Year 3 | | | 5,000 | |
| Expected unit sales | 7,000 | 7,000 | 7,000 | |
| Expected selling price | × $12 | × $12 | × $12 | |
| Total expected sales | $84,000 | $84,000 | $84,000 | $252,500 |
| Cost of goods sold: | | | | |
| From Year 1 | $73,500 | $31,500 | | |
| From Year 2 | | 42,000 | $21,000 | |
| From Year 3 | | | 52,500 | |
| Total expected CGS | $73,500 | $73,500 | $73,500 | $220,500 |
| Gross margin | $10,500 | $10,500 | $10,500 | $ 31,500 |

c. **Extended normal costing** applies the use of a normalized rate to direct costs as well as to manufacturing overhead.

   d.   The following table summarizes the use of rates in the three costing methods described:

|  | Direct Materials | Direct Labor | Manufacturing Overhead |
|---|---|---|---|
| Actual Costing | Actual | Actual | Actual |
| Normal Costing | Actual | Actual | Budgeted |
| Extended Normal Costing | Budgeted | Budgeted | Budgeted |

4.   Overhead rates may be computed at the **plant-wide** level.

   a.   This method has the benefit of simplicity but may result in inaccurate cost assignments when the incurrence of overhead costs and allocation bases (activity bases or cost drivers) do not have a uniform relationship throughout the plant.

      1)   For example, products may not all be processed in the same way, or departments may be dissimilar.

   b.   Some processes within the plant may be labor intensive, and others may be machine intensive.

      1)   Thus, rates may be calculated more accurately at the **departmental** level when these conditions are true.

   c.   However, neither plant-wide nor departmental rates may achieve the desired accuracy, especially in automated environments.

      1)   For this reason, **activity-based costing systems** have been developed that calculate multiple overhead rates based on multiple cost drivers and cost pools (see subunit 4.2).

5.   Stop and review!  You have completed the outline for this subunit.  Study multiple-choice questions 6 through 17 beginning on page 142.

## 3.3 ALLOCATION OF SERVICE DEPARTMENT COSTS

1.   **Service (support) department costs** are considered part of overhead (indirect costs). Thus, they cannot feasibly be traced to cost objects and therefore must be allocated to the operating departments that use the services.

   a.   When service departments also render services to each other, their costs may be allocated to each other before allocation to operating departments.

2.   Four criteria are used to allocate costs.

   a.   **Cause and effect** should be used if possible because of its objectivity and acceptance by operating management.

   b.   **Benefits received** is the most frequently used alternative when a cause-and-effect relationship cannot be determined.

      1)   However, it requires an assumption about the benefits of costs, for example, that advertising which promotes the company but not specific products was responsible for increased sales by the various divisions.

   c.   **Fairness** is sometimes mentioned in government contracts but appears to be more of a goal than an objective allocation base.

   d.   **Ability to bear** (based on profits) is usually unacceptable because of its dysfunctional effect on managerial motivation.

3.  **Three methods** of service department allocation are in general use.

   a.   The **direct method** is the simplest.

   1)   The direct method allocates service department costs directly to the producing departments without regard for services rendered by service departments to each other.

   2)   Service department costs are allocated to production departments based on an allocation base appropriate to each service department's function.

   3)   EXAMPLE:

   a)   A company has the following service department costs and allocation bases:

| Service Department | Costs to Be Allocated | Allocation Base |
|---|---|---|
| Information Technology | $120,000 | CPU cycles |
| Custodial Services | 40,000 | Floor space |
| Total | $160,000 | |

   b)   The production departments have the following preallocation costs and allocation base amounts:

| Production Department | Preallocation Costs | CPU Cycles Used | % | Floor Space in Sq. Ft. | % |
|---|---|---|---|---|---|
| Department A | $300,000 | 60,000,000 | 62.5% | 56,000 | 70.0% |
| Department B | 200,000 | 36,000,000 | 37.5% | 24,000 | 30.0% |
| Totals | $500,000 | 96,000,000 | 100.0% | 80,000 | 100.0% |

   c)   The direct method allocates the service department costs to the production departments as follows:

| | Service Departments | | Production Departments | | |
|---|---|---|---|---|---|
| | Information Technology | Custodial Services | Department A | Department B | Total |
| Totals before allocation | $120,000 | $40,000 | $300,000 | $200,000 | $660,000 |
| Allocate IT (62.5%, 37.5%) | (120,000) | | 75,000 | 45,000 | 0 |
| Allocate Custodial (70.0%, 30.0%) | | (40,000) | 28,000 | 12,000 | 0 |
| Totals after allocation | $ 0 | $ 0 | $403,000 | $257,000 | $660,000 |

   b.   The **step** or **step-down method** allocates some of the costs of services rendered by service departments to each other.

   1)   The step method derives its name from the procedure involved: The service departments are allocated in order, from the one that provides the most service to other service departments down to the one that provides the least.

   2)   EXAMPLE:

   a)   The services that each service department provides the other must be ascertained:

| Service Department | CPU Cycles Used | % | Floor Space in Sq. Ft. | % |
|---|---|---|---|---|
| Information Technology | 196,000,000 | 98.0% | 20,000 | 80.0% |
| Custodial Services | 4,000,000 | 2.0% | 5,000 | 20.0% |
| Totals | 200,000,000 | 100.0% | 25,000 | 100.0% |

b)    Looking just at reciprocal service department activity, custodial services provides 20% of its services to information technology but IT only provides 2% of its services to custodial. Thus, custodial will be allocated first.

c)    The next step is to determine the relative proportions of the three departments that will receive the first allocation (the second allocation will only be distributed to the two production departments, whose allocation bases were determined under the direct method on the preceding page).

| Allocate Custodial Services: | Floor Space in Sq. Ft. | % |
|---|---|---|
| To Department A | 56,000 | 56.0% |
| To Department B | 24,000 | 24.0% |
| To Information Technology | 20,000 | 20.0% |
| Totals | 100,000 | 100.0% |

d)    The step-down allocation is performed as follows:

| | Service Departments | | Production Departments | | |
|---|---|---|---|---|---|
| | Custodial Services | Information Technology | Department A | Department B | Total |
| Totals before allocation | $40,000 | $120,000 | $300,000 | $200,000 | $660,000 |
| Allocate Custodial (20.0%, 56.0%, 24.0%) | (40,000) | 8,000 | 22,400 | 9,600 | 0 |
| Totals after first allocation | $      0 | $128,000 | $322,400 | $209,600 | $660,000 |
| Allocate IT (62.5%, 37.5%) | | (128,000) | 80,000 | 48,000 | 0 |
| Totals after allocation | | $      0 | $402,400 | $257,600 | $660,000 |

c.    The **reciprocal method** is the most complex and the most theoretically sound of the three. It is also known as the simultaneous solution method, cross allocation method, matrix allocation method, or double distribution method.

1)    The reciprocal method recognizes services rendered by all service departments to each other.

2)    EXAMPLE:

a)    The reciprocal method requires calculating the allocation base amounts for information technology, i.e., the service department that was not allocated to the other service department under the step method.

| Allocate Information Technology: | CPU Cycles Used | % |
|---|---|---|
| To Department A | 60,000,000 | 60.0% |
| To Department B | 36,000,000 | 36.0% |
| To Custodial Services | 4,000,000 | 4.0% |
| Totals | 100,000,000 | 100.0% |

b)    Use linear algebra to calculate fully reciprocated information technology costs (FRITC) and fully reciprocated custodial services costs (FRCSC):

FRITC = Preallocation IT costs + (FRCSC × Portion of custodial effort used by IT)
       = $120,000 + (FRCSC × 20%)

FRCSC = Preallocation custodial costs + (FRITC × Portion of IT effort used by custodial)
       = $40,000 + (FRITC × 4%)

c) These algebraic equations can be solved simultaneously.

$$
\begin{aligned}
\text{FRITC} &= \$120{,}000 + (\text{FRCSC} \times 20\%) \\
&= \$120{,}000 + \{[\$40{,}000 + (\text{FRITC} \times 4\%)] \times 20\%\} \\
&= \$120{,}000 + [(\$40{,}000 + .04\text{FRITC}) \times .2] \\
&= \$120{,}000 + \$8{,}000 + .008\text{FRITC} \\
.992\text{FRITC} &= \$128{,}000 \\
\text{FRITC} &= \$129{,}032
\end{aligned}
$$

$$
\begin{aligned}
\text{FRCSC} &= \$40{,}000 + (\text{FRITC} \times 4\%) \\
&= \$40{,}000 + (\$129{,}032 \times .04\%) \\
&= \$40{,}000 + \$5{,}161 \\
&= \$45{,}161
\end{aligned}
$$

d) The reciprocal allocation is performed as follows:

| | Service Departments | | Production Departments | | |
| --- | --- | --- | --- | --- | --- |
| | Custodial Services | Information Technology | Department A | Department B | Total |
| Totals before allocation | $40,000 | $120,000 | $300,000 | $200,000 | $ 660,000 |
| Allocate Custodial Services | (45,161) | | | | (45,161) |
| (20.0%, 56.0%, 24.0%) | | 9,032 | 25,290 | 10,839 | 45,161 |
| Allocate Information Technology | | (129,032) | | | (129,032) |
| (4.0%, 60.0%, 36.0%) | 5,161 | | 77,419 | 46,452 | 129,032 |
| Totals after allocation | $     0 | $     0 | $402,710 | $257,290 | $ 660,000 |

4. Some service department cost allocation methods involve a **dual-rate method**, i.e., variable costs from a service department allocated using one rate and fixed costs allocated using another. The examples in this section employed a single rate.

5. Stop and review! You have completed the outline for this subunit. Study multiple-choice questions 18 through 31 beginning on page 147.

## 3.4 CORE CONCEPTS

### Job-Order Costing

- Job-order costing is concerned with **accumulating costs by specific job**.
- A **subsidiary ledger** tracks costs for each job.
- Work-in-process is not affected when actual overhead costs are incurred. Instead, overhead is applied to each job based on a **predetermined overhead rate** for the year.

### Overhead Costs and Normal Costing

- In job-order costing, the use of a predetermined overhead rate often results in the **over- or underapplication of overhead**. If this difference is **immaterial**, it can be closed directly to cost of goods sold. If it is **material**, it should be allocated based on the relative values of work-in-process, finished goods, and cost of goods sold.
- During **times of low production**, per-unit overhead charges will skyrocket. To prevent the resulting distortions in the financial statements, **normal costing** derives the overhead application rate by looking at several years at a time, not just one.
- **Extended normal costing** applies the use of a normalized rate to direct costs as well as to manufacturing overhead.

## Allocation of Service Department Costs

- **Three methods** of service department allocation are in general use.

- The **direct method** is the simplest. It involves allocating service department costs directly to the producing departments **without regard** for services rendered by service departments to each other.

- The **step** or **step-down method** allocates **some** of the costs of services rendered by service departments to each other.

- The **reciprocal method** is the most complex and the most theoretically sound of the three. It recognizes services rendered by **all** service departments to each other.

## QUESTIONS

### 3.1 Job-Order Costing

**1.** Felicity Corporation manufactures a specialty line of dresses using a job-order costing system. During January, the following costs were incurred in completing job J-1:

| | |
|---|---|
| Direct materials | $27,400 |
| Direct labor | 9,600 |
| Administrative costs | 2,800 |
| Selling costs | 11,200 |

Factory overhead was applied at the rate of $50 per direct labor hour, and job J-1 required 400 direct labor hours. If job J-1 resulted in 4,000 good dresses, the cost of goods sold per unit is

A. $9.25

B. $14.25

C. $14.95

D. $17.75

**Answer (B) is correct.** *(Publisher)*
**REQUIRED:** The cost of goods sold per unit using job-order costing.
**DISCUSSION:** Cost of goods sold is based on the manufacturing costs incurred in production. It does not include selling or general and administrative expenses. Manufacturing costs consist of direct materials, $27,400; direct labor, $9,600; and overhead, $20,000 (400 direct labor hours × $50 per hour). The total of these three cost elements is $57,000. Dividing the $57,000 of total manufacturing costs by the 4,000 units produced results in a per-unit cost of $14.25.
Answer (A) is incorrect because $9.25 fails to include overhead. Answer (C) is incorrect because $14.95 includes administrative costs. Answer (D) is incorrect because $17.75 includes selling and administrative costs.

**2.** Lucy Sportswear manufactures a specialty line of T-shirts using a job-order costing system. During March, the following costs were incurred in completing job ICU2: direct materials, $13,700; direct labor, $4,800; administrative, $1,400; and selling, $5,600. Overhead was applied at the rate of $25 per machine hour, and job ICU2 required 800 machine hours. If job ICU2 resulted in 7,000 good shirts, the cost of goods sold per unit would be

A. $6.50

B. $6.30

C. $5.70

D. $5.50

**Answer (D) is correct.** *(CMA, adapted)*
**REQUIRED:** The cost of goods sold per unit using job-order costing.
**DISCUSSION:** Cost of goods sold is based on the manufacturing costs incurred in production but does not include selling or general and administrative expenses. Manufacturing costs equal $38,500 [$13,700 DM + $4,800 DL + (800 hours × $25) OH]. Thus, per-unit cost is $5.50 ($38,500 ÷ 7,000 units).
Answer (A) is incorrect because $6.50 includes selling and administrative expenses. Answer (B) is incorrect because $6.30 includes selling costs. Answer (C) is incorrect because $5.70 includes administrative expenses.

**3.** Which method of measuring the costs to be assigned to products or services uses budgeted rates for direct costs but applies those rates to the actual quantities of the inputs?

A. Actual costing.

B. Normal costing.

C. Extended normal costing.

D. Standard costing.

Answer (C) is correct. *(Publisher)*

**REQUIRED:** The cost measurement method that uses budgeted rates for direct costs but applies those rates to the actual quantities of the inputs.

**DISCUSSION:** Extended normal costing assigns both direct costs (such as labor and materials) and overhead to cost objects by using budgeted rates. The direct cost assigned equals the budgeted rate times the actual amount of the direct-cost input. The overhead assigned equals the budgeted rate times the actual amount of whichever driver or other base is used for cost assignment purposes. The use of budgeted rates for overhead as well as direct costs may be helpful to avoid fluctuations during the year. It is also helpful when some direct costs, such as direct labor, may not be known until year-end.

Answer (A) is incorrect because actual costing uses only actual direct and overhead costs. Answer (B) is incorrect because normal costing uses budgeted rates only for overhead costs. Answer (D) is incorrect because standard costing applies budgeted rates to the standard (not actual) inputs allowed.

**4.** Job-order costs are most useful for

A. Determining inventory valuation using LIFO.

B. Estimating the overhead costs included in transfer prices.

C. Controlling indirect costs of future production.

D. Determining the cost of a specific project.

Answer (D) is correct. *(Publisher)*

**REQUIRED:** The best purpose for job-order costing.

**DISCUSSION:** Job-order costs are used in determining the costs of a specific, clearly identifiable job or project. In contrast, process costing averages the costs of all production.

Answer (A) is incorrect because LIFO is equally applicable to either job-order costing or process costing. Answer (B) is incorrect because process costing is equally useful for the estimation of overhead. Answer (C) is incorrect because control of costs does not vary between job-order and process-costing systems.

**5.** A shipbuilding company employing 30 workers constructs custom-built yachts. Which of the following is an appropriate product-costing method for this operation?

A. Process costing.

B. Variable cost transfer pricing.

C. Job-order costing.

D. Step-down allocation of costs.

Answer (C) is correct. *(Publisher)*

**REQUIRED:** The appropriate costing method for a custom-built product.

**DISCUSSION:** The job-order cost system of accounting is appropriate when producing products with individual characteristics such as in the manufacturing of custom-built yachts. The unique aspect of job-order costing is the identification of costs to specific units of a particular job.

Answer (A) is incorrect because process costing is more appropriate for the continuous manufacture of similar products. Answer (B) is incorrect because transfer pricing is used when a company transfers products between two decentralized divisions. Answer (D) is incorrect because the step-down method allocates service department costs to the users of the services.

## 3.2 Overhead Costs and Normal Costing

**6.** Units of production is an appropriate overhead allocation base when

- A. Several well-differentiated products are manufactured.
- B. Direct labor costs are low.
- C. Direct material costs are large relative to direct labor costs incurred.
- D. Only one product is manufactured.

Answer (D) is correct. *(CMA, adapted)*
**REQUIRED:** The situation in which units of production is an appropriate overhead allocation base.
**DISCUSSION:** Allocating overhead on the basis of the number of units produced is usually not appropriate. Costs should be allocated on the basis of some plausible relationship between the cost object and the incurrence of the cost, preferably cause and effect. Overhead costs may be incurred regardless of the level of production. When multiple products are involved, the number of units of production may bear no relationship to the incurrence of the allocated cost. If overhead is correlated with machine hours but different products require different quantities of that input, the result may be an illogical allocation. However, if a firm manufactures only one product, this allocation method may be acceptable because all costs are to be charged to the single product.
Answer (A) is incorrect because the number of units of production may have no logical relationship to overhead when several different products are made. Answer (B) is incorrect because a low level of direct labor costs means that fixed overhead is substantial, and an appropriate cost driver should be used to make the allocation. Answer (C) is incorrect because the allocation should be made on the basis of the appropriate cost drivers without regard to the relationship between direct materials and labor costs.

**7.** Generally, individual departmental rates rather than a plantwide rate for applying manufacturing overhead are used if

- A. A company wants to adopt a standard cost system.
- B. A company's manufacturing operations are all highly automated.
- C. Manufacturing overhead is the largest cost component of its product cost.
- D. The manufactured products differ in the resources consumed from the individual departments in the plant.

Answer (D) is correct. *(CMA, adapted)*
**REQUIRED:** The circumstance in which individual departmental overhead application rates are used.
**DISCUSSION:** Overhead is usually assigned to products based on a predetermined rate or rates. The activity base for overhead allocation should have a high correlation with the incurrence of overhead. Given only one cost driver, one overhead application rate is sufficient. If products differ in the resources consumed in individual departments, multiple rates are preferable.
Answer (A) is incorrect because a standard cost system can be based on individual or multiple application rates. Answer (B) is incorrect because whether production is machine intensive affects the nature but not necessarily the number of cost drivers. Answer (C) is incorrect because a single plant-wide application rate is acceptable, even with high overhead, if all overhead is highly correlated with a single application base.

**8.** A manufacturer allocates overhead to jobs in process using direct labor costs, direct materials costs, and machine hours. The overhead application rates for the current year are

100% of direct labor
20% of direct materials
$117 per machine hour

A particular production run incurred the following costs:

Direct labor, $8,000
Direct materials, $2,000
A total of 140 machine hours were required for the production run.

What is the total cost charged to the production run?

- A. $18,000
- B. $18,400
- C. $34,780
- D. None of the answers are true.

Answer (C) is correct. *(CIA, adapted)*
**REQUIRED:** The total cost for a production run given overhead application rates.
**DISCUSSION:** The total cost is $34,780. It consists of direct labor ($8,000), direct materials ($2,000), and overhead ($24,780). The overhead applied is calculated as follows:

| | | |
|---|---|---|
| $8,000 of direct labor × 100% | = | $ 8,000 |
| $2,000 of direct materials × 20% | = | 400 |
| 140 machine hours × $117 | = | 16,380 |
| | | $24,780 |

Answer (A) is incorrect because $18,000 includes only $8,000 for overhead (based on 100% of direct labor). Answer (B) is incorrect because $18,400 includes only $8,400 for overhead (based on 100% of direct labor and 20% of direct materials). Answer (D) is incorrect because total cost is $34,780.

**9.** The appropriate method for the disposition of underapplied or overapplied overhead of a manufacturer

   A. Is to cost of goods sold only.

   B. Is to finished goods inventory only.

   C. Is apportioned to cost of goods sold and finished goods inventory.

   D. Depends on the significance of the amount.

Answer (D) is correct. *(CMA, adapted)*
   **REQUIRED:** The appropriate treatment of underapplied or overapplied overhead at the end of a period.
   **DISCUSSION:** Overapplied or underapplied overhead should be disposed of at the end of an accounting period by transferring the balance either to cost of goods sold (if the amount is not material) or to cost of goods sold, finished goods inventory, and work-in-process inventory. Theoretically, the allocation is preferred, but, because the amount is usually immaterial, the entire balance is often transferred directly to cost of goods sold. Thus, the entry depends upon the significance of the amount.

**10.** Pane Company uses a job costing system and applies overhead to products on the basis of direct labor cost. Job No. 75, the only job in process on January 1, had the following costs assigned as of that date: direct materials, $40,000; direct labor, $80,000; and factory overhead, $120,000. The following selected costs were incurred during the year:

Traceable to jobs:

| | | |
|---|---:|---:|
| Direct materials | $178,000 | |
| Direct labor | 345,000 | $523,000 |

Not traceable to jobs:

| | | |
|---|---:|---:|
| Factory materials and supplies | $ 46,000 | |
| Indirect labor | 235,000 | |
| Plant maintenance | 73,000 | |
| Depreciation on factory equipment | 29,000 | |
| Other factory costs | 76,000 | $459,000 |

Pane's profit plan for the year included budgeted direct labor of $320,000 and overhead of $448,000. Assuming no work-in-process on December 31, Pane's overhead for the year was

   A. $11,000 overapplied.

   B. $24,000 overapplied.

   C. $11,000 underapplied.

   D. $24,000 underapplied.

Answer (B) is correct. *(CMA, adapted)*
   **REQUIRED:** The extent to which overhead was under- or overapplied.
   **DISCUSSION:** Pane applies overhead to products on the basis of direct labor cost. The rate is 1.4 ($448,000 budgeted OH ÷ $320,000 budgeted DL cost). Thus, $483,000 (1.4 × $345,000 actual DL cost) of overhead was applied, of which $24,000 ($483,000 − $459,000 actual OH) was overapplied.
   Answer (A) is incorrect because $11,000 equals the difference between budgeted and actual overhead. Answer (C) is incorrect because $11,000 equals the difference between budgeted and actual overhead. Answer (D) is incorrect because the overhead was overapplied.

Questions 11 through 14 are based on the following information.

Northcoast Manufacturing Company, a small manufacturer of parts used in appliances, has just completed its first year of operations. The company's controller, Vic Trainor, has been reviewing the actual results for the year and is concerned about the application of factory overhead. Trainor is using the following information to assess its manufacturing operations.

- Northcoast's equipment consists of several machines with a combined cost of $2,200,000 and no residual value. Each machine has an output of five units of product per hour and a useful life of 20,000 hours.
- Selected actual data of Northcoast's operations for the year just ended is presented in the opposite column.

| Products manufactured | 650,000 units |
|---|---|
| Machine use | 130,000 hours |
| Direct labor usage | 35,000 hours |
| Labor rate | $15 per hour |
| Total overhead | $1,130,000 |
| Cost of goods sold | $1,720,960 |
| Finished goods inventory (at year-end) | $430,240 |
| Work-in-process inventory (at year-end) | $0 |

- Total overhead is applied to direct labor cost using a predetermined plant-wide rate.
- The budgeted activity for the year included 20 employees, each working 1,800 productive hours per year to produce 540,000 units of product. The machines are highly automated, and each employee can operate two to four machines simultaneously. Normal activity is for each employee to operate three machines. Machine operators are paid $15 per hour.
- Budgeted overhead costs for the past year for various levels of activity are shown in the table below.

### Northcoast Manufacturing Company
### Budgeted Annual Costs for Total Overhead

| | | | |
|---|---|---|---|
| Units of product | 360,000 | 540,000 | 720,000 |
| Labor hours | 30,000 | 36,000 | 42,000 |
| Machine hours | 72,000 | 108,000 | 144,000 |
| | | | |
| Total overhead costs | | | |
| Plant supervision | $ 70,000 | $ 70,000 | $ 70,000 |
| Plant rent | 40,000 | 40,000 | 40,000 |
| Equipment depreciation | 288,000 | 432,000 | 576,000 |
| Maintenance | 42,000 | 51,000 | 60,000 |
| Utilities | 144,600 | 216,600 | 288,600 |
| Indirect material | 90,000 | 135,000 | 180,000 |
| Other costs | 11,200 | 16,600 | 22,000 |
| Total | $685,000 | $961,200 | $1,236,600 |

**11.** What is the predetermined overhead application rate for the year?

A. 1.78

B. 1.83

C. 2.09

D. 2.15

Answer (A) is correct.  *(Publisher)*
**REQUIRED:** The predetermined overhead application rate.
**DISCUSSION:** The predetermined overhead application rate is found by dividing the total budgeted overhead by the budgeted direct labor cost. Hence, the predetermined overhead application rate is 1.78 [$961,200 ÷ (36,000 × $15)].
Answer (B) is incorrect because 1.83 results from dividing total budgeted overhead by the actual direct labor cost.
Answer (C) is incorrect because 2.09 results from dividing total actual overhead by the budgeted direct labor cost. Answer (D) is incorrect because 2.15 results from dividing total actual overhead by the actual direct labor cost.

**12.** How much is overhead overapplied/ underapplied?

A. $195,500 overapplied.

B. $168,800 overapplied.

C. $168,800 underapplied.

D. $195,500 underapplied.

Answer (D) is correct.  *(Publisher)*
**REQUIRED:** The amount of overhead overapplied/ underapplied.
**DISCUSSION:** The amount of overhead overapplied/ underapplied is found by subtracting the actual incurred overhead from the actual applied overhead. The actual applied overhead is $934,500 [(35,000 hours × $15) × 1.78]. Thus, the amount of underapplied overhead is $195,500 ($934,500 – $1,130,000).
Answer (A) is incorrect because $195,500 is the amount underapplied. Answer (B) is incorrect because $168,800 results from subtracting actual incurred overhead from total budget overhead. Answer (C) is incorrect because $168,800 results from subtracting actual incurred overhead from total budget overhead.

**13.** What is the amount of underapplied overhead allocated to cost of goods sold?

- A. $0
- B. $39,100
- C. $156,400
- D. $195,500

Answer (C) is correct. *(Publisher)*
**REQUIRED:** The amount of underapplied overhead allocated to cost of goods sold.
**DISCUSSION:** Because the amount of underapplied overhead is considered material, the proper accounting treatment is to prorate this amount to work-in-process, finished goods inventory, and the cost of goods sold. Thus, the ending balances must be added together to get $2,151,200 ($1,720,960 + $430,240). The amount of underapplied overhead is then multiplied by .8 ($1,720,960 ÷ $2,151,200) to arrive at the amount of underapplied overhead allocated to cost of goods sold, or $156,400.
Answer (A) is incorrect because $0 is the amount allocated to work-in-process inventory. Answer (B) is incorrect because $39,100 is the amount allocated to finished goods inventory. Answer (D) is incorrect because $195,500 is the amount of overhead underapplied.

**14.** If machine hours were used as the application base, what would be Northcoast's predetermined overhead rate?

- A. $10.46 per machine hour.
- B. $8.90 per machine hour.
- C. $8.69 per machine hour.
- D. $7.39 per machine hour.

Answer (B) is correct. *(Publisher)*
**REQUIRED:** The predetermined overhead rate.
**DISCUSSION:** The predetermined overhead rate is found by dividing total budget overhead by budgeted machine hours. Thus, the budgeted overhead of $961,200 is divided by the budgeted machine hours of 108,000. The predetermined overhead rate is therefore $8.90 per machine hour.
Answer (A) is incorrect because $10.46 per machine hour results from dividing the actual overhead by the budgeted machine hours. Answer (C) is incorrect because $8.69 per machine hour results from dividing the actual overhead by the actual machine hours. Answer (D) is incorrect because $7.39 per machine hour results from dividing budgeted overhead by the actual machine hours.

**15.** During the current accounting period, a manufacturing company purchased $70,000 of raw materials, of which $50,000 of direct materials and $5,000 of indirect materials were used in production. The company also incurred $45,000 of total labor costs and $20,000 of other manufacturing overhead costs. An analysis of the work-in-process control account revealed $40,000 of direct labor costs. Based upon the above information, what is the total amount accumulated in the overhead control account?

- A. $25,000
- B. $30,000
- C. $45,000
- D. $50,000

Answer (B) is correct. *(CIA, adapted)*
**REQUIRED:** The total amount accumulated in the overhead control account.
**DISCUSSION:** Overhead consists of all costs, other than direct materials and direct labor, that are associated with the manufacturing process. It includes both fixed and variable costs. The overhead control account should have the following costs:

| | |
|---|---|
| Indirect materials | $ 5,000 |
| Indirect labor ($45,000 – $40,000) | 5,000 |
| Other overhead | 20,000 |
| Total overhead | $30,000 |

Answer (A) is incorrect because $25,000 excludes the indirect materials. Answer (C) is incorrect because $45,000 is the total labor cost. Answer (D) is incorrect because $50,000 is the direct materials cost.

Questions 16 and 17 are based on the following information.

Nash Glassworks Company has budgeted fixed manufacturing overhead of $100,000 per month. The company uses absorption costing for both external and internal financial reporting purposes. Budgeted overhead rates for cost allocations for the month of April using alternative unit output denominator levels are shown in the next column.

| Capacity Levels | Budgeted Denominator Level (units of output) | Budgeted Overhead Cost Rate |
|---|---|---|
| Theoretical | 1,500,000 | $.0667 |
| Practical | 1,250,000 | .0800 |
| Normal | 775,000 | .1290 |
| Master-budget | 800,000 | .1250 |

Actual output for the month of April was 800,000 units of glassware.

**16.** When Nash Glassworks Company allocates fixed costs, management will select a capacity level to use as the denominator volume. All of the following are appropriate as the capacity level that approximates actual volume levels except

A. Normal capacity.

B. Expected annual activity.

C. Theoretical capacity.

D. Master-budget capacity.

Answer (C) is correct. *(CMA, adapted)*
REQUIRED: The item not an approximation of actual volume levels.
DISCUSSION: Theoretical (ideal) capacity is the maximum capacity given continuous operations with no holidays, downtime, etc. It assumes perfect efficiency at all times. Consequently, it can never be attained and is not a reasonable estimate of actual volume.
Answer (A) is incorrect because normal capacity is the long-term average level of activity that will approximate demand over a period that includes seasonal, cyclical, and trend variations. Answer (B) is incorrect because expected annual activity is an approximation of actual volume levels for a specific year. Answer (D) is incorrect because master-budget capacity is the expected level of activity used for budgeting for a given year.

**17.** The choice of a production volume level as a denominator in the computation of fixed overhead rates can significantly affect reported net income. Which one of the following statements is true for Nash Glassworks Company if its beginning inventory is zero, production exceeded sales, and variances are adjustments to cost of goods sold? The choice of

A. Practical capacity as the denominator level will result in a lower net income amount than if master-budget capacity is chosen.

B. Normal capacity as the denominator level will result in a lower net income amount than if any other capacity volume is chosen.

C. Master-budget capacity as the denominator level will result in a lower net income amount than if theoretical capacity is chosen.

D. Practical capacity as the denominator level will result in a higher net income amount than if normal capacity is chosen.

Answer (A) is correct. *(CMA, adapted)*
REQUIRED: The true statement about choosing a denominator volume for computing fixed overhead application rates.
DISCUSSION: The choice of practical rather than master budget capacity as the denominator level will result in a lower absorption costing net income. Practical capacity is the maximum level at which output is produced efficiently, with an allowance for unavoidable interruptions, for example, for holidays and scheduled maintenance. Because this level will be higher than master-budget (expected) capacity, its use will usually result in the underapplication of fixed overhead. For example, given costs of $100,000 and master-budget capacity of 800,000 units, $.125 per unit is the application rate. If practical capacity is 1,250,000 units, the application rate is $.08 per unit. If actual production is 800,000 units, fixed overhead will not be over- or underapplied given the use of master-budget capacity. However, there will be $36,000 (450,000 units × $.08) of underapplied fixed overhead if practical capacity is the denominator level. Consequently, given that the beginning inventory is zero and that production exceeded sales, less fixed overhead will be inventoried at the lower practical capacity rate than at the master-budget rate. Thus, master-budget net income will be greater.
Answer (B) is incorrect because a normal capacity rate results in a larger ending inventory and a greater net income than a theoretical or practical capacity rate. Answer (C) is incorrect because the master-budget rate exceeds the theoretical capacity rate. It results in a greater ending inventory and a greater net income. Answer (D) is incorrect because a practical capacity rate results in a lower ending inventory and a lower net income than a normal capacity rate.

## 3.3 Allocation of Service Department Costs

**18.** In allocating factory service department costs to producing departments, which one of the following items would most likely be used as an activity base?

A. Units of product sold.

B. Salary of service department employees.

C. Units of electric power consumed.

D. Direct materials usage.

Answer (C) is correct. *(CMA, adapted)*
**REQUIRED:** The item most likely used as an activity base when allocating factory service department costs.
**DISCUSSION:** Service department costs are considered part of factory overhead and should be allocated to the production departments that use the services. A basis reflecting cause and effect should be used to allocate service department costs. For example, the number of kilowatt hours used by each producing department is probably the best allocation base for electricity costs.
Answer (A) is incorrect because making allocations on the basis of units sold may not meet the cause-and-effect criterion. Answer (B) is incorrect because the salary of service department employees is the cost allocated, not a basis of allocation. Answer (D) is incorrect because making allocations on the basis of materials usage may not meet the cause-and-effect criterion.

Questions 19 and 20 are based on the following information. The Photocopying Department provides photocopy services for both Departments A and B and has prepared its total budget using the following information for next year:

| | |
|---|---|
| Fixed costs | $100,000 |
| Available capacity | 4,000,000 pages |
| Budgeted usage | |
| Department A | 1,200,000 pages |
| Department B | 2,400,000 pages |
| Variable cost | $0.03 per page |

**19.** Assume that the single-rate method of cost allocation is used and the allocation base is budgeted usage. How much photocopying cost will be allocated to Department B in the budget year?

A. $72,000

B. $122,000

C. $132,000

D. $138,667

Answer (D) is correct. *(CMA, adapted)*
**REQUIRED:** The service cost allocated to Department B using a single rate based on budgeted usage.
**DISCUSSION:** Department B is budgeted to use 66 2/3% of total production (2,400,000 ÷ 3,600,000), so it should be allocated fixed costs of $66,667 ($100,000 × 66 2/3%). The variable cost allocation is $72,000 (2,400,000 pages × $.03 per page), and the total allocated is therefore $138,667 ($66,667 + $72,000).
Answer (A) is incorrect because $72,000 is the variable cost allocation. Answer (B) is incorrect because $122,000 assumes that fixed costs are allocated equally between A and B. Answer (C) is incorrect because $132,000 assumes fixed costs are allocated at a per-page rate based on available capacity ($100,000 ÷ 4,000,000 pages = $.025 per page), not on budgeted usage ($100,000 ÷ 3,600,000 pages = $.0278 per page).

**20.** Assume that the dual-rate cost allocation method is used, and the allocation basis is budgeted usage for fixed costs and actual usage for variable costs. How much cost would be allocated to Department A during the year if actual usage for Department A is 1,400,000 pages and actual usage for Department B is 2,100,000 pages?

A. $42,000

B. $72,000

C. $75,333

D. $82,000

Answer (C) is correct. *(CMA, adapted)*
**REQUIRED:** The service cost allocated to Department A if a dual-rate allocation method is used.
**DISCUSSION:** Based on budgeted usage, Department A should be allocated 33 1/3% [1,200,000 pages ÷ (1,200,000 pages + 2,400,000 pages)] of fixed costs, or $33,333 ($100,000 × 33 1/3%). The variable costs are allocated at $.03 per unit for 1,400,000 pages, or $42,000. The sum of the fixed and variable elements is $75,333.
Answer (A) is incorrect because $42,000 equals the variable costs allocated to Department A. Answer (B) is incorrect because $72,000 is the allocation to Department B using a single rate. Answer (D) is incorrect because $82,000 assumes fixed costs are allocated at a per-page rate based on actual usage ($100,000 ÷ 3,500,000 pages = $.0286 per page).

**21.** A company has two service departments (S1 and S2) and two production departments (P1 and P2). Departmental data for January were as follows:

|  | S1 | S2 |
|---|---|---|
| Costs incurred: | $27,000 | $18,000 |
| Service provided to: |  |  |
| S1 | -- | 20% |
| S2 | 10% | -- |
| P1 | 50% | 30% |
| P2 | 40% | 50% |

What are the total allocated service department costs to P2 if the company uses the reciprocal method of allocating its service department costs? (Round calculations to the nearest whole number.)

A. $19,800

B. $21,949

C. $22,500

D. $23,051

Answer (D) is correct. *(CIA, adapted)*
**REQUIRED:** The total allocated service department costs to P2.
**DISCUSSION:** The reciprocal method allocates service department costs to other service departments as well as to production departments by means of simultaneous equations, as shown below. Thus, total service cost allocated to P2 is $23,051 [($31,224 × 40%) + ($21,122 × 50%)].

$$S1 = \$27,000 + .2S2$$
$$\phantom{S1} = \$27,000 + [.2(\$18,000 + .1S1)]$$
$$\phantom{S1} = \$27,000 + \$3,600 + .02S1$$
$$.98S1 = \$30,600$$
$$S1 = \$31,224$$

$$S2 = \$18,000 + .1(\$31,224)$$
$$\phantom{S2} = \$18,000 + \$3,122$$
$$S2 = \$21,122$$

Answer (A) is incorrect because $19,800 equals the sum of 40% of S1's preallocation costs and 50% of S2's preallocation costs. Answer (B) is incorrect because $21,949 is the total service cost allocated to P1. Answer (C) is incorrect because $22,500 equals the average of the preallocation costs of S1 and S2.

---

Questions 22 through 26 are based on the following information. The managers of Rochester Manufacturing are discussing ways to allocate the cost of service departments, such as Quality Control and Maintenance, to the production departments. To aid them in this discussion, the controller has provided the following information:

|  | Quality Control | Maintenance | Machining | Assembly | Total |
|---|---|---|---|---|---|
| Budgeted overhead costs before allocation | $350,000 | $200,000 | $400,000 | $300,000 | $1,250,000 |
| Budgeted machine hours | -- | -- | 50,000 | -- | 50,000 |
| Budgeted direct labor hours | -- | -- | -- | 25,000 | 25,000 |
| Budgeted hours of service: |  |  |  |  |  |
| Quality Control | -- | 7,000 | 21,000 | 7,000 | 35,000 |
| Maintenance | 10,000 | -- | 18,000 | 12,000 | 40,000 |

**22.** If Rochester Manufacturing uses the direct method of allocating service department costs, the total service costs allocated to the assembly department would be

A. $80,000

B. $87,500

C. $120,000

D. $167,500

Answer (D) is correct. *(CMA, adapted)*
**REQUIRED:** The total service costs allocated to the Assembly Department using the direct method.
**DISCUSSION:** Under the direct method, service department costs are allocated directly to the production departments, with no allocation to other service departments. The total budgeted hours of service by the Quality Control Department to the two production departments is 28,000 (21,000 + 7,000). Given that the Assembly Department is expected to use 25% (7,000 ÷ 28,000) of the total hours budgeted for the production departments, it will absorb 25% of total quality control costs ($350,000 × 25% = $87,500). The total budgeted hours of service by the Maintenance Department to the production departments is 30,000 (18,000 + 12,000). The Assembly Department is expected to use 40% (12,000 ÷ 30,000) of the total maintenance hours budgeted for the production departments. Thus, the Assembly Department will be allocated 40% of the $200,000 of maintenance costs, or $80,000. The total service department costs allocated to the Assembly Department is $167,500 ($87,500 + $80,000).

**23.** Using the direct method, the total amount of overhead allocated to each machine hour at Rochester Manufacturing would be

A. $2.40

B. $5.25

C. $8.00

D. $15.65

Answer (D) is correct. *(CMA, adapted)*
**REQUIRED:** The total overhead allocated to each machine hour.
**DISCUSSION:** Machining uses 75% (21,000 ÷ 28,000) of the total quality control hours and 60% (18,000 ÷ 30,000) of the total maintenance hours budgeted for the production departments. Under the direct method, it will therefore be allocated $262,500 ($350,000 × 75%) of quality control costs and $120,000 ($200,000 × 60%) of maintenance costs. In addition, Machining is expected to incur another $400,000 of overhead costs. Thus, the total estimated Machining overhead is $782,500 ($262,500 + $120,000 + $400,000), and the overhead cost per machine hour is $15.65 ($782,500 ÷ 50,000 hours).

**24.** If Rochester Manufacturing uses the step-down method of allocating service costs beginning with quality control, the maintenance costs allocated to the assembly department would be

A. $70,000

B. $108,000

C. $162,000

D. $200,000

Answer (B) is correct. *(CMA, adapted)*
**REQUIRED:** The maintenance costs allocated to the Assembly Department if the step-down method is applied beginning with quality control costs.
**DISCUSSION:** The step-down method allocates service costs to both service and production departments but does not involve reciprocal allocations among service departments. Accordingly, Quality Control will receive no allocation of maintenance costs. The first step is to allocate quality control costs to the Maintenance Department. Maintenance is expected to use 20% (7,000 ÷ 35,000) of the available quality control hours and will be allocated $70,000 ($350,000 × 20%) of quality control costs. Thus, total allocable maintenance costs equal $270,000 ($70,000 + $200,000). The Assembly Department is estimated to use 40% (12,000 ÷ 30,000) of the available maintenance hours. Consequently, it will be allocated maintenance costs of $108,000 ($270,000 × 40%).

**25.** If Rochester Manufacturing uses the reciprocal method of allocating service costs, the total amount of quality control costs (rounded to the nearest dollar) to be allocated to the other departments would be

A. $284,211

B. $336,842

C. $350,000

D. $421,053

Answer (D) is correct. *(CMA, adapted)*
**REQUIRED:** The total quality control costs to be allocated to the other departments using the reciprocal method.
**DISCUSSION:** The reciprocal method involves mutual allocations of service costs among service departments. For this purpose, a system of simultaneous equations is necessary. The total costs for the Quality Control Department consist of $350,000 plus 25% (10,000 hours ÷ 40,000 hours) of maintenance costs. The total costs for the Maintenance Department equal $200,000 plus 20% (7,000 hours ÷ 35,000 hours) of quality control costs. These relationships can be expressed by the following equations:

$$Q = \$350,000 + .25M$$
$$M = \$200,000 + .2Q$$

To solve for Q, the second equation can be substituted into the first as follows:

$$Q = \$350,000 + .25(\$200,000 + .2Q)$$
$$Q = \$350,000 + \$50,000 + .05Q$$
$$.95Q = \$400,000$$
$$Q = \$421,053$$

**26.** If Rochester Manufacturing decides not to allocate service costs to the production departments, the overhead allocated to each direct labor hour in the Assembly Department would be

A. $3.20

B. $3.50

C. $12.00

D. $16.00

Answer (C) is correct. *(CMA, adapted)*
**REQUIRED:** The overhead cost per direct labor hour in the Assembly Department if no service costs are allocated to production departments.
**DISCUSSION:** With no allocation of service department costs, the only overhead applicable to the Assembly Department is the $300,000 budgeted for that department. Hence, the overhead cost applied per direct labor hour will be $12 ($300,000 budgeted overhead ÷ 25,000 hours).

Questions 27 and 28 are based on the following information. M&P Tool has three service departments that support the production area. Outlined below is the estimated overhead by department for the upcoming year.

| Service Departments | Estimated Overhead | Number of Employees |
| --- | --- | --- |
| Receiving | $25,000 | 2 |
| Repair | 35,000 | 2 |
| Tool | 10,000 | 1 |
| Production Departments | | |
| Assembly | | 25 |
| Bolting | | 12 |

The Repair Department supports the greatest number of departments, followed by the Tool Department. Overhead cost is allocated to departments based upon the number of employees.

**27.** Using the direct method of allocation, how much of the Repair Department's overhead will be allocated to the Tool Department?

A. $0

B. $875

C. $7,000

D. $11,667

Answer (A) is correct. *(CMA, adapted)*
REQUIRED: The Repair Department costs allocated to the Tool Department under the direct method.
DISCUSSION: The direct method allocates service department costs directly to the producing departments without recognition of services provided among the service departments. Hence, no service cost is allocated to the Tool Department because it is a service department.

**28.** Using the step-down method of allocation, the allocation from the Repair Department to the Tool Department would be

A. $0

B. $875

C. $7,000

D. $11,667

Answer (B) is correct. *(CMA, adapted)*
REQUIRED: The allocation from the Repair Department to the Tool Department using the step-down method.
DISCUSSION: Under the step-down method, service costs are allocated to all departments. However, no reciprocal allocations among service departments are performed. The process usually begins with the department that provides the greatest percentage of its services to other service departments. Thus, the Repair Department is the logical starting point. Given that service costs are allocated to each department (service or production) on the basis of its proportion of employees (excluding employees in the allocating department), the allocation of the Repair Department's overhead to the Tool Department is $875 {$35,000 × [1 employee ÷ (1 + 2 + 25 + 12)]}.
Answer (A) is incorrect because, under the step-down method, other service departments share in the allocation of costs. Answer (C) is incorrect because this amount is far greater than could be allocated to a service department with one employee. Answer (D) is incorrect because this amount is far greater than could be allocated to a service department with one employee.

Questions 29 and 30 are based on the following information. Fabricating and Finishing are the two production departments of a manufacturing company. Building Operations and Information Services are service departments that provide support to the two production departments as well as to each other. The company employs departmental overhead rates in the two production departments to allocate the service department costs to the production departments. Square footage is used to allocate building operations, and computer time is used to allocate information services. The costs of the service departments and relevant operating data for the departments are as follows:

|  | Building Operations | Information Services | Fabricating | Finishing |
|---|---|---|---|---|
| Costs: | | | | |
| Labor and benefit costs | $200,000 | $ 300,000 | | |
| Other traceable costs | 350,000 | 900,000 | | |
| Total | $550,000 | $1,200,000 | | |
| Operating Data: | | | | |
| Square feet occupied | 5,000 | 10,000 | 16,000 | 24,000 |
| Computer time (in hours) | 200 | | 1,200 | 600 |

**29.** If the company employs the direct method to allocate the costs of the service departments, then the amount of building operations costs allocated to Fabricating would be

A. $140,000

B. $160,000

C. $176,000

D. $220,000

Answer (D) is correct. *(CIA, adapted)*
   **REQUIRED:** The amount of building operations costs allocated to Fabricating under the direct method.
   **DISCUSSION:** The direct method does not allocate service costs to other service departments. Hence, the allocation base is the square footage in the two production departments. Fabricating's share is 40% (16,000 ÷ 40,000) of the total cost incurred by Building Operations, or $220,000 ($550,000 × 40%).
   Answer (A) is incorrect because $140,000 is 40% of other traceable costs. Answer (B) is incorrect because $160,000 assumes an allocation base of 55,000 square feet. Answer (C) is incorrect because $176,000 assumes an allocation base of 50,000 square feet, the base that would be used under the step method if the costs of building operations are allocated first.

**30.** If the company employs the step method to allocate the costs of the service departments and if information services costs are allocated first, then the total amount of service department costs (Information Services and Building Operations) allocated to finishing would be

A. $657,000

B. $681,600

C. $730,000

D. $762,000

Answer (D) is correct. *(CIA, adapted)*
   **REQUIRED:** The total service department costs allocated to Finishing under the step method.
   **DISCUSSION:** The step method of service department cost allocation is a sequential (but not a reciprocal) process. These costs are allocated to other service departments as well as to users. The process usually begins with the service department that renders the greatest percentage of its services to other service departments. If the $1,200,000 of information services costs is allocated first, the allocation base is 2,000 computer hours (200 + 1,200 + 600). Thus, $120,000 [$1,200,000 × (200 ÷ 2,000)] will be allocated to Building Operations and $360,000 [$1,200,000 × (600 ÷ 2,000)] to Finishing. The total of the building operations costs to be allocated to production equals $670,000 ($550,000 + $120,000). The allocation base will be 40,000 square feet because no costs are allocated back to Information Services. Accordingly, the total of service costs allocated to Finishing equals $762,000 {$360,000 + [$670,000 × (24,000 ÷ 40,000)]}.
   Answer (A) is incorrect because $657,000 results from allocating building operations costs first. Also, the information services costs are allocated using total computer hours. Answer (B) is incorrect because $681,600 results from allocating building operations costs to Information Services. Answer (C) is incorrect because $730,000 allocates the costs of both service departments according to the direct method rather than the step method.

**31.** When allocating service department costs to production departments, the method that does not consider different cost behavior patterns is the

A. Step method.

B. Reciprocal method.

C. Direct method.

D. Single-rate method.

Answer (D) is correct.   *(CMA, adapted)*
**REQUIRED:** The method of service department cost allocation that does not consider cost behavior patterns.
**DISCUSSION:** The single-rate method combines fixed and variable costs. However, dual rates are preferable because they allow variable costs to be allocated on a different basis from fixed costs.
Answer (A) is incorrect because the step method can be used on a single- or dual-rate basis. Answer (B) is incorrect because the reciprocal method can be used on a single- or dual-rate basis. Answer (C) is incorrect because the direct method can be used on a single- or dual-rate basis.

---

Use Gleim's *CMA Test Prep* for interactive testing with **over 2,000 additional multiple-choice questions!**

# STUDY UNIT FOUR
# PROCESS COSTING AND OTHER
# COST ACCUMULATION SYSTEMS

(16 pages of outline)

This study unit is the **last of three** on **cost management**. The relative weight assigned to this major topic in Part 2 of the exam is **25%** at **skill level C** (all six skill types required). The three study units are

Study Unit 2: Cost Management Terminology and Concepts
Study Unit 3: Job-Order Costing, Overhead Costs, and Service Department Allocation
Study Unit 4: Process Costing and Other Cost Accumulation Systems

After studying the outlines and answering the multiple-choice questions in this study unit, you will have the skills necessary to address the following topics listed in the IMA's Learning Outcome Statements:

Part 2 -- Section B.3. Accumulation systems

For each cost accumulation system identified (process costing, activity-based costing, life-cycle costing), the candidate should be able to:

a. define the nature of the system, understand the cost flows of the system, and recognize its appropriate use
b. calculate inventory values and cost of goods sold
c. understand how to account for normal and abnormal spoilage
d. understand the strategic value of cost information regarding products and services, pricing, overhead allocations, and other issues
e. understand the benefits and limitations of each cost accumulation system

For these specific cost accumulation systems, the candidate should be able to:

f. understand the concept of equivalent units in process costing and calculate the value of equivalent units
g. define the elements of activity-based costing such as cost pool, cost driver, resource driver, activity driver, and value-added activity
h. calculate product cost using an activity-based system and compare and analyze the results with costs calculated using a traditional system
i. understand the concept of the life-cycle costing and the strategic value of including upstream costs, manufacturing costs, and downstream costs
j. recognize that operation costing is a hybrid cost system utilizing characteristics of both job costing and process costing and identify industry settings where operation costing is appropriate
k. demonstrate an understanding of backflush costing and describe why it is appropriate in a just-in-time setting where manufacturing cells are utilized

Part 2 -- Section B.4. Overhead costs

The candidate should be able to:

NOTE:  Statements a. through j. are covered in Study Unit 3.

k.    compare and contrast traditional overhead allocation with activity-based overhead allocation

l.    calculate overhead expense in an activity-based setting and describe the benefits derived from activity-based overhead allocation

NOTE:  Statements m. and n. are covered in Study Unit 3.

## 4.1 PROCESS COSTING

1.    Process cost accounting is used to assign costs to inventoriable goods or services.  It is applicable to **relatively homogeneous products** that are mass produced on a continuous basis (e.g., refined oil).

    a.    Where job-order costing uses subsidiary ledgers to keep track of specific jobs, process costing typically has a **work-in-process account for each department** through which the production of output passes.

    b.    Process costing is an averaging process that calculates the average cost of all units:

        1)    Costs are accumulated for a cost object that consists of a large number of similar units of goods or services;

        2)    Work-in-process is stated in terms of equivalent units;

        3)    Unit costs are established.

    c.    Unlike job-order costing, processing is continuous.  The creation of products goes on without the initiation of a specific sales order.

    d.    As in job-order costing, the physical inputs required for the production process are obtained from suppliers.

| | | |
|---|---|---|
| Raw materials | $XXX | |
|     Accounts payable | | $XXX |

    e.    Direct materials are used by the first department in the process.

| | | |
|---|---|---|
| Work-in-process -- Department A | $XXX | |
|     Raw materials | | $XXX |

    f.    The products move from one department to the next.

| | | |
|---|---|---|
| Work-in-process -- Department B | $XXX | |
|     Work-in-process -- Department A | | $XXX |

    g.    The second department adds more direct materials.

| | | |
|---|---|---|
| Work-in-process -- Department B | $XXX | |
|     Raw materials | | $XXX |

    h.    Direct labor costs incurred for the period are recorded.

| | | |
|---|---|---|
| Work-in-process -- Department A | $XXX | |
| Work-in-process -- Department B | XXX | |
|     Wages payable | | $XXX |

    i.    Owing to the uniform nature of process costing, **actual manufacturing overhead** can be charged rather than an applied rate as in job-order.

        1)    Therefore, there is no contra-account for manufacturing overhead to hold amounts applied.

            a)    The issue of over- and underapplied overhead therefore does not usually arise under process costing unless a standard costing system is used (see subunit 3.2).

2) The same journal entries as in job-order are used when indirect costs are paid.

| | | |
|---|---|---|
| Manufacturing overhead | $XXX | |
|     Property taxes payable | | $XXX |

| | | |
|---|---|---|
| Manufacturing overhead | $XXX | |
|     Prepaid insurance | | $XXX |

| | | |
|---|---|---|
| Manufacturing overhead | $XXX | |
|     Accumulated depreciation -- factory equipment | | $XXX |

3) The actual amounts incurred are charged to each production department's work-in-process.

| | | |
|---|---|---|
| Work-in-process -- Department A | $XXX | |
| Work-in-process -- Department B | XXX | |
|     Manufacturing overhead | | $XXX |

j. When **spoilage** is identified, the accounting treatment is the same as under job-order costing (see subunit 3.1).

k. When processing is finished in the last department, all the costs are transferred to finished goods.

| | | |
|---|---|---|
| Finished goods | $X,XXX | |
|     Work-in-process -- Department B | | $X,XXX |

l. As products are sold, the costs are transferred to cost of goods sold.

| | | |
|---|---|---|
| Cost of goods sold | $X,XXX | |
|     Finished goods | | $X,XXX |

2. The following diagram depicts the flow of cost accumulation in a process costing system:

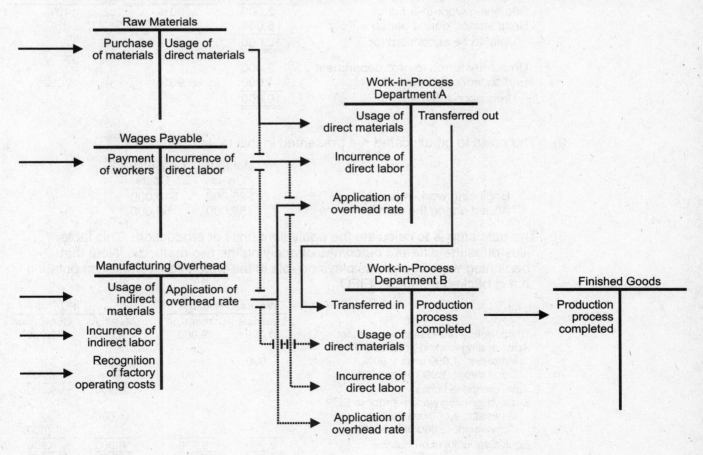

3.   Some units remain unfinished at the end of the period.  For each department to adequately account for the costs attached to its unfinished units, the units must be restated in terms of **equivalent units of production (EUP)**.

    a.   An equivalent unit of production is the set of inputs required to manufacture one physical unit.

        1)   The EUP conversion is a two-phase process:  First, the **equivalent units** are determined, then the **per-unit cost** is calculated.

        2)   The two calculations are made separately for materials and conversion cost (transferred-in costs are by definition 100% complete).  Conversion costs are assumed to be uniformly incurred.

    b.   Two methods of calculating EUP are in common use:  weighted-average and FIFO.

        1)   Under the **weighted-average method**, units in beginning work-in-process inventory are treated as if they were started and completed during the current period.  Beginning work-in-process is therefore not included in the EUP calculation.

        2)   Under the **first-in, first-out (FIFO) method**, units in beginning work-in-process inventory are part of the EUP calculation.  The calculation is thus more complex than weighted-average but tends to be more accurate.

    c.   EXAMPLE:  A department of a manufacturing concern is preparing its cost reports for the month.

        1)   The first step is to prepare a quantity schedule:

| | Units | Completed for Materials | Completed for Conversion |
|---|---|---|---|
| Beginning work-in-process | 2,000 | 80% | 40% |
| Units started during period | 8,000 | | |
| Units to be accounted for | 10,000 | | |
| | | | |
| Units transferred to next department | 9,000 | | |
| Ending work-in-process | 1,000 | 90% | 70% |
| Units accounted for | 10,000 | | |

        2)   The costs to be allocated are presented in this table:

| | Materials Costs | Conversion Costs |
|---|---|---|
| Beginning work-in-process | $25,000 | $10,000 |
| Added during the month | 55,000 | 50,000 |

        3)   The next step is to calculate the equivalent units of production.  This table illustrates the different outcomes of applying the two methods.  Note that beginning work-in-process plays no role in the weighted-average computation but is backed out under FIFO.

| | Weighted-Average | | FIFO | |
|---|---|---|---|---|
| | Materials | Conversion | Materials | Conversion |
| Units transferred to next department | 9,000 | 9,000 | 9,000 | 9,000 |
| Add:  ending work-in-process FUP | | | | |
|   Materials:  1,000 units × 90% | 900 | | 900 | |
|   Conversion:  1,000 units × 70% | | 700 | | 700 |
| Total completed units | | | 9,900 | 9,700 |
| Less:  beginning work-in-process EUP | | | | |
|   Materials:  2,000 units × 80% | | | (1,600) | |
|   Conversion:  2,000 units × 40% | | | | (800) |
| Equivalent units of production | 9,900 | 9,700 | 8,300 | 8,900 |

4) Once the equivalent units have been calculated, the per-unit costs under each of the two methods can be derived.

a) Under the **weighted-average** method, **all materials and conversion costs** are averaged in, both those incurred in the current period and those in beginning work-in-process.

Materials costs: $\dfrac{\$25,000 + \$55,000}{9,900 \text{ EUP}}$ = $8.08

Conversion costs: $\dfrac{\$10,000 + \$50,000}{9,700 \text{ EUP}}$ = $6.19

Total unit cost under weighted-average $14.27

b) Under the **FIFO** method, **only the costs incurred in the current period** are included in the calculation.

Materials costs: $\dfrac{\$55,000}{8,300 \text{ EUP}}$ = $6.63

Conversion costs: $\dfrac{\$50,000}{8,900 \text{ EUP}}$ = $5.62

Total unit cost under first-in, first-out $12.24

4. Stop and review! You have completed the outline for this subunit. Study multiple-choice questions 1 through 45 beginning on page 169.

## 4.2 ACTIVITY-BASED COSTING

1. **Activity-based costing (ABC)** attaches costs to activities rather than to physical goods.

   a. ABC is a refinement of a basic costing system. It may be used by manufacturing, service, or retailing entities and in **job-order or process costing systems**.

   b. It has been popularized because of the rapid advance of technology, which has led to a significant increase in the incurrence of indirect costs and a consequent need for more accurate cost assignment.

   c. ABC is one means of improving a cost system to avoid what has been called **peanut-butter costing**.

      1) Inaccurately averaging or spreading costs like peanut butter over products or service units that use different amounts of resources results in product-cost cross-subsidization.

      2) **Product-cost cross-subsidization** is the condition in which the miscosting of one product causes the miscosting of other products.

2. The peanut-butter effect of using a traditional costing system can be summarized as follows:

   a. Direct labor and direct materials are traced to products or service units.

   b. A single pool of indirect costs (overhead) is accumulated for a given organizational unit.

   c. Indirect costs from the pool are assigned using an allocative (rather than a tracing) procedure, such as using a single overhead rate for an entire department, e.g., $3 of overhead for every direct labor hour.

      1) The effect is an averaging of costs that may result in significant inaccuracy when products or service units do not use similar amounts of resources.

3.  If ABC is used, however:

    a.  The multiple activities that use resources classified as overhead are identified.

        1)  An **activity** is a set of work actions undertaken within the entity.

    b.  A cost pool is established for each activity.

        1)  **Cost pools** contain **cost elements**, which are amounts paid for resources used by an activity.

        2)  Each cost pool should be **homogeneous**; that is, each should consist of costs that have substantially similar relationships with the driver or other base used for assignment to cost objects.

    c.  The costs in each pool are assigned based on a cost driver specific to the activity.

        1)  A **cost driver** is a factor or event that changes an activity's total cost; it is also the means used to assign costs to activities and to reassign those costs to other activities, products, or services.

            a)  Thus, a cost driver may be a **resource driver**, a measure of resources consumed by an activity, such as the square footage it occupies.

            b)  An **activity driver** is a measure of the demands made on an activity by next-stage cost objects, such as the number of parts in a product used to measure an assembly activity.

        2)  Each driver must have a **cause-and-effect relationship** (not simply a high positive correlation) with the activity for which it is being used as the allocation base.

            a)  If a driver cannot feasibly be identified, overhead is assigned to products or services using an allocative procedure.

4.  **Cost objects** are the intermediate and final dispositions of cost pools.

    a.  A cost object may be a job, product, process, activity, service, or anything else for which a cost measure is desired.

    b.  Intermediate cost objects receive temporary accumulations of costs as the cost pools move from their originating points to the final cost objects.

        1)  For example, work-in-process is an intermediate cost object, and finished salable goods are final cost objects.

5.  Because ABC attempts to refine costing by assigning costs to **activities rather than to organizational units**, ABC requires identification of the activities that consume resources.

    a.  Design of an ABC system starts with process value analysis, a comprehensive understanding of how an organization generates its output.

        1)  A **process value analysis** involves a determination of which activities that use resources are value-adding or nonvalue-adding and how the latter may be reduced or eliminated.

        2)  A **value-adding activity** contributes to customer satisfaction or meets a need of the entity. The perception is that it cannot be omitted without a loss of the quantity, quality, or responsiveness of output demanded by the entity or its customers.

        3)  A **nonvalue-adding activity** does not make such a contribution. It can be eliminated, reduced, or redesigned without impairing the quantity, quality, or responsiveness of the product or service desired by customers or the entity.

    b.  The linkage of product costing and continuous improvement of processes is **activity-based management (ABM)**. It encompasses driver analysis, activity analysis, and performance measurement.

6.   Once an ABC system has been designed:

    a.   Costs may be assigned to the identified activities.

    b.   Costs of related activities that can be reassigned using the same driver or other base are combined in homogeneous cost pools.

    c.   An overhead rate is calculated for each pool.

7.   The next step, as in traditional methods, is to assign costs to next-stage cost objects.

    a.   In other words, cost assignment is a two-step process:

        1)   Costs are accumulated for an activity based on the resources it can be directly observed to use and on the resources it can be assumed to use based on its consumption of **resource drivers**.

        2)   Costs are reassigned to next-stage cost objects on the basis of **activity drivers**.

8.   An essential element of ABC is **driver analysis**, which emphasizes the search for the cause-and-effect relationship between an activity and its consumption of resources and an activity and the demands made on it by a cost object.

    a.   For this purpose, activities and their drivers often have been classified in accounting literature as follows:

        1)   **Unit-level** (volume-related) activities occur when a unit is produced, e.g., direct labor and direct materials activities. Drivers are direct labor hours or dollars, machine hours, and units of output.

        2)   **Batch-level** activities occur when a batch of units is produced, e.g., ordering, setup, or materials handling. Drivers may include number or duration of setups, orders processed, number of receipts, weight of materials handled, or number of inspections.

        3)   **Product- or service-level** (product- or service-sustaining) activities provide support of different kinds to different types of output, e.g., engineering changes, inventory management, or testing. Drivers may include design time, testing time, number of engineering change orders, or number of categories of parts.

        4)   **Facility-level** (facility-sustaining) activities concern overall operations, e.g., management of the physical plant, personnel administration, or security arrangements. Drivers may include any of those used at the first three levels.

    b.   In **SMA 4X**, "Value-Chain Analysis for Assessing Competitive Advantage" (issued 1996), the IMA has identified two types of cost drivers relevant to **strategic planning**:

        1)   **Structural cost drivers** are organizational factors that determine the economic structure driving the cost of a firm's products.

            a)   Structural cost drivers reflect a firm's long-term decisions, which position the firm in its industry and marketplace.

            b)   The structural cost drivers are

                i)    The scale of the firm's operations
                ii)   The experience level of the firm
                iii)  The level of technology used within the firm
                iv)   The complexity of the firm's operations

        2)   **Executional cost drivers** capture a firm's operational decisions on how best to employ its resources to achieve its objectives.

            a)   Executional drivers are determined by management policy, style, and culture.

        b)    Examples of executional cost drivers are

            i)     Workforce involvement
            ii)    Existence of a quality assurance program
            iii)   Capacity utilization
            iv)   Relations with suppliers

9.    Using the four-level driver-analysis model, activities are grouped, and drivers are determined for the activities.

    a.    Within each grouping of activities, the cost pools for activities that can use the same driver are combined into homogeneous cost pools.

        1)    In contrast, traditional systems assign costs largely on the basis of unit-level drivers.

    b.    A difficulty in applying ABC is that, although the first three levels of activities pertain to specific products or services, facility-level activities do not.

        1)    Thus, **facility-level costs** are not accurately assignable to products or services. The theoretically sound solution may be to treat these costs as **period costs**.

        2)    Nevertheless, organizations that apply ABC ordinarily assign them to products or services to obtain a full-absorption cost suitable for external financial reporting in accordance with GAAP.

10.   As the foregoing discussion indicates, an **advantage** of ABC is that overhead costs are accumulated in **multiple cost pools** related to activities instead of in a single pool for a department, process, plant, or company.

    a.    ABC also is more likely than a traditional system to assign costs to activities and reassign them to next-stage cost objects using a base that is highly correlated with the resources consumed by activities or with the demands placed on activities by cost objects.

    b.    **Process value analysis** provides information for eliminating or reducing nonvalue-adding activities (e.g., scheduling production, moving components, waiting for the next operating step, inspecting output, or storing inventories).

        1)    The result is therefore not only more accurate cost assignments, especially of overhead, but also better cost control and more efficient operations.

    c.    A disadvantage of ABC is that it may still be relatively more costly to implement because of the more detailed information required.

        1)    Another disadvantage is that ABC-based costs of products or services **may not conform with GAAP**; for example, ABC may assign research costs to products but not such traditional product costs as plant depreciation, insurance, or taxes.

11.   Organizations most likely to benefit from using ABC are those with products or services that vary significantly in volume, diversity of activities, and complexity of operations; relatively high overhead costs; or operations that have undergone major technological or design changes.

    a.    However, service organizations may have some difficulty in implementing ABC because they tend to have relatively high facility-level costs that are difficult to assign to specific service units.

    b.    They also engage in many nonuniform human activities for which information is not readily accumulated.

    c.    Moreover, output measurement is more problematic in service than in manufacturing entities.

    d.    Nevertheless, ABC has been adopted by various insurers, banks, railroads, and healthcare providers.

12. Direct labor (hours or dollars) has long been the most common **base for allocating overhead** because of the simplicity of the calculation, but it is not always relevant.

   a. Companies now use dozens of different allocation bases depending upon how activity affects overhead costs. One company reported that it used 37 different bases to allocate overhead, some of which were averages of several activities.

   b. In principle, a separate overhead account or subsidiary ledger account should be used for each type of overhead.

   c. In the past, "people were cheap and machines were expensive." This meant that direct labor was ordinarily a larger component of total production cost than overhead and was the activity that drove (caused) overhead costs.

      1) Due to the lowered cost of computers and robotics and the expansion of employee benefits ("machines are cheap and people are expensive"), overhead is more likely to be a large component of total production cost, with direct labor often a small percentage.

      2) Most overhead costs vary in proportion to product diversity and the complexity of an operation.

         a) Direct labor is not a cost driver for most overhead costs.

      3) Allocating a very large cost (overhead) using a very small cost (direct labor) as a base is irrational.

         a) A small change in direct labor on a product can make a significant difference in total production cost, an effect that may rest on an invalid assumption about the relationship of the cost and the allocation base.

   d. As previously noted, ABC is more useful when overhead costs are relatively high.

      1) Also, the more diverse a company's line of products or services or the more significant the volume differences among its products or services, the more beneficial ABC will be.

      2) Simple averaging procedures such as direct-labor-based costing are valid only when products or services are absolutely uniform. For example, a simple allocation basis in a factory with large and small machines and high-priced and low-cost labor that work together would not be very exact.

13. EXAMPLE: A company produces two similar products. Raw materials costs are $20 per unit, direct labor is $70 per unit, and manufacturing overhead totals $20,000. The company produces 1,000 units of Product 1 and 100 units of Product 2.

   a. Using direct labor as the allocation base, costs are as follows:

| | Product 1 | Product 2 | Total |
|---|---|---|---|
| Raw materials | $ 14,000 | $ 1,400 | |
| Direct labor | 70,000 | 7,000 | |
| Overhead {$20,000 × [$70,000 ÷ ($70,000 + $7,000)]} | 18,182 | | |
| Overhead {$20,000 × [$7,000 ÷ ($70,000 + $7,000)]} | | 1,818 | |
| Total costs | $102,182 | $10,218 | $112,400 |
| | | | |
| Cost per unit | $102.18 | $102.18 | |

Alternatively, assume that the overhead represents setup costs, with equal setup times required for the products. Thus, the $20,000 would be allocated equally under an ABC system. The ABC costs would be as follows:

| | Product 1 | Product 2 | Total |
|---|---|---|---|
| Raw materials | $14,000 | $ 1,400 | |
| Direct labor | 70,000 | 7,000 | |
| Overhead ($20,000 × 50%) | 10,000 | | |
| Overhead ($20,000 × 50%) | | 10,000 | |
| Total costs | $94,000 | $18,400 | $112,400 |
| | | | |
| Cost per unit | $94.00 | $184.00 | |

Because of the low volume of Product 2, the difference between the traditional allocation base and ABC is significant. If the company were selling Product 2 at $150 each (resulting in an apparent unit profit of $47.82 based on the direct-labor-based cost), it would lose money on every sale.

b.  As the example above illustrates, differences in volume can distort cost allocations even when overhead is relatively low. The distortion is worse when overhead is a higher proportion of total costs. Assume that direct labor costs are only $10 per unit and that overhead totals $140,000. The traditional allocation results in the following costs:

| | Product 1 | Product 2 | Total |
|---|---|---|---|
| Raw materials | $ 14,000 | $ 1,400 | |
| Direct labor | 10,000 | 1,000 | |
| Overhead {$140,000 × [$10,000 ÷ ($10,000 + $1,000)]} | 127,273 | | |
| Overhead {$140,000 × [$1,000 ÷ ($10,000 + $1,000)]} | | 12,727 | |
| Total costs | $151,273 | $15,127 | $166,400 |
| | | | |
| Cost per unit | $151.27 | $151.27 | |

Using the ABC system, the allocation of overhead setup costs based on equal setup times would result in the following production costs:

| | Product 1 | Product 2 | Total |
|---|---|---|---|
| Raw materials | $14,000 | $ 1,400 | |
| Direct labor | 10,000 | 1,000 | |
| Overhead ($140,000 × 50%) | 70,000 | | |
| Overhead ($140,000 × 50%) | | 70,000 | |
| Total costs | $94,000 | $72,400 | $166,400 |
| | | | |
| Cost per unit | $94.00 | $724.00 | |

Thus, the combination of relatively high overhead and a substantial difference in product volume results in unit costs for Product 1 and Product 2 that are 38% lower and 379% higher, respectively, than those computed using the traditional method.

c.  The practical effect of this difference can be illustrated in a competitive bid situation for Product 1. A manager using direct-labor-based cost would bid some amount slightly greater than $151.27 and, after losing, would then wonder how a competitor could make a profit with a bid just over $100. The ABC system provides more relevant costing figures.

14. Companies use ABC because of its ability to solve costing problems that conventional cost accounting either creates or fails to address.

a.  These problems include suboptimal pricing, poor allocation of costs, and incorrect direction by management.

b.   For example, if overhead is allocated at 700% of direct labor, managers may try to reduce direct labor costs by $1 to reduce the amount of overhead allocated by $7.

1)   But the better decision may be to ignore direct labor and concentrate on such cost-cutting efforts as eliminating setups, engineering changes, and movement of materials.

15.  Stop and review!  You have completed the outline for this subunit.  Study multiple-choice questions 46 through 63 beginning on page 185.

## 4.3 LIFE-CYCLE COSTING

1.   A life-cycle approach to budgeting estimates a product's revenues and expenses over its entire sales life cycle beginning with research and development, proceeding through the introduction and growth stages into the maturity stage, and finally into the harvest or decline stage.

a.   Accordingly, **life-cycle costing** takes a long-term view of the entire cost life cycle, also known as the **value chain**.

Value Chain for a Manufacturer

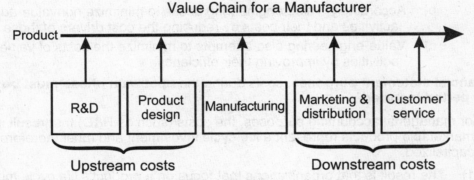

b.   This information is important for pricing decisions because revenues must cover costs incurred in each stage of the value chain, not just production.

2.   Life-cycle costing emphasizes the relationships among costs incurred at different value-chain stages, for example, the effect of reduced design costs on future customer-service costs.

a.   Because it makes a distinction between **incurring costs** (actually using resources) and **locking in (designing in) costs**, life-cycle costing highlights the potential for cost reduction activities during the upstream phase of the value chain.

b.   It is in this phase that the greatest opportunity exists to minimize downstream costs. Indeed, it has been **estimated that 90% or more of costs are committed** (not incurred) before production begins.

3.   In contrast, traditional approaches focus on cost control (as opposed to cost reduction) during production and treat pre- and postproduction (upstream and downstream) costs as period costs that are largely ignored in determining the profitability of specific products.

a.   Other costs that traditional methods ignore are the **after-purchase costs** (operating, support, repair, and disposal) incurred by customers.

b.   Accordingly, **whole-life cost** is a concept closely associated with life-cycle cost.

1)   Whole-life cost equals the life-cycle cost plus after-purchase costs.

2)   Attention to the reduction of all whole-life costs through analysis and management of all value-chain activities is a powerful competitive tool because of the potential for increasing customer satisfaction.

c. Life-cycle and whole-life cost concepts are associated with target costing and target pricing.

1) A firm may determine that market conditions require that a product sell at a given **target price**.

2) Hence, a **target cost** can be determined by subtracting the desired unit profit margin from the target price.

3) The cost reduction objectives of life-cycle and whole-life cost management can therefore be determined using target costing.

d. **Value engineering** is a means of reaching targeted cost levels.

1) Value engineering is a systematic approach to assessing all aspects of the value chain cost buildup for a product.

    a) The purpose is to minimize costs without reducing customer satisfaction.

2) For this purpose, distinguishing between value-adding and nonvalue-adding activities is useful.

    a) A value-adding activity contributes to customer value or satisfies a need of the entity. A nonvalue-adding activity does not make such a contribution.

    b) Accordingly, value engineering seeks to minimize nonvalue-adding activities and their costs by reducing the cost drivers of those activities.

    c) Value-engineering also attempts to minimize the costs of value-adding activities by improving their efficiency.

4. For **financial statement purposes**, costs during the **upstream phase must be expensed in the period incurred**.

a. For managerial accounting purposes, the costs (such as R&D) that result in marketable products represent a life-cycle investment and must therefore be capitalized.

1) The result is that organizations that focus on a product's life cycle must develop an accounting system consistent with GAAP for financial reporting purposes.

2) However, it should allow for capitalization and subsequent allocation of upstream costs for managerial accounting purposes.

b. Essentially, life-cycle costing requires the accumulation of all costs over a product's lifetime, from inception of the idea to the abandonment of the product.

1) These costs are then allocated to production on an expected unit-of-output basis.

c. The **internal income statement** for a product will report total sales for all periods, minus all expenses to date.

1) A risk reserve may be established as an account contra to the capitalized costs.

2) The reserve consists of any deferred product costs that might not be recovered if sales are less than planned.

d. The overall **advantage** of life-cycle costing is that it provides a better measure for evaluating the performance of product managers.

1) Traditional financial statements, however, might report that certain products were extremely profitable because upstream costs were expensed in previous periods.

2) For example, if a substantial investment is made in the development of a new product, but that product quickly becomes obsolete due to new technology, how worthwhile was the investment?

3) Life-cycle costing combines all costs and revenues for all periods to provide a better view of a product's overall performance.

5. Stop and review! You have completed the outline for this subunit. Study multiple-choice questions 64 through 70 beginning on page 192.

## 4.4 OPERATION COSTING

1. **Operation costing** is a **hybrid** of job-order costing and process costing that emphasizes physical processes (operations) for cost management and control purposes.

   a. Operation costing is appropriate **when similar products are produced in different models or styles** or otherwise have distinctive traits.

      1) Operation costing is often used for such items as clothes, shoes, electronics, and jewelry.

   b. Operation costing is used by firms that produce batches of similar units that are subject to selected processing steps (operations).

      1) Different batches may pass through different sets of operations, but all units are processed identically within a given operation.

      2) Operation costing also may be appropriate when different materials are processed through the same basic operations, such as the woodworking, finishing, and polishing of different product lines of furniture.

   c. Operation costing accumulates total conversion costs and determines a **unit conversion cost** (total conversion cost ÷ total units passing through the operation) for each operation as in process costing.

      1) Production is controlled using work orders, and direct materials costs are charged specifically to products as in job-order systems.

      2) Cost classifications are not necessarily limited to direct materials and conversion costs, and the costs within each classification may be assigned using the more appropriate of job costing or process costing.

      3) More work-in-process accounts are needed because one is required for each operation.

2. Stop and review! You have completed the outline for this subunit. Study multiple-choice questions 71 through 76 beginning on page 195.

## 4.5 BACKFLUSH COSTING

1. **Backflush costing** is often used by firms that have adopted a **just-in-time (JIT)** production philosophy.

   a. A JIT system **treats carrying inventory as a nonvalue-adding activity**.

      1) Hence, components are made available just in time to be used in the production process.

      2) Backflush costing **complements JIT** because it simplifies costing.

   b. A traditional system tracks costs as they are incurred (sequential tracking), but backflush costing delays recording of some cost information.

      1) Backflush costing treats the detailed recording of inventory data as a nonvalue-adding activity.

      2) **Work-in-process is usually eliminated**, journal entries to inventory accounts may be delayed until the time of product completion or even the time of sale, and standard costs are used to assign costs to units when journal entries are made, that is, to "flush" costs out of the system to the points at which inventories remain.

c.   Backflush costing works well with JIT systems because of the simplification of production, which is reflected in the use of **manufacturing cells**.

1)   These cells are groups of machines and workers producing a given type of product.

2)   Each worker can operate and maintain the machines, perform set-up activities, make quality inspections, and move work-in-process within the cell.

3)   The result is **less need for central support departments**, placement of materials and tools close to the point of use, savings of space, and greater production flexibility.

4)   A further benefit is that a JIT system allows for identification of more direct costs and therefore minimizes overhead allocations.

a)   For the same reason, backflush costing also complements activity-based costing (ABC).

d.   **One variation of backflush costing** records raw materials inventory at standard cost when it is purchased.

1)   Because materials arrive just in time for processing, an entry to a separate materials inventory account is unnecessary.

| | | |
|---|---|---|
| Raw and in-process inventory | $XXX | |
| Materials price variance (dr. or cr.) | XXX | |
|     Accounts payable | | $XXX |

2)   Conversion costs (direct labor and overhead) are recorded when incurred at their actual amounts.

| | | |
|---|---|---|
| Conversion costs | $XXX | |
|     Salaries and wages payable, etc. | | $XXX |

3)   The entry for the transfer to finished goods is where backflush costing gets its name. Because costs have not been accumulated sequentially during production, these costs must be "flushed out" once production is complete.

| | | |
|---|---|---|
| Finished goods (standard cost) | $XXX | |
|     Raw and in-process inventory (standard cost) | | $XXX |
|     Conversion costs (standard cost) | | XXX |

a)   This one entry summarizes the effect of all the sequential entries of a traditional costing system that do not get made in backflush costing.

4)   After a count, raw and in-process inventory is adjusted for the materials efficiency variance (debit or credit).

a)   This variance is recorded for the difference between actual usage and standard usage for the amount of goods finished.

5)   The under- or overapplied conversion costs (debit conversion costs applied and credit conversion costs control) are usually closed to cost of goods sold instead of being prorated because the amounts tend to be small.

6)   The final entry is the same as under a traditional costing system.

| | | |
|---|---|---|
| Cost of goods sold | $XXX | |
|     Finished goods | | $XXX |

e. **A greater departure from traditional methods** is to recognize the sale but not the completion of units.

1) In this variation of backflush costing, only one inventory account is used (inventory control) instead of two (raw and in-process inventory and finished goods).

2) The entry at the time of the acquisition of direct materials is:

| | | |
|---|---|---|
| Inventory control | $XXX | |
| Materials price variance (dr. or cr.) | XXX | |
|    Accounts payable | | $XXX |

3) As described in d.2) on the previous page, actual conversion costs are debited to a control account.

4) Under this method, no finished goods inventory is carried at all.

| | | |
|---|---|---|
| Cost of goods sold | $XXX | |
|    Inventory control | | $XXX |
|    Conversion costs | | XXX |

5) As described in d.5) on the previous page, under- or overapplied conversion costs are recognized by debiting conversion costs applied and crediting conversion costs control with, typically, a debit or credit to cost of goods sold.

6) All conversion costs are period costs in this version of backflush costing.

7) If recognition of a direct materials efficiency variance is desired, a physical count is made, and the difference between what is on hand and what should be on hand is the variance for which inventory is adjusted.

f. **Another possibility** is to eliminate entries to a materials inventory account altogether.

1) Accordingly, finished goods are debited when completed (with credits to accounts payable, etc., and to overhead applied) and credited when sold, but no other inventory entries are made.

g. **Yet another variation** of backflush costing records costs (direct materials, direct labor, and overhead) directly in cost of goods sold.

1) At the end of the period, the standard costs of the ending work-in-process and finished goods inventories are flushed back from cost of goods sold (debit WIP and FG, credit CGS).

h. Backflush costing may undervalue inventory and is therefore **inconsistent with GAAP** except when the difference is not material or an adjustment is made. Another criticism is that the lack of sequential tracking leaves an inadequate audit trail.

2. Stop and review! You have completed the outline for this subunit. Study multiple-choice questions 77 through 83 beginning on page 197.

## 4.6 CORE CONCEPTS

Process Costing

- Process cost accounting is applicable to **relatively homogeneous products** that are **mass produced** on a continuous basis (e.g., refined oil).
- Costs are accumulated **department by department**, not job by job.
- Costs are grouped by **direct materials** and **conversion costs** (direct labor and overhead).
- **Two methods** for accumulating costs and valuing inventory are in common use.
- Under **weighted-average**, beginning work-in-process inventory is not considered.  Under **first-in, first-out**, beginning work-in-process inventory is taken into account.

Activity-Based Costing

- Activity-based costing attaches costs to **activities rather than to physical goods**.  It may be used by manufacturing, service, or retailing entities and in job-order or process costing systems.
- Activity-based costing **prevents the inappropriate spreading of costs** over products or service units that use different amounts of resources (peanut-butter costing).
- **Cost pools** are established for each activity and **cost drivers** are associated with each pool.

Life-Cycle Costing

- The life-cycle approach to costing considers the revenues and costs associated with a product over its **entire life cycle**, rather than just the costs associated with manufacturing.
- Life-cycle costing considers costs attaching in **every stage of the value chain**, beginning with R&D and ending with product phaseout.
- Life-cycle costing makes a distinction between costs that are **incurred** (i.e., at the time resources are used) and costs that are **locked in** (i.e., committed to by the company owing to the product's design).

Operation Costing

- Operation costing is a **hybrid** of job-order and process costing.  It is appropriate when similar products are produced in different models or styles or otherwise have distinctive traits.
- Operation costing accumulates total conversion costs and determines a **unit conversion cost** for each operation as in process costing.

Backflush Costing

- Backflush costing **rejects the traditional sequential method** of accumulating costs as products move through the manufacturing process.
- When production is complete, certain journal entries are made to **"flush" the costs out of the system** that would have been recorded earlier in the process under a traditional system.

## QUESTIONS

### 4.1 Process Costing

**1.** Smile Labs develops 35mm film using a four-step process that moves progressively through four departments. The company specializes in overnight service and has the largest drug store chain as its primary customer. Currently, direct labor, direct materials, and overhead are accumulated by department. The cost accumulation system that best describes the system Smile Labs is using is

   A. Operation costing.

   B. Activity-based costing.

   C. Job-order costing.

   D. Process costing.

Answer (D) is correct. *(CMA, adapted)*
   **REQUIRED:** The type of costing system that accumulates costs by department.
   **DISCUSSION:** Process costing is used to assign costs to similar products that are mass produced on a continuous basis. Costs are accumulated by departments or cost centers rather than by jobs. Process costing is an averaging process that calculates the average cost of all units.
   Answer (A) is incorrect because operation costing is used for goods that undergo some similar and some dissimilar processes. Direct materials are costed on a job-order basis, whereas a unit conversion cost is determined for each operation. Answer (B) is incorrect because ABC emphasizes activities as the basic cost objects. It establishes cost pools for the activities and then reassigns those costs to other cost objects (e.g., products) on the basis of their consumption of the related cost drivers. Answer (C) is incorrect because job-order costing accumulates costs by job rather than by department.

**2.** Which one of the following alternatives correctly classifies the business application to the appropriate costing system?

| | Job Costing System | Process Costing System |
|---|---|---|
| A. | Wallpaper manufacturer | Oil refinery |
| B. | Aircraft assembly | Public accounting firm |
| C. | Paint manufacturer | Retail banking |
| D. | Print shop | Beverage manufacturer |

Answer (D) is correct. *(CMA, adapted)*
   **REQUIRED:** The appropriate matching of business applications with costing systems.
   **DISCUSSION:** A job costing system is used when products differ from one customer to the next, that is, when products are heterogeneous. A process costing system is used when similar products are mass produced on a continuous basis. A print shop, for example, would use a job costing system because each job will be unique. Each customer provides the specifications for the product desired. A beverage manufacturer, however, would use a process costing system because homogenous units are produced continuously.
   Answer (A) is incorrect because a wallpaper manufacturer would use a process costing system. Answer (B) is incorrect because a public accounting firm would use a job costing system. Answer (C) is incorrect because a paint manufacturer would use a process costing system.

**3.** The cost of goods manufactured for Toddler Toys for the year 2000 was $860,000. Beginning work-in-process inventory was $50,000. Ending work-in-process was $60,000. If the beginning finished goods inventory was $500,000 and the ending finished goods inventory was $990,000, what was the cost of goods sold for the year?

   A. $360,000

   B. $370,000

   C. $490,000

   D. $1,350,000

Answer (B) is correct. *(Publisher)*
   **REQUIRED:** The cost of goods sold.
   **DISCUSSION:** Beginning finished goods inventory ($500,000) + cost of goods manufactured ($860,000) – ending finished goods inventory ($990,000) = cost of goods sold ($370,000). The work-in-process inventories are irrelevant.
   Answer (A) is incorrect because $360,000 results from subtracting the difference between beginning and ending work-in-process inventories from the cost of goods sold. Answer (C) is incorrect because $490,000 represents the difference between beginning and ending inventories. Answer (D) is incorrect because $1,350,000 is the result of reversing the treatment of beginning and ending finished goods inventories.

**4.** If the beginning balance for May of the materials inventory account was $27,500, the ending balance for May is $28,750, and $128,900 of materials were used during the month, the materials purchased during the month cost

   A. $101,400

   B. $127,650

   C. $130,150

   D. $157,650

Answer (C) is correct. *(CMA, adapted)*
   **REQUIRED:** The materials purchased during the month.
   **DISCUSSION:** Purchases equals usage adjusted for the inventory change. Hence, purchases equals $130,150 ($128,900 used – $27,500 BI + $28,750 EI).
   Answer (A) is incorrect because $101,400 assumes zero ending inventory. Answer (B) is incorrect because $127,650 results from reversing the treatment of beginning and ending inventories. Answer (D) is incorrect because $157,650 assumes zero beginning inventory.

**5.** If the beginning monthly balance of materials inventory was $37,000, the ending balance was $39,500, and $257,800 of materials were used, the cost of materials purchased during the month was

A. $255,300

B. $257,800

C. $260,300

D. $297,300

Answer (C) is correct.  *(Publisher)*
REQUIRED: The materials purchased during the month.
DISCUSSION: Materials used equals beginning inventory, plus purchases, minus ending inventory. Given that purchases are not known, the calculation is as follows:

$$\$37,000 + P - \$39,500 = \$257,800$$
$$P = \$257,800 + \$39,500 - \$37,000$$
$$P = \$260,300$$

Answer (A) is incorrect because $255,300 transposed the ending and beginning inventory amounts. Answer (B) is incorrect because $257,800 is the amount of materials used without regard to changes in inventory levels. Answer (D) is incorrect because $297,300 fails to consider the beginning inventory.

---

Questions 6 through 10 are based on the following information.

Madtack Company's beginning and ending inventories for the month of November are

| | November 1 | November 30 |
|---|---|---|
| Direct materials | $ 67,000 | $ 62,000 |
| Work-in-process | 145,000 | 171,000 |
| Finished goods | 85,000 | 78,000 |

Production data for the month of November follows:

| | |
|---|---|
| Direct labor | $200,000 |
| Actual overhead | 132,000 |
| Direct materials purchased | 163,000 |
| Transportation in | 4,000 |
| Purchase returns and allowances | 2,000 |

Madtack uses one overhead control account and charges overhead to production at 70% of direct labor cost. The company does not formally recognize over/underapplied overhead until year-end.

---

**6.** Madtack Company's prime cost for November is

A. $370,000

B. $168,000

C. $363,000

D. $170,000

Answer (A) is correct.  *(CMA, adapted)*
REQUIRED: The prime cost.
DISCUSSION: Prime costs are defined as direct materials and direct labor. The first step is to calculate the cost of raw materials used during the month:

| | |
|---|---|
| Beginning materials inventory | $ 67,000 |
| Plus purchases | 163,000 |
| Plus transportation in | 4,000 |
| Minus purchase returns | (2,000) |
| Materials available for use | $232,000 |
| Minus ending materials inventory | (62,000) |
| Materials used | $170,000 |

Adding the $170,000 of materials used to the $200,000 of direct labor results in a total of $370,000 for prime costs.
Answer (B) is incorrect because $168,000 equals purchases of materials adjusted for the change in inventories. Answer (C) is incorrect because $363,000 incorporates the change in finished goods inventories. Answer (D) is incorrect because $170,000 equals the materials used.

---

**7.** Madtack Company's total manufacturing cost for November is

A. $502,000

B. $503,000

C. $363,000

D. $510,000

Answer (D) is correct.  *(CMA, adapted)*
REQUIRED: The total manufacturing costs for the month.
DISCUSSION: Total manufacturing costs consist of materials, labor, and overhead. Total prime costs were $370,000. Overhead applied was $140,000 ($200,000 of direct labor × 70%). Thus, total manufacturing cost is $510,000 ($170,000 + $200,000 + $140,000).
Answer (A) is incorrect because $502,000 is based on actual overhead. Answer (B) is incorrect because $503,000 incorporates the change in finished goods inventories.
Answer (C) is incorrect because $363,000 excludes overhead but includes the change in finished goods inventory.

**8.** Madtack Company's cost of goods transferred to finished goods inventory for November is

A. $469,000

B. $477,000

C. $495,000

D. $484,000

Answer (D) is correct. *(CMA, adapted)*
**REQUIRED:** The cost of goods transferred to finished goods inventory during the month.
**DISCUSSION:** Total manufacturing costs consist of materials, labor, and overhead. That amount is then adjusted for the change in work-in-process inventories to arrive at the cost of goods transferred to finished goods. Total manufacturing cost was $510,000. Thus, the cost of goods transferred to finished goods inventory is $484,000 ($510,000 + $145,000 – $171,000).
Answer (A) is incorrect because $469,000 uses actual overhead and adjusts the figures for the change in finished goods inventory. Answer (B) is incorrect because $477,000 includes the change in finished goods inventory in the calculation. Answer (C) is incorrect because $495,000 uses materials purchased rather than materials used and also fails to adjust properly for transportation in.

**9.** Madtack Company's cost of goods sold for November is

A. $484,000

B. $491,000

C. $502,000

D. $476,000

Answer (B) is correct. *(CMA, adapted)*
**REQUIRED:** The cost of goods sold for the month.
**DISCUSSION:** The cost of goods sold section of the income statement is below.

| | |
|---|---:|
| Beginning finished goods inventory | $ 85,000 |
| Add: Cost of goods manufactured | 484,000 |
| Goods available for sale | $569,000 |
| Minus: Ending finished goods inventory | (78,000) |
| Cost of goods sold | $491,000 |

Answer (A) is incorrect because $484,000 is the cost of goods manufactured. Answer (C) is incorrect because $502,000 is based on cost of goods manufactured of $495,000. Answer (D) is incorrect because $476,000 is based on actual overhead costs and fails to adjust for the change in finished goods inventories.

**10.** Madtack Company's net charge to overhead control for the month of November is

A. $8,000 debit, overapplied.

B. $8,000 debit, underapplied.

C. $8,000 credit, overapplied.

D. $8,000 credit, underapplied.

Answer (C) is correct. *(CMA, adapted)*
**REQUIRED:** The net charge to the overhead control account for the month.
**DISCUSSION:** The overhead control account would have been debited for $132,000 of actual overhead. Credits would have totaled $140,000 representing 70% of direct labor costs of $200,000. Hence, the $140,000 credit exceeds the $132,000 debit. Overhead was overapplied by $8,000.
Answer (A) is incorrect because an overapplication of overhead is represented by a credit in the overhead control account. Answer (B) is incorrect because the overhead was overapplied for the month. Answer (D) is incorrect because the overhead was overapplied for the month.

Questions 11 through 17 are based on the following information.

Rebel Corporation uses a process-costing system. Products are manufactured in a series of three departments. The following data relate to Department Two for the month of February:

| | |
|---|---|
| Beginning work-in-process (70% complete) | 10,000 units |
| Goods started in production | 80,000 units |
| Ending work-in-process (60% complete) | 5,000 units |

The beginning work-in-process was valued at $66,000, consisting of $20,000 of transferred-in costs, $30,000 of materials costs, and $16,000 of conversion costs. Materials are added at the beginning of the process; conversion costs are added evenly throughout the process. Costs added to production during February were

| | |
|---|---|
| Transferred-in | $16,000 |
| Materials used | 88,000 |
| Conversion costs | 50,000 |

All preliminary and final calculations are rounded to two decimal places.

**11.** Under the weighted-average method, how much conversion cost did Rebel Corporation transfer out of Department Two during February?

A. $69,259

B. $63,750

C. $66,000

D. $64,148

Answer (B) is correct.  *(Publisher)*
**REQUIRED:** The conversion cost transferred out under the weighted-average method.
**DISCUSSION:** For conversion costs, the equivalent-unit calculation under the weighted-average method is as follows:

| | |
|---|---|
| Beginning WIP | 10,000 units × 100% = 10,000 |
| Started and completed | 75,000 units × 100% = 75,000 |
| Ending WIP | 5,000 units × 60% = 3,000 |
| | 88,000 |

The conversion costs consisted of $16,000 in beginning inventory and $50,000 incurred during the month, for a total of $66,000. Unit conversion cost is therefore $.75 ($66,000 ÷ $88,000 EU). Thus, the total conversion cost transferred was $63,750 [(10,000 units in BWIP + 80,000 units started – 5,000 units in EWIP) × $.75].
Answer (A) is incorrect because $69,259 results from using the equivalent units calculated under FIFO (81,000) in determining the unit conversion cost under the weighted-average method. Answer (C) is incorrect because $66,000 equals the total conversion costs to be accounted for. Answer (D) is incorrect because $64,148 is the conversion cost transferred out under a FIFO assumption.

**12.** Under the weighted-average method, how much materials cost did Rebel Corporation transfer out of Department Two during February?

A. $88,000

B. $93,500

C. $111,350

D. $112,500

Answer (C) is correct.  *(Publisher)*
**REQUIRED:** The materials cost transferred out under the weighted-average method.
**DISCUSSION:** For materials, the equivalent-unit calculation under the weighted-average method is

| | |
|---|---|
| Beginning WIP | 10,000 units × 100% = 10,000 |
| Started and completed | 75,000 units × 100% = 75,000 |
| Ending WIP | 5,000 units × 100% = 5,000 |
| | 90,000 |

The materials costs consisted of $30,000 in beginning inventory and $88,000 incurred during the month, for a total of $118,000. The equivalent unit cost of materials is therefore $1.31 ($118,000 ÷ 90,000 EU). Total materials cost transferred is $111,350 (85,000 units transferred × $1.31).
Answer (A) is incorrect because $88,000 is the materials costs incurred during the month. Answer (B) is incorrect because $93,500 results from using a unit cost based on the FIFO method. Answer (D) is incorrect because $112,500 is the materials cost transferred out under FIFO.

**13.** Under the weighted-average method, what is the total of equivalent units for transferred-in costs for the month?

A. 75,000 units.

B. 80,000 units.

C. 81,000 units.

D. 90,000 units.

Answer (D) is correct.  *(Publisher)*
**REQUIRED:** The equivalent units for transferred-in costs under the weighted-average method.
**DISCUSSION:** The equivalent units for transferred-in costs are calculated in the same way as those for materials added at the beginning of the process. The equivalent-unit calculation under the weighted-average method is

| | | |
|---|---|---|
| Beginning WIP | 10,000 units × 100% = | 10,000 |
| Started and completed | 75,000 units × 100% = | 75,000 |
| Ending WIP | 5,000 units × 100% = | 5,000 |
| | | 90,000 |

Answer (A) is incorrect because 75,000 units is the amount started and completed during the month; it ignores the impact of inventories. Answer (B) is incorrect because 80,000 units is based on the FIFO method. Answer (C) is incorrect because 81,000 units is based on the equivalent units for conversion costs calculated under the FIFO method.

**14.** Assume that the company uses the first-in, first-out (FIFO) method of inventory valuation. Under FIFO, how much conversion cost did Rebel Corporation transfer out of Department Two during February?

A. $63,750

B. $64,360

C. $66,000

D. $74,500

Answer (B) is correct.  *(Publisher)*
**REQUIRED:** The conversion cost transferred out under the FIFO method.
**DISCUSSION:** For conversion costs, the equivalent-unit calculation under the FIFO method is

| | | |
|---|---|---|
| Beginning WIP | 10,000 units × 30% = | 3,000 |
| Started and completed | 75,000 units × 100% = | 75,000 |
| Ending WIP | 5,000 units × 60% = | 3,000 |
| | | 81,000 |

The conversion cost includes $16,000 in beginning inventory, all of which would have been transferred out. The $50,000 incurred during the month is divided by the 81,000 equivalent units to arrive at a unit cost for the current period of $.62. Given that 78,000 equivalent units (85,000 physical units transferred out – 7,000 EU in BWIP completed in the prior period) of current-period production were completed and transferred, the total conversion cost transferred out was $64,360 [$16,000 BWIP + ($.62 × 78,000 FIFO EU)].
Answer (A) is incorrect because $63,750 is based on the weighted-average method. Answer (C) is incorrect because $66,000 equals total conversion costs incurred. Answer (D) is incorrect because $74,500 is based on the weighted-average unit cost per equivalent unit.

**15.** Assuming the company uses the FIFO method of inventory valuation, conversion costs included in the ending work-in-process inventory equal

A. $1,860

B. $2,250

C. $3,100

D. $5,500

Answer (A) is correct.  *(Publisher)*
**REQUIRED:** The conversion cost included in ending inventory under the FIFO method.
**DISCUSSION:** The FIFO unit conversion cost for the current period is $.62. Moreover, ending work-in-process consists of 3,000 equivalent units of conversion cost (5,000 physical units × 60%). Accordingly, the conversion cost in the ending work-in-process inventory consists of $1,860 (3,000 EU × $.62) of current-period cost. The conversion cost incurred in the prior period and attached to the beginning work-in-process inventory is deemed to have been transferred out.
Answer (B) is incorrect because $2,250 is based on the weighted-average method. Answer (C) is incorrect because $3,100 is based on the equivalent units for materials. Answer (D) is incorrect because $5,500 is the amount of materials cost in the ending work-in-process inventory.

**16.** Refer to the information on the preceding page(s). Assume that the company uses the first-in, first-out (FIFO) method of inventory valuation. Under FIFO, how much materials cost did Rebel Corporation transfer out of Department Two during February?

A.    $88,000

B.    $111,350

C.    $112,500

D.    $114,615

Answer (C) is correct.    *(Publisher)*
    **REQUIRED:** The materials cost transferred out under FIFO.
    **DISCUSSION:** For materials, the equivalent-unit calculation under the FIFO method is

| | | |
|---|---|---|
| Beginning WIP | 10,000 units × 0% = | 0 |
| Started and completed | 75,000 units × 100% = | 75,000 |
| Ending WIP | 5,000 units × 100% = | 5,000 |
| | | 80,000 |

The materials cost includes $30,000 in beginning inventory, all of which would have been transferred out. The $88,000 incurred during the month is divided by the 80,000 equivalent units to arrive at a unit cost for the current period of $1.10. Thus, given that 75,000 equivalent units (85,000 physical units transferred out – 10,000 EU in BWIP completed in the prior period) of current-period production were completed and transferred, total materials cost transferred out equals $112,500 [$30,000 BWIP + (75,000 FIFO EU × $1.10)].
    Answer (A) is incorrect because $88,000 is the amount of materials costs incurred during the month. Answer (B) is incorrect because $111,350 is based on the weighted-average method. Answer (D) is incorrect because $114,615 is based on the equivalent units for conversion costs.

**17.** Refer to the information on the preceding page(s). Assuming the company uses the FIFO method of inventory valuation, what amount of materials cost is included in the ending work-in-process inventory?

A.    $1,860

B.    $3,300

C.    $5,500

D.    $6,450

Answer (C) is correct.    *(Publisher)*
    **REQUIRED:** The materials cost left in ending work-in-process inventory under FIFO.
    **DISCUSSION:** The unit cost of materials under FIFO is $1.10. Because the 5,000 units in ending work-in-process inventory are 100% complete as to materials, its materials cost consists of $5,500 (5,000 EU × $1.10) of current-period costs. Materials costs incurred in the prior period and attached to the beginning work-in-process inventory are deemed to have been transferred out.
    Answer (A) is incorrect because $1,860 is the amount of conversion costs. Answer (B) is incorrect because $3,300 assumes that materials are added proportionately throughout the process. Answer (D) is incorrect because $6,450 is based on the unit cost under the weighted-average method.

Questions 18 and 19 are based on the following information.

A sporting goods manufacturer buys wood as a direct material for baseball bats. The Forming Department processes the baseball bats, and the bats are then transferred to the Finishing Department where a sealant is applied. The Forming Department began manufacturing 10,000 "Casey Sluggers" during the month of May. There was no beginning inventory.

Costs for the Forming Department for the month of May were as follows:

| | |
|---|---|
| Direct materials | $33,000 |
| Conversion costs | 17,000 |
| Total | $50,000 |

A total of 8,000 bats were completed and transferred to the Finishing Department; the remaining 2,000 bats were still in the forming process at the end of the month. All of the Forming Department's direct materials were placed in process, but, on average, only 25% of the conversion cost was applied to the ending work-in-process inventory.

**18.** The cost of the units transferred to the Finishing Department is

A. $50,000

B. $40,000

C. $53,000

D. $42,400

Answer (D) is correct. *(CMA, adapted)*
**REQUIRED:** The cost of the units transferred to the Finishing Department.
**DISCUSSION:** The total equivalent units for raw materials equals 10,000 because all materials for the ending work-in-process had already been added to production. Hence, the materials cost per unit was $3.30 ($33,000 ÷ 10,000). For conversion costs, the total equivalent units equals 8,500 [8,000 completed + (2,000 in EWIP × 25%)]. Thus, the conversion cost was $2.00 per unit ($17,000 ÷ 8,500). The total cost transferred was therefore $42,400 [8,000 units × ($3.30 + $2.00)].
Answer (A) is incorrect because a portion of the total costs is still in work-in-process. Answer (B) is incorrect because $40,000 assumes that work-in-process is 100% complete as to conversion costs. Answer (C) is incorrect because $53,000 exceeds the actual costs incurred during the period. Given no beginning inventory, the amount transferred out cannot exceed the costs incurred during the period.

**19.** The cost of the work-in-process inventory in the Forming Department at the end of May is

A. $10,000

B. $2,500

C. $20,000

D. $7,600

Answer (D) is correct. *(CMA, adapted)*
**REQUIRED:** The cost of the work-in-process inventory.
**DISCUSSION:** The equivalent units for raw materials would be 10,000 (8,000 + 2,000) since the work-in-process is 100% complete as to materials. Therefore, dividing the $33,000 by 10,000 units results in a unit cost for materials of $3.30. The equivalent units for conversion costs would be 8,500 units [8,000 + (2,000 units × .25)]. Dividing the $17,000 of conversion costs by 8,500 equivalent units results in a unit cost of $2 per bat. Therefore, the total cost of goods transferred out would be $5.30, consisting of $3.30 for materials and $2 for conversion costs. Multiplying $5.30 times the 8,000 bats completed results in a total transfer of $42,400. Consequently, the cost of the ending work-in-process must have been $7,600 ($50,000 total costs incurred − $42,400).
Answer (A) is incorrect because $10,000 assumes that work-in-process inventory is 100% complete as to conversion costs. Answer (B) is incorrect because $2,500 assumes that work-in-process inventory is 100% complete as to conversion costs and that 500 bats are in inventory. Answer (C) is incorrect because $20,000 assumes that work-in-process is 100% complete as to conversion costs and that 6,000 units were transferred out.

Questions 20 through 23 are based on the following information.

Levittown Company employs a process cost system for its manufacturing operations. All direct materials are added at the beginning of the process and conversion costs are added proportionately. Levittown's production quantity schedule for November is reproduced in the next column.

| | Units |
|---|---|
| Work-in-process on November 1 | |
| (60% complete as to conversion costs) | 1,000 |
| Units started during November | 5,000 |
| Total units to account for | 6,000 |
| | |
| Units completed and transferred out | |
| from beginning inventory | 1,000 |
| Units started and completed during November | 3,000 |
| Work-in-process on November 30 | |
| (20% complete as to conversion costs) | 2,000 |
| Total units accounted for | 6,000 |

**20.** Using the FIFO method, the equivalent units for direct materials for November are

A. 5,000 units.

B. 6,000 units.

C. 4,400 units.

D. 3,800 units.

Answer (A) is correct. *(CMA, adapted)*
**REQUIRED:** The equivalent units for direct materials under the FIFO method.
**DISCUSSION:** The computation of equivalent units for a period using the FIFO method of process costing includes only the conversion costs and material added to the product in that period and excludes any work done in previous periods. Accordingly, FIFO equivalent units include work and material to complete BWIP, plus work and material to complete units started this period, minus work and material needed to complete EWIP. Given that all materials are added at the beginning of the process, only those units started during November would have received materials in that month. Because 5,000 units were started, the equivalent units for direct materials equal 5,000.
Answer (B) is incorrect because 6,000 is the total units to account for. Answer (C) is incorrect because 4,400 equals units completed and transferred out from BI plus units started and completed in November plus 20% of work-in-process on November 30 (1,000 + 3,000 + 400). Answer (D) is incorrect because 3,800 is not the equivalent units for direct materials. Only those units started during November would have received materials in that month. Therefore, equivalent units for direct materials equal 5,000.

**21.** Using the FIFO method, the equivalent units for conversion costs for November are

A. 3,400 units.

B. 3,800 units.

C. 4,000 units.

D. 4,400 units.

Answer (B) is correct. *(CMA, adapted)*
**REQUIRED:** The equivalent units for conversion costs under the FIFO method.
**DISCUSSION:** Given that BWIP (1,000 units) was already 60% complete, 400 equivalent units were needed for completion. In addition, 3,000 units were started and completed during the period. The 2,000 units in EWIP equal 400 equivalent units since they are 20% complete. Total equivalent units are 3,800 (400 + 3,000 + 400).
Answer (A) is incorrect because 3,400 units consist of the units started and completed during November plus the 20% of work-in-process complete as to conversion costs (3,000 + 400). Answer (C) is incorrect because 4,000 units consist of the units started and completed in November and the units completed and transferred out from BI (3,000 + 1,000). Answer (D) is incorrect because 4,400 units consist of the units started and completed in November, plus the units completed and transferred out from BI plus the 20% of work-in-process complete as to conversion costs (3,000 + 1,000 + 400).

**22.** Using the weighted-average method, the equivalent units for direct materials for November are

   A.  3,400 units.

   B.  4,400 units.

   C.  5,000 units.

   D.  6,000 units.

Answer (D) is correct. *(CMA, adapted)*
   **REQUIRED:** The equivalent units for direct materials using the weighted-average method.
   **DISCUSSION:** The difference between the weighted-average and FIFO methods of process costing is how BWIP is handled. FIFO makes a distinction between the costs in BWIP and the costs of goods started this period. Weighted average does not. Thus, when there is no BWIP, there is no difference between the two costing methods. Because 6,000 units have been started (1,000 BWIP + 5,000 started this period), and all materials are added at the beginning of the process, equivalent units for materials equal 6,000.
   Answer (A) is incorrect because 3,400 units equals units started and completed in November plus 20% of ending work-in-process (3,000 + 400). Answer (B) is incorrect because 4,400 units equals units started and completed in November plus units completed and transferred out from BI plus 20% of ending work-in-process (3,000 + 1,000 + 400). Answer (C) is incorrect because 5,000 is the number of units started in November.

**23.** Using the weighted-average method, the equivalent units for conversion costs for November are

   A.  3,400 units.

   B.  3,800 units.

   C.  4,000 units.

   D.  4,400 units.

Answer (D) is correct. *(CMA, adapted)*
   **REQUIRED:** The equivalent units for conversion costs using the weighted-average method.
   **DISCUSSION:** Under the weighted-average method, work in the previous period on the beginning inventories is included along with the work added this period. Thus, the only difference between the FIFO calculations and the weighted-average calculation is the equivalent units for the beginning inventory. The 4,000 completed units (1,000 BWIP + 3,000 started this period) equal 4,000 equivalent units. The 2,000 units in EWIP are equivalent to 400 units (2,000 units × 20% complete). Thus, there are 4,400 conversion cost equivalent units.
   Answer (A) is incorrect because 3,400 units consist of the units started and completed in November plus the 20% of work-in-process complete as to conversion costs (3,000 + 400). Answer (B) is incorrect because 3,800 units equal the 400 units in BWIP needed for completion plus the units started and completed in November plus the 20% of work-in-process complete as to conversion costs (400 + 3,000 + 400). Answer (C) is incorrect because 4,000 units equal the units completed and transferred out from BI plus units started and completed during November (1,000 + 3,000).

**24.** Which of the following is a period cost rather than a product cost of a manufacturer?

   A.  Direct materials.

   B.  Variable overhead.

   C.  Fixed overhead.

   D.  Abnormal spoilage.

Answer (D) is correct. *(Publisher)*
   **REQUIRED:** The period cost.
   **DISCUSSION:** Materials, labor, and overhead (both fixed and variable) are examples of product costs. Abnormal spoilage is an example of a period cost. Abnormal spoilage is not inherent in a production process and should not be categorized as a product cost. Abnormal spoilage should be charged to a loss account in the period that detection of the spoilage occurs.
   Answer (A) is incorrect because direct materials are product costs. Answer (B) is incorrect because variable overhead is a product cost. Answer (C) is incorrect because fixed overhead is a product cost.

Questions 25 and 26 are based on the following information.

A company employs a process costing system for its two-department manufacturing operation using the first-in, first-out (FIFO) inventory method. When units are completed in Department 1, they are transferred to Department 2 for completion. Inspection takes place in Department 2 immediately before the direct materials are added, when the process is 70% complete with respect to conversion. The specific identification method is used to account for lost units.

The number of defective units (that is, those failing inspection) is usually below the normal tolerance limit of 4% of units inspected. Defective units have minimal value, and the company sells them without any further processing for whatever it can. Generally, the amount collected equals, or slightly exceeds, the transportation cost. A summary of the manufacturing activity for Department 2, in units for the current month, is presented in the next column.

| | Physical Flow (output units) |
|---|---|
| Beginning inventory (60% complete with respect to conversion) | 20,000 |
| Units transferred in from Department 1 | 180,000 |
| Total units to account for | 200,000 |
| | |
| Units completed in Department 2 during the month | 170,000 |
| Units found to be defective at inspection | 5,000 |
| Ending inventory (80% complete with respect to conversion) | 25,000 |
| Total units accounted for | 200,000 |

**25.** The equivalent units for direct materials for the current month would be

   A. 175,000 units.

   B. 181,500 units.

   C. 195,000 units.

   D. 200,000 units.

Answer (C) is correct.  *(CIA, adapted)*
**REQUIRED:** The equivalent units for direct materials for the current month.
**DISCUSSION:** The equivalent units for direct materials equals 195,000 units (20,000 BWIP + 150,000 units started and completed + 25,000 EWIP). This calculation recognizes that direct materials had not been added to beginning inventory (60% complete) and spoiled units (70% complete), but that ending inventory (80% complete) includes direct materials.
Answer (A) is incorrect because 175,000 units does not include 20,000 units from BWIP. Answer (B) is incorrect because 181,500 units includes 150,000 units plus 40% of BWIP, 80% of EWIP, and 70% of the defective units. Answer (D) is incorrect because 200,000 units includes 100% of the defective units.

**26.** The units that failed inspection during the current month would be classified as

   A. Abnormal spoilage.

   B. Normal scrap.

   C. Normal reworked units.

   D. Normal waste.

Answer (B) is correct.  *(CIA, adapted)*
**REQUIRED:** The classification of units that failed inspection.
**DISCUSSION:** The units that failed inspection are classified as normal scrap because they have minimal value and can be sold without further reworking. The defective units are less than the 4% tolerance limit for normal spoilage. Scrap can be sold, disposed of, or reused.
Answer (A) is incorrect because abnormal spoilage is not a normal result of efficient operations. In this case, the percentage of spoiled units is within the normal tolerance limit. Answer (C) is incorrect because reworked units are defective units that require further processing for them to be sold. This company does not rework defective units. Answer (D) is incorrect because waste has no monetary value and may have a disposal cost associated with it.

A company uses a process costing system in which all materials are added at the beginning of the first process. Conversion costs are added evenly throughout the process. During the past month, 10,000 units were started in production, and 8,000 were completed and transferred to the next department. There were no beginning inventories. The ending inventories were 70% complete at the end of the month. The company uses a weighted-average method for inventory valuation.

**27.** If materials used in production cost $15,000 and conversion costs incurred were $25,000, what amount of inventory (rounded) was transferred to the next department?

A. $32,000

B. $33,280

C. $36,280

D. $40,000

Answer (B) is correct. *(Publisher)*
**REQUIRED:** The cost of goods transferred to the next department in a process costing system.
**DISCUSSION:** The equivalent units of materials equal 10,000 because all materials are added at the beginning of the process, and 10,000 units were started. The equivalent units of conversion costs equal 9,400 [8,000 units completed + (2,000 units in ending inventory × 70%)]. The unit cost of materials is $1.50 ($15,000 ÷ 10,000 EU). The unit cost of conversion is $2.66 ($25,000 ÷ 9,400 EU). Thus, the cost of goods transferred was $33,280 [8,000 units × ($1.50 + $2.66)].
Answer (A) is incorrect because $32,000 is based on 10,000 equivalent units of conversion costs. Answer (C) is incorrect because $36,280 assumes transfer of 10,000 units of materials. Answer (D) is incorrect because $40,000 equals total costs incurred in production.

**28.** If materials used in production cost $15,000 and conversion costs incurred were $25,000, what is the value (rounded) of the ending work-in-process inventory in the first processing department?

A. $6,720

B. $8,000

C. $3,720

D. $0

Answer (A) is correct. *(Publisher)*
**REQUIRED:** The ending work-in-process inventory.
**DISCUSSION:** The cost transferred out was $33,280. Hence, the ending inventory must equal the production costs for the month (given no beginning inventories), minus costs transferred out, or $6,720 [($15,000 materials + $25,000 conversion cost) – $33,280].
Answer (B) is incorrect because $8,000 assumes that ending work-in-process contains 2,000 equivalent units of conversion costs. Answer (C) is incorrect because $3,720 assumes that ending work-in-process contains only conversion costs. Answer (D) is incorrect because some units remain in work-in-process.

**29.** Assume that this company uses first-in, first-out (FIFO) for inventory costing instead of the weighted-average inventory valuation. If materials used in production cost $15,000 and conversion costs incurred were $25,000, what amount of inventory (rounded) was transferred to the next department under FIFO?

A. $32,000

B. $33,280

C. $36,280

D. $40,000

Answer (B) is correct. *(Publisher)*
**REQUIRED:** The cost of goods transferred to the next department in a process costing system if FIFO is used.
**DISCUSSION:** The only difference between weighted average and FIFO relates to the beginning inventories. Because there were no beginning inventories in this problem, the two valuation methods produce the same results. The equivalent units of materials equal 10,000 because all materials are added at the beginning of the process, and 10,000 units were started. The equivalent units of conversion costs equal 9,400 [8,000 units completed + (2,000 units in ending inventory × 70%)]. The unit cost of materials is $1.50 ($15,000 ÷ 10,000 EU). The unit cost of conversion is $2.66 ($25,000 ÷ 9,400 EU). Therefore, the cost of goods transferred using the FIFO method for inventory costing is $33,280 [8,000 units × ($1.50 + $2.66)].
Answer (A) is incorrect because $32,000 is based on 10,000 equivalent units of conversion costs. Answer (C) is incorrect because $36,280 assumes transfer of 10,000 units of materials. Answer (D) is incorrect because $40,000 equals total costs incurred in production.

Questions 30 through 37 are based on the following information.

Albany Mining Corporation uses a process costing system for its ore extraction operations. The following information pertains to work-in-process inventories and operations for the month of May:

| | Units | Completion % | |
| | | Materials | Conversion |
| --- | --- | --- | --- |
| BWIP on May 1 | 32,000 | 60% | 20% |
| Started in production | 200,000 | | |
| Completed production | 184,000 | | |
| EWIP on May 31 | 48,000 | 90% | 40% |

Costs for the month were as follows:

| | BWIP | Incurred in May |
| --- | --- | --- |
| Direct materials | $54,560 | $ 468,000 |
| Direct labor | 20,320 | 182,880 |
| Factory overhead | 15,240 | 391,160 |
| | $90,120 | $1,042,040 |

**30.** Under the FIFO method, the equivalent units of materials are

A. 195,200 units.

B. 208,000 units.

C. 214,400 units.

D. 227,200 units.

Answer (B) is correct.  *(Publisher)*
REQUIRED: The equivalent units of materials under FIFO.
DISCUSSION: Under the FIFO method, equivalent units are determined based only on work performed during the current period. They include work performed to complete BWIP, work on units started and completed during the period, and work done on EWIP. Thus, total FIFO equivalent units of materials are

| BWIP | 32,000 units × 40% = | 12,800 |
| --- | --- | --- |
| Started and completed | | |
| (184,000 – 32,000 in BWIP) | 152,000 units ×100% = | 152,000 |
| EWIP | 48,000 units × 90% = | 43,200 |
| Total equivalent units | | 208,000 |

Answer (A) is incorrect because 195,200 units omits the 12,800 equivalent units of work on BWIP during the current period.  Answer (C) is incorrect because 214,400 units assumes that BWIP was 40% complete.  Answer (D) is incorrect because 227,200 units is based on the weighted-average method.

**31.** Under the FIFO method, the equivalent units of conversion cost are

A. 171,200 units.

B. 177,600 units.

C. 184,000 units.

D. 196,800 units.

Answer (D) is correct.  *(Publisher)*
REQUIRED: The equivalent units of conversion cost under FIFO.
DISCUSSION: Under FIFO, equivalent units are determined based only on work performed during the current period. They include work performed to complete BWIP, work on units started and completed during the period, and work done on EWIP. Thus, total FIFO equivalent units of conversion cost are

| BWIP | 32,000 units × 80% = | 25,600 |
| --- | --- | --- |
| Started and completed | | |
| (184,000 – 32,000 in BWIP) | 152,000 units ×100% = | 152,000 |
| EWIP | 48,000 units × 40% = | 19,200 |
| Total equivalent units | | 196,800 |

Answer (A) is incorrect because 171,200 units omits work on BWIP.  Answer (B) is incorrect because 177,600 units omits work on EWIP.  Answer (C) is incorrect because 184,000 equals the physical units completed.

**32.** Under the FIFO method, the equivalent unit cost of materials for May is

A. $2.06

B. $2.25

C. $2.30

D. $2.51

Answer (B) is correct.  *(Publisher)*
REQUIRED: The equivalent-unit cost of materials under FIFO.
DISCUSSION: The FIFO equivalent units of materials equal 208,000. Accordingly, unit cost of materials under FIFO is $2.25 ($468,000 materials cost in May ÷ 208,000 EU).
Answer (A) is incorrect because $2.06 results from dividing May's costs by the equivalent units calculated under the weighted-average method.  Answer (C) is incorrect because $2.30 is the weighted-average cost per equivalent unit.
Answer (D) is incorrect because $2.51 equals total materials cost divided by FIFO equivalent units of materials.

**33.** Using the FIFO method, the equivalent unit conversion cost for May is

A. $2.92

B. $3.00

C. $3.10

D. $3.23

Answer (A) is correct. *(Publisher)*
**REQUIRED:** The equivalent-unit conversion cost under FIFO.
**DISCUSSION:** The FIFO equivalent units of conversion cost equal 196,800. Conversion cost incurred during May was $574,040 ($182,880 DL + $391,160 FOH). Hence, the equivalent-unit conversion cost under FIFO is $2.92 ($574,040 ÷ 196,800).
Answer (B) is incorrect because $3.00 is the cost per equivalent unit under the weighted-average method. Answer (C) is incorrect because $3.10 equals total conversion cost divided by FIFO equivalent units of conversion cost. Answer (D) is incorrect because $3.23 assumes EWIP is 0% complete as to conversion cost.

**34.** Under the FIFO method, the total cost of units in the ending work-in-process inventory at May 31 is

A. $153,264

B. $154,800

C. $155,424

D. $156,960

Answer (A) is correct. *(Publisher)*
**REQUIRED:** The total cost of units in EWIP under FIFO.
**DISCUSSION:** Under FIFO, the equivalent-unit materials cost is $2.25, and the EWIP contains 43,200 equivalent units of materials. The equivalent-unit conversion cost is $2.92, and the EWIP contains 19,200 equivalent units of conversion cost. Consequently, EWIP equals $153,264 [(43,200 × $2.25) + (19,200 × $2.92)].
Answer (B) is incorrect because $154,800 is based on a FIFO calculation for materials and a weighted-average calculation for conversion cost. Answer (C) is incorrect because $155,424 is based on a weighted-average calculation for materials and a FIFO calculation for conversion cost. Answer (D) is incorrect because $156,960 is based on the unit costs under the weighted-average method.

**35.** Using the weighted-average method, the equivalent unit cost of materials for May is

A. $2.06

B. $2.25

C. $2.30

D. $2.51

Answer (C) is correct. *(Publisher)*
**REQUIRED:** The equivalent-unit cost of materials under the weighted-average method.
**DISCUSSION:** The weighted-average method averages the work done in the prior period with the work done in the current period. The two layers of units to analyze are those completed during the period and those still in EWIP. The units completed totaled 184,000. The equivalent units of materials in EWIP equaled 43,200 (48,000 physical units × 90%). Hence, the total equivalent units of materials equaled 227,200 (184,000 + 43,200). The materials cost in BWIP is combined in the weighted-average calculation with the materials cost incurred during the current period. The equivalent-unit materials cost is therefore $2.30 [($54,560 BWIP + $468,000 incurred in May) ÷ 227,200 EU].
Answer (A) is incorrect because $2.06 is based on weighted-average equivalent units and FIFO costs. Answer (B) is incorrect because $2.25 is the cost based on the FIFO method. Answer (D) is incorrect because $2.51 equals total materials costs divided by FIFO equivalent units of materials.

**36.** Using the weighted-average method, the total cost of the ending work-in-process inventory at May 31 is

A. $153,264

B. $154,800

C. $155,424

D. $156,960

Answer (D) is correct. *(Publisher)*
**REQUIRED:** The total cost of the EWIP under the weighted-average method.
**DISCUSSION:** Given a weighted-average assumption, the unit materials cost was $2.30, and the unit conversion cost was $3.00. Furthermore, the equivalent units for materials equaled 43,200 (48,000 physical units × 90%), and the equivalent units for conversion cost equaled 19,200 (48,000 physical units × 40%). The total weighted-average cost of EWIP was therefore $156,960 [(43,200 EU of materials × $2.30) + (19,200 EU of conversion cost × $3.00)].
Answer (A) is incorrect because $153,264 is the FIFO EWIP. Answer (B) is incorrect because $154,800 is based on a FIFO calculation for materials and a weighted-average calculation for conversion cost. Answer (C) is incorrect because $155,424 is based on a weighted-average calculation for materials and a FIFO calculation for conversion cost.

**37.** Refer to the information on the preceding page(s). Under the weighted-average method, the equivalent unit conversion cost for May is

   A. $2.92

   B. $3.00

   C. $3.10

   D. $3.31

**Answer (B) is correct.**  *(Publisher)*
**REQUIRED:**  The equivalent-unit conversion cost under the weighted-average method.
**DISCUSSION:**  The weighted-average method averages the work performed in the prior period with the work done in the current period.  The two layers of units to analyze are those completed during the period and those still in EWIP.  The units completed totaled 184,000.  The 48,000 units in EWIP are 40% complete as to conversion cost, the equivalent of 19,200 units.  Thus, total equivalent units for conversion cost under the weighted-average method equaled 203,200.  Moreover, the conversion cost in BWIP is combined in the weighted-average calculation with the conversion cost incurred during the current period.  The equivalent-unit conversion cost is therefore $3.00 [($20,320 DL in BWIP + $15,240 FOH in BWIP + $182,880 DL in May + $391,160 FOH in May) ÷ 203,200].
    Answer (A) is incorrect because $2.92 is the FIFO unit cost.  Answer (C) is incorrect because $3.10 is based on FIFO equivalent units and weighted-average cost.  Answer (D) is incorrect because $3.31 results from omitting the equivalent units in EWIP.

---

Questions 38 through 45 are based on the following information.

Kimbeth Manufacturing uses a process cost system to manufacture Dust Density Sensors for the mining industry.  The following information pertains to operations for the month of May.

| | Units |
|---|---|
| Beginning work-in-process inventory, May 1 | 16,000 |
| Started in production during May | 100,000 |
| Completed production during May | 92,000 |
| Ending work-in-process inventory, May 31 | 24,000 |

The beginning inventory was 60% complete for materials and 20% complete for conversion costs.  The ending inventory was 90% complete for materials and 40% complete for conversion costs.

Costs pertaining to the month of May are as follows:

• Beginning inventory costs are materials, $54,560; direct labor, $20,320; and overhead, $15,240.
• Costs incurred during May are materials used, $468,000; direct labor, $182,880; and overhead, $391,160.

---

**38.** Using the first-in, first-out (FIFO) method, the equivalent units of production (EUP) for materials are

   A. 97,600 units.

   B. 104,000 units.

   C. 107,200 units.

   D. 108,000 units.

**Answer (B) is correct.**  *(CMA, adapted)*
**REQUIRED:**  The equivalent units of production for materials under FIFO.
**DISCUSSION:**  Under FIFO, EUP are based solely on work performed during the current period.  The EUP equals the sum of the work done on the beginning work-in-process inventory, units started and completed in the current period, and the ending work-in-process inventory.  Given that beginning work-in-process was 60% complete as to materials, the current period is charged for 6,400 EUP (16,000 units × 40%).  Because 92,000 units were completed during the period, 76,000 (92,000 – 16,000 in BWIP) must have been started and completed during the period.  They represent 76,000 EUP.  Finally, the EUP for ending work-in-process equal 21,600 (24,000 units × 90%).  Thus, total EUP for May are 104,000 (6,400 + 76,000 + 21,600).
    Answer (A) is incorrect because 97,600 units omits the 6,400 EUP added to beginning work-in-process.  Answer (C) is incorrect because 107,200 units assumes beginning work-in-process was 40% complete.  Answer (D) is incorrect because 108,000 units equals the sum of the physical units in beginning work-in-process and the physical units completed.

**39.** Using the FIFO method, the equivalent units of production for conversion costs are

    A. 85,600 units.

    B. 88,800 units.

    C. 95,200 units.

    D. 98,400 units.

Answer (D) is correct. *(CMA, adapted)*
    **REQUIRED:** The equivalent units of production for conversion costs under FIFO.
    **DISCUSSION:** The beginning inventory was 20% complete as to conversion costs. Hence, 12,800 EUP (16,000 units × 80%) were required for completion. EUP for units started and completed equaled 76,000 [(92,000 completed units − 16,000 units in BWIP) × 100%]. The work done on ending work-in-process totaled 9,600 EUP (24,000 units × 40%). Thus, total EUP for May are 98,400 (12,800 + 76,000 + 9,600).
    Answer (A) is incorrect because 85,600 units omits the work done on beginning work-in-process. Answer (B) is incorrect because 88,800 units omits the work done on ending work-in-process. Answer (C) is incorrect because 95,200 units assumes the beginning work-in-process was 40% complete as to conversion costs.

**40.** Using the FIFO method, the equivalent unit cost of materials for May is

    A. $4.12

    B. $4.50

    C. $4.60

    D. $4.80

Answer (B) is correct. *(CMA, adapted)*
    **REQUIRED:** The equivalent unit cost of materials under FIFO.
    **DISCUSSION:** Under the FIFO method, EUP for materials equal 104,000 [(16,000 units in BWIP × 40%) + (76,000 units started and completed × 100%) + (24,000 units in EWIP × 90%)]. Consequently, the equivalent unit cost of materials is $4.50 ($468,000 total materials cost in May ÷ 104,000 EUP).
    Answer (A) is incorrect because $4.12 is based on EUP calculated under the weighted-average method. Answer (C) is incorrect because $4.60 is the weighted-average cost per equivalent unit. Answer (D) is incorrect because $4.80 omits the 6,400 EUP added to beginning work-in-process.

**41.** Using the FIFO method, the equivalent unit conversion cost for May is

    A. $5.65

    B. $5.83

    C. $6.00

    D. $6.20

Answer (B) is correct. *(CMA, adapted)*
    **REQUIRED:** The conversion cost per equivalent unit under FIFO.
    **DISCUSSION:** Under the FIFO method, EUP for conversion costs equal 98,400 [(16,000 units in BWIP × 80%) + (76,000 units started and completed × 100%) + (24,000 units in EWIP × 40%)]. Conversion costs incurred during the current period equal $574,040 ($182,880 DL + $391,160 FOH). Hence, the equivalent unit cost for conversion costs is $5.83 ($574,040 ÷ 98,400).
    Answer (A) is incorrect because $5.65 is based on EUP calculated under the weighted-average method. Answer (C) is incorrect because $6.00 is the cost per equivalent unit calculated under the weighted-average method. Answer (D) is incorrect because $6.20 results from combining conversion costs for May with those in beginning work-in-process and dividing by 98,400 EUP.

**42.** Using the FIFO method, the total cost of units in the ending work-in-process inventory at May 31 is

    A. $153,168

    B. $154,800

    C. $155,328

    D. $156,960

Answer (A) is correct. *(CMA, adapted)*
    **REQUIRED:** The total cost of units in ending work-in-process under FIFO.
    **DISCUSSION:** The FIFO costs per equivalent unit for materials and conversion costs are $4.50 and $5.83, respectively. EUP for materials in ending work-in-process equal 21,600 (24,000 × 90%). Thus, total FIFO materials cost is $97,200 (21,600 EUP × $4.50). EUP for conversion costs in ending work-in-process equal 9,600 (24,000 × 40%). Total conversion costs are therefore $55,968 (9,600 EUP × $5.83). Consequently, total work-in-process costs are $153,168 ($97,200 + $55,968).
    Answer (B) is incorrect because $154,800 is based on a FIFO calculation for materials and a weighted-average calculation for conversion costs. Answer (C) is incorrect because $155,328 is based on a weighted-average calculation for materials and a FIFO calculation for conversion costs. Answer (D) is incorrect because $156,960 is the weighted-average cost of ending work-in-process.

**43.** Refer to the information on the preceding page(s). Using the weighted-average method, the equivalent unit cost of materials for May is

- A. $4.12
- B. $4.50
- C. $4.60
- D. $5.02

Answer (C) is correct. *(CMA, adapted)*
**REQUIRED:** The weighted-average equivalent unit cost for materials.
**DISCUSSION:** The weighted-average method averages the work done in the prior period with the work done in the current period. There are two layers of units to analyze: those completed during the period, and those still in ending inventory. The units completed totaled 92,000. The 24,000 ending units are 90% complete as to materials, so EUP equal 21,600. Hence, total EUP for materials are 113,600 (92,000 + 21,600). The total materials costs incurred during the period and accumulated in beginning work-in-process is $522,560 ($468,000 + $54,560). Thus, weighted-average unit cost is $4.60 ($522,560 ÷ 113,600 EUP).
Answer (A) is incorrect because $4.12 equals materials costs for May divided by weighted-average EUP. Answer (B) is incorrect because $4.50 is the equivalent unit cost based on the FIFO method. Answer (D) is incorrect because $5.02 is based on a FIFO calculation of equivalent units and a weighted-average calculation of costs.

**44.** Refer to the information on the preceding page(s). Using the weighted-average method, the equivalent unit conversion cost for May is

- A. $5.65
- B. $5.83
- C. $6.00
- D. $6.20

Answer (C) is correct. *(CMA, adapted)*
**REQUIRED:** The weighted-average conversion cost per equivalent unit.
**DISCUSSION:** The weighted-average method does not distinguish between the work done in the prior period and the work done in the current period. Accordingly, the 92,000 completed units represent 92,000 weighted-average EUP. The 24,000 units in ending work-in-process are 40% complete as to conversion costs, so they equal 9,600 EUP. Hence, total EUP for conversion costs are 101,600 (92,000 + 9,600). The sum of the conversion costs accumulated in beginning work-in-process and incurred during the period is $609,600 ($20,320 + $15,240 + $182,880 + $391,160). Thus, weighted-average unit cost is $6.00 ($609,600 ÷ 101,600 EUP).
Answer (A) is incorrect because $5.65 omits the conversion costs in beginning work-in-process. Answer (B) is incorrect because $5.83 is the equivalent unit conversion cost based on FIFO. Answer (D) is incorrect because $6.20 is based on a FIFO calculation of equivalent units and a weighted-average calculation of costs.

**45.** Refer to the information on the preceding page(s). Using the weighted-average method, the total cost of the units in the ending work-in-process inventory at May 31 is

- A. $99,360
- B. $153,168
- C. $154,800
- D. $156,960

Answer (D) is correct. *(CMA, adapted)*
**REQUIRED:** The ending work-in-process.
**DISCUSSION:** The weighted-average costs per equivalent unit for materials and conversion costs are $4.60 and $6.00, respectively. EUP for materials in ending work-in-process equal 21,600 (24,000 × 90%). Thus, total weighted-average materials cost is $99,360 (21,600 × $4.60). EUP for conversion costs in ending work-in-process equal 9,600 (24,000 units × 40%). Total conversion costs are therefore $57,600 (9,600 EUP × $6.00). Consequently, total ending work-in-process costs are $156,960 ($99,360 + $57,600).
Answer (A) is incorrect because $99,360 is the weighted-average cost of materials in ending work-in-process. Answer (B) is incorrect because $153,168 is the FIFO cost of ending work-in-process. Answer (C) is incorrect because $154,800 is based on a FIFO calculation for materials and a weighted-average calculation for conversion costs.

## 4.2 Activity-Based Costing

**46.** Cost allocation is the process of assigning indirect costs to a cost object. The indirect costs are grouped in cost pools and then allocated by a common allocation base to the cost object. The base that is employed to allocate a homogeneous cost pool should

- A. Have a cause-and-effect relationship with the cost items in the cost pool.

- B. Assign the costs in the pool uniformly to cost objects even if the cost objects use resources in a nonuniform way.

- C. Be a nonfinancial measure (e.g., number of setups) because a nonfinancial measure is more objective.

- D. Have a high correlation with the cost items in the cost pool as the sole criterion for selection.

Answer (A) is correct. *(CIA, adapted)*
**REQUIRED:** The characteristic of a base used to allocate a homogeneous cost pool.
**DISCUSSION:** A cost allocation base is the common denominator for systematically correlating indirect costs and a cost object. The cost driver of the indirect costs is ordinarily the allocation base. In a homogeneous cost pool, all costs should have the same or a similar cause-and-effect relationship with the cost allocation base.
Answer (B) is incorrect because, if an allocation base uniformly assigns costs to cost objects when the cost objects use resources in a nonuniform way, the base is smoothing or spreading the costs. Smoothing can result in undercosting or overcosting of products, with adverse effects on product pricing, cost management and control, and decision making. Answer (C) is incorrect because financial measures (e.g., sales dollars and direct labor costs) and nonfinancial measures (e.g., setups and units shipped) can be used as allocation bases. Answer (D) is incorrect because high correlation between the cost items in a pool and the allocation base does not necessarily mean that a cause-and-effect relationship exists. Two variables may move together without such a relationship. The perceived relationship between the cost driver (allocation base) and the indirect costs should have economic plausibility and high correlation.

**47.** A company with three products classifies its costs as belonging to five functions: design, production, marketing, distribution, and customer services. For pricing purposes, all company costs are assigned to the three products. The direct costs of each of the five functions are traced directly to the three products. The indirect costs of each of the five business functions are collected into five separate cost pools and then assigned to the three products using appropriate allocation bases. The allocation base that will most likely be the best for allocating the indirect costs of the distribution function is

- A. Number of customer phone calls.

- B. Number of shipments.

- C. Number of sales persons.

- D. Dollar sales volume.

Answer (B) is correct. *(CIA, adapted)*
**REQUIRED:** The allocation base that will most likely be the best for allocating the indirect costs of the distribution function.
**DISCUSSION:** The number of shipments is an appropriate cost driver. A cause-and-effect relationship may exist between the number of shipments and distribution costs.
Answer (A) is incorrect because the number of customer phone calls has little relation to distribution. It is probably more closely related to customer service. Answer (C) is incorrect because the number of sales persons is not related to distribution. It is more closely related to marketing. Answer (D) is incorrect because the dollar sales volume is not necessarily related to distribution. It is more likely related to marketing.

**48.** Activities, their drivers, and their costs may be classified as unit-level, batch-level, product-level, and facility-level. If activity-based costing information is prepared for internal purposes, which costs are most likely to be treated as period costs?

- A. Unit-level.

- B. Batch-level.

- C. Product-level.

- D. Facility-level.

Answer (D) is correct. *(Publisher)*
**REQUIRED:** The level of costs in an ABC analysis most likely to be treated as period costs.
**DISCUSSION:** A difficulty in applying ABC is that, although the first three levels of activities pertain to specific products or services, facility-level activities do not. Thus, facility-level costs are not accurately assignable to products. The theoretically sound solution may be to treat these costs as period costs. Nevertheless, organizations that apply ABC ordinarily assign them to products to obtain a full absorption cost suitable for external financial reporting in accordance with GAAP. However, for internal purposes, facility-level costs should be treated as period costs to avoid distorting decisions about cost efficiency, pricing, and profitability.
Answer (A) is incorrect because unit-level costs relate to particular products (or services). Answer (B) is incorrect because batch-level costs relate to particular products (or services). Answer (C) is incorrect because product-level costs relate to particular products (or services).

**49.** Process value analysis is a key component of activity-based management that links product costing and

- A. Reduction of the number of cost pools.
- B. Continuous improvement.
- C. Accumulation of heterogeneous cost pools.
- D. Overhead rates based on broad averages.

Answer (B) is correct.    *(Publisher)*
    **REQUIRED:** The element of process value analysis.
    **DISCUSSION:** Design of an ABC system starts with process value analysis, a comprehensive understanding of how an organization generates its output. It involves a determination of which activities that use resources are value-adding or nonvalue-adding and how the latter may be reduced or eliminated. This linkage of product costing and continuous improvement of processes is activity-based management (ABM). It encompasses driver analysis, activity analysis, and performance measurement.
    Answer (A) is incorrect because ABC tends to increase the number of cost pools and drivers used. Answer (C) is incorrect because ABC's philosophy is to accumulate homogeneous cost pools. Thus, the cost elements in a pool should be consumed by cost objects in proportion to the same driver. Homogenizing cost pools minimizes broad averaging of costs that have different drivers. Answer (D) is incorrect because ABC's philosophy is to accumulate homogeneous cost pools. Thus, the cost elements in a pool should be consumed by cost objects in proportion to the same driver. Homogenizing cost pools minimizes broad averaging of costs that have different drivers.

**50.** Nile Co. is a manufacturer whose cost assignment and product costing procedures follow activity-based costing principles. Activities have been identified and classified as being either value-adding or nonvalue-adding as to each product. Which of the following activities used in Nile's production process is nonvalue-adding?

- A. Design engineering activity.
- B. Heat treatment activity.
- C. Drill press activity.
- D. Raw materials storage activity.

Answer (D) is correct.    *(CPA, adapted)*
    **REQUIRED:** The nonvalue-adding activity.
    **DISCUSSION:** Analysis by activity provides for better cost control because of identification of nonvalue-adding activities. A value-added activity contributes to customer satisfaction or meets a need of the entity. A nonvalue-adding activity does not make such a contribution. It can be eliminated, reduced, or redesigned without impairing the quantity, quality, or responsiveness of the product or service desired by customers or the entity. For example, raw materials storage may be greatly reduced or eliminated in a just-in-time (JIT) production system without affecting customer value.
    Answer (A) is incorrect because design engineering activity adds value to products in the production process. Answer (B) is incorrect because heat treatment activity adds value to products in the production process. Answer (C) is incorrect because drill press activity adds value to products in the production process.

**51.** The series of activities in which customer usefulness is added to the product is the definition of

- A. A value chain.
- B. Process value analysis.
- C. Integrated manufacturing.
- D. Activity-based costing.

Answer (A) is correct.    *(CMA, adapted)*
    **REQUIRED:** The series of activities in which customer usefulness is added to the product.
    **DISCUSSION:** Value-chain analysis for assessing competitive advantage is an integral part of the strategic planning process. Value-chain analysis is a continuous process of gathering, evaluating, and communicating information for business decision making. A value chain depicts how customer value accumulates along a chain of activities that lead to an end product or service. A value chain consists of the activities required to research and develop, design, produce, market, deliver, and support its product. Extended value-chain analysis expands the view of the parties involved to include those upstream (e.g., suppliers) and downstream (e.g., customers).
    Answer (B) is incorrect because process value analysis relates to a single process. Answer (C) is incorrect because computer-integrated manufacturing uses computers to control all aspects of manufacturing in a single location. Answer (D) is incorrect because ABC identifies the activities associated with cost incurrence and the drivers of those activities. Costs are then assigned to cost objects based on the demands they make on activities.

**52.** The use of activity-based costing normally results in

- A. Substantially greater unit costs for low-volume products than is reported by traditional product costing.

- B. Substantially lower unit costs for low-volume products than is reported by traditional product costing.

- C. Decreased setup costs being charged to low-volume products.

- D. Equalizing setup costs for all product lines.

Answer (A) is correct. *(CMA, adapted)*
**REQUIRED:** The true statement about ABC.
**DISCUSSION:** ABC differs from traditional product costing because it uses multiple allocation bases and therefore allocates overhead more accurately. The result is that ABC often charges low-volume products with more overhead than a traditional system. For example, the cost of machine setup may be the same for production runs of widely varying sizes. This relationship is reflected in an ABC system that allocates setup costs on the basis of the number of setups. However, a traditional system using an allocation base such as machine hours may underallocate setup costs to low-volume products. Many companies adopting ABC have found that they have been losing money on low-volume products because costs were actually higher than originally thought.
    Answer (B) is incorrect because low-volume products are usually charged with greater unit costs under ABC. Answer (C) is incorrect because greater setup costs are usually charged to low-volume products under ABC. Answer (D) is incorrect because setup costs will not be equalized unless setup time is equal for all products.

**53.** Because of changes that are occurring in the basic operations of many firms, all of the following represent trends in the way indirect costs are allocated except

- A. Treating direct labor as an indirect manufacturing cost in an automated factory.

- B. Using throughput time as an application base to increase awareness of the costs associated with lengthened throughput time.

- C. Preferring plant-wide application rates that are applied to machine hours rather than incurring the cost of detailed allocations.

- D. Using several machine cost pools to measure product costs on the basis of time in a machine center.

Answer (C) is correct. *(CMA, adapted)*
**REQUIRED:** The item not a trend in the way indirect costs are being allocated.
**DISCUSSION:** With the automation of factories and the corresponding emphasis on activity-based costing (ABC), companies are finding new ways of allocating indirect factory overhead. One change is that plant-wide application rates are being used less often because a closer matching of costs with cost drivers provides better information to management. ABC results in a more accurate application of indirect costs because it provides more refined data. Instead of a single cost goal for a process, a department, or even an entire plant, an indirect cost pool is established for each identified activity. The related cost driver, the factor that changes the cost of the activity, is also identified.
    Answer (A) is incorrect because computerization has decreased the amount of direct labor to the point that some companies are treating direct labor as an indirect factory overhead cost. Answer (B) is incorrect because throughput time (the rate of production over a stated time), clearly drives (influences) costs. Answer (D) is incorrect because multiple cost pools are preferable. They permit a better matching of indirect costs with cost drivers.

**54.** Multiple or departmental overhead rates are considered preferable to a single or plantwide overhead rate when

- A. Manufacturing is limited to a single product flowing through identical departments in a fixed sequence.

- B. Various products are manufactured that do not pass through the same departments or use the same manufacturing techniques.

- C. Cost drivers, such as direct labor, are the same over all processes.

- D. Individual cost drivers cannot accurately be determined with respect to cause-and-effect relationships.

Answer (B) is correct. *(CMA, adapted)*
**REQUIRED:** The situation in which multiple or departmental overhead rates are considered preferable.
**DISCUSSION:** Multiple rates are appropriate when a process differs substantially among departments or when products do not go through all departments or all processes. The trend in cost accounting is toward activity-based costing, which divides production into numerous activities and identifies the cost driver(s) most relevant to each. The result is a more accurate tracing of costs.
    Answer (A) is incorrect because one rate may be cost beneficial when a single product proceeds through homogeneous processes. Answer (C) is incorrect because, if cost drivers are the same for all processes, multiple rates are unnecessary. Answer (D) is incorrect because individual cost drivers for all relationships must be known to use multiple application rates.

**55.** Davis Corporation has used a traditional cost accounting system to apply quality control costs uniformly to all products at a rate of 15% of direct labor cost. Monthly direct labor cost for its main product is $30,000. In an attempt to distribute quality control costs more equitably, Davis is considering activity-based costing (ABC). The monthly data shown below have been gathered for the main product. The three activities are (1) incoming materials inspection, (2) in-process inspection, and (3) product certification. Costs are to be allocated to each activity on the basis of cost drivers.

| Activity | Cost Driver | Cost Rate | Quantity for Main Product |
|---|---|---|---|
| (1) | Number of types of materials | $12 per type | 12 types |
| (2) | Number of units | $0.14 per unit | 17,500 units |
| (3) | Number of orders | $77 per order | 30 orders |

The monthly quality control cost assigned to the main product using ABC is

A. $150 per order.

B. $404 lower than using the traditional system.

C. $4,500

D. $404 higher than using the traditional system.

Answer (D) is correct.    *(Publisher)*
**REQUIRED:** The monthly quality control cost assigned to the main product using ABC.
**DISCUSSION:** ABC assigns overhead costs on the basis of multiple cost drivers instead of only one driver. Using the three cost drivers in the question produces the following calculation:

| | |
|---|---|
| Number of types of materials (12 × $12) | $  144 |
| Number of units (17,500 × $.14) | 2,450 |
| Number of orders (30 × $77) | 2,310 |
| Total | $4,904 |

Under the old method of allocation based on direct labor, the allocated amount would have been 4,500 ($30,000 × 15%), or $404 lower than under ABC.
Answer (A) is incorrect because $150 per order equals $4,500 divided by 30 orders. Answer (B) is incorrect because ABC yields an allocation $404 higher than the traditional system. Answer (C) is incorrect because $4,500 is the quality control cost under the traditional system.

**56.** Which of the following statements about activity-based costing is false?

A. Activity-based costing is useful for allocating marketing and distribution costs.

B. Activity-based costing is more likely to result in major differences from traditional costing systems if the firm manufactures only one product rather than multiple products.

C. In activity-based costing, cost drivers are what cause costs to be incurred.

D. Activity-based costing differs from traditional costing systems in that products are cross-subsidized.

Answer (B) is correct.    *(CIA, adapted)*
**REQUIRED:** The false statement about activity-based costing (ABC).
**DISCUSSION:** ABC determines the activities that will serve as cost objects and then accumulates a cost pool for each activity using the appropriate activity base (cost driver). It is a system that may be employed with job order or process costing methods. Thus, when there is only one product, the allocation of costs to the product is trivial. All of the cost is assigned to the one product; the particular method used to allocate the costs does not matter.
Answer (A) is incorrect because marketing and distribution costs should be allocated to specific products. Answer (C) is incorrect because ABC determines the activities that will serve as cost objects and then accumulates a cost pool for each activity using the appropriate activity base (cost driver). Answer (D) is incorrect because, under ABC, a product is allocated only those costs that pertain to its production; that is, products are not cross-subsidized.

Questions 57 and 58 are based on the following information.

Zeta Company is preparing its annual profit plan. As part of its analysis of the profitability of individual products, the controller estimates the amount of overhead that should be allocated to the individual product lines from the information given as follows:

|  | Wall Mirrors | Specialty Windows |
| --- | --- | --- |
| Units produced | 25 | 25 |
| Material moves per product line | 5 | 15 |
| Direct labor hours per unit | 200 | 200 |
| Budgeted materials handling costs |  | $50,000 |

**57.** Under a costing system that allocates overhead on the basis of direct labor hours, the materials handling costs allocated to one unit of wall mirrors would be

A. $1,000

B. $500

C. $2,000

D. $5,000

Answer (A) is correct. *(CMA, adapted)*
   **REQUIRED:** The amount of materials handling costs allocated to one unit of wall mirrors when direct labor hours is the activity base.
   **DISCUSSION:** If direct labor hours are used as the allocation base, the $50,000 of costs is allocated over 400 hours of direct labor. Multiplying the 25 units of each product times 200 hours results in 5,000 labor hours for each product, or a total of 10,000 hours. Dividing $50,000 by 10,000 hours results in a cost of $5 per direct labor hour. Multiplying 200 hours times $5 results in an allocation of $1,000 of overhead per unit of product.
   Answer (B) is incorrect because $500 is the allocation based on number of material moves. Answer (C) is incorrect because $2,000 assumes that all the overhead is allocated to the wall mirrors. Answer (D) is incorrect because $5,000 assumes overhead of $250,000.

**58.** Under activity-based costing (ABC), the materials handling costs allocated to one unit of wall mirrors would be

A. $1,000

B. $500

C. $1,500

D. $2,500

Answer (B) is correct. *(CMA, adapted)*
   **REQUIRED:** The amount of materials handling costs allocated to one unit of wall mirrors under ABC.
   **DISCUSSION:** An activity-based costing (ABC) system allocates overhead costs on the basis of some causal relationship between the incurrence of cost and activities. Because the moves for wall mirrors constitute 25% (5 ÷ 20) of total moves, the mirrors should absorb 25% of the total materials handling costs. Thus, $12,500 ($50,000 × 25%) is allocated to mirrors. The remaining $37,500 is allocated to specialty windows. Dividing the $12,500 by 25 units produces a cost of $500 per unit of mirrors.
   Answer (A) is incorrect because $1,000 uses direct labor as the allocation basis. Answer (C) is incorrect because $1,500 is the allocation per unit of specialty windows. Answer (D) is incorrect because $2,500 is not based on the number of material moves.

Questions 59 and 60 are based on the following information.
Believing that its traditional cost system may be providing misleading information, an organization is considering an activity based costing (ABC) approach. It now employs a full cost system and has been applying its manufacturing overhead on the basis of machine hours.

The organization plans on using 50,000 direct labor hours and 30,000 machine hours in the coming year. The following data show the manufacturing overhead that is budgeted.

| Activity | Cost Driver | Budgeted Activity | Budgeted Cost |
|---|---|---|---|
| Material handling | No. of parts handled | 6,000,000 | $ 720,000 |
| Setup costs | No. of setups | 750 | 315,000 |
| Machining costs | Machine hours | 30,000 | 540,000 |
| Quality control | No. of batches | 500 | 225,000 |
| Total manufacturing overhead cost: | | | $1,800,000 |

Cost, sales, and production data for one of the organization's products for the coming year are as follows:

| Prime costs: | |
|---|---|
| Direct material cost per unit | $4.40 |
| Direct labor cost per unit | |
| .05 DLH @ $15.00/DLH | .75 |
| Total prime cost | $5.15 |

| Sales and production data: | |
|---|---|
| Expected sales | 20,000 units |
| Batch size | 5,000 units |
| Setups | 2 per batch |
| Total parts per finished unit | 5 parts |
| Machine hours required | 80 MH per batch |

**59.** If the organization uses the traditional full cost system, the cost per unit for this product for the coming year would be

A. $5.39
B. $5.44
C. $6.11
D. $6.95

Answer (C) is correct. *(CIA, adapted)*
REQUIRED: The unit cost under traditional full costing.
DISCUSSION: Given that manufacturing overhead is applied on the basis of machine hours, the overhead rate is $60 per hour ($1,800,000 ÷ 30,000) or $.96 per unit [(80 machine hours per batch × $60) ÷ 5,000 units per batch]. Accordingly, the unit full cost is $6.11 ($5.15 unit prime cost + $.96).
Answer (A) is incorrect because $5.39 assumes that 80 machine hours are required for the total production of 20,000 units. Answer (B) is incorrect because $5.44 is based on the machining overhead rate ($18). Answer (D) is incorrect because $6.95 is based on the direct labor hour manufacturing overhead rate.

**60.** If the organization employs an activity based costing system, the cost per unit for the product described for the coming year would be

A. $6.00
B. $6.08
C. $6.21
D. $6.30

Answer (D) is correct. *(CIA, adapted)*
REQUIRED: The unit cost under the ABC system.
DISCUSSION: Materials handling cost per part is $.12 ($720,000 ÷ 6,000,000), cost per setup is $420 ($315,000 ÷ 750), machining cost per hour is $18 ($540,000 ÷ 30,000), and quality cost per batch is $450 ($225,000 ÷ 500). Hence, total manufacturing overhead applied is $22,920 [(5 parts per unit × 20,000 units × $.12) + (4 batches × 2 setups per batch × $420) + (4 batches × 80 machine hours per batch × $18) + (4 batches × $450)]. The total unit cost is $6.296 [$5.15 prime cost + ($22,920 ÷ 20,000 units) overhead].
Answer (A) is incorrect because $6.00 assumes one setup per batch and 80 total machine hours. Answer (B) is incorrect because $6.08 assumes that only 80 machine hours were used. Answer (C) is incorrect because $6.21 assumes one setup per batch.

**61.** New-Rage Cosmetics has used a traditional cost accounting system to apply quality control costs uniformly to all products at a rate of 14.5% of direct labor cost. Monthly direct labor cost for Satin Sheen makeup is $27,500. In an attempt to distribute quality control costs more equitably, New-Rage is considering activity-based costing. The monthly data shown in the chart below have been gathered for Satin Sheen makeup.

| Activity | Cost Driver | Cost Rates | Quantity for Satin Sheen |
|---|---|---|---|
| Incoming material inspection | Type of material | $11.50 per type | 12 types |
| In-process inspection | Number of units | $0.14 per unit | 17,500 units |
| Product certification | Per order | $77 per order | 25 orders |

The monthly quality control cost assigned to Satin Sheen makeup using activity-based costing is

A. $88.64 per order.

B. $525.50 lower than the cost using the traditional system.

C. $8,500.50

D. $525.50 higher than the cost using the traditional system.

Answer (D) is correct. *(CMA, adapted)*
**REQUIRED:** The monthly quality control cost assigned using activity-based costing.
**DISCUSSION:** ABC identifies the causal relationship between the incurrence of cost and activities, determines the drivers of the activities, establishes cost pools related to the drivers and activities, and assigns costs to ultimate cost objects on the basis of the demands (resources or drivers consumed) placed on the activities by those cost objects. Hence, ABC assigns overhead costs based on multiple allocation bases or cost drivers. Under the traditional, single-base system, the amount allocated is $3,987.50 ($27,500 × 14.5%). Under ABC, the amount allocated is $4,513 [(12 × $11.50) + (17,500 × $.14) + (25 × $77)], or $525.50 more than under the traditional system.
Answer (A) is incorrect because the ABC assignment of $4,513 is at a rate of $180.52 for each of the 25 orders. Answer (B) is incorrect because ABC yields a higher allocation. Answer (C) is incorrect because the total is $4,513 on the ABC basis.

**62.** Factory Company makes two products, X and Z. X is being introduced this period, and Z has been in production for 2 years. For the period about to begin, 1,000 units of each product are to be manufactured. Assume that the only relevant overhead item is the cost of engineering change orders; that X and Z are expected to require eight and two change orders, respectively; that X and Z are expected to require 2 and 3 machine hours, respectively; and that the cost of a change order is $600. If Factory applies engineering change order costs on the basis of machine hours, the cross-subsidy per unit arising from this peanut-butter costing approach is

A. $1.20

B. $2.40

C. $3.60

D. $4.80

Answer (B) is correct. *(Publisher)*
**REQUIRED:** The cross-subsidy per unit.
**DISCUSSION:** ABC is one means of improving a cost system to avoid what has been called peanut-butter costing. Inaccurately averaging or spreading costs like peanut butter over products or service units that use different amounts of resources results in product-cost cross-subsidization. This term describes the condition in which the miscosting of one product causes the miscosting of other products. In a traditional system, direct labor and direct materials are traced to products or service units, a single pool of costs (overhead) is accumulated for a given organizational unit, and these costs are then assigned using an allocative rather than a tracing procedure. The effect is an averaging of costs that may result in significant inaccuracy when products or service units do not use similar amounts of resources. The total change order cost is $6,000 [(8 + 2) × $600], the cost per machine hour is $1.20 {$6,000 ÷ [(2 × 1,000) + (3 × 1,000)] hours}, and the unit costs assigned on a machine-hour basis to X and Z are $2.40 (2 hours × $1.20) and $3.60 (3 hours × $1.20), respectively. However, if the change order costs are traced directly to X and Z, the unit costs assigned will be $4.80 [(8 orders × $600) ÷ 1,000 units] and $1.20 [(2 orders × $600) ÷ 1,000 units], respectively. Hence, the unit amount by which machine-hour-based assignment overcosts Z and undercosts X (the cross-subsidy) is $2.40 ($3.60 – $1.20 or $4.80 – $2.40).
Answer (A) is incorrect because $1.20 is the unit cost per machine hour or the unit cost directly attributable to Z. Answer (C) is incorrect because $3.60 is the unit cost assigned to Z on the machine-hour basis. Answer (D) is incorrect because $4.80 is the unit cost assigned to X on a direct-tracing basis.

**63.** ALF Co. is an assisted-living facility that provides services in the form of residential space, meals, and other occupant assistance (OOA) to its occupants. ALF currently uses a traditional cost accounting system that defines the service provided as assisted living, with service output measured in terms of occupant days. Each occupant is charged a daily rate equal to ALF's annual cost of providing residential space, meals, and OOA divided by total occupant days. However, an activity-based costing (ABC) analysis has revealed that occupants' use of OOA varies substantially. This analysis determined that occupants could be grouped into three categories (low, moderate, and high usage of OOA) and that the activity driver of OOA is nursing hours. The driver of the other activities is occupant days. The following quantitative information was also provided:

| Occupant Category | Annual Occupant Days | Annual Nursing Hours |
|---|---|---|
| Low usage | 36,000 | 90,000 |
| Medium usage | 18,000 | 90,000 |
| High usage | 6,000 | 120,000 |
| | 60,000 | 300,000 |

The total annual cost of OOA was $7.5 million, and the total annual cost of providing residential space and meals was $7.2 million. Accordingly, the ABC analysis indicates that the daily costing rate should be

A.  $182.50 for occupants in the low-usage category.

B.  $145.00 for occupants in the medium-usage category.

C.  $245.00 for occupants in the high-usage category.

D.  $620.00 for all occupants.

Answer (A) is correct.  *(Publisher)*
**REQUIRED:** The true statement about daily costing rates based on an ABC analysis.
**DISCUSSION:** This service organization produces three "products" (the three occupant categories), and the "units produced" equal occupant days. According to the ABC analysis, production involves two activities: (1) provision of residential space and meals and (2) OOA. The drivers of these activities are occupant days and nursing hours, respectively. Thus, the cost pool rate for the first activity (residential space and meals) is $120 per occupant day ($7,200,000 ÷ 60,000 days), and the cost pool rate for the second activity (OOA) is $25 ($7,500,000 ÷ 300,000 hours). The total cost for providing services to occupants in the low-usage category is $6,570,000 [(36,000 days × $120) + (90,000 hours × $25)]. The daily cost rate for these occupants is therefore $182.50 ($6,570,000 ÷ 36,000 occupant days).
Answer (B) is incorrect because $145.00 equals the sum of the cost pool rates ($120 + $25). Answer (C) is incorrect because $245 equals the rate per day for medium-usage occupants. Answer (D) is incorrect because $620 is the rate per day for high-usage occupants.

## 4.3 Life-Cycle Costing

**64.** Life-cycle costing

A.  Is sometimes used as a basis for cost planning and product pricing.

B.  Includes only manufacturing costs incurred over the life of the product.

C.  Includes only manufacturing cost, selling expense, and distribution expense.

D.  Emphasizes cost savings opportunities during the manufacturing cycle.

Answer (A) is correct.  *(CMA, adapted)*
**REQUIRED:** The true statement about life-cycle costing.
**DISCUSSION:** Life-cycle costing estimates a product's revenues and expenses over its expected life cycle. This approach is especially useful when revenues and related costs do not occur in the same periods. It emphasizes the need to price products to cover all costs, not just those for production. Hence, costs are determined for all value-chain categories: upstream (R&D, design), manufacturing, and downstream (marketing, distribution, and customer service). The result is to highlight upstream and downstream costs in the cost planning process that often receive insufficient attention.
Answer (B) is incorrect because the life-cycle model includes the upstream (R&D and design) and downstream (marketing, distribution, and customer service) elements of the value chain as well as manufacturing costs. Answer (C) is incorrect because the life-cycle model includes the upstream (R&D and design) and downstream (marketing, distribution, and customer service) elements of the value chain as well as manufacturing costs. Answer (D) is incorrect because life-cycle costing emphasizes the significance of locked-in costs, target costing, and value engineering for pricing and cost control. Thus, cost savings at all stages of the life cycle are important.

**65.** Target pricing

    A. Is more effective when applied to mature, long-established products.

    B. Considers short-term variable costs and excludes fixed costs.

    C. Is often used when costs are difficult to control.

    D. Is a pricing strategy used to create competitive advantage.

Answer (D) is correct.  *(CMA, adapted)*
    **REQUIRED:** The definition of target pricing.
    **DISCUSSION:** Target pricing and costing may result in a competitive advantage because it is a customer-oriented approach that focuses on what products can be sold at what prices. It is also advantageous because it emphasizes control of costs prior to their being locked in during the early links in the value chain. The company sets a target price for a potential product reflecting what it believes consumers will pay and competitors will do. After subtracting the desired profit margin, the long-run target cost is known. If current costs are too high to allow an acceptable profit, cost-cutting measures are implemented or the product is abandoned. The assumption is that the target price is a constraint.
    Answer (A) is incorrect because target pricing is used on products that have not yet been developed. Answer (B) is incorrect because target pricing considers all costs in the value chain. Answer (C) is incorrect because target pricing can be used in any situation, but it is most likely to succeed when costs can be well controlled.

**66.** In target costing,

    A. The market price of the product is taken as a given.

    B. Only raw materials, labor, and variable overhead cannot exceed a threshold target.

    C. Only raw materials cannot exceed a threshold target.

    D. Raw materials are recorded directly to cost of goods sold.

Answer (A) is correct.  *(CMA, adapted)*
    **REQUIRED:** The true statement about target costing.
    **DISCUSSION:** Target costing begins with a target price, which is the expected market price given the company's knowledge of its customers and competitors. Subtracting the unit target profit margin determines the long-term target cost. If this cost is lower than the full cost, the company may need to adopt comprehensive cost-cutting measures. For example, in the furniture industry, certain price points are popular with buyers: a couch might sell better at $400 than at $200 because consumers question the quality of a $200 couch and thus will not buy the lower-priced item. The result is that furniture manufacturers view $400 as the target price of a couch, and the cost must be lower.
    Answer (B) is incorrect because all product cost categories are addressed by target costing. Answer (C) is incorrect because all product cost categories are addressed by target costing. Answer (D) is incorrect because the manner in which raw materials costs are accounted for is irrelevant.

**67.** A company's product has an expected 4-year life cycle from research, development, and design through its withdrawal from the market. Budgeted costs are

| | |
|---|---|
| Upstream costs (R&D, design) | $2,000,000 |
| Manufacturing costs | 3,000,000 |
| Downstream costs (marketing, distribution, customer service) | 1,200,000 |
| After-purchase costs | 1,000,000 |

The company plans to produce 200,000 units and price the product at 125% of the whole-life unit cost. Thus, the budgeted unit selling price is

    A. $15

    B. $31

    C. $36

    D. $45

Answer (D) is correct.  *(Publisher)*
    **REQUIRED:** The unit selling price.
    **DISCUSSION:** Whole-life costs include after-purchase costs (operating, support, repair, and disposal) incurred by customers as well as life-cycle costs (R&D, design, manufacturing, marketing, distribution, and research). Hence, the budgeted unit whole-life cost is $36 [($2,000,000 + $3,000,000 + $1,200,000 + $1,000,000) ÷ 200,000 units], and the budgeted unit selling price is $45 ($36 × 125%).
    Answer (A) is incorrect because $15 is the budgeted unit manufacturing cost. Answer (B) is incorrect because $31 is the budgeted unit life-cycle cost. Answer (C) is incorrect because $36 is the budgeted unit whole-life cost.

Questions 68 through 70 are based on the following information.

A company that uses life cycle costing is considering the manufacture of a product with a 5-year life cycle that will require spending $1,000,000 for R&D and $2,000,000 for design and testing. Annual fixed and unit variable costs for the product and projected average annual unit sales at three selling prices are given below:

| | | | Sales Price | | |
| | Fixed | Variable | $ 750 | $ 900 | $1,125 |
|---|---|---|---|---|---|
| Production costs | $1,500,000 | $100 | | | |
| Marketing and distribution costs | 1,500,000 | 100 | | | |
| Customer service costs | 180,000 | 40 | | | |
| Unit average annual sales | | | 8,000 | 6,000 | 4,800 |

At the highest price, R&D costs will increase by $500,000 and design and testing costs by $1,000,000. Moreover, fixed customer service costs will rise by $30,000 per year, and variable customer service costs will rise by $25 per unit. At the lowest price, fixed marketing and distribution costs will decrease by $30,000 per year.

**68.** At a unit price of $750, the life cycle costs are

A. $7,620,000

B. $8,070,000

C. $27,000,000

D. $28,350,000

Answer (D) is correct.  *(Publisher)*
**REQUIRED:** The life cycle costs at a unit price of $750.
**DISCUSSION:** Life cycle costs include upstream (R&D and design and testing) and downstream (marketing and distribution and customer service) costs over the product's 5-year life cycle. At a unit price of $750, upstream costs equal $3,000,000 ($1,000,000 + $2,000,000). Fixed costs of production and the fixed downstream costs equal $15,750,000 [($1,500,000 + $1,500,000 + $180,000 − $30,000) × 5 years], and variable costs of production and variable downstream costs equal $9,600,000 [8,000 units × ($100 + $100 + $40) × 5 years]. Accordingly, the life cycle costs at a price of $750 equal $28,350,000 ($3,000,000 + $15,750,000 + $9,600,000).
Answer (A) is incorrect because $7,620,000 is the life cycle cost for 1 year at a unit price of $900. Answer (B) is incorrect because $8,070,000 is the life cycle cost for 1 year at a unit price of $750. Answer (C) is incorrect because $27,000,000 is the sales revenue for the life cycle at a unit price of $1,125.

**69.** At a unit price of $900, the life cycle costs are

A. $18,900,000

B. $26,100,000

C. $26,910,000

D. $28,350,000

Answer (B) is correct.  *(Publisher)*
**REQUIRED:** The life cycle costs at a unit price of $900.
**DISCUSSION:** At a unit price of $900, upstream costs equal $3,000,000 ($1,000,000 + $2,000,000). Fixed costs of production and the fixed downstream costs equal $15,900,000 [($1,500,000 + $1,500,000 + $180,000) × 5 years], and variable costs of production and the variable downstream costs equal $7,200,000 [6,000 units × ($100 + $100 + $40) × 5 years]. Thus, the life cycle costs at a price of $900 equal $26,100,000 ($3,000,000 + $15,900,000 + $7,200,000).
Answer (A) is incorrect because $18,900,000 omits the variable costs. Answer (C) is incorrect because $26,910,000 equals the life-cycle costs at a unit price of $1,125. Answer (D) is incorrect because $28,350,000 equals the life-cycle costs at a unit price of $750.

**70.** Which unit sales price should be selected to obtain the maximum profit over the product's 5-year life cycle?

A. $750

B. $900

C. $1,125

D. No profit can be earned.

Answer (A) is correct.  *(Publisher)*
**REQUIRED:** The maximum profit over the product's 5-year life cycle.
**DISCUSSION:** Life cycle costs include upstream (R&D and design and testing) and downstream (marketing and distribution and customer service) costs over the product's 5-year life cycle. At a unit price of $750, upstream costs equal $3,000,000 ($1,000,000 + $2,000,000). Fixed costs of production and the fixed downstream costs equal $15,750,000 [($1,500,000 + $1,500,000 + $180,000 − $30,000) × 5 years], and variable costs of production and variable downstream costs equal $9,600,000 [8,000 units × ($100 + $100 + $40) × 5 years]. Accordingly, the life cycle costs at a price of $750 equal $28,350,000 ($3,000,000 + $15,750,000 + $9,600,000). Sales revenue at this price is $30,000,000 (8,000 units × $750 × 5 years). Hence, profit at a price of $750 is $1,650,000 ($30,000,000 − $28,350,000).
Answer (B) is incorrect because $900,000 is the profit at a unit price of $900. Answer (C) is incorrect because $90,000 is the profit at a unit price of $1,125. Answer (D) is incorrect because a profit of $1,650,000 is earned at a price of $750.

## 4.4 Operation Costing

**71.** Three commonly employed systems for product costing are job-order costing, operation costing, and process costing. Match the type of production environment with the costing method used.

| | Job-Order Costing | Operation Costing | Process Costing |
|---|---|---|---|
| A. | Auto repair | Clothing manufacturing | Oil refining |
| B. | Loan processing | Drug manufacturing | Custom printing |
| C. | Custom printing | Paint manufacturing | Paper manufacturing |
| D. | Engineering design | Auto assembly | Motion picture production |

Answer (A) is correct.  *(CIA, adapted)*
**REQUIRED:** The proper matching of the type of production environment with the costing method used.
**DISCUSSION:** Job-order costing is appropriate when producing products with individual characteristics. Process costing should be used to assign costs to similar products that are mass produced on a continuous basis. Operation costing is a hybrid of job-order and process costing systems. It is used by companies that manufacture goods that undergo some similar and some dissimilar processes. Operation costing accumulates total conversion costs and determines a unit conversion cost for each operation. However, direct materials costs are charged specifically to products as in job-order systems. Operation costing is appropriate for clothing manufacturing. Thus, job-order costing is appropriate for auto repair, operation costing for clothing manufacturing, and process costing for oil refining.
Answer (B) is incorrect because custom printing requires job-order costing. Answer (C) is incorrect because process costing should be used for paint manufacturing. Answer (D) is incorrect because job-order costing is appropriate for motion picture production.

**72.** An operation costing system is

A. Identical to a process costing system except that actual cost is used for manufacturing overhead.

B. The same as a process costing system except that materials are allocated on the basis of batches of production.

C. The same as a job order costing system except that materials are accounted for in the same way as they are in a process costing system.

D. The same as a job order costing system except that no overhead allocations are made since actual costs are used throughout.

Answer (B) is correct.  *(CMA, adapted)*
**REQUIRED:** The definition of an operation costing system.
**DISCUSSION:** Operation costing is a hybrid of job-order and process costing systems wherein materials are allocated on the basis of batches of production. It is used by companies that manufacture goods that undergo some similar and some dissimilar processes. Operation costing accumulates total conversion costs and determines a unit conversion cost for each operation. However, direct materials costs are charged specifically to products or batches as in job-order systems.
Answer (A) is incorrect because operation costing differs from process costing in the treatment of materials. Answer (C) is incorrect because operation costing differs from process costing in the treatment of materials. Answer (D) is incorrect because overhead allocations are made in operation costing.

Questions 73 through 76 are based on the following information.

Gregg Industries manufactures molded chairs. The three models of molded chairs, which are all variations of the same design, are Standard (can be stacked), Deluxe (with arms), and Executive (with arms and padding). The company uses batch manufacturing and has an operation costing system.

Gregg has an extrusion operation and subsequent operations to form, trim, and finish the chairs. Plastic sheets are produced by the extrusion operation, some of which are sold directly to other manufacturers. During the forming operation, the remaining plastic sheets are molded into chair seats and the legs are added; the standard model is sold after this operation. During the trim operation, the arms are added to the deluxe and executive models and the chair edges are smoothed. Only the executive model enters the finish operation where the padding is added. All of the units produced are subject to the same steps within each operation, and no units are in process at the end of the period. The units of production and direct materials costs were as follows:

| | Units Produced | Extrusion Materials | Form Materials | Trim Materials | Finish Materials |
|---|---|---|---|---|---|
| Plastic sheets | 5,000 | $ 60,000 | | | |
| Standard model | 6,000 | 72,000 | $24,000 | | |
| Deluxe model | 3,000 | 36,000 | 12,000 | $ 9,000 | |
| Executive model | 2,000 | 24,000 | 8,000 | 6,000 | $12,000 |
| | 16,000 | $192,000 | $44,000 | $15,000 | $12,000 |

Manufacturing costs applied during the month were:

| | Extrusion Operation | Form Operation | Trim Operation | Finish Operation |
|---|---|---|---|---|
| Direct labor | $152,000 | $60,000 | $30,000 | $18,000 |
| Overhead | 240,000 | 72,000 | 39,000 | 24,000 |

**73.** The unit cost of a standard model is

A. $36.50

B. $52.50

C. $69.30

D. $96.30

Answer (B) is correct. *(CMA, adapted)*
REQUIRED: The unit cost of a standard model using operation costing.
DISCUSSION: A standard model passes through the extrusion and form operations. Thus, its unit cost includes the materials and conversion costs for both operations. The unit materials and conversion costs for the extrusion operation are $12.00 ($192,000 ÷ 16,000 units) and $24.50 [($152,000 + $240,000) ÷ 16,000 units], respectively. The unit materials and conversion costs for the form operation are $4.00 [$44,000 ÷ (16,000 – 5,000) units] and $12.00 [($60,000 + $72,000) ÷ (16,000 – 5,000) units], respectively. Accordingly, the unit cost of a standard model is $52.50 ($12.00 + $24.50 + $4.00 + $12.00).
Answer (A) is incorrect because $36.50 is the unit cost of a plastic sheet. Answer (C) is incorrect because $69.30 is the unit cost of a deluxe model. Answer (D) is incorrect because $96.30 is the unit cost of an executive model.

**74.** The unit cost of a deluxe model is

A. $52.50

B. $55.50

C. $66.30

D. $69.30

Answer (D) is correct. *(CMA, adapted)*
REQUIRED: The unit cost of a deluxe model using operation costing.
DISCUSSION: A deluxe model passes through the extrusion, form, and trim operations, so its unit cost equals that of the standard model plus the unit costs incurred in the trim operation. The unit materials and conversion costs for the trim operation are $3.00 [$15,000 ÷ (16,000 – 11,000) units] and $13.80 [($30,000 + $39,000) ÷ (16,000 – 11,000) units], respectively. Hence, the unit cost of a deluxe model is $69.30 ($52.50 + $3.00 + $13.80).
Answer (A) is incorrect because $52.50 is the unit cost of a standard model. Answer (B) is incorrect because $55.50 excludes the conversion cost incurred in the trim operation. Answer (C) is incorrect because $66.30 excludes the materials cost incurred in the trim operation.

**75.** The total product cost of the executive model is

A. $182,500

B. $192,600

C. $207,900

D. $315,000

Answer (B) is correct. *(CMA, adapted)*
    **REQUIRED:** The total product cost of the executive model using operation costing.
    **DISCUSSION:** An executive model passes through all four operations. Thus, its unit cost equals that of the deluxe model plus the unit costs incurred in the finish operation. The unit cost of the deluxe model is $69.30. The unit materials and conversion costs for the finish operation are $6.00 [$12,000 ÷ (16,000 – 14,000) units] and $21.00 [($18,000 + $24,000) ÷ (16,000 – 14,000) units], respectively. Consequently, the unit cost of the executive model is $96.30 ($69.30 + $6.00 + $21.00), and the total product cost is $192,600 (2,000 units × $96.30).
    Answer (A) is incorrect because $182,500 is the total product cost of the plastic sheets. Answer (C) is incorrect because $207,900 is the total product cost of the deluxe model. Answer (D) is incorrect because $315,000 is the total product cost of the standard model.

**76.** Assume that 1,000 units of the deluxe model remained in work-in-process at the end of the period and that these units were 100% complete as to materials and 60% complete as to trim operation conversion. What is the balance of work-in-process?

A. $42,000

B. $64,500

C. $69,000

D. $69,300

Answer (B) is correct. *(CMA, adapted)*
    **REQUIRED:** The balance of work-in-process using operation costing.
    **DISCUSSION:** Given that 5,000 units (16,000 – 11,000) entered the trim operation, they consisted of 2,000 deluxe units and 2,000 executive units that were complete as to materials and trim operation conversion and 1,000 deluxe units that were complete as to materials and 60% complete as to trim operation conversion. Accordingly, the equivalent units of production for materials in the trim operation equaled 5,000 (5,000 physical units × 100%). However, the EUP for trim operation conversion equaled 4,600 [(2,000 × 100%) + (2,000 × 100%) + (1,000 × 60%)]. Because total conversion cost for the trim operation was $69,000, the conversion cost per equivalent unit was $15.00 ($69,000 ÷ 4,600), and the total trim operation conversion cost in work-in-process was $9,000 (1,000 physical units × $15 per EUP × 60% completed as to conversion). Moreover, the work-in-process is complete as to all materials costs for the first three operations and the conversion costs for the first two operations. The unit materials and conversion costs for the extrusion operation are $12.00 ($192,000 ÷ 16,000 units) and $24.50 ($392,000 ÷ 16,000 units), respectively. The unit materials and conversion costs for the form operation are $4.00 [$44,000 ÷ (16,000 – 5,000) units] and $12.00 [$132,000 ÷ (16,000 – 5,000) units]. The total cost of work-in-process is therefore $64,500 {$9,000 + [1,000 units × ($12.00 + $4.00 + $3.00 + $24.50 + $12.00)]}.
    Answer (A) is incorrect because $42,000 equals the conversion costs in the finish operation. Answer (C) is incorrect because $69,000 equals the conversion costs in the trim operation. Answer (D) is incorrect because $69,300 is the cost of 1,000 completed deluxe units.

## 4.5 Backflush Costing

**77.** Backflush costing is most likely to be used when

A. Management desires sequential tracking of costs.

B. A just-in-time production philosophy has been adopted.

C. The company carries significant amounts of inventory.

D. Actual production costs are debited to work-in-process.

Answer (B) is correct. *(Publisher)*
    **REQUIRED:** The true statement about backflush costing.
    **DISCUSSION:** Backflush costing is often used with a JIT system because it minimizes the effort devoted to accounting for inventories. It delays much of the accounting for production costs until the completion of production or even the sale of goods. Backflush costing is most appropriate when inventories are low or when the change in inventories is minimal, that is, when most production costs for a period flow into cost of goods sold.
    Answer (A) is incorrect because traditional systems track costs as units pass through each step of production. Answer (C) is incorrect because backflush costing is inconsistent with the full-costing requirement of GAAP. The larger the inventories or the change therein, the greater the discrepancy. Moreover, larger inventories require more detailed information. Answer (D) is incorrect because backflush costing eliminates the work-in-process account.

Questions 78 through 82 are based on the following information.

A company that manufactures a single product uses backflush costing. At the beginning of the period, there were no inventories. During the period, 40,000 units were produced, of which 39,000 were sold. The standard unit direct materials and conversion costs for the period were $30 and $18, respectively. The actual unit direct materials and conversion costs for the period were $29 and $20, respectively. Furthermore, any under- or overapplied conversion cost is not prorated between cost of goods sold and finished goods, but materials price variances are recognized. Materials efficiency variances should be disregarded.

The following additional information is also available for the period:

| Direct materials purchased (actual cost of materials sufficient to produce 42,000 units) | $1,218,000 |
|---|---|
| Direct materials used (standard cost) | 1,200,000 |
| Conversion costs incurred (actual cost) | 800,000 |

**78.** Assume the company's backflush accounting system records the purchase of direct materials and the completion and sale of finished goods. The entry for the purchase of direct materials is

A.
| Inventory control | $1,260,000 | |
| Accounts payable control | | $1,260,000 |

B.
| Raw and in-process inventory control | $1,218,000 | |
| Accounts payable control | | $1,218,000 |

C.
| Raw and in-process inventory control | $1,260,000 | |
| Accounts payable control | | $1,218,000 |
| Direct materials price variance | | 42,000 |

D. No entry.

Answer (C) is correct. *(Publisher)*
**REQUIRED:** The entry to record the purchase of direct materials.
**DISCUSSION:** The company records the purchase of direct materials and recognizes direct materials variances. It also records the completion and sale of finished goods. Hence, the only inventory account omitted is work-in-process, and the direct materials purchases are debited to raw and in-process inventory control, an account that includes direct materials that are both not yet in process and in-process. Because the company recognizes direct materials variances, the direct materials price variance is recorded at the time of purchase, and the raw and in-process inventory is carried at standard cost. Accordingly, the debit to raw and in-process inventory is $1,260,000 (42,000 units that can be produced with the materials purchased × $30 standard DM cost per output unit), the credit to accounts payable or other relevant accounts is $1,218,000 (actual cost), and the favorable direct materials price variance is therefore $42,000 ($1,260,000 standard cost – $1,218,000 actual cost).
Answer (A) is incorrect because the direct materials price variance should be credited. Answer (B) is incorrect because the direct materials price variance should be credited, and the inventory should be carried at standard cost. Answer (D) is incorrect because the company's backflush system records the purchase of inventory.

**79.** Assume the company's backflush accounting system records the purchase of direct materials and the completion and sale of finished goods. The entry to record finished goods is

A.
| Finished goods control | $1,920,000 | |
| Raw and in-process inventory control | | $1,200,000 |
| Conversion costs applied | | 720,000 |

B.
| Finished goods control | $1,960,000 | |
| Raw and in-process inventory control | | $1,160,000 |
| Conversion costs applied | | 800,000 |

C.
| Finished goods control | $2,000,000 | |
| Accounts payable control | | $1,200,000 |
| Conversion costs control | | 800,000 |

D. No entry.

Answer (A) is correct. *(Publisher)*
**REQUIRED:** The entry to record the completion of goods.
**DISCUSSION:** In this version of backflush costing, the cost of finished goods completed during the period is recorded at their standard cost of $1,920,000 [40,000 units × ($30 DM + $18 CC per unit)]. Raw and in-process inventory is credited for its standard cost of $1,200,000 (40,000 units × $30), and conversion costs applied is credited for $720,000 (40,000 units × $18 standard cost per output unit).
Answer (B) is incorrect because this entry is at actual cost. Answer (C) is incorrect because the credits should be to raw and in-process inventory control and to conversion costs applied at standard cost. Answer (D) is incorrect because the company's backflush system records the completion of goods.

**80.** Assume the company's backflush accounting system records the purchase of direct materials and the completion and sale of finished goods. The entry to record under- or overapplied conversion costs is

A.
| | | |
|---|---|---|
| Conversion costs applied | $720,000 | |
| Cost of goods sold | 78,000 | |
| Finished goods | 2,000 | |
| Conversion costs control | | $800,000 |

B.
| | | |
|---|---|---|
| Conversion costs applied | $800,000 | |
| Cost of goods sold | | $ 80,000 |
| Conversion costs control | | 720,000 |

C.
| | | |
|---|---|---|
| Conversion costs control | $800,000 | |
| Cost of goods sold | | $ 78,000 |
| Finished goods | | 2,000 |
| Conversion costs applied | | 720,000 |

D.
| | | |
|---|---|---|
| Conversion costs applied | $720,000 | |
| Cost of goods sold | 80,000 | |
| Conversion costs control | | $800,000 |

Answer (D) is correct. *(Publisher)*
**REQUIRED:** The entry to record under- or overapplied conversion costs.
**DISCUSSION:** Conversion costs control is initially debited for actual conversion costs ($800,000). Conversion costs applied is initially credited for standard conversion costs (40,000 units × $18 = $720,000). Thus, when under- or overapplied conversion costs are recorded, those entries are reversed. The balancing entry is to cost of goods sold because it is given that any under- or overapplication is not prorated. Given that the amount applied was less than the amount incurred, cost of goods sold should be debited for $80,000 ($800,000 – $720,000).
Answer (A) is incorrect because it is given that the underapplication of conversion costs is not prorated between cost of goods sold and finished goods. Answer (B) is incorrect because the amounts applied and actually incurred are reversed. Answer (C) is incorrect because conversion costs are under-, not overapplied, and the underapplied amount is not prorated. Moreover, the amount actually incurred is credited, and the amount applied is debited.

**81.** Assume the company's backflush accounting system records the purchase of direct materials and the sale but not the completion of finished goods. The entry to record the sale of finished goods is

A.
| | | |
|---|---|---|
| Cost of goods sold | $1,872,000 | |
| Finished goods control | | $1,872,000 |

B.
| | | |
|---|---|---|
| Cost of goods sold | $1,872,000 | |
| Inventory control | | $1,170,000 |
| Conversion costs applied | | 702,000 |

C.
| | | |
|---|---|---|
| Inventory control | $1,911,000 | |
| Cost of goods sold | | $1,911,000 |

D.
| | | |
|---|---|---|
| Cost of goods sold | $1,911,000 | |
| Accounts payable control | | $1,131,000 |
| Conversion costs applied | | 780,000 |

Answer (B) is correct. *(Publisher)*
**REQUIRED:** The entry to record the sale of finished goods.
**DISCUSSION:** In this version of backflush costing, the completion of finished goods is not recognized; a single inventory account records the direct materials in the direct materials inventory, in work-in-process, and in finished goods; and all conversion costs are period costs because they are never recorded in a work-in-process or finished goods account. Accordingly, the standard cost of units sold is debited to cost of goods sold in the amount of $1,872,000 [39,000 units sold × ($30 DM + $18 CC per unit)]. The balancing credits at standard cost are to inventory control for $1,170,000 (39,000 units × $30 DM per unit) and conversion costs applied for $702,000 (39,000 units × $18 CC per unit).
Answer (A) is incorrect because this entry would be made if the completion of finished goods were recorded. Answer (C) is incorrect because $1,911,000 is the cost of goods sold if the standard unit direct materials and conversion costs were $29 and $20, respectively. Answer (D) is incorrect because $1,911,000 is the cost of goods sold if the standard unit direct materials and conversion costs were $29 and $20, respectively.

**82.** Refer to the information on the preceding page(s). Assume the company's backflush accounting system records the purchase of direct materials and the sale but not the completion of finished goods. The entry to record under- or overapplied conversion costs is

A.  Conversion costs
    applied                    $720,000
    Cost of goods sold          80,000
      Conversion costs
      control                              $800,000

B.  Conversion costs
    control                    $800,000
      Cost of goods sold                   $ 80,000
      Conversion costs
      applied                               720,000

C.  Conversion costs
    applied                    $702,000
    Cost of goods sold          98,000
      Conversion costs
      control                              $800,000

D.  Conversion costs
    control                    $800,000
      Cost of goods sold                   $ 98,000
      Conversion costs
      applied                               702,000

Answer (C) is correct.   *(Publisher)*
**REQUIRED:** The entry to record under- or overapplied conversion costs.
**DISCUSSION:** Because the completion of finished goods is not recognized, no conversion costs are inventoried. Thus, conversion costs are initially recorded by debits to a control account when incurred, and conversion costs are applied by a credit entry only when goods are sold. The under- or over-application of conversion costs is therefore recognized by closing the control and applied accounts (credit and debit, respectively) and by debiting or crediting the difference to cost of goods sold. No proration of this amount is possible because no finished goods account is maintained. Consequently, the entry is to debit conversion costs applied for $702,000 (39,000 units × $18 standard CC per unit), to credit conversion costs control for the $800,000 actually incurred, and to debit cost of goods sold for the $98,000 difference.
Answer (A) is incorrect because this entry assumes that a finished goods account is used. Answer (B) is incorrect because this entry is the inverse of the entry when a finished goods account is used. Answer (D) is incorrect because this entry is the inverse of the proper entry.

**83.** Key Co. changed from a traditional manufacturing operation with a job-order costing system to a just-in-time operation with a backflush costing system. What is(are) the expected effect(s) of these changes on Key's inspection costs and recording detail of costs tracked to jobs in process?

|   | Inspection Costs | Detail of Costs Tracked to Jobs |
|---|---|---|
| A. | Decrease | Decrease |
| B. | Decrease | Increase |
| C. | Increase | Decrease |
| D. | Increase | Increase |

Answer (A) is correct.   *(CPA, adapted)*
**REQUIRED:** The effects of changing to a JIT operation with backflush costing.
**DISCUSSION:** In a JIT system, materials go directly into production without being inspected. The assumption is that the vendor has already performed all necessary inspections. The minimization of inventory reduces the number of suppliers, storage costs, transaction costs, etc. Backflush costing eliminates the traditional sequential tracking of costs. Instead, entries to inventory may be delayed until as late as the end of the period. For example, all product costs may be charged initially to cost of sales, and costs may be flushed back to the inventory accounts only at the end of the period. Thus, the detail of cost accounting is decreased.

Use Gleim's *CMA Test Prep* for interactive testing with **over 2,000 additional multiple-choice questions!**

# STUDY UNIT FIVE
# OVERVIEW OF INFORMATION SYSTEMS AND SYSTEMS DEVELOPMENT AND DESIGN

(12 pages of outline)

This study unit is the **first of three** on **information management**. The relative weight assigned to this major topic in Part 2 of the exam is **15%** at **skill level A** (two skill types required). The three study units are:

Study Unit 5: Overview of Information Systems and Systems Development and Design
Study Unit 6: Technology of Information Systems
Study Unit 7: Electronic Commerce and Other Topics

After studying the outlines and answering the multiple-choice questions in this study unit, you will have the skills necessary to address the following topics listed in the IMA's Learning Outcome Statements:

Part 2 – Section C.1.  Nature and purpose of an information system

The candidate should be able to:

a. identify the different types of business information systems, e.g., transaction processing, management information, decision support, etc.

b. recognize that information systems support the business functions of accounting, finance, marketing, operations management, and human resources

c. identify and define the two basic ways that transaction processing systems process data; i.e., (i) batch processing and (ii) real-time processing

d. recognize that management information systems provide information and support the day-to-day decision-making needs of management

Part 2 – Section C.2.  Systems development and design

The candidate should be able to:

a. recognize that most computer-based information systems are conceived, designed, and implemented using a systematic development process

b. recognize that end-users and information technology specialists should design information systems based on an analysis of an organization's information requirements

c. define a systems development life cycle (SDLC) and understand that the SDLC involves activities that are highly related and interdependent

d. outline the steps of an SDLC and explain how they are related

e. recognize that systems feasibility studies should encompass cost/benefit analyses which include both tangible and intangible benefits

f. identify both the tangible and intangible benefits of a cost/benefit analysis

## 5.1 NATURE AND PURPOSE OF AN INFORMATION SYSTEM

1.    A **system** is a regularly interacting or interdependent group of items (subsystems) forming a unified whole.

    a.    Every system, such as a business, is in turn part of a larger system, such as a national economy.

        1)    The **boundary** of a system defines its operational limits and separates it from the **environment**.

        2)    A system performs its processing functions within the boundary.

            a)    **Inputs** flow into and **outputs** flow out of the system through the boundary.

            b)    A boundary shared with another system is an **interface**.

    b.    To attain the system's objectives, it must have regulatory mechanisms, called **controls**, to prevent, detect, and correct deviations from standards. The three basic types of control systems are:

        1)    **Feedback control systems**, which gather information after the occurrence of an event, evaluate it and initiate action to improve future activities, for example, cost variances in a standard costing system.

        2)    **Feedforward control systems**, which anticipate potential variations from plans so that adjustments can be made to prevent problems either before they occur or before they become too serious, for example, a cash budget.

        3)    **Preventive control systems**, which prevent an unwanted event from occurring, for example, separation of duties and organization independence.

2.    An **information system** performs four major tasks:

    a.    **Input**. The system must acquire (capture) data from within or without the entity.

    b.    **Transformation**. Raw materials (**data**) are converted into knowledge useful for decision making (**information**).

    c.    **Output**. The ultimate purpose of the system is **communication of results** to internal or external users.

    d.    **Storage**. Before, during, and after processing, data must be temporarily or permanently stored, for example, in **files or databases**.

3.    Information systems have evolved to serve the needs of **users at all levels** of the organizational hierarchy.

    a.    Each of the systems described here, in increasing level of aggregation, delivers information in a different form to serve the needs of a particular user group.

4.    At the **operational level**, the ongoing routine operations of an organization are supported by a **transaction processing system (TPS)**.

    a.    A transaction is a single, discrete event that can be captured by an information system, e.g., the movement of raw materials from storage to production, the taking of a reservation, the recording of a new employee's personal data, or the sale of a piece of merchandise.

    b.    A transaction processing system therefore captures the fundamental data that reflect the economic life of an organization.

        1)    These raw data eventually feed a firm's financial statements and flow to other systems that provide decision-makers with information aggregated at the appropriate level.

5. At the **knowledge level**, two types of systems are used.

     a. **Office automation systems (OASs)** are used by clerical personnel to speed the storage, retrieval, and dissemination of communication within and without the organization. Typical applications include word processing, spreadsheets, digital document storage, and desktop publishing.

     b. **Knowledge work systems (KWSs)** are used by technical personnel in specialized fields such as engineering, graphics, medical diagnosis, scientific inquiry, and market research.

6. At the **management level**, managers get the information they need for analysis, planning, control, and decision making from a **management information system (MIS)**.

     a. The goal of an MIS is to provide operational summary data and exception reports derived from input from the TPS.

        1) These reports are periodic and ordinarily concern problems that are highly structured. Hence, an MIS tends to have only minor analytical capacities.

     b. MISs may be classified by function or by activity.

        1) **Functions** include:

           a) Marketing -- sales analysis, forecasting, and planning

           b) Manufacturing -- production planning, cost control, and quality control

           c) Logistics -- planning and control of purchasing and inventory management

           d) Personnel -- planning for human resources and employee evaluation

           e) Finance and accounting -- capital budgeting, financial analysis, and cost analysis

           f) Information processing -- systems development planning and cost/benefit analysis

        2) **Activities** include:

           a) Strategic planning -- setting overall organizational objectives and drafting strategic plans

           b) Management control -- budgeting and resource allocation

           c) Operational control -- detailed scheduling of operations and performance supervision, receipts and disbursements, ordering and shipping

     c. An **accounting information system (AIS)** is a subsystem of an MIS that processes routine, highly structured financial and transactional data relevant to managerial as well as financial accounting. An AIS is concerned with

        1) Transactions with external parties (e.g., customers, suppliers, governments, owners, and creditors) reflected in financial statements prepared in conformity with GAAP, and

        2) The internal activities recorded in the cost accounting system and the preparation of related reports and analyses (e.g., production reports, pro forma financial statements, budgets, and cost-volume-profit analyses).

        3) The major components of an AIS are the

           a) **General ledger systems**, including general ledger accounting, budgeting, responsibility accounting, cost allocation, and profitability determination

           b) **Cash receipts and disbursements systems**, including payroll, accounts receivable, and accounts payable

           c) **Production systems**, including materials inventory, work-in-process, quality control, cost estimation, and scheduling

           d) **Marketing**, including finished goods, order processing, and marketing (sales) analysis

7.   Also at the management level, **decision support systems (DSSs)** were devised to overcome the "shotgun" approach of the MIS.  A DSS focuses on a single managerial problem.

   a.   A DSS is an interactive system that is useful in solving semistructured and unstructured problems, that is, those requiring a top-management or middle-management decision maker to exercise judgment and to control the process.

      1)   A DSS **does not automate a decision** or provide structured information flows but rather allows for certain aspects of the problem to be preprogrammed and provides tools for an end user to employ in applying insight and judgment.

      2)   The system must be interactive to permit the user to explore the problem by using the computational capacities, models, assumption, data resources, and display graphics of the DSS.

      3)   Thus, a DSS is an ad hoc, quick-response system initiated and operated by the end users.  Its components are language, processing, and knowledge systems.

         a)   A DSS may make use of statistical and financial analysis tools, other management science models, and graphics software.

         b)   **Spreadsheet software** can be a simple type of DSS.

            i)   Information and formulas are the basis for the model of a decision entered into the cells of the spreadsheet.  By varying the inputs, the decision maker can perform a what-if or sensitivity analysis of a problem.

         c)   A data-driven DSS exploits advanced database technology to analyze vast amounts of data.

            i)   One approach is **online analytical processing (OLAP)**, or **multidimensional data analysis**, which allows a user to view multiple perspectives of the same data.

            ii)   Another approach is **data mining**, which allows a user to discover hidden relationships in the data, such as associations (links to a given event), sequences of events, classifications (descriptions of the group to which an item belongs), or clusters (new groupings not previously known).

               •   Discovery of these relationships may lead to formulation of rules useful in forecasting and decision making.  Typical applications of data mining are identification of potential customers and purchasing patterns.

            iii)   A **group DSS** may also be designed to aid in the collaborative solution of unstructured problems.  It includes not only communications software but also electronic questionnaires, brainstorming tools, voting or prioritizing tools, idea organizers, a group dictionary, etc.

8.   At the **strategic level**, high-level decision makers get the information they need to set, and monitor progress toward, the organization's long-term objectives from an **executive information system (EIS)**, also called an **executive support system (ESS)**.

   a.   An EIS gives immediate information about an organization's critical success factors.

   b.   The information in an EIS comes from sources both within and without the organization, including information from nontraditional computer sources.

      1)   An EIS should have the ability to provide overviews, often in graphical format, or to **drill down** to the detailed data.

      2)   An EIS can be used on computers of all sizes.

      c.    An EIS assists senior managers in

          1)    Tracking the organization's performance
          2)    Sensing the organization's environment
          3)    Forecasting
          4)    Identifying problems
          5)    Identifying opportunities

9.    The following table summarizes the various systems discussed.

| Organizational Level | System Type | Typical Users | Examples |
|---|---|---|---|
| Strategic | Executive support system (ESS) | President, vice presidents, chief officers | Long-term sales and profit trends, marketing forecasting, budgeting system |
| Management | Decision support system (DSS) | Middle managers | Inventory level control, production scheduling |
|  | Management information system (MIS) |  | Sales trends, expense monitoring |
| Knowledge | Knowledge work system (KWS) | Accountants, engineers, designers | CAD/CAM, drug interaction, weather modeling |
|  | Office automation system (OAS) | Administrative assistants | Word processing, spreadsheets |
| Operational | Transaction processing system (TPS) | Operational managers, bookkeepers, reservation agents | Payroll, accounts payable, accounts receivable, cash receipts |

10.    The tremendous variety of forms that information systems can take and the diverse needs of users have led to the concept of **information resources management (IRM)**, which takes a global view of the information holdings and needs of an organization.

      a.    This view is promoted by the Information Resources Management Association of Hershey, PA (http://www.irma-international.org/).

11.    Stop and review! You have completed the outline for this subunit. Study multiple-choice questions 1 through 11 beginning on page 213.

# 5.2 PROCESSING MODES

1.    **Batch processing** is the accumulation and grouping of transactions for processing on a **delayed basis**.

      a.    The batch approach is suitable for applications that can be processed at intervals.

      b.    It is typical of older systems or of applications that involve large volumes of similar items, e.g., payroll, sales, inventory, and billing.

2.    **Online processing** involves direct communication with the computer, giving the system the capability to handle transactions **as they are entered**. An online system permits both immediate posting (updating) and inquiry of master files as transactions occur.

      a.    **Real-time processing** involves processing an input record and receiving the output soon enough to affect a current decision-making process. In a real-time system, the user interacts with the system to control an ongoing activity.

      b.    **Online, real-time systems** usually permit access to the main computer from multiple remote terminals.

          1)    A common example of an online, real-time application is an airline reservation system, which is constantly updated from moment to moment and must be available all the time.

3.  **Batch and online modes** are commonly **combined** in a single application.

    a.  Most such systems permit continuous **entry** of transactions throughout the workday in **online mode** and periodic **posting** of the transactions to the master files in **batch mode**.

    b.  Such a combination provides the advantages of system availability throughout the day with the efficiencies of batch update.

    c.  Inquiry processing in a database system can be the result of either batch or real-time processing. However, inquiry users cannot make changes to the records retrieved.

4.  **Service bureaus** perform batch processing for subscribers.

    a.  This off-site mode of processing requires a user to prepare input and then transport it to the bureau, with attendant loss of time and increase in security problems.

        1)  Employing a service bureau is one means of **outsourcing**.

    b.  Hiring a **facilities management organization** is another means of outsourcing.

        1)  A facilities management organization operates and manages the client's internal data processing activity.

        2)  It may manage hardware, software, system development, system maintenance, and staffing.

        3)  The facilities manager may own all of the hardware and software and employ all the personnel.

5.  A **totally centralized system** is one in which all processing and systems development are done at a single data processing center. This arrangement is typical of older (mainframe) systems.

    a.  All processing is done by one large computer.

    b.  Remote users are serviced via data communications channels between themselves and the center.

    c.  Terminals at the remote sites are usually dumb terminals (providing communications only, with no stand-alone processing capabilities).

    d.  Requests for development of new systems are submitted for the consideration of the centralized systems development group.

    e.  The centralized staff is large.

    f.  Advantages of total centralization arise primarily from the economies of scale permitted and the strengthening of control.

6.  In **totally decentralized systems**, data processing functions are independently developed at each remote site. Each site has its own smaller computer and its own staff.

    a.  In a completely decentralized system, each computer stands alone, independent of any centralized or other computer.

    b.  The primary advantages of a decentralized system are that

        1)  The individual units' personnel identify more closely with the system.
        2)  Development projects are more easily accepted and meet local needs better.

7.  Totally centralized and totally decentralized systems represent two ends of a **continuum**.

    a.  The essential activities surrounding information systems are

        1)  Planning
        2)  Systems development
        3)  Programming
        4)  Operations

    b.  Any of these four functions may range along the continuum, anywhere from total centralization to total decentralization.

8. **Downsizing** consists of moving organization-wide applications to mid-range or networked computers.

   a. The purpose is to reduce costs by using less expensive systems that are more versatile than larger, more expensive systems.

9. The advent of cheaper and smaller computers has permitted the development of a hybrid of centralization and decentralization called **distributed processing**.

   a. In a distributed system, the decision is not whether an application should run centrally or locally, but rather, which **parts of the application** are better performed by small local computers and which parts are better performed at some other, possibly centralized, site.

      1) This optimal distribution of processing tasks must strike a balance between performing processes on the most appropriate platform and minimizing traffic over the communications network that connects the platforms.

      2) EXAMPLE: In processing a sales order, order entry may be handled by a terminal. Upon the completion of the sales order, the terminal will transmit it to a server in a local warehouse. This computer will determine whether the item is available by interrogating an inventory file at the organization's manufacturing plant. If the item is available, the paperwork is produced locally at the warehouse, and the clerk at the terminal is notified. If it is not available, the plant's computer determines the probable delay before the item is available. This information is transmitted via the local warehouse computer to the terminal. If this delay is acceptable to the customer, the production paperwork is performed at the plant. Thus, the actual processing of the order entry is shared by the terminal, the warehouse server, and the manufacturing plant computer.

   b. An advantage of distributed processing is **fail-soft protection**, i.e., the ability to shut down nonessential processes and continue essential ones during times of hardware or software failure.

   c. **Cooperative processing** is a system in which computers in a distributed processing network can share the use of application programs belonging to another end user.

      1) The system assigns different machines the functions they perform best in executing a transaction-based application program.

      2) For example, a personal computer might be used to enter and validate data for the application, and a large server might handle file input and output.

10. Stop and review! You have completed the outline for this subunit. Study multiple-choice questions 12 through 20 beginning on page 216.

## 5.3 SYSTEMS DEVELOPMENT AND DESIGN

1. Developing a computer-based information system is a creative and demanding task that can and should produce economic benefits for an organization.

   a. However, systems development can be a disaster, with labor and financial resources being expended with no observable return and perhaps even a system that cannot be completed.

      1) Positive results are more frequently obtained if the process is **formally structured, documented, and subject to management controls**.

   b. Systems development should be overseen by an **information systems steering committee** consisting of top-level managers representing the functional areas of the organization, such as information systems, accounting, and marketing.

      1) The steering committee provides overall guidance for information systems activities to assure that goals are consistent with those of the organization.

    2)    Thus, the steering committee establishes priorities for implementing applications and either performs or approves high-level planning.

    3)    **Business process reengineering** is systems development that involves a complete rethinking of how business functions are performed to provide value to customers, that is, radical innovation instead of mere improvement and a disregard for current jobs, hierarchies, and reporting relationships.

        a)    The total quality management (TQM) philosophy and developments in information technology are enablers of reengineering, but the human resource dimension also must be considered.

2.    Three approaches to developing new information systems are common.

    a.    **Prototyping** is an approach that involves creating a working model of the system requested, demonstrating it for the user, obtaining feedback, and making changes to the underlying code.

        1)    This process repeats through several iterations until the user is satisfied with the system's functionality.

        2)    Formerly, this approach was derided as being wasteful of resources and tending to produce unstable systems, but with vastly increased processing power and high-productivity development tools, prototyping can, in some cases, be an efficient means of systems development.

    b.    **End user development** is employed when personnel of the end user department have the necessary skills to generate a system without major assistance from IT.

        1)    The existence of software development tools makes it possible for those who are not IT professionals to build working systems.

        2)    This approach has the advantage of having the actual users of the system being the ones who build it.

        3)    The risk of end user development is that the system may be redundant, poorly documented, and not properly tested.

    c.    By far the the most common methodology for building new information systems is the **systems development life-cycle (SDLC) approach.**

        1)    The SDLC approach is highly structured and, if properly followed, can help an organization deploy maintainable, well-documented systems with the functionality that was intended.

3.    The steps in the systems development life-cycle are as follows:

    a.    The **project definition phase** includes

        1)    Preparing the project proposal
        2)    Determining project priority
        3)    Submitting the proposal for approval

    b.    A **feasibility study** consists of

        1)    An investigation of the current system
        2)    Determination of the information and processing requirements
        3)    Evaluation of the possible applications of computer data processing
        4)    Selection of the best option
        5)    An evaluation of the proposed design choice's cost effectiveness and impact on the organization

           a)    A feasibility study must therefore consider technical, operational, and economic feasibility. The design choice must be within the range of available technology, meet the operational needs of users and otherwise be acceptable to them, and have a favorable cost-benefit ratio.

c.   A **cost-benefit analysis** is the analysis tool to use in selecting the best system alternative.

1)   Feasibility studies should include an analysis of the cost-benefit ratio of any system alternatives.

2)   In many cases, the best possible system may not be cost effective.

3)   Thus, once the decision makers have determined that two or more system alternatives are acceptable, the cost-benefit relationship should be used to select the best system for a particular application.

d.   The **project initiation phase** includes:

1)   Promptly informing managers and employees about the project

2)   Assembling the project team (possibly including systems analysts, programmers, accountants, and users)

3)   Training selected personnel to improve necessary skills and enhance communication among team members

4)   Establishing project controls (e.g., by implementing a project scheduling technique such as PERT)

e.   **Systems analysis** is the process of learning how a system functions, determining the needs of users, and developing the logical requirements of a proposed system.

1)   A systems analysis requires a survey of the existing system, the organization itself, and the organization's environment to determine (among other things) whether a new system is needed.

2)   The survey results determine not only what, where, how, and by whom activities are performed but also why, how well, and whether they should be done at all.

3)   Ascertaining the problems and informational needs of decision makers is the next step.

4)   The **systems analyst** must consider the entity's key success variables (factors that determine its success or failure), the decisions currently being made and those that should be made, the factors important in decision making (timing, relation to other decisions, etc.), the information needed for decisions, and how well the current system makes those decisions.

5)   Finally, the systems analysis should establish the requirements of a system that will meet user needs.

f.   The process of developing specifications for the components of a system is **systems design**.

1)   Detailed systems design involves developing specifications regarding input, processing, internal controls and security measures, programs, procedures, output, and databases.

2)   The three major activities of systems design are user interface design, data design, and process design.

3)   Systems design determines how information requirements will be met.

4)   It concerns how users will interact with the system to meet their needs, how data will be organized, and the formulation of processing steps.

5)   This step involves work by specialists to develop specifications for

a)   Work flow and programs (but not coding)
b)   Controls and points where they should be implemented
c)   Hardware
d)   Security measures, including backup
e)   Data communications
f)   Quality assurance testing for the balance of the development process

g.   An important tool in structured analysis and design is the **data flow diagram**.

    1)   Data flow diagrams use four basic symbols to show how data flow to, from, and within the system and the processes that manipulate the data.

    2)   A data flow diagram can be used to depict lower-level details as well as higher-level processes.

    3)   A system can be divided into subsystems, and each subsystem can be further subdivided at levels of increasing detail.

h.   **Flowcharting** is another aid in the system development process.

    1)   A flowchart is a pictorial representation of the definition, analysis, or solution of a problem in which symbols are used to depict operations, data flow, equipment, etc.

    2)   Flowcharts may be created for a system, program, or document.

    3)   The best method of displaying the flow of data and the information processing of a system is a system flowchart.

        a)   A **system flowchart** is a pictorial representation of an information system at the macro level.  It emphasizes inputs, processing steps, and outputs but not the details of execution.

    4)   Other means of documenting the decision logic reflected in systems are matrices (presentations of pairs of conditions and resulting actions), decision tables, decision trees, and pseudocode.

i.   **Physical database design** depends on the existing system.

    1)   New files or a new database may have to be designed.

    2)   Modifying an existing database may be feasible.

    3)   If the existing database provides for the new application, modification may not be necessary.

j.   **Program development** entails coding programs in accordance with the specifications in the physical design phase and then testing the results.

    1)   **Structured programming** divides the system's set of programs into discrete modules by functional specifications.

        a)   The objective is to create modules that are independent logical units, each of which has one entry and one exit point.

        b)   This reduces the complexity resulting from instructions that jump back and forth among different sections of the program (called "spaghetti code").

        c)   Data sharing among modules should also be minimized.

    2)   Each module can be coded by a separate team to

        a)   Facilitate security because no one group knows the complete set of programs

        b)   Expedite the development process because several programming teams can work simultaneously

        c)   Facilitate maintenance because a change or patch need only be module-specific, a less complicated procedure than fitting a patch to a complex, multifunction program

k.   **Procedure development** includes writing technical manuals, forms, and other materials for all persons who will use, maintain, or otherwise work with the system.

l.   **Installation and operation** are the final phases of the SDLC.

1)   Training and educating system users is important not only for proper use of the system but also to offset the resistance of users whose jobs may have been substantially changed.

2)   Acceptance testing by users of inputs, outputs, programs, and procedures is necessary to determine that the new system meets their needs.

3)   Systems conversion is the final testing and switchover.

a)   **Parallel operation** is the operation of the old and new systems simultaneously until satisfaction is obtained that the new system is operating as expected.

b)   **Pilot operation** (modular or phase-in conversion) is the conversion to the new or modified system by module or segment, e.g., one division, department, function, or branch of the company at a time. One disadvantage is the extension of the conversion time.

4)   Systems follow-up or post-implementation evaluation is a subsequent review of the efficiency and effectiveness of the system after it has operated for a substantial time (e.g., 1 year).

m.   **Errors** can be corrected most easily and clearly when they are found at an early stage of systems development. Their correction becomes more costly as the life cycle progresses.

n.   **Systems maintenance** must be undertaken by systems analysts and applications programmers continuously throughout the life of a system.

1)   Maintenance is the redesign of the system and programs to meet new needs or to correct design flaws.

2)   Ideally, these changes should be made as part of a regular program of preventive maintenance.

4.   Some factors to consider in evaluating the **cost-benefit analysis** are:

a.   **Tangible benefits** identified in the cost-benefit analysis might include reduced

1)   Maintenance, rental, and operating costs
2)   Personnel
3)   Investment in hardware and software
4)   Age of accounts receivables
5)   Investment in inventory (because of increased turnover)

b.   **Intangible benefits** identified in the cost-benefit analysis might include

1)   Improved control over information-processing activities
2)   Less time spent by operating management on data-related activities
3)   Better decision making
4)   Increased emphasis on long-range planning
5)   Higher employee morale

c.   **Tangible costs** identified in the cost-benefit analysis might include those for

1)   Maintenance, personnel, and operations
2)   Training and orientation
3)   Lease or purchase of new hardware and software
4)   Site preparation
5)   Design

    d.   **Intangible costs** identified in the cost-benefit analysis might include those for
        1)   Negative effects on employee morale, resulting in decreased productivity
        2)   Negative effects on customers, resulting in decreased business
        3)   Decreased control of the information system by operating management
        4)   Increased centralized control of the information system
        5)   Increased specialization in information processing
        6)   Increased potential cost for breakdowns as system becomes centralized

5.   Stop and review!  You have completed the outline for this subunit.  Study multiple-choice
     questions 21 through 34 beginning on page 219.

## 5.4  CORE CONCEPTS

### Nature and Purpose of an Information System

- An information system performs four major tasks:  **input**, **transformation**, **output**, and **storage**.
- Each **organizational level** uses information systems appropriate to its functions.
- At the **strategic** level, high-level executives use **executive support systems**.
- At the **management** level, middle managers use **decision support systems** and **management information systems**.
- At the **knowledge** level, knowledge workers such as engineers and accountants use **knowledge work systems** and **office automation systems**.
- At the **operational** level, operational managers and bookkeepers use **transaction processing systems**.

### Processing Modes

- **Batch processing** is the accumulation and grouping of transactions for processing on a **delayed basis**.
- **Online processing** involves direct communication with the computer, giving the system the capability to handle transactions **as they are entered**.
- **Real-time processing** involves processing an input record and **receiving the output** soon enough to affect a current decision-making process.

### Systems Development and Design

- Positive results are more frequently obtained if the systems development process is **formally structured, documented, and subject to management controls**.
- The typical **steps in the systems development process** are project definition, feasibility study, cost-benefit analysis, project initiation, existing system analysis, new system design, physical database design, program development, installation and operation, and system maintenance.

# QUESTIONS

## 5.1 Nature and Purpose of an Information System

**1.** Feedback, feedforward, and preventive controls are important types of control systems and procedures for an accounting information system. Which one of the following is in the correct order of feedback, feedforward, and preventive control systems?

    A. Cash budgeting, capital budgeting, and hiring qualified employees.

    B. Cash budgeting, cost accounting variances, and separation of duties.

    C. Cost accounting variances, separation of duties, and cash planning.

    D. Cost accounting variances, cash budgeting, and organizational independence.

Answer (D) is correct. *(CMA, adapted)*
    **REQUIRED:** The correct order of feedback, feedforward, and preventive control systems.
    **DISCUSSION:** A feedback control system gathers information after the occurrence of an event, evaluates it, and initiates action to improve future activities. For example, calculation of variances in a standard cost accounting system is a feedback control. A feedforward control anticipates potential variations from plans so that adjustments can be made to prevent problems either before they occur or before they become too serious. A cash budget is an example of a feedforward control because it anticipates cash needs and allows for the provision of resources to meet those needs. A preventive control prevents an unwanted event from occurring. Separation of duties and organizational independence are examples of preventive controls because certain unwanted events are impossible if these controls are properly implemented.
    Answer (A) is incorrect because cash budgeting is a feedforward control. Answer (B) is incorrect because cash budgeting is a feedforward control, and variance analysis is a feedback control. Answer (C) is incorrect because separation of duties is a preventive control, but cash planning is not.

**2.** Many organizations supplement feedback control systems with feedforward control systems. The major goal of most feedforward control systems is

    A. The prediction of potential variations from plans so that adjustments can be made to prevent problems before they occur or become significant.

    B. The prediction of potential variations from budgets so that variance analysis can be performed on problems that become significant.

    C. To provide complete information by use of system controls on computer input.

    D. To make predictions about any future event in the organization.

Answer (A) is correct. *(CMA, adapted)*
    **REQUIRED:** The major goal of most feedforward control systems.
    **DISCUSSION:** A feedforward system anticipates problems and strives for timely prevention rather than after-the-fact correction. Planning is a related concept. Preventive maintenance is an example of a feedforward control.
    Answer (B) is incorrect because variance analysis is a feedback control. Answer (C) is incorrect because the goal of feedforward systems is to predict variations before they occur, not to provide information by use of system controls on computer input. Answer (D) is incorrect because feedforward controls are concerned with variations that will lead to problems, not with predicting all future events.

**3.** Which one of the following is not considered a typical risk associated with outsourcing (the practice of hiring an outside company to handle all or part of the data processing)?

    A. Inflexibility.

    B. Loss of control.

    C. Loss of confidentiality.

    D. Less availability of expertise.

Answer (D) is correct. *(CMA, adapted)*
    **REQUIRED:** The item that is not considered a typical risk associated with outsourcing.
    **DISCUSSION:** Some companies have outsourced their data processing function because of the economies provided, superior service quality, avoidance of changes in the organization's information system infrastructure, cost predictability, the freeing up of human and financial capital, avoidance of fixed costs, and the greater expertise offered by outside vendors. The risks of outsourcing include the inflexibility of the relationship, the loss of control, the vulnerability of important information, and often the dependency on a single vendor.

**4.** Which one of the following terms best describes a decision support system (DSS)?

- A. Management reporting system.
- B. Formalized system.
- C. Interactive system.
- D. Accounting information system.

Answer (C) is correct.   *(CMA, adapted)*
**REQUIRED:**  The best description of a DSS.
**DISCUSSION:**  A decision support system is an interactive system that is useful in solving semistructured and unstructured problems, that is, those requiring a top-management or middle-management decision maker to exercise judgment and to control the process.  A DSS does not automate a decision or provide structured information flows but rather provides tools for an end user to employ in applying insight and judgment.  The system must be interactive to permit the user to explore the problem by using the computational capacities, models, assumptions, data resources, and display graphics of the DSS.

Answer (A) is incorrect because a management reporting system provides structured, routine information flows. Answer (B) is incorrect because the required flexibility of a DSS means that it cannot be highly formalized or structured. Answer (D) is incorrect because an accounting information system processes routine, highly structured financial and transactional data relevant for accounting purposes.

**5.** Which one of the following statements about an executive information system (EIS) is false?  The EIS

- A. Provides top executives with immediate and easy access to information in a highly interactive format.
- B. Helps executives monitor business conditions in general and assists in strategic planning to control and operate the company.
- C. Is designed to accept data from many different sources; to combine, integrate, and summarize the data; and to display this data in a format that is easy to understand and use.
- D. Is likely to be one of the most widely used and the largest of the information subsystems in a business organization.

Answer (D) is correct.   *(CMA, adapted)*
**REQUIRED:**  The false statement regarding an executive information system (EIS).
**DISCUSSION:**  An EIS focuses on strategic (long-range) objectives and gives immediate information about an organization's critical success factors.  The information in an EIS comes from sources both within and without the organization.  An EIS is typically used only by executives at the highest levels within the organization; as a result, it is not widely used within the organization.  Information provided is often highly aggregated, but the details supporting the aggregated data are accessible.

**6.** An executive information system (EIS) has all of the following characteristics except

- A. Focusing on obtaining strategic objectives.
- B. Giving immediate information about an organization's critical success factors.
- C. Providing information from nontraditional computer sources.
- D. Providing advice and answers to top management from a knowledge-based system.

Answer (D) is correct.   *(CMA, adapted)*
**REQUIRED:**  The item that is not a characteristic of an executive information system (EIS).
**DISCUSSION:**  An EIS serves the needs of top management for transaction processing (primarily inquiries and support for decisions), operational control, managerial control, and strategic planning.  Top management needs access to the database and decision models, the use of large amounts of summarized internal and especially external data, and the capacity for ad hoc analysis.  Thus, an EIS focuses on strategic (long-range) objectives and gives immediate information about a firm's critical success factors.  Information is typically supplied from nontraditional computer sources.  However, an EIS program can be used on computers of all sizes.  An EIS is not a program for providing top management with advice and answers from a knowledge-based (expert) system.

Answer (A) is incorrect because an EIS does focus on obtaining strategic objectives.  Answer (B) is incorrect because an EIS gives immediate information about an organization's critical (strategic) success factors.  Answer (C) is incorrect because an EIS does not use traditional computer sources.

**7.** How is an accounting information system (AIS) distinguished from a management information system (MIS)?

    A. An AIS deals with financial information; an MIS handles all other information.

    B. An AIS may be either manual or computer based; an MIS is computer based.

    C. An AIS is a subsystem within an MIS.

    D. An AIS is control oriented; an MIS is used exclusively for planning.

Answer (C) is correct. *(CMA, adapted)*
    **REQUIRED:** The difference between an AIS and an MIS.
    **DISCUSSION:** An information system transforms raw data into knowledge useful for decision making. An MIS provides information for management decisions. An AIS is a subsystem of an MIS and processes financial and transactional data relevant to managerial decisions as well as financial accounting.
    Answer (A) is incorrect because an MIS provides financial information; an AIS is a subsystem within an MIS that is not limited to financial information. Answer (B) is incorrect because an AIS is a subsystem within an MIS which is an integrated user-machine system that includes computer hardware and software. Answer (D) is incorrect because both types of systems are used to provide a wide range of information to management.

**8.** In an information system environment, many organizations combine key data processing cycles related to accounting and finance. Traditionally, these cycles are

    A. Cash receipts, cash disbursements, and capital budgeting.

    B. Capital budgeting and financial reporting.

    C. Cash receipts and cash disbursements.

    D. Cash receipts, cash disbursements, capital budgeting, and financial reporting.

Answer (D) is correct. *(CMA, adapted)*
    **REQUIRED:** The key data processing cycles related to accounting and finance.
    **DISCUSSION:** An entity's financing and investing function, including capital budgeting, concerns the management of financial assets, acquisition and disposal of fixed assets, issuance of stock, payment of dividends, and borrowing. The accounting function manages the entity's financial records, accounts for the flow of funds (e.g., cash disbursements and receipts), and prepares financial statements for external reporting purposes. These functions are readily combined for data processing purposes. For example, the process of developing a budget may be divided into operating and financial (cash disbursements, cash receipts, capital budget, pro forma balance sheet, and cash flows statement) components linked by the pro forma income statement.
    Answer (A) is incorrect because the financial reporting cycle is omitted. Answer (B) is incorrect because the cash receipts and cash disbursements cycles are omitted. Answer (C) is incorrect because the capital budgeting and financial reporting cycles are omitted.

**9.** An accounting information system (AIS) must include certain source documents in order to control purchasing and accounts payable. For a manufacturing organization, the best set of documents should include

    A. Purchase requisitions, purchase orders, inventory reports of goods needed, and vendor invoices.

    B. Purchase orders, receiving reports, and inventory reports of goods needed.

    C. Purchase orders, receiving reports, and vendor invoices.

    D. Purchase requisitions, purchase orders, receiving reports, and vendor invoices.

Answer (D) is correct. *(CMA, adapted)*
    **REQUIRED:** The best set of documents to be included in an AIS to control purchasing and accounts payable.
    **DISCUSSION:** An AIS is a subsystem of a management information system that processes financial and transactional data relevant to managerial and financial accounting. The AIS supports operations by collecting and sorting data about an organization's transactions. An AIS is concerned not only with external parties but also with the internal activities needed for management decision making at all levels. An AIS is best suited to solve problems when reporting requirements are well defined. A manufacturer has well-defined reporting needs for routine information about purchasing and payables. Purchase requisitions document user department needs, and purchase orders provide evidence that purchase transactions were appropriately authorized. A formal receiving procedure segregates the purchasing and receiving functions and establishes the quantity, quality, and timeliness of goods received. Vendor invoices establish the liability for payment and should be compared with the foregoing documents.
    Answer (A) is incorrect because receiving reports should be included. Answer (B) is incorrect because requisitions and vendor invoices should be included. Answer (C) is incorrect because purchase requisitions should be included.

**10.** Which one of the following statements about an accounting information system (AIS) is false?

A. AIS supports day-to-day operations by collecting and sorting data about an organization's transactions.

B. The information produced by AIS is made available to all levels of management for use in planning and controlling an organization's activities.

C. AIS is best suited to solve problems where there is great uncertainty and ill-defined reporting requirements.

D. AIS is often referred to as a transaction processing system.

Answer (C) is correct.    *(CMA, adapted)*
**REQUIRED:** The false statement about an accounting information system (AIS).
**DISCUSSION:** An AIS is a subsystem of a management information system that processes financial and transactional data relevant to managerial and financial accounting. The AIS supports operations by collecting and sorting data about an organization's transactions. An AIS is concerned not only with external parties, but also with the internal activities needed for management decision making at all levels. An AIS is best suited to solve problems when reporting requirements are well defined. A decision support system is a better choice for problems in which decision making is less structured.

**11.** Which one of the following features is least likely to apply to the transaction processing cycle of an accounting information system?

A. Data records are chiefly historical in nature.

B. Most of the sources of data are an organization's recurring transactions.

C. Data are usually financial in nature.

D. Data records are the basis of predictive systems.

Answer (D) is correct.    *(CMA, adapted)*
**REQUIRED:** The feature that is least likely to apply to the transaction processing cycle of an AIS.
**DISCUSSION:** An AIS is a subsystem of a management information system that processes financial and transactional data relevant to managerial and financial accounting. The AIS supports operations by collecting and sorting historical data about an organization's transactions. An AIS is concerned not only with external parties but also with the internal activities needed for management decision making at all levels. An AIS is best suited to solve problems when reporting requirements are well defined. An AIS does not typically use records based on predictive systems, which would be a feature of a decision support system.

## 5.2 Processing Modes

**12.** Batch processing

A. Is not used by most businesses because it reduces the audit trail.

B. Processes individual transactions as they occur.

C. Allows users to inquire about groups of information contained in the system.

D. Accumulates transaction records into groups for processing against the master file.

Answer (D) is correct.    *(CMA, adapted)*
**REQUIRED:** The true statement about batch processing.
**DISCUSSION:** Batch processing is the accumulation and grouping of transactions for processing on a delayed basis. The batch approach is suitable for applications that can be processed against the master file at intervals and involve large volumes of similar items, such as payroll, sales, inventory, and billing.
Answer (A) is incorrect because batch processing provides as much of an audit trail as any computerized operation. Answer (B) is incorrect because individual transactions are grouped into batches, and the entire batch is processed together. Answer (C) is incorrect because batch processing refers to the input of data, not inquiry.

**13.** Transaction processing systems frequently support the inquiry of online database users. Inquiry processing includes all of the following characteristics except that

A. Either batch or real-time processing may be used.

B. It is dependent on the use of telecommunication networks and database management query languages.

C. Responses are in a prespecified format displayed on the end user's terminal.

D. End users are allowed to make changes to the records retrieved.

Answer (D) is correct.    *(CMA, adapted)*
**REQUIRED:** The item not a characteristic of inquiry processing.
**DISCUSSION:** Inquiry processing in a database system can be the result of either batch or real-time processing. An inquiry system requires the use of sophisticated hardware and software, including a database query language. Responses are in a prespecified format. End users receive responses concerning the results of transaction activities but are not allowed to make changes to the records retrieved.
Answer (A) is incorrect because either batch or real-time processing may be used to query a database system.
Answer (B) is incorrect because a query system is dependent on the use of telecommunication networks and database management query languages. Answer (C) is incorrect because responses are in a prespecified format.

**14.** The concept of timeliness of data availability is most relevant to

    A. Payroll systems.

    B. General ledger systems.

    C. Manual systems.

    D. Online systems.

Answer (D) is correct. *(CMA, adapted)*
    **REQUIRED:** The systems in which the concept of timeliness of data availability is most relevant.
    **DISCUSSION:** An online processing system is in direct communication with the computer, giving it the capability to handle transactions as they are entered. An online system permits both immediate posting (updating) and inquiry of master files as transactions occur. In an online system, data are immediately available to users upon entry. Timeliness is not necessarily an element of any system unless it is online.

**15.** A system that has several computers connected for communication and data transmission purposes but also enables each computer to process its own data is known as a

    A. Distributed data processing network.

    B. Centralized network.

    C. Decentralized network.

    D. Multidrop network.

Answer (A) is correct. *(CMA, adapted)*
    **REQUIRED:** The type of system having several computers connected for communication and data transmission purposes but also enabling each computer to process its own data.
    **DISCUSSION:** Distributed processing is characterized by a merger of computer and telecommunications technology. Distributed systems permit not only remote access to a computer but also the performance of local processing at local sites. The result is greater flexibility in systems design and the possibility of an optimal distribution of processing tasks.
    Answer (B) is incorrect because, in a centralized network, processing occurs in one location. Answer (C) is incorrect because, in a pure decentralized system, the nodes are not interconnected. Answer (D) is incorrect because a multidrop network provides links for each terminal to a single communications line connected to a central processing unit; only one terminal can send or receive messages at a time.

**16.** An interactive system environment is best characterized by

    A. Data files with records arranged sequentially.

    B. The processing of groups of data at regular intervals.

    C. Sorting the transaction file before processing.

    D. The processing of data immediately on input.

Answer (D) is correct. *(CMA, adapted)*
    **REQUIRED:** The characteristic of an interactive system environment.
    **DISCUSSION:** In an interactive (inquiry) system, users employ interactive terminals to converse directly with the system. The system is characterized by online entry and processing, direct access, and timesharing.
    Answer (A) is incorrect because an interactive system requires direct access files. Answer (B) is incorrect because an interactive system permits immediate, online processing of single transactions. Answer (C) is incorrect because the transaction file does not have to be sorted before processing.

**17.** In traditional information systems, computer operators are generally responsible for backing up software and data files on a regular basis. In distributed or cooperative systems, ensuring that adequate backups are taken is the responsibility of

    A. User management.

    B. Systems programmers.

    C. Data entry clerks.

    D. Tape librarians.

Answer (A) is correct. *(CIA, adapted)*
    **REQUIRED:** The persons responsible for ensuring that adequate backups are taken in distributed or cooperative systems.
    **DISCUSSION:** In distributed or cooperative systems, the responsibility for ensuring that adequate backups are taken is the responsibility of user management. The systems are under the control of users, not a central information processing department.
    Answer (B) is incorrect because distributed environments have no systems programmers comparable to those at central sites for traditional systems. Answer (C) is incorrect because distributed environments may not have data entry clerks. Users typically perform their own data entry. Answer (D) is incorrect because, in distributed environments, there are no tape librarians.

**18.** The system that permits the computers in a distributed processing network to share the use of another end-user's application program is

    A.  Electronic data interchange.

    B.  Interactive processing.

    C.  Executive support system.

    D.  Cooperative processing.

Answer (D) is correct.  *(CMA, adapted)*
    **REQUIRED:**  The system that permits the computers in a distributed processing network to share the use of another end-user's application program.
    **DISCUSSION:**  Cooperative processing is a system whereby computers in a distributed processing network can share the use of application programs belonging to another end user.  The system assigns different machines the functions they perform best in executing a transaction-based application program.  For example, a microcomputer might be used to enter and validate data for the application, and a mainframe might handle file input and output.
    Answer (A) is incorrect because EDI is the communication of electronic documents directly from a computer in one entity to a computer in another entity.  Answer (B) is incorrect because interactive processing does not allow for the use of another end-user's application programs.  Answer (C) is incorrect because an executive support system focuses on strategic objectives and gives immediate information about an organization's critical success factors.

**19.** An insurance company that has adopted cooperative processing is planning to implement new standard software in all its local offices.  The new software has a fast response time, is very user friendly, and was developed with extensive user involvement.  The new software captures, consolidates, edits, validates, and finally transfers standardized transaction data to the headquarters mainframe.  Local managers, who were satisfied with existing locally written microcomputer applications, opposed the new approach because they anticipated

    A.  Increased workloads.

    B.  Centralization of all processing tasks.

    C.  More accountability.

    D.  Less computer equipment.

Answer (C) is correct.  *(CIA, adapted)*
    **REQUIRED:**  The reason for opposing introduction of new software.
    **DISCUSSION:**  Cooperative processing implies a tighter coupling than previously existed between the microcomputers and the mainframe.  The result may threaten the managers' perceived autonomy by increasing the control exercised by headquarters and therefore the accountability of local managers.
    Answer (A) is incorrect because, given that only existing systems would be converted, the transaction volume would likely remain relatively constant.  Answer (B) is incorrect because, in a cooperative processing environment, different computers execute different parts of an application.  Answer (D) is incorrect because, compared with mainframe-only processing, cooperative processing typically requires more computer equipment at distributed locations.

**20.** Today, organizations are using personal computers for data presentation because personal computer use compared to mainframe use is more

    A.  Controllable.

    B.  Conducive to data integrity.

    C.  Reliable.

    D.  Cost effective.

Answer (D) is correct.  *(CIA, adapted)*
    **REQUIRED:**  The reason for using personal computers for data presentation.
    **DISCUSSION:**  In cooperative processing, personal computers are more cost effective than mainframes for data entry and presentation.  They are better suited to frequent screen updating and graphical user interfaces.
    Answer (A) is incorrect because personal computer use is less controllable than mainframe use.  Answer (B) is incorrect because the difficulty of control in a personal computer environment threatens data integrity.  Answer (C) is incorrect because, given their decades of refinement, mainframes are usually more reliable than personal computers.

## 5.3 Systems Development and Design

**21.** The three major activities of systems design are

    A.  User interface design, data manipulation, and output analysis.

    B.  Process design, output design, and output analysis.

    C.  User interface design, data design, and process design.

    D.  Data design, input validation, and processing.

**Answer (C) is correct.** *(CMA, adapted)*
**REQUIRED:** The three major activities of systems design.
**DISCUSSION:** Systems design determines how information requirements will be met. It concerns how users will interact with the system to meet their needs, how data will be organized, and the formulation of processing steps.
Answer (A) is incorrect because data manipulation is not a part of systems design; it is an operational activity that occurs after a system has been installed. Answer (B) is incorrect because output analysis occurs after a system has been installed. Answer (D) is incorrect because input validation and processing are operational activities.

**22.** Ordinarily, the analysis tool for the systems analyst and steering committee to use in selecting the best system alternative is

    A.  Pilot testing.

    B.  User selection.

    C.  Decision tree analysis.

    D.  Cost-benefit analysis.

**Answer (D) is correct.** *(CMA, adapted)*
**REQUIRED:** The analysis tool to use in selecting the best system alternative.
**DISCUSSION:** Feasibility studies should include an analysis of the cost-benefit ratio of any system alternatives. In many cases, the best possible system may not be cost effective. Thus, once the decision makers have determined that two or more systems alternatives are acceptable, the cost-benefit relationship should be used to select the best system for a particular application.
Answer (A) is incorrect because pilot testing determines only whether a system works, not how efficient it is in a particular application. Answer (B) is incorrect because users may not have the necessary systems knowledge to make a decision. Answer (C) is incorrect because decision tree analysis is probably more sophisticated than is necessary in choosing between a few systems alternatives.

**23.** In the systems development cycle, coding is

    A.  A form of testing and debugging.

    B.  Part of the detailed design phase.

    C.  Part of the data flow diagram.

    D.  A form of program maintenance.

**Answer (B) is correct.** *(CMA, adapted)*
**REQUIRED:** The true statement about coding in the system development cycle.
**DISCUSSION:** According to one paradigm for the life-cycle approach, the detailed design phase is part of the implementation of the system. Detailed design includes coding programs in accordance with the specifications established in the physical design phase. Testing the results is the next phase.
Answer (A) is incorrect because coding occurs prior to testing and debugging. Answer (C) is incorrect because data flows need to be known before coding can begin. Answer (D) is incorrect because program maintenance is the redesign of programs to meet new needs or to correct design flaws.

**24.** In determining the need for system changes, several types of feasibility studies can be made. The most commonly recognized feasibility studies are

    A.  Legal, environmental, and economic.

    B.  Environmental, operational, and economic.

    C.  Technical, economic, legal, and practical.

    D.  Technical, operational, and economic.

**Answer (D) is correct.** *(CMA, adapted)*
**REQUIRED:** The most commonly recognized types of system change feasibility studies.
**DISCUSSION:** A feasibility study consists of an investigation of the current system, determination of the information and processing requirements, evaluation of the possible applications of computer data processing, selection of the best option, and an evaluation of the proposed design choice's cost effectiveness and impact on the organization. A feasibility study must therefore consider technical, operational, and economic feasibility. The design choice must be within the range of available technology, meet the operational needs of users and otherwise be acceptable to them, and have a favorable cost-benefit ratio.
Answer (A) is incorrect because an information system is unlikely to have a significant effect on the environment. Answer (B) is incorrect because an information system is unlikely to have a significant effect on the environment. Answer (C) is incorrect because legal issues are least likely to be a concern in systems development.

**25.** Two phases of systems planning are project definition and project initiation. All of the following are steps in the project initiation phase except

   A. Preparing the project proposal.

   B. Informing managers and employees of the project.

   C. Assembling the project team.

   D. Training selected personnel.

Answer (A) is correct. *(CMA, adapted)*
   **REQUIRED:** The step not a part of the project initiation phase of systems planning.
   **DISCUSSION:** The project initiation phase includes promptly informing managers and employees about the project, assembling the project team (possibly including systems analysts, programmers, accountants, and users), training selected personnel to improve necessary skills and enhance communication among team members, and establishing project controls (e.g., by implementing a project scheduling technique such as PERT). Preparing the project proposal is a part of the project definition phase, as are feasibility studies, determining project priority, and submitting the proposal for approval.
   Answer (B) is incorrect because informing managers and employees of the project is a component of the project initiation phase. Answer (C) is incorrect because assembling the project team is a component of the project initiation phase. Answer (D) is incorrect because training selected personnel is a component of the project initiation phase.

**26.** Systems analysts are the personnel within an organization who are responsible for the development of the company's information system. Which one of the following functions are least likely to be performed by a systems analyst?

   A. Design of computer applications.

   B. Preparation of specifications for computer programming.

   C. Developing, coding, and testing computer programs.

   D. Examining user information requirements.

Answer (C) is correct. *(CMA, adapted)*
   **REQUIRED:** The function least likely to be performed by a systems analyst.
   **DISCUSSION:** A systems analyst plans and designs computer applications. This is often accomplished with the assistance of systems flowcharts. Systems analysis usually involves examining user information requirements, surveying the existing system, and preparing specifications for computer programming. The concept of systems analysis, however, does not include the development, coding, and testing of individual computer programs. The work of the systems analyst provides the design specifications that will guide the preparation of specific programs by programmers. In a good system of internal control, the systems analyst should not perform programming tasks or have access to computer equipment, production programs, data files, or input-output controls.
   Answer (A) is incorrect because systems analysts design computer applications. Answer (B) is incorrect because analysts prepare specifications for computer programmers. Answer (D) is incorrect because the systems analyst must examine user information requirements to learn what type of application is needed.

**27.** The least risky strategy for converting from a manual to a computerized accounts receivable system would be a

   A. Direct conversion.

   B. Parallel conversion.

   C. Pilot conversion.

   D. Database conversion.

Answer (B) is correct. *(CMA, adapted)*
   **REQUIRED:** The least risky strategy for converting from a manual to a computerized accounts receivable system.
   **DISCUSSION:** The least risky strategy of converting from a manual to a computerized system is a parallel conversion in which the old and new systems are operated simultaneously until satisfaction is obtained that the new system is operating as expected. Slightly more risky is a pilot conversion in which the new system is introduced by module or segment.
   Answer (A) is incorrect because direct conversion is more risky than a parallel conversion. Answer (C) is incorrect because pilot conversion is more risky than a parallel conversion. Answer (D) is incorrect because database conversion is more risky than a parallel conversion.

**28.** Workwell Company operates in several regions, with each region performing its data processing in a regional data center. The corporate management information systems (MIS) staff has developed a database management system to handle customer service and billing. The director of MIS recommended that the new system be implemented in the Southwestern Region to ascertain if the system operates in a satisfactory manner. This type of conversion is called a

A. Parallel conversion.

B. Direct conversion.

C. Prototype conversion.

D. Pilot conversion.

Answer (D) is correct. *(CMA, adapted)*
**REQUIRED:** The type of systems conversion process in which a new system is first implemented in one subunit of the organization.
**DISCUSSION:** A modular conversion approach entails switching to the new or improved system in organizational (division, region, product line, etc.) segments or system segments (accounts receivable, database, etc.). A pilot conversion is one in which the final testing and switchover are accomplished at one segment or division of the company.
Answer (A) is incorrect because parallel conversion operates the old and new systems simultaneously. Answer (B) is incorrect because direct conversion involves immediate conversion to the new system throughout the organization. Answer (C) is incorrect because a prototype conversion involves developing and putting into operation successively more refined versions of the system until sufficient information is obtained to produce a satisfactory design.

**29.** The graphic portrayal of the flow of data and the information processing of a system, including computer hardware, is best displayed in a

A. Data-flow diagram.

B. System flowchart.

C. Gantt chart.

D. Decision table.

Answer (B) is correct. *(CMA, adapted)*
**REQUIRED:** The best method of displaying the flow of data and the information processing of a system.
**DISCUSSION:** A system flowchart is a pictorial representation of an information system at the macro level. It emphasizes inputs, processing steps, and outputs but not the details of execution.
Answer (A) is incorrect because a data-flow diagram would show only where data goes, not the total system. Answer (C) is incorrect because a Gantt chart is a bar chart used to monitor the progress of large projects. Answer (D) is incorrect because a decision table is used to show the various possibilities available in a given decision situation.

**30.** Errors are most costly to correct during

A. Programming.

B. Conceptual design.

C. Analysis.

D. Implementation.

Answer (D) is correct. *(CMA, adapted)*
**REQUIRED:** The time when errors are most costly to correct.
**DISCUSSION:** Errors can be corrected most easily and clearly when they are found at an early stage of systems development. Their correction becomes more costly as the life cycle progresses. Because implementation is the last stage of the process listed, errors are most costly to correct when discovered at the implementation stage.
Answer (A) is incorrect because error correction at the programming level would be less costly than at the implementation stage. Answer (B) is incorrect because error correction at the conceptual design level would be less costly than at the implementation stage. Answer (C) is incorrect because error correction at the analysis level would be less costly than at the implementation stage.

**31.** The process of monitoring, evaluating, and modifying a system as needed is referred to as

A. Systems analysis.

B. Systems feasibility study.

C. Systems maintenance.

D. Systems implementation.

Answer (C) is correct. *(CMA, adapted)*
**REQUIRED:** The term for the process of monitoring, evaluating, and modifying a system.
**DISCUSSION:** Systems maintenance must be undertaken by systems analysts and applications programmers continuously throughout the life of a system. Maintenance is the redesign of the system and programs to meet new needs or to correct design flaws. Ideally, these changes should be made as part of a regular program of preventive maintenance.
Answer (A) is incorrect because systems analysis is the process of determining user problems and needs, surveying the organization's present system, and analyzing the facts. Answer (B) is incorrect because a feasibility study determines whether a proposed system is technically, operationally, and economically feasible. Answer (D) is incorrect because systems implementation involves training and educating system users, testing, conversion, and follow-up.

**32.** The process of developing specifications for hardware, software, manpower, data resources, and information products required to develop a system is referred to as

- A. Systems analysis.
- B. Systems feasibility study.
- C. Systems maintenance.
- D. Systems design.

Answer (D) is correct.  *(CMA, adapted)*
REQUIRED: The process of developing specifications for the components of a system.
DISCUSSION: Detailed systems design involves developing specifications regarding input, processing, internal controls and security measures, programs, procedures, output, and databases.
Answer (A) is incorrect because systems analysis is the process of learning how the current system functions, determining the needs of users, and developing the logical requirements of a proposed system.  Answer (B) is incorrect because a feasibility study determines the technical, operational, and economic feasibility of a system.  Answer (C) is incorrect because systems maintenance is the process of monitoring, evaluating, and modifying a system.

**33.** The process of learning how the current system functions, determining the needs of users, and developing the logical requirements of a proposed system is referred to as

- A. Systems maintenance.
- B. Systems analysis.
- C. Systems feasibility study.
- D. Systems design.

Answer (B) is correct.  *(CMA, adapted)*
REQUIRED: The term referring to the process of learning how a system functions, determining the needs of users, and developing the logical requirements of a proposed system.
DISCUSSION: A systems analysis requires a survey of the existing system, the organization itself, and the organization's environment to determine (among other things) whether a new system is needed.  The survey results determine not only what, where, how, and by whom activities are performed but also why, how well, and whether they should be done at all.  Ascertaining the problems and informational needs of decision makers is the next step.  The systems analyst must consider the entity's key success variables (factors that determine its success or failure), the decisions currently being made and those that should be made, the factors important in decision making (timing, relation to other decisions, etc.), the information needed for decisions, and how well the current system makes those decisions.  Finally, the systems analysis should establish the requirements of a system that will meet user needs.
Answer (A) is incorrect because maintenance is the final stage of the life cycle in that it continues throughout the life of the system; maintenance includes the redesign of the system and programs to meet new needs or to correct design flaws.  Answer (C) is incorrect because the systems feasibility study does not involve the process of learning how the current system works.  Answer (D) is incorrect because systems design is the process of developing a system to meet specified requirements.

**34.** An information system (IS) project manager is currently in the process of adding a systems analyst to the IS staff.  The new systems analyst will be involved with testing the new computerized system.  At which stage of the systems development life-cycle will the analyst be primarily used?

- A. Cost-benefit analysis.
- B. Requirements definition.
- C. Flowcharting.
- D. Implementation.

Answer (D) is correct.  *(CMA, adapted)*
REQUIRED: The stage of the systems development life-cycle involving testing of a new system.
DISCUSSION: The systems development life-cycle approach is the oldest methodology applied to the development of medium or large information systems.  The cycle is analytically divisible into stages:  investigation, analysis, systems design, implementation, and maintenance.  Testing, training, and conversion occur in the installation and operation, or implementation, stage of the life-cycle.
Answer (A) is incorrect because cost-benefit analysis is a part of the feasibility study conducted early in the life-cycle.  Answer (B) is incorrect because requirements are defined during the analysis or systems study stage.  Answer (C) is incorrect because flowcharting is a necessary activity in all early stages of the life-cycle.

# STUDY UNIT SIX
# TECHNOLOGY OF INFORMATION SYSTEMS

(18 pages of outline)

This study unit is the **second of three** on **information management**. The relative weight assigned to this major topic in Part 2 of the exam is **15%** at **skill level A** (two skill types required). The three study units are

Study Unit 5: Overview of Information Systems and Systems Development and Design
Study Unit 6: Technology of Information Systems
Study Unit 7: Electronic Commerce and Other Topics

After studying the outlines and answering the multiple-choice questions in this study unit, you will have the skills necessary to address the following topics listed in the IMA's Learning Outcome Statements:

Part 2 – Section C.3. Technology of Information Systems

The candidate should be able to:

a. recognize that the use of telecommunications systems allows companies to move data from distant points, generally at lower costs

b. demonstrate an understanding of the different types of communications networks being used in business environments

c. describe wide area networks and local area networks

d. demonstrate an understanding of client/server networks

e. recognize that software applications, such as spreadsheets, generally reside on the client computer, while the databases and related software are stored on the server computers

f. distinguish between mainframe systems and client/server applications and identify the advantages and disadvantages of each

g. demonstrate an understanding of a database management system and describe its characteristics

h. distinguish between a flat database and a relational database

i. demonstrate an understanding of a relational database system

j. demonstrate an understanding of decision support systems, how they operate, and the types of decisions that these systems support

k. recognize that artificial intelligence encompasses other applications including expert systems, fuzzy logic, neural networks, etc., and can capture management reasoning in software

l. define an expert system and its capabilities

m. demonstrate how to use a spreadsheet for business analysis, planning, and modeling

n. construct a spreadsheet used for accounting reporting or analysis purposes

o.   analyze a spreadsheet report and determine which formulas are causing errors, and how to correct the formulas

p.   describe the Internet and identify the components of the Internet's backbone

q.   demonstrate an understanding of the uses of "browser" software

r.   define the term intranet

s.   identify how intranets enable companies to share expertise among their organizational units

t.   define virtual private network

## 6.1   DATA COMMUNICATIONS, NETWORKS, AND CLIENT/SERVER SYSTEMS

1.   Large **mainframe computers** dominated the electronic data processing field in its first decades.

   a.   Mainframes were arranged so that all processing and data storage were done in a single, central location.

   b.   Communication with the mainframe was accomplished with the use of **dumb terminals**, simple keyboard-and-monitor combinations with no processing power (i.e., no CPU) of their own.

2.   The next stage in the evolution of networking was to connect computers not in different rooms of a building, but in separate buildings and eventually separate countries.

   a.   This required converting the **digital signal** used internally by the computer into an **analog signal** suitable for transmission over ordinary telephone lines.

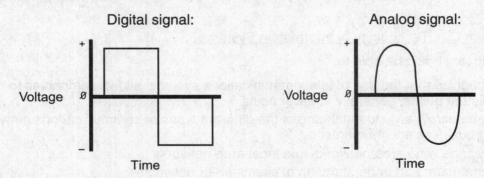

Digital signal:          Analog signal:

   1)   This conversion is necessary because when a digital signal travels more than about 10 feet, it starts to lose its shape and eventually resembles an analog signal.  By that point it has become completely unusable.

   b.   In all-digital networks, such as LANs (see item 4. on the next page) and connections between dumb terminals and mainframes, **repeaters** are placed every so often to revive the digital signal and return it to its full square-wave shape.

   1)   This is obviously not an option with the existing telephone network and its hundreds of thousands of miles of wire.

   2)   The solution is simply to convert the computer's digital signal into an analog signal (**modulation**), send it over the phone line, then reconvert it to a digital signal at the other end (**demodulation**).

   3)   The device that performs these conversion and reconversion functions is a **modem** (short for modulator-demodulator).

   c.   The introduction of the modem allowed organizations to begin moving information between locations in purely electronic format, eliminating the need for the passage of physical documents.  The potential for **cost savings** in this technology was obvious.

3.   Improvements in technology have led to increasing **decentralization** of information processing.

    a.   The mainframe-style computer was the only arrangement available in the early days of data processing. International Business Machines (now called IBM) dominated the marketplace.

        1)   Mainframes are still in use at large institutions such as governments, banks, insurance companies, and universities. However, remote connections to them are usually through desktop computers rather than through dumb terminals.

        2)   In the 1980s, the **minicomputer** gave organizations the ability to perform data processing without the high cost and large dedicated facilities of a mainframe. Digital Equipment Corporation (DEC) and Hewlett-Packard (HP) dominated this market.

        3)   As minicomputers evolved, the concept of distributed processing arose.

            a)   **Distributed processing** involves the decentralization of processing tasks and data storage and assigning these functions to multiple computers, often in separate locations.

            b)   This allowed for a drastic reduction in the amount of communications traffic because data that were needed locally could reside locally.

        4)   In 1981, IBM introduced the **Personal Computer (PC)**. This designation quickly lost its status as a brand name and became a generic term for almost any computer smaller than a minicomputer.

    b.   During the 1980s, desktop computers, and the knowledge needed to build information systems, became widespread throughout the organization.

        1)   In the early part of this period, the only means of moving data from one computer to another was the laborious process of copying the data to a diskette and physically carrying it to the destination computer. This method of connecting computers was called **sneakernet**, after the footwear involved.

        2)   It was clear that a reliable way of wiring office computers together would lead to tremendous gains in productivity.

4.   This need led to the development of the **local area network (LAN)**. A LAN is any interconnection between devices in a single office or building.

    a.   Very small networks with few devices can be connected using a **peer-to-peer** arrangement, where every device is directly connected to every other.

        1)   Peer-to-peer networks become increasingly difficult to administer with each added device.

    b.   The most cost-effective and easy-to-administer arrangement for LANs uses the client/server model.

        1)   **Client/server networks** differ from peer-to-peer networks in that the devices play more specialized roles. Client processes (initiated by the individual user) request services from server processes (maintained centrally).

        2)   In a client/server arrangement, **servers** are centrally located and devoted to the functions that are needed by all network users.

            a)   Examples include mail servers (to handle electronic mail), application servers (to run application programs), file servers (to store databases and make user inquiries more efficient), Internet servers (to manage access to the Internet), and web servers (to host websites).

            b)   Whether a device is **classified as a server** is not determined by its hardware configuration, but rather by the **function it performs**. A simple desktop computer can be a server.

3)  Technically, a **client** is any object that uses the resources of another object. Thus, a client can be either a device or a software program.

    a)  In common usage, however, "client" refers to a device that requests services from a server. This understanding of the term encompasses anything from a powerful graphics workstation to a personal data assistant (PDA), such as a Palm Pilot or a Blackberry.

    b)  A client device normally displays the user interface and enables data entry, queries, and the receipt of reports. Moreover, many applications, e.g., word processing and spreadsheet software, run on the client computer.

4)  The key to the client/server model is that **it runs processes on the platform most appropriate to that process while attempting to minimize traffic over the network.**

5)  **Security** for client-server systems may be more difficult than in a highly centralized system because of the numerous access points.

5.  Networks can be classified by their **geographical extent** and protocol. A **protocol** is a set of rules for message transmission among the devices in the network.

    a.  A **local area network (LAN)** is the type of network with which most modern office workers are familiar. A LAN connects devices within a single location.

        1)  A LAN can use a **bounded medium** (cable) or an **unbounded medium** (wireless).

        2)  Each device is linked to the LAN by means of a **network interface card (NIC)**.

        3)  As a LAN grows, it can be divided into **segments**. Segmenting improves speed by segregating traffic flow. The segments of a LAN are connected by **hubs**.

        4)  LANs are connected by **bridges** and **gateways**.

    b.  A **wide area network (WAN)** connects devices over geographically separated locations, such as buildings in an office park.

        1)  A WAN must provide far more robust error correction and data routing techniques than a LAN.

        2)  The grouping of data into addressable **packets** is what makes WANs possible. **Switches** are devices that carry out this function.

    c.  WANs come in many varieties.

        1)  **Integrated Services Digital Network (ISDN)** provides international standards for voice, video, and data communications over existing telephone lines.

            a)  The Basic level of ISDN allows up to eight devices to be connected to a single telephone circuit. The circuit has a total bandwidth of 144 kilobits per second (Kbps).

            b)  The significantly more powerful Primary level of ISDN has a total bandwidth of 1.544 Mbps.

        2)  **Private networks** are dedicated facilities, e.g., satellites, microwave transmitters, or telephone lines, leased from a **common carrier**. Hence, no dial-up access is required, and security is enhanced.

            a)  A **private branch exchange (PBX)** is a special computer at a company facility used to store, hold, transfer, and redial telephone calls.

                i)  A PBX can carry both voice and data and can switch digital data among computers and office equipment, e.g., printers, copiers, and fax machines. A PBX uses telephone lines, so its data transmission capacity is limited.

3) **Public-switched networks** use public telephone lines.

    a) This arrangement may be the most economical, but data transmission may be of lower quality, no connection may be available, and security measures may be ineffective.

4) **Value-added networks (VANs)** are private networks that transmit the data of subscribing entities.

    a) One of the most important uses of a VAN is for electronic data interchange (EDI) (see subunit 7.1).

    b) To compete with the Internet, these third-party networks add value by providing error detection and correction services, electronic mailbox facilities for EDI purposes, EDI translation, and security for e-mail and data transmissions.

5) **Virtual private networks (VPNs)** emerged as a relatively inexpensive way to solve the problem of the high cost of leased lines.

    a) A company connects each office or LAN to a local Internet service provider and routes data through the Internet, using shared, low-cost public bandwidth as the communications backbone.

    b) The success of VPNs depends on the development of secure encryption products that protect data while in transit across the Internet.

d. The proliferation of wide area networks is owing to the promulgation of **connectivity standards for open systems**.

1) **Open systems** mean that the devices made by one manufacturer will work with those of another. This is in contrast to **closed** or **proprietary systems**, in which one vendor's products will not work with any other's.

2) The most important conceptual work for data communications is the **Open Systems Interconnect (OSI) Reference Model**, published in 1983 by the International Organization for Standardization (ISO).

    a) The OSI Reference Model, sometimes called the Seven-Layer Model, is not a set of specific protocols. It is, rather, **simply a framework** to which designers of networking hardware and software can refer to make sure their designs address all the necessary tasks of networking.

e. A development in the late 1990s called the **thin client** explicitly mimics the old mainframe-and-terminal model.

1) The client machine may have very little processing power and no hard drive but a robust graphical interface.

2) Essentially all processing and data storage are done on the servers. Just enough of an application is downloaded to the client to run it.

3) One advantage of this architecture is the large amount of IT staff time and effort saved that formerly went to configuring and troubleshooting desktop machines.

6. Stop and review! You have completed the outline for this subunit. Study multiple-choice questions 1 through 13 beginning on page 240.

## 6.2 DATABASE MANAGEMENT SYSTEMS

1. A **database** is a series of related files combined to minimize redundancy of data items.

   a. A single integrated system allows for improved data accessibility.

   b. When systems within the organization are not integrated, they not only may contain different data but also may define and update data in inconsistent ways.

      1) Thus, determining the location of data and ensuring their consistency are more difficult.

   c. EXAMPLE: The various files related to human resources in the conventional record systems of most organizations include payroll, work history, and permanent personnel data.

      1) An employee's name must appear in each of these files when they are stored and processed separately. The result is redundancy.

      2) When data are combined in a database, each data item is usually stored only once.

   d. The data are stored physically on **direct-access storage devices** (e.g., magnetic disks). They are also stored for efficient access.

      1) The most frequently accessed items are placed in the physical locations permitting the fastest access.

      2) When these items were stored in separate files under older file-oriented systems, the physical locations were usually similar to the logical structure of the data. Items that logically belonged together were stored in physical proximity to one another.

   e. A **logical data model** is a user view. It is the way a user describes the data and defines their interrelationships based on the user's needs, without regard to how the data are physically stored.

2. To understand the vast improvement in performance brought about by database technology, it is helpful to review the development of file structures.

   a. The early mainframe computers used **flat files**, meaning that all the records, and all the data elements within each record, followed one behind the other. Much early mainframe storage was on magnetic tape, which naturally stored data in this fashion.

   b. EXAMPLE: Here are two records excerpted from a tape file:

| Record | Customer | Street | City | Order_Nbr | Part_Nbr_1 | Qty_1 | Price_1 | Ext_1 | Part_Nbr_2 | Qty_2 | Price_2 | Ext_2 |
|---|---|---|---|---|---|---|---|---|---|---|---|---|
| 116385 | Zeno's Paradox Hardware | 10515 Prince Avenue | Athens, GA | 19742133 | A316 | 3 | $0.35 | $1.05 | G457 | 12 | $1.15 | $13.80 |

(Many intervening records)

| Record | Customer | Street | City | Order_Nbr | Part_Nbr_1 | Qty_1 | Price_1 | Ext_1 |
|---|---|---|---|---|---|---|---|---|
| 122406 | Zeno's Paradox Hardware | 10515 Prince Avenue | Athens, GA | 19742259 | A316 | 4 | $0.35 | $1.40 |

   c. Two inefficiencies are apparent at once in this method of accessing data:

      1) The customer's address has to be stored with every order the customer places, taking up much unnecessary storage.

      2) All intervening records must be read and skipped over in order to find both records pertaining to this customer.

3. Database technology overcame these two difficulties. There are three main ways of organizing a database.

   a. A **tree** or **hierarchical structure** arranges data in a one-to-many relationship in which each record has one antecedent but may have an unlimited number of subsequent records.

1) EXAMPLE: One customer, many orders; one order, many parts.

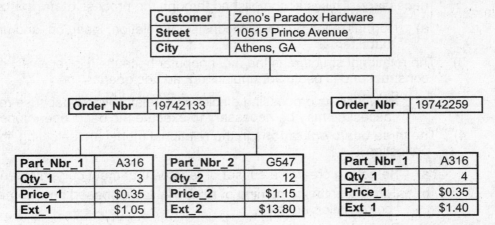

2) Because the records are not stored one after the other, a tree database structure stores a pointer with each record. The **pointer** is the storage address of the next record.

3) The tree structure cuts down on data redundancy, but retains the necessity of searching every record to fulfill a query. Thus, like the flat file, adding new records is awkward and ad hoc queries are inefficient.

b. The **network structure** connects every record in the database with every other record.

1) This was an attempt to make queries more efficient. However, the huge number of cross-references inherent in this structure makes maintenance far too complex.

c. A **relational structure** organizes data in a conceptual arrangement.

1) An individual data item is called a **field**, **column**, or **attribute** (e.g., name, date, amount).

    a) Related fields are brought together in a **record**, **row**, or **tuple** (e.g., for a single sales transaction).

    b) Multiple records make up a **file**, **table**, or **relation** (e.g., sales).

    c) Tables can be **joined** or **linked** based on common fields rather than on high-overhead pointers or linked lists as in other database structures.

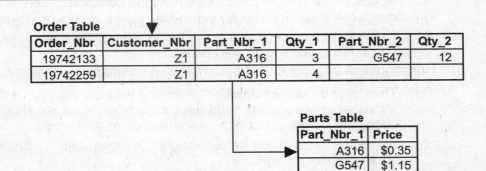

2) Note that in a relational structure, each data element is stored as few times as necessary. This is accomplished through the process of **normalization**.

    a) Normalization prevents inconsistent deletion, insertion, and updating of data items.

3) The relational structure is the most popular because it is relatively easy to construct and is useful for unplanned, ad hoc queries.

    a) However, its processing efficiency is relatively low because many accesses may be necessary to execute the basic operations.

4) The three **basic operations** in the relational model are selecting, joining, and projecting.

    a) **Selecting** creates a subset of records that meet certain criteria.

    b) **Joining** is the combining of relational tables based on a common field or combination of fields.

    c) **Projecting** results in the requested subset of columns from the table. This operation creates a new table containing only the required information.

5) **Cardinality** expresses the bounds (a minimum and a maximum) of the association between related entities.

    a) For example, a college class must have a minimum of 3 students and can have a maximum of 59. The student-class relationship has a cardinality limit expressed as (3, 59).

d. The data in a database are subject to the constraint of **referential integrity**.

1) This means that if data are collected about something, all preexisting conditions regarding it must be met; thus, for a payment voucher to exist, a vendor must also exist.

e. A **distributed database** is stored in two or more physical sites using either replication or partitioning.

1) The **replication** or **snapshot** technique creates duplicates to be stored at multiple locations.

    a) Changes are periodically copied and sent to each location. If a database is small, storing multiple copies may be cheaper than retrieving records from a central site.

2) **Fragmentation** or **partitioning** stores specific records where they are most needed.

    a) For example, a financial institution may store a particular customer's data at the branch where (s)he usually transacts his/her business. If the customer executes a transaction at another branch, the pertinent data are retrieved via communications lines.

    b) One variation is the **central index**. A query to this index obtains the location in a remote database where the complete record is to be found.

    c) Still another variation is the **ask-the-network distributed database**. In this system, no central index exists. Instead, the remote databases are polled to locate the desired record.

3) Updating data in a distributed system may require special protocols.

    a) Thus, a **two-phase commit** disk-writing protocol is used. If data are to be updated in two places, databases in both locations are cleared for updating before either one performs (commits) the update.

    b) In the first phase, both locations agree to the update. In the second phase, both perform the update.

f.   A **deadly embrace (deadlock)** occurs when each of two transactions has a lock on a single data resource.

    1)   When deadly embraces occur, the DBMS must have an algorithm for undoing the effects of one of the transactions and releasing the data resources it controls so that the other transaction can run to completion.

    2)   Then, the other transaction is restarted and permitted to run to completion.

    3)   If deadly embraces are not resolved, response time worsens or the system eventually fails.

4.   A **database management system (DBMS)** is an integrated set of computer programs that create the database, maintain the elements, safeguard the data from loss or destruction, and make the data available to applications programs and inquiries.

a.   The DBMS allows programmers and designers to work independently of the physical and logical structure of the database.

    1)   Before the development of DBMSs, programmers and systems designers needed to consider the logical and physical structure of the database with the creation of every new application. This was extremely time consuming and therefore expensive.

b.   The **schema** is a description of the overall logical structure of the database using **data-definition language**, which is the connection between the logical and physical structures of the database.

    1)   A **subschema** describes a particular user's (application's) view of a part of the database using data definition language.

c.   A fundamental characteristic of databases is that applications are independent of the database structure; when writing programs or designing applications to use the database, only the name of the desired item is necessary.

d.   A data item is identified using the **data manipulation language**, after which the DBMS locates and retrieves the desired item(s).

    1)   The data manipulation language is used to add, delete, retrieve, or modify data or relationships.

e.   The physical structure of the database can be completely altered without having to change any of the programs using the data items. Thus, different users may define different views of the data (subschemas).

5.   **Other Database Concepts**

a.   The **database administrator (DBA)** is the individual who has overall responsibility for developing and maintaining the database and for establishing controls to protect its integrity.

    1)   Thus, only the DBA should be able to update data dictionaries. In small systems, the DBA may perform some functions of a DBMS. In larger applications, the DBA uses a DBMS as a primary tool.

b.   The **data dictionary** is a file, either computer or manual, that describes both the physical and logical characteristics of every data element in a database.

    1)   The data dictionary includes, for example, the name of the data element (e.g., employee name, part number), the amount of disk space required to store the data element (in bytes), and what kind of data is allowed in the data element (e.g., alphabetic, numeric).

        a)   The data dictionary also provides a mapping from the data element to every application where it is updated and vice versa.

      2) Thus, the data dictionary contains the size, format, usage, meaning, and ownership of every data element as well as what persons, programs, reports, and functions use the data element.

      3) In an advanced data dictionary, a change in a data element automatically changes related programs.

  c. The **database mapping facility** is software that is used to evaluate and document the structure of the database.

  d. The **data control language** specifies the privileges and security rules governing database users.

  e. **Data command interpreter languages** are symbolic character strings used to control the current state of DBMS operations.

6. Storing all related data on one storage device creates **security problems**.

  a. Should hardware or software malfunctions occur, or unauthorized access be achieved, the results could be disastrous.

  b. Greater emphasis on security is required to provide backup and restrict access to the database.

      1) For example, the system may employ **dual logging**, that is, use of two transaction logs written simultaneously on separate storage media.

      2) It may also use a snapshot technique to capture data values before and after transaction processing.

      3) The files that store these values can be used to reconstruct the database in the event of data loss or corruption.

  c. The responsibility for creating, maintaining, securing, and restricting access to the database belongs to the database administrator.

  d. A DBMS includes security features. Thus, a specified user's access may be limited to certain data fields or logical views depending on the individual's assigned duties.

7. Databases and the associated DBMS permit efficient storage and retrieval of data for formal system applications.

  a. They also permit increased ad hoc accessing of data (e.g., to answer inquiries for data not contained in formal system outputs) as well as updating of files by transaction processing.

  b. These increased capabilities, however, result in increased cost because they require

      1) The use of sophisticated hardware (direct-access devices)
      2) Sophisticated software (the DBMS)
      3) Highly trained technical personnel (database administrator, staff)
      4) Increased security controls

8. An **object-oriented database** is a response to the need to store not only numbers and characters but also graphics and multimedia applications.

  a. Translating these data into tables and rows is difficult. However, in an object-oriented database, they can be stored, along with the procedures acting on them, within an object.

9. In a **hypermedia database**, blocks of data are organized into nodes that are linked in a pattern determined by the user so that an information search need not be restricted to the predefined organizational scheme. A node may contain text, graphics, audio, video, or programs.

  a. Hybrid systems containing object-oriented and relational database capabilities have also been developed.

10. Advanced database systems provide for **online analytical processing (OLAP)**, also called multidimensional data analysis, which is the ability to analyze large amounts of data from numerous perspectives. OLAP is an integral part of the data warehouse concept (see subunit 7.5).

11. Stop and review! You have completed the outline for this subunit. Study multiple-choice questions 14 through 26 beginning on page 244.

## 6.3 DECISION SUPPORT SYSTEMS

1. **Decision support systems (DSSs)** were devised to overcome the "shotgun" approach of management information systems (see item 6. in subunit 5.1). A DSS focuses on a single managerial problem.

    a. A DSS is an interactive system that is useful in **solving semistructured and unstructured problems**, that is, those requiring a top-management or middle-management decision maker to exercise judgment and to control the process.

        1) A DSS **does not automate a decision** or provide structured information flows but rather allows for certain aspects of the problem to be preprogrammed and provides tools for an end user to employ in applying insight and judgment.

        2) The system must be interactive to permit the user to explore the problem by using the computational capacities, models, assumption, data resources, and display graphics of the DSS.

        3) Thus, a DSS is an ad hoc, quick-response system initiated and operated by the end users. Its components are language, processing, and knowledge systems.

            a) A DSS may make use of statistical and financial analysis tools, other management science models, and graphics software. It may also use both procedural and nonprocedural languages.

2. The types of decision support systems include the following:

    a. A **model-driven DSS** is often a stand-alone system designed to assist in answering a narrowly defined set of questions, such as a system for scheduling surgical teams to have people with the correct skill sets available at all times.

        1) The question is formulated ahead of time and the DSS offers various solutions.

    b. A **data-driven DSS** draws on an organization's vast store of data records to present trends and relationships, such as actual vs. budgeted gross margin for all retail locations for the past 24 months.

        1) Such vast amounts of data are usually supplied by a data warehouse (see subunit 7.5). The question is not formulated ahead of time; once the user sees the data, certain courses of action may be suggested.

    c. A **document-driven DSS** provides a decision maker with unstructured information in the form of optically-stored documents, such as a collection of title deeds for perusal by a loan officer looking for customers who might want second mortgages.

    d. A **knowledge-driven DSS** uses stored facts and rules to produce a solution to a highly structured problem, e.g., a GPS-based trip-planning system.

3. Stop and review! You have completed the outline for this subunit. Study multiple-choice questions 27 and 28 beginning on page 248.

## 6.4 ARTIFICIAL INTELLIGENCE AND EXPERT SYSTEMS

1. **Artificial intelligence (AI)** is computer software designed to perceive, reason, and understand.

   a. AI is largely based on powerful **reasoning capabilities**. However, most human decision making hinges on **knowledge** (i.e., remembering relationships between variables based on experience).

      1) Human reasoning is extremely complex, based on deduction, induction, intuition, emotion, and biochemistry, resulting in a range of possible outcomes.

      2) Digital (binary) computer reasoning, on the other hand, is based entirely on if-then processes (also known as production and situation-action rules), in which every operation has exactly two outcomes (yes/no, on/off, true/false, one/zero).

2. The advantage of AI in a business environment is that, relative to human experts, they

   a. Can work 24 hours a day

   b. Will not become ill, die, or be hired away

   c. Are extremely fast processors of data, especially if numerous rules (procedures) must be evaluated

3. In the business arena, emphasis has been on the particular form of AI termed **expert systems**. Expert systems rely on a computer's ability to think and make decisions in a human way.

   a. An expert system is an interactive system that asks a series of questions and uses knowledge gained from a human expert to analyze answers and come to a decision.

   b. Expert systems were originally developed to make decisions in areas that did not have enough human experts to make decisions. Some of the earliest expert systems were used by doctors to diagnose diseases.

   c. Experimental work is being done with expert systems in taxation, financial accounting, managerial accounting, and auditing.

4. An expert system can be separated into **six components**: knowledge database, domain database, database management system, inference engine, user interface, and knowledge acquisition facility. The knowledge database and domain database together are the knowledge domain.

   a. The **knowledge database** contains the rules used when making certain decisions. The facts about the relevant topic are contained in the **domain database**.

      1) They are used as a basis for comparison when the system matches a pattern of events or facts with a decision situation.

   b. The **inference engine** is the heart of the expert system's processing. It performs the deductive thinking and logic portion of the processing.

      1) The inference engine uses **rules** from the knowledge database, **facts** from the domain database, and **user input**.

   c. Rather than use algorithms as in typical computer programs, expert systems employ symbolic processing based on heuristics.

      1) **Algorithms** are predefined procedures in which the programmer has prescribed exactly how (s)he wants to arrive at a solution.

      2) By contrast, a **heuristic** procedure is an exploratory problem-solving technique that uses self-education methods, e.g., the evaluation of feedback, to improve performance.

         a) Heuristic systems are often very interactive and provide explanations of their problem-solving behavior.

5.  An expert system is developed using a **continuous process of revision**. As new knowledge or decision-making strategies become available, prior systems must be revised.

    a.  The most time-consuming and costly part of developing an expert system is **gathering knowledge** from experts and decision makers.

6.  The development of artificial intelligence and its subfield, expert systems, has been identified by the **AICPA Future Issues Committee** as one of the major concerns facing the accounting profession.

    a.  By using expert systems, accountants can perform their duties in less time and with more uniformity. An expert system makes it more likely that different decision makers will come to the same conclusions given the same set of facts.

        1)  An expert system is useful in **applying financial accounting standards** in a consistent manner when preparing financial statements or performing audits.

        2)  Expert systems make **compliance with tax laws** much easier because all rules can be programmed into the computer. Tax planning has also benefited from the use of expert systems.

        3)  For **management control**, expert systems can be used to supplement management information systems by providing models of decisions used for planning and control.

        4)  For **auditing**, an expert system can be used to choose an audit program, select a test sample type and size, determine the level of error, perform analytical procedures, and then make a judgment decision based on the findings.

7.  Expert systems are becoming so simple that virtually anyone can develop them, even without knowledge of computer programming.

    a.  This result is accomplished through the use of programs known as **shells**. An expert system shell is a flexible system that provides the framework for developing a customized expert system.

        1)  It is quite advantageous for a company that wishes to take its own expert knowledge and design an expert system to fit its needs.

8.  Other areas of research in AI include the following:

    a.  **Fuzzy logic systems** deal with imprecise data and problems that have many solutions.

        1)  Fuzzy logic, a departure from classical two-valued sets and logic, uses soft **linguistic system variables** (e.g., large, hot, or tall) and a **continuous range of truth values** rather than strict binary (true/false) decisions and assignments.

            a)  Formally, fuzzy logic is a structured, model-free estimator that approximates a function through linguistic input/output associations.

        2)  **Fuzzy rule-based systems** apply these methods to solve many types of real-world problems, especially when a system is difficult to model, when it is controlled by a human operator or expert, or when ambiguity or vagueness is common.

        3)  **Fuzzy set theory** allows objects to belong partly to multiple sets.

            a)  Fuzzy logic is useful for describing the vagueness of things in the real world, where belonging to a set is really a matter of degree.

            b)  An object's **membership value**, or degree to which it belongs to a set, can be any number between one and zero.

   4)    Fuzzy logic is particularly useful in the design of industrial controls, in data retrieval, and in systems in which the user is not intimately familiar with all the data.

   a)    It is also useful when absolute accuracy is costly or judgments of value must be synthesized from multiple inputs.

   5)    Fuzzy logic has emerged as a profitable tool for the controlling of subway systems and complex industrial processes, as well as for household and entertainment electronics, diagnosis systems, and other expert systems.

   6)    The key benefits of a fuzzy design are simplified and reduced development cycle, ease of implementation, and more user-friendly and efficient performance.

   b.    **Neural networks** learn from their mistakes by changing their knowledge databases when informed of the accuracy of their decisions.

   c.    **Genetic algorithms** (adaptive computation) are problem-solving methods that use evolutionary processes, that is, the model of living things adapting through reproduction, mutation, and natural selection.

   d.    **Intelligent agents** are programs that apply a built-in or learned knowledge base to execute a specific, repetitive, and predictable task, for example, showing a computer user how to perform a task or searching web sites for particular financial information.

9.    Stop and review!  You have completed the outline for this subunit.  Study multiple-choice questions 29 through 34 beginning on page 249.

## 6.5 SPREADSHEETS

1.    **Spreadsheet software** was the first "killer app" for the desktop computer, meaning it was the first piece of software to work extremely well at a given task, thus gaining wide appeal for the hardware.

   a.    The software package that accomplished this was VisiCalc for the Apple II in 1979.  It turned the desktop computer into a serious business tool.

   b.    Lotus 1-2-3 and Quattro Pro were successful successors to VisiCalc.  Microsoft Excel is currently the most popular desktop spreadsheet package.

2.    The power of spreadsheets comes from their ability to perform arithmetic operations on large amounts of data, to quickly report on these results, and to perform what-if operations (the latter being a **simple type of DSS**).

   a.    A spreadsheet consists of **rows** and **columns** that intersect to form **cells**.

   1)    Values and formulas can be entered in the cells.  The combination of values and formulas form the basis for a decision model.

   2)    By varying the inputs, the decision maker can perform a what-if or sensitivity analysis of a problem.  Thus, business analysis, planning, and modeling is facilitated.

   b.    Spreadsheets generally reside on a client computer, while databases and related software are stored on server computers.

3. **Errors** are common in spreadsheets, and they are not always obvious because they are embedded in formulas which lie "behind the scenes."

   a. EXAMPLE: The following is an amortization schedule for a bond with a $5,000 face value issued at a discount. There must be an erroneous formula somewhere because the ending net carrying amount after 5 years does not equal the face amount.

**Columns**

| | A | B | C | D | E | F | G |
|---|---|---|---|---|---|---|---|
| **1** | | | Times: | Equals: | Minus: | Equals: | |
| **2** | Year | Beginning Net Carrying Amount | Effective Rate | Interest Expense | Cash Paid | Discount Amortized | Ending Net Carrying Amount |
| **3** | 1 | $4,601 | 8% | $368 | $300 | $68 | $4,669 |
| **Rows 4** | 2 | $4,669 | 8% | $374 | $300 | $74 | $4,743 |
| **5** | 3 | $4,743 | 8% | $379 | $300 | $79 | $4,822 |
| **6** | 4 | $4,822 | 8% | $386 | $300 | $86 | $4,736 |
| **7** | 5 | $4,736 | 8% | $379 | $300 | $79 | $4,815 |
| **8** | Totals | | | $1,886 | $1,500 | $386 | |

      1) The first step is to rework the arithmetic of the final column. Each cell in column G should contain a value equal to the beginning carrying amount for the period from column B plus the discount amortized that period from column F.

| | Column B | | Column F | | Column G | |
|---|---|---|---|---|---|---|
| Year 1 | $4,601 | + | $68 | = | $4,669 | OK |
| Year 2 | $4,669 | + | $74 | = | $4,743 | OK |
| Year 3 | $4,743 | + | $79 | = | $4,822 | OK |
| Year 4 | $4,822 | + | $86 | = | $4,736 | Incorrect |

      2) An examination of cell G6 reveals that, unlike the other cells in column G, it instructs the computer to subtract cell F6 from B6 rather than adding them.

   b. **Two common ways** in which errors are introduced into spreadsheets are

      1) User confusion over relative and absolute cell addressing when replicating a formula from one cell to another.

         a) Relative addressing involves having the destination cell receive its data from other cells in the same "pattern" as the cell that was copied from.

         b) Absolute addressing involves having the destination cell receive its data from cells that the user specifies.

      2) Copy-and-paste operations carried out with insufficient attention.

   c. The "invisible" nature of spreadsheet formulas makes errors easy to overlook.

      1) **The computer cannot catch these errors**. All the computer can do is carry out the instructions it is given. It is up to the user to ensure that the computer receives the correct instructions.

4. Stop and review! You have completed the outline for this subunit. Study multiple-choice questions 35 through 38 beginning on page 251.

## 6.6 INTERNET AND INTRANET

1. The **Internet** is a **network of networks** all over the world.

   a. The Internet is descended from the original ARPANet, a product of the Defense Department's Advanced Research Projects Agency (ARPA), introduced in 1969. The idea was to have a network that could not be brought down during an enemy attack by bombing a single central location.

      1) ARPANet connected computers at universities, corporations, and government.
      2) In view of the growing success of the Internet, ARPANet was retired in 1990.

   b. The Internet facilitates inexpensive communication and information transfer among computers, with gateways allowing mainframe computers to interface with personal computers.

      1) Very high-speed **Internet backbones** carry signals around the world and meet at **network access points**.

   c. Most Internet users obtain connections through **Internet service providers (ISPs)** that in turn connect either directly to a backbone or to a larger ISP with a connection to a backbone.

      1) The topology of the backbone and its interconnections may once have resembled a spine with ribs connected along its length but is now almost certainly more like a fishing net wrapped around the world with many circular paths.

2. The Internet was initially restricted to e-mail and text-only documents.

   a. In the 1980s, English computer scientist Tim Berners-Lee conceived the idea of allowing users to click on a word or phrase (a **hyperlink**) on their screens and having another document automatically be displayed.

   b. Berners-Lee created a simple coding mechanism called **hypertext markup language (HTML)** to perform this function. He also created a set of rules called **hypertext transfer protocol (HTTP)** to allow hyperlinking across the Internet rather than on just a single computer. He then created a piece of software, called a **browser**, that allowed users to read HTML from any brand of computer. The result was the **World Wide Web** (often simply called "the Web").

      1) As the use of HTML and its successor languages spread, it became possible to display rich graphics and streaming audio and video in addition to text.

      2) **Extensible markup language (XML)** was developed by an international consortium and released in 1998 as an open standard usable with many programs and platforms.

         a) XML codes all information in such a way that a user can determine not only **how it should be presented** but also **what it is**, i.e., all computerized data may be tagged with identifiers.

         b) Unlike HTML, XML uses **codes that are extensible, not fixed**. Thus, if an industry can agree on a set of codes, software for that industry can be written that incorporates those codes.

   c. With the explosive growth of the World Wide Web in the 1990s, whole **new distribution channels** opened up for businesses. Consumers can browse a vendor's catalog using the rich graphics of the Web, initiate an order, and remit payment, all from the comfort of their homes.

      1) An organization's **presence** on the Web is constituted in its **website**. The website consists of a **home page**, the first screen encountered by users, and subsidiary **web pages** (screens constructed using HTML or a similar language).

        2)    Every page on the World Wide Web has a unique address, recognizable by any web-enabled device, called a **universal resource locator (URL)**. However, just because the address is recognizable doesn't mean it's accessible to every user -- security is a major feature of any organization's website.

3.    An **intranet** permits sharing of information throughout an organization by applying Internet connectivity standards and Web software (e.g., browsers) to the organization's internal network.

    a.    An intranet addresses the connectivity problems faced by organizations that have many types of computers. It is ordinarily restricted to those within the organization and to outsiders after appropriate identification.

    b.    An **extranet** consists of the linked intranets of two or more organizations, for example, of a supplier and its customers. It typically uses the public Internet as its transmission medium but requires a password for access.

4.    Stop and review! You have completed the outline for this subunit. Study multiple-choice questions 39 and 40 on page 252.

## 6.7 CORE CONCEPTS

### Data Communications, Networks, and Client-Server Systems

- **Decentralization** has been the theme throughout the electronic data processing era. Originally, highly centralized mainframe computers were the only option.
- The development of the **local area network** (LAN) allowed for huge productivity gains by allowing workers to share information without the need for the high expense and specialized staff of a mainframe.
- In a **client/server network**, the devices play specialized roles. This configuration allows for each function in the network to be performed by the most appropriate hardware platform.
- A **client** is any device that uses the resources of another object, whether that other object be another device or a software program.
- A **server** is a device or program that provides services for other devices and programs.
- Public switched networks, value-added networks, and virtual private networks are possible configurations for **wide area networks** (WAN), i.e., networks used by organizations that span more than a single building.

### Database Management Systems

- A **database** is a series of related files combined to **minimize redundancy** of data items.
- Early solutions such as **flat files** and **network databases** were **awkward to maintain** and required high machine overhead.
- The **relational database** has been the most cost-effective architecture. Relational databases employ **normalization techniques** to ensure that data items are stored with as little redundancy as possible. Also, relational databases have very powerful search features.
- A **database management system** is an **integrated set of computer programs** that centralize and greatly ease the tasks of administering the database.
- A **database administrator** is the individual with overall responsibility for developing and maintaining the database and for establishing controls to protect its integrity.

### Decision Support Systems

- A **decision support system** (DSS) is an interactive system that is useful in solving **semistructured and unstructured problems**, that is, those requiring a decision-maker to exercise judgment and to control the process.
- Model-driven, data-driven, document-driven, and knowledge-driven are possible **configurations** for decision support systems.

## Artificial Intelligence and Expert Systems

- **Artificial intelligence** (AI) is computer software designed to perceive, reason, and understand.
- In the business arena, emphasis has been on the particular form of AI termed **expert systems**. Expert systems rely on a computer's ability to think and make decisions in a human way.

## Spreadsheets

- The power of spreadsheets comes from their ability to perform arithmetic operations on **large amounts of data**, to **quickly report** these results, and to perform **what-if operations**.
- **Errors** are common in spreadsheets, and they are not always obvious because they are embedded in formulas which lie "behind the scenes."

## Internet and Intranet

- The **Internet** is a **network of networks** all over the world.
- The Internet facilitates **inexpensive communication and information transfer** among computers, with gateways allowing mainframe computers to interface with personal computers.
- An **intranet** permits sharing of information throughout an organization by applying Internet connectivity standards and Web software (e.g., browsers) to the organization's internal network.

## QUESTIONS

### 6.1 Data Communications, Networks, and Client/Server Systems

**1.** The use of message encryption software

A. Guarantees the secrecy of data.

B. Requires manual distribution of keys.

C. Increases system overhead.

D. Reduces the need for periodic password changes.

Answer (C) is correct. *(CIA, adapted)*
   **REQUIRED:** The effect of message encryption software.
   **DISCUSSION:** Encryption software uses a fixed algorithm to manipulate plain text and an encryption key (a set of random data bits used as a starting point for application of the algorithm) to introduce variation. The machine instructions necessary to encrypt and decrypt data constitute system overhead. As a result, processing speed may be slowed.
   Answer (A) is incorrect because no encryption approach absolutely guarantees the secrecy of data. Answer (B) is incorrect because keys may also be distributed electronically via secure key transporters. Answer (D) is incorrect because periodic password changes are needed. Passwords are the typical means of validating users' access to unencrypted data.

**2.** An insurance firm uses a wide area network (WAN) to allow agents away from the home office to obtain current rates and client information and to submit approved claims using notebook computers and dial-in modems. In this situation, which of the following methods would provide the best data security?

A. Dedicated phone lines.

B. Call-back features.

C. Frequent changes of user IDs and passwords.

D. End-to-end data encryption.

Answer (D) is correct. *(CIA, adapted)*
   **REQUIRED:** The best data security method for a wide area network.
   **DISCUSSION:** Encryption of data is a security procedure in which a program encodes data prior to transmission and another program decodes the data after transmission. Encoding is important when confidential data that can be electronically monitored are transmitted between geographically separated locations.
   Answer (A) is incorrect because dedicated phone lines are not available to agents in the field. Answer (B) is incorrect because call-back features are used to authenticate the user but do not otherwise protect the transmitted data. Answer (C) is incorrect because frequent changes of user IDs and passwords are used to authenticate the user but do not otherwise protect the transmitted data.

**3.** Which of the following is false with respect to client-server networks?

A. A client-server network divides processing of an application between a client machine on a network and a server.

B. In a client-server network, many applications reside on the client computer.

C. The server customarily manages peripheral hardware and controls access to shared databases.

D. A client-server network can cope with only 12 or fewer clients at a time.

**Answer (D) is correct.** *(Publisher)*
**REQUIRED:** The false statement about client-server networks.
**DISCUSSION:** A client-server network can cope with thousands of clients at a time. They can access the server over the Internet from anywhere at any time with no time-related charges.

**4.** An electronic meeting conducted between several parties at remote sites is referred to as

A. Teleprocessing.

B. Interactive processing.

C. Telecommuting.

D. Teleconferencing.

**Answer (D) is correct.** *(CMA, adapted)*
**REQUIRED:** The process of holding an electronic meeting between several parties at remote sites.
**DISCUSSION:** Conducting an electronic meeting among several parties at remote sites is teleconferencing. It can be accomplished by telephone or electronic mail group communication software. Videoconferencing permits the conferees to see each other on video screens. The practice has grown in recent years as companies have attempted to cut their travel costs.
Answer (A) is incorrect because teleprocessing refers to connections in an online system. Answer (B) is incorrect because interactive processing allows users to converse directly with the system. It requires online processing and direct access to stored information. Answer (C) is incorrect because telecommuting refers to the practice of individuals working out of their homes by communicating with their office via the computer.

**5.** Large organizations often have their own telecommunications networks for transmitting and receiving voice, data, and images. Very small organizations, however, are unlikely to be able to make the investment required for their own networks and are more likely to use

A. Public switched lines.

B. Fast-packet switches.

C. Standard electronic mail systems.

D. The Internet.

**Answer (A) is correct.** *(CIA, adapted)*
**REQUIRED:** The telecommunications networks likely to be used by small organizations.
**DISCUSSION:** Companies can use public switched lines (phone lines) on a per-transmission basis. This option is the most cost-effective way for low-volume users to conduct telecommunications.
Answer (B) is incorrect because fast-packet switches receive transmissions from various devices, break the data into packets, and route them over a network to their destination. They are typically installed by telecommunication utility companies and other large companies that have their own networks. Answer (C) is incorrect because electronic mail systems do not allow for voice and image transmissions. Answer (D) is incorrect because the Internet does not provide telephone connections.

**6.** A local area network (LAN) is best described as a(n)

A. Computer system that connects computers of all sizes, workstations, terminals, and other devices within a limited proximity.

B. System to allow computer users to meet and share ideas and information.

C. Electronic library containing millions of items of data that can be reviewed, retrieved, and analyzed.

D. Method to offer specialized software, hardware, and data handling techniques that improve effectiveness and reduce costs.

**Answer (A) is correct.** *(CMA, adapted)*
**REQUIRED:** The best description of a local area network (LAN).
**DISCUSSION:** A LAN is a local distributed computer system, often housed within a single building. Computers, communication devices, and other equipment are linked by dedicated channels. Special software facilitates efficient data communication among the hardware devices.
Answer (B) is incorrect because a LAN is more than a system to allow computer users to share information; it is an interconnection of a computer system. Answer (C) is incorrect because a LAN is not a library. Answer (D) is incorrect because a LAN does not require specialized hardware.

**7.** Which of the following networks provides the least secure means of data transmission?

   A. Value-added.

   B. Public-switched.

   C. Local area.

   D. Private.

**Answer (B) is correct.**  *(CIA, adapted)*
   **REQUIRED:** The network that provides the least secure means of data transmission.
   **DISCUSSION:** Public-switched networks are wide area networks that use public telephone lines. This arrangement may be the most economical, but data transmission may be of lower quality, no connection may be available, and security measures may be ineffective.
   Answer (A) is incorrect because value-added carriers provide data security and error detection and correction procedures. Answer (C) is incorrect because local area networks inherently limit data transmission exposures. Answer (D) is incorrect because private networks provide security through limited access and dedicated facilities.

**8.** If a system does not have a mainframe computer or a file server but does processing within a series of personal computers, the network is a(n)

   A. Offline processing system.

   B. Expert system.

   C. Direct access system.

   D. Peer-to-peer system.

**Answer (D) is correct.**  *(CIA, adapted)*
   **REQUIRED:** The system in which processing is done within a series of personal computers.
   **DISCUSSION:** A local area network is a user-controlled network that operates without the assistance of a common carrier. It can have several personal computers attached to a host computer, can be linked as part of several LANs that may or may not communicate with a host computer, or can be connected together but not connected to a host computer (stand alone). A peer-to-peer network operates without a mainframe or file server.
   Answer (A) is incorrect because offline processing occurs when devices are not directly connected to the computer. Answer (B) is incorrect because expert systems are information systems that provide diagnostic and problem solving through the use of structured software and expert experience. Answer (C) is incorrect because direct access refers to the method for storing and retrieving data within a database.

**9.** Which of the following is considered to be a server in a local area network (LAN)?

   A. The cabling that physically interconnects the nodes of the LAN.

   B. A device that stores program and data files for users of the LAN.

   C. A device that connects the LAN to other networks.

   D. A workstation that is dedicated to a single user on the LAN.

**Answer (B) is correct.**  *(CIA, adapted)*
   **REQUIRED:** The server in a local area network.
   **DISCUSSION:** A file server is a computer in a network that operates as a librarian. It stores programs and data files for users of the LAN and manages access to them.
   Answer (A) is incorrect because the cabling that interconnects the nodes of the LAN is the telecommunications link. Answer (C) is incorrect because a device that connects the LAN to other networks is a network gateway. Answer (D) is incorrect because a workstation dedicated to a single user of the LAN is a client.

**10.** When connecting two or more electronic mail systems, which of the following is a major security issue?

   A. Inability to encrypt messages going between network gateways.

   B. Loss of critical text within messages.

   C. Inability of receiving users to automatically acknowledge receipt of messages.

   D. Inability to keep backup copies of messages.

**Answer (A) is correct.**  *(CIA, adapted)*
   **REQUIRED:** The major security issue when connecting two or more electronic mail systems.
   **DISCUSSION:** Loss of confidentiality is a major risk of an e-mail system. Inability to encrypt messages going between network gateways is a major security issue. A gateway is a means of connecting otherwise incompatible networks, nodes, or devices. It performs this function by converting one set of communication protocols to another. Accordingly, even if all systems are secured, an unsecured gateway can be a security exposure.
   Answer (B) is incorrect because loss of critical text within messages is a less serious concern than loss of confidentiality. Answer (C) is incorrect because inability of receiving users to automatically acknowledge receipt of messages is a less serious concern than loss of confidentiality. Answer (D) is incorrect because inability to keep backup copies of messages is a less serious concern than loss of confidentiality.

**11.** A company has a very large, widely dispersed internal audit department. Management wants to implement a computerized system to facilitate communications among auditors. The specifications require that auditors have the ability to place messages in a central electronic repository where all auditors can access them. The system should facilitate finding information on a particular topic. Which type of system would best meet these specifications?

- A. Electronic data interchange (EDI).

- B. Electronic bulletin board system (BBS).

- C. Fax/modem software.

- D. Private branch exchange (PBX).

Answer (B) is correct. *(CIA, adapted)*
**REQUIRED:** The best system to facilitate communications among auditors.
**DISCUSSION:** Bulletin board systems function as a centralized information source and message switching system for a particular interest group. Users review and leave messages for other users, and communicate with other users on the system at the same time.
Answer (A) is incorrect because EDI is for the electronic transmission of business information and electronic mail, but it does not offer central repositories that store messages for many parties to read. Answer (C) is incorrect because, although fax/modem software can store images of faxes received, it does not meet the criterion of ease of access to information on a particular topic. Answer (D) is incorrect because a PBX is a telecommunications system that routes calls to particular extensions within an organization.

**12.** In distributed data processing, a ring network

- A. Has all computers linked to a host computer, and each linked computer routes all data through the host computer.

- B. Links all communication channels to form a loop, and each link passes communications through its neighbor to the appropriate location.

- C. Attaches all channel messages along one common line with communication to the appropriate location via direct access.

- D. Organizes itself along hierarchical lines of communication usually to a central host computer.

Answer (B) is correct. *(CMA, adapted)*
**REQUIRED:** The true statement about a ring network in a distributed data processing system.
**DISCUSSION:** In a distributed system, an organization's processing needs are examined in their totality. The decision is not whether an application should be done centrally or locally but, rather, which parts are better performed by small local computers as intelligent terminals and which parts are better performed at some other, possibly centralized, site. The key distinction between decentralized and distributed systems is the interconnection among the nodes. A ring network links communication channels to form a loop. Each link passes communications through its neighbor to the appropriate location.
Answer (A) is incorrect because a star network routes all data through the host computer. Answer (C) is incorrect because a bus network attaches all channel messages along one common line with communication to the appropriate location via direct access. Answer (D) is incorrect because a tree configuration is organized along hierarchical lines to a host computer.

**13.** Information processing made possible by a network of computers dispersed throughout an organization is called

- A. Online processing.

- B. Interactive processing.

- C. Time sharing.

- D. Distributed data processing.

Answer (D) is correct. *(CMA, adapted)*
**REQUIRED:** The method of information processing by dispersed computers.
**DISCUSSION:** Distributed processing is characterized by a merger of computer and telecommunications technology. Distributed systems permit not only remote access to a computer but also the performance of local processing at local sites. The result is greater flexibility in systems design and the possibility of an optimal distribution of processing tasks.
Answer (A) is incorrect because online processing is a method of processing data that permits both immediate posting (updating) and inquiry of master files as transactions occur. Answer (B) is incorrect because interactive processing is a method of processing data immediately upon input. Answer (C) is incorrect because time sharing is the processing of a program by the CPU until an input or output operation is required. In time sharing, the CPU spends a fixed amount of time on each program.

## 6.2   Database Management Systems

**14.** In a database, there are often conditions that constrain database records. For example, a sales order cannot exist unless the corresponding customer exists. This kind of constraint is an example of

- A. Normalization.
- B. Entity integrity.
- C. Internal schema.
- D. Referential integrity.

Answer (D) is correct.   *(CIA, adapted)*
**REQUIRED:** The constraint exemplified by prohibiting preparation of a sales order unless it references an existing customer.
**DISCUSSION:** The data in a database are subject to the constraint of referential integrity. Thus, if data are collected about something, e.g., a payment voucher, all reference conditions regarding the data must be met. Thus, for a voucher to exist, a vendor must also exist.
Answer (A) is incorrect because normalization is the practice of decomposing database relations to remove data field redundancies and thus reduce the likelihood of update anomalies. Answer (B) is incorrect because, in a database, entity integrity means that each thing or relationship in the database is uniquely identified by a single key value. Answer (C) is incorrect because, in a database, the internal schema describes the ways the data are physically organized on the disk.

**15.** All of the following are methods for distributing a relational database across multiple servers except

- A. Snapshot (making a copy of the database for distribution).
- B. Replication (creating and maintaining replica copies at multiple locations).
- C. Normalization (separating the database into logical tables for easier user processing).
- D. Fragmentation (separating the database into parts and distributing where they are needed).

Answer (C) is correct.   *(CIA, adapted)*
**REQUIRED:** The item not a method for distributing a relational database across multiple servers.
**DISCUSSION:** A distributed database is stored in two or more physical sites. The two basic methods of distributing a database are partitioning and replication. However, normalization is a process of database design, not distribution. Normalization is the term for determining how groups of data items in a relational structure are arranged in records in a database. This process relies on "normal forms"; that is, conceptual definitions of data records and specified design rules. Normalization is intended to prevent inconsistent updating of data items. It is a process of breaking down a complex data structure by creating smaller, more efficient relations, thereby minimizing or eliminating the repeating groups in each relation.
Answer (A) is incorrect because the snapshot technique makes duplicates to be stored at multiple locations. Changes are periodically copied and sent to each location. If a database is small, storing multiple copies may be cheaper than retrieving records from a central site. Answer (B) is incorrect because the replication technique makes duplicates to be stored at multiple locations. Changes are periodically copied and sent to each location. If a database is small, storing multiple copies may be cheaper than retrieving records from a central site. Answer (D) is incorrect because fragmentation or partitioning stores specific records where they are most needed. For example, a financial institution may store a particular customer's data at the branch where (s)he usually transacts his/her business. If the customer executes a transaction at another branch, the pertinent data are retrieved via communications lines.

**16.** In a database system, locking of data helps preserve data integrity by permitting transactions to have control of all the data needed to complete the transactions. However, implementing a locking procedure could lead to

- A. Inconsistent processing.
- B. Rollback failures.
- C. Unrecoverable transactions.
- D. Deadly embraces (retrieval contention).

Answer (D) is correct.   *(CIA, adapted)*
**REQUIRED:** The potential disadvantage of a locking procedure.
**DISCUSSION:** In a distributed processing system, the data and resources a transaction may update or use should be held in their current status until the transaction is complete. A deadly embrace occurs when two transactions need the same resource at the same time. If the system does not have a method to cope with the problem efficiently, response time worsens or the system eventually fails. The system should have an algorithm for undoing the effects of one transaction and releasing the resources it controls so that the other transaction can run to completion.
Answer (A) is incorrect because inconsistent processing occurs when a transaction has different effects depending on when it is processed. Data locking ensures consistent processing. Answer (B) is incorrect because rollback failure is the inability of the software to undo the effects of a transaction that could not be run to completion. A rollback failure is not caused by data locking. However, data locking may lead to situations in which rollback is required. Answer (C) is incorrect because unrecoverable transactions are not a typical symptom of locking procedures.

**17.** In data modeling and database design, the nature and extent of a relationship between two entities is the

- A. Domain.
- B. Subschema.
- C. Cardinality.
- D. Referential path.

Answer (C) is correct.   *(CMA, adapted)*
**REQUIRED:** The nature and extent of a relationship between two entities.
**DISCUSSION:** Cardinality expresses the bounds (a minimum and a maximum) of the association between related entities. For example, assuming the entities are (1) the number of students and (2) a college class, a cardinality limit of (3, 59) for the class entity in the student-class relationship means that a class may contain from 3 to 59 students. The minimum cardinality means that an occurrence of the entity on one side of the relation (the class) must be linked to at least three instances of the entity on the other side (the number of students). The maximum cardinality means that an occurrence of the class entity must be linked to no more than 59 instances of the student entity.
Answer (A) is incorrect because the domain is the set of possible values of an attribute of one particular entity.
Answer (B) is incorrect because subschema is a particular user's (application's) view of a part of the database using data definition language. Answer (D) is incorrect because a referential path is the connection between an unspecified number of relations connected by a chain of referential constraints.

**18.** One advantage of a database management system (DBMS) is

- A. The responsibility and control assumed by each organizational unit for its own data.
- B. The decrease in the cost of the data processing department as users become responsible for establishing their own data handling techniques.
- C. A decreased vulnerability because the database management system has numerous security controls to prevent disasters.
- D. The independence of the data from the application programs, which allows the programs to be developed for the user's specific needs without concern for data capture problems.

Answer (D) is correct.   *(CMA, adapted)*
**REQUIRED:** The advantage of a DBMS.
**DISCUSSION:** A fundamental characteristic of databases is that applications are independent of the database structure; when writing programs or designing applications to use the database, only the name of the desired item is necessary. Programs can be developed for the user's specific needs without concern for data capture problems. Reference can be made to the items using the data manipulation language, after which the DBMS takes care of locating and retrieving the desired items. The physical or logical structure of the database can be completely altered without having to change any of the programs using the data items; only the schema requires alteration.
Answer (A) is incorrect because each organizational unit develops programs to make use of elements of a broad database. Answer (B) is incorrect because data handling techniques are still the responsibility of the data processing department; it is the use of the data that is departmentalized. Answer (C) is incorrect because the DBMS is no safer than any other database system.

**19.** A flat file structure is used in database management systems (DBMS) when

A. A complex network structure is employed.

B. A network based structure is used and a complex database schema is developed.

C. A simple network structure is employed.

D. A relational database model is selected for use.

Answer (D) is correct.   *(CMA, adapted)*
**REQUIRED:** The situation in which a flat file structure is used with a DBMS.
**DISCUSSION:** A flat file structure is used with a relational database model. A relational structure organizes data in conceptual tables. One relation (table or file) can be joined together or related to another without pointers or linked lists if each contains one or more of the same fields (also known as columns or attributes). The relational structure is expected to become the most popular structure because it is relatively easy to construct.
Answer (A) is incorrect because a complex network structure requires something more intricate than a flat file structure. Answer (B) is incorrect because a network structure reduces redundancy by arranging data through development of many-to-many relationships; that is, each item may have multiple antecedent as well as successive relationships, which would preclude a flat file structure. Answer (C) is incorrect because a network structure reduces redundancy by arranging data through development of many-to-many relationships; that is, each item may have multiple antecedent as well as successive relationships, which would preclude a flat file structure.

**20.** The database approach to systems and the resulting concept of database management systems have several unique characteristics not found in traditional systems, specifically file-oriented systems. Which one of the following statements does not apply to database-oriented systems?

A. Database systems have data independence; that is, the data and the programs are maintained separately except during processing.

B. Database systems contain a data definition language that helps describe each schema and subschema.

C. The database administrator is the part of the software package that instructs the operating aspects of the program when data are retrieved.

D. A primary goal of database systems is to minimize data redundancy.

Answer (C) is correct.   *(CMA, adapted)*
**REQUIRED:** The statement that does not apply to database-oriented systems.
**DISCUSSION:** A database management system (DBMS) involves an integrated set of computer programs that create the database, maintain the elements, safeguard the data from loss or destruction, and make the data available to application programs and inquiries. In a database system, the data and programs are maintained separately except during processing. The DBMS contains a description of the logical and physical structure of the database called the schema. The schema is the description of the structure or organization of the database using data description (definition) language. A primary goal of a DBMS is to minimize data redundancy, and user interface is enhanced through increased accessibility and flexibility. The system is administered by a database administrator who is a person with overall responsibility for developing and maintaining the database.

**21.** The financial accounting database has several critical relationships that must be properly maintained if the system is to function in an orderly manner. Which one of the following statements about the financial accounting database is false?

A. The general ledger is a master file in which a record is maintained for each and every account in the organization's accounting system.

B. Subsidiary ledgers are master files containing accounting records by specific account categories.

C. Cash disbursements journals are complete records of each transaction that reduces cash.

D. Transaction records include cross-reference between general ledger files, subsidiary account numbers, and source document numbers.

Answer (C) is correct.   *(CMA, adapted)*
**REQUIRED:** The false statement about the financial accounting database.
**DISCUSSION:** Although most cash disbursements are recorded in cash disbursements journals, such transactions can also be recorded in other journals, primarily the general journal.
Answer (A) is incorrect because the general ledger is a master file with a record for every account. Answer (B) is incorrect because subsidiary ledgers are master files containing accounting records by specific account categories. Answer (D) is incorrect because transaction records contain cross-references.

**22.** In an overall description of a database, the names of data elements, their characteristics, and their relationship to each other are defined by using a

    A. Data definition language.

    B. Data control language.

    C. Data manipulation language.

    D. Data command interpreter language.

Answer (A) is correct. *(CIA, adapted)*
    **REQUIRED:** The language used to define a database.
    **DISCUSSION:** The data definition language defines the database structure and content, especially the schema (the description of the entire database) and subschema (logical views of the database). The schema specifies characteristics such as the names of the data elements contained in the database and their relationship to each other. The subschema defines the logical data views required for applications. Thus, it limits the data elements and functions available to each application.
    Answer (B) is incorrect because the data control language specifies the privileges and security rules governing database users. Answer (C) is incorrect because data manipulation language provides application programs with a means of interacting with the database to add, retrieve, modify, or delete data or relationships. Answer (D) is incorrect because data command interpreter languages are symbolic character strings used to control the current state of database management system operations.

**23.** The increased use of database processing systems makes managing data and information a major information service function. Because the databases of an organization are used for many different applications, they are coordinated and controlled by a database administrator. The functions of a database administrator are

    A. Data input preparation, database design, and database operations.

    B. Database design, database operation, and database security.

    C. Database design, database operation, and equipment operations.

    D. Database design, software support, and database security.

Answer (B) is correct. *(CMA, adapted)*
    **REQUIRED:** The functions of a database administrator.
    **DISCUSSION:** A database administrator (DBA) is the person who has overall responsibility for developing, designing, controlling, and maintaining the database. The DBA manages all database functions including design and maintenance of the schema that describes the structure of the database. The DBA also assigns user passwords and establishes other security measures. Control of changes in data items and in the programs that use the database is another responsibility of the DBA.
    Answer (A) is incorrect because the user is responsible for input preparation. Answer (C) is incorrect because the manager of the EDP department is responsible for equipment (hardware) operations. Answer (D) is incorrect because the systems programming group is responsible for software support.

**24.** To trace data through several application programs, an auditor needs to know what programs use the data, which files contain the data, and which printed reports display the data. If data exist only in a database system, the auditor could probably find all of this information in a

    A. Data dictionary.

    B. Database schema.

    C. Data encryptor.

    D. Decision table.

Answer (A) is correct. *(CIA, adapted)*
    **REQUIRED:** The information source in a database needed to trace data through several application programs.
    **DISCUSSION:** The data dictionary is a file (possibly manual but usually computerized) in which the records relate to specified data items. It contains definitions of data items, the list of programs used to process them, and the reports in which data are found. Only certain persons or entities are permitted to retrieve data or to modify data items. Accordingly, these access limitations are also found in the data dictionary.
    Answer (B) is incorrect because the schema describes the structure of the database. Answer (C) is incorrect because an encryptor encodes data. Answer (D) is incorrect because a decision table is a type of logic diagram that presents in matrix form the decision points and related actions reflected in a computer program.

**25.** All of the following are characteristic of computer machine language except

A. Internal binary code.

B. Hexadecimal code.

C. Assembly language.

D. On/off electrical switches.

Answer (C) is correct. *(CMA, adapted)*

**REQUIRED:** The item not characteristic of machine language.

**DISCUSSION:** An assembly language program may be written in one of several languages that use mnemonic codes, not the binary code in which a machine language program is written. In the hierarchy of programming languages, assembly language is one level higher than machine language. Machine language is a programming language made up of instructions that a computer can directly recognize and execute.

Answer (A) is incorrect because machine language is internally stored in binary form (the only characters used in binary notation are 0 and 1). Answer (B) is incorrect because machine language uses binary code for internal purposes but printing out (dumping) the contents of storage can be done more efficiently if the printout is expressed in a number system with a base of 8 (actual) or 6 (hexadecimal). Answer (D) is incorrect because on/off electrical switches correspond to the binary digits 0 and 1 in which machine language is written.

**26.** A software tool infrequently used to select or access items in the database is most likely a(n)

A. Report generator.

B. Program generator.

C. Application generator.

D. Query utility program.

Answer (D) is correct. *(CMA, adapted)*

**REQUIRED:** The software tool infrequently used to select or access items in a database.

**DISCUSSION:** Utility programs are service programs that perform certain standard tasks, such as sorting, merging, copying, and printing file dumps. A query utility program could be used to access items in a database. However, such programs would not be used in normal operational circumstances. A query language permits interactive searching of a database. Data may be read and reorganized but not altered.

Answer (A) is incorrect because a report generator is frequently used. It generates reports based on special requirements by users, often in conjunction with query language. Answer (B) is incorrect because program generators allow the user to create application programs based on requirements entered in a specific format. They differ from query languages because they permit data to be written or altered. Answer (C) is incorrect because an application generator is frequently used.

## 6.3 Decision Support Systems

**27.** Which group of characteristics best describes decision support systems?

A. Analytical models, specialized databases, and interactive computer-based modeling processes.

B. Analytical models, specialized databases, interactive computer-based modeling processes, and the decision maker's own insights and judgments.

C. Analytical models, programming models, application models, and interactive computer-based modeling processes.

D. Expert systems, model-based information, electronic data interchange, and the decision maker's own insights and judgments.

Answer (B) is correct. *(CMA, adapted)*

**REQUIRED:** The characteristics that best describe decision support systems.

**DISCUSSION:** Decision support systems (DSS) were devised to overcome the "shotgun" approach of the MIS. They are useful for semistructured problems such as those requiring the decision maker to exercise judgment in controlling the process but allowing for certain aspects of the problem to be preprogrammed. A DSS does not automate a decision but rather provides tools for the user to employ in applying his or her own insight and judgment. The system should be interactive to permit the user to explore the problem by using the computational capacities, models, and data resources of the DSS.

Answer (A) is incorrect because the decision-maker's insight and judgment are important aspects of a DSS. Answer (C) is incorrect because a DSS does not include programming models. Answer (D) is incorrect because a DSS is not an expert system. An expert system actually makes the decision, whereas a DSS merely aids the decision maker.

**28.** Which of the following is the best example of the use of a decision support system (DSS)?

A. A manager uses a personal-computer-based simulation model to determine whether one of the company's ships would be able to satisfy a particular delivery schedule.

B. An auditor uses a generalized audit software package to retrieve several purchase orders for detailed vouching.

C. A manager uses the query language feature of a database management system (DBMS) to compile a report showing customers whose average purchase exceeds $2,500.

D. An auditor uses a personal-computer-based word processing software package to modify an internal control questionnaire for a specific audit engagement.

Answer (A) is correct. *(CIA, adapted)*

**REQUIRED:** The best example of the use of a decision support system.

**DISCUSSION:** A decision support system (DSS) assists middle- and upper-level managers in long-term, nonroutine, and often unstructured decision making. The system contains at least one decision model, is usually interactive, dedicated, and time-shared, but need not be real-time. It is an aid to decision making, not the automation of a decision process. The personal-computer-based simulation model is used to provide interactive problem solving (i.e., scheduling) assistance, the distinguishing feature of a DSS.

Answer (B) is incorrect because the generalized audit software package does not provide interactive problem solving assistance in retrieving the purchase orders, and thus is not a DSS. Answer (C) is incorrect because the query feature of a DBMS does not provide interactive problem solving assistance in compiling the report, and thus is not a DSS. Answer (D) is incorrect because the word processing software package does not provide interactive problem solving assistance to the auditor, and thus is not a DSS.

## 6.4 Artificial Intelligence and Expert Systems

**29.** Expert systems consist of

A. Software packages with the ability to make judgment decisions.

B. A panel of outside consultants.

C. Hardware designed to make judgment decisions.

D. Hardware and software used to automate routine tasks.

Answer (A) is correct. *(CIA, adapted)*

**REQUIRED:** The definition of expert systems.

**DISCUSSION:** Artificial intelligence and its subfield, expert systems, have been identified by the AICPA Future Issues Committee as one of the major issues the accounting profession will face in the future. Expert systems attempt to permit a computer to think and make decisions in a human way. An expert system is an interactive system that asks a series of questions and uses knowledge gained from a human expert to analyze answers and come to a decision, that is, to exercise judgment. They were originally developed to make decisions in areas that did not have enough human experts to make decisions. Some of the earliest expert systems were used by doctors to diagnose diseases.

Answer (B) is incorrect because expert systems do not require outside consultants. Answer (C) is incorrect because hardware does not make judgment decisions. Answer (D) is incorrect because automation of routine tasks is not the purpose of expert systems.

**30.** Which one of the following incorporates making the best decisions possible, using a logical approach to solving problems, using reasoning, having the capability to learn, and allowing subjective inputs and outputs?

A. Expert systems.

B. Decision support systems.

C. Multi-networking.

D. Neural networks.

Answer (A) is correct. *(CMA, adapted)*

**REQUIRED:** The item based on a logical approach to making the best decisions possible by using reasoning, learning, and allowing subjective inputs and outputs.

**DISCUSSION:** An expert system is software designed to perceive, reason, and understand. An expert system is an interactive system that asks a series of questions and uses knowledge gained from a human expert to analyze answers and come to a decision. The system is developed by using a continuous process of revision. As new knowledge or decision-making strategies become available, prior systems must be revised.

Answer (B) is incorrect because decision support systems are extensions of the MIS concept that are primarily useful for semistructured problems, such as those requiring the decision maker to exercise judgment in controlling the process but allowing for certain aspects of the problem to be preprogrammed. A decision support system does not automate a decision but rather provides tools for the user to employ in applying his/her own insight and judgment. Answer (C) is incorrect because multi-networking involves using multiple networks with the same computer. Answer (D) is incorrect because neural networks, although similar to expert systems, can learn from making mistakes.

**31.** Prudent managers will recognize the limits within which expert systems can be effectively applied. An expert system would be most appropriate to

A. Compensate for the lack of certain technical knowledge within the organization.

B. Help make customer-service jobs easier to perform.

C. Automate daily managerial problem-solving.

D. Emulate human expertise for strategic planning.

Answer (B) is correct.   *(CIA, adapted)*
**REQUIRED:** The appropriate use for an expert system.
**DISCUSSION:** Expert systems allow even small companies to perform activities and provide services previously only available from larger firms. The use of expert systems has helped to improve the quality of customer service in applications such as maintenance and scheduling by automating them and making them easy to perform.
Answer (A) is incorrect because expert systems codify and apply existing knowledge, but they do not create knowledge that is lacking. Answer (C) is incorrect because expert systems do best in automating lower-level clerical functions. Answer (D) is incorrect because expert systems concern problems with relatively few possible outcomes that are all known in advance.

**32.** The processing in knowledge-based systems is characterized by

A. Algorithms.

B. Deterministic procedures.

C. Heuristics.

D. Simulations.

Answer (C) is correct.   *(CIA, adapted)*
**REQUIRED:** The characteristic of processing in knowledge-based systems.
**DISCUSSION:** Knowledge-based (expert) systems contain a knowledge base for a limited domain of human expertise and inference procedures for the solution of problems. They use symbolic processing based on heuristics rather than algorithms. A heuristic procedure is an exploratory problem-solving technique that uses self-education, e.g., the evaluation of feedback, to improve performance. These systems are interactive and provide explanations of their problem-solving behavior.
Answer (A) is incorrect because algorithms are defined procedures used in typical computer programs. Answer (B) is incorrect because deterministic procedures permit no uncertainty in outcomes. Answer (D) is incorrect because simulations are computer programs that permit experimentation with logical and mathematical models.

**33.** A bank implemented an expert system to help account representatives consolidate the bank's relationships with each customer. The expert system has

A. A sequential control structure.

B. Distinct input/output variables.

C. A knowledge base.

D. Passive data elements.

Answer (C) is correct.   *(CIA, adapted)*
**REQUIRED:** The component of an expert system.
**DISCUSSION:** An expert system relies on a computer's ability to make decisions in a human way. There are six components to the expert system: knowledge base, domain database, database management system, inference engine, user interface, and knowledge acquisition facility. The knowledge base contains the rules used when making decisions.
Answer (A) is incorrect because traditional programs, e.g., in COBOL, have sequential control structures; expert systems do not. Answer (B) is incorrect because traditional programs, not expert systems, have distinct input/output variables. Answer (D) is incorrect because traditional programs, not expert systems, have passive data elements.

**34.** For which of the following applications would the use of a fuzzy logic system be the most appropriate artificial intelligence (AI) choice?

A. Assigning airport gates to arriving airline flights.

B. Forecasting demand for spare auto parts.

C. Ventilating expressway tunnels.

D. Diagnosing computer hardware problems.

Answer (C) is correct.   *(CIA, adapted)*
**REQUIRED:** The most appropriate use for fuzzy logic.
**DISCUSSION:** Fuzzy logic is a superset of conventional (Boolean) logic that has been extended to handle the concept of partial truth. Because they use nonspecific terms (membership functions) characterized by well-defined imprecision, fuzzy logic systems can create rules to address problems with many solutions. Fuzzy logic can be used when values are approximate or subject and data are incomplete or ambiguous. These systems have been applied successfully to applications such as ventilating expressway tunnels, backing a tractor-trailer into a parking space, reducing power usage in an air conditioner, selecting companies for business combinations, or detecting fraud in medical insurance claims.
Answer (A) is incorrect because assigning airport gates to arriving airline flights requires an expert system that uses precise data for quick and consistent decisions. Answer (B) is incorrect because neural networks provide the technology to undertake sophisticated forecasting and analysis. They emulate the processing patterns of the brain and therefore can learn from experience. Answer (D) is incorrect because diagnosing problems with computer hardware requires an expert system.

## 6.5 Spreadsheets

Questions 35 through 38 are based on the following information. This information illustrates the use of a spreadsheet for accounting purposes. The Promo Company is preparing a strategic plan for the next 2 years. Promo has assumed that sales will increase by 10% annually. Management further assumes that, if an additional $10,000 advertising program is undertaken in 20X3, sales could increase by an additional 10% in 20X3. Direct materials, direct labor, and variable manufacturing overhead costs increase at the same rate as sales. Variable selling expenses are expected to increase 10% annually, except for the additional advertising program noted above. Ron Quinn, financial analyst, prepared the following spreadsheet (thousands of dollars).

| | A | B | C | D |
|---|---|---|---|---|
| | | 20X1 | 20X2 | 20X3 |
| 1 | Net sales | $500.0 | $550.0 | $660.0 |
| 2 | Direct materials | 200.0 | 220.0 | 242.0 |
| 3 | Direct labor | 50.0 | 55.0 | 60.5 |
| 4 | Selling expenses -- variable | 30.0 | 43.0 | 46.3 |
| 5 |      -- fixed | 8.0 | 8.0 | 8.0 |
| 6 | Manufacturing overhead | | | |
| 7 |     Variable | 10.0 | 11.0 | 13.2 |
| 8 |     Fixed | 20.0 | 20.0 | 20.0 |
| 9 | Administration expenses -- fixed | 10.0 | 10.0 | 10.0 |
| 10 | Operating income | 172.0 | 183.0 | 260.0 |
| 11 | Contribution margin | | | |

Promo's management is surprised that the forecasted operating income increases by only 6.4% in 20X2 but by 42.1% in 20X3.

**35.** To better understand the forecasted data, Promo Company's management has requested that Ron Quinn add contribution margin onto a new line (row 11). The formula for the cell B11 should be

A. +B1 – SUM (B2:B9).

B. +B1 – B2 – B3.

C. +B1 – SUM (B2:B5).

D. +B1 – B2 – B3 – B4 – B7.

Answer (D) is correct. *(CMA, adapted)*
REQUIRED: The formula for cell B11.
DISCUSSION: The contribution margin equals operating revenues minus all variable operating expenses. Consequently, it equals net sales minus direct materials, direct labor, variable selling expenses, and variable manufacturing overhead (+B1 – B2 – B3 – B4 – B7).
Answer (A) is incorrect because fixed expenses are disregarded when calculating the contribution margin.
Answer (B) is incorrect because all variable operating expenses should be subtracted. Answer (C) is incorrect because variable manufacturing overhead but not fixed selling expenses should be subtracted.

**36.** Promo Company's management has requested that Ron Quinn review the 20X2 data and explain why only a 6.4% increase in operating income is forecasted. Quinn has determined that an error exists in cell

A. C1.

B. C2.

C. C3.

D. C4.

Answer (D) is correct. *(CMA, adapted)*
REQUIRED: The error in a cell for 20X2.
DISCUSSION: Variable selling expenses for 20X2 should be 110% of those for 20X1, or $33 (1.1 × $30). The additional $10,000 advertising program does not occur until 20X3.
Answer (A) is incorrect because 110% of $500 equals $550. Answer (B) is incorrect because 110% of $200 equals $220. Answer (C) is incorrect because 110% of $50 equals $55.

**37.** In reviewing the 20X3 data, Ron Quinn has found formula errors in which of the following cells?

A. D1 and D2.

B. D1 and D3.

C. D2 and D7.

D. D2 and D3.

Answer (D) is correct. *(CMA, adapted)*
REQUIRED: The formula errors for 20X3.
DISCUSSION: Management assumes that, if an additional $10,000 advertising program is undertaken in 20X3, sales would increase an additional 10% (to 20%) in 20X3. Direct materials, direct labor, and variable manufacturing overhead increase at the same rate as sales. Accordingly, cell D2 (direct materials) should be $264 (1.2 × $220 for 20X2), and cell D3 (direct labor) should be $66 (1.2 × $55 for 20X2).
Answer (A) is incorrect because cell D1 (net sales) equals $660 (1.2 × $550 for 20X2). Answer (B) is incorrect because cell D1 (net sales) equals $660 (1.2 × $550 for 20X2). Answer (C) is incorrect because cell D7 (variable manufacturing overhead) equals $13.2 (1.2 × $11.0 for 20X2).

**38.** Assume that Ron Quinn wants to adjust fixed manufacturing overhead to include 5% annual inflation. The new formula for cell C8 should be

    A. +B8 + 5.

    B. +B8 × 1.05.

    C. +B8 × 5.

    D. +B8 + 0.05.

Answer (B) is correct. *(CMA, adapted)*
    **REQUIRED:** The new formula for cell C8.
    **DISCUSSION:** Fixed manufacturing overhead is presumed to change only with inflation, that is, with the value of the unit of measure. Hence, C8 should equal $21 ($20 for 20X1 × 1.05 inflation rate).
    Answer (A) is incorrect because +B8 + 5 equals only $20,005. Answer (C) is incorrect because +B8 × 5 equals $100,000, a 400% increase. Answer (D) is incorrect because +B8 + 0.05 equals only $20,000.05.

## 6.6 Internet and Intranet

**39.** The linked networks throughout the world that facilitate information transfer among computers and form the basis of the Internet are sometimes called

    A. Internet backbone.

    B. Intranet.

    C. Virtual private network.

    D. Client-server model.

Answer (A) is correct. *(Publisher)*
    **REQUIRED:** The name for the linked networks that serve as the foundation of the Internet.
    **DISCUSSION:** The Internet backbone is the name given to the interconnected networks that form the basis of the Internet. At one time, the networks may have looked like the backbone of a fish, but now with the many interconnected relationships among networks throughout the world, the model looks more like a fishnet than a backbone.
    Answer (B) is incorrect because an intranet permits a company to share information through a LAN that applies Internet connectivity standards and web software. Answer (C) is incorrect because a virtual private network is a means of providing a secure connection through an otherwise insecure Internet. Answer (D) is incorrect because a client-server model divides the processing of an application between a client machine on a network and a server.

**40.** Which of the following is a means of searching for information on the Internet?

    A. Browser software.

    B. Routers.

    C. Virtual private network.

    D. Wide area network.

Answer (A) is correct. *(Publisher)*
    **REQUIRED:** The means of searching for information on the Internet.
    **DISCUSSION:** Browser software is a program that accesses information on the Internet. Examples of browsers include Netscape and Internet Explorer.
    Answer (B) is incorrect because a router is used to route data packets from one LAN or WAN to another. Answer (C) is incorrect because a virtual private network is a means of providing a secure connection through an otherwise insecure Internet. Answer (D) is incorrect because a WAN provides data communication and file sharing among remote offices. It is an enterprise-wide communications network that allows signals to be transmitted from a LAN via a public or private line to other LANs in distant locations.

---

Use Gleim's *CMA Test Prep* for interactive testing with **over 2,000 additional multiple-choice questions!**

# STUDY UNIT SEVEN
# ELECTRONIC COMMERCE AND OTHER TOPICS

(11 pages of outline)

This study unit is the **last of three** on **information management**. The relative weight assigned to this major topic in Part 2 of the exam is **15%** at **skill level A** (two skill types required). The three study units are

Study Unit 5: Overview of Information Systems and Systems Development and Design
Study Unit 6: Technology of Information Systems
Study Unit 7: Electronic Commerce and Other Topics

After studying the outlines and answering the multiple-choice questions in this study unit, you will have the skills necessary to address the following topics listed in the IMA's Learning Outcome Statements:

<u>Part 2 – Section C.4. Electronic commerce</u>

The candidate should be able to:

a. define and identify major characteristics of electronic data interchange (EDI)
b. explain how EDI differs from Internet-based electronic commerce applications
c. define business-to-business (B2B) commerce and its characteristics
d. summarize the importance of the Internet for B2B commerce
e. demonstrate an understanding of how B2B electronic commerce has affected the industrial supply chain
f. demonstrate an understanding of other e-commerce technologies, including online transaction processing (OLTP) and electronic funds transfer (EFT)

<u>Part 2 – Section C.5. Integrated enterprise-wide data model</u>

The candidate should be able to:

a. define enterprise-wide planning (ERP) and its characteristics
b. recognize that ERP is reliant on an enterprise-wide database
c. describe an enterprise-wide database (data warehouse)
d. demonstrate an understanding of how data warehousing facilitates data mining
e. define data marts
f. define online analytical processing

## 7.1 ELECTRONIC DATA INTERCHANGE

1. **E-business** is an umbrella term referring to all methods of conducting business electronically. This can include strictly internal communications as well as nonfinancial dealings with outside parties (e.g., contract negotiations).

   a. **E-commerce** is a narrower term referring to financial transactions with outside parties, e.g., the purchase and sale of goods and services.

      1) E-commerce comes in two basic varieties, **business-to-business (B2B)** (see subunit 7.2) and **business-to-consumer (B2C).**

      2) E-business and e-commerce are sometimes considered to be synonymous.

2. Because e-commerce transactions cross the boundaries of the enterprise, security is of primary concern.

   a. **Security issues** include

      1) The correct identification of the transacting parties **(authentication)**
      2) Determination of who may rightfully make binding agreements **(authorization)**
      3) Protecting the **confidentiality and integrity** of information
      4) Assuring the trustworthiness of listed **prices and discounts**
      5) Providing **evidence** of the transmission and receipt of documents
      6) Guarding against **repudiation** by the sender or recipient
      7) The proper extent of **verification** of payment data
      8) The best **method of payment** to avoid wrongdoing or disagreements
      9) **Lost or duplicated** transactions
      10) Determining who bears the **risk of fraud**

   b. **Responses to security issues** include

      1) **Encryption** and associated authentication methods, preferably by physically secure hardware rather than software
      2) Numerical **sequencing** to identify missing or false messages
      3) The capacity of the host computer to **avoid downtime and repel attacks**
      4) **Nonrepudiation** methods, such as **digital certificates**, which prove origination and delivery so that parties cannot disclaim responsibility for sending or receiving a message

         a) Sellers and buyers routinely provide acknowledgements and confirmations, respectively, in a website dialogue to avoid later disputes.

         b) In EDI (see item 3. below), control over nonrepudiation is achieved by sequencing, encryption, and authentication.

      5) Adherence to **legal requirements**, such as privacy statutes
      6) Documenting **trading agreements**, especially the terms of trade and methods of authorization and authentication
      7) Agreements for **end-to-end security** and availability with providers of information services and value-added networks (see item 5.b. on the next page)
      8) **Disclosure** by public trading systems of their terms of business

3. **Electronic data interchange (EDI)** is the leading method of carrying on e-commerce.

   a. EDI involves the communication of data in format agreed to by the parties directly from a computer in one entity to a computer in another entity, for example, to order goods from a supplier or to transfer funds.

   b. EDI was the first step in the evolution of e-business.

      1) Successful EDI implementation begins with mapping the work processes and flows that support achievement of the organization's objectives.

      2) EDI was developed to enhance just-in-time (JIT) inventory management.

  c. **Advantages** of EDI include reduction of clerical errors, speed of transactions, and the elimination of repetitive clerical tasks, such as document preparation, processing, and mailing.

  d. **Disadvantages** of EDI include the following:

   1) Information may be insecure.

    a) Thus, end-to-end data encryption should be used to protect data during EDI.

   2) Data may be lost.

   3) Transmissions to trading partners may fail.

   4) EDI is less standardized and more costly than Internet-based commerce, which ordinarily uses XML.

    a) EDI requires programming expertise and leased telephone lines or the use of a value-added or third-party network, whereas XML is simple and easy to understand.

  e. An extension of EDI is computer-stored records, which can be less expensive than traditional physical file storage.

4. **Terms and components** of EDI include the following:

  a. **Standards** concern procedures to convert written documents into a standard electronic document-messaging format to facilitate EDI.

  b. **Conventions** are the procedures for arranging data elements in specified formats for various accounting transactions, e.g., invoices, materials releases, and advance shipment notices.

  c. A **data dictionary** prescribes the meaning of data elements, including specification of each transaction structure.

  d. **Transmission protocols** are rules used to determine how each electronic envelope is structured and processed by the communications devices.

   1) Normally, a group of accounting transactions is combined in an electronic envelope and transmitted into a communications network.

   2) Rules are required for the separation and transmission of envelopes.

5. **Methods of communication** between computers include the following:

  a. A **point-to-point system** requires the use of dedicated computers by all parties.

   1) Each computer must be designed to be compatible with the other(s). This system is very similar to a network within one company. Dedicated lines or modems are used.

  b. **Value-added networks (VANs)** are private, third-party providers of common interfaces between organizations.

   1) Subscribing to a VAN eliminates the need for one organization to establish direct computer communication with a trading partner.

   2) VANs provide translation of the sender's protocol (data configuration) to the receiver's protocol. Thus, the sender and receiver do not have to conform to the same standards, conventions, and protocols.

   3) Moreover, VANs eliminate the need for dedicated computers waiting for incoming messages.

   4) In addition, VANs store messages so companies can batch outgoing and incoming messages.

   c.   An **extranet** is another means of carrying on e-commerce.

      1)   Extranets rely on the established communications protocols of the Internet. Thus, the expensive, specialized equipment needed for EDI is unnecessary.

      2)   **Firewalls**, special combinations of hardware and software (see item 2.d. under subunit 7.2), provide security.

      3)   The extranet approach is based on less formal agreements between the trading partners than in EDI and requires the sending firm to format the documents into the format of the receiving firm.

6.   The use of EDI has certain **implications for control**.

   a.   EDI eliminates the paper documents, both internal and external, that are the traditional basis for many controls, including internal and external auditing.

   b.   Moreover, an organization that has reengineered its processes to take full advantage of EDI may have eliminated even the electronic equivalents of paper documents.

      1)   For example, the buyer's **point-of-sale (POS)** system may directly transmit information to the seller, which delivers on a JIT basis. Purchase orders, invoices, and receiving reports are eliminated and replaced with

         a)   Evaluated receipts settlements (authorizations for automatic periodic payment);

         b)   A long-term contract establishing quantities, prices, and delivery schedules;

         c)   Production schedules;

         d)   Advance ship notices; and

         e)   Payments by EFT.

   c.   Accordingly, auditors must seek new forms of evidence to support assertions about EDI transactions, whether it exists at the client organization, the trading partner, or a third party, such as a VAN.

      1)   Examples of such evidence are

         a)   The authorized paper purchase contract,

         b)   An electronic completed production schedule image, and

         c)   Internal and external evidence of evaluated receipts settlements sent to the trading partner.

      2)   Auditors must evaluate digital signatures and reviews when testing controls.

      3)   Auditors may need to consider other subsystems when testing a particular subsystem. Thus, production cycle evidence may be needed to test the expenditure cycle.

7.   Stop and review! You have completed the outline for this subunit. Study multiple-choice questions 1 through 9 beginning on page 264.

## 7.2 BUSINESS-TO-BUSINESS

1. **Business-to-business commerce (B2B)** is not limited to EDI and other direct links between businesses but also involves activities within the broader electronic market.

   a. B2B involves working with vendors, distributors, and other businesses over the Internet.

   b. There are two types of B2B companies:

      1) **Vertical companies** work at all levels within an industry and mostly earn their revenues from advertising on a specialized sector or from transaction fees from the e-commerce they may host.

         a) Websites of vertical companies are the most likely to contain such community features as industry news, articles, and discussion groups.

      2) **Horizontal companies** operate across numerous industries.

         a) They provide products, goods, materials, or services that are not specific to a particular industry or company.

   c. **Benefits of B2B** include

      1) Reduced purchasing costs. Purchasing products online saves time, and electronically processing an order simplifies the ordering process.

      2) Increased market efficiency. By using the Internet, companies have easy access to price quotes from various suppliers. Buyers are more likely to get a better price, given the increased number of suppliers.

      3) Greater market intelligence. B2B provides producers with better insights into the demand levels in any given market.

      4) Decreased inventory levels. Companies can make better use of their inventory and raw materials. The Internet allows companies using JIT manufacturing techniques to achieve better control of their operations, for example, by more precise coordination of delivery of raw materials. It also allows companies to use less working capital to do the same amount of work, which allows those funds to be invested elsewhere.

   d. The overriding principle of online B2B is that it can make companies more efficient. Increased efficiency means lower costs, which is a goal that interests every company. Thus, the potential of B2B online commerce is enormous.

2. The most important control is to install an organization-wide **network security policy**. This is particularly true when an organization engages in electronic commerce.

   a. The policy should seek to ensure the following:

      1) **Availability** is the ability of the intended and authorized users to access computer resources to meet organizational goals.

      2) **Confidentiality** is assurance of the secrecy of information that could adversely affect the organization if revealed to the public or competitors.

      3) **Integrity** is maintained by preventing the unauthorized or accidental modification of programs or data.

   b. The network security plan should, at the very least, include a user account management system, installation of an Internet firewall, and methods, such as encryption, to ensure that only the intended user receives the information and that the information is complete and accurate.

    c.   **User account management** involves installing a system to ensure that

        1)   New accounts are added correctly and assigned only to authorized users.

        2)   Old and unused accounts are removed promptly.

        3)   Passwords are changed periodically, and employees are educated on how to choose a password that cannot be easily guessed (e.g., a password of at least six characters including both letters and numerals).

    d.   A **firewall** is a combination of hardware and software that separates an internal network from an external network (e.g., the Internet) and prevents passage of specific types of traffic.

        1)   A firewall identifies names, Internet protocol (IP) addresses, applications, etc., and compares them with programmed access rules.

        2)   A firewall may have any of the following features:

            a)   A **packet-filtering system** examines each incoming IP packet.

            b)   A **proxy server** maintains copies of web pages to be accessed by specified users. Outsiders are directed there, and more important information is not available from this access point.

            c)   An **application gateway** limits traffic to specific applications.

            d)   A **circuit-level gateway** is a filter that connects an internal device, e.g., a network printer, with an outside TCP/IP port. It can identify a valid TCP session.

            e)   **Stateful inspection** stores information about the state of a transmission and uses it as background for evaluating messages from similar sources.

        3)   Firewall systems ordinarily produce **reports** on organization-wide Internet use, exception reports for unusual usage patterns, and system penetration-attempt reports. These reports are very helpful as a method of continuous monitoring, or logging, of the system.

            a)   Firewalls do not provide adequate protection against **computer viruses**. Thus, an organization should include one or more virus controls in its network security policy.

  3.   Stop and review! You have completed the outline for this subunit. Study multiple-choice questions 10 through 15 beginning on page 267.

## 7.3 OTHER E-COMMERCE TECHNOLOGIES

  1.   **Online transaction processing (OLTP)** is an ambiguous term that is used in two senses.

    a.   OLTP can refer to almost any electronic means by which businesses deal with consumers.

        1)   Home banking, automated teller machines (ATMs), and the purchase of airline tickets over the Internet are examples of online transaction processing.

    b.   OLTP can also refer to a computer-based transaction processing system (TPS) (see item 4. under subunit 5.1).

    c.   Whichever sense of the phrase is meant, the key to any OLTP system is **instantaneous update** of the database.

        1)   A **powerful DBMS** (see subunit 6.2) is needed to negotiate between many users who are simultaneously accessing the system and possibly even trying to update the same data elements.

        2)   **Reliable, high-speed communications links** are also vital. The system must be able to adapt to many levels of transaction volume.

2. **Electronic funds transfer (EFT)** is the movement of cash from one bank to another by purely electronic means.

   a. EFT transaction costs are lower than for manual systems because documents and human intervention are eliminated from the transactions process.

      1) EFT is thus a crucial part of making B2B so beneficial to the trading partners; invoices can be paid without any paperwork.

   b. A typical application of EFT is the direct deposit of payroll checks in employees' accounts or the automatic withdrawal of payments for cable and telephone bills, mortgages, etc.

      1) Extremely large amounts of money are moved each day through EFT.

3. Stop and review! You have completed the outline for this subunit. Study multiple-choice questions 16 and 17 beginning on page 268.

## 7.4 ENTERPRISE RESOURCE PLANNING SYSTEMS

1. **Enterprise resource planning (ERP)** is the latest phase in the development of computerized systems for managing organizational resources.

   a. ERP is intended to integrate enterprise-wide information systems by creating **one database** linked to all of an organization's applications.

   b. ERP connects all functional subsystems (human resources, the financial accounting system, production, marketing, distribution, purchasing, receiving, order processing, shipping, etc.) and also connects the organization with its suppliers and customers.

      1) Thus, ERP facilitates demand analysis and materials requirements planning.

      2) By decreasing lead times, it improves just-in-time inventory management.

      3) Even more importantly, ERP's coordination of all operating activities permits flexible responses to shifts in supply and demand.

   c. Because ERP software is costly and complex, it is usually installed only by the largest enterprises, but mid-size organizations are increasingly likely to buy ERP software.

      1) Major ERP packages include R/3 from SAP AG and Oracle e-Business Suite, PeopleSoft, and JD Edwards EnterpriseOne, all from Oracle Corp.

   d. The disadvantages of ERP are its **extent and complexity**, which make implementation difficult and costly.

   e. The benefits of ERP may significantly derive from the required **business process reengineering**.

      1) Using ERP software that reflects the **best practices** forces the linked subunits in the organization not only to redesign and improve their processes but also to conform to one standard.

      2) An organization may wish to undertake a reengineering project before choosing ERP software.

         a) The project should indicate what best practices already exist in the organization's processes. This approach may be preferable for a unique enterprise in a highly differentiated industry.

      3) The processes reflected in the ERP software may differ from the organization's.

         a) In this case, the better policy is usually to change the organization's processes.

         b) Customizing ERP software is expensive and difficult, and it may result in bugs and awkwardness in adopting upgrades.

f. In the **traditional ERP system**, subsystems share data and coordinate their activities.

    1) Thus, if marketing receives an order, it can quickly verify that inventory is sufficient to notify shipping to process the order.

    2) Otherwise, production is notified to manufacture more of the product, with a consequent automatic adjustment of output schedules.

    3) If materials are inadequate for this purpose, the system will issue a purchase order.

    4) If more labor is needed, human resources will be instructed to reassign or hire employees.

    5) The foregoing business processes (and others) should interact seamlessly in an ERP system. Moreover, the current generation of ERP software also provides the capability for smooth (and instant) interaction with the business processes of external parties.

g. The subsystems in a traditional ERP system are internal to the organization. Hence, they are often called **back-office** functions.

    1) The information produced is principally (but not exclusively) intended for internal use by the organization's managers.

2. The current generation of ERP software (**ERP II**) has added **front-office** functions.

    a. These connect the organization with customers, suppliers, owners, creditors, and strategic allies (e.g., the members of a trading community or other business association).

    b. Accordingly, an ERP II system has the following interfaces with its back-office functions:

        1) **Supply-chain management** applications for an organization focus on relationships extending from its suppliers to its final customers. Issues addressed include distribution channels, warehousing and other logistical matters, routing of shipments, and sales forecasting.

            a) In turn, one organization's supply chain is part of a **linked chain** of multiple organizations. This chain connects the producers of raw materials, processors of those materials, entities that make intermediate goods, assemblers of final products, wholesalers, retailers, and ultimate consumers.

            b) Supply chain management involves a **two-way exchange of information**. For example, a customer may be able to track the progress of its order, and the supplier may be able to monitor the customer's inventory. Thus, the customer has better information about order availability, and the supplier knows when the customer's inventory needs replenishment.

            c) An **advanced planning and scheduling system** may be an element of a supply chain management application for a manufacturer. It controls the flow of material and components within the chain. Schedules are created given projected costs, lead times, and inventories.

        2) **Customer relationship management (CRM)** applications extend to customer service, finance-related matters, sales, and database creation and maintenance.

            a) Integration of data is helpful in better understanding customer needs, such as product preference or location of retail outlets. Thus, the organization may be able to optimize its sales forecasts, product line, and inventory levels.

            b) **Business intelligence (BI)** involves examining data from both within and without the organization in order to draw conclusions about the enterprise's environment.

       c)    **Partner relationship management** applications connect the organization not only with such partners as customers and suppliers but also with owners, creditors, and strategic allies (for example, other members of a joint venture).

       d)    **Collaborative business partnerships** may arise between competitors or different types of organizations, such as a manufacturer partnering with an environmental group.

          i)    Special software may be helpful to the partners in sharing information, developing a common strategy, and measuring performance.

3.    The following are the main elements of the **architecture** of an ERP system:

    a.    Current ERP systems have a **client-server configuration** with scores, hundreds, or even thousands of client (user) computers.

       1)    So-called **thin clients** (see item 5.e. in subunit 6.1) have little processing ability, but **fat clients** may have substantial processing power.

       2)    The system may have multiple servers to run applications and contain databases.

       3)    The network architecture may be in the form of a **local area network** or **wide-area network** (see item 5. in subunit 6.1), or users may connect with the server(s) via the **Internet**.

       4)    An ERP system may use almost any of the available **operating systems** and **database management systems**.

    b.    An advantage of an ERP system is the elimination of data redundancy through the use of a central, enterprise-wide database.

       1)    When an organization has separate systems for its different functions (called **stovepipe systems**), a data element, such as price, has to be updated wherever it is stored.

          a)    Failure of even one function to update a data element causes a loss of **data integrity**. Considerable inefficiency arises when different organizational subunits (IT, production, marketing, accounting, etc.) have different data about prices and inventory availability.

       2)    Under an ERP system, every data element is, in principle, stored once (also called normalization; see item 3.c.2) in subunit 6.2), and all functions have access to it.

          a)    Thus, when a data element such as price is updated in the central database, the change is effectively made for all functions. The result is data integrity.

4.    An organization may not have the resources, desire, or need for an ERP system with the greatest degree of integration (e.g., SAP R/3).

    a.    An alternative to a comprehensive system is a **best-of-breed approach**. Thus, an organization might install a traditional ERP system from one vendor and add e-commerce and other extended applications from separate niche vendors.

    b.    An organization that adopts this approach needs to use **middleware**, that is, software that permits different applications to communicate and exchange data. This type of middleware is called an **extended application interface**.

    c.    An ERP system that extends to customers, suppliers, and others uses **Internet portals**. In this case, a portal is a website through which authorized external users may gain access to the organization's ERP.

       1)    Portals provide links to related websites and services (e.g., newsletters, e-mail, and e-commerce capabilities).

5.    Stop and review!  You have completed the outline for this subunit.  Study multiple-choice questions 18 through 23 beginning on page 269.

## 7.5  DATA WAREHOUSING AND DATA MINING

1.    A **data warehouse** is a central database for transaction-level data from more than one of the organization's systems.

    a.    Data warehouses are very large and require that transaction records be converted to a standard format.

        1)    The ability of the data warehouse to report on data from more than one system makes it a very powerful tool for ad hoc queries.

        2)    The data warehouse can also be accessed using analytical and graphics tools, a technique called **online analytical processing (OLAP)**.

            a)    An important component of OLAP is **drill-down analysis**, in which the user is first presented with the data at an aggregate level and then can display successive levels of detail for a given date, region, product, etc., until finally reaching the original transactions.

        3)    A data warehouse is strictly a query-and-reporting system.  It is not used to carry on the enterprise's routine operations.

            a)    In other words, a data warehouse does not take the place of a transaction processing system (TPS) (see item 4. in subunit 5.1).

            b)    Rather, a data warehouse gets its input from the various transaction processing systems in the organization.

            c)    A data warehouse is optimized for data retrieval and reporting.  A TPS is optimized for data entry.

    b.    A **data mart** is a subset of an enterprise-wide data warehouse.

        1)    A data mart is designed primarily to address a specific function or department's needs, whereas a data warehouse is generally meant to address the needs of the entire enterprise.

    c.    A data warehouse enables **data mining**, i.e., the search for unexpected relationships between data.

        1)    The classic example of the use of data mining was the discovery by convenience stores that diapers and beer often appeared on the same sales transaction in the late evening.

        2)    Special software and a large amount of processing power are needed for effective data mining.

2.    Stop and review!  You have completed the outline for this subunit.  Study multiple-choice questions 24 through 29 beginning on page 271.

## 7.6 CORE CONCEPTS

<u>Electronic Data Interchange</u>

- **E-business** is an umbrella term referring to all methods of conducting business electronically.
- **E-commerce** is a narrower term referring to financial transactions with outside parties, e.g., the purchase and sale of goods and services.
- **Electronic data interchange** (EDI) is the leading method of carrying on e-commerce. It involves the communication of data in standardized format directly from a computer in one entity to a computer in another entity.
- EDI services are often provided by third-party communications vendors through services known as **value-added networks** (VANs).

<u>Business-to-Business</u>

- **Business-to-business** (B2B) involves communications with vendors, distributors, and other businesses over the Internet.
- **Benefits** of working with suppliers and business customers over the Internet include reduced purchasing costs and increased market efficiency.

<u>Other E-Commerce Technologies</u>

- **Electronic funds transfer** (EFT) is the movement of cash from one bank to another by purely electronic means.

<u>Enterprise Resource Planning Systems</u>

- **Enterprise resource planning** (ERP) is intended to integrate enterprise-wide information systems by creating one database linked to all of an organization's applications.

<u>Data Warehousing and Data Mining</u>

- A **data warehouse** is a central database for transaction-level data from more than one of the organization's systems.
- A **data mart** is subset of an enterprise-wide data warehouse.
- A data warehouse enables **data mining**, i.e., the search for unexpected relationships between data.

## QUESTIONS

### 7.1 Electronic Data Interchange

1. Which of the following is likely to be a benefit of electronic data interchange (EDI)?

A. Increased transmission speed of actual documents.

B. Improved business relationships with trading partners.

C. Decreased liability related to protection of proprietary business data.

D. Decreased requirements for backup and contingency planning.

Answer (B) is correct.    *(CIA, adapted)*
   **REQUIRED:** The benefit of EDI.
   **DISCUSSION:** Electronic data interchange is the electronic transfer of documents between businesses. EDI was developed to enhance just-in-time (JIT) inventory management. Advantages include speed, reduction of clerical errors, and elimination of repetitive clerical tasks and their costs. Improved business relationships result because of the mutual benefits conferred by EDI. Accordingly, some organizations require EDI.
   Answer (A) is incorrect because EDI transmits document data, not the actual document. Answer (C) is incorrect because liability for protection of a trading partner's proprietary business data is a major risk that must be addressed by the control structure. Answer (D) is incorrect because backup and contingency planning requirements are not diminished by use of EDI.

2. The emergence of electronic data interchange (EDI) as standard operating practice increases the risk of

A. Unauthorized third-party access to systems.

B. Systematic programming errors.

C. Inadequate knowledge bases.

D. Unsuccessful system use.

Answer (A) is correct.    *(CIA, adapted)*
   **REQUIRED:** The risk increased by the emergence of EDI as standard operating practice.
   **DISCUSSION:** EDI is the communication of electronic documents directly from a computer in one entity to a computer in another entity. EDI for business documents between unrelated parties has the potential to increase the risk of unauthorized third-party access to systems because more outsiders will have access to internal systems.
   Answer (B) is incorrect because systematic programming errors are the result of misspecification of requirements or lack of correspondence between specifications and programs. Answer (C) is incorrect because inadequate knowledge bases are a function of lack of care in building them. Answer (D) is incorrect because a benefit of EDI is to improve the efficiency and effectiveness of system use.

3. A control a company could use to detect forged EDI messages is to

A. Acknowledge all messages initiated externally with confirming messages.

B. Permit only authorized employees to have access to transmission facilities.

C. Delay action on orders until a second order is received for the same goods.

D. Write all incoming messages to a write-once/read-many device for archiving.

Answer (A) is correct.    *(CIA, adapted)*
   **REQUIRED:** The control to detect forged electronic data interchange messages.
   **DISCUSSION:** If the company acknowledges messages initiated externally, the alleged sender would have the opportunity to recognize that it had not sent the message and could notify the company of the potential forgery. Then corrective action can be taken by the company.
   Answer (B) is incorrect because permitting only authorized employees to have access to transmission facilities controls for unauthorized access to the facilities but would not detect forged EDI messages. Answer (C) is incorrect because delaying action on orders until a second order is received for the same goods defeats the purpose of using EDI, namely, rapid communication followed by rapid response. Answer (D) is incorrect because writing all incoming messages to a write-once/read-many device is a good practice, but it will not detect forgeries.

**4.** Before sending or receiving EDI messages, a company should

A. Execute a trading partner agreement with each of its customers and suppliers.

B. Reduce inventory levels in anticipation of receiving shipments.

C. Demand that all its suppliers implement EDI capabilities.

D. Evaluate the effectiveness of its use of EDI transmissions.

Answer (A) is correct. *(CIA, adapted)*
**REQUIRED:** The process that should be performed before sending or receiving electronic data interchange messages.
**DISCUSSION:** Before sending or receiving EDI messages, a company should execute a trading partner agreement with its customers and suppliers. All parties should understand their responsibilities, the messages each will initiate, how they will interpret messages, the means of authenticating and verifying the completeness and accuracy of messages, the moment when the contract between the parties is effective, the required level of security, etc.
Answer (B) is incorrect because the company may intend to reduce inventory levels, but that intention is unrelated to the timing of its first EDI messages. Answer (C) is incorrect because the company may want to demand or encourage all its customers and suppliers to implement EDI capabilities, but that request is independent of sending and receiving messages. Answer (D) is incorrect because it is not possible to evaluate the effectiveness of EDI transmissions until after they occur.

**5.** The best approach for minimizing the likelihood of software incompatibilities leading to unintelligible messages is for a company and its customers to

A. Acquire their software from the same software vendor.

B. Agree to synchronize their updating of EDI-related software.

C. Agree to use the same software in the same ways indefinitely.

D. Each write their own version of the EDI-related software.

Answer (B) is correct. *(CIA, adapted)*
**REQUIRED:** The best approach for minimizing the likelihood of software incompatibilities leading to unintelligible messages.
**DISCUSSION:** EDI entails the exchange of common business data converted into standard message formats. Thus, two crucial requirements are that the participants agree on transaction formats and that translation software be developed to convert messages into a form understandable by other companies. Thus, if one company changes its software, its trading partners must also do so.
Answer (A) is incorrect because the company and its customers may obtain their EDI-related software from the same vendor but still have software incompatibility problems if they do not synchronize their installation of updated versions. Answer (C) is incorrect because, as business requirements change, it may not be possible to use the same software in the same ways indefinitely. Answer (D) is incorrect because, even if the company and its customers each write their own versions, synchronization problems will arise from updates.

**6.** In a review of an EDI application using a third-party service provider, the auditor should

I. Ensure encryption keys meet ISO standards.

II. Determine whether an independent review of the service provider's operation has been conducted.

III. Verify that only public-switched data networks are used by the service provider.

IV. Verify that the service provider's contracts include necessary clauses, such as the right to audit.

A. I and II.

B. I and IV.

C. II and III.

D. II and IV.

Answer (D) is correct. *(CIA, adapted)*
**REQUIRED:** The auditor's procedures in a review of an EDI application.
**DISCUSSION:** An auditor should review trading partner agreements and contracts with third-party service providers. These documents should contain necessary clauses and appropriately limit liabilities. Moreover, legal counsel should have reviewed the agreements or contracts. An auditor should also determine whether the third-party service provider's operations and controls have been independently reviewed (for example, by public accountants).
Answer (A) is incorrect because using a third-party service provider does not require encryption. Answer (B) is incorrect because using a third-party service provider does not require encryption. Answer (C) is incorrect because use of public-switched data networks is not a requirement of EDI.

**7.** After implementing EDI with suppliers, a company discovered a dramatic increase in the prices it paid the single supplier of some special materials for its primary product line. After consulting with the supplier, the company determined that the supplier had assumed the risk of not having inventory and raised its prices accordingly since the company was the only buyer for the special materials. The best approach for managing inventory in this situation is for the company to

    A. Give the supplier more information about expected use of the materials.

    B. Demand that the supplier reduce the prices of the materials.

    C. Find another supplier to replace the one charging higher prices.

    D. Change its product line so the special materials are no longer needed.

Answer (A) is correct. *(CIA, adapted)*
    **REQUIRED:** The best approach for managing inventory when the supplier increases its price to compensate for the higher risk of not having inventory.
    **DISCUSSION:** If the company gives the supplier more information about use of the materials, the supplier may be able to plan its production more effectively. It could then reduce its inventory of the materials and its inventory costs, thus permitting it to charge a lower price.
    Answer (B) is incorrect because the company could demand that the supplier reduce the price of the materials, but the supplier could then decline to supply them. Answer (C) is incorrect because other suppliers may also charge a high price. Answer (D) is incorrect because, if the special materials are needed in the primary product line, it is unlikely that the company would discontinue that line before investigating alternatives, e.g., working with the supplier to help the supplier manage its inventory.

**8.** If the cycle time for manual purchase orders is 25 days, composed of 4 days of preparation, 3 days in the mail, 14 days in process at the supplier, and 4 days for delivery of raw materials, the shortest possible cycle time if a company fully implemented EDI with suppliers would be

    A. 21 days.

    B. 18 days.

    C. 4 days.

    D. 1 day.

Answer (C) is correct. *(CIA, adapted)*
    **REQUIRED:** The shortest possible time for the purchase order cycle when an EDI is implemented.
    **DISCUSSION:** The full implementation of an EDI system will eliminate the manufacturer's preparation time for purchase orders, the days in the mail, and processing by the supplier. The only time required will be the 4 days for physical delivery. An EDI system allows for the computer-to-computer exchange of transaction documents such as purchase orders, invoices, and shipping documents. It eliminates the printing and handling of paper by one party and the input of data by the other.
    Answer (A) is incorrect because a cycle time of 21 days does not include reductions possible by using EDI to eliminate mail time and supplier processing time. Answer (B) is incorrect because a cycle time of 18 days does not include reductions possible by using EDI to eliminate supplier processing time. Answer (D) is incorrect because the cycle time cannot be reduced below the delivery time of 4 days with implementation of EDI alone. More efficient transportation would be required.

**9.** An Internet firewall is designed to provide adequate protection against which of the following?

    A. A computer virus.

    B. Unauthenticated logins from outside users.

    C. Insider leaking of confidential information.

    D. A Trojan horse application.

Answer (B) is correct. *(Publisher)*
    **REQUIRED:** The protection provided by an Internet firewall.
    **DISCUSSION:** A firewall is a device that separates two networks and prevents passage of specific types of network traffic while maintaining a connection between the networks. Generally, an Internet firewall is designed to protect a system from unauthenticated logins from outside users, although it may provide several other features as well.
    Answer (A) is incorrect because a firewall cannot adequately protect a system against computer viruses. Answer (C) is incorrect because industrial spies need not leak information through the firewall. A telephone or floppy disk are much more common means of sharing confidential information. Answer (D) is incorrect because a firewall cannot adequately protect against a Trojan horse (a program, such as a game, that appears friendly but that actually contains applications destructive to the computer system) or any other program that can be executed in the system by an internal user.

## 7.2 Business-to-Business

**10.** Which of the following is not an advantage of business-to-business (B2B)?

    A. Reduced purchasing costs.

    B. Reduced information technology costs.

    C. Increased market efficiency.

    D. Decreased inventory levels.

**Answer (B) is correct.** *(Publisher)*
    **REQUIRED:** The factor which is not an advantage of business-to-business (B2B).
    **DISCUSSION:** Instituting a B2B system requires large initial outlays for equipment, software, and training.
    Answer (A) is incorrect because purchasing products online saves time, and electronically processing an order simplifies the ordering process. Answer (C) is incorrect because, by using the Internet, companies have easy access to price quotes from various suppliers. Buyers are more likely to get a better price, given the increased number of suppliers. Answer (D) is incorrect because companies can make better use of their inventory and raw materials if they participate in B2B.

**11.** The best description of a firewall is

    A. An item of hardware that helps an organization increase network security.

    B. A strict policy concerning password controls such as length of password and expiration period.

    C. A combination of hardware and software that separates an internal network from an external network.

    D. The set of protocols that enables electronic data interchange.

**Answer (C) is correct.** *(Publisher)*
    **REQUIRED:** The best description of a firewall.
    **DISCUSSION:** A firewall is a combination of hardware and software that separates an internal network from an external network. It identifies names, Internet protocol (IP) addresses, applications, etc., and compares them with programmed access rules.
    Answer (A) is incorrect because a firewall consists of both hardware and software. Answer (B) is incorrect because a firewall is a combination of hardware and software that separates an internal network from an external network. Answer (D) is incorrect because a firewall is a combination of hardware and software that separates an internal network from an external network.

**12.** Business-to-business (B2B) can best be described as

    A. The communication of data in a standardized format directly from a computer in one entity to a computer in another entity.

    B. Working with vendors, distributors, and other businesses over the Internet.

    C. An arrangement offered to businesses by private, third-party providers of common interfaces.

    D. An umbrella term referring to all methods of conducting business electronically.

**Answer (B) is correct.** *(Publisher)*
    **REQUIRED:** The best description of business-to-business (B2B).
    **DISCUSSION:** Business-to-business (B2B) is working with vendors, distributors, and other businesses over the Internet.
    Answer (A) is incorrect because electronic data interchange (EDI) is the communication of data in a standardized format directly from a computer in one entity to a computer in another entity. Answer (C) is incorrect because a value-added network (VAN) is a private, third-party provider of common interfaces between organizations. Answer (D) is incorrect because e-business is an umbrella term referring to all methods of conducting business electronically.

**13.** What is the most important control for a company engaged in business-to-business (B2B)?

    A. Firewall.

    B. Proxy server.

    C. Network security policy.

    D. User account management system.

**Answer (C) is correct.** *(Publisher)*
    **REQUIRED:** The understanding of network security policy and what it encompasses.
    **DISCUSSION:** A network security policy is the most important control for a company engaged in B2B. This policy should include a user account management system and a firewall.
    Answer (A) is incorrect because a firewall is a component of a network security policy. Answer (B) is incorrect because a proxy server is a component of a firewall and a firewall is a component of a network security policy. Answer (D) is incorrect because a network security policy should include a user account management system.

**14.** A network security policy should seek to ensure all of the following EXCEPT:

- A. Firewall.
- B. Availability.
- C. Integrity.
- D. Confidentiality.

**Answer (A) is correct.** *(Publisher)*
**REQUIRED:** What a network security policy should seek to ensure.
**DISCUSSION:** A network security policy is the most important control for company engaged in B2B. This policy should ensure availability, confidentiality, and integrity. Availability is the ability of the intended and authorized users to access computer resources to meet organizational goals. Confidentiality is assurance of the secrecy of information that could adversely affect the organization if revealed to the public or competitors. Integrity is maintained by preventing the unauthorized or accidental modification of programs or data.
Answer (B) is incorrect because a network policy should ensure availability. Answer (C) is incorrect because a network policy should ensure integrity. Answer (D) is incorrect because a network policy should ensure confidentiality.

**15.** A firewall may have any of the following features EXCEPT:

- A. Packet-filtering system.
- B. Denial switch.
- C. Stateful inspection.
- D. Circuit-level gateway.

**Answer (B) is correct.** *(Publisher)*
**REQUIRED:** The features of a firewall.
**DISCUSSION:** A firewall may have any of the following features:

1. A packet-filtering system examines each incoming IP packet.
2. A proxy server maintains copies of web pages to be accessed by specified users. Outsiders are directed there, and more important information is not available from this access point.
3. An application gateway limits traffic to specific applications.
4. A circuit-level gateway is a filter that connects an internal device, e.g., a network printer, with an outside TCP/IP port. It can identify a valid TCP session.
5. Stateful inspection stores information about the state of a transmission and uses it as background for evaluating messages from similar sources.

A denial switch is a fictitious term and is not a feature of a firewall.
Answer (A) is incorrect because a packet-filtering system can be a feature of a firewall. Answer (C) is incorrect because stateful inspection can be a feature of a firewall. Answer (D) is incorrect because a circuit-level gateway can be a feature of a firewall.

## 7.3 Other E-Commerce Technologies

**16.** Which of the following risks is not greater in an electronic funds transfer (EFT) environment than in a manual system using paper transactions?

- A. Unauthorized access and activity.
- B. Duplicate transaction processing.
- C. Higher cost per transaction.
- D. Inadequate backup and recovery capabilities.

**Answer (C) is correct.** *(CIA, adapted)*
**REQUIRED:** The risk not greater in an EFT environment than in a manual system using paper transactions.
**DISCUSSION:** EFT is a service provided by financial institutions worldwide that is based on EDI technology. EFT transaction costs are lower than for manual systems because documents and human intervention are eliminated from the transactions process.
Answer (A) is incorrect because unauthorized access and activity is a risk specific to EFT. Answer (B) is incorrect because inaccurate transaction processing (including duplication) is a risk specific to EFT. Answer (D) is incorrect because inadequate backup and recovery capabilities is a risk specific to EFT.

**17.** Which of the following is a risk that is higher when an electronic funds transfer (EFT) system is used?

A. Improper change control procedures.

B. Unauthorized access and activity.

C. Insufficient online edit checks.

D. Inadequate backups and disaster recovery procedures.

Answer (B) is correct. *(CIA, adapted)*
**REQUIRED:** The higher risk in an EFT system.
**DISCUSSION:** Unauthorized access to money transfer activities or data is an inherent and unique risk of EFT systems. An unauthorized person may attempt to read, alter, or delete information in data files or to enter authorized fund transfers. Hence, in the financial services industry, protection of confidential customer transactions is especially important. Moreover, unauthorized transfers subject a financial institution to a direct risk of serious loss.
Answer (A) is incorrect because improper change control procedures is a risk common to all information technology environments. This risk is not higher than the risk for other systems. Answer (C) is incorrect because insufficient online edit checks is a risk common to all information technology environments. This risk is not higher than the risk for other systems. Answer (D) is incorrect because inadequate backups and disaster recovery procedures is a risk common to all information technology environments. This risk is not higher than the risk for other systems.

## 7.4 Enterprise Resource Planning Systems

**18.** In a traditional ERP system, the receipt of a customer order may result in

I. Customer tracking of the order's progress

II. Automatic replenishment of inventory by a supplier

III. Hiring or reassigning of employees

IV. Automatic adjustment of output schedules

A. I, II, and IV only.

B. I and III only.

C. III and IV only.

D. I, II, III, and IV.

Answer (C) is correct. *(Publisher)*
**REQUIRED:** The possible effects of receipt of a customer order by a traditional ERP system.
**DISCUSSION:** The traditional ERP system is one in which subsystems share data and coordinate their activities. Thus, if marketing receives an order, it can quickly verify that inventory is sufficient to notify shipping to process the order. Otherwise, production is notified to manufacture more of the product, with a consequent automatic adjustment of output schedules. If materials are inadequate for this purpose, the system will issue a purchase order. If more labor is needed, human resources will be instructed to reassign or hire employees. However, the subsystems in a traditional ERP system are internal to the organization. Hence, they are often called back-office functions. The information produced is principally (but not exclusively) intended for internal use by the organization's managers.
The current generation of ERP software (ERP II) has added front-office functions. Consequently, ERP II but not traditional ERP is capable of customer tracking of the order's progress and automatic replenishment of inventory by a supplier.

**19.** An enterprise resource planning (ERP) system integrates the organization's computerized subsystems and may also provide links to external parties. An advantage of ERP is that

A. The reengineering needed for its implementation should improve business processes.

B. Customizing the software to suit the unique needs of the organization will facilitate upgrades.

C. It can be installed by organizations of all sizes.

D. The comprehensiveness of the system reduces resistance to change.

Answer (A) is correct. *(Publisher)*
**REQUIRED:** The advantage of ERP.
**DISCUSSION:** The benefits of ERP may significantly derive from the business process reengineering that is needed for its implementation. Using ERP software that reflects the best practices forces the linked subunits in the organization not only to redesign and improve their processes but also to conform to one standard.
Answer (B) is incorrect because the disadvantages of ERP are its extent and complexity, which make customization of the software difficult and costly. Answer (C) is incorrect because ERP software is costly and complex. It is usually installed only by the largest enterprises. Answer (D) is incorrect because implementing an ERP system is likely to encounter significant resistance because of its comprehensiveness.

**20.** What are the possible characteristics of a client-server configuration in a current ERP system?

I.   Thin clients, local area network, single server
II.  Fat clients, wide area network, multiple servers
III. Fat clients, connection via Internet, single server

    A. I, II, and III.

    B. II and III only.

    C. II only.

    D. I only.

Answer (A) is correct. *(Publisher)*
**REQUIRED:** The elements of a client-server configuration in a current ERP system.
**DISCUSSION:** Current ERP systems have a client-server configuration with, possibly, scores or hundreds of client (user) computers. Clients may be thin or fat. So-called thin clients have little processing ability, but fat clients may have substantial processing power. The system may have multiple servers to run applications and contain databases. The network architecture may be in the form of a local area network (LAN) or wide area network (WAN), or users may connect with the server(s) via the Internet. An ERP system may use almost any of the available operating systems and database management systems.
Answer (B) is incorrect because an ERP system also may have thin clients connected via a LAN. Answer (C) is incorrect because an ERP system also may have thin clients connected via a LAN or the Internet with one server. Answer (D) is incorrect because an ERP system also may have fat clients connected via a WAN or the Internet to multiple servers.

**21.** A principal advantage of an ERP system is

    A. Program-data dependence.

    B. Data redundancy.

    C. Separate data updating for different functions.

    D. Centralization of data.

Answer (D) is correct. *(Publisher)*
**REQUIRED:** The principal advantage of an ERP system.
**DISCUSSION:** An advantage of an ERP system is the elimination of data redundancy through the use of a central database. In principle, information about an item of data is stored once, and all functions have access to it. Thus, when the item (such as a price) is updated, the change is effectively made for all functions. The result is reliability (data integrity).
Answer (A) is incorrect because an ERP system uses a central database and a database management system. A fundamental characteristic of a database is that applications are independent of the physical structure of the database. Writing programs or designing applications to use the database requires only the names of desired data items, not their locations. Answer (B) is incorrect because an ERP system eliminates data redundancy. Answer (C) is incorrect because an ERP system is characterized by one-time data updating for all organizational functions.

**22.** The current generation of ERP software (ERP II) may include an advanced planning and scheduling system that

    A. Determines the location of retail outlets.

    B. Connects the organization with other members of a joint venture.

    C. Controls the flow of a manufacturer's materials and components through the supply chain.

    D. Permits tracking of orders by customers.

Answer (C) is correct. *(Publisher)*
**REQUIRED:** The function of an advanced planning and scheduling system.
**DISCUSSION:** An advanced planning and scheduling system may be an element of a supply chain management application for a manufacturer. It controls the flow of materials and components within the chain. Schedules are created given projected costs, lead times, and inventories.
Answer (A) is incorrect because customer relationship management applications in ERP II extend to customer service, finance-related matters, sales, and database creation and maintenance. Integrated data are helpful in better understanding customer needs, such as product preference or location of retail outlets. Answer (B) is incorrect because partner relationship management applications connect the organization not only with such partners as customers and suppliers but also with owners, creditors, and strategic allies (for example, other members of a joint venture). Answer (D) is incorrect because an advanced planning scheduling system is used by a manufacturer to control flows through the supply chain. Other software permits customers to obtain information about order availability.

**23.** The current generation of ERP software (ERP II) has added such front-office functions as

A. Inventory control.

B. Human resources.

C. Purchasing.

D. Customer service.

Answer (D) is correct. *(Publisher)*
**REQUIRED:** The front-office function addressed by ERP II.
**DISCUSSION:** The current generation of ERP software (ERP II) has added front-office functions. Customer relationship management applications in ERP II extend to customer service, finance-related matters, sales, and database creation and maintenance. Integrated data are helpful in better understanding customer needs, such as product preference or location of retail outlets. Thus, the organization may be able to optimize its sales forecasts, product line, and inventory levels.
Answer (A) is incorrect because inventory control is a back-office function. Answer (B) is incorrect because human resources is a back-office function. Answer (C) is incorrect because purchasing is a back-office function.

## 7.5 Data Warehousing and Data Mining

**24.** A data warehouse is

A. An integral feature of an enterprise resource planning system.

B. A tool for managers to get the information they need for analysis, planning, control, and decision making.

C. A comprehensive system to satisfy the reporting needs of all users in the organization.

D. A central database for transaction-level data from more than one of an organization's systems.

Answer (D) is correct. *(Publisher)*
**REQUIRED:** The best description of a data warehouse.
**DISCUSSION:** A data warehouse is a central database for transaction-level data from more than one of an organization's systems.
Answer (A) is incorrect because a data warehouse is not a component of an enterprise resource planning (ERP) system. Answer (B) is incorrect because a tool for managers to get the information they need for analysis, planning, control, and decision making is a management information system (MIS). Answer (C) is incorrect because no single system can satisfy the reporting needs of all users in a large, complex, modern organization.

**25.** Data mining is

A. The search for unexpected relationships between data.

B. The creation of a subset of the organization's data warehouse.

C. The process of putting data into standardized formats for transmission between organizations.

D. Replacing an organization's current transaction processing system with a streamlined system.

Answer (A) is correct. *(Publisher)*
**REQUIRED:** The definition of data mining.
**DISCUSSION:** Data mining is the search for unexpected relationships between data.
Answer (B) is incorrect because a subset of the organization's data warehouse is a data mart. Answer (C) is incorrect because putting data in a standardized format for transmission between organizations is a necessary part of electronic data interchange (EDI). Answer (D) is incorrect because it is a nonsense answer.

**26.** Smith Company has three computer systems named MacArthur, Patton, and Eisenhower, which are the computers for the sales, R&D, and IT departments, respectively. Which computer system is the data warehouse:

A. MacArthur.

B. Patton.

C. Eisenhower.

D. Insufficient information.

Answer (C) is correct. *(Publisher)*
**REQUIRED:** The computer system which is the best example of a data warehouse.
**DISCUSSION:** A data warehouse holds data for multiple departments and multiple sets of users. Since different departments upload their information to one central database, the IT department typically maintains the database. Thus, the Eisenhower system is the data warehouse.
Answer (A) is incorrect because the MacArthur system is the sales department's computer system. Answer (B) is incorrect because the Patton system is the R&D department's computer. Answer (D) is incorrect because the question states the Eisenhower computer system is maintained by the IT department.

**27.** Smith Company has three computer systems named MacArthur, Patton, and Eisenhower, which are the computers for the sales, R&D, and IT departments, respectively. The MacArthur and Patton systems maintain data for a period of three years, but the Eisenhower maintains its data indefinitely. If the sales department wishes to begin a direct mail campaign to all previous customers who purchased beer and diapers, it will need to _____ the _____ system.

    A. Data retrieve, MacArthur.

    B. Data retrieve, Eisenhower.

    C. Data mine, MacArthur.

    D. Data mine, Eisenhower.

Answer (D) is correct.  *(Publisher)*
    **REQUIRED:** The knowledge of what data mining means and the computer system where data mining would take place.
    **DISCUSSION:** Data mining is the search for unexpected relationships between data. A data warehouse is a central database that maintains more than one organization's system. Since the IT department maintains the data warehouse, the Eisenhower system is the system that is data mined.
    Answer (A) is incorrect because data retrieve is not a generally accepted term. Furthermore, the data warehouse is the Eisenhower system, not the MacArthur system. Answer (B) is incorrect because data retrieve is not a generally accepted term. Answer (C) is incorrect because the data warehouse is the Eisenhower system, not the MacArthur system.

**28.** Smith Company has three computer systems named MacArthur, Patton, and Eisenhower, which are the computers for the sales, R&D, and IT departments, respectively. MacArthur and Patton systems maintain data for a period of three years, but the Eisenhower maintains its data indefinitely. The MacArthur and Patton systems upload their information to the Eisenhower system at 12:01 a.m. each day. The Eisenhower computer most likely has multiple

    A. Data segregation.

    B. Data marts.

    C. Data warehouses.

    D. Data mining.

Answer (B) is correct.  *(Publisher)*
    **REQUIRED:** The knowledge of what a data mart is.
    **DISCUSSION:** The data warehouse is a central database that maintains more than one organization's system. A data mart is a subset of an enterprise-wide data warehouse. Therefore, one could expect the Eisenhower system, which is the data warehouse, to have multiple data marts.
    Answer (A) is incorrect because data segregation is not a generally accepted term. Answer (C) is incorrect because a data warehouse is a central database that maintains more than one organization's system. The Eisenhower system is the data warehouse. Answer (D) is incorrect because data mining is the search for unexpected relationships between data.

**29.** Smith Company's central warehousing computer has the following accounts in the purchasing department's data mart EXCEPT:

    A. Accounts payable.

    B. Cost of goods manufactured.

    C. Finished goods inventory.

    D. Vendor lists.

Answer (C) is correct.  *(Publisher)*
    **REQUIRED:** The knowledge of what a data mart contains.
    **DISCUSSION:** The data warehouse is a central database that maintains more than one organization's system. A data mart is a subset of an enterprise-wide data warehouse. Each organization has a data mart that is designed primarily to address a specific function or department's needs. The purchasing department is responsible for purchasing the materials for a firm. The purchasing department most likely does not need to know the value of finished goods inventory. However, the purchasing department would need to have information concerning accounts payable, cost of goods manufactured, and vendor lists.
    Answer (A) is incorrect because the purchasing department would need the data subset of accounts payable. Answer (B) is incorrect because the purchasing department would need the data subset of cost of goods manufactured. Answer (D) is incorrect because the purchasing department would need the data subset of vendor lists.

---

Use Gleim's ***CMA Test Prep*** for interactive testing with **over 2,000 additional multiple-choice questions!**

# STUDY UNIT EIGHT
# COST AND VARIANCE MEASURES

(23 pages of outline)

This study unit is the **first of three** on **performance measurement**. The relative weight assigned to this major topic in Part 2 of the exam is **20%** at **skill level C** (all six skill types required). The three study units are

Study Unit 8:   Cost and Variance Measures

Study Unit 9:   Responsibility Accounting and Financial Measures

Study Unit 10: The Balanced Scorecard and Quality Considerations

After studying the outlines and answering the multiple-choice questions in this study unit, you will have the skills necessary to address the following topics listed in the IMA's Learning Outcome Statements:

Part 2 – Section D.1. Cost and variance measures

The candidate should be able to:

a. recognize that performance against operational goals can be measured by a variety of methods including measures based on revenue, manufacturing costs, non-manufacturing costs, and profit depending on the type of center or unit being measured.

b. recognize that performance evaluation measures should be directly related to the factors that drive the element being measured, e.g., cost drivers and revenue drivers

c. prepare a performance analysis by comparing actual results to the master budget and calculating favorable and unfavorable variances from budget

d. identify the benefits and limitations of measuring performance by comparing actual results to the master budget

e. prepare a flexible budget based on actual sales (output) volume

f. determine the sales-volume variance and the sales-price variance by comparing the flexible budget to the master (static) budget

g. determine the flexible-budget variance by comparing actual results to the flexible budget

h. investigate the flexible-budget variance to determine individual differences between actual and budgeted input prices and input quantities

i. define a standard cost system and identify the reasons for adopting a standard cost system

j. demonstrate an understanding of price (rate) variances and calculate the price variances related to direct material and direct labor inputs

k. demonstrate an understanding of efficiency (usage) variances and calculate the efficiency variances related to direct material and direct labor inputs

l. demonstrate an understanding of spending and efficiency variances as they relate to fixed and variable overhead

m. recognize the significance of a sales-mix variance and its impact on revenue and contribution margin

n.   demonstrate an understanding that the efficiency (usage) variances can be further analyzed as mix and yield variances

o.   recognize that a mix variance results from using direct material and/or labor inputs in a ratio that differs from standard specifications and calculate a mix variance

p.   recognize that a yield variance results because the yield (output) obtained differs from the one expected on the basis of input and calculate a yield variance

q.   analyze variances, identify causes, and recommend corrective actions

## 8.1 STATIC AND FLEXIBLE BUDGETING

1.   **Standard costing** is a system designed to alert management when the actual costs of production differ significantly from target ("standard") costs.

   a.   **Standard costs** are predetermined, attainable unit costs.

   1)   Standard costs are usually established for direct materials, direct labor, manufacturing overhead, and nonmanufacturing (selling and administrative) costs. See item 3.b. under subunit 1.1.

2.   Standard costs are compared to actual results and the differences are calculated. These differences are referred to as **variances**.

   a.   A **favorable variance** occurs when actual costs are less than standard costs. An **unfavorable variance** occurs when the actual costs are greater than standard.

   b.   Variance analysis is an important tool of the management accountant because it assigns responsibility.

   1)   Variance analysis enables **management by exception**, the practice of giving attention primarily to significant deviations from expectations (whether favorable or unfavorable).

   a)   Attending to operations not performing within expected limits is likely to yield the best ratio of the benefits of investigation to costs.

   c.   The significance of variances depends not only on their amount but also on their direction, frequency, and trend. Moreover, variances may signify that standards need to be reevaluated.

   1)   Management is signaled that corrective action may be needed.

   d.   The purpose of identifying and assigning responsibility for variances is to determine who is likely to have information that will enable management to find solutions.

   1)   The constructive approach is to promote learning and continuous improvement in manufacturing operations, not to assign blame. However, information about variances may be useful in evaluating managers' performance.

3.   The starting point for variance analysis is the **static budget variance**.

   a.   The static budget variance measures the difference between the static (master) budget amount and the actual results. It constitutes the **total variance to be explained**.

   b.   The static budget variance consists of two components:

   1)   The **flexible budget variance** measures the difference between the actual results and the amount expected for the achieved level of activity (the flexible budget).

   2)   The **sales volume variance** measures the difference between the static budget and the amount expected for the achieved level of activity (the flexible budget).

c. This **three-way variance analysis** can be computed for any of the elements of operating income except fixed overhead.

| | | |
|---|---|---|
| Revenue | | $X,XXX |
|   Direct materials | $XXX | |
|   Direct labor | XXX | |
|   Variable manufacturing overhead | XXX | |
|   Variable nonmanufacturing costs | <u>XXX</u> | |
| Total variable costs | | <u>(X,XXX)</u> |
| Contribution margin | | $X,XXX |
|   Fixed manufacturing overhead* | $XXX | |
|   Fixed nonmanufacturing costs | <u>XXX</u> | |
| Total fixed costs | | <u>(X,XXX)</u> |
| Operating income | | $X,XXX |

*The treatment of fixed manufacturing overhead variances is different from that of the other variances. See item 3. under subunit 8.5.

4. Another hierarchy can be used to explore the factors giving rise to the variances.

  a. Static budget variance (in both hierarchies, this is the total variance to be explained).

    1) Revenue variance

    2) Direct materials variance

      a) The **direct materials price variance** (also called the **rate** or **spending variance**) is that portion of the total direct materials variance arising solely from a difference in the prices of inputs.

      b) The **direct materials quantity variance** (also called an **efficiency** or **usage variance**) is that portion of the total direct materials variance arising solely from a difference in the quantity of inputs.

        i) The **direct materials mix variance** measures the effects on total input cost of changes in the proportions of various inputs.

        ii) The **direct materials yield variance** measures the effect of varying the total input while holding constant the input mix and the weighted-average unit price.

    3) Direct labor variance

      a) Direct labor rate variance

      b) Direct labor efficiency variance

        i) Direct labor mix variance

        ii) Direct labor yield variance

    4) Variable manufacturing overhead variance

      a) Variable manufacturing overhead spending variance

      b) Variable manufacturing overhead efficiency variance

    5) Fixed manufacturing overhead variance

      a) Fixed manufacturing overhead spending variance

      b) Fixed manufacturing overhead production volume variance

    6) Variable nonmanufacturing overhead variance

      a) Variable nonmanufacturing overhead spending variance

      b) Variable nonmanufacturing overhead efficiency variance

    7) Fixed nonmanufacturing overhead variance

      a) Fixed nonmanufacturing overhead spending variance

      b) Fixed nonmanufacturing overhead production volume variance

5.  The following steps are executed in the calculation of variances:

    a.  The **static budget** is prepared before the budget period begins and is left unchanged.

        1)  The static budget reflects the **expected levels** of production, input prices, labor costs, overhead costs, selling and administrative costs, etc.

        2)  Each element of the static budget is calculated using the appropriate driver.

    b.  The **actual results** are prepared after the budget period ends.

        1)  The actual results reflect the revenues that were **actually earned** and the costs that were **actually incurred**.

        2)  The drivers are therefore adjusted to the amounts actually encountered.

    c.  The **flexible budget** activity level is determined after the budget period ends.

        1)  The flexible budget reflects the revenues that **should have been earned** and the costs that **should have been incurred** given the achieved levels of production.

        2)  The drivers are therefore the same as those used in the actual results.

    d.  The variances are calculated by comparing the three reports.

6.  **Comprehensive example of variance calculation:**

    a.  A manufacturer whose sole product is a line of dog food has selected the following drivers for the elements of operating income:

| Element | Driver | Budgeted Units for Month |
|---|---|---|
| -- | Tons manufactured | 800 |
| Revenues | Tons sold | 700 |
| Direct materials | Input tons consumed | 1,000 |
| Direct labor | Direct labor hours | 900 |
| Manufacturing overhead | Machine hours | 200 |
| Nonmanufacturing costs | Tons sold | 700 |

    b.  The static budget is prepared as follows:

|  |  |  | Static Budget |
|---|---|---|---|
| Revenues | 700 tons sold @ $220 per ton |  | $154,000 |
| Less variable costs: |  |  |  |
| Direct materials | 1,000 tons used @ $54.00 per ton | $54,000 |  |
| Direct labor | 900 labor hours @ $17.20 per hour | 15,480 |  |
| Variable mfg. overhead | 200 machine hours @ $48.00 per hour | 9,600 |  |
| Variable S&A | 700 tons sold @ $6.00 per ton | 4,200 |  |
| Total variable costs |  |  | (83,280) |
| Contribution margin |  |  | $ 70,720 |
| Less fixed costs: |  |  |  |
| Fixed mfg. overhead | 200 machine hours @ $40.00 per hour | $ 8,000 |  |
| Fixed S&A | 700 tons sold @ $5.00 per ton | 3,500 |  |
| Total fixed costs |  |  | (11,500) |
| Operating income |  |  | $ 59,220 |

c.   During the month, the company experienced different market conditions from what was expected. Actual results are reported as follows:

|  |  |  | Actual Results |
|---|---|---|---|
| Revenues | 660 tons sold @ $240 per ton |  | $158,400 |
| Less variable costs: |  |  |  |
| Direct materials | 1,078 tons used @ $50.00 per ton | $53,900 |  |
| Direct labor | 932 labor hours @ $17.30 per hour | 16,124 |  |
| Variable mfg. overhead | 195 machine hours @ $48.00 per hour | 9,360 |  |
| Variable S&A | 660 tons sold @ $6.00 per ton | 3,960 |  |
| Total variable costs |  |  | (83,344) |
| Contribution margin |  |  | $ 75,056 |
| Less fixed costs: |  |  |  |
| Fixed mfg. overhead | Actual costs incurred | $ 9,496 |  |
| Fixed S&A | Actual costs incurred | 4,000 |  |
| Total fixed costs |  |  | (13,496) |
| Operating income |  |  | $ 61,560 |

d.   The next step is to prepare the flexible budget using actual drivers with budgeted revenues and costs. Note that standard costs and prices are used.

|  |  |  | Flexible Budget |
|---|---|---|---|
| Revenues | 660 tons sold @ $220 (standard) per ton |  | $145,200 |
| Less variable costs: |  |  |  |
| Direct materials | 1,078 tons used @ $54.00 per ton | $58,212 |  |
| Direct labor | 932 labor hours @ $17.20 per hour | 16,030 |  |
| Variable mfg. overhead | 195 machine hours @ $48.00 per hour | 9,360 |  |
| Variable S&A | 660 tons sold @ $6.00 per ton | 3,960 |  |
| Total variable costs |  |  | (87,562) |
| Contribution margin |  |  | $ 57,638 |
| Less fixed costs: |  |  |  |
| Fixed mfg. overhead | Same as static budget | $ 8,000 |  |
| Fixed S&A | Same as static budget | 3,500 |  |
| Total fixed costs |  |  | (11,500) |
| Operating income |  |  | $ 46,138 |

e.   The variances can now be calculated. Positive variances are favorable.

|  | Actual Results | Flexible Budget Variances | Flexible Budget | Sales Volume Variances | Static Budget |
|---|---|---|---|---|---|
| Revenues | $158,400 | $ 13,200 | $145,200 | $ (8,800) | $154,000 |
| Less variable costs: |  |  |  |  |  |
| Direct materials | $ 53,900 | $ 4,312 | $ 58,212 | $ (4,212) | $ 54,000 |
| Direct labor | 16,124 | (94) | 16,030 | (550) | 15,480 |
| Variable mfg. overhead | 9,360 | 0 | 9,360 | 240 | 9,600 |
| Variable S&A | 3,960 | 0 | 3,960 | 240 | 4,200 |
| Total variable costs | $ 83,344 | $ 4,218 | $ 87,562 | $ (4,282) | $ 83,280 |
| Contribution margin | $ 75,056 | $17,418 | $ 57,638 | $(13,082) | $ 70,720 |
| Less fixed costs: |  |  |  |  |  |
| Fixed mfg. overhead | $ 9,496 | $ (1,496) | $ 8,000 | $ 0 | $ 8,000 |
| Fixed S&A | 4,000 | (500) | 3,500 | 0 | 3,500 |
| Total fixed costs | $ 13,496 | $ (1,996) | $ 11,500 | $ 0 | $ 11,500 |
| Operating income | $ 61,560 | $15,422 | $ 46,138 | $(13,082) | $ 59,220 |

f.    Note that the sum of the flexible budget variance and sales volume variances for any of the elements equals the static budget variance for that element.

    1)    This example uses operating income:

| | | | | |
|---|---|---|---|---|
| Flexible budget variance | $ 15,422 | Actual results | $ 61,560 | |
| Sales volume variance | (13,082) | Less: static budget | 59,220 | |
| Static budget variance | $ 2,340 F | Static budget variance | $ 2,340 | F |

7.    Stop and review! You have completed the outline for this subunit. Study multiple-choice questions 1 through 6 beginning on page 295.

## 8.2 DIRECT MATERIALS VARIANCES

1.    The variances calculated above for direct materials can be combined as follows to produce a single **total direct materials variance**.

    EXAMPLE:

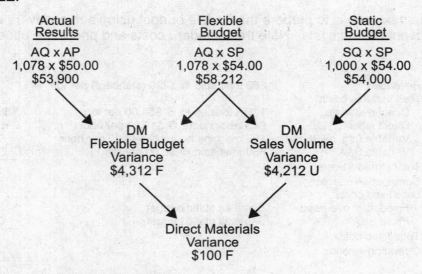

| Actual Results | Flexible Budget | Static Budget |
|---|---|---|
| AQ x AP | AQ x SP | SQ x SP |
| 1,078 x $50.00 | 1,078 x $54.00 | 1,000 x $54.00 |
| $53,900 | $58,212 | $54,000 |

DM Flexible Budget Variance $4,312 F

DM Sales Volume Variance $4,212 U

Direct Materials Variance $100 F

2.    The unit costs were derived as follows.

    EXAMPLE:

    a.    The company's production process involves combining horse meat, beef by-products, and cereal. Within certain limits, any of these raw materials can be substituted for one of the others.

    b.    The month's production is budgeted for the following inputs, mix percentages, and costs:

| | Budgeted Total Input Tons | Budgeted Mix | Budgeted Input Portion Tons | Budgeted Input Price per Ton | Total Standard Cost per Production Run |
|---|---|---|---|---|---|
| Horse meat | 1,000 | 30% | 300 | $50 | $15,000 |
| Beef | 1,000 | 50% | 500 | $70 | 35,000 |
| Cereal | 1,000 | 20% | 200 | $20 | 4,000 |
| Totals | | 100% | 1,000 | | $54,000 |

    c.    The standard direct materials cost per ton of input is therefore $54.00 ($54,000 ÷ 1,000 tons). Note that this was the standard cost used in preparing the static budget.

d. At month end, the following actual price and usage data were compiled:

| | Actual Input Tons | Actual Input Price per Ton | Total Actual Cost of Inputs | Actual Mix |
|---|---|---|---|---|
| Horse meat | 360 | $48 | $17,280 | 33.40% |
| Beef | 530 | $62 | 32,860 | 49.17% |
| Cereal | 188 | $20 | 3,760 | 17.44% |
| Totals | 1,078 | | $53,900 | 100.00% |

e. The actual direct materials cost per ton of input is therefore $50.00 rounded ($53,900 ÷ 1,078 tons). Note that this was the cost used in preparing the actual results report.

f. The total materials variance for the month is therefore $100 F ($54,000 – $53,900). Note that this is the same total variance as the one derived in item 1 on the previous page.

3. Besides the breakdown presented on the previous page (flexible budget variance vs. sales volume variance), another useful way of subdividing the total variance for direct materials is to break it down into a materials price variance and a materials quantity (or efficiency) variance.

a. The **materials price variance** measures the deviation of the actual price incurred for raw materials from the price expected (holding quantity constant). Note that, when determining a price variance, the actual cost of the materials is ignored because the only concern is the amount of variance that would have occurred given no quantity variance.

b. The **materials quantity variance** measures the deviation of the actual amount of raw materials used from the amount expected (holding price constant). Note that, when determining a quantity variance, the actual cost of the materials is ignored because the only concern is the amount of variance that would have occurred given no price variance.

c. EXAMPLE:

| | Actual Input Tons | Actual Input Price per Ton | AQ x AP | Actual Input Tons | Budgeted Input Price per Ton | AQ x SP | Budgeted Input Tons | Budgeted Input Price per Ton | SQ x SP |
|---|---|---|---|---|---|---|---|---|---|
| Horse meat: | 360 | $48 | $17,280 | 360 | $50 | $18,000 | 300 | $50 | $15,000 |
| Beef: | 530 | $62 | 32,860 | 530 | $70 | 37,100 | 500 | $70 | 35,000 |
| Cereal: | 180 | $20 | 3,760 | 188 | $20 | 3,760 | 200 | $20 | 4,000 |
| Totals | 1,078 | | $53,900 | 1,078 | | $58,860 | 1,000 | | $54,000 |

DM Price Variance $4,960 F

DM Quantity Variance $4,860 U

Direct Materials Variance $100 F

d. A **favorable** materials quantity variance indicates that the workers are using less than the standard quantity of materials.

1) A favorable quantity variance may therefore result from workers being unusually efficient or from the production of lower quality products.

    e.   An **unfavorable** materials quantity variance is usually caused by waste, shrinkage, or theft.

        1)   An unfavorable quantity variance may be the responsibility of the production department supervisor because the excess usage occurred while the materials were under that person's supervision.

4.   In some production processes, inputs are **substitutable**, e.g., a baker of pecan pies may use pecans from Florida rather than from Georgia as market conditions shift.

    a.   Whenever inputs are substitutable, the direct materials quantity variance can be split into two component variances:

        1)   The **direct materials mix variance** measures the deviation of the cost of the actual mix of raw materials used from the mix expected (holding quantity constant).

        2)   The **direct materials yield variance** measures the deviation of the cost of the actual amount of raw materials used from the amount expected (holding price constant).

    b.   First, the actual mix of each input must be determined.

        EXAMPLE:

| | Actual Input Tons | Actual Input Price per Ton | Total Actual Cost of Inputs | Actual Mix |
|---|---|---|---|---|
| Horse meat | 360 | $48 | $17,280 | 33.40% |
| Beef | 530 | $62 | 32,860 | 49.17% |
| Cereal | 188 | $20 | 3,760 | 17.44% |
| Totals | 1,078 | | $53,900 | 100.00% |

    c.   Now the mix and yield variances for direct materials can be derived.

        EXAMPLE:

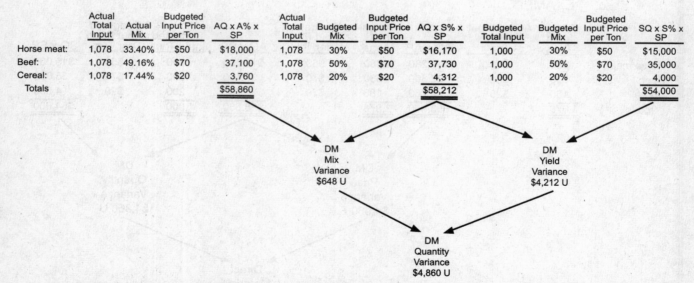

| | Actual Total Input | Actual Mix | Budgeted Input Price per Ton | AQ x A% x SP | Actual Total Input | Budgeted Mix | Budgeted Input Price per Ton | AQ x S% x SP | Budgeted Total Input | Budgeted Mix | Budgeted Input Price per Ton | SQ x S% x SP |
|---|---|---|---|---|---|---|---|---|---|---|---|---|
| Horse meat: | 1,078 | 33.40% | $50 | $18,000 | 1,078 | 30% | $50 | $16,170 | 1,000 | 30% | $50 | $15,000 |
| Beef: | 1,078 | 49.16% | $70 | 37,100 | 1,078 | 50% | $70 | 37,730 | 1,000 | 50% | $70 | 35,000 |
| Cereal: | 1,078 | 17.44% | $20 | 3,760 | 1,078 | 20% | $20 | 4,312 | 1,000 | 20% | $20 | 4,000 |
| Totals | | | | $58,860 | | | | $58,212 | | | | $54,000 |

DM Mix Variance $648 U

DM Yield Variance $4,212 U

DM Quantity Variance $4,860 U

5.   Stop and review! You have completed the outline for this subunit. Study multiple-choice questions 7 through 22 beginning on page 297.

## 8.3 DIRECT LABOR VARIANCES

1. Except for terminology, the labor and materials variances are identical.

   EXAMPLE:

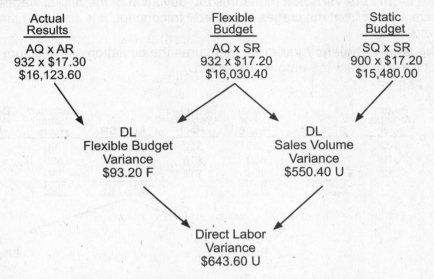

| Actual Results | Flexible Budget | Static Budget |
|---|---|---|
| AQ x AR | AQ x SR | SQ x SR |
| 932 x $17.30 | 932 x $17.20 | 900 x $17.20 |
| $16,123.60 | $16,030.40 | $15,480.00 |

DL Flexible Budget Variance $93.20 F

DL Sales Volume Variance $550.40 U

Direct Labor Variance $643.60 U

2. Most production processes require labor of various skill levels.

   a. EXAMPLE:

      1) The dog food production line involves workers at the apprentice, technician, and master levels.

      2) The month's production run is budgeted for the following labor inputs:

| | Budgeted Total Labor Hours | Budgeted Mix | Budgeted Labor Portion Hours | Budgeted Labor Rate per Hour | Total Standard Cost per Production Run |
|---|---|---|---|---|---|
| Master | 900 | 10% | 90 | $22 | $ 1,980 |
| Technician | 900 | 70% | 630 | $18 | 11,340 |
| Apprentice | 900 | 20% | 180 | $12 | 2,160 |
| Totals | | 100% | 900 | | $15,480 |

      3) The standard direct labor cost per ton of input is therefore $17.20 ($15,480 ÷ 900 tons). Note that this was the standard cost used in preparing the static budget.

      4) At month end, the following actual wage and hour data were compiled:

| | Actual Labor Hours | Actual Input Wage per Hour | Total Actual Cost of Direct Labor | Actual Mix |
|---|---|---|---|---|
| Master | 86 | $22 | $ 1,892 | 9.23% |
| Technician | 680 | $18 | 12,240 | 72.96% |
| Apprentice | 166 | $12 | 1,992 | 17.81% |
| Totals | 932 | | $16,124 | 100.00% |

      5) The actual direct labor cost per hour is therefore $17.30 rounded ($16,124 ÷ 932 hours). Note that this was the cost used in preparing the actual results report.

      6) The total labor variance for the month is therefore $644 U rounded ($15,480 – $16,124). Note that this is the same total variance as the one derived in item 1. above.

3.   Besides the breakdown presented on the previous page (flexible budget variance vs. sales volume variance), another useful way of subdividing the total variance for direct labor is to break it down into a labor rate variance and a labor efficiency variance.

    a.   The **labor rate variance** measures the deviation of the actual wages incurred for direct labor from the wages expected.  In concept, it is similar to the materials price variance.

    b.   The **labor efficiency variance** measures the deviation of the actual amount of labor consumed from the amount expected.

    c.   EXAMPLE:

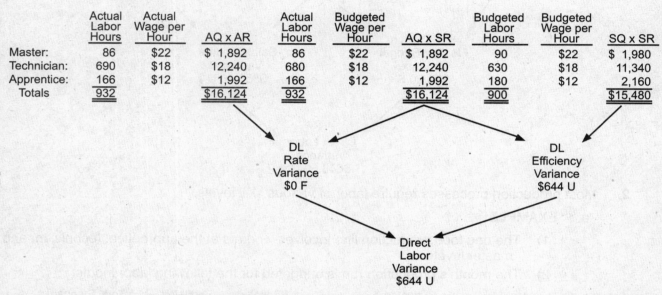

| | Actual Labor Hours | Actual Wage per Hour | AQ x AR | Actual Labor Hours | Budgeted Wage per Hour | AQ x SR | Budgeted Labor Hours | Budgeted Wage per Hour | SQ x SR |
|---|---|---|---|---|---|---|---|---|---|
| Master: | 86 | $22 | $ 1,892 | 86 | $22 | $ 1,892 | 90 | $22 | $ 1,980 |
| Technician: | 690 | $18 | 12,240 | 680 | $18 | 12,240 | 630 | $18 | 11,340 |
| Apprentice: | 166 | $12 | 1,992 | 166 | $12 | 1,992 | 180 | $12 | 2,160 |
| Totals | 932 | | $16,124 | 932 | | $16,124 | 900 | | $15,480 |

DL Rate Variance $0 F

DL Efficiency Variance $644 U

Direct Labor Variance $644 U

    d.   A **favorable** labor efficiency variance indicates that the workers have been expending less than the standard number of labor hours.

       1)   A favorable variance may therefore result from workers being unusually efficient or from the production of lower quality products.

    e.   An **unfavorable** labor efficiency variance may be caused by workers' taking unauthorized work breaks.  It may also be caused by production delays resulting from materials shortages or inferior materials.

4.   The actual mix of labor skill levels can vary just as the mix of direct materials can vary.

    a.   The direct labor efficiency variance can be split into two component variances:

       1)   The **direct labor mix variance** measures the deviation of the cost of the actual mix of wage rates used from the mix expected.

       2)   The **direct labor yield variance** measures the deviation of the cost of the actual amount of labor expended from the amount expected.

    b.   First, the actual mix of each rate must be determined.

    EXAMPLE:

| | Actual Labor Hours | Actual Input Wage per Hour | Total Actual Cost of Direct Labor | Actual Mix |
|---|---|---|---|---|
| Master | 86 | $22 | $ 1,892 | 9.23% |
| Technician | 680 | $18 | 12,240 | 72.96% |
| Apprentice | 166 | $12 | 1,992 | 17.81% |
| Totals | 932 | | $16,124 | 100.00% |

   c.   Now the mix and yield variances for direct labor can be calculated.

      EXAMPLE:

| | Actual Total Hours | Actual Mix | Budgeted Wage per Hour | AQ x A% x SR | Actual Total Hours | Budgeted Mix | Budgeted Wage per Hour | AQ x A% x SR | Budgeted Total Hours | Budgeted Mix | Budgeted Wage per Hour | SQ x S% x SR |
|---|---|---|---|---|---|---|---|---|---|---|---|---|
| Master: | 932 | 9.23% | $22 | $ 1,892 | 932 | 10% | $22 | $ 2,050 | 900 | 10% | $22 | 1,980 |
| Technician: | 932 | 72.96% | $18 | 12,240 | 932 | 70% | $18 | 11,743 | 900 | 70% | $18 | 11,340 |
| Apprentice: | 932 | 17.81% | $12 | 2,237 | 932 | 20% | $12 | 2,237 | 900 | 20% | $12 | 2,160 |
| Totals | | | | $16,030 | | | | $16,030 | | | | $15,480 |

DL Mix Variance $94 U

DL Yield Variance $550 U

DL Efficiency Variance $644 U

5.   Stop and review! You have completed the outline for this subunit. Study multiple-choice questions 23 through 31 beginning on page 303.

## 8.4 PARTIAL AND TOTAL FACTOR PRODUCTIVITY

1.   **Productivity measures** are related to the efficiency, mix, and yield variances.

   a.   Productivity is the relationship between outputs and inputs (including the mix of inputs). The higher this ratio, the greater the productivity.

2.   A **partial productivity** measure is the **ratio of output quantity to input quantity** for a single factor of production.

   a.   For example:

      1)   Direct materials: 500 tons of nails ÷ 504 tons of steel = 0.9921

      2)   Direct labor: 1 nuclear submarine ÷ 5,000,000 hours = 0.0000002

      3)   Capital: $2,000,000,000 of vehicles produced ÷ $1,500,000,000 plant = 1.33

   b.   Partial productivity measures are useful when compared over time, among different productive facilities, or with benchmarks.

      1)   A partial productivity measure **comparing results over time** determines whether the actual relationship between inputs and outputs has improved or deteriorated.

2) EXAMPLE: A manufacturer expended the following inputs to produce 100,000 units of product:

| Input | Current Year Input Quantity | Current Year Partial Factor Productivity (CY Output ÷ CY Input) |
|---|---|---|
| R&D hours | 200 | 500 |
| Direct material units | 420,000 | 0.238 |
| Direct labor hours | 5,500 | 18.182 |
| Machine hours | 12,000 | 8.333 |
| Marketing and distribution hours | 24,000 | 4.167 |

a) The productivity for each factor using the same output but the prior year's inputs can be calculated:

| Input | Prior Year Input Quantity | Prior Year Partial Factor Productivity (CY Output ÷ PY Input) |
|---|---|---|
| R&D hours | 600 | 167 |
| Direct material units | 460,000 | 0.217 |
| Direct labor hours | 5,800 | 17.241 |
| Machine hours | 10,800 | 9.259 |
| Marketing and distribution hours | 24,000 | 4.167 |

b) A comparison of the results reveals whether productivity has improved or deteriorated for each input factor:

| Input | Change in Productivity | Percentage Change |
|---|---|---|
| R&D hours | 333 | 200.0% |
| Direct material units | 0.021 | 9.5% |
| Direct labor hours | 0.940 | 5.5% |
| Machine hours | -0.926 | -10.0% |
| Marketing and distribution hours | 0.000 | 0.0% |

c. A disadvantage of a partial productivity measure is that it relates output to a single factor of production and therefore does not consider substitutions among input factors.

3. **Total factor productivity** ratios are calculated to compensate for the narrowness of partial productivity measures. Total productivity is the **ratio of output to the cost of all inputs used**.

   a. This ratio will increase from one period to the next as technological improvements permit greater output to be extracted from a given amount and mix of inputs. Use of a less costly input mix also increases the ratio.

   b. EXAMPLE:

   1) The manufacturer incurred the following input costs to produce the 100,000 units of output:

| Input | Current Year Input Quantity | Current Year Input Prices | CY Input Cost at CY Prices |
|---|---|---|---|
| R&D hours | 200 | $45.75 | $    9,150 |
| Direct material units | 420,000 | $ 1.10 | 462,000 |
| Direct labor hours | 5,500 | $28.20 | 155,100 |
| Machine hours | 12,000 | $ 0.60 | 7,200 |
| Marketing and distribution hours | 24,000 | $35.50 | 852,000 |
| | | | $1,485,450 |

   2) Total factor productivity for the current year is therefore:

$$100,000 \div \$1,485,450 = 0.067319$$

3) The cost for each factor using the same input quantity but the prior year's prices can be calculated:

| Input | Current Year Input Quantity | Current Year Input Prices | CY Input Cost at CY Prices |
|---|---|---|---|
| R&D hours | 600 | $45.75 | $    27,450 |
| Direct material units | 460,000 | $  1.10 | 506,000 |
| Direct labor hours | 5,800 | $28.20 | 163,560 |
| Machine hours | 10,800 | $  0.60 | 6,480 |
| Marketing and distribution hours | 24,000 | $35.50 | 852,000 |
| | | | $1,555,490 |

4) Total factor productivity for the prior year is therefore:

$$100,000 \div \$1,555,490 = 0.064288$$

5) Overall then, productivity improved from the prior year:

$$0.067319 - 0.064288 = 0.003031$$

4. **Stop and review!** You have completed the outline for this subunit. Study multiple-choice questions 32 through 36 beginning on page 306.

## 8.5 OVERHEAD VARIANCES

1. A manufacturing concern's **total overhead variance** is composed of variable and fixed portions.

   a. EXAMPLE:

     1) The company has determined that it incurs $48 of variable overhead and $40 of fixed overhead for every machine hour.

     2) Thus, the company has budgeted for $9,600 of variable overhead (200 machine hours × $48) and $8,000 of fixed overhead (200 machine hours × $40). Note that these were the amounts used in preparing the static budget report.

2. The **variable portion** of the total overhead variance can be calculated the same way as direct materials and direct labor.

   a. Note that these variances are not referred to as "flexible-budget" and "sales-volume" variances. There is no need for two separate breakdowns because there is no "mix" aspect to variable overhead.

   EXAMPLE:

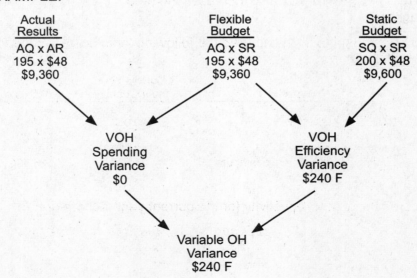

3.    The **fixed portion** of the total overhead variance has two components, but they are not combined.

    a.    Just as with variable overhead, the fixed overhead **spending variance** is derived by comparing the actual costs incurred with the flexible budget.

        1)    Note that for fixed overhead, the **flexible and static budgets are the same**. This is because fixed costs are by their nature unchanging within the relevant range of the budgeting cycle. The same amount of fixed costs must be covered regardless of machine usage or output level.

    b.    For the same reason, fixed overhead lacks an efficiency component.

        1)    Instead, a **production volume variance** is calculated.

            a)    EXAMPLE: First, the budgeted machine hours per budgeted unit of output is calculated (200 hours ÷ 700 tons = 0.2857 hours per ton).

            b)    This figure is then multiplied by the actual unit output and the fixed overhead application rate.

                $0.2857$ hours per ton × $660$ tons × $40$ per hour = $7,543

            c)    The flexible/static budget amount is then subtracted from the result to arrive at the production volume variance.

                Production volume variance = $7,543 − $8,000 = $457 U

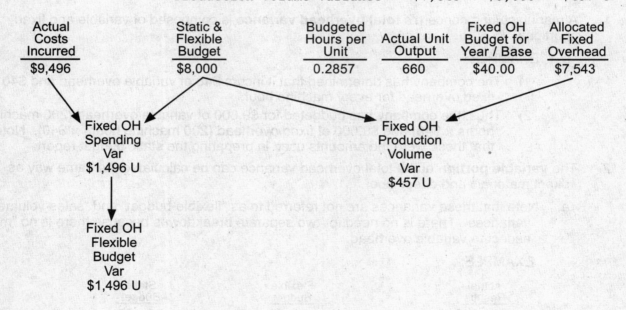

4. Integrated overhead variance analysis combines the variable and fixed portions of the overhead variance to allow simplified scrutiny.

    a. **Four-way overhead variance analysis** includes all four intermediate variances calculated on the previous two pages.

        1) EXAMPLE:

| 4-Way Analysis | Spending Variance | Efficiency Variance | Production Volume Variance |
|---|---|---|---|
| Variable OH | $0 | $240 F | -- |
| Fixed OH | $1,496 U | -- | $457 U |

    b. **Three-way overhead variance analysis** combines the variable spending and fixed budget variances into a single spending variance and reports the other two variances separately.

        1) EXAMPLE:

| 3-Way Analysis | Spending Variance | Efficiency Variance | Production Volume Variance |
|---|---|---|---|
| Total OH | $1,496 U | $240 F | $457 U |

    c. **Two-way overhead variance analysis** combines the spending and efficiency variances into a single flexible variance and reports the volume variance separately.

        1) EXAMPLE:

| 2-Way Analysis | Flexible Budget Variance | Production Volume Variance |
|---|---|---|
| Total OH | $1,256 U | $457 U |

        2) The flexible variance in 2-way analysis is also called the **controllable variance**. It is the portion of the total not attributable to the volume variance.

### 5.    Comprehensive example:

| | STANDARD COSTS | ACTUAL COSTS |
|---|---|---|
| **DIRECT MATERIALS** | 600,000 units of materials at $2.00 each | 700,000 units at $1.90 |
| **DIRECT LABOR** | 60,000 hours allowed for actual output at $7 per hour | 65,000 hours at $7.20 |
| **OVERHEAD** | $8.00 per direct labor hour on normal capacity of 50,000 direct labor hours: | |
| | $6.00 for variable overhead | $396,000 variable |
| | $2.00 for fixed overhead | $130,000 fixed |

**MATERIALS VARIANCES**

Price

$$
\begin{aligned}
AQ \times (SP - AP) &= \text{Actual quantity} \times (\text{Standard price} - \text{Actual price}) \\
&= 700{,}000 \text{ units} \times (\$2.00 - \$1.90) \\
&= 700{,}000 \times \$0.10 \\
&= \$70{,}000 \text{ F}
\end{aligned}
$$

Quantity

$$
\begin{aligned}
(SQ - AQ) \times SP &= (\text{Standard quantity} - \text{Actual quantity}) \times \text{Standard price} \\
&= (600{,}000 \text{ units} - 700{,}000 \text{ units}) \times \$2.00 \\
&= -100{,}000 \times \$2.50 \\
&= \$200{,}000 \text{ U}
\end{aligned}
$$

**LABOR VARIANCES**

Rate

$$
\begin{aligned}
AQ \times (SP - AP) &= \text{Actual hours} \times (\text{Standard rate} - \text{Actual rate}) \\
&= 65{,}000 \text{ hours} \times (\$7.00 - \$7.20) \\
&= 65{,}000 \times -\$0.20 \\
&= \$13{,}000 \text{ U}
\end{aligned}
$$

Efficiency

$$
\begin{aligned}
(SQ - AQ) \times SP &= (\text{Standard hours} - \text{Actual hours}) \times \text{Standard rate} \\
&= (65{,}000 \text{ hours} - 60{,}000 \text{ hours}) \times \$7.00 \\
&= -5{,}000 \times \$7.00 \\
&= \$35{,}000 \text{ U}
\end{aligned}
$$

**VARIABLE OVERHEAD VARIANCES**

Spending

$$
\begin{aligned}
(AQ \times SP) - AC &= (\text{Actual hours} \times \text{Standard rate}) - \text{Actual costs incurred} \\
&= (65{,}000 \times \$6.00) - \$396{,}000 \\
&= \$390{,}000 - \$396{,}000 \\
&= \$6{,}000 \text{ U}
\end{aligned}
$$

Efficiency

$$
\begin{aligned}
(SQ - AQ) \times SP &= (\text{Standard hours} - \text{Actual hours}) \times \text{Standard rate} \\
&= (60{,}000 - 65{,}000) \times \$6.00 \\
&= -5{,}000 \times \$6.00 \\
&= \$30{,}000 \text{ U}
\end{aligned}
$$

**FIXED OVERHEAD VARIANCES**

Budget

$$
\begin{aligned}
\text{Amount applied} - \text{Actual costs incurred} &= \$100{,}000 - \$130{,}000 \\
&= \$30{,}000 \text{ U}
\end{aligned}
$$

Volume

$$
\begin{aligned}
(\text{Standard hours allowed for actual output} \times \text{Standard rate}) - \\
\text{Actual costs incurred} &= (60{,}000 \text{ hours} \times \$2.00) - \$100{,}000 \\
&= \$120{,}000 - \$100{,}000 \\
&= \$20{,}000 \text{ F}
\end{aligned}
$$

**NET MANUFACTURING VARIANCE     $224,000**

|  | Actual Output at Actual Input and Cost | Actual Output at Standard Input and Cost |
|---|---|---|
| Materials | $1,330,000 | $1,200,000 |
| Labor | 468,000 | 420,000 |
| Variable overhead | 396,000 | 360,000 |
| Fixed overhead | 130,000 | 120,000 |
| Net unfavorable variance |  | 224,000 |
|  | $2,324,000 | $2,324,000 |

6. Stop and review! You have completed the outline for this subunit. Study multiple-choice questions 37 through 70 beginning on page 308.

## 8.6 VARIANCES IN THE LEDGER ACCOUNTS

1. Variances usually do not appear on the financial statements of a firm. They are recorded in the ledger accounts but are only used for managerial control.

2. When standard costs are recorded in inventory accounts, direct labor and materials variances are also recorded.

   a. **Direct labor** is recorded as a liability at actual cost, but it is ordinarily charged to work-in-process control at its standard cost for the standard quantity used.

      1) The direct labor rate and efficiency variances are recognized at that time.

   b. **Direct materials**, on the other hand, should be debited to materials control at standard prices at the time of purchase.

      1) The purpose is to isolate the purchase price variance as soon as possible.

         a) The **purchase price variance** is a nonmanufacturing variance which measures the deviation of the amount paid to purchase raw materials during a period from the amount expected to be paid.

         b) The general formula is **PPV = AQ × (SP − AP)**. Stating the formula in this way produces a positive result when the variance is favorable.

      2) When direct materials are used, they are debited to work-in-process at the standard cost for the standard quantity; the materials quantity variance is recognized at that time. Note that unfavorable variances are debts (like expenses), while favorable variances are credits.

         a)  
         | | | |
         |---|---|---|
         | Materials control (AQ × SP) | $XXX | |
         | Direct materials purchase price variance (dr or cr) | XXX | |
         |     Accounts payable (AQ × AP) | | $XXX |

         b)  
         | | | |
         |---|---|---|
         | Work-in-process control (SQ × SP) | $XXX | |
         | Direct materials quantity variance (dr or cr) | XXX | |
         | Direct labor rate variance (dr or cr) | XXX | |
         | Direct labor efficiency variance (dr or cr) | XXX | |
         |     Materials control (AQ × SP) | | $XXX |
         |     Wages payable (AQ × AP) | | XXX |

  c. Overhead costs are treated as follows:

   1) Actual overhead costs are debited to **overhead control** and credited to accounts payable, wages payable, etc.

     Overhead control (actual)          $XXX
       Wages payable (actual)             $XXX
       Accounts payable (actual)           XXX

   2) Applied overhead is credited to overhead control or to an **overhead applied** account and debited to work-in-process control.

     Work-in-process control (standard)     $XXX
       Overhead applied (standard)           $XXX

   3) The simplest method of recording the overhead variances is to wait until year-end. The variances can then be recognized separately when the overhead control and overhead applied accounts are closed (by a credit and a debit, respectively). The balancing debits or credits are to the variance accounts.

     Overhead applied (standard)         $XXX
     Variable overhead spending variance (dr or cr)  XXX
     Variable overhead efficiency variance (dr or cr)  XXX
     Fixed overhead budget variance (dr or cr)    XXX
     Fixed overhead volume variance (dr or cr)    XXX
       Overhead control (actual)          $XXX

   4) The result of the foregoing entries is that work-in-process contains standard costs only.

3. **Immaterial variances** are customarily closed to cost of goods sold or income summary.

  a. **Material variances** may be prorated. A simple approach is to allocate the total net variance to work-in-process, finished goods, and cost of goods sold based on the balances in those accounts.

  b. More complex methods of allocation are possible.

   1) Direct materials and labor might be transferred to work-in-process at their actual quantities. In that case, the direct materials quantity and direct labor efficiency variances might be recognized when goods are transferred from work-in-process to finished goods.

   2) The direct materials price variance might be isolated at the time of transfer to work-in-process.

   3) The difficulty with these methods is that they delay the recognition of variances. Early recognition is desirable for control purposes.

4. Stop and review! You have completed the outline for this subunit. Study multiple-choice questions 71 through 77 beginning on page 321.

## 8.7 SALES VARIANCES

1.    Variance analysis is not only a tool of the manufacturing divisions, but also a method used to judge the effectiveness of the selling departments.

   a.   If a firm's sales differ from the amount budgeted, the difference could be attributable to either the **sales price variance** or the **sales volume variance** (sum of the sales quantity and mix variances).

   b.   The analysis of these variances concentrates on **contribution margins** because fixed costs are assumed to be constant.

   c.   EXAMPLE:  A firm has budgeted sales of 10,000 units of its sole product at $17 per unit.  Variable costs are expected to be $10 per unit and fixed costs are budgeted at $50,000.  A comparison of budgeted to actual results is as follows:

| | Budget Computation | Budget Amount | Actual Computation | Actual Amount |
|---|---|---|---|---|
| Sales | 10,000 units @ $17/unit | $170,000 | 11,000 units @ $16/unit | $176,000 |
| Variable costs | 10,000 units @ $10/unit | (100,000) | 11,000 units @ $10/unit | (110,000) |
| Contribution margin | | $ 70,000 | | $ 66,000 |
| Fixed costs | | (50,000) | | (50,000) |
| Operating income | | $ 20,000 | | $ 16,000 |
| | | | | |
| Unit contribution margin | $70,000/10,000 units | = $7 | $66,000/11,000 units | = $6 |

   1)   Although sales were greater than predicted, the contribution margin is less than expected.

   a)   The discrepancy can be analyzed in terms of the sales price variance and the sales volume variance.

   2)   For a single-product firm, the **sales price variance** is the change in the contribution margin attributable solely to the change in selling price (holding quantity constant).

   a)   In the example, the actual selling price of $16 per unit is $1 less than expected.  Thus, the sales price variance is $11,000 U (11,000 actual units sold × $1).

   3)   For the single product, the **sales volume variance** is the change in contribution margin caused by the difference between the actual and budgeted volume (holding price constant).

   a)   In the example, it equals $7,000 F (1,000-unit increase in volume × $7 budgeted UCM).

   4)   The sales mix variance is zero because the firm sells only one product.  Hence, the sales volume variance equals the sales quantity variance.

   5)   The sales price variance ($11,000 U) combined with the sales volume variance ($7,000 F) equals the total change in the contribution margin ($4,000 U).

   d.   A similar analysis may be done for **cost of goods sold**.

   1)   The average production cost per unit is used instead of the average unit selling price, but the quantities for production volume are the same.

   2)   Accordingly, the overall variation in gross profit is the sum of the variation in revenue plus the variation in cost of goods sold.

2.    If a company produces two or more products, the **multiproduct sales variances** reflect not only the effects of the change in total unit sales, but also any difference in the mix of products sold.

    a.    The **multiproduct sales price variance** may be calculated as in the single-product case for each product. The results are then added.

        1)    An alternative is to multiply the actual total units sold times the difference between the following:

            a)    The weighted-average price based on actual units sold at actual unit prices.

            b)    The weighted-average price based on actual units sold at budgeted prices.

    b.    The **multiproduct sales volume variance** may be calculated the same as the single-product case for each product. The results are then added.

        1)    An alternative is to determine the difference between the following:

            a)    Actual total unit sales times the budgeted weighted-average UCM for the actual mix.

            b)    Budgeted total unit sales times the budgeted weighted-average UCM for the planned mix.

    c.    The multiproduct sales volume variance may be broken down into the sales quantity and sales mix variances.

        1)    The **sales quantity variance**, which equals the sales volume variance for a single-product company, is the difference between the budgeted contribution margin based on actual unit sales and the budgeted contribution margin based on expected sales, assuming that the budgeted sales mix is constant.

            a)    One way to calculate this variance is to multiply the budgeted UCM for each product times the difference between the budgeted unit sales of the product and its budgeted percentage of actual total unit sales. The results are then added.

                i)    An alternative is to multiply the difference between total actual unit sales and the total expected unit sales by the budgeted weighted-average UCM based on the expected mix.

        2)    The **sales mix variance** is the difference between the budgeted contribution margin for the actual mix and actual total quantity of products sold and the budgeted contribution margin for the expected mix and actual total quantity of products sold.

            a)    One way to calculate this variance is to multiply the budgeted UCM for each product times the difference between actual unit sales of the product and its budgeted percentage of actual total unit sales. The results are then added.

                i)    An alternative is to multiply total actual unit sales times the difference between the budgeted weighted-average UCM for the expected mix and the budgeted weighted-average UCM for the actual mix.

d. **Comprehensive example:**

|  | Plastic | Metal | Total |
|---|---|---|---|
| Budgeted selling price per unit | $6.00 | $10.00 | |
| Budgeted variable cost per unit | 3.00 | 7.50 | |
| Budgeted contribution margin per unit | $3.00 | $ 2.50 | |
| | | | |
| Budgeted unit sales | 300 | 200 | 500 |
| Budgeted mix percentage | 60% | 40% | 100% |
| Actual units sold | 260 | 260 | 520 |
| Actual selling price per unit | $6.00 | $9.50 | |

1) As shown below (000 omitted), the **total contribution margin variance** was $100 unfavorable ($130 unfavorable sales price variance – $30 favorable sales volume variance).

     **Sales price variance:**
       Plastic 260 × ($6.00 – $6.00)      $ 0
       Metal 260 × ($10 – $9.50)      (130)    $130 unfavorable
     **Sales volume variance:**
       Plastic (260 – 300) × $3.00      $(120)
       Metal (260 – 200) × $2.50      150    $ 30 favorable
     **Total contribution margin variance**      $100 unfavorable

2) The sales volume variance may be broken down as follows: Sales quantity variance:

     **Sales quantity variance:**
       Plastic [(520 × .6) – 300] × $3.00      $ 36
       Metal [(520 × .4) – 200] × $2.50      20    $ 56 favorable
     **Sales mix variance:**
       Plastic [260 – (520 × .6)] × $3.00      $(156)
       Metal [260 – (520 × .4)] × $2.50      130    $ 26 unfavorable
     **Sales volume variance**      $ 30 favorable

e. The sales quantity variance may be broken down into the market size and market share variances.

   1) The **market size variance** measures the effect on the contribution margin of the difference between the actual market size in units and the budgeted market size in units, assuming the market share percentage and the budgeted weighted-average UCM are constant.

     a) It equals the budgeted market share percentage, times the difference between the actual market size in units and the budgeted market size in units, times the budgeted weighted-average UCM.

   2) The **market share variance** measures the effect on the contribution margin of the difference between the actual and budgeted market share percentages, assuming the actual market size in units and the budgeted weighted-average UCM are constant.

     a) It equals the difference between the actual market share percentage and the budgeted market share percentage, times the actual market size in units, times the budgeted weighted-average UCM.

   3) EXAMPLE: Assume that a company's budgeted and actual market sizes and market shares are as follows:

| | Budget | Actual |
|---|---|---|
| Market size in units | 60,000 | 50,000 |
| Market share | 9% | 10% |

a)  Assuming a budgeted weighted-average UCM of $3, the market size variance is $2,700 U [(60,000 units – 50,000 units) × 9% × $3]. The variance is unfavorable because market size diminished.

b)  The market share variance is $1,500 F [50,000 units × $3 × (10% – 9%)]. The variance is favorable because market share increased. Thus, the sales quantity variance is $1,200 U ($2,700 U – $1,500 F).

3.  Stop and review! You have completed the outline for this subunit. Study multiple-choice questions 78 through 92 beginning on page 324.

## 8.8 CORE CONCEPTS

### Static and Flexible Budgeting

- The starting point for variance analysis is the **static budget variance**, which measures the difference between the static (master) budget amount and the actual results.
- The static budget variance consists of **two components**:
  - The **flexible budget variance** measures the difference between the actual results and the amount expected for the achieved level of activity (the flexible budget).
  - The **sales volume variance** measures the difference between the static budget and the amount expected for the achieved level of activity (the flexible budget).
- This **three-way variance analysis** can be computed for any of the elements of operating income.

### Direct Materials Variances

- Besides the three-way breakdown (static budget variance/flexible budget variance/sales volume variance), the direct materials variance can also be decomposed into the **materials price variance** and the **materials quantity variance**.
- The materials quantity variance can be further broken down into the **direct materials mix variance** and the **direct materials yield variance**.

### Direct Labor Variances

- Besides the three-way breakdown (static budget variance/flexible budget variance/sales volume variance), the direct labor variance can also be decomposed into the **labor rate variance** and the **labor efficiency variance**.
- The labor efficiency variance can be further broken down into the **direct labor mix variance** and the **direct labor yield variance**.

### Partial and Total Factor Productivity

- A partial productivity measure is the **ratio** of output quantity to input quantity for a **single factor of production**.
- Total productivity is the **ratio** of output to the cost of **all inputs used**.

### Overhead Variances

- A manufacturing concern's total overhead variance is composed of **variable and fixed portions**.
- Besides the three-way breakdown (static budget variance/flexible budget variance/sales volume variance), the **variable overhead variance** can also be decomposed into the **variable overhead spending variance** and the **variable overhead efficiency variance**.
- In the standard three-way breakdown, the **sales volume variance component** of the **fixed overhead variance** is **always $0** because fixed costs are by their nature unchanging within the relevant range of the budgeting cycle.
- The flexible budget variance component can be decomposed into a **fixed overhead spending variance** and a **fixed overhead volume variance**.

## Variances in the Ledger Accounts

- Variances usually **do not appear** on the **financial statements**. They are recorded in the ledger accounts but are only used for **managerial control**.

## Sales Variances

- If a firm's **sales differ from the amount budgeted**, the difference could be attributable to either the sales price variance or the sale volume variance.
- For a single-product firm, the **sales price variance** is the change in the contribution margin attributable solely to the change in selling price.
- For a single-product firm, the **sales volume variance** is the change in the contribution margin caused by the difference between the actual and budgeted volume.
- If a company produces two or more products, the **multiproduct sales variances** reflect not only the effects of the change in total unit sales but also any difference in the mix of products sold.

## QUESTIONS

### 8.1 Static and Flexible Budgeting

**1.** In a responsibility accounting system, a feedback report that focuses on the difference between budgeted amounts and actual amounts is an example of

A. Management by exception.

B. Assessing blame.

C. Granting rewards to successful managers.

D. Ignoring other variables for which the budgeted goals were met.

Answer (A) is correct. *(Publisher)*
**REQUIRED:** The term for feedback reports that focus on differences between budgeted and actual amounts.
**DISCUSSION:** A responsibility accounting system should have certain controls that provide for feedback reports indicating deviations from expectations. Management may then focus on those deviations (exceptions) for either reinforcement or correction.
Answer (B) is incorrect because the responsibility accounting system should not be used exclusively to assess blame.
Answer (C) is incorrect because the responsibility accounting system should not be used exclusively to give rewards.
Answer (D) is incorrect because feedback reports concentrate on deviations, but not to the total exclusion of other budgeted variables.

**2.** The difference between the actual amounts and the flexible budget amounts for the actual output achieved is the

A. Production volume variance.

B. Flexible budget variance.

C. Sales volume variance.

D. Standard cost variance.

Answer (B) is correct. *(CMA, adapted)*
**REQUIRED:** The term for the difference between the actual amounts and the flexible budget amounts.
**DISCUSSION:** A flexible budget is prepared at the end of the budget period when the actual results are available. A flexible budget reflects the revenues that should have been earned and costs that should have been incurred given the achieved levels of production and sales. The difference between the flexible budget and actual figures is known as the flexible budget variance.
Answer (A) is incorrect because the production volume variance equals under- or overapplied fixed overhead.
Answer (C) is incorrect because the sales volume variance is the difference between the flexible budget amount and the static budget amount. Answer (D) is incorrect because a standard cost variance is not necessarily based on a flexible budget.

**3.** The purpose of identifying manufacturing variances and assigning their responsibility to a person/department should be to

A. Use the knowledge about the variances to promote learning and continuous improvement in the manufacturing operations.

B. Trace the variances to finished goods so that the inventory can be properly valued at year-end.

C. Determine the proper cost of the products produced so that selling prices can be adjusted accordingly.

D. Pinpoint fault for operating problems in the organization.

Answer (A) is correct.   *(CMA, adapted)*
**REQUIRED:** The purpose of identifying and assigning responsibility for manufacturing variances.
**DISCUSSION:** The purpose of identifying and assigning responsibility for variances is to determine who is likely to have information that will enable management to find solutions. The constructive approach is to promote learning and continuous improvement in manufacturing operations, not to assign blame. However, information about variances may be useful in evaluating managers' performance.
Answer (B) is incorrect because, depending on a cost-benefit determination, variances either are adjustments of cost of goods sold or are allocated among the inventory accounts and cost of goods sold. Moreover, the accounting issues are distinct from supervisory considerations. Answer (C) is incorrect because selling prices are based on much more than the cost of production; for instance, competitive pressure is also a consideration. Answer (D) is incorrect because, by itself, pinpointing fault is not an appropriate objective. Continuous improvement is the ultimate objective.

**4.** Which of the following management practices involves concentrating on areas that deserve attention and placing less attention on areas operating as expected?

A. Management by objectives.

B. Responsibility accounting.

C. Benchmarking.

D. Management by exception.

Answer (D) is correct.   *(CIA, adapted)*
**REQUIRED:** The management practice that concentrates on areas needing attention.
**DISCUSSION:** Management by exception gives significant attention only to those areas in which material deviations from expectations occur. Consequently, management focuses resources where the greatest returns from supervisory effort may be achieved.
Answer (A) is incorrect because, in MBO, a manager and his/her subordinates jointly formulate the subordinates' objectives and the plans for attaining them. Answer (B) is incorrect because, in a responsibility accounting system, managers are evaluated only on the basis of factors they control. Answer (C) is incorrect because benchmarking is the practice of identifying, studying, and building upon the best practices in the industry or in the world.

**5.** A manufacturing firm planned to manufacture and sell 100,000 units of product during the year at a variable cost per unit of $4.00 and a fixed cost per unit of $2.00. The firm fell short of its goal and only manufactured 80,000 units at a total incurred cost of $515,000. The firm's manufacturing cost variance was

A. $85,000 favorable.

B. $35,000 unfavorable.

C. $5,000 favorable.

D. $5,000 unfavorable.

Answer (C) is correct.   *(CMA, adapted)*
**REQUIRED:** The manufacturing cost variance.
**DISCUSSION:** The company planned to produce 100,000 units at $6 each ($4 variable + $2 fixed cost), or a total of $600,000, consisting of $400,000 of variable costs and $200,000 of fixed costs. Total production was only 80,000 units at a total cost of $515,000. The flexible budget for a production level of 80,000 units includes variable costs of $320,000 (80,000 units × $4). Fixed costs would remain at $200,000. Thus, the total flexible budget costs are $520,000. Given that actual costs were only $515,000, the variance is $5,000 favorable.
Answer (A) is incorrect because $85,000 favorable is based on a production level of 100,000 units. Answer (B) is incorrect because the variance is favorable. Answer (D) is incorrect because the variance is favorable.

**6.** The efficiency variance for either direct labor or materials can be divided into

A. Spending variance and yield variance.

B. Yield variance and price variance.

C. Volume variance and mix variance.

D. Yield variance and mix variance.

Answer (D) is correct.   *(CMA, adapted)*
**REQUIRED:** The components into which a direct labor or materials efficiency variance can be divided.
**DISCUSSION:** A direct labor or materials efficiency variance is calculated by multiplying the difference between standard and actual usage times the standard cost per unit of input. The efficiency variances can be divided into yield and mix variances. These variances are calculated only when the production process involves combining several materials or classes of labor in varying proportions (when substitutions are allowable in combining resources).
Answer (A) is incorrect because a spending variance is not the same as an efficiency variance. Answer (B) is incorrect because a price variance is not the same as an efficiency variance. Answer (C) is incorrect because a volume variance is based on fixed costs, and an efficiency variance is based on variable costs.

## 8.2  Direct Materials Variances

**7.** A favorable materials price variance coupled with an unfavorable materials usage variance most likely results from

A. Machine efficiency problems.

B. Product mix production changes.

C. The purchase and use of higher-than-standard quality materials.

D. The purchase of lower than standard quality materials.

Answer (D) is correct.   *(CMA, adapted)*
**REQUIRED:** The cause of a favorable materials price variance coupled with an unfavorable materials usage variance.
**DISCUSSION:** A favorable materials price variance is the result of paying less than the standard price for materials. An unfavorable materials usage variance is the result of using an excessive quantity of materials. If a purchasing manager were to buy substandard materials to achieve a favorable price variance, an unfavorable quantity variance could result from using an excessive amount of poor quality materials.
Answer (A) is incorrect because machine efficiency problems do not explain the price variance. Answer (B) is incorrect because a change in product mix does not explain the price variance. Answer (C) is incorrect because materials of higher-than-standard quality are more likely to cause an unfavorable price variance and a favorable quantity variance.

**8.** Under a standard cost system, the materials efficiency variances are the responsibility of

A. Production and industrial engineering.

B. Purchasing and industrial engineering.

C. Purchasing and sales.

D. Sales and industrial engineering.

Answer (A) is correct.   *(CMA, adapted)*
**REQUIRED:** The function(s) responsible for the materials efficiency (quantity) variance.
**DISCUSSION:** The materials efficiency variance is the difference between actual and standard quantities used in production, times the standard price. An unfavorable materials efficiency variance is usually caused by wastage, shrinkage, or theft. Thus, it may be the responsibility of the production department because excess usage would occur while the materials are in that department. In addition, industrial engineering may play a role because it is responsible for design of the production process.
Answer (B) is incorrect because purchasing rarely can control the materials efficiency variance. Answer (C) is incorrect because sales has no effect on the materials efficiency variance. Answer (D) is incorrect because sales has no effect on the materials efficiency variance.

Questions 9 and 10 are based on the following information.

Blaster, Inc., a manufacturer of portable radios, purchases the components from subcontractors to use to assemble into a complete radio. Each radio requires three units each of Part XBEZ52, which has a standard cost of $1.45 per unit. During May, Blaster experienced the following with respect to Part XBEZ52.

|  | Units |
|---|---|
| Purchases ($18,000) | 12,000 |
| Consumed in manufacturing | 10,000 |
| Radios manufactured | 3,000 |

**9.** During May, Blaster, Inc. incurred a purchase price variance of

A. $450 unfavorable.

B. $450 favorable.

C. $500 favorable.

D. $600 unfavorable.

Answer (D) is correct. *(CMA, adapted)*
REQUIRED: The purchase price variance.
DISCUSSION: The standard cost per part is $1.45. The actual cost was $18,000 for 12,000 parts, or $1.50 each. Thus, the price variance is $600 unfavorable [12,000 parts × ($1.45 – $1.50)].
Answer (A) is incorrect because $450 unfavorable equals the standard quantity needed for the actual output times the $.05 unfavorable price variance per part. Answer (B) is incorrect because the variance is unfavorable, and $450 is the amount of the variance that relates only to the standard input for the actual output. Answer (C) is incorrect because the variance is unfavorable. Furthermore, the variance is based on the quantity purchased, not the quantity consumed. [Note: The materials price variance is sometimes isolated at the time of transfer to production.]

**10.** During May, Blaster, Inc. incurred a materials efficiency variance of

A. $1,450 unfavorable.

B. $1,450 favorable.

C. $4,350 unfavorable.

D. $4,350 favorable.

Answer (A) is correct. *(CMA, adapted)*
REQUIRED: The materials efficiency variance.
DISCUSSION: Standard usage was three parts per radio at $1.45 each. For a production level of 3,000 units, the total materials needed equaled 9,000 parts, but materials actually used totaled 10,000 parts. Thus, the variance is $1,450 unfavorable [(9,000 standard usage – 10,000 actually used) × $1.45 standard cost per part].
Answer (B) is incorrect because the variance is unfavorable. The actual quantity used exceeded the standard input allowed. Answer (C) is incorrect because $4,350 unfavorable assumes that 12,000 parts were consumed. Answer (D) is incorrect because $4,350 favorable assumes that 12,000 parts were consumed and that the variance is favorable.

**11.** Garland Company uses a standard cost system. The standard for each finished unit of product allows for 3 pounds of plastic at $0.72 per pound. During December, Garland bought 4,500 pounds of plastic at $0.75 per pound, and used 4,100 pounds in the production of 1,300 finished units of product. What is the materials purchase price variance for the month of December?

A. $117 unfavorable.

B. $123 unfavorable.

C. $135 unfavorable.

D. $150 unfavorable.

Answer (C) is correct. *(CMA, adapted)*
REQUIRED: The materials purchase price variance.
DISCUSSION: The materials purchase price variance equals the quantity purchased multiplied by the difference between the standard price and the actual price, or $135 unfavorable [4,500 lbs. × ($.75 – $.72)].
Answer (A) is incorrect because $117 unfavorable is based on the standard input for 1,300 units. Answer (B) is incorrect because $123 unfavorable is based on the actual quantity used. Answer (D) is incorrect because $150 unfavorable is based on the assumption that 5,000 lbs. were purchased.

**12.** Which one of the following variances is most controllable by the production control supervisor?

A. Materials price variance.

B. Materials usage variance.

C. Variable overhead spending variance.

D. Fixed overhead budget variance.

Answer (B) is correct. *(CMA, adapted)*
**REQUIRED:** The variance that is most controllable by the production control supervisor.
**DISCUSSION:** The production control supervisor has the most control over the materials usage variance. The materials usage variance measures the excess amount of materials used over the amount specified in the standards. The materials usage (or materials quantity) variance, when unfavorable, is often attributable to waste, shrinkage, or theft in the production areas. The excess usage occurs under the supervision of the production department.
Answer (A) is incorrect because the materials price variance can be greatly influenced by the purchasing manager.
Answer (C) is incorrect because the variable overhead spending variance is both a quantity and a price variance. Prices paid are not controllable by the production control supervisor. Answer (D) is incorrect because fixed overhead variances usually cannot be controlled by the manufacturing departments.

---

Questions 13 and 14 are based on the following information. The controller for Durham Skates is reviewing the production cost report for July. An analysis of direct materials costs reflects an unfavorable flexible budget variance of $25. The plant manager believes this is excellent performance on a flexible budget for 5,000 units of direct materials. However, the production supervisor is not pleased with this result because she claims to have saved $1,200 in materials cost on actual production using 4,900 units of direct materials. The standard materials cost is $12 per unit. Actual materials used for the month amounted to $60,025.

---

**13.** The actual average cost per unit for materials was

A. $12.00

B. $12.01

C. $12.24

D. $12.25

Answer (D) is correct. *(CMA, adapted)*
**REQUIRED:** The actual average cost per unit for materials.
**DISCUSSION:** Dividing the actual cost of $60,025 by the 4,900 units used results in an average cost of $12.25 per unit.
Answer (A) is incorrect because $12 is the standard cost. Answer (B) is incorrect because $12.01 is based on the budgeted usage. Answer (C) is incorrect because $12.24 equals the $60,000 standard cost for 5,000 units divided by 4,900 units.

**14.** If the direct materials variance is investigated further, it will reflect a price variance of

A. Zero.

B. $1,200 favorable.

C. $1,225 unfavorable.

D. $2,500 favorable.

Answer (C) is correct. *(CMA, adapted)*
**REQUIRED:** The direct materials price variance.
**DISCUSSION:** The price variance equals the actual quantity times the difference between the actual price and the standard price. The actual price is $12.25, and the standard price is $12 (given). Thus, the price variance is $1,225 unfavorable [4,900 units × ($12.00 standard – $12.25 actual)].
Answer (A) is incorrect because a price variance exists. The actual price paid was greater than the standard allowed.
Answer (B) is incorrect because the variance is unfavorable.
Answer (D) is incorrect because the variance is unfavorable.

**15.** In a standard cost system, the investigation of an unfavorable materials usage variance should begin with the

A. Production manager only.

B. Plant controller only.

C. Purchasing manager only.

D. Production manager or the purchasing manager.

Answer (D) is correct. *(CMA, adapted)*
**REQUIRED:** The place to begin investigating an unfavorable materials usage (quantity) variance.
**DISCUSSION:** An unfavorable materials quantity variance is usually caused by waste, shrinkage, or theft. Alternatively, an unfavorable variance could be attributable to the purchasing department's not buying the proper quality of materials in an attempt to achieve a favorable material price variance. Thus, either the production manager or the purchasing manager could be responsible for a material usage variance.
Answer (A) is incorrect because both the purchasing manager and the production manager could be at fault.
Answer (B) is incorrect because the plant controller is at too high a level for an investigation of a materials usage variance.
Answer (C) is incorrect because both the purchasing manager and the production manager could be at fault.

Questions 16 through 18 are based on the following information. ChemKing uses a standard costing system in the manufacture of its single product. The 35,000 units of direct materials in inventory were purchased for $105,000, and two units of direct materials are required to produce one unit of final product. In November, the company produced 12,000 units of product. The standard allowed for materials was $60,000, and the unfavorable quantity variance was $2,500.

**16.** ChemKing's standard price for one unit of direct materials is

A. $2.00

B. $2.50

C. $3.00

D. $5.00

Answer (B) is correct. *(CMA, adapted)*
**REQUIRED:** The standard price for one unit of direct materials.
**DISCUSSION:** Given that the company produced 12,000 units with a total standard cost for direct materials of $60,000, the standard cost must be $5.00 ($60,000 ÷ 12,000 units) per unit of finished product. Because each unit of finished product requires two units of direct materials, the standard unit cost for direct materials must be $2.50.
Answer (A) is incorrect because the unit standard cost is $2.50. Answer (C) is incorrect because $3 is the actual cost per unit of direct materials. Answer (D) is incorrect because $5 is the total standard cost of direct materials for each unit of finished product.

**17.** The units of direct materials used to produce November output totaled

A. 12,000 units.

B. 12,500 units.

C. 23,000 units.

D. 25,000 units.

Answer (D) is correct. *(CMA, adapted)*
**REQUIRED:** The number of units of direct materials used to produce November output.
**DISCUSSION:** The company produced 12,000 units of output, each of which required two units of direct materials. Thus, the standard input allowed for direct materials was 24,000 units at a standard cost of $2.50 each. An unfavorable quantity variance signifies that the actual quantity used was greater than the standard input allowed. The direct materials quantity variance equals the difference between standard and actual quantities times the standard price per unit. Consequently, because 1,000 ($2,500 U ÷ $2.50) additional units were used, the actual total quantity must have been 25,000 units (24,000 standard + 1,000).
Answer (A) is incorrect because 12,000 units is the number of units of finished product. Answer (B) is incorrect because 12,500 units assumes that each unit of finished product includes only one unit of direct materials. Answer (C) is incorrect because 23,000 units assumes a favorable quantity variance.

**18.** The direct materials price variance for the units used in November was

A. $2,500 unfavorable.

B. $11,000 unfavorable.

C. $12,500 unfavorable.

D. $3,500 unfavorable.

Answer (C) is correct. *(CMA, adapted)*
**REQUIRED:** The direct materials price variance for the units used in November.
**DISCUSSION:** The price variance equals actual quantity times the difference between the actual and standard prices. Actual usage and the standard price were 25,000 units and $2.50, respectively. Actual price was $3.00 ($105,000 total cost ÷ 35,000 units purchased). Consequently, the direct materials price variance is $12,500 unfavorable [25,000 units × ($2.50 – $3.00)].
Answer (A) is incorrect because $2,500 unfavorable is the direct materials quantity variance. Answer (B) is incorrect because the price variance is $12,500, or $.50 per unit. Answer (D) is incorrect because the price variance is $12,500, or $.50 per unit.

**19.** Tower Company planned to produce 3,000 units of its single product, Titactium, during November. The standard specifications for one unit of Titactium include 6 pounds of materials at $.30 per pound. Actual production in November was 3,100 units of Titactium. The accountant computed a favorable direct materials purchase price variance of $380 and an unfavorable direct materials quantity variance of $120. Based on these variances, one could conclude that

A. More materials were purchased than were used.

B. More materials were used than were purchased.

C. The actual cost of materials was less than the standard cost.

D. The actual usage of materials was less than the standard allowed.

Answer (C) is correct. *(CMA, adapted)*
**REQUIRED:** The meaning of a favorable direct materials purchase price variance and an unfavorable direct materials quantity variance.
**DISCUSSION:** The direct materials purchase price variance may be isolated at the time of purchase or at the time of transfer to production. It equals the actual quantity of materials purchased or transferred times the difference between the standard and actual unit prices. Hence, a favorable direct materials purchase price variance means that materials were purchased at a price less than the standard price.
Answer (A) is incorrect because no variance relates quantity purchased to quantity used. Answer (B) is incorrect because no variance relates quantity purchased to quantity used. Answer (D) is incorrect because the unfavorable quantity variance indicates that more materials were used than allowed by the standards. The direct materials quantity variance equals the standard unit price times the difference between the standard quantity allowed for the actual output and the actual quantity used.

**20.** David Rogers, purchasing manager at Fairway Manufacturing Corporation, was able to acquire a large quantity of direct materials from a new supplier at a discounted price. Marion Conner, inventory supervisor, is concerned because the warehouse has become crowded and some things had to be rearranged. Brian Jones, vice president of production, is concerned about the quality of the discounted materials. However, the Engineering Department tested the new materials and indicated that they are of acceptable quality. At the end of the month, Fairway experienced a favorable direct materials usage variance, a favorable direct labor usage variance, and a favorable direct materials price variance. The usage variances were solely the result of a higher yield from the new material. The favorable direct materials price variance is considered the responsibility of the

A. Purchasing manager.

B. Inventory supervisor.

C. Vice president of production.

D. Engineering manager.

Answer (A) is correct. *(CMA, adapted)*
**REQUIRED:** The person responsible for a direct materials price variance.
**DISCUSSION:** A direct materials price variance is the actual quantity used times the difference between the standard and actual prices. It is normally considered the responsibility of the purchasing manager because no one else has an opportunity to influence the price. In this case, the purchasing manager obtained the discount that led to the favorable price variance.
Answer (B) is incorrect because an inventory supervisor has no influence over the price paid for materials. Answer (C) is incorrect because the vice president receives the materials without knowing the price. Answer (D) is incorrect because the engineering manager is concerned only with the quality of the materials.

Questions 21 and 22 are based on the following information.

A company produces a gasoline additive. The standard costs and input for a 500-liter batch of the additive are presented below.

| Chemical | Standard Input Quantity in Liters | Standard Cost per Liter | Total Cost |
|---|---|---|---|
| Echol | 200 | $.200 | $ 40.00 |
| Protex | 100 | .425 | 42.50 |
| Benz | 250 | .150 | 37.50 |
| CT-40 | 50 | .300 | 15.00 |
| | 600 | | $135.00 |

The quantities purchased and used during the current period are shown below. A total of 140 batches were made during the current period.

| Chemical | Quantity Purchased (Liters) | Total Purchase Price | Quantity Used (Liters) |
|---|---|---|---|
| Echol | 25,000 | $ 5,365 | 26,600 |
| Protex | 13,000 | 6,240 | 12,880 |
| Benz | 40,000 | 5,840 | 37,800 |
| CT-40 | 7,500 | 2,220 | 7,140 |
| Total | 85,500 | $19,665 | 84,420 |

**21.** What is the direct materials mix variance for this operation?

A. $294 favorable.

B. $388.50 favorable.

C. $94.50 unfavorable.

D. $219.50 favorable.

Answer (B) is correct. *(Publisher)*
**REQUIRED:** The direct materials mix variance.
**DISCUSSION:** The direct materials mix variance equals the difference between the budgeted weighted-average standard unit cost for the budgeted mix and the budgeted weighted-average standard unit cost for the actual mix times the actual total quantity used. This variance is favorable if the standard weighted-average cost for the actual mix is less than the standard weighted-average cost for the budgeted mix. The standard mix weighted-average standard unit cost is $.225 per liter ($135 standard total cost ÷ 600 liters). The standard cost of the actual quantity used was $18,606 (see below). Thus, the actual mix weighted-average standard unit cost was $.220398 ($18,606 ÷ 84,420 liters used), and the mix variance was $388.50 favorable [84,420 liters × ($.225 – $.220398)].

$$26,600 \times \$.200 = \$ 5,320.00$$
$$12,880 \times .425 = 5,474.00$$
$$37,800 \times .150 = 5,670.00$$
$$7,140 \times .300 = 2,142.00$$
$$\$18,606.00$$

Answer (A) is incorrect because $294 favorable is the materials quantity variance. Answer (C) is incorrect because $94.50 unfavorable is the direct materials yield variance. Answer (D) is incorrect because $219.50 favorable is based on the actual mix of purchases.

**22.** What is the direct materials yield variance for this operation?

A. $294.50 favorable.

B. $388.50 favorable.

C. $94.50 unfavorable.

D. $219.50 favorable.

Answer (C) is correct. *(Publisher)*
**REQUIRED:** The direct materials yield variance.
**DISCUSSION:** The direct materials yield variance equals the difference between the actual input and the standard input allowed for the actual output times the budgeted weighted-average standard cost per input unit at the standard mix. The standard input for the actual output was 84,000 liters (140 batches × 600 liters per batch). The standard mix budgeted weighted-average standard unit cost is $.225 per liter ($135 total cost ÷ 600 liters). Thus, the yield variance is $94.50 unfavorable [(84,000 liters allowed – 84,420 liters used) × $.225].

Answer (A) is incorrect because $294.50 favorable is the direct materials quantity variance. Answer (B) is incorrect because $388.50 favorable is the direct materials mix variance. Answer (D) is incorrect because $219.50 favorable is based on the actual mix of purchases.

## 8.3 Direct Labor Variances

**23.** An unfavorable direct labor efficiency variance could be caused by a(n)

A. Unfavorable variable overhead spending variance.

B. Unfavorable direct materials usage variance.

C. Unfavorable fixed overhead volume variance.

D. Favorable variable overhead spending variance.

Answer (B) is correct. *(CMA, adapted)*
**REQUIRED:** The possible cause of an unfavorable direct labor efficiency variance.
**DISCUSSION:** An unfavorable direct labor efficiency variance indicates that actual hours exceeded standard hours. Too many hours may have been used because of inefficiency on the part of employees, excessive coffee breaks, machine down-time, inadequate materials, or materials of poor quality that required excessive rework. An unfavorable direct materials usage variance might be related to an unfavorable labor efficiency variance. Working on a greater quantity of direct materials may require more direct labor time.
Answer (A) is incorrect because the variable overhead spending variance may be affected by, but does not affect, a direct labor efficiency variance. It equals the difference between actual variable overhead, which includes indirect but not direct labor, and the variable overhead applied based on the standard rate and the actual activity level, which may or may not be measured in direct labor hours. Thus, the effect of an unfavorable direct labor efficiency variance is to decrease an unfavorable variable overhead spending variance or to increase a favorable variable overhead spending variance. Answer (C) is incorrect because the fixed overhead volume variance does not affect, and is not affected by, a direct labor efficiency variance. It equals the difference between budgeted fixed overhead and the fixed overhead applied based on the standard rate and the standard input (e.g., direct labor) allowed for the actual output. Answer (D) is incorrect because the variable overhead spending variance may be affected by, but does not affect, a direct labor efficiency variance. It equals the difference between actual variable overhead, which includes indirect but not direct labor, and the variable overhead applied based on the standard rate and the actual activity level, which may or may not be measured in direct labor hours. Thus, the effect of an unfavorable direct labor efficiency variance is to decrease an unfavorable variable overhead spending variance or to increase a favorable variable overhead spending variance.

**24.** The inventory control supervisor at Wilson Manufacturing Corporation reported that a large quantity of a part purchased for a special order that was never completed remains in stock. The order was not completed because the customer defaulted on the order. The part is not used in any of Wilson's regular products. After consulting with Wilson's engineers, the vice president of production approved the substitution of the purchased part for a regular part in a new product. Wilson's engineers indicated that the purchased part could be substituted providing it was modified. The units manufactured using the substituted part required additional direct labor hours resulting in an unfavorable direct labor efficiency variance in the Production Department. The unfavorable direct labor efficiency variance resulting from the substitution of the purchased part in inventory is best assigned to the

A. Sales manager.

B. Inventory supervisor.

C. Production manager.

D. Vice president of production.

Answer (D) is correct. *(CMA, adapted)*
**REQUIRED:** The person most responsible for an unfavorable direct labor efficiency variance caused by a part substitution.
**DISCUSSION:** An unfavorable direct labor efficiency variance is normally charged to the production manager, the person with the most control over the amount and kinds of direct labor used. However, that individual is not responsible. (S)he was told to use the nonconforming part that required extra labor time. Thus, the variance should be charged to the vice president of production, the individual who most influenced the incurrence of the cost.
Answer (A) is incorrect because the sales manager did not make the substitution decision. Answer (B) is incorrect because the inventory supervisor did not make the substitution decision. Answer (C) is incorrect because the production manager did not make the substitution decision.

**25.** Under a standard cost system, direct labor price variances are usually not attributable to

A. Union contracts approved before the budgeting cycle.

B. Labor rate predictions.

C. The use of a single average standard rate.

D. The assignment of different skill levels of workers than planned.

Answer (A) is correct.    *(CMA, adapted)*
**REQUIRED:** The factor that usually does not affect the direct labor price variance.
**DISCUSSION:** The direct labor price (rate) variance is the actual hours worked times the difference between the standard rate and the actual rate paid. This difference may be attributable to (1) a change in labor rates since the establishment of the standards, (2) using a single average standard rate despite different rates earned among different employees, (3) assigning higher-paid workers to jobs estimated to require lower-paid workers (or vice versa), or (4) paying hourly rates, but basing standards on piecework rates (or vice versa). The difference should not be caused by a union contract approved before the budgeting cycle because such rates would have been incorporated into the standards.
Answer (B) is incorrect because predictions about labor rates may have been inaccurate. Answer (C) is incorrect because using a single average standard rate may lead to variances if some workers are paid more than others and the proportions of hours worked differ from estimates. Answer (D) is incorrect because assigning higher paid (and higher skilled) workers to jobs not requiring such skills leads to an unfavorable variance.

**26.** Normal Company produced 600 units of one of its products last year. The standard for labor hours allowed was 2 hours per unit at a standard rate of $6 per hour. Actual hours worked amounted to 1,230 hours. The labor rate variance was $246 unfavorable, and the labor efficiency variance was $180 unfavorable. What was the actual direct labor cost for the period?

A. $7,134

B. $7,200

C. $7,380

D. $7,626

Answer (D) is correct.    *(Publisher)*
**REQUIRED:** The actual direct labor costs for the period.
**DISCUSSION:** The standard direct labor cost for 1,230 actual hours at $6 per hour equals $7,380. The rate variance of $246 was unfavorable, which means that the actual cost was $246 higher than the standard cost, or $7,626 ($7,380 + $246).
Answer (A) is incorrect because $7,134 assumes a favorable rate variance. Answer (B) is incorrect because $7,200 is based on the efficiency variance rather than the rate variance. Answer (C) is incorrect because $7,380 is the standard cost for actual hours. It does not adjust for the unfavorable rate variance.

**27.** The following is a standard cost variance analysis report on direct labor cost for a division of a manufacturing company.

| Job | Actual Hours at Actual Wages | Actual Hours at Standard Wages | Standard Hours at Standard Wages |
|-----|------------------------------|--------------------------------|----------------------------------|
| 213 | $ 3,243 | $ 3,700 | $ 3,100 |
| 215 | 15,345 | 15,675 | 15,000 |
| 217 | 6,754 | 7,000 | 6,600 |
| 219 | 19,788 | 18,755 | 19,250 |
| 221 | 3,370 | 3,470 | 2,650 |
| Totals | $48,500 | $48,600 | $46,600 |

What is the total flexible budget direct labor variance for the division?

A. $100 favorable.

B. $1,900 unfavorable.

C. $1,900 favorable.

D. $2,000 unfavorable.

Answer (B) is correct.    *(CIA, adapted)*
**REQUIRED:** The total flexible budget direct labor variance for the division.
**DISCUSSION:** The total flexible budget direct labor variance equals the difference between total actual direct labor cost and standard direct labor cost (standard hours × standard rate) allowed for the actual output. It combines the direct labor rate and efficiency variances. For this company, the variance is $1,900 U ($46,600 standard wages at standard hours – $48,500 actual wages at actual hours).
Answer (A) is incorrect because the direct labor rate variance is $100 F ($48,500 – $48,600). Answer (C) is incorrect because the total labor variance is unfavorable. Answer (D) is incorrect because the direct labor efficiency variance is $2,000 U.

**28.** Tub Co. uses a standard cost system. The following information pertains to direct labor for product B for the month of October:

- Standard hours allowed for actual production: 2,000
- Actual rate paid per hour: $8.40
- Standard rate per hour: $8.00
- Direct labor efficiency variance: $1,600 U

What were the actual hours worked?

   A. 1,800

   B. 1,810

   C. 2,190

   D. 2,200

Answer (D) is correct. *(CPA, adapted)*
   **REQUIRED:** The actual hours worked.
   **DISCUSSION:** The standard hours allowed equaled 2,000, and the direct labor efficiency variance was $1,600 unfavorable. Thus, actual hours exceeded standard hours. The direct labor efficiency variance equals the excess hours times the standard rate ($8 per hour). Given that the variance is $1,600, 200 excess hours ($1,600 ÷ $8) must have been worked. Thus, 2,200 actual hours (2,000 standard + 200 excess) were worked.
   Answer (A) is incorrect because the 200-hour difference between actual and standard hours should be added to, not subtracted from, the standard hours allowed. Answer (B) is incorrect because the difference between actual and standard hours must be determined using the standard rate per hour. The efficiency variance was also incorrectly treated as favorable and subtracted from the standard hours. Answer (C) is incorrect because the difference between standard and actual hours must be determined using the standard rate per hour.

**29.** The flexible budget for the month of May was for 9,000 units with direct materials at $15 per unit. Direct labor was budgeted at 45 minutes per unit for a total of $81,000. Actual output for the month was 8,500 units with $127,500 in direct materials and $77,775 in direct labor expense. The direct labor standard of 45 minutes was maintained throughout the month. Variance analysis of the performance for the month of May shows a(n)

   A. Favorable direct materials usage variance of $7,500.

   B. Favorable direct labor efficiency variance of $1,275.

   C. Unfavorable direct labor efficiency variance of $1,275.

   D. Unfavorable direct labor price variance of $1,275.

Answer (D) is correct. *(CMA, adapted)*
   **REQUIRED:** The result of variance analysis based on a flexible budget for direct labor and materials.
   **DISCUSSION:** The standard cost for direct materials is $127,500 (8,500 units × $15). Thus, no variance arose with respect to direct materials. Because direct labor for 9,000 units was budgeted at $81,000, the unit direct labor cost is $9. Thus, the direct labor budget for 8,500 units is $76,500, and the total direct labor variance is $1,275 ($77,775 − $76,500). Because the actual cost is greater than the budgeted amounts, the $1,275 variance is unfavorable. Given that the actual time per unit (45 minutes) was the same as that budgeted, no direct labor efficiency variance was incurred. Hence, the entire $1,275 unfavorable variance must be attributable to the direct labor rate (or price) variance.
   Answer (A) is incorrect because no direct materials variance occurred. The actual cost was equal to the budgeted cost for direct materials. Answer (B) is incorrect because no direct labor efficiency variance occurred. Budgeted hours were identical to actual hours for 8,500 units. Answer (C) is incorrect because no direct labor efficiency variance occurred. Budgeted hours were identical to actual hours for 8,500 units.

Questions 30 and 31 are based on the following information.

A company's standard direct labor rates in effect for the fiscal year ending June 30 and standard hours allowed for the output in April are

| | Standard DL Rate per Hour | Standard DLH Allowed for Output |
|---|---|---|
| Labor class III | $8.00 | 500 |
| Labor class II | 7.00 | 500 |
| Labor class I | 5.00 | 500 |

The wage rates for each labor class increased January 1 under the terms of a new union contract. The standard wage rates were not revised. The actual direct labor hours (DLH) and the actual direct labor rates for April were as follows:

| | Actual Rate | Actual DLH |
|---|---|---|
| Labor class III | $8.50 | 550 |
| Labor class II | 7.50 | 650 |
| Labor class I | 5.40 | 375 |

**30.** What is the direct labor yield variance (rounded)?

A. $500

B. $320

C. $820

D. $515

Answer (A) is correct. *(Publisher)*
REQUIRED: The direct labor yield variance for April.
DISCUSSION: The direct labor yield variance is the difference between budgeted and actual hours times the budgeted weighted-average rate for the planned mix. Total hours worked were 1,575 (550 + 650 + 375), standard hours allowed equaled 1,500 (500 + 500 + 500), and the budgeted weighted-average rate for the planned mix was $6.67 {[(500 × $8) + (500 × $7) + (500 × $5)] ÷ 1,500 standard DLH}. Thus, the variance is $500 unfavorable ($6.67 × 75).
Answer (B) is incorrect because $320 is the direct labor mix variance. Answer (C) is incorrect because $820 is the direct labor efficiency variance. Answer (D) is incorrect because $515 is based on the budgeted weighted-average rate for the actual mix.

**31.** What is the direct labor mix variance (rounded)?

A. $50.00

B. $320.00

C. $66.67

D. $500.00

Answer (B) is correct. *(Publisher)*
REQUIRED: The direct labor mix variance for April.
DISCUSSION: The direct labor mix variance is the difference between the budgeted weighted-average rates for the actual and planned mixes, times the actual labor inputs. The budgeted weighted-average rate for the planned mix is $6.67 (see preceding question). The budgeted weighted-average rate for the actual mix is $6.873 [(550 × $8) + (650 × $7) + (375 × $5) ÷ 1,575 actual DLH]. Thus, the direct labor mix variance is $320 [($6.873 − 6.67) × 1,575].
Answer (A) is incorrect because $50.00 is the variance for labor class II only [($7 − $6.67) × (650 DLH − 500 DLH)]. Answer (C) is incorrect because $66.67 is the variance for labor class III only [($8 − $6.67) × (550 DLH − 500 DLH)]. Answer (D) is incorrect because $500 is the direct labor yield variance.

## 8.4 Partial and Total Factor Productivity

**32.** A manufacturing cell's partial productivity can be measured using data on

A. Inventory shrinkage.

B. Inventory turnover.

C. Direct materials usage.

D. Scrap.

Answer (C) is correct. *(CIA, adapted)*
REQUIRED: The data used in measuring a manufacturing cell's partial productivity.
DISCUSSION: A partial productivity measure is the ratio of output quantity to input quantity for a single factor of production (e.g., materials, labor, capital). Partial productivity measures, for example, the number of finished units per direct labor hour or per pound of direct materials, are useful when compared over time among different production facilities or with benchmarks. A partial productivity measure comparing results over time determines whether the actual relationship between inputs and outputs has improved or deteriorated.
Answer (A) is incorrect because inventory shrinkage measures the effectiveness of internal control. Answer (B) is incorrect because inventory turnover measures the efficiency of asset usage. Answer (D) is incorrect because scrap is neither an input nor a good output.

**33.** The quantity of output divided by the quantity of one input equals

A. Gross margin.

B. Residual income.

C. Practical capacity.

D. Partial productivity.

Answer (D) is correct. *(Publisher)*
**REQUIRED:** The cost accounting term.
**DISCUSSION:** Partial productivity equals the quantity of output divided by the quantity of one input.
Answer (A) is incorrect because gross margin (profit) is the difference between sales and the absorption cost of goods sold. It should be contrasted with contribution margin (sales – variable costs) and profit margin (income ÷ revenue). Answer (B) is incorrect because residual income is the excess of the return on an investment over a targeted amount equal to an imputed interest charge on invested capital. The rate used is ordinarily the weighted-average cost of capital. Some enterprises prefer to measure managerial performance in terms of the amount of residual income rather than the percentage ROI. The principle is that the enterprise is expected to benefit from expansion as long as residual income is earned. Using a percentage ROI approach, expansion might be rejected if it lowered ROI even though residual income would increase. Answer (C) is incorrect because practical capacity is the maximum level at which output is produced efficiently. It allows for unavoidable delays in production for maintenance, holidays, etc. Use of practical capacity as a denominator value usually results in underapplied overhead because it always exceeds the actual use of capacity.

---

Questions 34 and 35 are based on the following information. Fabro, Inc. produced 1,500 units of Product RX-6 last week. The inputs to the production process for Product RX-6 were as follows:

> 450 pounds of Direct Material A at a cost of $1.50 per pound
> 300 pounds of Direct Material Z at a cost of $2.75 per pound
> 300 labor hours at a cost of $15.00 per hour

---

**34.** What is the total factor productivity for Product RX-6?

A. 2.00 units per pound.

B. 5.00 units per hour.

C. 0.25 units per dollar input.

D. 0.33 units per dollar input.

Answer (C) is correct. *(CMA, adapted)*
**REQUIRED:** The total factor productivity.
**DISCUSSION:** Total factor productivity equals units of output divided by the cost of all inputs. It varies with output levels, input prices, input quantities, and input mix. Hence, the total factor productivity equals 0.25 units per dollar input {1,500 units ÷ [(450 pounds of A × $1.50) + (300 pounds of Z × $2.75) + (300 hours × $15)]}.
Answer (A) is incorrect because the total factor productivity is measured in units of output per dollar of input. Answer (B) is incorrect because the total factor productivity is measured in units of output per dollar of input. Answer (D) is incorrect because 0.33 units per dollar input is based only on labor costs. All input costs should be included.

**35.** What is the best productivity measure for the first-line supervisor in Fabro, Inc.'s production plant?

A. 5.00 units per labor hour.

B. $2.00 per pound.

C. 0.33 units per dollar input.

D. $15.00 per labor hour.

Answer (A) is correct. *(CMA, adapted)*
**REQUIRED:** The best productivity measure for the first-line supervisor in the production plant.
**DISCUSSION:** A first-line supervisor's primary job is employee supervision, so his/her productivity should be measured on the basis of output per labor hour. Thus, 5 units per labor hour expended (1,500 units ÷ 300 labor hours) measures productivity based on the factor over which the first-line supervisor has the most control.
Answer (B) is incorrect because a first-line supervisor normally does not control the price paid for either direct materials or labor. Answer (C) is incorrect because the first-line supervisor does not control the prices paid for direct materials or labor. Accordingly, output per dollar of input is not a meaningful measure. Answer (D) is incorrect because a first-line supervisor normally does not control the price paid for either direct materials or labor.

**36.** The total factor productivity ratio

A. Will decrease from one period to the next as technological improvements permit greater output to be extracted from a given amount and mix of inputs.

B. Is the ratio of output to the cost of all inputs used.

C. Relates output to a single factor of production and does not consider substitutions among input factors.

D. Will decrease if a less costly input mixture is used.

Answer (B) is correct.  *(Publisher)*
**REQUIRED:** The true statement about a total factor productivity ratio.
**DISCUSSION:** A total factor productivity ratio is the ratio of output to the cost of all inputs used. Such a measure is considered superior to a partial productivity measure, which is the ratio of output quantity to input quantity for a single factor of production (e.g., materials, labor, capital). A disadvantage of a partial productivity measure is that it relates output to a single factor of production and therefore does not consider substitutions among input factors. The total factor productivity ratio will increase from one period to the next as technological improvements permit greater output to be extracted from a given amount and mix of inputs. Use of a less costly input mix also increases the ratio.
Answer (A) is incorrect because the ratio will increase with technological improvements. Answer (C) is incorrect because the ratio incorporates all factors of production into a single ratio. Answer (D) is incorrect because the ratio will increase if less costly inputs are used.

## 8.5 Overhead Variances

**37.** If overhead is applied on the basis of units of output, the variable overhead efficiency variance will be

A. Zero.

B. Favorable, if output exceeds the budgeted level.

C. Unfavorable, if output is less than the budgeted level.

D. A function of the direct labor efficiency variance.

Answer (A) is correct.  *(CMA, adapted)*
**REQUIRED:** The effect on the variable overhead efficiency variance.
**DISCUSSION:** The variable overhead efficiency variance equals the product of the variable overhead application rate and the difference between the standard input for the actual output and the actual input. Hence, the variance will be zero if variable overhead is applied on the basis of units of output because the difference between actual and standard input cannot be recognized.
Answer (B) is incorrect because the variance will be zero. Answer (C) is incorrect because the variance will be zero. Answer (D) is incorrect because the correlation between the variable overhead and direct labor efficiency variances occurs only when overhead is applied on the basis of direct labor.

---

Questions 38 through 41 are based on the following information.

Ardmore Enterprises uses a standard cost system in its small appliance division. The standard cost of manufacturing one unit of Zeb is as follows:

| | |
|---|---|
| Direct materials -- 60 pounds at $1.50 per pound | $ 90 |
| Direct labor -- 3 hours at $12 per hour | 36 |
| Overhead -- 3 hours at $8 per hour | 24 |
| Total standard cost per unit | $150 |

The budgeted variable overhead rate is $3 per direct labor hour, and the budgeted fixed overhead is $27,000 per month. During May, Ardmore produced 1,650 units of Zeb compared with a normal capacity of 1,800 units. The actual cost per unit was as follows:

| | |
|---|---|
| Direct materials (purchased and used) -- | |
| 58 pounds at $1.65 per pound | $ 95.70 |
| Direct labor -- 3.1 hours at $12 per hour | 37.20 |
| Overhead -- $39,930 per 1,650 units | 24.20 |
| Total actual cost per unit | $157.10 |

---

**38.** The total direct materials quantity variance for May is

A. $14,355 favorable.

B. $14,355 unfavorable.

C. $4,950 favorable.

D. $4,950 unfavorable.

Answer (C) is correct.  *(CMA, adapted)*
**REQUIRED:** The direct materials quantity variance.
**DISCUSSION:** The direct materials quantity variance equals the difference between the standard and actual quantities times the standard price. Hence, the favorable direct materials quantity variance is $4,950 [1,650 units × (60 standard pounds – 58 actual pounds) × $1.50 standard].
Answer (A) is incorrect because $14,355 is the amount of the direct materials price variance. Answer (B) is incorrect because $14,355 is the amount of the direct materials price variance. Answer (D) is incorrect because a favorable variance exists. The standard amount for the actual output exceeded the actual amount.

**39.** The direct materials price variance for May is

A. $14,355 unfavorable.

B. $14,850 unfavorable.

C. $14,355 favorable.

D. $14,850 favorable.

Answer (A) is correct.  *(CMA, adapted)*
    **REQUIRED:** The direct materials price variance.
    **DISCUSSION:** The direct materials price variance equals the actual quantity used times the difference between the standard and actual price per unit. Thus, the unfavorable direct materials price variance is $14,355 [1,650 units × 58 actual pounds × ($1.50 standard price – $1.65 actual price)].
    Answer (B) is incorrect because $14,850 is based on the standard unit quantity, not the actual quantity. Answer (C) is incorrect because the price variance is unfavorable. The actual price is greater than the standard price. Answer (D) is incorrect because $14,850 is based on the standard unit quantity, not the actual quantity.

**40.** The direct labor rate variance for May is

A. $1,920 favorable.

B. $0

C. $4,950 unfavorable.

D. $4,950 favorable.

Answer (B) is correct.  *(CMA, adapted)*
    **REQUIRED:** The direct labor rate variance.
    **DISCUSSION:** The direct labor rate variance equals the actual hours used times the difference between the standard and actual rates. Consequently, the direct labor rate variance is zero [1,650 units × 3.1 actual hours × ($12 per hour standard rate – $12 per hour actual rate)].
    Answer (A) is incorrect because $1,920 is the amount of the flexible budget overhead variance. Answer (C) is incorrect because $4,950 is the amount of the direct materials quantity variance. Answer (D) is incorrect because $4,950 is the amount of the direct materials quantity variance.

**41.** The flexible budget overhead variance for May is

A. $3,270 unfavorable.

B. $3,270 favorable.

C. $1,920 unfavorable.

D. $1,920 favorable.

Answer (D) is correct.  *(CMA, adapted)*
    **REQUIRED:** The flexible budget overhead variance.
    **DISCUSSION:** The flexible budget overhead variance is the difference between actual overhead costs and the flexible budget amount for the actual output. Standard total fixed costs at any level of production are $27,000. Standard variable overhead is $9 per unit (3 labor hours × $3). Thus, total standard variable overhead is $14,850 for the actual output (1,650 units × $9), and the total flexible budget amount is $41,850 ($27,000 FOH + $14,850 VOH). Accordingly, the favorable flexible budget variance is $1,920 favorable ($41,850 flexible budget amount – $39,930 actual amount).
    Answer (A) is incorrect because $3,270 is the flexible budget amount for an output of 1,800 units. Answer (B) is incorrect because $3,270 is the flexible budget amount for an output of 1,800 units. Answer (C) is incorrect because a favorable variance exists. Actual overhead is less than the standard overhead at the actual production level.

**42.** Variable overhead is applied on the basis of standard direct labor hours. If, for a given period, the direct labor efficiency variance is unfavorable, the variable overhead efficiency variance will be

A. Favorable.

B. Unfavorable.

C. Zero.

D. The same amount as the direct labor efficiency variance.

Answer (B) is correct.  *(CMA, adapted)*
    **REQUIRED:** The effect on the variable overhead efficiency variance.
    **DISCUSSION:** If variable overhead is applied to production on the basis of direct labor hours, both the variable overhead efficiency variance and the direct labor efficiency variance will be calculated on the basis of the same number of hours. If the direct labor efficiency variance is unfavorable, the overhead efficiency variance will also be unfavorable because both variances are based on the difference between standard and actual direct labor hours worked.
    Answer (A) is incorrect because both efficiency variances are based on the same number of hours worked. Thus, if one is unfavorable, the other will also be unfavorable. Answer (C) is incorrect because both efficiency variances are based on the same number of hours worked. Thus, if one is unfavorable, the other will also be unfavorable. Answer (D) is incorrect because the amount of the variances will be different depending on the amount of the costs anticipated and actually paid.

Questions 43 through 47 are based on the following information.

Water Control, Inc. manufactures water pumps and uses a standard cost system. The standard overhead costs per water pump are based on direct labor hours and are as follows:

Variable overhead (4 hours at $8 per hour)    $32
Fixed overhead (4 hours at $5* per hour)       20
    Total overhead cost per unit               $52

* Based on a capacity of 100,000 direct labor hours per month.

The following information is available for the month of November:

- 22,000 pumps were produced although 25,000 had been scheduled for production.
- 94,000 direct labor hours were worked at a total cost of $940,000.
- The standard direct labor rate is $9 per hour.
- The standard direct labor time per unit is four hours.
- Variable overhead costs were $740,000.
- Fixed overhead costs were $540,000.

**43.** The fixed overhead spending variance for November was

A. $40,000 unfavorable.

B. $70,000 unfavorable.

C. $460,000 unfavorable.

D. $240,000 unfavorable.

Answer (A) is correct. *(CMA, adapted)*
**REQUIRED:** The fixed overhead spending variance.
**DISCUSSION:** The fixed overhead spending (budget) variance is the difference between budgeted and actual fixed overhead. Actual fixed overhead was $540,000. Budgeted fixed overhead was $5 per hour based on a capacity of 100,000 direct labor hours per month, or $500,000. Because these costs are fixed, the budgeted fixed overhead is the same at any level of production. Hence, the variance is $40,000 unfavorable ($500,000 – $540,000).
Answer (B) is incorrect because $70,000 unfavorable is the difference between actual fixed overhead and the product of the standard rate and the actual direct labor hours. Answer (C) is incorrect because $460,000 unfavorable is the volume variance. Answer (D) is incorrect because $240,000 unfavorable is the difference between actual variable overhead and budgeted fixed overhead.

**44.** The variable overhead spending variance for November was

A. $60,000 favorable.

B. $12,000 favorable.

C. $48,000 unfavorable.

D. $40,000 unfavorable.

Answer (B) is correct. *(CMA, adapted)*
**REQUIRED:** The variable overhead spending variance.
**DISCUSSION:** The variable overhead spending variance is the difference between actual variable overhead and the variable overhead based on the standard rate and the actual activity level. Thus, the variable overhead spending variance was $12,000 favorable [(94,000 actual hours × $8 standard rate) – $740,000 actual cost].
Answer (A) is incorrect because $60,000 favorable is based on 100,000 hours, not the actual hours of 94,000. Answer (C) is incorrect because $48,000 unfavorable is the variable overhead efficiency variance. Answer (D) is incorrect because $40,000 unfavorable is the fixed overhead spending variance.

**45.** The variable overhead efficiency variance for November was

A. $48,000 unfavorable.

B. $60,000 favorable.

C. $96,000 unfavorable.

D. $200,000 unfavorable.

Answer (A) is correct. *(CMA, adapted)*
**REQUIRED:** The variable overhead efficiency variance.
**DISCUSSION:** The variable overhead efficiency variance equals the standard price ($8 an hour) times the difference between the actual hours and the standard hours allowed for the actual output. Thus, the variance is $48,000 unfavorable {[(22,000 units produced × 4 standard hours per unit) – 94,000 actual hours] × $8}.
Answer (B) is incorrect because $60,000 favorable is the variable overhead spending variance calculated based on capacity, not actual hours. Answer (C) is incorrect because $96,000 unfavorable is based on the difference between standard hours allowed for the actual output and capacity hours. Answer (D) is incorrect because $200,000 unfavorable is the excess of actual direct labor costs over actual variable overhead costs.

**46.** The direct labor price variance for November was

A. $54,000 unfavorable.

B. $94,000 unfavorable.

C. $60,000 favorable.

D. $148,000 unfavorable.

Answer (B) is correct. *(CMA, adapted)*
REQUIRED: The direct labor price (rate) variance.
DISCUSSION: The direct labor price variance equals actual labor hours times the difference between standard and actual labor rates. The actual direct labor cost was $940,000 for 94,000 hours, or $10 per hour. The standard rate was $9 per hour. Thus, the variance is $94,000 unfavorable [94,000 hours × ($9 − $10)].
Answer (A) is incorrect because $54,000 unfavorable is the direct labor efficiency variance. Answer (C) is incorrect because $60,000 favorable equals the actual rate times the difference between capacity and actual hours. Answer (D) is incorrect because $148,000 unfavorable is the total direct labor variance.

**47.** The direct labor efficiency variance for November was

A. $108,000 favorable.

B. $120,000 favorable.

C. $60,000 favorable.

D. $54,000 unfavorable.

Answer (D) is correct. *(CMA, adapted)*
REQUIRED: The direct labor efficiency variance.
DISCUSSION: The direct labor efficiency variance equals the difference between standard and actual hours times the standard rate. Hence, the variance is $54,000 unfavorable {[(22,000 units × 4 standard hours per unit) × 94,000 hours] × $9}. The variance is unfavorable because the actual hours exceeded the standard hours.
Answer (A) is incorrect because $108,000 favorable is based on the difference between standard and capacity hours. Answer (B) is incorrect because $120,000 favorable is based on the actual rate and the difference between standard hours and capacity. Answer (C) is incorrect because $60,000 favorable is based on the actual rate and the difference between actual hours and capacity.

**48.** The variance in an absorption costing system that measures the departure from the denominator level of activity that was used to set the fixed overhead rate is the

A. Spending variance.

B. Efficiency variance.

C. Production volume variance.

D. Flexible budget variance.

Answer (C) is correct. *(CMA, adapted)*
REQUIRED: The difference between actual production and the denominator level of production.
DISCUSSION: A denominator level of activity must be used to establish the standard cost (application rate) for fixed overhead. The production volume variance is the difference between budgeted fixed costs and the standard cost per unit of input times the standard units of input allowed for the actual production.
Answer (A) is incorrect because the fixed overhead spending variance is the difference between actual fixed costs and budgeted costs. Answer (B) is incorrect because the efficiency variance is applicable to variable overhead. Answer (D) is incorrect because the flexible budget variance is the difference between actual and budgeted amounts in a flexible budget.

Questions 49 through 53 are based on the following information.

Funtime, Inc. manufactures video game machines. Market saturation and technological innovations have caused pricing pressures which have resulted in declining profits. To stem the slide in profits until new products can be introduced, an incentive program has been developed to reward production managers who contribute to an increase in the number of units produced and effect cost reductions.

The managers have responded to the pressure of improving manufacturing in several ways. The video game machines are put together by the Assembly Group which requires parts from both the Printed Circuit Boards (PCB) and the Reading Heads (RH) groups. To attain increased production levels, the PCB and RH groups commenced rejecting parts that previously would have been tested and modified to meet manufacturing standards. Preventive maintenance on machines used in the production of these parts has been postponed with only emergency repair work being performed to keep production lines moving.

The more aggressive Assembly Group production supervisors have pressured maintenance personnel to attend to their machines at the expense of other groups. This has resulted in machine downtime in the PCB and RH groups that, when coupled with demands for accelerated parts delivery by the Assembly Group, has led to more frequent parts rejections and increased friction among departments.

Funtime operates under a standard cost system. The standard costs for video game machines are as follows:

| Cost Item | Standard Cost per Unit | | |
| --- | --- | --- | --- |
| | Quantity | Cost | Total |
| Direct Materials | | | |
| Housing unit | 1 | $20 | $ 20 |
| Printed circuit boards | 2 | 15 | 30 |
| Reading heads | 4 | 10 | 40 |
| Direct labor hours | | | |
| Assembly group | 2 | 8 | 16 |
| PCB group | 1 | 9 | 9 |
| RH group | 1.5 | 10 | 15 |
| Variable overhead hours | 4.5 | 2 | 9 |
| Total standard cost per unit | | | $139 |

Funtime prepares monthly performance reports based on standard costs. Presented below is the contribution report for May when production and sales both reached 2,200 units.

Funtime, Inc.
Contribution Report
For the Month of May

| | Budget | Actual | Variance |
| --- | --- | --- | --- |
| Units | 2,000 | 2,200 | 200F |
| Revenue | $400,000 | $440,000 | $40,000F |
| Variable costs | | | |
| Direct materials | 180,000 | 220,400 | 40,400U |
| Direct labor | 80,000 | 93,460 | 13,460U |
| Variable overhead | 18,000 | 18,800 | 800U |
| Total variable costs | 278,000 | 332,660 | 54,660U |
| Contribution margin | $122,000 | $107,340 | $14,660U |

Funtime's top management was surprised by the unfavorable contribution to overall corporate profits despite the increased sales in May. Jack Rath, cost accountant, was assigned to identify the reasons for the unfavorable contribution results as well as the individuals or groups responsible. After review, Rath prepared the Usage Report presented below.

Funtime, Inc.
Usage Report
For the Month of May

| Cost Item | Quantity | Actual Cost |
| --- | --- | --- |
| Direct materials | | |
| Housing units | 2,200 units | $ 44,000 |
| Printed circuit boards | 4,700 units | 75,200 |
| Reading heads | 9,200 units | 101,200 |
| Direct labor | | |
| Assembly | 3,900 hours | 31,200 |
| Printed circuit boards | 2,400 hours | 23,760 |
| Reading heads | 3,500 hours | 38,500 |
| Variable overhead | 9,900 hours | 18,800 |
| Total variable cost | | $332,660 |

Rath reported that the PCB and RH groups supported the increased production levels but experienced abnormal machine downtime, causing the idling of workers that required the use of overtime to keep up with the accelerated demand for parts. The idle time was charged to direct labor. Rath also reported that the production managers of these two groups resorted to parts rejections, as opposed to testing and modification procedures formerly applied. Rath determined that the Assembly Group met management's objectives by increasing production while using lower than standard hours.

**49.** What is the total direct materials price variance?

A. $346,500 favorable.

B. $346,500 unfavorable.

C. $13,900 favorable.

D. $13,900 unfavorable.

Answer (D) is correct. *(Publisher)*

**REQUIRED:** The total direct materials price variance.

**DISCUSSION:** The total direct materials price variance is found by multiplying the difference between the standard price and the actual price by the actual quantity. The actual price is calculated by dividing actual cost by actual quantity. Thus, the actual prices are $20 per unit ($44,000 ÷ 2,200) for housing units, $16 per unit ($75,200 ÷ 4,700) for printed circuit boards, and $11 per unit ($101,200 ÷ 9,200) for reading heads. Thus, total direct materials price variance is

| | | | |
|---|---|---|---|
| Housing units: | 2,200 × ($20 − $20) = | $ | 0 |
| Printed circuit boards: | 4,700 × ($15 − $16) = | | 4,700 U |
| Reading heads: | 9,200 × ($10 − $11) = | | 9,200 U |
| | | | $13,900 U |

Answer (A) is incorrect because $346,500 favorable results from using the standard cost per unit for each direct material, and by reversing the order of subtraction. Answer (B) is incorrect because $346,500 unfavorable results from using the standard cost per unit for each direct material. Answer (C) is incorrect because the price variance is unfavorable when the actual price is greater than the standard price.

**50.** What is the total direct materials quantity variance?

A. $8,500 unfavorable.

B. $8,500 favorable.

C. $9,200 unfavorable.

D. $9,200 favorable.

Answer (A) is correct. *(Publisher)*

**REQUIRED:** The total direct materials quantity variance.

**DISCUSSION:** The total direct materials quantity variance is found by multiplying the difference between the standard quantity and actual quantity by the standard price. Standard quantities are calculated by multiplying the actual units by the standard quantity per unit. The standard quantities are 2,200 parts (2,200 × 1) for housing units, 4,400 parts (2,200 × 2) for printed circuit boards, and 8,800 parts (2,200 × 4) for reading heads. Thus, the total direct materials quantity variance is

| | | | |
|---|---|---|---|
| Housing units: | (2,200 − 2,200) × $20 = | $ | 0 |
| Printed circuit boards: | (4,400 − 4,700) × $15 = | | 4,500 U |
| Reading heads: | (8,800 − 9,200) × $10 = | | 4,000 U |
| | | | $8,500 U |

Answer (B) is incorrect because $8,500 favorable results from reversing the order of subtraction. Answer (C) is incorrect because $9,200 unfavorable results from multiplying by the actual price. Answer (D) is incorrect because $9,200 favorable results from multiplying by the actual price and reversing the order of subtraction.

**51.** What is the variable overhead efficiency variance?

A. $0

B. $900 unfavorable.

C. $9,900 unfavorable.

D. $9,900 favorable.

Answer (A) is correct. *(Publisher)*

**REQUIRED:** The variable overhead efficiency variance.

**DISCUSSION:** The variable overhead efficiency variance is found by multiplying the difference between standard hours and actual hours by the standard rate. The number of standard hours is calculated by multiplying the actual units by the standard hours per unit. Thus, the number of standard hours is 9,900 ($2,200 × 4.5 hours per unit), and the variable overhead efficiency variance is $0 [(9,900 − 9,900) × $2].

Answer (B) is incorrect because $900 unfavorable results from multiplying by the budgeted number of units, 2,000, instead of actual, 2,200. Answer (C) is incorrect because $9,900 unfavorable results from using a standard hours per unit rate of 9 hours and reversing the order of subtraction. Answer (D) is incorrect because $9,900 favorable results from using a standard hours per unit rate of 9 hours.

**52.** Refer to the information on the preceding page(s). What is the variable overhead spending variance?

A. $1,000 unfavorable.

B. $1,000 favorable.

C. $1,800 unfavorable.

D. $1,800 favorable.

Answer (B) is correct. *(Publisher)*
REQUIRED: The variable overhead spending variance.
DISCUSSION: The variable overhead spending variance is found by subtracting actual variable overhead from the product of actual hours and the standard rate. Accordingly, the variable overhead spending variance is $1,000 favorable [(9,900 × $2) – $18,800].
Answer (A) is incorrect because $1,000 unfavorable results from reversing the order of subtraction. Answer (C) is incorrect because $1,800 unfavorable results from using the budgeted variable overhead and by reversing the order of subtraction. Answer (D) is incorrect because $1,800 favorable results from using the budgeted variable overhead.

**53.** Refer to the information on the preceding page(s). What is the contribution margin volume variance?

A. $9,800 unfavorable.

B. $9,800 favorable.

C. $12,200 favorable.

D. $14,660 unfavorable.

Answer (C) is correct. *(Publisher)*
REQUIRED: The contribution margin volume variance.
DISCUSSION: The contribution margin volume variance is found by multiplying budgeted unit contribution by the difference between actual units and budgeted units. The budgeted unit contribution is $61 ($122,000 ÷ 2,000 units). Thus, the variance is $12,200 favorable [(2,200 actual units – 2,000 budgeted units) × $61 per unit].
Answer (A) is incorrect because $9,800 unfavorable results from multiplying by the actual unit contribution and reversing the order of subtraction. Answer (B) is incorrect because $9,800 favorable results from multiplying by the actual unit contribution. Answer (D) is incorrect because $14,660 unfavorable is the variance between budgeted and actual contribution margins.

**54.** The production volume variance is due to

A. Inefficient or efficient use of direct labor hours.

B. Efficient or inefficient use of variable overhead.

C. Difference from the planned level of the base used for overhead allocation and the actual level achieved.

D. Excessive application of direct labor hours over the standard amounts for the output level actually achieved.

Answer (C) is correct. *(CMA, adapted)*
REQUIRED: The cause of the production volume variance.
DISCUSSION: The production volume variance (also called an idle capacity variance) is a component of the total overhead variance. It is the difference between budgeted fixed costs and the product of the standard fixed cost per unit of input times the standard units of input allowed for the actual output. Thus, the production volume variance equals under- or overapplied fixed overhead. This variance results when actual activity differs from the activity base used to calculate the fixed overhead application rate.
Answer (A) is incorrect because the direct labor efficiency variance relates to inefficient or efficient use of direct labor hours. Answer (B) is incorrect because the variable overhead efficiency variance relates to efficient or inefficient use of variable overhead. Answer (D) is incorrect because the volume variance is related to overhead application, not direct labor.

Questions 55 and 56 are based on the following information. Tiny Tykes Corporation had the following activity relating to its fixed and variable overhead for the month of July:

Actual costs
| | |
|---|---|
| Fixed overhead | $120,000 |
| Variable overhead | 80,000 |

Flexible budget
(Actual output achieved ×
budgeted rate)
| | |
|---|---|
| Variable overhead | 90,000 |

Applied
(Standard input allowed for actual
output achieved × budgeted rate)
| | |
|---|---|
| Fixed overhead | 125,000 |
| Variable overhead spending variance | 2,000 F |
| Production volume variance | 5,000 U |

**55.** If the budgeted rate for applying variable overhead was $20 per direct labor hour, how efficient or inefficient was Tiny Tykes Corporation in terms of using direct labor hours as an activity base?

A. 100 direct labor hours inefficient.

B. 100 direct labor hours efficient.

C. 400 direct labor hours inefficient.

D. 400 direct labor hours efficient.

Answer (D) is correct. *(CMA, adapted)*
**REQUIRED:** The efficiency variance stated in terms of direct labor hours.
**DISCUSSION:** The variable overhead spending and efficiency variances are the components of the total variable overhead variance. Given that actual variable overhead was $80,000 and the flexible budget amount was $90,000, the total variance is $10,000 favorable. If the overhead spending variance is $2,000 favorable, the efficiency variance must be $8,000 favorable ($10,000 total – $2,000 spending). At a rate of $20 per hour, this variance is equivalent to 400 direct labor hours ($8,000 ÷ $20).
Answer (A) is incorrect because the variances are favorable. Answer (B) is incorrect because 100 direct labor hours are equivalent to the spending variance (100 hours × $20 = $2,000). Answer (C) is incorrect because the variances are favorable.

**56.** The fixed overhead efficiency variance is

A. $3,000 favorable.

B. $3,000 unfavorable.

C. $5,000 favorable.

D. Never a meaningful variance.

Answer (D) is correct. *(CMA, adapted)*
**REQUIRED:** The fixed overhead efficiency variance.
**DISCUSSION:** Variable overhead variances can be subdivided into spending and efficiency components. However, fixed overhead variances do not have an efficiency component because fixed costs, by definition, are not related to changing levels of output. Fixed overhead variances are typically subdivided into a budget (or fixed overhead spending) variance and a volume variance.
Answer (A) is incorrect because efficiency variances are applicable to variable costs. Answer (B) is incorrect because efficiency variances are applicable to variable costs. Answer (C) is incorrect because efficiency variances are applicable to variable costs.

Questions 57 through 61 are based on the following information. Nanjones Company manufactures a line of products distributed nationally through wholesalers. Presented below are planned manufacturing data for the year and actual data for November of the current year. The company applies overhead based on planned machine hours using a predetermined annual rate.

| | Planning Data | | | Data for November |
|---|---|---|---|---|
| | Annual | November | | |
| Fixed overhead | $1,200,000 | $100,000 | Direct labor hours (actual) | 4,200 |
| Variable overhead | $2,400,000 | $220,000 | Direct labor hours (plan based on output) | 4,000 |
| Direct labor hours | 48,000 | 4,000 | Machine hours (actual) | 21,600 |
| Machine hours | 240,000 | 22,000 | Machine hours (plan based on output) | 21,000 |
| | | | Fixed overhead | $101,200 |
| | | | Variable overhead | $214,000 |

**57.** The predetermined overhead application rate for Nanjones Company is

A. $5.00

B. $25.00

C. $10.00

D. $15.00

Answer (D) is correct. *(CMA, adapted)*
**REQUIRED:** The predetermined overhead application rate.
**DISCUSSION:** The predetermined overhead application rate is $15 [($1,200,000 FOH + $2,400,000 VOH) ÷ 240,000 machine hours].
Answer (A) is incorrect because $5 is the fixed overhead application rate. Answer (B) is incorrect because $25 is the fixed overhead per labor hour. Answer (C) is incorrect because $10 is the variable portion of the overhead application rate.

**58.** The total amount of overhead applied to production for November was

A. $316,200

B. $315,000

C. $320,000

D. $300,000

Answer (B) is correct. *(CMA, adapted)*
**REQUIRED:** The total amount of overhead applied to production for the month.
**DISCUSSION:** Overhead is applied on the basis of planned machine hours. The predetermined overhead application rate is $15 [($1,200,000 FOH + $2,400,000 VOH) ÷ 240,000 machine hours]. Thus, total overhead applied was $315,000 (21,000 planned machine hours based on output × $15).
Answer (A) is incorrect because the total overhead applied was $315,000 based on 21,000 hours at $15 per hour. Answer (C) is incorrect because the total overhead applied was $315,000 based on 21,000 hours at $15 per hour. Answer (D) is incorrect because $300,000 is based on planned direct labor hours at $75 per hour.

**59.** The amount of over- or underapplied variable manufacturing overhead for November was

A. $6,000 overapplied.

B. $4,000 underapplied.

C. $20,000 overapplied.

D. $6,000 underapplied.

Answer (B) is correct. *(CMA, adapted)*
**REQUIRED:** The amount of over- or underapplied variable overhead for the month.
**DISCUSSION:** Variable overhead applied in November was $210,000 [21,000 planned machine hours based on output × ($2,400,000 planned annual VOH ÷ 240,000 planned machine hours)]. Because the applied overhead was less than actual ($214,000), underapplied variable overhead equaled $4,000.
Answer (A) is incorrect because the overhead was underapplied. Answer (C) is incorrect because the overhead was underapplied. Answer (D) is incorrect because $6,000 is based on the 22,000 machine hours planned for November rather than the planned hours for actual output.

**60.** The variable overhead spending variance for November was

A. $2,000 favorable.

B. $6,000 favorable.

C. $14,000 unfavorable.

D. $6,000 unfavorable.

Answer (A) is correct. *(CMA, adapted)*
**REQUIRED:** The variable overhead spending variance.
**DISCUSSION:** The variable overhead spending variance equals the difference between actual variable overhead and the product of the actual input and the budgeted application rate. At a variable overhead application rate (standard cost) of $10 per machine hour ($2,400,000 ÷ 240,000 hours), the total standard cost for the 21,600 actual hours was $216,000. Given actual costs of $214,000, the favorable variance is $2,000.
Answer (B) is incorrect because $6,000 is based on planned machine hours of 22,000. Answer (C) is incorrect because the variance is favorable. Answer (D) is incorrect because the variance is favorable.

**61.** The fixed overhead volume variance for November was

   A. $1,200 unfavorable.

   B. $5,000 unfavorable.

   C. $10,000 favorable.

   D. $5,000 favorable.

Answer (D) is correct. *(CMA, adapted)*
   **REQUIRED:** The fixed overhead volume variance.
   **DISCUSSION:** The fixed overhead volume (production volume or idle capacity) variance is the difference between budgeted fixed costs and the product of the standard fixed overhead cost per unit of input and the standard units of input allowed for the actual output. Budgeted fixed costs for the month were $100,000. The standard cost of actual output was $105,000 [21,000 machine hours planned for actual output × ($1,200,000 planned annual FOH ÷ 240,000 planned annual machine hours) FOH application rate]. Hence, the fixed overhead volume variance was $5,000 favorable. It was favorable because the budget for fixed overhead was less than the amount applied to jobs. An overapplication of fixed overhead suggests that output exceeded expectations.
   Answer (A) is incorrect because the variance was favorable. Answer (B) is incorrect because the variance was favorable. Answer (C) is incorrect because $10,000 is based on 22,000 planned machine hours.

**62.** Coach Corporation is considering which capacity measure is appropriate to use as the denominator level of activity when applying fixed overhead to units produced. Assume that Coach selects direct labor hours as the cost driver and the following additional data are available from the prior year:

|  | Hours |
|---|---|
| Standard direct labor hours for normal capacity | 200,000 |
| Standard direct labor hours allowed for units produced in the prior year | 210,000 |
| Standard direct labor hours for the master budget capacity | 220,000 |

Which of the following capacity measures for the denominator-level of activity would have resulted in an unfavorable volume variance?

   A. Both normal capacity and master budget capacity.

   B. Neither normal capacity nor master budget capacity.

   C. Normal capacity only.

   D. Master budget capacity only.

Answer (D) is correct. *(CMA, adapted)*
   **REQUIRED:** The capacity measures for the denominator-level of activity that would have resulted in an unfavorable volume variance.
   **DISCUSSION:** The volume (production volume or idle capacity) variance is the amount of under- or overapplied fixed overhead. It is the difference between budgeted fixed overhead and the amount applied based on a predetermined rate and the standard input allowed for actual output. It measures the use of capacity rather than specific cost outlays. The predetermined rate equals the budgeted overhead divided by a measure of capacity. Consequently, when the standard input allowed for actual output exceeds the budgeted capacity, fixed overhead is overapplied, and the volume variance is favorable. If the master budget capacity is the denominator value, the volume variance is unfavorable. Conversely, when the standard input allowed for actual output is less than the budgeted capacity, fixed overhead is underapplied, and the volume variance is unfavorable. If the normal capacity is the denominator value, the volume variance is favorable.
   Answer (A) is incorrect because the standard input for the actual output exceeds normal capacity. Thus, use of normal capacity results in a favorable volume variance. Answer (B) is incorrect because the standard input for the actual output exceeds normal capacity. Thus, use of normal capacity results in a favorable volume variance. Answer (C) is incorrect because use of master budget capacity results in an unfavorable variance.

Questions 63 through 69 are based on the following information.

PortCo Products is a divisionalized furniture manufacturer. The divisions are autonomous segments, with each division being responsible for its own sales, costs of operations, working capital management, and equipment acquisition. Each division serves a different market in the furniture industry. Because the markets and products of the divisions are so different, there have never been any transfers between divisions.

The Commercial Division manufactures equipment and furniture that is purchased by the restaurant industry. The division plans to introduce a new line of counter and chair units that feature a cushioned seat for the counter chairs. John Kline, the division manager, has discussed the manufacturing of the cushioned seat with Russ Fiegel of the Office Division. They both believe a cushioned seat currently made by the Office Division for use on its deluxe office stool could be modified for use on the new counter chair. Consequently, Kline has asked Russ Fiegel for a price for 100-unit lots of the cushioned seat. The following conversation took place about the price to be charged for the cushioned seats:

Fiegel: "John, we can make the necessary modifications to the cushioned seat easily. The direct materials used in your seat are slightly different and should cost about 10% more than those used in our deluxe office stool. However, the direct labor time should be the same because the seat fabrication operation basically is the same. I would price the seat at our regular rate--full cost plus 30% markup."

Kline: "That's higher than I expected, Russ. I was thinking that a good price would be your variable manufacturing costs. After all, your capacity costs will be incurred regardless of this job."

Fiegel: "John, I'm at capacity. By making the cushion seats for you, I'll have to cut my production of deluxe office stools. Of course, I can increase my production of economy office stools. The direct labor time freed by not having to fabricate the frame or assemble the deluxe stool can be shifted to the frame fabrication and assembly of the economy office stool. Fortunately, I can switch my labor force between these two models of stools without any loss of efficiency. As you know, overtime is not a feasible alternative in our community. I'd like to sell it to you at variable cost, but I have excess demand for both products. I don't mind changing my product mix to the economy model if I get a good return on the seats I make for you. Here are my standard costs for the two stools and a schedule of my overhead."

Kline: "I guess I see your point, Russ, but I don't want to price myself out of the market. Maybe we should talk to Corporate to see if they can give us any guidance."

| Office Division Standard Costs and Prices | | | |
|---|---|---|---|
| | Deluxe Office Stool | | Economy Office Stool |
| Direct materials | | | |
| Framing | $ 8.15 | | $ 9.76 |
| Cushioned seat | | | |
| Padding | 2.40 | | -- |
| Vinyl | 4.00 | | -- |
| Molded seat (purchased) | -- | | 6.00 |
| Direct labor | | | |
| Frame fabrication (.5 × $7.50 per DLH) | 3.75 | (.5 × $7.50 per DLH) | 3.75 |
| Cushion fabrication (.5 × $7.50 per DLH) | 3.75 | | -- |
| Assembly* (.5 × $7.50 per DLH) | 3.75 | (.5 × $7.50 per DLH) | 2.25 |
| Overhead (1.5 DLH × $12.80 per DLH) | 19.20 | (.8 DLH × $12.80 per DLH) | 10.24 |
| Total standard cost | $45.00 | | $32.00 |
| Selling price (30% markup) | $58.50 | | $41.60 |

*Attaching seats to frames and attaching rubber feet.

| Office Division Overhead Budget | | |
|---|---|---|
| Overhead Item | Nature | Amount |
| Supplies | Variable--at current market prices | $ 420,000 |
| Indirect labor | Variable | 375,000 |
| Supervision | Nonvariable | 250,000 |
| Power | Use varies with activity; rates are fixed | 180,000 |
| Heat and light | Nonvariable--light is fixed regardless of production while heat/ air conditioning varies with fuel charges | 140,000 |
| Property taxes and insurance taxes | Nonvariable--any change in amounts/ rates is independent of production | 200,000 |
| Depreciation | Fixed dollar total | 1,700,000 |
| Employee benefits | 20% of supervision, direct and indirect labor | 575,000 |
| Total overhead | | $3,840,000 |
| Capacity in DLH | | 300,000 |
| Overhead rate per DLH | | $    12.80 |

**63.** What amount of employee benefits is associated with direct labor costs?

- A.  $675,000
- B.  $75,000
- C.  $450,000
- D.  $500,000

Answer (C) is correct.  *(Publisher)*
**REQUIRED:** The amount of employee benefits that is associated with direct labor costs.
**DISCUSSION:** The total employee benefits include 20% of supervision and direct and indirect labor costs. To find the amount associated with direct labor, 20% of supervision and indirect labor costs are subtracted from total employee benefits {$575,000 − [($250,000 + $375,000) × 20%]}, or $450,000.
Answer (A) is incorrect because 20% of supervision and indirect labor costs need to be subtracted from total employee benefits to determine the employee benefits associated with direct labor costs. Answer (B) is incorrect because $75,000 is the result of deducting 80% of supervision and indirect labor costs from total employee benefits. Answer (D) is incorrect because 20% of supervision also needs to be deducted.

**64.** What is the variable overhead rate?

A. $7.80 per hr.

B. $11.25 per hr.

C. $5.17 per hr.

D. $5.00 per hr.

Answer (D) is correct. *(Publisher)*
    **REQUIRED:** The variable overhead rate.
    **DISCUSSION:** To determine the variable overhead rate, all variable amounts must be totaled ($1,500,000) and divided by the capacity in DLH (300,000).

| | Total | Per DLH |
|---|---|---|
| Supplies | $ 420,000 | $1.40 |
| Indirect labor | 375,000 | 1.25 |
| Power | 180,000 | .60 |
| Employee benefits: | | |
|   20% direct labor | 450,000 | 1.50 |
|   20% indirect labor | 75,000 | .25 |
|   Total | $1,500,000 | $5.00 |

    Answer (A) is incorrect because $7.80 per hr. is the fixed overhead rate per direct labor hour. Answer (B) is incorrect because the variable overhead rate is determined by dividing variable expenses (supplies, indirect labor, power, and direct and indirect labor benefits) by direct labor hours. Answer (C) is incorrect because $5.17 per hr. incorrectly includes supervision benefits of $50,000.

**65.** What is the transfer price per 100-unit lot based on variable manufacturing costs to produce the modified cushioned seat?

A. $1,329

B. $1,869

C. $789

D. $1,986

Answer (A) is correct. *(Publisher)*
    **REQUIRED:** The transfer price based on the variable manufacturing cost.
    **DISCUSSION:** The variable manufacturing cost to produce a 100-unit lot is 100 times the sum of direct materials, direct labor, and variable overhead per seat.

| | | |
|---|---|---|
| Cushion materials: | | |
|   Padding | $2.40 | |
|   Vinyl | 4.00 | |
|     Total cushion materials | $6.40 | |
| Cost increase 10% (given) | ×1.10 | |
|   Cost of cushioned seat | | $7.04 |
| | | |
| Cushion fabrication labor ($7.50 per DLH × .5 DLH) | | 3.75 |
| Variable overhead ($5.00 per DLH × .5 DLH) | | 2.50 |
| Total variable cost per cushioned seat | | $13.29 |
| Total variable cost per 100-unit lot | | $1,329 |

    Answer (B) is incorrect because $1,869 is the transfer price plus the opportunity cost of $540 of the Office Division. Answer (C) is incorrect because $789 is the transfer price minus the opportunity cost of $540 of the Office Division. Answer (D) is incorrect because the transfer price based on the variable manufacturing costs is $1,329.

**66.** What is the fixed manufacturing overhead rate?

A. $7.80 per hr.

B. $11.25 per hr.

C. $5.17 per hr.

D. $5.00 per hr.

Answer (A) is correct. *(Publisher)*
    **REQUIRED:** The fixed overhead rate.
    **DISCUSSION:** Total fixed overhead is $2,340,000 (see below). It is divided by the 300,000-hour level of activity to determine the $7.80 hourly rate.

| | |
|---|---|
| Supervision | $ 250,000 |
| Heat and light | 140,000 |
| Property taxes and insurance | 200,000 |
| Depreciation | 1,700,000 |
| Benefits (20% of supervision) | 50,000 |
| | $2,340,000 |

    Answer (B) is incorrect because the fixed overhead rate is determined by dividing fixed expenses (supervision, heat and light, property taxes and insurance, depreciation, and supervision benefits) by direct labor hours. Answer (C) is incorrect because $5.17 per hr. incorrectly includes supervision benefits of $50,000. Answer (D) is incorrect because $5.00 per hr. is the variable overhead rate per hour.

**67.** Refer to the information on the preceding page(s). How many economy office stools can be produced with the labor hours currently used to make 100 deluxe stools?

    A.  80

    B.  125

    C.  100

    D.  150

Answer (B) is correct.  *(Publisher)*
    **REQUIRED:** The economy stools that can be produced in the time spent to make 100 deluxe stools.
    **DISCUSSION:** The labor hours used in cushion fabrication will be used to make the modified cushioned seat. Thus, the labor time freed by not making deluxe stools equals the frame fabrication and assembly time only. The number of economy office stools that can be produced is 125.

| | |
|---|---|
| Labor hours to make 100 deluxe stools (1.5 × 100) | 150  hrs. |
| Minus: Labor hours to make 100 cushioned seats (cushion fabrication .5 × 100) | (50) hrs. |
| Labor hours available for economy stool | 100  hrs. |
| Labor hours to make one economy stool | ÷ .8  hrs. |
| Stools produced by extra labor in economy stool production (100 ÷ .8 hr.) | 125  stools |

    Answer (A) is incorrect because the total hours available for economy stools needs to be divided by the .8 hr. required to make an economy stool. Answer (C) is incorrect because the total hours available for economy stools needs to be divided by the .8 hr. required to make an economy stool. Answer (D) is incorrect because 150 is the number of hours required to make 100 deluxe stools before considering the hours required to make 100 cushioned seats.

**68.** Refer to the information on the preceding page(s). When computing the opportunity cost for the deluxe office stool, what is the contribution margin per unit produced?

    A.  $25.20

    B.  $15.84

    C.  $13.56

    D.  $33.30

Answer (A) is correct.  *(Publisher)*
    **REQUIRED:** The contribution margin per unit of the deluxe office stool.
    **DISCUSSION:** The contribution margin per unit is equal to the selling price minus the variable costs. Variable costs per unit for the deluxe office stool equal $33.30 and the selling price is $58.50. Thus, the contribution margin is $25.20 per unit ($58.50 − $33.30). The total standard cost is $45.00, which includes $11.70 of fixed overhead (1.5 hr. × $7.80), and the variable costs are $33.30 ($45.00 − $11.70).
    Answer (B) is incorrect because $15.84 is the contribution margin of the economy office stool. Answer (C) is incorrect because variable costs of $33.30 need to be deducted from the sales price of $58.50. Answer (D) is incorrect because $33.30 is the variable cost that must be subtracted from the sales price to yield the contribution margin.

**69.** Refer to the information on the preceding page(s). What is the opportunity cost of the Office Division if 125 economy stools can be made in the time required for 100 deluxe stools?

    A.  $789

    B.  $1,869

    C.  $1,329

    D.  $540

Answer (D) is correct.  *(Publisher)*
    **REQUIRED:** The opportunity cost of the Office Division.
    **DISCUSSION:** Opportunity cost is the benefit of the next best opportunity forgone. The opportunity cost here is the contribution margin forgone by shifting production to the economy office stool ($2,520 − $1,980 = $540).

| | Deluxe | | Economy |
|---|---|---|---|
| Selling price | $58.50 | | $41.60 |
| Costs | | | |
|   Materials | $14.55 | | $15.76 |
|   Labor ($7.50 × 1.5) | 11.25 | ($7.50 × .8) | 6.00 |
|   Variable overhead ($5 × 1.5) | 7.50 | ($5 × .8) | 4.00 |
|   Fixed overhead | -- | | -- |
| Total costs | $33.30 | | $25.76 |
| Unit CM | $25.20 | | $15.84 |
| Units produced | × 100 | | × 125 |
| Total CM | $2,520 | | $1,980 |

    Answer (A) is incorrect because $789 is the transfer price of $1,329 minus the opportunity cost of $540 of the Office Division. Answer (B) is incorrect because $1,869 is the transfer price of $1,329 plus the opportunity cost of $540 of the Office Division. Answer (C) is incorrect because $1,329 is the transfer price, not the opportunity cost of the Office Division.

**70.** Which one of the following variances is of least significance from a behavioral control perspective?

A. Unfavorable direct materials quantity variance amounting to 20% of the quantity allowed for the output attained.

B. Unfavorable direct labor efficiency variance amounting to 10% more than the budgeted hours for the output attained.

C. Favorable direct labor rate variance resulting from an inability to hire experienced workers to replace retiring workers.

D. Fixed overhead volume variance resulting from management's decision midway through the fiscal year to reduce its budgeted output by 20%.

Answer (D) is correct. *(CMA, adapted)*
**REQUIRED:** The variance of least significance from a behavioral control perspective.
**DISCUSSION:** Most variances are of significance to someone who is responsible for that variance. However, a fixed overhead volume variance is often not the responsibility of anyone other than top management. The fixed overhead volume variance equals the difference between budgeted fixed overhead and the amount applied (standard input allowed for the actual output × standard rate). It can be caused by economic downturns, labor strife, bad weather, or a change in planned output. Thus, a fixed overhead volume variance resulting from a top management decision to reduce output has fewer behavioral implications than other variances.
Answer (A) is incorrect because an unfavorable direct materials quantity variance affects production management and possibly the purchasing function. It may indicate an inefficient use of materials or the use of poor quality materials. Answer (B) is incorrect because an unfavorable direct labor efficiency variance reflects upon production workers who have used too many hours. Answer (C) is incorrect because a favorable direct labor rate variance related to hiring is a concern of the human resources function. The favorable rate variance might be more than offset by an unfavorable direct labor efficiency variance or a direct materials quantity variance (if waste occurred).

## 8.6 Variances in the Ledger Accounts

**71.** Company Z uses a standard cost system that carries materials at actual price until they are transferred to the work-in-process account. In project A, 500 units of X were used at a cost of $10 per unit. Standards require 450 units to complete this project. The standard price is established at $9 per unit. What is the proper journal entry?

A.
| Work-in-process | $4,950 | |
|---|---|---|
| Direct materials price variance | 500 | |
|   Direct materials quantity variance | | $  450 |
|   Inventory | | 5,000 |

B.
| Work-in-process | $5,950 | |
|---|---|---|
|   Direct materials price variance | | $  500 |
|   Direct materials quantity variance | | 450 |
|   Inventory | | 5,000 |

C.
| Work-in-process | $4,050 | |
|---|---|---|
| Direct materials price variance | 500 | |
| Direct materials quantity variance | 450 | |
|   Inventory | | $5,000 |

D.
| Work-in-process | $5,000 | |
|---|---|---|
|   Inventory | | $5,000 |

Answer (C) is correct. *(Publisher)*
**REQUIRED:** The journal entry to record direct materials issued and related variances.
**DISCUSSION:** The entry to record direct materials used is to debit work-in-process at standard prices and standard quantities (450 units × $9 = $4,050). In this question, all direct materials variances are recorded at the time work-in-process is charged. The direct materials price variance and the direct materials quantity variance must be calculated. The project used more units at a higher price than estimated, so both variances will be unfavorable (debits). The direct materials quantity variance is $450 U [(500 – 450) × $9]. The direct materials price variance is $500 U [500 units × ($10 – $9)]. Inventory is credited for the actual prices and actual quantities (500 × $10 = $5,000).
Answer (A) is incorrect because the unfavorable direct materials quantity variance should be a debit. Answer (B) is incorrect because the unfavorable direct materials price and quantity variances should be debits. Answer (D) is incorrect because this entry fails to record the variances.

**72.** If a project required 50 hours to complete at a cost of $10 per hour but should have taken only 45 hours at a cost of $12 per hour, what is the proper entry to record the costs?

A.  Work-in-process                          $540
    Direct labor efficiency variance           60
       Direct labor price variance                    $100
       Accrued payroll                                 500

B.  Wage expense                             $440
    Direct labor efficiency variance           60
       Accrued payroll                                $500

C.  Work-in-process                          $460
    Direct labor price variance               100
       Direct labor efficiency variance               $ 60
       Accrued payroll                                 500

D.  Work-in-process                          $500
       Accrued payroll                                $500

Answer (A) is correct.  *(Publisher)*
   **REQUIRED:** The journal entry to record accrued payroll and direct labor cost variances.
   **DISCUSSION:** The entry to record accrued payroll is to charge work-in-process at the standard wage rate times the standard number of hours and to credit accrued payroll for the actual payroll dollar amount. The project required more hours but a lower wage rate than estimated. Hence, the direct labor efficiency variance will be unfavorable (a debit). The direct labor price variance will be favorable (a credit).

Direct labor efficiency variance $(50 - 45) \times \$12$  =  $\$ 60$ U
Direct labor price variance $50 \times (\$12 - \$10)$  =  $\$100$ F

   Answer (B) is incorrect because this entry omits the price variance and fails to inventory the labor costs. Answer (C) is incorrect because this entry would be the proper entry if the hourly rate were greater than estimated, but hours worked were less. Answer (D) is incorrect because the direct labor variances must be recognized.

**73.** Omega Company would have applied $32,500 of fixed overhead if capacity usage had equaled the master budget. Given that amount, that 2,000 standard hours (the normal volume) were allowed for the actual output, that actual fixed overhead equaled the budgeted amount, and that overhead was applied at a rate of $15 per hour, what is the entry to close the fixed overhead accounts?

A.  Fixed overhead control           $30,000
    Production volume variance          2,500
       Fixed overhead applied                    $32,500

B.  Cost of goods sold               $32,500
       Fixed overhead control                    $32,500

C.  Work-in-process                  $30,000
    Overhead price variance             2,500
       Fixed overhead applied                    $32,500

D.  Fixed overhead applied           $30,000
    Production volume variance          2,500
       Fixed overhead control                    $32,500

Answer (D) is correct.  *(Publisher)*
   **REQUIRED:** The year-end journal entry to close the fixed overhead accounts.
   **DISCUSSION:** The entry is to debit fixed overhead applied and credit fixed overhead control for their respective balances. The difference is attributable solely to the production volume variance because the budget (spending) variance is zero (actual fixed overhead = the budgeted amount). The volume variance is unfavorable because fixed overhead is underapplied. The underapplication (the unfavorable volume variance debited) is $2,500 [(2,000 hours × $15 per hour) – $32,500 budgeted fixed factory overhead].
   Answer (A) is incorrect because the normal balances in the overhead applied and overhead control accounts are a credit and a debit, respectively. Hence, the closing entries must be the reverse. Answer (B) is incorrect because the fixed overhead applied account must be closed with a debit entry. Answer (C) is incorrect because this entry does not close the overhead accounts.

**74.** Assume price variances are recorded at the time of purchase. What is the journal entry to record a direct materials price variance if materials are purchased at $5 per unit for $650 and their standard price is $4 per unit?

A.  Inventory                       $650
       Accounts payable                      $650

B.  Inventory                       $520
    Direct materials price variance   130
       Accounts payable                      $650

C.  Inventory                       $520
    Work-in-process                   130
       Cash                                  $650

D.  Finished goods                  $520
    Direct materials price variance   130
       Cash                                  $650

Answer (B) is correct.  *(Publisher)*
   **REQUIRED:** The journal entry to record a direct materials price variance at the time of purchase.
   **DISCUSSION:** The entry at the time of purchase is to charge inventory for $520, which is the actual quantity purchased ($650 ÷ $5 per unit = 130 units) times the standard unit price ($4). Accounts payable is credited for $650 (actual quantity × actual price). The difference between the actual and standard prices is the price variance. Because the actual price exceeded the standard, the price variance is debited for the difference. The price variance is $130 [130 units × ($5 – $4)] unfavorable.
   Answer (A) is incorrect because this entry assumes the price variance is not recorded at time of purchase. Answer (C) is incorrect because the variance should be charged to a separate account, not work-in-process. Answer (D) is incorrect because materials should be debited to inventory.

Questions 75 through 77 are based on the following information. Alpha Company paid janitors $5 per hour to clean the production area. It initially set the standard cost of janitorial work at $4.50 per hour, and 530 hours were worked by the janitors.

**75.** What is the proper journal entry to account for this expense for the month of June if 530 hours were worked by the janitors?

A. Salaries expense        $2,650
   Payroll                      $2,650

B. Variable overhead control    $2,650
   Variable overhead applied       $2,650

C. Variable overhead control    $2,650
   Payroll payable               $2,650

D. Variable overhead applied    $2,650
   Payroll payable               $2,650

Answer (C) is correct. *(Publisher)*
**REQUIRED:** The journal entry to record the actual variable overhead incurred.
**DISCUSSION:** The entry to record actual variable overhead incurred (530 hours × $5 = $2,650) is to charge the variable overhead control account. A corresponding credit is made to accounts payable or any other appropriate account.
Answer (A) is incorrect because actual indirect production costs are debited to overhead control. Answer (B) is incorrect because overhead application is usually based on standard rates and a given activity base, not amounts actually incurred. Overhead is applied by crediting overhead control (or a separate applied overhead account) and debiting work-in-process. Answer (D) is incorrect because the variable overhead is debited to variable overhead control, not variable overhead applied.

**76.** What is the appropriate entry to record the application of the hours worked by the janitors?

A. Work-in-process         $2,385
   Variable overhead applied       $2,385

B. Work-in-process         $2,385
   Variable overhead control       $2,385

C. Work-in-process         $2,385
   Variable overhead control     265
   Variable overhead applied       $2,650

D. Cost of goods sold       $2,385
   Variable overhead applied       $2,385

Answer (A) is correct. *(Publisher)*
**REQUIRED:** The journal entry to record the application of variable overhead.
**DISCUSSION:** The entry to record the application of variable overhead is to charge the work-in-process account and enter a corresponding credit to the variable overhead applied account for the amount of overhead computed using the predetermined overhead rate (530 × $4.50 = $2,385).
Answer (B) is incorrect because overhead control is debited for overhead incurred. Answer (C) is incorrect because the overhead application is at $4.50, not $5.00, per hour. Answer (D) is incorrect because the goods to which these costs apply are in process.

**77.** What entry accounts for the recognition of the variance that occurred? Assume that this was the only variable overhead variance.

A. Variable overhead applied    $2,650
   Variable overhead control       $2,385
   Variance summary           265

B. Variable overhead applied    $2,385
   Variable overhead spending
     variance                  265
       Variable overhead control    $2,650

C. Variable overhead applied    $2,385
   Variable overhead efficiency
     variance                  265
       Variable overhead control    $2,650

D. Variable overhead control    $2,385
   Variable spending variance    265
       Variable overhead applied     $2,650

Answer (B) is correct. *(Publisher)*
**REQUIRED:** The journal entry to record the isolation of the variance.
**DISCUSSION:** The spending variance is recognized by a debit, given that more was spent for that activity than was estimated. The entry to record the unfavorable variable overhead spending variance is to charge the variable overhead spending variance account for the appropriate amount. The variable overhead applied account is charged for its balance. The variable overhead control account is credited for its balance. These entries will result in a zero balance in both the applied and the control accounts assuming that no variable overhead efficiency variance existed.
Answer (A) is incorrect because the variance is a debit to a spending variance account, not a credit to a variance summary. Answer (C) is incorrect because the variance is a spending variance resulting from the excess of an actual cost over a standard cost, not an efficiency variance. Answer (D) is incorrect because variable overhead applied is debited and variable overhead control is credited to close out the accounts.

## 8.7 Sales Variances

**78.** The variance that arises solely because the quantity actually sold differs from the quantity budgeted to be sold is

    A. Static budget variance.

    B. Master budget increment.

    C. Sales mix variance.

    D. Sales volume variance.

**Answer (D) is correct.**  *(CMA, adapted)*
    **REQUIRED:** The variance that arises solely when actual sales differ from budgeted sales.
    **DISCUSSION:** If a firm's sales differ from the amount budgeted, the difference could be attributable either to the sales price variance or the sales volume variance. The sales volume variance is the change in contribution margin caused by the difference between the actual and budgeted sales volumes.
    Answer (A) is incorrect because a static budget variance is the difference between actual costs or revenues and those budgeted on a static budget. Answer (B) is incorrect because a master budget increment is an increase in a budgeted figure on the firm's master budget. Answer (C) is incorrect because the sales mix variance is caused when a company's actual sales mix is different from the budgeted sales mix.

**79.** In analyzing company operations, the controller of the Jason Corporation found a $250,000 favorable flexible-budget revenue variance. The variance was calculated by comparing the actual results with the flexible budget. This variance can be wholly explained by

    A. The total flexible budget variance.

    B. The total sales volume variance.

    C. The total static budget variance.

    D. Changes in unit selling prices.

**Answer (D) is correct.**  *(CMA, adapted)*
    **REQUIRED:** The cause of a favorable flexible-budget revenue variance.
    **DISCUSSION:** Variance analysis can be used to judge the effectiveness of selling departments. If a firm's sales differ from the amount budgeted, the difference may be attributable to either the sales price variance or the sales volume (quantity) variance. Changes in unit selling prices may account for the entire variance if the actual quantity sold is equal to the quantity budgeted. None of the revenue variance is attributed to the sales volume variance because no such variance exists when a flexible budget is used. The flexible budget is based on the level of sales at actual volume.
    Answer (A) is incorrect because the total flexible budget variance includes items other than revenue. Answer (B) is incorrect because the sales volume variance represents the change in contribution margin caused by a difference between actual and budgeted units sold. However, given a flexible budget, there is no difference between budgeted and actual units sold. By definition, a flexible budget's volume is identical to actual volume. Answer (C) is incorrect because the total static budget variance includes many items other than revenue.

**80.** The sales volume variance is partly a function of the unit contribution margin (UCM). For a single-product company, it is

    A. The difference between actual and master budget sales volume, times actual UCM.

    B. The difference between flexible budget and actual sales volume, times master budget UCM.

    C. The difference between flexible budget and master budget sales volume, times actual UCM.

    D. The difference between flexible budget and master budget sales volume, times master budget UCM.

**Answer (D) is correct.**  *(CIA, adapted)*
    **REQUIRED:** The definition of sales volume variance.
    **DISCUSSION:** For a single-product company, the sales volume variance is the difference between the actual and budgeted sales quantities times the budgeted UCM. If the company sells two or more products, the difference between the actual and budgeted product mixes must be considered. In that case, the sales volume variance equals the difference between (1) actual total unit sales times the budgeted weighted-average UCM for the actual mix and (2) budgeted total unit sales times the budgeted weighted-average UCM for the planned mix.
    Answer (A) is incorrect because budgeted, not actual, UCM is used to calculate this variance. Answer (B) is incorrect because the flexible budget volume is the actual volume, resulting in a zero variance. Answer (C) is incorrect because budgeted, not actual, UCM is used to calculate this variance.

**81.** For a company that produces more than one product, the sales volume variance can be divided into which two of the following additional variances?

   A. Sales price variance and flexible budget variance.

   B. Sales mix variance and sales price variance.

   C. Sales quantity variance and sales mix variance.

   D. Sales mix variance and production volume variance.

Answer (C) is correct. *(CMA, adapted)*
   **REQUIRED:** The components of the sales volume variance.
   **DISCUSSION:** The sales volume variance can be divided into the sales quantity variance and the sales mix variance. The sales quantity variance is the change in contribution margin caused by the difference between actual and budgeted volume, assuming that budgeted sales mix, unit variable costs, and unit sales prices are constant. Thus, it equals the sales volume variance when the sales mix variance is zero. In a multiproduct firm, the sales mix variance is a variance caused by a sales mix that differs from that budgeted. For example, even when the sales quantity is exactly as budgeted, an unfavorable sales mix variance can be caused by greater sales of a low-contribution product at the expense of lower sales of a high-contribution product.
   Answer (A) is incorrect because the sales price variance is a separate variance and is not a component of the sales volume variance. Answer (B) is incorrect because the sales price variance is a separate variance and is not a component of the sales volume variance. Answer (D) is incorrect because the production volume variance is a fixed overhead variance. It is not related to the sales volume variance.

**82.** The sales quantity variance is partly a function of the unit contribution margin (UCM). It equals

   A. Actual units × (budgeted weighted-average UCM for planned mix − budgeted weighted-average UCM for actual mix).

   B. (Actual units − master budget units) × budgeted weighted-average UCM for the planned mix.

   C. Budgeted market share percentage × (actual market size in units − budgeted market size in units) × budgeted weighted-average UCM.

   D. (Actual market share percentage−budgeted market share percentage) × actual market size in units × budgeted weighted-average UCM.

Answer (B) is correct. *(Publisher)*
   **REQUIRED:** The definition of the sales quantity variance.
   **DISCUSSION:** The sales volume variance equals the difference between the flexible budget contribution margin for the actual volume and that included in the master budget. Its components are the sales quantity and sales mix variances. The sales quantity variance focuses on the firm's aggregate results. It assumes a constant product mix and an average contribution margin for the composite unit. It equals the difference between actual and budgeted unit total sales, times the budgeted weighted-average UCM for the planned mix.
   Answer (A) is incorrect because this equation defines the sales mix variance. Answer (C) is incorrect because this equation defines the market size variance. Answer (D) is incorrect because this equation defines the market share variance.

**83.** The sales mix variance is partly a function of the unit contribution margin (UCM). It equals

   A. Actual units × (budgeted weighted-average UCM for planned mix − budgeted weighted-average UCM for actual mix).

   B. (Actual units − master budget units) × budgeted weighted-average UCM for planned mix.

   C. Budgeted market share percentage × (actual market size in units − budgeted market size in units) × budgeted weighted-average UCM.

   D. (Actual market share percentage − budgeted market share percentage) × actual market size in units × budgeted weighted-average UCM.

Answer (A) is correct. *(Publisher)*
   **REQUIRED:** The definition of the sales mix variance.
   **DISCUSSION:** The sales mix variance may be viewed as a sum of variances. For each product in the mix, the difference between actual units sold and its budgeted percentage of the actual total unit sales is multiplied by the budgeted UCM for the product. The results are added to determine the mix variance. An alternative is to multiply total actual units sold by the difference between the budgeted weighted-average UCM for the planned mix and that for the actual mix.
   Answer (B) is incorrect because this equation defines the sales quantity variance. Answer (C) is incorrect because this equation defines the market size variance. Answer (D) is incorrect because this equation defines the market share variance.

**84.** The market size variance is partly a function of the unit contribution margin (UCM). It equals

A. Actual units × (budgeted weighted-average UCM for planned mix − budgeted weighted-average UCM for actual mix).

B. (Actual units − master budget units) × budgeted weighted-average UCM for the planned mix.

C. Budgeted market share percentage × (actual market size in units − budgeted market size in units) × budgeted weighted-average UCM.

D. (Actual market share percentage − budgeted market share percentage) × actual market size in units × budgeted weighted-average UCM.

Answer (C) is correct.  *(Publisher)*
**REQUIRED:** The definition of the market size variance.
**DISCUSSION:** The components of the sales quantity variance are the market size variance and the market share variance. The market size variance gives an indication of the change in contribution margin caused by a change in the market size. The market size and market share variances are relevant to industries in which total level of sales and market share are known, e.g., the automobile industry. The market size variance measures the effect of changes in an industry's sales on an individual company, and the market share variance analyzes the impact of a change in market share.
Answer (A) is incorrect because this equation defines the sales mix variance. Answer (B) is incorrect because this equation defines the sales quantity variance. Answer (D) is incorrect because this equation defines the market share variance.

Questions 85 through 89 are based on the following information.

Folsom Fashions sells a line of women's dresses. Folsom's performance report for November follows.

The company uses a flexible budget to analyze its performance and to measure the effect on operating income of the various factors affecting the difference between budgeted and actual operating income.

|  | Actual | Budget |
|---|---|---|
| Dresses sold | 5,000 | 6,000 |
| Sales | $235,000 | $300,000 |
| Variable costs | (145,000) | (180,000) |
| Contribution margin (CM) | 90,000 | 120,000 |
| Fixed costs | (84,000) | (80,000) |
| Operating income | $  6,000 | $ 40,000 |

**85.** The effect of the sales quantity variance on the contribution margin for November is

A. $30,000 unfavorable.

B. $18,000 unfavorable.

C. $20,000 unfavorable.

D. $15,000 unfavorable.

Answer (C) is correct.  *(CMA, adapted)*
**REQUIRED:** The effect of the sales quantity variance on the contribution margin.
**DISCUSSION:** The sales quantity variance is the difference between the actual and budgeted units, times the budgeted unit CM.

$$\left(5{,}000 - 6{,}000\right) \times \frac{\$120{,}000}{6{,}000} = \$20{,}000 \; U$$

Answer (A) is incorrect because $30,000 is the difference between the actual and budgeted contribution margins. Answer (B) is incorrect because $18,000 equals the difference between actual and budgeted unit sales times the actual unit CM. Answer (D) is incorrect because $15,000 is the sales price variance.

**86.** The sales price variance for November is

A. $30,000 unfavorable.

B. $18,000 unfavorable.

C. $20,000 unfavorable.

D. $15,000 unfavorable.

Answer (D) is correct.  *(CMA, adapted)*
**REQUIRED:** The amount of the sales price variance for the month.
**DISCUSSION:** The sales price variance is the actual number of units sold (5,000), times the difference between budgeted selling price ($300,000 ÷ 6,000) and actual selling price ($235,000 ÷ 5,000).

$$\left(\$50 - \$47\right) \times 5{,}000 = \$15{,}000 \; U$$

Answer (A) is incorrect because $30,000 is the difference between the actual and budgeted contribution margins. Answer (B) is incorrect because $18,000 equals the difference between actual and budgeted unit sales times the actual unit CM. Answer (C) is incorrect because $20,000 is the sales quantity variance.

**87.** The variable cost flexible budget variance for November is

    A. $5,000 favorable.

    B. $5,000 unfavorable.

    C. $4,000 favorable.

    D. $4,000 unfavorable.

Answer (A) is correct. *(CMA, adapted)*
    **REQUIRED:** The variable cost flexible budget variance.
    **DISCUSSION:** The variable cost flexible budget variance is equal to the difference between actual variable costs and the product of the actual quantity sold and the budgeted unit variable cost ($180,000 ÷ 6,000 = $30).

$$\bigl(\$30 \times 5{,}000\bigr) - \$145{,}000 = \$5{,}000 \ F$$

    Answer (B) is incorrect because the variance is favorable. Answer (C) is incorrect because $4,000 is the amount of the fixed cost variance. Answer (D) is incorrect because $4,000 is the amount of the fixed cost variance.

**88.** The fixed cost variance for November is

    A. $5,000 favorable.

    B. $5,000 unfavorable.

    C. $4,000 favorable.

    D. $4,000 unfavorable.

Answer (D) is correct. *(CMA, adapted)*
    **REQUIRED:** The fixed cost variance for the month.
    **DISCUSSION:** The fixed cost variance equals the difference between actual fixed costs and budgeted fixed costs.

$$\$84{,}000 - \$80{,}000 = \$4{,}000 \ U$$

    Answer (A) is incorrect because $5,000 is the variable cost variance. Answer (B) is incorrect because $5,000 is the variable cost variance. Answer (C) is incorrect because the variance is unfavorable.

**89.** What additional information is needed for Folsom to calculate the dollar impact of a change in market share on operating income for November?

    A. Folsom's budgeted market share and the budgeted total market size.

    B. Folsom's budgeted market share, the budgeted total market size, and average market selling price.

    C. Folsom's budgeted market share and the actual total market size.

    D. Folsom's actual market share and the actual total market size.

Answer (C) is correct. *(CMA, adapted)*
    **REQUIRED:** The additional information necessary for a market share variance calculation.
    **DISCUSSION:** A change in market share reflects a change in relative competitiveness. To isolate the effect on operating income of an increase or a decrease in market share, the company must know its budgeted and actual market shares, the actual size of the market for November, and the budgeted weighted-average unit contribution margin. Such computations may help Folsom to determine whether its decline in sales resulted from a loss of competitiveness or a shrinkage of the market.
    Answer (A) is incorrect because Folsom will need to know the actual total market size. Answer (B) is incorrect because Folsom will need to know the actual total market size. Answer (D) is incorrect because Folsom will need to know the budgeted market share.

Questions 90 and 91 are based on the following information.

Clear Plus, Inc. manufactures and sells boxes of pocket protectors. The static master budget and the actual results for May appear in the opposite column.

| | Actuals | Static Budget |
|---|---|---|
| Unit sales | 12,000 | 10,000 |
| Sales | $132,000 | $100,000 |
| Variable costs of sales | 70,800 | 60,000 |
| Contribution margin | 61,200 | 40,000 |
| Fixed costs | 32,000 | 30,000 |
| Operating income | $ 29,200 | $ 10,000 |

**90.** The operating income for Clear Plus, Inc. using a flexible budget for May is

A. $12,000

B. $19,200

C. $30,000

D. $18,000

Answer (D) is correct.  *(CMA, adapted)*
   **REQUIRED:** The flexible budget operating income.
   **DISCUSSION:** A flexible budget is prepared after the budget period has ended and actual sales and costs are known. Assuming that unit sales price ($100,000 ÷ 10,000 units = $10) and variable costs of sales ($60,000 ÷ 10,000 unit = $6) and total fixed costs ($30,000) do not change, a flexible budget may be prepared for the actual sales level (12,000 units). Hence, the budgeted contribution margin (sales – variable costs of sales) equals $48,000 [(12,000 units × $10) – (12,000 units × $6)]. The operating income is therefore $18,000 ($48,000 CM – $30,000 FC).
   Answer (A) is incorrect because $12,000 assumes that all costs are variable. Answer (B) is incorrect because $19,200 is based on actual variable costs. Answer (C) is incorrect because $30,000 is based on actual sales revenues.

**91.** Which one of the following statements concerning Clear Plus, Inc.'s actual results for May is correct?

A. The flexible budget variance is $8,000 favorable.

B. The sales price variance is $32,000 favorable.

C. The sales volume variance is $8,000 favorable.

D. The flexible budget variable cost variance is $10,800 unfavorable.

Answer (C) is correct.  *(CMA, adapted)*
   **REQUIRED:** The true statement about the actual results.
   **DISCUSSION:** The sales volume variance is the change in contribution margin caused by the difference between the actual and budgeted volume. It equals the budgeted unit contribution margin times the difference between actual and expected volume, or $8,000 [(12,000 – 10,000) × ($10 – $6)]. The sales volume variance is favorable because actual sales exceeded budgeted sales.
   Answer (A) is incorrect because the flexible budget variance is $11,200 favorable ($29,200 actual operating income – $18,000 flexible budget operating income). Answer (B) is incorrect because the sales price variance is $12,000 [$132,000 actual sales – (12,000 units sold × $10)]. Answer (D) is incorrect because the total projected variable costs at the actual sales level equal $72,000 (12,000 units × $6). Thus, the variable cost variance is $1,200 favorable ($72,000 – $70,800 actual).

**92.** The market share variance is partly a function of the unit contribution margin (UCM). It equals

A. Actual units × (budgeted weighted-average UCM for planned mix – budgeted weighted-average UCM for actual mix).

B. (Actual units – master budget units) × budgeted weighted-average UCM for the planned mix.

C. Budgeted market share percentage × (actual market size in units – budgeted market size in units) × budgeted weighted-average UCM.

D. (Actual market share percentage – budgeted market share percentage) × actual market size in units × budgeted weighted-average UCM.

Answer (D) is correct.  *(Publisher)*
   **REQUIRED:** The definition of the market share variance.
   **DISCUSSION:** The market share variance gives an indication of the amount of contribution margin gained (forgone) because of a change in the market share.
   Answer (A) is incorrect because this equation defines the sales mix variance. Answer (B) is incorrect because this equation defines the sales quantity variance. Answer (C) is incorrect because this equation defines the market size variance.

# STUDY UNIT NINE
# RESPONSIBILITY ACCOUNTING AND
# FINANCIAL MEASURES

(15 pages of outline)

This study unit is the **second of three** on **performance measurement**. The relative weight assigned to this major topic in Part 2 of the exam is **20%** at **skill level C** (all six skills types required). The three study units are

Study Unit 8:   Cost and Variance Measures
Study Unit 9:   Responsibility Accounting and Financial Measures
Study Unit 10: The Balanced Scorecard and Quality Considerations

After studying the outlines and answering the multiple-choice questions in this study unit, you will have the skills necessary to address the following topics listed in the IMA's Learning Outcome Statements:

Part 2 – Section D.1. Cost and variance measures

The candidate should be able to:

a.   recognize that performance against operational goals can be measured by a variety of methods, including measures based on revenue, manufacturing costs, nonmanufacturing costs, and profit, depending on the type of center or unit being measured

b.   recognize that performance evaluation measures should be directly related to the factors that drive the element being measured, e.g., cost drivers and revenue drivers

Part 2 – Section D.2. Responsibility centers and reporting segments

The candidate should be able to:

a.   recognize that responsibility centers (strategic business units) represent effective units for performance evaluation

b.   identify and explain the different types of responsibility centers

c.   demonstrate an understanding of contribution reporting as used for performance evaluation

d.   analyze a contribution report and evaluate performance

e.   recognize that organizations may evaluate performance on the basis of segments, such as product lines, geographical areas, or other meaningful segments

f.   demonstrate an understanding that the allocation of common costs among segments can be an issue in performance evaluation

g.   identify methods for allocating common costs, such as stand-alone cost allocation and incremental cost allocation

h.   define transfer pricing and identify the objectives of transfer pricing

i.   identify the methods for determining transfer prices and list the advantages and disadvantages of each method

j.   recognize how transfer pricing is affected by business issues, such as the presence of outside suppliers and the opportunity costs associated with capacity usage

   k.    demonstrate an understanding of how special issues, such as tariffs, exchange rates, and the availability of materials and skills, affect performance evaluation in multinational companies

   l.    demonstrate an understanding of how special issues, such as taxes, currency restrictions, and expropriation risk, affect transfer pricing in multinational companies

   m.    recognize the role that timely feedback reporting plays in linking planning, control, and performance evaluations

   n.    recognize that performance measurement reports should be tailored to the audience and level of management to which they are directed

## Part 2 – Section D.3. Financial measures

The candidate should be able to:

   a.    demonstrate an understanding of the issues involved in determining product profitability, business unit profitability, and customer profitability, including cost measurement, cost allocation, investment measurement, and valuation

   b.    calculate product-line profitability, business unit profitability, and customer profitability given a set of data and assumptions

   c.    evaluate customers and products on the basis of profitability and identify ways to improve profitability and/or drop unprofitable customers and products

   d.    define and calculate return on investment

   e.    calculate return on investment based on the Dupont Model and describe how this model enhances basic return on investment calculations

   f.    analyze and interpret return on investment calculations and evaluate performance on the basis of the analysis

   g.    define and calculate residual income

   h.    analyze and interpret residual income calculations and evaluate performance on the basis of the analysis

   i.    compare and contrast the benefits and limitations of return on investment and residual income as measures of performance

   j.    define and calculate economic value added (EVA®)

   k.    demonstrate an understanding of how economic value added differs from return on investment and residual income measures

   l.    recognize that market value added is another measure of performance

   m.    demonstrate an understanding that several factors, such as revenue and expense recognition policies, may affect the measurement of income and reduce comparability among business units and companies

   n.    demonstrate an understanding that several factors, such as inventory measurement policies, joint asset sharing, and overall asset measurement, may affect the measurement of investment and reduce comparability among business units and companies

   o.    recognize that some organizations evaluate performance on the basis of cash flow return on investment

   p.    compare and contrast cash flow return on investment with return on investment

   q.    demonstrate an understanding of the effect international operations can have on performance measurement

## 9.1 RESPONSIBILITY CENTERS

1. Managerial performance ordinarily should be evaluated based on factors that can be influenced by the manager, such as revenues, costs, or investment.

   a. For example, a **controllable cost** may be defined as one directly regulated by a specific manager at a given level of production within a given time span or one that the manager can significantly influence.

2. A well-designed responsibility accounting system establishes **responsibility centers** (also called **strategic business units**) for the purpose of encouraging managerial effort to attain organizational objectives, motivating managers to make decisions consistent with those objectives, and providing a basis for determining managerial compensation.

   a. A **cost center**, e.g., a maintenance department, is responsible for costs only.

      1) Cost drivers are the relevant performance measures.

      2) A disadvantage of a cost center is the potential for cost shifting, for example, replacement of variable costs for which a manager is responsible with fixed costs for which (s)he is not.

         a) Another disadvantage is that long-term issues may be disregarded when the emphasis is on, for example, annual cost amounts.

         b) Yet another issue is allocation of service department costs to cost centers.

      3) Service centers exist primarily and sometimes solely to provide specialized support to other organizational subunits. They are usually operated as cost centers.

   b. A **revenue center**, e.g., a sales department, is responsible for revenues only.

      1) Revenue drivers are the relevant performance measures. They are factors that influence unit sales, such as changes in prices and products, customer service, marketing efforts, and delivery terms.

   c. A **profit center**, e.g., an appliance department in a retail store, is responsible for revenues and expenses.

   d. An **investment center**, e.g., a branch office, is responsible for revenues, expenses, and invested capital.

      1) The advantage of an investment center is that it permits an evaluation of performance that can be compared with that of other responsibility centers or other potential investments on a return on investment basis, i.e., on the basis of the effectiveness of asset usage.

3. Controllability is not an absolute basis for responsibility. More than one manager may influence a cost, and responsibility may be assigned based on knowledge about its incurrence rather than ability to control it directly.

   a. Accordingly, a successful system is dependent upon the proper delegation of responsibility and the commensurate authority.

4. The purpose of a responsibility system is to motivate management performance that adheres to overall company objectives (goal congruence).

   a. **Goal congruence** is promoted by encouraging cooperation among organizational functions (production, marketing, and support) by influencing managers to think of their products or services as salable outside the firm, and by encouraging managers to find new methods of earning profits.

   b. **Suboptimization** occurs when one segment of a firm takes action that is in its own best interests but is detrimental to the firm as a whole.

5. Stop and review! You have completed the outline for this subunit. Study multiple-choice questions 1 through 14 beginning on page 343.

## 9.2 CONTRIBUTION AND SEGMENT REPORTING

1.  The **contribution margin (CM) approach** to performance evaluation is emphasized in responsibility accounting because it focuses on **controllability**.

    a.  Fixed costs are much less controllable than variable costs, so the contribution margin (sales – all variable costs) may be a fairer basis for evaluation than gross margin (also called gross profit), which equals sales minus cost of sales.

2.  The CM approach is also useful for making **disinvestment decisions** about whether product lines and business units should be continued or whether particular customers or geographic areas should continue to be served.

    a.  This approach lends itself to the **relevant revenue and relevant cost analysis** required for disinvestment decisions.

    b.  Relevant revenues and costs are all expected future amounts that will vary among the possible decision choices.

        1)  For example, the allocated common costs and other fixed costs that will not be affected by disinvestment would be excluded from the analysis.

    c.  The relevant revenues and costs analysis must address all the ramifications of the decision to disinvest.

        1)  For example, discontinuing one product may affect sales of other products, and currently nonprofitable service to certain customers may be justified by their future profit potential.

    d.  Still another issue is **opportunity cost**. Disinvestment is often justified when alternative uses of resources are more profitable but not when idle capacity may result.

3.  The following is an example of a CM income statement:

| | | |
|---|---:|---:|
| Sales | | $150,000 |
| Variable manufacturing costs | | (40,000) |
|    Manufacturing contribution margin | | $110,000 |
| Variable selling and administrative costs | | (20,000) |
|    Contribution margin | | $ 90,000 |
| Controllable fixed costs: | | |
|    Manufacturing | $30,000 | |
|    Selling and administrative | 25,000 | (55,000) |
| Short-run performance margin | | $ 35,000 |
| Traceable fixed costs: | | |
|    Depreciation | $10,000 | |
|    Insurance | 5,000 | (15,000) |
| Segment margin | | $ 20,000 |
| Allocated common costs | | (10,000) |
|    Net income | | $ 10,000 |

    a.  Controllable (discretionary) costs are characterized by uncertainty about the relationship between input (the costs) and the value of the related output. Examples are advertising and research costs.

    b.  A segment is a product line, geographical area, or other meaningful subunit of the organization.

    c.  Committed costs result when a going concern holds fixed assets (property, plant, and equipment). Examples are insurance, long-term lease payments, and depreciation.

    d.  Profit margin is net income divided by sales. It shows the percentage of sales dollars resulting in net income (return on investment).

4.    Allocation of **central administration costs** is a fundamental issue in responsibility accounting.  It is usually made based on budgeted revenue or contribution margin.

    a.    If allocation is based on actual sales or contribution margin, responsibility centers that increase their sales (or CM) will be charged with increased overhead.

    b.    If central administrative or other fixed costs are not allocated, responsibility centers might reach their revenue (or CM) goals without covering all fixed costs (which is necessary to operate in the long run).

    c.    Allocation of overhead, however, is motivationally negative; central administrative or other fixed costs may appear noncontrollable and be unproductive.

    d.    A much preferred alternative is to budget a certain amount of CM earned by each responsibility center to the central administration based on negotiation.

        1)    The intended result is for each unit to see itself as contributing to the success of the overall entity rather than carrying the weight (cost) of central administration.

        2)    Central administration can then make the decision whether to expand, divest, or close responsibility centers.

5.    The responsibility for internal reports is management's.  Management may direct the accountant to provide a report in any format deemed suitable for the decision process.

6.    Stop and review!  You have completed the outline for this subunit.  Study multiple-choice questions 15 through 18 beginning on page 347.

## 9.3 COMMON COSTS

1.    **Common costs** are the costs of products, activities, facilities, services, or operations shared by two or more cost objects.

    a.    The term **joint costs** is frequently used to describe the common costs of a single process that yields two or more joint products.

2.    The difficulty with common costs is that they are **indirect costs** whose allocation may be arbitrary.

    a.    A direct **cause-and-effect relationship** between a common cost and the actions of the cost object to which it is allocated is desirable.

        1)    Such a relationship promotes acceptance of the allocation by managers who perceive the fairness of the procedure, but identification of cause and effect may not be feasible.

    b.    An alternative allocation criterion is the **benefit received**.

        1)    For example, advertising costs that do not relate to particular products may increase sales of all products.

        2)    Allocation based on the increase in sales by organizational subunits is likely to be accepted as equitable despite the absence of clear cause-and-effect relationships.

    c.    Two specific approaches to common cost allocation are in general use.

        1)    EXAMPLE:  The proportionate costs of servicing three customers are presented in the table below.  The common cost of providing service to these customers is $8,000.

|  | Cost of Servicing | % |
|---|---|---|
| Luciano | $ 7,000 | 70% |
| Ratzinger | 2,000 | 20% |
| Wojtyla | 1,000 | 10% |
| Total | $10,000 | 100% |

      2)    The **stand-alone method** allocates a common cost to each cost object on a proportionate basis:

|  | Total Cost to Be Allocated | Allocation % | Allocated Cost |
|---|---|---|---|
| Luciano | $8,000 | 70% | $5,600 |
| Ratzinger | 8,000 | 20% | 1,600 |
| Wojtyla | 8,000 | 10% | 800 |
| Total |  | 100% | $8,000 |

      3)    The **incremental method** allocates the common cost up to the amount of each cost object's traceable cost total:

|  | Traceable Cost | Allocated Cost |
|---|---|---|
| Luciano | $ 7,000 | $7,000 |
| Ratzinger | 2,000 | 1,000 |
| Wojtyla | 1,000 | 0 |
| Total | $10,000 | $8,000 |

3.    Cost allocation is necessary for making economic decisions, e.g., the price to charge for a product, whether to make or buy a part, or whether to divest a segment.

    a.    Cost allocation is also necessary for external financial reporting and for calculation of reimbursements, such as those involved in governmental contracting.

    b.    Furthermore, cost allocation serves as a **motivator**.

      1)    For example, designers of products may be required to include downstream costs, such as servicing and distribution, in their cost projections to fix their attention on how their efforts affect the total costs of the company.

      2)    Another typical example of the motivational effects of cost allocation is that it tends to encourage marketing personnel to emphasize products with large contribution margins.

4.    A persistent problem in large organizations is the treatment of the costs of headquarters and other **central support costs**. Such costs are frequently allocated.

    a.    Research has shown that central support costs are allocated to departments or divisions for the following reasons:

      1)    The allocation reminds managers that support costs exist and that the managers would incur these costs if their operations were independent.

      2)    The allocation reminds managers that profit center earnings must cover some amount of support costs.

      3)    Departments or divisions should be motivated to use central support services appropriately.

      4)    Managers who must bear the costs of central support services that they do not control may be encouraged to exert pressure on those who do. Thus, they may be able to restrain such costs indirectly.

5.    Negative behavioral effects may arise from arbitrary cost allocations.

    a.    Managers' morale may suffer when allocations depress operating results.

    b.    Dysfunctional conflict may arise among managers when costs controlled by one are allocated to others.

    c.    Resentment may result if cost allocation is perceived to be arbitrary or unfair.

        1)    For example, an allocation on an ability-to-bear basis, such as operating income, penalizes successful managers and rewards underachievers and may therefore have a demotivating effect.

6.    Stop and review!  You have completed the outline for this subunit.  Study multiple-choice questions 19 through 21 on page 349.

## 9.4 TRANSFER PRICING

1.    **Transfer prices** are the amounts charged by one segment of an organization for goods and services it provides to **another segment of the same organization**.

    a.    Transfer prices are used by profit and investment centers (a cost center's costs are allocated to producing departments).

        1)    The problem is the determination of the transfer price when one responsibility center purchases from another.

        2)    In a decentralized system, each responsibility center theoretically may be completely separate.

           a)    Thus, Division A should charge the same price to Division B as would be charged to an outside buyer.

           b)    The reason for decentralization is to motivate managers, and the best interests of Division A may not be served by giving a special discount to Division B if the goods can be sold at the regular price to outside buyers.  However, having A sell at a special price to B may be to the company's advantage.

2.    A transfer price should permit a segment to operate as an independent entity and achieve its goals while functioning in the best interests of the company.  Hence, transfer pricing should motivate managers by encouraging goal congruence and managerial effort.

    a.    **Motivation** is the desire of managers to attain a specific goal and the commitment to accomplish the goal.  Managerial motivation is therefore a combination of goal congruence and managerial effort.

    b.    **Goal congruence** takes place when a manager's individual goals align with those of the organization.

        1)    Performance is assumed to be optimized when the parties understand that personal and segmental goals should be consistent with those of the organization.

    c.    **Managerial effort** is the extent to which a manager attempts to accomplish a goal.

        1)    Managerial effort may include psychological as well as physical commitment to a goal.

3.    Transfer prices can be determined in a number of ways.  They may be based on

    a.    A **market price**, assuming that a market exists

    b.    **Differential outlay cost plus opportunity cost to the seller**

        1)    For example, if a good costing $4 can be sold for $10, the outlay cost is $4 and the seller's opportunity cost is $6 (given no idle capacity).

    c.    **Full absorption cost**

        1)    Full-cost price includes materials, labor, and full allocation of manufacturing overhead.

d. **Cost plus a lump sum or a markup percentage**

   1) Cost may be either the standard or the actual cost. The former has the advantage of isolating variances. Actual costs give the selling division little incentive to control costs.

   2) A cost-based price ignores market prices and may not promote long-term efficiencies.

e. **Negotiation**

   1) A negotiated price may result when organizational subunits are free to determine the prices at which they buy and sell internally. Hence, a transfer price may simply reflect the best bargain that the parties can strike between themselves.

   2) The transfer price need not be based directly on particular market or cost information.

   3) A negotiated price may be especially appropriate when market prices are subject to rapid fluctuation.

4. The **choice of a transfer pricing policy** (which type of transfer price to use) is normally decided by top management at the corporate level. The decision will typically include consideration of the following:

   a. **Goal congruence factors**

      1) The transfer price should promote the goals of the company as a whole.

   b. **Segmental performance factors**

      1) The segment making the transfer should be allowed to recover its incremental cost plus its opportunity cost of the transfer. The opportunity cost is the benefit forgone by not selling to an outsider.

         a) For this purpose, the transfer should be at market price.

         b) The selling manager should not lose income by selling within the company.

      2) Properly allocating revenues and expenses through appropriate transfer pricing also facilitates evaluation of the performance of the various segments.

   c. **Negotiation factors**

      1) If the purchasing segment could purchase the product or service outside the company, it should be permitted to negotiate the transfer price.

      2) The purchasing manager should not have to incur greater costs by purchasing within the company.

   d. **Capacity factors**

      1) If Division A has excess capacity, it should be used for producing products for Division B. If Division A is operating at full capacity and selling its products at the full market price, profitable work should not be abandoned to produce for Division B.

   e. **Cost structure factors**

      1) If Division A has excess capacity and an opportunity arises to sell to Division B at a price in excess of the variable cost, the work should be performed for Division B because a contribution to cover the fixed costs will result.

   f. **Tax factors**

      1) A wide range of tax issues on the interstate and international levels may arise, e.g., income taxes, sales taxes, value-added taxes, inventory and payroll taxes, and other governmental charges.

     2)    In the international context, exchange rate fluctuations, threats of expropriation, and limits on transfers of profits outside the host country are additional concerns.

        a)    Thus, because the best transfer price may be a low one because of the existence of tariffs or a high one because of the existence of foreign exchange controls, the effect may be to skew the performance statistics of management.

        b)    The high transfer price may result in foreign management appearing to show a lower return on investment than domestic management, but the ratio differences may be negated by the fact that a different transfer pricing formula is used.

5.    **EXAMPLE:**

    a.    Division A produces a small part at a cost of $6 per unit. The regular selling price is $10 per unit. If Division B can use the part in its production, the cost to the company (as a whole) will be $6.

    b.    Division B has another supplier who will sell the item to B at $9.50 per part. Division B wants to buy the $9.50 part from the outside supplier instead of the $10 part from Division A, but making the part for $6 is in the company's best interest.

    c.    What amount should Division A charge Division B?

        1)    The answer is complicated by many factors. For example, if Division A has excess capacity, B should be charged a lower price. If it is operating at full capacity, B should be charged $10.

        2)    Also consider what portion of Division A's costs is fixed. For example, if a competitor offered to sell the part to B at $5 each, can Division A advantageously sell to B at a price lower than $5? If Division A's $6 total cost is composed of $4 of variable costs and $2 of fixed costs, it is beneficial for all concerned for A to sell to B at a price less than $5. Even at a price of $4.01, the parts would be providing a contribution margin to cover some of A's fixed costs.

6.    **Dual pricing** is another internal price-setting alternative.

    a.    For example, the seller could record the transfer to another segment at the usual market price that would be paid by an outsider. The buyer, however, would record a purchase at the variable cost of production.

        1)    Each segment's reported performance is improved by the use of a dual-pricing scheme.

        2)    The company would benefit because variable costs would be used for decision-making purposes. In a sense, variable costs would be the relevant price for decision-making purposes, but the regular market price would be used for evaluation of production divisions.

    b.    However, under a dual-pricing system, the profit for the company will be less than the sum of the profits of the individual segments.

        1)    In effect, the seller is given a corporate subsidy under the dual-pricing system.

        2)    The dual-pricing system is rarely used because the incentive to control costs is reduced.

            a)    The seller is assured of a high price, and the buyer is assured of an artificially low price. Thus, neither manager must exert much effort to show a profit on segmental performance reports.

7.    Stop and review! You have completed the outline for this subunit. Study multiple-choice questions 22 through 36 beginning on page 350.

## 9.5 FINANCIAL MEASURES

1.  **Product profitability analysis** allows management to determine whether a product is providing any coverage of fixed costs.

    EXAMPLE:

    a.  At first glance, a dairy operation appears to be comfortably profitable.

    | | |
    |---|---:|
    | Sales | $540,000 |
    | Variable Costs | 312,000 |
    | Contribution margin | $228,000 |
    | Other traceable costs: | |
    | Marketing | 116,000 |
    | R&D | 18,000 |
    | Product line margin | $ 94,000 |
    | Fixed costs | 24,000 |
    | Operating income | $ 70,000 |

    b.  A product profitability analysis shows an entirely different picture. Two product lines are losing money, and one is not even covering its own variable costs.

    | | Milk | Cream | Cottage Cheese | Total |
    |---|---:|---:|---:|---:|
    | Sales | $300,000 | $ 60,000 | $180,000 | $540,000 |
    | Variable costs | 110,000 | 62,000 | 140,000 | 312,000 |
    | Contribution margin | $190,000 | $ (2,000) | $ 40,000 | $228,000 |
    | Other traceable costs: | | | | |
    | Marketing | 66,000 | 10,000 | 40,000 | 116,000 |
    | R&D | 8,000 | 4,000 | 6,000 | 18,000 |
    | Product line margin | $116,000 | $(16,000) | $ (6,000) | $ 94,000 |
    | Fixed costs | | | | 24,000 |
    | Operating income | | | | $ 70,000 |

2.  **Business unit profitability analysis** performs the same function on the segment level.

    a.  EXAMPLE: A business unit profitability analysis for a company that provides research services allows management to see which branch offices are the most profitable.

    | | Sacramento | Omaha | Albany | Jacksonville | Total |
    |---|---:|---:|---:|---:|---:|
    | Sales | $1,200,000 | $800,000 | $2,000,000 | $4,600,000 | $8,600,000 |
    | Variable costs of sales | 800,000 | 460,000 | 1,400,000 | 3,200,000 | 5,860,000 |
    | Other variable costs | 256,000 | 176,000 | 320,000 | 544,000 | 1,296,000 |
    | Contribution margin | $ 144,000 | $164,000 | $ 280,000 | $ 856,000 | $1,444,000 |
    | Traceable fixed costs | 150,000 | 100,000 | 160,000 | 220,000 | 630,000 |
    | Business unit margin | $ (6,000) | $ 64,000 | $ 120,000 | $ 636,000 | $ 814,000 |
    | Nontraceable fixed costs | | | | | 200,000 |
    | Operating income | | | | | $ 614,000 |

3.  **Customer profitability analysis** enables a firm to make decisions about whether to continue servicing a given customer.

    a.  EXAMPLE: At first glance, it appears that the two unprofitable customers should be dropped.

|  | Gonzales | Abdullah | Patel | Kawanishi | Total |
|---|---|---|---|---|---|
| Sales | $10,000 | $40,000 | $62,000 | $22,000 | $134,000 |
| Cost of goods sold | 7,200 | 26,000 | 41,000 | 18,100 | 92,300 |
| Other relevant costs | 1,000 | 2,200 | 4,400 | 4,100 | 11,700 |
| Customer margin | $ 1,800 | $11,800 | $16,600 | $ (200) | $ 30,000 |
| Allocated fixed costs | 2,000 | 6,000 | 8,800 | 4,000 | 20,800 |
| Operating income | $ (200) | $ 5,800 | $ 7,800 | $(4,200) | $ 9,200 |

    b.  Dropping Kawanishi makes sense. However, Gonzales is contributing to the coverage of fixed costs, costs which would have to be shifted to the other customers if Gonzales were dropped.

4.  **Return on investment (ROI)** is the key performance measure of an investment center.

    a.  The well-known **DuPont method** of financial planning and control decomposes ROI into **total assets turnover** and **profit margin**. This formula emphasizes that ROI may be explained in terms of the efficiency of asset management and the profit margin.

$$\frac{Sales}{Total\ assets} \times \frac{Net\ income}{Sales} = \frac{Net\ income}{Total\ assets}$$

    b.  A variant of the DuPont formula is **return on equity**, which equals total assets turnover, times the profit margin, times the equity multiplier (also known as the financial leverage ratio).

$$\frac{Sales}{Total\ assets} \times \frac{Net\ income}{Sales} \times \frac{Total\ assets}{Equity} = \frac{Net\ income}{Equity}$$

    c.  A major problem with ROI is that a responsibility center with a high ROI may not accept a profitable investment if its ROI is less than the center's targeted ROI.

5.  **Residual income** is the excess of the return on an investment over a targeted amount equal to an imputed interest charge on invested capital.

    a.  The rate is ordinarily the weighted-average cost of capital, but it may be an arbitrary hurdle rate.

    b.  Projects with a positive residual income should be accepted, and projects with a negative residual income should be rejected.

    c.  Residual income is often touted as superior to ROI. It may be more consistent with maximizing profits.

6.  **Economic value added (EVA®)** is a more specific version of residual income.

    a.  The ideas behind EVA® have been around for a long time, but the concept has been trademarked by the consulting firm Stern, Stewart & Co.

    b.  In the EVA® equation, after-tax operating income equals [earnings before interest and taxes × (1.0 − the tax rate)]. The after-tax, weighted-average cost of capital is determined based on the fair values of debt and equity. EVA® equals:

$$After\text{-}tax\ OI - [After\text{-}tax\ WACC \times (Total\ assets - Current\ liabilities)]$$

    c.    EVA® represents a business unit's true **economic profit** primarily because a charge for the cost of equity capital is implicit in the cost of capital.

        1)    The cost of equity is an opportunity cost, that is, the return that could have been obtained on the best alternative investment of similar risk.

        2)    Hence, EVA® measures the marginal benefit obtained by using resources in a particular way. It is useful for determining whether a segment of a business is increasing **shareholder value**.

    d.    EVA® differs from accounting income not only because it subtracts the cost of equity but also because it makes certain other adjustments.

        1)    For example, R&D costs may be capitalized and amortized over five years for EVA® purposes, and true economic depreciation rather than the amount used for accounting or tax purposes may be recognized. Adjustments will vary from firm to firm.

    e.    EVA® is one of several methods for measuring managerial performance regarding creation of shareholder value.

        1)    The **equity spread** calculates equity value creation by multiplying beginning equity capital by the difference between the return on equity (net income ÷ equity) and the percentage cost of equity.

        2)    **Total shareholder return** equals the change in the stock price plus dividends per share, divided by the initial stock price.

        3)    The most straightforward calculation of **market value added** determines the wealth created during a stated period as the difference between the market value of equity (shares outstanding × market price) and the adjusted equity supplied by shareholders. Debt is assumed to equal its book value in this version of MVA because of the difficulty of estimating its market value.

           a)    The equity supplied must be adjusted for any adverse past changes in book value, such as writeoffs for extraordinary losses.

           b)    MVA reflects the evaluation of the firm's future performance by the securities markets.

           c)    MVA does not consider dividend payment performance or the returns on alternative uses of capital.

           d)    A standardized measure can be calculated by dividing the current period's MVA by the adjusted equity value at the end of the prior period.

7.    **Investment bases** must be compared to ensure comparability of the results of entities of different sizes.

    a.    Different **attributes** of financial information may be used to measure the elements of the investment base.

        1)    Historical cost
        2)    Replacement cost
        3)    Market value
        4)    Present value

    b.    **Alternative income measurements** are

        1)    Net income
        2)    Net income adjusted for price level changes
        3)    Cash flow
        4)    Earnings before interest and taxes (EBIT)

c. **Invested capital** may be defined in various ways, for example, as

    1) Total assets available

    2) Total assets employed, which excludes assets that are idle, such as vacant land

    3) Working capital plus other assets, which excludes current liabilities (i.e., capital provided by short-term creditors)

      a) This investment base assumes that the manager controls short-term credit.

    4) Equity, which includes an allocated portion of long-term liabilities

      a) One problem with this investment base is that, although it has the advantage of emphasizing return to owners, it reflects decisions at different levels of the entity: short-term liabilities incurred by the responsibility center and long-term liabilities controlled at the corporate level.

8. The **cash flow return on investment (CFROI)** is a measure reflecting the belief that cash generation is the truest way to evaluate a firm in the long run.

    a. Broadly speaking, CFROI is sustainable cash flow divided by the cash invested.

    b. CFROI may be stated as an **internal rate of return (IRR)** over the economic life of the firm's assets.

      1) The difference (the CFROI spread) between the IRR (the rate at which the net present value of cash flows is zero) and the real cost of capital is a measure of the firm's ability to create value.

    c. Focusing on cash avoids the effects of choices of accounting policies and other stratagems (e.g., off-balance-sheet financing using operating leases) for managing earnings.

      1) Moreover, CFROI adjusts for the effects of inflation and depreciation.

    d. The complicated calculation is generally made for a period of at least 5 years so that long-term average economic conditions are considered in the forecast.

    e. The determination of CFROI requires

      1) Restating financial statement information into current dollars

      2) Estimating cash flows, including outlays for taxes, in current dollars after making inflation adjustments for monetary and near-monetary assets

      3) Forecasting the useful lives of assets and the residual values of nondepreciable and nonamortizable assets at the end of the forecast period

9. The comparability of performance measures may be affected by differences in the **accounting policies** used by different business units.

    a. For example, policies regarding depreciation, decisions to capitalize or expense, inventory flow assumptions, and revenue recognition can lead to comparability issues for performance measures.

      1) These differences may be heightened for the business units of a **multinational enterprise**.

    b. **Issues other than accounting policy** may also affect comparability.

      1) Differences in the tax systems in the jurisdictions where business units operate

      2) The presence of extraordinary items of profit or loss

      3) Allocation of common costs

      4) The varying availability of resources

    c.    Other issues face business units operating in **foreign countries**:

        1)    Changes in foreign currency exchange rates and inflation rates

        2)    Limitations on repatriation of earnings and investments imposed by the government of a foreign operation's host country

        3)    Threats of expropriation of assets held in foreign countries

        4)    The imposition of tariffs, import-export duties, and price controls

    d.    In addition, **nonfinancial performance measures** are important for day-to-day control in assessing the quality of processes and products.

        1)    Some nonfinancial performance indicators include rework, outgoing quality level, returned merchandise, total setup time, customer report card, competitive rank, and on-time delivery.

10.    Stop and review!  You have completed the outline for this subunit.  Study multiple-choice questions 37 through 58 beginning on page 355.

## 9.6 CORE CONCEPTS

### Responsibility Centers

- A well-designed responsibility accounting system establishes **responsibility centers** (also called **strategic business units**) for the purpose of encouraging managerial effort to attain organizational objectives.
- A **cost center**, e.g., a maintenance department, is responsible for costs only.
- A **revenue center**, e.g., a sales department, is responsible for revenues only.
- A **profit center**, e.g., an appliance department in a retail store, is responsible for revenues and expenses.
- An **investment center**, e.g., a branch office, is responsible for revenues, expenses, and invested capital.

### Contribution and Segment Reporting

- The contribution approach to performance evaluation is emphasized in responsibility accounting because it focuses on **controllability**.
- The **contribution margin** income statement focuses on **relevant revenues and costs**.

### Common Costs

- **Common costs** are the costs of products, activities, facilities, services, or operations shared by two or more cost objects.
- Two specific approaches to common cost allocation are in general use, the **stand-alone method** and the **incremental method**.

### Transfer Pricing

- **Transfer prices** are the amounts charged by one segment of an organization for goods and services it provides to **another segment of the same organization**.
- A transfer price should permit a segment to operate as an independent entity and achieve its goals while functioning in the **best interests of the company**.
- Hence, transfer pricing should **motivate managers** by encouraging goal congruence and managerial effort.

## Financial Measures

- **Product profitability analysis** allows management to determine whether a product is providing any coverage of fixed costs.
- **Business unit profitability analysis** performs the same function on the segment level.
- **Customer profitability analysis** enables a firm to make decisions about whether to continue servicing a given customer.
- **Return on investment, residual income**, and **economic value added** (EVA®) are all useful measures for segment profitability analysis.

## QUESTIONS

### 9.1 Responsibility Centers

**1.** Fairmount, Inc. uses an accounting system that charges costs to the manager who has been delegated the authority to make the decisions incurring the costs. For example, if the sales manager accepts a rush order that will result in higher-than-normal manufacturing costs, these additional costs are charged to the sales manager because the authority to accept or decline the rush order was given to the sales manager. This type of accounting system is known as

A. Responsibility accounting.

B. Functional accounting.

C. Reciprocal allocation.

D. Transfer price accounting.

Answer (A) is correct. *(CMA, adapted)*
**REQUIRED:** The system in which additional costs are charged to the manager with authority for their incurrence.
**DISCUSSION:** In a responsibility accounting system, managerial performance should be evaluated only on the basis of those factors directly regulated (or at least capable of being significantly influenced) by the manager. For this purpose, operations are organized into responsibility centers. Costs are classified as controllable and noncontrollable, which implies that some revenues and costs can be changed through effective management. If a manager has authority to incur costs, a responsibility accounting system will charge them to the manager's responsibility center. However, controllability is not an absolute basis for establishment of responsibility. More than one manager may be able to influence a cost, and responsibility may be assigned on the basis of knowledge about the incurrence of a cost rather than the ability to control it.
Answer (B) is incorrect because functional accounting allocates costs to functions regardless of responsibility. Answer (C) is incorrect because reciprocal allocation is a means of allocating service department costs. Answer (D) is incorrect because transfer price accounting is a means of charging one department for products acquired from another department in the same organization.

**2.** In responsibility accounting, a center's performance is measured by controllable costs. Controllable costs are best described as including

A. Direct material and direct labor only.

B. Only those costs that the manager can influence in the current time period.

C. Only discretionary costs.

D. Those costs about which the manager is knowledgeable and informed.

Answer (B) is correct. *(CMA, adapted)*
**REQUIRED:** The elements of controllable costs.
**DISCUSSION:** Control is the process of making certain that plans are achieving the desired objectives. A controllable cost is one that is influenced by a specific responsible manager at a given level of production within a given time span. For example, fixed costs are often not controllable in the short run.
Answer (A) is incorrect because many overhead costs are also controllable. Answer (C) is incorrect because controllable costs need not be discretionary. Discretionary costs are characterized by uncertainty about the relationship between input and the value of the related output; they may or may not be controllable. Answer (D) is incorrect because controllable costs are those over which a manager has control; the manager may be informed or know about costs that (s)he cannot directly regulate or influence.

**3.** A segment of an organization is referred to as a service center if it has

A. Responsibility for developing markets and selling the output of the organization.

B. Responsibility for combining the raw materials, direct labor, and other factors of production into a final output.

C. Authority to make decisions affecting the major determinants of profit including the power to choose its markets and sources of supply.

D. Authority to provide specialized support to other units within the organization.

Answer (D) is correct.  *(CMA, adapted)*
   **REQUIRED:** The definition of a service center.
   **DISCUSSION:** A service center exists primarily and sometimes solely to provide specialized support to other units within the organization. Service centers are usually operated as cost centers.
   Answer (A) is incorrect because a service center has no responsibility for developing markets or selling. Answer (B) is incorrect because a production center is engaged in manufacturing. Answer (C) is incorrect because a profit center can choose its markets and sources of supply.

**4.** The least complex segment or area of responsibility for which costs are allocated is a(n)

A. Profit center.

B. Investment center.

C. Contribution center.

D. Cost center.

Answer (D) is correct.  *(CMA, adapted)*
   **REQUIRED:** The least complex segment or area of responsibility for which costs are allocated.
   **DISCUSSION:** A cost center is a responsibility center that is accountable only for costs. The cost center is the least complex type of segment because it has no responsibility for revenues or investments.
   Answer (A) is incorrect because a profit center is a segment responsible for both revenues and costs. A profit center has the authority to make decisions concerning markets and sources of supply. Answer (B) is incorrect because an investment center is a responsibility center that is accountable for revenues (markets), costs (sources of supply), and invested capital. Answer (C) is incorrect because a contribution center is responsible for revenues and variable costs, but not invested capital.

**5.** The budgeting process that uses management by objectives and input from the individual manager is an example of the application of

A. Flexible budgeting.

B. Human resource management.

C. Responsibility accounting.

D. Capital budgeting.

Answer (C) is correct.  *(CMA, adapted)*
   **REQUIRED:** The type of system in which the budgeting process uses MBO and input from individual managers.
   **DISCUSSION:** Managerial performance should ideally be evaluated only on the basis of those factors controllable by the manager. Managers may control revenues, costs, or investments in resources. A well-designed responsibility accounting system establishes responsibility centers within the organization. However, controllability is not an absolute basis for establishment of responsibility. More than one manager may be able to influence a cost, and responsibility may be assigned on the basis of knowledge about the incurrence of a cost rather than the ability to control it. Management by objectives (MBO) is a related concept. It is a behavioral, communications-oriented, responsibility approach to employee self-direction. Under MBO, a manager and his/her subordinates agree upon objectives and the means of attaining them. The plans that result are reflected in responsibility accounting and in the budgeting process.
   Answer (A) is incorrect because flexible budgeting is the process of preparing a series of multiple budgets for varying levels of production or sales. Answer (B) is incorrect because human resource management is the process of managing personnel. Answer (D) is incorrect because capital budgeting is a means of evaluating long-term investments.

**6.** Which of the following techniques would be best for evaluating the management performance of a department that is operated as a cost center?

- A. Return on assets ratio.
- B. Return on investment ratio.
- C. Payback method.
- D. Variance analysis.

Answer (D) is correct. *(CIA, adapted)*
**REQUIRED:** The best method for evaluating a cost center.
**DISCUSSION:** A cost center is a responsibility center that is responsible for costs only. Of the alternatives given, variance analysis is the only one that can be used in a cost center. Variance analysis involves comparing actual costs with predicted or standard costs.
Answer (A) is incorrect because return on assets cannot be computed for a cost center. The manager is not responsible for revenue (return) or the assets available. Answer (B) is incorrect because return on investment cannot be computed for a cost center. The manager is not responsible for revenue (return) or the assets available. Answer (C) is incorrect because the payback method is a means of evaluating alternative investment proposals.

**7.** Responsibility accounting defines an operating center that is responsible for revenue and costs as a(n)

- A. Profit center.
- B. Revenue center.
- C. Division.
- D. Operating unit.

Answer (A) is correct. *(CMA, adapted)*
**REQUIRED:** The name given to a responsibility center that is responsible for both revenue and costs.
**DISCUSSION:** A profit center is responsible for both revenues and costs, whereas a cost center is responsible only for costs.
Answer (B) is incorrect because a revenue center is responsible only for revenues, not costs. Answer (C) is incorrect because a division can be any type of responsibility center. Answer (D) is incorrect because an operating unit can be organized as any type of center.

**8.** Decentralized firms can delegate authority and yet retain control and monitor managers' performance by structuring the organization into responsibility centers. Which one of the following organizational segments is most like an independent business?

- A. Revenue center.
- B. Profit center.
- C. Cost center.
- D. Investment center.

Answer (D) is correct. *(CMA, adapted)*
**REQUIRED:** The organizational segment most like an independent business.
**DISCUSSION:** An investment center is the organizational type most like an independent business because it is responsible for its own revenues, costs incurred, and capital invested. The other types of centers do not incorporate all three elements.
Answer (A) is incorrect because a revenue center is responsible only for revenue generation, not for costs or capital investment. Answer (B) is incorrect because a profit center is responsible for revenues and costs but not for invested capital. Answer (C) is incorrect because a cost center is evaluated only on the basis of costs incurred. It is not responsible for revenues or invested capital.

**9.** The basic purpose of a responsibility accounting system is

- A. Budgeting.
- B. Motivation.
- C. Authority.
- D. Variance analysis.

Answer (B) is correct. *(CMA, adapted)*
**REQUIRED:** The basic purpose of a responsibility accounting system.
**DISCUSSION:** The basic purpose of a responsibility accounting system is to motivate management to perform in a manner consistent with overall company objectives. The assignment of responsibility implies that some revenues and costs can be changed through effective management. The system should have certain controls that provide for feedback reports indicating deviations from expectations. Higher-level management may focus on those deviations for either reinforcement or correction.
Answer (A) is incorrect because budgeting is an element of a responsibility accounting system, not the basic purpose. Answer (C) is incorrect because authority is an element of a responsibility accounting system, not the basic purpose. Answer (D) is incorrect because analysis of variances is an element of a responsibility accounting system, not the basic purpose.

**10.** A successful responsibility accounting reporting system is dependent upon

A. The correct allocation of controllable variable costs.

B. Identification of the management level at which all costs are controllable.

C. The proper delegation of responsibility and authority.

D. A reasonable separation of costs into their fixed and variable components since fixed costs are not controllable and must be eliminated from the responsibility report.

Answer (C) is correct. *(CMA, adapted)*
**REQUIRED:** The factor upon which a successful responsibility accounting system is dependent.
**DISCUSSION:** Managerial performance should ideally be evaluated only on the basis of those factors controllable by the manager. Managers may control revenues, costs, and/or investments in resources. However, controllability is not an absolute. More than one manager may be able to influence a cost, and managers may be accountable for some costs they do not control. In practice, given the difficulties of determining the locus of controllability, responsibility may be assigned on the basis of knowledge about the incurrence of a cost rather than the ability to control it. Accordingly, a successful system is dependent upon the proper delegation of responsibility and the commensurate authority.
Answer (A) is incorrect because fixed costs may also be controllable, and some costs not controllable may need to be assigned. Answer (B) is incorrect because knowledge about the incurrence of a cost rather than controllability may in practice be an appropriate basis for delegation of responsibility. Answer (D) is incorrect because fixed costs can be controllable.

**11.** Rockford Manufacturing Corporation uses a responsibility accounting system in its operations. Which one of the following items is least likely to appear in a performance report for a manager of one of Rockford's assembly lines?

A. Direct labor.

B. Materials.

C. Repairs and maintenance.

D. Depreciation on the manufacturing facility.

Answer (D) is correct. *(CMA, adapted)*
**REQUIRED:** The item least likely to appear on a performance report for an assembly line manager.
**DISCUSSION:** A well-designed responsibility accounting system establishes responsibility centers within an organization. In a responsibility accounting system, managerial performance should be evaluated only on the basis of those factors directly regulated (or at least capable of being significantly influenced) by the manager. Thus, a manager of an assembly line is responsible for direct labor, materials, repairs and maintenance, and supervisory salaries. The manager is not responsible for depreciation on the manufacturing facility. (S)he is not in a position to control or influence capital budgeting decisions.
Answer (A) is incorrect because direct labor is controllable by the production manager. Answer (B) is incorrect because materials are controllable by the production manager. Answer (C) is incorrect because repairs and maintenance are controllable by the production manager.

**12.** Sherman Company uses a performance reporting system that reflects the company's decentralization of decision making. The departmental performance report shows one line of data for each subordinate who reports to the group vice president. The data presented show the actual costs incurred during the period, the budgeted costs, and all variances from budget for that subordinate's department. Sherman is using a type of system called

A. Contribution accounting.

B. Cost-benefit accounting.

C. Flexible budgeting.

D. Responsibility accounting.

Answer (D) is correct. *(CMA, adapted)*
**REQUIRED:** The system in which each manager's performance report shows the costs actually incurred in the manager's department.
**DISCUSSION:** In a responsibility accounting system, managerial performance should be evaluated only on the basis of those factors directly regulated (or at least capable of being significantly influenced) by the manager. For this purpose, operations are organized into responsibility centers. Costs are classified as controllable and noncontrollable, which implies that some revenues and costs can be changed through effective management. If a manager has authority to incur costs, a responsibility accounting system will charge those costs to the manager's responsibility center.
Answer (A) is incorrect because contribution accounting is a method of control in which only variable costs are matched with revenues. Answer (B) is incorrect because cost-benefit accounting is a nonsense term referring to matching costs and benefits. Answer (C) is incorrect because flexible budgeting prepares budgets for multiple levels of operations.

**13.** Overtime conditions and pay were recently set by the human resources department. The production department has just received a request for a rush order from the sales department. The production department protests that additional overtime costs will be incurred as a result of the order. The sales department argues that the order is from an important customer. The production department processes the order. To control costs, which department should never be charged with the overtime costs generated as a result of the rush order?

A. Human resources department.

B. Production department.

C. Sales department.

D. Shared by production department and sales department.

Answer (A) is correct. *(CIA, adapted)*
**REQUIRED:** The department that is never charged with overtime generated by a rush order.
**DISCUSSION:** The sales department should be responsible for the overtime costs because it can best judge whether the additional cost of the rush order is justified. The production department also may be held responsible for the overtime costs because charging the full overtime cost to the sales department would give the production department no incentive to control these costs. However, the human resources department would never be charged with the overtime costs because it has no effect on the incurrence of production overtime.
Answer (B) is incorrect because, to control costs, the production department may be charged with the overtime costs. Answer (C) is incorrect because, to control costs, the sales department may be charged with the overtime costs. Answer (D) is incorrect because the sales department and the production department may be charged with the overtime costs.

**14.** The format for internal reports in a responsibility accounting system is prescribed by

A. Generally accepted accounting principles.

B. The Financial Accounting Standards Board.

C. The American Institute of Certified Public Accountants.

D. Management.

Answer (D) is correct. *(Publisher)*
**REQUIRED:** The source of authority for the format of internal reports.
**DISCUSSION:** The responsibility for internal reports is management's. Management may direct the accountant to provide a report in any format deemed suitable for the decision process. The accountant should work closely with management to make these reports an effective communication device regarding the firm and its decisions.
Answer (A) is incorrect because generally accepted accounting principles concern external financial reporting, not internal reporting. Answer (B) is incorrect because the Financial Accounting Standards Board is concerned with external financial reporting, not internal reporting. Answer (C) is incorrect because the American Institute of Certified Public Accountants is concerned with external financial reporting, not internal reporting.

## 9.2 Contribution and Segment Reporting

**15.** The segment margin of the Wire Division of Lerner Corporation should not include

A. Net sales of the Wire Division.

B. Fixed selling expenses of the Wire Division.

C. Variable selling expenses of the Wire Division.

D. The Wire Division's fair share of the salary of Lerner Corporation's president.

Answer (D) is correct. *(CMA, adapted)*
**REQUIRED:** The item not included in a statement showing segment margin.
**DISCUSSION:** Segment margin is the contribution margin for a segment of a business minus fixed costs. It is a measure of long-run profitability. Thus, an allocation of the corporate officers' salaries should not be included in segment margin because they are neither variable costs nor fixed costs that can be rationally allocated to the segment. Other items that are often not allocated include corporate income taxes, interest, company-wide R&D expenses, and central administration costs.
Answer (A) is incorrect because sales of the division would appear on the statement. Answer (B) is incorrect because the division's fixed selling expenses are separable fixed costs. Answer (C) is incorrect because variable costs of the division are included.

**16.** Which one of the following firms is likely to experience dysfunctional motivation on the part of its managers due to its allocation methods?

A. To allocate depreciation of forklifts used by workers at its central warehouse, Shahlimar Electronics uses predetermined amounts calculated on the basis of the long-term average use of the services provided.

B. Manhattan Electronics uses the sales revenue of its various divisions to allocate costs connected with the upkeep of its headquarters building. It also uses ROI to evaluate the divisional performances.

C. Rainier Industrial does not allow its service departments to pass on their cost overruns to the production departments.

D. Tashkent Auto's MIS is operated out of headquarters and serves its various divisions. Tashkent's allocation of the MIS-related costs to its divisions is limited to costs the divisions will incur if they were to outsource their MIS needs.

Answer (B) is correct. *(CMA, adapted)*
**REQUIRED:** The firm most likely to experience dysfunctional motivation on the part of its managers.
**DISCUSSION:** Managerial performance ordinarily should be evaluated only on the basis of those factors controllable by the manager. If a manager is allocated costs that (s)he cannot control, dysfunctional motivation can result. In the case of allocations, a cause-and-effect basis should be used. Allocating the costs of upkeep on a headquarters building on the basis of sales revenue is arbitrary because cost may have no relationship to divisional sales revenues. Consequently, divisional ROI is reduced by a cost over which a division manager has no control. Furthermore, the divisions with the greatest sales are penalized by receiving the greatest allocation.
Answer (A) is incorrect because allocating depreciation on the basis of long-term average use is a reasonable basis of allocation. This basis is controllable by the division managers and reflects a causal relationship. Answer (C) is incorrect because a service department's cost overruns may not be attributable to any activities of production departments. Answer (D) is incorrect because market-based allocations of costs of services are reasonable applications of the cause-and-effect principle.

**17.** Consider the following information for Richardson Company for the prior year.

- The company produced 1,000 units and sold 900 units, both as budgeted.

- There were no beginning or ending work-in-process inventories and no beginning finished goods inventory.

- Budgeted and actual fixed costs were equal, all variable manufacturing costs were affected by production volume only, and all variable selling costs were affected by sales volume only.

- Budgeted per unit revenues and costs were as follows:

|  | Per unit |
| --- | --- |
| Sales price | $100 |
| Direct materials | 30 |
| Direct labor | 20 |
| Other variable manufacturing costs | 10 |
| Fixed selling costs | 5 |
| Variable selling costs | 12 |
| Fixed selling costs ($33,600 total) | 4 |
| Fixed administrative costs ($1,800 total) | 2 |

The contribution margin earned by Richardson for the prior year was

A. $25,200

B. $28,000

C. $31,500

D. $35,000

Answer (A) is correct. *(CMA, adapted)*
**REQUIRED:** The contribution margin.
**DISCUSSION:** The CM equals revenues minus all variable costs expensed. Given no WIP and no beginning finished goods, the CM was $25,200 [900 units × ($100 − $30 − $20 − $10 − $12)]. The variable costs of producing the units not sold are included in ending inventory, rather than in the CM. The fixed costs are also excluded from computation of the CM.
Answer (B) is incorrect because $28,000 results from assuming the sale of 1,000 units. Answer (C) is incorrect because $31,500 results from assuming a UCM of $35. This computation includes fixed unit selling costs of $5 but excludes the $12 per unit variable selling costs. Answer (D) is incorrect because $35,000 results from assuming a UCM of $35 and sales of 1,000 units.

**18.** When using a contribution margin format for internal reporting purposes, the major distinction between segment manager performance and segment performance is

    A. Unallocated fixed cost.

    B. Direct variable costs of producing the product.

    C. Direct fixed cost controllable by the segment manager.

    D. Direct fixed cost controllable by others.

Answer (D) is correct. *(CMA, adapted)*
    **REQUIRED:** The major distinction between segment manager performance and segment performance.
    **DISCUSSION:** Control of costs accounts for the major difference between segment manager performance and segment performance. Segment performance is based on all costs directly attributable to the segment. Segment manager performance is based on all costs directly controllable by the segment manager. All variable costs ordinarily meet the criteria for both measures. The difference usually arises because a fixed cost is directly attributable to a segment but is not controllable by the manager. For example, a profit center manager may have no control over fixed costs of the segment.
    Answer (A) is incorrect because unallocated fixed costs do not affect either performance measure. Answer (B) is incorrect because direct variable costs affect both performance measures. Answer (C) is incorrect because direct fixed costs controllable by others do not affect either of the performance measures.

### 9.3 Common Costs

**19.** Common costs are

    A. Direct costs.

    B. Current costs.

    C. Controllable costs.

    D. Indirect costs.

Answer (D) is correct. *(Publisher)*
    **REQUIRED:** The nature of common costs.
    **DISCUSSION:** Common costs are the cost of products, activities, facilities, services, or operations shared by two or more cost objects. They are indirect costs because they cannot be traced to a particular cost object in an economically feasible manner. Hence, they must be allocated.
    Answer (A) is incorrect because direct costs can be traced to a particular cost object in an economically feasible manner. Answer (B) is incorrect because current cost is an attribute used to measure assets. Answer (C) is incorrect because controllable costs can be influenced by a particular manager.

**20.** Managers are most likely to accept allocations of common costs based on

    A. Cause and effect.

    B. Ability to bear.

    C. Fairness.

    D. Benefits received.

Answer (A) is correct. *(Publisher)*
    **REQUIRED:** The criterion most likely to result in acceptable allocations of common costs.
    **DISCUSSION:** The difficulty with common costs is that they are indirect costs whose allocation may be arbitrary. A direct cause-and-effect relationship between a common cost and the actions of the cost object to which it is allocated is desirable. Such a relationship promotes acceptance of the allocation by managers who perceive the fairness of the procedure, but identification of cause and effect may not be feasible.
    Answer (B) is incorrect because allocation using an ability-to-bear criterion punishes successful managers and rewards underachievers. Answer (C) is incorrect because fairness is an objective rather than a criterion. Moreover, fairness may be interpreted differently by different managers. Answer (D) is incorrect because the benefits-received criterion is preferable when a cause-effect relationship cannot be feasibly identified.

**21.** A large corporation allocates the costs of its headquarters staff to its decentralized divisions. The best reason for this allocation is to

    A. More accurately measure divisional operating results.

    B. Improve divisional management's morale.

    C. Remind divisional managers that common costs exist.

    D. Discourage any use of central support services.

Answer (C) is correct. *(Publisher)*
    **REQUIRED:** The best reason for allocating headquarters costs.
    **DISCUSSION:** The allocation reminds managers that support costs exist and that the managers would incur these costs if their operations were independent. The allocation also reminds managers that profit center earnings must cover some amount of support costs.
    Answer (A) is incorrect because an arbitrary allocation may skew operating results. Answer (B) is incorrect because the allocation may create resentment and conflict. Answer (D) is incorrect because efficient use of central support services should be encouraged.

## 9.4 Transfer Pricing

**22.** The price that one division of a company charges another division for goods or services provided is called the

- A. Market price.
- B. Transfer price.
- C. Outlay price.
- D. Distress price.

**Answer (B) is correct.** *(CIA, adapted)*
**REQUIRED:** The price that one division of a company charges another for goods or services provided.
**DISCUSSION:** A transfer price is the price charged by one segment of an organization for a product or service supplied to another segment of the same organization.
Answer (A) is incorrect because market price is an approach to determine a transfer price. Answer (C) is incorrect because outlay price is an approach to determine a transfer price. Answer (D) is incorrect because distress price is an approach to determine a transfer price.

**23.** The most fundamental responsibility center affected by the use of market-based transfer prices is a(n)

- A. Production center.
- B. Investment center.
- C. Cost center.
- D. Profit center.

**Answer (D) is correct.** *(CMA, adapted)*
**REQUIRED:** The most fundamental responsibility center affected by the use of market-based transfer prices.
**DISCUSSION:** Transfer prices are often used by profit centers and investment centers. Profit centers are the more fundamental of these two centers because investment centers are responsible not only for revenues and costs but also for invested capital.
Answer (A) is incorrect because a production center may be a cost center, a profit center, or even an investment center. Transfer prices are not used in a cost center. Transfer prices are used to compute profitability, but a cost center is responsible only for cost control. Answer (B) is incorrect because an investment center is not as fundamental as a profit center. Answer (C) is incorrect because transfer prices are not used in a cost center.

**24.** Transfer pricing should encourage goal congruence and managerial effort. In a decentralized organization, it should also encourage autonomous decision making. Managerial effort is

- A. The desire and the commitment to achieve a specific goal.
- B. The extent to which individuals have the authority to make decisions.
- C. The extent of the attempt to accomplish a specific goal.
- D. The sharing of goals by supervisors and subordinates.

**Answer (C) is correct.** *(Publisher)*
**REQUIRED:** The definition of managerial effort.
**DISCUSSION:** Managerial effort is the extent to which a manager attempts to accomplish a goal. Managerial effort may include psychological as well as physical commitment to a goal.
Answer (A) is incorrect because motivation is the desire and the commitment to achieve a specific goal. Answer (B) is incorrect because autonomy is the extent to which individuals have the authority to make decisions. Answer (D) is incorrect because goal congruence is the sharing of goals by supervisors and subordinates.

**25.** Goal congruence is

- A. The desire and the commitment to achieve a specific goal.
- B. The sharing of goals by supervisors and subordinates.
- C. The extent to which individuals have the authority to make decisions.
- D. The extent of the attempt to accomplish a specific goal.

**Answer (B) is correct.** *(Publisher)*
**REQUIRED:** The definition of goal congruence.
**DISCUSSION:** Goal congruence is agreement on the goals of the organization and/or the segment by both supervisors and subordinates. Performance is assumed to be optimized when there is an understanding that personal and segmental goals be consistent with those of the organization.
Answer (A) is incorrect because motivation is the desire and the commitment to achieve a specific goal. Answer (C) is incorrect because autonomy is the extent to which individuals have the authority to make decisions. Answer (D) is incorrect because managerial effort is the extent of the attempt to accomplish a specific goal.

**26.** Motivation is

A. The desire and the commitment to achieve a specific goal.

B. The sharing of goals by supervisors and subordinates.

C. The extent to which individuals have the authority to make decisions.

D. The extent of the attempt to accomplish a specific goal.

Answer (A) is correct. *(Publisher)*
REQUIRED: The definition of motivation.
DISCUSSION: Motivation is the desire to attain a specific goal (goal congruence) and the commitment to accomplish the goal (managerial effort). Managerial motivation is therefore a combination of managerial effort and goal congruence.
Answer (B) is incorrect because goal congruence is the sharing of goals by supervisors and subordinates. Answer (C) is incorrect because autonomy is the extent to which individuals have the authority to make decisions. Answer (D) is incorrect because managerial effort is the extent of the attempt to accomplish a specific goal.

**27.** In theory, the optimal method for establishing a transfer price is

A. Flexible budget cost.

B. Incremental cost.

C. Budgeted cost with or without a markup.

D. Market price.

Answer (D) is correct. *(CMA, adapted)*
REQUIRED: The optimal method for establishing a transfer price.
DISCUSSION: Transfer prices are the amounts charged by one segment of an organization for goods and services it provides to another segment within the organization. Transfer prices should promote congruence of subunit goals with those of the organization, subunit autonomy, and managerial effort. Although no rule exists for determining the transfer price that meets these criteria in all situations, a starting point is to calculate the sum of the additional outlay costs and the opportunity cost to the supplier. Given no idle capacity and a competitive external market (all goods transferred internally can be sold externally), the sum of the outlay and opportunity costs will be the market price.
Answer (A) is incorrect because using flexible budget cost as a transfer price provides no motivation to the seller to control costs and no reward for selling internally when an external market exists. Answer (B) is incorrect because using incremental cost as a transfer price provides no motivation to the seller to control costs and no reward for selling internally when an external market exists. Answer (C) is incorrect because market price is preferable to a budgeted or actual cost with or without a markup (unless the markup equals the profit earned by selling externally).

**28.** A limitation of transfer prices based on actual cost is that they

A. Charge inefficiencies to the department that is transferring the goods.

B. Can lead to suboptimal decisions for the company as a whole.

C. Must be adjusted by some markup.

D. Lack clarity and administrative convenience.

Answer (B) is correct. *(CIA, adapted)*
REQUIRED: The limitation of transfer prices based on actual cost.
DISCUSSION: The optimal transfer price of a selling division should be set at a point that will have the most desirable economic effect on the firm as a whole while at the same time continuing to motivate the management of every division to perform efficiently. Setting the transfer price based on actual costs rather than standard costs would give the selling division little incentive to control costs.
Answer (A) is incorrect because inefficiencies are charged to the buying department. Answer (C) is incorrect because, by definition, cost-based transfer prices are not adjusted by some markup. Answer (D) is incorrect because cost-based transfer prices provide the advantages of clarity and administrative convenience.

**29.** Outlay cost plus opportunity cost is

A. The retail price.

B. The price representing the cash outflows of the supplying division plus the contribution to the supplying division from an outside sale.

C. The price usually set by an absorption-costing calculation.

D. The price set by charging for variable costs plus a lump sum or an additional markup, but less than full markup.

Answer (B) is correct.   *(Publisher)*
   **REQUIRED:** The definition of outlay cost plus opportunity cost.
   **DISCUSSION:** At this price, the supplying division is indifferent as to whether it sells internally or externally. Outlay cost plus opportunity cost therefore represents a minimum acceptable price for a seller. However, no transfer price formula is appropriate in all circumstances.
   Answer (A) is incorrect because the retail price is the definition of the market price, assuming an arm's-length transaction. Answer (C) is incorrect because full cost is the price usually set by an absorption-costing calculation. Answer (D) is incorrect because the variable-cost-plus price is the price set by charging for variable costs plus a lump sum or an additional markup, but less than full markup.

**30.** Variable-cost-plus price is

A. The price on the open market.

B. The price representing the cash outflows of the supplying division plus the contribution to the supplying division from an outside sale.

C. The price set by charging for variable costs plus a lump sum or an additional markup, but less than full markup.

D. The price usually set by an absorption costing calculation.

Answer (C) is correct.   *(Publisher)*
   **REQUIRED:** The definition of variable-cost-plus price.
   **DISCUSSION:** The variable-cost-plus price is the price set by charging for variable cost plus either a lump sum or an additional markup but less than the full markup price. This permits top management to enter the decision process and dictate that a division transfer at variable cost plus some appropriate amount.
   Answer (A) is incorrect because the price on the open market is the definition of the market price. Answer (B) is incorrect because outlay cost plus opportunity cost is the price representing the cash outflows of the supplying division plus the contribution to the supplying division from an outside sale. Answer (D) is incorrect because the full-cost price is the price usually set by an absorption-costing calculation.

**31.** Full-cost price is

A. The price on the open market.

B. The price representing the cash outflows of the supplying division plus the contribution to the supplying division from an outside sale.

C. The price usually set by an absorption-costing calculation.

D. The price set by charging for variable costs plus a lump sum or an additional markup, but less than full markup.

Answer (C) is correct.   *(Publisher)*
   **REQUIRED:** The definition of full-cost price.
   **DISCUSSION:** Full-cost price is the price usually set by an absorption-costing calculation and includes materials, labor, and a full allocation of manufacturing overhead. This full-cost price may lead to dysfunctional behavior by the supplying and receiving divisions, e.g., purchasing from outside sources at a slightly lower price that is substantially above the variable costs of internal production.
   Answer (A) is incorrect because the market price is the price on the open market. Answer (B) is incorrect because the outlay cost plus opportunity cost is the price representing the cash outflows of the supplying division plus the contribution to the supplying division from an outside sale. Answer (D) is incorrect because the variable-cost-plus price is the price set by charging for variable costs plus a lump sum or an additional markup, but less than full markup.

**32.** An appropriate transfer price between two divisions of The Stark Company can be determined from the following data:

Fabricating Division:

| | |
|---|---|
| Market price of subassembly | $50 |
| Variable cost of subassembly | $20 |
| Excess capacity (in units) | 1,000 |

Assembling Division:

| | |
|---|---|
| Number of units needed | 900 |

What is the natural bargaining range for the two divisions?

A. Between $20 and $50.

B. Between $50 and $70.

C. Any amount less than $50.

D. $50 is the only acceptable price.

Answer (A) is correct. *(CMA, adapted)*

**REQUIRED:** The natural bargaining range for the transfer price.

**DISCUSSION:** An ideal transfer price should permit each division to operate independently and achieve its goals while functioning in the best interest of the overall company. Transfer prices can be determined in a number of ways, including normal market price, negotiated price, variable costs, or full absorption costs. The capacity of the Selling Division is often a determinant of the ideal transfer price. If the Fabricating Division had no excess capacity, it would charge the Assembling Division the regular market price. However, if the Fabricating Division has excess capacity of 1,000 units, negotiation is possible because any transfer price greater than the variable cost of $20 would absorb some of its fixed costs and result in increased divisional profits. Thus, any price between $20 and $50 is acceptable to the Fabricating Division. Any price under $50 is acceptable to the Assembling Division because that is the price that would be paid to an outside supplier.

Answer (B) is incorrect because the Assembling Division would not pay more than the market price of $50. Answer (C) is incorrect because Fabricating will not be willing to accept less than its variable cost of $20. Answer (D) is incorrect because Fabricating should be willing to accept any price between $20 and $50.

**33.** A carpet manufacturer maintains a retail division consisting of stores stocking its brand and other brands, and a manufacturing division that makes carpets and pads. An outside market exists for carpet padding material in which all padding produced can be sold. The proper transfer price for padding transferred from the manufacturing division to the retail division is

A. Variable manufacturing division production cost.

B. Variable manufacturing division production cost plus allocated fixed factory overhead.

C. Variable manufacturing division production cost plus variable selling and administrative cost.

D. The market price at which the retail division could purchase padding.

Answer (D) is correct. *(CIA, adapted)*

**REQUIRED:** The proper transfer price for padding transferred from the manufacturing division to the retail division.

**DISCUSSION:** The three basic criteria that the transfer pricing system in a decentralized company should satisfy are to: (1) provide information allowing central management to evaluate divisions with respect to total company profit and each division's contribution to profit, (2) stimulate each manager's efficiency without losing each division's autonomy, and (3) motivate each divisional manager to achieve his/her own profit goal in a manner contributing to the company's success. The market price should be used as the transfer price to avoid waste and maximize efficiency in a competitive economy (an outside market in which all padding produced can be sold). This price also measures the product's profitability and the division managers' performance in a competitive environment.

Answer (A) is incorrect because the market price will better achieve the goals of a transfer pricing system. The selling division would not have as strong an incentive to control costs if some variant of actual cost is used. The efficiency of the purchasing division is also promoted when it must treat the selling division as if it were an independent vendor. Answer (B) is incorrect because the market price will better achieve the goals of a transfer pricing system. The selling division would not have as strong an incentive to control costs if some variant of actual cost is used. Answer (C) is incorrect because the market price will better achieve the goals of a transfer pricing system. The selling division would not have as strong an incentive to control costs if some variant of actual cost is used.

Questions 34 through 36 are based on the following information.

Parkside, Inc. has several divisions that operate as decentralized profit centers. Parkside's Entertainment Division manufactures video arcade equipment using the products of two of Parkside's other divisions. The Plastics Division manufactures plastic components, one type that is made exclusively for the Entertainment Division, while other less complex components are sold to outside markets. The products of the Video Cards Division are sold in a competitive market; however, one video card model is also used by the Entertainment Division.

The actual costs per unit used by the Entertainment Division are presented below.

|  | Plastic Components | Video Cards |
|---|---|---|
| Direct material | $1.25 | $2.40 |
| Direct labor | 2.35 | 3.00 |
| Variable overhead | 1.00 | 1.50 |
| Fixed overhead | .40 | 2.25 |
| Total cost | $5.00 | $9.15 |

The Plastics Division sells its commercial products at full cost plus a 25% markup and believes the proprietary plastic component made for the Entertainment Division would sell for $6.25 per unit on the open market. The market price of the video card used by the Entertainment Division is $10.98 per unit.

**34.** A per-unit transfer price from the Video Cards Division to the Entertainment Division at full cost, $9.15, would

- A. Allow evaluation of both divisions on a competitive basis.
- B. Satisfy the Video Cards Division's profit desire by allowing recovery of opportunity costs.
- C. Provide no profit incentive for the Video Cards Division to control or reduce costs.
- D. Encourage the Entertainment Division to purchase video cards from an outside source.

Answer (C) is correct. *(CMA, adapted)*
REQUIRED: The effect of a full-cost transfer price.
DISCUSSION: A transfer price is the amount one segment of an organization charges another segment for a product. The selling division should be allowed to recover its incremental cost plus the opportunity cost of the transfer. Hence, in a competitive market, the seller should be able to charge the market price. Using full cost as a transfer price provides no incentive to the seller to control production costs.
Answer (A) is incorrect because evaluating the seller is difficult if it can pass along all costs to the buyer. Answer (B) is incorrect because transfers at full cost do not allow for a seller's profit. Answer (D) is incorrect because a full-cost transfer is favorable to the buyer. It is lower than the market price.

**35.** Assume that the Entertainment Division is able to purchase a large quantity of video cards from an outside source at $8.70 per unit. The Video Cards Division, having excess capacity, agrees to lower its transfer price to $8.70 per unit. This action would

- A. Optimize the profit goals of the Entertainment Division while subverting the profit goals of Parkside, Inc.
- B. Allow evaluation of both divisions on the same basis.
- C. Subvert the profit goals of the Video Cards Division while optimizing the profit goals of the Entertainment Division.
- D. Optimize the overall profit goals of Parkside, Inc.

Answer (D) is correct. *(CMA, adapted)*
REQUIRED: The impact of lowering the transfer price to match an outside seller's price.
DISCUSSION: If the selling division has excess capacity, it should lower its transfer price to match the outside offer. This decision optimizes the profits of the company as a whole by allowing for use of capacity that would otherwise be idle.
Answer (A) is incorrect because this action is congruent with the goals of Parkside. The use of idle capacity enhances profits. Answer (B) is incorrect because the transfer is at a loss (relative to full cost) to the selling division, although the company as a whole will benefit. Answer (C) is incorrect because the buying division is indifferent as to whether to purchase internally or externally.

**36.** Assume that the Plastics Division has excess capacity and it has negotiated a transfer price of $5.60 per plastic component with the Entertainment Division. This price will

A. Cause the Plastics Division to reduce the number of commercial plastic components it manufactures.

B. Motivate both divisions as estimated profits are shared.

C. Encourage the Entertainment Division to seek an outside source for plastic components.

D. Demotivate the Plastics Division causing mediocre performance.

Answer (B) is correct. *(CMA, adapted)*
**REQUIRED:** The effect of using a negotiated transfer price that is greater than full cost but less than market price.
**DISCUSSION:** Given that the Plastics Division (the seller) has excess capacity, transfers within the company entail no opportunity cost. Accordingly, the transfer at the negotiated price will improve the performance measures of the transferor. Purchasing internally at below the market price also benefits the transferee, so the motivational purpose of transfer pricing is achieved. The goal congruence purpose is also achieved because the internal transaction benefits the company.
Answer (A) is incorrect because this arrangement creates no disincentive for the selling division. It will make a profit on every unit transferred. Answer (C) is incorrect because the market price charged by outside sources is higher than the negotiated price. Answer (D) is incorrect because, given idle capacity, selling at any amount in excess of variable cost should motivate the selling division.

## 9.5 Financial Measures

**37.** In evaluating an investment center, top management should concentrate on

A. Dollar sales.

B. Net income.

C. Profit percentages.

D. Return on investment.

Answer (D) is correct. *(Publisher)*
**REQUIRED:** The area on which management should concentrate in evaluating an investment center.
**DISCUSSION:** Each investment center of a business should be evaluated based upon return on investment to judge operating performance. ROI is comparable to calculations made both within and without a particular organization. Management may review the investment opportunities available within or without the firm. In essence, net income is stated as a proportion of investment capital (resources required).
Answer (A) is incorrect because dollar sales do not give a measure of operating performance based on resources required. Answer (B) is incorrect because net income does not give a measure of operating performance based on resources required. Answer (C) is incorrect because profit percentages do not give a measure of operating performance based on resources required.

**38.** The return on investment calculation considers only the following components:

$$S = \text{Sales}$$
$$I = \text{Investment}$$
$$NI = \text{Net income}$$

Which of the following formulas best describes the return on investment calculation?

A. $(I \div S) \times (S \div NI) = I \div NI$.

B. $(S \div I) \times (NI \div S) = NI \div I$.

C. $(I \div S) \times (NI \div S) = (I \times NI) \times (S \times S)$.

D. $(S \div I) \times (S \div NI) = (S \times S) \div (I \times NI)$.

Answer (B) is correct. *(Publisher)*
**REQUIRED:** The formula for return on investment.
**DISCUSSION:** The first term in the formula for return on investment is the number of times investment capital has turned over through the sales mechanism $(S \div I)$. This amount is multiplied by the net income expressed as a percentage of sales $(NI \div S)$ to give the return on investment $(NI \div I)$. The basic formula for return on investment is therefore

$$(S \div I) \times (NI \div S) = NI \div I.$$

Answer (A) is incorrect because $I \div NI$ is the reciprocal of return on investment. Answer (C) is incorrect because sales must be divided by investment $(S \div I)$ to determine the number of times investment capital has turned over, which results in $NI \div I$ as return on investment. Answer (D) is incorrect because net income must be expressed as a percentage of sales $(NI \div S)$, which results in $NI \div I$ as return on investment.

**39.** A firm earning a profit can increase its return on investment by

   A. Increasing sales revenue and operating expenses by the same dollar amount.

   B. Decreasing sales revenues and operating expenses by the same percentage.

   C. Increasing investment and operating expenses by the same dollar amount.

   D. Increasing sales revenues and operating expenses by the same percentage.

Answer (D) is correct.  *(CMA, adapted)*
   **REQUIRED:** The means by which a profitable company can increase its return on investment (ROI).
   **DISCUSSION:** ROI equals income divided by invested capital. If a company is already profitable, increasing sales and expenses by the same percentage will increase ROI. For example, if a company has sales of $100 and expenses of $80, its net income is $20. Given invested capital of $100, ROI is 20% ($20 ÷ $100). If sales and expenses both increase 10% to $110 and $88, respectively, net income increases to $22. ROI will then be 22% ($22 ÷ $100).
   Answer (A) is incorrect because increasing sales and expenses by the same dollar amount will not change income or ROI. Answer (B) is incorrect because decreasing revenues and expenses by the same percentage will reduce income and lower ROI. Answer (C) is incorrect because increasing investment and operating expenses by the same dollar amount will lower ROI. The higher investment increases the denominator, and the increased expenses reduce the numerator.

**40.** Which one of the following statements pertaining to the return on investment (ROI) as a performance measurement is false?

   A. When the average age of assets differs substantially across segments of a business, the use of ROI may not be appropriate.

   B. ROI relies on financial measures that are capable of being independently verified, while other forms of performance measures are subject to manipulation.

   C. The use of ROI may lead managers to reject capital investment projects that can be justified by using discounted cash flow models.

   D. The use of ROI can make it undesirable for a skillful manager to take on troubleshooting assignments such as those involving turning around unprofitable divisions.

Answer (B) is correct.  *(CMA, adapted)*
   **REQUIRED:** The false statement about ROI as a performance measurement.
   **DISCUSSION:** Return on investment is the key performance measure in an investment center. ROI is a rate computed by dividing a segment's income by the invested capital. ROI is therefore subject to the numerous possible manipulations of the income and investment amounts. For example, a manager may choose not to invest in a project that will yield less than the desired rate of return, or (s)he may defer necessary expenses.
   Answer (A) is incorrect because ROI can be misleading when the quality of the investment base differs among segments. Answer (C) is incorrect because managers may reject projects that are profitable (a return greater than the cost of capital), but would decrease ROI. For example, the managers of a segment with a 15% ROI may not want to invest in a new project with a 10% ROI, even though the cost of capital might be only 8%. Answer (D) is incorrect because the use of ROI does not reflect the relative difficulty of tasks undertaken by managers.

**41.** Which one of the following items would most likely not be incorporated into the calculation of a division's investment base when using the residual income approach for performance measurement and evaluation?

   A. Fixed assets employed in division operations.

   B. Land being held by the division as a site for a new plant.

   C. Division inventories when division management exercises control over the inventory levels.

   D. Division accounts payable when division management exercises control over the amount of short-term credit used.

Answer (B) is correct.  *(CMA, adapted)*
   **REQUIRED:** The item most likely not incorporated into the calculation of a division's investment base.
   **DISCUSSION:** An evaluation of an investment center is based upon the return on the investment base. These assets include plant and equipment, inventories, and receivables. Most likely, however, an asset, such as land, that is being held by the division as a site for a new plant would not be included in the investment base because it is not currently being used in operations. Total assets in use rather than total assets available is preferable when the investment center has been forced to carry idle assets.
   Answer (A) is incorrect because fixed operating assets are controlled by the division manager and contribute to profits. Answer (C) is incorrect because inventories are operating assets that contribute to profits and are controlled by the division manager. Answer (D) is incorrect because the level of accounts payable is an operating decision that should be considered in the evaluation of the division manager.

**42.** One approach to measuring divisional performance is return on investment. Return on investment is expressed as operating income

A. Divided by the current year's capital expenditures plus cost of capital.

B. Minus imputed interest charged for invested capital.

C. Divided by fixed assets.

D. Divided by total assets.

Answer (D) is correct. *(CMA, adapted)*
**REQUIRED:** The method of calculating return on investment (ROI).
**DISCUSSION:** ROI is calculated by dividing income by invested capital. It is a key performance measure of an investment center. Invested capital may be defined in various ways, such as shareholders' equity, total assets available, or total assets employed (which excludes assets that are idle). Total assets available is the measure that assumes the manager will use all assets without regard to financing.
Answer (A) is incorrect because ROI is based on all assets, not just current investment expenditures. Answer (B) is incorrect because the calculation of ROI does not adjust for imputed interest on invested capital. Answer (C) is incorrect because the denominator would not be limited to fixed assets.

**43.** Charlie's Service Co. is a service center. For the month of June, Charlie's had the following operating statistics:

| | |
|---|---|
| Sales | $750,000 |
| Operating income | 25,000 |
| Net profit after taxes | 8,000 |
| Total assets available | 500,000 |
| Shareholders' equity | 200,000 |
| Cost of capital | 6% |

Charlie's has a

A. Return on investment of 3.33%.

B. Residual income of $(5,000).

C. Return on investment of 6%.

D. Residual income of $(20,000).

Answer (B) is correct. *(Publisher)*
**REQUIRED:** The true statement about the company's operating performance.
**DISCUSSION:** Residual income is the excess of the actual ROI in dollars over a targeted amount equal to an imputed interest charge on invested capital. The rate used is ordinarily the weighted-average cost of capital. Some entities measure managerial performance in terms of the amount of residual income rather than the percentage ROI. Assuming the investment base is defined as total assets available, Charlie's targeted amount is $30,000 ($500,000 total assets × 6% cost of capital). Assuming that operating income of $25,000 is the ROI in dollars, residual income was $(5,000). This result is consistent with defining the numerator of the ROI calculation (Income ÷ Investment) as operating income. However, it might also be defined as net profit after taxes (net income). Moreover, the ROI denominator may be defined variously, e.g., total assets available, total assets employed, working capital plus other assets, or shareholders' equity.
Answer (A) is incorrect because the return on sales was 3.33%. Answer (C) is incorrect because 6% is the cost of capital. Answer (D) is incorrect because $(20,000) assumes that ROI in dollars is $25,000 (operating income) and that the targeted amount is $45,000 ($750,000 × 6% of sales).

**44.** Listed below is selected financial information for the Western Division of the Hinzel Company for last year.

| Account | Amount (thousands) |
|---|---|
| Average working capital | $ 625 |
| General and administrative expenses | 75 |
| Net sales | 4,000 |
| Average plant and equipment | 1,775 |
| Cost of goods sold | 3,525 |

If Hinzel treats the Western Division as an investment center for performance measurement purposes, what is the before-tax return on investment (ROI) for last year?

A. 34.78%

B. 22.54%

C. 19.79%

D. 16.67%

Answer (D) is correct. *(CMA, adapted)*
**REQUIRED:** The before-tax ROI for an investment center.
**DISCUSSION:** An investment center is responsible for revenues, expenses, and invested capital. Given average plant and equipment of $1,775 and average working capital of $625, the net investment is $2,400. Before-tax profit is $400 ($4,000 sales – $3,525 cost of goods sold – $75 general expenses). If before-tax ROI equals before-tax profit divided by net investment, the answer is 16.67% ($400 ÷ $2,400).
Answer (A) is incorrect because 34.78% results from subtracting working capital from plant and equipment in calculating the net investment. Answer (B) is incorrect because 22.54% fails to include average working capital in the total for the net investment. Answer (C) is incorrect because 19.79% results from not subtracting general and administrative expenses in the calculation of before-tax profit.

**45.** The segment margin of an investment center after deducting the imputed interest on the assets used by the investment center is known as

A. Return on investment.

B. Residual income.

C. Operating income.

D. Return on assets.

Answer (B) is correct.   *(CMA, adapted)*
**REQUIRED:** The segment margin of an investment center after imputed interest on the assets used has been deducted.
**DISCUSSION:** Residual income is the excess of the amount of return on investment (ROI) over a targeted amount equal to an imputed interest charge on invested capital. The rate used to impute the interest is usually the weighted-average cost of capital. The advantage of using residual income rather than percentage ROI is that the former emphasizes maximizing an amount instead of a percentage. Managers are encouraged to accept projects with returns exceeding the cost of capital even if the investments reduce the percentage ROI.
Answer (A) is incorrect because this ROI computation does not subtract imputed interest on capital used from the investment base. Answer (C) is incorrect because operating income equals operating revenues minus operating costs. Answer (D) is incorrect because this ROI computation does not subtract imputed interest on capital used from the investment base.

**46.** The imputed interest rate used in the residual income approach to performance evaluation can best be described as the

A. Average lending rate for the year being evaluated.

B. Historical weighted-average cost of capital for the company.

C. Target return on investment set by the company's management.

D. Average return on investments for the company over the last several years.

Answer (C) is correct.   *(CMA, adapted)*
**REQUIRED:** The true statement about the imputed interest rate used in the residual income approach to performance evaluation.
**DISCUSSION:** Residual income is the excess of the return on an investment over a targeted amount equal to an imputed interest charge on invested capital. The rate used is ordinarily set as a target return by management but is often equal to the weighted average cost of capital. Some enterprises prefer to measure managerial performance in terms of the amount of residual income rather than the percentage ROI because the firm will benefit from expansion as long as residual income is earned.
Answer (A) is incorrect because the cost of equity capital must also be incorporated into the imputed interest rate. Answer (B) is incorrect because the current weighted-average cost of capital must be used. Answer (D) is incorrect because the rate should be based on cost of capital, not investment returns of preceding years.

**47.** James Webb is the general manager of the Industrial Product Division, and his performance is measured using the residual income method. Webb is reviewing the following forecasted information for his division for next year:

| Category | Amount (thousands) |
| --- | --- |
| Working capital | $ 1,800 |
| Revenue | 30,000 |
| Plant and equipment | 17,200 |

If the imputed interest charge is 15% and Webb wants to achieve a residual income target of $2,000,000, what will costs have to be in order to achieve the target?

A. $9,000,000

B. $10,800,000

C. $25,150,000

D. $25,690,000

Answer (C) is correct.   *(CMA, adapted)*
**REQUIRED:** The maximum costs consistent with meeting a residual income target.
**DISCUSSION:** Residual income is the excess of the amount of the ROI over a targeted amount equal to an imputed interest charge on invested capital. If a manager has $19,000,000 of invested capital ($17,200,000 of plant and equipment + $1,800,000 of working capital), a 15% imputed interest charge equals $2,850,000. Adding $2,000,000 of residual income to the imputed interest results in a target profit of $4,850,000. This profit can be achieved if costs are $25,150,000 ($30,000,000 revenue – $4,850,000 profit).
Answer (A) is incorrect because this level of cost would result in a residual income greater than $2,000,000. Answer (B) is incorrect because this level of cost would result in a residual income greater than $2,000,000. Answer (D) is incorrect because $25,690,000 results from subtracting working capital from plant and equipment in determining invested capital.

**48.** REB Service Co. is a computer service center. For the month, REB had the following operating statistics:

| | |
|---|---|
| Sales | $450,000 |
| Operating income | 25,000 |
| Net profit after taxes | 8,000 |
| Total assets | 500,000 |
| Shareholders' equity | 200,000 |
| Cost of capital | 6% |

Based on the above information, which one of the following statements is true? REB has a

A. Return on investment of 4%.

B. Residual income of $(5,000).

C. Return on investment of 1.6%.

D. Residual income of $(22,000).

Answer (B) is correct. *(CMA, adapted)*
**REQUIRED:** The true statement about the company's performance.
**DISCUSSION:** Return on investment is commonly calculated by dividing pretax income by total assets available. Residual income is the excess of the return on investment over a targeted amount equal to an imputed interest charge on invested capital. The rate used is ordinarily the weighted-average cost of capital. Some companies measure managerial performance in terms of the amount of residual income rather than the percentage return on investment. Because REB has assets of $500,000 and a cost of capital of 6%, it must earn $30,000 on those assets to cover the cost of capital. Given that operating income was only $25,000, it had a negative residual income of $5,000.
Answer (A) is incorrect because, although the firm's return on equity investment was 4%, its return on all funds invested was 5% ($25,000 pretax operating income ÷ $500,000). Answer (C) is incorrect because ROI is commonly based on before-tax income. Answer (D) is incorrect because $(22,000) equals the difference between net profit after taxes and targeted income.

**49.** Residual income is a better measure for performance evaluation of an investment center manager than return on investment because

A. The problems associated with measuring the asset base are eliminated.

B. Desirable investment decisions will not be neglected by high-return divisions.

C. Only the gross book value of assets needs to be calculated.

D. The arguments about the implicit cost of interest are eliminated.

Answer (B) is correct. *(CMA, adapted)*
**REQUIRED:** The reason residual income is a better measure of performance evaluation than return on investment.
**DISCUSSION:** Residual income is the excess of the amount of the ROI over a targeted amount equal to an imputed interest charge on invested capital. The advantage of using residual income rather than percentage ROI is that the former emphasizes maximizing a dollar amount instead of a percentage. Managers of divisions with a high ROI are encouraged to accept projects with returns exceeding the cost of capital even if those projects reduce the department's ROI.
Answer (A) is incorrect because the methods use the same asset base. Answer (C) is incorrect because the methods use the same asset base. Answer (D) is incorrect because use of the residual income method requires a knowledge of the cost of capital; thus, arguments about the implicit cost of interest may escalate with use of the residual income method.

**50.** Assume Avionics Industrials reported at year-end that operating income before taxes for the year equaled $2,400,000. Long-term debt issued by Avionics has a coupon rate equal to 6%, and its cost of equity is 8%. The book value of the debt currently equals its fair value, and the book value of the equity capital for Avionics is $900,000 less than its fair value. Current assets are listed at $2,000,000 and long-term assets equal $9,600,000. The claims against those assets are in the form of $1,500,000 in current liabilities and $2,200,000 in long-term liabilities. The income tax rate for Avionics is 30%. What is the economic value added (EVA®)?

A. $731,240

B. $948,760

C. $1,668,760

D. $1,680,000

Answer (B) is correct. *(Publisher)*
**REQUIRED:** The economic value added (EVA®).
**DISCUSSION:** EVA® equals after-tax operating income minus the product of the after-tax weighted-average cost of capital (WACC) and an investment base equal to total assets minus current liabilities. After-tax operating income and after-tax weighted-average cost of capital (WACC) are not given and must be calculated. WACC is an after-tax rate determined using the fair values of the sources of long-term funds. Because interest is tax deductible, the coupon rate on long-term debt must be adjusted. The appropriate cost of debt for WACC calculations is 4.2% [(1.0 − 0.3 tax rate) × 0.06]. The given equity rate of 8% is not adjusted because distributions to shareholders are not deductible. The fair value of long-term debt is given as $2,200,000. The book value of equity equals total assets minus total liabilities, or $7,900,000. Thus, the fair value of equity is $8,800,000 ($7,900,000 book value + $900,000). The WACC is then calculated as follows:

$$WACC = \frac{[(\$2,200,000 \ FV \ of \ LT \ debt) \times (.042)] + [(\$8,800,000 \ FV \ of \ equity) \times (0.08)]}{(\$2,200,000 + \$8,800,000)} = 7.24\%$$

After-tax operating income equals operating income multiplied by 1 minus the tax rate, or $1,680,000. Hence, EVA® is equal to $948,760 {($1,680,000) − [$10,100,000 × (0.0724)]}.
Answer (A) is incorrect because $731,240 is the cost of capital. Answer (C) is incorrect because income taxes must be deducted from operating income to compute EVA®. Answer (D) is incorrect because $1,680,000 is the after-tax operating income.

Questions 51 and 52 are based on the following information. Edith Carolina, president of the Deed Corporation, requires a minimum return on investment of 8% for any project to be undertaken by her company. The company is decentralized, and leaves investment decisions up to the discretion of the division managers as long as the 8% return is expected to be realized. Michael Sanders, manager of the Cosmetics Division, has had a return on investment of 14% for his division for the past 3 years and expects the division to have the same return in the coming year. Sanders has the opportunity to invest in a new line of cosmetics which is expected to have a return on investment of 12%.

**51.** If the Deed Corporation evaluates managerial performance using residual income based on the corporate minimum required rate of return, what will be the preference for taking on the proposed cosmetics line by Edith Carolina and Michael Sanders?

|    | Carolina | Sanders |
|----|----------|---------|
| A. | Accept   | Reject  |
| B. | Reject   | Accept  |
| C. | Accept   | Accept  |
| D. | Reject   | Reject  |

Answer (C) is correct. *(CMA, adapted)*
**REQUIRED:** The preferences of the company and the division manager regarding a project with an ROI greater than the minimum return but less than the normal return if the manager is evaluated based on residual income.
**DISCUSSION:** Residual income is the excess of the return on an investment over a targeted amount, which is equal to an imputed interest charge on invested capital (in this case, 8%). The rate is usually the weighted-average cost of capital. Some enterprises prefer to measure managerial performance in terms of the amount of residual income rather than the percentage ROI. The principle is that the enterprise is expected to benefit from expansion as long as residual income is earned. Using a percentage ROI approach, expansion might be rejected if it lowered ROI, even though residual income would increase. Using residual income, both Carolina and Sanders would accept the new project because residual income will increase if a 12% return is earned when the target ROI is only 8%.

**52.** If the Deed Corporation evaluates managerial performance using return on investment, what will be the preference for taking on the proposed cosmetics line by Edith Carolina and Michael Sanders?

|    | Carolina | Sanders |
|----|----------|---------|
| A. | Accept   | Reject  |
| B. | Reject   | Accept  |
| C. | Accept   | Accept  |
| D. | Reject   | Reject  |

Answer (A) is correct. *(CMA, adapted)*
**REQUIRED:** The preferences of the company and the division manager regarding a project with an ROI greater than the minimum return but less than the normal return.
**DISCUSSION:** A company with an 8% ROI threshold should obviously accept a project yielding 12% because the company's overall ROI would increase. The manager being evaluated on the basis of ROI who is already earning 14% will be unwilling to accept a 12% return on a new project because the overall ROI for the division would decline slightly. This absence of goal congruence suggests a weakness in ROI-based performance evaluation.

**53.** The following forecasted information is available for a manufacturing division for next year:

| Category            | Amount (thousands) |
|---------------------|--------------------|
| Working capital     | $ 1,800            |
| Revenue             | 30,000             |
| Plant and equipment | 17,200             |

To establish a standard of performance for the division's manager using the residual income approach, four scenarios are being considered.

|   | Imputed Interest | Target Residual Income |
|---|------------------|------------------------|
| 1 | 15%              | $2,000,000             |
| 2 | 12%              | 1,500,000              |
| 3 | 18%              | 1,250,000              |
| 4 | 10%              | 2,500,000              |

Which scenario assumes the lowest maximum cost?

A. Scenario 1.

B. Scenario 2.

C. Scenario 3.

D. Scenario 4.

Answer (A) is correct. *(Publisher)*
**REQUIRED:** The lowest maximum cost consistent with meeting a residual income target.
**DISCUSSION:** Residual income is the excess of the amount of the ROI over a targeted amount equal to an imputed interest charge on invested capital. If a manager has $19,000,000 of invested capital ($17,200,000 of plant and equipment + $1,800,000 of working capital), a 15% imputed interest charge equals $2,850,000. Adding $2,000,000 of residual income to the imputed interest results in a target profit of $4,850,000. This profit can be achieved if costs are $25,150,000 ($30,000,000 revenue – $4,850,000 profit).
Answer (B) is incorrect because Scenario 2 requires maximum costs of $26,220,000 to reach the target. Answer (C) is incorrect because Scenario 3 requires maximum costs of $25,330,000 to reach the target. Answer (D) is incorrect because Scenario 4 requires maximum costs of $25,600,000 to reach the target.

Questions 54 and 55 are based on the following information.

Dzyubenko Co. reported these data at year-end:

| | |
|---|---|
| Pre-tax operating income | $ 4,000,000 |
| Current assets | 4,000,000 |
| Long-term assets | 16,000,000 |
| Current liabilities | 2,000,000 |
| Long-term liabilities | 5,000,000 |

The long-term debt has an interest rate of 8%, and its fair value equaled its book value at year-end. The fair value of the equity capital is $2 million greater than its book value. Dzyubenko's income tax rate is 25%, and its cost of equity capital is 10%.

**54.** What is the weighted-average cost of capital (WACC) to be used in the economic value added (EVA®) calculation?

A. 8%

B. 8.89%

C. 9%

D. 10%

Answer (C) is correct. *(Publisher)*
**REQUIRED:** The WACC to be used in an EVA® calculation.
**DISCUSSION:** The WACC is an after-tax rate determined using the fair values of the sources of long-term funds. Thus, the appropriate cost of debt is 6% [(1.0 − .25 tax rate) × .08] because interest is tax deductible. However, the given equity rate (10%) is not adjusted because distributions to shareholders are not deductible. The fair value of long-term debt is given as $5 million. The book value of equity must be $13 million ($20 million of assets − $7 million of liabilities), and its fair value is $15 million ($13 million + $2 million). Accordingly, the WACC is 9%:

$$WACC = \frac{(\$5 \ million \ FV \ of \ LT \ debt \times .06) + (\$15 \ million \ FV \ of \ equity \times 10\%)}{(\$5 \ million + \$15 \ million)}$$

$$= \frac{\$300,000 + \$1.5 \ million}{\$20 \ million}$$

$$= .09$$

Answer (A) is incorrect because 8% is the pre-tax cost of debt. Answer (B) is incorrect because 8.89% is based on the book value of equity. Answer (D) is incorrect because 10% is the cost of equity.

**55.** The EVA® is

A. $1,380,000

B. $1,620,000

C. $1,830,000

D. $3,000,000

Answer (A) is correct. *(Publisher)*
**REQUIRED:** The EVA®.
**DISCUSSION:** EVA® equals after-tax operating income minus the product of the after-tax WACC and an investment base equal to total assets minus current liabilities. Thus, EVA® is $1,380,000 {[$4 million × (1.0 − .25)] − [($20 million total assets − $2 million current liabilities) × .09 after-tax WACC]}.
Answer (B) is incorrect because $1,620,000 is the required return on the investment base. Answer (C) is incorrect because $1,830,000 is based on the assumption that $13 million is the investment base. Answer (D) is incorrect because $3,000,000 is the after-tax operating income.

Questions 56 through 58 are based on the following information. Semibar Co. reports net income of $630,000. The information below for the year just ended is also available:

| | January 1 | December 31 |
|---|---|---|
| Shareholders' equity | $4,200,000 | $4,480,000 |
| Share price | $25 | $30 |
| Shares outstanding | 400,000 | 400,000 |
| Cost of equity | 10% | 10% |
| Dividends per share | | $1.00 |

**56.** Equity value creation is

A. $630,000

B. $448,000

C. $420,000

D. $210,000

Answer (D) is correct. *(Publisher)*
**REQUIRED:** The equity value creation.
**DISCUSSION:** The equity spread calculates equity value creation by multiplying beginning equity capital by the difference between the return on equity (net income ÷ average equity) and the percentage cost of equity. Thus, the equity value creation is $210,000 {[($630,000 ÷ $4,200,000) – 10%] × $4,200,000}.
Answer (A) is incorrect because $630,000 is net income. Answer (B) is incorrect because $448,000 is 10% of ending shareholders' equity. Answer (C) is incorrect because $420,000 is 10% of beginning shareholders' equity.

**57.** The market value added (MVA) is

A. $2,000,000

B. $1,720,000

C. $400,000

D. $280,000

Answer (B) is correct. *(Publisher)*
**REQUIRED:** The market value added.
**DISCUSSION:** MVA is the difference between the market value of equity (shares outstanding × share price) and the equity supplied by shareholders. Hence, MVA equals $1,720,000 {[(400,000 shares × $30) – $4,480,000 SE at 12/31] – [(400,000 shares × $25) – $4,200,000 SE at 1/1]}.
Answer (A) is incorrect because $2,000,000 equals 400,000 shares times the increase in the share price. Answer (C) is incorrect because $400,000 is the amount of dividends paid. Answer (D) is incorrect because $280,000 is the increase in equity.

**58.** The total shareholder return is

A. 24%

B. 20%

C. 16.67%

D. 4%

Answer (A) is correct. *(Publisher)*
**REQUIRED:** The total shareholder return.
**DISCUSSION:** The total shareholder return is the sum of the change in the stock price and dividends per share, divided by the initial stock price. It equals 24% {[($30 – $25) + $1] ÷ $25}.
Answer (B) is incorrect because 20% is based on a denominator equal to the ending share price. Answer (C) is incorrect because 16.67% ignores dividends and is based on a denominator equal to the ending share price. Answer (D) is incorrect because 4% ignores the share price change.

Use Gleim's *CMA Test Prep* for interactive testing with **over 2,000 additional multiple-choice questions!**

# STUDY UNIT TEN
# THE BALANCED SCORECARD AND
# QUALITY CONSIDERATIONS

(17 pages of outline)

This study unit is the **last of three** on **performance measurement**. The relative weight assigned to this major topic in Part 2 of the exam is **20%** at **skill level C** (all six skill types required). The three study units are

Study Unit 8:   Cost and Variance Measures
Study Unit 9:   Responsibility Accounting and Financial Measures
Study Unit 10:  The Balanced Scorecard and Quality Considerations

After studying the outlines and answering the multiple-choice questions in this study unit, you will have the skills necessary to address the following topics listed in the IMA's Learning Outcome Statements:

Part 2 – Section D.4. Balanced scorecard

The candidate should be able to:

a.   define the concept of a balanced scorecard and identify its components
b.   define critical success factors and recognize the importance of these factors in evaluating a firm
c.   identify financial measures, such as operating income, revenue growth, revenues from new products, gross margin percentage, cost reductions, economic value added (EVA®), return on investment, etc.
d.   identify customer satisfaction measures, such as market share, retention, response time, delivery performance, defects, lead time, etc.
e.   identify internal business process measures, such as new product introductions, technological capability, cycle time, etc.
f.   identify innovation and learning measures, such as employee skill sets, organizational learning, industry leadership, etc.
g.   describe the characteristics of successful implementation and use of a balanced scorecard
h.   analyze and interpret a balanced scorecard and evaluate performance on the basis of the analysis

Part 2 – Section D.5. Quality considerations

The candidate should be able to:

a.   identify the core principles (critical factors) of total quality management
b.   identify the opportunity costs associated with poor quality management
c.   demonstrate an understanding of the role that communication and training play in successful total quality management programs
d.   describe the relationship between quality management and productivity and explain why misconceptions about this relationship can lead to poor decisions

e.    demonstrate an understanding of methods to analyze quality problems, such as control charts, Pareto diagrams, and cause-and-effect (fishbone) diagrams

f.    identify the relationship between compensation systems and total quality management systems

g.    identify the purpose of quality audits and gap analyses

h.    define quality as it relates to customer expectations

i.    define conformance as it relates to quality and identify the characteristics of goalpost quality conformance and absolute quality conformance

j.    describe and identify the components of the costs of quality commonly referred to as prevention costs, appraisal costs, internal failure costs, and external failure costs

## 10.1 THE BALANCED SCORECARD

1.    The trend in performance evaluation is the **balanced scorecard** approach to managing the implementation of the firm's strategy.

   a.    The balanced scorecard is an accounting report that connects the firm's critical success factors to measurements of its performance.

      1)    **Critical success factors (CSFs)** are specific, measurable financial and nonfinancial elements of a firm's performance that are vital to its competitive advantage.

   b.    A firm identifies its CSFs by means of a **SWOT analysis** that addresses internal factors (its strengths and weaknesses) and external factors (its opportunities and threats).

      1)    The firm's greatest strengths are its **core competencies**, which are functions the company performs especially well. These are the basis for its competitive advantages and strategy.

      2)    **Strengths and weaknesses** are internal resources or a lack thereof, for example, technologically advanced products, a broad product mix, capable management, leadership in R&D, modern production facilities, and a strong marketing organization.

      3)    **Opportunities and threats** arise from such externalities as government regulation, advances in technology, and demographic changes. They may be reflected in such competitive conditions as

         a)    Raising or lowering of barriers to entry into the firm's industry by competitors

         b)    Changes in the intensity of rivalry within the industry, for example, because of overcapacity or high exit barriers

         c)    The relative availability of substitutes for the firm's products or services

         d)    Bargaining power of customers, which tends to be greater when switching costs are low and products are not highly differentiated

         e)    Bargaining power of suppliers, which tends to be higher when suppliers are few

      4)    The SWOT analysis tends to highlight the basic factors of cost, quality, and the speed of product development and delivery.

   c.    Once the firm has identified its CSFs, it must establish specific, measurable ways for each CSF that are both relevant to the success of the firm and reliably stated.

      1)    Thus, the balanced scorecard varies with the strategy adopted by the firm.

         a)    For example, product differentiation or cost leadership either in a broad market or a narrowly focused market (a focus strategy). These measures provide a basis for implementing the firm's competitive strategy.

      2) The scorecard should include **lagging indicators** (such as output and financial measures) and **leading indicators** (such as many types of nonfinancial measures).

         a) The latter should be used only if they are predictors of ultimate financial performance.

      3) The scorecard should permit a determination of whether certain objectives are being achieved at the expense of others.

         a) For example, reduced spending on customer service may improve short-term financial results at a significant cost that is revealed by a long-term decline in customer satisfaction measures.

      4) By providing measures that are **nonfinancial** as well as financial, long-term as well as short-term, and internal as well as external, the balanced scorecard de-emphasizes short-term financial results and focuses attention on CSFs.

2. A typical balanced scorecard classifies objectives into one of four perspectives on the business:

  a. **Financial**

    1) **CSFs** may be sales, fair value of the firm's stock, profits, and liquidity.

    2) **Measures** may include sales, projected sales, accuracy of sales projections, new product sales, stock prices, operating earnings, earnings trend, revenue growth, gross margin percentage, cost reductions, economic value added, return on investment (or any of its variants), cash flow coverage and trends, turnover (assets, receivables, and inventory), and interest coverage.

  b. **Customer satisfaction**

    1) **CSFs** may be customer satisfaction, dealer and distributor relationships, marketing and selling performance, prompt delivery, and quality.

    2) **Measures** may include customer retention rate, returns, complaints, survey results, coverage and strength of distribution channels, market research results, training of marketing people, sales trends, market share and its trend, on-time delivery rate, service response time and effectiveness, and warranty expense.

  c. **Internal business processes**

    1) **CSFs** may be quality, productivity (an input-output relationship), flexibility of response to changing conditions, operating readiness, and safety.

    2) **Measures** may include rate of defects, amounts of scrap and rework, returns, survey results, field service reports, warranty costs, vendor defect rate, cycle (lead) time, labor and machine efficiency, setup time, scheduling effectiveness, downtime, capacity usage, maintenance, and accidents and their results.

  d. **Learning and growth**

    1) **CSFs** may be development of new products, promptness of their introduction, human resource development, morale, and competence of the work force.

    2) **Measures** may include new products marketed, number of design changes, patents and copyrights registered, R&D personnel qualifications, actual versus planned shipping dates, hours of training, skill set levels attained, personnel turnover, personnel complaints and survey results, financial and operating results, technological capabilities, organizational learning, and industry leadership.

3.    EXAMPLE of a balanced scorecard.

a.    Each **objective** is associated with one or more **measures** that permit the organization to gauge progress toward the objective.

b.    Note that achievement of the objectives in each **perspective** makes it possible to achieve the objectives in the next higher perspective.

---

**Financial Perspective**

    **Objective:** Increase shareholder value      **Measures:** Increase in common stock price
                                                     Reliability of dividend payment

**Customer Perspective**

    **Objective:** Increase customer satisfaction      **Measures:** Greater market share
                                                     Higher customer retention rate
                                                     Positive responses to surveys

**Internal Business Process Perspective**

    **Objective:** Improve product quality      **Measures:** Achievement of zero defects

    **Objective:** Improve internal processes      **Measures:** Reduction in delivery cycle time
                                                     Smaller cost variances

**Learning and Growth Perspective**

    **Objective:** Increase employee confidence      **Measures:** Number of suggestions to
                                                       improve processes
                                                     Positive responses to surveys

    **Objective:** Increase employee competence      **Measures:** Attendance at internal and external
                                                       training seminars

---

4.    The **development and implementation** of a comprehensive balanced scorecard requires active support and participation by senior management. This involvement will in turn assure the cooperation of lower-level managers in the identification of objectives, appropriate measures, targeted results, and methods of achieving the results.

a.    The scorecard should contain measures at the detail level that permits everyone to understand how his/her efforts affect the firm's results.

b.    The scorecard and the strategy it represents must be communicated to all managers and used as a basis for compensation decisions.

c.    The following are **problems in implementation** of the balanced scorecard approach:

1)    Using too many measures, with a consequent loss of focus on CSFs

2)    Failing to evaluate personnel on nonfinancial as well as financial measures

3)    Including measures that will not have long-term financial benefits

4)    Not understanding that subjective measures (such as customer satisfaction) are imprecise

5)    Trying to achieve improvements in all areas at all times

6)    Not being aware that the hypothesized connection between nonfinancial measures and ultimate financial success may not continue to be true

5.    Stop and review! You have completed the outline for this subunit. Study multiple-choice questions 1 through 3 on page 380.

## 10.2 CONTROL AND FEEDBACK

1. The success of a performance measurement and control system is determined by its effectiveness in getting people to modify their performance.

   a. When a budget or other plan is interpreted as inflexible, the manager might act in ways contrary to the company's best interest in a misguided effort to meet the proposed criteria.

2. The classical approach assumes people will act to correct their behavior when ordered to do so, but, in practice, individuals may resist formal controls for many reasons:

   a. Control procedures highlight things people do poorly, thus damaging their self-esteem.

   b. People tend to avoid unpleasant situations.

   c. The goals of a control system may not be accepted as worthwhile by an employee.

      1) Employees may believe that the stated standard of performance is too high.

      2) Established standards of performance may be considered irrelevant to accomplishment of what an individual regards as the primary job objective.

   d. An individual may resent the assignment of control authority to another individual or group. The assignment of responsibility for failure to achieve objectives may be dysfunctional for the organization.

      1) The pressure to conform to plans, when exerted by management accountants, may have a negative effect on performance.

      2) But the same feedback from someone inside the operational unit may be a motivator for higher performance.

   e. When informal group norms differ from control objectives, members of the group may resist the controls.

3. Human reactions to **feedback** should be considered in setting performance standards and designing control systems.

   a. The nature of the feedback should motivate employees to improve their performance and reach the planned objectives, rather than offend or intimidate them.

   b. The timing, form, and content of the information on deviations should be considered in order to obtain maximum compliance by those affected.

4. Modern behavioral theory provides for some measure of **self-control** at the lowest possible level (i.e., increased participation by the employees).

   a. Self-control appears to be more effective than the traditional approach, which emphasizes centralized flow of control information toward top management and the use of outside staff control groups.

   b. A participative approach to standard setting is more apt to obtain acceptance of the standards by the employees whose performance will be measured.

5. **Decentralized decision making** is beneficial because it creates greater responsiveness to the needs of the customers, suppliers, and employees. Furthermore, greater authority enhances managerial morale and development.

   a. The disadvantage of decentralization is that there may be a duplication of effort and a lack of goal congruence.

6.  Effective **management control** requires performance measurement and feedback. This process affects allocation of resources to organizational subunits. It also affects decisions about managers' compensation, advancement, and future assignments.

    a.  Furthermore, evaluating their performance serves to motivate managers to optimize the measures in the performance evaluation model. However, that model may be inconsistent with the organization's model for managerial decision making.

        1)  To achieve goal congruence, the models should be synchronized. For example, if senior management wishes to maximize results over the long term, subordinates should be evaluated over the long term.

        2)  Unfortunately, information systems seldom provide information on the outcomes of individual decisions, and senior managers may be unaware of desirable options not chosen. Moreover, performance feedback usually applies to specific responsibility centers for specific periods. The result is that use of the same criteria for decision making and managerial evaluation may be difficult.

7.  Feedback regarding managerial performance may take the form of **financial and nonfinancial measures** that may be **internally or externally generated**. Moreover, different measures have a long-term or short-term emphasis.

    a.  An example of an external financial measure is stock price.

    b.  Examples of external nonfinancial measures are market share, customer satisfaction, and delivery performance.

    c.  Examples of internal financial measures are cost variances, return on investment, residual income, return on sales, and other financial ratios.

    d.  Examples of internal nonfinancial measures are product quality, new product development time, and manufacturing lead time (cycle time).

8.  Many forms of performance feedback are based on **accounting information**. The particular measures to be chosen are dependent on a five-stage process:

    a.  Senior management must determine what measure is consistent with its objectives.

    b.  The elements of the measure must be specified; e.g., calculation of residual income requires a definition of the items to be included in investment. A manager will therefore be motivated to avoid actions that increase the investment base.

    c.  The basis for determining the dollar values of the elements of the measure also must be specified. For example, in a residual income calculation based on an investment base defined as total assets, present value, current cost, current disposal price, or historical cost may be the attribute used to specify the dollar value of the investment.

        1)  **Historical cost** creates comparability issues because returns on significantly depreciated assets may be higher than those on newer assets that have been acquired using inflated dollars. Thus, otherwise similarly situated managers may report different operating results. Moreover, managers may be reluctant to replace aging assets.

    d.  A standard must be established to provide a basis for comparison.

        1)  One issue is the difficulty of the standard.

        2)  A second issue is whether individual managers should have unique performance goals. Because different managers may face widely varying problems, establishing challenging but attainable goals tailored to individual circumstances is preferable.

    e.  The frequency of performance feedback depends on many factors, such as the nature of the information, its cost, the design of the accounting information system, the level of management receiving the feedback, and the usefulness of the information.

9.  Organizational mechanisms for performance feedback should satisfy the behavioral criteria of goal congruence and managerial effort. However, they should not encroach on the desired level of autonomy granted to a subunit manager.

10. Senior management should be aware of the limitations of accrual-accounting measures. For example, cash-based and accrual-based measures may yield different results, so a manager may reject a project with a positive net present value because its effect on accounting income is initially negative.

11. Some companies try to motivate employees by providing **employee-benefit statements** that show all of the components of the employer's distributions for the benefit of the employee. For example, in addition to salary, the benefit statement would show the employer's contributions to Social Security, health and life insurance premiums paid, pension contributions, and the values of other fringe benefits provided.

12. Stop and review! You have completed the outline for this subunit. Study multiple-choice questions 4 through 14 beginning on page 381.

## 10.3 QUALITY CONSIDERATIONS

1.  Establishing a **definition of quality** is difficult, and any single definition will have weaknesses.

    a.  Consequently, multiple perspectives should be maintained: attributes of the product (performance, serviceability, durability, etc.), customer satisfaction, conformity with manufacturing specifications, and value (relation of quality and price).

    b.  One of the dimensions of quality is **conformance**, or how well a product and its components meet applicable standards.

        1)  The traditional view is that conforming products are those with characteristics that lie within an acceptable specified range of values that includes a target value.

            a)  This view also regards a certain percentage of defective (nonconforming) units as acceptable.

        2)  The traditional view was superseded by the **zero-defects (goalpost conformance)** approach that sought to eliminate all nonconforming output.

            a)  An extension of this approach is the **robust quality (absolute quality conformance)** concept. Its goal is to reach the target value in every case for the reason that hidden quality costs occur when output varies from the target even though the units are within specifications.

2.  American companies became concerned with quality issues in the late 1970s and early 1980s when Japanese manufacturers presented a formidable competitive challenge.

    a.  To provide guidelines for implementing a quality program, the IMA issued its **Statement of Management Accounting (SMA) 4R**, *Practices and Techniques: Managing Quality Improvements*, in 1993.

        1)  SMA 4R is the basis for these outlines.

3.  Various management processes, tools, and measures should be adopted.

    a.  **Policy deployment** is the systematic planning of corporate objectives and the detailed ways in which organizational subunits will approach the accomplishment of their related goals. The purpose is goal congruence.

b. **Quality function deployment** ensures that customer requirements are translated into design requirements at each step in product development. It is an umbrella concept most useful in an environment in which the Plan-Do-Check-Act Cycle is used at all levels.

1) The **Plan-Do-Check-Act Cycle (PDCA)** (the Deming Wheel) is a "management-by-fact" or scientific-method approach to continuous improvement.

a) PDCA creates a process-centered environment because it involves studying the current process, collecting and analyzing data to identify causes of problems, planning for improvement, and deciding how to measure improvement (Plan).

b) The plan is then implemented on a small scale if possible (Do).

c) The next step is to determine what happened (Check).

d) If the experiment was successful, the plan is fully implemented (Act).

e) The cycle is then repeated using what was learned from the preceding cycle.

c. **Kaizen** is a Japanese word for the continuous pursuit of improvement in every aspect of organizational operations.

1) For example, a budget prepared on the kaizen principle projects costs based on future improvements. The possibility of such improvements must be determined, and the cost of implementation and the savings therefrom must be estimated.

d. **Employee involvement** means training and empowering employees to harness their creativity for problem solving and to stress management's complete commitment to quality.

1) Thus, decision making should be pushed down to employees who understand customer preferences as well as the production or service processes of the organization.

2) As a consequence of employee empowerment, the performance measurement and compensation systems should be redesigned accordingly to reward employees responsible for quality improvements.

3) **Quality circles** are used to obtain input from employees and to locate the best perspective on problem solving.

e. **Suppliers' management** is the careful selection of suppliers and the cultivation of long-term relationships based on the consistent ability to meet mutual expectations.

f. **Competitive benchmarking** "involves continuously evaluating the practices of best-in-class organizations and adapting company processes to incorporate the best of these practices."

g. **Quality training** familiarizes all employees with the means for preventing, detecting, and eliminating nonquality. These continuous educational processes are tailored to the appropriate groups.

h. **Reward and recognition** for quality improvement should be group-oriented and based on quality measures.

i. **Customer retention** is a vitally important measure of service quality because loyal customers spend more, refer new customers, and are less costly to service.

j. **Statistical and other quantitative methods** are used to identify quality problems.

4. SMA 4R lists four categories of **costs of quality**: prevention, appraisal, internal failure, and external failure. An organization should attempt to minimize its total cost of quality.

   a. **Conformance costs** include prevention and appraisal, which are both financial measures of internal performance.

      1) **Prevention** attempts to avoid defective output. These costs include preventive maintenance, employee training, review of equipment design, and evaluation of suppliers.

      2) **Appraisal** embraces such activities as statistical quality control programs, inspection, and testing.

   b. **Nonconformance costs** include costs of internal failure (a financial measure of internal performance) and external failure costs (a financial measure of customer satisfaction).

      1) **Internal failure** costs occur when defective products are detected before shipment.

         a) Examples are scrap, rework, tooling changes, downtime, redesign of products or processes, lost output, reinspection and retesting, expediting of operations after delays, lost learning opportunities, and searching for and correcting problems.

      2) The costs of **external failure** or **lost opportunity** include lost profits from a decline in market share as dissatisfied customers make no repeat purchases, return products for refunds, cancel orders, and communicate their dissatisfaction to others.

         a) Thus, external failure costs are incurred for customer service complaints; rejection, return, repair, or recall of products or services; warranty obligations; products liability claims; and customer losses.

         b) **Environmental costs** are also external failure costs, e.g., fines for nonadherence to environmental law and loss of customer goodwill.

            i) To minimize environmental damage and its resulting costs, the International Organization for Standardization has issued **ISO 14000** standards to promote the reduction of environmental damage by an organization's products, services, and operations and to develop environmental auditing and performance evaluation systems.

      3) **Quality cost indices** may be calculated to measure the cost of maintaining a given level of quality, for example, total quality costs divided by direct labor costs.

      4) **Nonfinancial measures of internal performance** may include manufacturing cycle efficiency (value-added production time ÷ total throughput time), ratio of good output to total output, defects per product line, the half-life method (time required to reduce the defect ratio by 50%), and new product development time.

      5) **Nonfinancial measures of customer satisfaction** may include delivery cycle time (total time from receipt of order until delivery), percentage of defective goods shipped, customer complaints, customer response time, on-time deliveries, survey data, and market share.

      6) **Nonquantitative factors** must also be considered. For example, an emphasis on quality improves competitiveness, enhances employee expertise, and generates goodwill.

    c.  **Quality and productivity** do not necessarily have an inverse relationship.

       1)  Traditionally, the optimal level of quality costs has been deemed to occur where the conformance cost curve intercepts the nonconformance cost curve, which corresponds to the minimum point on the total cost curve. Thus, beyond some point, incurrence of further prevention and appraisal costs is not cost beneficial.

       2)  However, the modern robust quality view is that this relationship does not always hold. Improving quality and reducing costs in each category may be possible if the most efficient prevention methods are applied.

          a)  For example, selection of a supplier meeting high quality standards regarding defect rates and delivery times may drive down not only failure costs but also the prevention and appraisal costs incurred when supplier performance was less reliable.

5.    **Management of time** is important to any quality improvement program.

    a.  **Product development and delivery time** is a crucial factor in the competitive equation. A company that is first in the market with a new product has obvious advantages.

       1)  Reducing development time is also important because product life cycles are becoming shorter.

       2)  Organizations need to respond quickly and flexibly to new technology, changes in consumer tastes, and competitive challenges.

    b.  One financial measure of product development is **breakeven time**, which is the time from management approval of the project to the time when the cumulative present value of its cash inflows equals the cumulative present value of the investment cash outflows.

       1)  The most popular method of determining breakeven time calculates the time required for the present value of the cumulative cash flows to equal zero.

          a)  An alternative that results in a longer breakeven time is to consider the time required for the present value of the cumulative cash inflows to equal the present value of all the expected future cash outflows.

    c.  **Customer-response time** is the delay from placement of an order to delivery of the good or service.

       1)  **Response time** is a function of time drivers, e.g., uncertainty about arrivals of customers in the queue and bottlenecks (points at which capacity is reached or exceeded).

          a)  Response time consists of order receipt time (delay between the placement of an order and its readiness for setup), manufacturing cycle time (delay from the moment the order is ready for setup to its completion), and order delivery time.

       2)  **Manufacturing cycle (throughput) time** equals order waiting time plus manufacturing time.

       3)  **Queuing (waiting-line) theory** is a group of mathematical models for systems involving waiting lines.

          a)  The objective of queuing theory is to minimize the total cost of the system, including both service and waiting costs, for a given rate of arrivals.

          b)  Mathematical solutions are available for simple systems having unscheduled random arrivals. For other systems, simulation must be used to find a solution.

6. Several **techniques for analyzing quality problems** are available.

  a. **Statistical quality control** is a method of determining whether the shipment or production run of units lies within acceptable limits.

    1) It is also used to determine whether production processes are out of control.

    2) **Statistical control charts** are graphic aids for monitoring the status of any process subject to random variations.

      a) Originally developed to control the quality of production processes, they also have applications of direct interest to the management accountant, for example, unit cost of production, direct labor hours used, ratio of actual expenses to budgeted expenses, number of calls by sales personnel, and total accounts receivable.

      b) The chart consists of three horizontal lines plotted on a horizontal time scale.

      c) The center line represents the average or mean value for the process being controlled.

      d) The other two lines are the upper control limit (UCL) and the lower control limit (LCL).

      e) The processes are measured periodically, and the values are plotted on the chart (X).

        i) If the value falls within the control limits, no action is taken.

        ii) If the value falls outside the limits, the process is considered out of control, and an investigation is made for possible corrective action.

      f) Another advantage of the chart is that it makes trends visible.

      g) EXAMPLE:

Unit Cost      X      May's results are out of control.

$1.05 ---------------------------- UCL
         X
$1.00 _____
    X
$0.95 ---------------------------- LCL
  March    April    May

    3) **P charts** are based on an attribute (acceptable/not acceptable) rather than a measure of a variable. Specifically, it shows the percentage of defects in a sample.

    4) **C charts** are also attribute control charts. They show defects per item.

    5) An **R chart** shows the range of dispersion of a variable, such as size or weight.

    6) An **X-bar chart** shows the sample mean for a variable.

  b. Variations in the value of some process parameter may have several causes.

    1) **Random variations** occur by chance. Present in virtually all processes, they are not correctable because they will not repeat themselves in the same manner. Excessively narrow control limits will result in many investigations of what are simply random fluctuations.

    2) **Implementation deviations** occur because of human or mechanical failure to achieve target results.

    3) **Measurement variations** result from errors in the measurements of actual results.

4)   **Model fluctuations** can be caused by errors in the formulation of a decision model.

5)   **Prediction variances** result from errors in forecasting data used in a decision model.

c.   **Bar charts** (bar graphs) are a two-dimensional (variables plotted on x and y axes) graphic means of quantitative comparison by using bars or rectangles with lengths proportional to the measure of the data or things being compared.  Bar charts may be vertical (column charts) or horizontal.

1)   **Pareto analysis** is based on the concept that about 80% of results or effects are caused by about 20% of people or events.

a)   Thus, managers should concentrate on the relatively few people or events that have the most significant effects.

2)   **Pareto diagrams** are bar charts in which the frequencies of the various types of adverse conditions that may occur in a given process are depicted.

a)   For example, an auditor might construct a Pareto diagram of the types and numbers of control deviations found in the receiving department.  The tallest (or longest) bar signifies the most common type of problem.

d.   A **histogram** is a bar chart used to depict a frequency distribution.

1)   It is used to create a graphic representation of the results of repeated measurements of a single variable, with the class intervals on the horizontal axis and the frequency (or relative frequency) of occurrence on the vertical axis.

2)   EXAMPLE:  A histogram of the number of occurrences of various net cash flows is given below.  Cash flows between $0 and $1,000 occurred on 5 days; cash flows between $1,000 and $2,000 also occurred on 5 days; cash flows between −$2,000 and −$3,000 occurred on 3 days, etc.

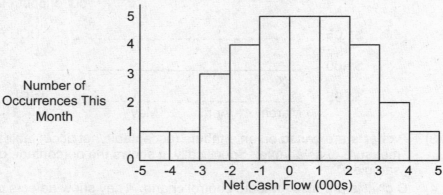

e.   A **fishbone diagram** (also called a **cause-and-effect diagram** or an **Ishikawa diagram**) is a total quality management process improvement technique that is useful in studying causation (why the actual and desired situations differ).

1)   This format organizes the analysis of causation and helps to identify possible interactions among causes.

2)   The head of the skeleton represents the statement of the problem.

3)   The principal classifications of causes are represented by lines (bones) drawn diagonally from the heavy horizontal line (the spine).

4)   Smaller horizontal lines are added in their order of probability in each classification.

5)  EXAMPLE:

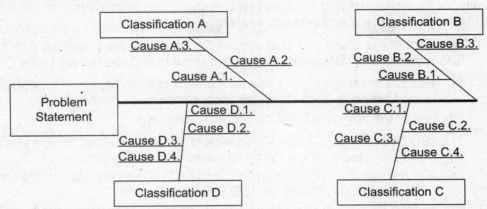

f.  The **Taguchi quality loss function** is a measure of the departure from absolute quality conformance (robust quality).

1)  It is based on the principle that quality losses occur even when items are within specified limits or tolerances. Thus, any variation from a quality target for a characteristic results in hidden quality costs.

2)  The basic formula is

$$L = k\,(x - T)^2$$

Where: L = the quality costs per unit
k = a constant based on the entity's external failure cost experience
x = actual measure of the quality variable
T = target value of the quality variable

a)  The estimate of the constant is

$$k = c \div d^2$$

Where: c = the loss at a specification limit
d = the difference between the target value and the specification limit

b)  The following is the graph of a Taguchi loss function (the quality cost at the target value is $0):

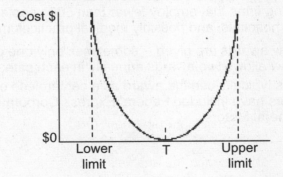

7.   In 1987, the International Organization for Standardization (ISO) introduced **ISO 9000**, a "family" of 11 standards and technical reports that provide guidance for establishing and maintaining a **quality management system**.

   a.   The intent of the standards is to ensure the quality of the **process, not the product**. The marketplace determines whether a product is good or bad.

      1)   For this reason, the ISO deems it unacceptable for phrases referring to ISO certification to appear on individual products or packaging.

   b.   Only one of the standards is a certification standard.

      1)   **ISO 9001:2000**, *Quality Management Systems – Requirements*, is the standard that provides a model for quality assurance programs.

      2)   For this reason, "ISO 9001:2000 certified" is the only acceptable formulation. There is no such thing as "ISO 9000 certification."

   c.   Though they do not have the force of law, these standards do carry weight because, if a company fails to gain ISO 9001:2000 certification, it risks not being able to find customers for its products.

      1)   Some companies are obtaining ISO 9001:2000 certification out of fear that the European Union (EU) will require compliance with the standards in an attempt to restrict imports.

   d.   ISO 9000 has given birth to a new industry of consultants who advise companies on how to meet the standards and obtain registration.

      1)   These consultants conduct quality audits to help companies determine whether they have a sufficiently adequate quality system to apply for ISO 9001:2000 certification.

      2)   Once a company applies for certification, licensed independent auditors come in and conduct another quality audit.

8.   The U.S. Congress created the **Malcolm Baldridge National Quality Award** in 1987 to encourage quality among American companies. The award was named for President Ronald Reagan's first Secretary of Commerce, who was killed in a rodeo accident.

   a.   The Baldridge Award and ISO 9000 registration promote an awareness of quality as a vital competitive element.

   b.   Applicants for the Baldridge Award are grouped into three categories: the manufacturing group, the service group, and the small business group (service or manufacturing firms that employ fewer than 500 people). Officials say that a category for schools, hospitals, and possibly medical practices may be added soon.

      1)   Very few awards are given -- sometimes only one per year in each category. The law allows two awards annually in each category.

      2)   Winners typically use the award as a centerpiece of their advertising campaigns. Winners have included Federal Express Corporation and the Cadillac Division of General Motors.

    c.    Judges look to seven performance areas in selecting winners. These areas are

        1)    Senior executive leadership and dedication to quality,

        2)    Information and analysis demonstrating that the firm has measured its quality performance,

        3)    Strategic quality planning, including goal setting and how goals have been achieved,

        4)    Human resource development and management, including the authority of employees to deviate from established procedures if it will improve quality or customer service,

        5)    Management of process quality, with emphasis on procedures to look across departmental lines to improve quality,

        6)    Quality and operational results focusing on objective data, including customer reports, that show that a company is achieving continuous improvement, and

        7)    Customer satisfaction, the most heavily weighted of the criteria. Knowledge of the customer and responsiveness to customer needs are particularly important.

    d.    The quality audit is the key to the award.

        1)    A **quality audit** is a systematic examination to determine whether quality activities and related results comply with planned arrangements and whether these arrangements are implemented effectively and are suitable to achieve objectives.

        2)    Companies must audit their operations using the Baldridge standards to measure their quality and productivity.

    e.    Annually, thousands of companies request the application forms for the Baldridge Award.

        1)    One important reason is to obtain copies of the quality-audit program that accompanies the forms.

        2)    The detailed audit program is then used by companies to conduct self audits of their quality systems. In other words, a quality audit is a self-improvement tool; the objective is to find out where quality can be improved.

9.    One of the first steps in implementing an improved **quality management system (QMS)** is to compare the current QMS to the requirements of the ISO 9000 or Baldridge standards.

    a.    This procedure is most commonly called a **gap analysis**. Many consultants can assist with the analysis, or companies may choose to do it themselves.

        1)    It is important to understand what the gap analysis involves and what information it will provide.

        2)    The most important tool for the gap analysis is the gap checklist or audit program, which is a list of the requirements in the standards written in question format.

            a)    The quality auditor uses the list to compare the QMS that is in place with the requirements.

            b)    A well-designed checklist will provide the auditor with recommendations about what documents to look for, examples of what will meet the requirements, and other guidance for auditing in accordance with the standards.

            c)    The audit checklist should also give the auditor a place to document what was observed that did not meet the standards.

10.    Stop and review! You have completed the outline for this subunit. Study multiple-choice questions 15 through 35 beginning on page 384.

## 10.4 TOTAL QUALITY MANAGEMENT

1. The emergence of the **total quality management (TQM)** concept is one of the most significant developments in managerial accounting.

   a. TQM was developed in the mid-1940s by statistician W. Edwards Deming, who aided Japanese industry in its recovery from World War II.

   b. The Deming Prize is awarded by the Union of Japanese Scientists and Engineers for outstanding contributions to the study or application of TQM.

2. **TQM** recognizes that quality improvement can increase revenues and decrease costs significantly. The following are TQM's **core principles** or **critical factors**:

   a. Emphasis on the **customer**

      1) Satisfaction of external customers
      2) Satisfaction of internal customers
      3) Requirements for external suppliers
      4) Requirements for internal suppliers

   b. **Continuous improvement** as a never-ending process, not a destination.

   c. **Engaging every employee** in the pursuit of total quality because avoidance of defects in products or services and satisfaction of external customers requires that all internal customers be satisfied.

3. **TQM** is a **comprehensive approach** to quality.

   a. It treats the pursuit of quality as a **basic organizational function** that is as important as production or marketing.

   b. TQM is the continuous pursuit of quality in every aspect of organizational activities through a philosophy of doing it right the first time, employee training and empowerment, promotion of teamwork, improvement of processes, and attention to satisfaction of customers, both internal and external.

      1) TQM emphasizes the supplier's relationship with the customer, identifies customer needs, and recognizes that everyone in a process is at some time a customer or supplier of someone else, either within or without the organization.

      2) Thus, TQM begins with external customer requirements, identifies internal customer-supplier relationships and requirements, and establishes requirements for external suppliers.

      3) Organizations tend to be vertically organized, but TQM requires strong horizontal linkages.

   c. The management of quality is not limited to quality management staff, engineers, production personnel, etc.

      1) The role of **management accountants** includes assisting in designing and operating quality information, measurement, and reporting systems.

         a) In particular, they can contribute to problem solving through measuring and reporting quality costs.

4. **Implementation of TQM** cannot be accomplished by application of a formula, and the process is lengthy and difficult. The following phases are typical:

   a. Establishing an executive-level quality council of senior managers with strong involvement by the CEO.

   b. Providing quality training programs for senior managers.

   c.   Conducting a quality audit to evaluate the success of the process for gathering background information to develop the strategic quality improvement plan.

      1)   The quality audit also may identify the best improvement opportunities and the organization's strengths and weaknesses compared with its benchmarked competitors.

   d.   Preparing a gap analysis to ascertain what is necessary to bridge the gap between the organization and the quality leaders in its industry and to establish a database for the development of the strategic quality improvement plan.

   e.   Developing strategic quality improvement plans for the short and long term.

   f.   Conducting employee communication and training programs.

   g.   Establishing quality teams, which ensure that goods and services conform to specifications.

   h.   Creating a measurement system and setting goals.

   i.   Revising compensation, appraisal, and recognition systems.

   j.   Reviewing and revising the entire effort periodically.

5.   Stop and review!  You have completed the outline for this subunit.  Study multiple-choice questions 36 through 41 beginning on page 391.

## 10.5  CORE CONCEPTS

### The Balanced Scorecard

- The balanced scorecard is an accounting report that **connects** the firm's critical success factors to **measurements of its performance**.
- A typical balanced scorecard includes measures in **four categories**:  financial, customer satisfaction, internal business processes, and learning and innovation.

### Control and Feedback

- The success of a performance measurement and control system is determined by its effectiveness in getting people to **modify their performance**.
- **Decentralized decision making** is beneficial because it creates greater responsiveness to the needs of the customers, suppliers, and employees.

### Quality Considerations

- SMA 4R lists four categories of **costs of quality**:  prevention, appraisal, internal failure, and external failure.  An organization should attempt to minimize its total cost of quality.
- Several **graphical techniques** are available for tracking quality improvements.  Some examples are statistical control charts, histograms, fishbone (Ishikawa) diagrams, and Taguchi quality loss function charts.
- In 1987, the International Organization for Standardization (ISO) introduced **ISO 9000**, a "family" of 11 standards and technical reports that provide guidance for establishing and maintaining a **quality management system**.

### Total Quality Management

- TQM recognizes that quality improvement can **increase revenues and decrease costs** significantly.  It is a **comprehensive approach** to quality.
- TQM's **core principles** are emphasis on the customer, continuous improvement, and engaging every employee.

## QUESTIONS

### 10.1  The Balanced Scorecard

**1.** Using the balanced scorecard approach, an organization evaluates managerial performance based on

    A.  A single ultimate measure of operating results, such as residual income.

    B.  Multiple financial and nonfinancial measures.

    C.  Multiple nonfinancial measures only.

    D.  Multiple financial measures only.

**Answer (B) is correct.**  *(Publisher)*
**REQUIRED:**  The nature of the balanced scorecard approach.
**DISCUSSION:**  The trend in managerial performance evaluation is the balanced scorecard approach.  Multiple measures of performance permit a determination as to whether a manager is achieving certain objectives at the expense of others that may be equally or more important.  These measures may be financial or nonfinancial and usually include items in four categories:  profitability; customer satisfaction; innovation; and efficiency, quality, and time.

**2.** On a balanced scorecard, which of the following would not be an example of a customer satisfaction measure?

    A.  Market share.

    B.  Economic value added.

    C.  Response time.

    D.  Customer retention.

**Answer (B) is correct.**  *(Publisher)*
**REQUIRED:**  The measure that is not an element of customer satisfaction on a balanced scorecard.
**DISCUSSION:**  Customer satisfaction measures include market share, retention, response time, delivery performance, number of defects, and lead time.  Economic value added, or EVA®, is a profitability measure.
    Answer (A) is incorrect because market share is a customer satisfaction measure.  Answer (C) is incorrect because response time is a customer satisfaction measure.  Answer (D) is incorrect because customer retention is a customer satisfaction measure.

**3.** On a balanced scorecard, which is more of an internal process measure than an external-based measure?

    A.  Cycle time.

    B.  Profitability.

    C.  Customer satisfaction.

    D.  Market share.

**Answer (A) is correct.**  *(Publisher)*
**REQUIRED:**  The measure that is more internal-process related on a balanced scorecard.
**DISCUSSION:**  Cycle time is the manufacturing time to complete an order.  Thus, cycle time is strictly related to internal processes.  Profitability is a combination of internal and external considerations.  Customer satisfaction and market share are related to how customers perceive a product and how competitors react.
    Answer (B) is incorrect because profitability is a measure that includes external considerations.  Answer (C) is incorrect because customer satisfaction is a measure that includes external considerations.  Answer (D) is incorrect because market share is a measure that includes external considerations.

## 10.2 Control and Feedback

**4.** Which one of the following organizational policies is most likely to result in undesirable managerial behavior?

A. Patel Chemicals sponsors television coverage of cricket matches between national teams representing India and Pakistan. The expenses of such media sponsorship are not allocated to its various divisions.

B. Joe Walk, the chief executive officer of Eagle Rock Brewery, wrote a memorandum to his executives stating, "Operating plans are contracts and they should be met without fail."

C. The budgeting process at Madsen Manufacturing starts with operating managers providing goals for their respective departments.

D. Fullbright Lighting holds quarterly meetings of departmental managers to consider possible changes in the budgeted targets due to changing conditions.

Answer (B) is correct.  *(CMA, adapted)*
**REQUIRED:** The organization policy most likely to result in undesirable managerial behavior.
**DISCUSSION:** Control is the process of making certain that plans are achieving the desired objectives. A budget is one of the most common control devices. It is a plan for the future; it is not a contract. To interpret a budget or other plan to be as inflexible as a contract may encourage a manager to act in ways contrary to the company's best interest in a misguided effort to meet the criteria proposed.
Answer (A) is incorrect because, if the costs are not allocated to individual managers, they have no reason to object to the allocation. Answer (C) is incorrect because participatory budgeting obtains the support of those involved and is likely to foster desirable behavior. Answer (D) is incorrect because changing budget targets as conditions change results in setting fairer performance goals.

**5.** Which of the following is the best example of why an employee may resist modifying his/her performance to meet the goals set by a control system?

A. The control system highlights the things that the employee does well.

B. The employee believes that the control system sets the standard of performance too high.

C. People tend to avoid pleasant situations.

D. The control system establishes a standard of performance that the employee considers relevant to what (s)he regards as their primary job objective.

Answer (B) is correct.  *(Publisher)*
**REQUIRED:** The best example of why an employee may resist modifying his/her performance to reach stated goals.
**DISCUSSION:** The success of a control system is determined by its effectiveness in motivating people to modify their performance. The goals of a control system may be met with resistance if they are not accepted by the employee. For example, an employee may resist changing his/her performance when (s)he believes that the stated standard of performance is set too high.
Answer (A) is incorrect because employee resistance is most likely to occur when a control procedure highlights the things an employee does poorly, thus damaging his/her self-esteem. Answer (C) is incorrect because people tend to avoid unpleasant situations. Answer (D) is incorrect because the goals of a control system will most likely not be accepted by an employee when the established standards of performance are considered irrelevant to the accomplishment of what an employee regards as the primary job objective.

**6.** Which of the following statements regarding human reactions to feedback is false?

A. Feedback should motivate employees to improve their performance.

B. The timing and content of feedback should be considered.

C. The nature of feedback should be to intimidate, rather than to offend employees.

D. Human reactions to feedback should be considered in designing control systems.

Answer (C) is correct.  *(Publisher)*
**REQUIRED:** The false statement regarding human reactions to feedback.
**DISCUSSION:** Human reactions to feedback should be considered in setting performance standards and designing control systems. However, the nature of feedback should motivate employees to improve their performance and reach the planned objectives, rather than to offend or to intimidate them. Furthermore, the timing, form, and content of the feedback on deviations should be considered in order to obtain maximum compliance by the affected employees.

**7.** Which one of the following will not occur in an organization that gives managers throughout the organization maximum freedom to make decisions?

- A. Cause individual managers to regard the managers of other segments as they do external parties.

- B. Encourage more effective solutions to operational problems.

- C. Eliminate having two divisions of the organization with competing models.

- D. Reduce the delays in securing approval for the introduction of new products.

Answer (C) is correct.   *(CMA, adapted)*
    **REQUIRED:** The event that will not occur in an organization that gives managers maximum freedom to make decisions.
    **DISCUSSION:** Decentralization is beneficial because it creates greater responsiveness to the needs of local customers, suppliers, and employees. Managers at lower levels are more knowledgeable about local markets and the needs of customers, etc. A decentralized organization is also more likely to respond flexibly and quickly to changing conditions, for example, by expediting the introduction of new products. Furthermore, greater authority enhances managerial morale and development. Disadvantages of decentralization include duplication of effort and lack of goal congruence. Therefore, decentralization will increase the chance that two divisions of the same organization will have competing models that both aim for the same market segments.
    Answer (A) is incorrect because, when segments are autonomous, other segments are regarded as external parties, e.g., as suppliers, customers, or competitors. Answer (B) is incorrect because decentralizing decision-making authority leads to more effective solutions to operational problems. Solutions will come from the individuals with the greatest knowledge of the operations involved. Answer (D) is incorrect because a decentralized organization is more likely to respond quickly to changing conditions. Therefore, decentralization should result in a reduction of the delays in securing approval for the introduction of new products.

**8.** Managerial performance may be measured in many ways. For example, an internal nonfinancial measure is

- A. Market share.

- B. Delivery performance.

- C. Customer satisfaction.

- D. Manufacturing lead time.

Answer (D) is correct.   *(Publisher)*
    **REQUIRED:** The internal nonfinancial measure.
    **DISCUSSION:** Feedback regarding managerial performance may take the form of financial and nonfinancial measures that may be internally or externally generated. Moreover, different measures have a long-term or short-term emphasis. Examples of internal nonfinancial measures are product quality, new product development time, and manufacturing lead time (cycle time).
    Answer (A) is incorrect because market share is an external nonfinancial measure. Answer (B) is incorrect because delivery performance is an external nonfinancial measure. Answer (C) is incorrect because customer satisfaction is an external nonfinancial measure.

**9.** Many forms of performance feedback are based on accounting information. For example, a divisional manager may be evaluated based on return on investment (income ÷ investment). One step in the process of developing a performance measure based on accounting information is to determine the basis for stating the measure in terms of dollars. Thus, if ROI is the chosen measure, and investment is defined as total assets, comparability issues are most likely to arise when the attribute used to calculate total assets is

- A. Current cost.

- B. Current disposal price.

- C. Historical cost.

- D. Present value.

Answer (C) is correct.   *(Publisher)*
    **REQUIRED:** The attribute most likely to create comparability problems.
    **DISCUSSION:** Historical cost creates comparability issues because returns on significantly depreciated assets may be higher than those on newer assets that have been acquired using inflated dollars. Thus, otherwise similarly situated managers may report different operating results. Moreover, managers may be reluctant to replace aging assets.
    Answer (A) is incorrect because current cost is an attempt to remedy the theoretical deficiencies of historical cost by presenting more accurate balance sheet values. Answer (B) is incorrect because current disposal price is an attempt to remedy the theoretical deficiencies of historical cost by presenting more accurate balance sheet values. Answer (D) is incorrect because present value is an attempt to remedy the theoretical deficiencies of historical cost by presenting more accurate balance sheet values.

**10.** An organization's managerial decision-making model for capital budgeting is based on the net present value of discounted cash flows. The same organization's managerial performance evaluation model is based on annual divisional return on investment. Which of the following is true?

A. Divisional managers are likely to maximize the measures in the decision-making model.

B. Divisional managers are likely to maximize the measures in the performance evaluation model.

C. The manager has an incentive to accept a project with a positive net present value that initially has a negative effect on net income.

D. The use of models with different criteria promotes goal congruence.

Answer (B) is correct. *(Publisher)*
**REQUIRED:** The true statement about use of different models for decision making and managerial evaluation.
**DISCUSSION:** Effective management control requires performance measurement and feedback. This process affects allocation of resources to organizational subunits. It also affects decisions about managers' compensation, advancement, and future assignments. Furthermore, evaluating their performance serves to motivate managers to optimize the measures in the performance evaluation model. However, that model may be inconsistent with the organization's model for managerial decision making.
Answer (A) is incorrect because self-interest provides an incentive to maximize the measures used in performance evaluation. Answer (C) is incorrect because a manager evaluated on the basis of annual ROI has an interest in maximizing short-term net income, not long-term NPV. Answer (D) is incorrect because the models should be synchronized so that the goals of the organization and the manager are congruent.

**11.** Which of the following is an example of a feedback control?

A. Preventive maintenance.

B. Inspection of completed goods.

C. Close supervision of production-line workers.

D. Measuring performance against a standard.

Answer (B) is correct. *(Publisher)*
**REQUIRED:** The example of a feedback control.
**DISCUSSION:** Feedback controls obtain information about completed activities. They permit improvement in future performance by learning from past mistakes. Thus, corrective action occurs after the fact. Inspection of completed goods is an example of a feedback control.
Answer (A) is incorrect because preventive maintenance is a feedforward control because it attempts to anticipate and prevent problems. Answer (C) is incorrect because the close supervision of production-line workers is a concurrent control because it adjusts an ongoing process. Answer (D) is incorrect because measuring performance against a standard is a general aspect of control.

**12.** The steps in a typical control process include

1. Selecting strategic control points at which to gather information about activities being performed
2. Accumulating, classifying, and recording data samples
3. Observing the work or collecting samples of data
4. Determining whether performance is satisfactory
5. Reviewing and revising standards
6. Reporting significant deviations to managers concerned

What is the correct order of these steps?

A. 1, 3, 2, 4, 6, 5

B. 1, 2, 3, 4, 5, 6

C. 1, 3, 4, 2, 6, 5

D. 1, 3, 4, 2, 5, 6

Answer (A) is correct. *(Publisher)*
**REQUIRED:** The proper sequence of steps in a typical control process.
**DISCUSSION:** The proper sequence of steps in a typical control process is as follows:

1. Selecting strategic control points at which to gather information about activities being performed
2. Observing the work or collecting samples of data
3. Accumulating, classifying, and recording data samples
4. Comparing samples with predetermined quality, schedule, and cost standards
5. Determining whether performance is satisfactory
6. Reporting significant deviations to managers concerned
7. Determining, by repeating the above steps, whether action taken is effective in correcting reported deviations (follow-up)
8. Reviewing and revising standards

Answer (B) is incorrect because observation must occur before classifying and recording data samples. Answer (C) is incorrect because data must be recorded before comparisons can occur. Answer (D) is incorrect because data must be recorded before comparisons can occur.

**13.** Control devices may be

|  | Quantitative | Qualitative |
|---|---|---|
| A. | Yes | Yes |
| B. | Yes | No |
| C. | No | Yes |
| D. | No | No |

**Answer (A) is correct.**  *(Publisher)*
**REQUIRED:** The form of control devices.
**DISCUSSION:** Control devices may be either qualitative or quantitative. Budgets, schedules, quotas, and charts are examples of quantitative control devices. Job instructions, quality-control standards, and employment criteria are qualitative control devices.

**14.** Which of the following statements regarding effective control systems is false?

A. Excessive controls are costly in time and money.

B. Outdated information is inappropriate.

C. Controls should measure the performance of all areas.

D. Controls should be simple.

**Answer (C) is correct.**  *(Publisher)*
**REQUIRED:** The false statement regarding effective control systems.
**DISCUSSION:** An effective control system should be meaningful. Therefore, controls should be in place to measure performance only in important areas. Excessive controls in minor areas are not economical because the added benefits do not outweigh the loss of time and money.
Answer (A) is incorrect because effective controls should be economical because excessive controls are costly in time and money. Answer (B) is incorrect because effective controls need to be timely because outdated information may be unreliable. Answer (D) is incorrect because effective controls need to be simple enough that the people using the control can understand.

## 10.3 Quality Considerations

**15.** A traditional quality control process in manufacturing consists of mass inspection of goods only at the end of a production process. A major deficiency of the traditional control process is that

A. It is expensive to do the inspections at the end of the process.

B. It is not possible to rework defective items.

C. It is not 100% effective.

D. It does not focus on improving the entire production process.

**Answer (D) is correct.**  *(CIA, adapted)*
**REQUIRED:** The major deficiency of a traditional quality control process.
**DISCUSSION:** The process used to produce the goods is not thoroughly reviewed and evaluated for efficiency and effectiveness. Preventing defects and increasing efficiency by improving the production process raises quality standards and decreases costs.
Answer (A) is incorrect because other quality control processes can also be expensive. Answer (B) is incorrect because reworking defective items may be possible although costly. Answer (C) is incorrect because no quality control system will be 100% effective.

**16.** Which of the following is a false statement regarding quality audits?

A. A quality audit is a requirement for ISO 9001:2000 certification.

B. A quality audit is a requirement for the Baldridge Award.

C. A quality audit program is related to gap analysis.

D. An annual quality audit is mandatory for those who have become ISO 9001:2000 certified.

**Answer (D) is correct.**  *(Publisher)*
**REQUIRED:** The false statement with respect to quality audits.
**DISCUSSION:** A quality audit is required for an organization to become ISO 9001:2000 certified. Once certification has been achieved, an annual audit is not required.
Answer (A) is incorrect because a quality audit is required to become ISO 9001:2000 certified. Answer (B) is incorrect because a quality audit is part of the Baldridge Award process. Answer (C) is incorrect because a quality audit is designed to measure the gap between specified standards and a company's quality system.

**17.** The most important component of quality control is

A. Ensuring goods and services conform to the design specifications.

B. Satisfying upper management.

C. Conforming with ISO-9001:2000 specifications.

D. Determining the appropriate timing of inspections.

Answer (A) is correct. *(CIA, adapted)*

**REQUIRED:** The most important component of quality control.

**DISCUSSION:** The intent of quality control is to ensure that goods and services conform to the design specifications. Whether the focus is on feedforward, feedback, or concurrent control, the emphasis is on ensuring product or service conformity.

Answer (B) is incorrect because quality control is geared towards satisfying the customer, not upper management. Answer (C) is incorrect because ensuring the conformance with ISO-9001:2000 specifications is a component of a compliance audit, not quality control. Answer (D) is incorrect because determining the appropriate timing of inspections is only one step towards approaching quality control. Consequently, it is not the primary component of the quality control function.

**18.** The cost of scrap, rework, and tooling changes in a product quality cost system is categorized as a(n)

A. Training cost.

B. External failure cost.

C. Internal failure cost.

D. Prevention cost.

Answer (C) is correct. *(CMA, adapted)*

**REQUIRED:** The categorization of the cost of scrap, rework, and tooling changes in a product quality cost system.

**DISCUSSION:** According to SMA 4R, internal failure costs are incurred when detection of defective products occurs before shipment. Examples of internal failure costs are scrap, rework, tooling changes, and downtime.

Answer (A) is incorrect because training costs are prevention costs. Answer (B) is incorrect because the costs of external failure, such as warranty expense, product liability, and customer ill will, arise when problems are discovered after products have been shipped. Answer (D) is incorrect because prevention costs are incurred to avoid defective output. Examples include preventive maintenance, employee training, review of equipment design, and evaluation of suppliers.

**19.** The four categories of costs associated with product quality costs are

A. External failure, internal failure, prevention, and carrying.

B. External failure, internal failure, prevention, and appraisal.

C. External failure, internal failure, training, and appraisal.

D. Warranty, product liability, training, and appraisal.

Answer (B) is correct. *(CMA, adapted)*

**REQUIRED:** The categories of product quality costs.

**DISCUSSION:** SMA 4R lists four categories of quality costs: prevention, appraisal, internal failure, and external failure (lost opportunity). Costs of prevention include attempts to avoid defective output, including employee training, review of equipment design, preventive maintenance, and evaluation of suppliers. Appraisal costs include quality control programs, inspection, and testing. Internal failure costs are incurred when detection of defective products occurs before shipment, including scrap, rework, tooling changes, and downtime. External failure costs are incurred after the product has been shipped, including the costs associated with warranties, product liability, and customer ill will.

Answer (A) is incorrect because carrying cost is not one of the elements of quality costs. Answer (C) is incorrect because training costs are not a category of quality costs. Answer (D) is incorrect because warranty, product liability, and training are not cost categories identified by SMA 4R.

**20.** The cost of statistical quality control in a product quality cost system is categorized as a(n)

A. Internal failure cost.

B. Training cost.

C. External failure cost.

D. Appraisal cost.

Answer (D) is correct. *(CMA, adapted)*

**REQUIRED:** The cost category that includes statistical quality control.

**DISCUSSION:** The following are the four categories of quality costs: prevention, appraisal, internal failure, and external failure (lost opportunity). Appraisal costs include quality control programs, inspection, and testing. However, some authorities regard statistical quality and process control as preventive activities because they not only detect faulty work but also allow for adjustment of processes to avoid future defects.

Answer (A) is incorrect because internal failure costs arise after poor quality has been found; statistical quality control is designed to detect quality problems. Answer (B) is incorrect because statistical quality control is not a training cost. Answer (C) is incorrect because external failure costs are incurred after the product has been shipped, including the costs associated with warranties, product liability, and customer ill will.

**21.** Listed below are selected line items from the Cost of Quality Report for Watson Products for last month.

| Category | Amount |
|---|---|
| Rework | $ 725 |
| Equipment maintenance | 1,154 |
| Product testing | 786 |
| Product repair | 695 |

What is Watson's total prevention and appraisal cost for last month?

   A. $786

   B. $1,154

   C. $1,940

   D. $2,665

Answer (C) is correct.  *(CMA, adapted)*
   **REQUIRED:** The total prevention and appraisal costs.
   **DISCUSSION:** The costs of prevention and appraisal are conformance costs that serve as financial measures of internal performance. Prevention costs are incurred to prevent defective output. These costs include preventive maintenance, employee training, review of equipment design, and evaluation of suppliers. Appraisal costs are incurred to detect nonconforming output. They embrace such activities as statistical quality control programs, inspection, and testing. The equipment maintenance cost of $1,154 is a prevention cost. The product testing cost of $786 is an appraisal cost. Their sum is $1,940.
   Answer (A) is incorrect because $786 is the appraisal cost. Answer (B) is incorrect because $1,154 is the prevention cost. Answer (D) is incorrect because $2,665 includes rework, an internal failure cost.

**22.** All of the following are generally included in a cost-of-quality report except

   A. Warranty claims.

   B. Design engineering.

   C. Supplier evaluations.

   D. Lost contribution margin.

Answer (D) is correct.  *(CMA, adapted)*
   **REQUIRED:** The item that does not normally appear in a cost-of-quality report.
   **DISCUSSION:** A cost-of-quality report includes most costs related to quality, including the costs of external failure, internal failure, prevention, and appraisal. Lost contribution margins from poor product quality are external failure costs that normally do not appear on a cost-of-quality report because they are opportunity costs. Opportunity costs are not usually recorded by the accounting system, thereby understating the costs of poor quality. Lost contribution margins from reduced sales, market share, and sales prices are external failure costs that are also not usually included in a cost-of-quality report.
   Answer (A) is incorrect because the costs of warranty claims are readily measurable external failure costs captured by the accounting system. Answer (B) is incorrect because the costs of design engineering are prevention costs that are usually included in cost-of-quality reports. Answer (C) is incorrect because the costs of supplier evaluations are prevention costs that are usually included in cost-of-quality reports.

**23.** Conformance is how well a product and its components meet applicable standards. According to the robust quality concept,

   A. A certain percentage of defective units is acceptable.

   B. Units are acceptable if their characteristics lie within an acceptable range of values.

   C. The goal is for all units to be within specifications.

   D. Every unit should reach a target value.

Answer (D) is correct.  *(Publisher)*
   **REQUIRED:** The true statement about robust quality.
   **DISCUSSION:** Conformance is how well a product and its components meet applicable standards. The traditional view is that conforming products are those with characteristics that lie within an acceptable specified range of values that includes a target value. This view also regarded a certain percentage of defective (nonconforming) units as acceptable. The traditional view was superseded by the zero-defects approach that sought to eliminate all nonconforming output. An extension of this approach is the robust quality concept. Its goal is to reach the target value in every case. The reason is that hidden quality costs occur when output varies from the target even though the units are within specifications.
   Answer (A) is incorrect because the traditional view of quality treats a certain number of defective units as acceptable. Answer (B) is incorrect because the traditional view of quality treats a unit as acceptable if it is within a range of specified values. Answer (C) is incorrect because the robust quality concept is an extension of the zero-defects approach. The goal of robust quality is in every case to reach a target value, not merely a range of acceptable values.

**24.** The Plan-Do-Check-Act (PDCA) Cycle is a quality tool devised by W.E. Deming. It is best described as

    A. A "management-by-fact" approach to continuous improvement.

    B. An ongoing evaluation of the practices of best-in-class organizations.

    C. The translation of customer requirements into design requirements.

    D. The responsibility of every employee, work group, department, or supplier to inspect the work.

Answer (A) is correct. *(Publisher)*
    **REQUIRED:** The best description of PDCA.
    **DISCUSSION:** PDCA is a "management-by-fact" or scientific method approach to continuous improvement. PDCA creates a process-centered environment because it involves studying the current process, collecting and analyzing data to identify causes of problems, planning for improvement, and deciding how to measure improvement (Plan). The plan is then implemented on a small scale if possible (Do). The next step is to determine what happened (Check). If the experiment was successful, the plan is fully implemented (Act). The cycle is then repeated using what was learned from the preceding cycle.
    Answer (B) is incorrect because competitive benchmarking is an ongoing evaluation of the practices of best-in-class organizations. Answer (C) is incorrect because quality deployment is the translation of customer requirements into design requirements. Answer (D) is incorrect because the "quality at the source" concept emphasizes the responsibility of every employee, work group, department, or supplier to inspect the work.

**25.** Which of the following quality costs are nonconformance costs?

    A. Systems development costs.

    B. Costs of inspecting in-process items.

    C. Environmental costs.

    D. Costs of quality circles.

Answer (C) is correct. *(Publisher)*
    **REQUIRED:** The nonconformance costs.
    **DISCUSSION:** Nonconformance costs include internal and external failure costs. External failure costs include environmental costs, e.g., fines for violations of environmental laws and loss of customer goodwill.
    Answer (A) is incorrect because systems development costs are prevention (conformance) costs. Answer (B) is incorrect because costs of inspecting in-process items are appraisal (conformance) costs. Answer (D) is incorrect because costs of quality circles are prevention (conformance) costs.

**26.** According to the robust quality concept,

    A. The minimum point on the total quality cost curve occurs when conformance cost per unit equals nonconformance cost per unit.

    B. Improving quality requires tradeoffs among categories of quality costs.

    C. Beyond some point, incurrence of prevention and appraisal costs is not cost beneficial.

    D. Costs in all categories of quality costs may be reduced while improving quality.

Answer (D) is correct. *(Publisher)*
    **REQUIRED:** The robust quality view about quality costs.
    **DISCUSSION:** The optimal level of quality costs traditionally has been deemed to occur where the conformance cost curve intercepts the nonconformance cost curve, which corresponds to the minimum point on the total cost curve. Thus, beyond some point, incurrence of prevention and appraisal costs is not cost beneficial. However, the modern robust quality view is that this relationship does not always hold. Improving quality and reducing costs in each category may be possible if the most efficient prevention methods are applied. For example, selection of a supplier meeting high quality standards regarding defect rates and delivery times may drive down not only failure costs but also the prevention and appraisal costs incurred when supplier performance was less reliable.

**27.** Quality costing is similar in service and manufacturing organizations. Nevertheless, the differences between these organizations have certain implications for quality management. Thus,

    A. Direct labor costs are usually a higher percentage of total costs in manufacturing organizations.

    B. External failure costs are relatively greater in service organizations.

    C. Quality improvements resulting in more efficient use of labor time are more likely to be accepted by employees in service organizations.

    D. Poor service is less likely to result in loss of customers than a faulty product.

Answer (B) is correct. *(Publisher)*
    **REQUIRED:** The true statement distinguishing quality considerations in service and manufacturing organizations.
    **DISCUSSION:** External failure costs arise when problems occur after delivery. They occur because products or services are nonconforming or otherwise do not satisfy customers. External failure costs in service enterprises are even more important than in manufacturing environments. Faulty goods sometimes may be reworked or replaced to a customer's satisfaction, but poor service tends to result in a loss of customers.
    Answer (A) is incorrect because direct labor costs are usually a higher percentage of total costs in service organizations. Answer (C) is incorrect because service activities are usually more labor intensive than in modern manufacturing environments. Thus, more efficient labor usage is more likely to be viewed as a threat to employee job security in service organizations. Answer (D) is incorrect because the bad will resulting from poor service may be even more likely than a defective product to result in loss of customers.

**28.** When evaluating projects, breakeven time is best described as

A. Annual fixed costs ÷ monthly contribution margin.

B. Project investment ÷ annual net cash inflows.

C. The point at which cumulative cash inflows on a project equal total cash outflows.

D. The point at which discounted cumulative cash inflows on a project equal discounted total cash outflows.

Answer (D) is correct.   *(CMA, adapted)*
**REQUIRED:** The definition of breakeven time.
**DISCUSSION:** Breakeven time evaluates the rapidity of new product development. The usual calculation determines the period beginning with project approval that is required for the discounted cumulative cash inflows to equal the discounted cumulative cash outflows. However, it may also be calculated as the point at which discounted cumulative cash inflows on a project equal discounted total cash outflows. The concept is similar to the payback period, but it is more sophisticated because it incorporates the time value of money. It also differs from the payback method because the period covered begins at the outset of a project, not when the initial cash outflow occurs.
Answer (A) is incorrect because it is related to breakeven point, not breakeven time. Answer (B) is incorrect because the payback period equals investment divided by annual undiscounted net cash inflows. Answer (C) is incorrect because the payback period is the period required for total undiscounted cash inflows to equal total undiscounted cash outflows.

**29.** Management of a company is attempting to build a reputation as a world-class manufacturer of quality products. Which of the following measures would not be used by the firm to measure quality?

A. The percentage of shipments returned by customers because of poor quality.

B. The number of parts shipped per day.

C. The number of defective parts per million.

D. The percentage of products passing quality tests the first time.

Answer (B) is correct.   *(CIA, adapted)*
**REQUIRED:** The measure not used for quality measurement.
**DISCUSSION:** The number of parts shipped per day would most likely be used as a measure of the effectiveness and efficiency of shipping procedures, not the quality of the product. This measure does not consider how many of the parts are defective.
Answer (A) is incorrect because the percentage of shipments returned measures quality by the number of defective units. Answer (C) is incorrect because the number of defective parts per million measures quality by the number of defective units. Answer (D) is incorrect because the percentage of products passing quality tests the first time measures quality by the number of nondefective products.

**30.** Quality cost indices are often used to measure and analyze the cost of maintaining a given level of quality. One example of a quality cost index, which uses a direct labor base, is computed as

$$Quality\ cost\ index\ =$$

$$\frac{Total\ quality\ costs}{Direct\ labor\ costs} \times 100$$

The following quality cost data were collected for May and June:

|  | May | June |
|---|---|---|
| Prevention costs | $  4,000 | $  5,000 |
| Appraisal costs | 6,000 | 5,000 |
| Internal failure costs | 12,000 | 15,000 |
| External failure costs | 14,000 | 11,000 |
| Direct labor costs | 90,000 | 100,000 |

Based upon these cost data, the quality cost index

A. Decreased 4 points from May to June.

B. Was unchanged from May to June.

C. Increased 10 points from May to June.

D. Decreased 10 points from May to June.

Answer (A) is correct.   *(CIA, adapted)*
**REQUIRED:** The change, if any, in the quality cost index.
**DISCUSSION:** The index for May was 40% [($4,000 + $6,000 + $12,000 + $14,000) ÷ $90,000], and the index for June was 36% [($5,000 + $5,000 + $15,000 + $11,000) ÷ $100,000].
Answer (B) is incorrect because the index decreased. Answer (C) is incorrect because the increase in prevention costs was 10% of the increase in labor costs. Answer (D) is incorrect because the decrease in appraisal costs was 10% of the increase in labor costs.

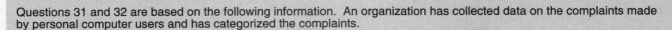

Questions 31 and 32 are based on the following information. An organization has collected data on the complaints made by personal computer users and has categorized the complaints.

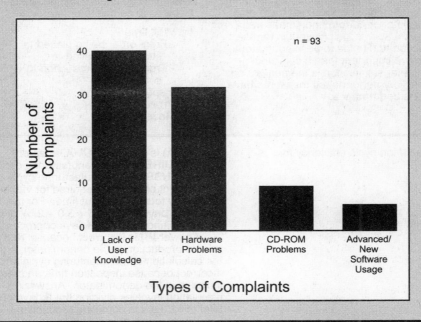

**31.** Using the information collected, the organization should focus on

A. The total number of personal computer complaints that occurred.

B. The number of computer complaints associated with CD-ROM problems and new software usage.

C. The number of computer complaints associated with the lack of user knowledge and hardware problems.

D. The cost to alleviate all computer complaints.

Answer (C) is correct. *(CIA, adapted)*
REQUIRED: The organization's focus based on the data.
DISCUSSION: Complaints based on lack of user knowledge and hardware problems are by far the most frequent according to this chart. Consequently, the company should devote its resources primarily to these issues.
Answer (A) is incorrect because more detailed information is not available. The Pareto diagram does not focus on the total quantity of computer complaints. Answer (B) is incorrect because complaints about CD-ROMs and software are infrequent. Answer (D) is incorrect because cost information is not provided.

**32.** The chart displays

A. The arithmetic mean of each computer complaint.

B. The relative frequency of each computer complaint.

C. The median of each computer complaint.

D. The absolute frequency of each computer complaint.

Answer (D) is correct. *(CIA, adapted)*
REQUIRED: The information provided by the chart.
DISCUSSION: This Pareto diagram depicts the frequencies of complaints in absolute terms. It displays the actual number of each type of complaint.
Answer (A) is incorrect because the chart does not display arithmetic means of each type of complaint. Answer (B) is incorrect because the chart does not display relative frequencies of each type of complaint. Answer (C) is incorrect because the chart does not display medians of each type of complaint.

Questions 33 and 34 are based on the following information.

Wolk Corporation is a highly automated manufacturing firm. The vice president of finance has decided that traditional standards are inappropriate for performance measures in an automated environment. Labor is insignificant in terms of the total cost of production and tends to be fixed, material quality is considered more important than minimizing material cost, and customer satisfaction is the number one priority. As a result, delivery performance measures have been chosen to evaluate performance.

The following information is considered typical of the time involved to complete orders:

- Wait time:
  - From order being placed to start of production — 10.0 days
  - From start of production to completion — 5.0 days
- Inspection time — 1.5 days
- Process time — 3.0 days
- Move time — 2.5 days

**33.** What is the manufacturing cycle efficiency for this order?

A. 25.0%

B. 13.6%

C. 37.5%

D. 69.2%

Answer (A) is correct. *(CMA, adapted)*
**REQUIRED:** The manufacturing cycle efficiency statistic.
**DISCUSSION:** Manufacturing cycle efficiency is defined as the quotient of the time required for value-added production time divided by total throughput time. For this order, the total lead time is 12 days (5.0 + 1.5 + 3.0 + 2.5), and the manufacturing cycle efficiency is 25% (3 days of processing ÷ 12).
Answer (B) is incorrect because 13.6% includes the 10 days prior to production in the denominator, a period not included in the calculation of manufacturing cycle efficiency. Answer (C) is incorrect because inspection time and move time should be included in the denominator. Answer (D) is incorrect because the calculation involves dividing the 3 days of processing time by the total of 12 days to complete production.

**34.** What is the delivery cycle time for this order?

A. 7 days.

B. 12 days.

C. 15 days.

D. 22 days.

Answer (D) is correct. *(CMA, adapted)*
**REQUIRED:** The delivery cycle time for the order.
**DISCUSSION:** The delivery cycle time is defined as the entire time from receipt of the order until delivery of the order. This period equals 22 days (10.0 + 5.0 + 1.5 + 3.0 + 2.5).
Answer (A) is incorrect because 7 days excludes the wait time. Answer (B) is incorrect because 12 days ignores the 10 days of the waiting period prior to the start of production. Answer (C) is incorrect because 15 days incorporates the wait time but not the production periods.

**35.** Quality Company produces a component of a machine. The target value for a key dimension of the component is 100 millimeters (mm). The quality loss per unit if the key dimension is measured at precisely the upper or lower specification limit (100 mm ± 1 mm) is estimated to be $10. The following are the measures of a sample of four units:

| Unit | Measurement |
|------|-------------|
| 1 | 99 |
| 2 | 101 |
| 3 | 99.5 |
| 4 | 100.5 |

The Quality Company produces 1,000 of the components. Based on the sample, the estimated quality loss is

A. $625

B. $6,250

C. $10,000

D. $25,000

Answer (B) is correct. *(Publisher)*
**REQUIRED:** The estimated quality loss.
**DISCUSSION:** The quality loss constant (k) in the Taguchi quality loss function equation is $10 [$10 loss at the specification limit ÷ $(1 \text{ mm})^2$]. Accordingly, the quality loss for the sample may be determined as follows:

| Unit | Measurement in mm | Actual – Target $(x - T)$ | $(x - T)^2$ | $k(x - T)^2$ |
|------|-------------------|---------------------------|-------------|--------------|
| 1 | 99 | −1 | 1 | $10.00 |
| 2 | 101 | +1 | 1 | 10.00 |
| 3 | 99.5 | −.5 | .25 | 2.50 |
| 4 | 100.5 | +.5 | .25 | 2.50 |
| | | | 2.50 | $25.00 |

The average per unit quality loss for the sample is $6.25 ($25 ÷ 4). Consequently, the total estimated loss for 1,000 components is $6,250.
Answer (A) is incorrect because $625 equals $.625 times 1,000 units. Answer (C) is incorrect because $10,000 equals $10 times 1,000 units. Answer (D) is incorrect because $25,000 is based on the total loss for the sample ($25), not the unit average loss ($6.25).

## 10.4 Total Quality Management

> Questions 36 and 37 are based on the following information. The management and employees of a large household goods moving company decided to adopt total quality management (TQM) and continuous improvement (CI). They believed that, if their company became nationally known as adhering to TQM and CI, one result would be an increase in the company's profits and market share.

**36.** The primary reason for adopting TQM was to achieve

A. Greater customer satisfaction.

B. Reduced delivery time.

C. Reduced delivery charges.

D. Greater employee participation.

**Answer (A) is correct.** *(CIA, adapted)*
**REQUIRED:** The primary reason for adopting TQM.
**DISCUSSION:** TQM is an integrated system that anticipates, meets, and exceeds customers' needs, wants, and expectations.
Answer (B) is incorrect because reduced delivery time is one of many potential activities that needs improvement. Answer (C) is incorrect because reduced delivery charges is one of many potential activities that needs improvement. Answer (D) is incorrect because increased employee participation is necessary to achieve TQM, but it is not the primary purpose for establishing the program.

**37.** Quality is achieved more economically if the company focuses on

A. Appraisal costs.

B. Prevention costs.

C. Internal failure costs.

D. External failure costs.

**Answer (B) is correct.** *(CIA, adapted)*
**REQUIRED:** The necessary focus for achieving quality more economically.
**DISCUSSION:** Prevention attempts to avoid defective output. Prevention costs include preventive maintenance, employee training, review of equipment design, and evaluation of suppliers. Prevention is less costly than detection and correction of defective output. It is also ordinarily less costly than the combined costs of appraisal, internal failure, and external failure.

**38.** Under a total quality management (TQM) approach

A. Measurement occurs throughout the process, and errors are caught and corrected at the source.

B. Quality control is performed by highly trained inspectors at the end of the production process.

C. Upper management assumes the primary responsibility for the quality of the products and services.

D. A large number of suppliers are used in order to obtain the lowest possible prices.

**Answer (A) is correct.** *(CIA, adapted)*
**REQUIRED:** The true statement about total quality management.
**DISCUSSION:** Total quality management emphasizes quality as a basic organizational function. TQM is the continuous pursuit of quality in every aspect of organizational activities. One of the basic tenets of TQM is doing it right the first time. Thus, errors should be caught and corrected at the source.
Answer (B) is incorrect because total quality management emphasizes discovering errors throughout the process, not inspection of finished goods. Answer (C) is incorrect because all members of the organization assume responsibility for quality of the products and services. Answer (D) is incorrect because the total quality management philosophy recommends limiting the number of suppliers to create a strong relationship.

**39.** Which of the following is a characteristic of total quality management (TQM)?

A. Management by objectives.

B. On-the-job training by other workers.

C. Quality by final inspection.

D. Education and self-improvement.

**Answer (D) is correct.** *(CIA, adapted)*
**REQUIRED:** The characteristic of TQM.
**DISCUSSION:** According to management theorist W.E. Deming's well-known 14 points, education and self-improvement are essential. Knowledge is opportunity. Hence, continuous improvement should be everyone's primary career objective.
Answer (A) is incorrect because one of the 14 points recommends elimination of numerical quotas. MBO causes aggressive pursuit of numerical quotas. Answer (B) is incorrect because informal learning from coworkers serves to entrench bad work habits. One of the 14 points stresses proper training of everyone. Answer (C) is incorrect because another of the 14 points states that quality by final inspection is unnecessary if quality is built in from the start.

**40.** In which of the following organizational structures does total quality management (TQM) work best?

    A.  Hierarchal.

    B.  Teams of people from the same specialty.

    C.  Teams of people from different specialties.

    D.  Specialists working individually.

**Answer (C) is correct.**  *(CIA, adapted)*
    **REQUIRED:** The structure in which TQM works best.
    **DISCUSSION:** TQM advocates replacement of the traditional hierarchal structure with teams of people from different specialties. This change follows from TQM's emphasis on empowering employees and teamwork. Employees should have proper training, necessary information, and the best tools; be fully engaged in the decision process; and receive fair compensation. If such empowered employees are assembled in teams of individuals with the required skills, TQM theorists believe they will be more effective than people performing their tasks separately in a rigid structure.
    Answer (A) is incorrect because hierarchal organization stifles TQM. Answer (B) is incorrect because TQM works best with teams of people from different specialties. Answer (D) is incorrect because teamwork is essential for TQM.

**41.** In year 2, a manufacturing company instituted a total quality management (TQM) program producing the following report:

Summary Cost of Quality Report (000s)

|  | Year 1 | Year 2 | % Change |
|---|---|---|---|
| Prevention costs | $   200 | $   300 | +50 |
| Appraisal costs | 210 | 315 | +50 |
| Internal failure costs | 190 | 114 | –40 |
| External failure costs | 1,200 | 621 | –48 |
| Total quality costs | $1,800 | $1,350 | –25 |

On the basis of this report, which one of the following statements is most likely true?

    A.  An increase in conformance costs resulted in a higher quality product and therefore resulted in a decrease in nonconformance costs.

    B.  An increase in inspection costs was solely responsible for the decrease in quality costs.

    C.  Quality costs such as scrap and rework decreased by 48%.

    D.  Quality costs such as returns and repairs under warranty decreased by 40%.

**Answer (A) is correct.**  *(CMA, adapted)*
    **REQUIRED:** The true statement about a report prepared by a company using a TQM program.
    **DISCUSSION:** TQM emphasizes the supplier's relationship with the customer, and recognizes that everyone in a process is at some time a customer or supplier of someone else, either within or without the organization. The costs of quality include costs of conformance and costs of nonconformance. Costs of conformance include prevention costs and appraisal (inspection) costs. Nonconformance costs are composed of internal failure costs and external failure costs, such as lost opportunity. Conformance costs (prevention and appraisal) increased substantially, whereas the nonconformance costs (internal and external failure) decreased. Hence, the increase in conformance costs resulted in a higher quality product.
    Answer (B) is incorrect because prevention costs also increased substantially, which could also have led to higher quality products. Answer (C) is incorrect because scrap and rework are internal failure costs, which decreased by 40%. Answer (D) is incorrect because returns and repairs are external failure costs, which decreased by 48%.

---

Use Gleim's **CMA Test Prep** for interactive testing with **over 2,000 additional multiple-choice questions**!

# STUDY UNIT ELEVEN
# OVERVIEW OF EXTERNAL FINANCIAL REPORTING

(16 pages of outline)

This study unit is the **first of ten** on **external financial reporting**. The relative weight assigned to this major topic in Part 2 of the exam is **25%** at **skill level B** (four skill types required). The ten study units are

Study Unit 11:   Overview of External Financial Reporting
Study Unit 12:   Overview of Financial Statements
Study Unit 13:   Cash and Receivables
Study Unit 14:   Inventories and Investments
Study Unit 15:   Long-Lived Assets
Study Unit 16:   Liabilities
Study Unit 17:   Equity and Revenue Recognition
Study Unit 18:   Other Income Statement Items
Study Unit 19:   Business Combinations and Derivatives
Study Unit 20:   SEC Requirements and the Annual Report

After studying the outlines and answering the multiple-choice questions in this study unit, you will have the skills necessary to address the following topics listed in the IMA's Learning Outcome Statements:

Part 2 – Sections E.1. Objectives of external financial reporting; and E.2. Financial accounting fundamentals

The candidate should be able to:

a.   identify the objectives of external financial reporting, i.e., providing information on resources and obligations, comprehensive income, and cash flow

b.   identify and demonstrate an understanding of basic accounting assumptions and conventions, including going concern, historical cost, accrual accounting, and conservatism

c.   demonstrate an understanding of recognition and measurement concepts

d.   differentiate between realization and recognition

e.   identify financial statement elements for each of the financial statements

## 11.1 CONCEPTUAL FRAMEWORK UNDERLYING FINANCIAL ACCOUNTING

1. The Financial Accounting Standards Board (FASB) promulgated its **Statements of Financial Accounting Concepts (SFACs)** to provide accountants with "a framework of fundamentals on which financial accounting and reporting standards could be based."

   a. Six SFACs are extant. They are:

      1) SFAC 1 – Objectives of Financial Reporting by Business Enterprises (Nov 1978)
      2) SFAC 2 – Qualitative Characteristics of Accounting Information (May 1980)
      3) SFAC 4 – Objectives of Financial Reporting by Nonbusiness Organizations (Dec 1980)
      4) SFAC 5 – Recognition and Measurement in Financial Statements of Business Enterprises (Dec 1984)
      5) SFAC 6 – Elements of Financial Statements (Dec 1985)
      6) SFAC 7 – Using Cash Flow Information and Present Value in Accounting Measurements (Feb 2000)

   b. SFACs 1, 6, 5, and 7 are covered in this study unit. SFAC 2 is covered in Gleim's *CMA Review, Part 1*, subunit 16.2. SFAC 4 is not relevant to the CMA Exam. (SFAC 3 was replaced by SFAC 6.)

   c. Note that **SFACs do not establish GAAP**. They provide a theoretical framework; they do not decide specific accounting and reporting questions.

2. *Objectives of Financial Reporting by Business Enterprises* **(SFAC 1)**, issued November 1978.

   a. **Scope of financial reporting**

      1) The objectives extend to all means of "general purpose external financial reporting by business enterprises" (financial reporting).

         a) "The objectives stem primarily from the needs of external users who lack the authority to prescribe the information they want..."

      2) "**Financial statements** are a central feature of financial reporting. They are a principal means of communicating accounting information to those outside an enterprise."

         a) "**Financial reporting** includes not only financial statements but also other means of communicating information that relates, directly or indirectly, to the information provided by the accounting system."

            i) Annual reports, prospectuses, other filings with the SEC, news releases, and letters to shareholders are examples of reports that may include financial statements, other financial information, and non-financial information.

         b) "...financial reporting and financial statements have essentially the same objectives..."

      3) "Financial statements are often audited by independent accountants for the purpose of enhancing confidence in their reliability."

         a) However, information included in financial reporting is often not subject to outside scrutiny.

b. **Environmental context of objectives**

1) "Financial reporting is not an end in itself but is intended to provide information that is **useful in making business and economic decisions** – for making reasoned choices among alternative uses of scarce resources in the conduct of business and economic activities."

2) "The function of financial reporting is to provide information that is useful to those who make economic decisions about business enterprises and about investments in or loans to business enterprises."

c. **Characteristics and limitations of information provided**

1) "The information provided by financial reporting

   a) Is primarily financial in nature – it is generally quantified and expressed in **units of money**."

   b) Pertains to **individual business enterprises**... rather than to industries or an economy as a whole..."

   c) Often results from **approximate, rather than exact, measures**. The measures commonly involve numerous estimates, classifications, summarizations, judgments, and allocations."

   d) Largely reflects the financial effects of transactions and **events that have already happened**."

   e) Involves a cost to provide and use, and generally the **benefits** of the information provided should be expected to **at least equal the cost involved**."

2) "Financial reporting is but **one source of information** needed by those who make economic decisions about business enterprises."

d. **Objectives – General considerations**

1) "The objectives begin with a broad focus on information that is **useful in investment and credit decisions**..."

   a) However, these are not the only parties to whom the objectives apply. "To the contrary, information that satisfies the objectives should be useful to all who are interested in an enterprise's future capacity to pay or in how investors or creditors are faring."

2) "The role of financial reporting in the economy is to provide information that is useful in making business and economic decisions, not to determine what those decisions should be."

3) "The role of financial reporting requires it to provide **evenhanded, neutral, or unbiased** information."

e. **Objective – Information useful in investment and credit decisions**

1) "Financial reporting should provide information that is **useful to present and potential investors and creditors** and other users in making rational investment, credit, and other similar decisions."

2) "The information should be comprehensible to those who have a reasonable understanding of business and economic activities and who are willing to study the information with reasonable diligence."

3) "Efforts may be needed to increase the understandability of financial information. **Cost-benefit considerations** may indicate that information understood or used by only a few should not be provided."

f.   **Objective – Information useful in assessing cash flow prospects**

    1)   "Financial reporting should provide information to help present and potential investors and creditors and other users assess the amounts, timing, and uncertainty of **prospective cash receipts**..."

    2)   "Investors, creditors, and others need information to help them form rational expectations about those prospective cash receipts and assess the risk that the amounts or timing of the receipts **may differ from expectations**..."

g.   **Objective – Information about enterprise resources, claims to those resources, and changes in them**

    1)   "Financial reporting should

        a)   Provide information about the **economic resources** of an enterprise, the **claims to those resources**..., and the **effects of transactions**, events, and circumstances that change resources and claims to those resources."

        b)   Provide information about an enterprise's economic resources, obligations, and owners' equity.  That information helps investors, creditors, and others identify the enterprise's financial strengths and weaknesses and assess its **liquidity and solvency**."

           i)   However, "...financial accounting is not designed to measure directly the value of an enterprise."

        c)   Provide information about an enterprise's **performance during a period**."

           i)   "The primary focus of financial reporting is information about an enterprise's performance provided by measures of **earnings and its components**."

               •   "Financial statements that show only cash receipts and payments during a short period, such as a year, cannot adequately indicate whether or not an enterprise's performance is successful."

               •   "... **accrual accounting** generally provides a better indication of enterprise performance than information about current cash receipts and payments."

           ii)   "Investors and creditors ordinarily invest in or lend to enterprises that they expect to continue in operation – an expectation that is familiar to accountants as **'the going concern' assumption**.  Information about the past is usually less useful in assessing prospects for an enterprise's future if the enterprise is in liquidation or is expected to enter liquidation."

        d)   Provide information about how an enterprise **obtains and spends cash** ... and about other factors that may affect an enterprise's liquidity or solvency."

        e)   Provide information about how management of an enterprise has discharged its **stewardship responsibility to owners** (stockholders) for the use of enterprise resources entrusted to it."

           i)   "Financial reporting, and especially financial statements, usually cannot and does not separate management performance from enterprise performance."

        f)   Include **explanations and interpretations** to help users understand financial information provided."

           i)   "Investors, creditors, and others are aided in evaluating estimates and judgmental information by explanations of underlying assumptions or methods used..."

3. ***Elements of Financial Statements (SFAC 6)***, issued December 1985.

   a. SFAC 6 applies to business enterprises and not-for-profit entities.

     1) The elements defined are those that relate to measuring the performance and status of an entity based on information provided by accrual accounting.

   b. The following elements reflect resources and claims thereto at a **moment in time**:

     1) **Assets** are "probable future economic benefits obtained or controlled by a particular entity as a result of past transactions or events."

       a) A valuation allowance changes the carrying amount of an asset. It is not a separate asset or a liability.

     2) **Liabilities** are "probable future sacrifices of economic benefits arising from present obligations of a particular entity to transfer assets or provide services to other entities in the future as a result of past transactions or events."

       a) A valuation account, e.g., bond premium or discount, changes the carrying amount of a liability.

     3) **Equity or net assets** is "the residual interest in the assets of an entity that remains after deducting its liabilities."

       a) Equity of a business enterprise, in contrast with the net assets of a non-profit entity, is changed by investments by, and distributions to, owners.

   c. The following elements describe transactions, events, and circumstances during **intervals of time** (the first three apply only to business enterprises):

     1) **Investments by owners** are "increases in equity of a particular business enterprise resulting from transfers to it from other entities of something valuable to obtain or increase ownership interests (or equity) in it."

     2) **Distributions to owners** are "decreases in equity of a particular business enterprise resulting from transferring assets, rendering services, or incurring liabilities by the enterprise to owners."

       a) A distribution to owners decreases equity (the ownership interest).

     3) **Comprehensive income** is "the change in equity of a business enterprise during a period from transactions and other events and circumstances from nonowner sources." It excludes changes in equity resulting from investments by and distributions to owners.

       a) Comprehensive income and the financial statements are based on the **financial capital maintenance** concept; comprehensive income is a return on, not a return of, financial capital.

       b) Comprehensive income **differs from measures of net income** in current practice.

         i) Comprehensive income encompasses certain changes in equity recognized in the equity section of the balance sheet but not in the income statement, such as

           • Changes in the fair values of available-for-sale securities
           • Foreign currency translation adjustments
           • The excess of an additional pension liability over any prior service cost

       c) Comprehensive income also differs from **earnings** as defined in SFAC 5, as earnings is sometimes used in current practice as a synonym for net income.

         i) "Earnings is a measure of entity performance during a period ... Comprehensive income is a broad measure of the effects of transactions and other events on an entity..."

    d)    **Statement of Financial Accounting Standards (SFAS) 130**, *Reporting Comprehensive Income*, requires that all items recognized under current standards as components of comprehensive income be reported in a financial statement displayed with the same prominence as the other statements.

    4)    **Revenues** are "inflows or other enhancements of assets of an entity or settlements of its liabilities (or a combination of both) from delivering or producing goods, rendering services, or other activities that constitute the entity's ongoing major or central operations."

    5)    **Expenses** are "outflows or other using up of assets or incurrences of liabilities (or a combination of both) from delivering or producing goods, rendering services, or carrying out other activities that constitute the entity's ongoing major or central operations."

    6)    **Gains (losses)** are increases (decreases) in equity "from peripheral or incidental transactions of an entity and from all other transactions and other events and circumstances affecting the entity except those that result from revenues (expenses) or investments by (distributions to) owners."

  d.    Nine of the ten elements described in SFAC 6 make up three of the four **basic financial statements**:

    1)    **Statement of Financial Position ("Balance Sheet")**

        a)    Assets
        b)    Liabilities
        c)    Equity
        d)    Investments by owners

    2)    **Statement of Income**

        a)    Revenues
        b)    Gains
        c)    Expenses
        d)    Losses

    3)    **Statement of Retained Earnings**

        a)    Distributions to owners

    4)    SFAS 103 requires that the components of comprehensive income be displayed in the financial statements. Other than reporting net income as one of the components, no particular format is required. Thus, an enterprise may display comprehensive income on a separate statement, combined with the statement of income, or in some other manner.

        a)    Comprehensive income

  e.    The following table summarizes all changes in equity:

| Transactions and other events and circumstances affecting a business enterprise during a period | | | |
|---|---|---|---|
| **Changes in assets and liabilities not accompanied by changes in equity** | **Changes in assets and liabilities accompanied by changes in equity** | | **Changes within equity that do not affect assets or liabilities** |
| • Exchanges of assets for assets<br>• Exchanges of liabilities for liabilities<br>• Acquisitions of assets by incurring liabilities<br>• Settlements of liabilities by transferring assets | **Comprehensive income** | **Changes in equity from transfers between enterprise and its owners** | |
| | • Revenues<br>• Gains<br>• Expenses<br>• Losses | • Investments by owners<br>• Distributions to owners | |

4. ***Recognition and Measurement in Financial Statements of Business Enterprises*** **(SFAC 5)**, issued December 1984.

    a. Recognition criteria determine whether and when items should be incorporated into the financial statements, either initially or as changes in existing items.

        1) Four **fundamental recognition criteria** apply to all recognition issues. However, each is subject to the pervasive cost-benefit constraint and the materiality threshold.

            a) The item must meet the definition of an **element** of financial statements.

            b) It must have a relevant **attribute** measurable with sufficient reliability (**measurability**).

            c) The information about it must be capable of making a difference in user decisions (**relevance**).

            d) The information must be representationally faithful, verifiable, and neutral (**reliability**).

        2) **Revenue recognition principle.** According to the revenue recognition principle, revenues and gains should be recognized when (1) realized or realizable and (2) earned.

            a) Revenues and gains are **realized** when goods or services have been exchanged for cash or claims to cash.

            b) Revenues and gains are **realizable** when goods or services have been exchanged for assets that are readily convertible into cash or claims to cash.

            c) Revenues are **earned** when the earning process has been substantially completed and the entity is entitled to the resulting benefits or revenues.

                i) **Gains** ordinarily do not involve an earning process. Thus, the significant criterion for recognition of gains is being realized or realizable.

            d) The two conditions are usually met when goods are delivered or services are rendered, that is, at the time of sale, which is customarily the **time of delivery**.

            e) As a reflection of the profession's conservatism, **expenses and losses** have historically been subject to less stringent recognition criteria than revenues and gains.

                i) Expenses and losses are not subject to the realization criterion.

                ii) Rather, expenses and losses are recognized when a **consumption of economic benefits** occurs during the entity's primary activities or when an **impairment** of the ability of existing assets to provide future benefits has occurred.

                    • An expense or loss also may be recognized when a **liability** has been incurred or increased without the receipt of corresponding benefits; a probable and reasonably estimable contingent loss is an example.

                iii) Long-lived assets, such as equipment, buildings, and intangible assets, are **depreciated or amortized** over their useful lives. Natural resources are **depleted** -- usually on a units-of-production basis.

3) The following are exceptions to the basic revenue recognition rules:

    a) Revenues from long-term contracts may be recognized using the **percentage-of-completion method**.

        i) This method allows for revenue to be recognized **before delivery** at various stages of the contract, although the entire job is not complete.

    b) **Completion of production** or a **change in prices** is an appropriate basis for recognition **before delivery** if products or other assets are readily realizable, e.g., precious metals and some agricultural products.

    c) Recognition of revenues or gains or losses is appropriate in **nonmonetary transactions**, including exchanges and nonreciprocal transactions (e.g., contributions received or given). However, fair values must be reasonably determinable.

    d) If the collectibility of assets is relatively uncertain, revenues and gains may be recognized **after delivery,** as cash is received using the **installment sales method** or the **cost recovery method**.

    e) Revenues from, for example, interest and rent, may be recognized based on the passage of time.

4) Recognition of revenues, expenses, gains, losses, and changes in related assets and liabilities involves, among other things, the application of the **pervasive expense recognition principles**: associating cause and effect, systematic and rational allocation, and immediate recognition.

    a) SFAC 6 defines matching, a term that has been given a variety of meanings in accounting literature, as essentially synonymous with **associating cause and effect**.

        i) **Matching** "is simultaneous or combined recognition of the revenues and expenses that result directly and jointly from the same transactions or other events." Such a direct relationship is found when revenue for sales of goods is recognized in the same period as the cost of goods sold.

    b) **Systematic and rational allocation** procedures do not directly relate costs and revenues but are applied when a causal relationship is "generally, but not specifically, identified."

        i) This expense recognition principle is appropriate when

            • An asset provides benefits over several periods (its estimated useful life),

            • The asset is used up as a result of events affecting the entity, and

            • The expense resulting from such wastage is indirectly (not directly and traceably) related to specific revenues and particular periods.

        ii) The usual example is depreciation.

    c) **Immediate recognition** is the applicable principle when costs cannot be directly or feasibly related to specific revenues, and their benefits are used up in the period in which they are incurred. Utilities expense is a common example.

b. Different **measurement attributes** of assets and liabilities are used in current practice.

    1) **Historical cost** is the acquisition price of an asset and is ordinarily adjusted subsequently for amortization (which includes depreciation) or other allocations. It is the relevant attribute for plant assets and most inventories.

    2) **Historical proceeds** is the cash or equivalent that is actually received when an obligation was created and may be subsequently amortized. It is the relevant attribute for liabilities incurred to provide goods or services to customers.

        a) An example is a magazine subscription.

    3) **Current (replacement) cost** is the cash or equivalent that would have to be paid for a current acquisition of the same or an equivalent asset.

        a) Inventory valued at the lower of cost or market may reflect current cost.

    4) **Current market value (exit value)** is the cash or equivalent realizable by selling an asset in an orderly liquidation (not in a forced sale). It is used to measure some marketable securities, e.g., those held by investment companies or assets expected to be sold at below their carrying amount.

        a) Certain liabilities, such as those incurred by writers of options who do not own the underlying assets, also are measured at current market value.

        b) More commonly, current market value is used when the lower-of-cost-or-market rule is applied to inventories and marketable securities.

    5) **Net realizable value** is the cash or equivalent expected to be received for an asset in the due course of business, minus the costs of completion and sale. It is used to measure short-term receivables and some inventories, for example, damaged inventories.

        a) Net realizable value is distinct from liquidation value, which is the appropriate valuation of assets and liabilities when the going-concern assumption no longer holds.

    6) **Net settlement value** is the cash or equivalent that the entity expects to pay to satisfy an obligation in the due course of business. It is used to measure such items as trade payables and warranty obligations.

        a) Net settlement value ignores present value considerations. The amounts that will be realized in a liquidation are usually less than those that would have been received in the due course of business.

    7) **Present value** is in theory the most relevant method of measurement because it incorporates time value of money concepts.

        a) Determination of the present value of an asset or liability requires discounting at an appropriate interest rate the related future cash flows expected to occur in the due course of business.

        b) In practice, it is currently used only for long-term receivables and payables (but see SFAC 7).

c. **Nominal units of money** are expected to continue as the measurement scale in current practice.

    1) The use of monetary units unadjusted for changes in purchasing power is not ideal, but it has the virtue of simplicity and does not result in excessive distortion if inflation or deflation is relatively low.

5.    ***Using Cash Flow Information and Present Value in Accounting* Measurements (SFAC 7)**, issued February 2000.

    a.    Accounting measurements ordinarily use an observable amount determined by market forces but, absent such a measurement, **estimated cash flows** often serve as a measure of an asset or a liability.

        1)    Thus, SFAC 7 establishes a framework that uses cash flows for measurements at initial recognition, for fresh-start measurements, and for applications of the interest method of allocation.

    b.    An **estimated cash flow** is a future amount, whether paid or received.

        1)    A **fresh-start measurement** occurs in a period subsequent to initial recognition. It results in a carrying amount not based on prior amounts or accounting treatments.

            a)    An example is the reporting of trading securities at fair value at each balance sheet date.

        2)    An **interest method of allocation** uses present value in the absence of a fresh-start measurement to calculate the periodic change in the carrying amount of an asset or liability.

    c.    SFAC 7 also states principles for the use of present value, especially when the amounts of future cash flows or their timing are uncertain, and describes the objective of present value.

        1)    **Present value** is a current measure of an estimated cash flow after discounting.

        2)    The present value of \$1 due or payable in n periods and discounted at interest rate i is $\$1 \div (1 + i)^n$.

    d.    The **scope of SFAC 7** is limited to **measurement matters**. It does not concern recognition issues or determine when fresh-start measurements should be used.

    e.    The **objective of present value measurement** is to distinguish the economic differences between sets of future cash flows that may vary in amount, timing, and uncertainty.

    f.    For initial recognition and fresh-start purposes, present value is based on an observable measurement attribute.

        1)    Absent observed transaction prices, the present value measurement should encompass the elements of a **market price** if one existed (fair value).

        2)    **Fair value** is the amount at which an "asset (or liability) could be bought (or incurred) or sold (or settled) in a current transaction between willing parties, that is, other than in a forced or liquidation sale."

    g.    The **market** finally determines asset and liability values.

        1)    However, if management's estimates are the sole source of information, the objective is still to estimate the likely market price if a market existed.

    h.    A **measurement based on present value** should **reflect uncertainty** so that variations in risks are incorporated. Accordingly, the following are the necessary elements of a present value measurement:

        1)    Estimates of future cash flows
        2)    Expected variability of their amount and timing
        3)    The time value of money (risk-free interest rate)
        4)    The price of uncertainty inherent in an asset or liability
        5)    Other factors, such as lack of liquidity or market imperfections

i. The **traditional approach** to calculating present value employs one set of estimated cash flows and one interest rate.

1) This approach is expected to continue to be used in many cases, for example, when contractual cash flows are involved.

2) However, SFAC 7 describes the **expected cash flow (ECF)** approach, which is applicable in more complex circumstances, such as when no market or no comparable item exists for an asset or liability.

   a) The **ECF** results from multiplying each possible estimated amount by its probability and adding the products.

   b) The ECF approach emphasizes **explicit assumptions** about the possible estimated cash flows and their probabilities.

      i) The traditional method merely includes those uncertainties in the choice of interest rate.

      ii) Moreover, by allowing for a range of possibilities, the ECF method permits the use of expected present value when the timing of cash flows is uncertain.

   c) **Expected present value** is the sum of present values of estimated cash flows discounted using the same interest rate and weighted according to their probabilities.

3) The **cost-benefit constraint** applies to the use of the expected cash flow approach.

4) Many pricing tools, for example, the **Black-Scholes option-pricing model**, have been developed to estimate fair value. If such a model includes the elements of present value with an objective of fair value, it is consistent with SFAC 7.

5) Fair value should include an **adjustment for risk** (the price of the uncertainty of cash flows) if it is identifiable, measurable, and significant. But, if a reliable estimate of a market risk premium cannot be obtained, discounting expected cash flows at the risk-free rate may provide the best estimate of fair value.

   a) Measurements of present value occur under conditions of **uncertainty**; the cash flows are estimates rather than known amounts.

      i) Thus, as long as the uncertainty persists, the accounting entity is **at risk**, and it will require a risk premium to accept uncertainty.

   b) The inclusion of uncertainty and risk in a measurement is intended to reflect the **market's treatment** of assets and liabilities with uncertain cash flows.

      i) If a market price is not observable, a present value measurement may be the best available means of estimating a price.

   c) Finance theory provides various methods for estimating the **risk premium**.

      i) For example, **portfolio theory** states that the risk of a given asset depends on its effect on the total risk of a portfolio of assets.

   d) Measurement using estimates is inherently imprecise, but **reliability** of accounting information should be weighted against its **relevance**.

      i) Use of ECF techniques may result in sufficient reliability and greater relevance than the use of undiscounted measurements.

j.    The purpose of a present value measurement of the **fair value of a liability** "is to estimate the value of the assets required currently to (a) settle the liability with the holder or (b) transfer the liability to an entity of comparable credit standing."

   1)    Measurement of certain liabilities, for example, bonds payable, involves the same process as that used for assets. The measure of such a liability is the price at which another entity is willing to hold it as an asset.

      a)    Some liabilities, however, are not typically held as salable assets by the obligee, for example, liabilities for warranties or environmental cleanup.

         i)    Liabilities of this kind are sometimes assumed by a third person.
         ii)   In this case, the estimate of the liability would be the estimate of the price a third person would have to be paid to assume the liability.

   2)    The entity's **credit standing** is always incorporated into initial and fresh-start measurements of liabilities.

      a)    Credit standing affects the price an entity is willing to pay to hold another entity's liability as an asset.

      b)    The effect of credit standing on liability measures is ordinarily reflected in **interest rate adjustments**; improved creditworthiness allows an entity to borrow at a lower rate.

k.    Present value is a feature of **interest methods of allocation**.

   1)    A typical example is amortization of the discount or premium on bonds.

      a)    Unlike a fresh-start measurement, an accounting allocation does not attempt to reflect all factors that cause change in an asset or liability. It represents merely the consumption of assets or the reduction of liabilities, that is, the change in a reported amount corresponding to the change in the present value of a set of future cash flows.

   2)    Because no allocation method, whether or not interest-based, is preferable in every situation, the FASB will choose whether to require an interest method of allocation on a project-by-project basis.

   3)    An interest method is most likely relevant when

      a)    The transaction is a borrowing and a lending
      b)    Similar assets or liabilities are allocated using an interest method
      c)    The asset or liability has closely related estimated cash flows
      d)    The initial measurement was at present value

   4)    Application of an interest method requires careful definition of

      a)    The **cash flows** (e.g., promised cash flows, expected cash flows, or another definition)
      b)    The **interest rate**
      c)    The **application of the interest rate**
      d)    The reporting of **changes in the amount or timing** of estimated cash flows

   5)    **Changes in estimated cash flows** may result in a fresh-start measurement or in a change in the plan of amortization.

      a)    If remeasurement is not done, a change in the scheme may be effected by

         i)    Prospectively determining a new effective rate given the carrying amount and the remaining cash flows.
         ii)   Retrospectively determining a new effective rate given the original carrying amount, actual cash flows, and the newly estimated cash flows and using it to adjust the current carrying amount.

        iii)   Adjusting the carrying amount to the present value of the remaining cash flows discounted at the original rate.

- The FASB prefers this catch-up approach.

6. Stop and review! You have completed the outline for this subunit. Study multiple-choice questions 1 through 28 beginning on page 409.

## 11.2 ASSUMPTIONS, PRINCIPLES, AND LIMITATIONS

1. Certain **assumptions** underlie the environment in which the reporting entity operates. These assumptions were not promulgated by an official body. They have developed over time and are generally recognized by the accounting profession.

   a. **Economic-entity assumption.** Every business is a separate entity. The affairs of the business are kept separate from the personal affairs of the owners.

   b. **Going-concern (business continuity) assumption.** Unless stated otherwise, every business is assumed to be a going concern that will continue operating indefinitely. As a result, liquidation values are not important because it is assumed that the company is not going to be liquidated in the near future.

   c. **Monetary-unit (unit-of-money) assumption.** Accounting records are kept in terms of money. Using money as the unit of measure is the best way of providing economic information to users of financial statements. Also, the changing purchasing power of the monetary unit is assumed not to be significant.

   d. **Periodicity (time period) assumption.** Even though the most accurate way to measure an entity's results of operations is to wait until it liquidates and goes out of business, this method is not followed. Instead, financial statements are prepared periodically throughout the life of a business to ensure the timeliness of information. The periodicity assumption necessitates the use of estimates in the preparation of financial statements.

2. Certain **principles** provide guidelines that the accountant follows when recording financial information.

   a. The **revenue recognition** and **matching principles** were formally incorporated by the FASB as recognition and measurement concepts (see item 4. in subunit 11.1). Two additional principles are described below.

   b. **Historical cost principle.** Transactions are recorded at cost because that is the most objective determination of value. It is a reliable measure.

   c. **Full-disclosure principle.** Financial statement users should be able to assume that anything they need to know about a company is reported in the financial statements. As a result, many notes are typically presented with the financial statements to provide information that is not shown on the face of the statements. However, full disclosure is not a substitute for reporting in accordance with GAAP.

3. The measurements made in financial statements do not necessarily represent the true worth of a firm or its segments. The following are common **limitations of financial statements**:

   a. The measurements are made in nominal units of money; therefore, qualitative aspects of a firm and changes in the value of the unit of measures are not reflected.

   b. Information supplied by financial reporting involves estimation, classification, summarization, judgment, and allocation.

   c. Financial statements primarily reflect transactions and events that have already occurred. Consequently, they are usually based on historical cost.

d.    Only transactions and events involving an entity being reported upon are reflected in that entity's financial reports. However, transactions and events of other entities, e.g., unconsolidated but affiliated entities and competitors, may be very important.

e.    Financial statements are based on the going-concern assumption. If that assumption is invalid, the appropriate attribute for measuring financial statement items is liquidation value, not historical cost, fair value, net realizable value, etc.

f.    The reporting entity may have off-balance-sheet liabilities, for example, obligations under pension plans and operating leases.

4.    The **historical cost assumption** places certain **limitations on financial statements**.

a.    As previously mentioned, most transactions and events reported on financial statements are recorded at their amounts on the dates of the transactions or events. Many assets previously acquired are recorded on the balance sheet at their historical cost.

b.    When the fair values of these assets significantly change after the acquisition date, the balance sheet presentation of the assets becomes significantly less relevant in determining the company's worth.

c.    Over time, discrepancies develop between current and the historical costs.

1)    For example, the replacement cost and the carrying amount of assets will diverge.

2)    Moreover, the value of the unit of measure (the dollar for U.S. firms) will also change.

3)    Accordingly, comparisons between prior years and between competing firms become less meaningful.

5.    The following are three major **limitations of segment reporting**:

a.    The definition of a reportable segment has been changed by the FASB to reflect an **operating-segment approach** to reporting.

1)    Nevertheless, what represents a segment still varies widely among firms and industries.

b.    **Common-cost allocations** between related entities are subject to management manipulation.

1)    Many different allocation bases exist, allowing management to choose the one with the most benefits to a particular segment. Comparability of firms is again impaired.

c.    **Transfer pricing** has the same limitations as cost allocation. Transfer prices tend to be set to benefit particular segments and are also subject to management manipulation.

6.    Certain **constraints (doctrines)** circumscribe the process of recognition in the financial statements.

a.    The **cost-benefit** and **materiality constraints** were formally incorporated by the FASB as qualitative characteristics of financial reporting (see Gleim's *CMA Review, Part 1*, items 1.f. and 1.g. in subunit 16.2). Two additional doctrines are described below and on the next page.

b.    **Industry practices constraint.** Occasionally, GAAP are not followed in an industry because adherence to them would generate misleading or unnecessary information.

1)    For instance, banks and insurance companies typically valued marketable equity securities at market value even before the issuance of **SFAS 115**, *Accounting for Certain Investments in Debt and Equity Securities*. Market value and liquidity are most important to these industries.

c. **Conservatism constraint.** Conservatism is "a prudent reaction to uncertainty to try to ensure that uncertainties and risks inherent in business situations are adequately considered" (SFAC 2).

   1) The conservatism doctrine originally directed accountants, when faced with two or more acceptable choices, to report the lowest amount for an asset or income.

      a) However, conservatism does not condone introducing bias into the financial statements through a deliberate understatement of net assets and net income.

   2) Thus, if estimates of future amounts to be paid or received differ but are **equally likely**, conservatism requires using the **least optimistic estimate**.

      a) However, if the estimates are **not equally likely**, conservatism does not necessarily require use of the estimate that results in understatement rather than the **estimate that is the most likely**.

   3) The application of the lower-of-cost-or-market rule to inventories is an example of the use of the conservatism constraint.

7. The following table summarizes the conceptual framework underlying financial accounting:

**Objectives**
**(11.1, Item 2)**
Provide Information
- That is useful in investment and credit decisions
- That is useful in assessing cash-flow prospects
- About enterprise resources, claims to those resources, and changes in them

| **Qualitative Characteristics** **CMA Review, Part 1, Subunit 16.2** | **Elements of Financial Statements** **(11.1, item 3)** |
|---|---|
| Pervasive constraint: Benefits > Costs; User-specific qualities: Understandability, Decision Usefulness; Primary decision-specific qualities: Relevance, Feedback value, Predictive value, Timeliness, Reliability, Verifiability, Neutrality, Representational faithfulness; Secondary and interactive qualities: Comparability, Consistency; Threshold for recognition: Materiality | Assets, Liabilities, Equity, Investments by owners, Distributions to owners, Comprehensive income, Revenues, Expenses, Gains, Losses |

**Recognition and Measurement Concepts**

| **Assumptions** **(11.2, item 1)** | **Principles** **(11.2, item 2)** | **Constraints** **(11.2, item 6)** |
|---|---|---|
| Economic entity | Historical cost | Cost-benefit |
| Going concern | Revenue recognition | Materiality |
| Monetary unit | Matching | Industry practice |
| Periodicity | Full disclosure | Conservatism |

8. Stop and review! You have completed the outline for this subunit. Study multiple-choice questions 29 through 33 on page 418.

## 11.3 CORE CONCEPTS

<u>Conceptual Framework underlying Financial Accounting</u>

- The Financial Accounting Standards Board (FASB) promulgated its **Statements of Financial Accounting Concepts (SFACs)** to provide accountants with "a framework of fundamentals on which financial accounting and reporting standards could be based."

- SFAC 1 asserts that "financial reporting is not an end in itself but is intended to provide **information that is useful in making business and economic decisions...**"

- SFAC 6 lists the **ten elements of financial statements** as assets, liabilities, equity, investments by owners, distributions to owners, comprehensive income, revenues, expenses, gains, and losses.

- Nine of the ten elements (all but comprehensive income) make up three of the **four basic financial statements**: the statement of financial position, the statement of income, and the statement of retained earnings. The fourth statement is the statement of cash flows which draws its elements from the other statements.

- SFAC 5 describes the **revenue recognition principle**, that revenues and gains should be recognized when (1) realized or realizable and (2) earned.

- SFAC 7 asserts that the objective of **present value measurement** is to distinguish the economic differences between sets of **future cash flows** that may vary in amount, timing, and uncertainty.

<u>Assumptions, Principles, and Limitations</u>

- Certain **assumptions** underlie the environment in which the reporting entity operates. These assumptions were not promulgated by an official body. They are the economic-entity, going-concern, monetary-unit, and periodicity.

- Certain **principles** provide guidelines that the accountant follows when recording financial information. They are revenue recognition, matching, historical cost, and full-disclosure.

- Certain **constraints** circumscribe the process of recognition in the financial statements. They are cost-benefit, materiality, industry practice, and conservatism.

- Three **limitations** must be borne in mind when using GAAP-based financial statements: the use of operating segments, the allocation of common costs, and transfer pricing.

## QUESTIONS

### 11.1 Conceptual Framework Underlying Financial Accounting

**1.** A publicly held corporation is required to have its financial statements audited by an independent external auditor. The three purposes of these financial statements are to provide useful information (a) for credit and investment decisions, (b) about the firm's resources, and (c) for

    A. Determining the impact of inflation.

    B. Long-lived asset replacements.

    C. Assessing market values of assets.

    D. Evaluating prospective cash flows.

Answer (D) is correct. *(CMA, adapted)*
    **REQUIRED:** The third purpose of financial statements.
    **DISCUSSION:** According to SFAC 1, *Objectives of Financial Reporting by Business Enterprises*, "Financial reporting should provide information to help present and potential investors and creditors and other users in assessing the amounts, timing, and uncertainty of prospective cash receipts from dividends or interest and the proceeds from the sale, redemption, or maturity of securities or loans. Because investors' and creditors' cash flows are related to enterprise cash flows, financial reporting should provide information to help investors, creditors, and others assess the amounts, timing, and uncertainty of prospective net cash inflows to the related enterprise."
    Answer (A) is incorrect because the company is not required to present information about the effects of price level changes. Answer (B) is incorrect because such information will be communicated if the three broad purposes stated in SFAC 1 are satisfied. Answer (C) is incorrect because required financial statements for the most part reflect historical costs.

**2.** According to SFAC 1, *Objectives of Financial Reporting by Business Enterprises*,

    A. External users have the ability to prescribe information they want.

    B. Information is always based on exact measures.

    C. Financial reporting is usually based on industries or the economy as a whole.

    D. Financial accounting does not directly measure the value of a business enterprise.

Answer (D) is correct. *(Publisher)*
    **REQUIRED:** The true statement about the objectives of financial reporting.
    **DISCUSSION:** Financial reporting furnishes information that helps to identify the financial strengths and weaknesses of an enterprise, to assess its liquidity and solvency, and to evaluate its performance during a period of time. However, financial accounting does not directly measure the value of an enterprise, although it may provide information to those who wish to do so.
    Answer (A) is incorrect because some external users (e.g., taxing authorities) have the authority to obtain desired information, but most do not. The objectives are based on the needs of the latter class of users. Answer (B) is incorrect because financial information involves estimation and judgment. Answer (C) is incorrect because financial reporting is usually based on individual entities.

**3.** The accounting system should be designed

    A. To meet external reporting requirements.

    B. To balance management information needs with the cost of obtaining that information.

    C. To eliminate fraud by accounting personnel.

    D. By persons not directly involved with the system, such as consultants.

Answer (B) is correct. *(CMA, adapted)*
    **REQUIRED:** The true statement about the design of an internal accounting and reporting system.
    **DISCUSSION:** One of the characteristics and limitations of the kind of information that financial reporting can provide is that the information is provided and used at a cost (see SFAC 1). All accounting information is subject to two quantitative constraints: materiality and cost-benefit. If a reasonable person relying on the information would not have changed his/her judgment as a result of an omission or misstatement, it is not considered material. The cost-benefit constraint states that the benefits of information must exceed the cost of obtaining it.
    Answer (A) is incorrect because the first objective of the internal accounting and reporting system must be to provide relevant and reliable information for management decision making. Answer (C) is incorrect because the control of fraud is only an objective to the extent that the system is cost beneficial. Answer (D) is incorrect because those who best know the information needs should design the system.

**4.** A company with total assets of $100,000,000 and net income of $9,000,000 purchases staplers with an estimated life of 10 years for $1,000. In connection with the purchase, the company debits miscellaneous expense. This scenario is most closely associated with which of the following concepts or principles?

- A. Materiality and going concern.
- B. Relevance and neutrality.
- C. Reliability and comparability/consistency.
- D. Materiality and cost-benefit.

Answer (D) is correct. *(CIA, adapted)*
**REQUIRED:** The concepts or principles most closely associated with the choice of an accounting method.
**DISCUSSION:** In principle, wasting assets should be capitalized and depreciated. However, the effect on the financial statements of expensing rather than capitalizing and depreciating the staplers is clearly not material given that they cost $1,000 and the company has total assets of $100,000,000. The cost-benefit concept is tied to materiality, and relates to the cost of information. Specifically, the cost of producing the information about depreciation expense over 10 years for the staplers probably is higher than the benefits of the information for decision making. Thus, the expedient procedure of expensing the $1,000 should be followed.
Answer (A) is incorrect because the going-concern principle relates to circumstances in which there is doubt as to the viability of the enterprise. Answer (B) is incorrect because SFAC 2 identifies relevance and reliability as the two primary qualities that make accounting information useful for decision making. Relevance is the capacity of information to make a difference in the user's decision. Reliability provides assurance that the information is reasonably free from error and bias, and that it represents what it purports to represent. Neutrality is an ingredient of reliability. Answer (C) is incorrect because reliability relates to using reproducible accounting numbers, such as historical cost to record assets. Comparability/consistency relates to using the same accounting principles from period to period. Comparability (including consistency) is an interactive quality that relates to both primary qualities of relevance and reliability.

**5.** If the going-concern assumption is no longer valid for a company,

- A. Land held as an investment would be valued at its liquidation value.
- B. All prepaid assets would be completely written off immediately.
- C. Total contributed capital and retained earnings would remain unchanged.
- D. The allowance for uncollectible accounts would be eliminated.

Answer (A) is correct. *(CMA, adapted)*
**REQUIRED:** The true statement about a situation in which the going-concern assumption is not valid.
**DISCUSSION:** Under the going-concern, or business continuity, assumption, a financial statement user is to presume that a company will continue operating indefinitely in the absence of indications to the contrary. The essence of this assumption is that liquidation values are not used in the financial statements because the firm is unlikely to liquidate in the near future. When the going-concern assumption is not valid, it is necessary to make appropriate disclosures and to report assets at their liquidation values. For instance, land would no longer be reported at cost but at its liquidation value.
Answer (B) is incorrect because some prepaid assets may have a liquidation value. For example, supplies can be sold and prepaid insurance can be redeemed. Answer (C) is incorrect because capital would change to equalize the write-downs and write-ups on the asset side of the balance sheet. Answer (D) is incorrect because the allowance would still exist because many of the accounts may never be paid.

**6.** According to SFAC 5, revenues of an entity are normally measured by the exchange values of the assets or liabilities involved. Recognition of revenue does not occur until

- A. The revenue is realized and assured of collection.
- B. The revenue is realized or realizable and earned.
- C. Products or services are exchanged for cash or claims to cash.
- D. The entity has substantially accomplished what it agreed to do.

Answer (B) is correct. *(CMA, adapted)*
**REQUIRED:** The timing of the recognition of revenue.
**DISCUSSION:** Recognition is the process of recording an item in the financial records. Revenue should not be recognized until it is (1) realized or realizable and (2) earned. Revenues are realized in an exchange for cash or claims to cash. Revenues are realizable when "related assets received or held are readily convertible to known amounts of cash or claims to cash." Revenues are earned "when the entity has substantially accomplished what it must do to be entitled to the benefits represented by the revenues" (SFAC 5).
Answer (A) is incorrect because absolute assurance of collectibility is not required. Answer (C) is incorrect because some exchange may occur before the earning process is substantially complete. Answer (D) is incorrect because recognition also requires that revenue be realized or realizable as well as earned.

Question 7 is based on the following information.

Randolf Castell opened a small general store in 1946. A cousin, Alfred Bedford, served as a bookkeeper and office manager while Castell concentrated on operations. The business prospered and each of Castell's three sons joined their father in the business. In fact, as each son finished school, Castell opened a new store and put the son in charge. In time, each son began to specialize:# one in hardware, another in dry goods, and the third in furniture. Further expansion took place, and the business was incorporated as Four Castles, Inc., with all of the stock being held by the family. Castell closed his original store to serve as president and concentrate on administration.

As Four Castles prospered and more stores opened, the company needed additional capital. Bedford suggested "going public" but pointed out that this required accounting and reporting procedures with which he was unfamiliar. Therefore, a trained and qualified accountant was hired as controller. The new controller has had to provide explanations to Castell and Bedford on the accounting and reporting requirements of public companies.

**7.** Four Castles' records have been kept on the tax basis of accounting to eliminate the need to maintain a second set of records. When the tax basis allowed for a choice between cash and accrual bases of accounting, the firm employed the cash basis. Neither the tax basis nor the cash basis of accounting is generally acceptable for the financial statements of a publicly held corporation such as Four Castles. The accrual basis of accounting must be used so that

A. Specific expenses are related to specific revenues.

B. Expenses of a time period are related to revenues of the same time period.

C. Expenses and related revenues are expressed in terms of economic reality.

D. Necessary time-period allocations of long-lived costs are made on a systematic or rational basis.

Answer (B) is correct. *(CMA, adapted)*
**REQUIRED:** The reason the accrual basis of accounting must be used.
**DISCUSSION:** According to SFAC 1, "Accrual accounting attempts to record the financial effects on an enterprise of transactions and other events and circumstances that have cash consequences for an enterprise in the periods in which those transactions, events, and circumstances occur rather than only in the periods in which cash is received or paid by the enterprise."
Answer (A) is incorrect because perfect matching of expenses with revenues is often impossible. Answer (C) is incorrect because the accrual basis is principally used to match the occurrence and the effects of transactions. Economic reality is more difficult to express in historical cost/nominal dollar financial statements. Answer (D) is incorrect because it is a function of matching (depreciation is an allocation).

**8.** According to SFAC 5, the concepts of earnings and comprehensive income have the same broad components, but they are not the same because certain classes of gains and losses are included in comprehensive income but are excluded from earnings. One of the items included in comprehensive income but excluded from earnings is

A. A gain on discontinued operations.

B. Changes in market values of marketable equity securities classified as noncurrent assets.

C. A loss from the obsolescence of a material amount of inventory.

D. An extraordinary gain.

Answer (B) is correct. *(CMA, adapted)*
**REQUIRED:** The item included in comprehensive income but not earnings.
**DISCUSSION:** SFAC 5 defines earnings as a measure of entity performance during a period similar to, but distinct from, present net income. It excludes certain accounting adjustments of prior periods that are recognized in the current period. Comprehensive income is "a broad measure of the effects of transactions and other events on an entity, including all recognized changes in equity (net assets) of the entity during a period from transactions and other events and circumstances except those resulting from investments by owners and distribution to owners." Certain gains and losses included in comprehensive income (referred to as "cumulative accounting adjustments" and "other nonowner changes in equity") are excluded from earnings.
Answer (A) is incorrect because a gain on discontinued operations is included in both earnings and comprehensive income. Answer (C) is incorrect because a loss from the obsolescence of a material amount of inventory is included in both earnings and comprehensive income. Answer (D) is incorrect because an extraordinary gain is included in both earnings and comprehensive income.

**9.** In December year 1, catalogues were printed for use in a special promotion in January year 2. The catalogues were delivered by the printer on December 13, year 1, with an invoice for $70,000 attached. Payment was made in January year 2. The $70,000 should be reported as a deferred cost at the December 31, year 1 balance sheet date because of the

A.   Matching principle.

B.   Revenue recognition principle.

C.   Objectivity principle.

D.   Cost principle.

Answer (A) is correct.   *(CIA, adapted)*
**REQUIRED:** The principle dictating that costs be deferred.
**DISCUSSION:** Matching is the simultaneous or combined recognition of revenues and expenses resulting directly and jointly from the same transactions or other events. Expenses should be associated with the revenues that they help to create. Because the catalogues are still on hand at the balance sheet date, they will not contribute to the earning process until the next period. Hence, the cost should be deferred and matched with the revenues of the following period.
Answer (B) is incorrect because the revenue recognition principle determines the period in which revenue is recognized. Answer (C) is incorrect because the objectivity principle indicates that, to the extent possible, accounting data should be unbiased and verifiable. Answer (D) is incorrect because the cost principle states that cost is the usual basis for recording most assets and liabilities.

**10.** The practice of recording advanced payments from customers as a liability is an example of applying the

A.   Going-concern assumption.

B.   Monetary-unit assumption.

C.   Historic cost principle.

D.   Revenue recognition principle.

Answer (D) is correct.   *(CIA, adapted)*
**REQUIRED:** The assumption or principle justifying recording advance receipts as liabilities.
**DISCUSSION:** Revenue should not be recognized until it is realized or realizable and earned. Thus, if the amounts received in cash have not yet been earned, they should be recorded as liabilities of the company.
Answer (A) is incorrect because the going-concern assumption is that the business will have an indefinite life. Answer (B) is incorrect because the monetary-unit assumption is that money is the common denominator by which economic activity is conducted, and that the monetary unit provides an appropriate basis for accounting measurement and analysis. Answer (C) is incorrect because the historical cost principle is the requirement that most assets and liabilities be accounted for and reported on the basis of acquisition price.

**11.** A company provides fertilization, insect control, and disease control services for a variety of trees, plants, and shrubs on a contract basis. For $50 per month, the company will visit the subscriber's premises and apply appropriate mixtures. If the subscriber has any problems between the regularly scheduled application dates, the company's personnel will promptly make additional service calls to correct the situation. Some subscribers elect to pay for an entire year because the company offers an annual price of $540 if paid in advance. For a subscriber who pays the annual fee in advance, the company should recognize the related revenue

A.   When the cash is collected.

B.   Evenly over the year as the services are performed.

C.   At the end of the contract year after all of the services have been performed.

D.   At the end of the fiscal year.

Answer (B) is correct.   *(CIA, adapted)*
**REQUIRED:** The appropriate timing of revenue recognition.
**DISCUSSION:** In accordance with SFAC 5, revenues should be recognized when they are realized or realizable and earned. Revenues are realized when products, merchandise, or other assets are exchanged for cash or claims to cash. Revenues are realizable when related assets received or held are readily convertible to known amounts of cash or claims to cash. Revenues are earned when the entity has substantially accomplished what it must do to be entitled to the benefits represented by the revenues. The most common time at which these two conditions are met is when the product or merchandise is delivered or services are rendered to customers. In the situation presented, the performance of the service (monthly spraying) is so significant to completing the earning process that revenue should not be recognized until delivery occurs. At the time of performing the service (monthly spraying and any special visits), the revenue has been realized and earned and should be recognized.
Answer (A) is incorrect because the revenue has not been earned when the cash is collected. Answer (C) is incorrect because revenue from services rendered is recognized when the services have been performed. A portion of the services is performed monthly. Thus, a portion of the related revenue should be recognized monthly rather than when the contract year or the fiscal year is complete. Answer (D) is incorrect because revenue from services rendered is recognized when the services have been performed. A portion of the services is performed monthly. Thus, a portion of the related revenue should be recognized monthly rather than when the contract year or the fiscal year is complete.

**12.** On February 1, year 1, a computer software firm agrees to program a software package. Twelve payments of $10,000 on the first of each month are to be made, with the first payment March 1, year 1. The software is accepted by the client June 1, year 2. How much year 1 revenue should be recognized?

A. $0

B. $100,000

C. $110,000

D. $120,000

Answer (A) is correct. *(CIA, adapted)*
**REQUIRED:** The revenue recognized in the year in which payments begin if delivery occurs in the next period.
**DISCUSSION:** Revenue is recognized when it is realized or realizable and the earning process is substantially complete. Delivery is the usual time at which recognition is appropriate. Because delivery occurred in year 2, no revenue should be recognized in year 1.

**13.** Although a transfer of ownership has not occurred, the percentage-of-completion method is acceptable under the revenue recognition principle because

A. The assets are readily convertible into cash.

B. The production process can be readily divided into definite stages.

C. Cash has been received from the customer.

D. The earning process is completed at various stages.

Answer (D) is correct. *(CMA, adapted)*
**REQUIRED:** The reason percentage-of-completion is acceptable as a means of revenue recognition.
**DISCUSSION:** SFAC 5 states that revenue should be recognized when it is both realized or realizable and earned. If a project is contracted for before production and covers a long time period in relation to reporting periods, revenues may be recognized by a percentage-of-completion method as they are earned (as production occurs), provided reasonable estimates of results at completion and reliable measures of progress are available. Thus, contractors traditionally use the percentage-of-completion method because some revenue can be recognized during each period of the production process. In a sense, the earning process is completed in various stages; thus, revenues should be recorded in each stage.
Answer (A) is incorrect because, depending upon the terms of the contract, the assets may not be readily convertible into cash. Answer (B) is incorrect because, on a large construction project, the production process often cannot be easily divided into definite stages. Answer (C) is incorrect because cash is sometimes not received until the project is completed.

**14.** In SFAC 5, *Recognition and Measurement in Financial Statements of Business Enterprises*, several alternatives have been identified for measuring items on the statement of financial position. Which of the following alternatives may be used?

|   | Present Value | Current Cost | Net Realizable Value |
|---|---|---|---|
| A. | No | No | No |
| B. | No | Yes | Yes |
| C. | Yes | Yes | No |
| D. | Yes | Yes | Yes |

Answer (D) is correct. *(CMA, adapted)*
**REQUIRED:** The acceptable attribute(s) for measuring items in the balance sheet.
**DISCUSSION:** According to SFAC 5, items appearing in financial statements may, under certain circumstances, be measured by different attributes. The attributes used in current practice are historical cost (historical proceeds), current cost, current market value, net realizable (settlement) value, and the present value of future cash flows. For example, the present value of future cash flows is used to value long-term payables; current cost is the method used to measure and report some inventories; and net realizable value is used to measure short-term receivables.

**15.** Recognition is the process of formally recording and reporting an item in the financial statements. In order for a revenue item to be recognized, it must be all of the following except

   A.  Measurable.

   B.  Relevant.

   C.  Material.

   D.  Realized or realizable.

Answer (C) is correct.  *(CMA, adapted)*
   **REQUIRED:**  The characteristic not required for recognition of revenue.
   **DISCUSSION:**  Recognition means incorporating transactions into the accounting system so as to report them in the financial statements as assets, liabilities, revenues, expenses, gains, or losses.  When items meet the criteria for recognition, disclosure by other means is not a substitute for recognition in the financial statements.  The four fundamental recognition criteria are (1) the item meets the definition of an element of financial statements, (2) the item has an attribute measurable with sufficient reliability, (3) the information is relevant, and (4) the information is reliable (SFAC 5).  In addition, revenue should be recognized when it is realized or realizable and earned.  Materiality is not a recognition criterion.  An immaterial item that meets the criteria for recognition may be recognized.

**16.** The mining industry frequently recognizes revenue using the completion-of-production method. This method is acceptable under the revenue recognition principle for all of the following reasons except that

   A.  Production costs can be readily determined.

   B.  Sales prices are reasonably assured.

   C.  Assets are readily realizable.

   D.  Units are interchangeable.

Answer (A) is correct.  *(CMA, adapted)*
   **REQUIRED:**  The reason that does not justify recognizing mining revenue at the completion of the production process.
   **DISCUSSION:**  Recognizing revenue at the time goods are produced is appropriate when the assets are readily realizable (convertible) because they are salable at reliably determinable prices without significant effort.  Readily realizable assets are fungible and quoted prices are available in an active market that can rapidly absorb the quantity produced (SFAC 5).  Examples include some agricultural products and rare minerals.  That production costs can be readily determined is not a justification for immediate recognition.  Production costs can be readily determined for almost any product manufactured.
   Answer (B) is incorrect because recognition at the time of production is appropriate if assets are readily realizable, i.e., if they are salable at reliably determinable prices without significant effort.  Answer (C) is incorrect because recognition at the time of production is appropriate if assets are readily realizable, i.e., if they are salable at reliably determinable prices without significant effort.  Answer (D) is incorrect because interchangeability (fungibility) is a requirement for recognition at the time of production.

Questions 17 through 20 are based on the following information.

According to SFAC 5, *Recognition and Measurement in Financial Statements of Business Enterprises*, items reported in financial statements must meet certain criteria and are measured by different attributes, depending on the nature of the item.

**17.** In order for an event to be recognized in the financial statements, it must be

   A.  Relevant, reliable, and measurable.

   B.  Relevant, reliable, and useful.

   C.  Relevant, reliable, and timely.

   D.  Reliable, useful, and measurable.

Answer (A) is correct.  *(CMA, adapted)*
   **REQUIRED:**  The criteria for recognition in the financial statements.
   **DISCUSSION:**  SFAC 5 states that an item and information about the item should be recognized when the following four fundamental recognition criteria are met:  (1) The item meets the definition of an element of financial statements; (2) it has a relevant attribute measurable with sufficient reliability (measurability); (3) the information about the item is capable of making a difference in user decisions (relevance); and (4) the information is representationally faithful, verifiable, and neutral (reliability).
   Answer (B) is incorrect because usefulness is not one of the criteria for recognition stated in SFAC 5.  Answer (C) is incorrect because timeliness is not a criterion for recognition under SFAC 5.  Answer (D) is incorrect because usefulness is not one of the criteria for recognition stated in SFAC 5.

**18.** Long-term payables are measured using

A. Historical cost.

B. Current market value.

C. Net realizable value.

D. Present value of future cash flows.

Answer (D) is correct. *(CMA, adapted)*
**REQUIRED:** The measurement attribute for long-term payables.
**DISCUSSION:** Under SFAC 5, long-term payables and receivables are measured and reported at the present, or discounted, value of future cash flows. For payables, this amount is the present value of future cash outflows expected to be required to satisfy the liability in due course of business.

Answer (A) is incorrect because historical cost, although used for many types of assets and liabilities, is not permitted for valuation of long-term payables under SFAC 5. Answer (B) is incorrect because current market value measures liabilities for certain marketable commodities and securities, e.g., obligations of writers of options or sellers of shares who do not own the underlying assets. Answer (C) is incorrect because net realizable value is the undiscounted amount of cash into which an asset is expected to be converted in due course of business minus direct costs necessary to make that conversion. Net settlement value is the equivalent term for liabilities but is applicable only to short-term payables.

**19.** Damaged inventory is measured using

A. Historical cost.

B. Current cost.

C. Net realizable value.

D. Present value of future cash flows.

Answer (C) is correct. *(CMA, adapted)*
**REQUIRED:** The measurement attribute for damaged inventory.
**DISCUSSION:** Net realizable value is the undiscounted amount of cash into which an asset is expected to be converted in due course of business, minus the direct costs necessary to make that conversion. Short-term receivables and damaged inventories are examples of assets commonly valued at net realizable value.

Answer (A) is incorrect because historical cost is not appropriate for damaged inventories. They are likely to be worth less than their original cost. Answer (B) is incorrect because current or replacement cost is the cash equivalent that would have to be paid if the same assets were acquired currently. The company is unlikely to purchase damaged goods, so current cost is irrelevant. Answer (D) is incorrect because the present value of future cash flows is not appropriate. The company presumably will sell the goods soon.

**20.** Land currently used in the business is measured at

A. Historical cost.

B. Current cost.

C. Current market value.

D. Net realizable value.

Answer (A) is correct. *(CMA, adapted)*
**REQUIRED:** The measurement attribute for land.
**DISCUSSION:** Land is normally carried in the accounting records at historical cost. According to SFAC 5, historical cost is the amount of cash or its equivalent paid to acquire an asset. Historical cost is the attribute at which assets such as property, plant, and equipment are measured.

Answer (B) is incorrect because current or replacement cost is difficult to measure for an asset such as land. Some inventories are carried at current cost. Answer (C) is incorrect because current market value is used to measure certain investments, such as trading securities. Answer (D) is incorrect because net realizable value is applicable only to assets that are to be disposed of in the near future. Land does not meet that criterion.

**21.** All of the following are acceptable methods for recognizing revenue from service transactions except the

    A. Collection method.

    B. Specific-performance method.

    C. Completed-performance method.

    D. Accretion method.

Answer (D) is correct.  *(CMA, adapted)*
    **REQUIRED:** The method of revenue recognition that is not acceptable for service transactions.
    **DISCUSSION:** The accretion method records revenue as the product grows. For example, it is theoretically feasible to record a timber company's revenue as the trees grow because the product is increasing in value each year. This kind of phenomenon does not occur in the service industries. Hence, the accretion method is not applicable.
    Answer (A) is incorrect because, although the cash basis is theoretically acceptable only when the collection is not assured, the method has traditionally been used in many service industries. Answer (B) is incorrect because revenue may meet the criteria of being realized or realizable and earned when specific performance of a service has occurred. Answer (C) is incorrect because it is valid to record service revenue at the completion of performance.

**22.** Based on SFAC 5, *Recognition and Measurement in Financial Statements of Business Enterprises*, a complete set of financial statements for a period should show all of the following except the

    A. Financial position at the end of the period.

    B. Earnings for the period.

    C. Comprehensive income for the period.

    D. Management discussion and analysis.

Answer (D) is correct.  *(CMA, adapted)*
    **REQUIRED:** The item that is not a part of a complete set of financial statements.
    **DISCUSSION:** According to SFAC 5, a complete set of financial statements includes a balance sheet, an earnings (net income) statement, a cash flow statement, a statement of comprehensive income, and an explanation of investments by, and distributions to, owners during the period. Management's discussion and analysis of financial condition and results of operations is included in the Basic Information Package (BIP) required as part of the Integrated Disclosure System used in filings with the Securities and Exchange Commission.
    Answer (A) is incorrect because reporting of financial position at the end of the period is required by SFAC 5. Answer (B) is incorrect because earnings for the period is required by SFAC 5. Answer (C) is incorrect because comprehensive income for the period is required by SFAC 5.

**23.** Amortization of intangible assets, such as copyrights or patents, is the accounting process of

    A. Determining the cash flow from operations for the current period.

    B. Systematically allocating the cost of the intangible asset to the periods of use.

    C. Accumulating a fund for the replacement of the asset at the end of its useful life.

    D. Systematically reflecting the change in general price levels over the current period.

Answer (B) is correct.  *(CMA, adapted)*
    **REQUIRED:** The meaning of amortization.
    **DISCUSSION:** SFAC 6 defines amortization as "the accounting process of reducing an amount by periodic payments or write-downs. Specifically, amortization is the process of reducing a liability recorded as a result of a cash receipt by recognizing revenues or reducing an asset recorded as a result of a cash payment by recognizing expenses or costs of production." Amortization is a means of allocating an initial cost to the periods that benefit from that cost. It is similar to depreciation, a term associated with long-lived tangible assets, and depletion, which is associated with natural resources.
    Answer (A) is incorrect because amortization is an allocation process that is not cash-based. Answer (C) is incorrect because no funding is associated with amortization. Answer (D) is incorrect because amortization has nothing to do with changes in price levels.

**24.** Inventory valued at the lower-of-cost-or-market is never valued using which measurement attribute?

A. Historical cost.

B. Current cost.

C. Present value.

D. Net realizable value.

Answer (C) is correct. *(Publisher)*
**REQUIRED:** The measurement attribute never used with the lower-of-cost-or-market method.
**DISCUSSION:** Present value is not used for valuing assets under the lower-of-cost-or-market method. Present value incorporates time-value-of-money concepts into an asset valuation by discounting future cash flows at the appropriate interest rate. The lower-of-cost-or-market method values an asset at historical cost unless the market value of the asset is less than original cost. The value used for market is subject to ceiling and floor amounts.
Answer (A) is incorrect because historical cost is used unless the asset's market value is lower. Answer (B) is incorrect because current (replacement) cost is used to measure market value. Answer (D) is incorrect because the market valuation is subject to ceiling and floor values. The ceiling is NRV, and the floor is NRV minus a normal profit.

**25.** The appropriate attribute to use when selling assets in an orderly liquidation is

A. Historical cost.

B. Current cost.

C. Net realizable value.

D. Current market value.

Answer (D) is correct. *(CMA, adapted)*
**REQUIRED:** The attribute to use when selling assets in an orderly liquidation.
**DISCUSSION:** According to SFAC 5, current market value (exit value) is used to measure the cash or equivalent that is realizable when selling assets in an orderly liquidation.

**26.** The assets of a company forced into liquidation should be shown on the balance sheet at their

A. Undepreciated historical cost.

B. Current market value.

C. Net realizable value.

D. Current cost.

Answer (C) is correct. *(CIA, adapted)*
**REQUIRED:** The valuation of the assets of a liquidating company.
**DISCUSSION:** When forced liquidation of a company is imminent and the going-concern assumption is no longer valid, the most appropriate valuation method for assets is net realizable value, which is the estimated selling price upon disposal minus costs of disposal.
Answer (A) is incorrect because a going concern should report assets at their undepreciated historical cost. When liquidation appears imminent historical cost is inappropriate for balance sheet reporting. Answer (B) is incorrect because a company facing liquidation is expected to dispose of its assets in a "forced" or "distressed" sale. Current market value (exit value) may occur if the liquidation is orderly. Answer (D) is incorrect because current cost is appropriate only when the going-concern assumption is applicable and the effects of changing prices are to be measured and reported in the financial statements.

**27.** According to SFAC 7, *Using Cash Flow Information and Present Value in Accounting Measurements*, the objective of present value is to estimate fair value when used to determine accounting measurements for

| | Initial-Recognition Purposes | Fresh-Start Purposes |
|---|---|---|
| A. | No | No |
| B. | Yes | Yes |
| C. | Yes | No |
| D. | No | Yes |

Answer (B) is correct. *(Publisher)*
**REQUIRED:** The objective of present value in initial-recognition and fresh-start measurements.
**DISCUSSION:** SFAC 7 states that the objective of present value in initial-recognition or fresh-start measurements is to estimate fair value. "Present value should attempt to capture the elements that taken together would comprise a market price if one existed, that is, fair value." A present value measurement includes five elements: estimates of cash flows, expectations about their variability, the time value of money (the risk-free interest rate), the price of uncertainty inherent in an asset or liability, and other factors (e.g., illiquidity or market imperfections). Fair value encompasses all these elements using the estimates and expectations of participants in the market.

**28.** The expected cash flow approach to measuring present value promulgated by SFAC 7

    A. Uses a single set of estimated cash flows.

    B. Is limited to assets and liabilities with contractual cash flows.

    C. Focuses on explicit assumptions about the range of expected cash flows and their respective probabilities.

    D. Focuses on the single most likely amount or best estimate.

Answer (C) is correct.  *(Publisher)*
    **REQUIRED:** The nature of the expected cash flow approach.
    **DISCUSSION:** The traditional approach to calculating present value employs one set of estimated cash flows and one interest rate. This approach is expected to continue to be used in many cases, for example, when contractual cash flows are involved. However, SFAC 7 describes the expected cash flow approach, which is applicable in more complex circumstances, such as when no market or no comparable item exists for an asset or liability. The expected cash flow results from multiplying each possible estimated amount by its probability and adding the products. The expected cash flow approach emphasizes explicit assumptions about the possible estimated cash flows and their probabilities. The traditional method merely includes those uncertainties in the choice of interest rate. Moreover, by allowing for a range of possibilities, the expected cash flow method permits the use of present value when the timing of cash flows is uncertain.
    Answer (A) is incorrect because the traditional present value measurement approach uses a single set of estimated cash flows and a single interest rate. Answer (B) is incorrect because the expected cash flow approach may also apply when the timing of cash flows is uncertain or when nonfinancial assets and liabilities are to be measured and no market or comparable item exists for them. Answer (D) is incorrect because some current accounting applications use the estimated mode (single most likely amount or best estimate), but the expected cash flow approach arrives at an estimated mean by probabilistically weighting a range of possible estimated amounts.

## 11.2 Assumptions, Principles, and Limitations

**29.** Limitations of the statement of financial position include all of the following except

    A. The use of historical cost for valuing assets and liabilities.

    B. Inclusion of information on capital maintenance.

    C. Exclusion of some economic resources and obligations.

    D. The use of estimates in the determination of certain items.

Answer (B) is correct.  *(CMA, adapted)*
    **REQUIRED:** The item not a limitation of the statement of financial position (balance sheet).
    **DISCUSSION:** The basic financial statements are prepared using the concept of financial capital maintenance. A return on financial capital results only if the financial (money) amount of net assets at the end of the period exceeds the amount at the beginning. Hence, inclusion of information on capital mainten-ance is a fundamental approach to financial reporting, not a limitation (SFAC 5).
    Answer (A) is incorrect because historical cost may not be an accurate valuation of a balance sheet item. Changing prices and other factors are not recognized in the basic financial state-ments. Answer (C) is incorrect because not all assets and liabilities are included in the balance sheet; for example, certain contingencies and pension obligations are not included. Answer (D) is incorrect because measurement in financial statements tends to be approximate rather than exact. Estimates are commonly used to determine reported amounts, e.g., depreciation and present value.

**30.** In accounting for inventories, generally accepted accounting principles require departure from the historical cost principle when the utility of inventory has fallen below cost. This rule is known as the "lower-of-cost-or-market" rule. "Market" as defined here means

    A. Original cost minus allowance for obsolescence.

    B. Original cost plus normal profit margin.

    C. Replacement cost of the inventory.

    D. Original cost minus cost to dispose.

Answer (C) is correct.  *(CMA, adapted)*
    **REQUIRED:** The meaning of the term "market."
    **DISCUSSION:** In the phrase "lower-of-cost-or-market," the term "market" means the replacement cost of the inventory as determined in the market in which the company buys its inventory, not the market in which it sells to customers. Market is limited to a ceiling amount equal to net realizable value and a floor amount equal to net realizable value minus a normal profit margin.
    Answer (A) is incorrect because the market value is not a cost. Answer (B) is incorrect because the floor amount is net realizable value minus a normal profit margin. Answer (D) is incorrect because original cost minus cost to dispose equals net realizable value.

**31.** A Midwestern public utility reports noncurrent assets as the first item on its statement of financial position. This practice is an example of the

A. Going-concern assumption.

B. Conservatism.

C. Economic-entity assumption.

D. Industry practice constraint.

Answer (D) is correct. *(CMA, adapted)*
**REQUIRED:** The reason a public utility reports noncurrent assets as the first item on the balance sheet.
**DISCUSSION:** Assets are normally listed in the order of their importance, with current assets typically being the most important. For a public utility, the physical plant is the most important asset. Thus, public utilities often report their noncurrent assets as the first item on the balance sheet. This departure from the customary presentation in accordance with GAAP is justified by the peculiarities of the industry.
Answer (A) is incorrect because the assumed continuity of the business is the basis for reporting financial statement items at other than liquidation value. Answer (B) is incorrect because conservatism is a prudent reaction to uncertainty. For example, if different estimates are available and none is more likely than another, the least optimistic should be used. However, conservatism is not a bias toward understatement. Answer (C) is incorrect because the affairs of an economic entity are distinct from those of its owners.

**32.** A newly acquired plant asset is to be depreciated over its useful life. The rationale for this process is the

A. Economic-entity assumption.

B. Monetary-unit assumption.

C. Materiality assumption.

D. Going-concern assumption.

Answer (D) is correct. *(CIA, adapted)*
**REQUIRED:** The rationale for depreciating a plant asset.
**DISCUSSION:** A basic feature of financial accounting is that the business entity is assumed to be a going concern in the absence of evidence to the contrary. The going-concern concept is based on the empirical observation that many enterprises have an indefinite life. The reporting entity is assumed to have a life long enough to fulfill its objectives and commitments and therefore to depreciate wasting assets over their useful lives.
Answer (A) is incorrect because the economic-entity assumption provides that economic activity can be identified with a particular unit of accountability. Answer (B) is incorrect because the monetary-unit assumption provides that all transactions and events can be measured in terms of a common denominator, for instance, the dollar. Answer (C) is incorrect because the materiality assumption simply implies that items of insignificant value can be expensed rather than capitalized and depreciated or amortized.

**33.** The accounting measurement that is not consistent with the going concern concept is

A. Historical cost.

B. Realization.

C. The transaction approach.

D. Liquidation value.

Answer (D) is correct. *(CMA, adapted)*
**REQUIRED:** The accounting measurement inconsistent with the going concern concept.
**DISCUSSION:** Financial accounting principles assume that a business entity is a going concern in the absence of evidence to the contrary. The concept justifies the use of depreciation and amortization schedules, and the recording of assets and liabilities using attributes other than liquidation value.
Answer (A) is incorrect because historical cost is part of the basic structure of accrual accounting. Answer (B) is incorrect because realization is part of the basic structure of accrual accounting. Answer (C) is incorrect because the transaction approach is part of the basic structure of accrual accounting.

---

Use Gleim's *CMA Test Prep* for interactive testing with **over 2,000 additional multiple-choice questions!**

# STUDY UNIT TWELVE
# OVERVIEW OF FINANCIAL STATEMENTS

(27 pages of outline)

This study unit is the **second of ten** on **external financial reporting**. The relative weight assigned to this major topic in Part 2 of the exam is **25%** at **skill level B** (four skill types required). The ten study units are

Study Unit 11: Overview of External Financial Reporting
Study Unit 12: Overview of Financial Statements
Study Unit 13: Cash and Receivables
Study Unit 14: Inventories and Investments
Study Unit 15: Long-Lived Assets
Study Unit 16: Liabilities
Study Unit 17: Equity and Revenue Recognition
Study Unit 18: Other Income Statement Items
Study Unit 19: Business Combinations and Derivatives
Study Unit 20: SEC Requirements and the Annual Report

After studying the outlines and answering the multiple-choice questions in this study unit, you will have the skills necessary to address the following topics listed in the IMA's Learning Outcome Statements:

Part 2 – Section E.3.  Financial statements and statement users

For the Statement of Financial Position (balance sheet), the Statement of Earnings (income statement), Statement of Cash Flows, and the Statement of Changes in Shareholders' Equity, the candidate should be able to:

    a.   identify the users of these financial statements and their needs
    b.   demonstrate an understanding of the purposes and uses of each statement
    c.   identify the major components and classifications of each statement
    d.   identify the limitations of each statement
    e.   identify statement information that requires supplemental disclosure in the body of the statement or in the footnotes
    f.   recognize the correct format of financial information in each statement
    g.   calculate and classify components of each financial statement

Part 2 – Section E.4.  Recognition, measurement, valuation, and disclosure

For the subtopic listed, the candidate should be able to:

1.  define the subtopic and describe the characteristics of its components
2.  demonstrate an understanding of appropriate valuation techniques for the components of each subtopic
3.  demonstrate an understanding of the appropriate accounting conventions for the components of each subtopic
4.  compare and contrast valuation techniques and accounting methods
5.  show the correct financial statement presentation
6.  identify the appropriate disclosure requirements in the body of the financial statements and/or in the footnotes

Comprehensive income

    a.  define comprehensive income and other comprehensive income
    b.  identify the three alternative ways that other comprehensive income may be displayed in the financial statements
    c.  calculate comprehensive income

## 12.1 BASIC FINANCIAL STATEMENTS AND THEIR USERS

1.  The **basic financial statements** consist of the following:

    a.  Statement of financial position ("balance sheet")
    b.  Statement of income
    c.  Statement of retained earnings
    d.  Statement of cash flows

2.  Disclosures of **changes in equity** and in the number of shares of equity securities are necessary whenever financial position and results of operations are presented.

    a.  These disclosures may occur in the basic statements, in the notes thereto, or in separate statements [Accounting Principles Board (APB) **Opinion No. 12**, *Omnibus Opinion – 1967*].
    b.  **Comprehensive income** must be displayed in a financial statement given the same prominence as the other statements, but no specific format is required.

3.  The basic financial statements and notes of a business enterprise serve as vehicles for achieving the **objectives of financial reporting**.

    a.  **Supplementary information** (e.g., on changing prices) and various other means of financial reporting (such as management's discussion and analysis) are also useful.
    b.  The basic financial statements **complement** each other.

        1)  They describe different aspects of the same transactions.
        2)  More than one statement is necessary to provide information for a specific economic decision.

    c.  The **elements** of one statement **articulate** (are interrelated) with those of other statements.

        1)  The **balance sheet** reports assets, liabilities, equity, and investments by owners **at a moment in time**.

            a)  The **statement of income** and **statement of retained earnings** report revenues, expenses, gains, losses, and distributions to owners **over a period of time**.

2) The elements in the first group are changed by those in the second group and are their cumulative result:

| | |
|---|---|
| Beginning balance | (Balance sheet) |
| +/– Changes during the period | (Statements of income and retained earnings) |
| Ending balance | (Balance sheet) |

3) Accordingly, financial statements that report the first type of elements articulate with those reporting the second type and vice versa.

4) The **notes** are considered part of the basic financial statements.

    a) They amplify or explain information recognized in the statements and are an integral part of statements prepared in accordance with GAAP.

    b) Notes should not be used to correct improper presentations.

4. **Users of financial statements** may directly or indirectly have an economic interest in a specific business. Users with direct interests usually invest in or manage the business, and users with indirect interests advise, influence, or represent users with direct interests.

    a. Users with **direct interests** include

        1) Investors or potential investors
        2) Suppliers and creditors
        3) Employees
        4) Management

    b. Users having **indirect interests** include

        1) Financial advisers and analysts
        2) Stock markets or exchanges
        3) Regulatory authorities

5. The users of financial statements also may be grouped by their relation to the business.

    a. **Internal users** use financial statements to make decisions affecting the operations of the business. These users include management, employees, and the board of directors.

        1) Management needs financial statements to assess financial strengths and deficiencies, to evaluate performance results and past decisions, and to plan for future financial goals and steps toward accomplishing them.

        2) Employees want financial information to negotiate wages and fringe benefits based on the increased productivity and value they provide to a profitable firm.

    b. **External users** use financial statements to determine whether doing business with the firm will be beneficial.

        1) Investors need information to decide whether to increase, decrease, or obtain an investment in a firm.

        2) Creditors need information to determine whether to extend credit and under what terms.

        3) Financial advisers and analysts need financial statements to help investors evaluate particular investments.

        4) Stock exchanges need financial statements to evaluate whether to accept a firm's stock for listing or whether to suspend the stock's trading.

        5) Regulatory agencies may need financial statements to evaluate the firm's conformity with regulations and to determine price levels in regulated industries.

6. Stop and review! You have completed the outline for this subunit. Study multiple-choice questions 1 through 6 beginning on page 448.

## 12.2 STATEMENT OF FINANCIAL POSITION

1. The **statement of financial position (balance sheet)** "provides information about an entity's assets, liabilities, and equity and their relationships to each other at a moment in time." It helps users to assess "the entity's liquidity, financial flexibility, profitability, and risk" (SFAC 5).

   a. The **elements** of the balance sheet make up a detailed presentation of the basic accounting equation for a business enterprise:

   *Assets = Liabilities + Equity*

   1) The equation is based on the proprietary theory. The owners' equity in an enterprise (residual interest) is what remains after the economic obligations of the enterprise are subtracted from its economic resources.

   b. Some variation of the following system of **classification** is used by most enterprises:

   | Assets | Liabilities |
   |---|---|
   | Current assets | Current liabilities |
   | Noncurrent assets | Noncurrent liabilities |
   |   Long-term investments and funds | |
   |   Property, plant, and equipment | Equity |
   |   Intangible assets | Contributed capital |
   |   Other noncurrent assets | Retained earnings |
   |   Deferred charges | Accumulated other |
   | |   comprehensive income |

   1) Assets are usually presented in descending order of liquidity; for example, inventory (a current asset) is more liquid than property, plant, and equipment.

   2) Liabilities are shown in ascending order of nearness to maturity. Trade payables (a current liability) will appear before bonds payable (a long-term liability).

   3) Items in the equity section are presented in descending order of permanence, e.g., common stock before retained earnings.

   c. The **format** of the balance sheet is not standardized, and any method that promotes full disclosure and understandability is acceptable.

   1) The **account (or horizontal) form** presents assets on the left and liabilities and equity on the right.

   2) The **report (or vertical) form** is also commonly used. It differs from the account form only in that liabilities and equity are below rather than beside assets.

2. **The Resource Structure**

   a. **Current assets** consist of "cash and other assets or resources commonly identified as reasonably expected to be realized in cash or sold or consumed during the normal operating cycle of the business" [Accounting Research Bulletin (ARB) 43, Ch. 3A].

   1) The **operating cycle** is the average time between the acquisition of resources and the final receipt of cash from their sale as the culmination of the entity's revenue-generating activities.

   a) If the operating cycle is less than a year, 1 year is the basis for defining current and noncurrent assets.

   2) Current assets include cash and cash equivalents; inventories; receivables; certain trading, available-for-sale, and held-to-maturity securities; and prepaid expenses.

b. **Noncurrent assets** are those which do not qualify as current.

1) **Long-term investments and funds** include a variety of nonoperating investments and funds intended to be held beyond the longer of 1 year or the operating cycle. The assets typically included are

a) Advances or investments in securities made to control or influence another entity and other securities not classified as current

b) Restricted funds, for example, funds earmarked to retire long-term debt, satisfy pension obligations, or pay for the acquisition or construction of noncurrent assets

c) Cash surrender value of life insurance policies

d) Capital assets not used in current operations, such as idle facilities or land held for a future plant site or for speculative purposes

2) **Property, plant, and equipment (PPE)** consist of tangible items used in operations.

a) PPE are recorded at cost and are shown net of accumulated depreciation if depreciable. They include

i) Land and depletable natural resources, e.g., oil and gas reserves

ii) Buildings, machinery, equipment, furniture, fixtures, leasehold improvements, land improvements, leased assets held under capital leases, and other depreciable assets

3) **Intangible assets** are defined by **SFAS 142**, *Goodwill and Other Intangible Assets*, as nonfinancial assets without physical substance.

a) Examples are patents, copyrights, trademarks, trade names, franchises, and purchased goodwill.

4) **Other noncurrent assets** include noncurrent assets not readily classifiable elsewhere. Accordingly, there is little uniformity of treatment. Among the items typically reported as other assets are

a) Long-term receivables arising from unusual transactions, e.g., loans to officers or employees and sales of capital assets

b) Bond issue costs

c) Machinery rearrangement costs (also classifiable as PPE)

d) Long-term prepayments

e) Deferred tax assets arising from interperiod tax allocation

5) The category **deferred charges** (long-term prepayments) appears on some balance sheets.

a) Many of these items, for example, bond issue costs and rearrangement costs, which involve long-term prepayments, are frequently classified as other assets.

3. **The Financing Structure**

a. **Current liabilities** are "obligations whose liquidation is reasonably expected to require the use of existing resources properly classifiable as current assets, or the creation of other current liabilities" (ARB 43, Ch. 3A).

1) This classification includes the following:

a) Payables for items **entering into the operating cycle**, for example, those incurred to obtain materials and supplies to be used in producing goods or services for sale.

b) Payables arising from operations **directly related to the operating cycle**, such as accrued wages, salaries, rentals, royalties, and taxes.

    c)   **Collections made in advance** of delivering goods or performing services, e.g., ticket sales revenue or magazine subscription revenue.

    d)   **Other obligations** expected to be liquidated in the ordinary course of business during the longer of 1 year or the operating cycle.

        i)   These include short-term notes given to acquire capital assets, payments required under sinking-fund provisions, payments on the current portion of serial bonds, and agency obligations incurred by the collection of assets on behalf of third parties.

    e)   **Estimated amounts** expected to be required within a relatively short time to pay known obligations even though

        i)   The amount can only be approximated, e.g., accrual of bonus payments, or

        ii)   The specific payee has not been designated, for example, in the case of warranties for repair of products already sold.

    f)   Obligations that, by their terms, are **due on demand** within the longer of 1 year or the operating cycle. Liquidation need not be expected.

    g)   Long-term obligations **callable at the balance sheet date** because of the debtor's violation of the debt agreement or long-term obligations that will become callable if the violation is not cured within a specified grace period.

  2)   Current liabilities require the use of current assets or the creation of other current liabilities and therefore do not include

    a)   **Short-term obligations intended to be refinanced** on a long-term basis when the ability to consummate the refinancing has been demonstrated.

        i)   This ability is demonstrated by a post-balance-sheet-date issuance of long-term debt or by entering into a financing agreement that meets certain criteria.

    b)   Debts to be paid from funds accumulated in accounts classified as **noncurrent assets**.

        i)   Hence, a liability for bonds payable in the next period will not be classified as current if payment is to be from a noncurrent fund.

  b.   **Noncurrent liabilities** include the noncurrent portions of the following:

    1)   Long-term notes and bonds payable

      a)   Any unamortized premium or discount should be separately disclosed in the presentation of bonds payable.

    2)   Liabilities under capital leases
    3)   Pension obligations
    4)   Deferred tax liability arising from interperiod tax allocation
    5)   Obligations under product or service warranty agreements
    6)   Advances for long-term commitments to provide goods or services
    7)   Advances from affiliated entities
    8)   Deferred revenue

  c.   **Equity** of a business enterprise is the residual after total liabilities are deducted from total assets.

    1)   Equity is divided into capital contributed by owners, retained earnings, and accumulated other comprehensive income (all comprehensive income items not included in net income).

    a)   **Treasury stock** recorded at cost is a deduction from total equity, not an asset. Treasury stock recorded at par is a direct reduction of the pertinent contributed capital account, e.g., common stock or preferred stock.

4. A **bankrupt entity** about to be liquidated is not a going concern.

    a. A **statement of affairs** prepared as of a specific date presents assets and liabilities of the debtor at **liquidation values**, with carrying amounts shown on a memorandum basis.

    b. Some critics argue that the balance sheet's reliance on historical costs (rather than liquidation values) is a limitation of the statement.

5. Stop and review! You have completed the outline for this subunit. Study multiple-choice questions 7 through 17 beginning on page 449.

## 12.3 STATEMENT OF INCOME AND STATEMENT OF RETAINED EARNINGS

1. The results of operations are reported in the income statement (statement of earnings) on the **accrual basis** using an approach oriented to historical transactions.

    a. The traditional income statement reports revenues from, and expenses of, the entity's major activities and gains and losses from other activities. The statement provides information about performance over an interval of time.

        *Revenues – Expenses + Gains – Losses = Income or Loss*

        1) Revenue and expense accounts are temporary (**nominal**) accounts that are periodically closed to permanent (**real**) accounts. The accountant need not close each revenue and expense transaction directly to capital.

        2) **Income or loss** is closed to **retained earnings** at the end of the period.

        3) Revenue is a part of **continuing operations**. Thus, discontinued operations and extraordinary items are reported separately.

2. **Transactions Included in Income**

    a. **APB 9**, *Reporting the Results of Operations*, prescribes the **all-inclusive approach** with some modifications.

        1) All transactions **affecting the net change in equity during the period** are included with these exceptions:

            a) Transactions with owners
            b) Prior-period adjustments
            c) Items reported initially in other comprehensive income
            d) Transfers to and from appropriated retained earnings
            e) Adjustments made in a quasi-reorganization

        2) The net income reported in this way over the life of the entity reflects the sum of the periodic net incomes, including the nonrecurring items that are an appropriate part of the earnings history.

            a) An additional advantage of the all-inclusive approach is that manipulation is less likely. Thus, the income statement will be less subject to variation caused by differences in judgment.

            b) The utility of the statement as a predictor of future income is not impaired if full disclosure of unusual, irregular, or nonrecurring items is made and an appropriate format is used.

    b. No authoritative accounting pronouncement allows the use of the **current operating performance** concept of income.

        1) The current operating performance concept emphasizes the ordinary, normal, recurring operations of the entity during the current period. Inclusion of extraordinary items or prior-period adjustments is believed to impair the significance of net income.

### 3.     Income Statement Format

a.     Three formats are commonly used for presentation of income or loss from continuing operations.

1)     The **single-step income statement** provides one grouping for revenue items and one for expense items. The single step is the one subtraction necessary to arrive at net income.

Bonilla Company
Income Statement
For Year Ended December 31, 200X

| | | |
|---|---|---|
| Revenues | | |
| Net sales | $XXX | |
| Other revenues | XXX | |
| Gains | XXX | |
| Total revenues | | $ XXX |
| Expenses | | |
| Costs of goods sold | $XXX | |
| Selling and administrative expenses | XXX | |
| Interest expense | XXX | |
| Losses | XXX | |
| Income tax expense | XXX | |
| Total expenses | | XXX |
| Net income | | $ XXX |
| Earnings per common share | | $ Y.YY |

2) The **multiple-step income statement** matches operating revenues and expenses in a section separate from nonoperating items, enhancing disclosure by presenting intermediary totals rather than one net income figure.

Willis Company
Income Statement
For Year Ended December 31, 200X

| | | | |
|---|---|---|---|
| Revenues: | | | |
| Gross sales | | | $ XXX |
| Less: Sales discounts | | $XXX | |
| Sales returns and allowances | | XXX | XXX |
| Net sales | | | $ XXX |
| Cost of Goods Sold: | | | |
| Beginning inventory | | $XXX | |
| Purchases | $XXX | | |
| Less: Purchase returns and discounts | XXX | | |
| Net purchases | $XXX | | |
| Transportation-in | XXX | XXX | |
| Goods available for sale | | $XXX | |
| Less: Ending inventory | | XXX | |
| Cost of goods sold | | | XXX |
| Gross profit | | | $ XXX |
| Operating Expenses: | | | |
| Selling expenses: | | | |
| Sales salaries and commissions | $XXX | | |
| Freight-out | XXX | | |
| Travel | XXX | | |
| Advertising | XXX | | |
| Office supplies | XXX | XXX | |
| Administrative expenses: | | | |
| Executive salaries | XXX | | |
| Professional salaries | XXX | | |
| Wages | XXX | | |
| Depreciation | XXX | | |
| Office supplies | XXX | XXX | |
| Total operating expenses | | | XXX |
| Income from operations | | | $ XXX |
| Other Revenues and Gains: | | | |
| Dividend revenue | | $XXX | XXX |
| Other Expenses and Losses: | | | |
| Interest expense | | $XXX | |
| Loss on disposal of equipment | | XXX | XXX |
| Income before taxes * | | | $ XXX |
| Income taxes | | | XXX |
| Net income * | | | $ XXX |
| Earnings per common share | | | $ Y.YY |

\* If discontinued operations were being reported, these captions would have been "Income from continuing operations before taxes" and "Income from continuing operations," respectively.

3)    The **condensed income statement** includes only the section totals of the multiple-step format.

Marzullo Company
Income Statement
For Year Ended December 31, 200X

| | | |
|---|---:|---:|
| Net sales | | $ XXX |
| Cost of goods sold | | XXX |
| Gross profit | | $ XXX |
| Selling expenses | $XXX | |
| Administrative expenses | XXX | XXX |
| Income from operations | | $ XXX |
| Other revenues and gains | | XXX |
| Other expenses and losses | | XXX |
| Income before taxes * | | $ XXX |
| Income taxes | | XXX |
| Net income * | | $ XXX |
| | | |
| Earnings per common share | | $ Y.YY |

* If discontinued operations were being reported, these captions would have been "Income from continuing operations before taxes" and "Income from continuing operations," respectively.

b.    When an enterprise reports discontinued operations or extraordinary items, these must be presented in a separate section after income from continuing operations.

1)    Because these items are reported after the presentation of income taxes, they must be shown **net of tax**.

2)    **Discontinued operations** are reported in two components:

a)    Income or loss from operations of the division from the first day of the reporting period until the date of disposal

b)    Gain or loss on the disposal of the divisions

3)    **Extraordinary items** must meet two criteria:

a)    To be considered extraordinary, an item must be **both unusual in nature and infrequent in occurrence** in the environment in which the entity operates.

b)    Write-downs of receivables and inventories, translation of foreign currency amounts, disposal of a segment, sale of productive assets, effects of strikes, and accruals on long-term contracts can never be considered extraordinary.

4)    Appropriate earnings per share amounts must be disclosed, either on the face of the statement or in the accompanying notes.

5) EXAMPLE:

| | | |
|---|---|---|
| Income from continuing operations | | $XXX |
| Discontinued operations: | | |
| Income from operations of divested division, net of applicable income taxes of $XX | $XXX | |
| Loss on disposal of divested division, net of applicable income taxes of $XX | XXX | XXX |
| Income before extraordinary item | | $ XXX |
| Extraordinary item: | | |
| Loss from volcanic eruption, net of applicable income taxes of $XX | | XXX |
| Net income | | $ XXX |
| | | |
| Per share of common stock: | | |
| Income from continuing operations | | $Y.YY |
| Income from operations of divested division, net of tax | | Y.YY |
| Loss on disposal of divested division, net of tax | | (Y.YY) |
| Income before extraordinary item | | $Y.YY |
| Extraordinary loss, net of tax | | (Y.YY) |
| Net income | | $Y.YY |

c. **Cost of goods sold** equals cost of goods manufactured (or purchases for a retailer) adjusted for the change in finished goods inventory. Adding beginning inventory to purchases produces goods available for sale.

1) **Cost of goods manufactured** is equivalent to a retailer's purchases. It equals all manufacturing costs incurred during the period, plus beginning work-in-process, minus ending work-in-process. It also may be stated as cost of goods sold, plus ending finished goods inventory, minus beginning finished goods inventory.

d. Other expenses

1) **Selling expenses** are those incurred in selling or marketing.

a) Examples include sales representatives' salaries, rent for sales department, commissions, and traveling expense; advertising; sales department salaries and expenses; samples; and credit and collection costs. Shipping costs are also often classified as selling costs.

2) **General and administrative expenses** are incurred for the direction of the enterprise as a whole and are not related wholly to a specific function, e.g., selling or manufacturing.

a) They include accounting, legal, and other fees for professional services; officers' salaries; insurance; wages of office staff; miscellaneous supplies; and office occupancy costs.

3) **Interest expense** is recognized based on the passage of time. In the case of bonds, notes, and capital leases, the **effective interest method** is used.

4. APB 9 states that the income statement and the **statement of retained earnings** (presented separately or combined) are designed to broadly reflect the results of operations.

a. Most entities report changes in retained earnings in a **statement of equity (changes in equity)** or a separate statement.

b. The statement of retained earnings consists of beginning retained earnings, plus or minus any prior-period adjustments (net of tax); net income (loss); dividends paid or declared; and certain other rare items, e.g., quasi-reorganizations. The final amount is ending retained earnings.

c. EXAMPLE:

| | |
|---|---:|
| Retained earnings, Jan. 1, as originally reported | $XXX |
| Correction for overstatement of depreciation expense in prior period | XXX |
| Retained earnings, Jan. 1, as restated | $XXX |
| Net income | XXX |
| Cash dividends paid | (XXX) |
| Retained earnings, Dec. 31 | $XXX |

d. The retained earnings balance is sometimes divided into **appropriated** and **unappropriated** amounts.

e. A **quasi-reorganization** eliminates a deficit in retained earnings through reductions in other capital accounts. It accomplishes in a simpler way the same purpose as a legal reorganization. Elimination of the deficit permits a company to pay dividends.

5. **Comprehensive Income**

a. **SFAS 130**, *Reporting Comprehensive Income*, applies to enterprises issuing a full set of financial statements if they have items of **other comprehensive income (OCI)**. However, the terms "comprehensive income" and "OCI" are not required.

1) SFAS 130 divides comprehensive income into net income and OCI. Under existing accounting standards, OCI is classified separately into

a) Foreign currency items (translation adjustments; gains and losses on a hedge of a net investment in a foreign operation, which are accounted for as if they were translation adjustments; and gains and losses on derivatives designated, qualifying, and effective as hedging instruments in foreign currency cash flow hedges).

b) Minimum pension liability adjustments.

c) Unrealized gains and losses on available-for-sale securities, except those that are hedged items in a fair value hedge.

d) The effective portions (minus amounts reclassified into earnings) of gains or losses on derivatives designated and qualifying as hedges of the exposure to variability in the cash flows of a recognized asset or liability or of a forecasted transaction.

b. Comprehensive income and its components must be displayed in a financial statement given the same prominence as other statements.

1) No specific format is specified, but SFAS 130 encourages an enterprise to display the components of OCI and comprehensive income below net income.

2) Regardless of the format, net income must be presented as a component of comprehensive income in the statement.

3) Among the **possible formats** for reporting comprehensive income are

a) A separate statement of comprehensive income
b) A combined statement of income and comprehensive income
c) A statement of changes in equity

4) Each component of OCI is displayed net of tax, or one amount is shown for the aggregate tax effect on OCI, but the tax effect on each component must be disclosed.

c. The total of OCI for a period is transferred to a component of equity separate from retained earnings and additional paid-in capital.

1) The accumulated balance for each classification in that component must be disclosed in the balance sheet, a statement of changes in equity, or the notes.

d. **Reclassification adjustments** are made for each component of OCI except minimum pension liability adjustments.

1) Their purpose is to avoid double counting when an item included in net income was also included in OCI for the same or a prior period.

a) For example, if a gain or loss on available-for-sale securities is realized in the current period, the prior recognition of an unrealized holding gain or loss must be eliminated from OCI.

e. A total for comprehensive income is reported in interim-period condensed statements.

f. SFAS 130 does not apply to not-for-profit organizations.

6. Stop and review! You have completed the outline for this subunit. Study multiple-choice questions 18 through 32 beginning on page 453.

## 12.4 STATEMENT OF CASH FLOWS

1. If a business enterprise or not-for-profit organization reports financial position and results of operations, it must present a statement of cash flows for any period for which results of operations are presented (**SFAS 95**, *Statement of Cash Flows*).

a. However, defined benefit pension plans, certain other employee benefit plans, and certain highly liquid investment companies are exempt.

b. SFAS 95 states, "Financial statements shall not report an amount of cash flow per share." The per-share amount may improperly imply that the cash flow is an alternative to net income as a performance measure.

2. The primary purpose of a statement of cash flows is to provide relevant **information about the cash receipts and payments of an entity** during a period. A secondary purpose is to provide information about investing and financing activities.

a. If used with information in the other financial statements, the statement of cash flows should help investors, creditors, donors, and others to assess the entity's ability to generate positive future net cash flows, meet its obligations, and pay dividends.

b. Cash flow information also helps users to assess

1) The entity's needs for external financing

2) The reasons for differences between income and associated cash receipts and payments

3) The cash and noncash aspects of investing and financing activities

a) Information about **noncash investing and financing activities** that affect recognized assets or liabilities but do not directly affect cash flow for the period must be disclosed.

i) These transactions are excluded from the body of the statement to avoid undue complexity and detraction from the objective of providing information about cash flows.

ii) Examples include converting debt to equity, obtaining assets by assuming liabilities or entering into a capital lease, obtaining a building or investment asset by receiving a gift, and exchanging a noncash asset or liability for another.

3.  The **changes in cash and in cash equivalents** during the period are to be explained in a statement of cash flows.

    a.  If an entity invests its cash in excess of immediate needs in short-term, highly liquid investments (cash equivalents), it should use the descriptive term "cash and cash equivalents." Otherwise, the term "cash" is acceptable. Terms such as "funds" or "quick assets" may not be used.

        1)  **Cash equivalents** are readily convertible to known amounts of cash and are so near their maturity that they present insignificant risk of changes in value because of changes in interest rates.

            a)  Thus, an exchange of cash for cash equivalents has no effect on the statement of cash flows.

        2)  Usually, only investments with original maturities of 3 months or less qualify as cash equivalents.

            a)  Examples are money market funds, commercial paper, and treasury bills.

        3)  However, not all qualifying investments must be classified as cash equivalents.

            a)  An entity should establish and consistently apply a policy concerning which qualifying investments are to be treated as cash equivalents.

4.  A statement of cash flows reports the cash effects of operating activities, investing activities, and financing activities during the period.

    a.  **Cash flows from operating activities** include all transactions and other events not classified as investing and financing activities.

        1)  In general, the cash effects of transactions and other events that enter into the **determination of income** are to be classified as operating activities.

            a)  Cash flows from operating activities include cash receipts from interest on loans and dividends on equity securities.

            b)  They also include cash payments to employees and suppliers; to governments for taxes, duties, and fees; and to lenders for interest.

        2)  **SFAS 102**, *Statement of Cash Flows-Exemption of Certain Enterprises and Classification of Cash Flows from Certain Securities Acquired for Resale*, classifies as operating items cash flows from certain securities and other assets acquired for resale and carried at market value in a trading account (e.g., by banks, brokers, and dealers in securities), or from loans acquired for resale and carried at lower of cost or market.

            a)  Moreover, **SFAS 115**, *Accounting for Certain Investments in Debt and Equity Securities*, states that cash flows from purchases, sales, and maturities of **trading securities** are cash flows from operating activities.

        3)  The cash flows from operating activities section may be presented in **one of two formats**.

            a)  The FASB encourages use of the direct method.

                i)  However, **if the direct method is used**, a separate reconciliation in the form of the **indirect method must be provided** in a separate schedule. Therefore, use of the indirect method is more efficient.

                ii) Net cash flow from operations will be the same under either method.

                iii) The other two sections of the statement of cash flows are identical regardless of which method was chosen for presentation of cash flows from operating activities.

4) The **indirect method** is the simpler of the two. Accrual-basis net income is adjusted for noncash transactions to arrive at net cash flows from operating activities.

    a) Common categories of items that must be **added back** to accrual-basis net income are:

        i) **Decreases in current assets** (inventories, receivables, prepaid expenses)

        ii) **Increases in current liabilities** (accounts payable)

        iii) **Expenses involving no outlay of cash** (depreciation, amortization of bond discount, losses on disposal of assets)

    b) Common categories of items that must be **deducted from** accrual-basis net income are:

        i) **Increases in current assets** (inventories, receivables, prepaid expenses)

        ii) **Decreases in current liabilities** (accounts payable)

        iii) **Revenues involving no receipt of cash** (amortization of bond premium, gains on disposal of assets)

5) The **direct method** calculates net cash flow from operations by netting major classes of gross operating cash receipts against major classes of operating cash payments.

    a) At a minimum, the following classes are included in a direct presentation:

        i) Cash collected from customers, including lessees, licensees, and the like

        ii) Interest and dividends received (excluding those donor-restricted for long-term purposes)

        iii) Other operating cash receipts, if any

        iv) Cash paid to employees and other suppliers of goods or services, including suppliers of insurance, advertising and the like

        v) Interest paid

        vi) Income taxes paid

        vii) Other operating cash payments, if any

b. **Cash flows from investing activities** include making and collecting loans and acquiring and disposing of debt or equity instruments and property, plant, and equipment and other productive assets, that is, assets held for or used in the production of goods or services (other than the materials held in inventory).

    1) Investing activities exclude transactions in cash equivalents and in certain loans or other debt or equity instruments acquired specifically for resale.

    2) Cash flows from purchases, sales, and maturities of **available-for-sale** and **held-to-maturity securities** are cash flows from investing activities and are reported gross for each classification of security in the cash flows statement (SFAS 115).

   c.    **Cash flows from financing activities** include the issuance of stock, the payment of dividends, treasury stock transactions, the issuance of debt, and the repayment or other settlement of debt obligations.

      1)   They also include receiving restricted resources that by donor stipulation must be used for long-term purposes.

      2)   Cash flows from **derivative instruments** accounted for as fair value or cash flow hedges may be classified in the same category as the flows from the hedged item, provided that this policy is disclosed.

          a)   However, if hedge accounting is discontinued, subsequent cash flows are classified in accordance with the nature of the instrument (SFAS 104 and SFAS 133).

5.    In general, cash inflows and outflows should be reported separately at gross amounts. In certain instances, however, the **netted** amounts of related cash receipts and payments may provide sufficient information for certain classes of cash flows.

   a.    If the turnover of an item is quick, amounts are large, and the maturity is short, or if the entity is essentially holding or disbursing cash for customers, net reporting is proper.

      1)   Examples are demand deposits of a bank and customer accounts payable of a broker-dealer.

      2)   SFAS 104 permits banks, savings institutions, and credit unions to report net cash receipts and payments for deposits, time deposits, and loans.

6.    SFAS 95 also requires translation of **foreign currency cash flows**.

   a.    A weighted-average exchange rate may be used if the result is substantially the same as would be obtained by using the rates in effect when the flows occurred.

   b.    The effect of exchange rate fluctuations must be separately reported as part of the reconciliation of cash and cash equivalents.

7.    **EXTENDED EXAMPLE:**

---

**Information Relating to year 2 Activities**

- Net income for year 2 was $690,000.
- Cash dividends of $240,000 were declared and paid in year 2.
- Equipment costing $400,000 with a $150,000 carrying amount was sold on January 1, year 2 for $150,000 in cash.
- A long-term investment was sold in year 2 for $135,000.
- 10,000 common shares were issued in year 2 for $22 a share.
- Short-term investments consist of Treasury bills maturing on 6/30/year 3. They are not cash equivalents because their maturities are not 3 months or less.
- The provision for year 2 income taxes was $210,000.
- The accounts receivable balance at the beginning and end of year 2 were net of allowances for bad debts of $50,000 and $60,000 respectively. Dice wrote off $40,000 of bad debts during year 2. The only transactions affecting accounts receivable and the allowance were credit sales, collections, write-offs, and recognition of bad debt expense.
- During year 2, Dice constructed a plant asset. The accumulated expenditures during the year included $11,000 of capitalized interest.
- Dice accounts for its interest in the Thrice Corp. under the equity method. Its equity in Thrice's year 2 earnings was $25,000. At the end of year 2, Dice received a $10,000 cash dividend from Thrice.

| | December 31, | |
|---|---|---|
| **Assets** | Year 2 | Year 1 |
| Cash | $ 195,000 | $ 100,000 |
| Short-term investments | 300,000 | 0 |
| Accounts receivable (net) | 480,000 | 510,000 |
| Inventory | 680,000 | 600,000 |
| Prepaid expenses | 15,000 | 20,000 |
| Long-term investments | 215,000 | 300,000 |
| Plant assets | 1,700,000 | 1,000,000 |
| Accumulated depreciation | (450,000) | (450,000) |
| Intangible assets | 90,000 | 100,000 |
|    Total assets | $3,225,000 | $2,180,000 |
| **Liabilities and Equity** | | |
| Accounts payable | $ 825,000 | $ 720,000 |
| Interest payable | 15,000 | 10,000 |
| Income tax payable | 20,000 | 30,000 |
| Short-term debt | 325,000 | 0 |
| Deferred taxes | 250,000 | 300,000 |
| Common stock, $10 par | 800,000 | 700,000 |
| Additional paid-in capital | 370,000 | 250,000 |
| Retained earnings | 620,000 | 170,000 |
| Total equities | $3,225,000 | $2,180,000 |

a. **Operating activities section -- indirect method**

1) The following computations are required to determine **net cash provided by operations** ($905,000, as shown in the reconciliation on the next page):

a) **Depreciation**. In year 2, Dice must have recognized $250,000 of depreciation [$450,000 accumulated depreciation at 12/31/year 2 – ($450,000 accumulated depreciation at 12/31/year 1 – $250,000 accumulated depreciation on equipment sold on 1/1/year 2)]. The depreciation and the $10,000 ($100,000 at 12/31/year 1 – $90,000 at 12/31/year 2) amortization of intangible assets should be added to net income because both are noncash items included in net income.

b) **Cost of goods sold**. The adjustment from cost of goods sold (an accrual accounting amount) to cash paid to suppliers requires two steps: from CGS to purchases and from purchases to cash paid to suppliers. The $80,000 ($680,000 – $600,000) increase in inventory is a deduction from net income because it indicates that purchases were $80,000 greater than the cost of goods sold amount used to compute net income.

c) **Accounts payable**. The $105,000 ($825,000 – $720,000) increase in accounts payable is an addition to net income. It indicates that cash disbursements to suppliers were $105,000 less than purchases. The net effect of the changes in inventory and accounts payable is that cash paid to suppliers was $25,000 less than CGS.

d) **Accounts receivable**. The net accounts receivable balance declined by $30,000 ($510,000 – $480,000), implying that cash collections exceeded net income. Given that sales, collections, write-offs, and recognition of bad debt expense were the only relevant transactions, $30,000 should be added to net income. Use of the change in net accounts receivable as a reconciliation adjustment is a short-cut method. It yields the same net adjustment to net income as separately including the effects of the change in gross accounts receivable [($510,000 + $50,000 bad debt allowance) – ($480,000 + $60,000 bad debt allowance) = an addition of $20,000], bad debt expense (a noncash item resulting in an addition of $50,000), and bad debt write-offs (a deduction of $40,000 to reflect that write-offs did not result in collections).

e) **Prepaid expenses**. The $5,000 decrease signifies that noncash expenses were recognized and should be added back to net income.

f) **Dividends received**. Earnings of an affiliate accounted for under the equity method are debited to the investment account and credited to net income. A cash dividend from the affiliate is debited to cash and credited to the investment account. Thus, an adjustment reducing net income by $15,000 ($25,000 earnings – $10,000 cash dividend) for undistributed earnings is necessary.

g) **Long-term investments**. A $100,000 ($300,000 + $25,000 equity in affiliate's earnings – $10,000 cash dividend – $215,000) decrease in the long-term investments account occurred when these investments were sold for $135,000. The resulting $35,000 gain was included in the determination of net income. The cash effect is properly classified as an investing activity, and the $35,000 should be subtracted from net income to remove it from the operating section. SFAS 115 is not applicable because the Thrice investment is accounted for under the equity method.

h) **Interest payable**. Interest payable increased by $5,000, which represents a noncash expense and a reconciling addition to net income. The interest capitalized is ignored for reconciliation purposes because it is not reported as interest expense in the income statement or as interest paid in the statement of cash flows or in related disclosures. The $11,000 of capitalized interest is included in the capitalized cost of the plant asset.

i) **Income tax payable**. Income tax payable decreased by $10,000, giving rise to a reconciling deduction from net income because tax expense was less than cash paid for taxes.

j) **Deferred taxes**. Deferred taxes decreased by $50,000. This reconciling deduction from net income resulted when temporary differences reversed and cash payments for taxes exceeded tax expense.

| Reconciliation of Net Income to Net Operating Cash Flow | | |
| --- | --- | --- |
| Net income for year 2 | $690,000 | |
| Depreciation | 250,000 | a) |
| Amortization | 10,000 | a) |
| Inventory | (80,000) | b) |
| Accounts payable | 105,000 | c) |
| Accounts receivable (net) | 30,000 | d) |
| Prepaid expenses | 5,000 | e) |
| Undistributed earnings of an affiliate | (15,000) | f) |
| Gain on sale of investments | (35,000) | g) |
| Interest payable | 5,000 | h) |
| Income tax payable | (10,000) | i) |
| Deferred taxes | (50,000) | j) |
| Net operating cash flow | $905,000 | |

b. **Investing activities section**

1) The $300,000 increase in short-term investments indicates that a purchase occurred.

2) The balance sheet further indicates that plant assets increased by $700,000 ($1,700,000 – $1,000,000). Moreover, plant assets (equipment) costing $400,000 were sold. Thus, the cost of constructing the plant asset must have equaled $1,100,000 [$1,700,000 ending plant assets balance – ($1,000,000 beginning balance – $400,000 cost of equipment sold)].

3) The cash flows from investing activities include the cash effects of the sale of equipment and the long-term investments, the purchases of short-term investments (assuming they are held-to-maturity or available-for-sale securities), and the construction of a plant asset. The equipment was sold for $150,000 and the long-term investments for $135,000. Thus, the net cash used in investing activities was $1,115,000.

| | | |
| --- | --- | --- |
| Purchases: | | |
| Short-term investments | $ (300,000) | a) |
| Plant assets | (1,100,000) | b) |
| Sales: | | |
| Equipment | 150,000 | c) |
| Long-term investments | 135,000 | c) |
| Net investing cash flow | $(1,115,000) | |

c. **Financing activities section**

1) Dice Corp.'s year 2 financing activities included the issuance of short-term debt ($325,000 – $0 = $325,000), the issuance of common stock and the recording of additional paid-in capital [($800,000 – $700,000) + ($370,000 – $250,000) = $220,000], and the payment of cash dividends ($240,000). The net cash provided by these financing activities was $305,000.

| | | |
|---|---|---|
| Short-term debt | $ 325,000 | a) |
| Common stock | 220,000 | a) |
| Cash dividends | (240,000) | a) |
| Net financing cash flow | $ 305,000 | |

d. **Preparing the statement**

1) According to Dice Corp.'s balance sheets, the **net change in cash** was an increase of $95,000 ($195,000 – $100,000).

   a) This amount reconciles with the net cash provided by (used in) operating, investing, and financing activities ($905,000 – $1,115,000 + $305,000 = $95,000).

2) Dice Corp. had no noncash financing and investing transactions in year 2 to be reported in supplemental disclosures.

3) If Dice Corp. uses the indirect method to present its statement of cash flows, the interest paid (excluding amounts capitalized) and income taxes paid must be reported in **supplemental disclosures**. Interest paid cannot be calculated here because interest expense is not given in the example.

4) Income taxes paid were $270,000 ($210,000 provision for income taxes + $50,000 decrease in deferred taxes + $10,000 decrease in income tax payable).

---

Dice Corp.
Statement of Cash Flows -- Indirect Method
for the Year Ended December 31, Year 2
Increase (Decrease) in Cash and Cash Equivalents

| | | |
|---|---|---|
| Operating cash flows: | | |
| Net income for year 2 | $ 690,000 | |
| Depreciation | 250,000 | |
| Amortization | 10,000 | |
| Inventory | (80,000) | |
| Accounts payable | 105,000 | |
| Accounts receivable (net) | 30,000 | |
| Prepaid expenses | 5,000 | |
| Undistributed earnings of an affiliate | (15,000) | |
| Gain on sale of investments | (35,000) | |
| Interest payable | 5,000 | |
| Income tax payable | (10,000) | |
| Deferred taxes | (50,000) | |
| Net cash provided by operating activities | | $ 905,000 |
| Investing cash flows: | | |
| Proceeds from sale of equipment | $ 150,000 | |
| Proceeds from sale of long-term investments | 135,000 | |
| Payments for short-term investments | (300,000) | |
| Payments for plant assets | (1,100,000) | |
| Net cash used in investing activities | | (1,115,000) |
| Financing cash flows: | | |
| Proceeds from short-term debt | $ 325,000 | |
| Proceeds from issuing common stock | 220,000 | |
| Dividends paid | (240,000) | |
| Net cash provided by financing activities | | 305,000 |
| Net increase | | $ 95,000 |
| Beginning balance | | 100,000 |
| Ending balance | | $ 195,000 |

e.   **Operating activities section -- direct method**

1)   Had the statement of cash flows on the previous page employed the direct method rather than the indirect method, the operating activities section would have looked like the following:

Cash flows from operating activities:

| | |
|---|---:|
| Cash collected from customers | $ 7,790,000 |
| Cash paid to employees and suppliers | (6,520,000) |
| Dividend from affiliate | 10,000 |
| Interest received | 30,000 |
| Interest paid | (135,000) |
| Income taxes paid | (270,000) |
| Net cash provided by operating activities | $905,000 |

a)   **Cash collected from customers** may be determined by adjusting sales for the changes in customer receivables.

i)   This calculation requires information similar to that used in an indirect presentation to reconcile net income to net operating cash flow: total operating receivables (which are usually separate from those for interest and dividends), bad debt write-offs, and any other noncash entries in customer accounts.

b)   **Cash paid to employees and suppliers** of goods and services may be determined by adjusting cost of goods sold and expenses (excluding interest, income tax, and depreciation) for the changes in inventory, prepaid expenses, and operating payables.

i)   This calculation is also similar to the process used in reconciling net income to net operating cash flow. It requires that operating payables and expenses be separated from interest and income tax payable.

c)   Dividends received, not the amount of equity-based earnings recognized in net income, is included.

d)   Interest income is adjusted for changes in interest receivable.

e)   Interest expense is adjusted for changes in interest payable. Interest capitalized is not considered in determining interest paid because it is included in payments for plant assets, not in interest expense.

f)   Income taxes paid equaled tax expense adjusted for the changes in deferred taxes and in taxes payable.

8.   Stop and review! You have completed the outline for this subunit. Study multiple-choice questions 33 through 67 beginning on page 458.

## 12.5   SELECTED DISCLOSURES

1.   **APB 22**, *Disclosure of Accounting Policies*, requires that all significant accounting policies of a reporting entity be disclosed as an integral part of its financial statements.

a.   Disclosure of significant accounting policies is required when

1)   A selection has been made from existing acceptable principles, such as alternative depreciation methods or inventory valuation methods.

2)   A policy is unique to the industry in which the entity operates, even if the policy is predominately followed in that industry.

3)   GAAP have been applied in an unusual or innovative way.

    b. Certain items are explicitly listed in APB 22 as **commonly required disclosures** in a summary of significant accounting policies.

        1) These items include the basis of consolidation, depreciation methods, amortization of intangible assets, inventory pricing, recognition of profit on long-term construction-type contracts, and recognition of revenue from franchising and leasing operations.

        2) APB 22 recognizes that financial statement disclosure of accounting policies should not duplicate details presented elsewhere in the financial statements.

            a) For example, the summary of significant policies should not contain the composition of plant assets or inventories or the maturity dates of long-term debt. Instead, the summary can refer to details about matters that are presented elsewhere in the financial statements.

    c. According to SFAS 95, an enterprise must disclose its policy for determining which items are cash equivalents.

2. **APB 28**, *Interim Financial Reporting*, requires certain minimum disclosures of interim data by public companies.

    a. The list of specific required items is as follows: sales or gross revenues; provisions for income taxes; extraordinary items; cumulative effect of accounting changes; net income; comprehensive income; basic and diluted EPS; seasonal revenues, costs, or expenses; significant changes in estimates or provisions for income taxes; disposal of a component of an entity; unusual or infrequent items; contingent items; changes in accounting principles or estimates; significant changes in financial position; certain disclosures about reportable operating segments; and certain information about stock-based employee compensation cost if awards are outstanding that are accounted for at intrinsic value, not fair value.

    b. If condensed balance sheet or cash flow data are not presented, significant changes in liquid assets, net working capital, long-term liabilities, or equity should be disclosed.

    c. Interim financial statements are considered a part of the annual period. Only a few modifications to the criteria for the recognition of revenue and expense for annual reporting purposes are permitted.

    d. **Revenue recognition criteria** are the same as for annual statements.

    e. Modifications of expense recognition are inconsequential.

        1) **Gross profit methods** may be used to estimate inventory.

        2) Declines in inventory value may be ignored if they are temporary.

        3) **Liquidation of LIFO base-period inventory** may be accounted for at current prices if the inventory will be replaced prior to year-end.

    f. The main concern is to prorate nonrecurring annual charges equitably to interim periods, e.g., year-end bonuses, vacation pay, major repairs.

        1) Seasonal variations should be disclosed in notes or by use of 12-month or year-to-date statements. Extraordinary items are reported separately in the interim period in which they occur.

    g. Taxes are based on the **estimated annual effective tax rate** after all tax-planning tools are implemented and include the effects of credits, special deductions, etc.

        1) This rate also includes the effect of any expected year-end valuation allowance for deferred tax assets related to originating deductible temporary differences and carryforwards during the year (FASB Interpretation No. 18 and SFAS 109).

        2) Each interim period's tax (benefit) is the estimated annual effective tax rate times year-to-date "ordinary" income (loss), minus tax (benefit) recognized in prior interim periods. "Ordinary" means excluding unusual or infrequent items and items not reported in continuing operations.

3)   SFAS 109, which amended APB 28 and FASB Interpretation No. 18, provides that a **tax benefit** is recognized for a loss arising early in the year if the benefits are expected to be (a) realized during the year or (b) recognizable as a **deferred tax asset** at year-end.

a)   A tax benefit is recognized for a loss arising in an interim period if realization is more likely than not.

b)   A **valuation allowance** must be recognized if it is likely that some portion of a deferred tax asset will not be realized.

c)   These principles are applied in determining the estimated tax benefit of an ordinary loss for the fiscal year used to calculate the annual effective tax rate and year-to-date tax benefit of a loss.

4)   Taxes on all items other than continuing operations are determined at incremental rates.  Thus, their marginal effect on taxes is calculated.

h.   **Accounting changes in interim periods** are governed by **SFAS 154**, *Accounting Changes and Error Corrections*.

1)   A change in accounting principle in an interim period should be effected by **retrospective application** unless determination of the cumulative effect or the period-specific effects is impracticable.

a)   The period-specific effects of the change are adjustments to the individual periods reported.  Beginning balances of the first period reported are adjusted to reflect the cumulative effects of the change on all prior periods.

b)   The **impracticability exception** that is available for annual financial statements **may not be used** for interim periods preceding the period of the change.

i)   When retrospective application to interim periods preceding the period of the change is impracticable, the change may only be made at the beginning of a **subsequent** fiscal year.

2)   All disclosures required for accounting changes in annual statements are required in interim statements.

3.   **SFAS 47**, *Disclosure of Long-Term Obligations*, requires disclosure of commitments under unconditional purchase obligations associated with suppliers.

a.   Such obligations are commitments to transfer funds in the future for fixed or minimum amounts of goods or services at fixed or minimum prices.

b.   Disclosure of the following information for **recorded obligations** for each of the 5 years following the date of the latest balance sheet presented is required:

1)   The aggregate amount of payments for unconditional purchase obligations

2)   The aggregate amount of maturities and sinking-fund requirements for all long-term borrowings

c.   If an unconditional purchase obligation is **not recorded** in the balance sheet, certain disclosures are required, including

1)   The nature and term of the obligation

2)   The variable components of the obligation

3)   The amounts purchased under the obligation for each period an income statement is presented

4)   The amount of the fixed and determinable portion of the obligation at the latest balance sheet date and, if determinable, for each of the 5 succeeding fiscal years

4. **SFAS 57**, *Related Party Disclosures*, requires the disclosure of material related-party transactions other than compensation arrangements (officers' salaries and expenses), expense allowances, and other similar items in the ordinary course of business.

   a. According to SFAS 57, related-party transactions include transactions between

      1) A parent and its subsidiaries
      2) Subsidiaries of a common parent
      3) An enterprise and employee trusts managed by or under the trusteeship of the enterprise's management
      4) An enterprise and its principal owners, management, or members of their immediate families
      5) Affiliates
      6) An enterprise and its equity-based investees
      7) An enterprise and any other entity if one party can significantly influence the other to the extent that one party may be prevented from fully pursuing its own interests
      8) Parties, all of which can be significantly influenced by another party

   b. SFAS 57 requires disclosure of

      1) The nature of the relationship involved
      2) A description of the transactions for each period an income statement is presented and such other information as is deemed necessary to an understanding of the effects of the transactions
      3) The dollar amounts of transactions for each period an income statement is presented and the effects of any change in the method of establishing their terms
      4) Amounts due from or to related parties as of the date of each balance sheet, including the terms of settlement
      5) Certain tax information required by SFAS 109 if the enterprise is part of a group that files a consolidated tax return

5. **SFAS 107**, *Disclosures about Fair Value of Financial Instruments*, requires certain entities to disclose the fair value of financial instruments, whether or not they are recognized in the balance sheet, if it is feasible to estimate such fair values.

   a. If estimating fair value is not feasible, disclosures include information pertinent to estimating the fair value of the financial instrument or class of financial instruments, such as the carrying amount, effective interest rate, and maturity.

      1) The reasons that estimating the fair value is not practicable should also be disclosed.

   b. Under **SFAS 126**, disclosures are optional if the entity is nonpublic, has total assets of less than $100 million, and has not held or issued any derivative financial instruments other than loan commitments during the reporting period.

   c. SFASs 107 and 133 define a **financial instrument** as cash, evidence of an ownership interest in an entity, or a contract that both

      1) Imposes on one entity a contractual obligation

         a) To deliver cash or another financial instrument to a second entity or
         b) To exchange other financial instruments on potentially unfavorable terms with the second entity, and

      2) Conveys to that second entity a contractual right

         a) To receive cash or another financial instrument from the first entity or
         b) To exchange other financial instruments on potentially favorable terms with the first entity.

    d.    **Quoted market prices**, if available, are the best evidence of the fair value.

    e.    Ordinarily, disclosures should not net the fair values of financial instruments even if they are of the same class or are related, e.g., by a risk management strategy.

        1)    However, exceptions are made for **rights of setoff** and for **master netting arrangements** executed with the same counterparty (in regard to such items as forward contracts, interest-rate swaps, currency swaps, and options).

    f.    **Credit risk** is the risk of accounting loss from a financial instrument because of the possibility that a loss may occur from the failure of another party to perform according to the terms of a contract.

        1)    In most instances, an entity must disclose all significant **concentrations of credit risk** arising from all financial instruments, whether from one counterparty or groups.

            a)    Group concentrations arise when multiple counterparties have similar activities and economic characteristics that would cause their ability to meet obligations to be similarly affected by changes in conditions. Disclosures include

                i)    Information about the shared activity, region, or economic characteristic that identifies the concentration.

                ii)    The maximum loss due to credit risk if parties failed completely to perform and the security, if any, proved to be of no value.

                iii)    The policy of requiring security, information about access to that security, and the nature and a brief description of the security.

                iv)    The policy of entering into master netting arrangements to mitigate the credit risk, information about them, and a description of the terms, including the extent to which they reduce the maximum amount of loss.

    g.    SFAS 107 encourages, but does not require, disclosure of quantitative information about the **market risks** of financial instruments that is consistent with the way an entity manages those risks.

6.    **AICPA Statement of Position (SOP) 94-6**, *Disclosure of Certain Significant Risks and Uncertainties*, is an important pronouncement on disclosures.

    a.    Required disclosures include risks and uncertainties at the balance sheet date that could significantly affect reported amounts in the near term, that is, within 1 year of the balance sheet date.

    b.    One set of disclosures concerns risks and uncertainties relating to the **nature of operations**.

        1)    Thus, entities must disclose their major products or services, principal markets, and the locations of those markets.

        2)    They should also disclose all industries in which they operate, the relative importance of each, and the basis for determining the relative importance, e.g., assets, revenue, or earnings. However, this set of disclosures need not be quantified.

    c.    A second type of disclosures concerns the **use of estimates** in the preparation of financial statements. Financial statements should explain that conformity with GAAP requires management to use numerous estimates.

    d.    A third category of disclosures concerns certain **significant estimates** used to value assets, liabilities, or contingencies.

        1)    Disclosures are required when the estimated effects of a condition, situation, or set of circumstances at the balance sheet date are subject to a **reasonable possibility** of change in the near term and the effects will be material.

        2)    The effect of using a different estimate determines materiality.

        3)    The nature of the uncertainty, that it is reasonably possible, and that the estimate may change in the near term are to be disclosed.

        4)    If an estimate is of a **loss contingency** covered by SFAS 5, the disclosure should include the estimated range of loss or a statement that an estimate cannot be made.

        5)    Factors making an estimate sensitive to change may be, but need not be, disclosed.

        6)    If an entity is not required to make disclosures about certain significant estimates because it has employed **risk-reduction techniques**, it is encouraged to disclose the uncertainty and the risk-reduction techniques.

    e.    A fourth set of disclosures concerns **current vulnerability due to concentrations**, for example, when entities fail to diversify.

        1)    Disclosure is necessary if management knows prior to issuance of the statements that

            a)    The concentration exists at the balance sheet date,

            b)    It makes the entity vulnerable to a near-term **severe impact**, and

            c)    Such impact is at least **reasonably possible** in the near term.

        2)    Disclosable concentrations include those in

            a)    The volume of business with a given customer, supplier, lender, grantor, or contributor;

            b)    Revenue from given products, services, or fund-raising events;

            c)    The available suppliers of materials, labor, services, or rights (e.g., licenses) used in operations; and

            d)    The market or geographic area where the entity operates.

        3)    A **severe impact** may result from loss of all or a part of a business relationship, price or demand changes, loss of a patent, changes in the availability of a resource or right, or the disruption of operations in a market or geographic area.

            a)    Furthermore, it is always reasonably possible in the near term that any customer, grantor, or contributor will be lost and that operations located in another country will be disrupted.

        4)    For concentrations of labor subject to **collective bargaining**, disclosure should include the percentage of employees covered by a collective bargaining agreement and the percentage covered by an agreement that will expire within 1 year.

            a)    For concentrations of operations in another country, disclosure should include the carrying amounts of net assets and the areas they are located.

7.  **AICPA Professional Auditing Standard AU 560**, *Subsequent Events*, concerns certain material events or transactions that occur after the balance sheet date and prior to the issuance of the financial statements. The events addressed by AU 560 are those that require adjustment of, or disclosure in, the statements.

    a.  Subsequent events affecting the realization of assets (such as receivables and inventories) or the settlement of estimated liabilities ordinarily require **adjustment**. They usually reflect the resolution of conditions that existed over a relatively long period.

    b.  One type of subsequent event provides additional evidence about **conditions at the date of the balance sheet** and affects the estimates inherent in statement preparation.

        1)  An example is a loss on an uncollectible receivable as a result of a customer's bankruptcy.

        2)  The financial statements should be **adjusted** for any changes in estimates resulting from such events.

    c.  A second type of subsequent event provides evidence about **conditions that did not exist at the date of the balance sheet** but that arose subsequent to that date. Some of these events require **disclosure** but not adjustment.

        1)  Examples of subsequent events requiring only disclosure include

            a)  Sale of a bond or capital stock issue

            b)  Purchase of a business

            c)  Settlement of litigation when the precipitating event occurred after the balance sheet date

            d)  Loss of plant or inventories as a result of fire or flood

            e)  Losses on receivables resulting from conditions (e.g., a customer's major casualty) arising after the balance sheet date

        2)  Some events of the second type may be so significant that the most appropriate disclosure is to supplement the historical statements with **pro forma financial data**.

8.  Stop and review! You have completed the outline for this subunit. Study multiple-choice questions 68 through 86 beginning on page 470.

## 12.6 CORE CONCEPTS

Basic Financial Statements and Their Users

- The **elements** of one statement **articulate** (are interrelated) with those of other statements.
- The **balance sheet** reports assets, liabilities, equity, and investments by owners **at a moment in time**.
- The statement of income and statement of retained earnings report revenues, expenses, gains, losses, and distributions to owners **over a period of time**.
- The elements of the **balance sheet** are **changed by** those on the **income statement** and are their cumulative result.

Statement of Financial Position

- The statement of financial position (balance sheet) "provides information about an entity's **assets, liabilities, and equity** and their relationships to each other at a moment in time."
- The items in the balance sheet represent the **resources** of the entity and **claims** to those resources.

Statement of Income and Statement of Retained Earnings

- The items in the statements of income and retained earnings represent the **effects of transactions** and other events and circumstances that result in changes in the entity's resources and claims to those resources.
- The statement of income can be presented in the **single-step**, **multi-step**, or **condensed** format.
- The results of **discontinued operations** and the effects of **extraordinary items** are presented **separately** after income from continuing operations.

Statement of Cash Flows

- The primary purpose of a statement of cash flows is to provide relevant information about the **cash receipts and payments** of an entity during a period.
- Cash flows are classified as being from **operating** activities, **investing** activities, or **financing** activities.
- Cash flows from **operating activities** can be displayed using the **direct method** (income statement approach) or the **indirect method** (reconciliation approach).
- If the **direct method** is used for reporting operating activities, a **reconciliation** that mimics the indirect method **must be disclosed**.

Selected Disclosures

- An entity must **disclose** all significant **accounting policies** as an integral part of its financial statements.
- **Accounting policies** so disclosed cover matters such as reporting of accounting changes and error corrections, long-term obligations, the fair values of financial instruments, and significant risks and uncertainties.

## QUESTIONS

### 12.1 Basic Financial Statements and Their Users

**1.** The basic financial statements include a

A. Balance sheet, income statement, statement of retained earnings, and statement of changes in retained earnings.

B. Statement of financial position, income statement, statement of retained earnings, and statement of changes in retained earnings.

C. Balance sheet, statement of financial position, income statement, and statement of changes in retained earnings.

D. Statement of financial position, income statement, statement of cash flows, and statement of retained earnings.

Answer (D) is correct. *(CMA, adapted)*
**REQUIRED:** The statements included in the basic financial statements.
**DISCUSSION:** Under GAAP, the basic required statements are the statements of financial position, income, cash flows, and retained earnings. Changes in equity must be disclosed in the basic statements, the notes, or a separate statement. A statement of cash flows is now a required part of a full set of financial statements of all business entities (both publicly held and privately held) (SFAS 95). Moreover, comprehensive income must be displayed in a financial statement given the same prominence as other statements, but no specific format is required as long as net income is displayed as a component of comprehensive income in the statement.

**2.** What are the disclosure requirements with respect to changes in capital accounts other than retained earnings and changes in other equity data?

A. When the income statement and balance sheet are presented, all changes in the capital accounts and changes in the number of shares of equity securities must be disclosed.

B. When the balance sheet is presented, all changes in the capital accounts must be disclosed.

C. When the income statement is presented, all changes in the capital accounts and changes in the number of shares of equity securities must be disclosed.

D. Changes in the number of shares of equity securities must be disclosed when a balance sheet is presented, but there is no specific disclosure requirement with respect to the capital accounts other than retained earnings.

Answer (A) is correct. *(Publisher)*
**REQUIRED:** The disclosure requirements with respect to changes in capital accounts other than retained earnings and changes in other equity data.
**DISCUSSION:** APB 12, *Omnibus Opinion-1967*, requires disclosure both of changes in the separate accounts appearing in equity (in addition to retained earnings) and of changes in the number of shares of equity securities when both the balance sheet and the income statement are presented. This disclosure may be in separate statements, the basic financial statements, or the notes.
Answer (B) is incorrect because the requirement applies only when both the balance sheet and the income statement are presented. Answer (C) is incorrect because the requirement applies only when both the balance sheet and the income statement are presented. Answer (D) is incorrect because there is a specific disclosure requirement with respect to the changes in the capital accounts.

**3.** A primary objective of external financial reporting is

A. Direct measurement of the value of a business enterprise.

B. Provision of information that is useful to present and potential investors, creditors, and others in making rational financial decisions regarding the enterprise.

C. Establishment of rules for accruing liabilities.

D. Direct measurement of the enterprise's stock price.

Answer (B) is correct. *(CMA, adapted)*
**REQUIRED:** The primary objective of external financial reporting.
**DISCUSSION:** According to the FASB's Statement of Financial Accounting Concepts (SFAC) 1, the objectives are to provide information that (1) is useful to present and potential investors, creditors, and others in making rational financial decisions regarding the enterprise; (2) helps those parties in assessing the amounts, timing, and uncertainty of prospective cash receipts from dividends or interest and the proceeds from sale, redemption, or maturity of securities or loans; and (3) concerns the economic resources of an enterprise, the claims thereto, and the effects of transactions, events, and circumstances that change its resources and claims thereto.
Answer (A) is incorrect because SFAC 1 states that financial reporting is not designed to measure directly the value of a business. Answer (C) is incorrect because, while rules for accruing liabilities are a practical concern, the establishment of such rules is not a primary objective of external reporting. Answer (D) is incorrect because the objectives of financial accounting are unrelated to the measurement of stock prices; stock prices are a product of stock market forces.

**4.** Notes to financial statements are beneficial in meeting the disclosure requirements of financial reporting. The notes should not be used to

    A. Describe significant accounting policies.

    B. Describe depreciation methods employed by the company.

    C. Describe principles and methods peculiar to the industry in which the company operates, when these principles and methods are predominantly followed in that industry.

    D. Correct an improper presentation in the financial statements.

Answer (D) is correct. *(CMA, adapted)*
    **REQUIRED:** The improper use of notes in financial statements.
    **DISCUSSION:** Financial statement notes should not be used to correct improper presentations. The financial statements should be presented correctly on their own. Notes should be used to explain the methods used to prepare the financial statements and the amounts shown.

**5.** Financial statement users with a direct economic interest in a specific business include

    A. Financial advisers.

    B. Regulatory bodies.

    C. Stock markets.

    D. Suppliers.

Answer (D) is correct. *(Publisher)*
    **REQUIRED:** The financial statement users with direct economic interests.
    **DISCUSSION:** Users with direct interests include investors or potential investors, suppliers and creditors, employees, and management.
    Answer (A) is incorrect because financial advisers have indirect interests. Answer (B) is incorrect because regulatory bodies have indirect interests. Answer (C) is incorrect because stock markets have indirect interests.

**6.** Which of the following is not a need of financial statement users?

    A. Financial advisers and analysts need financial statements to help investors evaluate particular investments.

    B. Stock exchanges need financial statements to set a firm's stock price.

    C. Regulatory agencies need financial statements to evaluate price changes for regulated industries.

    D. Employees need financial information to negotiate wages and fringe benefits.

Answer (B) is correct. *(Publisher)*
    **REQUIRED:** The item not a need of financial statement users.
    **DISCUSSION:** Investors' purchases and sales set stock prices. Stock exchanges need financial statements to evaluate whether to accept a firm's stock for listing or whether to suspend trading in the stock.
    Answer (A) is incorrect because financial advisers use financial statements for evaluating investments. Answer (C) is incorrect because regulatory agencies use financial statements for rate making. Answer (D) is incorrect because employees use financial statements for labor negotiations.

## 12.2 Statement of Financial Position

**7.** The primary purpose of the statement of financial position is to reflect

    A. The fair value of the firm's assets at some moment in time.

    B. The status of the firm's assets in case of forced liquidation of the firm.

    C. The success of a company's operations for a given amount of time.

    D. Items of value, debt, and net worth.

Answer (D) is correct. *(CMA, adapted)*
    **REQUIRED:** The primary purpose of the statement of financial position.
    **DISCUSSION:** The balance sheet presents three major financial accounting elements: assets (items of value), liabilities (debts), and equity (net worth). According to SFAC 6, *Elements of Financial Statements*, assets are probable future economic benefits resulting from past transactions or events. Liabilities are probable future sacrifices of economic benefits arising from present obligations as a result of past transactions or events. Equity is the residual interest in the assets after deduction of liabilities.
    Answer (A) is incorrect because the measurement attributes of assets include but are not limited to fair value. Answer (B) is incorrect because financial statements reflect the going concern assumption. Hence, they usually do not report forced liquidation values. Answer (C) is incorrect because the income statement provides this type of information.

**8.** A statement of financial position allows investors to assess all of the following except

A. The efficiency with which enterprise assets are used.

B. The liquidity and financial flexibility of the enterprise.

C. The capital structure of the enterprise.

D. The net realizable value of enterprise assets.

Answer (D) is correct.  *(CMA, adapted)*
**REQUIRED:** The attribute not assessable using a statement of financial position.
**DISCUSSION:** Assets are usually measured at original historical cost in a statement of financial position, although some exceptions exist. For example, some short-term receivables are reported at their net realizable value. Thus, the statement of financial position cannot be relied upon to assess NRV.
Answer (A) is incorrect because efficiency of asset use is assessed by calculating liquidity, leverage, and asset management ratios. These ratios require balance sheet data. Answer (B) is incorrect because liquidity and financial flexibility are assessed by calculating liquidity, leverage, and asset management ratios. These ratios require balance sheet data. Answer (C) is incorrect because the capital structure of the enterprise is reported in the equity section of the statement of financial position.

**9.** The accounting equation (assets − liabilities = equity) reflects the

A. Entity point of view.

B. Fund theory.

C. Proprietary point of view.

D. Enterprise theory.

Answer (C) is correct.  *(CMA, adapted)*
**REQUIRED:** The concept on which the basic accounting equation is based.
**DISCUSSION:** The equation is based on the proprietary theory. Equity in an enterprise is what remains after the economic obligations of the enterprise are deducted from its economic resources.
Answer (A) is incorrect because the entity concept limits accounting information to that related to a specific entity (possibly not the same as the legal entity). Answer (B) is incorrect because fund theory stresses that assets equal obligations (equity and liabilities are sources of assets). Answer (D) is incorrect because the enterprise concept stresses ownership of the assets; that is, the emphasis is on the credit side of the balance sheet.

**10.** Karen's Crafts, Inc. has the following accounts included in its December 31 trial balance:

| | |
|---|---|
| Accounts payable | $250,000 |
| Discount on bonds payable | 34,000 |
| Wages payable | 29,000 |
| Interest payable | 14,000 |
| Bonds payable | |
| (Issued 1/1/1996; due 1/1/2016) | 500,000 |
| Income taxes payable | 26,000 |

What amount of current liabilities will be reported on Karen's December 31 statement of financial position?

A. $285,000

B. $319,000

C. $353,000

D. $819,000

Answer (B) is correct.  *(Publisher)*
**REQUIRED:** The total of current liabilities.
**DISCUSSION:** Current liabilities consist of those debts that will have to be paid in the coming year or the normal operating cycle, whichever period is longer. Examples include accounts payable, wages payable, interest payable, and income taxes payable. Bonds payable and its contra account, discount on bonds payable, would both be shown under the long-term liability classification. The total current liabilities would be $319,000 ($250,000 + $29,000 + $14,000 + $26,000).
Answer (A) is incorrect because the discount on bonds payable is erroneously deducted from the total. Answer (C) is incorrect because $353,000 includes discount on bonds payable. Answer (D) is incorrect because $819,000 includes bonds payable.

**11.** Perry Mansfield Corporation has the following accounts included in its December 31 trial balance:

| | |
|---|---|
| Accounts receivable | $110,000 |
| Inventories | 250,000 |
| Patents | 90,000 |
| Prepaid insurance | 19,500 |
| Accounts payable | 72,000 |
| Cash | 28,000 |

What amount of current assets should Perry Mansfield include in its statement of financial position at December 31?

A. $335,500

B. $388,000

C. $407,500

D. $479,500

Answer (C) is correct. *(Publisher)*
**REQUIRED:** The amount of current assets.
**DISCUSSION:** Current assets consist of cash, certain marketable securities, receivables, inventories, and prepaid expenses. Adding these elements together produces a total of $407,500 ($28,000 cash + $110,000 receivables + $250,000 inventories + $19,500 prepaid insurance).
Answer (A) is incorrect because deducting accounts payable from the current assets results in the amount of working capital, rather than the total of current assets. Answer (B) is incorrect because it fails to include prepaid insurance in the total. Answer (D) is incorrect because it erroneously includes accounts payable.

**12.** According to SFAS 78, *Classification of Obligations That Are Callable by the Creditor,* long-term obligations that are or will become callable by the creditor because of the debtor's violation of a provision of the debt agreement at the balance sheet date should be classified as

A. Long-term liabilities.

B. Current liabilities unless the debtor goes bankrupt.

C. Current liabilities unless the creditor has waived the right to demand repayment for more than 1 year from the balance sheet date.

D. Contingent liabilities until the violation is corrected.

Answer (C) is correct. *(CMA, adapted)*
**REQUIRED:** The classification of long-term debt callable because of the debtor's violation of a loan agreement.
**DISCUSSION:** In these circumstances, the obligation should be classified as current. However, the debt need not be reclassified if the violation will be cured within a specified grace period or if the creditor formally waives or subsequently loses the right to demand repayment for a period of more than a year from the balance sheet date. Also, reclassification is not required if the debtor expects and has the ability to refinance the obligation on a long-term basis.
Answer (A) is incorrect because SFAS 78 requires classification as a current liability. Answer (B) is incorrect because bankruptcy is not an exception. Answer (D) is incorrect because SFAS 78 concerns callable, not contingent, liabilities.

**13.** Abernathy Corporation uses a calendar year for financial and tax reporting purposes and has $100 million of mortgage bonds due on January 15, year 2. By January 10, year 2, Abernathy intends to refinance this debt with new long-term mortgage bonds and has entered into a financing agreement that clearly demonstrates its ability to consummate the refinancing. This debt is to be

A. Classified as a current liability on the statement of financial position at December 31, year 1.

B. Classified as a long-term liability on the statement of financial position at December 31, year 1.

C. Retired as of December 31, year 1.

D. Considered off-balance-sheet debt.

Answer (B) is correct. *(CMA, adapted)*
**REQUIRED:** The balance sheet treatment of maturing long-term debt that is to be refinanced on a long-term basis.
**DISCUSSION:** SFAS 6 states that short-term obligations expected to be refinanced should be reported as current liabilities unless the firm both plans to refinance and has the ability to refinance the debt on a long-term basis. The ability to refinance on a long-term basis is evidenced by a post-balance-sheet date issuance of long-term debt or a financing arrangement that will clearly permit long-term refinancing.
Answer (A) is incorrect because the company intends to refinance the debt on a long-term basis. Answer (C) is incorrect because the debt has not been retired. Answer (D) is incorrect because the debt is on the balance sheet.

**14.** Lister Company intends to refinance a portion of its short-term debt in year 2 and is negotiating a long-term financing agreement with a local bank. This agreement would be noncancelable and would extend for a period of 2 years. The amount of short-term debt that Lister Company can exclude from its statement of financial position at December 31, year 1

A. May exceed the amount available for refinancing under the agreement.

B. Depends on the demonstrated ability to consummate the refinancing.

C. Is reduced by the proportionate change in the working capital ratio.

D. Is zero unless the refinancing has occurred by year-end.

Answer (B) is correct. *(CMA, adapted)*
**REQUIRED:** The amount of short-term debt excluded from the current section of the balance sheet.
**DISCUSSION:** If an enterprise intends to refinance short-term obligations on a long-term basis and demonstrates an ability to consummate the refinancing, the obligations should be excluded from current liabilities and classified as noncurrent (SFAS 6, *Classification of Short-Term Obligations Expected to Be Refinanced*). The ability to consummate the refinancing may be demonstrated by a post-balance-sheet-date issuance of a long-term obligation or equity securities, or by entering into a financing agreement that meets certain criteria. These criteria are that the agreement does not expire within 1 year, it is noncancelable by the lender, no violation of the agreement exists at the balance sheet date, and the lender is financially capable of honoring the agreement.
Answer (A) is incorrect because the amount excluded cannot exceed the amount available for refinancing. Answer (C) is incorrect because SFAS 6 has no provision for adjustments or reductions. Answer (D) is incorrect because the refinancing need not have occurred if the firm intends and demonstrates an ability to consummate such refinancing.

**15.** When treasury stock is accounted for at cost, the cost is reported on the balance sheet as a(n)

A. Asset.

B. Reduction of retained earnings.

C. Reduction of additional paid-in-capital.

D. Unallocated reduction of equity.

Answer (D) is correct. *(CMA, adapted)*
**REQUIRED:** The reporting of treasury stock.
**DISCUSSION:** Treasury stock is a corporation's own stock that has been reacquired but not retired. The entry to record the acquisition of treasury stock accounted for at cost is to debit a contra equity account and to credit cash. In the balance sheet, treasury stock recorded at cost is subtracted from the total of the capital stock balances, additional paid-in capital, retained earnings, and accumulated other comprehensive income. It is not allocated. If treasury stock is recorded at par, it is a direct reduction of common stock, not total equity.
Answer (A) is incorrect because treasury stock is not an asset. A corporation cannot own itself. Answer (B) is incorrect because treasury stock accounted for at cost is subtracted from the total of the other equity accounts. Answer (C) is incorrect because treasury stock accounted for at cost is subtracted from the total of the other equity accounts.

**16.** When a company was in the process of closing its original store, no accounting notice of the liquidation values of the discontinued store's assets were considered in the accounting records. The accountant did not make any entries until the assets were disposed of because the company was still a going concern. However, when liquidation of a business is foreseen but not yet accomplished, a different financial statement is prepared. This statement is known as the

A. Statement of liquidation.

B. Charge and discharge statement.

C. Statement of realization.

D. Statement of affairs.

Answer (D) is correct. *(CMA, adapted)*
**REQUIRED:** The additional financial statement that is prepared when a company is in the process of liquidation.
**DISCUSSION:** A statement of affairs is prepared for a company in the process of liquidation. It reflects the financial condition of the company on a going out of business rather than a going concern basis. Liquidation value instead of historical cost is used to value assets. Moreover, assets are not classified as current or noncurrent but according to the extent to which they are subject to secured claims. Liabilities are shown based on categories of creditors, and shareholders' equity may become shareholders' deficiency because a liquidating company may have a negative net worth.
Answer (A) is incorrect because the statement prepared by the trustee in bankruptcy to reconcile the book amounts to his/her administration of the estate is the statement of realization and liquidation. Answer (B) is incorrect because a charge and discharge statement is prepared by the personal representative of a decedent's estate. Answer (C) is incorrect because the statement prepared by the trustee in bankruptcy to reconcile the book amounts to his/her administration of the estate is the statement of realization and liquidation.

**17.** Felicity Company has the following accounts included in its December 31 trial balance:

| | |
|---|---:|
| Treasury stock | $ 48,000 |
| Retained earnings | 141,000 |
| Trademarks | 32,000 |
| Preferred stock | 175,000 |
| Common stock | 50,000 |
| Deferred income taxes | 85,000 |
| Additional paid-in capital | 196,000 |
| Accumulated depreciation | 16,000 |

What amount of equity will be reported on Felicity's December 31 statement of financial position?

A. $373,000

B. $514,000

C. $562,000

D. $610,000

Answer (B) is correct. *(Publisher)*
**REQUIRED:** The total equity.
**DISCUSSION:** Equity consists of contributed capital, retained earnings, and other comprehensive income. Equity accounts may therefore include retained earnings, preferred stock, common stock, and additional paid-in capital. Moreover, treasury stock is a contra account in the equity section of the balance sheet. The total is $514,000 ($141,000 + $175,000 + $50,000 + $196,000 − $48,000 of treasury stock).
Answer (A) is incorrect because retained earnings should be included in equity. Answer (C) is incorrect because $562,000 results from a failure to deduct treasury stock. Answer (D) is incorrect because treasury stock should be deducted from, not added to, equity.

## 12.3 Statement of Income and Statement of Retained Earnings

**18.** An income statement for a business prepared under the current operating performance concept would include only the recurring earnings from its normal operations and

A. No other items.

B. Any extraordinary items.

C. Any prior-period adjustments.

D. Any gains or losses from extinguishment of debt.

Answer (A) is correct. *(CMA, adapted)*
**REQUIRED:** The items included in a current operating performance income statement.
**DISCUSSION:** The current operating performance concept emphasizes the ordinary, normal, recurring operations of the entity during the current period. Inclusion of extraordinary items or prior-period adjustments is believed to impair the significance of net income. The current operating performance concept is not consistent with GAAP.
Answer (B) is incorrect because extraordinary items are excluded under the current operating performance concept. Answer (C) is incorrect because prior-period adjustments are excluded under the current operating performance concept. Answer (D) is incorrect because gains and losses from extinguishment of debt are extraordinary.

**19.** The major distinction between the multiple-step and single-step income statement formats is the separation of

A. Operating and nonoperating data.

B. Income tax expense and administrative expenses.

C. Cost of goods sold expense and administrative expenses.

D. The effect on income taxes due to extraordinary items and the effect on income taxes due to income before extraordinary items.

Answer (A) is correct. *(CIA, adapted)*
**REQUIRED:** The major distinction between the multiple-step and single-step income statement formats.
**DISCUSSION:** Within the income from continuing operations classification, the single-step income statement provides one grouping for revenue items and one for expense items. The single-step is the one subtraction necessary to arrive at income from continuing operations prior to the effect of income taxes. In contrast, the multiple-step income statement matches operating revenues and expenses separately from nonoperating items. This format emphasizes subtotals such as gross margin, operating income, and nonoperating income within presentation of income from continuing operations.

**20.** In a multiple-step income statement for a retail company, all of the following are included in the operating section except

A. Sales.

B. Cost of goods sold.

C. Dividend revenue.

D. Administrative and selling expenses.

Answer (C) is correct. *(CMA, adapted)*
**REQUIRED:** The item excluded from the operating section of a multiple-step income statement of a retailer.
**DISCUSSION:** The operating section of a retailer's income statement includes all revenues and costs necessary for the operation of the retail establishment, e.g., sales, cost of goods sold, administrative expenses, and selling expenses. Dividend revenue, however, is classified under other revenues. In a statement of cash flows, cash dividends received are considered an operating cash flow.
Answer (A) is incorrect because sales is part of the normal operations of a retailer. Answer (B) is incorrect because cost of goods sold is part of the normal operations of a retailer. Answer (D) is incorrect because administrative and selling expenses are part of the normal operations of a retailer.

**21.** In Hopkins Co.'s Year 3 single-step income statement, the section titled *Revenues* consisted of the following:

| | | |
|---|---|---|
| Net sales revenue | | $187,000 |
| Results from discontinued operations: | | |
|   Income from operations of | | |
|    component (including gain on | | |
|    disposal of $21,600) | $18,000 | |
|    Income tax | (6,000) | 12,000 |
| Interest revenue | | 10,200 |
| Gain on sale of equipment | | 4,700 |
| Cumulative change in Year 1 and Year 2 | | |
|   income due to change in depreciation | | |
|   method (net of $750 tax effect) | | 1,500 |
| Total revenues | | $215,400 |

In the revenues section of the Year 3 income statement, Hopkins should have reported total revenues of

A. $217,800

B. $215,400

C. $203,700

D. $201,900

Answer (D) is correct. *(Publisher)*
**REQUIRED:** The total revenues under GAAP.
**DISCUSSION:** Revenue is a component of income from continuing operations. Results of discontinued operations is a classification in the income statement separate from continuing operations. The cumulative effect of a change in accounting principle is not reported in the income statement. Hence, total revenues were $201,900 ($215,400 – $12,000 results from discontinued operations – $1,500 cumulative-effect type change). Alternatively, total revenues consist of net sales of $187,000, plus interest revenue of $10,200, plus gain on sale of equipment (which is not an extraordinary item) of $4,700.
Answer (A) is incorrect because $217,800 equals $215,400 reported total revenues, plus the $2,400 loss from operations of the segment. Answer (B) is incorrect because $215,400 improperly includes the results from discontinued operations and the cumulative-effect type change. Answer (C) is incorrect because $203,700 improperly subtracts interest revenue and does not adjust for the results from discontinued operations.

**22.** When reporting extraordinary items,

A. Each item (net of tax) is presented on the face of the income statement separately as a component of net income for the period.

B. Each item is presented exclusive of any related income tax.

C. Each item is presented as an unusual item within income from continuing operations.

D. All extraordinary gains or losses that occur in a period are summarized as total gains and total losses, then offset to present the net extraordinary gain or loss.

Answer (A) is correct. *(CMA, adapted)*
**REQUIRED:** The true statement about the reporting of extraordinary items.
**DISCUSSION:** Extraordinary items should be presented net of tax after discontinued operations. APB 30 states, "Descriptive captions and the amounts for individual extraordinary events or transactions should be presented, preferably on the face of the income statement, if practicable; otherwise, disclosure in related notes is acceptable."
Answer (B) is incorrect because extraordinary items are to be reported net of the related tax effect. Answer (C) is incorrect because extraordinary items are not reported in the continuing operations section of the income statement. Answer (D) is incorrect because each extraordinary item is to be reported separately.

**23.** Which one of the following items is included in the determination of income from continuing operations?

A. Discontinued operations.

B. Extraordinary loss.

C. Cumulative effect of a change in an accounting principle.

D. Unusual loss from a write-down of inventory.

Answer (D) is correct. *(CMA, adapted)*
REQUIRED: The item included in the computation of income from continuing operations.
DISCUSSION: APB 30 specifies certain items that ordinarily are not to be treated as extraordinary gains and losses. Rather, they are included in the determination of income from continuing operations. These gains and losses include those from write-downs of receivables and inventories, translation of foreign currency amounts, disposal of a business segment, sale of productive assets, strikes, and accruals on long-term contracts. A write-down of inventory is therefore included in the computation of income from continuing operations.
Answer (A) is incorrect because discontinued operations are reported separately from income from continuing operations. Answer (B) is incorrect because extraordinary loss is reported separately from income from continuing operations. Answer (C) is incorrect because a cumulative effect of a change in an accounting principle is not reported in the income statement.

**24.** SFAS 128, *Earnings per Share*, requires which of the following policies regarding presentation of extraordinary items?

A. Earnings-per-share amounts should be presented in a separate schedule.

B. Extraordinary items should be presented as an aggregate amount.

C. Income taxes applicable to extraordinary items should be presented in a separate schedule.

D. Earnings-per-share amounts should be presented on the face of the income statement or in the notes.

Answer (D) is correct. *(Publisher)*
REQUIRED: The presentation of EPS amounts for extraordinary items.
DISCUSSION: Basic and diluted per-share amounts for extraordinary items are presented either on the face of the income statement or in the related notes. Prior to the issuance of SFAS 128, APB 15 required presentation of EPS amounts for income before extraordinary items and net income on the face of the income statement.
Answer (A) is incorrect because EPS amounts may be presented either on the face of the income statement or in the notes. Answer (B) is incorrect because extraordinary items should be presented individually, rather than in the aggregate, and on the face of the income statement, if practicable; otherwise, disclosure in related notes is acceptable (APB 30). Answer (C) is incorrect because income taxes applicable to extraordinary items should be presented on the face of the income statement or in a related note.

**25.** Brett Corporation had retained earnings of $529,000 at January 1 of the current year. Net income for the year was $2,496,000, and cash dividends of $750,000 were declared and paid. Another $50,000 of dividends were declared late in December, but were unpaid at year-end. Brett's ending balance of its statement of retained earnings is

A. $1,696,000

B. $2,225,000

C. $2,275,000

D. $3,025,000

Answer (B) is correct. *(Publisher)*
REQUIRED: The year-end balance of retained earnings.
DISCUSSION: Dividends declared but not paid reduce retained earnings. Thus, the year-end balance of retained earnings is calculated as follows:

| | | |
|---|---|---|
| January 1 balance | | $ 529,000 |
| Net income | | 2,496,000 |
| Retained earnings available | | $3,025,000 |
| Dividends | $750,000 | |
| | 50,000 | (800,000) |
| Year-end balance | | $2,225,000 |

Answer (A) is incorrect because $1,696,000 does not include the beginning balance. Answer (C) is incorrect because $2,275,000 results from a failure to deduct the dividend that was unpaid; such a dividend would be a liability of the corporation. Answer (D) is incorrect because $3,025,000 results from a failure to deduct dividends.

**26.** The changes in account balances of the Samson Corporation during the year are presented below:

|  | Increase |
|---|---|
| Assets | $356,000 |
| Liabilities | 108,000 |
| Capital stock | 240,000 |
| Additional paid-in capital | 24,000 |

Assuming there are no charges to retained earnings other than for a dividend payment of $52,000, the net income for the year should be

A. $16,000

B. $36,000

C. $52,000

D. $68,000

Answer (B) is correct. *(Publisher)*
REQUIRED: The net income for the year given the increase in assets, liabilities, and paid-in capital.
DISCUSSION: To calculate net income, the dividend payment ($52,000) should be added to the increase in assets ($356,000). The excess of this sum ($408,000) over the increase in liabilities ($108,000) gives the total increase in owners' equity ($300,000). The excess of this amount over the combined increases in the capital accounts ($264,000) equals the increase in retained earnings ($36,000) arising from net income.
Answer (A) is incorrect because $16,000 is the excess of the sum of the increases in the capital accounts other than retained earnings over the increase in net assets. Answer (C) is incorrect because $52,000 is the dividend. Answer (D) is incorrect because $68,000 equals the sum of the dividend and the excess of the sum of the increases in the capital accounts other than retained earnings over the increase in net assets.

**27.** When a business enterprise provides a full set of general-purpose financial statements reporting financial position, results of operations, and cash flows, comprehensive income and its components should

A. Appear as a part of discontinued operations, extraordinary items, and cumulative effect of a change in accounting principle.

B. Be reported net of related income tax effects, in total and individually.

C. Appear in a supplemental schedule in the notes to the financial statements.

D. Be displayed in a financial statement that has the same prominence as other financial statements.

Answer (D) is correct. *(CPA, adapted)*
REQUIRED: The presentation of comprehensive income and its components.
DISCUSSION: If an enterprise that reports a full set of financial statements has items of other comprehensive income (OCI), it must display comprehensive income and its components in a financial statement having the same prominence as the other statements included in the full set. No particular format is required, but net income must be displayed as a component of comprehensive income in that statement.
Answer (A) is incorrect because discontinued operations and extraordinary items are components of net income, which is itself a component of comprehensive income. The cumulative effect of a change in accounting principle is not reported in the income statement. Answer (B) is incorrect because the components of OCI are displayed either (1) net of related tax effects or (2) before the related tax effects with one amount shown for the aggregate tax effect related to the total of OCI. No amount is displayed for the tax effect related to total comprehensive income. Answer (C) is incorrect because comprehensive income and its components must be displayed in a financial statement given the same prominence as other financial statements included in the full set of financial statements.

---

Questions 28 through 30 are based on the following information. The Horatio Company's beginning and ending inventories for the fiscal year ended September 30, year 2 are

|  | Oct. 1, year 1 | Sept. 30, year 2 |
|---|---|---|
| Materials | $30,000 | $44,000 |
| Work-in-process (WIP) | 80,000 | 70,000 |
| Finished goods | 16,000 | 24,000 |

Production data for the fiscal year ended September 30, year 2 are

| Materials purchased | $160,000 |
|---|---|
| Purchase discounts taken | 2,000 |
| Direct labor | 200,000 |
| Manufacturing overhead | 150,000 |

---

**28.** The cost of goods manufactured (CGM) for the year ended September 30, year 2 is

A. $484,000

B. $494,000

C. $504,000

D. $518,000

Answer (C) is correct. *(Publisher)*
REQUIRED: The CGM.
DISCUSSION: CGM equals all manufacturing costs incurred during the period, plus BWIP, minus EWIP. Materials used equals $144,000 ($30,000 BI + $160,000 purchased – $2,000 discounts – $44,000 EI). Thus, manufacturing costs incurred during the period equal $494,000 ($144,000 materials used + $200,000 DL + $150,000 OH), and CGM equals $504,000 ($494,000 + $80,000 BWIP – $70,000 EWIP).
Answer (A) is incorrect because $484,000 results from reversing the effect of the change in WIP. Answer (B) is incorrect because $494,000 does not consider the change in WIP. Answer (D) is incorrect because $518,000 does not consider the change in materials inventory.

**29.** The cost of goods sold (CGS) for the year ended September 30, year 2 is

   A. $500,000

   B. $504,000

   C. $508,000

   D. $496,000

Answer (D) is correct. *(Publisher)*
**REQUIRED:** The CGS.
**DISCUSSION:** CGS equals CGM adjusted for the change in finished goods inventory. CGM equals all manufacturing costs incurred during the period, plus BWIP, minus EWIP. Materials used equals $144,000 ($30,000 BI + $160,000 purchased – $2,000 discounts – $44,000 EI). Thus, manufacturing costs incurred during the period equal $494,000 ($144,000 materials used + $200,000 DL + $150,000 OH), and CGM equals $504,000 ($494,000 + $80,000 BWIP – $70,000 EWIP). Accordingly, CGS is $496,000 ($504,000 CGM + $16,000 BFG – $24,000 EFG).
    Answer (A) is incorrect because $500,000 results from reversing the treatment of purchase discounts. Answer (B) is incorrect because $504,000 is the CGM. Answer (C) is incorrect because $508,000 results from assuming that no beginning or ending inventories of materials, WIP, or finished goods existed.

**30.** The total value of inventory to be reported on the balance sheet at September 30, year 2 is

   A. $44,000

   B. $70,000

   C. $24,000

   D. $138,000

Answer (D) is correct. *(Publisher)*
**REQUIRED:** The total year-end inventory.
**DISCUSSION:** The ending inventory consists of three elements: materials of $44,000, WIP of $70,000, and finished goods of $24,000, a total of $138,000.
    Answer (A) is incorrect because $44,000 is the ending materials inventory. Answer (B) is incorrect because $70,000 is the EWIP. Answer (C) is incorrect because $24,000 is the finished goods inventory.

**31.** Which of the following items should be reported as a component of other comprehensive income (OCI)?

   A. Unrealized loss on an investment classified as a trading security.

   B. Unrealized loss on an investment classified as an available-for-sale security.

   C. Realized loss on an investment classified as an available-for-sale security.

   D. Cumulative effect of a change in accounting principle.

Answer (B) is correct. *(Publisher)*
**REQUIRED:** The item properly classified as a component of OCI.
**DISCUSSION:** Comprehensive income includes all changes in equity (net assets) of a business entity except those changes resulting from investments by owners and distributions to owners. Comprehensive income includes two major categories: net income and OCI. Net income includes the results of operations classified as income from continuing operations, discontinued operations, and extraordinary items. Components of comprehensive income not included in the determination of net income are included in OCI; for example, unrealized gains and losses on available-for-sale securities (except those that are hedged items in a fair value hedge).
    Answer (A) is incorrect because unrealized gains and losses on trading securities are components of net income. Answer (C) is incorrect because realized gains and losses on available-for-sale securities are components of net income. Answer (D) is incorrect because the cumulative effect of a change in accounting principle is not reported in the income statement.

**32.** On December 31, year 3, the last day of its fiscal year, Roark Company purchased 2,000 shares of available-for-sale securities at a price of $10 per share. These securities had a fair value of $24,000 and $30,000 on December 31, year 4 and December 31, year 5, respectively. No dividends were paid, and all of the securities were sold on December 31, year 5. OCI recognizes all holding gains and losses on available-for-sale securities before recognizing realized gain. If OCI's tax rate is 25%, the total after-tax effect on comprehensive income in year 5 of the foregoing transactions was

A. $10,000

B. $7,500

C. $4,500

D. $3,000

Answer (C) is correct. *(Publisher)*
**REQUIRED:** The total after-tax effect on comprehensive income of a sale of available-for-sale securities in year 5.
**DISCUSSION:** Roark paid $20,000 for the shares. Thus, its after-tax holding gain in year 4 was $3,000 [($24,000 fair value – $20,000) × (1.0 – .25 tax rate)]. Because the shares were classified as available-for-sale, the $3,000 holding gain was included in OCI, not net income. Roark's after-tax holding gain in year 5 was $4,500 [($30,000 – $24,000) × (1.0 – .25)]. Moreover, its realized after-tax gain in year 5 included in net income was $7,500 [($30,000 – $20,000) × (1.0 – .25)]. The recognition of these amounts in year 4 and year 5 necessitates a reclassification adjustment to prevent double counting. This adjustment to OCI is equal to, but opposite in sign from, the realized gain recognized in net income. Accordingly, the after-tax effect on comprehensive income in year 5 of the sale of the available-for-sale securities is $4,500 ($7,500 realized gain + $4,500 holding gain – $7,500 reclassification adjustment).
Answer (A) is incorrect because $10,000 is the pre-tax realized gain recognized in net income in year 5. Answer (B) is incorrect because $7,500 is the amount of the reclassification adjustment and the realized after-tax gain. Answer (D) is incorrect because $3,000 is the after-tax holding gain in year 4.

## 12.4 Statement of Cash Flows

**33.** When preparing the statement of cash flows, companies are required to report separately as operating cash flows all of the following except

A. Interest received on investments in bonds.

B. Interest paid on the company's bonds.

C. Cash collected from customers.

D. Cash dividends paid on the company's stock.

Answer (D) is correct. *(CMA, adapted)*
**REQUIRED:** The item not reported separately as an operating cash flow on a statement of cash flows.
**DISCUSSION:** Under SFAS 95, a statement of cash flows should report as operating activities all transactions and other events not classified as investing or financing activities. In general, the cash flows from transactions and other events that enter into the determination of income are to be classified as operating. Cash receipts from sales of goods and services, from interest on loans, and from dividends on equity securities are from operating activities. Cash payments to suppliers for inventory; to employees for wages; to other suppliers and employees for other goods and services; to governments for taxes, duties, fines, and fees; and to lenders for interest are also from operating activities. However, distributions to owners (cash dividends on a company's own stock) are cash flows from financing, not operating, activities.
Answer (A) is incorrect because interest received from investments is an operating cash flow. Answer (B) is incorrect because interest paid on bonds is an operating cash flow. Answer (C) is incorrect because customer collections is an operating cash flow.

**34.** A statement of cash flows is intended to help users of financial statements

A. Evaluate a firm's liquidity, solvency, and financial flexibility.

B. Evaluate a firm's economic resources and obligations.

C. Determine a firm's components of income from operations.

D. Determine whether insiders have sold or purchased the firm's stock.

Answer (A) is correct. *(CMA, adapted)*
**REQUIRED:** The reason companies are required to prepare a statement of cash flows.
**DISCUSSION:** The primary purpose of a statement of cash flows is to provide information about the cash receipts and payments of an entity during a period. If used with information in the other financial statements, the statement of cash flows should help users to assess the entity's ability to generate positive future net cash flows (liquidity), its ability to meet obligations (solvency) and pay dividends, the need for external financing, the reasons for differences between income and cash receipts and payments, and the cash and noncash aspects of the investing and financing activities.
Answer (B) is incorrect because the statement of cash flows deals with only one resource -- cash. Answer (C) is incorrect because the income statement shows the components of income from operations. Answer (D) is incorrect because the identity of stock buyers and sellers is not shown.

**35.** A financial statement includes all of the following items: net income, depreciation, operating activities, and financing activities. What financial statement is this?

A. Balance sheet.

B. Income statement.

C. Statement of cash flows.

D. Statement of changes in equity.

Answer (C) is correct. *(CIA, adapted)*
**REQUIRED:** The financial statement that includes net income, depreciation, operating activities, and financing activities.
**DISCUSSION:** A statement of cash flows is a required financial statement. Its primary purpose is to provide information about cash receipts and payments by reporting the cash effects of an enterprise's operating, investing, and financing activities. Related disclosures report the effects of noncash investing and financing activities. Because the statement or a separate schedule reconciles net income and net operating cash flow, depreciation, a noncash expense, is included in the presentation.
Answer (A) is incorrect because the balance sheet does not include periodic net income or depreciation expense. Answer (B) is incorrect because the income statement does not have captions for operating and financing activities. Answer (D) is incorrect because equity does not include captions for operating and investing activities, depreciation, and net income.

**36.** Which of the following items is specifically included in the body of a statement of cash flows?

A. Operating and nonoperating cash flow information.

B. Conversion of debt to equity.

C. Acquiring an asset through a capital lease.

D. Purchasing a building by giving a mortgage to the seller.

Answer (A) is correct. *(CMA, adapted)*
**REQUIRED:** The information specifically included within the body of a statement of cash flows.
**DISCUSSION:** SFAS 95 excludes all noncash transactions from the body of the statement of cash flows to avoid undue complexity and detraction from the objective of providing information about cash flows. Information about all noncash financing and investing activities affecting recognized assets and liabilities shall be reported in related disclosures.

**37.** A statement of cash flows is to be presented in general purpose external financial statements by which of the following?

A. Publicly held business enterprises only.

B. Privately held business enterprises only.

C. All business enterprises.

D. All business enterprises and not-for-profit organizations.

Answer (D) is correct. *(Publisher)*
**REQUIRED:** The entities required to present a statement of cash flows.
**DISCUSSION:** SFAS 95 as amended by SFAS 117 requires a statement of cash flows as part of a full set of financial statements of all business entities (both publicly held and privately held) and not-for-profit organizations. Defined benefit pension plans, certain other employee benefit plans, and certain highly liquid investment companies, however, are exempted from this requirement by SFAS 102.

**38.** Select the combination below that explains the impact of credit card interest incurred and paid during the period on (1) equity on the balance sheet and (2) the statement of cash flows.

| | (1) Effect of Equity on Balance Sheet | (2) Reflected on Statement of Cash Flows as a(n) |
|---|---|---|
| A. | Decrease | Financing outflow |
| B. | Decrease | Operating outflow |
| C. | No effect | Financing outflow |
| D. | No effect | Operating outflow |

Answer (B) is correct. *(CIA, adapted)*
**REQUIRED:** The effect of interest expense on the balance sheet and cash flow statement.
**DISCUSSION:** Credit card interest incurred is classified as interest expense on the income statement, which in turn reduces equity on the balance sheet by reducing retained earnings. Cash payments to lenders and other creditors for interest, e.g., credit card interest payments, are to be classified on the statement of cash flows as an outflow of cash from operating activities.

**39.** Which of the following related cash transactions should be disclosed as gross amounts of cash receipts and cash payments rather than as net amounts?

A. The purchase and sale of fixed assets.

B. Changes in cash and cash equivalents.

C. The purchase and sale of federal funds.

D. The receipts and payments from demand deposits.

Answer (A) is correct. *(Publisher)*
**REQUIRED:** The related receipts and payments that should be classified as gross amounts.
**DISCUSSION:** In general, cash inflows and cash outflows from operating, investing, and financing activities should be reported separately at gross amounts in a statement of cash flows. In certain instances, however, the net amount of related cash receipts and cash payments may provide sufficient information about particular classes of cash flows. For example, SFAS 104 permits banks, saving institutions, and credit unions to report net amounts for (1) the placement and withdrawal of deposits with other financial institutions, (2) the acceptance and repayment of time deposits, and (3) the making of loans to customers and the collection of principal.
Answer (B) is incorrect because changes in cash and cash equivalents are classes of related cash flows that may be presented as net amounts. Answer (C) is incorrect because the purchase and sale of federal funds is a class of related cash flows that may be presented as net amounts. Answer (D) is incorrect because the receipts and payments from demand deposits are classes of related cash flows that may be presented as net amounts.

**40.** The following information was taken from the accounting records of Oak Corporation for the year ended December 31:

| | |
|---|---:|
| Proceeds from issuance of preferred stock | $4,000,000 |
| Dividends paid on preferred stock | 400,000 |
| Bonds payable converted to common stock | 2,000,000 |
| Payment for purchase of machinery | 500,000 |
| Proceeds from sale of plant building | 1,200,000 |
| 2% stock dividend on common stock | 300,000 |
| Gain on sale of plant building | 200,000 |

The net cash flows from investing and financing activities that should be presented on Oak's statement of cash flows for the year ended December 31 are, respectively,

A. $700,000 and $3,600,000.

B. $700,000 and $3,900,000.

C. $900,000 and $3,900,000.

D. $900,000 and $3,600,000.

Answer (A) is correct. *(CMA, adapted)*
**REQUIRED:** The respective net cash flows from investing and financing activities.
**DISCUSSION:** Investing activities include the lending of money and the collecting of those loans, and the acquisition, sale, or other disposal of securities that are not cash equivalents and of productive assets that are expected to generate revenue over a long period of time. Financing activities include (1) the issuance of stock, (2) the payment of dividends, (3) treasury stock transactions, (4) the issuance of debt, (5) the receipt of donor-restricted resources to be used for long-term purposes, and (6) the repayment or other settlement of debt obligations. Investing activities would include the purchase of machinery and the sale of a building. The net inflow from these activities is $700,000 ($1,200,000 – $500,000). Financing activities include the issuance of preferred stock and the payment of dividends. The net inflow is $3,600,000 ($4,000,000 – $400,000). The conversion of bonds into common stock and the stock dividend do not affect cash.
Answer (B) is incorrect because the stock dividend has no effect on cash flows from financing activities. Answer (C) is incorrect because the gain on the sale of the building is double counted in determining the net cash flow from investing activities. Answer (D) is incorrect because the gain on the sale of the building is double counted in determining the net cash flow from investing activities.

**41.** In the statement of cash flows, the payment of common share dividends appears in the <List A> activities section as a <List B> of cash.

| | List A | List B |
|---|---|---|
| A. | Operating | Source |
| B. | Financing | Use |
| C. | Investing | Use |
| D. | Investing | Source |

Answer (B) is correct. *(CIA, adapted)*
**REQUIRED:** The treatment of cash dividends in a statement of cash flows.
**DISCUSSION:** Financing activities include, among other things, obtaining resources from owners and providing them with a return on, and a return of, their investment. Consequently, the payment of cash dividends to providers of common equity financing is a use of cash that appears in the financing section of the statement of cash flows.

**42.** Frazier Company reported current net income of $161,000. During the year, accounts receivable increased by $14,000 and accounts payable increased by $10,500. Inventories declined by $8,000. Depreciation expense was $40,000. Net cash provided by operating activities is

A. $165,000

B. $189,500

C. $205,500

D. $212,500

Answer (C) is correct. *(Publisher)*
**REQUIRED:** The net cash provided by operating activities.
**DISCUSSION:** The net income of $161,000 must be adjusted by noncash expenses (such as depreciation) and the amount of changes in current assets. The calculation would be:

| | |
|---|---:|
| Net income | $161,000 |
| Depreciation expense | 40,000 |
| Increase in receivables | (14,000) |
| Increase in payables | 10,500 |
| Decrease in inventories | 8,000 |
| | $205,500 |

Answer (A) is incorrect because $165,000 results from a failure to add back depreciation -- a noncash expense. Answer (B) is incorrect because $189,500 results from deducting the inventory change rather than adding it. Answer (D) is incorrect because $212,500 results from reversing the treatment of receivables and payables.

**43.** With respect to the content and form of the statement of cash flows,

A. The pronouncements covering the cash flow statement encourage the use of the indirect method.

B. The indirect method adjusts ending retained earnings to reconcile it to net cash flows from operations.

C. The direct method of reporting cash flows from operating activities includes disclosing the major classes of gross cash receipts and gross cash payments.

D. The reconciliation of the net income to net operating cash flow need not be presented when using the direct method.

Answer (C) is correct. *(CMA, adapted)*
**REQUIRED:** The true statement about the content and form of the statement of cash flows.
**DISCUSSION:** SFAS 95 encourages use of the direct method of reporting major classes of operating cash receipts and payments, but the indirect method may be used. The minimum disclosures of operating cash flows under the direct method are cash collected from customers, interest and dividends received, other operating cash receipts, cash paid to employees and other suppliers of goods or services, interest paid, income taxes paid, and other operating cash payments.
Answer (A) is incorrect because SFAS 95 encourages use of the direct method. Answer (B) is incorrect because the indirect method reconciles net income with the net cash flow from operations. Answer (D) is incorrect because the reconciliation is required regardless of the method used.

**44.** The statement of cash flows may be presented in either a direct or an indirect (reconciliation) format. In which of these formats would cash collected from customers be presented as a gross amount?

| | Direct | Indirect |
|---|---|---|
| A. | No | No |
| B. | No | Yes |
| C. | Yes | Yes |
| D. | Yes | No |

Answer (D) is correct. *(R. O'Keefe)*
**REQUIRED:** The format in which cash collected from customers would be presented as a gross amount.
**DISCUSSION:** The statement of cash flows may report cash flows from operating activities in either an indirect (reconciliation) or a direct format. The direct format reports the major classes of operating cash receipts and cash payments as gross amounts. The indirect presentation reconciles net income to the same amount of net cash flow from operations that would be determined in accordance with the direct method. To arrive at net operating cash flow, the indirect method adjusts net income by removing the effects of (1) all deferrals of past operating cash receipts and payments, (2) all accruals of expected future operating cash receipts and payments, (3) all financing and investing activities, and (4) all noncash operating transactions.

Questions 45 through 47 are based on the following information.

Royce Company had the following transactions during the fiscal year ended December 31, year 2:

- Accounts receivable decreased from $115,000 on December 31, year 1 to $100,000 on December 31, year 2.
- Royce's board of directors declared dividends on December 31, year 2 of $.05 per share on the 2.8 million shares outstanding, payable to shareholders of record on January 31, year 3. The company did not declare or pay dividends for fiscal year 1.

- Sold a truck with a net book value of $7,000 for $5,000 cash, reporting a loss of $2,000.
- Paid interest to bondholders of $780,000.
- The cash balance was $106,000 on December 31, year 1 and $284,000 on December 31, year 2.

**45.** Royce Company uses the direct method to prepare its statement of cash flows at December 31, year 2. The interest paid to bondholders is reported in the

- A. Financing section, as a use or outflow of cash.
- B. Operating section, as a use or outflow of cash.
- C. Investing section, as a use or outflow of cash.
- D. Debt section, as a use or outflow of cash.

Answer (B) is correct. *(CMA, adapted)*
**REQUIRED:** The proper reporting of interest paid.
**DISCUSSION:** Payment of interest on debt is considered a cash outflow from an operating activity, although repayment of debt principal is a financing activity.
Answer (A) is incorrect because interest paid on bonds is an operating cash flow. Answer (C) is incorrect because investing activities include the lending of money and the acquisition, sale, or other disposal of securities that are not cash equivalents and the acquisition, sale, or other disposal of long-lived productive assets. Answer (D) is incorrect because SFAS 95 does not provide for a debt section.

**46.** Royce Company uses the indirect method to prepare its year 2 statement of cash flows. It reports a(n)

- A. Source or inflow of funds of $5,000 from the sale of the truck in the financing section.
- B. Use or outflow of funds of $140,000 in the financing section, representing dividends.
- C. Deduction of $15,000 in the operating section, representing the decrease in year-end accounts receivable.
- D. Addition of $2,000 in the operating section for the $2,000 loss on the sale of the truck.

Answer (D) is correct. *(CMA, adapted)*
**REQUIRED:** The correct presentation of an item on a statement of cash flows prepared under the indirect method.
**DISCUSSION:** The indirect method determines net operating cash flow by adjusting net income. Under the indirect method, the $5,000 cash inflow from the sale of the truck is shown in the investing section. A $2,000 loss was recognized and properly deducted to determine net income. This loss, however, did not require the use of cash and should be added to net income in the operating section.
Answer (A) is incorrect because, under the provisions of SFAS 95, the $5,000 inflow would be shown in the investing section. Answer (B) is incorrect because no outflow of cash dividends occurred in year 2. Answer (C) is incorrect because the decrease in receivables should be added to net income.

**47.** The total of cash provided (used) by operating activities plus cash provided (used) by investing activities plus cash provided (used) by financing activities is

- A. Cash provided of $284,000.
- B. Cash provided of $178,000.
- C. Cash used of $582,000.
- D. Equal to net income reported for fiscal year ended December 31, year 2.

Answer (B) is correct. *(CMA, adapted)*
**REQUIRED:** The net total of cash provided and used.
**DISCUSSION:** The total of cash provided (used) by the three activities (operating, investing, and financing) should equal the increase or decrease in cash for the year. During year 2, the cash balance increased from $106,000 to $284,000. Thus, the sources of cash must have exceeded the uses by $178,000.
Answer (A) is incorrect because $284,000 is the ending cash balance, not the change in the cash balance; it ignores the beginning balance. Answer (C) is incorrect because the cash balance increased during the year. Answer (D) is incorrect because net income must be adjusted for noncash expenses and other accruals and deferrals.

Questions 48 through 50 are based on the following information. Heniser Corporation engaged in the following cash transactions during the current year:

| | |
|---|---|
| Sale of land and building | $280,000 |
| Purchase of treasury stock | 140,000 |
| Purchase of land | 137,000 |
| Payment of cash dividend | 185,000 |
| Purchase of equipment | 153,000 |
| Issuance of common stock | 247,000 |
| Retirement of bonds | 200,000 |

**48.** Heniser's net cash provided (used) by investing activities is

A. $280,000

B. $(10,000)

C. $(210,000)

D. $(350,000)

Answer (B) is correct. *(Publisher)*
**REQUIRED:** The net cash provided (used) by investing activities.
**DISCUSSION:** Investing activities include making and collecting loans and acquiring and disposing of debt or equity instruments; property, plant, and equipment; and other productive assets. The calculation is

| | |
|---|---|
| Sale of land and building | $ 280,000 |
| Purchase of land | (137,000) |
| Purchase of equipment | (153,000) |
| Net cash provided (used) | $ (10,000) |

Answer (A) is incorrect because $280,000 results from a failure to deduct the uses of cash. Answer (C) is incorrect because $(210,000) results from deducting the retirement of bonds. Answer (D) is incorrect because $(350,000) results from deducting the purchase of treasury stock, which would be a financing activity, not an investing activity.

**49.** Heniser's net cash provided (used) by financing activities is

A. $247,000

B. $(78,000)

C. $(138,000)

D. $(278,000)

Answer (D) is correct. *(Publisher)*
**REQUIRED:** The net cash provided (used) by financing activities.
**DISCUSSION:** Financing activities include the issuance of stock, the payment of dividends, treasury stock transactions, and the issuance and repayment of debt. They also include receiving restricted resources that are donor-stipulated for long-term purposes. The calculation is

| | |
|---|---|
| Issuance of common stock | $ 247,000 |
| Purchase of treasury stock | (140,000) |
| Payment of cash dividend | (185,000) |
| Retirement of bonds | (200,000) |
| Cash provided (used) | $(278,000) |

Answer (A) is incorrect because $247,000 results from a failure to deduct the uses of cash. Answer (B) is incorrect because $(78,000) results from a failure to deduct the retirement of bonds. Answer (C) is incorrect because $(138,000) results from a failure to deduct for the purchase of treasury stock.

**50.** Heniser's net cash flow, assuming that it reported net cash provided by operating activities of $400,000, is

A. $112,000

B. $252,000

C. $392,000

D. $688,000

Answer (A) is correct. *(Publisher)*
**REQUIRED:** The overall net cash flow.
**DISCUSSION:** A statement of cash flows reports cash flows from operating activities, investing activities, and financing activities. Combining the $400,000 of cash provided by operating activities with the $10,000 use for investing activities and $278,000 use for financing activities results in a net source of cash of $112,000 ($400,000 – $10,000 – $278,000).

Answer (B) is incorrect because $252,000 results from a failure to deduct the purchase of treasury stock. Answer (C) is incorrect because $392,000 results from adding rather than deducting the treasury stock purchase. Answer (D) is incorrect because $688,000 results from adding the uses of cash rather than deducting them.

**51.** Depreciation expense is added to net income under the indirect method of preparing a statement of cash flows in order to

A. Report all assets at gross carrying amount.

B. Ensure depreciation has been properly reported.

C. Reverse noncash charges deducted from net income.

D. Calculate net carrying amount.

Answer (C) is correct.  *(CMA, adapted)*
**REQUIRED:** The reason depreciation expense is added to net income under the indirect method.
**DISCUSSION:** The indirect method begins with net income and then removes the effects of past deferrals of operating cash receipts and payments, accruals of expected future operating cash receipts and payments, and net income items not affecting operating cash flows (e.g., depreciation).
Answer (A) is incorrect because assets other than cash are not shown on the statement of cash flows. Answer (B) is incorrect because depreciation is recorded on the income statement. On the statement of cash flows, depreciation is added back to net income because it was previously deducted on the income statement. Answer (D) is incorrect because net carrying amount of assets is reported on the balance sheet, not the statement of cash flows.

**52.** In reconciling net income on an accrual basis to net cash provided by operating activities, what adjustment is needed to net income because of (1) an increase during the period in prepaid expenses and (2) the periodic amortization of premium on bonds payable?

|   | (1) Increase in Prepaid Expenses | (2) Amortization of Premium on Bonds Payable |
|---|---|---|
| A. | Add | Add |
| B. | Add | Deduct |
| C. | Deduct | Add |
| D. | Deduct | Deduct |

Answer (D) is correct.  *(CIA, adapted)*
**REQUIRED:** The adjustments to reconcile accrual basis net income to cash provided by operating activities.
**DISCUSSION:** An increase in prepaid expenses indicates that cash outlays for expenses exceeded the related expense incurred; thus, net income exceeded net cash provided by operations and a deduction is needed in the reconciliation. Also, the amortization of premium on bonds payable causes a reduction of interest expense but does not increase cash; therefore, net income exceeds net cash from operating activities, and a deduction is needed in the reconciliation.

**53.** In its statement of cash flows issued for the year ending June 30, Prince Company reported a net cash inflow from operating activities of $123,000. The following adjustments were included in the supplementary schedule reconciling cash flow from operating activities with net income:

| | |
|---|---|
| Depreciation | $38,000 |
| Increase in net accounts receivable | 31,000 |
| Decrease in inventory | 27,000 |
| Increase in accounts payable | 48,000 |
| Increase in interest payable | 12,000 |

Net income is

A. $29,000

B. $41,000

C. $79,000

D. $217,000

Answer (A) is correct.  *(Publisher)*
**REQUIRED:** The net income given cash flow from operating activities and reconciling adjustments.
**DISCUSSION:** To derive net income from net cash inflow from operating activities, various adjustments are necessary. The depreciation of $38,000 should be subtracted because it is a noncash item included in the determination of net income. The increase in net accounts receivable of $31,000 should be added because it signifies that sales revenue was greater than the cash collections from customers. The increase in accounts payable should be subtracted because it indicates that purchases were $48,000 greater than cash disbursements to suppliers. The second step of the transformation from cash paid to suppliers to cost of goods sold is to subtract the decrease in inventory. This change means that cost of goods sold was $27,000 greater than purchases. The $12,000 increase in interest payable should also be subtracted because it indicates that interest expense was greater than the cash paid to the lenders. Thus, the net adjustment to net cash inflow from operating activities is – $94,000 (– $38,000 + $31,000 – $27,000 – $48,000 – $12,000). Net income is $29,000 ($123,000 net cash inflow – $94,000 net adjustment).
Answer (B) is incorrect because the increase in interest payable is not subtracted. Answer (C) is incorrect because depreciation and the increase in interest payable are not subtracted. Answer (D) is incorrect because depreciation, the increase in accounts payable, the decrease in inventory, and the increase in interest payable should be subtracted, and the increase in net accounts receivable should be added.

---

Questions 54 through 56 are based on the following information.

Northern Exposure, Inc. had the following transactions during the year just ended:

| | |
|---|---:|
| Proceeds from sale of land and building | $450,000 |
| Purchase of common stock | 60,000 |
| Purchase of land for cash | 45,000 |
| Payment of cash dividend | 90,000 |
| Purchase of equipment for cash | 120,000 |
| Issuance of preferred stock | 66,000 |
| Cash repurchase of bonds | 100,000 |
| Issuance of a 5% common stock dividend | 50,000 |
| Recording of an asset and a liability for a capital lease | 100,000 |

Northern Exposure, Inc. reported current net income of $290,000. During the year, accounts receivable increased by $22,000 and accounts payable decreased by $5,500. Depreciation expense was $20,000. Inventories increased by $11,000.

---

**54.** Northern Exposure's net cash provided by operating activities is

A. $271,500

B. $293,500

C. $310,000

D. $348,500

Answer (A) is correct. *(Publisher)*
**REQUIRED:** The net cash provided by operating activities.
**DISCUSSION:** The net income of $290,000 must be adjusted for depreciation expense and changes in current assets. The calculation is

| | |
|---|---:|
| Net income | $290,000 |
| Depreciation expense | 20,000 |
| Increase in receivables | (22,000) |
| Decrease in payables | (5,500) |
| Increase in inventories | (11,000) |
| | $271,500 |

Answer (B) is incorrect because $293,500 is the result of adding the inventory increase rather than deducting it.
Answer (C) is incorrect because $310,000 occurs by failing to adjust for the changes in current assets. Answer (D) is incorrect because $348,500 is the result of reversing the treatment of all of the current asset changes.

**55.** Northern Exposure's net cash provided (used) by investing activities is

A. $185,000

B. $225,000

C. $285,000

D. $351,000

Answer (C) is correct. *(Publisher)*
**REQUIRED:** The net cash provided by investing activities.
**DISCUSSION:** Investing activities include buying and selling investments and property, plant, and equipment. However, entering into a capital lease is a noncash investing activity. The calculation is

| | |
|---|---:|
| Sale of land and building | $ 450,000 |
| Purchase of land | (45,000) |
| Purchase of equipment | (120,000) |
| | $ 285,000 |

Answer (A) is incorrect because $185,000 results from deducting the retirement of bonds, which is a financing activity. Answer (B) is incorrect because $225,0000 results from deducting the purchase of common stock, which is a financing activity. Answer (D) is incorrect because $351,000 results from adding in the issuance of preferred stock, which is a financing activity.

**56.** Northern Exposure's net cash provided (used) by financing activities is

A. $66,000

B. $(24,000)

C. $(84,000)

D. $(184,000)

Answer (D) is correct.    *(Publisher)*
   **REQUIRED:** The net cash provided (used) by financing activities.
   **DISCUSSION:** Financing activities include the issuance of stock, payment of dividends, treasury stock transactions, and the issuance and retirement of debt. They also include receiving restricted resources that are donor-stipulated to be used for long-term purposes. However, the stock dividend is a noncash financing activity. The calculation is

| | |
|---|---:|
| Issuance of preferred stock | $ 66,000 |
| Purchase of common stock | (60,000) |
| Payment of cash dividend | (90,000) |
| Repurchase of bonds | (100,000) |
| Cash provided (used) | $(184,000) |

   Answer (A) is incorrect because $66,000 results from a failure to deduct the uses of cash. Answer (B) is incorrect because $(24,000) results from a failure to deduct the purchase of common stock and the retirement of bonds. Answer (C) is incorrect because $(84,000) results from a failure to deduct the retirement of bonds.

**57.** Appalachian Outfitters, Inc., a mail order supplier of camping gear, is putting together its current year statement of cash flow. A comparison of the company's year-end balance sheet with the prior year's balance sheet shows the following changes from a year ago.

### Assets

| | |
|---|---:|
| Cash & marketable securities | $ (600) |
| Accounts receivable | 200 |
| Inventories | (100) |
| Gross fixed assets | 4,600 |
| Accumulated depreciation | (500) |
| Total | $3,600 |

### Liabilities & Net Worth

| | |
|---|---:|
| Accounts payable | $ 250 |
| Accruals | 50 |
| Long-term note | (300) |
| Long-term debt | 1,400 |
| Common stock | 0 |
| Retained earnings | 2,200 |
| Total | $3,600 |

The firm's payout ratio is 20%. During the current year, net cash provided by operations amounted to

A. $2,900

B. $3,050

C. $3,450

D. $4,050

Answer (C) is correct.    *(CMA, adapted)*
   **REQUIRED:** The net cash provided by operations.
   **DISCUSSION:** The net profit after taxes equals the change in retained earnings divided by 1 minus the dividend payout ratio, or $2,750 [$2,200 ÷ (1 − .2)]. Adjusting this amount for noncash items yields the net cash provided by operations. Depreciation is a noncash expense that should be added. To adjust for the difference between cost of goods sold and purchases, the inventory decrease is added (CGS exceeded purchases). To adjust for the difference between purchases and cash paid to suppliers, the increase in accounts payable is also added (purchases exceeded cash paid to suppliers). The increase in accounts receivable is subtracted because it indicates that accrued revenues were greater than cash collections. Finally, the increase in accrued liabilities is added. Thus, the net cash provided by operations is $3,450 ($2,750 + $500 + $100 + $250 − $200 + $50).
   Answer (A) is incorrect because $2,900 excludes the adjustments for depreciation and accruals of liabilities other than accounts payable. Answer (B) is incorrect because $3,050 excludes the adjustments for inventory, accounts payable, and accruals. Answer (D) is incorrect because $4,050 results from adding the $600 decrease in cash and marketable securities.

**58.** The following data were extracted from the financial statements of a company for the year ended December 31:

| | |
|---|---|
| Net income | $70,000 |
| Depreciation expense | 14,000 |
| Amortization of intangible assets | 1,000 |
| Decrease in accounts receivable | 2,000 |
| Increase in inventories | 9,000 |
| Increase in accounts payable | 4,000 |
| Increase in plant assets | 47,000 |
| Increase in contributed capital | 31,000 |
| Decrease in short-term notes payable | 55,000 |

There were no disposals of plant assets during the year. Based on the above, a statement of cash flows will report a net increase in cash of

A. $11,000

B. $17,000

C. $54,000

D. $69,000

Answer (A) is correct. *(CIA, adapted)*
REQUIRED: The net increase in cash as reported on the statement of cash flows.
DISCUSSION: Depreciation and amortization are noncash expenses and are added to net income. A decrease in receivables indicates that cash collections exceed sales on an accrual basis, so it is added to net income. To account for the difference between cost of goods sold (a deduction from income) and cash paid to suppliers, a two-step adjustment of net income is necessary. The difference between cost of goods sold and purchases is the change in inventory. The difference between purchases and the amount paid to suppliers is the change in accounts payable. Accordingly, the conversion of cost of goods sold to cash paid to suppliers requires deducting the inventory increase and adding the accounts payable increase. An increase in plant assets indicates an acquisition of plant assets, causing a decrease in cash, so it is deducted. An increase in contributed capital represents a cash inflow and is added to net income. A decrease in short-term notes payable is deducted from net income because it reflects a cash outflow. Thus, cash increased by $11,000 ($70,000 NI + $14,000 + $1,000 + $2,000 – $9,000 + $4,000 – $47,000 + $31,000 – $55,000).
Answer (B) is incorrect because $17,000 results from subtracting the amortization and the decrease in receivables and adding the increase in inventories. Answer (C) is incorrect because $54,000 results from adjusting net income for the increase in plant assets and the increase in contributed capital only. Answer (D) is incorrect because $69,000 results from not making the adjustments for receivables, inventories, notes payable, and accounts payable.

**59.** The net income for Cypress, Inc. was $3,000,000 for the year ended December 31. Additional information is as follows:

| | |
|---|---|
| Depreciation on fixed assets | $1,500,000 |
| Gain from cash sale of land | 200,000 |
| Increase in accounts payable | 300,000 |
| Dividends paid on preferred stock | 400,000 |

The net cash provided by operating activities in the statement of cash flows for the year ended December 31 should be

A. $4,200,000

B. $4,500,000

C. $4,600,000

D. $4,800,000

Answer (C) is correct. *(CMA, adapted)*
REQUIRED: The net cash provided by operations.
DISCUSSION: Net operating cash flow may be determined by adjusting net income. Depreciation is an expense not directly affecting cash flows that should be added back to net income. The increase in accounts payable is added to net income because it indicates that an expense has been recorded but not paid. The gain on the sale of land is an inflow from an investing, not an operating, activity and should be subtracted from net income. The dividends paid on preferred stock are cash outflows from financing, not operating, activities and do not require an adjustment. Thus, net cash flow from operations is $4,600,000 ($3,000,000 + $1,500,000 – $200,000 + $300,000).
Answer (A) is incorrect because $4,200,000 equals net cash provided by operating activities minus the $400,000 financing activity. Answer (B) is incorrect because $4,500,000 equals net income, plus depreciation. Answer (D) is incorrect because $4,800,000 equals net income, plus depreciation, plus the increase in accounts payable.

**60.** In the indirect presentation of cash flows from operating activities in a statement of cash flows, net income of a business enterprise is adjusted for noncash revenues, gains, expenses, and losses to determine the cash flows from operating activities. A reconciliation of net cash flows from operating activities to net income

A. Must be reported in the statement of cash flows.

B. Must be presented separately in a related disclosure.

C. May be either reported in the statement of cash flows or presented separately in a related disclosure.

D. Need not be presented.

Answer (C) is correct. *(Publisher)*
REQUIRED: The proper reporting of a reconciliation of net cash flows from operating activities to net income.
DISCUSSION: When an indirect presentation of net cash flows from operating activities is made, a reconciliation with net income must be provided for all noncash revenues, gains, expenses, and losses. This reconciliation may be either reported in the statement of cash flows or provided separately in related disclosures, with the statement of cash flows presenting only the net cash flows from operating activities.
Answer (A) is incorrect because the reconciliation may be presented in a related disclosure. Answer (B) is incorrect because the reconciliation may be reported in the statement of cash flows. Answer (D) is incorrect because a reconciliation must be reported in an indirect presentation of the statement of cash flows.

**61.** All of the following should be classified under the operating section in a statement of cash flows except a

A. Decrease in inventory.

B. Depreciation expense.

C. Decrease in prepaid insurance.

D. Purchase of land and building in exchange for a long-term note.

Answer (D) is correct. *(CMA, adapted)*
**REQUIRED:** The item not classified as an operating item in a statement of cash flows.
**DISCUSSION:** Operating activities include all transactions and other events not classified as investing and financing activities. Operating activities include producing and delivering goods and providing services. Cash flows from such activities are usually included in the determination of net income. However, the purchase of land and a building in exchange for a long-term note is an investing activity. Because this transaction does not affect cash, it is reported in related disclosures of noncash investing and financing activities.

**62.** Which one of the following transactions should be classified as a financing activity in a statement of cash flows?

A. Purchase of equipment.

B. Purchase of treasury stock.

C. Sale of trademarks.

D. Payment of interest on a mortgage note.

Answer (B) is correct. *(CMA, adapted)*
**REQUIRED:** The transaction classified as a financing activity.
**DISCUSSION:** Under SFAS 95, financing activities are defined to include the issuance of stock, the payment of dividends, the receipt of donor-restricted resources to be used for long-term purposes, treasury stock transactions (purchases or sales), the issuance of debt, the repayment of amounts borrowed, obtaining and paying for other resources obtained from creditors on long-term credit.
Answer (A) is incorrect because the purchase of equipment is an investing activity. Answer (C) is incorrect because the sale of trademarks, like the sale of any long-lived asset, is an investing activity. Answer (D) is incorrect because the payment of interest on a mortgage note is an operating activity.

**63.** All of the following should be classified as investing activities except

A. Cash outflows to purchase manufacturing equipment.

B. Cash inflows from the sale of bonds of other entities.

C. Cash outflows to creditors for interest.

D. Cash inflows from the sale of a manufacturing plant.

Answer (C) is correct. *(CMA, adapted)*
**REQUIRED:** The item not an investing activity.
**DISCUSSION:** Under SFAS 95, investing activities are defined to include the lending of money and the collecting of those loans. They also include the acquisition, sale, or other disposal of securities that are not cash equivalents and of productive assets that are expected to generate revenue over a long period of time. However, interest payments to creditors are cash flows from operating activities.

**64.** When using the indirect method to prepare a statement of cash flows, which one of the following should be deducted from net income when determining net cash flows from operating activities?

A. An increase in accrued liabilities.

B. Amortization of premiums on bonds payable.

C. A loss on the sale of plant assets.

D. Depreciation expense.

Answer (B) is correct. *(CMA, adapted)*
**REQUIRED:** The item deducted from net income to determine net cash flows from operating activities.
**DISCUSSION:** The indirect method reconciles the net income of a business with the net operating cash flow. The indirect method removes the effects of all past deferrals of operating cash receipts and payments, all accruals of expected future operating cash receipts and payments, and all items not affecting operating cash flows to arrive at the net cash flow from operating activities. Hence, the amortization of the premium on bonds payable is deducted from net income in the reconciliation because it represents a noncash decrease in interest expense (an increase in net income).
Answer (A) is incorrect because an increase in accrued liabilities reflects an increase in noncash expenses and is added to net income. Answer (C) is incorrect because a loss on the sale of plant assets is from an investing activity. Thus, it should be added to net income to determine net operating cash flow. Answer (D) is incorrect because depreciation is a noncash expense that should be added to net income.

**65.** Metro, Inc. reported current net income of $150,000. Changes occurred in several balance sheet accounts during the year as follows:

| | |
|---|---|
| Investment in Videogold, Inc. stock, carried on the equity basis | $5,500 increase |
| Accumulated depreciation, caused by major repair to projection equipment | 2,100 decrease |
| Premium on bonds payable | 1,400 decrease |
| Deferred income tax liability (long-term) | 1,800 increase |

In Metro's current cash flow statement, the reported net cash provided by operating activities should be

  A. $150,400

  B. $148,300

  C. $144,900

  D. $142,800

Answer (C) is correct. *(CPA, adapted)*
  **REQUIRED:** The reported net cash provided by operating activities.
  **DISCUSSION:** The increase in the equity-based investment reflects the investor's share of the investee's net income after adjustment for dividends received. Hence, this increase is a noncash revenue and should be subtracted in the reconciliation of net income to net operating cash inflow. A major repair provides benefits to more than one period and therefore should not be expensed. One method of accounting for a major repair is to charge accumulated depreciation if the useful life of the asset has been extended, with the offsetting credit to cash, a payable, etc. However, the cash outflow, if any, is from an investing activity. The item has no effect on net income and no adjustment is necessary. Amortization of bond premium means that interest expense is less than cash paid out for interest, and should be subtracted in the reconciliation. The increase in the deferred tax liability is a noncash item that reduces net income and should be added in the reconciliation. Accordingly, net cash provided by operations is $144,900 ($150,000 – $5,500 – $1,400 + $1,800).
  Answer (A) is incorrect because $150,400 results from omitting the adjustment for the equity-based investment. Answer (B) is incorrect because $148,300 results from omitting the adjustment for the equity-based investment and improperly subtracting the decrease in accumulated depreciation. Answer (D) is incorrect because $142,800 results from improperly subtracting the decrease in accumulated depreciation.

**66.** Disclosure of information about significant concentrations of credit risk is required for

  A. Most financial instruments.

  B. Financial instruments with off-balance-sheet credit risk only.

  C. Financial instruments with off-balance-sheet market risk only.

  D. Financial instruments with off-balance-sheet risk of accounting loss only.

Answer (A) is correct. *(CPA, adapted)*
  **REQUIRED:** The financial instruments for which disclosure of significant concentrations of credit risk is required.
  **DISCUSSION:** SFAS 107 requires the disclosure of information about the fair value of financial instruments, whether recognized or not (certain nonpublic entities and certain instruments, such as leases and insurance contracts, are exempt from the disclosure requirements). SFAS 107 also requires disclosure of all significant concentrations of credit risk for most financial instruments (except for obligations for deferred compensation, certain instruments of a pension plan, insurance contracts, warranty obligations and rights, and unconditional purchase obligations).

**67.** During the current year, Beck Co. purchased equipment for cash of $47,000, and sold equipment with a $10,000 carrying value for a gain of $5,000. How should these transactions be reported in Beck's statement of cash flows?

  A. Cash outflow of $32,000.

  B. Cash outflow of $42,000.

  C. Cash inflow of $5,000 and cash outflow of $47,000.

  D. Cash inflow of $15,000 and cash outflow of $47,000.

Answer (D) is correct. *(CPA, adapted)*
  **REQUIRED:** The reporting of a purchase and a sale of equipment in a statement of cash flows.
  **DISCUSSION:** Investing activities include making and collecting loans and acquiring and disposing of debt or equity instruments and property, plant, and equipment and other productive assets, that is, assets held for or used in the production of goods or services (other than the materials held in inventory). Thus, the cash effects of purchases and sales of equipment should be reported in the investing cash flows section of the statement of cash flows. Moreover, cash inflows and outflows ordinarily are not netted. They should be reported separately at gross amounts. Accordingly, Beck should report a cash inflow of $15,000 ($10,000 carrying value + $5,000 gain) for the sale of equipment and a $47,000 outflow for the purchase. In adjusting accrual-based net income to net operating cash flow, the $5,000 gain on the sale of equipment should be subtracted to prevent double counting.
  Answer (A) is incorrect because cash inflows and outflows ordinarily are not netted. Answer (B) is incorrect because an outflow of $42,000 assumes netting and a $5,000 inflow. Answer (C) is incorrect because the cash inflow was $15,000. Beck received the $10,000 carrying value and a $5,000 gain.

## 12.5 Selected Disclosures

**68.** Which of the following should be disclosed in the summary of significant accounting policies?

    A.  Valuation method used for work-in-process inventory.

    B.  Interest capitalized for the period.

    C.  Adequacy of pension plan assets in relation to vested benefits.

    D.  Depreciation charges for the period.

Answer (A) is correct. *(CIA, adapted)*
    **REQUIRED:** The item that should be disclosed in the summary of significant accounting policies.
    **DISCUSSION:** APB 22 requires that all significant accounting principles and methods that involve selection from among alternatives, are peculiar to a given industry, or are innovative or unusual applications be specifically identified and described in an initial note to the financial statements or in a separate summary. The disclosure should include accounting principles adopted and the method of applying them. This summary of significant accounting policies should not duplicate other facts to be disclosed elsewhere in the statements. The valuation method for inventory is an example of an accounting method (policy) that should be disclosed.

**69.** The accounting profession has adopted various standards to be followed when reporting inventory in the financial statements. All of the following are required to be reported in the financial statements or disclosed in notes to the financial statements except for

    A.  Inventory detail, such as raw materials, work-in-process, and finished goods.

    B.  Significant financing agreements, such as product financing arrangements and pledging of inventories.

    C.  The basis upon which inventory amounts are stated.

    D.  Unrealized profit on inventories.

Answer (D) is correct. *(CMA, adapted)*
    **REQUIRED:** The item not a required disclosure about inventory.
    **DISCUSSION:** APB 22 requires disclosure of accounting policies in a separate summary of significant policies or as the first note to the financial statements. The disclosure should specify accounting principles adopted and the method of applying those principles. Examples include inventory valuation methods; inventory details, such as the mix of finished goods, work-in-progress, and raw materials; methods used in determining costs; and any significant financing agreements, such as leases, related party transactions, product financing arrangements, firm purchase commitments, pledging of inventories, and involuntary liquidation of LIFO layers. Unrealized profit on inventories is not reported because the company usually has no assurance that the inventories will be sold.

**70.** APB 22, *Disclosure of Accounting Policies*, recommends that when financial statements are issued, information identifying the accounting policies adopted by the reporting entity should be presented as part of the financial statements. All of the following are required to be disclosed with respect to accounting policies except the

    A.  Depreciation methods used for plant assets.

    B.  Inventory valuation and costing methods.

    C.  Accounting for long-term construction contracts.

    D.  Estimated lives of depreciable assets.

Answer (D) is correct. *(CMA, adapted)*
    **REQUIRED:** The item that is not a required disclosure by APB 22.
    **DISCUSSION:** APB 22 requires disclosure of accounting policies in a separate summary of significant accounting policies or in the initial note to the financial statements. The disclosures should identify the principles followed and the methods of applying them that materially affect the statements. Moreover, the disclosures should encompass principles and methods involving a selection from acceptable alternatives, accounting principles peculiar to a particular industry, and innovative or unusual applications of GAAP. However, the disclosures should not repeat details presented elsewhere, e.g., the estimated lives of depreciable assets.

**71.** A company is required to disclose in a note to the financial statements the

    A.  Names of the members of the board of directors.

    B.  Method of inventory valuation used.

    C.  Market value of fixed assets.

    D.  Five highest paid employees.

Answer (B) is correct. *(CMA, adapted)*
    **REQUIRED:** The information that must be disclosed in the notes to financial statements.
    **DISCUSSION:** APB 22 requires disclosure of accounting policies in a separate summary of significant accounting policies or as the initial note to the financial statements. The disclosure should emphasize selection of alternative accounting principles, accounting principles peculiar to a particular situation or industry, and innovative or unusual applications. The disclosure should include accounting principles adopted and the method of applying them. Examples include depreciation and amortization methods, inventory valuation methods, consolidation methods, and franchising and leasing activities.
    Answer (A) is incorrect because the names of directors are not shown in the notes. Answer (C) is incorrect because there is no requirement to show the market value of fixed assets. Answer (D) is incorrect because the IRS requires not-for-profit organizations to identify the five highest paid employees.

**72.** Publicly traded companies must report all of the following interim financial data except

    A. Basic and diluted earnings per share for each period presented.

    B. Summarized information on sales, income taxes, extraordinary items, effect of change in accounting principles, net income, and comprehensive income.

    C. A condensed balance sheet, income statement, and statement of cash flows for each interim period presented.

    D. The disposal of a component of an entity, extraordinary items, and unusual or infrequently occurring items.

Answer (C) is correct. *(CMA, adapted)*
    **REQUIRED:** The item not a required disclosure by publicly traded companies in interim financial data.
    **DISCUSSION:** APB 28 does not require presentation of interim income statements, statements of financial position, or statements of cash flows. Although interim financial statements may be presented, minimum disclosures required when a publicly held company does issue summarized financial information include

1) Sales or gross revenues, provision for income taxes, extraordinary items, cumulative effect of changes in accounting principles, net income, and comprehensive income
2) Basic and diluted EPS
3) Seasonal revenues, costs, or expenses
4) Significant changes in estimates or provisions for income taxes
5) Disposal of a component of an entity
6) Unusual, or infrequent items
7) Contingent items
8) Changes in accounting principles or estimates
9) Significant changes in financial position
10) Certain information about reportable operating segments
11) Certain information about defined benefit pension and other postretirement benefit plans required by SFAS 132(R)

**73.** A public company has made a justifiable change in accounting principle during the second interim period of the entity's fiscal year. It is practicable to determine all of the effects of the change. In the interim report provided for that period,

    A. Net income of the first interim period need not be restated.

    B. No cumulative effect of the change is to be included in the net income of the second period.

    C. Justification for the change need not be disclosed because such disclosure will normally be included in the annual report.

    D. No disclosure is required for effects on any subsequent interim period.

Answer (B) is correct. *(Publisher)*
    **REQUIRED:** The proper treatment of a change in accounting principle in the second interim period.
    **DISCUSSION:** Per SFAS 154, a change in accounting principle in an interim period should be effected by retrospective application unless determination of the cumulative effect or the period-specific effects is impracticable. The period-specific effects of the change are adjustments to the individual periods reported. Beginning balances of the first period reported are adjusted to reflect the cumulative effects of the change on all prior periods. The impracticability exception that is available for annual financial statements may not be used for interim periods preceding the period of the change. When retrospective application to interim periods preceding the period of the change is impracticable, the change may only be made at the beginning of a subsequent year.
    Answer (A) is incorrect because net income of the first interim period must be restated. Answer (C) is incorrect because, for all changes in accounting principle, disclosure of the nature of, and justification for, the accounting change should be made in the statements of the period of change. Answer (D) is incorrect because, for each postchange interim period of the fiscal year of the change, the effect on income from continuing operations, net income, and related per-share amounts must be disclosed for that interim period.

**74.** The following information is applicable to a change in accounting principle made in the second quarter of the year from FIFO to LIFO. The firm is able to apply the new principle retrospectively. For all relevant periods, prices have risen. The effect of the change is limited to the effects on the inventory balance and income tax provisions (a 40% tax rate).

| Period | Net Income on the Basis of FIFO | Gross Effect of Change | Gross Effect Minus Income Taxes |
|---|---|---|---|
| Prior to 1st Qtr | $6,262,000 | $300,000 | $180,000 |
| 1st Qtr | 1,032,400 | 60,000 | 36,000 |
| 2nd Qtr | 1,282,400 | 60,000 | 36,000 |
| 3rd Qtr | 1,298,600 | 90,000 | 54,000 |
| 4th Qtr | 1,164,800 | 120,000 | 72,000 |

Net income for the first quarter should be restated as

A. $1,068,400

B. $1,032,400

C. $816,400

D. $996,400

**Answer (D) is correct.** *(Publisher)*
**REQUIRED:** The restated net income for the first quarter resulting from a change in an accounting principle made in the second quarter.
**DISCUSSION:** Per SFAS 154, a change in accounting principle in an interim period should be effected by retrospective application unless determination of the cumulative effect or the period-specific effects is impracticable. The period-specific effects of the change are adjustments to the individual periods reported. Beginning balances of the first period reported are adjusted to reflect the cumulative effects of the change on all prior periods. Accordingly, given the period-specific effects for the first quarter, restated net income based on retrospective application is $996,400 ($1,032,400 – $36,000 gross after-tax effect of applying the new principle). Changing to LIFO when prices are rising decreases net income.
Answer (A) is incorrect because $1,068,400 results from adding, not subtracting, the gross effect minus income taxes. Given rising prices, the change to LIFO lowers after-tax income. Answer (B) is incorrect because first quarter net income must be adjusted. Answer (C) is incorrect because $816,400 results from subtracting the cumulative after-tax effect on prior periods as well as the adjustment for the first quarter.

**75.** APB 28, *Interim Financial Reporting*, provides guidelines for interim reporting that state firms

A. May use the gross profit method for interim inventory pricing although a different inventory method is used for annual reporting.

B. Must determine income tax expense by applying progressive tax rates to income on a quarterly basis.

C. May prorate extraordinary items over four quarters.

D. Need not disclose basic and diluted earnings per share each quarter.

**Answer (A) is correct.** *(CMA, adapted)*
**REQUIRED:** The true statement about interim reporting.
**DISCUSSION:** APB 28 requires companies to use basically the same reporting methods for interim and annual financial statements. However, one exception is that the gross profit method may be used for interim inventory valuation even though it is not used for year-end statements.
Answer (B) is incorrect because tax expense is based on the expected annual effective rate after all credits and special deductions have been considered. Answer (C) is incorrect because an extraordinary item is to be reported in the interim period in which the gain or loss occurred. Answer (D) is incorrect because SFAS 128 requires that basic and diluted EPS be reported by an entity with a complex capital structure if it has publicly traded common stock or potential common stock.

**76.** When interim financial statements are prepared, they should be prepared

A. Employing the same accounting principles used for annual reports.

B. Without determining estimated income tax expense.

C. Quarterly only, not on a monthly basis.

D. Containing only operating income data.

**Answer (A) is correct.** *(CMA, adapted)*
**REQUIRED:** The provisions to be followed in the preparation of interim financial statements.
**DISCUSSION:** With few exceptions, APB 28, *Interim Financial Reporting*, specifies that interim statements are to follow the same principles as those for annual reports. APB 28 views each interim period primarily as an integral part of an annual period. Certain principles and practices used for annual reporting, however, may require modification at interim dates so interim reports may relate more closely to the results of operations for the annual period.
Answer (B) is incorrect because tax expense is to be recorded based on the expected annual effective rate after all tax-planning tools are implemented (according to FASB Interpretation No. 18). Answer (C) is incorrect because interim periods of any length may be used. Answer (D) is incorrect because APB 28 requires interim statements to be similar to annual reports, including such items as extraordinary gains and losses and the effects of changes in accounting principle. The all-inclusive income statement approach is required by GAAP for both annual and interim statements.

**77.** SFAS 47, *Disclosure of Long-Term Obligations*, resulted in identifying disclosure requirements for long-term obligations as a group. The Financial Accounting Standards Board believed that a particular group of long-term obligations frequently was not disclosed adequately. Thus, this statement was specifically addressed to

   A.  Loss contingencies.

   B.  Noncancelable purchase obligations.

   C.  Severance pay.

   D.  Pension plans.

Answer (B) is correct. *(CMA, adapted)*
   **REQUIRED:** The type of obligation specifically addressed by SFAS 47.
   **DISCUSSION:** SFAS 47 requires disclosure of unconditional purchase obligations associated with suppliers' financing arrangements and future payments required by long-term debt and redeemable stock agreements. Unconditional purchase obligations are commitments to transfer funds in the future for fixed or minimum amounts of goods or services at fixed or minimum prices. SFAS 47 provides the standards of accounting for an unconditional purchase obligation that was negotiated as part of the financing arrangement for facilities that will provide contracted goods or services or for costs related to those goods or services, has a remaining term of more than 1 year, and is either noncancelable or cancelable only under specific terms.
   Answer (A) is incorrect because loss contingencies are liabilities covered by SFAS 5. Answer (C) is incorrect because severance pay is a form of deferred compensation, a topic not addressed by SFAS 47. Answer (D) is incorrect because pension liabilities are covered by SFASs 87 and 88.

**78.** SFAS 47, *Disclosure of Long-Term Obligations*, does not apply to an unconditional purchase obligation that is cancelable under which of the following conditions?

   A.  Upon the occurrence of a remote contingency.

   B.  With the permission of the other party.

   C.  If a replacement agreement is signed between the same parties.

   D.  Upon payment of a nominal penalty.

Answer (D) is correct. *(Publisher)*
   **REQUIRED:** The condition excluding unconditional purchase obligation coverage by SFAS 47.
   **DISCUSSION:** SFAS 47 provides the standards of accounting for an unconditional purchase obligation that

1) Was negotiated as part of the financing arrangement
2) Has a remaining term of more than 1 year
3) Is either noncancelable or cancelable only under specific terms

Excluded from these terms and from the provisions of SFAS 47 is a purchase obligation cancelable upon the payment of a nominal penalty.

**79.** If an unconditional purchase obligation is not presented in the balance sheet, certain disclosures are required. A disclosure that is not required is

   A.  The nature and term of the obligation.

   B.  The variable components of the obligation.

   C.  The imputed interest necessary to reduce the unconditional purchase obligation to its present value.

   D.  The amounts purchased under the obligation for each period an income statement is presented.

Answer (C) is correct. *(Publisher)*
   **REQUIRED:** The item not required to be disclosed if an unconditional purchase obligation is not recognized in the balance sheet.
   **DISCUSSION:** When an unconditional purchase obligation is not recorded in the balance sheet, SFAS 47 encourages, but does not require, the disclosure of the amount of imputed interest necessary to reduce the unconditional purchase obligation to its present value. The other disclosures are explicitly required by SFAS 47 when an unconditional purchase obligation is not recorded in the balance sheet.

**80.** In accordance with SFAS No. 47, *Disclosure of Long-Term Obligations,* for unconditional purchase obligations not recorded on the purchaser's statement of financial position, all of the following disclosures are required except for the

   A.  Nature and term of the obligations.

   B.  Total amount of the fixed and determinable portion of the obligations at the financial statement date and for each of the next 5 years.

   C.  Nature of any variable portions of the obligations.

   D.  Sources of funds used for payments.

Answer (D) is correct. *(CMA, adapted)*
   **REQUIRED:** The item not a required disclosure regarding unconditional purchase obligations not recorded on the purchaser's balance sheet.
   **DISCUSSION:** SFAS 47 requires disclosure of unconditional purchase obligations associated with suppliers' financing arrangements (e.g., in the form of take-or-pay and throughput contracts) and future payments required by long-term debt and redeemable stock agreements. Unrecorded unconditional purchase obligations are those requiring payment for future goods or services and are not cancelable or, if so, provide for a substantial penalty. Disclosures required for unrecorded obligations include the nature and term of the item, fixed and determinable payments in total and for each of the next 5 years, the nature of any variable payments, and amounts purchased in the periods for which an income statement is being prepared. Sources of funds to be used for payments need not be disclosed.

**81.** The Financial Accounting Standards Board has provided guidance on disclosures of transactions between related parties, for example, transactions between subsidiaries of a common parent. SFAS 57, *Related Party Disclosures*, requires all of the following disclosures except

- A. The nature of the relationship involved.
- B. A description of the transactions for each period an income statement is presented.
- C. The dollar amounts of transactions for each period an income statement is presented.
- D. The effect on the cash flow statement for each period a cash flow statement is presented.

Answer (D) is correct.  *(CMA, adapted)*
**REQUIRED:** The related-party transaction disclosure not required by SFAS 57.
**DISCUSSION:** SFAS 57 requires disclosure of related-party transactions except for compensation agreements, expense allowances, and transactions eliminated in consolidated working papers. Required disclosures include the relationship(s) of the related parties; a description and dollar amounts of transactions for each period presented and the effects of any change in the method of establishing their terms; and amounts due to or from the related parties and, if not apparent, the terms and manner of settlement. The effect on the cash flow statement need not be disclosed.
Answer (A) is incorrect because disclosure of the nature of the relationship involved is required. Answer (B) is incorrect because disclosure of a description of the transactions for each period an income statement is presented is required. Answer (C) is incorrect because disclosure of the dollar amounts of transactions for each period an income statement is presented is required.

**82.** SFAS 107, *Disclosures about Fair Value of Financial Instruments*, requires all entities to disclose the fair value of all financial instruments for which it is practicable to estimate fair value. Which of the following is a financial instrument?

- A. Merchandise inventory.
- B. Deferred subscriptions revenue.
- C. A note payable in U.S. Treasury bonds.
- D. A warranty payable.

Answer (C) is correct.  *(Publisher)*
**REQUIRED:** The definition of a financial instrument.
**DISCUSSION:** SFAS 107 defines a financial instrument as cash, evidence of an ownership interest in an entity, or a contract that both (1) imposes on one entity a contractual obligation (A) to deliver cash or another financial instrument to a second entity or (B) to exchange other financial instruments on potentially unfavorable terms with the second entity, and (2) conveys to that second entity a contractual right (A) to receive cash or another financial instrument from the first entity or (B) to exchange other financial instruments on potentially favorable terms with the first entity. A note payable in U.S. Treasury bonds gives the holder the contractual right to receive, and imposes on the issuer the contractual obligation to deliver, bonds that are themselves financial instruments. Thus, given that one entity has a contractual obligation to deliver another financial instrument and the second entity has a contractual right to receive another financial instrument, the note payable in U.S. Treasury bonds meets the definition of a financial instrument.
Answer (A) is incorrect because, although the sale of inventory could result in the receipt of cash, the holder of the inventory has no current contractual right to receive cash. Answer (B) is incorrect because this obligation will result in the delivery of goods or services. Answer (D) is incorrect because this obligation will result in the delivery of goods or services.

**83.** Whether recognized or unrecognized in an entity's financial statements, disclosure of the fair values of the entity's financial instruments is required when

- A. Estimating those values is practicable.
- B. The entity maintains accurate cost records.
- C. Aggregated fair values are material to the entity.
- D. Individual fair values are material to the entity.

Answer (A) is correct.  *(CPA, adapted)*
**REQUIRED:** The circumstances in which disclosure of the fair values of the entity's financial instruments is required.
**DISCUSSION:** SFAS 107, *Disclosures about Fair Value of Financial Instruments*, as amended by SFAS 133, requires certain entities to disclose the fair value of financial instruments, whether or not they are recognized in the balance sheet, if it is practicable to estimate such fair values. If estimating fair value is not practicable, disclosures include information pertinent to estimating the fair value of the financial instrument or class of financial instruments, such as the carrying amount, effective interest rate, and maturity. The reasons that estimating the fair value is not practicable should also be disclosed.
Answer (B) is incorrect because the disclosure requirement is based on a practicability standard, not record keeping. Answer (C) is incorrect because the disclosure requirement is based on a practicability standard, not materiality. Answer (D) is incorrect because the disclosure requirement is based on a practicability standard, not materiality.

**84.** According to AICPA SOP 94-6, *Disclosure of Certain Significant Risks and Uncertainties*, financial statements must disclose significant risks and uncertainties. The required disclosures include

    A.  Quantified comparisons of the relative importance of the different businesses in which the entity operates.

    B.  Information about a significant estimate used to value an asset only if it is probable that the financial statement effect of a condition existing at the balance sheet date will change materially in the near term.

    C.  Risk-reduction techniques that have successfully mitigated losses.

    D.  Vulnerability due to a concentration if a near-term severe impact is at least reasonably possible.

Answer (D) is correct. *(Publisher)*
    **REQUIRED:** The required disclosure.
    **DISCUSSION:** The current vulnerability due to concentrations must be disclosed if certain conditions are met. Disclosure is necessary if management knows prior to issuance of the statements that the concentration exists at the balance sheet date, it makes the entity vulnerable to a near-term severe impact, and such impact is at least reasonably possible in the near term. A severe impact may result from loss of all or a part of a business relationship, price or demand changes, loss of a patent, changes in the availability of a resource or right, or the disruption of operations in a market or geographic area.
    Answer (A) is incorrect because disclosures about the nature of operations need not be quantified. Answer (B) is incorrect because a material financial statement effect need only be reasonably possible in the near term. Answer (C) is incorrect because the criteria for required disclosures about significant estimates may not be met if the entity has successfully employed risk-reduction techniques. In these circumstances, disclosure of those techniques is encouraged but not required.

**85.** Subsequent events include which of the following?

  I.  Events that provide evidence about conditions that exist at the date of the balance sheet, that affect the estimates inherent in statement preparation.

  II.  Events that provide evidence about conditions that did not exist at the date of the balance sheet.

    A.  I only.

    B.  II only.

    C.  Both I and II.

    D.  Neither I nor II.

Answer (C) is correct. *(Publisher)*
    **REQUIRED:** The events that are subsequent events.
    **DISCUSSION:** AICPA Professional Auditing Standard AU 560, *Subsequent Events*, concerns certain material events or transactions that occur after the balance sheet date and prior to the issuance of the financial statements. One type of subsequent event provides evidence about conditions that exist at the date of the balance sheet that affect the estimates inherent in statement preparation. Another type of subsequent event provides evidence about conditions that did not exist at the date of the balance sheet.

**86.** Zero Corp. suffered a loss that would have a material effect on its financial statements on an uncollectible trade account receivable due to a customer's bankruptcy. This occurred suddenly due to a natural disaster ten days after Zero's balance sheet date but one month before the issuance of the financial statements. Under these circumstances,

| | The Financial Statements Should Be Adjusted | The Event Requires Financial Statement Disclosure, but No Adjustment | The Auditor's Report Should Be Modified for a Lack of Consistency |
|---|---|---|---|
| A. | Yes | No | No |
| B. | Yes | No | Yes |
| C. | No | Yes | Yes |
| D. | No | Yes | No |

Answer (D) is correct. *(CPA, adapted)*
    **REQUIRED:** The effect on the financial statements and the auditor's report.
    **DISCUSSION:** Certain subsequent events may provide additional evidence about conditions at the date of the balance sheet and affect estimates inherent in the preparation of statements. These events require adjustment by the client in the financial statements at year-end. Other subsequent events provide evidence about conditions not existing at the date of the balance sheet but arising subsequent to that date and affecting the interpretation of the year-end financial statements. These events may require disclosure in notes to the financial statements but do not require adjustment of the financial statement balances. Thus, in this case, the financial statements should not be adjusted, but disclosure should be made in the notes. The auditor's report is unaffected.

---

Use Gleim's *CMA Test Prep* for interactive testing with **over 2,000 additional multiple-choice questions**!

# STUDY UNIT THIRTEEN
# CASH AND RECEIVABLES

(14 pages of outline)

This study unit is the **third of ten** on **external financial reporting**. The relative weight assigned to this major topic in Part 2 of the exam is **25%** at **skill level B** (four skill types required). The ten study units are

Study Unit 11: Overview of External Financial Reporting
Study Unit 12: Overview of Financial Statements
Study Unit 13: Cash and Receivables
Study Unit 14: Inventories and Investments
Study Unit 15: Long-Lived Assets
Study Unit 16: Liabilities
Study Unit 17: Equity and Revenue Recognition
Study Unit 18: Other Income Statement Items
Study Unit 19: Business Combinations and Derivatives
Study Unit 20: SEC Requirements and the Annual Report

After studying the outlines and answering the multiple-choice questions in this study unit, you will have the skills necessary to address the following topics listed in the IMA's Learning Outcome Statements:

Part 2 – Section E.4. Recognition, measurement, valuation, and disclosure

For each of the subtopics listed, the candidate should be able to:

1. define the subtopic and describe the characteristics of its components

2. demonstrate an understanding of appropriate valuation techniques for the components of each subtopic

3. demonstrate an understanding of the appropriate accounting conventions for the components of each subtopic

4. compare and contrast valuation techniques and accounting methods

5. show the correct financial statement presentation

6. identify the appropriate disclosure requirements in the body of the financial statements and/or in the footnotes

Cash and marketable securities

    a.   subtopic components: cash, cash equivalents, marketable (trading) securities
    b.   determine when cash is restricted

Accounts receivable

    a.   subtopic components: current, noncurrent, trade, and nontrade receivables; trade discounts, cash (sales) discounts, sales returns and allowances, net realizable value, promissory note, factoring receivables, write-offs, and collection of write-offs
    b.   identify issues related to the valuation of accounts receivable
    c.   calculate cash discounts using both the gross method and the net method

d.   identify two methods of recording uncollectibles and describe why the allowance method is the generally accepted approach

e.   calculate the allowance for uncollectibles using both the percentage-of-sales (income statement) approach and the percentage-of-receivables (balance sheet) approach

f.   discount a long-term note using the time value of money tables and indicate its correct valuation at time of sale

g.   calculate the interest revenue and discount amortized for each time period of the note

h.   define imputed interest rate

i.   demonstrate an understanding of receivables when they are used as collateral

j.   distinguish between receivables sold on a with recourse basis and those sold on a without recourse basis

## 13.1 CASH, CASH EQUIVALENTS, AND MARKETABLE SECURITIES

1.   **Nature of Cash**. Cash is the first item presented in the assets section of the balance sheet. It is ready money, the most liquid of assets.

   a.   Cash itself is ordinarily classified as a **current asset**.

      1)   Per ARB 43, Chapter 3A, current assets are "reasonably expected to be realized in cash or sold or consumed during the normal operating cycle of the business."

      2)   However, even though not actually set aside in special accounts, cash that is "clearly to be used in the near future for the liquidation of long-term debts, payments to sinking funds, or for other similar purposes should be excluded from current assets."

   b.   For the sake of simplicity, **nominal units of money** provide the measurement scale; that is, changes in purchasing power over time are not recognized in standard financial statements.

   c.   On the **balance sheet**, only one cash account is presented. It reflects all unrestricted cash.

2.   **Items of Cash**. To be classified as cash, an asset must be readily available for use by the business and can have no restrictions placed on its use.

   a.   The cash account on the balance sheet should consist of

      1)   Coin and currency on hand, including petty cash and change funds
      2)   Demand deposits (checking accounts)
      3)   Time deposits (savings accounts)
      4)   Near-cash assets, such as undeposited checks

3.   **Cash Equivalents**. These are short-term, highly liquid investments.

   a.   Cash equivalents have these characteristics:

      1)   They are readily convertible into known amounts of cash.
      2)   They are so near maturity that interest rate risk is insignificant.
      3)   They generally have an original maturity of 3 months or less.

   b.   Common examples are Treasury bills, money market funds, and short-term commercial paper.

4.   **Restricted Cash**. Cash amounts designated for special uses should be separately presented. Restricted and unrestricted amounts are often held in separate bank accounts.

   a.   Examples are bond sinking funds and new building funds.

   b.   The nature of the use will determine whether such an amount will be classified as **current** or **noncurrent**.

      1)   A bond sinking fund to redeem noncurrent bond debt is noncurrent; the amount to be used to redeem bonds currently redeemable is a current asset.

5.   **Compensating Balances**.  As part of an agreement regarding either an existing loan or the provision of future credit, a borrower may be required to keep an average or minimum amount on deposit with the lender.

   a.   This compensating balance increases the borrower's effective interest rate.
   b.   The SEC's recommended reporting solution depends on the duration of the lending arrangement and the nature of the restriction.

      1)   If the balance relates to a **short-term agreement** and is legally restricted, it is separately reported among the cash and cash equivalent as a **current asset**.
      2)   If the balance relates to a **long-term agreement**, the legally restricted balance is noncurrent and should be separately classified in either the **investments** or **other assets** section.
      3)   When the entity has a compensating balance agreement but the use of the balance is **not restricted**, the agreement should be disclosed in the **notes to the statements**.

6.   **Trading securities** (formerly called marketable securities).  This designation is for "debt and equity securities that are bought and held principally for the purpose of selling them in the near term" (SFAS 115).

   a.   Trading securities are bought and held primarily for sale in the near future.  They are purchased and sold frequently.
   b.   Each trading security is initially recorded at cost but is subsequently measured at **fair value** at each balance sheet date.

      1)   Quoted market prices are easy to obtain and are the most reliable and verifiable measure of fair value.

   c.   **Unrealized holding gains and losses** on trading securities are included in **earnings**.

      1)   A holding gain or loss is the net change in fair value during the period, not including recognized dividends or interest not received.

7.   Stop and review!  You have completed the outline for this subunit.  Study multiple-choice questions 1 through 8 beginning on page 491.

## 13.2 ACCOUNTS RECEIVABLE

1.   **Definition**.  A receivable is an asset recognized to reflect a claim against another party for the receipt of money, goods, or services.  For most accounting purposes, the claim is one expected to be settled in cash.

2.   **Classifications**

   a.   **Current vs. noncurrent**

      1)   A receivable is a **current** asset if it is reasonably expected to be collected within the longer of 1 year or the entity's normal operating cycle.
      2)   Otherwise, it should be classified as **noncurrent**.

   b.   **Trade vs. nontrade**

      1)   **Trade receivables**, which constitute the majority of receivables, arise from credit sales to customers as part of the ordinary revenue-producing activities of an entity.

         a)   They are normally **unsecured** and most often noninterest-bearing, but charges are added to revolving charge accounts and installment receivables.
         b)   Forfeiture of a cash discount because of delayed payment is an implicit means of charging interest on trade receivables.

2) **Nontrade receivables** includes all receivables not classified as trade receivables. They may include

   a) Lease receivables
   b) Deposits to guarantee payment or to cover possible loss
   c) Advances to shareholders, directors, officers, et al.
   d) Subscriptions for the entity's securities
   e) Tax refunds
   f) Claims for insurance proceeds or amounts arising from litigation
   g) Interest, dividends, rent, or royalties accrued

3) Trade receivables are further classified into accounts and notes.

c. **Accounts vs. notes**

1) **Accounts receivable** are often short-term, unsecured, and informal credit arrangements (open accounts). Most trade receivables are accounts.

   a) However, **installment accounts receivable** may involve long-term arrangements and be evidenced by formal promissory notes.

2) **Notes receivable** are evidenced by a formal instrument, such as a promissory note. A formal document provides its holder with a stronger legal status than does an account receivable.

   a) In a **note**, the maker (debtor) usually promises to pay to the order of a second party (creditor) a fixed amount of money at a definite time.

   b) Most notes bear **interest** (explicitly or implicitly) because they represent a longer-term borrowing than an account receivable.

d. One type of claim that does not constitute a receivable is for unsold goods on **consignment**.

1) The consignor retains title to these goods and should report them in inventory at cost, not in receivables at their sales price.

3. **Discounts**

a. **Trade discounts** are used to differentiate alternative prices among different classes of customers.

1) EXAMPLE:

   a) An item with a list price of $1,000 might be subject to a 40% trade discount when selling to a wholesale customer. Thus, $400 is deducted from the list price in arriving at the actual selling price of $600. Only the $600 is recorded. The accounts do not reflect trade discounts.

   b) Some sellers will offer chain-trade discounts, such as 40%, 10%, which means certain classes of buyers receive both a 40% discount and a 10% discount.

      i) In the previous example, the $600 would be further reduced by another $60 to bring the actual selling price down to $540. All journal entries on the buyer's and seller's books would be for $540 with no indication of the original list price or the discount.

2) In summary, trade discounts are nothing more than a means of calculating the sales price; they are not recorded.

    b.   **Cash discounts (sales discounts)** are a means of accelerating cash collection by rewarding customers for early payment.

        1)   The **gross method** accounts for receivables at their face amount. It is used when customers are not expected to pay soon enough to take the discount.

            a)   If the customer does pay within the discount period, the discount is recorded and classified as an offset to sales in the income statement.

        2)   The **net method** records receivables net of the applicable cash (sales) discount allowed for early payment. It is used when customers are expected to pay within the discount period.

            a)   If the payment is not received during the discount period, a miscellaneous revenue account, such as sales discounts forfeited, is credited when the payment is received.

        3)   EXAMPLE:

            a)   An item is sold with terms of 2/10, n/30 (i.e., 2% discount if payment made within 10 days, entire balance due in 30 days).

|  | Gross Method | Net Method |
|---|---|---|
| Accounts receivable | $1,000 | $980 |
|    Sales | $1,000 | $980 |

            b)   Payment is received within the discount period.

|  | Gross Method | Net Method |
|---|---|---|
| Cash | $ 980 | $980 |
| Sales discounts | 20 | |
|    Accounts receivable | $1,000 | $980 |

            c)   Payment is received after the discount period.

|  | Gross Method | Net Method |
|---|---|---|
| Cash | $1,000 | $980 |
|    Accounts receivable | $1,000 | $980 |
| | | |
| Cash | | $ 20 |
|    Sales discounts forfeited | | $ 20 |

4.   **Sales returns and allowances**. A provision must be made for the return of merchandise because of product defects, customer dissatisfaction, etc.

    a.   If returns are **immaterial**, the usual accounting is to debit the contra-revenue account and credit accounts receivable at the time of the adjustment.

        1)   This method is disallowed for tax purposes.

    b.   If the amounts are **material**, however, the method described above will be inconsistent with the matching principle when the sale and the return occur in different periods.

        1)   Accordingly, an **allowance** should be established at the end of the period for material estimated sales returns.

    c.   Whichever case applies, the journal entry is the same:

| | | |
|---|---|---|
| Sales returns and allowances | $XXX | |
|    Accounts receivable | | $XXX |

    d.   The balance sheet presentation is

| | | |
|---|---|---|
| Gross sales | $X,XXX | |
| Less: sales returns and allowances | (XXX) | |
|    Net sales | | $X,XXX |

5.   **Valuation of receivables**.  There are two approaches to accounting for bad debts:  the direct write-off method and the allowance method.

    a.   The **direct write-off method** expenses bad debts when they are determined to be uncollectible.

        1)   The direct write-off method is subject to manipulation because timing is at the discretion of management.  It is **not acceptable under GAAP**.

    b.   The **allowance method** systematically records bad debt expense as a percentage of either sales or the level of accounts receivable on an annual basis.  The allowance method is **acceptable under GAAP**.

        1)   The periodic journal entry to **record bad debt expense** is

| | | |
|---|---|---|
| Bad debt expense | $XXX | |
|     Allowance for doubtful accounts | | $XXX |

        2)   As accounts receivable are written off, they are charged to the allowance account.

| | | |
|---|---|---|
| Allowance for doubtful accounts | $XXX | |
|     Accounts receivable | | $XXX |

            a)   Note that the write-off of a particular bad debt has **no effect on expenses**; also, there is **no effect on working capital** because the asset account and the contra account are reduced by equal amounts.

    c.   **Two approaches** to calculating the amount charged to bad debt expense are available under the allowance method.

        1)   Under the **income-statement approach**, bad debts are considered a function of sales on account, embodying the **matching principle**.

            a)   Periodic bad debt expense is computed as a **percentage of sales**.

            b)   EXAMPLE:  A company has the following account balances at year-end:

| | Debit | Credit |
|---|---|---|
| Accounts receivable | $100,000 | |
| Allowance for doubtful accounts | 1,600 | |
| Sales on credit | | $500,000 |

            c)   Based on its experience, the company expects bad debts to average 2% of sales.  Hence, the estimated expense is $10,000 ($500,000 × 2%).  The year-end adjusting journal entry is

| | | |
|---|---|---|
| Bad debt expense | $ 10,000 | |
|     Allowance for doubtful accounts | | $ 10,000 |

            d)   Because the allowance account previously had a debit balance, the new credit balance is $8,400.  The balance sheet presentation is

| | | |
|---|---|---|
| Accounts receivable (gross) | $100,000 | |
|     Less:  allowance for doubtful accounts | (8,400) | |
| Accounts receivable (net) | | $ 91,600 |

        2)   Under the **balance-sheet approach**, bad debt expense is a function of both sales and collections, reporting accounts receivable at their **net realizable value (NRV)**.

            a)   The allowance is periodically adjusted to reflect a **percentage of accounts receivable**.

b) An enterprise rarely experiences a single rate of uncollectibility on all its accounts. For this reason, firms using the balance-sheet approach to estimate bad debt expense generally prepare an **aging schedule** of accounts receivable.

c) EXAMPLE: The company prepares the following aging schedule of its accounts receivable:

| Balance Range | Less than 30 Days | 31 - 60 Days | 61- 90 Days | Over 90 Days | Total Balances |
|---|---|---|---|---|---|
| $0 - $100 | $ 5,000 | $ 200 | $ 100 | $ 100 | $ 5,400 |
| $100 - $1,000 | 8,000 | 3,800 | | | 11,800 |
| $1,000 - $5,000 | 20,000 | 2,000 | 1,900 | | 23,900 |
| $5,000 - $10,000 | 38,000 | | 8,000 | 900 | 46,900 |
| Over $10,000 | | 12,000 | | | 12,000 |
| Totals | $71,000 | $18,000 | $10,000 | $1,000 | $100,000 |

d) The company then applies different percentages to each stratum based on experience:

| Aging Strata | Balance | Estimated Percent Uncollectible | Ending Balance in Allowance Account |
|---|---|---|---|
| Less than 30 days | $ 71,000 | 2% | $1,420 |
| 30 - 60 days | 18,000 | 12% | 2,160 |
| 60 - 90 days | 10,000 | 15% | 1,500 |
| Over 90 days | 1,000 | 20% | 200 |
| Total | $100,000 | | $5,280 |

e) Because the allowance account currently has a debit balance of $1,600, the following journal entry is required to establish the proper valuation:

| | | |
|---|---|---|
| Bad debt expense | $  6,880 | |
| Allowance for doubtful accounts | | $  6,880 |

f) The balance sheet presentation is

| | | |
|---|---|---|
| Accounts receivable (gross) | $100,000 | |
| Less: allowance for doubtful accounts | (5,280) | |
| Accounts receivable (net) | | $94,720 |

3) Occasionally a customer will pay on an **account previously written off**.

a) The first entry is to reestablish the account for the amount the customer has agreed to pay (any remainder remains written off):

| | | |
|---|---|---|
| Accounts receivable | $XXX | |
| Allowance for doubtful accounts | | $XXX |

b) The second entry records the receipt of cash.

| | | |
|---|---|---|
| Cash | $XXX | |
| Accounts receivable | | $XXX |

c) The net effect of these entries is to return the amount written off to the allowance account to absorb future write-offs.

i) The assumption is that the original write-off entry was in error and that another account(s) is(are) uncollectible.

6. **Disposition of receivables**. Companies often use their accounts receivables as financing tools, either selling them to improve cash flow or as collateral for loans.

   a. **Factoring**. In order to improve liquidity, a company will sometimes sell its accounts receivable to a third party who assumes the responsibility of collection.

      1) If the factoring is **with recourse**, the factor can require the seller of the receivables to pay for any accounts that turn out to be uncollectible.

         a) If the factoring is **without recourse**, the factor assumes all the risks and rewards of collection.

      2) The seller receives money that can be immediately reinvested into new inventories. The company can offset the fee charged by the factor by eliminating its bad debts, credit department, and accounts receivable staff.

      3) The factor usually receives a high financing fee (at least two points above prime), plus a fee for doing the collection. Furthermore, the factor can often operate more efficiently than its clients because of the specialized nature of its services.

      4) EXAMPLE: A factor charges a 2% fee plus an interest rate of 18% on all monies advanced to the company. Monthly sales are $100,000, and the factor advances 90% of the receivables submitted after deducting the 2% fee and the interest. Credit terms are net 60 days. What is the cost to the company of this arrangement?

         | | |
         |---|---:|
         | Amount of receivable submitted | $100,000 |
         | Minus: 10% reserve | (10,000) |
         | Minus: 2% factor's fee | (2,000) |
         | Amount accruing to the company | $ 88,000 |
         | Minus: 18% interest for 60 days | (2,640) |
         | Amount to be received immediately | $ 85,360 |

         a) The company will also receive the $10,000 reserve at the end of the 60-day period if it has not been absorbed by sales returns and allowances. Thus, the total cost to the company to factor the sales for the month is $4,640 ($2,000 factor fee + interest of $2,640). Assuming that the factor has approved the customers' credit in advance, the seller will not absorb any bad debts.

      5) The journal entry to record the preceding transaction is

         | | | |
         |---|---:|---:|
         | Cash | $85,360 | |
         | Equity in factored receivables | 10,000 | |
         | Factor fee expense | 2,000 | |
         | Prepaid interest | 2,640 | |
         | Accounts receivable | | $100,000 |

      6) One common form of factoring is the **credit card sale**. The retailer benefits by prompt receipt of cash and avoidance of bad debts and other costs. In return, the credit card company charges a fee.

         a) Two methods of accounting for credit card sales may be necessary depending upon the reimbursement method used.

            i) If the credit card company pays after submission of credit card receipts, the retailer initially records a receivable. After payment, it credits the receivable, debits cash, and debits service charge expense.

            ii) If the credit card company establishes a banking arrangement whereby the retailer's checking account is increased by the direct deposit of credit card receipts, no receivable is recognized. Instead, the journal entry would be a debit to cash, a debit to service charge expense, and a credit to sales.

    b.　**Pledging**.  A pledge (a general assignment) is the use of receivables as collateral (security) for a loan.

        1)　The borrower agrees to use collections of receivables to repay the loan.  Upon default, the lender can sell the receivables to recover the loan proceeds.

        2)　Because a pledge is a relatively informal arrangement, it is not reflected in the accounts, although disclosure should be made in the financial statements either in a note or parenthetically.  The loan itself is recorded in the normal way.

    c.　**Assignment**.  An assignment (a specific assignment) is a more formal borrowing arrangement (**secured borrowing**).  The assignor (borrower) signs a promissory note and financing agreement, and specific receivables serve as **collateral**.

        1)　Specific assignment permits the assignee (lender) to reduce its risk by accepting only accounts with a high probability of collection.

        2)　Occasionally, the debtors are notified to make payments to the assignee, but most assignments are not on a notification basis.

            a)　The loan is at a specified percentage of the face amount of the collateral, and interest and service fees are charged to the assignor.

        3)　Assigned accounts receivable may be segregated from other accounts receivable (debit accounts receivable assigned, credit receivable) on the balance sheet.

            a)　The note payable is reported in the liability section.

    d.　**Securitization** is the transfer of a portfolio of financial assets (e.g., trade receivables, mortgage loans, automobile loans, or credit card receivables) to a **special-purpose entity (SPE)**, often a trust, and the sale of beneficial interests in SPE to investors.

        1)　The proceeds of the sale of these interests are paid to the transferor.  Amounts of interest and principal collected on the securitized assets are paid to the investors in accordance with the legal agreement that established the SPE.

  7.　Stop and review!  You have completed the outline for this subunit.  Study multiple-choice questions 9 through 24 beginning on page 494.

## 13.3 NOTES RECEIVABLE

  1.　**Definition**

    a.　A **note receivable** is a debt evidenced by a two-party writing, i.e., a **promissory note**, and thus follows the laws concerning negotiable instruments.

        1)　A negotiable instrument must therefore be in writing, signed by the maker (the promisor), and contain an unconditional promise to pay a sum certain to the payee at a definite time.

    b.　Notes stand in contrast to accounts receivable, which are more informal promises to pay.

        1)　New customers, high-risk customers, or those needing an extension for the time of payment are among those from whom a vendor might require a note.

    c.　Notes with maturities of **three months or less** are generally classified as short-term and are treated as **cash equivalents**.

        1)　Short-term notes are usually recorded at **face value less allowances**, i.e., because the interest implicit in the maturity amount is immaterial, no interest revenue is recognized.

d. Notes with maturities **longer than three months** are considered **long-term** and the creditor must recognize an **interest component** of revenue.

1) **APB 21**, *Interest on Receivables and Payables*, mandates that receivables be recorded at the **present value of the expected future cash flows** and that any difference between the proceeds and the face amount, if material, must be recognized as a premium or discount and amortized.

2. **The Time Value of Money**

a. A quantity of money to be received or paid in the future is worth less than the same amount now. The difference, called **the time value of money**, is measured in terms of interest calculated using the appropriate **discount rate**.

1) Interest is the "price of money," i.e., the amount paid by a borrower to a lender for the privilege of borrowing the funds.

b. Standard tables have been developed to facilitate the calculation of present values. Each entry in one of these tables represents the factor by which any dollar amount can be modified to obtain its present value.

c. The **present value (PV) of an amount** is the value today of some future payment.

1) It equals the future payment times the present value of $1 (a factor found in a standard table) for the given number of periods and interest rate.

| | Present Value | | |
| No. of Periods | 6% | 8% | 10% |
| --- | --- | --- | --- |
| 1 | 0.943 | 0.926 | 0.909 |
| 2 | 0.890 | 0.857 | 0.826 |
| 3 | 0.840 | 0.794 | 0.751 |
| 4 | 0.792 | 0.735 | 0.683 |
| 5 | 0.747 | 0.681 | 0.621 |

a) EXAMPLE: The present value of $1,000 to be received in 3 years, discounted at 8%, is $794 ($1,000 × 0.794).

d. An **ordinary annuity (annuity in arrears)** is a series of payments occurring at the end of each period. In an **annuity due (annuity in advance)** the payments are made (received) at the beginning of each period.

1) The **PV of an ordinary annuity** is the value today of a series of equal payments extending into the future. Note that these values are simply the aggregates of the values in the single-amount table.

| | Present Value | | |
| No. of Periods | 6% | 8% | 10% |
| --- | --- | --- | --- |
| 1 | 0.943 | 0.926 | 0.909 |
| 2 | 1.833 | 1.783 | 1.736 |
| 3 | 2.673 | 2.577 | 2.487 |
| 4 | 3.465 | 3.312 | 3.170 |
| 5 | 4.212 | 3.993 | 3.791 |

a) EXAMPLE: The present value of an ordinary annuity of four payments of $1,000 each, discounted at 10%, is $3,170 ($1,000 × 3.170).

e. When a company accepts an **interest-bearing note**, the note is recorded at the sum of (1) the present value of the principal and (2) the present value of the interest payments.

3. **Accepting a Note at a Premium**

a. EXAMPLE: A company agrees to accept, in return for merchandise, a 3-year, $100,000 note bearing 8% interest paid annually. The company's effective interest rate is 6%. Since the note's stated rate exceeds the effective rate, the note will be issued at a premium.

b.    The company records the note at its present value, which consists of a single payment of $100,000 in three years and 3 payments of interest of $8,000 each.  These payment streams are discounted at the company's effective rate (five decimal places are used for increased accuracy).

| | |
|---|---|
| Present value of principal ($100,000 × 0.83962) | $ 83,962 |
| Present value of interest ($8,000 × 2.67301) | 21,384 |
| Present value of note | $105,346 |

c.    The entry to record the note is thus

| | | |
|---|---|---|
| Note receivable | $100,000 | |
| Premium on note receivable | 5,346 | |
| Sales | | $105,346 |

d.    The premium on the note is amortized using the effective interest method as follows.  Observe that on the note's maturity date, its carrying amount equals its face amount.

| | | Times: | Equals: | Minus: | Equals: | |
|---|---|---|---|---|---|---|
| Year | Beginning Net Carrying Amount | Effective Rate | Interest Revenue | Cash Received | Premium Amortized | Ending Net Carrying Amount |
| 1 | $105,346 | 6% | $ 6,321 | $ 8,000 | $(1,679) | $103,667 |
| 2 | $103,667 | 6% | 6,220 | 8,000 | (1,780) | $101,887 |
| 3 | $101,887 | 6% | 6,113 | 8,000 | (1,887) | $100,000 |
| | | | $18,654 | $24,000 | $(5,346) | |

e.    The table provides the amounts for each year-end's journal entries:

Year 1

| | | |
|---|---|---|
| Cash | $8,000 | |
| Premium on note receivable | | $1,679 |
| Interest revenue | | 6,321 |

Year 2

| | | |
|---|---|---|
| Cash | $8,000 | |
| Premium on note receivable | | $1,780 |
| Interest revenue | | 6,220 |

Year 3

| | | |
|---|---|---|
| Cash | $8,000 | |
| Premium on note receivable | | $1,887 |
| Interest revenue | | 6,113 |

| | | |
|---|---|---|
| Cash | $100,000 | |
| Note receivable | | $100,000 |

4.    **Accepting a Note at a Discount**

a.    EXAMPLE:  In the above scenario, assume that instead, the note bore 6% interest, while the company's effective rate was 8%.  Since the stated rate is less than the effective rate, the note will be issued at a discount.

b.    The company records the note at its present value:

| | |
|---|---|
| Present value of principal ($100,000 × 0.79383) | $79,383 |
| Present value of interest ($6,000 × 2.57710) | 15,463 |
| Present value of note | $94,846 |

c.    The entry to record the note is thus

| | | |
|---|---|---|
| Note receivable | $100,000 | |
| Discount on note receivable | | $ 5,154 |
| Sales | | 94,846 |

d.    The discount on the note is amortized using the effective interest method as follows.
Observe that, on the note's maturity date, its carrying amount equals its face
amount.

| Year | Beginning Net Carrying Amount | Times: Effective Rate | Equals: Interest Revenue | Minus: Cash Received | Equals: Discount Amortized | Ending Net Carrying Amount |
|------|-------------------------------|-----------------------|--------------------------|----------------------|----------------------------|----------------------------|
| 1 | $94,846 | 8% | $ 7,588 | $ 6,000 | $1,588 | $ 96,434 |
| 2 | $96,434 | 8% | 7,715 | 6,000 | 1,715 | $ 98,148 |
| 3 | $98,148 | 8% | 7,852 | 6,000 | 1,852 | $100,000 |
| | | | $23,154 | $18,000 | $5,154 | |

e.    The table provides the amounts for each year-end's journal entry:

Year 1
Cash                                        $6,000
Discount on note receivable          1,588
    Interest revenue                                      $7,588

Year 2
Cash                                        $6,000
Discount on note receivable          1,715
    Interest revenue                                      $7,715

Year 3
Cash                                        $6,000
Discount on note receivable          1,852
    Interest revenue                                      $7,852

Cash                                     $100,000
    Note receivable                                      $100,000

5.    **Discounting Notes Receivable**

a.    When a note receivable is **discounted** (i.e., **sold**, usually at a bank), the gain or loss
on disposition of the note must be calculated.

b.    The holder is borrowing the maturity amount (principal + interest at maturity) of the
note.  The bank usually collects the maturity amount from the maker of the note.

c.    Thus, the steps in discounting are to

1)    Compute the total interest receivable on the note (face amount × stated rate ×
note term).

2)    Compute the maturity amount (face amount + total interest receivable).

3)    Compute the accrued interest receivable (face amount × stated rate × note term
elapsed).

4)    Compute the bank's discount (maturity amount × bank's discount rate × note
term remaining).

5)    Compute the cash proceeds (maturity amount – the bank's discount).

6)    Compute the carrying amount of the note (face amount + accrued interest
receivable).

       7)   Compute the gain or loss (proceeds – carrying amount).

           a)   If a gain results, the entry is

| | | |
|---|---|---|
| Cash | $XXX | |
|    Gain on sale of note receivable | | $XXX |
|    Note receivable | | XXX |
|    Interest receivable | | XXX |

           b)   If a loss results, the entry is

| | | |
|---|---|---|
| Cash | $XXX | |
| Loss on sale of note receivable | XXX | |
|    Note receivable | | $XXX |
|    Interest receivable | | $XXX |

   d.   If a note is discounted **with recourse**, the note must be disclosed as a **contingent liability**.

       1)   If the maker dishonors the note, the bank will collect from the entity that discounted the note.

           a)   Alternatively, the credit in the previous entry is sometimes made to **notes receivable discounted**, a contra-asset account.

   e.   When computing yearly interest, the day the note is received, made, etc., is not included, but the last day of the note is counted.

       1)   EXAMPLE: A 30-day note dated January 17 matures on February 16. There are 14 days (31 – 17) left in January, and 16 days must be counted in February for a 30-day note. Accordingly, the maturity date is February 16.

6.   **Noninterest-bearing notes**.

   a.   The term "noninterest-bearing" is misleading because it is used to describe **two circumstances**: (1) when a note bears implicit interest only (no stated interest) and (2) when no actual interest is charged (the cash proceeds equal the face amount).

   b.   When a note is noninterest-bearing in the latter sense or when it bears interest at a rate that is unreasonable in the circumstances, APB 21 requires an interest rate to be **imputed** (estimated).

   c.   In these circumstances, the transaction should be recorded at the more clearly determinable of the fair value of the property, goods, or services; fair value of the note; or discounted value of future payments based on an imputed rate of interest.

       1)   If the present value of a note with no stated rate or an unreasonable rate must be determined by discounting future payments using an imputed rate, the prevailing rate for similar instruments of issuers with similar credit ratings normally helps determine the appropriate rate.

       2)   The stated rate may be less than the effective (or imputed) rate because the lender has received other stated (or unstated) rights and privileges as part of the bargain. The difference between the respective present values of the note computed at the stated rate and at the effective or imputed rate should be accounted for as the cost of the rights or privileges obtained.

7.   Stop and review! You have completed the outline for this subunit. Study multiple-choice questions 25 through 43 beginning on page 499.

## 13.4 CORE CONCEPTS

<u>Cash, Cash Equivalents, and Marketable Securities</u>

- To be classified as **cash**, an asset must **be readily available** for use by the business and can have no restrictions placed on its use.
- **Short-term, highly liquid** investments, such as Treasury bills and money market funds, are referred to as **cash equivalents**.
- **Trading (marketable) securities** are ones that "are bought and held primarily for sale in the near future."

<u>Accounts Receivable</u>

- A **receivable** is a current asset if it is expected to be collected within the longer of one year or the operating cycle.
- The **gross method** reports receivables at their face amount. It is used when **customers are not expected** to pay soon enough to take the discount allowed for early payment.
- The **net method** reports receivables net of the applicable cash discount. It is used when **customers are expected** to pay within the discount period.
- The method acceptable under GAAP for recording bad debt expense is the **allowance method**. Under the allowance method, bad debt expense does not change when a particular account is determined to be uncollectible.
- The **income statement** approach to the allowance method matches **bad debt expense** to the period in which the revenue was earned.
- The **balance-sheet approach** to the allowance method views **bad debt expense** as a function of both sales and collections, reporting accounts receivable at their net realizable value.
- Accounts receivable can be **disposed of** by being factored (sold), pledged (collateralized), assigned, or securitized.

<u>Notes Receivable</u>

- A **note receivable** has sounder legal standing than an account receivable because it is evidenced by a **written acknowledgment** of the debt.
- Notes receivable should be reported at their face amount **net of any premium or discount** arising from a difference between the note's stated rate of interest and the market rate.

## QUESTIONS

### 13.1 Cash, Cash Equivalents, and Marketable Securities

**1.** On a company's December 31, year 1 balance sheet, which of the following items should be included in the amount reported as cash?

I.  A check payable to the company, dated January 2, year 2, in payment of a sale made in December year 1.

II. A check drawn on the company's account, payable to a vendor, dated and recorded in the company's books on December 31, year 1 but not mailed until January 10, year 2.

    A. I only.

    B. II only.

    C. I and II only.

    D. Neither I nor II.

Answer (B) is correct. *(CIA, adapted)*
**REQUIRED:** The item(s) to be included in the amount reported as cash at year-end.
**DISCUSSION:** The check payable to the company is dated after the balance sheet date, so the amount of the check should be reported as a receivable in the December 31, year 1 balance sheet. The check drawn on the company's account was dated and recorded in the company books in year 1 but not mailed until after the financial statement date. Thus, the amount of the check should be included in both the amount reported as cash and the amount reported as accounts payable in the company's December 31, year 1 balance sheet. Control of cash requires a proper cutoff of cash receipts and cash disbursements.
Answer (A) is incorrect because the check payable to the company is a receivable. Answer (C) is incorrect because the check payable to the company is a receivable. Answer (D) is incorrect because the check drawn on the company's account was dated and recorded in the company's books in year 1, so it should be included in both the amount reported as cash and the amount reported as accounts payable.

**2.** The following information pertains to a checking account of a company at July 31:

| | |
|---|---:|
| Balance per bank statement | $40,000 |
| Interest earned for July | 100 |
| Outstanding checks | 3,000 |
| Customers' checks returned for insufficient funds | 1,000 |
| Deposit in transit | 5,000 |

At July 31, the company's correct cash balance is

    A. $41,100

    B. $41,000

    C. $42,100

    D. $42,000

Answer (D) is correct. *(CIA, adapted)*
**REQUIRED:** The correct cash balance.
**DISCUSSION:** The correct cash balance is $42,000 ($40,000 cash balance per bank statement + $5,000 deposit in transit – $3,000 checks outstanding). The $100 interest earned and the $1,000 NSF checks are reflected in the $40,000 bank balance.
Answer (A) is incorrect because $41,100 mistakenly includes the $100 interest and subtracts the $1,000 of NSF checks, amounts already reflected in the bank statement balance. Answer (B) is incorrect because $41,000 is computed by subtracting the $1,000 of NSF checks, an amount already reflected in the bank statement balance. Answer (C) is incorrect because $42,100 includes the $100 interest, an amount already reflected in the bank statement balance.

**3.** The following information pertains to Grey Co. at December 31, 20X2:

| | |
|---|---:|
| Checkbook balance | $12,000 |
| Bank statement balance | 16,000 |
| Check drawn on Grey's account, payable to a vendor, dated and recorded 12/31/X2 but not mailed until 1/10/X3 | 1,800 |

On Grey's December 31, 20X2 balance sheet, what amount should be reported as cash?

    A. $12,000

    B. $13,800

    C. $14,200

    D. $16,000

Answer (B) is correct. *(CPA, adapted)*
**REQUIRED:** The amount of cash that should be reported on the balance sheet.
**DISCUSSION:** The cash account on the balance sheet should consist of (1) coin and currency on hand, (2) demand deposits (checking accounts), (3) time deposits (savings accounts), and (4) near-cash assets (e.g., deposits in transit or checks written to creditors but not yet mailed). Thus, the cash balance should be $13,800 ($12,000 checkbook balance + $1,800 check drawn but not mailed). The checkbook balance should be used because it more closely reflects the amount of cash that is unrestricted as of the balance sheet date.
Answer (A) is incorrect because $12,000 excludes the check that was recorded but not mailed. Answer (C) is incorrect because $14,200 equals the bank statement balance minus the check not mailed. Answer (D) is incorrect because $16,000 is the bank statement balance.

**4.** Castillo Co. had the following balances at December 31, 20X2:

| | |
|---|---:|
| Cash in checking account | $ 35,000 |
| Cash in money market account | 75,000 |
| U.S. Treasury bill, purchased 11/1/20X2, maturing 1/31/20X3 | 350,000 |
| U.S. Treasury bill, purchased 12/1/20X2, maturing 3/31/20X3 | 400,000 |

Castillo treats all highly liquid investments with a maturity of three months or less when purchased as cash equivalents. What amount should Castillo report as cash and cash equivalents in its December 31, 20X2, balance sheet?

A. $110,000

B. $385,000

C. $460,000

D. $860,000

**Answer (C) is correct.** *(CPA, adapted)*
**REQUIRED:** The balance of cash and cash equivalents.
**DISCUSSION:** Cash is an asset that must be readily available for use by the business. It normally consists of (1) coin and currency on hand, (2) demand deposits (checking accounts), (3) time deposits (savings accounts), and (4) near-cash assets (e.g., money market accounts). In this case, cash equivalents include investments with original maturities of 3 months or less. The original maturity is the date on which the obligation becomes due. Accordingly, the amount to be reported as cash and cash equivalents is $460,000 ($35,000 + $75,000 + $350,000).
Answer (A) is incorrect because $110,000 excludes the T-bill maturing on 1/31/20X3. Answer (B) is incorrect because $385,000 excludes the cash in the money market account. Answer (D) is incorrect because $860,000 includes the T-bill maturing on 3/31/20X3.

**5.** Ral Corp.'s checkbook balance on December 31, 20X2 was $5,000. In addition, Ral held the following items in its safe on that date:

| | |
|---|---:|
| Check payable to Ral Corp., dated January 2, 20X3, in payment of a sale made in December 20X2, not included in December 31 checkbook balance | $2,000 |
| Check payable to Ral Corp., deposited December 15 and included in December 31 checkbook balance, but returned by bank on December 30 stamped "NSF." The check was redeposited on January 2, 20X3 and cleared on January 9. | 500 |
| Check drawn on Ral Corp.'s account, payable to a vendor, dated and recorded in Ral's books on December 31, but not mailed until January 10, 20X3 | 300 |

The proper amount to be shown as cash on Ral's balance sheet at December 31, 20X2 is

A. $4,800

B. $5,300

C. $6,500

D. $6,800

**Answer (A) is correct.** *(CPA, adapted)*
**REQUIRED:** The amount to be recorded as cash on the year-end balance sheet.
**DISCUSSION:** The December 31 checkbook balance is $5,000. The $2,000 check dated January 2, 20X3 is properly not included in this balance because it is not negotiable at year-end. The $500 NSF check should not be included in cash because it is a receivable. The $300 check that was not mailed until January 10 should be added to the balance. This predated check is still within the control of the company and should not decrease the cash account. Consequently, the cash balance to be reported on the December 31, 20X2 balance sheet is $4,800.

| | |
|---|---:|
| Balance per checkbook | $5,000 |
| Add: Predated check | 300 |
| Deduct: NSF check | (500) |
| Cash balance 12/31/X2 | $4,800 |

Answer (B) is incorrect because $5,300 does not include deduction of the NSF check. Answer (C) is incorrect because $6,500 includes the postdated check but not the predated check. Answer (D) is incorrect because $6,800 includes the postdated check.

Questions 6 through 8 are based on the following information.  On January 1, a company establishes a petty cash account and designates one employee as petty cash custodian.  The original amount included in the petty cash fund is $500, and it will be used to make small cash disbursements.  The fund will be replenished on the first of each month, after the petty cash custodian presents receipts for disbursements to the general cashier.  The following disbursements are made in January.  The balance in the petty cash box at the end of January is $163.

|                  |       |
|------------------|-------|
| Office supplies  | $173  |
| Postage          | 112   |
| Entertainment    | 42    |

**6.** Who is responsible, at all times, for the amount of the petty cash fund?

A. The president of the company.

B. The general office manager.

C. The general cashier.

D. The petty cash custodian.

Answer (D) is correct.  *(CIA, adapted)*
**REQUIRED:** The person responsible for the petty cash fund.
**DISCUSSION:** The duties of the petty cash custodian include obtaining signed receipts for cash disbursements and requesting reimbursement from the general cashier.  Consequently, the petty cash custodian is responsible for the petty cash fund (both cash and signed receipts) at all times.

**7.** Which of the following is not an appropriate procedure for controlling the petty cash fund?

A. The petty cash custodian files receipts by category of expenditure after their presentation to the general cashier, so that variations in different types of expenditures can be monitored.

B. Surprise counts of the fund are made from time to time by a superior of the petty cash custodian to determine that the fund is being accounted for satisfactorily.

C. The petty cash custodian obtains signed receipts from each individual to whom petty cash is paid.

D. Upon receiving petty cash receipts as evidence of disbursements, the general cashier issues a company check to the petty cash custodian, rather than cash, to replenish the fund.

Answer (A) is correct.  *(CIA, adapted)*
**REQUIRED:** The inappropriate procedure for controlling the petty cash fund.
**DISCUSSION:** It would be inappropriate for the petty cash custodian to retain the petty cash receipts because the receipts could be used for a second reimbursement.  The receipts should be canceled or mutilated after submission for reimbursement.
   Answer (B) is incorrect because surprise counts may deter fraudulent activity.  Answer (C) is incorrect because requiring signed receipts is an appropriate control procedure.  The signed receipts provide documentation of cash transactions.  Answer (D) is incorrect because reimbursement by company check is an appropriate control procedure.  It is unwise to have excessive amounts of cash readily available.

**8.** The entry required at the end of January is:

A.
| | | |
|---|---|---|
| Office supplies expense | $173 | |
| Postage expense | 112 | |
| Entertainment expense | 42 | |
| Cash | | $327 |

B.
| | | |
|---|---|---|
| Office supplies expense | $173 | |
| Postage expense | 112 | |
| Entertainment expense | 42 | |
| Petty cash | | $327 |

C.
| | | |
|---|---|---|
| Office supplies expense | $173 | |
| Postage expense | 112 | |
| Entertainment expense | 42 | |
| Cash over and short | 10 | |
| Cash | | $337 |

D.
| | | |
|---|---|---|
| Office supplies expense | $173 | |
| Postage expense | 112 | |
| Entertainment expense | 42 | |
| Cash | | $317 |
| Cash over and short | | 10 |

Answer (C) is correct.  *(CIA, adapted)*
**REQUIRED:** The entry for petty cash fund disbursements.
**DISCUSSION:** Each expense item is recognized, cash is credited for the total expenditures plus the cash shortage ($173 + $112 + $42 + $10 = $337), and the discrepancy is debited to the cash over and short account.  The discrepancy is the original balance of the fund, minus total documented expenditures, minus the ending balance of the fund ($500 – $327 – $163 = $10).
   Answer (A) is incorrect because this entry does not recognize that $10 is missing from the petty cash fund.  Answer (B) is incorrect because this entry credits petty cash rather than cash and does not recognize that $10 is missing from the petty cash fund.  Answer (D) is incorrect because this entry credits the cash account for the wrong amount ($317 rather than $337) and credits the cash over and short account rather than debiting it.

## 13.2 Accounts Receivable

**9.** Bad debt expense must be estimated in order to satisfy the matching principle when expenses are recorded in the same periods as the related revenues. In estimating the provision for doubtful accounts for a period, companies generally accrue

A. Either an amount based on a percentage of total sales or an amount based on a percentage of accounts receivable after adjusting for any balance in the allowance for doubtful accounts.

B. A percentage of total sales.

C. Either an amount based on a percentage of credit sales or an amount based on a percentage of accounts receivable after adjusting for any balance in the allowance for doubtful accounts.

D. An amount equal to last year's bad debt expense.

Answer (C) is correct. *(CMA, adapted)*
**REQUIRED:** The true statement about the accrual entry for bad debts.
**DISCUSSION:** The allowance method records bad debt expense systematically as a percentage of either sales or the level of accounts receivable. The latter calculation considers the amount already existing in the allowance account. The credit is to a contra asset (allowance) account. As accounts receivable are written off, they are charged to the allowance account.
Answer (A) is incorrect because credit sales should be used instead of total sales. Answer (B) is incorrect because credit sales are preferred to total sales, and the ending balance in receivables can also be used as the basis for estimating bad debts. Answer (D) is incorrect because each year's bad debt expense should be matched with its revenues.

**10.** Oxford Company sold $300,000 of its accounts receivables without recourse to a factoring agency. The purchaser assessed a finance charge of 5%. It also retained 5% to cover adjustments (sales returns, discounts, etc.). Oxford should record

A. A debit to cash of $300,000.

B. A credit to accounts receivable of $300,000.

C. A credit to liability on transferred accounts receivable of $300,000.

D. Interest expense of $15,000.

Answer (B) is correct. *(Publisher)*
**REQUIRED:** The journal entry to record a sale of accounts receivable on a nonrecourse basis.
**DISCUSSION:** The entry to record a nonrecourse sale of receivables is to debit cash for the proceeds of the sale [$300,000 × (100% − 5% − 5%) = $270,000], debit a receivable from the factor for the proceeds retained to cover probable adjustments (5% × $300,000 = $15,000), and credit accounts receivable for the face value of the receivables transferred ($300,000). The difference of $15,000 (the finance charge) is debited to a loss on sale of receivables.
Answer (A) is incorrect because cash is debited for $270,000. Answer (C) is incorrect because the company will have no contingent liability. The accounts were transferred without recourse. Answer (D) is incorrect because the company did not borrow money; it sold an asset. Thus, "interest expense" is not an appropriate term.

**11.** At January 1, 20X2, Jamin Co. had a credit balance of $260,000 in its allowance for uncollectible accounts. Based on past experience, 2% of Jamin's credit sales have been uncollectible. During 20X2, Jamin wrote off $325,000 of uncollectible accounts. Credit sales for 20X2 were $9 million. In its December 31, 20X2 balance sheet, what amount should Jamin report as allowance for uncollectible accounts?

A. $115,000

B. $180,000

C. $245,000

D. $440,000

Answer (A) is correct. *(CPA, adapted)*
**REQUIRED:** The allowance for uncollectible accounts.
**DISCUSSION:** The beginning balance in the allowance account is $260,000, write-offs equal $325,000, and bad debt expense is $180,000 ($9,000,000 × .02). Thus, the ending balance in the allowance account is $115,000.

| Allowance | | | |
|---|---|---|---|
| | | $260,000 | 1/1/X2 |
| Write-offs | $325,000 | 180,000 | Bad debt exp. |
| | | $115,000 | 12/31/X2 |

Answer (B) is incorrect because $180,000 equals the bad debt expense ($9,000,000 × .02). Answer (C) is incorrect because $245,000 results from debiting $180,000 instead of crediting the allowance account for that amount. Answer (D) is incorrect because $440,000 ignores the write-offs.

**12.** Ward Co. estimates its uncollectible accounts expense to be 2% of credit sales. Ward's credit sales for 20X2 were $1 million. During 20X2, Ward wrote off $18,000 of uncollectible accounts. Ward's allowance for uncollectible accounts had a $15,000 balance on January 1, 20X2. In its December 31, 20X2 income statement, what amount should Ward report as uncollectible accounts expense?

A. $23,000

B. $20,000

C. $18,000

D. $17,000

Answer (B) is correct. *(CPA, adapted)*
REQUIRED: The uncollectible accounts expense as a percentage of sales.
DISCUSSION: When bad debt expense is estimated on the basis of net credit sales, a cost (bad debt expense) is being directly associated with a revenue of the period (net credit sales). Thus, uncollectible accounts expense is $20,000 ($1,000,000 credit sales × 2%).
Answer (A) is incorrect because $23,000 assumes that $20,000 is the required ending balance in the allowance account (expense = write-offs + the change in the allowance).
Answer (C) is incorrect because $18,000 equals the write-offs for 20X2. Answer (D) is incorrect because $17,000 is the ending balance in the allowance account.

**13.** An internal auditor is deriving cash flow data based on an incomplete set of facts. Bad debt expense was $2,000. Additional data for this period follow:

| | |
|---|---|
| Net income | $100,000 |
| Accounts receivable beginning balance | 5,000 |
| Allowance for bad debts beginning balance | (500) |
| Accounts receivable written off | 1,000 |
| Increase in net accounts receivable (after subtraction of allowance for bad debts) | 30,000 |

How much cash was collected from accounts receivable this period?

A. $67,000

B. $68,500

C. $68,000

D. $70,000

Answer (D) is correct. *(CIA, adapted)*
REQUIRED: The cash collected on accounts receivable.
DISCUSSION: The cash collected equals net income adjusted for the change in net accounts receivable (gross A/R – allowance for bad debts). An increase in net accounts receivable implies that cash collected was less than net income. Hence, cash collected was $70,000 ($100,000 – $30,000 increase in net A/R). Write-offs (debit the allowance, credit A/R) do not affect the computation of cash collected because the allowance and gross accounts receivable are reduced by the same amount. Moreover, recognition of bad debt expense (debit bad debt expense, credit the allowance) is not included in this calculation because it is already reflected in the net accounts receivable balance.
Answer (A) is incorrect because $67,000 results from subtracting the writeoffs and the bad debt expense from the sum of net income and beginning net accounts receivable.
Answer (B) is incorrect because $68,500 assumes a zero balance in the beginning allowance account and deducts bad debt expense from the sum of net income and beginning net accounts receivable. Answer (C) is incorrect because $68,000 deducts bad debt expense from the sum of net income and beginning net accounts receivable.

**14.** An analysis of a company's $150,000 accounts receivable at year-end resulted in a $5,000 ending balance for its allowance for uncollectible accounts and a bad debt expense of $2,000. During the past year, recoveries on bad debts previously written off were correctly recorded at $500. If the beginning balance in the allowance for uncollectible accounts was $4,700, what was the amount of accounts receivable written off as uncollectible during the year?

A. $1,200

B. $1,800

C. $2,200

D. $2,800

Answer (C) is correct. *(CIA, adapted)*
REQUIRED: The amount of accounts receivable written off during the year.
DISCUSSION: Under the allowance method, uncollectible accounts are written off by a debit to the allowance account and a credit to accounts receivable. The $500 of recovered bad debts is accounted for by a debit to accounts receivable and a credit to the allowance account. The $2,000 bad debt expense is also credited to the allowance account. The amount of accounts receivable written off as uncollectible is $2,200 [$5,000 ending allowance – ($4,700 beginning allowance + $500 recoveries + $2,000 bad debt expense)].
Answer (A) is incorrect because $1,200 results from subtracting the recoveries instead of adding them. Answer (B) is incorrect because $1,800 results from subtracting bad debt expense from the allowance account. Answer (D) is incorrect because $2,800 results from subtracting the recoveries and bad debt expense from the allowance account.

Questions 15 through 17 are based on the following information. Madison Corporation uses the allowance method to measure its accounts receivable and is making the annual adjustments at fiscal year end, November 30. The proportion of uncollectible accounts is estimated based on past experience, which indicates 1.5% of net credit sales will be uncollectible. Total sales for the year were $2,000,000, of which $200,000 were cash transactions. Madison has determined that the Norris Corporation accounts receivable balance of $10,000 is uncollectible and will write off this account before year-end adjustments are made. Listed below are Madison's account balances at November 30 prior to any adjustments and the $10,000 write-off.

| | |
|---|---:|
| Sales | $2,000,000 |
| Accounts receivable | 750,000 |
| Sales discounts | 125,000 |
| Allowance for doubtful accounts | 16,500 |
| Sales returns and allowances | 175,000 |
| Bad debt expense | 0 |

**15.** The entry to write off Norris Corporation's accounts receivable balance of $10,000 will

A. Increase total assets and decrease net income.

B. Decrease total assets and net income.

C. Have no effect on total assets and decrease net income.

D. Have no effect on total assets and net income.

Answer (D) is correct. *(CMA, adapted)*
REQUIRED: The effect of an entry to write off accounts receivable.
DISCUSSION: If a company uses the allowance method, the write-off of a receivable has no effect on total assets. The journal entry involves a debit to the allowance account (a contra asset) and a credit to accounts receivable (an asset). The net effect is that the asset section is both debited and credited for the same amount. Thus, there will be no effect on either total assets or net income.

**16.** After a suggestion from the company's external auditors, Madison wishes to value its accounts receivable using the balance sheet approach. The chart below presents the aging of the accounts receivable subsidiary ledger accounts at November 30.

| Account | Total Balance | Less than 60 days | 61-90 days | 91-120 days | Greater than 120 days |
|---|---|---|---|---|---|
| Arcadia | $ 50,000 | $ 50,000 | | | |
| Dawson | 128,000 | 90,000 | $ 38,000 | | |
| Gracelon | 327,000 | 250,000 | 77,000 | | |
| Prentiss | 25,000 | | | | $25,000 |
| Strauss | 210,000 | | | $210,000 | |
| Total | $740,000 | $390,000 | $115,000 | $210,000 | $25,000 |
| % uncollectible | | 1% | 5% | 15% | 40% |

If Madison has already written off the $10,000 uncollectible account and recorded the November 30 entry for bad debt expense using the allowance method, the final entry to the related accounts to adjust to the balance sheet approach of valuing accounts receivable is

A. Debit allowance for doubtful accounts for $22,150 and credit bad debt expense for $22,150.

B. Debit allowance for doubtful accounts for $12,150 and credit sales for $12,150.

C. Credit accounts receivable for $12,150 and debit bad debt expense for $12,150.

D. Credit allowance for doubtful accounts for $22,150 and debit bad debt expense for $22,150.

Answer (D) is correct. *(CMA, adapted)*
REQUIRED: The entry needed to change to the balance sheet approach to recording bad debts.
DISCUSSION: The balance sheet approach emphasizes asset valuation. Hence, it determines the amount that should be in the allowance (valuation) account to absorb future bad debts. This process may be accomplished by preparing an aging schedule and multiplying each column by the expected uncollectibility rate.

| Receivables | Rate | Expected Bad Debt |
|---|---|---|
| $390,000 | 1% | $ 3,900 |
| 115,000 | 5% | 5,750 |
| 210,000 | 15% | 31,500 |
| 25,000 | 40% | 10,000 |
| | | $51,150 |

Accordingly, the allowance account should have a credit balance of $51,150. If a company uses the allowance method, the write-off of a receivable involves a debit to the allowance account (a contra asset) and a credit to accounts receivable (an asset). Thus, the $10,000 uncollectible account write-off will decrease the allowance account by $10,000. Under the allowance method, the entry to provide for bad debts is to debit bad debt expense and credit the allowance account. Net credit sales were $1,500,000 ($1,800,000 – $125,000 of discounts – $175,000 of returns). Thus, the expected bad debt expense is $22,500 ($1,500,000 × 1.5%). This amount is recorded regardless of the balance remaining in the allowance account from previous periods. The net effect is that the allowance account is increased by $22,500. Thus, after recording these two entries, the allowance account balance was $29,000 ($16,500 beginning balance – $10,000 written off + $22,500 adjustment). The allowance account should have a $51,150 credit balance. Hence, the necessary correction is to debit bad debt expense and credit (increase) the allowance for $22,150 ($51,150 – $29,000).

**17.** As a result of the November 30 adjusting entry to provide for bad debts, the allowance for doubtful accounts will

    A.  Increase by $30,000.

    B.  Increase by $25,500.

    C.  Increase by $22,500.

    D.  Decrease by $22,500.

Answer (C) is correct. *(CMA, adapted)*
    **REQUIRED:** The effect on the allowance account of the year-end adjusting entry for bad debt expense.
    **DISCUSSION:** The entry is to debit bad debt expense and credit the allowance account. Net credit sales were $1,500,000 ($1,800,000 – $125,000 of discounts – $175,000 of returns). Thus, the expected bad debt expense is $22,500 ($1,500,000 × 1.5%). This amount is recorded regardless of the balance remaining in the allowance account from previous periods. The net effect is that the allowance account is increased by $22,500.

**18.** A government has just levied $140,000 in taxes and estimates that $14,000 of the taxes will never be collected. The journal entry of the government at the time the taxes are levied is:

    A.  Tax revenue        $140,000
           Tax receivable            $140,000

    B.  Tax receivable    $140,000
           Tax revenue             $140,000

    C.  Tax revenue         $126,000
           Allowance for
             uncollectible taxes  $ 14,000
             Tax receivable          $140,000

    D.  Tax receivable    $140,000
           Tax revenue             $126,000
           Allowance for
             uncollectible taxes    $ 14,000

Answer (D) is correct. *(CIA, adapted)*
    **REQUIRED:** The journal entry required at the time the taxes are levied.
    **DISCUSSION:** Tax receivable is debited for the full amount of the taxes levied. Only the portion of the taxes levied that is expected to be collected is credited to tax revenue. The uncollectible portion is credited to an allowance for uncollectible taxes.
    Answer (A) is incorrect because tax receivable should be debited and tax revenue credited. Also, only the portion of the taxes levied that is expected to be collected should be credited to tax revenue, with the remainder credited to an allowance for uncollectible taxes. Answer (B) is incorrect because only the portion of the taxes levied that is expected to be collected should be credited to tax revenue, with the remainder credited to an allowance for uncollectible taxes. Answer (C) is incorrect because tax revenue and allowance for uncollectible taxes are credited and tax receivable is debited.

**19.** Wren Company had the following account balances at December 31, 20X2:

| | |
|---|---|
| Accounts receivable | $ 900,000 |
| Allowance for doubtful accounts | |
|   (before any provision for 20X2 | |
|   doubtful accounts expense) | 16,000 |
| Credit sales for 20X2 | 1,750,000 |

Wren is considering the following methods of estimating doubtful accounts expense for 20X2:

    • Based on credit sales at 2%
    • Based on accounts receivable at 5%

What amount should Wren charge to doubtful accounts expense under each method?

| | Percentage of Credit Sales | Percentage of Accounts Receivable |
|---|---|---|
| A. | $51,000 | $45,000 |
| B. | $51,000 | $29,000 |
| C. | $35,000 | $45,000 |
| D. | $35,000 | $29,000 |

Answer (D) is correct. *(CPA, adapted)*
    **REQUIRED:** The amount charged to doubtful accounts expense under each method.
    **DISCUSSION:** Doubtful accounts expense is estimated in two ways. The first, which emphasizes asset valuation, is based on an aging of the receivables to determine the balance in the allowance for uncollectible accounts. Bad debt expense is the amount necessary to adjust the allowance account to this estimated balance. The second, which emphasizes income measurement, recognizes bad debt expense as a percentage of sales. The corresponding credit is to the allowance for uncollectible accounts. Under the first method, if doubtful accounts are estimated to be 5% of gross accounts receivable, the allowance account should have a balance of $45,000 ($900,000 × 5%), and the entry is to debit doubtful accounts expense and credit the allowance for $29,000 ($45,000 – $16,000 existing balance). Under the second method, bad debt expense is $35,000 ($1,750,000 × 2%).
    Answer (A) is incorrect because $51,000 equals 2% of credit sales plus the balance of the allowance account, and $45,000 equals 5% of gross accounts receivable. Answer (B) is incorrect because $51,000 equals 2% of credit sales plus the balance of the allowance account. Answer (C) is incorrect because $45,000 equals 5% of gross accounts receivable.

**20.** One of the conditions necessary to recognize a transfer of receivables with recourse as a sale is that the

A. Transferee surrenders control of the receivables but retains a beneficial interest.

B. Transferor has derecognized all assets sold.

C. The transferor is not both entitled and obligated to repurchase the receivables.

D. Transferred assets are isolated from the transferee.

Answer (C) is correct.  *(CMA, adapted)*
**REQUIRED:** The condition for recognizing a transfer of receivables with recourse as a sale.
**DISCUSSION:** The transferor of a financial asset surrenders control and the transaction is treated as a sale only if three conditions are met: (1) The assets have been isolated from the transferor (i.e., they are beyond the reach of the transferor and its creditors); (2) neither a regular transferee nor a holder of a beneficial interest in a qualifying special-purpose entity (e.g., certain trusts) is subject to a condition that both constrains its right to pledge or exchange those interests and provides more than a trivial benefit to the transferor; and (3) the transferor does not maintain effective control over the transferred assets through certain repurchase or redemption agreements or the ability unilaterally to cause the holder to return specific assets (SFAS 140).
Answer (A) is incorrect because the transferor must surrender control. Answer (B) is incorrect because the transferee must have the unconstrained right to pledge or exchange the receivables. Answer (D) is incorrect because the transferred assets must be isolated from the transferor.

**21.** On March 31, 20X2, Vale Co. had an unadjusted credit balance of $1,000 in its allowance for uncollectible accounts. An analysis of Vale's trade accounts receivable at that date revealed the following:

| Age | Amount | Estimated Uncollectible |
|---|---|---|
| 0 - 30 days | $60,000 | 5% |
| 31 - 60 days | 4,000 | 10% |
| Over 60 days | 2,000 | $1,400 |

What amount should Vale report as allowance for uncollectible accounts in its March 31, 20X2 balance sheet?

A. $4,800

B. $4,000

C. $3,800

D. $3,000

Answer (A) is correct.  *(CPA, adapted)*
**REQUIRED:** The amount in the allowance for uncollectible accounts based on an aging schedule.
**DISCUSSION:** The aging schedule determines the balance in the allowance for uncollectible accounts. Of the accounts that are no more than 30 days old, the amount uncollectible is $3,000 ($60,000 × 5%). Accounts that are 31-60 days old and over 60 days old have estimated uncollectible balances of $400 ($4,000 × 10%) and $1,400, respectively. Hence, the amount that should be in the allowance for uncollectible accounts is $4,800 ($3,000 + $400 + $1,400). The $1,000 balance already in the account is disregarded because the aging schedule determines the balance that should be in the account.
Answer (B) is incorrect because $4,000 equals the existing balance plus the estimated uncollectible amount for the newest receivables. Answer (C) is incorrect because $3,800 is the credit to the allowance account. Answer (D) is incorrect because $3,000 is the estimated uncollectible amount for the newest receivables.

**22.** If a transfer of receivables with recourse qualifies to be recognized as a sale, the proceeds from the sale are

A. Accounted for as a secured borrowing.

B. Recorded at fair value for the assets obtained and liabilities incurred.

C. Recorded at the historical cost of the assets obtained.

D. Reduced by the fair value of the recourse obligation.

Answer (D) is correct.  *(CMA, adapted)*
**REQUIRED:** The interest rate used in estimating the selling price of receivables.
**DISCUSSION:** When a transfer of receivables with recourse meets the criteria to be accounted for as a sale, the proceeds of the sale are reduced by the fair value of the recourse obligation. When the transfer does not meet these criteria, the transfer is accounted for as a secured borrowing.

**23.** A company offers its customers credit terms of a 2% discount if paid within 10 days, or the full balance is due within 30 days (2/10, n/30). If some customers take advantage of the cash discount and others do not, which of the following accounts will appear on the income statement if the net method of recording receivables is employed?

|   | Sales Discounts | Sales Discounts Forfeited |
|---|---|---|
| A. | Yes | Yes |
| B. | Yes | No |
| C. | No | No |
| D. | No | Yes |

Answer (D) is correct.  *(CIA, adapted)*
    **REQUIRED:** The account(s) appearing on the income statement if the net method is used.
    **DISCUSSION:** The gross method accounts for receivables at their face value. If a discount is taken, a sales discount is recorded and classified as an offset to sales in the income statement to yield net sales. The net method records receivables net of the applicable discount. If the payment is not received during the discount period, an interest revenue account such as sales discounts forfeited is credited at the end of the discount period or when the payment is received. Accordingly, the application of the net method requires a sales discount forfeited but not a sales discount account.

**24.** A wholesaler purchased merchandise with a list price of $2,000 from a manufacturer. The purchase was subject to trade discounts of 30% and 10%. What is the proper journal entry to record the purchase transaction?

A. Debit purchases for $2,000 and credit accounts payable for $2,000.

B. Debit purchases for $1,200 and credit accounts payable for $1,200.

C. Debit purchases for $1,260 and credit accounts payable for $1,260.

D. Debit purchases for $2,000, credit accounts payable for $1,260, and credit trade discounts for $740.

Answer (C) is correct.  *(Publisher)*
    **REQUIRED:** The proper journal entry to record a purchase subject to a trade discount.
    **DISCUSSION:** First, the $2,000 list price will be reduced by the 30% trade discount to $1,400. Because of the second trade discount, this amount is then reduced by an additional 10%, or $140, leaving an actual price of $1,260 to be recorded in the accounts. Trade discounts are merely a means of calculating price; they are not recorded in the accounts.
    Answer (A) is incorrect because $2,000 is the list price, not the purchase price. Answer (B) is incorrect because $1,200 is calculated by deducting 40% from the $2,000 list price. Each discount should be calculated separately. Answer (D) is incorrect because trade discounts are not recorded in the accounts.

## 13.3 Notes Receivable

**25.** On Merf's April 30, 20X4 balance sheet, a note receivable was reported as a noncurrent asset, and its accrued interest for 8 months was reported as a current asset. Which of the following terms would fit Merf's note receivable?

A. Both principal and interest amounts are payable on August 31, 20X4 and August 31, 20X5.

B. Principal and interest are due December 31, 20X4.

C. Both principal and interest amounts are payable on December 31, 20X4 and December 31, 20X5.

D. Principal is due August 31, 20X5. Interest is due August 31, 20X4 and August 31, 20X5.

Answer (D) is correct.  *(CPA, adapted)*
    **REQUIRED:** The terms explaining classification of a note receivable as a noncurrent asset and its accrued interest as a current asset.
    **DISCUSSION:** A noncurrent note receivable is one that is not expected to be converted into cash within 1 year or 1 operating cycle, whichever is longer. Because the principal is due more than 1 year from the balance sheet date, it must be regarded as noncurrent. However, the accrued interest is a current asset because it is due in 4 months.

**26.** On August 15, 20X4, Benet Co. sold goods for which it received a note bearing the market rate of interest on that date. The 4-month note was dated July 15, 20X4. Note principal, together with all interest, is due November 15, 20X4. When the note was recorded on August 15, which of the following accounts increased?

A. Unearned discount.

B. Interest receivable.

C. Prepaid interest.

D. Interest revenue.

Answer (B) is correct. *(CPA, adapted)*
   **REQUIRED:** The account that increased when the note was recorded.
   **DISCUSSION:** Because the note bears interest at a reasonable rate, its present value at the date of issuance is the face amount. Hence, the note should be recorded at this amount. Interest receivable may also be debited and unearned interest revenue credited, although the simple alternative is to debit cash and credit interest revenue when payment is received.
   Answer (A) is incorrect because the note bears interest at the market rate. Thus, no discount from its face amount is recorded. Answer (C) is incorrect because no prepayment of interest has been made. Answer (D) is incorrect because interest revenue has not yet been earned.

**27.** On December 1, 20X4, Tigg Mortgage Co. gave Pod Corp. a $200,000, 12% loan. Pod received proceeds of $194,000 after the deduction of a $6,000 nonrefundable loan origination fee. Principal and interest are due in 60 monthly installments of $4,450, beginning January 1, 20X5. The repayments yield an effective interest rate of 12% at a present value of $200,000 and 13.4% at a present value of $194,000. What amount of accrued interest receivable should Tigg include in its December 31, 20X4 balance sheet?

A. $4,450

B. $2,166

C. $2,000

D. $0

Answer (C) is correct. *(CPA, adapted)*
   **REQUIRED:** The accrued interest receivable at year-end.
   **DISCUSSION:** Accrued interest receivable is always equal to the face amount times the nominal rate for the period of the accrual. Hence the accrued interest receivable is $2,000 [$200,000 × 12% × (1 ÷ 12)].
   Answer (A) is incorrect because $4,450 is the monthly installment. It includes principal as well as interest. Answer (B) is incorrect because $2,166 is based on a present value of $194,000 and an effective rate of 13.4%. It is the interest revenue from the loan. Answer (D) is incorrect because 1 month's interest should be accrued.

**28.** On December 1, 20X4, Money Co. gave Home Co. a $200,000, 11% loan. Money paid proceeds of $194,000 after the deduction of a $6,000 nonrefundable loan origination fee. Principal and interest are due in 60 monthly installments of $4,310, beginning January 1, 20X5. The repayments yield an effective interest rate of 11% at a present value of $200,000 and 12.4% at a present value of $194,000. What amount of income from this loan should Money report in its 20X4 income statement?

A. $0

B. $1,833

C. $2,005

D. $7,833

Answer (C) is correct. *(CPA, adapted)*
   **REQUIRED:** The amount of income from the loan at year-end.
   **DISCUSSION:** Under the effective-interest method, the effective rate of interest is applied to the net carrying amount of the receivable to determine the interest revenue. Thus, interest revenue from the loan, for the month of December, equals $2,005 [$194,000 × 12.4% × (1 ÷ 12)].
   Answer (A) is incorrect because one month's interest should be accrued. Answer (B) is incorrect because $1,833 is the accrued interest receivable, which equals the face amount times the nominal rate for the period [$200,000 × 11% × (1 ÷ 12)]. Answer (D) is incorrect because $7,833 equals the $6,000 origination fee plus the accrued interest receivable of $1,833.

**29.** Jole Co. lent $10,000 to a major supplier in exchange for a noninterest-bearing note due in three years and a contract to purchase a fixed amount of merchandise from the supplier at a 10% discount from prevailing market prices over the next 3 years. The market rate for a note of this type is 10%. On issuing the note, Jole should record

| | Discount on note receivable | Deferred charge |
|---|---|---|
| A. | Yes | Yes |
| B. | Yes | No |
| C. | No | Yes |
| D. | No | No |

Answer (A) is correct. *(CPA, adapted)*
   **REQUIRED:** The appropriate accounts to be used in recording the issuance of a noninterest-bearing note receivable.
   **DISCUSSION:** Absent established exchange prices or evidence of the note's market value, the present value of a note with no stated rate or an unreasonable rate should be determined by discounting future payments using an imputed rate. The prevailing rate for similar instruments of issuers with similar credit ratings normally helps determine the appropriate rate. The purpose is to approximate the rate in a similar transaction between independent parties. The stated interest rate may be less than the imputed rate because the lender has received other stated (or unstated) rights and privileges as part of the bargain. The difference between the respective present values of the note computed at the stated rate and at the imputed rate should be accounted for as the cost of the rights or privileges obtained. Jole Co. will record a discount on the note. In addition, because it has received the right to purchase merchandise at a discount from prevailing market prices, a deferred charge (prepaid purchases) also should be recorded at an amount equal to the discount.

**30.** On December 30, 20X4, Chang Co. sold a machine to Door Co. in exchange for a noninterest-bearing note requiring ten annual payments of $10,000. Door made the first payment on December 30, 20X4. The market interest rate for similar notes at date of issuance was 8%. Information on present value factors is as follows:

| Number of Periods | Present Value of $1 at 8% | Present Value of Ordinary Annuity of $1 at 8% |
|---|---|---|
| 9 | 0.50 | 6.25 |
| 10 | 0.46 | 6.71 |

In its December 31, 20X4 balance sheet, what amount should Chang report as note receivable?

   A. $45,000

   B. $46,000

   C. $62,500

   D. $67,100

Answer (C) is correct. *(CPA, adapted)*
   **REQUIRED:** The carrying amount of a noninterest-bearing note receivable at the date of issuance.
   **DISCUSSION:** The purchase agreement calls for a $10,000 initial payment and equal payments of $10,000 to be received at the end of each of the next 9 years. The amount reported for the receivable should consist of the present value of the nine future payments. The present value factor to be used is the present value of an ordinary annuity for nine periods at 8%, or 6.25. The note receivable should be recorded at $62,500 ($10,000 × 6.25).
   Answer (A) is incorrect because $45,000 results from multiplying $90,000 ($10,000 payments × 9 years) by 0.50. Answer (B) is incorrect because $46,000 results from multiplying the $100,000 total by 0.46. Answer (D) is incorrect because $67,100 results from using the present value of an ordinary annuity of $1 at 8% for 10 years instead of 9 years.

**31.** On July 1, Lee Co. sold goods in exchange for a $200,000 8-month noninterest-bearing note receivable. At the time of the sale, the note's market rate of interest was 12%. What amount did Lee receive when the note was discounted at 10% on September 1?

   A. $180,000

   B. $186,667

   C. $190,000

   D. $188,000

Answer (C) is correct. *(CPA, adapted)*
   **REQUIRED:** The amount received from discounting a noninterest-bearing note receivable.
   **DISCUSSION:** The maturity amount of a noninterest-bearing note receivable is its face amount. The discount fee is $10,000 [$200,000 maturity amount × 10% × (6 months ÷ 12)]. Thus, the proceeds equal $190,000 ($200,000 – $10,000).
   Answer (A) is incorrect because $180,000 assumes discounting for a full year. Answer (B) is incorrect because $186,667 assumes discounting for 8 months. Answer (D) is incorrect because $188,000 is based on a discount rate of 12%.

Questions 32 through 34 are based on the following information. On January 2, 20X4, Emme Co. sold equipment with a carrying amount of $480,000 in exchange for a $600,000 noninterest-bearing note due January 2, 20X7. There was no established exchange price for the equipment. The prevailing rate of interest for a note of this type at January 2, 20X4 was 10%. The present value of 1 at 10% for three periods is 0.75.

**32.** In Emme's 20X4 income statement, what amount should be reported as interest income?

A. $15,000

B. $45,000

C. $48,000

D. $60,000

Answer (B) is correct. *(CPA, adapted)*
**REQUIRED:** The interest income from a noninterest-bearing note received for property.
**DISCUSSION:** When a noninterest-bearing note is exchanged for property, and neither the note nor the property has a clearly determinable exchange price, the present value of the note should be the basis for recording the transaction. The present value is determined by discounting all future payments using an appropriately imputed interest rate. Emme Co. will receive $600,000 cash in 3 years. Assuming that 10% is the appropriate imputed rate of interest, the present value (initial carrying value) of the note at January 2, 20X4 was $450,000 ($600,000 × 0.75). Under the interest method, interest income for 2004 was $45,000 ($450,000 × 10%), and the entry is to debit the discount and credit interest income for that amount.
Answer (A) is incorrect because $15,000 is the difference between 10% of the face amount and 10% of the carrying amount. Answer (C) is incorrect because interest income is based on the present value of the note, not the carrying amount of the equipment. Answer (D) is incorrect because interest income is based on the carrying amount of the note, not the face amount.

**33.** In Emme's 20X4 income statement, what amount should be reported as gain (loss) on sale of equipment?

A. $(30,000)

B. $30,000

C. $120,000

D. $150,000

Answer (A) is correct. *(CPA, adapted)*
**REQUIRED:** The amount reported as gain (loss) on the sale of machinery.
**DISCUSSION:** Emme Co. sold equipment with a carrying amount of $480,000 and received a note with a present value of $450,000 ($600,000 × .75). Thus, Emme should report a $30,000 loss ($480,000 – $450,000).
Answer (B) is incorrect because the present value of the note is $30,000 less than the carrying amount surrendered. Answer (C) is incorrect because $120,000 is the difference between the face amount of the note and the carrying amount of the equipment. Answer (D) is incorrect because $150,000 is the discount (face amount – present value).

**34.** On June 1, 20X1, Yola Corp. lent Dale $500,000 on a 12% note, payable in five annual installments of $100,000 beginning January 2, 20X2. In connection with this loan, Dale was required to deposit $5,000 in a noninterest-bearing escrow account. The amount held in escrow is to be returned to Dale after all principal and interest payments have been made. Interest on the note is payable on the first day of each month beginning July 1, 20X1. Dale made timely payments through November 1, 20X1. On January 2, 20X2, Yola received payment of the first principal installment plus all interest due. At December 31, 20X1, Yola's interest receivable on the loan to Dale is

A. $0

B. $5,000

C. $10,000

D. $15,000

Answer (C) is correct. *(CPA, adapted)*
**REQUIRED:** The interest receivable on the loan at year-end.
**DISCUSSION:** Assuming the debtor made no payment on December 1, 2 months of interest should be accrued at year-end. Consequently, the interest receivable on the loan is $10,000 [$500,000 × 12% × (2 ÷ 12)].
Answer (A) is incorrect because $0 is the interest receivable on the loan on 1/2. Answer (B) is incorrect because $5,000 assumes 1 month interest is due. Answer (D) is incorrect because $15,000 assumes 3 months interest is due.

**35.** On December 31, Jet Co. received two $10,000 notes receivable from customers in exchange for services rendered. On both notes, interest is calculated on the outstanding principal balance at the annual rate of 3% and payable at maturity. The note from Hart Corp., made under customary trade terms is due in 9 months and the note from Maxx, Inc. is due in 5 years. The market interest rate for similar notes on December 31 was 8%. The compound interest factors to convert future values into present values at 8% follow:

Present value of $1 due in 9 months     .944
Present value of $1 due in 5 years       .680

At what amounts should these two notes receivable be reported in Jet's December 31 balance sheet?

| | Hart | Maxx |
|---|---|---|
| A. | $9,440 | $6,800 |
| B. | $9,652 | $7,820 |
| C. | $10,000 | $6,800 |
| D. | $10,000 | $7,820 |

**Answer (D) is correct.** *(CPA, adapted)*
**REQUIRED:** The amounts of the notes.
**DISCUSSION:** The presumption when a note is exchanged for services is that the interest rate is fair. If the rate is not stated or is unreasonable, the note and the services should be recorded at the fair value of the services or the market value of the note, whichever is more clearly determinable. Absent these values, the present value of the note should be the basis for recording both the note and the services. This present value is obtained by discounting all future payments on the note using an imputed rate (APB 21). The 3% rate on the Maxx note is unreasonable in light of the prevailing 8% rate for similar notes. This 5-year note should therefore be discounted at an imputed rate of 8%. Because annual interest on the principal is to be paid at maturity, the lump-sum payment due in 5 years is $11,500 {$10,000 + [($10,000 × 3%) interest × 5 years]}. The present value of this amount is $7,820 ($11,500 × .680). However, APB 21 does not apply to receivables from customers arising in the normal course of business that are due in customary trade terms not exceeding approximately 1 year. Thus, in practice, the Hart note is most likely to be reported at its face amount ($10,000).
Answer (A) is incorrect because the Hart note is short-term and is most likely to be reported without discounting. Moreover, the $6,800 value for the Maxx note does not include the discounted interest. Answer (B) is incorrect because a value of $9,652 (rounded) for the Hart note is a discounted amount. Answer (C) is incorrect because the $6,800 value for the Maxx note excludes the discounted interest due at maturity.

**36.** On July 1, 20X1, a company obtained a 2-year 8% note receivable for services rendered. At that time, the market rate of interest was 10%. The face amount of the note and the entire amount of the interest are due on June 30, 20X2. Interest receivable at December 31, 20X1, was

A. 5% of the face amount of the note.

B. 4% of the face amount of the note.

C. 5% of the July 1, 20X1 present amount of the amount due June 30, 20X2.

D. 4% of the July 1, 20X1 present amount of the amount due June 30, 20X2.

**Answer (B) is correct.** *(CPA, adapted)*
**REQUIRED:** The interest receivable at year-end.
**DISCUSSION:** Interest receivable is always equal to the face amount of a note times the coupon or nominal rate. Interest receivable for this note is therefore equal to the face amount times the 8% coupon rate for 6 months, which is the equivalent of the face amount of the note times 4%. Interest revenue is equal to the present value of the note times the market rate of interest for the interval of time the note was outstanding. The difference between the interest receivable and the interest revenue is recorded as an adjustment to the discount account.
Answer (A) is incorrect because 5% is the market rate for 6 months. Answer (C) is incorrect because interest receivable is always equal to the face amount of a note times the coupon or nominal rate. Answer (D) is incorrect because interest receivable is always equal to the face amount of a note times the coupon or nominal rate.

**37.** Rand, Inc. accepted from a customer a $40,000, 90-day, 12% interest-bearing note dated August 31. On September 30, Rand discounted the note at the Apex State Bank at 15%. However, the proceeds were not received until October 1. In Rand's September 30 balance sheet, the amount receivable from the bank, based on a 360-day year, includes accrued interest revenue of

A. $170

B. $300

C. $376

D. $462

**Answer (A) is correct.** *(CPA, adapted)*
**REQUIRED:** The accrued interest revenue recognized when a note is discounted.
**DISCUSSION:** As determined below, the interest received by Rand if it had held the 90-day note to maturity would have been $1,200. The discount fee charged on a note with a maturity amount of $41,200 ($40,000 face amount + $1,200 interest) discounted at 15% for 60 days is $1,030. The difference of $170 ($1,200 interest – $1,030 discount fee) should be reflected as accrued interest revenue at the balance sheet date because the cash proceeds were not received until the next period.

| | | |
|---|---|---|
| $40,000 × 12% × (90 ÷ 360) = | $1,200 | interest |
| $41,200 × 15% × (60 ÷ 360) = | (1,030) | discount fee |
| Accrued interest revenue | $ 170 | |

Answer (B) is incorrect because $300 assumes that interest is earned at 15% for 90 days and that the discount fee is $1,200. Answer (C) is incorrect because $376 assumes that the interest rate is also 12%. Answer (D) is incorrect because $462 assumes that interest is earned at 15% for 90 days.

**38.** Platt Co. has been forced into bankruptcy and liquidated. Unsecured claims will be paid at the rate of $.50 on the dollar. Maga Co. holds a noninterest-bearing note receivable from Platt in the amount of $50,000, collateralized by machinery with a liquidation value of $10,000. The total amount to be realized by Maga on this note receivable is

A. $35,000

B. $30,000

C. $25,000

D. $10,000

Answer (B) is correct.   *(CPA, adapted)*
REQUIRED: The amount to be realized from a liquidation claim.

DISCUSSION: The $50,000 note receivable is secured to the extent of $10,000. The remaining $40,000 is unsecured, and Maga will be paid on this claim at the rate of $.50 on the dollar.

| | |
|---|---|
| Secured claim | $10,000 |
| Unsecured ($40,000 × .5) | 20,000 |
| Amount realized | $30,000 |

Answer (A) is incorrect because $35,000 results from taking $.50 on the dollar for the entire amount of the note receivable and adding the amount that is secured. Answer (C) is incorrect because $25,000 results from multiplying $.50 times the full amount of the note. Answer (D) is incorrect because $10,000 is only the secured amount and does not take into effect the collection from the unsecured portion.

**39.** In Emme's 20X4 income statement, what amount should be reported as interest income?

A. $15,000

B. $45,000

C. $48,000

D. $60,000

Answer (B) is correct.   *(CPA, adapted)*
REQUIRED: The interest income from a noninterest-bearing note received for property.

DISCUSSION: When a noninterest-bearing note is exchanged for property, and neither the note nor the property has a clearly determinable exchange price, the present value of the note should be the basis for recording the transaction. The present value is determined by discounting all future payments using an appropriately imputed interest rate. Emme Co. will receive $600,000 cash in 3 years. Assuming that 10% is the appropriate imputed rate of interest, the present value (initial carrying value) of the note at January 2, 20X4 was $450,000 ($600,000 × 0.75). Under the interest method, interest income for 2004 was $45,000 ($450,000 × 10%), and the entry is to debit the discount and credit interest income for that amount.

Answer (A) is incorrect because $15,000 is the difference between 10% of the face amount and 10% of the carrying amount. Answer (C) is incorrect because interest income is based on the present value of the note, not the carrying amount of the equipment. Answer (D) is incorrect because interest income is based on the carrying amount of the note, not the face amount.

**40.** Roth, Inc. received from a customer a 1-year, $500,000 note bearing annual interest of 8%. After holding the note for 6 months, Roth discounted the note at Regional Bank at an effective interest rate of 10%. What amount of cash did Roth receive from the bank?

A. $540,000

B. $528,400

C. $513,000

D. $486,000

Answer (C) is correct.   *(CPA, adapted)*
REQUIRED: The amount of cash received when a note is discounted.

DISCUSSION: The maturity amount of the note is $540,000 [$500,000 face value + ($500,000 × 8%)]. The discount is $27,000 [$540,000 × 10% × (6 ÷ 12)]. Consequently, the proceeds equal $513,000 ($540,000 – $27,000).

Answer (A) is incorrect because $540,000 is the maturity value. Answer (B) is incorrect because $528,400 assumes a nominal rate of 10% and a discount rate of 8%. Answer (D) is incorrect because $486,000 results from discounting the note for 1 year.

**41.** Shep Co. has a receivable from its parent, Pep Co. Should this receivable be separately reported in Shep's balance sheet and in Pep's consolidated balance sheet?

| | Shep's Balance Sheet | Pep's Consolidated Balance Sheet |
|---|---|---|
| A. | Yes | No |
| B. | Yes | Yes |
| C. | No | No |
| D. | No | Yes |

Answer (A) is correct. *(CPA, adapted)*
**REQUIRED:** The treatment of an intercompany receivable in the balance sheet of a subsidiary and in the consolidated balance sheet.
**DISCUSSION:** In a consolidated balance sheet, reciprocal balances, such as receivables and payables, between a parent and a consolidated subsidiary should be eliminated in their entirety regardless of the portion of the subsidiary's stock held by the parent. However, intercompany transactions should not be eliminated from the separate financial statements of the entities.

**42.** A method of estimating uncollectible accounts that emphasizes asset valuation rather than income measurement is the allowance method based on

A. Aging the receivables.

B. Direct write-offs.

C. Gross sales.

D. Credit sales minus returns and allowances.

Answer (A) is correct. *(CPA, adapted)*
**REQUIRED:** The method of estimating uncollectible accounts that emphasizes asset valuation.
**DISCUSSION:** Under the allowance method, uncollectible accounts are estimated in two ways. The method that emphasizes asset valuation is based on an aging of the receivables to determine the balance in the allowance for uncollectible accounts. Bad debt expense is the amount necessary to adjust the allowance account to this estimated balance. The method emphasizing the income statement calculates bad debt expense as a percentage of sales.
Answer (B) is incorrect because the direct write-off method is not a means of estimation. Answer (C) is incorrect because an estimate based on gross sales focuses on the income statement. Answer (D) is incorrect because an estimate based on credit sales minus returns and allowances focuses on the income statement.

**43.** After being held for 30 days, a 90-day, 5% interest-bearing note receivable was discounted at a bank at 8%. The proceeds received from the bank upon discounting is the

A. Maturity amount minus the discount at 8%.

B. Maturity amount plus the discount at 8%.

C. Face amount minus the discount at 8%.

D. Face amount plus the discount at 8%.

Answer (A) is correct. *(CPA, adapted)*
**REQUIRED:** The proceeds from discounting a note receivable.
**DISCUSSION:** The cash proceeds from discounting the note will equal the maturity amount (face amount + interest at 5% for 90 days) minus the discount (maturity amount × 8% for 60 days).
Answer (B) is incorrect because the discount is subtracted. Answer (C) is incorrect because the maturity amount, not the face amount, of an interest-bearing note is the basis for determining the discount. Answer (D) is incorrect because the maturity amount, not the face amount, of an interest-bearing note is the basis for determining the discount.

Use Gleim's *CMA Test Prep* for interactive testing with **over 2,000 additional multiple-choice questions!**

# STUDY UNIT FOURTEEN
# INVENTORIES AND INVESTMENTS

(21 pages of outline)

This study unit is the **fourth of ten** on **external financial reporting**. The relative weight assigned to this major topic in Part 2 of the exam is **25%** at **skill level B** (four skill types required). The ten study units are

Study Unit 11: Overview of External Financial Reporting
Study Unit 12: Overview of Financial Statements
Study Unit 13: Cash and Receivables
Study Unit 14: Inventories and Investments
Study Unit 15: Long-Lived Assets
Study Unit 16: Liabilities
Study Unit 17: Equity and Revenue Recognition
Study Unit 18: Other Income Statement Items
Study Unit 19: Business Combinations and Derivatives
Study Unit 20: SEC Requirements and the Annual Report

After studying the outlines and answering the multiple-choice questions in this study unit, you will have the skills necessary to address the following topics listed in the IMA's Learning Outcome Statements:

Part 2 – Section E.4. Recognition, measurement, valuation, and disclosure

For each of the subtopics listed, the candidate should be able to:

1. define the subtopic and describe the characteristics of its components

2. demonstrate an understanding of appropriate valuation techniques for the components of each subtopic

3. demonstrate an understanding of the appropriate accounting conventions for the components of each subtopic

4. compare and contrast valuation techniques and accounting methods

5. show the correct financial statement presentation

6. identify the appropriate disclosure requirements in the body of the financial statements and/or in the footnotes

Inventories

   a. subtopic components: raw material inventory, work-in-process inventory, finished goods inventory, and merchandise inventory; perpetual, modified perpetual, and periodic inventory systems; cost of goods sold, cost of goods available for sale, goods in transit, and consigned goods

   b. identify issues in inventory valuation, including which goods to include, what costs to include, and which cost assumption to use

   c. identify the costs included in inventory

   d. differentiate between f.o.b. shipping point and f.o.b. destination

e.   demonstrate an understanding of special sale agreements, including sales with a buyback agreement (product financing arrangement), sales with high rates of returns, and sales on installment

f.   calculate and indicate the correct entries and financial statement presentation for purchase discounts using the gross method and using the net method

g.   identify accounting issues related to purchase commitments

h.   identify and compare cost flow assumptions used in accounting for inventories

i.   calculate ending inventory and cost of goods sold using the specific identification, average cost, first-in-first-out (FIFO), and last-in-first-out (LIFO) methods

j.   calculate the effect on income and on assets of using different inventory methods

k.   analyze the effects of inventory errors

l.   demonstrate an understanding of the LIFO reserve and LIFO liquidation

m.   calculate ending inventory and cost of goods sold using dollar-value LIFO

n.   identify advantages and disadvantages of the different inventory methods

o.   apply the lower of cost or market rule

p.   identify when inventories are valued at net realizable value

q.   demonstrate an understanding of the relative sales value method

r.   determine ending inventory by using the gross profit method and by using the retail inventory method

s.   recommend the inventory method and cost flow assumption that should be used given a set of facts and management goals

## Investments

a.   subtopic components:  debt securities:  held-to-maturity, trading, and available-for-sale securities; equity securities:  less than 20% holdings (available-for-sale and trading), between 20% and 50% holdings, and holdings more than 50%

b.   calculate discounts, premiums, and interest on debt securities using the effective interest method and utilizing time value of money tables

c.   define holding gain or loss

d.   compute the realized gain/loss on the sale of a debt or equity security

e.   calculate the securities fair value adjustment for available-for-sale and trading debt securities

f.   identify and describe the fair value method, equity method, and consolidated method for equity securities

g.   compare the equity method with the fair value method

h.   demonstrate an understanding of reclassification adjustments

i.   account for impairment of value and indicate the correct cost basis for the impaired security

j.   identify and describe the proper accounting for transfers of investment securities between categories

## 14.1 INVENTORIES

1.   **Definition**

a.   **ARB 43, Chapter 4**, *Inventory Pricing*, defines inventory as "the aggregate of those items of tangible personal property that

1)   Are held for sale in the ordinary course of business,

2)   Are in process of production for such sale, or

3)   Are to be currently consumed in the production of goods or services to be available for sale."

b.   Inventory does not include long-term assets subject to depreciation.

2. **Sources of Inventories**

   a. **Retailing.** A trading (retailing) concern purchases merchandise to be resold without substantial modification.

      1) Such entities may also maintain a supplies inventory.

      2) For a retailer, **cost of goods sold** essentially equals beginning merchandise inventory, plus purchases for the period, minus ending merchandise inventory.

         a) This amount equals purchases adjusted for the change in inventory.

   b. **Manufacturing.** A company that acquires goods for conversion into substantially different products has inventories of goods consumed directly or indirectly in production **(raw materials and supplies)**, goods in the course of production **(work-in-process)**, and goods awaiting sale **(finished goods)**.

      1) For a manufacturer, **cost of goods sold** essentially equals beginning finished goods, plus the cost of goods manufactured, minus ending finished goods.

      2) **Cost of goods manufactured** is equal to beginning-work-in-process, plus current manufacturing costs (direct materials and direct labor plus overhead), minus ending-work-in-process. Thus, it equals current manufacturing cost adjusted for the change in work-in-process.

3. **Goods Included in Inventory**

   a. Whether goods recently purchased or sold and currently in transit are properly included in inventory may be a function of the shipping terms in the relevant contract.

      1) The term **FOB (free on board) shipping point** means that title passes to the buyer at the time and place of shipment.

      2) The term **FOB destination** means that title passes when the goods arrive at their destination.

   b. Goods not physically on hand may properly be included in inventory, for example, goods on **consignment** (see item 7. under subunit 17.8).

   c. When inventories consist of more than one class of good, such as the typical case in which manufacturers maintain raw materials, work-in-process, and finished goods inventories, each class should be **shown separately on the balance sheet** or otherwise disclosed.

   d. The **cost of inventories** includes all costs necessary to transport the goods to the company, including not only the invoice price but also any freight or other delivery charges. Discounts should be deducted from the cost of the inventory.

      1) In a perpetual system, costs can be assigned to specified purchases.

      2) In a periodic system, transportation costs are usually debited to transportation-in (freight-in).

         a) Ordinarily, the balance in this account is closed to cost of goods sold (although allocation to cost of goods sold and ending inventory is theoretically preferable).

      3) Many companies believe that sales discounts for early payment are immaterial, so they deduct these discounts from overall purchases rather than the amounts assigned to individual inventory items.

   e. When **high rates of return** of goods sold are expected, the seller should recognize a sale if sales returns and allowances can be reasonably estimated. If a reasonable estimate cannot be made, the inventory account is not reduced.

      1) See also the **installment method**, item 3. under subunit 17.8.

4.    **Purchases**

    a.    In a **perpetual inventory system**, purchases are recorded directly in the inventory account.

        1)    When the purchase is made:

| | | |
|---|---|---|
| Inventory | $XXX | |
|    Accounts payable | | $XXX |

        2)    When a sale is made:

| | | |
|---|---|---|
| Cost of goods sold | $XXX | |
|    Inventory | | $XXX |

        3)    Under the **modified perpetual system**, dollar amounts of inventory are omitted from the perpetual records.  A physical count is usually done at least once a year, but some entities use statistical sampling and other estimation techniques.

    b.    In a **periodic inventory system**, a purchases account is used, and the beginning inventory balance is unchanged during the period.  Ending inventory is determined by a year-end physical count.

        1)    **Cost of goods** sold may be calculated as follows:

| | |
|---|---|
| Beginning inventory | $XXX |
|   Add:  Purchases | XXX |
| Goods available for sale | $XXX |
|     Less:  Ending inventory | (XXX) |
| Cost of goods sold | $XXX |

        2)    The entry to record cost of goods sold under a periodic inventory system is

| | | |
|---|---|---|
| Inventory (ending amount) | $XXX | |
| Cost of goods sold (residual amount) | XXX | |
|    Purchases (for the period) | | $XXX |
|    Inventory (beginning amount) | | XXX |

    c.    **Purchase returns and allowances** are also treated differently under the two systems.

        1)    In a periodic system, a contra-asset account is credited.

        2)    In a perpetual system, purchase is debited to inventory (accounts payable is credited), and returns and allowances are credited to the inventory account (accounts payable is then debited).

        3)    A return is recognized for goods returned to the seller.

        4)    The purchase returns and allowances account is a nominal account closed at year-end.

5.    **Cash Discounts**

    a.    **Cash discounts** are an incentive from the seller to encourage the buyer to pay early, thereby improving the seller's cash flow.  Two methods are available:

        1)    The **net method** is the theoretically correct treatment of cash discounts earned on the purchase of merchandise.  It records the cash price at the date of sale.

            a)    **Purchase discounts lost** are treated as a financing (interest) expense.

            b)    At year-end, purchase discounts lost are debited for each account payable for which the discount period has elapsed without payment.

        2)    The **gross method** ignores cash discounts.  It is more popular than the net method because of its simplicity (no adjusting entries are needed).

            a)    Discounts not taken are given no accounting recognition.

b) If payment is made within the discount period, **purchase discounts** (an account contra to purchases) is credited. Purchases, net of purchase discounts, are included in cost of goods sold.

c) If a **periodic system** is used in conjunction with the gross method, cost of goods sold may be calculated as follows:

| | |
|---|---|
| Beginning inventory | $XXX |
| Add: Purchases | XXX |
| Less: Purchase discounts | (XXX) |
| Less: Purchase returns and allowances | XXX |
| Add: Transportation-in | XXX |
| Goods available for sale | $XXX |
| Less: Ending inventory | (XXX) |
| Cost of goods sold | $XXX |

6. **Allocating Original Cost**

a. The **relative sales value method** is a means of allocating cost of common products or a group of items purchased together.

1) For instance, the lots in a real estate subdivision are measured at a percentage of the total cost, that is, the ratio of the sales value of an individual lot to the total estimated market sales of all the lots.

2) EXAMPLE: A real estate developer buys 100 acres for $200,000 and divides the land into two types of lots: 30 flat lots that will sell for $10,000 each and 70 hilly lots that will sell for $3,000 each. The original $200,000 purchase price is allocated on the basis of the relative sales values of the lots:

| | | | |
|---|---|---|---|
| 30 flat lots @ $10,000 ea. | = | $300,000 |
| 70 hilly lots @ $3,000 ea. | = | 210,000 |
| Total sales value | | $510,000 |

All flat lots: $200,000 × ($300,000 ÷ $510,000) = $117,647
All hilly lots: $200,000 × ($210,000 ÷ $510,000) = $ 82,353

Single flat lot: $117,647 ÷ 30 = $3,921.57
Single hilly lot: $82,353 ÷ 70 = $1,176.47

7. A **product financing arrangement** (sale with a buyback agreement) involves an apparent sale of inventory by a **sponsor** (a party seeking financing) coupled with a repurchase agreement.

a. In essence, the future reacquisition of the inventory is a return of collateral upon payment of a debt. The following are examples:

1) A buyer purchases a product that the sponsor agrees to repurchase.

2) The buyer is a separate entity established for the above purpose or is an existing credit grantor, trust, or nonbusiness entity.

3) The sponsor guarantees the debt of the buyer.

4) The financed product is to be used or sold by the sponsor.

b. **SFAS 49**, *Accounting for Product Financing Arrangements*, applies to a transaction in which a product is sold subject to repurchase of the product, of a substantially identical product, or of processed goods of which the product is a component.

1) The arrangement is treated as a borrowing if the financing arrangement requires the sponsor to purchase at specified prices, and the specified prices will fluctuate to cover changes in purchasing, financing, and holding costs (but the specified prices must not be otherwise subject to change).

   c.   The money received is accounted for as a liability rather than as a sale.

       1)   Financing and inventory holding costs are to be imputed. Usually, the selling price to the buyer is less than the repurchase price to cover these costs.

   d.   SFAS 49 is an attempt to prevent enterprises from reducing inventory (and inventory taxes) and increasing revenue and income through **parking transactions**.

       1)   In such transactions, an earning process has not been substantially completed because the sponsor still retains the risks and rewards of ownership even though title has passed to the apparent buyer.

8.   **Right of return.** When sales are made with the understanding that unsatisfactory goods may be returned, revenue and cost of sales nevertheless may be recognized and the goods removed from inventory when certain conditions exist.

   a.   If the conditions are met, a sale is recorded in the usual way. In addition, **estimated returns** (a contra revenue account) is debited and cost of sales and deferred gross margin are credited.

       1)   Inventory and deferred gross margin are debited and accounts receivable (or cash) is credited when returns are made.

   b.   If the conditions are not met, revenue and cost of sales are not recognizable until the right of return expires. The initial entry is to debit accounts receivable (or cash) and to credit inventory and deferred gross margin. Returns result in a reversal of this entry.

   c.   **SFAS 48**, *Revenue Recognition When Right of Return Exists*, prescribes the accounting when returns are expected to be material. It does not apply to the return of defective goods, such as under a warranty.

       1)   If revenue is to be recognized at the time of sale despite the existence of a right of return, any costs or losses anticipated are to be accounted for in accordance with **SFAS 5**, *Accounting for Contingencies*, and revenue and cost of sales are to be reduced to reflect expected returns as described above.

       2)   SFAS 48 prohibits revenue recognition at the time of sale when a right of return exists unless **six conditions** are met. If these conditions are not met, revenue recognition is deferred until they are met or the return privilege expires. The following are the conditions:

           a)   The seller's price is substantially fixed or determinable.

           b)   The buyer has paid or is obligated to pay, and the obligation is not contingent on resale.

           c)   The buyer's obligation is not changed in the event of theft, damage to, or destruction of the product.

           d)   The buyer has economic substance apart from the seller.

           e)   The seller is not substantially obligated to directly bring about resale.

           f)   The amount of future returns can be reasonably estimated.

9.   **Inventory Costing Methods -- Specific Identification**

   a.   **Specific identification** involves keeping individual cost records for every item in inventory. This is only practical when the number of items in inventory is small, such as automobiles, heavy equipment, yachts, or jewelry.

       1)   Specific identification at first appears to be the ideal costing method, since it allows for the exact matching of revenues and costs. This method is, however, seriously flawed because it allows for the manipulation of profits.

           a)   A manager can, at his/her discretion, sell one of several identical objects from inventory, each with a different cost, depending on the effect he/she wants to have on earnings.

10. **Inventory Costing Methods -- Average**

  a.  **Average** inventory costing comes in two varieties:

    1)  The **moving-average** method is used with **perpetual inventory** systems. A new average cost is calculated after each purchase.

      a)  EXAMPLE: A company had the following sales and purchases:

|  | Units | Times: Price | Equals: Extended | Inventory Balance | Divided By: Total Units | Equals: Per Unit Cost |
|---|---|---|---|---|---|---|
| Mar. 31 inventory | 1,000 | $12.50 | $ 12,500 | $12,500 | 1,000 | $12.50 |
| Apr. 14 purchase | 2,000 | $12.20 | $ 24,400 | $36,900 | 3,000 | $12.30 |
| Apr. 20 sale | (1,800) | $12.30 | $(22,140) | $14,760 | 1,200 | $12.30 |
| Apr. 24 purchase | 3,200 | $12.60 | $ 40,320 | $55,080 | 4,400 | $12.52 |
| Apr. 28 sale | (4,000) | $12.52 | $(50,080) | $ 5,000 | 400 | $12.50 |

      b)  The cost of goods sold may be calculated as follows:

| | |
|---|---|
| Beginning inventory | $12,500 |
| Add: purchases | 64,720 |
| Cost of goods available for sale | $77,220 |
| Less: ending inventory | (5,000) |
| Cost of goods sold | $72,220 |

    2)  The **weighted-average** method is used with **periodic inventory** systems. Because perpetual records are not kept, inventory cost is only calculated at the end of each period.

      a)  EXAMPLE:

|  | Units | Times: Price | Equals: Extended |
|---|---|---|---|
| Mar. 31 inventory | 1,000 | $12.50 | $12,500 |
| Apr. 14 purchase | 2,000 | $12.20 | 24,400 |
| Apr. 24 purchase | 3,200 | $12.60 | 40,320 |
| Total available | 6,200 | | $77,220 |
| Apr. 20 sale | (1,800) | | |
| Apr. 28 sale | (4,000) | | |
| Apr. 30 inventory | 400 | | |

      b)  The cost of goods sold may be calculated as follows:

| | | |
|---|---|---|
| Per unit cost | $77,220 ÷ 6,200 = | $12.45 |
| Ending inventory | 400 × $12.45 = | $4,980 |
| Cost of goods available for sale | | $77,220 |
| Less: ending inventory | | (4,980) |
| Cost of goods sold | | $72,240 |

    3)  Note that, while goods available for sale is identical under the two methods, cost of goods sold and ending inventory are not.

11. **Inventory Costing Methods -- FIFO**

  a.  **First-in, first-out (FIFO)** considers the first goods purchased to be the first goods sold.

    1)  Accordingly, ending inventory consists of the latest purchases. Cost of goods sold consists of costs carried over in beginning inventory and purchases during the current period.

    2)  The valuation will be the same regardless of whether the inventory is valued at the end of the period (a periodic system) or on a perpetual basis.

3)    EXAMPLE:

|  | Units | Times: Price | Equals: Extended | Inventory Consists of: | | |
|---|---|---|---|---|---|---|
|  |  |  |  | Units | Per Unit Cost | Balance |
| Mar. 31 inventory | 1,000 | $12.50 | $ 12,500 | 1,000 | $12.50 | $12,500 |
| Apr. 14 purchase | 2,000 | $12.20 | $ 24,400 | 1,000 | $12.50 | $12,500 |
|  |  |  |  | 2,000 | $12.20 | 24,400 |
|  |  |  |  | 3,000 |  | $36,900 |
| Apr. 20 sale | (1,000) | $12.50 | $(12,500) | 0 | $12.50 | $   0 |
|  | (800) | $12.20 | (9,760) | 1,200 | $12.20 | 14,640 |
|  | (1,800) |  | $(22,260) | 1,200 |  | $14,640 |
|  |  |  |  | 1,200 | $12.20 | $14,640 |
| Apr. 24 purchase | 3,200 | $12.60 | $ 40,320 | 3,200 | $12.60 | 40,320 |
|  |  |  |  | 4,400 |  | $54,960 |
| Apr. 28 sale | (1,200) | $12.20 | $(14,640) | 0 | $12.20 | $   0 |
|  | (2,800) | $12.60 | (35,280) | 400 | $12.60 | 5,040 |
|  | (4,000) |  | $(49,920) | 400 |  | $ 5,040 |

4)    Goods available for sale is identical to that calculated under the average methods, but ending inventory and cost of goods sold are different.

| Beginning inventory | $12,500 |
|---|---|
| Add:  purchases | 64,720 |
| Cost of goods available for sale | $77,220 |
| Less:  ending inventory | (5,040) |
| Cost of goods sold | $72,180 |

5)    While somewhat approximating the specific identification method's matching of cost flow to physical flow, FIFO does not possess the same potential for manipulation.

6)    An advantage of FIFO is that ending inventory is stated at approximately current replacement cost.  A disadvantage is that current revenues are matched to older costs.

12.  **Inventory Costing Methods -- LIFO**

a.  **Last-in, first-out (LIFO)** considers the most recent purchases to be sold first.

1)    Accordingly, ending inventory is priced at the cost of beginning inventory and the earliest purchases.

2) Periodic and perpetual systems will yield different results under LIFO.

    a) EXAMPLE of LIFO periodic:

        i) First, all purchases for the period are totaled:

| | Units | Times: Price | Equals: Extended |
|---|---|---|---|
| Mar. 31 inventory | 1,000 | $12.50 | $12,500 |
| Apr. 14 purchase | 2,000 | $12.20 | 24,400 |
| Apr. 24 purchase | 3,200 | $12.60 | 40,320 |
| Total available | 6,200 | | $77,220 |

        ii) Next, the period's sales are accounted for:

| | |
|---|---|
| Apr. 20 sale | (1,800) |
| Apr. 28 sale | (4,000) |
| All sales for month | (5,800) |

        iii) Lastly, the total sales is stripped out of the various layers:

| | Beg. Units | Inventory Consists of: Units Sold | End. Units | Per Unit Cost | Balance |
|---|---|---|---|---|---|
| Mar. 31 layer | 1,000 | (1,000) | 0 | $12.50 | $  0 |
| Apr. 14 layer | 2,000 | (2,000) | 0 | $12.20 | 0 |
| Apr. 24 layer | 3,200 | (2,800) | 400 | $12.60 | 5,040 |
| Totals | 6,200 | (5,800) | 400 | | $5,040 |

        iv) Goods available for sale is identical to that calculated under the other methods discussed, but ending inventory and cost of goods sold are different.

| | |
|---|---|
| Beginning inventory | $12,500 |
| Add: purchases | 64,720 |
| Cost of goods available for sale | $77,220 |
| Less: ending inventory | (5,040) |
| Cost of goods sold | $72,180 |

    b) EXAMPLE of LIFO perpetual:

| | Units | Times: Price | Equals: Extended | Units | Inventory Consists of: Per Unit Cost | Balance |
|---|---|---|---|---|---|---|
| Mar. 31 inventory | 1,000 | $12.50 | $ 12,500 | 1,000 | $12.50 | $12,500 |
| Apr. 14 purchase | 2,000 | $12.20 | $ 24,400 | 1,000 | $12.50 | $12,500 |
| | | | | 2,000 | $12.20 | 24,400 |
| | | | | 3,000 | | $36,900 |
| Apr. 20 sale | 0 | $12.50 | $  0 | 1,000 | $12.50 | $12,500 |
| | (1,800) | $12.20 | (21,960) | 200 | $12.20 | 2,440 |
| | (1,800) | | $(21,960) | 1,200 | | $14,940 |
| | | | | 1,000 | $12.50 | $12,500 |
| | | | | 200 | $12.20 | 2,440 |
| Apr. 24 purchase | 3,200 | $12.60 | 40,320 | 3,200 | $12.60 | 40,320 |
| | | | | 4,400 | | $55,260 |
| Apr. 28 sale | (600) | $12.50 | $ (7,500) | 400 | $12.50 | $ 5,000 |
| | (200) | $12.20 | (2,440) | 0 | $12.20 | 0 |
| | (3,200) | $12.60 | (40,320) | 0 | $12.60 | 0 |
| | (4,000) | | $(50,260) | 400 | | $ 5,000 |

i) Again, goods available for sale is the same, but ending inventory and cost of goods sold are different.

| | |
|---|---:|
| Beginning inventory | $12,500 |
| Add: purchases | 64,720 |
| Cost of goods available for sale | $77,220 |
| Less: ending inventory | (5,000) |
| Cost of goods sold | $72,220 |

3) A significant **advantage** of LIFO is its **matching of current revenues** with the most recent product costs.

    a) When prices are rising (which is most of the time), current costs are higher than older costs, resulting in lower income. The lower income means lower taxes.

        i) Thus, LIFO has traditionally been used as a tax-postponement tool.

    b) However, keeping LIFO records by product is extraordinarily time-consuming. Furthermore, it is rarely used for internal product pricing decisions.

        i) Thus, many firms use LIFO for external reporting and tax purposes and another method for internal costing.

    c) Companies that use two inventory costing methods often establish an inventory contra-account, sometimes called a **LIFO reserve**.

        i) At period end, it is adjusted to reflect the difference between LIFO and the internal costing method, called the **LIFO effect**.

| | | |
|---|---:|---:|
| Cost of goods sold | $XXX | |
| Allowance to reduce inventory to LIFO | | $XXX |

4) The building of inventory over time results in the creation of **LIFO layers**.

    a) EXAMPLE:

| | Units | Times: Price | Equals: Extended |
|---|---:|---:|---:|
| Year 5 layer | 1,600 | $74.25 | $118,800 |
| Year 4 layer | 1,500 | $59.40 | 89,100 |
| Year 3 layer | 1,350 | $49.50 | 66,825 |
| Year 2 layer | 1,200 | $45.00 | 54,000 |
| Year 1 (base) layer | 1,000 | $40.00 | 40,000 |
| Year 6 beg. inventory | 6,650 | | $368,725 |

    b) If **LIFO liquidation** takes place, however (i.e., the selling off of older, lower-cost layers), **distortions in net income** can result from matching current revenues against the older, lower costs.

        i) One way of counteracting LIFO liquidation is to treat substantially identical items of inventory as a single accounting unit called a **pool**.

        ii) Selling down inventory of one item in the pool can be compensated for by increasing the level of another item.

## 13. Inventory Costing Methods -- Dollar-value LIFO

    a. **Dollar-value LIFO** overcomes the shortcomings inherent in specific-good LIFO. The key is measuring inventory in terms of **total dollars rather than in units**.

    1) The **items** in a dollar-value LIFO pool **may be merely similar** rather than substantially identical. This makes the layers less subject to erosion than under specific goods pooled LIFO.

2) Dollar-value LIFO involves a **double-conversion process**.

    a) EXAMPLE: First, restate each period's ending inventory at its equivalent base-year value (year 1 is the base year) (the effects of inflation have been exaggerated for clarity):

| | At End-of-Year Price | Divided by: Price Index | At Base-Year Price |
|---|---|---|---|
| Year 1 ending inventory | $300,000 | 1.00 | $300,000 |
| Year 2 ending inventory | $374,000 | 1.10 | $340,000 |
| Year 3 ending inventory | $384,000 | 1.20 | $320,000 |
| Year 4 ending inventory | $455,000 | 1.30 | $350,000 |

    b) Second, determine the LIFO cost basis of each year's component of the ending balances.

| Year 1 Calculation: | At Base-Year Price | Times: Price Index | At LIFO Cost |
|---|---|---|---|
| Year 1 layer | $300,000 | 1.00 | $300,000 |
| Year 1 ending inventory | $300,000 | | $300,000 |

| Year 2 Calculation: | At Base-Year Price | Times: Price Index | At LIFO Cost |
|---|---|---|---|
| Year 1 layer | $300,000 | 1.00 | $300,000 |
| Year 2 layer | 40,000 | 1.10 | 44,000 |
| Year 2 ending inventory | $340,000 | | $344,000 |

    c) In any year when the balance goes down, a portion of the most recent year's layer must be stripped away and can never be replaced.

| Year 3 Calculation: | At Base-Year Price | Times: Price Index | At LIFO Cost |
|---|---|---|---|
| Year 1 layer | $300,000 | 1.00 | $300,000 |
| Year 2 layer | 20,000 | 1.10 | 22,000 |
| Year 3 ending inventory | $320,000 | | $322,000 |

| Year 4 Calculation: | At Base-Year Price | Times: Price Index | At LIFO Cost |
|---|---|---|---|
| Year 1 layer | $300,000 | 1.00 | $300,000 |
| Year 2 layer | 20,000 | 1.10 | 22,000 |
| Year 4 layer | 30,000 | 1.30 | 39,000 |
| Year 4 ending inventory | $350,000 | | $361,000 |

14. **Selecting an Inventory Costing Method**

    a. **ARB 43, Chapter 4** states that the major objective of an inventory costing method should be the most faithful representation of periodic income. This can be any of the methods discussed above, given varying circumstances.

    b. In general, when prices are rising, LIFO provides lower net income and the concomitant tax benefit.

    c. When the number of inventory items is few, specific identification is possible. However, it does subject earnings to management manipulation.

15. **Declines in Inventory Value**

    a. When inventory declines in value, the principle of historical cost is abandoned in favor of the constraint of conservatism.

    b. Because the asset has suffered a **permanent reduction in its ability to generate revenue**, it should no longer be reported on the balance sheet at its original cost.

        1) Goods can be impaired by damage, deterioration, obsolescence, changes in price levels, changes in demand, style changes, or other causes.

        2) Several alternatives to the historical-cost valuation methods discussed on the previous pages and above are available.

    c.   The **lower of cost or market (LCM)** rule requires that inventory be written down to its replacement value if its utility is no longer as great as its cost.

        1)   The loss should be recognized in the period in which it occurs, not the period in which the inventory is sold.

            a)   The LCM rule is applicable only to goods that will be sold in the ordinary course of business.  Damaged, obsolete, or deteriorated goods are usually carried at net realizable value in a separate account.

        2)   Market value should not exceed a **ceiling** equal to **net realizable value (NRV)**. This amount is the estimated selling price in the ordinary course of business minus reasonably predictable costs of completion and disposal.

            a)   Replacement cost does not accurately measure utility if the estimated sales price, reduced by the costs of completion and disposal, is lower, in which case the NRV more appropriately measures utility.

            b)   Reporting inventory above NRV overstates its utility and will result in a loss at the time of sale.

            c)   **NRV** can in some cases be chosen over lower of cost or market.

                i)   NRV can be used when two conditions apply:

                    •   There is a well-defined final market for the goods, and
                    •   There are no significant costs of disposal.

                ii)   Mined minerals is an example.

            d)   **Damaged inventories** should be reported at NRV.

        3)   Market should not be less than a **floor** equal to **NRV less a normal profit margin**.

            a)   If the inventory were written down to a replacement cost below this amount, an abnormal profit element (NRV – normal profit – replacement cost) would be included in revenue at the time of sale.

            b)   If cost will be recovered with an approximately normal profit upon sale in the ordinary course of business, no loss should be recognized even though replacement or production costs are lower.

        4)   Accordingly, the LCM rule results in measurement at original cost or current replacement cost.

            a)   **Designated market value** is thus replacement cost, not to be greater than NRV or less than NRV minus a normal profit.

    d.   Depending on the character and composition of the inventory, the LCM rule may properly be applied either **directly to each item** or to the **aggregate total of the inventory** (or, in some cases, to the total of the components of each major category).

        1)   The method should be the one that most clearly reflects periodic income.

        2)   Once inventory is written down, the reduced amount is the new cost basis, and a write-up will ordinarily not be permitted if prices increase.

        3)   LCM by item will always be equal to or less than the other LCM measurements, and LCM in total will always be equal to or greater than the other LCM valuations.

        4)   Most companies use **LCM by item**, and this method is **required for tax purposes**.

            a)   If dollar-value LIFO is employed, LCM should be applied to pools of items.
            b)   A company may not use LCM with LIFO for tax purposes.

5) EXAMPLE:

|  | Historical Cost | Replacement Cost | NRV | NRV Less Normal Profit | Designated Market Value | Lower of Cost or Market |
|---|---|---|---|---|---|---|
| Dowel screws | **$12.45** | $13.60 | $14.40 | $14.00 | $14.00 | $12.45 |
| Drywall screws | $15.15 | $12.00 | **$11.55** | $11.35 | **$11.55** | $11.55 |
| Machine screws | $16.00 | **$14.10** | $15.00 | $13.80 | **$14.10** | $14.10 |
| Metal screws | $10.30 | **$8.75** | $9.20 | $8.45 | **$8.75** | $8.75 |
| Wood screws | $8.90 | **$7.85** | $8.20 | $7.65 | **$7.85** | $7.85 |

6) Two methods are in common practice for recording LCM.

   a) Under the **direct method**, the loss is charged as a direct reduction of inventory.

| | | |
|---|---|---|
| Cost of goods sold | $XXX | |
| Inventory | | $XXX |

      i) This method has the theoretical drawback of charging a holding loss to an account that includes the costs of selling goods.

      ii) Also, inventory will be presented at LCM rather than at cost net of write-downs.

   b) Under the **allowance method**, which is the preferred technique, the loss is charged to a valuation account.

| | | |
|---|---|---|
| Holding loss on inventory | $XXX | |
| Allowance to reduce inventory to LCM | | $XXX |

      i) The unit costs in the subsidiary records need not be changed to agree with the control account.

7) Nontemporary market declines should be recognized in the **interim periods** in which they occur.

   a) **Recoveries** of these losses on the same inventory later in the fiscal year should be recognized as gains (but only to the extent of the previously recognized losses).

   b) If market declines can reasonably be **expected to be restored** by year-end, they **should not be recognized**.

16. Often an **estimate of inventory** is needed because taking a physical count of every item is impractical. Two methods are in common use.

  a. The **gross profit method** computes ending inventory given sales and a standard markup.

   1) The gross profit is subtracted from sales to determine cost of sales.

   2) This method is often used in the preparation of interim statements and when inventory has been destroyed or stolen.

     a) It is not, however, acceptable for tax purposes.

   3) EXAMPLE:

| | | |
|---|---|---|
| Beginning inventory | | $60,000 |
| Purchases | | 20,000 |
| Goods available for sale | | $80,000 |
| Sales (at selling price) | $50,000 | |
| Gross profit (20% of sales) | (10,000) | |
| Sales (at cost) | | 40,000 |
| Approximate inventory at cost | | $40,000 |

   4) A simple way to apply this method is to prepare the cost of goods sold section of an income statement and solve algebraically for the amounts not known.

b.    The **retail inventory method** converts ending inventory at retail to cost.

1)    The advantage of this method is that a physical inventory can be taken at retail.

2)    The **cost-retail ratio** used to convert retail to cost depends upon the flow assumption used.

a)    If a **weighted-average** flow is assumed, the cost ratio should be goods available at cost over goods available at retail.

b)    If **FIFO** is used, the cost ratio should be cost of purchases over purchases at retail.

c)    If **LIFO** is used, the cost of ending inventory depends on the cost of beginning inventory.

3)    If ending inventory is less than beginning inventory, the cost ratio should be cost of beginning inventory over beginning inventory at retail.

a)    Any increase (stated at retail) should be valued at the ratio of cost of purchases over purchases at retail.

4)    Also, the **lower-of-cost-or-market** concept may be applied to the retail method.

a)    In this approach, markups are added to beginning inventory and purchases at retail to obtain goods available at retail.

i)    Markdowns are not subtracted. This results in a higher denominator in the cost-retail ratio, which results in a lower ending inventory.

c.    COMPARATIVE EXAMPLE:

|  | Cost | Retail |
|---|---|---|
| Beginning inventory | $ 90,000 | $130,000 |
| Purchases | 330,000 | 460,000 |
| Markups |  | 10,000 |
| Markdowns |  | 40,000 |
| Sales |  | 480,000 |

1)    Ending inventory at retail is thus $80,000 ($130,000 + $460,000 + $10,000 − $40,000 − $480,000).

2)    The cost-retail ratio for the retail method under **weighted average** is 420 ÷ 560. Include both markups and markdowns in goods available at retail.

3)    The cost-retail ratio for the retail method under **FIFO** is 330 ÷ 430, assuming all markups and markdowns applied to goods purchased this period. Under FIFO, all inventory would come from current-period purchases.

4)    The cost-retail ratio for the retail method under **LIFO** is 90 ÷ 130 because ending inventory of $80,000 retail is less than beginning inventory of $130,000. If there had been an increase in inventory, the increment would be valued using a cost-retail ratio of 330 ÷ 430.

5)    The cost-retail ratio for the retail method under **LCM**, assuming weighted average, is 420 ÷ 600 because markups, not markdowns, are included in the calculation of the percentage. This method is typically used if LIFO is not used. The exclusion of markdowns from the ratio results in a valuation that approximates the lower of cost or market.

d. **Dollar-value LIFO** can also be used in conjunction with the retail inventory method.

1) EXAMPLE:

| | Cost | Retail |
|---|---|---|
| Beginning inventory | $12,000 | $ 16,800 |
| Purchases | 70,000 | 100,000 |
| Sales | | 90,000 |
| Ending inventory | | $ 26,800 |

a) The beginning price index was 100%; the year-end index is 134%.

b) The first step is to convert the year-end inventory to base-year prices: $26,800 ÷ 1.34 = $20,000.

c) Determine the increment: $20,000 − $16,800 = $3,200.

d) Convert the increment back to year-end prices: $3,200 × 134% = $4,288.

e) The next step is to convert the retail prices to cost and then add the layers:

| | |
|---|---|
| $16,800 × 100% (price index) × 71.43% (cost ratio) = | $12,000.24 |
| 3,200 × 134% (price index) × 70.00% (cost ratio) = | 3,001.60 |
| | $15,001.84 |

17. **Effect of Inventory Errors**

a. An error in stating year-end inventory will be reflected on the financial statements of two different years.

| Element | First Year | Second Year |
|---|---|---|
| Balance Sheet: | | |
| Beginning inventory | -- | Overstated |
| Ending inventory | Overstated | -- |
| Retained earnings | Understated | Overstated |
| Income Statement: | | |
| Cost of goods sold | Understated | Overstated |
| Operating income | Overstated | Understated |

b. The balance in retained earnings is correct at the end of the second year.

18. Stop and review! You have completed the outline for this subunit. Study multiple-choice questions 1 through 29 beginning on page 528.

## 14.2 INVESTMENTS (CURRENT AND LONG-TERM)

1. **Short-term investments** are **current assets**. They must be readily marketable and be intended to be converted into cash within the next year or operating cycle, whichever is longer. Bonds, other debt instruments, and stocks are typical examples of short-term investments.

a. When debt securities are purchased and the purchase price includes brokerage fees, these fees increase the accounting measurement of the debt securities.

1) **Accrued interest** arises when a debt security is bought or sold in between interest payments. If the purchase price includes accrued interest, the accrued interest does not increase the accounting measurement.

2) Discounts or premiums on debt securities (e.g., bonds) are not amortized if they are expected to be sold within 1 year.

b. When two or more classes of securities are purchased with a lump sum, the amount debited to each class is based on the **relative-sales-value method**.

   1) For instance, the purchase of $100,000 of debt securities and $200,000 of equity securities in the same company for a price of $295,000 is recorded by a debit to investment in debt securities for $98,333 = [$295,000 × (1 ÷ 3)] and a debit to investment in equity securities for $196,667 = [$295,000 × (2 ÷ 3)].

2. **SFAS 115**, *Accounting for Certain Investments in Debt and Equity Securities*, applies to investments in equity and debt securities.

   a. **Equity securities** are investments representing ownership interests, such as the stock of other companies.

      1) For SFAS 115 to apply to equity securities, they must have **readily determinable fair values**. Typically, this means there are quoted market prices available, such as a quoted per share price from the NYSE.

      2) In contrast, a closely held private company probably does not have readily determinable fair values attached to its share price. In this case, SFAS 115 does not apply, and the equity securities would be valued using the cost method.

   b. SFAS 115 does not apply to the following:

      1) Investments in equity securities accounted for under the equity method
      2) Investments in consolidated subsidiaries
      3) Most derivative instruments
      4) Enterprises with specialized accounting practices that include accounting for all investments at fair or market value
      5) Not-for-profit organizations

   c. **Debt securities** represent investments with credit relationships.

   d. When debt or equity securities are acquired, they should be classified as held-to-maturity, trading, or available-for-sale.

      1) **Held-to-maturity securities** are debt securities that the reporting enterprise has the positive intent and ability to hold to maturity.

         a) Held-to-maturity securities are reported at **amortized cost**.

         b) If a debt security is no longer considered being held to maturity because of changes in circumstances, it does not call "into question the intent to hold other debt securities to maturity in the future."

         c) Securities are deemed to be **held to maturity** when:

            i) The sale is near enough to the maturity or call date (e.g., within 3 months) so that interest rate risk (change in the market rate) does not have a significant effect on fair value

            ii) The sale is after collection of 85% or more of the principal

         d) If a debt security can **contractually be prepaid or otherwise settled** in such a way that the holder would not recover substantially all of the recorded investment, the security may not be classified as held-to-maturity.

            i) For example, if the issuing company is in a bankruptcy proceeding where it will not repay all of its obligations, then the company holding the debt securities cannot classify the debt as held-to-maturity.

         e) **Temporary declines** in the fair value of held-to-maturity investments below their amortized cost are not recognized because the assumption is that such declines will eventually reverse.

2) **Trading securities** can consist of debt securities and equity securities.

    a) Trading securities are bought and held primarily for sale in the near term. They are frequently purchased and sold.

    b) Each trading security is remeasured to fair value at each balance sheet date.

        i) At the balance sheet date, **unrealized holding gains and losses** on trading securities are included in earnings.

        ii) A **holding gain or loss** is the net change in fair value during the period, not including recognized dividends or interest not yet received.

    c) To retain historical cost in the accounts, a **valuation allowance** may be established for each security or at the portfolio level (if records for individual securities are maintained).

3) **Available-for-sale securities** include both debt securities and equity securities.

    a) The accounting is similar to trading securities.

    b) However, unrealized holding gains and losses, including those classified as current assets, are excluded from earnings and reported in **other comprehensive income (OCI)**. Tax effects are debited or credited directly to OCI.

        i) If the debt or equity security is a hedged item in a fair value hedge, then the unrealized holding gains and losses are included in net income, not other comprehensive income.

| | **Held to Maturity** | **Trading** | **Available-for-sale** |
|---|---|---|---|
| **Debt Securities:** | | | |
| Requirements | 1) The sale is near enough to the maturity or call date (e.g., within 3 months) so that interest rate risk (change in the market rate) does not have a significant effect on fair value | 1) Does not qualify as held-to-maturity | 1) All securities that do not qualify as held-to-maturity or trading |
| | 2) The collection of 85% or more of the principal has occurred | 2) Brought and held primarily for sale in the near term. They are frequently purchased and sold. | |
| Recognition of holding gains/losses | No | Yes | Yes |
| Unrealized holding gains/losses are recognized in | Not recognized | Net income | Other comprehensive income |
| Carrying amount reported at | Amortized cost | Fair value | Fair value |
| **Equity Securities:** | | | |
| Requirements | Never | 1) Brought and held primarily for sale in the near term. They are frequently purchased and sold. | 2) All equity securities that are held for sale in the near term except equity investments that are reported under the equity method or equity investments that require consolidation |
| | | 2) Readily determinable fair value | 2) Readily determinable fair value |
| Recognition of holding gains/losses | Not applicable | Yes | Yes |
| Unrealized holding gains/losses are recognized in | Not applicable | Net income | Other comprehensive income |
| Carrying amount reported at | Not applicable | Fair value | Fair value |

4) Income from **dividends and interest** for these types of securities, including amortization of premium or discount, continues to be included in earnings.

5) **Realized gains and losses** on trading, held-to-maturity, and available-for-sale securities also continue to be included in earnings.

6) **Transfers between categories** are at **fair value**.

    a) Unrealized holding gains and losses on securities transferred from the trading category will have already been recognized and are not reversed.

    b) The portion of unrealized holding gains and losses on securities transferred to the trading category (from either held-to-maturity or available-for-sale) not previously recognized in earnings is recognized in earnings immediately.

    c) The unrealized holding gain or loss on held-to-maturity securities transferred to the available-for-sale category is recognized in OCI.

    d) The unrealized holding gain or loss on the date of transfer for available-for-sale securities transferred to the held-to-maturity category continues to be reported in OCI.

        i) However, it is amortized as an adjustment of yield in the same manner as the amortization of any discount or premium. This amortization offsets or mitigates the effect on interest income of the amortization of the premium or discount.

        ii) Fair value accounting may result in a premium or discount when a debt security is transferred to the held-to-maturity category.

    e) Transfers between the held-to-maturity category and the trading category should be rare.

    f) **Reclassification adjustments** are made for each component of OCI affected by investments. The purpose of reclassification adjustments is to avoid double counting when an item included in net income was also included in OCI for the same or a prior period.

        i) For example, if a gain or loss on available-for-sale securities is realized in the current period, the prior recognition of an unrealized holding gain or loss must be eliminated from OCI.

7) **Impairment.** If a decline in fair value of an individual held-to-maturity or available-for-sale security below the amortized cost basis is **other than temporary**, the cost basis is written down to fair value as a **new cost basis**.

    a) The write-down is a **realized loss** and is included in earnings.

    b) The new cost basis is not affected by subsequent recoveries in fair value.

    c) Subsequent increases and decreases in the fair value of available-for-sale securities are included in OCI, except for other-than-temporary declines.

8) Individual trading, held-to-maturity, and available-for-sale securities may be classified as current or noncurrent.

9) **Cash flows** from trading securities are classified as operating items. Cash flows from available-for-sale and held-to-maturity securities are investing items.

10) The appropriateness of an investment's classification must be reassessed at each reporting date.

3. **The Equity Method of Accounting for Investments in Common Stock**

    a. Under **APB 18**, *The Equity Method of Accounting for Investments in Common Stock*, an investment in common stock enabling the investor to exercise **significant influence** over the operations and management of the investee should be accounted for by the equity method.

b.    When ownership of an investee reaches the level of **significant influence**, the investor must adopt the equity method.  A **20% or greater** ownership interest is rebuttably presumed to permit such influence.

1)    If the investee is in bankruptcy or if the investor does not enjoy significant influence due to the control lying with a majority owner, then the cost method should be used.

c.    If ownership by one entity, directly or indirectly, exceeds 50% of the outstanding voting interests of another entity, consolidated statements ordinarily should be prepared unless **control** does not rest with the majority owner (SFAS 94).

d.    Under the equity method, the **investment's carrying amount** is increased or decreased by the investor's proportionate share of earnings or losses.

1)    The adjusted share of the investee's earnings is accounted for as a debit, and losses and dividends are credits to the carrying amount of the investment on the investor's books.

2)    For example, if Company A owns 25% of Company B's stock and Company B has net income of $100,000, the journal entry for Company A would be:

| | | |
|---|---|---|
| Investment in Company B | $25,000 | |
| Earnings from Company B | | $25,000 |

e.    The investment's carrying amount is also reduced by any dividends received from the investee because the receipt of a **cash dividend** from the investee is treated as a return of an investment.  Thus, it is credited to the investment account but does not affect equity-based earnings.

1)    Continuing the example above, if Company B declares $60,000 in dividends to its shareholders, the journal entry for Company A is:

| | | |
|---|---|---|
| Cash | $15,000 | |
| Investment in Company B | | $15,000 |

f.    At the acquisition date, if the cost of the investment is different from the carrying amount of the net assets on the investee's books, amortization of this difference is required.

1)    The difference may be attributable wholly or in part to a difference between the **fair value and carrying amount of specific accounts**.

2)    If depreciable assets are understated, amortization of the excess of the fair value over the carrying amount must be recognized as an adjustment of the investment account.

3)    If there are differences due to real estate or inventory, these differences need to be adjusted when the investee sells these assets to avoid double counting.

a)    The excess fair value is already reflected in the investment balance and should not be counted again when the investor's share of the investee's earnings is debited to the investment account.

b)    The journal entry is to debit investment income for the excess profit and to credit the investment account.

4)    The difference between cost and the carrying amount may not be attributable wholly or in part to specific accounts, such as inventory or land.

a)    Accordingly, the excess of cost over the underlying equity in net assets that is not attributable to specific accounts should be treated as **goodwill**.

b)    This amount is not amortized.  The equity method investment (but not equity method goodwill itself) is **tested for impairment** under SFAS 142.

g.   If a company owns stock in an investee and either increases its ownership in the investee beyond 20% (or begins to enjoy significant influence) or decreases its ownership in the investee below 20% (or loses significant influence), then the investor must alter its method of recognizing its investment in the investee.

   1)   If the investor begins to enjoy significant influence over the investee, the investee must **retroactively adjust** the investment account as if the equity method had been in effect during all of the previous periods in which any percentage of ownership was held.

      a)   Thus, the investor must retroactively adjust the carrying amount of the investment, results of operations for current and prior periods presented, and retained earnings.

   2)   When an investor accounts for an investment by the equity method and then sells shares such that significant influence can no longer be presumed to be exerted, the **change from equity method** is accounted for on a prospective basis, i.e., no retroactive adjustment is made.

      a)   The carrying amount of the investment is unchanged, and subsequent dividends are accounted for as dividend income unless they are liquidating dividends.

h.   The investor's share of the investee's **extraordinary items** and **prior-period adjustments** are classified similarly by the investor if material.

i.   Use of the equity method is **discontinued** when the investment is reduced to zero by investee losses, unless the investor has committed to provide additional financial support to the investee.

4.   The **cost method** is used when the investor cannot exercise significant influence over the investee, and the equity securities do not have readily determinable fair values. Thus, it is the default method when the equity method and fair-value accounting are not applicable.

a.   Under the cost method, an investment in stock is initially recorded at cost, but subsequent unrealized changes in fair value are not recognized unless they represent **nontemporary declines**.

b.   Under both the cost and fair-value methods, **dividends** from an investee are accounted for by the investor as dividend income unless a liquidating dividend is received.

   1)   Intercompany transactions should be accounted for separately and in full.

c.   A **liquidating dividend** occurs when the total accumulated dividends received since the date of the acquisition exceed the investor's proportionate share of the investee's net accumulated earnings during that time.

   1)   A liquidating dividend reduces the carrying amount of the investment, not dividend income.

   2)   The dividends received that did not exceed the investor's share of the investee's earnings subsequent to the date of investment are **dividend revenue** under the cost method.

   3)   Because a liquidating dividend is a return of, not a return on, the investment, the investment amount also decreases under the cost method.

   4)   See item 4. under subunit 17.4 for a full description of liquidating dividends.

5.   Stop and review!  You have completed the outline for this subunit.  Study multiple-choice questions 30 through 40 beginning on page 538.

## 14.3 CORE CONCEPTS

<u>Inventories</u>

- Whether goods are **included in inventory** depends on the point at which **ownership passes**, i.e., FOB shipping point or FOB destination.
- The **net method** is the theoretically correct treatment of cash discounts available on the purchase of merchandise.
- The **gross method** ignores discounts. It is more popular because of its simplicity (no adjusting entries needed).
- **Inventory costing methods** include **specific identification** (used with very small inventories), **moving-average** (used with perpetual systems), **weighted-average** (used with periodic systems), **first-in, first-out** or FIFO (ending inventory is priced at approximately replacement cost), **last-in, first-out** or LIFO (matches current revenues with most current costs), and **dollar-value LIFO** (eliminates layer-liquidation distortions inherent in standard LIFO).
- When inventory **declines in value**, the principle of historical cost is abandoned in favor of the constraint of conservatism. The **lower of cost or market** rule (LCM) requires that inventory be written down to its replacement value.
- **Errors in ending inventory valuation** affect not just the current period financial statements, but also those of the following year.

<u>Investments (Current and Long-Term)</u>

- To be classified as **current**, an investment must be (a) readily marketable and (b) intended to be converted into cash within the next year or operating cycle.
- **Debt securities** are reported using a **three-way classification**: held-to-maturity, available-for-sale, and trading.
- **Equity securities** are classified as **either** available-for-sale or trading.
- When the **level of ownership** of another company reaches the level of significant influence **(presumed at 20%)**, the investor must adopt the **equity method** of accounting for the investment.
- When the level of ownership **exceeds 50%**, the financial statements of the two entities must be **consolidated**.

## QUESTIONS

### 14.1    Inventories

1.    The following inventory valuation errors have been discovered for Knox Corporation.

- The year 1 year-end inventory was overstated by $23,000.
- The year 2 year-end inventory was understated by $61,000.
- The year 3 year-end inventory was understated by $17,000.

The reported income before taxes for Knox was

| Year | Income Before Taxes |
|------|---------------------|
| Year 1 | $138,000 |
| Year 2 | 254,000 |
| Year 3 | 168,000 |

Reported income before taxes for year 1, year 2, and year 3, respectively, should have been

A.    $161,000, $170,000, and $212,000.

B.    $115,000, $338,000, and $124,000.

C.    $161,000, $338,000, and $90,000.

D.    $115,000, $338,000, and $212,000.

Answer (B) is correct.    *(CMA, adapted)*
    **REQUIRED:**  The reported income after correction of inventory errors.
    **DISCUSSION:**  Cost of sales equals beginning inventory, plus purchases or cost of goods manufactured, minus ending inventory.  Hence, over (under) statement of inventory affects cost of sales and income.  The year 1 pretax income was affected by the $23,000 year 1 overstatement of year-end inventory.  This error understated year 1 cost of sales and overstated pretax income.  The corrected income is $115,000 ($138,000 – $23,000).  The same $23,000 error caused year 2 income to be understated by overstating beginning inventory.  In addition, the $61,000 understatement of year 2 year-end inventory also caused year 2 income to be understated.  Thus, the corrected year 2 pretax income is $338,000 ($254,000 + $23,000 + $61,000).  The $61,000 understatement at the end of year 2 caused year 3 income to be overstated by understating beginning inventory.  Income for year 3 is understated by the $17,000 of year-end inventory understatement.  Accordingly, the corrected income is $124,000 ($168,000 – $61,000 + $17,000).
    Answer (A) is incorrect because year 1 income of $161,000 results from adding, not subtracting, the $23,000 overstatement of ending inventory.  Similarly, year 2 income of $170,000 results from subtracting, not adding, the $23,000 overstatement of beginning inventory and the $61,000 understatement of ending inventory.  Finally, year 3 income of $212,000 results from adding, not subtracting, the $61,000 understatement of beginning inventory and subtracting, not adding, the understatement of ending inventory.  Answer (C) is incorrect because year 3 income of $90,000 results from subtracting, not adding, the $17,000 understatement of ending inventory.  Answer (D) is incorrect because year 3 pre-tax income should be $124,000.

2.    All sales and purchases for the year at Ross Corporation are credit transactions.  Ross uses a perpetual inventory system and shipped goods that were correctly excluded from ending inventory.  However, in error, the sale was not recorded.  Which one of the following statements is correct?

A.    Accounts receivable was not affected, inventory was not affected, sales were understated, and cost of goods sold was understated.

B.    Accounts receivable was understated, inventory was not affected, sales were understated, and cost of goods sold was understated.

C.    Accounts receivable was understated, inventory was overstated, sales were understated, and cost of goods sold was overstated.

D.    Accounts receivable was understated, inventory was not affected, sales were understated, and cost of goods sold was not affected.

Answer (D) is correct.    *(CMA, adapted)*
    **REQUIRED:**  The effect on various related accounts resulting from a failure to record a sale when goods are shipped.
    **DISCUSSION:**  The failure to record a sale means that both accounts receivable and sales will be understated.  Because inventory was correctly counted, error has no effect on that account or on the cost of goods sold.
    Answer (A) is incorrect because accounts receivable will be understated and cost of goods sold will be unaffected.  Answer (B) is incorrect because cost of goods sold will be unaffected.  Answer (C) is incorrect because inventory and cost of goods sold will be unaffected.

**3.** During the year 1 year-end physical inventory count at Tequesta Corporation, $40,000 worth of inventory was counted twice. Assuming that the year 2 year-end inventory was correct, the result of the year 1 error was that

    A. Year 1 retained earnings was understated, and year 2 ending inventory was correct.

    B. Year 1 cost of goods sold was overstated, and year 2 income was understated.

    C. Year 1 income was overstated, and year 2 ending inventory was overstated.

    D. Year 1 cost of goods sold was understated, and year 2 retained earnings was correct.

Answer (D) is correct. *(CMA, adapted)*
    **REQUIRED:** The effect on year 1 and year 2 financial statements of a year 1 overstatement of inventory.
    **DISCUSSION:** The overstatement (double counting) of inventory at the end of year 1 caused year 1 cost of goods sold (BI + Purchases – EI) to be understated and both inventory and income to be overstated. The year 1 ending inventory equals year 2 beginning inventory. Thus, the same overstatement caused year 2 beginning inventory and cost of goods sold to be overstated and income to be understated. This is an example of a self-correcting error; by the end of year 2, the balance sheet is correct.
    Answer (A) is incorrect because the year 1 overstatement in inventory caused income and retained earnings to be overstated. Answer (B) is incorrect because year 1 costs were understated given that inventory was overstated. Answer (C) is incorrect because the year 2 ending inventory was given as correct.

**4.** An item of inventory purchased in year 1 for $25.00 was incorrectly written down to a current replacement cost of $17.50 in year 1. The item is currently selling in year 2 for $50.00, its normal selling price. Which one of the following statements is correct?

    A. The income for year 1 is overstated.

    B. The cost of sales for year 2 will be overstated.

    C. The income for year 2 will be overstated.

    D. The closing inventory of year 1 is overstated.

Answer (C) is correct. *(CMA, adapted)*
    **REQUIRED:** The effect of an inventory understatement.
    **DISCUSSION:** Because the inventory was written down incorrectly, the ending inventory value will be understated at the end of year 1. The understatement in ending inventory causes cost of goods sold to be overstated. The overstatement in cost of goods sold causes year 1 income to be understated. Conversely, the understatement in year 2 beginning inventory causes cost of goods sold for year 2 to be understated and income to be overstated.
    Answer (A) is incorrect because the year 1 income will be understated as a result of the understatement in ending inventory. Answer (B) is incorrect because the cost of goods sold for year 1 will be overstated, therefore causing the year 2 cost of goods sold to be understated. Answer (D) is incorrect because the closing inventory for year 1 will be understated since the inventory will be valued at $17.50 instead of the $25 correct figure.

**5.** All sales and purchases for the year at Ross Corporation are credit transactions. Ross shipped goods via FOB shipping point. In error, the goods were not recorded as a sale and were included in ending inventory. Which one of the following statements is correct?

    A. Accounts receivable was not affected, inventory was overstated, sales were understated, and cost of goods sold was understated.

    B. Accounts receivable was understated, inventory was not affected, sales were understated, and cost of goods sold was understated.

    C. Accounts receivable was understated, inventory was overstated, sales were understated, and cost of goods sold was overstated.

    D. Accounts receivable was understated, inventory was overstated, sales were understated, and cost of goods sold was understated.

Answer (D) is correct. *(CMA, adapted)*
    **REQUIRED:** The effects of a failure to record a sale of goods shipped FOB shipping point.
    **DISCUSSION:** The term "FOB shipping point" means that title passes to the buyer at the time and place of shipment. Thus, a sale should have been recorded at the time the goods were shipped. The result is that accounts receivable and sales will be understated because no entry was recorded. At the same time, inventory will be overstated because the goods that have been sold are still included in inventory. The overstatement in ending inventory will cause the cost of goods sold to be understated on the income statement.
    Answer (A) is incorrect because accounts receivable will be understated. Answer (B) is incorrect because inventory will be overstated. Answer (C) is incorrect because cost of goods sold will be understated due to the overstatement in inventory.

Questions 6 through 10 are based on the following information.

Thomas Engine Company is a wholesaler of marine engine parts. The activity of carburetor 2642J during the month of March is presented in the next column.

| Date | Balance or Transaction | Units | Unit Cost | Unit Sales Price |
|---|---|---|---|---|
| March 1 | Inventory | 3,200 | $64.30 | $86.50 |
| 4 | Purchase | 3,400 | 64.75 | 87.00 |
| 14 | Sales | 3,600 | | 87.25 |
| 25 | Purchase | 3,500 | 66.00 | 87.25 |
| 28 | Sales | 3,450 | | 88.00 |

**6.** If Thomas uses a first-in, first-out perpetual inventory system, the total cost of the inventory for carburetor 2642J at March 31 is

A. $196,115

B. $197,488

C. $201,300

D. $263,825

Answer (C) is correct.  *(CMA, adapted)*
**REQUIRED:** The total cost of ending inventory under the FIFO perpetual method.
**DISCUSSION:** The company began March with 3,200 units in inventory at $64.30 each. The March 4 purchase added 3,400 additional units at $64.75 each. Under the FIFO assumption, the 3,600 units sold on March 14 were the oldest units. That sale eliminated all of the 3,200 units priced at $64.30 and 400 of the units priced at $64.75, leaving an inventory of 3,000 units at $64.75 prior to the March 25 purchase. On March 25, 3,500 units were acquired at $66. The 3,450 units sold on March 28 were the 3,000 remaining units priced at $64.75 and 450 units priced at $66. Thus, the ending inventory consists of 3,050 units at $66 each, or $201,300. The answer would have been the same under the periodic FIFO method.
Answer (A) is incorrect because $196,115 is the answer under the periodic LIFO method. Answer (B) is incorrect because $197,488 is the is the answer under the LIFO method using the $64.75 cost of the March 4 purchase (instead of the beginning inventory cost). Answer (D) is incorrect because $263,825 is based on the $86.50 selling price at March 1, not the cost of the items.

**7.** If Thomas uses a last-in, first-out periodic inventory system, the total cost of the inventory for carburetor 2642J at March 31 is

A. $196,115

B. $197,488

C. $201,300

D. $268,400

Answer (A) is correct.  *(CMA, adapted)*
**REQUIRED:** The total cost of ending inventory under the LIFO periodic method.
**DISCUSSION:** The ending inventory consists of 3,050 units (beginning inventory plus purchases, minus sales). Under the periodic LIFO method, those units are valued at the oldest prices for the period, which is $64.30 of the beginning inventory. Multiplying $64.30 times 3,050 units produces a total inventory cost of $196,115.
Answer (B) is incorrect because $197,488 is the answer under the LIFO method but is based on the $64.75 cost of the March 4 purchase, instead of the beginning inventory cost. Answer (C) is incorrect because $201,300 is based on the FIFO method. Answer (D) is incorrect because $268,400 is based on the $88 selling price at the end of the month, not the cost.

**8.** If Thomas uses a last-in, first-out perpetual inventory system, the total cost of the inventory for carburetor 2642J at March 31 is

A. $196,200

B. $197,488

C. $263,863

D. $268,400

Answer (A) is correct.  *(CMA, adapted)*
**REQUIRED:** The cost of the ending inventory using the LIFO perpetual method.
**DISCUSSION:** Under the perpetual LIFO method, the company begins with 3,200 units at $64.30. To this is added the March 4 purchase of 3,400 units at $64.75. The March 14 sale uses all of the March 4 purchase and 200 of the original inventory units. Thus, the firm is left with 3,000 units at $64.30. The March 25 purchase of 3,500 at $66 is added to the previous 3,000 units. The March 28 sale of 3,450 units comes entirely from the March 25 purchase, leaving just 50 of those units at $66 each. Thus, at the end of the month, the inventory consists of two layers: 3,000 units at $64.30, or $192,900, and 50 units at $66, or $3,300. Adding the two layers together produces a total ending inventory of $196,200.
Answer (B) is incorrect because $197,488 is the answer under the periodic LIFO method but is based on the $64.75 cost of the March 4 purchase. Answer (C) is incorrect because $263,863 is based on the $86.50 selling price at March 1, not the cost of the items. Answer (D) is incorrect because $268,400 is based on the $88 selling price at month end, not the cost.

**9.** If Thomas uses a weighted-average periodic inventory system, the total cost of the inventory for carburetor 2642J at March 31 is

  A. $194,200

  B. $198,301

  C. $198,374

  D. $199,233

Answer (C) is correct.  *(CMA, adapted)*
  **REQUIRED:** The cost of the ending inventory under the weighted-average method.
  **DISCUSSION:** Under the weighted-average method, all inventory available for sale during the period is weighted, as follows, to determine the average cost per unit:

| | | | | |
|---|---|---|---|---|
| 3,200 | × | $64.30 | = | $205,760 |
| 3,400 | × | $64.75 | = | 220,150 |
| 3,500 | × | $66.00 | = | 231,000 |
| 10,100 | | | = | $656,910 |

Dividing the $656,910 total cost by the 10,100 available units produces an average unit cost of $65.04059.  Multiplying the unit cost times the 3,050 units in ending inventory produces a total cost at March 31 of $198,374.
  Answer (A) is incorrect because $194,200 ignores the March 25 purchase.  Answer (B) is incorrect because $198,301 is based on the unweighted average of the three unit purchase prices.  Answer (D) is incorrect because $199,233 is based on a perpetual moving average, not a periodic weighted average.

**10.** If Thomas uses a moving-average perpetual inventory system, the total cost of the inventory for carburetor 2642J at March 31 is

  A. $194,200

  B. $198,301

  C. $199,233

  D. $265,960

Answer (C) is correct.  *(CMA, adapted)*
  **REQUIRED:** The ending inventory cost using the perpetual moving-average basis.
  **DISCUSSION:** Under the perpetual moving-average method, the inventory is restated after every purchase and sale.  The unit cost will change after every purchase.  The calculations for the first purchase are as follows:

| | | | | |
|---|---|---|---|---|
| 3,200 | × | $64.30 | = | $205,760 |
| 3,400 | × | $64.75 | = | 220,150 |
| 6,600 | | | = | $425,910 |

The unit cost of $64.531818 was calculated by dividing the total inventory value of $425,910 by the 6,600 units.  After selling 3,600 units on March 14, the company would be left with 3,000 units at $64.531818, or $193,595.45.  This amount is added to the next purchase on March 25:

| | | | | |
|---|---|---|---|---|
| 3,000 | × | $64.531818 | = | $193,595.45 |
| 3,500 | × | $66.00 | = | 231,000.00 |
| 6,500 | | | = | $424,595.45 |

The unit cost of $65.322376 was calculated by dividing the $424,595.45 of total cost by the 6,500 available units.  Deducting the 3,450 units sold on March 28 leaves 3,050 ending units at $65.322376 each, for a total cost of $199,233.
  Answer (A) is incorrect because $194,200 ignores the March 25 purchase.  Answer (B) is incorrect because $198,301 is based on the unweighted average of the three unit purchase prices.  Answer (D) is incorrect because $265,960 is based on selling prices, not cost.

**11.** Walt Co. adopted the dollar-value LIFO inventory method as of January 1, when its inventory was valued at $500,000.  Walt's entire inventory constitutes a single pool.  Using a relevant price index of 1.10, Walt determined that its December 31 inventory was $577,500 at current-year cost, and $525,000 at base-year cost.  What was Walt's dollar-value LIFO inventory at December 31?

  A. $525,000

  B. $527,500

  C. $552,500

  D. $577,500

Answer (B) is correct.  *(CPA, adapted)*
  **REQUIRED:** The dollar-value LIFO inventory cost reported in the balance sheet.
  **DISCUSSION:** A price index for the current year may be calculated by dividing the ending inventory at current-year cost by the ending inventory at base-year cost.  This index is then applied to the current-year inventory layer stated at base-year cost.  Consequently, the index for the year is 1.1 ($577,500 ÷ $525,000), and the dollar-value LIFO cost at December 31 is $527,500 [$500,000 base layer + 1.1($525,000 − $500,000)].
  Answer (A) is incorrect because $525,000 is the base-year cost.  Answer (C) is incorrect because $552,500 results from using $525,000 as the base layer.  Answer (D) is incorrect because $577,500 is the year-end inventory at current cost.

Questions 12 and 13 are based on the following information.

Jensen Company uses a perpetual inventory system. The following purchases and sales were made during the month of May:

| Date | Activity | Description |
|---|---|---|
| May 1 | Balance | 100 units at $10 per unit |
| May 9 | Purchase | 200 units at $10 per unit |
| May 16 | Sale | 190 units |
| May 21 | Purchase | 150 units at $12 per unit |
| May 29 | Sale | 120 units |

**12.** If Jensen Company uses the first-in, first-out (FIFO) inventory cost flow assumption, the May 31 inventory is

A. $1,400

B. $1,460

C. $1,493

D. $1,680

Answer (D) is correct. *(CMA, adapted)*
**REQUIRED:** The inventory under the FIFO method.
**DISCUSSION:** The FIFO assumption is that the first units purchased are the first sold, so the ending inventory consists of the most recent units purchased. Thus, ending inventory consists of 140 units (100 beginning balance + 200 purchased – 190 sold + 150 purchased – 120 sold) from the May 21 purchase of 150 units. Its value is $1,680 ( 140 × $12). Under FIFO, the ending inventory is the same regardless of whether the inventory system is perpetual or periodic.
Answer (A) is incorrect because $1,400 is the cost under periodic LIFO. Answer (B) is incorrect because $1,460 is the cost under perpetual LIFO. Answer (C) is incorrect because $1,493 is the cost under the weighted-average method.

**13.** If Jensen Company uses the last-in, first-out (LIFO) inventory cost flow assumption, the May 31 inventory is

A. $1,400

B. $1,460

C. $1,493

D. $1,562

Answer (B) is correct. *(CMA, adapted)*
**REQUIRED:** The inventory under LIFO perpetual.
**DISCUSSION:** The LIFO assumption is that the last items purchased are the first sold. Moreover, the inventory must be restated after each purchase and sale of merchandise when the perpetual LIFO method is used. After the May 16 sale, the company held 110 units (100 beginning balance + 200 May 9 purchase – 190 May 16 sale) at a unit cost of $10. The May 21 purchase created a layer of 150 units at $12 per unit. Because the May 29 sale of 120 units is deemed to have come entirely from the layer created on May 21, the ending inventory of 140 units has two layers: 110 units at $10 and 30 units at $12. Ending inventory is therefore $1,460 [(110 × $10) + (30 × $12)].
Answer (A) is incorrect because $1,400 is the cost under periodic LIFO. Answer (C) is incorrect because $1,493 is the cost under the weighted-average method. Answer (D) is incorrect because $1,562 is the cost under the moving-average method.

**14.** The following FCL Corporation inventory information is available for the year ended December 31:

|  | Cost | Retail |
|---|---|---|
| Beginning inventory at 1/1 | $35,000 | $100,000 |
| Net purchases | 55,000 | 110,000 |
| Net markups |  | 15,000 |
| Net markdowns |  | 25,000 |
| Net sales |  | 150,000 |

The December 31 ending inventory at cost using the conventional (lower of average cost or market) retail inventory method equals

A. $17,500

B. $20,000

C. $27,500

D. $50,000

Answer (B) is correct. *(CMA, adapted)*
**REQUIRED:** The ending inventory using the conventional retail inventory method.
**DISCUSSION:** The conventional retail inventory method adds beginning inventory, net purchases, and markups (but not markdowns) to calculate a cost percentage. The purpose of excluding markdowns is to approximate a lower-of-average-cost-or-market valuation. The cost percentage is then used to reduce the retail price of the ending inventory to cost. FCL's cost-retail ratio is 40% ($90,000 ÷ $225,000), and ending inventory at cost is therefore $20,000 ($50,000 ending inventory at retail × 40%).

|  | Cost | Retail |
|---|---|---|
| Beginning inventory | $35,000 | $ 100,000 |
| Purchases | 55,000 | 110,000 |
| Markups |  | 15,000 |
| Total goods available | $90,000 | $ 225,000 |
| Sales |  | (150,000) |
| Markdowns |  | (25,000) |
| Calculated retail price of ending inventory |  | $  50,000 |

Answer (A) is incorrect because $17,500 is the ending inventory based on LIFO retail. Answer (C) is incorrect because $27,500 is based on FIFO retail. Answer (D) is incorrect because $50,000 is the ending inventory at retail.

Price's Food Market adopted the dollar-value LIFO method of inventory valuation at December 31, year 1. Inventory balances and price indices are shown in the next column.

| December 31 | Ending Inventory at End-of-Year Prices | Price Index at December 31 |
|---|---|---|
| Year 1 | $480,000 | 1.00 |
| Year 2 | 550,000 | 1.10 |
| Year 3 | 600,000 | 1.20 |

**15.** Price's Food Market's ending inventory as of December 31, year 2, computed by the dollar-value LIFO method, was

A. $480,000

B. $500,000

C. $502,000

D. $550,000

Answer (C) is correct. *(Publisher)*
**REQUIRED:** The inventory under the dollar-value LIFO method for year 2.
**DISCUSSION:** The year 2 ending inventory must be converted into base-year prices by dividing it by the year 2 price index of 1.10, resulting in an inventory value of $500,000 ($550,000 ÷ 1.10) at base-year prices. This amount consists of two layers: $480,000 purchased during the base year and $20,000 acquired in year 2. The latter amount must be converted back into year-end prices because the merchandise was not purchased during the base year. Accordingly, this $20,000 increment is multiplied by the price index for the current year. The result is an increment of $22,000 ($20,000 × 1.10). The total inventory is $502,000 ($480,000 + $22,000).
Answer (A) is incorrect because $480,000 is the inventory at the end of year 1. Answer (B) is incorrect because $500,000 is the year 2 inventory at base-year prices. Answer (D) is incorrect because $550,000 is the value at year-end prices.

**16.** Price's Food Market's ending inventory as of December 31, year 3, computed by the dollar-value LIFO method, is

A. $480,000

B. $500,000

C. $502,000

D. $600,000

Answer (C) is correct. *(Publisher)*
**REQUIRED:** The inventory under the dollar-value LIFO method for year 3.
**DISCUSSION:** The ending inventory at year-end prices must be converted into base-year prices by dividing it by the year 3 price index of 1.20, resulting in an inventory value of $500,000 ($600,000 ÷ 1.20) at base-year prices. This amount is the same as the inventory for year 2 at base-year prices. Thus, no increment was added during year 3. Consequently, the ending inventory for year 3 is the same as at the end of year 2, or $502,000. This amount consists of $480,000 of inventory purchased in year 1 and $22,000 purchased in year 2. Under LIFO, the assumption is that nothing is still on hand from year 3 purchases because the inventory is the same as at the end of the preceding year.
Answer (A) is incorrect because $480,000 was the inventory at the end of year 1. Answer (B) is incorrect because $500,000 is the year 3 inventory at base-year prices. Answer (D) is incorrect because $600,000 is the year 3 inventory at year-end prices.

Questions 17 through 22 are based on the following information. Farmers' Supply Company is a wholesaler of tractor parts. The activity of a particular type of mower blade during the month of May is presented below:

| Date | Activity | Units | Unit Cost | Unit Sales Price |
|------|----------|-------|-----------|------------------|
| May 1 | Beginning inventory | 6,400 | $64.30 | $86.50 |
| May 4 | Purchase | 6,800 | $64.75 | 87.00 |
| May 13 | Sales | 7,200 | | 87.25 |
| May 24 | Purchase | 7,000 | $66.00 | 87.25 |
| May 27 | Sales | 6,900 | | 88.00 |

**17.** If Farmers' uses a first-in, first-out (FIFO) perpetual inventory system, the total cost of the inventory for mower blades at May 31 is

A. $392,230

B. $394,975

C. $402,600

D. $536,800

Answer (C) is correct. *(Publisher)*
REQUIRED: The total cost of inventory at May 31 under the FIFO perpetual method.
DISCUSSION: The available inventory consisted of 20,200 units (6,400 BI + 6,800 May 4 purchase + 7,000 May 24 purchase), and 14,100 units (7,200 May 13 sale + 6,900 May 27 sale) were sold. Hence, ending inventory consists of 6,100 units. Under a FIFO assumption, these units are deemed to be from the last purchase. The ending inventory is therefore $402,600 (6,100 units × $66 unit cost of the May 24 purchase). The answer would have been the same in a periodic system, a statement that cannot be made for other inventory flow assumptions.
Answer (A) is incorrect because $392,230 is the inventory under the periodic LIFO method. Answer (B) is incorrect because $394,975 is the inventory under the periodic LIFO method using the $64.75 cost of the May 4 purchase. Answer (D) is incorrect because $536,800 is based on the $88 selling price at the end of the month.

**18.** If Farmers' uses a first-in, first-out (FIFO) periodic inventory system, the total cost of the inventory for mower blades at May 31 is

A. $392,230

B. $394,975

C. $402,600

D. $536,800

Answer (C) is correct. *(Publisher)*
REQUIRED: The total cost of inventory at May 31 under the FIFO periodic method.
DISCUSSION: The available inventory consisted of 20,200 units (6,400 BI + 6,800 May 4 purchase + 7,000 May 24 purchase), and 14,100 units (7,200 May 13 sale + 6,900 May 27 sale) were sold. Hence, ending inventory consists of 6,100 units. Under a FIFO assumption, these units are deemed to be from the last purchase. The ending inventory is therefore $402,600 (6,100 units × $66 unit cost of the May 24 purchase). The answer would have been the same in a perpetual system, a statement that cannot be made for other inventory flow assumptions.
Answer (A) is incorrect because $392,230 is the inventory under the periodic LIFO method. Answer (B) is incorrect because $394,975 is the inventory under the periodic LIFO method using the $64.75 cost of the May 4 purchase. Answer (D) is incorrect because $536,800 is based on the $88 selling price at the end of the month.

**19.** If Farmers' uses a last-in, first-out (LIFO) periodic inventory system, the total cost of the inventory for mower blades at May 31 is

A. $392,230

B. $394,975

C. $402,600

D. $536,800

Answer (A) is correct. *(Publisher)*
REQUIRED: The total cost of inventory at May 31 under the LIFO periodic method.
DISCUSSION: The ending inventory consists of 6,100 units (beginning inventory + purchases – sales). Under the periodic LIFO method, ending inventory is deemed to come from the beginning 6,400-unit inventory priced at $64.30 per unit. Thus, the inventory is $392,230 (6,100 × $64.30).
Answer (B) is incorrect because $394,975 is based on the $64.75 cost of the March 4 purchase. Answer (C) is incorrect because $402,600 is based on the FIFO method. Answer (D) is incorrect because $536,800 is based on the $88 selling price at the end of the month.

**20.** If Farmers' uses a last-in, first out (LIFO) perpetual inventory system, the total cost of the inventory for mower blades at May 31 is

A. $392,230

B. $392,400

C. $394,975

D. $402,600

Answer (B) is correct. *(Publisher)*
**REQUIRED:** The ending inventory using the perpetual LIFO method.
**DISCUSSION:** Under perpetual LIFO, the 7,200-unit sale on May 13 is deemed to have eliminated the 6,800-unit layer acquired on May 4 and to have reduced the 6,400-unit May 1 layer to 6,000 units. The 6,900-unit sale on May 27 reduced the 7,000-unit May 24 layer to 100 units. The ending inventory therefore has two layers under LIFO periodic: 6,000 units at $64.30 per unit and 100 units at $66.00 per unit, a total of $392,400.

Answer (A) is incorrect because $392,230 is the inventory under the LIFO periodic method. Answer (C) is incorrect because $394,975 is based on the $64.75 cost of the May 4 purchase. Answer (D) is incorrect because $402,600 is based on the FIFO method.

**21.** At May 31, if Farmers' uses a weighted-average inventory system, the total cost of the inventory for mower blades (assuming all calculations are rounded to two decimal places) is

A. $393,633

B. $396,622

C. $396,744

D. $398,467

Answer (C) is correct. *(Publisher)*
**REQUIRED:** The May 31 inventory under the weighted-average method.
**DISCUSSION:** Under the weighted-average periodic method, all inventory available for sale during the period is weighted to determine the average cost per unit.

| | | | |
|---|---|---|---|
| 6,400 | × $64.30 | = | $ 411,520 |
| 6,800 | × $64.75 | = | 440,300 |
| 7,000 | × $66.00 | = | 462,000 |
| 20,200 | | | $1,313,820 |

Thus, the weighted-average unit cost (rounded) is $65.04 ($1,313,820 ÷ 20,200 units). The total at March 31 is therefore $396,744 (6,100 units × $65.04).

Answer (A) is incorrect because $393,633 is based on the amount of the weighted-average unit cost immediately after the May 4 purchase. Answer (B) is incorrect because $396,622 is based on the unweighted average of the three unit purchase prices. Answer (D) is incorrect because $398,467 is based on a perpetual moving average.

**22.** At May 31, if Farmers' uses a moving-average inventory system, the total cost of the inventory for mower blades (assuming all calculations are rounded to two decimal places) is

A. $393,633

B. $396,622

C. $396,744

D. $398,452

Answer (D) is correct. *(Publisher)*
**REQUIRED:** The ending inventory using the moving-average method.
**DISCUSSION:** Under the perpetual moving-average method, the inventory is revalued after every purchase and sale. The calculations for the first purchase are as follows:

| Units | | Unit Cost | | |
|---|---|---|---|---|
| 6,400 | × | $64.30 | = | $411,520 |
| 6,800 | × | $64.75 | = | 440,300 |
| 13,200 | | | | $851,820 |

The unit cost is $64.53 (rounded) ($851,820 ÷ 13,200 units). After selling 7,200 units on May 13, the company had 6,000 units at $64.53, or $387,180. This amount is added to the next purchase on May 25:

| | | | | |
|---|---|---|---|---|
| 6,000 | × | $64.53 | = | $387,180 |
| 7,000 | × | $66.00 | = | 462,000 |
| 13,000 | | | | $849,180 |

The unit cost is $65.32 (rounded) ($849,180 ÷ 13,000 units). Subtracting the 6,900 units sold on May 27 leaves 6,100 units at $65.32 each, or $398,452.

Answer (A) is incorrect because $393,633 is based on the amount of the weighted-average unit cost immediately after the May 4 purchase. Answer (B) is incorrect because $396,622 is based on the unweighted average of the three unit purchase prices. Answer (C) is incorrect because $396,744 is based on a periodic weighted average.

Questions 23 and 24 are based on the following information. During January, Metro Co., which maintains a perpetual inventory system, recorded the following information pertaining to its inventory:

|  | Units | Unit Cost | Total Cost | Units on Hand |
|---|---|---|---|---|
| Balance on 1/1 | 1,000 | $1 | $1,000 | 1,000 |
| Purchased on 1/7 | 600 | 3 | 1,800 | 1,600 |
| Sold on 1/20 | 900 |  |  | 700 |
| Purchased on 1/25 | 400 | 5 | 2,000 | 1,100 |

**23.** Under the moving-average method, what amount should Metro report as inventory at January 31?

A. $1,300

B. $2,640

C. $3,225

D. $3,900

Answer (C) is correct.  *(CPA, adapted)*
**REQUIRED:** The ending inventory using the moving-average method.
**DISCUSSION:** The moving-average system is only applicable to perpetual inventories. It requires that a new weighted average be computed after every purchase. This moving average is based on remaining inventory held and the new inventory purchased. Based on the calculations below, the moving-average cost per unit for the 1/20 sale is $1.75, and the cost of goods sold (CGS) for January is $1,575 (900 units sold × $1.75). Thus, ending inventory is $3,225 ($1,000 beginning balance + $1,800 purchase on 1/7 – $1,575 CGS on 1/20 + $2,000 purchase on 1/25).

|  | Units | Moving-Average Cost/Unit | Total Cost |
|---|---|---|---|
| Balance 1/1 | 1,000 | $1.00 | $1,000 |
| Purchase 1/7 | 600 | 3.00 | 1,800 |
|  | 1,600 | $1.75 | $2,800 |

Answer (A) is incorrect because $1,300 is based on the periodic LIFO method. Answer (B) is incorrect because $2,640 is based on the weighted-average method. Answer (D) is incorrect because $3,900 is based on the FIFO method.

**24.** Under the LIFO method, what amount should Metro report as inventory at January 31?

A. $3,225

B. $1,300

C. $2,700

D. $3,900

Answer (C) is correct.  *(CPA, adapted)*
**REQUIRED:** The value of ending inventory using a LIFO perpetual system.
**DISCUSSION:** In a perpetual inventory system, purchases are directly recorded in the inventory account, and cost of goods sold (CGS) is determined as the goods are sold. Under LIFO, the latest goods purchased are assumed to be the first to be sold. Using LIFO perpetual, 600 of the 900 units sold on 1/20 are assumed to have come from the last purchase. Their cost was $1,800 (600 × $3). The remaining 300 came from the beginning balance at a cost of $300 (300 × $1). Hence, the total CGS for January was $2,100, and ending inventory must equal $2,700 ($1,000 beginning inventory + $1,800 purchase on 1/7 + $2,000 purchase on 1/25 – $2,100 CGS).
Answer (A) is incorrect because $3,225 is based on the moving-average method. Answer (B) is incorrect because $1,300 is based on the periodic LIFO method. Answer (D) is incorrect because $3,900 is based on the periodic FIFO method.

**25.** Brock Co. adopted the dollar-value LIFO inventory method as of January 1, 2002. A single inventory pool and an internally computed price index are used to compute Brock's LIFO inventory layers. Information about Brock's inventory follows:

| Date | Inventory At Base-Year Cost | At Current-Year Cost | At Dollar-Value LIFO |
|---|---|---|---|
| 1/1/02 | $40,000 | $40,000 | $40,000 |
| 2002 layer | 5,000 | 14,000 | 6,000 |
| 12/31/02 | 45,000 | 54,000 | 46,000 |
| 2003 layer | 15,000 | 26,000 | ? |
| 12/31/03 | $60,000 | $80,000 | ? |

What was Brock's dollar-value LIFO inventory at December 31, 2003?

- A. $80,000
- B. $74,000
- C. $66,000
- D. $60,000

**26.** Based on a physical inventory taken on December 31, Chewy Co. determined its chocolate inventory on a FIFO basis at $26,000 with a replacement cost of $20,000. Chewy estimated that, after further processing costs of $12,000, the chocolate could be sold as finished candy bars for $40,000. Chewy's normal profit margin is 10% of sales. Under the lower-of-cost-or-market rule, what amount should Chewy report as chocolate inventory in its December 31 balance sheet?

- A. $28,000
- B. $26,000
- C. $24,000
- D. $20,000

**27.** The following information is available for the Silver Company for the 3 months ended March 31 of this year:

| | |
|---|---|
| Merchandise inventory, January 1 of this year | $ 900,000 |
| Purchases | 3,400,000 |
| Freight-in | 200,000 |
| Sales | 4,800,000 |

The gross margin recorded was 25% of sales. What should be the merchandise inventory at March 31?

- A. $700,000
- B. $900,000
- C. $1,125,000
- D. $1,200,000

Answer (C) is correct. *(CPA, adapted)*
**REQUIRED:** The year-end dollar-value LIFO inventory.
**DISCUSSION:** To compute the ending inventory under dollar-value LIFO, the ending inventory stated in year-end or current-year cost must be restated at base-year cost. The layers at base-year cost are computed using a LIFO flow assumption and then weighted (multiplied) by the relevant indexes to price the ending inventory. The relevant price index for the 2003 layer is 1.33 1/3 ($80,000 current-year cost ÷ $60,000 base-year cost). The 2003 layer at base-year cost is multiplied by this index to translate it to the price in effect when the layer was added. Accordingly, the 2003 layer at dollar-value LIFO is $20,000 (1.33 1/3 × $15,000), and ending inventory is $66,000 ($46,000 at 12/31/02 + $20,000).
Answer (A) is incorrect because $80,000 is the current-year cost at year-end. Answer (B) is incorrect because $74,000 is the beginning inventory at current-year cost plus the 2003 layer at dollar-value LIFO. Answer (D) is incorrect because $60,000 is the base-year cost at year-end.

Answer (C) is correct. *(CPA, adapted)*
**REQUIRED:** The LCM value of inventory.
**DISCUSSION:** Market equals current replacement cost subject to maximum and minimum amounts. The maximum is net realizable value (NRV), and the minimum is NRV minus normal profit. When replacement cost is within this range, it is used as the market value. Cost is given as $26,000. NRV is $28,000 ($40,000 selling price – $12,000 additional processing costs), and NRV minus a normal profit equals $24,000 [$28,000 – ($40,000 × 10%)]. Because the lowest amount in the range ($24,000) exceeds replacement cost ($20,000), it is used as the market value. Because market ending value ($24,000) is less than cost ($26,000), it is also the ending inventory.
Answer (A) is incorrect because $28,000 is the NRV. Answer (B) is incorrect because $26,000 is the cost. Answer (D) is incorrect because $20,000 is the replacement cost.

Answer (B) is correct. *(CPA, adapted)*
**REQUIRED:** The estimated ending inventory using the gross profit method.
**DISCUSSION:** If the gross profit margin is 25% of sales, cost of goods sold equals 75% of sales. Ending inventory is equal to goods available for sale minus cost of goods sold.

| | |
|---|---|
| Beginning inventory | $ 900,000 |
| Purchases | 3,400,000 |
| Freight-in | 200,000 |
| Goods available for sale | $ 4,500,000 |
| CGS $4,800,000 × (1 – .25) | (3,600,000) |
| Ending inventory | $ 900,000 |

Answer (A) is incorrect because $700,000 does not include freight-in from the calculation. Answer (C) is incorrect because $1,125,000 is 25% of goods available for sale. Answer (D) is incorrect because $1,200,000 is the gross margin.

Questions 28 and 29 are based on the following information. Packard Corporation, which uses a periodic inventory system, overstated its inventory when it conducted its year-end count on December 31, Year 1. The ending inventory was actually $100,000, but due to double counting some items, the total counted came to $130,000.

**28.** What impact does this error have on the assets and income as reported on December 31, Year 1?

A. Assets are overstated and income is overstated.

B. Retained earnings are understated and cost of goods sold is understated.

C. Income is overstated and cost of goods sold is overstated.

D. Assets are understated and retained earnings is overstated.

Answer (A) is correct. *(Publisher)*
REQUIRED: The true statement about an overstatement of ending inventory.
DISCUSSION: An overstatement of ending inventory will cause assets to be overstated on the balance sheet. At the same time, cost of goods sold will be understated, leading to an overstatement of income and retained earnings.
Answer (B) is incorrect because retained earnings will be overstated. Answer (C) is incorrect because cost of goods sold is understated. Answer (D) is incorrect because assets are overstated.

**29.** What impact does this error have on the assets and income as reported on December 31, Year 2?

A. Assets are overstated and income is understated.

B. Assets are understated and income is overstated.

C. Cost of goods sold is overstated and income is understated.

D. Cost of goods sold is overstated and retained earnings is understated.

Answer (C) is correct. *(Publisher)*
REQUIRED: The true statement about an overstatement of beginning inventory on the financial statements at the end of Year 2.
DISCUSSION: The previous year's overstatement of inventory will cause the beginning inventory on the income statement to be overstated, thus leading to an overstatement of cost of goods sold. The cost overstatement causes income to be understated. Assets will be correct because inventory will have been recounted at the end of Year 2. Retained earnings will also be correct because the overstatement in Year 1 income would have been offset by the understatement in Year 2 income.
Answer (A) is incorrect because the assets will be correct. Answer (B) is incorrect because income will be understated and assets will be correct. Answer (D) is incorrect because retained earnings will be correct.

## 14.2 Investments (Current and Long-term)

**30.** An investment in trading securities is measured on the statement of financial position at the

A. Cost to acquire the asset.

B. Accumulated income minus accumulated dividends since acquisition.

C. Lower of cost or market.

D. Fair value.

Answer (D) is correct. *(CMA, adapted)*
REQUIRED: The means of valuing trading securities on the balance sheet.
DISCUSSION: Under SFAS 115, trading securities are those held principally for sale in the near term. They are classified as current and consist of debt securities and equity securities with readily determinable fair values. Unrealized holding gains and losses on trading securities are reported in earnings. Hence, these securities are reported at fair value, which is "the amount at which a financial instrument could be exchanged in a current transaction between willing parties, other than in a forced or liquidation sale."
Answer (A) is incorrect because cost is adjusted for changes in fair value. Answer (B) is incorrect because an equity-based investment is adjusted for the investor's share of the investee's earnings, minus dividends received. However, SFAS 115 does not apply to investments accounted for using the equity method. Answer (C) is incorrect because lower of cost or market was the measurement basis prescribed by SFAS 12, a pronouncement superseded by SFAS 115.

Questions 31 and 32 are based on the following information.

Information concerning Monahan Company's portfolio of debt securities at May 31, year 2 and May 31, year 3 is presented in the next column. All of the debt securities were purchased by Monahan during June, year 1. Prior to June, year 1, Monahan had no investments in debt or equity securities.

| As of May 31, Year 2 | Amortized Cost | Fair Value |
|---|---|---|
| Cleary Company bonds | $164,526 | $168,300 |
| Beauchamp Industry bonds | 204,964 | 205,200 |
| Morrow, Inc. bonds | 305,785 | 285,200 |
| Total | $675,275 | $658,700 |

| As of May 31, Year 3 | Amortized Cost | Fair Value |
|---|---|---|
| Cleary Company bonds | $152,565 | $147,600 |
| Beauchamp Industry bonds | 193,800 | 204,500 |
| Morrow, Inc. bonds | 289,130 | 291,400 |
| Total | $635,495 | $643,500 |

**31.** Assuming that the above securities are properly classified as available-for-sale securities under SFAS 115, *Accounting for Certain Investments in Debt and Equity Securities*, the unrealized holding gain or loss as of May 31, year 3 would be

A. Recognized as an $8,005 unrealized holding gain on the income statement.

B. Recognized in other comprehensive income by a year-end credit of $8,005.

C. Recognized in other comprehensive income by a year-end debit of $8,005.

D. Not recognized.

Answer (B) is correct. *(CMA, adapted)*
**REQUIRED:** The unrealized holding gain or loss on available-for-sale securities.
**DISCUSSION:** Available-for-sale securities include (1) equity securities with readily determinable fair values that are not classified as trading securities and (2) debt securities that are not classified as held-to-maturity or trading securities. Unrealized holding gains and losses are measured by the difference between recorded cost and fair value at year-end. They are excluded from earnings and reported in other comprehensive income. The balance is reported net of the tax effect. Thus, the difference at May 31, year 3 is $8,005 ($643,500 fair value – $635,495 amortized cost). This unrealized gain is reported as a credit to accumulated other comprehensive income.
Answer (A) is incorrect because unrealized gains and losses on available-for-sale securities do not appear on the income statement. Answer (C) is incorrect because gains are credits (increases in equity) and losses are debits (decreases in equity). Answer (D) is incorrect because SFAS 115 requires unrealized gains and losses on available-for-sale securities to be recorded in other comprehensive income.

**32.** Assuming that the securities are properly classified as held-to-maturity securities under SFAS 115, *Accounting for Certain Investments in Debt and Equity Securities*, the unrealized holding gain or loss as of May 31, year 2 would be

A. Recognized as an $8,005 unrealized holding gain on the income statement.

B. Recognized in other comprehensive income by a year-end credit of $8,005.

C. Recognized in other comprehensive income by a year-end debit of $8,005.

D. Not recognized.

Answer (D) is correct. *(CMA, adapted)*
**REQUIRED:** The proper financial statement treatment of held-to-maturity securities.
**DISCUSSION:** Debt securities that the reporting enterprise has the positive intent and ability to hold to maturity are classified as held-to-maturity. Held-to-maturity securities are reported at amortized cost. Under the provisions of SFAS 115, any unrealized gains or losses are not recognized.
Answer (A) is incorrect because unrealized gains and losses on held-to-maturity securities are not recorded. Answer (B) is incorrect because unrealized gains and losses on held-to-maturity securities are not recorded. Answer (C) is incorrect because unrealized gains and losses on held-to-maturity securities are not recorded.

Questions 33 and 34 are based on the following information.

On January 1, Boggs, Inc. paid $700,000 for 100,000 shares of Mattly Corporation representing 30% of Mattly's outstanding common stock. The following computation was made by Boggs.

| | |
|---|---|
| Purchase price | $700,000 |
| 30% equity in carrying amount of Mattly's net assets | 500,000 |
| Excess cost over carrying amount | $200,000 |

The excess cost over carrying amount was attributed to goodwill with an estimated useful life of 20 years. Mattly reported net income for the year ended December 31 of $300,000. Mattly Corporation had paid cash dividends of $100,000 on July 1.

**33.** If Boggs, Inc. exercised significant influence over Mattly Corporation and properly accounted for the long-term investment under the equity method, the amount of net investment revenue Boggs should report from its investment in Mattly is

A. $30,000

B. $60,000

C. $80,000

D. $90,000

Answer (D) is correct. *(CMA, adapted)*
**REQUIRED:** The net investment revenue reported using the equity method.
**DISCUSSION:** Under the equity method, Boggs should recognize 30% of Mattly's reported income of $300,000, or $90,000. Moreover, under SFAS 142, goodwill is not amortized. However, the equity method investment, not the equity method goodwill itself, may be tested for impairment. Thus, net investment income is $90,000. Dividends received from an investee must be recorded in the books of the investor as a decrease in the carrying amount of the investment and an increase in assets (cash).
Answer (A) is incorrect because $30,000 is the net investment revenue reported using the cost method. Answer (B) is incorrect because $60,000 equals 30% of the investee's net income minus 30% of the dividends paid. Answer (C) is incorrect because $80,000 assumes $10,000 of goodwill is amortized.

**34.** If Boggs, Inc. did not exercise significant influence over Mattly Corporation and properly accounted for the long-term investment under the cost method, the amount of net investment revenue Boggs should report from its investment in Mattly would be

A. $20,000

B. $30,000

C. $60,000

D. $90,000

Answer (B) is correct. *(CMA, adapted)*
**REQUIRED:** The net investment revenue reported using the cost method.
**DISCUSSION:** Under the fair value method or the cost method (the latter is appropriate if the equity method is not applicable, and the equity securities do not have readily determinable fair values), the investor records as revenue only the amount actually received as dividends. Boggs receives 30% of the $100,000 total dividend and records $30,000 of investment revenue.
Answer (A) is incorrect because $20,000 results from subtracting $10,000 of goodwill. Answer (C) is incorrect because $60,000 equals 30% of the investee's net income minus 30% of the dividends paid. Answer (D) is incorrect because $90,000 is the net investment revenue reported using the equity method.

**35.** An investment in available-for-sale securities is measured on the statement of financial position at the

A. Cost to acquire the asset.

B. Accumulated income less accumulated dividends since acquisition.

C. Fair value.

D. Par or stated value of the securities.

Answer (C) is correct. *(CMA, adapted)*
**REQUIRED:** The measurement of available-for-sale securities on the balance sheet.
**DISCUSSION:** According to SFAS 115, available-for-sale securities are investments in debt securities that are not classified as held-to-maturity or trading securities and in equity securities with readily determinable fair values that are not classified as trading securities. They are measured at fair value in the balance sheet.
Answer (A) is incorrect because cost is adjusted for changes in fair value. Answer (B) is incorrect because an equity-based investment is adjusted for the investor's share of the investee's earnings, minus dividends received. However, SFAS 115 does not apply to investments accounted for using the equity method. Answer (D) is incorrect because the par or stated value is an arbitrary amount.

**36.** Park Co. uses the equity method to account for its January 1, year 1 purchase of Tun, Inc.'s common stock. On January 1, year 1, the fair values of Tun's FIFO inventory and land exceeded their carrying amounts. How do these excesses of fair values over carrying amounts affect Park's reported equity in Tun's year 1 earnings?

| | Inventory Excess | Land Excess |
|---|---|---|
| A. | Decrease | Decrease |
| B. | Decrease | No effect |
| C. | Increase | Increase |
| D. | Increase | No effect |

Answer (B) is correct. *(CPA, adapted)*
**REQUIRED:** The effect on equity in investee earnings of the excess of the fair values of the investee's FIFO inventory and land over their carrying amounts.
**DISCUSSION:** The equity method of accounting requires the investor's proportionate share of the investee's reported net income to be adjusted for certain acquisition differentials. Thus, the difference at the date of acquisition of the investee's stock between the fair value and carrying amount of inventory is such an adjustment when the inventory is sold. A similar adjustment for land is required when the land is sold. Assuming that the FIFO inventory was sold in year 1 and the land was not, Park's proportionate share of Tun's reported net income is decreased by the inventory differential allocated at the date of acquisition.
Answer (A) is incorrect because the inventory excess decreases equity in the investee's earnings, but the land excess has no effect. Answer (C) is incorrect because the inventory excess decreases equity in the investee's earnings, but the land excess has no effect. Answer (D) is incorrect because the inventory excess decreases equity in the investee's earnings, but the land excess has no effect.

**37.** On January 2, year 1, Kean Co. purchased a 30% interest in Pod Co. for $250,000. On this date, Pod's equity was $500,000. The carrying amounts of Pod's net assets approximated their fair values, except for land, for which fair value exceeded its carrying amount by $200,000. Pod reported net income of $100,000 for year 1 and paid no dividends. Kean accounts for this investment using the equity method. In its December 31, year 1 balance sheet, what amount should Kean report as investment in subsidiary?

A. $210,000

B. $220,000

C. $276,000

D. $280,000

Answer (D) is correct. *(CPA, adapted)*
**REQUIRED:** The amount reported as investment in subsidiary under the equity method.
**DISCUSSION:** The purchase price is allocated to the fair value of the net assets acquired with the remainder allocated to goodwill. The fair value of Kean's 30% interest in Pod's net assets is $210,000 [($500,000 + $200,000) × 30%]. Equity method goodwill is $40,000 ($250,000 – $210,000). The equity method requires the investor's share of subsequent net income reported by the investee to be adjusted for the difference at acquisition between the fair value and the carrying amount of the investee's net assets when the net assets are sold or consumed in operations. The land is assumed not to be sold, and the goodwill is not amortized. Thus, Kean's share of Pod's net income is $30,000 ($100,000 declared income × 30%), and the investment account at year-end is $280,000 ($250,000 acquisition balance + $30,000 investment income).
Answer (A) is incorrect because $210,000 equals the fair value of the identifiable net assets acquired. Answer (B) is incorrect because $220,000 equals the price minus Kean's equity in Pod's net income. Answer (C) is incorrect because $276,000 assumes amortization of goodwill over 10 years.

**38.** Green Corp. owns 30% of the outstanding common stock and 100% of the outstanding noncumulative nonvoting preferred stock of Axel Corp. In year 1, Axel declared dividends of $100,000 on its common stock and $60,000 on its preferred stock. Green exercises significant influence over Axel's operations. What amount of dividend revenue should Green report in its income statement for the year ended December 31, year 1?

A. $0

B. $30,000

C. $60,000

D. $90,000

Answer (C) is correct. *(CPA, adapted)*
**REQUIRED:** The dividend revenue reported given declaration of common and preferred dividends by an investee.
**DISCUSSION:** An investment in common stock enabling the investor to exercise significant influence over the operations and management of the investee should be accounted for by the equity method. A 20% or greater ownership is presumed to permit such influence. Under the equity method, the receipt of a cash dividend from the investee should be credited to the investment account. It is a return of, not a return on, the investment. However, the equity method is not applicable to nonvoting stock. Thus, Green should report $60,000 of revenue when the preferred dividends are declared.
Answer (A) is incorrect because the preferred dividends should be credited to revenue. Answer (B) is incorrect because the cash dividends on common stock should be credited to the investment account. Answer (D) is incorrect because the cash dividends on common stock should be credited to the investment account.

**39.** Sage, Inc. bought 40% of Adams Corp.'s outstanding common stock on January 2, year 1 for $400,000. The carrying amount of the net assets at the purchase date totaled $900,000. Fair values and carrying amounts were the same for all items except for plant and inventory, for which fair values exceeded their carrying amounts by $90,000 and $10,000, respectively. The plant has an 18-year life. All inventory was sold during year 1. During year 1, Adams reported net income of $120,000 and paid a $20,000 cash dividend. What amount should Sage report in its income statement from its investment in Adams for the year ended December 31, year 1?

A. $48,000

B. $42,000

C. $36,000

D. $32,000

Answer (B) is correct. *(CPA, adapted)*
**REQUIRED:** The amount reported as investment income.
**DISCUSSION:** Sage holds 40% of the investee's stock and is assumed to exercise significant influence. It should therefore account for the investment on the equity basis by recognizing its proportionate share of the investee's net income. To determine the amount of investment income the investor should report, the investee's net income of $120,000 should be adjusted for the $10,000 excess of fair value over the carrying amount of the inventory acquired because this inventory was sold. The investee's reported net income also should be adjusted for the share of the difference between the fair value and carrying amount of the plant that has been consumed (depreciated), or $5,000 ($90,000 difference ÷ 18 years). No equity method goodwill exists because the $400,000 purchase price equals a proportionate share of the fair value of the net assets {[40% × ($900,000 + $90,000 + $10,000)] = $400,000}. Thus, Sage should report investment income of $42,000 [($120,000 − $10,000 − $5,000) × 40%].
Answer (A) is incorrect because $48,000 equals the proportionate share of the investee's reported net income. Answer (C) is incorrect because $36,000 adjusts the reported net income for the dividend disclosed and does not adjust for the plant depreciation. Answer (D) is incorrect because $32,000 includes a $10,000 adjustment for goodwill amortization. Goodwill is not amortized.

**40.** On January 1, year 1, Mega Corp. acquired 10% of the outstanding voting stock of Penny, Inc. On January 2, year 2, Mega gained the ability to exercise significant influence over financial and operating control of Penny by acquiring an additional 20% of Penny's outstanding stock. The two purchases were made at prices proportionate to the amounts assigned to Penny's net assets, which equaled their carrying amounts. For the years ended December 31, year 1 and year 2, Penny reported the following:

|                | Year 1    | Year 2    |
|----------------|-----------|-----------|
| Dividends paid | $200,000  | $300,000  |
| Net income     | 600,000   | 650,000   |

In year 2, what amounts should Mega report as current-year investment income and as an adjustment, before income taxes, to year 1 investment income?

|    | Year 2 Investment Income | Adjustment to Year 1 Investment Income |
|----|--------------------------|----------------------------------------|
| A. | $195,000                 | $160,000                               |
| B. | $195,000                 | $120,000                               |
| C. | $195,000                 | $40,000                                |
| D. | $105,000                 | $40,000                                |

Answer (C) is correct. *(CPA, adapted)*
**REQUIRED:** The amounts reported as current-year investment income and as an adjustment, before income taxes, to the previous year's investment income.
**DISCUSSION:** When ownership of an investee reaches the level of significant influence, the investor must adopt the equity method. The investor must also retroactively adjust the carrying amount of the investment, results of operations, and retained earnings as if the equity method had been in effect during all of the previous periods in which any percentage was held. Consequently, Mega should report year 2 investment income before taxes equal to $195,000 (30% × $650,000 net income reported by Penny for year 2). Ignoring taxes, it should retroactively adjust year 1 investment income by $40,000 [($600,000 investee net income in year 1 × 10% interest held in year 1) − ($200,000 dividends paid by investee in year 1 × 10%)].
Answer (A) is incorrect because $160,000 equals 30% of Penny's year 1 net income minus 10% of Penny's year 1 dividends. Answer (B) is incorrect because $120,000 equals 30% of Penny's year 1 net income minus 30% of Penny's year 1 dividends. Answer (D) is incorrect because $105,000 equals Mega's share of year 2 net income minus its share of dividends.

Use Gleim's ***CMA Test Prep*** for interactive testing with **over 2,000 additional multiple-choice questions**!

# STUDY UNIT FIFTEEN
# LONG-LIVED ASSETS

(25 pages of outline)

This study unit is the **fifth of ten** on **external financial reporting**. The relative weight assigned to this major topic in Part 2 of the exam is **25%** at **skill level B** (four skill types required). The ten study units are

Study Unit 11: Overview of External Financial Reporting
Study Unit 12: Overview of Financial Statements
Study Unit 13: Cash and Receivables
Study Unit 14: Inventories and Investments
Study Unit 15: Long-Lived Assets
Study Unit 16: Liabilities
Study Unit 17: Equity and Revenue Recognition
Study Unit 18: Other Income Statements
Study Unit 19: Business Combinations and Derivatives
Study Unit 20: SEC Requirements and the Annual Report

After studying the outlines and answering the multiple-choice questions in this study unit, you will have the skills necessary to address the following topics listed in the IMA's Learning Outcome Statements:

Part 2 – Section E.4. Recognition, measurement, valuation, and disclosure

For each of the subtopics listed, the candidate should be able to:

1. define the subtopic and describe the characteristics of its components

2. demonstrate an understanding of appropriate valuation techniques for the components of each subtopic

3. demonstrate an understanding of the appropriate accounting conventions for the components of each subtopic

4. compare and contrast valuation techniques and accounting methods

5. show the correct financial statement presentation

6. identify the appropriate disclosure requirements in the body of the financial statements and/or in the footnotes

Property, plant, and equipment

    a. subtopic components: land, buildings, equipment, and self-constructed assets; additions, improvements, replacements, reinstallations, and repairs; nonmonetary exchanges; depreciation; depletion; impairment

    b. calculate depreciation using the activity method, the straight-line method, the sum-of-the years'-digits method, declining-balance method, the group method, and the composite method

    c. calculate and record the gain or loss on the disposition of tangible assets

    d.   identify the basis on which tangible assets would be valued when payment is in the form of stock

    e.   demonstrate an understanding of the correct accounting treatment for interest costs incurred for the construction or acquisition of tangible assets

    f.   determine the effect on the financial statements of using different depreciation methods

    g.   recommend a depreciation method given a set of data and management goals

    h.   compute a depletion base given acquisition, exploration, development, and restoration costs

    i.   demonstrate an understanding of the write-off of resource cost

<u>Intangibles</u>

    a.   subtopic components: intangible assets: patents, copyrights, trademarks and trade names, leaseholds, franchises and licensees; purchased intangibles and internally-created intangibles; goodwill; internally-created goodwill and purchased goodwill; negative goodwill; amortization; research and development; start-up costs, initial operating losses, advertising costs, and computer software costs

    b.   demonstrate an understanding of the accounting for impairment of intangible assets

    c.   determine the effect on the financial statements of various intangible asset transactions

## 15.1 PROPERTY, PLANT, AND EQUIPMENT (PPE) – ACQUISITION AND VALUATION

1. **Definition**

    a.   PPE are **tangible**. The asset value is based on physical existence.

        1)   These assets are also known as fixed assets or plant assets.

    b.   PPE may be either **personal property** (something movable, e.g., equipment) or **real property** (such as land or a building).

    c.   PPE are used in the **ordinary operations** of an enterprise and are not held primarily for investment, resale, or inclusion in another product, although they are often sold.

        1)   Land held by developers is classified as an investment or inventory.

        2)   Intangible assets and natural resources also are operating assets.

    d.   PPE are **long-term**. They are not expected to be used up within 1 year or the normal operating cycle of the business, whichever is longer.

        1)   The cost of using up the service potential of PPE (except land) is systematically and rationally allocated by means of **depreciation**.

            a)   However, land may sustain a material loss in value, e.g., through soil erosion of agricultural property or a natural disaster (flood or earthquake).

        2)   Intangible assets and natural resources are also wasting assets. Allocation of their costs is known as **amortization** and **depletion**, respectively.

2. **Types of PPE in Addition to Land and Buildings**

    a.   **Land improvements**, such as landscaping, drainage, streets, street lighting, sewers, sidewalks, parking lots, driveways, fences, and rights-of-way.

    b.   **Machinery and equipment**, such as furniture, fixtures (personal property permanently attached to real property, such as a central heating system), and vehicles.

    c.   **Leaseholds and leasehold improvements.**

        1)   A leasehold (a lease) is a right to possess realty for a specified time. Leaseholds are treated as intangible assets (see item 7. under subunit 15.4).

        2)   Leasehold improvements include buildings constructed on, and other modifications made to, the leased property. They are classified as PPE.

      d.   **Natural resources**, including gold, silver, oil and gas, standing timber, coal, and other mineral deposits, are sometimes classified among PPE, but they are better treated as long-term inventories. They are held for direct resale or inclusion in other products.

           1)   Unlike natural resources, most items treated as PPE are not consumed in ordinary operations. They may deteriorate and become less efficient with use or the passage of time, but they remain otherwise unchanged.

      e.   **Internally constructed assets.**

      f.   **Miscellaneous items**, e.g., tools, patterns and dies, and returnable containers.

   3.   **Relevant Accounting Principles**

      a.   **Historical cost.** PPE "are reported at their historical cost, which is the amount of cash or its equivalent paid to acquire an asset" (SFAC 5).

           1)   The historical cost of an asset has also been defined to include "the costs necessarily incurred to bring it to the condition and location necessary for its intended use" (**SFAS 34**, *Capitalization of Interest Cost*).

           2)   Historical cost is adjusted for changes in utility, e.g., depreciation and impairment losses.

           3)   **Capital expenditures** for acquisition or subsequent enhancement of service potential (see item 8.) are included in the historical cost of an asset. They benefit more than one period.

               a)   A **revenue expenditure** (e.g., for routine maintenance) is excluded because it is deemed to benefit only the period in which it was made.

           4)   The price bargained for by the buyer and seller, however, is not the only component of historical cost.

               a)   Under the **full-cost principle**, the initial measurement of PPE should also embrace **all costs** necessary to **acquire** these assets, **transport** them to the sites of their intended use, and **prepare** them for operations.

                   i)   Freight-in (transportation-in), installation charges, renovation or reconditioning costs, expenses of tests and/or trial runs, and insurance and taxes during the pre-operations period are capitalizable.

                      ●   But depreciation is not recognized until PPE are placed in operation and begin to contribute economic benefits, that is, to participate in generating the revenues with which such costs should be matched [see item 4.d.1)].

      b.   **Matching.** In general, expenses, such as the decline in service potential of PPE, should be recognized at the time related revenues are earned.

           1)   Because no directly traceable relationship ordinarily exists between the consumption of service potential and specific revenues, the expense (depreciation) must be allocated to the periods expected to be benefited (the estimated useful life) in a systematic and rational manner (SFAC 6).

      c.   **Use of estimates.** Initial measurement and subsequent determination of the carrying amount of PPE inevitably require the use of judgment.

      d.   **Nonrecognition of unrealized gains.** **APB 6**, *Status of Accounting Research Bulletins*, states that "property, plant, and equipment should not be written up by an entity to reflect appraisal, market, or current values that are above cost to the entity."

4. **Initial Costs of Specific PPE**

   a. **Land.** The costs of acquiring and preparing land for its expected use are capitalized.

      1) The **price** should include not only the cash price but also any **encumbrances** assumed (such as mortgages or tax liens).

      2) The cost of land also includes **transaction costs**, e.g., surveying costs, legal fees, brokers' commissions, title insurance, and escrow fees.

      3) The cost of an **option to buy** land that is subsequently purchased is capitalized.

         a) But the costs of options, surveys, and other items related to land not purchased should be expensed.

      4) **Site preparation costs** [clearing, draining, filling, leveling the property, and razing existing buildings, minus any proceeds (such as timber sales)] are costs of the land, not of the building to be constructed on the land.

      5) Certain **permanent improvements** made by the entity, such as landscaping, have indefinite lives and are debited to the land account.

      6) **Other improvements** that may not have indefinite lives (sidewalks, roads, street lights, and sewers) may be paid for by the entity through special assessments levied by local governments, which undertake to maintain and replace them.

         a) Hence, these improvements should be debited to land cost because depreciation will not be recognized.

      7) Taxes, insurance costs, etc., incurred while holding land for investment should be capitalized if the asset is not generating revenue and expensed if it is.

   b. **Land improvements.** If driveways, parking lots, sidewalks, roads, fences, rights-of-way, etc., have limited lives and must be maintained and replaced by the owner, they should be debited to land improvements and depreciated.

   c. **Buildings.** The costs that are necessary to the purchase or construction of a building and that will result in future economic benefits should be capitalized. These include

      1) The **purchase price**, including any liens assumed by the purchase, etc.

      2) Costs of **renovation and preparation** of the structure for its expected use

      3) Costs of building permits for renovation or construction

      4) The expenses of **excavation** of the site to build the foundation (but not site preparation costs)

         a) The costs of razing an old building are debited to the land account when the land is purchased as a site for the new structure. These costs are an adjustment of the gain or loss on disposal if the old building was previously used in the entity's operations.

         b) The carrying amount of an existing building previously used in the entity's operations is not included in the cost of the new structure because that value will not produce future benefits.

      5) The materials, labor, and overhead **costs of construction**

   d. **Machinery and equipment**

      1) Costs include

         a) Purchase price
         b) Freight-in, handling, insurance, and storage until use begins
         c) Preparation, installation, and start-up costs, such as testing and trial runs
         d) Reconditioning used assets

      2) Proper categorization of these assets is important because of differences in depreciation methods and useful lives (especially for federal tax purposes).

         a) For example, a common error is to include fixtures in the building account rather than the equipment account.

e.   **Leasehold improvements**

1)   Leasehold improvements, such as buildings constructed on leased land, are accounted for in the same way as property to which title is held except that the term of the lease may limit the depreciation period.

a)   If the useful life of the asset extends beyond the lease term and renewal of the lease is likely, the amortization period may include all or part of the renewal period.

b)   If renewal is uncertain, the useful life is the remaining term, and the salvage value is the amount, if any, to be paid by the lessor to the lessee at the expiration of the lease.

5.   **Other Factors Affecting Initial Measurement**

a.   **Cash discounts.**  The issue is whether the discount should be considered in recording the cost, that is, whether the transaction should be recorded at its net or gross value.

1)   The **net method** is preferable because cost will reflect the cash price.

a)   A discount not taken will be charged to a discounts lost account.

2)   Under the **gross method**, discounts taken (but not lost) will be recorded.

b.   **Acquisition in exchange for a long-term obligation.**  If a note, mortgage, or other long-term obligation is given for an item of PPE, the fundamental accounting problem is to distinguish financing charges (interest expense) from the recorded cost of the asset (the cash-equivalent price).

c.   **Basket (lump-sum) purchases.**  When two or more assets with varying estimated useful lives are acquired for a single price, allocation of the cost is required.

1)   Only the common cost is allocated; capital expenditures related to a particular asset should be debited to that asset.

a)   For example, if inventory and equipment are purchased, the start-up costs for the equipment should not be apportioned to the inventory.

2)   The basis of allocation is relative fair value in accordance with current market prices, insurance appraisals, tax assessments, or other reasonable estimates.

a)   The seller's carrying amount is ordinarily not an acceptable means of allocation.

d.   **Issuance of an enterprise's own securities for PPE.**  The usual basis for valuation of this transaction is the fair value of the stock or other securities (if actively traded).

e.   **Donated assets.**  In general, **SFAS 116**, *Accounting for Contributions Received and Contributions Made*, requires contributions received to be recognized as revenues or gains in the period of receipt.  They are measured at fair value.

1)   SFAS 116 does not apply to **contributions by governmental units** to businesses or to tax exemptions, incentives, or abatements.

a)   Accordingly, a contribution from a governmental unit to a business may be credited to donated capital.

b)   However, SFAS 116 does not prohibit treating contributions by governmental entities as revenues or gains, and such treatment would be consistent with the accounting for contributions by nongovernmental entities and with the definition of comprehensive income given in SFAC 6.

6.  **Accounting for the Initial Costs of an Internally Constructed Asset (ICA).** The costs capitalized when productive assets are constructed may be direct (direct materials and direct labor) or indirect (overhead items, e.g., utilities, depreciation, insurance, taxes, and supplies).

    a.  Disagreement exists about **allocation of overhead**, especially those costs that are unaffected by production of an ICA.

        1)  Widely used methods are to capitalize the increase in overhead associated with the construction and to allocate part of normal overhead as well as the incremental overhead.

        2)  If production of an ICA used otherwise idle capacity, its cost probably should exclude fixed overhead.

    b.  An ICA should be capitalized at the lower of its fair value or its cost.

        1)  No gain is recognized in the year of construction because the acquisition of assets is ordinarily not considered the culmination of an earning process.

        2)  If cost exceeds fair value, however, the excess is expensed immediately to avoid overstating the asset.

7.  **Interest Capitalization.** A major issue in measuring the cost of an ICA is to account for interest costs incurred during construction. The applicable pronouncement is **SFAS 34**, *Capitalization of Interest Cost.*

    a.  **Reason for capitalization.** The costs necessary to bring an asset to the condition and location of its intended use are part of the historical cost. Interest incurred during construction is such a necessary cost.

        1)  An imputed cost of equity capital is not recognized.

    b.  **Assets qualifying for interest capitalization** include

        1)  Assets produced by the enterprise for its own use.

        2)  Assets produced for the enterprise by others for which deposits or progress payments have been made.

        3)  Assets produced for sale or lease as discrete projects, such as real estate developments or ships.

        4)  Equity-based investments. **SFAS 58**, *Capitalization of Interest Cost in Financial Statements That Include Investments Accounted for by the Equity Method,* states that the investee must have activities in progress necessary to commence its planned principal operations and be expending funds to obtain qualifying assets for its operations.

    c.  **Nonqualifying assets** include

        1)  Inventories routinely produced in large quantities on a repetitive basis

        2)  Assets in use or ready for their intended use in the earning activities of the enterprise

        3)  Assets not being used in the earning activities of the enterprise that are not undergoing the activities necessary to ready them for use

        4)  Idle land

    d.  **Amount of interest cost to be capitalized**

        1)  Interest cost includes interest on obligations with explicit interest rates (including amortization of issue costs and discount or premium), interest imputed on certain payables under APB 21, and interest on a capital lease.

        2)  Capitalizable interest is limited to the **amount theoretically avoidable** if expenditures for the assets had not been made, for example, the hypothetical interest saved by using the funds expended for the assets to repay existing borrowings or to avoid new borrowings.

3) Interest capitalized may not exceed the total incurred during the period.

4) Capitalized interest equals **average accumulated expenditures (AAE)** for the qualifying asset during the period times the interest rate(s).

    a) If a specific new borrowing outstanding during the period can be identified with the asset, the rate on that obligation may be applied.

    b) To the extent that AAE exceed the amount of specific new borrowings, a **weighted-average rate** must be applied that is based on other borrowings outstanding during the period. However, this rate may be applied to the entire AAE.

    c) Judgment must be exercised to determine the borrowings used to calculate the weighted-average rate and thereby to achieve the objective of a **reasonable measure** of capitalized interest.

5) Capitalization rates are applied to AAE (net of progress payment collections).

6) The **acquisition (capitalization) period** is the time required to carry out the activities necessary to bring a qualifying asset to the condition and location necessary for its intended use.

    a) The period begins and continues as long as expenditures for a qualifying asset are being made, activities necessary to make the asset ready for its intended use are in progress, and interest cost is being incurred.

    b) Interest capitalization ends if substantially all asset-related activities are suspended.

    c) Capitalization ends when the asset is substantially complete and ready for its intended use.

    d) Interest capitalization does not end merely because accounting principles require recognition of a value for the asset lower than acquisition cost.

7) Subsequent to capitalization, interest is not treated differently from other components of the cost of the qualifying asset.

8) **Interest earned** on borrowed funds is ordinarily not offset against interest cost to determine either capitalization rates or limitations on interest costs to be capitalized. Such income relates to investment, not acquisition, decisions.

  e. **Disclosures.** If no interest cost is capitalized, the amount incurred and expensed during the period should be reported. If some interest cost is capitalized, the total incurred and the amount capitalized should be disclosed.

8. **Subsequent Expenditures for PPE.** The issues regarding subsequent expenditures are to determine whether they should be expensed or capitalized and the accounting methods to be used.

  a. **Capitalizable expenditures** provide additional benefits by improving the quality of services rendered by the asset, extending its useful life, or increasing its output.

    1) These expenditures are matched through changes in depreciation schedules with revenues of the future periods expected to be benefited.

  b. **Revenue expenditures** maintain an asset's normal service capacity.

    1) These costs are recurring, not expected to benefit future periods, and expensed when incurred.

    2) An enterprise usually specifies a materiality threshold below which all costs are expensed, thereby avoiding the burden of depreciating immaterial amounts.

   c.  **Additions.** Substantial expenditures for extensions or expansions of existing assets are capitalized. An example is an additional story for a building.

      1)  If the addition is essentially a **separate asset**, it is recorded in a separate account and depreciated over its own useful life.

         a)  Otherwise, the addition should be debited to the original asset account and depreciated over the life of that asset.

      2)  If the original asset was constructed in anticipation of the addition, the costs related to changes in that asset should be capitalized.

         a)  However, costs of alterations in the original asset should be expensed if they could have been avoided by proper planning at an earlier time.

   d.  **Replacements and Improvements (Betterments).** A replacement substitutes a new component of an asset for a similar one, for example, a tile roof for a tile roof, but an improvement substitutes a better component, such as a more efficient heating system.

      1)  Given accounting recognition of the old component, e.g., recording a central air conditioning system separately from the building, the **substitution method** is applied. The old component is removed from the ledger, along with accumulated depreciation, and the cost of the new component is substituted. A gain or loss may be recognized.

         a)  The new component will be depreciated over the shorter of its useful life or that of the entire asset.

         b)  If the component replaced or improved has not been separately accounted for or if the old component has been modified, the substitution method is not used.

            i)  If the replacement or improvement augments the asset's service potential but does not extend its estimated useful life, the asset account is debited.

                •  The carrying amount of the old component is not removed, but this amount is ordinarily not material because the transaction will most often occur when the component is almost fully depreciated.

            ii)  If the replacement or improvement primarily extends the useful life without enhancing service potential, accumulated depreciation is debited as a recognition that the expenditure is a recovery of depreciation, not an increase in the quality of service.

   e.  **Rearrangements, Reinstallations, Relocations.** Rearranging the configuration of plant assets, reinstalling such assets, or relocating operations may entail material outlays that are separable from recurring expenses and provide probable future benefits.

      1)  The **substitution method** of accounting for these costs may be used if the original installation costs and accumulated depreciation are known.

      2)  Otherwise, the costs should be debited to a new account and amortized over the (usually brief) period benefited.

         a)  Some accountants treat this amount as an intangible asset, but others include it among the deferred charges, which are accounts with debit balances intended to be amortized that do not fall neatly within the definition of another asset category.

            i)  These balances are often presented as other assets.

3) **Relocation (moving) costs** are often expensed as incurred.

   a) But if these costs are incurred because of an unusual and infrequent event, such as a natural disaster, they may be included in an extraordinary loss.

f. **Repairs and Maintenance.** Routine, minor expenditures made to maintain the operating efficiency of PPE are ordinarily expensed as incurred. However, as the amounts involved become more significant and the benefits to future periods increase, treatment of a major repair as a replacement, etc., may be more appropriate.

1) Although a repair or maintenance cost should ordinarily be allocated to a single annual period only, its full recognition at the interim date when incurred may distort the interim statements. Accordingly, a repair or maintenance cost may be accounted for using an allowance method for interim reporting. This method entails

   a) Estimating the annual cost and allocating it to the interim periods

   b) Debiting an expense and crediting the allowance account for the amount allocated to each interim period

   c) Debiting the allowance and crediting cash, accounts payable, etc., for amounts actually expended

   d) In its theoretically preferable form, making an adjustment in the final interim period to reduce the year-end allowance to zero

   e) Presenting the allowance in the interim statements as an addition or offset to the related asset, i.e., as a valuation account

9. Stop and review! You have completed the outline for this subunit. Study multiple-choice questions 1 through 8 beginning on page 568.

## 15.2 PROPERTY, PLANT, AND EQUIPMENT (PPE) – DISPOSITION

1. **Disposals Other Than by Exchange**

a. Whatever the means of disposition, the following procedures must be followed:

1) Depreciation is recorded up to the time of disposal so that periodic depreciation expense is not understated, and the carrying amount of the asset is not overstated.

2) The asset's carrying amount is removed from the accounts by eliminating the asset, its accumulated depreciation, and any other valuation account.

3) Any consideration (proceeds) received is debited appropriately.

4) Gain or loss is usually included in the results of continuing operations as an ordinary item.

b. **Sale.** Accounting for a cash sale of PPE (including a scrap sale) is straightforward.

1) Depreciation, if any, is recognized to the date of sale, the carrying amount is removed from the books, the proceeds are recorded, and any gain or loss is recognized.

c. **Abandonment.** If an enterprise receives no proceeds in a retirement of the asset, no loss is recognized if it is fully depreciated. Otherwise, the carrying amount measures the loss.

1) An abandonment should be distinguished from a **contribution**, a transaction that is accounted for at fair value and may result in a gain as well as donation expense.

2) An abandonment or retirement may sometimes involve receipt of scrap value.

d. **Standby assets.** PPE may be taken out of service but not disposed of.

1) Standby assets retained for use in emergencies, as temporary replacements, or at times of maximum demand should be written down to residual value.

2) These assets are not depreciated when not in use.

3) If material, they are included in the other noncurrent assets section.

e. **Nonreciprocal transfer of a nonmonetary asset.** Such a transfer does not involve an exchange. It is ordinarily recorded at fair value whether it is to a shareholder or to another entity, and a gain or loss is recognized.

f. **Involuntary conversion.** An item of PPE is involuntarily converted when it is lost through a casualty (flood, earthquake, fire, etc.), expropriated (seized by a foreign government), or condemned (through the governmental power of eminent domain).

1) The accounting is the same as for other nonexchange dispositions.

2) The gain or loss on an involuntary conversion is reported in a separate caption of the income statement as an extraordinary item net of tax if it is unusual and infrequent in the environment in which the entity operates.

3) If a nonmonetary asset has been involuntarily converted to monetary assets (e.g., insurance proceeds), tax law may treat the gain as an adjustment of the basis of replacement property rather than as a currently taxable amount.

     a) **FASB Interpretation No. 30**, *Accounting for Involuntary Conversions of Nonmonetary Assets to Monetary Assets*, clarifies the financial accounting by requiring gain or loss recognition even though the enterprise reinvests or is required to reinvest the proceeds in replacement nonmonetary assets.

       i) Hence, the replacement property should be recorded at its cost. The involuntary conversion and replacement are not viewed as equivalent to a single exchange transaction between an enterprise and another entity.

2. **Exchanges of Nonmonetary Assets**

a. **APB 29**, *Accounting for Nonmonetary Transactions*, was amended by **SFAS 153**, *Exchanges of Nonmonetary Assets*. It applies to **nonreciprocal** transfers to or from owners and other parties. It also applies to nonmonetary exchanges. These are **reciprocal** transfers of nonmonetary assets that leave the transferor with no substantial continuing involvement in the assets relinquished. Thus, the usual risks and rewards of ownership are transferred.

1) **Monetary assets** and liabilities are assets and liabilities whose amounts are fixed in terms of units of currency by contract or otherwise, e.g., cash or payables. **Nonmonetary items** are all other items.

2) **Monetary transactions** are measured at the **fair value** of the assets involved, with gain or loss recognized immediately. Fair value of the assets given up generally is used unless the fair value of the assets received is more evident.

3) Accounting for **nonmonetary transactions** also should be based on **fair value**. However, accounting for nonmonetary transactions should be based on the **carrying amount** of the assets given up when the transaction is an exchange

     a) In which neither the fair value of the assets given up nor the fair value of the assets received is determinable within reasonable limits;

     b) Of inventory sold in the same line of business that is undertaken to facilitate sales to customers other than the parties to the exchange; or

        c)    That lacks commercial substance.

           i)    An exchange **lacks commercial substance** when an entity's cash flows are not expected to change significantly. Cash flows do not change significantly when (1) the configuration (risk, timing, and amount) of the entity's future cash flows is not expected to change significantly as a result of the exchange, or (2) the **entity-specific values** of the assets do not differ significantly.

    4)  **Boot.** In an exchange of nonmonetary assets that is not accounted for at fair value, if partial monetary consideration (boot) is received, a **proportionate amount of gain** is recognized by the recipient. However, the full amount of any **loss** is recognized as an adjustment of the carrying amount (the carryover basis).

        a)    The **entity paying the boot** does not recognize gain. It records the assets received at the sum of the boot plus the carrying amount of the assets transferred.

           i)    However, when this amount exceeds the fair value of the assets received, the assets received should be recorded at fair value, with the difference recognized as a loss.

        b)    The **recipient of boot** should recognize a gain to the extent that boot exceeds a proportionate share of the carrying amount of the assets surrendered.

           i)    The gain recognized equals the total potential gain (cash + fair value of assets received − carrying amount given up) times the ratio of

$$\frac{Boot}{Boot + Fair\ value\ of\ non\text{-}monetary\ assets\ received}$$

        c)    According to **Emerging Issues Task Force Issue 01-2**, the foregoing treatment of boot does not apply if it is at least 25% of the fair value of the exchange. In such a transaction, both parties should record a **monetary exchange** at fair value, with gains and losses recognized in full.

3.   **Impairment or Disposal of Long-Lived Assets**

    a.    **SFAS 144**, *Accounting for the Impairment or Disposal of Long-Lived Assets*, applies to the long-lived assets of an entity (a business enterprise or a not-for-profit organization) that are to be held and used or disposed of.

        1)  This pronouncement applies to a long-lived asset(s) included in a group with other assets and liabilities not subject to SFAS 144. The unit of accounting for such a long-lived asset is the group.

        2)  If a long-lived asset(s) is to be held and used, the **asset group** is the lowest level at which identifiable cash flows are largely independent of those of other groups.

        3)  If a long-lived asset(s) is to be disposed of by sale or otherwise, the **disposal group** constitutes assets to be disposed of together in one transaction and directly associated liabilities to be transferred in the same transaction (for example, warranties associated with an acquired customer base).

b.   **Long-Lived Assets to Be Held and Used**

1) **Impairment** of a long-lived asset (asset group) occurs when its carrying amount is greater than its fair value.

a)   However, a loss equal to this excess is recognized for the impairment only when the carrying amount is not **recoverable**, that is, when the carrying amount exceeds the sum of the **undiscounted cash flows** expected to arise from the use and disposition of the asset (asset group).

2) The **recoverability test** should be made when events or changes in circumstances provide indicators that the carrying amount may not be recoverable.

a)   **Goodwill** is included in an asset group only if the group is or includes a **reporting unit** (an operating segment or one level below as defined in SFAS 142).

i)   Estimated future cash flows used to test a lower-level asset group for recoverability are not adjusted for the exclusion of goodwill.

b)   The **carrying amounts** of assets (other than goodwill) and liabilities not covered by SFAS 144 that are part of an asset group are adjusted in accordance with other relevant GAAP prior to a test for recoverability.

c)   An impairment loss decreases only the carrying amounts of the long-lived assets in the group on a pro rata basis according to their relative carrying amounts.

i)   However, the carrying amount of a given long-lived asset is not reduced below its fair value if that fair value is determinable without undue cost and effort.

3) The carrying amount of a long-lived asset adjusted for an impairment loss is its **new cost basis**. A previously recognized impairment loss may not be reversed.

4) **Estimates of future cash flows** include only those directly associated with and expected to arise as a direct result of the use and disposition of the asset (asset group). However, the estimates do not include interest that will be recognized as an expense when incurred.

a)   The estimates must be based on the existing service potential at the time of the recoverability test, the entity's own reasonable assumptions about its use of the asset (asset group), and all available evidence.

b)   The estimates are made for the **remaining useful life** as determined from the perspective of the entity. The remaining useful life is that of the **primary asset** of the group, that is, the principal depreciable tangible asset or amortizable intangible asset that is the most significant component of the asset group for generating cash flows.

5) **Reporting.** A business enterprise (not-for-profit organization) reports an impairment loss in income from continuing operations before income taxes (income from continuing operations in the statement of activities). If a subtotal for "income from operations" is reported, the impairment loss is included.

c.   **Long-lived assets to be disposed of other than by sale.** If disposition is to be, for example, by abandonment, exchange, or a distribution to owners in a spinoff, the asset is classified as held and used until disposal.

d. **Long-lived assets to be disposed of by sale**

1) An asset (disposal group) is classified as **held for sale** when six conditions are met:

    a) A level of management with authority to approve the action has committed to a plan to sell.

    b) The asset is available for immediate sale in its current condition on usual and customary terms.

    c) Actions (such as actively seeking a buyer) have begun to complete the plan.

    d) Completion of sale within 1 year is probable. However, this condition need not be met if certain events or circumstances occur that the entity cannot control.

    e) The asset is actively marketed at a price reasonably related to current fair value.

    f) There is little likelihood of significant change in, or withdrawal of, the plan.

2) **Measurement** is at the **lower of carrying amount or fair value minus cost to sell**. If the asset (disposal group) is newly acquired, the carrying amount is the fair value minus cost to sell at the acquisition date.

    a) An asset classified as held for sale is not depreciated, but expenses related to the liabilities of a disposal group are accrued.

    b) **Costs to sell** are the incremental direct costs. They result directly from and are essential to the transaction and would not have been incurred but for the decision to sell.

    c) A loss is recognized for a write-down to fair value minus cost to sell. A **gain** is recognized for any subsequent increase but only to the extent of previously recognized losses for write-downs.

        i) The loss or gain adjusts only the carrying amount of a long-lived asset even if it is included in a disposal group.

3) **Changes to a plan of sale** may occur because of circumstances previously regarded as unlikely that result in a decision not to sell. In these circumstances, the asset (disposal group) is **reclassified as held and used**.

    a) A reclassified long-lived asset is **measured** individually at the lower of

        i) Carrying amount before the asset (disposal group) was classified as held for sale, minus any depreciation (amortization) that would have been recognized if it had always been classified as held and used, or

        ii) Fair value at the date of the decision not to sell.

    b) A **reclassification adjustment** to the carrying amount is included in income from continuing operations in the period of the decision not to sell. It is reported in the same income statement caption used to report a disposal loss, if any, recognized for an asset (disposal group) classified as held for sale that is not a component of an entity.

4) **Reporting.** If a **long-lived asset** is held for sale, it is reported separately in the balance sheet. If a **disposal group** is held for sale, its assets and liabilities are reported separately in the balance sheet and are not offset and presented as a single amount.

4. Stop and review! You have completed the outline for this subunit. Study multiple-choice questions 9 through 17 beginning on page 570.

## 15.3 PROPERTY, PLANT, AND EQUIPMENT (PPE) – DEPRECIATION AND DEPLETION

1. **Depreciation** is the process of systematically and rationally allocating the historical cost of the productive capacity of a tangible capital asset to the periods benefited. It is not a process of valuation. The periodic charge for depreciation is offset by a credit to **accumulated depreciation**, a contra-asset account.

   a. **Allocation** is defined broadly in SFAC 6 as "the accounting process of assigning or distributing an amount according to a plan or formula."

      1) Allocation includes amortization, which is defined as "the accounting process of reducing an amount by periodic payments or write-downs."

         a) Common examples of amortizations are depreciation and depletion. In practice, the term amortization is used narrowly to describe the write-down of intangible assets, such as a patent.

      2) **Systematic and rational allocation** is used when an asset benefits more than one period but a direct means of associating cause and effect is not available; that is, "allocation is applied if causal relations are generally, not specifically, identified" (SFAC 6).

   b. Depreciation is **not a cash expense** and therefore does not provide resources for the replacement of assets.

      1) Except to the extent that depreciation is tax deductible and therefore reduces cash outlays for taxes, it does not affect an enterprise's cash flows.

   c. The **straight-line** method is a simple time-based depreciation technique.

      1) The depreciable base (historical cost minus salvage value) is divided by the estimated useful life of the asset to arrive at periodic depreciation expense.

         a) Thus, depreciation expense is constant over the life of the asset. Fluctuations in usage and in maintenance charges are ignored.

      2) The carrying amount is dependent upon the length of time the asset is held rather than the amount of use.

   d. **Accelerated methods** were popularized when they became allowable on tax returns, but the same method need not be used for tax and financial statement purposes.

      1) Accelerated depreciation methods are time-based techniques that result in higher depreciation charges during the early periods of the asset's life.

      2) **Declining balance (DB)** is an accelerated method that determines periodic depreciation expense by multiplying some percentage (e.g., 200%, 150%, or 125%) of the carrying amount (NOT a depreciable base equal to cost minus salvage value) at the beginning of each period by the straight-line rate of depreciation.

         a) The carrying amount decreases by the depreciation recognized, and the result is the use of a constant rate against a declining balance.

         b) Salvage value is ignored in determining the carrying amount, but the asset is not depreciated below salvage value.

      3) **Sum-of-the-year's digits (SYD)** multiplies a constant depreciable base (cost − salvage value) by a declining fraction. It is a declining-rate, declining charge method.

         a) The SYD fraction's numerator is the number of years of the useful life (n) minus the prior years elapsed.

         b) The formula to compute the denominator is

$$\frac{n\ (n\ +\ 1)}{2}$$

e. **Activity-based methods** calculate depreciation as a function of an asset's use rather than the time it has been held.

    1) **Units-of-output** allocates cost based on production. As production varies, so will the credit to accumulated depreciation.

        a) Each unit is charged with a constant amount of depreciation equal to cost minus salvage value, divided by the total units expected to be produced.

        b) This technique is appropriate if obsolescence is not a cause of depreciation and the asset's output can be reasonably estimated.

        c) A variation is modified units of production (MUP), a technique that combines the straight-line and units-of-output methods.

            i) If depreciation is a function of output but a reasonable estimate of total output cannot be made, the periodic expense may be calculated using the straight-line method, but the estimate of the useful life employed each period will vary inversely with periodic output.

    2) **Services-used.** The reduction in service potential of an asset may be more clearly related to a measure of input or services used, e.g., machine hours, than the passage of time, obsolescence, or units produced.

        a) This technique is appropriate when output is indeterminable because specific output cannot be identified or the total cannot be estimated.

        b) Like the units-of-output method, the services-used method calculates a variable periodic depreciation expense based on a fixed charge per unit of activity.

f. **Group and composite depreciation.**

    1) These methods use **straight-line** techniques for an aggregate of assets.

        a) The **group method** relates to groups of similar assets with varying useful lives, and the **composite method** deals with dissimilar assets.

        b) These methods provide an efficient way to account for large numbers of depreciable assets. They also result in offsetting of under- and overstated depreciation estimates.

    2) These methods employ three components:

        a) Total depreciable cost (total acquisition cost – salvage value) for all the assets debited to a control account.

        b) A weighted-average estimated useful life (total depreciable cost ÷ total annual straight-line depreciation).

        c) A weighted-average depreciation rate based on cost (total annual straight-line depreciation ÷ total acquisition cost).

            i) A single accumulated depreciation account is also maintained.

    3) Early and late **retirements** are expected to offset each other.

        a) Thus, gains and losses on retirements of single assets are not recognized but are treated as **adjustments to accumulated depreciation**.

            i) The **journal entry** is to credit the asset at cost, debit cash for any proceeds received, and debit or credit accumulated depreciation for the difference.

        b) Periodic depreciation equals the weighted-average rate times the beginning balance of the asset account for the period; that is, depreciation is calculated based on the cost of assets in use during the period.

            i) **Prior-period retirements** are reflected in this balance.

    g.  **Depreciation for a fractional period** must be computed whenever an asset is acquired or disposed of other than at the beginning or end of a fiscal year.

        1)  Time-based methods most often compute depreciation to the nearest month of a partial year, but other conventions are also permitted.

        2)  A full year's depreciation may be recognized in the year of acquisition and none in the year of disposal or vice versa.

        3)  Depreciation may be recognized to the nearest full-year or the nearest half-year.

        4)  A half-year's depreciation may be recognized in both the year of acquisition and the year of disposal.

2.  **Depletion** is similar to depreciation in that it is an accounting process of allocating the historical cost of a tangible asset to the periods benefited by its uses.

    a.  The assets involved are **natural resources** (wasting assets), such as petroleum, timber, iron ore, gravel, or coal. They differ from depreciable assets (PPE) because they

        1)  Lose their separate character during extraction and consumption
        2)  Are produced only by natural processes
        3)  Are equivalent to inventories of raw material

    b.  **Calculating the depletion base** is complicated by the need to capitalize costs other than those incurred for acquisition.

        1)  One component of the depletion base is the **acquisition cost** of already discovered natural resources or of obtaining the right to search for them, including costs normally incurred to purchase land, such as legal fees and closing costs.

        2)  Two methods of accounting for **exploration costs** are permitted.

            a)  The **successful-efforts method** capitalizes only those exploration costs that lead to the location of resources that can be feasibly developed.

               i)  In the oil and gas industry, the cost of an exploratory well is temporarily capitalized until it is determined whether the effort is successful.

               ii)  A company using the successful-efforts method would then charge these costs to expense if production proves not to be feasible.

            b)  The **full-cost method** capitalizes the costs of both successful and unsuccessful efforts on the theory that the latter are necessary to the discovery of productive resources.

        3)  **Development costs** for extraction of natural resources must be incurred to construct buildings, drill wells or mine shafts, buy equipment, etc.

            a)  Intangible costs (e.g., for wells and shafts) are part of the depletion base.

            b)  Tangible assets, such as equipment, are needed to exploit natural resources.

               i)  These assets are separately capitalized and depreciated over their estimated useful lives or the life of the resource, whichever is shorter, if their usefulness is limited to the extraction of the particular resource.

               ii)  Tangible assets not limited in use to the exploitation of a particular resource should be depreciated over their useful lives.

               iii)  The cost of either kind of tangible asset, however, is ordinarily not included in the depletion base.

4) The depletion base must also be calculated with regard to the **residual value** of the property from which the natural resource is extracted.

   a) But any **restoration costs** before sale reduce the residual value (and increase the depletion base).

5) **Production costs** for extracting the resource (e.g., labor, materials, and overhead) are not included in the depletion base.

c. **Depletion calculations** are similar to those for usage-centered depreciation because the units-of-output (production) method is ordinarily used.

   1) The **depletion base** (capitalized costs of acquisition, exploration, and development, minus residual value adjusted for restoration costs) is divided by the units estimated to be economically recoverable to determine the **per-unit depletion rate**.

   2) Units extracted times the depletion rate equals **periodic depletion**.

      a) To the extent that extracted units are sold, **depletion expense** is debited.
      b) Unsold units are debited to an inventory account.
      c) Accumulated depletion or the natural resource asset account is credited.

   3) The calculation of depletion is straightforward, but estimating the amount of the recoverable resource is often extremely difficult.

      a) Changes in estimates may be frequent because price movements and new technology will affect the amounts that can be profitably extracted.

3. Stop and review! You have completed the outline for this subunit. Study multiple-choice questions 18 through 32 beginning on page 574.

## 15.4 INTANGIBLE ASSETS

1. **Intangible assets** are nonfinancial assets that lack physical substance. They often convey a right to do something that gives its holder some form of economic benefit.

   a. Some examples are

      1) Patents
      2) Copyrights
      3) Trademarks and trade names
      4) Leaseholds
      5) Franchises and licenses
      6) Goodwill
      7) Research and development
      8) Start-up costs
      9) Initial operating losses
      10) Advertising costs
      11) Computer software costs

   b. **SFAS 142**, *Goodwill and Other Intangible Assets*, applies to the initial recognition and measurement of intangible assets acquired with other assets or singly but not in a business combination.

      1) It also applies to the subsequent accounting for goodwill and other intangible assets acquired in a business combination.

2.   **Initial Recognition.**  If an intangible asset is acquired individually or with other assets but not in a business combination, it is initially recognized and measured at fair value.

   a.   The cost of a group of assets acquired other than in a business combination is allocated based on relative fair values, and goodwill is not recognized.

   b.   Cost is normally the more reliably measurable of the fair value of the consideration given or the fair value of the net assets acquired.

   c.   The costs of an **internally developed** intangible asset are **expensed when incurred** if one of the following applies:

      1)   The asset is not specifically identifiable,

      2)   The asset has an indeterminate life, or

      3)   The asset is inherent in a continuing business and related to the entity as a whole.

3.   **Subsequent to Recognition.**  The useful life of an asset is the period during which it is expected to contribute either directly or indirectly to the future cash flows of the reporting entity.

   a.   Among the considerations in **estimating useful life** are the reporting entity's expected use of the asset and

      1)   The useful life of a related asset or group of assets

      2)   Provisions based on law, regulation, or contract that may limit the useful life or that may permit renewal or extension without substantial cost

      3)   Economic factors, such as obsolescence, demand, or competition

      4)   Expenditures for maintenance

   b.   An intangible asset with a **finite useful life** to the reporting entity is amortized over that useful life.  If the useful life is finite but not precisely known, the best estimate is the amortization period.

      1)   The **pattern of consumption of economic benefits**, if it can be reliably ascertained, is reflected in the method of amortization.  Otherwise, the **straight-line method** is required.

      2)   The **amortizable amount** equals the amount initially assigned minus the **residual value**, which is the estimated fair value to the entity at the end of the asset's useful life, minus disposal costs.

         a)   The **residual value** is zero unless a third party has committed to purchase the asset, or it can be ascertained from an exchange transaction in an existing market for the asset that is expected to exist at the end of the useful life.

   c.   The useful life should be reevaluated each reporting period.

      1)   A change in the estimate results in a prospective change in amortization.

      2)   If a subsequent determination is made that the asset has an indefinite useful life, it is no longer amortized and is tested for impairment.

   d.   An amortized intangible asset is **reviewed for impairment** when events or changes in circumstances indicate that its carrying amount may not be recoverable.

      1)   An impairment loss is recognized only if the carrying amount is **not recoverable** and is greater than the asset's fair value.

      2)   Thus, the test for recognition is met if the sum of the undiscounted expected future cash flows from the asset is less than the carrying amount.

         a)   The measure of any **loss recognized** is the excess of that carrying amount over the fair value.  This loss is nonreversible, so the adjusted carrying amount is the new accounting basis.

e. An intangible asset with an **indefinite useful life** is not amortized.

    1) However, the useful life should be reevaluated each period. If it is found to be finite, the test for impairment described below is performed. The asset is then amortized prospectively.

    2) **Impairment loss.** A nonamortized intangible asset is **reviewed for impairment** annually or more often if events or changes in circumstances suggest that the asset is impaired. However, the impairment test does not consider recoverability.

        a) If the carrying amount exceeds the fair value of the asset, that excess is the recognized loss. This loss is nonreversible, so the adjusted carrying amount is the new accounting basis.

4. **Patents**

a. A patent is a right conferred upon application to, and approval by, the federal government (U.S. Patent and Trademark Office) for the exclusive use of an invention. Under the Patent Act, "Whoever invents or discovers any new and useful process, machine, manufacture, or composition of matter, or any new and useful improvement thereof, may obtain a patent therefor."

    1) **Utility patents** (the most common category) have a legal life ending 20 years after the application was filed. A patent for a design (as opposed to an invention) has a duration of 14 years.

    2) The initial capitalized cost of a **purchased patent** is normally the fair value of the consideration given, that is, its purchase price plus incidental costs, such as registration and attorneys' fees.

    3) **Internally developed patents** are less likely to be capitalized because related R&D costs must be expensed when incurred. Thus, only relatively minor costs can be capitalized, for example, patent registration fees and legal fees.

    4) The unrecovered costs of successful litigation involving patent infringement are capitalized because they will benefit future periods.

5. **Copyrights**

a. The federal Copyright Act provides broad rights to intellectual property consisting of "original works of authorship in any tangible medium of expression, now known or later developed."

    1) The author or publisher has exclusive extensive rights to reproduce, distribute, perform, display, and prepare derivative works from copyrighted material.

        a) Limited exceptions are allowed for library or archive reproduction and fair use for purposes of comment, criticism, news coverage, teaching, scholarship, or research.

        b) An **author's copyright** is for life plus 70 years.

        c) A **publisher's copyright** is for the earlier to expire of 95 years from publication or 120 years from creation.

    2) A similarity to patents is that legal fees, registration fees, litigation costs, and the purchase price can be capitalized, but internal R&D costs cannot.

6. **Trademarks**

    a.  A trademark or other mark (e.g., a service mark or certification mark) is a distinctive design, word, symbol, mark, picture, etc., affixed to a product or placed on a tag, label, container, or associated display and adopted by its seller or manufacturer to identify it.

    b.  A **trade name** is usually regarded as referring to a business and the goodwill it has generated, for example, Exxon.

    c.  Trademarks may be registered for renewable 10-year periods with the U.S. Patent and Trademark Office.

7. **Leaseholds** (or simply leases)

    a.  A lease gives a lessee the contractual right to hold and use certain property for a given period of time.

        1)  If the lessee has made **prepayments** on the lease, some accountants assert that these prepayments represent a deferred charge and should thus be reported as an intangible asset.

8. **Franchises and licenses**

    a.  A franchise is a contractual agreement by a franchisor (grantor of the franchise) to permit a franchisee (purchaser) to operate a certain business.

        1)  The **franchisee** should capitalize the initial fee and other expenditures, e.g., legal fees, necessary to acquire the franchise that will provide future benefits.

            a)  Future payments based on a percentage of revenues or for franchisor services are expensed as incurred. They benefit only the period of payment.

        2)  **Franchisor accounting.** **SFAS 45**, *Accounting for Franchise Fee Revenue*, states that franchise fee revenue should ordinarily be recognized, with a provision for uncollectible amounts, at the earliest time when the franchisor has substantially performed or satisfied all material services or conditions relating to the franchise sale.

    b.  **Licensing agreements** permit an enterprise to engage in a given activity, such as selling a well-known product, or to use rights (e.g., a patent) owned by others. For example, a broadcaster may secure the FCC's permission (classified by some authors as a franchise) to transmit on a given frequency within a certain area.

9. **Accounting for Goodwill Subsequent to Recognition**

    a.  **Goodwill** is the cost of an acquired entity minus the net amount assigned to assets acquired and liabilities assumed. It includes acquired intangible assets not meeting the criteria in SFAS 141 for asset recognition distinct from goodwill.

    b.  Goodwill is not amortized.

    c.  Goodwill of a reporting unit is tested for impairment each year at the same time, but different reporting units may be tested at different times.

        1)  **Potential impairment** of goodwill is deemed to exist only if the carrying amount (including goodwill) of a reporting unit is greater than its fair value.

        2)  Thus, accounting for goodwill is based on the units of the combined entity into which the acquired entity was absorbed. A **reporting unit** is an operating segment or a component thereof, that is, one level below an operating segment.

d.   If a potential impairment is found, the carrying amount of reporting-unit goodwill is compared with its implied fair value.

   1)   An impairment loss not exceeding the carrying amount of goodwill is then recognized equal to any excess of that carrying amount over the implied fair value. This loss is nonreversible.

   2)   The **implied fair value** of reporting-unit goodwill is estimated by allocating the fair value of the reporting unit to its assets and liabilities (including unrecognized intangible assets). The excess of that fair value over the amounts assigned equals the implied fair value.

e.   As part of testing goodwill for impairment at the acquisition date, all goodwill is divided among the reporting units that will benefit from the business combination.

   1)   The method used for this assignment should be reasonable, supportable, consistently applied, and consistent with the objectives of the assignment.

   2)   The assignment, in principle, should be done in the same manner as the determination of goodwill in a business combination.

      a)   However, if no assets or liabilities acquired or assumed are assigned to a reporting unit, the goodwill to be assigned equals the change in the fair value of the reporting unit as a result of the combination.

10.   **Equity Method Goodwill**

a.   According to **APB 18**, *The Equity Method of Accounting for Investments in Common Stock*, differences between the cost of an investment and the investor's equity in the net assets of the investee is allocated between two elements:

   1)   Goodwill

   2)   The difference between the carrying amount and fair value of those net assets at the acquisition date.

b.   Equity method investments continue to be reviewed for impairment under APB 18, not SFAS 142.

   1)   However, equity method goodwill is not amortized. Moreover, it is not separately reviewed for impairment because it is not separable from the investment.

11.   **Research and Development**

a.   **SFAS 2**, *Accounting for Research and Development Costs*, prescribes accounting for research and development (R&D).

   1)   **Research** is "planned search or critical investigation aimed at discovery of new knowledge with the hope that such knowledge will be useful in developing a new product or service or a new process or technique or in bringing about a significant improvement to an existing product or process."

   2)   **Development** is "the translation of research findings or other knowledge into a plan or design for a new product or process or for a significant improvement to an existing product or process whether intended for sale or use."

b.   R&D costs should be **expensed as incurred**, not capitalized as an intangible asset.

   1)   An **exception** is that expenditures for a tangible asset that has an alternative future use are capitalized. It is depreciated to R&D expense as it is used.

    c.    The following are typical examples of **activities included in R&D** unless conducted for others under a contract (reimbursable costs are not expensed):

        1)    Laboratory research aimed at discovery of new knowledge
        2)    Searching for applications of new research findings or using new technology
        3)    Conceptual formulation and design of possible product or process alternatives
        4)    Design, construction, and testing of preproduction prototypes and models

    d.    The following are typical examples of **activities not classified as R&D**:

        1)    Engineering follow-through in an early phase of commercial production
        2)    Routine, ongoing efforts to refine, enrich, or otherwise improve upon the qualities of an existing product
        3)    Adaptation of an existing capability to a particular requirement or customer's need as part of a continuing commercial activity
        4)    Seasonal or routine design changes to existing products
        5)    Legal work in connection with patent applications or litigation and the sale or licensing of patents

    e.    SFAS 2 does not cover R&D costs incurred under a contract for the benefit of others.

        1)    If R&D is performed for others, revenues and expenses should be recorded in the traditional manner. This assumes the risk has been transferred to others. If the risk is retained, i.e., if payment for R&D depends on the results, R&D expenditures performed for others should be expensed.

12.  **Start-up costs (organization costs) and initial operating losses** must be expensed as incurred, even for development stage companies.

13.  **Advertising Costs**

    a.    **AICPA Statement of Position (SOP) 93-7**, *Reporting on Advertising Costs*, states that most advertising costs should be expensed, either as incurred or when advertising first occurs.

        1)    The primary costs are production and communication.

            a)    Production includes idea development, copywriting, artwork, printing, hiring personnel (e.g., audio and video crews and actors), etc.
            b)    Communication requires use of magazines, radio, television, billboards, etc.

    b.    However, **direct response advertising** costs should be capitalized (deferred) if

        1)    The primary purpose is to elicit sales from customers who respond specifically to the advertising, and
        2)    Probable future economic benefits result.

    c.    An exception is made for expenditures **subsequent to recognition** of related revenue.

        1)    For example, if a magazine publisher advertises 1-year subscriptions, the company will receive subscriber certificates or application forms.

            a)    At the end of the first year, some percentage of the new subscribers will renew for another year, and then another, and so on.
            b)    Hence, the revenue in years 2, 3, etc., can be directly traced to the original advertising.
            c)    Because the revenues in later years are attributable to the advertising costs incurred in year 1, some of the costs should be matched with those years.

d. EXAMPLE: Assume a publisher spends $50,000 for an ad campaign offering 1-year subscriptions for $10 each that attracts 20,000 new subscribers. Based on the company's 5-year experience, about 50% of each year's subscribers will renew the following year. Thus, for its $50,000 expenditure, the company has essentially sold the following subscriptions:

| | |
|---|---:|
| Year 1 | 20,000 |
| Year 2 | 10,000 |
| Year 3 | 5,000 |
| Year 4 | 2,500 |
| Year 5 | 1,250 |
| Total | 38,750 |

1) The 20,000 subscriptions in the first year represent only 51.6129% (20,000 ÷ 38,750) of the total sales resulting from the ad campaign. As a result, the cost attributable to year 1 is $25,806.45 [$50,000 × (20,000 ÷ 38,750)], and the capitalized amount is $24,193.55 ($50,000 – $25,806.45). Accordingly, the entry to record the advertising expense for year 1 is

| | | |
|---|---:|---:|
| Advertising expense | $25,806.45 | |
| Future advertising benefits | 24,193.55 | |
| Cash | | $50,000.00 |

2) At the end of year 2, an adjusting entry is recorded to amortize the intangible asset recognized for future advertising benefits. The expense and amortization recognized for year 2 is $12,903.23 [$50,000 × (10,000 ÷ 38,750)].

| | | |
|---|---:|---:|
| Advertising expense | $12,903.23 | |
| Future advertising benefits | | $12,903.23 |

3) By the end of year 5, the entire $50,000 will be expensed. In practice, the amount allocated to years 4 and beyond is so small as to be immaterial, resulting in an arbitrary limitation of the useful life to fewer than 5 years.

14. **Computer Software Costs**

a. **SFAS 86**, *Accounting for the Costs of Computer Software to Be Sold, Leased, or Otherwise Marketed*, applies to software to be "sold, leased, or otherwise marketed as a separate product or as part of a product or process."

1) The reporting entity may

a) Develop and produce the software internally
b) Purchase the software from an external source

2) Definitions. A **computer software product** is either a

a) Computer software program or group of programs, or
b) **Product enhancement**, which is an improvement that extends the life or improves marketability of the original and usually requires a product design or possibly a redesign.

3) SFAS 86 **does not apply** to costs of software that an entity develops for its **own use** or contractually for others or to revenue recognition for marketed software.

4) **R&D costs** of computer software are all costs to establish technological feasibility. They are **expensed when incurred** (SFAS 2).

b. **Production costs of computer software.** The entity must capitalize production costs of product masters, including coding and testing costs, if they are incurred after technological feasibility is determined.

1) Once the product is available for general release, software costs can no longer be capitalized.

c.   **Purchased computer software.** If purchased software to be marketed has no alternative future use, the entity accounts for its cost as described on the previous page.

   1)   If purchased software to be marketed has an alternative future use, the entity capitalizes the costs when it purchases the software and accounts for it under GAAP, i.e., according to the alternative future use.

d.   **Amortization of capitalized software costs.** The general rule is to amortize capitalized software costs separately for each product.

   1)   For each product, the annual amortization is the GREATER of the amount determined using

      a)   The ratio of current gross revenues to the sum of current gross revenues and anticipated future gross revenues, or

      b)   The straight-line method over the remaining estimated economic life, including the current reporting period.

   2)   Amortization begins when the product is available for general release.

e.   **Evaluation of capitalized software costs.** At year-end, the unamortized cost of each software product must be compared with the net realizable value (NRV) of that software product.

   1)   Any excess of unamortized cost over NRV must be written off.

   2)   The NRV for each product is estimated future gross revenues, minus estimated future completion and disposal costs, minus maintenance and customer support costs.

   3)   After a write-down, the product's cost on the books is the NRV recorded at year-end, and the write-down cannot later be reversed.

f.   **AICPA SOP 98-1**, *Accounting for the Costs of Computer Software Developed or Obtained for Internal Use*, applies to all nongovernmental entities and does not amend other pronouncements.

   1)   Software is for **internal use** if it is intended solely to meet the entity's internal needs and, during its development or modification, no substantive plan exists for its external marketing. A joint development agreement is not a substantive marketing plan.

   2)   Software costs in the **preliminary project stage** are expensed as incurred.

   3)   During the **application development stage**, internal and external costs are capitalized.

   4)   During the **post-implementation/operation stage**, internal and external training costs and maintenance costs are expensed as incurred.

   5)   Internal costs for **upgrades and enhancements** are expensed or capitalized in accordance with the foregoing section.

   6)   When new software replaces old software, unamortized costs of the old software are expensed.

   7)   Capitalized costs are amortized on a straight-line basis over the useful life of the software unless another systematic and rational basis is more representative.

15.   **Deferred charges or other assets** is a catchall category, sometimes presented with intangible assets, that includes long-term prepayments not classified elsewhere.

   a.   Depending on the company, deferred charges may include prepaid expenses, plant rearrangement costs, and stock issue costs.

   b.   Such a classification has been criticized because many assets presented elsewhere, such as under property, plant, and equipment, are also deferred charges. That is, they are long-term prepayments that will be depreciated or amortized.

16.   Stop and review! You have completed the outline for this subunit. Study multiple-choice questions 33 through 49 beginning on page 580.

## 15.5 CORE CONCEPTS

Property, Plant, and Equipment – Acquisition and Valuation

- PPE may be either **personal property** (something movable, e.g., equipment) or **real property** (such as land or a building).
- PPE are reported at **historical cost** (net of applicable depreciation in the case of non-land PPE).
- **Site preparation costs**, such as razing old buildings, clearing, filling, and draining, are **costs of the land**, not of the building to be constructed on the land.
- The **cost of a building** includes any liens assumed and any costs of renovation and preparation.
- The **cost of machinery and equipment** includes the purchase price and all installation and start-up costs.
- **Improvements** made to property that is merely being leased, such as buildings constructed on leased land, are accounted for in the same way as property to which title is held (except that the depreciation period generally may not extend beyond the lease term).
- **Subsequent expenditures** are **capitalized** if they provide additional benefits by (a) improving the quality of services rendered by the asset, (b) extending the asset's useful life, or (c) increasing its output.

Property, Plant, and Equipment – Disposition

- When PPE is disposed of in a **partial monetary exchange** (i.e., boot is received), **gain must be recognized** in proportion of the amount of boot to the amount of total assets given up.
- When a long-lived asset is **impaired** (i.e., its fair value is less than its carrying amount), a **loss** equal to the excess is recognized if the amount is not recoverable.

Property, Plant, and Equipment – Depreciation and Depletion

- **Depreciation** is the process of systematically and rationally **allocating the historical cost** of the productive capacity of a tangible capital asset to the periods benefited. It is **not** a process of **valuation**.
- The **straight-line method** is the **simplest**. It allocates the asset's cost at a constant rate over its estimated useful life.
- **Accelerated methods** were popularized when they became allowable on **tax returns**, but the same method need not be used for tax and financial statement purposes. The two major ones are **declining balance** and **sum-of-the-years' digits**.
- **Activity-based methods**, such as **units-of-output**, calculate depreciation as a function of an **asset's use** rather than the time it has been held.
- **Depletion** is similar to depreciation, but the assets involved are **wasting assets**, such as natural resources (e.g., petroleum, timber, iron ore, etc.)

Intangible Assets

- **Intangible assets** are nonfinancial assets that **lack physical substance**. They often convey a right to do something that gives its holder some form of **economic benefits**, e.g., patents and copyrights.
- Intangible assets are **not depreciated**. Instead, they are periodically **reviewed for impairment** and written down to fair value.
- **Research and development costs** are expensed as incurred; they may **not** be capitalized.

## QUESTIONS

### 15.1 Property, Plant, and Equipment (PPE) – Acquisition and Valuation

**1.** Pearl Corporation acquired manufacturing machinery on January 1 for $9,000. During the year, the machine produced 1,000 units, of which 600 were sold. There was no work-in-process inventory at the beginning or at the end of the year. Installation charges of $300 and delivery charges of $200 were also incurred. The machine is expected to have a useful life of five years with an estimated salvage value of $1,500. Pearl uses the straight-line depreciation method. The original cost of the machinery to be recorded in Pearl's books is

A. $9,500

B. $9,300

C. $9,200

D. $9,000

Answer (A) is correct. *(CMA, adapted)*
**REQUIRED:** The original cost of the machinery to be recorded in the books.
**DISCUSSION:** The costs of fixed assets (plant and equipment) are all costs necessary to acquire these assets and to bring them to the condition and location required for their intended use. These costs include shipping, installation, pre-use testing, sales taxes, interest capitalization, etc. Thus, the original cost of the machinery to be recorded in the books is the sum of the purchase price, installation, and delivery charges, or $9,500 ($9,000 + $300 + $200).
Answer (B) is incorrect because $9,300 does not include the delivery charges. Answer (C) is incorrect because $9,200 omits the installation charges. Answer (D) is incorrect because $9,000 does not include the delivery and installation charges.

**2.** Lambert Company acquired a machine on October 1 that was placed in service on November 30. The cost of the machine was $63,000, of which $20,000 was given as a down payment. The remainder was borrowed at 12% annual interest. Additional costs included $2,500 for shipping, $4,000 for installation, $3,000 for testing, and $1,290 of interest on the borrowed funds. How much should be reported for this acquisition in the machine account on Lambert Company's statement of financial position as of November 30?

A. $63,000

B. $65,500

C. $69,500

D. $72,500

Answer (D) is correct. *(CMA, adapted)*
**REQUIRED:** The cost of the machine reported on the balance sheet.
**DISCUSSION:** The initial cost of a machine consists of all costs necessary to prepare it for operation. These include the purchase price minus any discounts ($63,000), shipping costs ($2,500), installation costs ($4,000), and pre-use testing ($3,000). Interest is capitalized only in the case of construction of assets for an enterprise's own use, and then only for the interest incurred during construction. Total acquisition cost is therefore $72,500.
Answer (A) is incorrect because $63,000 equals the price. Answer (B) is incorrect because $65,500 equals the price plus shipping. Answer (C) is incorrect because $69,500 equals the price plus shipping and installation.

**3.** A steel press machine is purchased for $50,000 cash and a $100,000 interest-bearing note payable. The cost to be recorded as an asset (in addition to the $150,000 purchase price) should include all of the following except

A. Freight and handling charges.

B. Insurance while in transit.

C. Interest on the note payable.

D. Assembly and installation costs.

Answer (C) is correct. *(CMA, adapted)*
**REQUIRED:** The expenditure not capitalized as part of the cost of a new fixed asset.
**DISCUSSION:** The capitalized cost of fixed assets includes all costs necessary to acquire them and to bring them to the condition and location required for their intended use. Costs of acquisition include shipping, assembly and installation, insurance while in transit, pre-use testing, trial runs, and sales taxes. Interest can also be a cost when assets are self constructed. However, capitalized interest is not a cost of acquisition when long-lived assets are purchased from outside vendors.

**4.** The value of property, plant, and equipment that is included in total assets on the statement of financial position is

A. Appraisal or market value.

B. Replacement cost.

C. Acquisition cost.

D. Cost minus accumulated depreciation.

Answer (D) is correct. *(CMA, adapted)*
**REQUIRED:** The value of PPE included in total assets.
**DISCUSSION:** Fixed assets are reported at their cost minus accumulated depreciation. The capitalized cost of fixed assets includes all costs necessary to acquire them and to bring them to the condition and location required for their intended use.
Answer (A) is incorrect because appraisal values are specifically excluded under ARB 43. Answer (B) is incorrect because replacement cost (current cost) is not acceptable for external financial reporting purposes. However, GAAP formerly required presentation of supplementary current cost information. Answer (C) is incorrect because acquisition cost should be reduced by periodic depreciation.

**5.** Samm Corp. purchased a plot of land for $100,000. The cost to raze a building on the property amounted to $50,000 and Samm received $10,000 from the sale of scrap materials. Samm built a new plant on the site at a total cost of $800,000 including excavation costs of $30,000. What amount should Samm capitalize in its land account?

A. $150,000

B. $140,000

C. $130,000

D. $100,000

Answer (B) is correct. *(CPA, adapted)*
**REQUIRED:** The amount reported as the cost of land.
**DISCUSSION:** The costs of acquiring and preparing land for its use are capitalized. Because the land was purchased to build a plant, the cost of razing the old building, minus any proceeds received from the sale of scrap materials, should be capitalized as part of the land account. Land should be reported at $140,000 ($100,000 + $50,000 – $10,000). The cost of construction of a building on the land, including the excavation costs, will be capitalized in the building account.
Answer (A) is incorrect because $150,000 results from not subtracting the proceeds of the scrap sale from the cost to raze the building. Answer (C) is incorrect because $130,000 equals the price of the land plus the excavation costs. Answer (D) is incorrect because $100,000 is the price of the land.

**6.** During 2002, Bay Co. constructed machinery for its own use and for sale to customers. Bank loans financed these assets both during construction and after construction was complete. How much of the interest incurred should be reported as interest expense in the 2002 income statement?

| | Interest Incurred for Machinery for Bay's Own Use | Interest Incurred for Machinery Held for Sale |
| --- | --- | --- |
| A. | All interest incurred | All interest incurred |
| B. | All interest incurred | Interest incurred after completion |
| C. | Interest incurred after completion | Interest incurred after completion |
| D. | Interest incurred after completion | All interest incurred |

Answer (D) is correct. *(CPA, adapted)*
**REQUIRED:** The interest incurred reported as interest expense.
**DISCUSSION:** In accordance with SFAS 34, interest should be capitalized for two types of assets: those constructed or otherwise produced for an enterprise's own use, including those constructed or produced by others, and those intended for sale or lease that are constructed or produced as discrete projects (e.g., ships). SFAS 58, *Capitalization of Interest Cost in Financial Statements That Include Investments Accounted For by the Equity Method*, adds equity based investments to the list of qualifying assets. An asset constructed for a company's own use qualifies for capitalization of interest if relevant expenditures have been made, activities necessary to prepare the asset for its intended use are in progress, and interest is being incurred. Thus, all other interest incurred, e.g., interest incurred for machinery held for sale and interest incurred after an asset has been completed, should be expensed.
Answer (A) is incorrect because all interest incurred for machinery held for sale and interest incurred for machinery for Bay's own use after completion should be expensed. Answer (B) is incorrect because all interest incurred for machinery held for sale and interest incurred for machinery for Bay's own use after completion should be expensed. Answer (C) is incorrect because all interest incurred for machinery held for sale and interest incurred for machinery for Bay's own use after completion should be expensed.

**7.** During January year 1, Yana Co. incurred landscaping costs of $120,000 to improve leased property. The estimated useful life of the landscaping is 15 years. The remaining term of the lease is 8 years, with an option to renew for an additional 4 years. However, Yana has not reached a decision with regard to the renewal option. In Yana's December 31, year 1 balance sheet, what should be the net carrying amount of landscaping costs?

A. $0

B. $105,000

C. $110,000

D. $112,000

Answer (B) is correct. *(CPA, adapted)*
**REQUIRED:** The net amount of leasehold improvements reported in the balance sheet.
**DISCUSSION:** General improvements to leased property should be capitalized as leasehold improvements and amortized in accordance with the straight-line method over the shorter of their expected useful life or the lease term. However, if the useful life of the asset extends beyond the lease term and renewal of the lease is likely, the amortization period may include all or part of the renewal period. If renewal is uncertain, the useful life is the remaining term, and the salvage value is the amount, if any, to be paid by the lessor to the lessee at the expiration of the lease. Consequently, the amortization period is the 8-year lease term, and the net carrying amount at December 31, year 1 of the landscaping costs incurred in January of year 1 is $105,000 [$120,000 × (7 years ÷ 8 years)].
Answer (A) is incorrect because land improvements with limited lives should be capitalized. Answer (C) is incorrect because $110,000 assumes that renewal for 4 years is likely. Answer (D) is incorrect because $112,000 assumes amortization over 15 years.

**8.** On July 1, Casa Development Co. purchased a tract of land for $1.2 million. Casa incurred additional costs of $300,000 during the remainder of the year in preparing the land for sale. The tract was subdivided into residential lots as follows:

| Lot Class | Number of Lots | Sales Price per Lot |
|-----------|----------------|---------------------|
| A | 100 | $24,000 |
| B | 100 | 16,000 |
| C | 200 | 10,000 |

Using the relative sales value method, what amount of costs should be allocated to the Class A lots?

A. $300,000

B. $375,000

C. $600,000

D. $720,000

Answer (C) is correct. *(CPA, adapted)*
**REQUIRED:** The amount of costs allocated using the relative sales value method.
**DISCUSSION:** The relative sales value method allocates cost based on the relative value of assets in a group. The total sales value of the lots is $6,000,000 [(100 × $24,000) + (100 × $16,000) + (200 × $10,000)]. Class A represents 40% of the total value ($2,400,000 ÷ $6,000,000). Total costs equal $1,500,000 ($1,200,000 + $300,000). Thus, the amount of costs allocated to Class A is $600,000 ($1,500,000 × .40).
Answer (A) is incorrect because $300,000 equals the additional costs incurred. Answer (B) is incorrect because $375,000 equals 25% of the total cost. Class A represents 25% of the lots but 40% of the total value. Answer (D) is incorrect because $720,000 equals 48% of the total cost. Class A's sales price per lot is 48% of the sum of the unit sales prices of Classes A, B, and C.

## 15.2 Property, Plant, and Equipment (PPE) – Disposition

**9.** SFAS 144, *Accounting for the Impairment or Disposal of Long-Lived Assets*, requires testing for possible impairment of a long-lived asset (asset group) that an entity expects to hold and use

A. At each interim and annual balance sheet date.

B. At annual balance sheet dates only.

C. Periodically.

D. Whenever events or changes in circumstances indicate that its carrying amount may not be recoverable.

Answer (D) is correct. *(Publisher)*
**REQUIRED:** The appropriate time for testing impairment of a long-lived asset (asset group) to be held and used.
**DISCUSSION:** A long-lived asset (asset group) to which SFAS 144 applies is tested for recoverability whenever events or changes in circumstances indicate that its carrying amount may not be recoverable. The carrying amount is not recoverable when it exceeds the sum of the undiscounted cash flows expected to result from the use and disposition of the asset (asset group). If the carrying amount is not recoverable, an impairment loss is recognized equal to the excess of the carrying amount over the fair value.

---

Questions 10 and 11 are based on the following information. Harper is contemplating exchanging a machine used in its operations for a similar machine on May 31 of the current year. Harper will exchange machines with either Austin Corporation or Lubin Company.

|  | Harper | Austin | Lubin |
|--|--------|--------|-------|
| Original cost of the machine | $162,500 | $180,000 | $150,000 |
| Accumulated depreciation through May 31 | 98,500 | 70,000 | 65,000 |
| Fair value at May 31 | 80,000 | 95,000 | 60,000 |

---

**10.** If Harper exchanges its used machine and $15,000 cash for Austin's used machine, the gain that Harper should recognize from this transaction for financial reporting purposes would be

A. $0

B. $2,526

C. $15,000

D. $16,000

Answer (A) is correct. *(CMA, adapted)*
**REQUIRED:** The gain recognized by Harper from a like-kind exchange if boot is given.
**DISCUSSION:** APB 29, *Accounting for Nonmonetary Transactions*, requires that an enterprise recognize losses but not gains on like-kind exchanges unless boot (cash) is received. The justification for this conservative view is that the exchange of similar nonmonetary assets is not the culmination of an earning process. Harper's used machine has a carrying amount of $64,000 ($162,500 cost – $98,500 accumulated depreciation). The carrying amount surrendered is thus $79,000 ($64,000 + $15,000 cash). The transaction is valued at the fair value of the consideration given ($80,000 + $15,000 = $95,000), a gain of $16,000 ($95,000 – $79,000). But gains may not be recognized on a like-kind exchange under APB 29 if boot is not received. The result for financial reporting purposes is a zero gain.

**11.** If Harper exchanges its used machine for Lubin's used machine and also receives $20,000 cash, the gain that Harper should recognize from this transaction for financial reporting purposes would be

A. $0

B. $4,000

C. $16,000

D. $25,000

Answer (C) is correct. *(CMA, adapted)*
**REQUIRED:** The gain recognized by Harper from a like-kind exchange with Lubin if boot is received.
**DISCUSSION:** In some circumstances, a portion of gains is recorded when boot (monetary assets) is received in the transaction, but the gain recognized cannot exceed the amount of boot received. If that had been the case here, the gain would have been recognized in the same proportion that the cash received bears to the total consideration received. Harper's used machine has a carrying amount of $64,000, and the fair value of the consideration received is $80,000 ($60,000 machine + $20,000 cash). Consequently, there is a gain is $16,000 ($80,000 – $64,000). Of the total consideration, cash is 25% ($20,000 ÷ $80,000). The recognized gain before 1986 would have been $4,000 ($16,000 total gain × 25%). However, EITF 86-29 requires that when boot is 25% or more of the total received, the entire amount of the gain, or $16,000, must be recognized.
Answer (A) is incorrect because there is a gain of $16,000. The boot is 25% or more of the value received, so the entire gain must be recognized. Answer (B) is incorrect because, under the provisions of EITF 86-29, the entire gain of $16,000 must be recognized. The boot received is 25% or more of the value received. Answer (D) is incorrect because the gain is $16,000.

**12.** On January 2, year 1, Clarinette Co. purchased assets for $400,000 that were to be depreciated over 5 years using the straight-line method with no salvage value. Taken together, these assets have identifiable cash flows that are largely independent of the cash flows of other asset groups. At the end of year 2, Clarinette, as the result of certain changes in circumstances indicating that the carrying amount of these assets may not be recoverable, tested them for impairment. It estimated that it will receive net future cash inflows (undiscounted) of $100,000 as a result of continuing to hold and use these assets, which had a fair value of $80,000 at the end of year 2. Thus, the impairment loss to be reported at December 31, year 2, is

A. $0

B. $140,000

C. $160,000

D. $400,000

Answer (C) is correct. *(Publisher)*
**REQUIRED:** The carrying amount given estimated future net cash inflows and the fair value.
**DISCUSSION:** The carrying amount at December 31, year 2 is $240,000 {$400,000 cost – [2 years – ($400,000 ÷ 5 years)]}, but the recoverable amount is only $100,000. Hence, the SFAS 144 test for recognition of an impairment loss has been met. This loss is measured by the excess of the carrying amount over the fair value. Clarinette should therefore recognize a loss of $160,000 ($240,000 – $80,000 fair value).
Answer (A) is incorrect because the test for recognition of impairment has been met. Answer (B) is incorrect because $140,000 is the excess of the carrying amount over the undiscounted future net cash inflows. Answer (D) is incorrect because $400,000 is the purchase price of the assets.

**13.** The guidance in SFAS 144, *Accounting for the Impairment or Disposal of Long-Lived Assets*, for the recognition and measurement of impairment losses on long-lived assets to be held and used applies to

    A.  Goodwill.

    B.  An asset group.

    C.  A financial instrument.

    D.  An intangible asset not being amortized.

Answer (B) is correct. *(Publisher)*
**REQUIRED:** The item to which SFAS 144 applies.
**DISCUSSION:** SFAS 144 applies to the long-lived assets of an entity (a business enterprise or a not-for-profit organization) that are to be held and used or disposed of. These assets include a lessee's capital leases, a lessor's long-lived assets subject to operating leases, and long-term prepaid assets. SFAS 144 applies to a long-lived asset(s) included in a group with other assets and liabilities not subject to SFAS 144. The unit of accounting for such a long-lived asset is the group. If a long-lived asset(s) is to be held and used, the asset group is the lowest level at which identifiable cash flows are largely independent of those of other groups. Under SFAS 144, if the carrying amount of a long-lived asset (asset group) is not recoverable, a loss equal to the excess of that carrying amount over the fair value is recognized.
Answer (A) is incorrect because SFAS 144 does not apply to goodwill, which is tested for impairment at the reporting unit level. If the fair value of the reporting unit is less than its carrying amount, a loss is measured equal to the excess of the carrying amount over the implied fair value of reporting unit goodwill (SFAS 142). Answer (C) is incorrect because SFAS 144 does not apply to financial assets, long-lived assets subject to pronouncements applicable to specialized industries (e.g., motion picture or broadcasting), and long-lived assets subject to other broadly applicable pronouncements (e.g., deferred tax assets or certain investments in debt and equity securities). Answer (D) is incorrect because SFAS 144 does not apply to an intangible asset not being amortized. However, under SFAS 142, a nonamortizable intangible asset is deemed to be impaired when its carrying amount exceeds its fair value. The measure of the impairment equals that excess (SFAS 144).

**14.** A long-lived asset is measured at the lower of carrying amount or fair value minus cost to sell if it is to be

  I.   Held for sale.
  II.  Abandoned.
  III. Exchanged for a similar productive asset.
  IV. Distributed to owners in a spinoff.

    A.  I only.

    B.  I and III only.

    C.  II, III, and IV only.

    D.  I, II, III, and IV.

Answer (A) is correct. *(Publisher)*
**REQUIRED:** The circumstances in which a long-lived asset is measured at the lower of carrying amount or fair value minus cost to sell.
**DISCUSSION:** Disposal of a long-lived asset may be other than by sale, e.g., by abandonment, exchange, or distribution to owners in a spinoff. When disposal is to be other than by sale, the asset continues to be classified as held and used until disposal. A long-lived asset to be held and used is measured at the lower of its carrying amount or fair value. The carrying amount of an asset classified as held and used is tested for recoverability when events or circumstances provide indicators that the carrying amount exceeds the sum of the undiscounted cash flows expected to arise from the use and disposition of the asset. If the carrying amount is not recoverable, the asset is measured at fair value, and an impairment loss (excess of carrying amount over fair value) is recognized. An asset that meets the criteria for classification as held for sale is measured at the lower of its carrying amount or fair value minus cost to sell.

**15.** Tera Corporation owns a plant that produces baubles for a specialized market niche. This plant is part of a an asset group that is the lowest level at which identifiable cash flows are largely independent of those of Tera's other holdings. The asset group includes long-lived assets X, Y, and Z, which are to be held and used. It also includes current assets and liabilities that are not subject to SFAS 144, *Accounting for the Impairment or Disposal of Long-Lived Assets.* The sum of the undiscounted cash flows expected to result from the use and eventual disposition of the asset group is $3,200,000, and its fair value is $2,900,000. The following are the carrying amounts of the assets and liabilities included in the asset group:

| | |
|---|---:|
| Current assets | $ 600,000 |
| Liabilities | (200,000) |
| Long-lived asset X | 1,500,000 |
| Y | 900,000 |
| Z | 600,000 |

If the fair value of X is determinable as $1,400,000 without undue cost and effort, what should be the carrying amount of Z?

- A. $440,000
- B. $500,000
- C. $600,000
- D. $660,000

Answer (A) is correct. *(Publisher)*
**REQUIRED:** The carrying amount of Z.
**DISCUSSION:** An impairment loss decreases only the carrying amounts of the long-lived assets in the group on a pro rata basis according to their relative carrying amounts. However, the carrying amount of a given long-lived asset is not reduced below its fair value if that fair value is determinable without undue cost and effort. Because the total carrying amount of the asset group of $3.4 million ($600,000 − $200,000 + $1,500,000 + $900,000 + $600,000) exceeds the $3.2 million sum of the undiscounted cash flows expected to result from the use and eventual disposition of the asset group, the carrying amount is not recoverable. Hence, an impairment loss equal to the excess of the total carrying amount of the group over its fair value ($3.4 million − $2.9 million = $500,000) must be recognized and allocated pro rata to the long-lived assets. The amounts allocated to X, Y, and Z are $250,000 [($1,500,000 ÷ $3,000,000) × $500,000], $150,000 [($900,000 ÷ $3,000,000) × $500,000], and $100,000 [($600,000 ÷ $3,000,000) × $500,000], respectively. The preliminary adjusted carrying amounts of X, Y, and Z are therefore $1,250,000 ($1,500,000 − $250,000), $750,000 ($900,000 − $150,000), and $500,000 ($600,000 − $100,000), respectively. However, the fair value of X determined without undue cost and effort is $1,400,000. Accordingly, $150,000 ($1,400,000 fair value of X − $1,250,000 preliminary adjusted carrying amount of X) must be reallocated to Y and Z. The amounts reallocated to Y and Z are $90,000 [($750,000 ÷ $1,250,000) × $150,000] and $60,000 [($500,000 ÷ $1,250,000) × $150,000], respectively. Thus, the carrying amount of Z should be $440,000 ($600,000 − $100,000 − $60,000).
Answer (B) is incorrect because $500,000 is the preliminary adjusted carrying amount of Z. Answer (C) is incorrect because $600,000 is the carrying amount of Z before reduction for a proportionate share of the impairment loss. Answer (D) is incorrect because $660,000 is the carrying amount of Z before reduction for a proportionate share of the impairment loss plus Z's share of the reallocated amount.

**16.** To determine whether an impairment loss must be recognized, estimates of future cash flows are used to test the recoverability of the carrying amount of a long-lived asset (asset group) to be held and used. The estimates of future cash flows for an asset group should be based on

- A. The service potential expected to exist at relevant times in the future.
- B. Assumptions developed by disinterested third parties.
- C. The remaining useful life of the primary asset of the group.
- D. All future expenditures exclusive of interest needed to produce the expected service potential if the asset group is under development.

Answer (C) is correct. *(Publisher)*
**REQUIRED:** The basis of cash flow estimates used in the recoverability test.
**DISCUSSION:** The estimates are made for the remaining useful life as determined from the perspective of the entity. The remaining useful life is that of the primary asset of the group, that is, the principal depreciable tangible asset or amortizable intangible asset that is the most significant component of the asset group for generating cash flows. Whether a given asset is primary is determined by such considerations as whether the other group assets would have been acquired without it, the cost of replacing it, and its useful life in relation to the other group assets. If the primary asset does not have the longest remaining useful life, estimates should assume the sale of the group at the end of the primary asset's remaining useful life.
Answer (A) is incorrect because the estimates of future cash flows are based on the existing service potential at the time of the test for recoverability, which is a function of the remaining useful life of the asset (asset group), ability to produce cash flows, and (for tangible assets) physical output. Answer (B) is incorrect because the estimates of future cash flows must be based on the entity's own assumptions about its use of the asset (asset group) and all available evidence. The assumptions must be reasonable in relation to other assumptions employed by the entity for other purposes for comparable periods. Answer (D) is incorrect because, if the asset (asset group) is under development, the cash flow estimates reflect all future expenditures necessary to produce the expected service potential. These expenditures include capitalizable interest.

**17.** If a long-lived asset satisfies the criteria for classification as held for sale,

    A. Its carrying amount is the cost at the acquisition date if the asset is newly acquired.

    B. It is not depreciated.

    C. Interest attributable to liabilities of a disposal group to which the asset belongs is not accrued.

    D. It is classified as held for sale even if the criteria are not met until after the balance sheet date but before issuance of the financial statements.

**Answer (B) is correct.** *(Publisher)*
    **REQUIRED:** The treatment of a long-lived asset that meets the criteria for classification as held for sale.
    **DISCUSSION:** A long-lived asset is not depreciated (amortized) while it is classified as held for sale and measured at the lower of carrying amount or fair value minus cost to sell. The reason is that depreciation (amortization) would reduce the carrying amount below fair value minus cost to sell. Furthermore, fair value minus cost to sell must be evaluated each period, so any future decline will be recognized in the period of decline.
    Answer (A) is incorrect because the carrying amount of a newly acquired long-lived asset classified as held for sale is its fair value minus cost to sell at the acquisition date. Answer (C) is incorrect because interest and other expenses attributable to liabilities of a disposal group to which the asset belongs are accrued. Answer (D) is incorrect because, if the criteria are not met until after the balance sheet date but before issuance of the financial statements, the long-lived asset continues to be classified as held and used in those statements.

## 15.3 Property, Plant, and Equipment (PPE) – Depreciation and Depletion

**18.** WD Mining Company purchased a section of land for $600,000 in year 1 to develop a zinc mine. The mine began operating in year 9. At that time, management estimated that the mine would produce 200,000 tons of quality ore. A total of 100,000 tons of ore was mined and processed from year 9 through December 31, year 16. During January year 17, a very promising vein was discovered. The revised estimate of ore still to be mined was 250,000 tons. Estimated salvage value for the mine land was $100,000 in both year 9 and year 17. Assuming that 10,000 tons of ore was mined in year 17, the computation WD Mining company should use to determine the amount of depletion to record in year 17 would be

    A. $\dfrac{\$600{,}000 - \$100{,}000}{450{,}000 \text{ tons}} \times 10{,}000 \text{ tons}$

    B. $\dfrac{\$600{,}000 - \$100{,}000}{350{,}000 \text{ tons}} \times 10{,}000 \text{ tons}$

    C. $\dfrac{\$600{,}000 - \$100{,}000 - \$250{,}000}{350{,}000 \text{ tons}} \times 10{,}000 \text{ tons}$

    D. $\dfrac{\$600{,}000 - \$100{,}000 - \$250{,}000}{250{,}000 \text{ tons}} \times 10{,}000 \text{ tons}$

**Answer (D) is correct.** *(CMA, adapted)*
    **REQUIRED:** The computation for determining the annual depletion.
    **DISCUSSION:** Because 50% of the original estimate of quality ore was recovered during the years year 9 through year 16, recorded depletion must have been $250,000 [($600,000 – $100,000 salvage value) × 50%]. In year 17, the earlier depletion of $250,000 is deducted from the $600,000 cost along with the $100,000 salvage value. The remaining depletable cost of $250,000 will be allocated over the 250,000 tons believed to remain in the mine. The $1 per ton depletion is then multiplied times the tons mined each year.
    Answer (A) is incorrect because the denominator should include only 250,000 tons. Also, this answer fails to deduct prior depletion. Answer (B) is incorrect because the denominator should include only 250,000 tons. Also, this answer fails to deduct prior depletion. Answer (C) is incorrect because the denominator should include only 250,000 tons.

**19.** In January, Vorst Co. purchased a mineral mine for $2,640,000 with removable ore estimated at 1.2 million tons. After it has extracted all the ore, Vorst will be required by law to restore the land to its original condition at an estimated cost of $180,000. Vorst believes it will be able to sell the property afterwards for $300,000. During the year, Vorst incurred $360,000 of development costs preparing the mine for production and removed and sold 60,000 tons of ore. In its current year income statement, what amount should Vorst report as depletion?

A. $135,000

B. $144,000

C. $150,000

D. $159,000

**Answer (B) is correct.** *(CPA, adapted)*
**REQUIRED:** The amount of depletion to be reported.
**DISCUSSION:** The depletion base is the purchase price of the land ($2,640,000), minus the value of the land after restoration ($300,000 – $180,000 = $120,000), plus any costs necessary to prepare the property for the extraction of ore ($360,000). This depletion base must be allocated over the 1.2 million tons of ore that the land is estimated to yield. Accordingly, Vorst's depletion charge per ton is $2.40 [($2,640,000 – $120,000 + $360,000) ÷ 1,200,000]. Vorst should report $144,000 (60,000 tons sold × $2.40) as depletion in its current year income statement.
Answer (A) is incorrect because $135,000 does not include the $180,000 restoration costs. Answer (C) is incorrect because $150,000 does not consider the restoration costs and the residual value of the land. Answer (D) is incorrect because $159,000 adds the $180,000 restoration cost instead of deducting the $120,000 net residual value of the land.

**20.** The factors primarily relied upon to determine the economic life of an asset are

A. Passage of time, asset usage, and obsolescence.

B. Tax regulations and SEC guidelines.

C. Tax regulations and asset usage.

D. SEC guidelines and asset usage.

**Answer (A) is correct.** *(CMA, adapted)*
**REQUIRED:** The factors primarily relied upon to determine the economic life of an asset.
**DISCUSSION:** Under the straight-line method, depreciation expense is a constant amount for each period of the estimated useful life of the asset. The straight-line method ignores fluctuations in the use of an asset and in maintenance and service charges. The book value is dependent upon the length of time the asset has been held rather than the amount of use. Physical wear and tear is a justification for an activity method of depreciation, e.g., depreciation based on hours of machine use. If technological developments are a primary factor in determining the period of use of an asset, a write-down method of depreciation based on market values may be appropriate.
Answer (B) is incorrect because the lives that are acceptable for tax purposes may not always be used for financial accounting purposes and because the SEC has not issued depreciation life guidelines. Answer (C) is incorrect because the lives that are acceptable for tax purposes may not always be used for financial accounting purposes and because the SEC has not issued depreciation life guidelines. Answer (D) is incorrect because the lives that are acceptable for tax purposes may not always be used for financial accounting purposes and because the SEC has not issued depreciation life guidelines.

Questions 21 through 23 are based on the following information.

Kruse Company acquired a company airplane on June 3, year 1. The following information relates to this purchase:

| | |
|---|---|
| Airplane cost | $123,750 |
| Estimated useful life in years | 6 |
| Estimated useful life in operating hours | 15,000 |
| Estimated residual value | $ 11,250 |

Actual hours flown in the year ended May 31,

| | |
|---|---|
| Year 2 | 1,984 |
| Year 3 | 2,800 |
| Year 4 | 1,690 |
| Year 5 | 1,824 |

**21.** The depreciation expense for the fiscal year ended May 31, year 5 using the units-of-output method for all years would be

A. $13,680

B. $14,880

C. $15,048

D. $18,750

Answer (A) is correct.  *(CMA, adapted)*
**REQUIRED:** The depreciation for the year ending May 31, year 5 based on units of output.
**DISCUSSION:** The depreciable cost of the plane is $112,500 ($123,750 cost – $11,250 residual value). Hence, the per-hour depreciation charge is $7.50 ($112,500 ÷ 15,000-hour useful life), and the total year 5 depreciation expense is $13,680 (1,824 hours × $7.50).
Answer (B) is incorrect because $14,880 is based on year 2 operations. Answer (C) is incorrect because $15,048 ignores the residual value of the airplane. Answer (D) is incorrect because $18,750 is based on the straight-line method.

**22.** The depreciation expense for the fiscal year ended May 31, year 3 using the double-declining-balance (DDB) method for all years would be

A. $17,188

B. $25,000

C. $27,500

D. $41,250

Answer (C) is correct.  *(CMA, adapted)*
**REQUIRED:** The depreciation for the year ending May 31, year 3 under the DDB method.
**DISCUSSION:** Under the DDB method, the depreciation percentage used is double the straight-line rate. For the airplane, the DDB rate is 33 1/3% [2 × (100% ÷ 6 years)]. In the first year, the DDB rate is applied to the initial cost of the asset (residual value is ignored). Thus, depreciation is $41,250 ($123,750 × 33 1/3%). This amount is subtracted from the initial cost to determine the new depreciable base. Accordingly, depreciation for the second year is $27,500 [($123,750 – $41,250) × 33 1/3%].
Answer (A) is incorrect because $17,188 is based on the straight-line percentage of 16 2/3%. Answer (B) is incorrect because $25,000 subtracted residual value from initial cost. Answer (D) is incorrect because $41,250 is the depreciation expense for the first year.

**23.** The depreciation expense for the fiscal year ended May 31, year 4 using the sum-of-the-years'-digits (SYD) method for all years would be

A. $17,679

B. $18,750

C. $21,429

D. $23,571

Answer (C) is correct.  *(CMA, adapted)*
**REQUIRED:** The depreciation for the year ending May 31, year 4 under the SYD method.
**DISCUSSION:** Under the SYD method, the depreciable base is $112,500 ($123,750 cost – $11,250 residual value). The annual depreciation rate equals the years remaining divided by the sum of the digits in the years of the asset's life. For a 6-year life, the denominator is 21 (1 + 2 + 3 + 4 + 5 + 6). Thus, third-year depreciation is $21,429 [$112,500 × (4 ÷ 21)].
Answer (A) is incorrect because $17,679 is based on the fourth-year rate and ignores residual value. Answer (B) is incorrect because $18,750 is based on the straight-line method. Answer (D) is incorrect because $23,571 ignores residual value.

Questions 24 through 26 are based on the following information. In year 1, Ace Industries made the strategic decision to upgrade its manufacturing facility and has since purchased the equipment listed below. The company uses a calendar year as its fiscal year and uses the half-year convention when determining depreciation expense.

* An extruding machine purchased on April 1, year 2 for $200,000. Installation costs were $40,000, and the machine has an estimated 8-year life with no expected salvage value.

* High-speed molding equipment placed in service July 1, year 2. This equipment cost $500,000, has an estimated 10-year life, and is reasonably expected to have a $50,000 salvage value.

* Computer-controlled assembly equipment purchased on August 1, year 3 for $800,000. This equipment has an estimated 8-year life with a salvage value of $60,000.

**24.** Using the straight-line depreciation method, Ace Industries' year 3 depreciation expense is

    A. $121,250

    B. $233,750

    C. $242,500

    D. $246,400

Answer (A) is correct.  *(CMA, adapted)*
    **REQUIRED:** The annual depreciation expense using the straight-line method.
    **DISCUSSION:** The extruding machine's depreciable base is $240,000 ($200,000 + $40,000 installation costs – $0 salvage), so the annual charge is $30,000 ($240,000 ÷ 8).  The molding equipment's depreciable base is $450,000 ($500,000 – $50,000 salvage).  Hence, annual depreciation is $45,000 ($450,000 ÷ 10).  The assembly equipment's depreciable base is $740,000 ($800,000 – $60,000 salvage), resulting in an annual charge of $92,500 ($740,000 ÷ 8).  However, given that year 3 is the first year of use, the half-year convention is applied.  Under this income tax convention, half a year's depreciation is recorded in the year of acquisition and in the year of disposal.  Accordingly, year 3 depreciation is $46,250 ($92,500 ÷ 2).  Total depreciation for the three types of equipment is $121,250 ($30,000 + $45,000 + $46,250).
    Answer (B) is incorrect because $233,750 is based on the double-declining-balance method and fails to consider installation costs.  Answer (C) is incorrect because $242,500 is based on the double-declining-balance method.  Answer (D) is incorrect because $246,400 is based on the composite method.

**25.** Using the double-declining-balance depreciation method, Ace Industries' year 3 depreciation expense is

    A. $121,250

    B. $233,750

    C. $242,500

    D. $246,400

Answer (C) is correct.  *(CMA, adapted)*
    **REQUIRED:** The annual depreciation expense using the double-declining-balance method.
    **DISCUSSION:** Under the double-declining-balance method, the depreciation rate is twice the straight-line rate, and salvage value is ignored initially.  The extruding machine is depreciated at a 25% rate because it has an 8-year life.  For year 2, depreciation based on the half-year convention is $30,000 {[($200,000 + $40,000 installation cost) × 25%] ÷ 2}.  The depreciation for year 3 is therefore $52,500 [($240,000 – $30,000) × 25%].  The molding equipment is depreciated at a 20% rate given its 10-year life, so year 2 depreciation based on the half-year convention is $50,000 [($500,000 × 20%) ÷ 2].  Accordingly, year 3 depreciation is $90,000 [($500,000 – $50,000) × 20%].  The assembly equipment is depreciated at a 25% rate based on an 8-year life.  Under the half-year convention, year 3 depreciation is $100,000 [($800,000 × 25%) ÷ 2].  Total depreciation expense is $242,500 ($52,500 + $90,000 + $100,000).
    Answer (A) is incorrect because $121,250 is the depreciation under the straight-line method.  Answer (B) is incorrect because $233,750 fails to consider installation costs.  Answer (D) is incorrect because $246,400 is based on the composite method.

**26.** Ace Industries has decided to simplify its record-keeping in year 4 by changing to composite depreciation for its manufacturing equipment.  The appropriate composite rate has been determined to be 16%.  If no additional equipment is purchased in year 4, Ace Industries' year 4 depreciation expense will be

    A. $121,250

    B. $233,750

    C. $242,500

    D. $246,400

Answer (D) is correct.  *(CMA, adapted)*
    **REQUIRED:** The depreciation expense for year 4 under the composite method of depreciation.
    **DISCUSSION:** The composite method of depreciation relates to groups of dissimilar assets with varying useful lives.  The depreciation rate applied is an average found by dividing the sum of the straight-line amounts (after allowance for salvage value) by the total cost.  The rate is applied to the total cost, and the group is depreciated to the salvage value (if no changes occur in the group).  Accordingly, year 4 composite depreciation is $246,400 [($240,000 + $500,000 + $800,000) × 16% given composite rate].
    Answer (A) is incorrect because $121,250 is the year 3 straight-line depreciation.  Answer (B) is incorrect because $233,750 is the year 3 DDB depreciation without regard to installation costs.  Answer (C) is incorrect because $242,500 is the DDB depreciation for year 3.

Questions 27 through 32 are based on the following information.

Felicity Company has the following information on one of its trucks purchased on January 1, year 1. No estimates were changed during the life of the truck.

| Truck cost | $100,000 |
|---|---|
| Useful life-years (estimated) | 5 years |
| Useful life-miles (estimated) | 100,000 |
| Estimated salvage value | $ 20,000 |
| Actual miles driven: Year 1 | 30,000 |
| Year 2 | 20,000 |
| Year 3 | 15,000 |
| Year 4 | 25,000 |
| Year 5 | 12,000 |

**27.** The year 3 depreciation expense for the truck using the sum-of-the-years'-digits (SYD) method was

A. $12,000

B. $16,000

C. $20,000

D. $26,667

Answer (B) is correct. *(Publisher)*
**REQUIRED:** The year 3 depreciation expense under the SYD method.
**DISCUSSION:** Under SYD, the amount depreciated is the original cost ($100,000) minus salvage value ($20,000), or $80,000. The portion expensed each year is based on a fraction, the denominator of which is the sum of the years of life of the asset. For an asset with a 5-year life, the denominator is 15 (5 + 4 + 3 + 2 + 1). The numerator is 5 in the first year, 4 in the second year, etc. The year 3 was the third year of the vehicle's life; thus, the fraction is 3 ÷ 15, and annual expense was $16,000 [$80,000 × (3 ÷ 15)].
Answer (A) is incorrect because $12,000 is based on the units-of-production method. Answer (C) is incorrect because $20,000 results from not deducting salvage value from the cost. Answer (D) is incorrect because $26,667 was the depreciation for the first year.

**28.** Assuming the company uses the double-declining-balance (DDB) method, the fiscal year 2 year-end accumulated depreciation was

A. $16,000

B. $24,000

C. $32,000

D. $64,000

Answer (D) is correct. *(Publisher)*
**REQUIRED:** The accumulated depreciation at the end of year 2 under the DDB method.
**DISCUSSION:** For an asset with a 5-year life, the straight-line rate is 20%. Under DDB, the applicable percentage is double the straight-line rate, or 40%. This rate is multiplied times the book value of the asset, which for the first year is the original cost. Hence, DDB depreciation was $40,000 ($100,000 × 40%) for year 1 and $24,000 [($100,000 − $40,000) × 40%] for year 2. Accumulated depreciation at the end of year 2 was therefore $64,000 ($40,000 + $24,000).
Answer (A) is incorrect because $16,000 is the difference between year 1 and year 2 depreciation expense. Answer (B) is incorrect because $24,000 is the depreciation expense for year 2. Answer (C) is incorrect because $32,000 is the first year's depreciation if salvage value were deducted to determine the depreciable amount.

**29.** Using the units-of-production method, what is the year 5 depreciation expense?

A. $8,000

B. $9,600

C. $10,000

D. $12,000

Answer (A) is correct. *(Publisher)*
**REQUIRED:** The depreciation expense for year 5.
**DISCUSSION:** Unit depreciation is calculated and then multiplied by the units produced in a given year. Unit depreciation is $.80 per mile [($100,000 cost − $20,000 salvage value) ÷ 100,000 miles]. For year 1 through year 4, the annual depreciation equaled the unit depreciation times the miles driven. For year 5, this must be modified because 90,000 (30,000 + 20,000 + 15,000 + 25,000) of the 100,000 miles of the estimated useful life have already been driven. Because only 10,000 miles of the useful life remain after year 4, year 5 depreciation is $8,000 (10,000 miles × $.80).
Answer (B) is incorrect because $9,600 assumes the full 12,000 miles driven in year 5 are eligible for depreciation. Answer (C) is incorrect because $10,000 assumes that depreciation is based on original cost without regard to salvage value. Answer (D) is incorrect because $12,000 is based on 12,000 miles and ignores salvage value.

**30.** If the company uses the half-year convention in recording depreciation, how much depreciation was recorded in year 1 under the sum-of-the-years'-digits (SYD) method?

A. $13,333

B. $16,667

C. $26,667

D. $33,333

Answer (A) is correct. *(Publisher)*

**REQUIRED:** The year 1 depreciation expense under the SYD method and the half-year convention.

**DISCUSSION:** Under SYD, the amount depreciated is the original cost ($100,000) minus salvage value ($20,000), or $80,000. The portion expensed each year equals the depreciable base times the SYD fraction (remaining years of useful life ÷ sum of the years' digits). The fraction for year 1 was 5 ÷ 15 [5 years remaining ÷ (5 + 4 + 3 + 2 + 1)], so annual expense was $26,667. However, the half-year convention reduced this amount to $13,333 ($26,667 × 50%).

Answer (B) is incorrect because $16,667 results from not subtracting salvage value. Answer (C) is incorrect because $26,667 does not consider the half-year convention. Answer (D) is incorrect because $33,333 does not consider either salvage value or the half-year convention.

**31.** If the company uses the half-year convention in recording depreciation, how much depreciation was recorded in year 2 under the sum-of-the-years'-digits (SYD) method?

A. $8,000

B. $10,667

C. $21,333

D. $24,000

Answer (D) is correct. *(Publisher)*

**REQUIRED:** The year 2 depreciation expense under the SYD method and the half-year convention.

**DISCUSSION:** Under SYD, the amount depreciated is the original cost ($100,000) minus salvage value ($20,000), or $80,000. The portion expensed each year equals the depreciable base times the SYD fraction. For year 1, this fraction was 5 ÷ 15 [5 years remaining ÷ (5 + 4 + 3 + 2 + 1)], and annual depreciation was $26,667 [80,000 × (5 ÷ 15)]. Under the half-year convention, $13,333 ($26,667 × 50%) of this amount was expensed in year 1. The remaining $13,333 was expensed during the first 6 months of year 2. The expense for the last 6 months of year 2 was half of the second year's depreciation, or $10,667 [$80,000 × 50% × (4 ÷ 15)]. Thus, total depreciation for year 2 was $24,000 ($13,333 + $10,667).

Answer (A) is incorrect because $8,000 is the units-of-production depreciation for year 5. Answer (B) is incorrect because $10,667 is the depreciation for the last half of year 2. Answer (C) is incorrect because $21,333 is the charge for the full second year of the asset's life.

**32.** Assuming the half-year convention was not used, the fiscal year 4 depreciation expense under the double-declining-balance (DDB) method was

A. $1,600

B. $6,912

C. $8,640

D. $14,400

Answer (A) is correct. *(Publisher)*

**REQUIRED:** The depreciation expense for year 4 under the DDB method.

**DISCUSSION:** For an asset with a 5-year life, the straight-line rate is 20%. Under DDB, the applicable percentage is double the straight-line rate, or 40%. This rate is multiplied by the book value of the asset, which for the first year is the original cost. Consequently, DDB depreciation was $40,000 ($100,000 × 40%) for year 1, $24,000 for year 2 [($100,000 − $40,000) × 40%], and $14,400 for year 3 [($100,000 − $40,000 − $24,000) × 40%]. Because accumulated depreciation through year 3 was $78,400 ($40,000 + $24,000 + $14,400), book value was $21,600 ($100,000 − $78,400), and year 4 depreciation (before considering salvage value) was $8,640 ($21,600 × 40%). However, the asset cannot be depreciated below its salvage value. Thus, the company cannot recognize more than $1,600 of depreciation expense ($21,600 − $20,000 salvage value) in year 4.

Answer (B) is incorrect because $6,912 is the amount that would be expensed if the depreciable base was net of the salvage value and the asset was depreciated below this salvage value. Answer (C) is incorrect because $8,640 assumes no salvage value. Answer (D) is incorrect because $14,400 is the expense for year 3.

## 15.4 Intangible Assets

**33.** A recognized intangible asset is amortized over its useful life

- A. Unless the pattern of consumption of the economic benefits of the asset is not reliably determinable.
- B. If that life is determined to be finite.
- C. Unless the precise length of that life is not known.
- D. If that life is indefinite but not infinite.

Answer (B) is correct. *(Publisher)*
**REQUIRED:** The circumstances in which a recognized intangible asset is amortized.
**DISCUSSION:** A recognized intangible asset is amortized over its useful life if that useful life is finite, that is, unless the useful life is determined to be indefinite. The useful life of an intangible asset is indefinite if no foreseeable limit exists on the period over which it will contribute, directly or indirectly, to the reporting entity's cash flows (SFAS 142).
Answer (A) is incorrect because an intangible asset is amortizable if its useful life is finite. If the pattern of consumption of the economic benefits of such an intangible asset is not reliably determinable, the straight-line amortization method is applied. Answer (C) is incorrect because, if the precise length of the useful life is not known, an intangible asset with a finite useful life is amortized over the best estimate of its useful life. Answer (D) is incorrect because a recognized intangible asset is not amortized if its useful life is indefinite.

**34.** Intangible assets acquired singly from other enterprises or individuals should be recorded at cost at date of acquisition. Cost may not be measured by which of the following?

- A. Net carrying amount of the previous owner.
- B. Amount of cash disbursed.
- C. Present value of amounts to be paid for liabilities incurred.
- D. Fair value of other assets distributed.

Answer (A) is correct. *(Publisher)*
**REQUIRED:** The method not allowed to measure cost of intangible assets.
**DISCUSSION:** If cash is the consideration given in an exchange transaction, the cash paid is the measure of the transaction. If noncash consideration (noncash assets, liabilities incurred, or equity interests issued) is given, the measurement is based on the more reliably measurable of the fair value of the consideration given or the fair value of the asset or net assets acquired (SFAS 142). Furthermore, the only objective of present value used in initial recognition and fresh-start measurements is to estimate fair value in the absence of a market price (SFAC 7). Consequently, only the carrying amount of the previous owner is not a proper measurement of cost.

**35.** Costs that are capitalized with regard to a patent include

- A. Legal fees of obtaining the patent, incidental costs of obtaining the patent, and costs of successful patent infringement suits.
- B. Legal fees of obtaining the patent, incidental costs of obtaining the patent, and research and development costs incurred on the invention that is patented.
- C. Legal fees of obtaining the patent, costs of successful patent infringement suits, and research and development costs incurred on the invention that is patented.
- D. Incidental costs of obtaining the patent, costs of successful and unsuccessful patent infringement suits, and the value of any signed patent licensing agreement.

Answer (A) is correct. *(CMA, adapted)*
**REQUIRED:** The proper items to be capitalized as part of the cost of a patent.
**DISCUSSION:** The cost should be amortized over the remaining legal life or useful life, whichever is shorter. In addition to the initial costs of obtaining a patent, legal fees incurred in the successful defense of a patent should be capitalized as part of the cost, whether it was internally developed or purchased from an inventor. The legal fees capitalized then should be amortized over the remaining useful life of the patent.
Answer (B) is incorrect because R&D costs must be expensed as incurred. Answer (C) is incorrect because R&D costs must be expensed as incurred. Answer (D) is incorrect because unsuccessful patent infringement suit costs should not be capitalized.

**36.** In accordance with generally accepted accounting principles, which of the following methods of amortization is required for amortizable intangible assets if the pattern of consumption of economic benefits is not reliably determinable?

    A. Sum-of-the-years'-digits.

    B. Straight-line.

    C. Units-of-production.

    D. Double-declining-balance.

Answer (B) is correct. *(CPA, adapted)*
    **REQUIRED:** The method of amortization of intangible assets if the pattern of consumption of economic benefits is not reliably determinable.
    **DISCUSSION:** The default method of amortization of intangible assets is the straight-line method (SFAS 142).

**37.** On June 30, year 5, Finn, Inc. exchanged 2,000 shares of Edlow Corp. $30 par value common stock for a patent owned by Bisk Co. The Edlow stock was acquired in year 1 at a cost of $50,000. At the exchange date, Edlow common stock had a fair value of $40 per share, and the patent had a net carrying amount of $100,000 on Bisk's books. Finn should record the patent at

    A. $50,000

    B. $60,000

    C. $80,000

    D. $100,000

Answer (C) is correct. *(CPA, adapted)*
    **REQUIRED:** The amount at which a patent should be recorded.
    **DISCUSSION:** When an intangible asset is acquired externally, it should be recorded at its cost at the date of acquisition. In an exchange transaction, cost is measured by the cash paid. Otherwise, the fair value of the more clearly evident of the consideration given or the asset acquired is the basis for measurement. The fair value of the assets given in return for the patent was $80,000 (2,000 shares of stock × $40 per share fair value). The $30 par value, the $25 per share ($50,000 ÷ 2,000 shares) acquisition cost, and the net carrying amount of the patent are not considered in determining fair value.
    Answer (A) is incorrect because $50,000 is the acquisition cost of the stock. Answer (B) is incorrect because $60,000 is the par value of the stock. Answer (D) is incorrect because $100,000 is the net carrying amount of the patent on the seller's books.

**38.** Which of the following costs of goodwill should be capitalized and amortized?

| | Maintaining Goodwill | Developing Goodwill |
|---|---|---|
| A. | Yes | No |
| B. | No | No |
| C. | Yes | Yes |
| D. | No | Yes |

Answer (B) is correct. *(CPA, adapted)*
    **REQUIRED:** The costs of goodwill that should be capitalized and amortized.
    **DISCUSSION:** SFAS 141, *Business Combinations*, requires that the cost of goodwill arising from a business combination be capitalized. SFAS 142 prohibits amortization of goodwill. Moreover, the cost of developing, maintaining, or restoring intangible assets (including goodwill) that are not specifically identifiable, have indeterminate useful lives, or are inherent in a continuing business and related to an enterprise as a whole should be expensed as incurred.
    Answer (A) is incorrect because costs of maintaining and developing goodwill should not be capitalized. Answer (C) is incorrect because costs of maintaining and developing goodwill should not be capitalized. Answer (D) is incorrect because costs of maintaining and developing goodwill should not be capitalized.

Questions 39 and 40 are based on the following information. In early year 1, Slash Publications conducted its annual advertising campaign wherein it sold 60,000 new one-year subscriptions to Slash Magazine. Based on similar ad campaigns during the past four years (the total extent of the company's experience with ad campaigns of this type), there is a 40% renewal rate each year. The ad campaign cost $100,000.

**39.** Based on the requirements of SOP 93-7, *Reporting on Advertising Costs*, how much of the $100,000 should be expensed during year 1?

A. $100,000

B. $38,424

C. $60,000

D. $61,576

Answer (D) is correct. *(Publisher)*
**REQUIRED:** The amount of advertising expense for the current year.
**DISCUSSION:** For its $100,000 expenditure, the company has essentially acquired the following sales (in number of subscriptions):

| | |
|---|---|
| Year 1 | 60,000 |
| Year 2 | 24,000 |
| Year 3 | 9,600 |
| Year 4 | 3,840 |
| Total | 97,440 |

Dividing the 97,440 of total sales by the 60,000 of sales applicable to the current year results in a percentage of 61.576%. Multiplying this percentage times the $100,000 expenditure results in an expense in year 1 of $61,576.
Answer (A) is incorrect because SOP 93-7 requires allocation of future advertising benefits when historical experience documents the existence of such benefits. Answer (B) is incorrect because $38,424 is the balance of the intangible asset account at the end of year 1. Answer (C) is incorrect because $60,000 is based on the non-renewal rate, rather than the total sales over four years.

**40.** Based on AICPA SOP 93-7, what is the balance of the intangible asset account, Future Advertising Benefits, on the balance sheet prepared at the end of year 2?

A. $0

B. $9,852

C. $13,793

D. $50,000

Answer (C) is correct. *(Publisher)*
**REQUIRED:** The balance of the intangible asset account at the end of year 2 after two years of amortization.
**DISCUSSION:** For its $100,000, the company acquired the following numbers of customers:

| | |
|---|---|
| Year 1 | 60,000 |
| Year 2 | 24,000 |
| Year 3 | 9,600 |
| Year 4 | 3,840 |
| Total | 97,440 |

By the end of year 2, the only customers' revenues remaining are those relating to year 3 (9,600 renewals) and year 4 (3,840 renewals), or a total of 13,440. Dividing the 13,440 by the original expectation of 97,440 results in 13.7931%. Multiplying 13.7931% times the initial $100,000 expenditure leaves $13,793 in the asset account to be amortized during the final two years of the asset's life.
Answer (A) is incorrect because AICPA SOP 93-7 requires the capitalization of advertising costs that have future benefits. Answer (B) is incorrect because $9,852 is the amount of amortization for year 3. Answer (D) is incorrect because $50,000 is based on years of life rather than units of benefit.

**41.** On September 1, year 1, for $4,000,000 cash and $2,000,000 notes payable, Norbend Corporation acquired the net assets of Crisholm Company, which had a fair value of $5,496,000 on that date. Norbend's management is of the opinion that the goodwill generated has an indefinite life. During the year-end audit for year 3 after all adjusting entries have been made, the goodwill is determined to be worthless. The amount of the write-off as of December 31, year 3 should be

A. $504,000

B. $478,800

C. $466,200

D. $474,600

Answer (A) is correct. *(CMA, adapted)*
**REQUIRED:** The goodwill write-off.
**DISCUSSION:** Given that the company paid $6,000,000 for net assets acquired with a fair value of $5,496,000, goodwill was $504,000. Under SFAS 142, *Goodwill and Other Intangible Assets*, purchased goodwill is not amortized but is tested annually for impairment.
Answer (B) is incorrect because goodwill is not amortized; however, it is tested annually for impairment. Answer (C) is incorrect because goodwill is not amortized; however, it is tested annually for impairment. Answer (D) is incorrect because goodwill is not amortized; however, it is tested annually for impairment.

**42.** During the current year, Orr Co. incurred the following costs:

| | |
|---|---|
| Research and development services performed by Key Corp. for Orr | $150,000 |
| Design, construction, and testing of preproduction prototypes and models | 200,000 |
| Testing in search for new products of process alternatives | 175,000 |

In its current year income statement, what should Orr report as research and development expense?

A. $150,000

B. $200,000

C. $350,000

D. $525,000

Answer (D) is correct. *(CPA, adapted)*
**REQUIRED:** The R&D expense.
**DISCUSSION:** Research is planned search or critical investigation aimed at discovery of new knowledge useful in developing a new product, service, process, or technique, or in bringing about a significant improvement to an existing product, etc. Development is translation of research findings or other knowledge into a plan or design for a new or improved product or process. R&D expenses include R&D performed under contract by others; design, construction, and testing of prototypes; and testing in search for new products (SFAS 2). Thus, all $525,000 should be expensed.
Answer (A) is incorrect because $150,000 does not include design, construction, and testing of preproduction prototypes or testing in search of new products. Answer (B) is incorrect because $200,000 does not include R&D performed under contract by others or testing in search for new products. Answer (C) is incorrect because $350,000 does not include testing in search for new products.

**43.** West, Inc. made the following expenditures relating to Product Y:

- Legal costs to file a patent on Product Y -- $10,000. Production of the finished product would not have been undertaken without the patent.
- Special equipment to be used solely for development of Product Y -- $60,000. The equipment has no other use and has an estimated useful life of 4 years.
- Labor and material costs incurred in producing a prototype model -- $200,000.
- Cost of testing the prototype -- $80,000.

What is the total amount of costs that will be expensed when incurred?

A. $280,000

B. $295,000

C. $340,000

D. $350,000

Answer (C) is correct. *(CPA, adapted)*
**REQUIRED:** The total amount of costs that will be expensed when incurred.
**DISCUSSION:** R&D costs are expensed as incurred. However, SFAS 2 specifically excludes legal work in connection with patent applications or litigation and the sale or licensing of patents from the definition of R&D. The legal costs of filing a patent should be capitalized. West's R&D costs include those incurred for the design, construction, and testing of preproduction prototypes. Moreover, the cost of equipment used solely for a specific project is also expensed immediately. Thus, the total amount of costs that will be expensed when incurred is $340,000.
Answer (A) is incorrect because $280,000 does not include the cost of the special equipment. Answer (B) is incorrect because $295,000 includes 1 year's straight-line depreciation on the special equipment instead of the full cost. Answer (D) is incorrect because $350,000 includes the legal costs of filing a patent.

**44.** On January 1, SOP Corp. incurred organization costs of $24,000. SOP is amortizing these costs so as to obtain the maximum allowable deduction for federal income tax purposes. For financial accounting purposes, what portion of the organization costs will SOP defer to years subsequent to the current year?

A. $23,400

B. $19,200

C. $4,800

D. $0

Answer (D) is correct. *(Publisher)*
**REQUIRED:** The deferred organization costs if amortization is the maximum allowable for tax purposes.
**DISCUSSION:** Organization costs are those incurred in the formation of a business entity. For federal income tax purposes, the minimum amortization period is 5 years. However, for financial accounting purposes, AICPA SOP 98-5 requires nongovernmental entities to expense all start-up costs and organization costs as incurred.

**45.** On December 31, year 1, Byte Co. had capitalized software costs of $600,000 with an economic life of four years. Sales for year 2 were 10% of expected total sales of the software. At December 31, year 2, the software had a net realizable value of $480,000. In its December 31, year 2 balance sheet, what amount should Byte report as net capitalized cost of computer software?

A. $432,000

B. $450,000

C. $480,000

D. $540,000

Answer (B) is correct. *(CPA, adapted)*
**REQUIRED:** The net capitalized cost of computer software at year-end.
**DISCUSSION:** SFAS 86, *Accounting for the Costs of Computer Software to Be Sold, Leased, or Otherwise Marketed*, applies to software to be "sold, leased, or otherwise marketed as a separate product or as part of a product or process." After technological feasibility has been established for a software product, all software production costs incurred until the product is available for general release to customers shall be capitalized and subsequently reported at the lower of unamortized cost or net realizable value. The amortization of capitalized software costs is determined separately for each product. The annual amortization is the greater of the amount determined using the ratio of current gross revenues to the sum of current gross revenues and anticipated future gross revenues, or the straight-line method over the remaining estimated economic life, including the current reporting period. At year-end, the unamortized cost of each software product must be compared with the net realizable value (NRV) of that software product. Any excess of unamortized cost over NRV must be written off. The amount of amortization under the straight-line method is used because it is greater than the amount determined using the 10% ratio of current sales to expected total sales. Thus, Byte Co. had an unamortized cost of software of $450,000 [$600,000 capitalized cost – ($600,000 ÷ 4)] at December 31, year 2. The $450,000 unamortized cost is lower than the $480,000 NRV, so $450,000 is the amount reported in the year-end balance sheet.
Answer (A) is incorrect because $432,000 equals the NRV at December 31, year 2 minus amortization calculated as 10% of NRV. Answer (C) is incorrect because $480,000 is the NRV at December 31, year 2. Answer (D) is incorrect because $540,000 assumes amortization at 10% with no adjustment for NRV.

**46.** Which advertising costs are most likely to be capitalized?

A. Costs of production.

B. Expenditures subsequent to recognition of related revenue.

C. Expenditures for idea development.

D. Costs of communication.

Answer (B) is correct. *(Publisher)*
**REQUIRED:** The capitalizable advertising costs.
**DISCUSSION:** AICPA SOP 93-7, *Reporting on Advertising Costs*, states that advertising costs should be expensed, either as incurred or when advertising first occurs. The primary costs are production and communication. However, direct response advertising costs should be capitalized (deferred) if the primary purpose is to elicit sales from customers who respond specifically to the advertising, and probable future economic benefits result. A second exception is for expenditures subsequent to recognition of related revenue. An example is a manufacturer's obligation to repay retailers for costs of advertising that involve the manufacturer's products. This type of cost should be accrued and expensed when related revenues are recognized.

Questions 47 and 48 are based on the following information. During 2004, Pitt Corp. incurred costs to develop and produce a routine, low-risk computer software product, as follows:

| | |
|---|---:|
| Completion of detail program design | $13,000 |
| Costs incurred for coding and testing to establish technological feasibility | 10,000 |
| Other coding costs after establishment of technological feasibility | 24,000 |
| Other testing costs after establishment of technological feasibility | 20,000 |
| Costs of producing product masters for training materials | 15,000 |
| Duplication of computer software and training materials from product masters (1,000 units) | 25,000 |
| Packaging product (500 units) | 9,000 |

**47.** In Pitt's December 31, 2004 balance sheet, what amount should be capitalized as software cost subject to amortization?

A. $54,000

B. $57,000

C. $59,000

D. $69,000

Answer (C) is correct. *(CPA, adapted)*
   **REQUIRED:** The amount capitalized as software cost subject to amortization.
   **DISCUSSION:** SFAS 86 specifies that costs incurred internally in creating a computer software product shall be charged to expense when incurred as research and development until technological feasibility has been established for the product. Thereafter, all software production costs incurred until the product is available for general release to customers shall be capitalized and subsequently reported at the lower of unamortized cost or net realizable value. Hence, the costs of completing the detail program design and establishing technological feasibility are expensed, the costs of duplicating software and training materials and packaging the product are inventoried, and the costs of coding and other testing after establishing technological feasibility and the costs of producing product masters are capitalized and amortized. The amount capitalized as software cost subject to amortization is therefore $59,000 ($24,000 + $20,000 + $15,000).
   Answer (A) is incorrect because $54,000 equals inventoriable costs plus the other testing costs. Answer (B) is incorrect because $57,000 is the sum of the costs expensed and the costs inventoried. Answer (D) is incorrect because $69,000 assumes the costs of coding and testing to establish feasibility are capitalized and amortized.

**48.** In Pitt's December 31, 2004 balance sheet, what amount should be reported in inventory?

A. $25,000

B. $34,000

C. $40,000

D. $49,000

Answer (B) is correct. *(CPA, adapted)*
   **REQUIRED:** The amount reported in inventory.
   **DISCUSSION:** Costs incurred internally in creating a computer software product shall be charged to expense when incurred as R&D until technological feasibility has been established. Thereafter, all software production costs incurred until the product is available for general release to customers shall be capitalized and amortized. The costs of duplicating the software, documentation, and training materials from the product masters and of physically packaging the product for distribution are capitalized as inventory (SFAS 86, *Accounting for the Costs of Computer Software to Be Sold, Leased, or Otherwise Marketed*). Hence, inventory should be reported at $34,000 ($25,000 duplication costs + $9,000 packaging costs).
   Answer (A) is incorrect because $25,000 excludes packaging costs. Answer (C) is incorrect because $40,000 excludes packaging costs but includes costs of producing product masters. Answer (D) is incorrect because $49,000 includes costs of producing product masters.

**49.** According to AICPA SOP 98-1, *Accounting for the Costs of Computer Software Developed or Obtained for Internal Use*, certain costs of internal-use software not qualifying as R&D costs should be capitalized in which stage(s), if any, of software development?

|   | Preliminary Project Stage | Application Development Stage | Post-Implementation/ Operation Stage |
|---|---|---|---|
| A. | Yes | Yes | Yes |
| B. | Yes | Yes | No |
| C. | No | Yes | No |
| D. | No | No | No |

Answer (C) is correct. *(Publisher)*
**REQUIRED:** The stage(s), if any, of development of internal-use software in which costs are capitalized.
**DISCUSSION:** AICPA SOP 98-1 states that certain internal and external development costs of internal-use software not qualifying as R&D costs should be expensed during the preliminary project and post-implementation/operation stages. However, they should be capitalized during the application development stage. Costs capitalizable include external direct costs of materials and services consumed, payroll and payroll-related costs for employees to the extent they spend time directly on the project, and interest costs. Furthermore, costs to develop or obtain software allowing for access or conversion of old data by a new system are also capitalized.

---

# STUDY UNIT SIXTEEN
# LIABILITIES

(28 pages of outline)

This study unit is the **sixth of ten** on **external financial reporting**. The relative weight assigned to this major topic in Part 2 of the exam is **25%** at **skill level B** (four skill types required). The ten study units are

Study Unit 11: Overview of External Financial Reporting
Study Unit 12: Overview of Financial Statements
Study Unit 13: Cash and Receivables
Study Unit 14: Inventories and Investments
Study Unit 15: Long-Lived Assets
Study Unit 16: Liabilities
Study Unit 17: Equity and Revenue Recognition
Study Unit 18: Other Income Statement Items
Study Unit 19: Business Combinations and Derivatives
Study Unit 20: SEC Requirements and the Annual Report

After studying the outlines and answering the multiple-choice questions in this study unit, you will have the skills necessary to address the following topics listed in the IMA's Learning Outcome Statements:

Part 2 – Section E.4. Recognition, measurement, valuation, and disclosure

For each of the subtopics listed, the candidate should be able to:

1. define the subtopic and describe the characteristics of its components

2. demonstrate an understanding of appropriate valuation techniques for the components of each subtopic

3. demonstrate an understanding of the appropriate accounting conventions for the components of each subtopic

4. compare and contrast valuation techniques and accounting methods

5. show the correct financial statement presentation

6. identify the appropriate disclosure requirements in the body of the financial statements and/or in the footnotes

Current liabilities

   a. subtopic components: current liability: notes payable, current maturities of long-term debt, short-term obligations expected to be refinanced, dividends payable, returnable deposits, unearned (or deferred) revenues, taxes payable, and employee-related liabilities; loss contingencies; warranty costs; premiums and coupons

   b. identify the classification issues of short-term debt expected to be refinanced

   c. identify the different types of employee-related liabilities

   d. apply both the expense warranty approach and the sales warranty approach

Long-term liabilities and bonds payable

a.   subtopic components:  long-term liabilities/debt:  bonds, long-term notes payable, mortgage notes payable, zero-interest-bearing notes, convertible debt

b.   calculate interest expense, interest payable, bond discount and premium using the straight-line method and the effective interest method (time value of money tables)

c.   identify the proper classification of bond discount and premium as an adjunct account

d.   define implicit interest rate and imputed interest

e.   account for notes issued for property, goods, and services

f.   calculate imputed fair value and note discount where the stated interest rate is unreasonable

g.   define off-balance sheet financing and identify different forms of this type of borrowing

h.   indicate the disclosure requirements for off-balance sheet financing

Inventories

g.   identify accounting issues related to purchase commitments

Part 2 – Section E.1. Objectives of external financial reporting; and E.2. Financial accounting fundamentals

NOTE:  Statements a. through e. are covered in Study Unit 11.

f.   special topics:  leases, pensions and other postretirement benefits, deferred income taxes

For each special topic, the candidate should be able to:

1.   define and describe its characteristics
2.   demonstrate a basic understanding of the relevant accounting issues
3.   describe the impact on a firm's financial statements

## 16.1 CURRENT LIABILITIES

1.   **Accounts payable**, commonly termed trade accounts payable, are liabilities; that is, they are probable future sacrifices of economic benefits arising from current obligations to transfer assets or to provide services in the future as a result of past transactions and events.  Accounts payable reflect the obligations to sellers that are incurred when an entity purchases inventory, supplies, or services on credit.

a.   Accounts payable should be recorded at their **settlement value**.

b.   Short-term liabilities, such as accounts payable, do not usually provide for a periodic payment of interest unless the accounts are not settled when due or payable.

1)   They also are usually not secured by collateral.

c.   Accounts payable are **current liabilities**.  They are reported before noncurrent liabilities in the balance sheet.

1)   **ARB 43, Chapter 3A**, *Current Assets and Current Liabilities*, defines a current liability as an obligation that will be either liquidated using current assets or replaced by another current liability.  All other liabilities are classified as noncurrent.

d.   **Purchases** and related accounts payable may be recorded using the gross method or the net method.

1)   The **gross method** records purchases and accounts payable without regard to purchase discounts available, for example, cash discounts for early payment.

a)   In a periodic system, purchase discounts taken are credited to a contra purchases account and closed to cost of goods sold.  In a perpetual system, they are credited to inventory.

2) The **net method** records purchases and accounts payable at the cash (discounted) price.

    a) The advantage of the net method is that it isolates purchase discounts lost, which are treated as financing charges.

e. The timing of recognition of accounts payable may depend on the **shipping terms**.

1) When goods are shipped **FOB shipping point**, title and risk of loss pass to the buyer at the time and place of shipment. Thus, the buyer records inventory and a payable at the time of shipment.

2) When goods are shipped **FOB destination**, title and risk of loss do not pass until the goods are duly tendered to the buyer at the destination. Hence, the buyer does not record inventory and a payable until that time.

2. A **note payable** is a debt evidenced by a two-party writing, i.e., a **promissory note**, and thus follows the laws concerning negotiable instruments.

a. A negotiable instrument must be in writing, signed by the maker (the promisor), and contain an unconditional promise to pay a sum certain to the payee at a definite time.

1) Notes stand in contrast to accounts payable, which are more informal promises to pay.

2) Notes with maturities of **three months or less** are generally classified as **short-term liabilities**.

    a) Short-term notes are usually recorded at **face value less allowances**, i.e., because the interest implicit in the maturity amount is immaterial, no interest expense is recognized.

3) Notes with maturities **longer than three months** are considered **long-term** and the debtor must recognize an **interest component** of expense (see item 3. under subunit 16.2).

3. **Current Maturities of Long-Term Debt**

a. Because current liabilities are defined as those that will be paid in the coming year or current operating cycle, any serial payments on long-term debt should be classified as current liabilities if they are to be paid in the coming year out of current resources.

b. If a sinking fund exists for purposes of making payment, the debt is classified as long term because it will not require the use of current resources.

4. **Refinancing**

a. **SFAS 6**, *Classification of Short-term Obligations Expected to Be Refinanced*, states that, if an enterprise intends to refinance short-term obligations on a long-term basis and demonstrates an ability to consummate the refinancing, the obligation should be excluded from current liabilities and classified as noncurrent.

1) The ability to consummate the refinancing may be demonstrated by a post-balance-sheet-date issuance of a long-term obligation or equity securities or by entering into a financing agreement that meets the following criteria:

    a) The agreement does not expire within the longer of 1 year or the operating cycle.

    b) It is noncancelable by the lender.

    c) No violation of the agreement exists at the balance sheet date.

    d) The lender is financially capable of honoring the agreement.

2) The amount of the short-term liability that is reclassified as a long-term liability should not exceed the amount available for refinancing.

b. **SFAS 78**, *Classification of Obligations That Are Callable by the Creditor*, states that long-term obligations callable because of the debtor's violation of the debt agreement at the balance sheet date are current liabilities.

    1) These obligations need not be classified as current if it is probable that a violation will be cured within a specified grace period.

        a) If the creditor formally waives the right to demand repayment for a period of more than a year from the balance sheet date, the debt need not be classified as current.

        b) The provisions of this statement also apply to debts that by their terms are callable within the year (or normal operating cycle, if longer).

    2) Reclassification is not required if the debtor expects and has the ability to refinance the obligation on a long-term basis.

5. **Dividends payable** become a liability once the dividends have been declared by the board of directors. The entry to record the declaration of a dividend is to debit retained earnings and credit dividends payable.

6. **Deposits and Other Advances**

    a. A deposit or other advance is a liability because it involves a probable future sacrifice of economic benefits arising from a current obligation of a particular entity to transfer assets or provide services to another entity in the future as a result of a past transaction (SFAC 6).

    b. An issue is whether deposits/advances are classified as current or noncurrent liabilities. They are current liabilities if they will be liquidated using current assets or be replaced by another current liability.

7. **Deferred Revenues**

    a. If the recognition criteria are not met, **amounts received in advance** are treated as liabilities (deferred revenues). Recognition is deferred until the obligation underlying the liability is partly or wholly satisfied.

    1) Cash received in advance may initially be created to a deferred revenue (liability) account. At the end of the accounting period, earned revenue is recognized with the following adjusting entry:

| | | |
|---|---|---|
| Deferred revenue | $XXX | |
|     Revenue | | $XXX |

        a) A reversing entry is not appropriate if advance receipts are initially credited to deferred revenue **(a permanent or real account).**

    2) If cash received in advance is initially credited to a revenue account, an adjusting entry is needed to credit a deferred revenue (liability) account for unearned amounts.

| | | |
|---|---|---|
| Revenue | $XXX | |
|     Deferred revenue | | $XXX |

        a) If this entry is reversed at the beginning of the next period, no entry will be needed to recognize revenue. This procedure keeps unearned revenue in the revenue account **(a temporary or nominal account)** except at the end of the period when statements are prepared.

8. **Taxes Payable**

    a. Accounting for deferred income taxes is explained in subunit 16.5.

    b. **Federal unemployment tax** and the **employer's share of FICA taxes** are expenses incurred as employees earn wages, but they are paid only on a periodic basis to the federal government. Accordingly, liabilities also should be accrued for both expenses, as well as for wages earned but not paid.

        1) **Income taxes withheld** and the **employee's share of FICA taxes** are accrued as withholding taxes (employee payroll deductions) and not as employer payroll taxes.

    c. **Property taxes** are usually expensed by monthly accrual over the fiscal period of the taxing authority.

    d. **Sales taxes** are levied on certain types of merchandise by most states.

        1) Ordinarily, the tax is paid by the customer purchasing the merchandise and is collected and remitted by the seller.

        2) Most states require quarterly or monthly filing of sales tax returns and remittance of taxes collected.

9. **Employee-related Liabilities**

    a. **SFAS 43**, *Accounting for Compensated Absences*, applies to employees' rights to receive compensation for future absences, such as vacations, sick leave, and holidays. It requires a liability accrual when four criteria are met:

        1) The payment of compensation is probable.
        2) The amount can be reasonably estimated.

            a) Otherwise, disclosure, but not recognition, is necessary.

        3) The benefits either vest or accumulate.

            a) Benefits vest if they are not contingent on future service.
            b) Sick pay benefits are accrued only if they vest.
            c) Benefits accumulate as earned, but unused rights may be carried forward to subsequent periods.

        4) The compensation relates to employees' services already rendered.

    b. **SFAS 112**, *Employers' Accounting for Postemployment Benefits*, applies the criteria in SFAS 43 to all postemployment benefits except those provided by pensions, postretirement benefit plans, certain deferred compensation arrangements, special or contractual termination agreements, and stock compensation plans.

        1) These benefits include, but are not limited to, salary continuation, supplemental unemployment benefits, severance benefits, disability-related benefits (including workers' compensation), job training and counseling, and continuation of benefits such as health care and life insurance coverage.

        2) If postemployment (and preretirement) benefits within the scope of SFAS 112 do not meet the criteria in SFAS 43, they are accounted for as **contingencies**.

10. **Loss contingencies**

    a. **SFAS 5**, *Accounting for Contingencies*, requires that a contingent loss be accrued (debit loss, credit liability or asset valuation allowance) when, based on information available prior to the issuance of the financial statements, two conditions are met: (1) It is **probable** that at a balance sheet date an asset has been impaired or a liability has been incurred, and (2) the amount of the loss can be **reasonably estimated**.

        1) If the loss is probable and can be reasonably estimated, it should be accrued if the amount is material.

        2) When the **reasonable estimate of loss is a range** and no amount within that range appears to be a better estimate than any other, the minimum of the range should be accrued.

        3) To prevent the financial statements from being misleading, **disclosure** of the nature of the accrual and, in some cases, the amount or the range of loss may be required.

b.  If both conditions are not met but the probability of the loss is at least **reasonably possible**, the nature of the contingency must be disclosed.

   1)  Also, an estimate of the loss or range of loss must be disclosed, or a statement must be included indicating that an estimate cannot be made.

   2)  An accrued loss and a loss that is disclosed but not accrued may arise from the same situation.

c.  Normally, loss contingencies are not disclosed if the probability of occurrence is **remote**.

   1)  For a debt guarantee, however, SFAS 5 requires that disclosure be made of a remote loss contingency.

      a)  This disclosure is required whether the guarantee is direct or indirect.

      b)  The essence of a guarantee is a **noncontingent obligation** to be ready to perform after the occurrence of a triggering event or condition. It is coupled with a **contingent obligation** to make payments if such an event or condition occurs. Thus, recognition of a liability at the inception of a guarantee is required even when it is not probable that payments will be made.

         i)   The **initial measurement**, the noncontingent obligation, ordinarily is at **fair value**. If a contingent loss and liability are also required to be recognized under SFAS 5, the liability recognized by the guarantor is the greater of the fair value measurement or the contingent liability amount.

         ii)  **Examples** are a standalone guarantee given for a premium (debit cash or a receivable), a standalone guarantee to an unrelated party without consideration (debit expense), or an operating lessee's guarantee of residual value (debit prepaid rent).

         iii) Many **disclosures** are required, such as the terms of the guarantee, how it arose, the triggering events, and maximum payments.

   2)  **Other remote loss contingencies** that should be disclosed are obligations of commercial banks under standby letters of credit and guarantees to repurchase receivables (or the related property) that were sold or assigned.

   3)  **General or unspecified business risks**, for example, those related to national and international economic conditions, require neither accrual nor disclosure.

d.  SFAS 5 also mentions the following possible loss contingencies:

   1)  Collectibility of receivables
   2)  Obligations related to product warranties or defects
   3)  Risk of loss from catastrophes
   4)  Threats of expropriation by a foreign government
   5)  Pending or threatened litigation
   6)  Actual or possible claims and assessments

e.  **Gain contingencies** should not be recognized until they are realized. For example, an award of damages in a lawsuit is not deemed to be realized if it is being appealed.

   1)  A gain contingency should be disclosed, but care should be taken to avoid misleading implications as to the likelihood of realization.

11. **Warranties**

a.  A warranty is a written guarantee of the integrity of a product or service and an undertaking by the seller to repair or replace a product, refund all or part of the price, or provide additional service. It is customarily offered for a limited time, such as 90 days.

    b.  If incurrence of warranty expense is probable, the amount can be reasonably estimated, and the amount is material, accrual accounting methods should be used.

        1)  Under the **expense warranty approach**, the total estimated warranty cost is debited to operating expense and credited to a liability in the year of sale.

            a)  This method is generally accepted when the warranty is not separable and is treated as a loss contingency.

        2)  The **sales warranty approach** is appropriate when the warranty and the product are separate, for example, when an extended warranty is sold in addition to the regular warranty.

            a)  Under this method, the warranty revenue is deferred and amortized over the term of the contract, usually on the straight-line basis. Any costs directly related to the contract, such as commissions, are also deferred and amortized.

## 12. Premiums and Coupons

    a.  Many sellers include box tops, stamps, rebates, coupons, special labels, etc., with merchandise that can be redeemed for premiums (cash or goods). The purpose is to increase sales.

    b.  In accordance with the principle of associating cause and effect (matching as defined in SFAC 6), the expense involved in making premium offers should be recognized in the same period as the related revenue.

        1)  Moreover, the premiums must be purchased and recorded as inventory, the expense of redemptions must be debited, and a liability for estimated redemptions must be credited at the end of the accounting period.

13.  Stop and review! You have completed the outline for this subunit. Study multiple-choice questions 1 through 23 beginning on page 614.

## 16.2 LONG-TERM LIABILITIES

### 1. Types of Bond Liabilities

    a.  A **bond** is a formal contractual agreement to pay an amount of money (face amount) at the maturity date plus interest at the stated rate at specific intervals. All of the terms of the agreement are stated in a document called an indenture.

    b.  Bonds may be classified as follows:

        1)  Securitization

            a)  **Mortgage bonds** are backed by specific assets, usually real estate.

            b)  **Debentures** are backed by the borrower's general credit but not by specific collateral.

            c)  **Collateral trust bonds** are backed by specific securities.

            d)  **Guaranty bonds** are guaranteed by a third party, e.g., the parent of the subsidiary that issued the bonds.

        2)  Maturity pattern

            a)  A **term bond** has a single maturity date at the end of its term.

            b)  A **serial bond** matures in stated amounts at regular intervals.

        3)  Ownership

            a)  **Registered bonds** are issued in the name of the owner. Interest payments are sent directly to the owner. When the owner sells registered bonds, the bond certificates must be surrendered and new certificates issued.

b) **Bearer bonds**, also called coupon bonds, are bearer instruments. Whoever presents the periodic interest coupons is entitled to payment.

4) Priority

a) **Subordinated debentures** and **second mortgage bonds** are junior securities with claims inferior to those of senior bonds.

5) Repayment provisions

a) **Income bonds** pay interest contingent on the debtor's profitability.

b) Some bond indentures require the issuer to establish a **sinking fund** (a long-term investment) to set aside assets for the repayment of interest and principal. The amounts transferred plus the revenue earned on the investments provide the necessary funds.

c) **Revenue bonds** are issued by governmental units and are payable from specific revenue sources.

d) **Participating bonds** share in excess earnings of the debtor as defined in the bond indenture.

6) Valuation

a) **Variable rate bonds** pay interest that is dependent on market conditions.

b) **Zero-coupon** or **deep-discount bonds** are noninterest-bearing. Because they are sold at less than their face amount, an interest rate is imputed.

c) **Commodity-backed bonds** are payable at prices related to a commodity such as gold.

7) Redemption provisions

a) **Callable bonds** may be repurchased by the issuer before maturity.

b) **Redeemable bonds** may be presented for payment by the creditor prior to the maturity date. The bonds usually are redeemable only after a specified period.

c) **Convertible bonds** may be converted into equity securities of the issuer at the option of the holder (buyer) under the conditions specified in the bond indenture.

2. **Issue of Bonds at a Premium or Discount**

a. The **proceeds received** from the sale of a bond equal the sum of the **present value** of the face amount and the present value of the interest payments (if the bond is interest-bearing).

b. When the **proceeds differ from the face amount**, the difference is a discount or premium.

1) Bonds are sold at a **premium** when the contract (stated) rate exceeds the market (effective) interest rate. The entry is

| | | |
|---|---|---|
| Cash | $XXX | |
| Premium on bonds payable | | $XXX |
| Bonds payable | | XXX |

2) Bonds are sold at a **discount** when the contract (stated) interest rate is less than the market (effective) interest rate. The entry is

| | | |
|---|---|---|
| Cash | $XXX | |
| Discount on bonds payable | XXX | |
| Bonds payable | | $XXX |

3) Whenever bonds are sold at a discount or premium, **APB 21**, *Interest on Receivables and Payables*, requires that the discount or premium be amortized using the **effective interest method**, also known as the **interest method** (unless the results of another method are not materially different).

   a) Under the interest method, interest expense changes every period, but the interest rate is constant.

   b) For a comprehensive illustration of the interest method, see item 3.d. under subunit 13.3.

c. When bonds are issued between interest payment dates, the buyer includes **accrued interest** in the purchase price.

d. **Interest expense** for a period is equal to the **carrying amount** of the bonds at the beginning of the period (face amount – unamortized discount or + unamortized premium) times the yield (market) interest rate.

   1) The **cash paid** for periodic interest is equal to the face amount of the bonds times the stated rate. It remains constant over the life of the bonds.

   2) The difference between interest expense and cash interest paid is the discount or premium **amortization**.

   3) Discount amortized, total interest expense, and the carrying amount of the bonds **increase** each period when amortizing a **discount**. The journal entry is

   | | | |
   |---|---|---|
   | Interest expense | $XXX | |
   | Discount on bonds payable | | $XXX |
   | Cash | | XXX |

   4) Premium amortized, total interest expense, and the carrying amount of the bonds **decrease** each period when amortizing a **premium**. The journal entry is

   | | | |
   |---|---|---|
   | Interest expense | $XXX | |
   | Premium on bonds payable | XXX | |
   | Cash | | $XXX |

e. At the **maturity date**, the discount or premium will be **fully amortized** to zero, and the net carrying amount of the bonds will equal the face amount.

f. Bond discount or premium appear as a direct subtraction from or addition to the face amount of the bonds payable in the **balance sheet** (APB 21).

3. **Long-term Notes Payable**

   a. **Notes payable** are essentially the same as bonds, except that a note is payable to a single creditor, whereas bonds are payable to thousands of creditors. In practice, notes are usually of shorter duration than bonds.

      1) Long-term notes, such as **mortgage notes**, that are payable in installments should be partially classified as a current liability to the extent of any payments due in the coming year. Those payments not due in the current year are classified as the long-term portion of the debt.

   b. The same provisions of APB 21 concerning the recognition of an interest component that apply to bonds payable (see item 2. on page 594) apply to notes payable.

      1) EXAMPLE: A company agrees to give, in return for merchandise, a 3-year, $100,000 note bearing 8% interest paid annually. The company's effective interest rate is 6%. Since the note's stated rate exceeds the effective rate, the note will be issued at a premium.

a)  The company records the note at its present value, which consists of a single payment of $100,000 in three years and 3 payments of interest of $8,000 each. These payment streams are discounted at the company's effective rate (five decimal places are used for increased accuracy).

| | |
|---|---:|
| Present value of principal ($100,000 × 0.83962) | $ 83,962 |
| Present value of interest ($8,000 × 2.67301) | 21,384 |
| Present value of note | $105,346 |

b)  The entry to record the note is thus

| | | |
|---|---:|---:|
| Inventory | $105,346 | |
|     Premium on note payable | | $ 5,346 |
|     Note payable | | 100,000 |

2)  Discount or premium, loan origination fees, etc., are amortized in accordance with the effective-interest method to arrive at a periodic interest expense that reflects a constant rate of interest when applied to the beginning balance.

3)  Discount or premium is not an asset or liability separable from the related note. A discount or premium is therefore reported in the balance sheet as a direct deduction from, or addition to, the face amount of the note (APB 21).

c.  **Noninterest-bearing notes.** A note may bear no explicit interest because interest is **implicit** in the maturity amount.

1)  The note's present value is determined using the lender's effective rate.

a)  If the present value of the note exceeds the fair value of the goods being received, a premium results and the entry is

| | | |
|---|---:|---:|
| Inventory | $XXX | |
|     Premium on notes payable | | $XXX |
|     Notes payable | | XXX |

i)  As the premium is amortized, the debit is to notes payable.

b)  If the fair value of the goods being received exceeds the present value of the note, a discount results and the entry is

| | | |
|---|---:|---:|
| Inventory | $XXX | |
| Discount on note payable | XXX | |
|     Notes payable | | $XXX |

i)  As the discount is amortized, the credit is to interest expense.

2)  Sometimes when a note is exchanged, the fair value of the goods cannot be readily determined and there is no secondary market for the note to aid in establishing its value.

a)  In these cases, an interest rate must be **imputed**. APB 21 requires the borrower's incremental rate to be used as a benchmark.

4.  **Conversion of Bonds**

a.  **APB 14**, *Convertible Debt and Debt Issued with Stock Purchase Warrants*, states that the debt and equity aspects of the convertible debt are inseparable. APB 14 states that all proceeds (usually cash) should be accounted for as debt (a liability) until conversion.

1)  The bond issue price (fair value) is affected, however, by the conversion feature.

b. Under the **book-value method** for recognizing the conversion of outstanding bonds payable to common stock, the stock issued is recorded at the carrying amount of the bonds (credit common stock and additional paid-in capital, debit the payable) at the time of issuance, with no recognition of gain or loss. This method is the most common and is generally accepted.

    1) Under the **market-value method**, the stock is recorded at the market value of the stock (or of the bonds). A gain or loss is recognized equal to the difference between the market value recorded and the carrying value of the bonds payable.

c. The carrying amount is based on all related accounts. Thus, the balances of unamortized bond premium or discount, unamortized issue costs, and the conversion costs should be considered adjustments of the net carrying amount at the time of conversion.

    1) Consequently, these items should be reflected as adjustments of the additional paid-in capital account.

d. According to **SFAS 84**, *Induced Conversions of Convertible Debt*, an issuer of a convertible security may attempt to induce prompt conversion of its convertible debt to equity securities by offering additional securities or other consideration as a sweetener.

    1) The additional consideration used to induce conversion should be reported as an ordinary expense. The amount equals the fair value of the securities or other consideration transferred in excess of the fair value of the securities that would have been issued under the original conversion privilege.

e. The treatment of gains or losses from early extinguishment of convertible debt is the same as for the retirement of ordinary debt.

5. **Purchase Commitments**

a. **SFAS 47**, *Disclosure of Long-Term Obligations*, requires disclosure of commitments **under unconditional purchase obligations** associated with suppliers.

    1) Such obligations are commitments to transfer funds in the future for fixed or minimum amounts of goods or services at fixed or minimum prices.

    2) SFAS 47 applies to an unconditional purchase obligation that

        a) Was negotiated as part of the financing arrangement for facilities that will provide contracted goods or services.

        b) Has a remaining term of more than 1 year.

        c) Is either noncancelable or cancelable only under terms that make continuation or replacement (but not cancelation) of the agreement reasonably assured.

            i) A purchase obligation cancelable upon the payment of a nominal penalty is not unconditional.

b. **Disclosure** of the following information is required for **recorded obligations** for each of the 5 years following the date of the latest balance sheet presented:

    1) The aggregate amount of payments for unconditional purchase obligations

    2) The aggregate amount of maturities and sinking-fund requirements for all long-term borrowings

c. If an unconditional purchase obligation is **not recorded**, certain **disclosures** are required. They include the following:

    1) The nature and term of the obligation

    2) The variable components of the obligation

3) The amounts purchased under the obligation for each period an income statement is presented

4) Amount of the fixed and determinable portion of the obligation at the latest balance sheet date and, if determinable, for each of the 5 succeeding fiscal years

d. When an unconditional purchase obligation is not recorded, SFAS 47 encourages, but does not require, the disclosure of the amount of **imputed interest** necessary to reduce the unconditional purchase obligation to its present value.

1) If known by the purchaser, the rate should be the initial effective interest rate of the debt that financed the facilities providing the contracted goods or services.

a) If the rate cannot be determined by the purchaser, the purchaser's incremental borrowing rate should be used.

6. **Off-balance-sheet financing**

a. It is to a company's advantage to improve its ratios by removing debt from the balance sheet. **Special purpose entities (SPEs)** are created to accomplish this goal.

1) For example, when a company wishes to construct a factory, large amounts of new debt must be taken on. A special purpose entity can be established solely to build and operate the new plant while absorbing the debt incurred during construction.

a) Once the plant is complete, the company will often establish a **take-or-pay** contract with the SPE. Under a take-or-pay arrangement, the company agrees to either buy all the output of the factory or to make guaranteed payments.

b) This way, the financial solvency of the SPE is assured and the company has acquired a steady source of supply without taking on a large debt burden.

b. In response to the accounting scandals involving abuse of off-balance-sheet arrangements, the FASB released **Interpretation No. 46 (revised December 2003)**, *Consolidation of Variable Interest Entities – an interpretation of ARB 51.*

1) **A variable interest entity (VIE)** is an off-balance-sheet arrangement that may take any legal form (e.g., corporation, partnership, limited liability company, or trust).

2) Variable interests are ownership, contractual, or monetary interests that vary with changes in the **fair value of the VIE's net assets** (excluding variable interests).

a) Examples are equity investments in a VIE that are at risk, subordinated debt or beneficial interests issued by the VIE, and guarantees of the VIE's assets or liabilities.

3) The **primary beneficiary (PB)** consolidates a VIE. An enterprise determines whether it is the PB when it **becomes involved** with the VIE.

a) The PB is an entity with variable interests that absorb a majority of the expected losses or receive a majority of the expected residual returns of the VIE. If different enterprises qualify under this criterion, the one that absorbs the majority of the expected losses is the PB.

b) **Reconsideration** of the decision to consolidate is indicated when, for example, expected losses or residual returns have been reallocated among the PB and unrelated parties, the PB disposes of its variable interests to unrelated parties, or the VIE issues new variable interests.

    c.    An entity must be consolidated as a VIE if, **by design**, any of three conditions exists.

        1)    The VIE is not properly capitalized, i.e., its **equity investment at risk** is insufficient to finance its operations without additional **subordinated financial support** from any parties.

            a)    Equity at risk equal to **less than 10%** of the VIE's total assets is rebuttably presumed to be insufficient. However, an entity may require equity at risk exceeding 10% of total assets to finance operations, e.g., if it faces high risk. Thus, the sufficiency threshold may exceed 10%.

        2)    As a group, the holders of equity at risk **lack** any one of the following characteristics of a **controlling financial interest**:

            a)    The ability based on voting or similar rights to make decisions significantly affecting the VIE's success,

            b)    An obligation to absorb expected losses, or

            c)    The right to receive expected residual returns.

        3)    Equity investors as a group lack the **voting rights** characteristic if

            a)    Voting rights of some investors are disproportionate to their obligations to absorb expected losses or their rights to receive expected returns of the VIE, and

            b)    Substantially all of the VIE's activities involve or are performed for an investor with disproportionately few voting rights.

    d.    Many traditional transactions have off-balance-sheet effects, for example,

        1)    Transfers of receivables with recourse accounted for as sales (see subunit 13.2)
        2)    Loss contingencies (see item 10. under subunit 16.1)
        3)    Unconditional purchase obligations (see item 5. under subunit 16.2)
        4)    Operating leases (see item 5. under subunit 16.3)
        5)    Deferred compensation arrangements (see subunit 16.4)

    e.    Many accounting pronouncements require **disclosures** about off-balance-sheet risk. Although a comprehensive listing is beyond the scope of this text, some of these disclosure provisions are included in the relevant study units.

7.    Stop and review! You have completed the outline for this subunit. Study multiple-choice questions 24 through 44 beginning on page 622.

## 16.3 LEASES

1.    **Definition**

    a.    A lease is an agreement whereby a **lessor (owner)** conveys the right to use specific property for a stated period to a **lessee** in exchange for a stated payment.

    b.    **SFAS 13**, *Accounting for Leases*, governs the accounting treatment, which is based on the **economic substance of the transaction**.

        1)    A lease may be, in effect, a financing agreement in which the lessor finances the purchase.

        2)    A lease may also be, in effect, a rental agreement.

2.    **Lessee's Accounting for Capital Leases**

    a.    A lessee classifies leases as capital leases or operating leases.

    b.    A **capital lease** transfers substantially all of the benefits and risks of ownership of the property.

        1)    It should be accounted for as the acquisition of an asset and the incurrence of an obligation by the lessee. The lessee then depreciates the asset and allocates the minimum lease payments between interest and reduction of the liability.

    2)    Each of the four criteria listed in SFAS 13 indicates that substantially all of the benefits and risks of ownership have been transferred.  A lease is classified as a capital lease by a lessee if, **at its inception**, any one of four criteria is satisfied:

        a)    The lease provides for the **transfer of ownership** of the leased property.

        b)    The lease contains a **bargain purchase option**.

        c)    The lease term is 75% or more of the **estimated economic life** of the leased property.

            i)    However, this criterion is inapplicable if the beginning of the lease term falls within the last 25% of the total estimated economic life.

        d)    The present value of the minimum lease payments (excluding executory costs) is at least 90% of the **fair value of the leased property**.

            i)    This criterion also is inapplicable if the beginning of the lease term falls within the last 25% of the total estimated economic life.

**3.    Lessee's Minimum Lease Payments**

    a.    Given a bargain purchase option, minimum lease payments have two components:  (1) minimum rental payments (excluding executory costs) and (2) the amount of the bargain purchase option.

        1)    If no bargain purchase option exists, minimum lease payments equal the sum of (a) the minimum rental payments, (b) the amount of residual value guaranteed by the lessee, and (c) any nonrenewal penalty imposed.

    b.    **Minimum rental payments** are the periodic amounts owed by the lessee, minus any amounts representing **executory costs** that will be borne by the lessor (insurance, maintenance, taxes, etc.).

    c.    The **residual value** is generally the estimated fair value of the leased property upon expiration of the lease.

        1)    All or part of this amount may be guaranteed by the lessee (or by an unrelated third party).  **FASB Interpretation No. 19**, *Lessee Guarantee of the Residual Value of Leased Property*, states that the amount of **guaranteed residual value** to be included in the determination of the lessee's minimum lease payments is the maximum deficiency the lessee is required to make good.

    d.    A **nonrenewal penalty** is "any payment that the lessee must make or can be required to make upon failure to renew or extend the lease at the expiration of the lease term, whether or not the payment would constitute a purchase of the leased property" (SFAS 13).

    e.    A **bargain purchase option** gives the lessee the right to purchase the leased property for a price sufficiently lower than its expected fair value at the exercise date that exercise "appears, at the inception of the lease, to be reasonably assured."

    f.    Future minimum lease payments as of the latest balance sheet presented must be **disclosed** in the aggregate and for **each of the 5 succeeding fiscal years**. This disclosure is required whether the lease is a capital or an operating lease.

**4.    Lessor's Accounting for Capital Leases**

    a.    Lessors also classify most leases as operating or capital leases using the capitalization criteria.

        1)    In addition, the lessor may not treat the lease as a capital lease unless **collectibility** of the remaining payments is reasonably predictable, and no material **uncertainties** exist regarding unreimbursable costs to be incurred by the lessor.

2) Lessors must then determine whether a capital lease is a direct financing or sales-type lease.

b. In a **direct financing lease**, the lessor does not recognize a manufacturer's or dealer's profit (loss).

1) The fair value of the leased property and its cost or carrying amount are the same at the inception of the lease.

a) The difference between the **gross investment** (minimum lease payments + unguaranteed residual value) and the cost or carrying amount is recorded as **unearned income**.

c. In a **sales-type lease**, the lessor recognizes **manufacturer's or dealer's profit (loss)**.

1) The fair value of the leased property at the lease's inception differs from its cost or carrying amount.

2) In the entry for a sales-type lease, the **asset** is credited for its cost or carrying amount.

a) **Cost of goods sold** is debited for the cost or carrying amount, plus any initial direct costs, minus the present value of any unguaranteed residual value (a continuing investment of the lessor).

b) **Lease payments receivable** is debited for the gross investment.

c) **Sales revenue** (price) is credited for the present value of the minimum lease payments.

d) **Unearned income** is credited for the difference between the gross investment (lease payments receivable) and the sum of the present values of its components discounted at the rate implicit in the lease.

e) The unearned income is amortized to income over the lease term using the **interest method** so as to produce a constant rate of return on the net investment. In the case of a sales-type lease, it equals the gross investment minus unearned income.

d. The following are the basic entries:

| Direct Financing Lease | | | Sales-Type Lease | | |
|---|---|---|---|---|---|
| Lease payments receivable | $XXX | | Cost of goods sold | $XXX | |
| Asset | | $XXX | Lease payments receivable | XXX | |
| Unearned income | | XXX | Sales revenue | | $XXX |
| | | | Unearned income | | XXX |
| | | | Asset | | XXX |

5. **Operating Leases**

a. Operating leases do not meet the criteria for capitalization.

1) They are transactions in which lessees rent the right to use lessor assets without acquiring a substantial portion of the benefits and risks of ownership of those assets.

2) Thus, a lessee does not record an asset and an obligation, and a lessor does not record a sale or financing, for an operating lease.

b. **Rent** is reported as income by the lessor or expense by the lessee in accordance with the lease agreement.

1) An accrual of rent expense is at settlement value, not present value. However, if rentals vary from a straight-line basis, the **straight-line basis** should be used unless another systematic and rational basis is more representative of the time pattern in which the use benefit from the property is reduced.

    c.    The lessor should report the leased property near property, plant, and equipment in the balance sheet and should depreciate the property according to its normal depreciation policy for owned assets.

        1)    Initial direct costs should be deferred and amortized by the lessor over the lease term in proportion to the recognition of rental income.

    6.    Stop and review! You have completed the outline for this subunit. Study multiple-choice questions 45 through 62 beginning on page 629.

## 16.4 PENSIONS AND OTHER POSTRETIREMENT BENEFITS

    1.    **SFAS 87**, *Employers' Accounting for Pensions*

        a.    SFAS 87 applies to any arrangement that is similar in substance to a pension plan, regardless of form, the method of financing, or whether the plan is written or implied by the well-defined practice of paying postretirement benefits.

            1)    A **defined benefit pension plan** specifies the future benefits to the retiree. Benefits are usually based on some combination of years of experience and salary level during the working years.

            2)    A **defined contribution plan** provides benefits in exchange for services, provides an account for each participant, and specifies how contributions are to be determined. Pension benefits depend only on contributions, returns on investment, and allocated forfeitures of other participants' benefits. Thus, employees have the benefit of gain and the risk of loss.

            3)    A **funded** pension plan is one that is supported by a separate fund created by the employer for the purpose of paying future pension benefits.

            4)    **Vesting** refers to the eligibility of an employee to receive pension benefits. An employee is fully vested when the right to receive benefits is no longer contingent upon future service. Some companies require employees to be employed for a year or more before they become vested.

            5)    A **qualified plan** meets the criteria for favorable tax treatment under the Internal Revenue Code.

        b.    SFAS 87 is based on the fundamental assumption that a **defined benefit pension plan** is part of an employee's compensation incurred when the services provided to the employer by the employee are rendered.

            1)    The defined pension benefit is provided in the form of deferred payments that are not precisely determinable.

                a)    These payments can only be estimated based on the plan benefit formula and relevant future events such as future compensation levels, mortality rates, ages at retirement, and vesting considerations.

        c.    SFAS 87 permits the delayed recognition of certain events, the reporting of a net cost, and the offsetting of assets and liabilities.

            1)    **Delayed recognition** means that certain changes in the pension obligation and in the value of the plan assets are not recognized as they occur. They are recognized on a systematic and gradual basis over subsequent periods.

            2)    **Net costing** means that various pension costs (service cost, interest, actuarial gains and losses, etc.) reflected in income are reported as one expense.

            3)    **Offsetting** means that the recognized values of the plan assets contributed to the plan are offset in the statement of financial position against the recognized liabilities.

d.　The **projected benefit obligation (PBO)** as of a date is equal to the actuarial present value of all benefits attributed by the pension benefit formula to employee services rendered prior to that date. The PBO is measured using assumptions as to future as well as past and current salary levels.

　　1)　The PBO at the end of a period is calculated as follows:

| | |
|---|---|
| Beginning PBO | $XXX |
| + Current service cost | XXX |
| + Prior service cost (retroactive benefits) | XXX |
| − Benefits paid | (XXX) |
| +/− Changes in assumption | XXX |
| Ending PBO | $XXX |

　　2)　The **accumulated benefit obligation (ABO)** is the present value of benefits accrued to date based on past and current compensation levels.

　　3)　Assumptions about discount (interest) rates must be made to calculate the PBO and the ABO.

　　　　a)　They reflect the rates at which benefits can be settled. In estimating these rates, it is appropriate to consider current prices of annuity contracts that could be used to settle pension obligations as well as the rates on high-quality fixed investments (SFAS 87).

e.　Annual pension expense is the **net periodic pension cost (NPPC)**. The required minimum NPPC to be recognized is calculated as follows:

| | |
|---|---|
| Service cost | $XXX |
| + Interest cost | XXX |
| − Return on plan assets | (XXX) |
| +/− Gains and losses | XXX |
| + Amortization of prior service cost | XXX |
| Net periodic pension cost | $XXX |

　　1)　**Service cost** is the present value of the future benefits earned by the employees in the current period (as calculated according to the plan's benefit formula). This amount is provided by the plan's actuary and is unaffected by the funded status of the plan.

　　2)　**Interest cost** is the increase in the PBO determined by multiplying the PBO at the beginning of the year by the current discount rate (e.g., the interest rate at which annuities could be purchased to settle pension obligations).

　　　　a)　This discount rate may change with changes in interest rates.

　　　　b)　The PBO and the discount rate are provided by the plan's actuary.

　　3)　The **actual return on plan assets** is based on the fair value of the plan assets at the beginning and end of the accounting period adjusted for contributions and payments during the period (FV at end of the period − FV at beginning of the period − contributions to the plan assets + benefits paid to the employees). The return on plan assets component (given that it is positive) decreases NPPC.

　　　　a)　The **expected return on plan assets** is the market-related value of the plan assets at the beginning of the period multiplied by the expected long-term rate of return.

          i)    Market-related value may be either fair value or a calculated value that recognizes changes in fair value systematically and rationally over no more than 5 years, such as a 5-year moving average.

- The purpose of spreading recognition of the changes in fair value is to reduce the volatility of the NPPC. For example, a company may choose to recognize 20% of the last 5 years' gains and losses each year.

    b)   The difference between the actual and the expected returns is ultimately included in the gain or loss component of NPPC, but gains and losses (e.g., the difference between the actual and the expected returns) are not required to be recognized in NPPC in the period when they occur.

        i)   Thus, the net effect on the required minimum NPPC is to decrease it by the amount of the expected, not the actual, return on plan assets. The current asset gain or loss, that is, the difference between the actual and expected returns, may be deferred.

4)   **Gains and losses** arise from changes in the amount of the PBO or plan assets that result from experience different from that expected and from changes in assumptions. SFAS 87 adopts a corridor approach to reduce the volatility of the NPPC caused by gains and losses.

    a)   The cumulative unrecognized net gain or loss at the beginning of the year is subject to required amortization in NPPC only to the extent it exceeds 10% of the greater of the PBO or the market-related value of plan assets. Thus, only the amount exceeding the 10% threshold need be amortized.

    b)   The minimum required amortization equals the excess described on the previous page divided by the average remaining service period of active employees expected to receive benefits.

    c)   Amortization of a net unrecognized gain (loss) decreases (increases) NPPC.

5)   **Amortization of prior service cost.** If a pension plan is amended to grant additional benefits for past periods of service, the cost of the retroactive benefits is allocated to the future periods of service of employees active at the date of the amendment who are expected to receive benefits.

    a)   The cost of retroactive benefits is the increase in the PBO at the date of the amendment and should be amortized by assigning an equal amount to each future period of service of each employee active at the date of the amendment who is expected to receive benefits. However, to reduce the burden of these allocation computations, any alternative amortization approach (e.g., averaging) that more rapidly reduces the unrecognized prior service cost is acceptable if applied consistently.

  f.   When funding is less than the NPPC, unfunded accrued pension cost is recorded as a credit to the **accrued pension cost** account. **Prepaid pension cost** (a debit) results from funding the plan in excess of the NPPC.

    1)   Assuming an unfunded ABO, the **total net liability** reported in the balance sheet equals the unfunded ABO (ABO – fair value of plan assets).

       a)   An **additional minimum pension liability** must be recognized if a portion of the ABO is unfunded and an asset has been recognized as prepaid pension cost or the existing liability (unfunded accrued pension cost) is less than the unfunded ABO.

          i)   Thus, the additional liability equals the unfunded ABO plus prepaid pension cost or minus accrued pension cost.

　　　　　　　ii)　Recognition of an additional liability has no effect on earnings.  An **intangible asset** is debited to the extent **unrecognized prior service cost** exists.  If that amount is not adequate, the remainder is reported in **other comprehensive income**.

　　　g.　SFAS 87 emphasizes accounting for a single-employer, defined benefit pension plan, but it also applies to defined contribution plans.

　　　　　1)　Under a **defined contribution plan**, the periodic pension cost reported by the employer is the contribution called for in that period.  The company reports an asset only if the contribution to the pension trust is greater than the defined, required contribution.  The company reports a liability only if the contribution is less than the required amount.

2.　**SFAS 106**, *Employers' Accounting for Postretirement Benefits Other Than Pensions*, applies principles similar to those of pension accounting.

　　　a.　SFAS 106 emphasizes an employer's accounting for a single-employer plan that defines the postretirement benefits other than pensions to be provided to employees **(other postretirement employee benefits or OPEB)**.

　　　　　1)　The OPEB are defined in terms of monetary amounts (e.g., a given dollar value of life insurance) or benefit coverage (e.g., amounts per day for hospitalization).

　　　　　　　a)　The amount of benefits depends on such factors as the benefit formula, the life expectancy of the retiree and any beneficiaries and covered dependents, and the frequency and significance of events (e.g., illnesses) requiring payments.

　　　　　2)　The costs are expensed over the **attribution period**, which begins on the date of hire unless the plan's benefit formula grants credit for service only from a later date.  The end of the period is the full eligibility date.

　　　　　3)　The basic elements of accounting for OPEB include the **expected postretirement benefit obligation (EPBO)**, which equals the **accumulated postretirement benefit obligation (APBO)** after the full eligibility date.

　　　　　　　a)　The EPBO for an employee is the actuarial present value at a given date of the OPEB expected to be paid.  Its measurement depends on the anticipated amounts and timing of future benefits, the costs to be incurred to provide those benefits, and the extent the costs are shared by the employee and others (such as governmental programs).

　　　　　　　b)　The APBO for an employee is the actuarial present value at a given date of the future benefits attributable to the employee's service as of that date.  Unlike the calculation of the ABO described in SFAS 87, the determination of the APBO (as well as of the EPBO and service cost) implicitly includes the consideration of **future salary progression** to the extent the benefit formula defines benefits as a function of future compensation levels.

　　　　　　　c)　SFAS 106 "requires that an employer's obligation for postretirement benefits expected to be provided to or for an employee be fully accrued by the date that employee attains full eligibility for all of the benefits, even if the employee is expected to render additional service beyond that date."

　　　　　　　　　i)　The **full eligibility date** is reached when the employee has rendered all the services necessary to earn all of the benefits expected to be received by that employee.

　　　　　　　　　ii)　Prior to that date, the EPBO exceeds the APBO.

　　　　　4)　Unlike SFAS 87, SFAS 106 does not require recognition of a minimum liability.

b.   The six possible components included in net periodic postretirement benefit cost (NPPBC) of an employer sponsoring a defined benefit health care plan are service cost, interest on the APBO, return on plan assets, amortization of unrecognized prior service cost, amortization of the transition obligation or asset, and the gain or loss component.

c.   **Net periodic postretirement benefit cost (NPPBC)** of an employer sponsoring a defined benefit health care plan is calculated as follows:

|   | | |
|---|---|---|
|   | Service cost | $XXX |
| + | Interest cost | XXX |
| + | Prior service cost | XXX |
| +/− | Amortization of transition obligation/asset | XXX |
| +/− | Gains and losses | XXX |
| +/− | Gains and losses from temporary deviations | XXX |
|   | Net periodic postretirement benefit cost | $XXX |

d.   **Service cost** is defined as the actuarial present value of benefits attributed to services rendered by employees during the period. It is the portion of the EPBO attributed to service in the period and is not affected by the level of funding.

e.   **Interest cost** reflects the change in the APBO during the period resulting solely from the passage of time. It equals the APBO at the beginning of the period times the assumed discount rate used in determining the present value of future cash outflows currently expected to be required to satisfy the obligation.

f.   **Prior service cost** is defined as the cost of benefit improvements attributable to plan participants' prior service pursuant to a plan amendment or a plan initiation that provides benefits in exchange for plan participants' prior service.

   1)   Ordinarily, it is recognized in NPPBC by assigning an equal amount to each remaining year of service to the full eligibility date of each participant active at the amendment date who was not yet fully eligible for benefits.

g.   The **gain or loss components** of NPPBC (SFAS 106) and NPPC (SFAS 87) are calculated similarly. Under SFAS 106, however, the employer may use a systematic method of amortization of unrecognized net gain or loss **other than the corridor approach**. The alternative is allowed if it results in amortization at least equal to the minimum determined under the corridor method.

   1)   Moreover, if an enterprise consistently recognizes gains and losses immediately, gains (losses) that do not offset previously recognized losses (gains) must first reduce any unrecognized transition obligation (asset).

      a)   The transition obligation (asset) represents an underlying unfunded (overfunded) APBO. The FASB believes that gains (losses) should not be recognized until the unfunded (overfunded) APBO is recognized.

h.   A **gain or loss from a temporary deviation** from the substantive plan is immediately recognized in income.

   1)   For example, under a plan's terms, an excess of benefit payments over the sum of the employer's cost and the employees' contributions for a year may be recovered from increased employees' contributions in the subsequent year. However, for the current year only, the employer may decide not to adjust contributions.

   2)   Delayed recognition is inappropriate because a temporary deviation is not deemed to provide future economic value and relates to benefits already paid.

3) If the deviation is other than temporary, that is, if the employer decides to continue to bear the burden of increased costs, the implication is that the substantive plan (the plan as understood by the parties, as opposed to the existing written plan) has been amended. An amendment would require accounting for prior service cost.

i. The initial application of SFAS 106 may result in a **transition asset or obligation**.

1) The transition amount is the difference between (1) the APBO and (2) the fair value of plan assets, plus any recognized accrued postretirement benefit cost, or minus any recognized prepaid postretirement benefit cost.

2) Unlike the accounting prescribed by SFAS 87, SFAS 106 permits employers to **elect immediate recognition** in income of the transition amount as the effect of a change in accounting principle.

3) The amount attributable to the effects of a plan initiation or benefit improvements adopted after 1990 is treated as **unrecognized prior service cost** and excluded from the transition amount immediately recognized.

4) If employers wish to amortize the transition amount on a delayed basis as part of the NPPBC, straight-line amortization over the average remaining service period of active plan participants is required unless

a) That period is less than 20 years, in which case a 20-year period may be elected, or

b) Almost all plan participants are inactive, in which case the average remaining life expectancy of those participants must be used.

3. Stop and review! You have completed the outline for this subunit. Study multiple-choice questions 63 through 72 beginning on page 635.

## 16.5 DEFERRED INCOME TAXES

1. **Scope and Principles**

a. **SFAS 109**, *Accounting for Income Taxes*, adopts the **asset and liability method** of accounting for income taxes.

1) It establishes standards of accounting and reporting for income taxes currently payable and for the tax consequences of

a) Revenues, expenses, gains, and losses included in taxable income of an earlier or later year than the year in which they are recognized in income for financial reporting purposes

b) Other events that create differences between the tax bases of assets and liabilities and their amounts for financial reporting purposes

c) Operating loss or tax credit carrybacks for refunds of taxes paid in prior years and carryforwards to reduce taxes payable in future years

2) SFAS 109 applies to

a) Taxes based on income, whether foreign, federal, state, or local

b) An enterprise's domestic and foreign operations that are consolidated, combined, or accounted for by the equity method

c) Foreign enterprises in preparing statements based on U.S. GAAP

3)   It does not address

    a)   The investment tax credit

    b)   Discounting future tax liabilities (recording them at their present value)

    c)   Income tax accounting for interim periods except for the

        i)   Standards for recognition of tax benefits

        ii)   Effects of enacted tax law changes

        iii)   Changes in valuation allowances

b.   **Interperiod tax allocation**.  Tax consequences are a transaction's or an event's effects on current and deferred income taxes.  Income taxes currently payable or refundable for a particular year usually include the tax consequences of most of the events recognized in the financial statements for the same year.

    1)   However, certain significant exceptions exist.  As a result, the tax consequences of some transactions or events may be recognized in income taxes currently payable or refundable in a year different from that in which their financial statement effects are recognized.  Moreover, some transactions or events may have tax consequences or financial-statement effects but never both.

        a)   Because of these differences, income taxes currently payable or refundable may differ from (exceed or be less than) income tax expense or benefit.  The accounting for these differences is interperiod tax allocation.

c.   **Objectives of SFAS 109.**  Accrual accounting should recognize taxes payable or refundable for the current year.

    1)   It should also recognize deferred tax liabilities and assets for the future tax consequences of events that have been previously recognized in the enterprise's financial statements or tax returns.

d.   Basic principles of income tax accounting

    1)   A current tax liability or asset is recognized for the estimated taxes payable or refundable on current-year tax returns.

    2)   A deferred tax liability or asset is recognized for the estimated future tax effects attributable to temporary differences and carryforwards.

    3)   Measurement of tax liabilities and assets is based on enacted tax law; the effects of future changes in that law are not anticipated.

    4)   A deferred tax asset is reduced by a valuation allowance if it is more likely than not that some portion will not be realized.

2.   **Temporary and Permanent Differences**

a.   Income reported in a GAAP-based income statement (calculated on the accrual basis) differs from income reported for tax purposes (calculated on the modified cash basis).

    1)   SFAS 109's asset-and-liability approach describes future income statement (and therefore, tax) consequences as arising from balance sheet valuations.

b.   A **temporary difference (TD)** arises when the recovery of an asset or the settlement of a liability has tax consequences.

    1)   TDs that result in **future taxable amounts** give rise to **deferred tax liabilities** in the balance sheet.

        a)   "Revenues or gains that are taxable after they are recognized in financial income," e.g., installment sales

        b)   "Expenses or losses that are deductible before they are recognized in financial income," e.g., property depreciated using MACRS

2) TDs that result in **future deductible amounts** give rise to **deferred tax assets** in the balance sheet.

   a) "Revenues or gains that are taxable before they are recognized in financial income," e.g., subscription revenues received

   b) "Expenses or losses that are deductible after they are recognized in financial income," e.g., warranty costs

3) Some TDs result from assets or liabilities that are recognized for tax purposes but not for financial reporting purposes.

   a) An example is organizational costs, which are deferred and amortized for tax purposes but, under **AICPA SOP 98-5**, *Reporting on the Costs of Start-Up Activities*, must be expensed when incurred for financial reporting purposes.

c. A **permanent difference (PD)** arises when a difference in tax and GAAP recognition does not result in a balance sheet item. It does **not** result in a deferred tax asset or liability. Among these are

   1) Items included in income for financial reporting purposes but not for tax purposes, e.g., state and municipal bond interest, proceeds from life insurance on key employees

   2) Items deducted from income for financial reporting purposes but not for tax purposes, e.g., premiums paid for life insurance on key employees, fines resulting from a violation of law

   3) Items deducted from income for tax purposes but not for financial reporting purposes, e.g., percentage depletion of natural resources, the dividends received deduction

3. **Recognition and Measurement**

   a. Because recovery of assets and settlement of liabilities are inherent assumptions of GAAP, accrual accounting must recognize deferred tax consequences of TDs (temporary differences).

      1) **Basic definitions**

         a) **Income tax expense or benefit** is the sum of the current tax expense or benefit and deferred tax expense or benefit.

         b) **Current tax expense or benefit** is the amount of taxes paid or payable (or refundable) for the year as determined by applying the enacted tax law to the taxable income or excess of deductions over revenues for that year.

         c) **Current tax liability** is equal to taxable income times the applicable tax rate.

         d) **Deferred tax expense or benefit** is the net change during the year in an enterprise's deferred tax liabilities and assets.

         e) A **deferred tax liability** records the deferred tax consequences attributable to taxable TDs. It is measured using the applicable enacted tax rate and provisions of the enacted tax law.

         f) A **deferred tax asset** records the deferred tax consequences attributable to deductible TDs and carryforwards. It is measured using the applicable enacted tax rate and provisions of the enacted tax law.

      2) A **valuation allowance** is a contra account to a deferred tax asset. It is used to reduce a deferred tax asset if the weight of the available evidence, both positive and negative, indicates that it is more likely than not (that is, the probability is more than 50%) that some portion will not be realized. The allowance should be sufficient to reduce the deferred tax asset to the amount that is more likely than not to be realized.

a)  Future realization of the tax benefit represented by a deferred tax asset ultimately depends on the existence of sufficient taxable income of the **proper character** (ordinary income or capital gain) within the **carryback and carryforward period**.

b)  The following are **sources of taxable income** permitting realization of the tax benefit of a deferred tax asset and therefore eliminating or reducing the need for a valuation allowance:

   i)   Reversals of taxable TDs
   ii)  Future taxable income without regard to reversing differences and carryforwards
   iii) Taxable income in the carryback period
   iv)  Tax-planning strategies, for example, those that accelerate taxable amounts to permit use of an expiring carryforward, change the character of income or loss, or switch from tax-exempt to taxable items of income

3)  **Determination of deferred taxes.**  The process below is followed for each taxpaying entity in each tax jurisdiction:

   a)  Identify TDs (types and amounts) and operating loss and tax credit carryforwards for tax purposes (nature and amounts, and length of the remaining carryforward period).
   b)  Measure the total deferred tax liability for taxable TDs using the applicable tax rate.
   c)  Measure the total deferred tax asset for deductible TDs and operating loss carryforwards using the applicable tax rate.
   d)  Measure deferred tax assets for each type of tax credit carryforward.
   e)  Recognize a valuation allowance if necessary.

4)  **Applicable tax rates.**  A deferred tax liability or asset is measured using the tax rate(s) expected to apply when the liability or asset is expected to be settled or realized.

   a)  The tax rate used in the measurement of deferred tax liabilities and assets is, in essence, a flat rate if graduated rates are not significant to the enterprise.  Otherwise, an average of the applicable graduated rates is used.

5)  The **basic entries** to record taxes in accordance with the asset and liability method required by SFAS 109 are as follows:

When a liability is recorded:

| | | |
|---|---|---|
| Income tax expense | $XXX | |
| Deferred income tax liability | | $XXX |
| Income tax payable | | XXX |

When an asset is recorded:

| | | |
|---|---|---|
| Income tax refundable | $XXX | |
| Deferred income tax asset | XXX | |
| Income tax payable | | $XXX |

4.  **Financial Statement Presentation.**  Deferred tax liabilities and assets should be separated into current and noncurrent components.  Whether an item is current or noncurrent usually depends on the classification of the related asset or liability.

a.  If a deferred tax item, including a deferred tax asset related to a carryforward, is not related to an asset or liability for financial reporting, it is classified based on the **expected reversal date** of the TD.

b. A **valuation allowance** for a particular tax jurisdiction is allocated pro rata between current and noncurrent deferred tax assets.

c. For a given tax-paying entity and within a specific jurisdiction, current deferred tax assets and liabilities are **netted**. Noncurrent deferred tax assets and liabilities are also offset and shown as a single amount.

5. **Basic Examples**

a. **Deferred tax liability**

1) For 2001, Pitou Co.'s pretax financial income is $520,000, and its taxable income is $500,000.

2) The $20,000 difference is attributable solely to an excess of tax depreciation over book depreciation that will result in future taxable amounts when the TD reverses.

3) Pitou's applicable tax rate is 34%. Given no beginning deferred tax amounts, the deferred tax liability is $6,800 ($20,000 taxable TD × 34%), and the deferred tax expense is also $6,800 ($6,800 year-end deferred tax liability – $0 balance at the beginning of the year).

4) Income tax payable (current tax expense) is $170,000 ($500,000 taxable income × 34%). Accordingly, income tax expense is $176,800 ($170,000 current tax expense + $6,800 deferred tax expense). The year-end entry is

| | | |
|---|---|---|
| Income tax expense | $176,800 | |
| Deferred income tax liability | | $ 6,800 |
| Income tax payable | | 170,000 |

5) For 2002, Pitou Co. has pretax financial income of $442,000 and taxable income of $450,000.

6) The difference reflects an $8,000 excess of book depreciation over tax depreciation.

7) There is no other difference between pretax financial income and taxable income. Hence, the taxable TD is reduced to $12,000 ($20,000 – $8,000), the year-end deferred tax liability is $4,080 ($12,000 × 34%), and the decrease in the deferred tax liability (the deferred tax benefit arising from reduction in the liability) is $2,720 ($6,800 at the beginning of the year – $4,080 at year-end).

8) Current tax expense (tax payable) is $153,000 ($450,000 taxable income × 34%). Consequently, total income tax expense for the year is $150,280 ($153,000 current tax expense – $2,720 deferred tax benefit). The year-end entry is

| | | |
|---|---|---|
| Income tax expense | $150,280 | |
| Deferred income tax liability | $ 2,720 | |
| Income tax payable | | 153,000 |

b. **Deferred tax asset**

1) Lunes Co. began operations in the year just ended. It has taxable income of $400,000 and pretax financial income of $385,000.

2) The difference is solely attributable to receipt of unearned subscription revenue (a liability) that was included as revenue in the tax return in the year of collection.

3) Lunes will recognize $9,000 of this unearned revenue as earned in its second year of operations and $6,000 in the third year.

4) The applicable tax rate is 34%. Thus, the deferred tax asset is $5,100 ($15,000 deductible TD × 34%), and the deferred tax benefit is also $5,100 ($5,100 year-end deferred tax asset – $0 balance at the beginning of the year). Income tax payable (current tax expense) is $136,000 ($400,000 taxable income × 34%).

5) Accordingly, income tax expense is $130,900 ($136,000 current tax expense – $5,100 deferred tax benefit). Based on the evidence (taxable income), no valuation allowance is required for the deferred tax asset. Thus, the year-end entry is

| | | |
|---|---|---|
| Income tax expense | $130,900 | |
| Deferred income tax asset | 5,100 | |
| Income tax payable | | $136,000 |

6) In its second year of operations, Lunes has taxable income of $600,000, with income tax payable (current tax expense) of $204,000 ($600,000 × 34%).

7) Taxable income and pretax financial income differ only in that $9,000 of unearned revenue collected in the preceding year is included in the determination of pretax financial income.

8) At the end of the second year, the deferred tax asset is therefore $2,040 [($15,000 – $9,000) × 34%], and the deferred tax expense (the decrease in the deferred tax asset) is $3,060 ($5,100 – $2,040).

9) Total income tax expense is $207,060 ($204,000 current tax expense + $3,060 deferred tax expense). Based on the evidence (taxable income), no valuation allowance is required for the deferred tax asset. Thus, the year-end entry is

| | | |
|---|---|---|
| Income tax expense | $207,060 | |
| Deferred income tax asset | | $   3,060 |
| Income tax payable | | 204,000 |

c. **Deferred tax asset – valuation allowance**

1) Mardi Co. has a $6,000 deductible TD at the end of its current year.

2) The applicable tax rate is 34%. Consequently, Mardi recorded a deferred tax asset of $2,040 ($6,000 × 34%). However, after weighing all the evidence, Mardi Co. has decided that it is more likely than not (more than 50% probable) that $4,000 of the deductible temporary difference will not be realized.

3) To reflect this determination, a valuation allowance (a contra account) should be credited. The offsetting debit is to income tax expense. The amount of the valuation allowance should be sufficient to reduce the deferred tax asset to the amount that is more likely than not to be realized.

4) Accordingly, Mardi should recognize a $1,360 valuation allowance to reduce the $2,040 deferred tax asset to $680 ($2,000 × 34%). The entry is

| | | |
|---|---|---|
| Income tax expense | $1,360 | |
| Deferred tax asset valuation allowance | | $1,360 |

6. Stop and review! You have completed the outline for this subunit. Study multiple-choice questions 73 through 94 beginning on page 639.

## 16.6 CORE CONCEPTS

Current Liabilities

- **Accounts payable** arise in the normal course of business to reflect obligations to suppliers. They are classified as current liabilities.
- The **gross method** reports payables at their face amount. It is used when **the company does not expect** to take advantage of any discount allowed for early payment.
- The **net method** reports payables net of the applicable discount. It is used when **the company expects** to pay within the discount period.
- A **note payable** is a debt acknowledged by a **written agreement**.
- Notes payable should be reported at their face amount **net of any premium or discount** arising from a difference between the note's stated rate of interest and the market rate.
- **Other current liabilities** which must be reported are current maturities of long-term debt, short-term obligations expected to be refinanced, deposits and advances received, deferred (unearned) revenues, taxes payable, employee-related liabilities (e.g., compensated absences), loss contingencies, warranty liabilities, and coupons issued.

Long-term Liabilities

- A **bond** is a **formal (long-term) contractual agreement** to pay an amount of money (the face amount) at the maturity date plus interest at the stated rate at specific intervals.
- Bonds should be reported at their face amount **net of any premium or discount** arising from a difference between the note's stated rate of interest and the market rate.
- Convertible debt issued with stock purchase warrants can be accounted for under the **book-value method** or the **market-value method**.
- A **variable interest entity** is an **off-balance-sheet** arrangement that may take any legal form. The **primary beneficiary consolidates** a variable interest entity.

Leases

- A lease is an agreement whereby a **lessor (owner) conveys** the right to use specific property for a stated period **to a lessee** in exchange for a stated payment.
- A **lessee** classifies leases as **capital leases** or **operating leases**.
- A **lessee** classifies a lease as a **capital lease** if **any of four criteria** are met at the inception of the lease: a transfer of ownership, a bargain purchase option, the lease term is 75% or more of the asset's estimated economic life, or the present value of the minimum lease payments is at least 90% of the fair value of the leased property.
- The **minimum lease payments** consist of the minimum rental payments and any bargain purchase option.
- A **lessor** determines whether a lease is classified as **capital** using the **same four criteria** as a lessee. A lessor further classifies all capital leases as either **direct financing leases** (lessor recognizes no dealer's profit) or **sales-type leases** (lessor recognizes dealer's profit).
- Leases that **do not meet** any of the four criteria for capitalization are classified as **operating leases** (by both lessors and lessees).

Pensions and Other Postretirement Benefits

- The **projected benefit obligation** of a **defined benefit plan** is measured using assumptions as to future as well as past and current salary levels.
- The **calculation of the projected benefit obligation** at the end of a period is as follows: beginning PBO plus current service cost, plus prior service cost, minus benefits paid, plus or minus changes in assumption.
- The **accumulated benefit obligation** is the present value of **benefits accrued to date** based on past and current compensation levels.

- The **calculation of the net periodic pension cost** for a period is as follows: service cost plus interest cost, minus return on plan assets, plus and minus gains and losses, plus amortization of prior service cost.
- The **total net liability** reported on the **balance sheet** is the unfunded accumulated benefit obligation minus the fair value of the plan assets.

## Deferred Income Taxes

- Deferred income taxes are the **tax effects** of a current period transaction that **will not be felt** until a later period.
- A **temporary difference** arises when the recovery of an asset or the settlement of a liability has tax consequences.
- Such differences that result in **future taxable amounts** give rise to **deferred tax liabilities** in the balance sheet (e.g., installment sales). Differences that result in **future deductible amounts** give rise to **deferred tax assets** (e.g., subscriptions revenues received).
- A **permanent difference** arises when a difference in tax and GAAP recognition does not result in a balance sheet item (e.g., state and municipal bond interest received). Such a difference does not result in a deferred tax asset or liability.

## QUESTIONS

### 16.1 Current Liabilities

1. On August 1, year 1, an enterprise issued 5-year bonds with a face amount of $10,000,000. The bonds carry a stated interest rate of 10% and interest is payable annually on July 31. Which is the appropriate classification of bonds payable and the related accrued interest payable on the December 31, year 5, balance sheet?

| Classification Table | | |
| --- | --- | --- |
| | Bonds Payable | Interest Payable |
| Classification A | Current liability | Current liability |
| Classification B | Current liability | Long-term liability |
| Classification C | Long-term liability | Current liability |
| Classification D | Long-term liability | Long-term liability |

    A. Classification A.

    B. Classification B.

    C. Classification C.

    D. Classification D.

Answer (A) is correct. *(CIA, adapted)*
**REQUIRED:** The appropriate classification of bonds payable and the related accrued interest payable on the balance sheet.
**DISCUSSION:** ARB 43, Chapter 3A, *Current Assets and Current Liabilities*, defines a current liability as an obligation that will be either liquidated using current assets or replaced by another current liability. SFAS 78, *Classification of Obligations That Are Callable by the Creditor*, amends ARB 43 to include the following as current liabilities: (1) obligations that, by their terms, are or will be due on demand within 1 year (or the operating cycle if longer), and (2) obligations that are or will be callable by the creditor within 1 year because of a violation of a debt covenant. At the balance sheet date, both the principal of the bonds and the interest accrued at the balance sheet date will be due within a year. These amounts are expected to require the use of current assets (there is no evidence to the contrary) and should be classified as current liabilities.
Answer (B) is incorrect because the interest payable should be classified as a current liability. It is due within a year after the balance sheet date. Answer (C) is incorrect because the balance of bonds payable should be classified as a current liability. The bonds are due within a year after the balance sheet date. Answer (D) is incorrect because both the balance of bonds payable and interest payable should be classified as current liabilities.

2. The selling price of a new company's units is $10,000 each. The buyers are provided with a 2-year warranty that is expected to cost the company $250 per unit in the year of the sale and $750 per unit in the year following the sale. The company sold 80 units in the first year of operation and 100 units in the second year. Actual payments for warranty claims were $10,000 and $65,000 in years one and two, respectively. The amount charged to warranty expense during the second year of operation is

    A. $25,000

    B. $65,000

    C. $85,000

    D. $100,000

Answer (D) is correct. *(CIA, adapted)*
**REQUIRED:** The amount charged to warranty expense during the second year of operation.
**DISCUSSION:** Under the accrual method, the total estimated warranty costs are charged to operating expense in the year of sale. The total estimated warranty cost per unit is $1,000 ($250 + $750). In year two, 100 units were sold, so the warranty expense recognized is $100,000.
Answer (A) is incorrect because $25,000 is the expected amount of warranty claims for the first year of second-year sales. Answer (B) is incorrect because $65,000 is the actual amount of claims in the second year. Answer (C) is incorrect because $85,000 is the expected amount of warranty claims in the second year.

**3.** Paxton Company started offering a 3-year warranty on its products sold after June 1, year 1. Paxton's actual sales for the year ended May 31, year 2 were $2,695,000. The total cost of the warranty is expected to be 3% of sales. The actual year 2 warranty expenditures were $31,500 in labor and $9,100 in parts. The amount of warranty expense that should appear on Paxton's income statement for the year ended May 31, year 2 is

A. $31,500

B. $40,250

C. $40,600

D. $80,850

Answer (D) is correct. *(CMA, adapted)*
    **REQUIRED:** The annual warranty expense.
    **DISCUSSION:** If warranty expense is expected to be 3% of sales, that amount should be recorded as an expense for the year. Consequently, the expense is $80,850 ($2,695,000 × 3%). The amount of cash expended during the year is irrelevant because the expense is expected to be paid over 3 years. A liability is credited for any portion of the expense not paid during year 2.
    Answer (A) is incorrect because $31,500 is the current year's outlay for labor. Answer (B) is incorrect because $40,250 is the liability accrued at year-end. Answer (C) is incorrect because $40,600 is the cash outlay for the current year.

**4.** An employee has the right to receive compensation for future paid leave, and the payment of compensation is probable. If the obligation relates to rights that vest but the amount cannot be reasonably estimated, the employer should

A. Accrue a liability with proper disclosure.

B. Not accrue a liability nor disclose the situation.

C. Accrue a liability; however, the additional disclosure is not required.

D. Not accrue a liability; however, disclosure is required.

Answer (D) is correct. *(CMA, adapted)*
    **REQUIRED:** The treatment of an obligation for future paid leave when the amount cannot be reasonably estimated.
    **DISCUSSION:** SFAS 43 lists four requirements that must be met before a liability is accrued for future compensated absences. These requirements are that the obligation must arise for past services, the employee rights must vest or accumulate, payment is probable, and the amount can be reasonably estimated. If the amount cannot be reasonably estimated, no liability should be recorded. However, the obligation should be disclosed.
    Answer (A) is incorrect because the conditions are not met for accrual of a liability. Answer (B) is incorrect because disclosure is required. Answer (C) is incorrect because the conditions are not met for accrual of a liability.

**5.** The Elam Company has reasonably estimated the following probable costs for the compensated absences of its employees:

| | |
|---|---|
| Vacation pay (vested) | $5,000 |
| Vacation pay (accumulated but not vested) | 3,000 |
| Sick pay (vested) | 4,000 |
| Sick pay (accumulated but not vested) | 2,000 |

The costs are attributable to services that have already been rendered. In accordance with SFAS 43, *Accounting for Compensated Absences,* the minimum amount that Elam must accrue as its liability for compensated absences is

A. $5,000

B. $8,000

C. $12,000

D. $14,000

Answer (C) is correct. *(Publisher)*
    **REQUIRED:** The minimum amount of liability to be accrued for compensated absences.
    **DISCUSSION:** Vacation pay and vested sick pay should be accrued as liabilities. Thus, the minimum accrual is $12,000 ($5,000 + $3,000 + $4,000).
    Answer (A) is incorrect because accumulated vacation pay and vested sick pay should be accrued. Answer (B) is incorrect because SFAS 43 also requires accrual of vested sick pay. Answer (D) is incorrect because SFAS 43 does not require accrual of nonvested sick pay.

**6.** Pine Company began operations on January 1, year 1. Pine employs 10 individuals who work 8-hour days and are paid hourly. Each employee earns 10 paid vacation days annually. Vacation days may be taken after January 1 of the year following the year in which they are earned. Additional information is as follows:

| Actual Hourly Wage Rate | | Vacation Days Used By Each Employee | |
|---|---|---|---|
| Year 1 | Year 2 | Year 1 | Year 2 |
| $8.00 | $8.00 | 0 | 8 |

The amounts of compensated absences liability that should have appeared on Pine's balance sheet at December 31, year 1 and year 2 were

A. $0 and $6,400.

B. $6,400 and $7,680.

C. $0 and $1,280.

D. $6,400 and $1,280

Answer (B) is correct. *(Publisher)*
**REQUIRED:** The liability for vacation pay at the end of year 1 and year 2.
**DISCUSSION:** Each employee earns 10 vacation days a year at $64 per day (8 hours × $8). Thus, for each employee, the annual expense is $640. The total for 10 workers is $6,400. Because no vacation days were used during year 1, the entire balance of $6,400 will be a liability at December 31. The workers will earn an additional 10 days of vacation during year 2, while using up eight days. Consequently, the liability will increase by two days during year 2, or $1,280 (2 days × 10 workers × $64). Adding the $1,280 to the $6,400 from the preceding year results in a year-end liability of $7,680.
Answer (A) is incorrect because accumulated vacation pay should be accrued for year 1. Answer (C) is incorrect because accumulated vacation pay should be accrued for year 1. Answer (D) is incorrect because the $6,400 liability from year 1 should be carried forward to year 2.

**7.** Case Cereal Co. frequently distributes coupons to promote new products. On October 1, Case mailed 1 million coupons for $.45 off each box of cereal purchased. Case expects 120,000 of these coupons to be redeemed before the December 31 expiration date. It takes 30 days from the redemption date for Case to receive the coupons from the retailers. Case reimburses the retailers an additional $.05 for each coupon redeemed. As of December 31, Case had paid retailers $25,000 related to these coupons, and had 50,000 coupons on hand that had not been processed for payment. What amount should Case report as a liability for coupons in its December 31 balance sheet?

A. $35,000

B. $29,000

C. $25,000

D. $22,500

Answer (A) is correct. *(CPA, adapted)*
**REQUIRED:** The liability for coupons at year-end.
**DISCUSSION:** The company pays $.50 ($.45 + $.05) for the redemption of a coupon, and it expects 120,000 to be redeemed at a total cost of $60,000 (120,000 × $.50). Given that payments of $25,000 have been made, the liability at year-end must be $35,000 ($60,000 – $25,000). The cost associated with the unprocessed coupons on hand does not reduce the liability because payment for these coupons has not yet been made.
Answer (B) is incorrect because $29,000 does not include the additional $.05 per coupon paid to retailers. Answer (C) is incorrect because $25,000 is the cost of the coupons on hand that have not yet been processed for payment. Case expects to receive additional redeemed coupons for 30 days after the balance sheet date. Answer (D) is incorrect because $22,500 equals $.45 times 50,000 coupons.

**8.** In December, Mill Co. began including one coupon in each package of candy that it sells and offering a toy in exchange for $.50 and five coupons. The toys cost Mill $.80 each. Sixty percent of the coupons will eventually be redeemed. During December, Mill sold 110,000 packages of candy, and no coupons were redeemed. In its December 31 balance sheet, what amount should Mill report as estimated liability for coupons?

A. $3,960

B. $10,560

C. $19,800

D. $52,800

Answer (A) is correct. *(CPA, adapted)*
**REQUIRED:** The amount to be reported as a liability for unredeemed coupons at year-end.
**DISCUSSION:** The liability for coupon redemptions is $3,960 {[(110,000 coupons issued ÷ 5 per toy) × ($.80 – $.50) set cost per toy × 60% redemption rate]}.
Answer (B) is incorrect because $10,560 does not include the $.50 paid by customers for the toy. Answer (C) is incorrect because $19,800 is based on the assumption one coupon can be redeemed for a toy. Answer (D) is incorrect because $52,800 assumes one coupon can be redeemed for a toy, and excludes the $.50 that customers must pay per toy.

**9.** During year 1, Rex Co. introduced a new product carrying a two-year warranty against defects. The estimated warranty costs related to dollar sales are 2% within 12 months following sale, and 4% in the second 12 months following sale. Sales and actual warranty expenditures for December 31, year 1 and year 2 are as follows:

| | Sales | Actual Warranty Expenditures |
|---|---|---|
| Year 1 | $ 600,000 | $ 9,000 |
| Year 2 | 1,000,000 | 30,000 |
| | $1,600,000 | $39,000 |

At December 31, year 2, Rex should report an estimated warranty liability of

A. $0

B. $39,000

C. $57,000

D. $96,000

Answer (C) is correct. *(CPA, adapted)*
**REQUIRED:** The estimated warranty liability at the end of the second year.
**DISCUSSION:** Because this product is new, the beginning balance in the estimated warranty liability account at the beginning of year 1 is $0. For year 1, the estimated warranty costs related to dollar sales are 6% (2% + 4%) of sales, or $36,000 ($600,000 × 6%). For year 2, the estimated warranty costs are $60,000 ($1,000,000 sales × 6%). These amounts are charged to warranty expense and credited to the estimated warranty liability account. This liability account is debited for expenditures of $9,000 and $30,000 in year 1 and year 2, respectively. Hence, the estimated warranty liability at 12/31/year 2 is $57,000.

| Estimated Warranty Liability | | |
|---|---|---|
| | $ 0 | 1/1/Year 1 |
| Year 1 expenditures $ 9,000 | 36,000 | Year 1 expense |
| Year 2 expenditures 30,000 | 60,000 | Year 1 expense |
| | $57,000 | 12/31/Year 2 |

Answer (A) is incorrect because all warranties have not expired. Answer (B) is incorrect because $39,000 equals the total warranty expenditures to date. Answer (D) is incorrect because $96,000 equals the total warranty expense to date.

**10.** Felicity Press received a total of $180,000 for 3-year subscriptions that began April 1, year 1. It recorded this amount as unearned revenue. Assuming Felicity records adjustments only at the end of the calendar year, the adjusting entry required to reflect the proper balances in the accounts at December 31, year 1 is to

A. Debit subscription revenue for $135,000 and credit unearned revenue for $135,000.

B. Debit unearned revenue for $135,000 and credit subscription revenue for $135,000.

C. Debit subscription revenue for $45,000 and credit unearned revenue for $45,000.

D. Debit unearned revenue for $45,000 and credit subscription revenue for $45,000.

Answer (D) is correct. *(Publisher)*
**REQUIRED:** The year-end adjusting entry for subscriptions revenue given an initial entry to unearned revenue.
**DISCUSSION:** The initial entry was to debit cash and credit unearned revenue, a liability account, for $180,000. The subscriptions were for 3 years, or 36 months, beginning April 1, year 1. Of this period, 25% (9 months ÷ 36 months) had elapsed as of December 31, year 1. Because the earning process for subscriptions revenue is completed in proportion to the delivery of the subscribed materials over the term of the agreement, Felicity should recognize 25% of the amounts received for subscriptions as revenue at December 31, year 1. The adjusting entry is to debit unearned revenue and credit subscription revenue for $45,000 ($180,000 × 25%). This entry reduces the liability balance to $135,000, representing the remaining 27 months of subscriptions.
Answer (A) is incorrect because debiting revenue and crediting unearned revenue assumes the initial entry was to a revenue account. Answer (B) is incorrect because $45,000, not $135,000, is the adjustment needed at year-end. Answer (C) is incorrect because debiting revenue and crediting unearned revenue assumes the initial entry was to a revenue account.

**11.** Flyn Press received a total of $180,000 for 3-year subscriptions that began April 1, year 1. It recorded this amount as subscription revenue. Assuming Flyn records adjustments only at the end of the calendar year, the adjusting entry required to reflect the proper balances in the accounts at December 31, year 1 is to

A. Debit subscription revenue for $135,000 and credit unearned revenue for $135,000.

B. Debit unearned revenue for $135,000 and credit subscription revenue for $135,000.

C. Debit subscription revenue for $45,000 and credit unearned revenue for $45,000.

D. Debit unearned revenue for $45,000 and credit subscription revenue for $45,000.

Answer (A) is correct. *(Publisher)*
**REQUIRED:** The year-end adjusting entry given an initial entry to a revenue account.
**DISCUSSION:** The company initially debited cash and credited subscription revenue, an income-statement account, for $180,000. Of this amount, $45,000 [$180,000 × (9 months ÷ 36 months)] had been earned by year-end. Because $45,000 should be the year-end subscription revenue amount, the adjusting entry is to debit subscription revenue and credit unearned revenue (a liability account) for $135,000 ($180,000 – $45,000).
Answer (B) is incorrect because debiting unearned revenue and crediting revenue assumes the initial entry was to an unearned revenue account. Answer (C) is incorrect because $135,000, not $45,000, is the necessary adjustment needed at year-end. Answer (D) is incorrect because debiting unearned revenue and crediting revenue assumes the initial entry was to an unearned revenue account.

**12.** Hopkins Corporation, a manufacturer of industrial fans, accounts for warranty costs under the accrual method. During November year 1, the company sold 500 units at $6,000 each. Each unit had a 1-year warranty. Based on past experience, the company expects future warranty costs to be $150 per unit. As of December 31, year 1, no journal entries involving warranty costs related to these units had been made, and no warranty costs were incurred during November or December. The year-end adjusting entry required at December 31, year 1 to account for estimated future warranty costs is to

A. Make no entry until costs are incurred.

B. Debit sales for $75,000 and credit unearned warranty revenue for $75,000.

C. Debit warranty expenses for $62,500 and credit estimated liability under warranties for $62,500.

D. Debit warranty expenses for $75,000 and credit estimated liability under warranties for $75,000.

Answer (D) is correct. *(Publisher)*
**REQUIRED:** The entry to record estimated future warranty costs.
**DISCUSSION:** When the warranty is inseparable from the item sold, warranty costs should be treated as a loss contingency to be accrued at the time of sale if their incurrence is probable and their amount can be reasonably estimated. The company sold 500 units, each of which is expected to result in warranty costs of $150. No warranty costs have yet been incurred, so the full $150 per unit should be accrued at year-end. The estimated expense is $75,000 (500 units × $150). The adjusting entry is therefore to debit warranty expense and credit estimated liability under warranties for $75,000.
Answer (A) is incorrect because, under GAAP, warranty costs should be accrued in the year of sale when the warranty is an integral part of the sale. Answer (B) is incorrect because the company is selling a product, not warranties. Thus, a liability and an expense must be accrued for the expected cost of servicing the products, not a liability for unearned revenue. Answer (C) is incorrect because a full year's expense should be recorded, not a prorated amount for the remaining 10 months in the warranty period.

**13.** Beginning January 1, year 1, Stone Company offered a 3-year warranty from date of sale on any of its products sold after January 1, year 1. The warranty offer was part of a program to increase sales. Meeting the terms of the warranty was expected to cost 4% of sales. Sales made under warranty in year 1 totaled $18 million, and 20% of the units sold were returned. These units were repaired or replaced at a cost of $130,000. The warranty expense reported on Stone's year 1 income statement is

A. $720,000

B. $202,000

C. $240,000

D. $130,000

Answer (A) is correct. *(Publisher)*
**REQUIRED:** The amount of warranty expense.
**DISCUSSION:** Given that warranty expense is expected to be 4% of sales, $720,000 ($18,000,000 × 4%) is recorded as an expense for year 1. How many units were returned in the current year and how much cash was expended for warranty repairs in the current year are not relevant because the warranty will last for 3 years. Warranty expense is recorded in the year of sale because warranty expense represents a selling cost.
Answer (B) is incorrect because $202,000 equals .4% of sales plus the cash outlay. Answer (C) is incorrect because the total cost is deducted in the year of the sale. It is not allocated over 3 years. Answer (D) is incorrect because $130,000 is the cash outlay in the current year.

**14.** The accrual of a contingent liability and the related loss should be recorded when the

A. Loss resulting from a future event may be material in relation to income.

B. Future vent that gives rise to the liability is unusual in nature and nonrecurring.

C. Amount of the loss resulting from the event is reasonably estimated and the occurrence of the loss is probable.

D. Event that gives rise to the liability is unusual and its occurrence is probable.

Answer (C) is correct. *(CMA, adapted)*
**REQUIRED:** The timing of the accrual of a contingent liability and the related loss.
**DISCUSSION:** SFAS 5 requires a contingent liability to be recorded, along with the related loss, when it is probable that an asset has been impaired or a liability has been incurred, and the amount of the loss can be reasonably estimated. The key words are "probable" and "reasonably estimated."
Answer (A) is incorrect because the loss must be probable and capable of estimation before it is recorded. Answer (B) is incorrect because the terms unusual and nonrecurring apply to extraordinary items, not contingencies. Answer (D) is incorrect because there is no requirement that a contingency be unusual.

**15.** A company is subject to warranty claims. It is estimated that between $1,000,000 and $3,000,000 will probably be paid out. No estimate of loss within this range is more likely than any other. The company should

    A. Make no journal entry at this time.

    B. Disclose only a possible loss.

    C. Defer a loss of $1,000,000 to $3,000,000.

    D. Accrue a loss of $1,000,000.

Answer (D) is correct. *(CIA, adapted)*
    **REQUIRED:** The proper treatment of an estimation of warranty claims.
    **DISCUSSION:** SFAS 5, *Accounting for Contingencies*, requires that a loss from contingencies be accrued when it is probable that, at a balance sheet date, an asset is overstated or a liability has been incurred and the amount of the loss can be reasonably estimated. According to FASB Interpretation No. 14, *Reasonable Estimation of the Amount of a Loss*, if the estimate is stated within a given range and no amount within that range appears to be a better estimate than any other, the minimum of the range should be accrued.
    Answer (A) is incorrect because GAAP require accrual of a $1,000,000 loss. Answer (B) is incorrect because the loss is probable. Answer (C) is incorrect because the loss is not deferred; it is accrued.

**16.** When reporting contingencies

    A. Guarantees of others' indebtedness are reported as a loss contingency only if the loss is considered imminent or highly probable.

    B. Disclosure of a loss contingency is to be made if there is a remote possibility that the loss has been incurred.

    C. Disclosure of a loss contingency must include a dollar estimate of the loss.

    D. A loss that is probable but not estimable must be disclosed with a notation that the amount of the loss cannot be estimated.

Answer (D) is correct. *(CMA, adapted)*
    **REQUIRED:** The true statement about reporting contingencies.
    **DISCUSSION:** SFAS 5 prescribes the accounting for contingencies. Contingencies are divided into three categories: probable (likely to occur), reasonably possible, and remote. When contingent losses are probable and the amount can be reasonably estimated, the amount of the loss should be charged against income. If the amount cannot be reasonably estimated but the loss is at least reasonably possible, full disclosure should be made, including a statement that an estimate cannot be made.
    Answer (A) is incorrect because SFAS 5 requires that a guarantee of another's indebtedness is to be disclosed even if the possibility of loss is remote. Moreover, the fair value of a noncontingent liability is recognized at the inception of the obligation to stand ready to perform during the term of the guarantee. Answer (B) is incorrect because remote contingencies ordinarily need not be disclosed. Answer (C) is incorrect because disclosure need not include an amount when that amount cannot be reasonably estimated.

**17.** A company has been sued for $100,000,000 for producing and selling an unsafe product. Attorneys for the company cannot predict the outcome of the litigation. In its financial statements, the company should

    A. Make the following journal entry, and disclose the existence of the lawsuit in a note.

        Estimated loss
          from litigation    $100,000,000
          Estimated liability
            from litigation loss    $100,000,000

    B. Disclose the existence of the lawsuit in a note without making a journal entry.

    C. Neither make a journal entry nor disclose the lawsuit in a note because bad publicity will hurt the company.

    D. Make the following journal entry, and disclose the existence of the lawsuit in a note.

        Cost of goods
          sold    $100,000,000
          Estimated liability
            from litigation loss    $100,000,000

Answer (B) is correct. *(CIA, adapted)*
    **REQUIRED:** The financial statement treatment of a possible loss from litigation.
    **DISCUSSION:** A contingency is "an existing condition, situation, or set of circumstances involving uncertainty as to possible gain or loss to an enterprise that will ultimately be resolved when one or more future events occur or fail to occur." The accounting treatment of loss contingencies is to charge estimated losses to income (and record the liability or asset impairment) when information available prior to issuance of financial statements indicates that it is probable that an asset had been impaired or a liability had been incurred (as of year-end) and the amount of loss can be reasonably estimated. If an accrual is not made, disclosure of the contingency should be made when there is a reasonable possibility that a loss will occur.
    Answer (A) is incorrect because a journal entry is made when the loss contingency is probable and reasonably estimable, not just possible. Answer (C) is incorrect because a disclosure must be made when a loss contingency is possible. Answer (D) is incorrect because a journal entry is made when the loss contingency is probable and reasonably estimable, not just possible.

**18.** For the past 3 months, Kenton, Inc. has been negotiating a labor contract with potentially significant wage increases. Before completing the year-end financial statements on November 30, Kenton determined that the contract was likely to be signed in the near future. Kenton has estimated that the effect of the new contract will cost the company either $100,000, $200,000, or $300,000. Also, Kenton believes that each estimate has an equal chance of occurring and that the likelihood of the new contract being retroactive to the fiscal year ended November 30 is probable. According to SFAS 5, Kenton should

A. Do nothing because no loss will occur if the contract is never signed.

B. Disclose each loss contingency amount in the notes to the November 30 financial statements.

C. Accrue $100,000 in the income statement, and disclose the nature of the contingency and the additional loss exposure.

D. Follow conservatism and accrue $300,000 in the income statement, and disclose the nature of the contingency.

Answer (C) is correct. *(CMA, adapted)*
**REQUIRED:** The proper action regarding the recording of a contingency under the provisions of SFAS 5.
**DISCUSSION:** SFAS 5 prescribes accounting for contingencies. Estimated losses from contingencies should be charged to income when information available prior to issuance of financial statements indicates that it is probable that an asset has been impaired or a liability has been incurred and the amount of loss can be reasonably estimated. "Probable" means that the future event is "likely" to occur. Moreover, if an estimate is stated within a given range, and no amount within the range appears to be a better estimate than any other, the minimum of the range should be accrued. Also, the nature of the contingency, the additional loss exposure, and the amount accrued should be disclosed.
Answer (A) is incorrect because a loss contingency should not be disregarded unless the chance of occurrence is remote. Answer (B) is incorrect because an event that will probably occur should be accrued in the financial statements. Answer (D) is incorrect because the minimum amount in the range should be accrued, unless another amount would give a more accurate estimate. Conservatism does not require accrual of the minimum estimate if another is the most likely.

**19.** Seller-Guarantor sold an asset with a carrying amount at the time of sale of $500,000 to Buyer for $650,000 in cash. Seller also provided a guarantee to Guarantee Bank of the $600,000 loan that Guarantee made to Buyer to finance the sale. The probability that Seller will become liable under the guarantee is remote. In a stand-alone arm's-length transaction with an unrelated party, the premium required by Seller to provide the same guarantee would have been $40,000. According to FASB Interpretation No. 45, *Guarantor's Accounting and Disclosure Requirements for Guarantees, Including Indirect Guarantees of the Indebtedness of Others*, the entry made by Seller at the time of the sale should include a

A. Gain of $150,000.

B. Noncontingent liability of $40,000.

C. Contingent liability of $600,000.

D. Loss of $450,000.

Answer (B) is correct. *(Publisher)*
**REQUIRED:** The entry made to reflect sale of an asset and the seller's guarantee of the buyer's debt.
**DISCUSSION:** No contingent liability results because the likelihood of payment by the guarantor is remote. However, a noncontingent liability is recognized at the inception of the seller's obligation to stand ready to perform during the term of the guarantee. This liability is initially measured at fair value. In a multiple-element transaction with an unrelated party, the fair value is estimated, for example, as the premium required by the guarantor to provide the same guarantee in a stand-alone arm's-length transaction with an unrelated party. The amount of that premium is given as $40,000. Hence, Seller debits cash for the total received ($650,000), credits the asset sold for its carrying amount ($500,000), credits the noncontingent liability for its estimated fair value ($40,000), and credits a gain for $110,000 ($650,000 – $500,000 – $40,000).
Answer (A) is incorrect because a gain of $150,000 assumes neither a noncontingent nor a contingent liability is recognized. Answer (C) is incorrect because no contingent liability is recognized. The likelihood of payment is remote, not probable. Answer (D) is incorrect because a loss of $450,000 assumes recognition of a contingent liability of $600,000.

**20.** During year 1, Smith Co. filed suit against West, Inc. seeking damages for patent infringement. At December 31, year 1, Smith's legal counsel believed that it was probable that Smith would be successful against West for an estimated amount in the range of $75,000 to $150,000, with all amounts in the range considered equally likely. In March year 2, Smith was awarded $100,000 and received full payment thereof. In its year 1 financial statements issued in February year 2, how should this award be reported?

A. As a receivable and revenue of $100,000.

B. As a receivable and deferred revenue of $100,000.

C. As a disclosure of a contingent gain of $100,000.

D. As a disclosure of a contingent gain of an undetermined amount in the range of $75,000 to $150,000.

Answer (D) is correct. *(CPA, adapted)*
**REQUIRED:** The reporting of a gain contingency.
**DISCUSSION:** In accordance with SFAS 5, gain contingencies should not be recognized until they are realized. A gain contingency should be disclosed, but care should be taken to avoid misleading implications as to the likelihood of realization. The disclosure should reflect the estimated range of the gain.

**21.** Lister Company intends to refinance a portion of its short-term debt next year and is negotiating a long-term financing agreement with a local bank. This agreement will be noncancelable and will extend for 2 years. The amount of short-term debt that Lister Company can exclude from its statement of financial position at December 31

A. May exceed the amount available for refinancing under the agreement.

B. Depends on the demonstrated ability to consummate the refinancing.

C. Must be adjusted by the difference between the present value and the market value of the short-term debt.

D. Is reduced by the proportionate change in the working capital ratio.

Answer (B) is correct. *(CMA, adapted)*
**REQUIRED:** The amount of short-term debt excluded.
**DISCUSSION:** If an enterprise intends to refinance short-term obligations on a long-term basis and demonstrates an ability to consummate the refinancing, the obligations should be excluded from current liabilities and classified as noncurrent (SFAS 6, *Classification of Short-Term Obligations Expected to Be Refinanced*). The ability to consummate the refinancing may be demonstrated by a post-balance-sheet-date issuance of a long-term obligation or equity securities, or by entering into a financing agreement that meets certain criteria. These criteria are that the agreement does not expire within 1 year, it is noncancelable by the lender, no violation of the agreement exists at the balance sheet date, and the lender is financially capable of honoring the agreement.
Answer (A) is incorrect because the amount excluded cannot exceed the amount available for refinancing. Answer (C) is incorrect because SFAS 6 has no provision for adjustments or reductions. Answer (D) is incorrect because SFAS 6 has no provision for adjustments or reductions.

**22.** A company has a $100,000 liability on the books. In 1 year, $110,000 will be due, including 10% interest. The company negotiates settlement of the debt today by exchanging $90,000 of customer receivables. What is the journal entry today?

| A. | Liability | $110,000 | |
| | Receivables | | $99,000 |
| | Gain | | 11,000 |
| | | | |
| B. | Liability | $100,000 | |
| | Receivables | | $99,000 |
| | Gain | | 1,000 |
| | | | |
| C. | Liability | $110,000 | |
| | Receivables | | $90,000 |
| | Gain | | 20,000 |
| | | | |
| D. | Liability | $100,000 | |
| | Receivables | | $90,000 |
| | Gain | | 10,000 |

Answer (D) is correct. *(CIA, adapted)*
**REQUIRED:** The journal entry to record settlement of a liability by exchanging customer receivables.
**DISCUSSION:** A troubled debt restructuring may occur as an asset exchange, as a modification of terms, or as a combination of these two methods. In this instance, the troubled debt restructuring is effected as an asset exchange. In such an exchange, the asset given up for the troubled debt must first be adjusted from its carrying amount to its fair value, with an ordinary gain or loss being recognized for the adjustment. The fair value of the asset provided must then be compared with the carrying amount of the troubled debt to determine the gain to be recognized on the exchange. In this question, one must assume that the carrying amount and fair value of the receivables are the same. Consequently, the liability should be debited for its $100,000 balance. Receivables with a $90,000 balance are given up, so that account should be credited. The difference is a gain. The liability and receivables should not be increased by the 10% interest rate.

**23.** At December 31, 20X2, a company had the following short-term obligations that were expected to be refinanced:

| | |
|---|---|
| 17% note payable | $140,000 |
| 15% note payable | $200,000 |

The 17% note payable was issued on October 1, 20X2 and matures on July 1, 20X3. The 15% note payable was issued on May 1, 20X2 and matures on May 1, 20X3. On February 1, 20X3, the $140,000 balance of the 17% note payable was refinanced by issuance of a long-term debt instrument. On February 7, 20X3, the company entered into a noncancelable agreement with a lender to refinance the 15% note payable on a long-term basis. On March 1, 20X3, the date of issuance of the December 31, 20X2 balance sheet, both parties are financially capable of honoring the agreement and there have been no violations of the provisions of the refinancing agreement. The total amount of short-term obligations that may be properly excluded from current liabilities on the company's December 31, 20X2 balance sheet is

- A. $0
- B. $140,000
- C. $200,000
- D. $340,000

Answer (D) is correct. *(CIA, adapted)*
**REQUIRED:** The total amount of short-term obligations that may be properly excluded from current liabilities.
**DISCUSSION:** Under SFAS 6, an enterprise is required to exclude a short-term obligation from current liabilities if the entity has the intent and ability to refinance it on a long-term basis. The ability to consummate the refinancing may be demonstrated either by (1) actually refinancing the short-term obligation by issuance of a long-term obligation or equity securities after the date of the balance sheet but before it is issued, or (2) entering into a financing agreement that clearly permits the enterprise to refinance the debt on a long-term basis. The ability to refinance the 17% note payable is demonstrated by the actual refinancing after the balance sheet date but before the date of issuance of the balance sheet. The ability to refinance the 15% note payable is demonstrated by the borrower's entering into a long-term, noncancelable financing agreement given that both parties are financially capable and no violations of its terms have occurred. Thus, $340,000 ($140,000 17% note + $200,000 15% note) may be excluded from current liabilities.
Answer (A) is incorrect because $340,000 may be excluded from current liabilities. Answer (B) is incorrect because the 15% note is also excluded from current liabilities. Answer (C) is incorrect because the 17% note is also excluded from current liabilities.

## 16.2 Long-Term Liabilities

Questions 24 and 25 are based on the following information. Tonya Corporation entered into a noncancelable, long-term contract with a supplier for the purchase of raw materials beginning in the calendar year 2. The contract price at December 31, year 1 was $1 million, and the fair value of the raw materials was $1,150,000. This amount was considered material.

**24.** Tonya Corporation's financial statements at December 31, year 2 should

- A. Include a contingent liability of $1 million.
- B. Disclose the purchase commitment.
- C. Include a liability of $1,150,000.
- D. Include a deferred liability of $1 million.

Answer (B) is correct. *(Publisher)*
**REQUIRED:** The proper accounting treatment of a purchase commitment on the year-end financial statements.
**DISCUSSION:** Purchase commitments ordinarily are not recognized because title has not passed to the buyer, but ARB 43 requires that losses on purchase commitments be recorded in the period in which they occur. Gains, however, should not be recorded. Thus, because a gain ($1,150,000 fair value – $1,000,000 price = $150,000 gain) is involved, the accounting treatment is to disclose the material purchase commitment but make no journal entry.
Answer (A) is incorrect because no liability is recorded as long as the contract is executory. When the other party performs under the contract, Tonya will incur an obligation and must then record a liability. Answer (C) is incorrect because no liability is recorded as long as the contract is executory. When the other party performs under the contract, Tonya will incur an obligation and must then record a liability. Answer (D) is incorrect because no liability is recognized until the other party performs.

**25.** Assume the goods were received and the market price of the raw materials is $900,000. If payment has not been remitted for this transaction, Tonya Corporation's financial statements at December 31, year 2 should report

    A. Nothing about this commitment.

    B. A liability of $1 million.

    C. A liability of $100,000.

    D. A liability of $900,000.

Answer (B) is correct. *(Publisher)*
    **REQUIRED:** The treatment of a loss on a purchase commitment.
    **DISCUSSION:** Tonya should debit inventory (purchases) for $900,000 (assuming this amount is the lower-of-cost-or-market valuation), debit a loss for $100,000 ($1,000,000 price – $900,000 fair value), and credit a liability for the $1 million agreed purchase price. If the goods had not been shipped by the seller, the entry would have been to debit an estimated loss and credit an estimated liability for $100,000. The subsequent entry when the goods are received would then be to debit inventory, debit the estimated liability, and credit a liability.
    Answer (A) is incorrect because the executed contract must be recorded. Answer (C) is incorrect because the entire $1 million liability must be recorded for the executed contract. If the contract were executory (unperformed), only the estimated loss and an equal liability would be recognized. Answer (D) is incorrect because $900,000 is the fair value of the inventory.

**26.** Careful reading of an annual report will reveal that off-balance-sheet debt includes

    A. Amounts due in future years under operating leases.

    B. Transfers of accounts receivable without recourse.

    C. Current portion of long-term debt.

    D. Amounts due in future years under capital leases.

Answer (A) is correct. *(CMA, adapted)*
    **REQUIRED:** The off-balance-sheet debt.
    **DISCUSSION:** Off-balance-sheet debt includes any type of liability that the company is responsible for but that does not appear on the balance sheet. The most common example is the amount due in future years on operating leases. Under SFAS 13, operating leases are not capitalized; instead, only the periodic payments of rent are reported when actually paid. Capital leases (those similar to a purchase) must be capitalized and reported as liabilities.
    Answer (B) is incorrect because transfers of accounts receivable without recourse do not create a liability for the company. This transaction is simply a transfer of receivables for cash. Answer (C) is incorrect because the current portion of long-term debt is reported on the balance sheet as a current liability. Answer (D) is incorrect because amounts due in future years under capital leases are required to be capitalized under SFAS 13.

**27.** Which of the following is not an example of off-balance-sheet financing?

    A. Transfers of receivables to third parties with recourse that are deemed to be sales.

    B. Guarantees of indebtedness.

    C. Unconditional purchase obligations.

    D. Capitalized leases.

Answer (D) is correct. *(CIA, adapted)*
    **REQUIRED:** The item not off-balance-sheet financing.
    **DISCUSSION:** Off-balance-sheet financing is debt that need not be recognized in the financial statements. One purpose is to improve the balance sheet by reducing the debt-equity ratio. Some common examples of off-balance-sheet financing are transfers of receivables with recourse accounted for as sales, project financing arrangements, take-or-pay contracts, unconditional purchase obligations, pension obligations (amounts in excess of the unfunded accumulated benefit obligation), and operating leases. Capitalized leases are recorded as financial commitments on the balance sheet and are not off-balance-sheet financing.
    Answer (A) is incorrect because, when transfers of receivables to third parties with recourse are deemed to be sales, they are not recorded as borrowings. Answer (B) is incorrect because guarantees of indebtedness result in loss contingencies that are disclosed but not accrued unless the loss is probable. Answer (C) is incorrect because an unconditional purchase commitment must be disclosed but not recorded at the time of the agreement.

**28.** If the market rate of interest is <List A> the coupon rate when bonds are issued, then the bonds will sell in the market at a price <List B> the face value, and the issuing firm will record a <List C> on bonds payable.

| | List A | List B | List C |
|---|---|---|---|
| A. | Equal to | Equal to | Premium |
| B. | Greater than | Greater than | Premium |
| C. | Greater than | Less than | Discount |
| D. | Less than | Greater than | Discount |

Answer (C) is correct. *(CIA, adapted)*
**REQUIRED:** The relationship of the market rate, the coupon rate, and the recording of a discount or premium.
**DISCUSSION:** If the market rate exceeds the coupon rate, the price of the bonds must decline to a level that equates the yield on the bonds with the market rate of interest. Accordingly, the bonds will be recorded by a debit to cash for the proceeds, a debit to discount on bonds payable, and a credit to bonds payable at face value.
Answer (A) is incorrect because, if the market rate equals the coupon rate, the bonds will not sell at a premium or discount. Answer (B) is incorrect because, if the market rate exceeds the coupon rate, the bond issue will sell at a discount. Answer (D) is incorrect because, if the market rate is less than the coupon rate, the bonds will sell at a price in excess of the face value. The issuing company will record a premium.

**29.** On January 1, a company issued a 10-year $500,000 bond at 96% of face value. The bond bears interest at 12%, payable on January 1 and July 1. The entry to record the issuance of the bond on January 1 would be

| | | | |
|---|---|---|---|
| A. | Cash | $480,000 | |
| | Bonds payable | | $480,000 |
| | | | |
| B. | Cash | $500,000 | |
| | Bonds payable | | $500,000 |
| | | | |
| C. | Cash | $480,000 | |
| | Discount on bonds | | |
| | payable | $ 20,000 | |
| | Bonds payable | | $500,000 |
| | | | |
| D. | Cash | $500,000 | |
| | Premium on | | |
| | bonds payable | | $ 20,000 |
| | Bonds payable | | $480,000 |

Answer (C) is correct. *(CIA, adapted)*
**REQUIRED:** The entry to record the issuance of the bond.
**DISCUSSION:** The company received $480,000 cash on the issuance of the bond. Its face value is $500,000, the amount to be paid at maturity. Hence, the credit to bonds payable is $500,000. The $20,000 difference is recorded as a discount on bonds payable (a debit) and is amortized over the life of the issue.
Answer (A) is incorrect because the entry to bonds payable is based on the face, or maturity, value of the bond issued. The difference between the amount received on issuance and the face value is recorded as a premium or discount on bonds payable. Answer (B) is incorrect because the discount should be recognized. Answer (D) is incorrect because the debit to cash is $480,000, a $20,000 discount should be debited, and the credit to bonds payable is $500,000.

**30.** A company issues 10-year bonds with a face value of $1,000,000, dated January 1 and bearing interest at an annual rate of 12% payable semiannually on January 1 and July 1. The full interest amount will be paid each due date. The market rate of interest on bonds of similar risk and maturity, with the same schedule of interest payments, is also 12%. If the bonds are issued on February 1, the amount the issuing company receives from the buyers of the bonds on that date is

A. $990,000

B. $1,000,000

C. $1,010,000

D. $1,020,000

Answer (C) is correct. *(CIA, adapted)*
**REQUIRED:** The amount received when bonds are issued subsequent to the date printed on the face of the bonds.
**DISCUSSION:** The amount the issuing company receives on February 1 is the face value of the issue plus 1 month of accrued interest, or $1,010,000 {$1,000,000 + [($1,000,000 × 12%) ÷ 12]}.
Answer (A) is incorrect because $990,000 is the result if 1 month of accrued interest is deducted from, rather than added to, the amount received. Answer (B) is incorrect because the purchasers must pay for the accrued interest from the last interest date to the issue date. They will receive 6 months' interest on July 1 despite holding the bonds for 5 months. Answer (D) is incorrect because $1,020,000 results from adding 2 months of accrued interest to the face value.

**31.** A bond issue sold at a premium is valued on the statement of financial position at the

A. Maturity value.

B. Maturity value plus the unamortized portion of the premium.

C. Cost at the date of investment.

D. Maturity value less the unamortized portion of the premium.

Answer (B) is correct. *(CMA, adapted)*
REQUIRED: The means of valuing a bond issue sold at a premium.
DISCUSSION: A bond liability is shown at its face value (maturity value), minus any related discount, or plus any related premium. Thus, a bond issued at a premium is shown at its maturity value plus the unamortized portion of the premium. The premium account is sometimes called an adjunct account because it is shown as an addition to another account.
Answer (A) is incorrect because the maturity value must be increased by any related unamortized premium. Answer (C) is incorrect because even a bond investment must be adjusted for the related premium or discount. Answer (D) is incorrect because the premium is added to the maturity value of a bond liability.

---

Questions 32 and 33 are based on the following information. On January 1, Matthew Company issued 7% term bonds with a face amount of $1,000,000 due in 8 years. Interest is payable semiannually on January 1 and July 1. On the date of issue, investors were willing to accept an effective interest rate of 6%.

---

**32.** The bonds were issued on January 1 at

A. A premium.

B. An amortized amount.

C. Carrying amount.

D. A discount.

Answer (A) is correct. *(CMA, adapted)*
REQUIRED: The true statement about the issuance of bonds.
DISCUSSION: Because the bonds sold for more than their face amount, they were sold at a premium. The premium adjusted the yield of the bonds to the effective rate (presumably, the market rate).
Answer (B) is incorrect because an amortized amount is the carrying amount of the bonds after at least one period's amortization has been recorded. Answer (C) is incorrect because carrying amount is the amount at which bonds appear on the financial statements, including any unamortized premium or discount. For a new issue of bonds, no carrying amount existed before issuance (i.e., they did not appear on the books). Answer (D) is incorrect because a discount arises when bonds are sold at less than their face amount.

**33.** Assume the bonds were issued on January 1 for $1,062,809. Using the effective interest amortization method, Matthew Company recorded interest expense for the 6 months ended June 30 in the amount of

A. $35,000

B. $70,000

C. $63,769

D. $31,884

Answer (D) is correct. *(CMA, adapted)*
REQUIRED: The interest expense for the first 6 months that the bonds are outstanding.
DISCUSSION: The annual interest cash outlay is $70,000 ($1,000,000 × 7% nominal rate), or $35,000 each semiannual period. Interest expense is less than $35,000, however, because the bonds were originally issued at a premium. That premium should be amortized over the life of the bond. Thus, interest expense for the first 6 months is $31,884 [$1,062,809 × 6% × (6 months ÷ 12 months)], and premium amortization is $3,116 ($35,000 – $31,884).
Answer (A) is incorrect because the $35,000 is the cash outlay. Answer (B) is incorrect because $70,000 is the cash outlay for a full year. Answer (C) is incorrect because $63,769 is the expense for the first year if interest is paid annually.

**34.** According to SFAS 78, *Classification of Obligations That Are Callable by the Creditor,* long-term obligations that are or will become callable by the creditor because of the debtor's violation of a provision of the debt agreement at the balance sheet date should be classified as

A. Long-term liabilities.

B. Current liabilities unless the debtor goes bankrupt.

C. Current liabilities unless the creditor has waived the right to demand repayment for more than 1 year from balance sheet date.

D. Contingent liabilities until the violation is corrected.

Answer (C) is correct.   *(CMA, adapted)*
**REQUIRED:** The classification of long-term debt.
**DISCUSSION:** In these circumstances, the obligation should be classified as current. However, the debt need not be reclassified if the violation will be cured within a specified grace period or if the creditor formally waives or subsequently loses the right to demand repayment for a period of more than a year from the balance sheet date. Also, reclassification is not required if the debtor expects and has the ability to refinance the obligation on a long-term basis.
Answer (A) is incorrect because SFAS 78 requires classification as a current liability. Answer (B) is incorrect because bankruptcy is not an exception. Answer (D) is incorrect because SFAS 78 concerns callable, not contingent, liabilities.

**35.** On July 1, 20X0, Eagle Corp. issued 600 of its 10%, $1,000 bonds at 99 plus accrued interest. The bonds are dated April 1, 20X0 and mature in 10 years. Interest is payable semiannually on April 1 and October 1. What amount did Eagle receive from the bond issuance?

A. $579,000

B. $594,000

C. $600,000

D. $609,000

Answer (D) is correct.   *(CPA, adapted)*
**REQUIRED:** The cash received from the issuance of a bond at a discount plus accrued interest.
**DISCUSSION:** The face amount of the bonds is $600,000 (600 bonds × $1,000 face value). Excluding interest, the proceeds from the issuance of the bonds were $594,000 ($600,000 × 99%). Accrued interest for three months was $15,000 [($600,000 face amount × 10% coupon rate × (3 ÷ 12)]. The net cash received from the issuance of the bonds was therefore equal to $609,000 ($594,000 bond proceeds + $15,000 accrued interest).
Answer (A) is incorrect because $579,000 results from subtracting the $15,000 of interest. Answer (B) is incorrect because $594,000 does not include accrued interest. Answer (C) is incorrect because $600,000 is the face amount of the bonds.

**36.** Hancock Co.'s December 31, 20X0 balance sheet contained the following items in the long-term liabilities section:

Unsecured

| | |
|---|---:|
| 9.375% registered bonds ($25,000 maturing annually beginning in 20X4) | $275,000 |
| 11.5% convertible bonds, callable beginning in 20X9, due in 20 years | 125,000 |

Secured

| | |
|---|---:|
| 9.875% guaranty security bonds, due in 20 years | $250,000 |
| 10.0% commodity backed bonds ($50,000 maturing annually beginning in 20X4) | 200,000 |

| | Serial Bonds | Debenture Bonds |
|---|---|---|
| A. | $475,000 | $400,000 |
| B. | $475,000 | $125,000 |
| C. | $450,000 | $400,000 |
| D. | $200,000 | $650,000 |

Answer (A) is correct.   *(CPA, adapted)*
**REQUIRED:** The total amounts of serial bonds and debenture bonds.
**DISCUSSION:** Serial bonds mature in installments at various dates. Debentures are unsecured bonds. The commodity-backed bonds and the registered bonds are serial bonds. They total $475,000 ($275,000 + $200,000). The registered bonds and the convertible bonds are debentures. They total $400,000 ($275,000 + $125,000).
Answer (B) is incorrect because the registered bonds are also debentures. Answer (C) is incorrect because the registered bonds, not the guaranty security bonds, are serial bonds. Answer (D) is incorrect because the registered bonds are serial bonds and the guaranty security bonds are not debentures.

**37.** On July 1, 20X0, after recording interest and amortization, York Co. converted $1 million of its 12% convertible bonds into 50,000 shares of $1 par value common stock. On the conversion date, the carrying amount of the bonds was $1.3 million, the fair value of the bonds was $1.4 million, and York's common stock was publicly trading at $30 per share. Using the book-value method, what amount of additional paid-in capital should York record as a result of the conversion?

    A.  $950,000

    B.  $1,250,000

    C.  $1,350,000

    D.  $1,500,000

Answer (B) is correct. *(CPA, adapted)*
    **REQUIRED:** The additional paid-in capital from conversion of bonds under the book-value method.
    **DISCUSSION:** Under the book-value method for recognizing the conversion of outstanding bonds payable to common stock, the stock issued is recorded at the carrying value of the bonds, with no recognition of a gain or loss. Accordingly, the conversion should be recorded at $1.3 million. However, this amount must be allocated between common stock and additional paid-in capital. The common stock account is always valued at par value; therefore, $50,000 (50,000 shares × $1) will be credited to common stock and $1,250,000 to additional paid-in capital.
    Answer (A) is incorrect because $950,000 equals the face amount of the bonds minus the par value of the stock. Answer (C) is incorrect because the carrying amount of the bonds is not increased by the par value of the stock. Answer (D) is incorrect because $1,500,000 is the fair value of the stock at the market price.

**38.** On March 1, 20X0, Fine Co. borrowed $10,000 and signed a two-year note bearing interest at 12% per annum compounded annually. Interest is payable in full at maturity on February 28, 20X2. What amount should Fine report as a liability for accrued interest at December 31, 20X1?

    A.  $0

    B.  $1,000

    C.  $1,200

    D.  $2,320

Answer (D) is correct. *(CPA, adapted)*
    **REQUIRED:** The amount of accrued interest liability.
    **DISCUSSION:** Given annual compounding, interest for the second year is calculated based on a carrying amount equal to the $10,000 principal plus the $1,200 ($10,000 × 12%) of first-year interest. Thus, accrued interest for the next 10 months is $1,120 {[($10,000 + $1,200) × 12%] × (10 months ÷ 12 months)}. Total accrued interest after 22 months is $2,320 ($1,200 + $1,120).
    Answer (A) is incorrect because interest is accrued annually. Answer (B) is incorrect because $1,000 is the 20X0 interest accrual. Answer (C) is incorrect because $1,200 is the interest for the first 12 months.

**39.** How will net income be affected by the amortization of a premium on bonds payable?

    A.  Interest expense is decreased, so net income is increased.

    B.  Interest expense is increased, so net income is decreased.

    C.  Interest revenue is increased, so net income is increased.

    D.  Interest revenue is decreased, so net income is decreased.

Answer (A) is correct. *(CIA, adapted)*
    **REQUIRED:** The effect on net income of the amortization of a premium on bonds payable.
    **DISCUSSION:** The entry is to debit interest expense, debit bond premium, and credit cash paid. Thus, the amortization of a premium on bonds payable reduces the interest expense, thereby increasing net income.
    Answer (B) is incorrect because the amortization of a premium on bonds payable reduces interest expense. Answer (C) is incorrect because interest revenue is not affected by the amortization of a premium on bonds payable. Answer (D) is incorrect because interest revenue is not affected by the amortization of a premium on bonds payable.

**40.** The effective-interest method and the straight-line method of amortizing a bond discount differ in that the effective-interest method results in

    A.  Higher total interest expense over the term of the bonds.

    B.  Escalating annual interest expense over the term of the bonds.

    C.  Shrinking annual interest expense over the term of the bonds.

    D.  Constant annual interest expense over the term of the bonds.

Answer (B) is correct. *(CIA, adapted)*
    **REQUIRED:** The difference between the effective-interest method and the straight-line method of amortizing a bond discount.
    **DISCUSSION:** Under the effective-interest method, interest expense for each period equals the effective interest rate times the carrying value of the bond issue. As the discount is amortized, the carrying value rises and interest expense increases.
    Answer (A) is incorrect because the two methods of amortization result in the same total interest expense over the term of the bonds. Answer (C) is incorrect because annual interest expense would decrease if a premium were being amortized. Answer (D) is incorrect because the straight-line method results in constant annual interest expense.

Questions 41 through 44 are based on the following information. On January 1, 20X2, Nichols Company issued 7% term bonds with a face amount of $2 million due January 1, 20Y0. Interest is payable semiannually on January 1 and July 1. On the date of issue, investors were willing to accept an effective interest rate of 6%.

**41.** Assume the bonds were issued on January 1, 20X2 for $2,125,618. Using the effective interest amortization method, Nichols Company recorded interest expense for the 6 months ended June 30, 20X2 in the amount of

- A.  $70,000
- B.  $140,000
- C.  $127,537
- D.  $63,769

Answer (D) is correct.  *(Publisher)*
**REQUIRED:** The interest expense for the first 6 months that the bonds are outstanding.
**DISCUSSION:** Given that the bonds paid interest at a 7% contract rate, the annual interest outlay is $140,000 on a $2 million issue, or $70,000 each semiannual period. Interest expense is less than $70,000, however, because the bonds were originally issued at a $125,618 premium. That premium, which existed because investors were willing to accept a 6% effective interest rate, should be amortized over the life of the bond. For a semiannual period, that 6% annual effective rate translates to a 3% semiannual rate. Hence, interest expense is $63,769 ($2,125,618 face value plus premium × 3%), the cash outlay is $70,000, and premium amortization is $6,231 ($70,000 – $63,769).
Answer (A) is incorrect because $70,000 is the semiannual cash outlay. Answer (B) is incorrect because $140,000 is the cash outlay for a full year. Answer (C) is incorrect because $127,537 would be the expense for the first year if interest were paid on an annual basis instead of semiannually.

**42.** Assume the bonds were issued on January 1, 20X2 for $2,125,618. Using the effective interest amortization method, Nichols Company recorded interest expense for the 6 months ended December 31, 20X2 in the amount of

- A.  $70,000
- B.  $140,000
- C.  $63,582
- D.  $63,769

Answer (C) is correct.  *(Publisher)*
**REQUIRED:** The interest expense for the second 6 months that the bonds are outstanding.
**DISCUSSION:** For a semiannual period, the 6% annual effective rate translates to a 3% semiannual rate. For the first 6-month period (ending June 30), interest expense was $63,769 ($2,125,618 face amount plus premium × 3%), the cash outlay was $70,000 [$2,000,000 × 7% × (6 ÷ 12)], and premium amortization was $6,231 ($70,000 – $63,769). The book value of the bond after 6 months was therefore $2,119,387 ($2,125,618 – $6,231). Consequently, for the second 6-month period (ending December 31, 20X2), interest expense was $63,582 ($2,119,387 × 3%).
Answer (A) is incorrect because $70,000 is the semiannual cash outlay. Answer (B) is incorrect because the $140,000 is the cash outlay for a full year. Answer (D) is incorrect because $63,769 is the expense for the 6-month period ended June 30, 20X2.

**43.** What is the carrying amount of the bonds after the payment of interest on January 1, 20X3?

- A.  $2,000,000
- B.  $2,125,618
- C.  $2,119,387
- D.  $2,112,969

Answer (D) is correct.  *(Publisher)*
**REQUIRED:** The carrying amount of the bonds after they have been outstanding for 1 year.
**DISCUSSION:** For a semiannual period, the 6% annual effective rate translates to a 3% semiannual rate. For the first 6-month period (ending June 30), interest expense was $63,769 ($2,125,618 face amount plus premium × 3%), the cash outlay was $70,000 [$2,000,000 × 7% × (6 ÷ 12)], and premium amortization was $6,231 ($70,000 – $63,769). The book value of the bond after 6 months was therefore $2,119,387 ($2,125,618 – $6,231). Consequently, for the second 6-month period (ending December 31, 20X2), interest expense was $63,582 ($2,119,387 × 3%), amortization was $6,418 ($70,000 – $63,582), and the year-end carrying amount was $2,112,969 ($2,119,387 – $6,418).
Answer (A) is incorrect because $2,000,000 is the face amount of the bonds. Answer (B) is incorrect because $2,125,618 is the issue price. Answer (C) is incorrect because $2,119,387 is the carrying amount after 6 months.

**44.** The bonds were issued on January 1, 20X2 at

A. A premium.

B. An amortized amount.

C. Carrying amount.

D. A discount.

Answer (A) is correct. *(Publisher)*
**REQUIRED:** The true statement about the bond issue.
**DISCUSSION:** Because the bonds sold for more than their face amount, they were issued at a premium. If they had been sold for less than their face amount, they would have been issued at a discount.
Answer (B) is incorrect because an amortized amount is the amount at which bonds appear on the books after at least one period's amortization has been recorded. Answer (C) is incorrect because the carrying amount is the amount at which bonds appear on the financial statements, net of any premium or discount. Given that these bonds were new, they did not have a carrying amount at the time of issuance (i.e., they did not appear on the books). Answer (D) is incorrect because a discount arises when bonds are sold at less than their face amount.

## 16.3 Leases

**45.** On January 1, Harrow Co., as lessee, signed a 5-year noncancelable equipment lease with annual payments of $100,000 beginning December 31. Harrow treated this transaction as a capital lease. The five lease payments have a present value of $379,000 at January 1, based on interest of 10%. What amount should Harrow report as interest for the year ended December 31?

A. $37,900

B. $27,900

C. $24,200

D. $0

Answer (A) is correct. *(CPA, adapted)*
**REQUIRED:** The interest to be recognized in the first year of a capital lease.
**DISCUSSION:** The lease liability at the inception of the lease is $379,000. Under the effective-interest method, the lease liability balance (the carrying amount) at the beginning of each year should be multiplied by the implicit interest rate to determine interest for that year. Accordingly, the interest expense for the first year is $37,900 ($379,000 × $10%).
Answer (B) is incorrect because $27,900 assumes the initial payment was made immediately. Answer (C) is incorrect because $24,200 is one-fifth of the total interest ($500,000 – $379,000 PV). Answer (D) is incorrect because interest must be accrued.

**46.** On January 1, year 1, Babson, Inc. leased two automobiles for executive use. The lease requires Babson to make five annual payments of $13,000 beginning January 1, year 1. At the end of the lease term, December 31, year 5, Babson guarantees the residual value of the automobiles will total $10,000. The lease qualifies as a capital lease. The interest rate implicit in the lease is 9%. Present value factors for the 9% rate implicit in the lease are as follows:

For an annuity due with 5 payments      4.240
For an ordinary annuity with 5 payments    3.890
Present value of $1 for 5 periods        0.650

Babson's recorded capital lease liability immediately after the first required payment should be

A. $48,620

B. $44,070

C. $35,620

D. $31,070

Answer (A) is correct. *(CPA, adapted)*
**REQUIRED:** The recorded capital lease liability immediately after the first required payment.
**DISCUSSION:** SFAS 13, *Accounting for Leases*, requires that the lessee record a capital lease as an asset and a liability at the present value of the minimum lease payments during the lease term. If no bargain purchase option exists, the minimum lease payments equal the sum of the minimum rental payments, the amount of guaranteed residual value, and any nonrenewal penalty imposed. Accordingly, the present value of the minimum lease payments, minus the first required payment, is $48,620 [($13,000 annual payment × 4.240 PV of an annuity due at 9% for 5 periods) + ($10,000 guaranteed residual value × .650 PV of $1 at 9% for 5 periods) – $13,000 first payment].
Answer (B) is incorrect because $44,070 is based on the interest factor for an ordinary annuity. Answer (C) is incorrect because $35,620 is based on deducting the first payment twice. Answer (D) is incorrect because $31,070 is based on the interest factor for an ordinary annuity and on deducting the first payment twice.

**47.** For a direct-financing lease, the gross investment (lease payments receivable) recorded by the lessor is equal to the

A. Present value of the minimum lease payments minus the unguaranteed residual value accruing to the lessor at the end of the lease term.

B. Lower of 90% of the present value of the minimum lease payments or the fair value of the leased asset.

C. Difference between the fair value of the leased asset and the unearned interest revenue.

D. Minimum lease payments plus the unguaranteed residual value accruing to the lessor at the end of the lease term.

Answer (D) is correct.    *(CMA, adapted)*
**REQUIRED:** The gross investment recorded by the lessor for a direct-financing lease.
**DISCUSSION:** For both sales-type and direct-financing leases, the lessor should record as the gross investment in the lease the amount of the minimum lease payments (which include periodic payments plus guaranteed residual value) plus any amounts of unguaranteed residual value. The net investment in the lease is equal to the gross investment, plus any unamortized initial direct costs, minus unearned income. The unguaranteed residual value is the expected value of the leased asset in excess of the guaranteed residual value at the end of the lease term (SFAS 13).
Answer (A) is incorrect because the gross investment is not adjusted for the time value of money. Answer (B) is incorrect because the gross investment is not adjusted for the time value of money or fair value. Answer (C) is incorrect because the gross investment is not adjusted for fair value.

**48.** Initial direct costs incurred by the lessor under a sales-type lease should be

A. Deferred and allocated over the economic life of the leased property.

B. Expensed in the period incurred.

C. Deferred and allocated over the term of the lease in proportion to the recognition of rental income.

D. Added to the gross investment in the lease and amortized over the term of the lease as a yield adjustment.

Answer (B) is correct.    *(CMA, adapted)*
**REQUIRED:** The accounting for initial direct costs in a sales-type lease.
**DISCUSSION:** SFAS 91, *Accounting for Nonrefundable Fees and Costs Associated with Originating or Acquiring Loans and Initial Direct Costs of Leases*, defines initial direct costs as having two components: (1) the lessor's external costs to originate a lease incurred in dealings with independent third parties and (2) the internal costs directly related to specified activities performed by the lessor for that lease. According to SFAS 13, in a sales-type lease, the cost, or carrying amount if different, plus any initial direct costs, minus the present value of any unguaranteed residual value, is charged against income in the same period that the present value of the minimum lease payments is credited to sales. The result is the recognition of a net profit or loss on the sales-type lease.
Answer (A) is incorrect because initial direct costs are considered an expense in the period of sale. Answer (C) is incorrect because they describe the proper treatment of initial direct costs in an operating lease and a direct financing lease, respectively. Answer (D) is incorrect because they describe the proper treatment of initial direct costs in an operating lease and a direct financing lease, respectively.

**49.** Howe Co. leased equipment to Kew Corp. on January 2, year 1 for an 8-year period expiring December 31, year 8. Equal payments under the lease are $600,000 and are due on January 2 of each year. The first payment was made on January 2, year 1. The list selling price of the equipment is $3,520,000 and its carrying cost on Howe's books is $2.8 million. The lease is appropriately accounted for as a sales-type lease. The present value of the lease payments at an imputed interest rate of 12% (Howe's incremental borrowing rate) is $3.3 million. What amount of profit on the sale should Howe report for the year ended December 31, year 1?

A. $720,000

B. $500,000

C. $90,000

D. $0

Answer (B) is correct.    *(CPA, adapted)*
**REQUIRED:** The amount of profit on a sales-type lease.
**DISCUSSION:** Howe Co., the lessor, should report a profit from a sales-type lease. The gross profit equals the difference between the sales price (present value of the minimum lease payments) and the cost. The cost for a sales-type lease is not the same as the fair value. Consequently, the profit on the sale equals $500,000 ($3,300,000 – $2,800,000).
Answer (A) is incorrect because $720,000 is the result of using the list selling price instead of the present value of the lease payments. Answer (C) is incorrect because $90,000 is one-eighth of the difference between the list price and the cost. Answer (D) is incorrect because a profit of $500,000 should be reported.

**50.** On January 1, Wren Company leased a building to Brill under an operating lease for 10 years at $50,000 per year, payable the first day of each lease year. Wren paid $15,000 to a real estate broker as a finder's fee. The annual depreciation on the building is $12,000. For the year, Wren incurred insurance and property tax expenses totaling $9,000. Wren's net rental income for the year should be

A. $27,500

B. $29,000

C. $35,000

D. $36,500

Answer (A) is correct. *(CPA, adapted)*
**REQUIRED:** The net rental income that should be recorded for the first year.
**DISCUSSION:** The net rental income is equal to the $50,000 annual payment minus any expenses to be recorded during the year. These expenses include $12,000 of depreciation, $9,000 for insurance and property taxes, and $1,500 ($15,000 ÷ 10 years) amortization of the finder's fee. The finder's fee is an initial direct cost that should be deferred and allocated over the lease term in proportion to the recognition of rental income (SFAS 13). It should therefore be recorded as a deferred charge and amortized using the straight-line method over the 10-year lease term. Accordingly, the net rental income for the year is $27,500.

| | |
|---|---|
| Rental income | $ 50,000 |
| Depreciation | (12,000) |
| Insurance and property tax expenses | (9,000) |
| Amortization | (1,500) |
| Net rental income | $ 27,500 |

Answer (B) is incorrect because $29,000 omits amortization of the finder's fee. Answer (C) is incorrect because $35,000 equals rental income minus the full finder's fee. Answer (D) is incorrect because $36,500 excludes insurance and property taxes from the computation.

**51.** Equipment covered by a lease agreement is expected by the lessor to have a residual value at the end of the lease term of $20,000. As part of the lease agreement, the lessee guarantees a residual value of $12,000. In the case of excessive usage, the guaranteed residual value is $18,000. What is the amount of guaranteed residual value that should be included in the calculation of the minimum lease payments?

A. $0

B. $12,000

C. $18,000

D. $20,000

Answer (B) is correct. *(Publisher)*
**REQUIRED:** The amount of guaranteed residual value to be included in minimum lease payments.
**DISCUSSION:** FASB Interpretation No. 19, *Lessee Guarantee of the Residual Value of Leased Property*, states that the amount of guaranteed residual value to be included in the determination of minimum lease payments is the "specified maximum deficiency that the lessee is obligated to make up." In these circumstances, that amount is materially lower than the expected salvage value. Consequently, the $12,000 guarantee should be included. The additional guarantee of $6,000 ($18,000 − $12,000) in the case of excessive usage is similar to a contingent rental payment. Because it is not determinable at the lease's inception, it is not a lessee guarantee of the residual value that is includible in the minimum lease payments.
Answer (A) is incorrect because the guaranteed residual value is included in the determination of minimum lease payments. Answer (C) is incorrect because the additional guarantee of $6,000 ($18,000 − $12,000) is not included. It is contingent and thus nondeterminable. Answer (D) is incorrect because the minimum lease payments include only guaranteed residual value.

**52.** On August 1, Jones Corporation leased property to Smith Company for a 5-year period. The annual $20,000 lease payment is payable at the end of each year. The expected residual value at the end of the lease term is $10,000. Jones Corporation's implicit interest rate is 12%. The cost of the property to Jones was $50,000, which is the fair value at the lease date. The present value of an ordinary annuity of 1 for five periods is 3.605. The present value of 1 at the end of five periods is .567. At the inception of the lease, the recorded gross investment is

A. $110,000

B. $100,000

C. $72,100

D. $90,000

Answer (A) is correct. *(J.O. Hall)*
**REQUIRED:** The amount to be recorded as gross investment at the inception of the lease.
**DISCUSSION:** For a direct financing or a sales-type lease, the lessor should record the gross investment in the lease at the undiscounted sum of the minimum lease payments (the total of the periodic payments and any guaranteed residual value, net of executory costs) and any unguaranteed residual value. Accordingly, the gross investment is the same regardless of whether any residual value is guaranteed. The five periodic payments of $20,000 equal $100,000. The expected residual value, including both guaranteed and unguaranteed portions, equals $10,000. Thus, the gross investment in this lease should be $110,000 ($100,000 + $10,000).
Answer (B) is incorrect because it fails to include the residual value in the gross investment. Answer (C) is incorrect because the annual lease payments should be recorded at their undiscounted value. Answer (D) is incorrect because the residual value is added to, not subtracted from, the undiscounted lease payments.

**53.** On December 1, Clark Company leased office space for 5 years at a monthly rental of $60,000. On that date, Clark paid the lessor the following amounts:

| | |
|---|---:|
| First month's rent | $ 60,000 |
| Last month's rent | 60,000 |
| Security deposit (refundable at lease expiration) | 80,000 |
| Installation of new walls and offices | 360,000 |

Clark's December expense relating to its use of this office space is

A. $60,000

B. $66,000

C. $126,000

D. $200,000

Answer (B) is correct. *(CPA, adapted)*
**REQUIRED:** The lessee's expense relating to an operating lease.
**DISCUSSION:** During the year, this operating lease was effective only for the month of December. The year's expenses therefore include the $60,000 monthly rent plus the $360,000 cost of the installation of the new walls and offices allocated over the 60 months of the rental agreement. Thus, the total December expense equals $66,000 [$60,000 + ($360,000 ÷ 60 months)].
Answer (A) is incorrect because $60,000 omits the allocation of the leasehold improvements. Answer (C) is incorrect because $126,000 includes the last month's rent. Answer (D) is incorrect because $200,000 includes the last month's rent and the security deposit and omits the allocation of the cost of the leasehold improvements.

**54.** Which of the following leases would be classified as a capital lease by the lessee?

| | Lease A | Lease B | Lease C | Lease D |
|---|---|---|---|---|
| Contains a bargain purchase option? | Yes | No | No | No |
| Lease term portion of the economic life of the leased property | 60% | 70% | 80% | 90% |
| Present value of the minimum lease payments as a portion of the fair value of the leased property | 60% | 70% | 80% | 90% |

A. Lease A only.

B. Lease B only.

C. Leases A, C, and D.

D. Leases C and D only.

Answer (C) is correct. *(CIA, adapted)*
**REQUIRED:** The lease(s) meeting a capitalization criterion.
**DISCUSSION:** SFAS 13, *Accounting for Leases*, states that a lease must be classified as a capital lease by a lessee if, at its inception, any one of the following criteria is met:

1. A lease provides for the transfer of ownership of the leased property.
2. The lease contains a bargain purchase option.
3. The lease term is 75% or more of the estimated economic life of the leased property.
4. The present value of the minimum lease payments (excluding executory costs) is at least 90% of the excess of the fair value of the leased property to the lessor at the inception of the lease over any related investment tax credit.

Lease A is a capital lease because the terms of the lease include a bargain purchase option. Leases C and D pass the economic life (75%) test, and lease D also passes the recovery of investment (90%) test.
Answer (A) is incorrect because Leases C and D are also capital leases. Answer (B) is incorrect because B is the only operating lease in the set. Answer (D) is incorrect because Lease A contains a bargain purchase option, so it qualifies as a capital lease.

**55.** Howell Corporation, a publicly traded corporation, is the lessee in a leasing agreement with Brandon, Inc. to lease land and a building. If the lease contains a bargain purchase option, Howell should record the land and the building as a(n)

A. Operating lease and capital lease, respectively.

B. Capital lease and operating lease, respectively.

C. Capital lease but recorded as a single unit.

D. Capital lease but separately classified.

Answer (D) is correct. *(CMA, adapted)*
**REQUIRED:** The accounting treatment of a lease agreement that contains a bargain purchase option.
**DISCUSSION:** A lessee records a lease as a capital lease if it meets any one of four criteria. Existence of a bargain purchase option is one of these criteria. If a lease involving land and a building contains a bargain purchase option or if the lease transfers ownership to the lessee at the end of its term, the lessee separately capitalizes the land and the building.
Answer (A) is incorrect because the bargain purchase option makes the lease a capital lease. Answer (B) is incorrect because the bargain purchase option makes the lease a capital lease. Answer (C) is incorrect because the land and the building should be recorded in separate accounts. The building is depreciable and the land is not.

**56.** Initial direct costs are incurred by the lessor and may be classified as incremental direct costs and internal direct costs. All of the following costs are examples of initial direct costs except the costs of

A. Closing the lease transaction.

B. Negotiating lease terms.

C. Establishing and monitoring credit policies.

D. Evaluating collateral and security arrangements.

Answer (C) is correct. *(CMA, adapted)*
**REQUIRED:** The item not an initial direct cost.
**DISCUSSION:** Under SFAS 91, initial direct costs have two components: (1) the lessor's external costs to originate a lease incurred in dealings with independent third parties and (2) the internal costs directly related to specified activities performed by the lessor for that lease, such as evaluating the lessee's financial condition; evaluating guarantees, collateral, and other security arrangements; negotiating lease terms; preparing and processing lease documents; and closing the transaction. Initial direct costs do not include the costs of advertising and other solicitation, servicing of existing leases, establishing and monitoring of credit policies, supervision, and administration.

**57.** Which of the following is not a required disclosure for lessors with regard to sales-type and direct financing leases at each balance sheet date?

A. Future minimum lease payments to be received for each of the next 5 years.

B. A general description of the assets out on lease.

C. Unearned income at the balance sheet date.

D. Unguaranteed residual values accruing to the benefit of the lessor.

Answer (B) is correct. *(Publisher)*
**REQUIRED:** The item not a required disclosure for lessors with regard to sales-type and direct financing leases at each balance sheet date.
**DISCUSSION:** The required disclosures for lessors with regard to sales-type and direct financing leases at each balance sheet date include the following:

1. Future minimum lease payments receivable with separate deductions for amounts representing executory costs and the uncollectible minimum lease payments receivable.
2. Unguaranteed residual values accruing to the benefit of the lessor.
3. Unearned income.
4. Future minimum lease payments to be received for each of the next 5 years, including information on total contingent rentals.
5. For direct financing leases only, the initial direct costs.

There is no requirement to provide a general description of the property leased out.

**58.** On January 1, Hook Oil Co. sold equipment with a carrying amount of $100,000 and a remaining useful life of 10 years to Maco Drilling for $150,000. Hook immediately leased the equipment back under a 10-year capital lease with a present value of $150,000. It will depreciate the equipment using the straight-line method. Hook made the first annual lease payment of $24,412 in December. In Hook's December 31 balance sheet, the unearned gain on the equipment sale should be

A. $50,000

B. $45,000

C. $25,588

D. $0

Answer (B) is correct. *(CPA, adapted)*
**REQUIRED:** The unearned gain on the equipment sale one year after a sale-leaseback transaction.
**DISCUSSION:** A profit or loss on the sale in a sale-leaseback transaction is ordinarily deferred and amortized in proportion to the amortization of the leased asset if the leaseback is classified as a capital lease. At 12/31, a gain proportionate to the lease amortization will be recognized [($150,000 – $100,000) ÷ 10 years = $5,000]. Hence, the deferred gain will be $45,000 ($50,000 – $5,000).

Answer (A) is incorrect because $50,000 is the total deferred gain at the inception of the lease. Answer (C) is incorrect because $25,588 is difference between the total deferred gain and the periodic lease payment. Answer (D) is incorrect because the seller-lessee has retained substantially all of the use of the property and should therefore defer gain.

Questions 59 and 60 are based on the following information.

On January 1, Plantation Restaurant is planning to enter as the lessee into the two lease agreements described in the columns to the right. Each lease is noncancelable, and Plantation does not receive title to either leased property during or at the end of the lease term. All payments required under these agreements are due on January 1 each year.

| Lessor | Hadaway, Inc. | Cutter Electronics |
| --- | --- | --- |
| Type of property | Oven | Computer |
| Yearly rental | $15,000 | $4,000 |
| Lease term | 10 years | 3 years |
| Economic life | 15 years | 5 years |
| Purchase option | None | $3,000 |
| Renewal option | None | None |
| Fair market value at inception of lease | $125,000 | $10,200 |
| Unguaranteed residual value | None | $2,000 |
| Lessee's incremental borrowing rate | 10% | 10% |
| Executory costs paid by | Lessee | Lessor |
| Annual executory costs | $800 | $500 |
| Present value factor at 10% (of an annuity due) | 6.76 | 2.74 |

**59.** Plantation Restaurant should treat the lease agreement with Hadaway, Inc. as a(n)

A. Capital lease with an initial asset value of $101,400.

B. Operating lease, charging $14,200 in rental expense and $800 in executory costs to annual operations.

C. Operating lease, charging the present value of the yearly rental expense to annual operations.

D. Operating lease, charging $15,000 in rental expense and $800 in executory costs to annual operations.

Answer (D) is correct. *(CMA, adapted)*
REQUIRED: The true statement about the lease.
DISCUSSION: The Hadaway lease is an operating lease with a $15,000 annual rental expense with annual executory costs of $800 to be paid by the lessee. An operating lease does not transfer the rights and risks of ownership to the lessee. The Hadaway lease is nothing more than a rental arrangement. SFAS 13 specifies that if any one of the following criteria is met, the lease is a capital lease: the lease transfers title to the lessee, the lease has a bargain purchase option, the lease term is 75% or more of the useful life of the leased asset, or the present value of the minimum lease payments is 90% or more of the asset's fair value. The Hadaway lease meets none of these four criteria.

Answer (A) is incorrect because the Hadaway lease does not meet any of the criteria of a capital lease. Answer (B) is incorrect because rental expense is $15,000. Answer (C) is incorrect because the actual cash outlay for rent, $15,000, is charged to expense.

**60.** Plantation Restaurant should treat the lease agreement with Cutter Electronics as a(n)

A. Capital lease with an initial asset value of $10,960.

B. Capital lease with an initial asset value of $10,200.

C. Operating lease, charging $3,500 in rental expense and $500 in executory costs to annual operations.

D. Capital lease with an initial asset value of $9,590.

Answer (D) is correct. *(CMA, adapted)*
REQUIRED: The true statement about the lease.
DISCUSSION: A capital lease is one in which many of the benefits and risks of ownership are transferred to the lessee. For accounting purposes, the lessee treats a capital lease as similar to the purchase of an asset. SFAS 13 specifies that, if the present value of the minimum lease payments (excluding executory costs) is 90% or more of the asset's fair value, the lease should be accounted for as a capital lease. Given that the executory costs associated with the lease are to be paid by the lessor, a portion of the lease rental price is for those costs, not for the asset. Executory costs include insurance, maintenance, and similar expenses. Consequently, the annual minimum lease payment equals the annual payment minus the executory costs, or $3,500 ($4,000 yearly rental – $500). The present value of the minimum lease payments is therefore $9,590 ($3,500 × 2.74), which is greater than 90% of the fair value of the asset. Thus, the lease should be capitalized. The appropriate amount of the initial asset value is the present value of the minimum lease payments calculated above.

Answer (A) is incorrect because the initial asset value cannot exceed the fair value of the leased asset. Moreover, $10,960 includes the present value of the executory costs. Answer (B) is incorrect because $10,200 is the fair value of the leased asset. Answer (C) is incorrect because the Cutter lease meets the criteria of a capital lease.

Questions 61 and 62 are based on the following information. Suki Corporation is the lessor in a lease arrangement with Idrol Associates. At the inception of the lease, Suki incurred legal fees and other initial direct costs for the preparation and processing of the lease contract that were considered material in amount.

**61.** Assuming the lease is classified as an operating lease by Suki Corporation, the initial direct costs should be

    A. Expensed in the year of incurrence by including them in cost of goods sold or by treating them as a selling expense.

    B. Deferred and recognized as a reduction in the interest rate implicit in the lease.

    C. Deferred and allocated over the lease term in proportion to the recognition of rental income.

    D. Deferred and carried on the statement of financial position until the end of the lease term.

Answer (C) is correct. *(CMA, adapted)*
**REQUIRED:** The lessor's accounting treatment of the initial direct costs of an operating lease.
**DISCUSSION:** SFAS 13, *Accounting for Leases*, requires lessors to capitalize the initial direct costs of an operating lease and allocate them over the term of the lease in proportion to the recognition of rental income.
Answer (A) is incorrect because the initial direct costs of a lease are to be deferred and matched against the future revenues from the lease. Answer (B) is incorrect because the initial direct costs are to be recognized separately. Answer (D) is incorrect because the initial direct costs are to be amortized over the term of the lease.

**62.** Assuming the lease is classified as a direct-financing capital lease by Suki Corporation, the initial direct costs should be

    A. Expensed in the year of incurrence by including them in cost of goods sold or by treating them as a selling expense.

    B. Deferred and recognized as a reduction in the interest rate implicit in the lease.

    C. Deferred and allocated over the lease term in proportion to the recognition of rental income.

    D. Deferred and carried on the statement of financial position until the end of the lease term.

Answer (B) is correct. *(CMA, adapted)*
**REQUIRED:** The lessor's treatment of initial direct costs of a direct-financing lease.
**DISCUSSION:** SFAS 98, *Accounting for Leases*, states that initial direct costs should be accounted for as an addition to the gross investment in a direct-financing lease. The net investment equals the gross investment, plus unamortized initial direct costs, minus unearned income (gross investment – carrying amount). The unearned income and the initial direct costs are amortized over the lease term to provide a constant rate of return on the net investment.
Answer (A) is incorrect because SFAS 13 does not permit the lessor to expense initial direct costs immediately unless a sales-type lease is involved. Answer (C) is incorrect because the treatment of the initial direct costs of direct-financing and operating leases differs. The former are accounted for as an addition to the gross investment. Answer (D) is incorrect because the costs are allocated over the period of the lease by means of increasing the cost of the investment in the lease.

## 16.4 Pensions and Other Postretirement Benefits

**63.** The Rice Company sponsors a defined benefit pension plan for its employees. At the beginning of Year 1, Rice had prepaid pension cost of $15,000, pension plan assets with a fair value of $50,000, and a projected benefit obligation (PBO) of $35,000. The accumulated benefit obligation (ABO) equals the PBO. The service cost for Year 1 was $45,000, and the amount funded was $40,000. The discount rate and the expected rate of return on plan assets were 10%. No amortization of prior service cost or previously unrecognized gains or losses is required to determine the minimum net periodic pension cost (NPPC). Thus, for Year 1, Rice reported

    A. Interest cost of $5,000.

    B. Prepaid pension cost of $15,000.

    C. NPPC of $43,500.

    D. Accrued pension cost of $16,500.

Answer (C) is correct. *(Publisher)*
**REQUIRED:** The true statement about pension reporting.
**DISCUSSION:** NPPC equals the sum of service cost and interest cost, minus the expected return on plan assets, or $43,500 [$45,000 + ($35,000 PBO × 10% discount rate) – ($50,000 fair value of plan assets × 10% expected rate of return)].
Answer (A) is incorrect because the interest cost component of NPPC is $3,500. Answer (B) is incorrect because prepaid pension cost is $11,500 [$15,000 – ($43,500 NPPC – $40,000 of funding)]. Answer (D) is incorrect because prepaid pension cost is $11,500 [$15,000 – ($43,500 NPPC – $40,000 of funding)].

**64.** According to SFAS 87, *Employer's Accounting for Pension Plans*, the projected benefit obligation (PBO) is best described as the

A. Present value of benefits accrued to date based on future salary levels.

B. Present value of benefits accrued to date based on current salary levels.

C. Increase in retroactive benefits at the date of the amendment of the plan.

D. Amount of the adjustment necessary to reflect the difference between actual and estimated actuarial returns.

**Answer (A) is correct.** *(CMA, adapted)*
**REQUIRED:** The best description of the PBO.
**DISCUSSION:** SFAS 87 defines the PBO as the actuarial present value of all future benefits attributable to past employee service at a moment in time. It is based on assumptions as to future compensation if the pension plan formula is based on future compensation.
Answer (B) is incorrect because the accumulated benefit obligation (ABO) is based only on current salary levels. Answer (C) is incorrect because prior service costs reflect the increase in retroactive benefits at the date of the amendment of the plan. Answer (D) is incorrect because the amortization of actuarial gains and losses is the amount of the adjustment necessary to reflect the difference between actual and estimated actuarial returns.

**65.** The following information pertains to Lee Corp.'s defined benefit pension plan for the current year:

| | |
|---|---|
| Service cost | $160,000 |
| Actual and expected gain on plan assets | 35,000 |
| Unexpected loss on plan assets related to a current year disposal of a subsidiary | 40,000 |
| Amortization of unrecognized prior service cost | 5,000 |
| Annual interest on pension obligation | 50,000 |

What amount should Lee report as pension expense in its current year income statement?

A. $250,000

B. $220,000

C. $210,000

D. $180,000

**Answer (D) is correct.** *(CPA, adapted)*
**REQUIRED:** The pension expense for the year.
**DISCUSSION:** The components of net periodic pension cost (NPPC) are: (1) service cost, (2) interest cost, (3) return on plan assets, (4) gain or loss to the extent recognized, and (5) amortization of any unrecognized prior service cost. Accordingly, the service cost, gain on plan assets, interest cost, and amortization of prior service cost are included in the computation. Gains and losses arising from changes in the PBO or plan assets resulting from experience different from that assumed and from changes in assumptions about discount rates, life expectancies, etc., are not required to be recognized when they occur. Accordingly, the unexpected loss on plan assets will be included in the net unrecognized gain or loss balance and will be eligible for amortization in the following year. NPPC is therefore $180,000 ($160,000 service cost – $35,000 actual and expected return on plan assets + $5,000 prior service cost amortization + $50,000 interest cost).
Answer (A) is incorrect because $250,000 results from adding, not subtracting, the expected gain on plan assets. Answer (B) is incorrect because $220,000 includes the unexpected loss. Answer (C) is incorrect because $210,000 includes the unexpected loss and subtracts instead of adding the amortization of prior service cost.

**66.** At the start of its current fiscal year, Emper Co. amended its defined benefit pension plan, resulting in an increase of $600,000 in the PBO. As of the date of the amendment, Emper had 50 employees. Ten employees are expected to leave at the end of each of the next 5 years (including the current year). The minimum amortization of prior service cost in the first year is

A. $80,000

B. $120,000

C. $160,000

D. $200,000

**Answer (D) is correct.** *(Publisher)*
**REQUIRED:** The minimum amortization of prior service cost.
**DISCUSSION:** Prior service cost is amortized by assigning an equal amount to each future period of service of each employee active at the date of the plan amendment who is expected to receive benefits under the plan. If all or almost all of a plan's participants are inactive, the prior service cost is amortized based on the remaining life expectancy of the participants. An alternative amortization approach, such as a straight-line method, that recognizes the cost of retroactive amendments more quickly is also permitted if used consistently. For Emper, total service years rendered during the 5-year period is 150 (50 + 40 + 30 + 20 + 10). The amortization fraction for the first year is thus 50/150, and the minimum amortization is $200,000 ($600,000 × 50/150).
Answer (A) is incorrect because 50, not 20, must be used as the numerator of the amortization fraction. Answer (B) is incorrect because the use of straight-line amortization over 5 years does not recognize the cost of retroactive amendments more quickly, so the method described above must be used. Answer (C) is incorrect because 50, not 40, must be used as the numerator of the amortization fraction for the first year.

**67.** The following information pertains to Gali Co.'s defined benefit pension plan for the year:

| | |
|---|---|
| Fair value of plan assets, beginning of year | $350,000 |
| Fair value of plan assets, end of year | 525,000 |
| Employer contributions | 110,000 |
| Benefits paid | 85,000 |

In computing pension expense, what amount should Gali use as actual return on plan assets?

- A. $65,000
- B. $150,000
- C. $175,000
- D. $260,000

**Answer (B) is correct.** *(CPA, adapted)*

**REQUIRED:** The actual return on plan assets.

**DISCUSSION:** The actual return on plan assets is based on the fair value of plan assets at the beginning and end of the accounting period adjusted for contributions and payments during the period. The actual return for Gali is $150,000 ($525,000 – $350,000 – $110,000 + $85,000).

Answer (A) is incorrect because $65,000 results when benefits paid to employees are not included. Answer (C) is incorrect because $175,000 is the change in the fair value of plan assets without adjustment for contributions or benefits paid. Answer (D) is incorrect because $260,000 does not deduct employer contributions.

**68.** Deerfield Corporation has the following information available regarding its pension plan:

| | May 31, Year 1 | May 31, Year 2 |
|---|---|---|
| Accumulated benefit obligation (ABO) | $180,000 | $280,000 |
| Projected benefit obligation (PBO) | 200,000 | 320,000 |
| Fair value of plan assets | 162,000 | 180,000 |
| Unrecognized prior service cost | 68,000 | 52,000 |
| Prepaid pension cost | 30,000 | -- |
| Accrued pension cost | -- | 88,000 |

In accordance with the requirements of SFAS 87, *Employers' Accounting for Pension Plans*, Deerfield's minimum liability at May 31, year 1 and year 2, respectively, was

- A. $38,000 and $140,000.
- B. $98,000 and $0.
- C. $48,000 and $12,000.
- D. $18,000 and $100,000.

**Answer (D) is correct.** *(CMA, adapted)*

**REQUIRED:** The minimum pension liability at the beginning and end of a period.

**DISCUSSION:** SFAS 87 requires the recording of a liability if the ABO is underfunded. Thus, if the ABO is greater than the fair value of plan assets, a net liability must be recognized. At May 31, year 1, the $180,000 ABO is $18,000 greater than the $162,000 fair value of plan assets. At May 31, year 2, a liability of $100,000 exists because the $280,000 ABO is $100,000 greater than the $180,000 fair value of plan assets.

Answer (A) is incorrect because $38,000 and $140,000 equal the excess of the PBO over the fair value of plan assets at May 31, year 1 and year 2, respectively. Answer (B) is incorrect because $98,000 is the sum of unrecognized prior service cost and prepaid pension cost, and $0 is the difference between the PBO at May 31, year 2 and the sum of the fair value of the plan assets, the unrecognized prior service cost, and the accrued pension cost. Answer (C) is incorrect because $48,000 is the amount of the entry at May 31, year 1 to record the additional liability needed to reflect the required minimum liability. It equals the excess of the ABO over the fair value of plan assets, plus the prepaid pension cost. The entry is to debit an intangible asset and to credit the additional liability for $48,000. At May 31, year 2, $12,000 equals the amount of the entry to record the additional liability ($280,000 ABO – $180,000 fair value of plan assets – $88,000 accrued pension cost).

**69.** The following information relates to the current year activity of the defined benefit pension plan of Twain Publishers, Ltd., a company whose stock is publicly traded:

| | |
|---|---|
| Service cost | $120,000 |
| Expected return on plan assets | 30,000 |
| Interest cost on pension benefit obligation | 40,000 |
| Amortization of actuarial loss | 10,000 |
| Amortization of prior service cost | 5,000 |

Twain's current year pension cost is

- A. $120,000
- B. $130,000
- C. $135,000
- D. $145,000

**Answer (D) is correct.** *(A. Oddo)*

**REQUIRED:** The net periodic pension cost (NPPC) for the year.

**DISCUSSION:** Components of NPPC are service cost, interest cost, the expected return on plan assets, and amortization of any (1) unrecognized prior service cost or (2) unrecognized net gain (loss). Service cost, interest cost, and the amortization of actuarial loss and prior service cost increase the net periodic pension cost. The expected return on plan assets decreases NPPC. Hence, NPPC is $160,000.

| | |
|---|---|
| Service cost | $120,000 |
| Return on plan assets | (30,000) |
| Interest cost | 40,000 |
| Amortization of actuarial loss | 10,000 |
| Amortization of prior service cost | 5,000 |
| Net periodic pension cost | $145,000 |

Answer (A) is incorrect because $120,000 includes only the service cost component. Answer (B) is incorrect because $130,000 excludes the amortization of prior service cost and the actual loss. Answer (C) is incorrect because $135,000 excludes the current year's amortization of the actuarial loss.

**70.** At end of the year, Penny Company's projected benefit obligation (PBO) was determined to be $1,500,000, which was $200,000 higher than had been expected. The market-related value of the defined benefit plan's assets was equal to its fair value of $1,250,000. No other gains and losses have occurred. If the average remaining service life is 20 years, the minimum required amortization of the unrecognized net gain (loss) in the next year will be

A. $20,000

B. $3,750

C. $2,500

D. $0

Answer (C) is correct. *(Publisher)*
**REQUIRED:** The minimum required amortization of unrecognized net gain (loss) next year.
**DISCUSSION:** At a minimum, amortization of the cumulative unrecognized net gain or loss (excluding asset gains and losses not yet reflected in market-related value) must be included as a component of NPPC for a year if, as of the beginning of the year, that unrecognized gain or loss exceeds 10% of the greater of the PBO or the market-related value (MRV) of plan assets. At year-end, Penny's PBO was $200,000 greater than estimated (a $200,000 liability loss). Because no other gain or loss has occurred, the unrecognized net loss to be amortized beginning next year is $200,000. The corridor amount is $150,000 (10% of the greater of $1,500,000 PBO or $1,250,000 MRV of plan assets). The amount outside the corridor is $50,000 ($200,000 – $150,000), and the amount to be amortized is thus $2,500 ($50,000 ÷ 20 years of average remaining service life).
Answer (A) is incorrect because $20,000 is the result of using the full $200,000 liability loss without regard to the corridor amount and assumes an amortization period of 10 years instead of 20. Answer (B) is incorrect because $3,750 is the result of using $125,000 ($1,250,000 plan assets × 10%) as the corridor amount instead of $150,000. Answer (D) is incorrect because $50,000 of the liability loss must be amortized over the average remaining service life beginning the year following the loss.

---

Questions 71 and 72 are based on the following information.

On November 30, the Board of Directors of Baldwin Corporation amended its pension plan giving retroactive benefits to its employees. The information to the right is provided at November 30:

| | |
|---|---:|
| Accumulated benefit obligation (ABO) | $825,000 |
| Projected benefit obligation (PBO) | 900,000 |
| Accrued pension cost | 112,500 |
| Plan assets (fair value) | 307,500 |
| Market-related asset value | 301,150 |
| Unrecognized prior service cost | 190,000 |
| Average remaining service life of employees | 10 years |
| Useful life of pension goodwill | 20 years |

**71.** Baldwin Corporation's minimum pension liability at November 30 is

A. $190,000

B. $405,000

C. $517,500

D. $523,850

Answer (C) is correct. *(CMA, adapted)*
**REQUIRED:** The minimum pension liability.
**DISCUSSION:** Under SFAS 87, a minimum liability must be recognized when the ABO exceeds the fair value of plan assets. Because the ABO exceeds the fair value of plan assets, the minimum liability to be recognized is $517,500 ($825,000 ABO – $307,500 FVPA).
Answer (A) is incorrect because $190,000 is the unrecognized prior service cost, which can be allocated to future periods. Answer (B) is incorrect because $405,000 is the additional liability to be recognized. Answer (D) is incorrect because $523,850 is based on the market-related asset value.

**72.** Using the straight-line method of amortization, the amount of prior service cost charged to expense during the year ended November 30 is

A. $9,500

B. $19,000

C. $30,250

D. $190,000

Answer (B) is correct. *(CMA, adapted)*
**REQUIRED:** The prior service cost expensed using the straight-line method.
**DISCUSSION:** Unrecognized prior service cost arises from the awarding of retroactive benefits resulting from plan initiation or amendments. Prior service cost is assigned to the future service periods of active employees using either a straight-line or another acceptable method of allocation. Given that the average remaining service life of the firm's employees is 10 years, the annual charge is $19,000 ($190,000 ÷ 10).
Answer (A) is incorrect because $9,500 is based on a 20-year amortization period. Answer (C) is incorrect because $30,250 equals the sum of unrecognized prior service cost and accrued pension cost, divided by 10 years. Answer (D) is incorrect because unrecognized prior service cost can be amortized over the remaining work life of employees; it does not have to be recorded entirely in the year of origination.

## 16.5 Deferred Income Taxes

**73.** Which one of the following temporary differences will result in a deferred tax asset?

A. Use of the straight-line depreciation method for financial statement purposes and the Modified Accelerated Cost Recovery System (MACRS) for income tax purposes.

B. Installment sale profits accounted for on the accrual basis for financial statement purposes and on a cash basis for income tax purposes.

C. Advance rental receipts accounted for on the accrual basis for financial statement purposes and on a cash basis for tax purposes.

D. Investment gains accounted for under the equity method for financial statement purposes and under the cost method for income tax purposes.

Answer (C) is correct. *(CMA, adapted)*
**REQUIRED:** The TD that will result in a deferred tax asset.
**DISCUSSION:** A deferred tax asset records the deferred tax consequences attributable to deductible temporary differences and carryforwards. Advance rental receipts accounted for on the accrual basis for financial statement purposes and on a cash basis for tax purposes would give rise to a deferred tax asset. The financial statements would report no income and no related tax expense because the rental payments apply to future periods. The tax return, however, would treat the rent as income when the cash was received, and a tax would be due in the year of receipt. Because the tax is paid prior to recording the income for financial statement purposes, it represents an asset that will be recognized as an expense when income is finally recorded.
Answer (A) is incorrect because using accelerated depreciation on the tax return results in a deferred tax liability. Answer (B) is incorrect because recognizing installment income on the financial statements but not the tax return results in a taxable temporary difference. Answer (D) is incorrect because recognizing investment gains on the financial statements earlier than they are recognized on the tax return gives rise to a deferred tax liability.

**74.** Barth and Garth, Inc. depreciate equipment over 15 years for financial purposes and over 7 years for tax purposes as prescribed by MACRS. As a result of this temporary difference, the deferred income taxes will be reported in its first year of use as a

A. Noncurrent asset.

B. Noncurrent liability.

C. Current liability.

D. Current asset.

Answer (B) is correct. *(Publisher)*
**REQUIRED:** The classification of deferred taxes arising from the excess of tax over book depreciation.
**DISCUSSION:** When a deferred tax liability or asset is related to an asset or a liability, its classification as current or noncurrent is based on the classification of the related item for financial reporting purposes. Because tax depreciation for the first year is greater than book depreciation, the tax basis of this noncurrent asset differs from (is less than) its book basis. The result is a taxable temporary difference. The deferred tax liability is classified as noncurrent because the related asset is noncurrent.
Answer (A) is incorrect because a temporary difference related to depreciable equipment results in a liability. Answer (C) is incorrect because depreciable equipment is classified as a noncurrent asset. Answer (D) is incorrect because depreciable equipment is classified as a noncurrent asset.

**75.** According to SFAS 109, *Accounting for Income Taxes*, when a company reports deferred tax assets and liabilities for two consecutive years, a deferred income tax benefit or expense should be reported equal to the

A. Decrease in the deferred tax assets.

B. Sum of the net changes in deferred tax assets and deferred tax liabilities.

C. Increase in the deferred tax liabilities.

D. Amount of the total income tax liability.

Answer (B) is correct. *(Publisher)*
**REQUIRED:** The method of determining deferred income tax expense or benefit.
**DISCUSSION:** The deferred tax expense or benefit recognized is the sum of the net changes in the deferred tax assets and deferred tax liabilities. The deferred income tax expense or benefit is aggregated with the income taxes currently payable or refundable to determine the amount of income tax expense or benefit for the year to be recorded in the income statement.
Answer (A) is incorrect because the deferred income tax expense or benefit is equal to the sum of the net changes in the deferred tax assets. Answer (C) is incorrect because the deferred income tax expense or benefit is equal to the sum of the net changes in the deferred tax assets. Answer (D) is incorrect because the total income tax liability includes both the current and deferred income tax expense or benefit for the year.

**76.** At the end of the current year, its first year of operation, the Fratzie Corporation reported $45,000 taxable income and $38,000 pretax financial income as a result of a single temporary difference. Because of uncertain economic times, the company believes that only 75% of the deductible temporary difference is more likely than not to be realized. The tax rate for the current year is 30%, and no change has been enacted for future years. On the year-end balance sheet, the deferred tax asset will be reported at a net balance of

    A. $7,000

    B. $5,250

    C. $2,100

    D. $1,575

Answer (D) is correct. *(Publisher)*
**REQUIRED:** The amount of deferred tax asset.
**DISCUSSION:** The deferred tax asset is based on the difference ($7,000) between taxable income ($45,000) and financial income ($38,000). However, there is an expectation only 75% of the tax benefit is more likely than not to be realized. Thus, the amount of the future deductible amounts will be $5,250 ($7,000 × 75%). The deferred tax asset is $1,575 ($5,250 × 30% enacted tax rate).
Answer (A) is incorrect because it represents a difference in income before application of the tax rate. Answer (B) is incorrect because it represents a difference in income before application of the tax rate. Answer (C) is incorrect because $2,100 is based on the full benefit without consideration that 25% of the benefit will never be realized.

**77.** West Corp. leased a building and received the $36,000 annual rental payment on June 15. The beginning of the lease was July 1, the current year. Rental income is taxable when received. West's tax rates are 30% for the current year and 40% thereafter. West had no other permanent or temporary differences. West determined that no valuation allowance was needed. What amount of deferred tax asset should West report in its December 31 balance sheet?

    A. $5,400

    B. $7,200

    C. $10,800

    D. $14,400

Answer (B) is correct. *(CPA, adapted)*
**REQUIRED:** The amount of deferred tax asset reported at year-end.
**DISCUSSION:** The $36,000 rental payment is taxable in full when received in the current year, but only $18,000 ($36,000 × 6/12) should be recognized in financial accounting income for the year. The result is a deductible temporary difference (deferred tax asset) arising from the difference between the tax basis ($0) of the liability for unearned rent and its reported amount in the year-end balance sheet ($36,000 − $18,000 = $18,000). The income tax payable for the current year based on the rental payment is $10,800 (30% tax rate for the current year × $36,000), the deferred tax asset is $7,200 (40% enacted tax rate applicable after the current year when the asset will be realized × $18,000 future deductible amount), and the income tax expense is $3,600 ($10,800 current tax expense − $7,200 deferred tax benefit). The deferred tax benefit equals the net change during the year in the enterprise's deferred tax liabilities and assets ($7,200 deferred tax asset recognized in the current year − $0).
Answer (A) is incorrect because $5,400 is based on a 30% tax rate. Answer (C) is incorrect because $10,800 is the income tax payable. Answer (D) is incorrect because $14,400 would be the income tax payable if the 40% tax rate applied in the current year.

**78.** In its current year income statement, Cere Co. reported income before income taxes of $300,000. Cere estimated that, because of permanent differences, taxable income for the year would be $280,000. During the year, Cere made estimated tax payments of $50,000, which were debited to income tax expense. Cere is subject to a 30% tax rate. What amount should Cere report as income tax expense?

    A. $34,000

    B. $50,000

    C. $84,000

    D. $90,000

Answer (C) is correct. *(CPA, adapted)*
**REQUIRED:** The amount to be reported for income tax expense.
**DISCUSSION:** Income tax expense or benefit is the sum of current tax expense or benefit and deferred tax expense or benefit. A deferred tax expense or benefit is the change in an entity's deferred tax assets and liabilities. However, a permanent difference does not result in a change in a deferred tax asset or liability. Thus, income tax expense equals current income tax expense, which is the amount of taxes paid or payable for the year. Income taxes payable for the year equal $84,000 ($280,000 taxable income × 30%).
Answer (A) is incorrect because $34,000 equals the $84,000 of income taxes payable minus the $50,000 of income taxes paid. Answer (B) is incorrect because $50,000 equals income taxes paid, not the total current income tax expense. Answer (D) is incorrect because $90,000 is equal to the reported income of $300,000 times the tax rate.

**79.** Based on its current operating levels, Glucose Corporation estimates that its annual level of taxable income in the foreseeable future will be $200,000 annually. Enacted tax rates for the tax jurisdiction in which Glucose operates are 15% for the first $50,000 of taxable income, 25% for the next $50,000 of taxable income, and 35% for taxable income in excess of $100,000. Which tax rate should Glucose use to measure a deferred tax liability or asset in accordance with SFAS 109?

    A. 15%

    B. 25%

    C. 27.5%

    D. 35%

**Answer (C) is correct.** *(Publisher)*
**REQUIRED:** The tax rate applicable to the measurement of a deferred tax liability or asset.
**DISCUSSION:** In measuring a deferred tax liability or asset, the objective is to use the enacted tax rate(s) expected to apply to taxable income in the periods in which the deferred tax liability or asset is expected to be settled or realized. If graduated tax rates are a significant factor for an enterprise, the applicable tax rate is the average graduated tax rate applicable to the amount of estimated future annual taxable income. As indicated, the applicable tax rate is 27.5% ($55,000 ÷ $200,000).

| Taxable Income | | Tax Rate | | |
|---|---|---|---|---|
| $ 50,000 | × | 15% | = | $ 7,500 |
| 50,000 | × | 25% | = | 12,500 |
| 100,000 | × | 35% | = | 35,000 |
| $200,000 | | | | $55,000 |

Answer (A) is incorrect because 15% is the tax rate for the first $50,000 of income. Answer (B) is incorrect because 25% is the tax rate for income over $50,000 but less than $100,000. Answer (D) is incorrect because 35% is the tax rate for income over $100,000.

**80.** In preparing its December 31 financial statements, Irene Corp. must determine the proper accounting treatment of a $180,000 loss carryforward available to offset future taxable income. There are no temporary differences. The applicable current and future income tax rate is 30%. Available evidence is not conclusive as to the future existence of sufficient taxable income to provide for the future realization of the tax benefit of the $180,000 loss carryforward. However, based on the available evidence, Irene believes that it is more likely than not that future taxable income will be available to provide for the future realization of only $100,000 of this loss carryforward. In its December 31 statement of financial condition, Irene should recognize what amounts?

| | Deferred Tax Asset | Valuation Allowance |
|---|---|---|
| A. | $0 | $0 |
| B. | $30,000 | $0 |
| C. | $54,000 | $24,000 |
| D. | $54,000 | $30,000 |

**Answer (C) is correct.** *(Publisher)*
**REQUIRED:** The amounts to be recognized as a deferred tax asset and related valuation allowance.
**DISCUSSION:** The applicable tax rate should be used to measure a deferred tax asset for an operating loss carryforward that is available to offset future taxable income. Irene should therefore recognize a $54,000 ($180,000 × 30%) deferred tax asset. A valuation allowance should be recognized to reduce the deferred tax asset if, based on the weight of the available evidence, the likelihood is more than 50% that some portion or all of a deferred tax asset will not be realized. Based on the available evidence, Irene believes that it is more likely than not that the tax benefit of $100,000 of the operating loss will be realized. Thus, the company should recognize a $24,000 valuation allowance to reduce the $54,000 deferred tax asset to $30,000 ($100,000 × 30%), the amount of the deferred tax asset that is more likely than not to be realized.

Answer (A) is incorrect because a deferred tax asset equal to $54,000 should be recognized and a valuation allowance should be recognized equal to $24,000 to reduce the deferred tax asset to $30,000. Answer (B) is incorrect because a deferred tax asset of $30,000 results from netting the valuation allowance against the deferred tax asset. Answer (D) is incorrect because $30,000 is the deferred tax asset, not the valuation allowance, after the two are netted.

Questions 81 and 82 are based on the following information.

Bearings Manufacturing Company, Inc. purchased a new machine on January 1, year 1, for $100,000. The company uses the straight-line depreciation method with an estimated equipment life of 5 years and a zero salvage value for financial statement purposes, and uses the 3-year, Modified Accelerated Cost Recovery System (MACRS) with an estimated equipment life of 3 years for income tax reporting purposes. Bearings is subject to a 35% marginal income tax rate.

Assume that the deferred tax liability at the beginning of the year is zero and that Bearings has a positive earnings tax position. The MACRS depreciation rates for 3-year equipment are shown below.

| Year | Rate |
|------|--------|
| 1 | 33.33% |
| 2 | 44.45 |
| 3 | 14.81 |
| 4 | 7.41 |

**81.** What is the deferred tax liability at December 31, year 1 (rounded to the nearest whole dollar)?

A. $7,000

B. $33,330

C. $11,666

D. $4,666

Answer (D) is correct. *(CMA, adapted)*
**REQUIRED:** The deferred tax liability assuming tax rates will not change.
**DISCUSSION:** For financial reporting purposes, the reported amount (cost – accumulated depreciation) of the machine at year-end, assuming straight-line depreciation and no salvage value, will be $80,000 [$100,000 cost – ($100,000 ÷ 5 years)]. The tax basis of this asset will be $66,670 [$100,000 – ($100,000 × 33.33%)]. A taxable temporary difference has arisen because the excess of the reported amount over the tax basis will result in a net future taxable amount over the recovery period. A taxable temporary difference requires recognition of a deferred tax liability. Assuming the 35% rate applies during the asset's entire life, the deferred tax liability equals the applicable enacted tax rate times the temporary difference, or $4,666 [($80,000 – $66,670) × 35%].
Answer (A) is incorrect because $7,000 is the tax benefit provided by the $20,000 depreciation expense on the books. Answer (B) is incorrect because $33,330 is the depreciation deduction on the tax return. Answer (C) is incorrect because $11,666 is the tax shield based on MACRS depreciation.

**82.** For Bearings Manufacturing Company, Inc., assume that the following new corporate income tax rates will go into effect:

| | |
|--------|-----|
| Years 2-4 | 40% |
| Year 5 | 45% |

What is the amount of the deferred tax asset/liability at December 31, year 1 (rounded to the nearest whole dollar)?

A. $9,000

B. $2,668

C. $0

D. $6,332

Answer (D) is correct. *(CMA, adapted)*
**REQUIRED:** The deferred tax liability assuming tax rates will change.
**DISCUSSION:** Because one tax rate is not applied to all relevant years, a more complex calculation is necessary because different rates will apply during the recovery period. During the years 2-4, book depreciation will equal $60,000 [3 × ($100,000 ÷ 5)], and tax depreciation will equal $66,670 (the tax basis at 12/31 year 1 will be recovered in full by 12/31 year 4). Based on the applicable enacted 40% tax rate, the net deferred tax asset for years 2-4 will be $2,668 [($66,670 – $60,000) × 40%]. However, the excess of book over tax depreciation in year 5 will be $20,000 ($20,000 – $0). Based on the applicable enacted 45% tax rate, the deferred tax liability for year 5 is $9,000 ($20,000 × 45%). Accordingly, the net deferred tax liability at December 31, year 1 is $6,332 ($9,000 – $2,668).
Answer (A) is incorrect because $9,000 is the deferred tax liability for year 1 reflecting the excess of book over tax depreciation. Answer (B) is incorrect because $2,668 is the deferred tax asset for years 2-4 resulting from the excess of tax over book depreciation during that period. Answer (C) is incorrect because a deferred tax liability of $6,332 is recorded for a taxable temporary difference.

**83.** Quinn Co. reported a net deferred tax asset of $9,000 in its December 31, 20X0 balance sheet. For 20X1, Quinn reported pretax financial statement income of $300,000. Temporary differences of $100,000 resulted in taxable income of $200,000 for 20X1. At December 31, 20X1, Quinn had cumulative taxable temporary differences of $70,000. Quinn's effective income tax rate is 30%. In its December 31, 20X1 income statement, what should Quinn report as deferred income tax expense?

A. $12,000

B. $21,000

C. $30,000

D. $60,000

Answer (C) is correct. *(CPA, adapted)*
**REQUIRED:** The deferred income tax expense.
**DISCUSSION:** Deferred tax expense or benefit is the net change in an entity's deferred tax liabilities and assets during the year. Quinn had a net deferred tax asset of $9,000 at the beginning of 20X1, and a net deferred tax liability of $21,000 ($70,000 × 30%) at the end of 20X1. The net change (a deferred tax expense in this case) is $30,000 ($9,000 reduction in the deferred tax asset + $21,000 increase in deferred tax liabilities).
Answer (A) is incorrect because $12,000 results from offsetting the deferred tax liability and the deferred tax asset. Answer (B) is incorrect because $21,000 is the deferred tax liability. Answer (D) is incorrect because $60,000 is the income tax expense for the year ($200,000 × .30).

**84.** As a result of differences between depreciation for financial reporting purposes and tax purposes, the financial reporting basis of Noor Co.'s sole depreciable asset, acquired in 2004, exceeded its tax basis by $250,000 at December 31. This difference will reverse in future years. The enacted tax rate is 30% for the current year and 40% for future years. Noor has no other temporary differences. In its December 31 balance sheet, how should Noor report the deferred tax effect of this difference?

A. As an asset of $75,000.

B. As an asset of $100,000.

C. As a liability of $75,000.

D. As a liability of $100,000.

Answer (D) is correct. *(CPA, adapted)*
**REQUIRED:** The deferred tax effect of the difference between the financial reporting basis and the tax basis.
**DISCUSSION:** The temporary difference arises because the excess of the reported amount of the depreciable asset over its tax basis will result in taxable amounts in future years when the reported amount is recovered. A taxable temporary difference results in a deferred tax liability. Because the enacted tax rate for future years is 40%, the deferred income tax liability is $100,000 ($250,000 × 40%).
Answer (A) is incorrect because the deferred income tax effect should be calculated using the 40% rate, and it is a liability. Answer (B) is incorrect because the deferred income tax effect is a liability. The temporary difference results in taxable, not deductible, amounts. Answer (C) is incorrect because $75,000 is based on the current year tax rate.

**85.** Taft Corp. uses the equity method to account for its 25% investment in Flame, Inc. During 20X0, Taft received dividends of $30,000 from Flame and recorded $180,000 as its equity in the earnings of Flame. Additional information follows:

- All the undistributed earnings of Flame will be distributed as dividends in future periods.
- The dividends received from Flame are eligible for the 80% dividends-received deduction.
- There are no other temporary differences.
- Enacted income tax rates are 30% for 20X0 and thereafter.

In its December 31, 20X0 balance sheet, what amount should Taft report for deferred income tax liability?

A. $9,000

B. $10,800

C. $45,000

D. $54,000

Answer (A) is correct. *(CPA, adapted)*
**REQUIRED:** The deferred income tax liability reported on the balance sheet.
**DISCUSSION:** According to SFAS 109, the deferred tax liability constitutes the "deferred tax consequences attributable to taxable temporary differences. A deferred tax liability is measured using the applicable enacted tax rate and provisions of the enacted tax law." Taft's recognition of $180,000 of equity-based earnings creates a temporary difference that will result in taxable amounts in future periods when dividends are distributed. The deferred tax liability arising from this temporary difference is measured using the 30% enacted tax rate and the dividends-received deduction. Accordingly, given that all the undistributed earnings will be distributed, a deferred tax liability of $9,000 [($180,000 equity – $30,000 dividends received) × 20% not deductible × 30% tax rate applicable after 20X0] should be reported.
Answer (B) is incorrect because $10,800 equals 30% of 20% of the equity in the earnings of Flame. Answer (C) is incorrect because $45,000 is the net increase in Taft's investment in Flame account under the equity method multiplied by the 30% tax rate. Answer (D) is incorrect because $54,000 equals 30% of $180,000.

**86.** Mill, which began operations on January 1, year 1, recognizes income from long-term construction contracts under the percentage-of-completion method in its financial statements and under the completed-contract method for income tax reporting. Income under each method follows:

| Year | Completed-Contract | Percentage-of-Completion |
|------|--------------------|--------------------------|
| 1 | $ -- | $300,000 |
| 2 | 400,000 | 600,000 |
| 3 | 700,000 | 850,000 |

There are no other temporary differences. If the applicable tax rate is 25%, Mill should report in its balance sheet at December 31, year 3, a deferred income tax liability of

A. $37,500

B. $105,000

C. $162,500

D. $195,000

Answer (C) is correct. *(CPA, adapted)*
**REQUIRED:** The deferred tax liability arising from differences in reporting income from long-term contracts.
**DISCUSSION:** In its financial statements issued through 12/31 year 3, Mill has reported $1,750,000 ($300,000 + $600,000 + $850,000) of income from long-term contracts. In its tax returns for the same period, it has reported $1,100,000 ($400,000 + $700,000) of income from the same sources. The result is a taxable temporary difference. Thus, Mill expects to have future taxable amounts of $650,000 and should recognize a deferred tax liability of $162,500 ($650,000 × 25% applicable tax rate).
Answer (A) is incorrect because $37,500 is the amount of the liability arising from the excess of percentage-of-completion over completed-contract revenue for year 1, assuming a 25% rate. Answer (B) is incorrect because $105,000 is the amount of the liability arising from the excess of percentage-of-completion over completed-contract revenue for years 2 and 3, assuming a 30% rate. Answer (D) is incorrect because $195,000 is based on a 30% rate.

**87.** When a change in the tax law or rates occurs, the effect of the change on a deferred tax liability or asset is

A. Not recognized.

B. Recognized as an adjustment as of the effective date of the change.

C. Recognized as an adjustment as of the enactment date of the change.

D. Recognized as a prior-period adjustment.

Answer (C) is correct. *(Publisher)*
**REQUIRED:** The effect on a deferred tax liability or asset of a change in the tax law or rates.
**DISCUSSION:** When a change in the tax law or rates occurs, the effect of the change on a deferred tax liability or asset is recognized as an adjustment in the period that includes the enactment date of the change. The adjustment is allocated to income from continuing operations. It is not treated as an extraordinary item.

**88.** On June 15, year 1, the county in which Mills Company operates enacted changes in the county's tax law. These changes are to become effective on January 1, year 2. They will have a material effect on the deferred tax accounts that Mills reported in accordance with SFAS 109. In which of the following interim and annual financial statements issued by Mills should the effect of the changes in tax law initially be reported?

A. The interim financial statements for the 3-month period ending June 30, year 1.

B. The annual financial statements for the year ending December 31, year 1.

C. The interim financial statements for the 3-month period ending September 30, year 1.

D. The annual financial statements for the year ending December 31, year 2.

Answer (A) is correct. *(Publisher)*
**REQUIRED:** The financial statements in which the effects of a change in tax law should initially be reported.
**DISCUSSION:** The effects of a change in tax law or rates initially should be included in income from continuing operations in the first financial statements issued for the period that includes the enactment date.
Answer (B) is incorrect because the effect should initially be reported in the first statements issued for the period that includes the enactment date. Answer (C) is incorrect because the period covered includes the effective date, not the enactment date. Answer (D) is incorrect because the period covered includes the effective date, not the enactment date.

**89.** In late summer, the Parker-Williams Partnership incorporated as a taxable entity. On September 7, the Dowdy Corporation, a taxable entity, changed its status to a partnership. In accordance with the provisions of SFAS 109, a deferred tax liability, based on temporary differences existing at the time of the change in the tax status of these enterprises, should

| | Parker-Williams | Dowdy |
|---|---|---|
| A. | Not be recognized | Not be eliminated |
| B. | Be recognized | Not be eliminated |
| C. | Be recognized | Be eliminated |
| D. | Not be recognized | Be eliminated |

Answer (C) is correct. *(Publisher)*
**REQUIRED:** The effect on two enterprises of changes in tax status.
**DISCUSSION:** When an enterprise such as Parker-Williams changes its status from a nontaxable partnership to a taxable corporation, a deferred tax liability or asset should be recognized for taxable or deductible temporary differences or carryforwards existing at the date of the tax status change. When a company such as Dowdy changes its status from a taxable to a nontaxable enterprise, any existing deferred tax liability or asset should usually be eliminated at the date of the tax status change. The effect of either recognizing or eliminating a deferred tax liability or asset should be allocated to continuing operations. It should not be treated as an extraordinary item.

**90.** When an enterprise is acquired in a business combination, a deferred tax liability or asset is recognized for the difference between the assigned amount and the tax basis of

A. Goodwill for which amortization is not tax deductible.

B. A leveraged lease.

C. Inventory.

D. Unallocated negative goodwill.

Answer (C) is correct. *(Publisher)*
**REQUIRED:** The effect on a deferred tax liability or asset of a business combination.
**DISCUSSION:** SFAS 109 requires that a deferred tax liability or asset be recognized for differences between the assigned amounts and the tax bases of assets and liabilities recorded when an enterprise is acquired in a business combination. The exceptions are for goodwill for which no tax deduction is allowed, unallocated excess over cost (negative goodwill), leveraged leases, and certain APB 23 differences. Accordingly, a difference between the assigned amount and the tax basis of inventory results in recognition of a deferred tax liability or asset in these circumstances. A deferred tax liability or asset is recognized if goodwill is tax deductible even though it is not amortizable on the financial statements. The reason is that tax deductible goodwill does not result in a permanent difference because it will eventually affect pretax financial income by being impaired, sold, or disposed of.

**91.** Which one of the following is true regarding disclosure of income taxes, including deferred taxes?

A. The manner of reporting the tax benefit of an operating loss carryforward or carryback is determined by the source of the income or loss in the current year.

B. The manner of reporting the tax benefit of an operating loss carryforward or carryback is determined by the source of expected future income that will result in realization of a deferred tax asset for an operating loss carryforward from the current year.

C. The tax benefit of an operating loss carryforward or carryback is disclosed only in a note to the financial statements.

D. The tax benefit of an operating loss carryforward or carryback is a component of net tax expense and is not separately disclosed.

Answer (A) is correct. *(CMA, adapted)*
**REQUIRED:** The true statement about disclosures relating to income taxes.
**DISCUSSION:** Under SFAS 109, with certain exceptions, the tax benefit of an operating loss carryforward is reported in the same manner as the source of the income offset by the carryforward in the current year. Similarly, the tax benefit of an operating loss carryback is reported in the same manner as the source of the current-year loss.
Answer (B) is incorrect because the manner of reporting is controlled by the source of the income or loss in the current year. Answer (C) is incorrect because the tax benefit is recorded. Answer (D) is incorrect because operating loss carryforwards and carrybacks should be separately disclosed.

**92.** For tax year 6, Windy Corporation had taxable income of $80,000 before using any of its net operating loss from year 5. Windy never elected to forgo the carryback of any of its losses since its incorporation in year 1. Windy's books and records reflect the following income (losses) since its incorporation:

| Year 1 | $20,000 |
|--------|---------|
| Year 2 | ($55,000) |
| Year 3 | $30,000 |
| Year 4 | $35,000 |
| Year 5 | ($50,000) |

What is the amount of taxable income Windy Corporation should report on its year 6 tax return?

A. $50,000

B. $60,000

C. $70,000

D. $80,000

Answer (B) is correct. *(Publisher)*
**REQUIRED:** The taxable income.
**DISCUSSION:** Under Sec. 172 of the Internal Revenue Code, a net operating loss (NOL) incurred in a tax year beginning after August 5, year 2 may be carried back 2 years and forward 20 years. An NOL incurred in earlier years can be carried back 3 years and forward 15 years. Absent an election to the contrary, the NOL must be carried to the earliest taxable year in the carryback period. The $55,000 NOL in year 2 is first carried back to offset the $20,000 of income in year 1. The $35,000 NOL carryover is then used to offset the $30,000 of income for year 3, leaving a $5,000 NOL carryover. The $5,000 carryover is used to reduce the year 4 income to $30,000. The $50,000 NOL in year 5 is first carried back to offset the remaining $30,000 of year 4 income. The result is a $20,000 NOL carryover that reduces the $80,000 of taxable income for year 6 to $60,000.
Answer (A) is incorrect because $50,000 is the NOL for year 5. Answer (C) is incorrect because $70,000 incorrectly uses a $10,000 NOL carryforward. Answer (D) is incorrect because $80,000 is the year 6 taxable income before using any of the year 5 NOL carryover.

**93.** For financial reporting purposes, it is considered generally acceptable to recognize benefits derived from the investment credit

A. Either over the life of the asset or in the year of acquisition.

B. Only as a reduction of income tax expense in the year of acquisition.

C. Only as a reduction in the cost of the asset.

D. Only over the life of the asset.

Answer (A) is correct. *(Publisher)*
**REQUIRED:** The proper accounting for the investment tax credit (ITC).
**DISCUSSION:** APB 4, *Accounting for the Investment Credit*, states that both the deferral and the flow-through methods of accounting for the investment tax credit are generally acceptable. The deferral method spreads the benefit of the ITC over the life of the asset either by reducing the cost of the asset or by treating it as deferred income to be amortized over the life of the asset. The flow-through method recognizes the ITC in the year of investment.
Answer (B) is incorrect because it is not the only acceptable method for financial accounting purposes. Answer (C) is incorrect because a reduction of the asset cost is in effect recognizing the credit over the life of the asset by reduced annual depreciation. It is not the only acceptable method. Answer (D) is incorrect because it is not the only acceptable method for financial accounting purposes.

**94.** The Stephens Company has a policy of deferring investment tax credits for accounting purposes. Investment tax credits of $100,000 were available on equipment that was purchased on January 1. The equipment has an estimated 10-year life. What is the amount of investment tax credits that should be credited to income for the calendar year?

A. $10,000

B. $14,286

C. $90,000

D. $100,000

Answer (A) is correct. *(CPA, adapted)*
**REQUIRED:** The ITC using the deferral method.
**DISCUSSION:** Under the cost reduction or deferral method of accounting for an ITC, the investment credits actually realized are deferred and amortized over the productive life of the acquired property. Because the $100,000 ITC is attributable to the purchase of equipment with a 10-year estimated useful life, 10% ($10,000) of the ITC should be credited to tax expense.
Answer (B) is incorrect because $14,286 results from amortizing the ITCs over 7 years. Answer (C) is incorrect because $90,000 is the amount of unused ITC. Answer (D) is incorrect because $100,000 results from expensing the entire credit in the current year.

---

Use Gleim's **CMA Test Prep** for interactive testing with **over 2,000 additional multiple-choice questions!**

# STUDY UNIT SEVENTEEN
# EQUITY AND REVENUE RECOGNITION

(27 pages of outline)

This study unit is the **seventh of ten** on **external financial reporting**. The relative weight assigned to this major topic in Part 2 of the exam is **25%** at **skill level B** (four skill types required). The ten study units are

Study Unit 11: Overview of External Financial Reporting
Study Unit 12: Overview of Financial Statements
Study Unit 13: Cash and Receivable
Study Unit 14: Inventories and Investments
Study Unit 15: Long-Lived Assets
Study Unit 16: Liabilities
Study Unit 17: Equity and Revenue Recognition
Study Unit 18: Other Income Statement Items
Study Unit 19: Business Combinations and Derivatives
Study Unit 20: SEC Requirements and the Annual Report

After studying the outlines and answering the multiple-choice questions in this study unit, you will have the skills necessary to address the following topics listed in the IMA's Learning Outcome Statements:

Part 2 – Section E.4. Recognition, measurement, valuation, and disclosure

For each of the subtopics listed, the candidate should be able to:

1. define the subtopic and describe the characteristics of its components

2. demonstrate an understanding of appropriate valuation techniques for the components of each subtopic

3. demonstrate an understanding of the appropriate accounting conventions for the components of each subtopic

4. compare and contrast valuation techniques and accounting methods

5. show the correct financial statement presentation

6. identify the appropriate disclosure requirements in the body of the financial statements and/or in the footnotes

Equity transactions and earnings per share

a. subtopic components: preferred stock and common stock; capital stock, additional paid-in capital and retained earnings; treasury stock (cost method and par value method); property dividends, scrip dividends; liquidating dividends; stock dividends (large and small); retained earnings

    b.    apply the accounting procedures for issuing shares of stock, including par value stock, no-par stock, stock sold on a subscription basis, lump sum sales, and stocks issued in noncash transactions

    c.    define stock options, warrants, and rights and recognize the correct presentation in the financial statements for these instruments

    d.    identify transactions that affect paid-in capital and those that affect retained earnings

    e.    infer the effect on shareholders' equity of large and small stock dividends

    f.    define stock split and distinguish from stock dividend

    g.    identify reasons for the appropriation of retained earnings

    h.    calculate earnings per share (basic and diluted)

## Revenues and expenses

    a.    apply the revenue recognition principle to various types of transactions

    b.    identify issues involved with revenue recognition at point of sale, including sales with buy-back agreements, sales when right of return exists, and trade loading (or channel stuffing)

    c.    identify instances where revenue is recognized before delivery

    d.    distinguish between percentage-of-completion and completed-contract methods for recognizing revenue

    e.    apply the percentage-of-completion and the completed-contract methods

    f.    compare and contrast the recognition of costs of construction, progress billings, collections, and gross profit recognized under the two long-term contract accounting methods

    g.    demonstrate an understanding of the proper accounting for losses on long-term contracts

    h.    identify instances where revenue is recognized after delivery

    i.    recognize the situations in which each of the following revenue recognition methods would be used: installment sales method, cost recovery method, and deposit method

    j.    demonstrate an understanding of the accounting procedures under the installment method, the cost recovery method, and the deposit method

    k.    define gains and losses and indicate the proper financial statement presentation

    l.    recognize the issues and concerns that have been identified with respect to revenue recognition practices

## Part 2 – Section E.1. Objectives of external financial reporting; and E.2. Financial accounting fundamentals

NOTE: Statements a. through e. are covered in Study Unit 11

    f.    Special topics: stock options

For each special topic, the candidate should be able to:

    1.    Define and describe its characteristics
    2.    Demonstrate a basic understanding of the relevant accounting issues
    3.    Describe the impact on a firm's financial statements

## 17.1 EQUITY

1.    **Equity** of a business enterprise consists of contributed capital, retained earnings, and accumulated other comprehensive income.

2.    An important concept is **legal capital**, which in many states is the par or stated value of preferred and common stock.

    a.    Par or stated value is an arbitrary amount per share established in the corporate charter.

    b.    Legal capital cannot be distributed to shareholders as dividends.

    c.    Legal capital also represents the maximum liability of the shareholders.

3. **Contributed capital** (paid-in capital) represents amounts invested by owners in exchange for stock (common or preferred).

    a. The stated capital (capital stock) shows the par or stated value of all shares issued and outstanding. If stock has no par or stated value, the amount received is reported.

        1) Amounts for common and preferred stock are separately listed.

    b. Paid-in capital in excess of par or stated value (additional paid-in capital) consists of the sources of contributed capital in excess of legal capital. These sources may include

        1) Amounts in excess of par or stated value received for the company's stock

        2) A debit item for receipts that are less than par or stated value, for example, discount on common stock

        3) Amounts attributable to treasury stock transactions

        4) Transfers at fair value from retained earnings upon the issuance of stock dividends

        5) Stock subscription defaults (if forfeiture is allowed)

    c. **Donated assets**. In general, **SFAS 116**, *Accounting for Contributions Received and Contributions Made*, requires that contributions received be recognized as revenues or gains in the period of receipt and as assets, decreases of liabilities, or expenses depending on their form. They are measured at fair value.

        1) **Contributions of the donee's stock**. **APB 9**, *Reporting the Results of Operations*, states that "adjustments or charges or credits resulting from transactions in the company's own capital stock" are excluded from the determination of net income or the results of operations.

            a) Thus, the receipt of a contribution of a company's own stock is recorded at fair value as increases in both additional paid-in capital and treasury stock. Because these accounts offset, the net effect on equity is $0.

        2) **Contributions by governmental entities**. SFAS 116 does not apply to tax exemptions, abatements, or incentives, or to transfers of assets from a government to a business enterprise.

            a) Hence, a credit to donated capital may be appropriate in these cases. Nevertheless, consistency suggests that these transactions also be accounted for in accordance with SFAS 116.

4. **Common Stock**

    a. The common shareholders are the **owners of the corporation**.

        1) Their rights as owners, although reasonably uniform, depend on the laws of the state in which the firm is incorporated.

        2) Equity ownership involves risk because holders of common stock are **not guaranteed a return** and are last in priority in a liquidation (residual interest).

            a) Shareholders' capital provides the cushion for creditors if any losses occur on liquidation.

    b. **Advantages**

        1) Common stock does not require a fixed dividend; i.e., dividends are paid from profits when available.

        2) Unlike debt, there is no fixed maturity date for repayment of the capital.

        3) The sale of common stock increases the firm's creditworthiness by providing it with more capital.

       4) Common stock is frequently more attractive to investors than debt because it grows in value with the success of the firm.

          a) The higher the common stock value, the more advantageous equity financing is over debt financing.

    c. **Disadvantages**

       1) Control (voting rights) is usually diluted as more common stock is sold.

       2) New common stock sales dilute earnings available to existing shareholders because of the greater number of shares outstanding.

       3) Underwriting costs are typically higher for common stock issues.

       4) Too much equity may raise the average cost of capital of the firm above its optimal level.

       5) Unlike cash dividends on preferred stock, common stock cash dividends are not tax-deductible by the firm.

5. **Shareholder Rights**

    a. Shareholders participate indirectly in corporate policy and management by **meeting annually and electing directors**.

       1) In addition, shareholders must approve fundamental changes:

          a) Amendments to the articles of incorporation or bylaws

          b) All actions of merger or consolidation

          c) Any proposal by directors to sell, lease, or exchange all or substantially all of the corporation's assets

       2) However, the shareholders have little control over the day-to-day operation of the corporation.

    b. **Voting rights**. The articles may provide for more or less than one vote per share.

       1) Usually, each shareholder is entitled to one vote for each share owned for each new director to be elected, i.e., straight voting. Shareholders also have the right to remove directors by vote.

       2) **Cumulative voting** is mandatory in almost 50% of the states that allow it.

          a) Cumulative voting entitles each shareholder who has one vote per share owned per director to accumulate votes and either give one candidate as many votes as the number of directors to be elected multiplied by the number of shares owned or distribute that number of votes among as many candidates as (s)he wishes.

          b) Number of directors to be elected × number of shares of the shareholder = number of votes the shareholder may allocate to any one or more candidates.

          c) Cumulative voting allows minority shareholders to obtain representation on the board if they own a certain minimum number of shares. It can preclude the holders of more than 50% of the voting stock from electing the entire board of directors.

       3) Different voting rights for different **classes of stock** are permitted. Thus, each class may have the right to elect one director. This results in class voting.

       4) A **voting agreement**, whereby shareholders contract how they will vote their shares, may be perpetual and secret.

       5) **Voting trusts**. Shareholders transfer their shares to one or more voting trustees in exchange for voting trust certificates. The trustees elect directors based on instructions from the shareholders.

          a) The term of a voting trust is initially limited to 10 years.

             i) Shareholders can agree to continue it beyond 10 years.

b) A voting trust indenture (document) must be made public, and copies must be available for inspection at the corporate offices.

6) A **proxy** is an authorization by a shareholder for someone else to vote the shares. Typically, a proxy must be written and is revocable at any time.

a) A proxy is effective for no more than 11 months, unless otherwise permitted by statute and specifically included in the writing or unless the proxy is coupled with an interest; e.g., the shares are collateral for a loan or the shareholder enters into a buy/sell agreement or a voting agreement. The proxy coupled with an interest may be irrevocable.

b) An otherwise irrevocable proxy is revocable by a bona fide purchaser of the shares who has no notice of the proxy.

c) A general proxy permits a holder to vote on all corporate proposals other than fundamental corporate changes. A limited proxy permits a holder to vote only on matters specified in the proxy.

c. Common shareholders may have **preemptive rights** to purchase any additional stock issuances in proportion to their current ownership percentages.

d. **Meetings**. Ordinarily, shareholders may act only at a meeting.

1) Annual shareholders' meetings are required and must be held at a time fixed in the bylaws. The purpose is to elect new directors and to conduct other necessary business. Lack of notice or defective notice voids action taken at the meeting.

2) Special shareholder meetings, e.g., to approve a merger, may be called by the board of directors, the owner(s) of at least 10% of the issued and outstanding common stock, or any other persons authorized in the articles of incorporation. Special meetings require written notice.

3) A quorum must be represented in person or by proxy to conduct business at a shareholders' meeting. A quorum is defined as a majority of shares outstanding. Most state statutes permit the articles to establish a greater percentage (supermajority).

4) Shareholders can act without a meeting if all shareholders entitled to vote consent in writing to the action.

6. **Preferred Stock**

a. **Advantages**

1) It is a form of equity and therefore builds the creditworthiness of the firm.
2) Control is still held by common shareholders.
3) Preferred stock is more flexible than bond issues because it has no maturity date or sinking fund schedule.
4) Superior earnings of the firm are usually still reserved for the common shareholders.

b. **Disadvantages**

1) Preferred stock cash dividends are not tax deductible and are paid with taxable income. The result is substantially greater cost relative to bonds.
2) In periods of economic difficulty, accumulated dividends may create major managerial and financial problems for the firm.

c. Typical provisions of preferred stock issues

1) **Priority** in assets and earnings. If the firm goes bankrupt, the preferred shareholders have priority over common shareholders.
2) **Cumulative dividends**.
3) **Convertibility**. Preferred stock issues may be convertible into common stock at the option of the shareholder.

4)    **Participation**.

5)    An issue of preferred stock that specifies that it will be redeemed within a few years (e.g., 5 to 10 years) is known as **transient preferred stock**.

d.    The **dividends received deduction**.  Holding common or preferred stock rather than bonds provides corporations a major tax advantage:  At least 70% of the dividends received is tax deductible, whereas all bond interest received is taxable.

7.    **Retained earnings** is increased by net income and decreased by net losses, dividends, and certain treasury stock transactions.

a.    Prior-period adjustments (error corrections) are taken directly to retained earnings.

8.    **Other Equity Accounts**

a.    Treasury stock.

b.    **Accumulated other comprehensive income** is a separate component of equity that reports items included in comprehensive income but excluded from the determination of net income.

9.    **Earnings per share** amounts must be disclosed for all periods for which an income statement or earnings summary is presented.  Because EPS disclosure is required on the face of the income statement and in the notes thereto, this topic is covered in Study Unit 18, "Other Income Statement Items."

10.    **SFAS 129**, *Disclosure of Information about Capital Structure*, applies to all entities.  It continues and consolidates previously existing guidance.

a.    Rights and privileges of outstanding securities must be disclosed along with information about shares issued.

b.    The equity section of the balance sheet should disclose information about liquidation preferences of preferred stock.

c.    Redemption requirements for the next 5 years must also be disclosed.

11.    Balance sheet presentation

Capital stock:

| | | |
|---|---:|---:|
| Preferred stock, $100 par value, 6% cumulative, 200,000 shares authorized, 200,000 issued and outstanding | $2,000,000 | |
| Common stock, no par, stated value $1 per share, 5,000,000 shares authorized, 3,000,000 issued and outstanding | 3,000,000 | |
| Common stock dividend distributable, 30,000 shares | 30,000 | |
| Total capital stock | | $5,030,000 |
| Additional paid-in capital: | | |
| Excess over par -- preferred | $   200,000 | |
| Excess over stated value -- common | 9,000,000 | |
| Total additional paid-in capital | | 9,200,000 |
| Total paid-in capital | | $14,230,000 |
| Retained earnings | | 6,000,000 |
| Total paid-in capital and retained earnings | | $20,230,000 |
| Treasury stock at cost, 100,000 shares, common | | (90,000) |
| Accumulated other comprehensive income | | 245,000 |
| Total stockholders' equity | | $20,050,000 |

12.    Stop and review!  You have completed the outline for this subunit.  Study multiple-choice questions 1 through 7 beginning on page 674.

## 17.2 ISSUANCE AND RETIREMENT OF STOCK

1. The **charter (articles of incorporation)** filed with the secretary of state of the state of incorporation indicates the **classes of stock** that may be issued and their **authorized amounts** in terms of shares or total dollar value.

    a. When authorized shares are issued, the effect is to increase the amount of that class of stock outstanding.

    b. If a company does not hold any stock as treasury stock, the number of shares of each type of stock may be determined by dividing the value allocated to each stock account by the related par value or stated value.

2. **Issuance of Stock**

    a. Stock, both common and preferred, can be issued with or without a **par value**.

    <u>With par value:</u>

    | | | |
    |---|---|---|
    | Cash | $150,000 | |
    | Common stock (100,000 shares @ $1 par) | | $100,000 |
    | Paid-in capital in excess of par -- common | | 50,000 |

    <u>Without par value:</u>

    | | | |
    |---|---|---|
    | Cash | $150,000 | |
    | Common stock (100,000 shares, no par value) | | $150,000 |

    1) A discount is unlikely but would be debited to stock discount.

3. **Stock Subscriptions**

    a. When stock is subscribed, the corporation recognizes an obligation to issue stock, and the subscriber undertakes the legal obligation to pay for the shares subscribed.

    1) At this date, if collection of the price is reasonably assured, the entry is:

    | | | |
    |---|---|---|
    | Stock subscriptions receivable | $40,000 | |
    | Preferred stock subscribed (2,000 shares @ $10 par) | | $20,000 |
    | Paid-in capital in excess of par -- preferred | | 20,000 |

    a) The **SEC** requires subscriptions receivable to be reported as a **contra equity** account unless collection has occurred before issuance of the financial statements. In that case, the account may be reported as an asset.

    2) When the subscription price is paid, the entries are:

    | | | |
    |---|---|---|
    | Cash | $40,000 | |
    | Stock subscriptions receivable | | $40,000 |
    | | | |
    | Preferred stock subscribed | $20,000 | |
    | Preferred stock (2,000 shares @ $10 par) | | $20,000 |

    a) Thus, additional paid-in capital is increased when the stock is subscribed and is not affected when the stock is subsequently issued.

    b. When a subscriber **defaults**, the entry to record the subscription must be reversed.

    1) State laws and corporate policies vary with regard to the treatment of defaults. The possibilities range from complete refund to complete forfeiture.

    2) To the extent that payment has been received and is forfeited, additional paid-in capital from stock subscription default is credited for the amount forfeited.

### 4.  Lump-Sum Sales

a.   The proceeds of the combined issuance of different classes of securities should be allocated based on the relative fair values of the securities **(proportional method)**.

   1)   EXAMPLE:  A company simultaneously issues common and preferred stock for the lump sum of $550,000.

| | |
|---|---:|
| Fair market value of common stock (200,000 shares @ $1.80) | $360,000 |
| Fair market value of preferred stock (10,000 shares @ $4.00) | 40,000 |
| Total fair market value | $400,000 |
| | |
| Allocated to common stock [$550,000 × ($360,000 ÷ $400,000)] | $495,000 |
| Allocated to preferred stock [$550,000 × ($40,000 ÷ $400,000)] | 55,000 |
| Total allocated capital | $550,000 |

b.   If the fair value of one of the classes of securities is not known, the other securities should be recorded at their fair values, with the remainder of the proceeds credited to the securities for which the fair value is not determinable **(incremental method)**.

   1)   EXAMPLE:  The company can determine the fair value of its common stock but not its preferred stock.

| | |
|---|---:|
| Total received | $550,000 |
| Fair market value of common stock (200,000 shares @ $1.80) | (360,000) |
| Allocated to preferred stock | $190,000 |

c.   If the fair value of none of the classes of securities is known, an arbitrary allocation may be necessary.

### 5.  Stock may be issued in exchange for **services or property** as well as for cash.

a.   The transaction should be recorded at the more clearly determinable of the fair values of the stock or the property or services received.

b.   The fair value used is that in effect at the date of the agreement.

### 6.  Retirement.  When stock is retired, cash (or treasury stock) is credited.  The stock account is debited for the par or stated value.

a.   Additional paid-in capital is debited to the extent additional paid-in capital exists from the original stock issuance.

   1)   Any remainder is debited to retained earnings or credited to additional paid-in capital from stock retirement.

b.   No gain or loss is reported on transactions with owners of an enterprise's own stock, but the transfer of nonmonetary assets in exchange for stock requires recognition of any **holding gain or loss** on the nonmonetary assets.

c.   Preferred stock may be subject to a **call provision**, that is, mandatory redemption at the option of the company at a specified price.

### 7.  Stop and review!  You have completed the outline for this subunit.  Study multiple-choice questions 8 through 12 beginning on page 676.

## 17.3 TREASURY STOCK

1. **Treasury stock** consists of shares of the entity's own stock reacquired for various purposes, e.g., mergers, stock options, stock dividends, or the elimination of a particular ownership interest. Treasury stock is commonly accounted for at cost, but the par value method is also acceptable.

2. The **cost method** of accounting for treasury stock transactions records the acquisition of treasury stock as a debit to a treasury stock account and a credit to cash. No other accounts are affected.

   a. When the treasury stock is subsequently reissued for cash at a price in **excess of acquisition cost**, the difference between the cash received and the carrying amount (acquisition cost) of the treasury stock is credited to an account titled "additional paid-in capital from treasury stock transactions" and not to "additional paid-in capital."

   b. If the treasury stock is subsequently reissued at **less than acquisition cost**, the deficiency is first treated as a reduction of additional paid-in capital related to previous reissuances of treasury stock of the same class.

      1) After additional paid-in capital from previous reissuances of treasury stock is reduced to a zero balance, the remaining debit is to retained earnings.

   c. Treasury stock accounted for at cost is a **contra equity account**. It is reported on the balance sheet as an unallocated reduction of total equity. Moreover, in most states, the cost of treasury stock is deemed to be a restriction of retained earnings.

   d. Treasury stock is **not an asset**, no dividends are paid on it, and no gains and losses are recognized on treasury stock transactions.

   e. If treasury stock is **permanently retired**, the treasury stock account is closed to the appropriate capital stock and other contributed capital accounts and, possibly, to retained earnings.

3. The **par value method** treats the acquisition of treasury stock as a constructive retirement and the resale as a new issuance.

   a. Upon **acquisition**, the entry originally made to issue stock is effectively reversed. Treasury stock at par value (a debit) is recorded as an offset to the contributed capital account representing issued shares of the same type, and the additional paid-in capital recorded when the stock was originally issued is removed.

      1) Any difference between the original issuance price and the reacquisition price is ordinarily adjusted through additional paid-in capital accounts and retained earnings. Hence, gains are credited to additional paid-in capital from treasury stock transactions, and losses are debited to the same account but only to the extent of prior gains.

         a) If the credit balance in the account is insufficient to absorb the loss, retained earnings will be debited for the remainder.

   b. Upon **subsequent reissuance**, the entry is to remove treasury stock at par value and reestablish additional paid-in capital for any excess of the reissuance price over par value.

      1) If the reissuance price is less than par, the debit is to an additional paid-in capital account or to retained earnings.

   c. Under the par value method, treasury stock is shown in the balance sheet as a direct reduction of common (preferred) stock, not of total equity.

4.    **Cost Method vs. Par Value Method**

a.    EXAMPLE:  A company has the following balances in its equity section on January 1:

Common stock, $10 par value, 200,000 shares outstanding    $2,000,000
Additional paid-in capital ($2 per share)                                      400,000
Retained earnings                                                               $2,000,000

April 15 – The company reacquired 30,000 shares for $20 per share:

| Cost Method | | | Par Value Method | | |
|---|---|---|---|---|---|
| Treasury stock (30,000 × $20) | $600,000 | | Treasury stock (30,000 × $10) | $300,000 | |
| Cash (same amount) | | $600,000 | Additional paid-in capital (30,000 × $2) | 60,000 | |
| | | | Retained earnings (remainder) | 240,000 | |
| | | | Cash (30,000 × $20) | | $600,000 |

July 28 – The company reissued 10,000 shares of treasury stock for $30 per share:

| Cost Method | | | Par Value Method | | |
|---|---|---|---|---|---|
| Cash (10,000 × $30) | $300,000 | | Cash (10,000 × $30) | $300,000 | |
| Treasury stock (10,000 × $20) | | $200,000 | Treasury stock (10,000 × $10) | | $100,000 |
| Paid-in capital from treasury stock | | | Paid-in capital from treasury stock | | |
| (remainder) | | 100,000 | (remainder) | | 200,000 |

October 2 – The company reissued 15,000 shares of treasury stock for $8 per share.

| Cost Method | | | Par Value Method | | |
|---|---|---|---|---|---|
| Cash (15,000 × $8) | $120,000 | | Cash (15,000 × $8) | $120,000 | |
| PiC from treasury stock (balance in | | | PiC from treasury stock (remainder) | 30,000 | |
| account) | 100,000 | | Treasury stock (15,000 × $10) | | $150,000 |
| Retained earnings (remainder) | 80,000 | | | | |
| Treasury stock (15,000 × $20) | | $300,000 | | | |

5.    Stop and review!  You have completed the outline for this subunit.  Study multiple-choice questions 13 through 19 beginning on page 678.

## 17.4  DIVIDENDS

1.    **Cash dividends** are distributed to shareholders in the form of cash.

a.    Dividends provide information about a company's health to the stock market.

1)    Thus, companies generally have an active policy strategy with respect to dividends.  In practice, dividends usually exhibit greater stability than earnings.

2)    A **residual dividend policy** will pay dividends only if earnings exceed the amount needed to support an optimal capital budget (i.e., a firm will pay higher dividends when it has fewer attractive investment opportunities).

b.    Once cash dividends are declared, they become a legal liability of the corporation.

1)    On the **date of declaration**, a portion of retained earnings must be reclassified.

Retained earnings                                    $XXX
    Dividends payable                                         $XXX

2)    On the **date of record**, no journal entry is recorded.  Anyone holding shares as of this date is entitled to the dividend.

3)    On the **date of payment**, the dividend is distributed.

Dividends payable                                    $XXX
    Cash                                                        $XXX

4)    Unlike stock dividends, cash dividends cannot be rescinded.

    c.   Because **preferred stock** is a hybrid of debt and equity, holders of preferred stock get **priority in the payment of dividends** over holders of common stock.

        1)   When a dividend payment date passes without a distribution being made, the unpaid dividends are said to be **in arrears**.

        2)   If the preferred stock is **cumulative**, dividends in arrears and the preferred dividends for the current period must be paid before common shareholders may receive dividends.

            a)   Dividends in arrears are not a liability of the company until they are declared and are not recognized in the financial statements.

            b)   However, the aggregate and per-share amounts of dividends in arrears should be disclosed on the face of the balance sheet or in the notes.

    d.   Some holders of preferred stock **share in cash dividends remaining** after preferred shareholders have been paid at the preference rate and common shareholders have been paid a basic return. Such preferred stock is referred to as **participating**.

        1)   **Fully participating** preferred stock shares equally in the remainder. The remainder is allocated in proportion to the par values of the outstanding shares.

        2)   **Partially participating** preferred stock receives an additional dividend up to a ceiling rate. Alternatively, a specified higher rate is paid on the common stock.

        3)   **Nonparticipating** preferred shareholders receive only the preference rate.

2.   **Property Dividends**

    a.   **APB 29**, *Accounting for Nonmonetary Transactions*, requires that certain nonreciprocal transfers of nonmonetary assets to owners be based on the **recorded amount** of the assets given up.

        1)   These transfers are made "in a spinoff or other form of reorganization or liquidation or in a plan that is in substance the rescission of a prior business combination." The recorded amount is determined after recognition of any impairment loss.

        2)   Other nonreciprocal transfers of nonmonetary assets to owners are recorded at **fair value** as of the declaration date.

            a)   If the property has appreciated, it should first be written up to fair value and a gain recognized:

| | | |
|---|---|---|
| Property A | $XXX | |
|    Gain on disposition of property | | $XXX |

            b)   A portion of retained earnings must then be reclassified:

| | | |
|---|---|---|
| Retained earnings | $XXX | |
|    Property dividend payable | | $XXX |

            c)   The property dividend is distributed:

| | | |
|---|---|---|
| Property dividend payable | $XXX | |
|    Property A | | $XXX |

3.   **Scrip dividends** may be declared when a corporation has sufficient retained earnings but is short of cash. Scrip is a form of **note payable**.

    a.   When a scrip dividend is declared, a portion of retained earnings must be reclassified:

| | | |
|---|---|---|
| Retained earnings | $XXX | |
|    Scrip dividend payable | | $XXX |

b.    Interest on the payable is incurred for the period from declaration to payment. Thus when the scrip dividend is paid, interest expense must be recognized.

| | | |
|---|---|---|
| Scrip dividend payable | $XXX | |
| Interest expense | XXX | |
| Cash | | $XXX |

4.    **Liquidating dividends** are distributions in excess of the corporation's retained earnings.

a.    Liquidating dividends are a **return of investment** rather than a return on investment.

1)    On the date of declaration, the balance in retained earnings is reclassified along with a portion of additional paid-in capital:

| | | |
|---|---|---|
| Retained earnings | $XXX | |
| Paid-in capital in excess of par -- common | XXX | |
| Dividends payable | | $XXX |

2)    On the date of record, no journal entry is recorded.

3)    On the date of payment, the dividend is distributed.

| | | |
|---|---|---|
| Dividends payable | $XXX | |
| Cash | | $XXX |

5.    A **stock dividend** is the issuance of a company's own common stock to its common shareholders for no consideration.

a.    The company is **capitalizing rather than distributing** a portion of retained earnings.

1)    Each shareholder's proportionate interest in the company and total book value remain unchanged.

b.    In a **small stock dividend** (i.e., one of less than 20%-25% of the common shares outstanding on the day of declaration), the amount reclassified from retained earnings must be the fair market value of the stock.

1)    EXAMPLE: A company has 100,000 shares of $1 par value common stock outstanding and $200,000 of retained earnings. The company declares a 10% stock dividend when the fair value of its shares is $12 per share.

2)    On the date of declaration, a portion of retained earnings is reclassified:

| | | |
|---|---|---|
| Retained earnings (10,000 shares @ $12 per share) | $120,000 | |
| Common stock dividend distributable (10,000 shares @ $1 par) | | $100,000 |
| Paid-in capital in excess of par -- common | | 20,000 |

3)    On the date of payment, the distribution is made:

| | | |
|---|---|---|
| Common stock dividend distributable | $120,000 | |
| Common stock | | $120,000 |

6.    A **stock split** is, like a stock dividend, the issuance of a company's own common stock to its common shareholders for no consideration.

a.    A stock split lowers the price of the stock and increases the number of shares outstanding, making it more attractive to investors.

1)    As with a stock dividend, each shareholder's proportionate interest in the company and total book value remain unchanged.

b.    **No journal entry** is recorded. No retained earnings are reclassified.

1)    A memorandum entry notes that the par or stated value of the stock has been reduced and that the number of shares outstanding has been increased.

c.    A **reverse stock split** reduces the number of shares outstanding and raises the per share price of those shares still outstanding.

7. A **large stock dividend**, i.e., one of more than 20%-25% of the common shares outstanding, is considered to more closely resemble a stock split than a stock dividend.

    a. This is described in **ARB 43, Chapter 7B** as a **split-up effected in the form of a dividend**.

        1) In such cases, the amount of retained earnings reclassified should only be the par value of the stock issued, not the market value as in a small stock dividend.

        2) EXAMPLE: A company has 100,000 shares of $1 par value common stock outstanding and $200,000 of retained earnings. The company declares a 50% stock dividend when the fair value of its shares is $12 per share.

        3) On the date of declaration, a portion of retained earnings is reclassified:

| | | |
|---|---|---|
| Retained earnings (50,000 shares @ $1 par) | $50,000 | |
|    Common stock dividend distributable | | $50,000 |

        4) On the date of payment, the distribution is made:

| | | |
|---|---|---|
| Common stock dividend distributable | $50,000 | |
|    Common stock | | $50,000 |

    b. Stock dividends are **revocable**. Nevertheless, undistributed stock dividends are normally reported in the equity section.

        1) At the declaration date, the debit is to retained earnings and the credits are to stock dividends distributable and additional paid-in capital.

8. Stop and review! You have completed the outline for this subunit. Study multiple-choice questions 20 through 40 beginning on page 680.

## 17.5 RETAINED EARNINGS

1. Few entries are made to retained earnings except to record annual income (loss) and the declaration of dividends. Occasionally, retained earnings will be affected by a prior-period adjustment or a treasury stock transaction.

2. **Appropriations of Retained Earnings**. Retained earnings is sometimes appropriated to a special account to disclose **management's intent** that some earnings retained in the business (not paid out in dividends) will be used for special purposes.

    a. A company may restrict (appropriate) retained earnings for such purposes as compliance with the terms of a bond indenture (bond contract), retention of assets for internally financed expansion, anticipation of losses, or adherence to legal restrictions (for example, a state law restricting retained earnings by an amount equal to the cost of treasury stock).

        1) Appropriation of retained earnings **does not set aside assets**.

            a) Rather, it has the effect of limiting the amount available for dividends.

            b) A formal entry (debit RE, credit RE appropriated) may be used, or the restriction may be disclosed in a note.

        2) According to APB 9, "transfers to and from accounts properly designated as appropriated retained earnings (such as general purpose contingency reserves or provisions for replacement costs of fixed assets)" are always excluded from the determination of net income.

            a) However, appropriation of retained earnings is permitted if it is reported within equity and is clearly identified (SFAS 5).

3. A **quasi-reorganization** is accomplished by closing the retained earnings account (which in a cumulative loss situation would have a debit balance). In subsequent years, any balance in retained earnings will be dated (e.g., the account may be titled "Retained Earnings Since December 31, 2001").

4. Stop and review! You have completed the outline for this subunit. Study multiple-choice questions 41 through 43 beginning on page 687.

## 17.6 STOCK OPTIONS, WARRANTS, AND RIGHTS

1. **Stock options** give certain employees the option to purchase common stock at a specified price for a specified period of time.

   a. The compensation expense for compensatory stock option plans should be recognized in the periods that the employee performs the service.

   b. **SFAS 123 (revised 2004)**, *Share-Based Payment*, requires that the cost of employee services performed in exchange for awards of share-based compensation normally is measured at the (1) **grant-date fair value** of the equity instruments issued or (2) **fair value of the liabilities** incurred.

2. **Stock warrants** (certificates evidencing options to buy stock at a given price within a certain period) not only may be issued to employees (as compensation) or to shareholders but also may be attached to bonds or preferred stock.

   a. The proceeds of securities issued with **detachable warrants** are allocated between the warrants and the securities based on their **relative fair values**.

      1) If the fair value of one but not the other is known, the proceeds are allocated incrementally. For example, if the fair value of the securities but not the warrants is known, the securities are recorded at fair value, and the remainder of the proceeds is assigned to the warrants.

   b. If warrants are not detachable, they are not accounted for separately.

3. A **preemptive right** safeguards a shareholder's proportionate ownership.

   a. Thus, it is the right to purchase a pro rata amount of a new issuance of the same class of stock before that stock can be offered to non-shareholders.

      1) However, many companies have eliminated the preemptive right because it may inhibit the large issuances of stock that are often needed in business combinations.

4. In a **rights offering**, each shareholder is issued a certificate or warrant that is an **option to buy** a certain number of shares at a fixed price.

   a. No journal entry is recorded when the rights are issued. A memorandum entry can be used to indicate the fact that rights have been issued.

   b. When the rights are exercised, the normal journal entry for the issue of new stock is recorded.

      1) Thus, if rights are allowed to lapse, contributed capital is unaffected.

   c. **Allocation**. The recipient of stock rights must allocate the carrying amount of the shares owned between those shares and the rights based on their relative fair values at the time the rights are received, for example, by debiting available-for-sale securities (rights) and crediting available-for-sale securities for the appropriate amount. The recipient then has three options: Exercise the rights, sell them, or let them expire.

      1) If the rights are **exercised**, the amount allocated to them becomes part of the carrying amount of the acquired shares.

      2) If the rights are **sold**, their carrying amount is credited, cash is debited, and a gain (loss) is credited (debited).

      3) If the rights **expire**, a loss is recorded.

   d. **Transaction costs** associated with the redemption of stock rights reduce equity.

5. Stop and review! You have completed the outline for this subunit. Study multiple-choice questions 44 through 49 beginning on page 688.

## 17.7 EARNINGS PER SHARE (EPS)

1. According to **SFAS 128**, *Earnings per Share*, **EPS** is the amount of earnings attributable to a share of common stock.

   a. Investors and analysts commonly use this ratio to measure the performance of an entity over an accounting period.

   b. SFAS 128 prescribes **two forms of EPS -- basic (BEPS)** and **diluted (DEPS)**. When a loss is reported, applicable loss-per-share figures are presented.

2. **BEPS** measures the entity's earnings performance during the reporting period based on common stock outstanding during all or part of the period. BEPS equals income available to common shareholders divided by the weighted-average number of shares of common stock outstanding.

   a. **Income available to common shareholders** is determined by subtracting from income from continuing operations (if that number is reported in the income statement) and net income the period's dividends declared on preferred stock and accumulated dividends for the period on cumulative preferred stock. When either a loss from continuing operations or a net loss is reported, dividends on preferred stock (if applicable) increase the amount of the loss.

      1) When a discontinued operation is not reported but the entity has an extraordinary item or an accounting change, the line item to be used in calculating the BEPS numerator is income before extraordinary item (or an accounting change) instead of income from continuing operations.

   b. **The weighted-average number of common shares outstanding** is determined by relating the portion of the reporting period that the shares were outstanding to the total time in the period. Weighting is necessary because some shares may have been issued or reacquired during the period.

3. **DEPS** measures the entity's earnings performance during the reporting period based on both common stock and dilutive potential common stock. Potential common stock is dilutive if its inclusion in the calculation of EPS results in a reduction of EPS (or an increase in loss per share).

   a. DEPS is computed by

      1) **Increasing the numerator of BEPS** for any dividends on convertible preferred stock and the after-tax interest related to any convertible debt.

      2) **Increasing the denominator of BEPS** to include the weighted-average number of additional shares of common stock that would have been outstanding if dilutive potential common stock had been issued.

         a) The numerator is also adjusted for other changes in income or loss, such as profit-sharing expenses, that would result from the assumed issuance of potential common stock.

   b. DEPS is based on the **most advantageous conversion rate or exercise price** from the perspective of the holder. Moreover, previously reported DEPS is not retroactively adjusted for subsequent conversions or subsequent changes in the market price of the common stock.

   c. The calculation of DEPS does not assume the conversion, exercise, or contingent issuance of **antidilutive** securities, i.e., securities that increase EPS or decrease loss per share amounts.

4. **Potential common stock** is a security or other contract that may entitle the holder to obtain common stock. Examples include convertible securities (convertible preferred stock and convertible debt), stock options and warrants (and their equivalents), and contingently issuable common stock.

   a. Option and warrant equivalents include nonvested stock granted to employees, stock purchase contracts, and partially paid stock subscriptions.

5. **Dilution**. In determining whether potential common stock is dilutive, each issue or series of issues is considered **separately and in sequence** from the most dilutive to the least dilutive. The issue with the lowest earnings per incremental share is included in DEPS before issues with higher earnings per incremental share. If the issue with the lowest earnings per incremental share is found to be dilutive with respect to BEPS, it is included in a trial calculation of DEPS. If the issue with the next lowest earnings per incremental share is dilutive with respect to the first trial calculation of DEPS, it is included in a new DEPS calculation. This process continues until all issues of potential common shares have been tested.

   a. If a discontinued operation, extraordinary item, or cumulative-effect accounting change is reported, the **control number** for determining whether potential common shares are dilutive is **income from continuing operations** adjusted for preferred dividends. Thus, if potential common shares have a dilutive effect on the calculation of DEPS for income from continuing operations, the same number of shares used to adjust the denominator for that calculation is used to adjust the denominator for the calculation of DEPS for all other reported earnings amounts.

      1) If a **loss from continuing operations** or a loss from continuing operations available to common shareholders is reported, potential common shares are not included in the calculation of DEPS for any reported earnings amount.

6. The **if-converted method** is used to determine the dilutive effect of **convertible securities**. Conversion is not assumed if the effect is antidilutive. The if-converted method assumes that the convertible securities were converted at the **beginning of the period or time of issuance**, if later. As a result, to arrive at the **DEPS denominator**, the BEPS denominator is increased by the weighted-average number of shares of common stock assumed to be issued.

   a. To determine the **DEPS numerator**, the BEPS numerator is increased by the dividends related to convertible preferred stock and by the after-tax amounts of interest related to convertible debt for which the denominator was increased. The BEPS numerator is also adjusted for other after-tax changes in income or loss, such as profit-sharing or royalty expenses, that would result from the assumed issuance of common shares.

7. The **treasury stock method** is used to determine the dilutive effect of **outstanding call options and warrants** issued by the reporting entity. Dilution occurs if the average market price for the period exceeds the exercise price.

   a. The treasury stock method assumes that

      1) The options and warrants were converted at the **beginning of the period or time of issuance**, if later.
      2) The **proceeds** were used to purchase common stock at the **average market price** during the period.
      3) To arrive at the **DEPS denominator**, the BEPS denominator is increased by the difference between the number of shares issued and the number of shares purchased.

   b. The **reverse treasury stock method** is used when the entity has entered into contracts to repurchase its own stock, for example, when it has **written put options**. When the contracts are in the money (the exercise price exceeds the average market price), the potential dilutive effect on EPS is calculated by

          1)   Assuming the issuance at the beginning of the period of sufficient shares to raise the proceeds needed to satisfy the contracts

          2)   Assuming those proceeds are used to repurchase shares

          3)   Including the excess of shares assumed to be issued over those assumed to be repurchased in the DEPS denominator

    c.   Options held by the entity on its own stock, whether they are puts or calls, are not included in the DEPS denominator because their effect is antidilutive.

8.   If the number of common shares outstanding changes because of a **stock dividend, a stock split, or a reverse stock split**, EPS amounts for all periods presented are adjusted retroactively to reflect the change in capital structure as if it had occurred at the beginning of the first period presented. Adjustments are made for such changes in capital structure even if they occur after the close of the current period but before the issuance of the financial statements.

9.   An entity with a **simple capital structure** must present BEPS amounts for both income from continuing operations and net income on the face of the income statement. An entity with a simple capital structure (only common stock outstanding) reports BEPS amounts only.

    a.   An entity with a complex capital structure (one with dilutive securities) presents BEPS and DEPS amounts for income from continuing operations and net income with equal prominence on the face of the income statement.

    b.   An entity that reports a **discontinued operation or an extraordinary item** reports the applicable BEPS and DEPS amounts for these components of income on the face of the income statement or in the notes to the financial statements.

10.   For all periods in which an income statement or earnings summary is presented, **disclosures** must include EPS data and the following items:

    a.   A reconciliation by individual security of the numerators and denominators of the BEPS and DEPS computations for income from continuing operations

    b.   The effect of preferred dividends on the BEPS numerator

    c.   Potential common shares not included in DEPS because their inclusion would have had an antidilutive effect in the periods reported

11.   If DEPS data are reported for at least one period, they are reported for all periods reported, even if they are equal to BEPS amounts.

12.   **Subsequent events**. For the latest period for which an income statement is presented, an entity must disclose any transaction occurring after the end of the most recent period but before the issuance of the financial statements that would have had a material effect on EPS had the transaction occurred prior to the balance sheet date.

13.   Stop and review! You have completed the outline for this subunit. Study multiple-choice questions 50 through 64 beginning on page 690.

## 17.8 REVENUE RECOGNITION

1.   **Revenue Recognition at the Point of Sale**

    a.   Revenues are normally recognized when they are **realized or realizable and earned**.

        1)   The revenue recognition criteria are ordinarily met at the **point of sale** (time of delivery of goods or services).

        2)   At this time, **title and risk of loss** usually pass to the buyer.

            a)   For example, if goods are shipped **FOB shipping point**, title and risk of loss to pass to the buyer at the point of shipment.

            b)   If the shipping term is **FOB destination**, title and risk of loss do not pass to the buyer until a tender of delivery is made at the destination.

    b.   **Exceptions** to this principle exist.

        1)   For example, revenue may be recognized at the point of production (before delivery) if an established market exists for fungible goods, such as precious metals or agricultural products.

            a)   Certain **gains**, for example, as a result of the increase in the fair value of trading securities, also may be recognized without being realized.

        2)   Revenue and profit may be recognized after the point of sale (after delivery) if considerable uncertainty exists about collection of the sales price. The installment method or cost-recovery method may be used in this case.

        3)   Certain multiperiod transactions, e.g., construction contracts, are accounted for by the percentage-of-completion method.

    c.   If the recognition criteria are not met, **amounts received in advance** are treated as liabilities (deferred revenues).

        1)   Recognition is deferred until the obligation underlying the liability is partly or wholly satisfied.

        2)   Cash received in advance may initially be credited to a deferred revenue (liability) account. At the end of the accounting period, earned revenue is recognized with the following **adjusting entry**:

| | | |
|---|---|---|
| Deferred revenue | $XXX | |
|     Revenue | | $XXX |

            a)   A **reversing entry** is not appropriate if advance receipts are initially credited to a deferred revenue account (a permanent or real account).

        3)   If cash received in advance is initially credited to a revenue account, an **adjusting entry** is needed to debit revenue and credit a deferred revenue (liability) account for unearned amounts.

| | | |
|---|---|---|
| Revenue | $XXX | |
|     Deferred revenue | | $XXX |

            a)   If this entry is reversed at the beginning of the next period, no entry will be needed to recognize revenue.

            b)   This procedure keeps unearned revenue in the revenue account (a temporary or nominal account) except at the end of the period when financial statements are prepared.

2.   **Cash- vs. Accrual-Basis Accounting**

    a.   **Accrual-basis accounting** records revenues and expenses in the periods when they are earned or incurred.

        1)   **Cash-basis accounting** records revenues when cash is received, and expenses when cash is paid.

    b.   Accrual-basis accounting uses **deferrals** to postpone recognition of revenues and expenses to subsequent periods if the related cash amounts are received or paid in a period prior to when they are earned or incurred.

        1)   **Accruals** are used to recognize revenues and expenses as earned or incurred in a period prior to when the related cash amounts are received or paid.

3.   The **installment method** recognizes income on a sale as the related receivable is collected.

    a.   This method is normally used when **collection is not reasonably assured** (when collection problems, i.e., bad debts, are subject to reasonable estimate, profit is usually recognized at the point of sale).

b.   The amount recognized each period is the **gross profit percentage** (gross profit ÷ selling price) on the sale multiplied by the cash collected.

   1)   In addition, interest income must be accounted for separately from the gross profit on the sale.

c.   If the goods sold are **repossessed** due to nonpayment, the goods' net realizable value, remaining deferred gross profit, and any loss are debited, and the remaining installment receivable credited.

d.   EXAMPLE: Assume that a TV costing $600 is sold on the installment basis for a price of $1,000 on November 1, year 1. A down payment of $100 was received and the remainder is due in nine monthly payments of $100 each. The entry for the sale is

| | | |
|---|---|---|
| Cash | $100 | |
| Installment receivable (year 1) | 900 | |
|     Inventory | | $600 |
|     Deferred gross profit (year 1) | | 400 |

   1)   In December when the first installment is received, the entry is

| | | |
|---|---|---|
| Cash | $100 | |
|     Installment receivable (year 1) | | $100 |

   2)   At December 31, the deferred gross profit must be adjusted to report the portion that has been earned. Given that 20% of the total price has been received, 20% of the gross profit has been earned. The entry is

| | | |
|---|---|---|
| Deferred gross profit (year 1) | $80 | |
|     Realized gross profit | | $80 |

   3)   Net income should include only the $80 realized gross profit for the period. The balance sheet should report a receivable of $800 minus the deferred gross profit of $320. Thus, the net receivable is $480.

   4)   In year 2, the remaining $800 is received, and the $320 balance of deferred gross profit is recognized. If only $400 were received in year 2 (if payments were extended), the December year 2 statements would report a $400 installment receivable and $160 of deferred gross profit.

   5)   If the TV in the example had to be repossessed because no payments after the down payment were made by the buyer, the used TV would be recorded at its net realizable value minus a resale profit. Assume that fair value at the time of repossession was only $500 because the TV had been damaged and that repair costs and sales commissions will amount to $100.

| | | |
|---|---|---|
| Inventory of used merchandise | $400 | |
| Deferred gross profit | 360 | |
| Loss on repossession | 140 | |
|     Installment receivable | | $900 |

   a)   The loss on repossession represents the difference between the $400 net realizable value ($500 fair value – $100 repair and sales costs) and the $540 book value ($900 remaining on the contract – $360 deferred gross profit) of the receivable.

   6)   Installment receivables are classified as **current assets** regardless of the due date. Even though the receivable may be due in more than 1 year, the stipulation that a current receivable is one that will be collected within the normal operating cycle makes installment receivables current assets.

   7)   Normally, an installment transaction has an **interest component**, and **APB 21**, *Interest on Receivables and Payables*, applies. The recognition of deferred gross profit is based on receipt of principal. The interest is imputed at the time of issuance and remains constant for the life of the installment.

4. The **cost-recovery method** may be used when receivables are collected over an extended period, considerable doubt exists as to collectibility, and a reasonable estimate of the loss cannot be made.

    a. Under the cost-recovery method, profit is recognized only after collections exceed the cost of the item sold. Subsequent amounts are treated entirely as revenues. This method is more conservative than the installment method.

    b. EXAMPLE: In year 1, Creditor Co. made a $100,000 sale accounted for using the cost-recovery method. The cost of the item sold was $70,000, and year 1 collections equaled $50,000. In year 2, collections equaled $25,000, and $10,000 of the receivable was determined to be uncollectible. As a result of these transactions, the net receivable (receivable – deferred profit) was $0 at the end of year 2. The following entries were made in year 1 and year 2:

Year 1

| | | |
|---|---:|---:|
| Receivable | $100,000 | |
|    Inventory | | $70,000 |
|    Deferred gross profit | | 30,000 |
| | | |
| Cash | $50,000 | |
|    Receivable | | $50,000 |

Year 2

| | | |
|---|---:|---:|
| Cash | $25,000 | |
| Deferred gross profit | 5,000 | |
|    Receivable | | $25,000 |
|    Realized gross profit | | 5,000 |
| | | |
| Deferred gross profit | $10,000 | |
|    Receivable | | $10,000 |

5. **Deposit Accounting**

    a. Customers are often charged for deposits, such as those on reusable containers.

    b. When cash deposits are paid, a liability must be established.

        1) When the containers are returned, the deposit is refunded and the liability debited.

        2) If the containers are not returned, the liability will be debited, the inventory credited, and a gain or loss recorded for the difference.

    c. Deposits are sometimes debited to trade receivables as part of the amounts due from customers.

        1) Because of the uncertainty about collection, the deposit receivable should be separately reported.

    d. **SFAS 66**, *Accounting for Sales of Real Estate*, requires that deposit accounting be used in circumstances in which a customer may cancel a land contract and receive a full refund.

        1) Thus, the transaction cannot be recorded as a sale until the specified period of time has passed.

        2) A liability is recorded when cash is received, and no revenue is recognized until the period has expired during which the customer may cancel.

6. **Long-Term Construction Contracts**

   a. The **completed-contract method** is used to account for a long-term contracted-for project when the percentage-of-completion method is inappropriate.

      1) Under the completed-contract method, all contract costs are deferred until the project is completed.

         a) Costs of completion are then matched with revenue. Revenue and gross profit are recognized only upon completion.

      2) All costs are deferred in a **construction-in-progress** (inventory) account that is closed to cost of sales when the project is completed.

   b. According to **AICPA SOP 81-1**, the **percentage-of-completion method** is presumed to be preferable.

      1) The percentage-of-completion method is used to recognize revenue on long-term contracts when the

         a) Extent of progress toward completion, contract revenue, and contract costs are reasonably estimable;

         b) Enforceable rights regarding goods or services to be provided, the consideration to be exchanged, and the terms of settlement are clearly specified; and

         c) Obligations of the parties are expected to be fulfilled.

   c. The percentage-of-completion method recognizes periodic **revenue or gross profit**.

      1) The components of gross profit under the percentage-of-completion method are:

         a) The estimated total revenue or gross profit

         b) The percentage of progress toward completion (the relationship of costs incurred to estimated total costs is the recommended but not the only basis for determining such progress)

         c) The revenue or gross profit recognized to date

      2) The **estimated total gross profit** equals the contract price minus the total estimated costs.

         a) The percentage completed times the total expected revenue or gross profit equals the total revenue or gross profit to be recognized to date.

         b) The revenue or gross profit recognized in prior periods is then subtracted from the total to date to determine the amount to be recognized in the current period.

      3) Under both the percentage-of-completion and completed-contract methods, the **full estimated loss** on any project is recognized as soon as it becomes apparent.

      4) When estimated revenue and costs are revised, a **change in accounting estimate** is recognized, and no retroactive restatement is necessary.

   d. EXAMPLE: A contractor agrees to build a bridge that will take 3 years to complete. The contract price is $2 million and expected total costs are $1.2 million.

|  | Year 1 | Year 2 | Year 3 |
|---|---|---|---|
| Costs incurred during each year | $300,000 | $600,000 | $550,000 |
| Costs expected in future | 900,000 | 600,000 | 0 |

      1) By the end of year 1, 25% ($300,000 ÷ $1,200,000) of expected costs has been incurred. Thus, the contractor will recognize 25% of the revenue or gross profit that will be earned on the project. The total gross profit is expected to be $800,000 ($2,000,000 − $1,200,000), so $200,000 (25% of $800,000) gross profit should be recognized in year 1.

2) At the end of year 2, total costs incurred are $900,000 ($300,000 + $600,000). Given that $600,000 is expected to be incurred in the future, the total expected cost is $1,500,000 ($900,000 + $600,000), and the estimate of gross profit is $500,000 ($2,000,000 contract price – $1,500,000 costs). If the project is 60% complete ($900,000 ÷ $1,500,000), $300,000 of cumulative gross profit should be recognized for years 1 and 2 (60% of $500,000). Because $200,000 was recognized in year 1, $100,000 should be recognized in year 2.

3) At the end of the third year, total costs are $1,450,000. Thus, the total gross profit is known to be $550,000. Because a total of $300,000 was recognized in years 1 and 2, $250,000 should be recognized in year 3.

4) Journal entries (assuming payment was made at the end of the contract):

|  |  | %-of-Completion | | Completed-Contract | |
|---|---|---|---|---|---|
| **Year 1:** | Construction in progress | $300,000 | | $300,000 | |
|  | Cash or accounts payable | | $300,000 | | $300,000 |
|  | | | | | |
|  | Construction in progress | $200,000 | | | |
|  | Construction gross profit | | $200,000 | | No entry |
|  | | | | | |
| **Year 2:** | Construction in progress | $600,000 | | $600,000 | |
|  | Cash or accounts payable | | $600,000 | | $600,000 |
|  | | | | | |
|  | Construction in progress | $100,000 | | | |
|  | Construction gross profit | | $100,000 | | No entry |
|  | | | | | |
| **Year 3:** | Construction in progress | $550,000 | | $550,000 | |
|  | Cash or accounts payable | | $550,000 | | $550,000 |
|  | | | | | |
|  | Cash | $2,000,000 | | $2,000,000 | |
|  | Construction in progress | | $1,750,000 | | $1,450,000 |
|  | Construction gross profit | | 250,000 | | 550,000 |

a) Ordinarily, **progress billings** are made and payments are received during the term of the contract.

   i) Accounts receivable is debited and progress billings is credited.

   ii) As cash is received, cash is debited and accounts receivable is credited. Neither billing nor the receipt of cash affects gross profit.

   iii) Moreover, billing, receipt of payment, and incurrence of cost have the same effects under both accounting methods.

b) If construction in progress (costs and recognized gross profit) exceeds total billings to date, the difference is reported as a **current asset**.

   i) If billings exceed construction in progress, the difference is reported as a **current liability**.

   ii) The **closing entry** is to debit progress billings and to credit construction in progress.

c) A variation on the foregoing entries is to credit periodic revenue for the gross amount.

   i) This practice requires a **debit to a nominal account** (a cost of revenue earned account that is similar to cost of goods sold) that equals the costs incurred in the current period.

   ii) For example, in year 1, instead of debiting construction in progress and construction gross profit for $200,000, the entry is

| | | |
|---|---|---|
| Construction in progress (gross profit) | $200,000 | |
| Construction expenses (a nominal account) | 300,000 | |
| Gross revenue | | $500,000 |

7. **Consignment Accounting**

a. A **consignment sale** is an arrangement between the owner of goods (consignor) and a sales agent (consignee). The consignee is expected to make his/her best efforts to sell the goods.

   1) **Title and risk of loss remain** with the consignor.
   2) **Sales are recorded** on the consignor's books only when the goods are sold to third parties by the consignee.
   3) Inventory shipped on consignment should therefore not be reported as a sale by a consignor but rather be included in **inventory**. Costs of transporting the goods to the consignee are inventoriable costs, not selling costs.
   4) The consignee records sales commissions when the goods are sold and at no time records the inventory as an asset.

b. **Consignor's Accounting**

   1) The initial shipment is recorded with a debit to **goods on consignment** and a credit to **inventory** for the cost of the merchandise.
   2) Receipts and expenses incurred by the consignee are recorded by debits to cash, commission expense, and cost of goods sold. Credits are to sales and goods on consignment.

c. **Consignee's Accounting**

   1) The **initial acquisition** of inventory is not recorded in the ledger accounts, although a supplementary memorandum entry may be made.
   2) **Sales** are recorded with a debit to cash (or accounts receivable) and credits to commission income and accounts payable to the consignor.
   3) Any **expenses** incurred on behalf of the consignor (such as freight-in or service costs) are reductions of the payable to the consignor.
   4) Payments to the consignor result in a debit to accounts payable and a credit to cash.

d. **Example Entries on the Books of the Consignor and Consignee**

   1) The consignor ships 100 units, costing $50 each, to a consignee:

| Consignor's Books | | Consignee's Books |
|---|---|---|
| Goods on consignment | $5,000 | Memorandum entry only |
|    Inventory |       $5,000 | |

   2) The consignee pays $120 for freight-in:

| Consignor's Books | | Consignee's Books | | |
|---|---|---|---|---|
| No entry | | Payable to consignor | $120 | |
| | |    Cash | | $120 |

   3) The consignee sells 80 units at $80 each. The consignee is to receive a 20% commission on all sales:

| Consignor's Books | Consignee's Books | | |
|---|---|---|---|
| No entry | Cash | $6,400 | |
| |    Payable to consignor | | $5,120 |
| |    Commission income | | 1,280 |

4)   The consignee sends a monthly statement to the consignor along with the balance owed. The cost of shipping goods to the consignee, including any such cost paid by the consignee, is recorded as a cost of consigned inventory by a debit to consigned goods out.

| Consignor's Books | | | Consignee's Books | | |
|---|---|---|---|---|---|
| Cash | $5,000 | | Payable to consignor | $5,000 | |
| Commission expense | 1,280 | | Cash | | $5,000 |
| Goods on consignment | 120 | | | | |
| Cost of good sold | 4,096 | | | | |
| Sales | | $6,400 | | | |
| Goods on consignment | | 4,096 | | | |

5)   The consignee may use **consignment in** rather than payable to consignor. Consignment in is a receivable/payable account.

6)   Goods on consignment is an account used in a perpetual or periodic inventory system when consignments are recorded in separate accounts.

a)   If the consignor uses a **perpetual inventory system**, the credit on shipment is to inventory.

b)   If the consignor uses a **periodic system**, the credit on shipment is to consignment shipments, a contra cost of sales account. The balance in the account is closed at the end of the period when the inventory adjustments are made.

8.   **Interest**. For a comprehensive discussion, see item 2. under subunit 13.3.

9.   **Product Financing Arrangements**

a.   These arrangements (sales with buyback agreements) involve an apparent sale of inventory by a **sponsor** (a party seeking financing) coupled with a repurchase agreement.

1)   In essence, the future reacquisition of the inventory is a return of collateral upon payment of a debt.

b.   Examples of these arrangements include:

1)   Sale of the product to another with an agreement by the seller to repurchase it
2)   The seller's establishment of a separate entity for these purpose(s)
3)   The seller's guarantee of the debt of the buyer
4)   The use or sale of the financed product by the seller

c.   **SFAS 49**, *Accounting for Product Financing Arrangements*, applies to a transaction in which a product is sold subject to repurchase of the product, of a substantially identical product, or of processed goods of which the product is a component.

1)   The arrangement is treated as a borrowing if the financing arrangement requires the sponsor to purchase at **specified prices**, and the specified prices will fluctuate to cover changes in purchasing, financing, and holding costs (but the specified prices must not be otherwise subject to change).

d.   The money received is accounted for as a liability rather than as a sale.

1)   Financing and inventory holding costs are to be imputed. Usually, the selling price to the buyer is less than the repurchase price to cover these costs.

e.   If another entity purchases inventory from a third party for repurchase by a sponsor, the sponsor-repurchaser should record an asset and a liability when the other entity makes the purchase.

f.   SFAS 49 is an attempt to prevent enterprises from reducing inventory (and inventory taxes) and increasing revenue and income through **parking transactions**.

1)   In such transactions, an earning process has not been substantially completed because the sponsor still retains the risks and rewards of ownership even though title has passed to the apparent buyer.

10. **Right of Return**

    a.  When sales are made with the understanding that unsatisfactory goods may be returned, revenue and cost of sales nevertheless may be recognized and the goods removed from inventory when certain conditions exist.

    b.  If the conditions are met, a sale is recorded in the usual way.

        1)  In addition, **estimated returns** (a contra revenue account) is debited and cost of sales and deferred gross margin are credited.

        2)  Inventory and deferred gross margin are debited and accounts receivable (or cash) is credited when returns are made.

    c.  If the conditions are not met, revenue and cost of sales are not recognizable until the right of return expires.

        1)  The initial entry is to debit accounts receivable (or cash) and to credit inventory and deferred gross margin. Returns result in a reversal of this entry.

    d.  **SFAS 48**, *Revenue Recognition When Right of Return Exists*, prescribes the accounting when returns are expected to be material. It does not apply to the return of defective goods, such as under a warranty.

        1)  If revenue is to be recognized at the time of sale despite the existence of a right of return, any costs or losses anticipated are to be accounted for in accordance with **SFAS 5**, *Accounting for Contingencies*, and revenue and cost of sales are to be reduced to reflect expected returns as described above.

        2)  SFAS 48 prohibits revenue recognition at the time of sale when a right of return exists unless **six conditions** are met. If these conditions are not met, revenue recognition is deferred until they are met or the return privilege expires. The following are the conditions:

            a)  The seller's price is substantially fixed or determinable.

            b)  The buyer has paid or is obligated to pay, and the obligation is not contingent on resale.

            c)  The buyer's obligation is not changed in the event of theft, damage to, or destruction of the product.

            d)  The buyer has economic substance apart from the seller.

            e)  The seller is not substantially obligated to directly bring about resale.

            f)  The amount of future returns can be reasonably estimated.

11. **Trade Loading**

    a.  This practice overstates operating revenues, earnings, and market share in the absence of a product financing arrangement or right of return.

    b.  The producing entity prematurely recognizes sales through influencing wholesalers (the "trade") to purchase more output than they can sell.

        1)  Hence, unless the practice can be repeated in following years, the loading of the "trade" will reduce the normal earnings of future years.

    c.  In the software industry, this is referred to as **channel stuffing**.

    d.  By any name, this invidious practice provides misleading, "window-dressed" results in the current period.

12. Stop and review! You have completed the outline for this subunit. Study multiple-choice questions 65 through 98 beginning on page 695.

## 17.9 CORE CONCEPTS

### Equity

- The **equity** of a business enterprise consists of contributed capital, retained earnings, and accumulated other comprehensive income.
- The **common shareholders** are the **owners** of a corporation. The issuance of common stock makes it easy for a business to **raise large amounts of capital** from many disparate parties.
- **Preferred stock** is a **hybrid** of debt and equity, i.e., holders stand higher in priority in bankruptcy than holders of common stock but lower than holders of debt. Also, preferred stock receives a **mandatory dividend**, similar to debt; the payment of dividends on common stock is residual, not mandatory.

### Issuance and Retirement of Stock

- If stock is issued with a **par or stated value**, amounts received upon sale are recorded as **paid-in capital in excess of par**.
- Likewise, when **stock subscriptions** are sold, paid-in capital in excess of par is credited for the amount received that exceeds the par or stated value of the stock subscribed.
- When **different classes of securities** are sold for a **lump sum**, the proceeds should be **allocated** based on the relative fair values of the securities (the **proportional method**). If the fair value of one of the classes of securities is not known, the others are recorded at their fair values and the remainder is credited to the securities for which the fair value is not known (the **incremental method**).
- **Gains and losses may not be recognized** on transactions in a company's **own stock**.

### Treasury Stock

- Treasury stock, i.e., **an entity's own stock reacquired** on the open market, is generally accounted for **at cost**, but the par value method is also acceptable.
- Under the **cost method**, additional paid-in capital is unaffected when treasury stock is acquired; under the **par value method**, additional paid-in capital is reduced.
- Under both methods, **paid-in capital from treasury stock** is recorded when treasury stock is **resold** above cost (under the cost method) or above par (under the par value method).

### Dividends

- Dividends provide information about **a company's health** to the stock market.
- The dividends on **cumulative preferred stock** accumulate during periods when no dividends are paid out. These must be paid before any dividends can be paid on common stock.
- Holders of **participating preferred stock** share in the cash dividends remaining after preferred shareholders have been paid at the preference rate and common shareholders have been paid a basic return.
- **Other types of dividends** are property dividends (distribution of tangible property), scrip dividends (distribution of notes payable), and stock dividends (distribution of the company's outstanding-but-unissued stock).
- A **stock split** is merely an increase in the number of outstanding shares; no journal entry is recorded.

Retained Earnings

- **Few entries** are made to retained earnings except to record annual income or loss and the declaration of dividends.
- Retained earnings is **sometimes appropriated** to a special account to disclose management's intent that some earnings retained in the business and not paid out as dividends will be used for special purposes. It is important to note that appropriating earnings does not set aside assets.

Stock Options, Warrants, and Rights

- **Stock options** give certain employees the option to purchase common stock at a specified price for a specified period of time.
- **Stock warrants** are certificates evidencing options to buy stock at a given price within a certain period. They may be issued to employees and shareholders and may be attached to bonds or preferred stock.
- In a **rights offering**, each shareholder is issued a certificate or warrant that is an option to buy a certain number of shares at a fixed price.

Earnings per Share (EPS)

- Earnings per share is presented in **two calculations**.
- **Basic earnings per share** is the income available to common shareholders divided by the **weighted-average number of shares** of common stock outstanding.
- **Diluted earnings per share** increases the numerator of the basic calculation for any **dividends on convertible preferred stock**, and increases the denominator to include the weighted-average number of additional shares of common stock that would have been outstanding if **dilutive potential common stock** had been issued.
- For purposes of determining the **degree of dilution**, the **if-converted method** is applied. The dilutive effect of all dilutive securities is considered to have been effective on the first day of the year.
- Earnings per share data is presented on the **income statement**.

Revenue Recognition

- Revenues are normally recognized when they are **realized or realizable and earned**.
- The **installment method** recognizes income on a sale as the related receivable is collected.
- The **cost-recovery method** may be used when receivables are collected over an extended period, considerable doubt exists as to collectibility, and a reasonable estimate of the loss cannot be made.
- Long-term construction contracts can be accounted for under the **completed-contract method**, but the **percentage-of-completion method** is preferable.
- The **percentage-of-completion method** recognizes periodic revenue or gross profit based upon the estimated total revenue or gross profit for the project, the percentage of the project completed, and the revenue or gross profit recognized to date.
- Ordinarily, **progress billings** are made and payments are received during the term of the contract. Construction in progress in excess of billings constitutes a **current asset**. Billings in excess of construction in progress constitute a **current liability**.
- When inventory is **consigned**, title and risk of loss remain with the consignor (owner of the goods). The consignor only **recognizes revenue** when the goods are **sold**.

## QUESTIONS

### 17.1 Equity

**1.** Issues of preferred stock that specify redemption of the issues over relatively short periods such as 5 to 10 years are called

    A.  Transient preferreds.

    B.  Short-term preferreds.

    C.  Preferred stock obligations.

    D.  Temporary preferreds.

Answer (A) is correct.  *(CIA, adapted)*

    **REQUIRED:** The term for issues of preferred stock that specify redemption of the issues over relatively short periods.

    **DISCUSSION:** Some preferred stock may be redeemed at a given time or at the option of the holder or otherwise at a time not controlled by the issuer. This feature makes preferred stock more nearly akin to debt, particularly in the case of transient preferred stock, which must be redeemed within a short time (e.g., 5 to 10 years). The SEC requires a separate presentation of redeemable preferred, nonredeemable preferred, and common stock.

    Answer (B) is incorrect because short-term preferreds is not a term in common usage. Answer (C) is incorrect because preferred stock obligations is not a term in common usage. Answer (D) is incorrect because temporary preferreds is not a term in common usage.

**2.** The following excerpt was taken from a company's financial statements: " . . . 10% convertible participating . . . $10,000,000." What is most likely being referred to?

    A.  Bonds.

    B.  Common stock.

    C.  Stock options.

    D.  Preferred stock.

Answer (D) is correct.  *(CIA, adapted)*

    **REQUIRED:** The securities most likely referred to as convertible participating.

    **DISCUSSION:** Preferred shareholders have priority over common shareholders in the assets and earnings of the enterprise. If preferred dividends are cumulative, any past preferred dividends must be paid before any common dividends. Preferred stock may also be convertible into common stock, and it may be participating. For example, 10% fully participating preferred stock will receive additional distributions at the same rates as other shareholders if dividends paid to all shareholders exceed 10%.

    Answer (A) is incorrect because bonds normally have a coupon yield stated in percentage and may be convertible but are not participating. Answer (B) is incorrect because common stock is not described as convertible or participating on the financial statements. Answer (C) is incorrect because common stock options are not participating and do not have a stated yield rate.

**3.** Unless the shares are specifically restricted, a holder of common stock with a preemptive right may share proportionately in all of the following except

    A.  The vote for directors.

    B.  Corporate assets upon liquidation.

    C.  Cumulative dividends.

    D.  New issues of stock of the same class.

Answer (C) is correct.  *(CMA, adapted)*

    **REQUIRED:** The item that is not a right of common shareholders.

    **DISCUSSION:** Common stock does not have the right to accumulate unpaid dividends. This right is often attached to preferred stock.

    Answer (A) is incorrect because common shareholders have the right to vote (although different classes of shares may have different privileges). Answer (B) is incorrect because common shareholders have the right to share proportionately in corporate assets upon liquidation (but only after other claims have been satisfied). Answer (D) is incorrect because common shareholders have the right to share proportionately in any new issues of stock of the same class (the preemptive right).

**4.** In comparing an investment in preferred stock to an investment in bonds, one substantial advantage to a corporation investing in preferred stock is the

- A. Taxable interest received.
- B. Voting power acquired.
- C. Set maturity date.
- D. Dividends received deduction.

Answer (D) is correct.  *(Publisher)*
**REQUIRED:** The major advantage associated with an investment in preferred stock rather than in bonds.
**DISCUSSION:** By investing in preferred stock instead of bonds, a corporation receives a significant tax advantage in the form of the dividends received deduction. Under the dividends received deduction, at least 70% of dividends received from preferred stock is deductible for tax purposes. With bonds, any interest received is fully taxable. Furthermore, the dividends received deduction also applies when a corporation holds an investment in common stock.
Answer (A) is incorrect because interest is not paid on preferred stock. Taxability of interest is a disadvantage of bonds. Answer (B) is incorrect because an investment in preferred stock usually does not confer voting rights. Answer (C) is incorrect because an investment in preferred stock does not include a maturity date.

**5.** Preferred and common stock differ in that

- A. Failure to pay dividends on common stock will not force the firm into bankruptcy, while failure to pay dividends on preferred stock will force the firm into bankruptcy.
- B. Common stock dividends are a fixed amount, while preferred stock dividends are not.
- C. Preferred stock has a higher priority than common stock with regard to earnings and assets in the event of bankruptcy.
- D. Preferred stock dividends are deductible as an expense for tax purposes, while common stock dividends are not.

Answer (C) is correct.  *(CIA, adapted)*
**REQUIRED:** The difference between preferred and common stock.
**DISCUSSION:** In the event of bankruptcy, the claims of preferred shareholders must be satisfied before common shareholders receive anything. The interests of common shareholders are secondary to those of all other claimants.
Answer (A) is incorrect because failure to pay dividends will not force the firm into bankruptcy, whether the dividends are for common or preferred stock. Only failure to pay interest will force the firm into bankruptcy. Answer (B) is incorrect because preferred dividends are fixed. Answer (D) is incorrect because neither common nor preferred dividends are tax deductible.

**6.** Which of the following is usually not a feature of cumulative preferred stock?

- A. Has priority over common stock with regard to earnings.
- B. Has priority over common stock with regard to assets.
- C. Has voting rights.
- D. Has the right to receive dividends in arrears before common stock dividends can be paid.

Answer (C) is correct.  *(CIA, adapted)*
**REQUIRED:** The item not usually a feature of cumulative preferred stock.
**DISCUSSION:** Preferred stock does not usually have voting rights. Preferred shareholders are usually given the right to vote for directors only if the company has not paid the preferred dividend for a specified period of time, such as ten quarters. Such a provision is an incentive for management to pay preferred dividends.
Answer (A) is incorrect because preferred stock has priority over common stock with regard to earnings, so dividends must be paid on preferred stock before they can be paid on common stock. Answer (B) is incorrect because preferred stock has priority over common stock with regard to assets. In the event of liquidation, for example, because of bankruptcy, the claims of preferred shareholders must be satisfied in full before the common shareholders receive anything. Answer (D) is incorrect because cumulative preferred stock has the right to receive any dividends not paid in prior periods before common stock dividends are paid.

**7.** At December 31, year 1, a corporation has the following account balances:

| | |
|---|---|
| Common stock ($10 par, 50,000 shares issued) | $500,000 |
| 8% preferred stock ($50 par, 10,000 shares issued) | 500,000 |
| Paid-in capital in excess of par on common stock | 640,000 |
| Paid-in capital in excess of par on preferred stock | 20,000 |
| Retained earnings | 600,000 |

The preferred stock is cumulative, nonparticipating, and has a call price of $55 per share. The journal entry to record the redemption of all preferred stock on January 2, year 2 pursuant to the call provision is

A.
| | | |
|---|---|---|
| Preferred stock | $500,000 | |
| Paid-in capital in excess of par: preferred | 20,000 | |
| Discount on preferred stock | 30,000 | |
| Cash | | $550,000 |

B.
| | | |
|---|---|---|
| Preferred stock | $500,000 | |
| Paid-in capital in excess of par: preferred | 20,000 | |
| Loss on redemption of preferred stock | 30,000 | |
| Cash | | $550,000 |

C.
| | | |
|---|---|---|
| Preferred stock | $500,000 | |
| Loss on redemption of preferred stock | 50,000 | |
| Retained earnings | 300,000 | |
| Cash | | $550,000 |
| Paid-in capital in excess of par: preferred | | 300,000 |

D.
| | | |
|---|---|---|
| Preferred stock | $500,000 | |
| Paid-in capital in excess of par: preferred | 20,000 | |
| Retained earnings | 30,000 | |
| Cash | | $550,000 |

**Answer (D) is correct.** *(CIA, adapted)*
**REQUIRED:** The journal entry to record the redemption of preferred stock pursuant to the call provision.
**DISCUSSION:** The exercise of the call provision resulted in the redemption of the 10,000 shares of preferred stock issued and outstanding at the call price of $550,000 (10,000 shares × $55 call price per share). To eliminate the carrying amount of the preferred stock and recognize the cash paid in this transaction, the required journal entry is to debit preferred stock for $500,000, debit paid-in capital in excess of par: preferred for $20,000, and credit cash for $550,000. The difference of $30,000 ($550,000 cash – $520,000 carrying amount of the preferred stock) is charged to retained earnings. No loss is reported because GAAP do not permit the recognition of a gain or loss on transactions involving a company's own stock.

---

## 17.2  Issuance and Retirement of Stock

**8.** The par value of common stock represents

A. The estimated fair value of the stock when it was issued.

B. The liability ceiling of a shareholder when a company undergoes bankruptcy proceedings.

C. The total value of the stock that must be entered in the issuing corporation's records.

D. The amount that must be recorded on the issuing corporation's record as paid-in capital.

**Answer (B) is correct.** *(CMA, adapted)*
**REQUIRED:** The amount represented by the par value of common stock.
**DISCUSSION:** Par value represents a stock's legal capital. It is an arbitrary amount assigned to stock before it is issued. Par value represents a shareholder's liability ceiling because, as long as the par value has been paid in to the corporation, the shareholders obtain the benefits of limited liability.
Answer (A) is incorrect because par value is rarely the same as fair value. Normally, fair value will be equal to or greater than par value, but there is no relationship between the two. Answer (C) is incorrect because all assets received for stock must be entered into a corporation's records. The amount received is very rarely the par value. Answer (D) is incorrect because all assets received for stock represent paid-in capital. Thus, paid-in capital may exceed par value.

**9.** On February 1 of the current year, King Corp., a newly formed company, had the following stock issued and outstanding:

- Common stock, no par, $1 stated value, 10,000 shares originally issued for $15 per share
- Preferred stock, $10 par value, 3,000 shares originally issued for $25 per share

King's February 1 statement of equity should report

| | Common Stock | Preferred Stock | Additional Paid-in Capital |
|---|---|---|---|
| A. | $150,000 | $30,000 | $45,000 |
| B. | $150,000 | $75,000 | $0 |
| C. | $10,000 | $75,000 | $140,000 |
| D. | $10,000 | $30,000 | $185,000 |

Answer (D) is correct. *(CPA, adapted)*
**REQUIRED:** The amounts of common stock, preferred stock, and additional paid-in capital to be reported.
**DISCUSSION:** The common stock was issued for a total of $150,000 (10,000 shares × $15). Of this amount, $10,000 (10,000 shares × $1 stated value) should be allocated to the common stock, with the remaining $140,000 ($150,000 – $10,000) credited to additional paid-in capital. The preferred stock was issued for $75,000 (3,000 shares × $25), of which $30,000 (3,000 shares × $10 par value) should be allocated to the preferred stock and $45,000 ($75,000 – $30,000) to additional paid-in capital. In the February 1 statement of equity, King therefore should report $10,000 in the common stock account, $30,000 in the preferred stock account, and $185,000 ($140,000 + $45,000) as additional paid-in capital.

**10.** Mouse Co. issued 1,000 shares of its $5 par common stock to Howe as compensation for 1,000 hours of legal services performed. Jason usually bills $160 per hour for legal services. On the date of issuance, the stock was trading on a public exchange at $140 per share. By what amount should the additional paid-in capital account increase as a result of this transaction?

- A. $135,000
- B. $140,000
- C. $155,000
- D. $160,000

Answer (A) is correct. *(CPA, adapted)*
**REQUIRED:** The increase in additional paid-in capital.
**DISCUSSION:** When stock is issued for property or services, the transaction is recorded at the fair value of the stock or of the property or services received. In this case, the fair value of the stock is used because it is more definite. The $140,000 should be allocated as follows: $5,000 (1,000 shares × $5 par) to common stock and $135,000 to additional paid-in capital.
Answer (B) is incorrect because $5,000 should be allocated to common stock. Answer (C) is incorrect because the fair value of the stock should be used to record the transaction.
Answer (D) is incorrect because the fair value of the stock should be used to record the transaction.

**11.** Purple Corp. had outstanding 2,000 shares of 11% preferred stock, $50 par. On August 8 of this year, Purple redeemed and retired 25% of these shares for $22,500. On that date, Purple's additional paid-in capital from preferred stock totaled $30,000. To record this transaction, Purple should debit (credit) its capital accounts as follows:

| | Preferred Stock | Additional Paid-In Capital | Retained Earnings |
|---|---|---|---|
| A. | $25,000 | $7,500 | $(10,000) |
| B. | $25,000 | -- | $(2,500) |
| C. | $25,000 | $(2,500) | -- |
| D. | $22,500 | -- | -- |

Answer (C) is correct. *(CPA, adapted)*
**REQUIRED:** The accounting for redemption and retirement of preferred stock.
**DISCUSSION:** Under the cost method, the entry to record a treasury stock purchase is to debit treasury stock at cost ($22,500) and credit cash. The entry to retire this stock is to debit preferred stock at par [(2,000 shares × 25%) × $50 = $25,000], debit additional paid-in capital from the original issuance ($30,000 × 25% = $7,500), credit treasury stock at cost ($22,500), and credit additional paid-in capital from stock retirement ($10,000). No entry to retained earnings is necessary.
Answer (A) is incorrect because, if the reacquisition price is less than the issuance price, a credit is made to additional paid-in capital, not retained earnings. Answer (B) is incorrect because, if the reacquisition price is less than the issuance price, a credit is made to additional paid-in capital, not retained earnings.
Answer (D) is incorrect because preferred stock must be debited for the par value of the retired shares.

**12.** The equity section of Smith Corporation's statement of financial position is presented below.

| | |
|---|---|
| Preferred stock, $100 par | $12,000,000 |
| Common stock, $5 par | 10,000,000 |
| Paid-in capital in excess of par | 18,000,000 |
| Retained earnings | 9,000,000 |
| Net worth | $49,000,000 |

The common shareholders of Smith Corporation have preemptive rights. If Smith Corporation issues 400,000 additional shares of common stock at $6 per share, a current holder of 20,000 shares of Smith Corporation's common stock must be given the option to buy

A. 1,000 additional shares.

B. 3,774 additional shares.

C. 4,000 additional shares.

D. 3,333 additional shares.

Answer (C) is correct.  *(CMA, adapted)*
**REQUIRED:** The new shares that a shareholder may buy given preemptive rights.
**DISCUSSION:** Common shareholders usually have preemptive rights, which means they have the right to purchase any new issues of stock in proportion to their current ownership percentages. The purpose of a preemptive right is to allow shareholders to maintain their current percentages of ownership. Given that Smith had 2,000,000 shares outstanding ($10,000,000 ÷ $5 par), an investor with 20,000 shares has a 1% ownership. Hence, this investor must be allowed to purchase 4,000 (400,000 shares × 1%) of the additional shares.
Answer (A) is incorrect because the investor would be allowed to purchase 1% of any new issues. Answer (B) is incorrect because preferred shareholders do not share in preemptive rights. Answer (D) is incorrect because preferred shareholders do not share in preemptive rights.

## 17.3 Treasury Stock

**13.** Corporations purchase their outstanding stock for all of the following reasons except to

A. Meet employee stock compensation contracts.

B. Increase earnings per share by reducing the number of shares outstanding.

C. Make a market in the stock.

D. Improve short-term cash flow.

Answer (D) is correct.  *(CMA, adapted)*
**REQUIRED:** The item not a reason for a company to buy treasury stock.
**DISCUSSION:** A corporation purchases its own stock to facilitate possible acquisitions, to allow shareholders to receive capital gains rather than dividends, to comply with employee stock compensation contracts, to avoid a hostile takeover, to increase EPS and book value per share, to support the market for the stock, to eliminate dissident shareholders, and to reduce the size of the business. The acquisition of treasury stock does not improve a company's short-term cash flow. Cash must be expended to purchase the shares.
Answer (A) is incorrect because one reason a corporation purchases its own stock is to meet employee stock option contracts. Answer (B) is incorrect because one reason a corporation purchases its own stock is to increase earnings per share by reducing the number of shares outstanding. Answer (C) is incorrect because one reason a corporation purchases its own stock is to support the market for its stock.

---

Questions 14 and 15 are based on the following information. On January 5, year 1, Norton Company issued 5,000 shares of common stock with a par value of $50. The proceeds received were at the issue price of $60 per share. On June 4, year 2, the company reacquired 500 shares at $57.50 per share.

---

**14.** Under the cost method of accounting for treasury stock, the amount debited to treasury stock is

A. $28,750

B. $25,000

C. $30,000

D. $3,750

Answer (A) is correct.  *(Publisher)*
**REQUIRED:** The amount debited to treasury stock under the cost method.
**DISCUSSION:** The cost method debits treasury stock for the amount paid. In this case, the cost is $57.50 per share, or $28,750 for 500 shares.
Answer (B) is incorrect because $25,000 is the aggregate par value of 500 shares. It is the amount debited to treasury stock under the par value method. Answer (C) is incorrect because $30,000 was the original issuance price of the reacquired shares. Answer (D) is incorrect because $3,750 is the amount paid in excess of par.

**15.** Under the par value method of accounting for treasury stock, the amount debited to treasury stock is

A. $28,750

B. $25,000

C. $30,000

D. $3,750

Answer (B) is correct. *(Publisher)*
**REQUIRED:** The amount debited to treasury stock under the par value method.
**DISCUSSION:** The par value method debits the par value of reacquired stock to treasury stock. The par value of 500 shares at $50 each is $25,000.
Answer (A) is incorrect because $28,750 is the cost of the treasury stock. This amount is debited to treasury stock under the cost method. Answer (C) is incorrect because $30,000 was the original issuance price of the reacquired shares. Answer (D) is incorrect because $3,750 is the amount paid in excess of par. It is debited to additional paid-in capital.

**16.** At December 31, year 1, a company had the following equity accounts:

| | |
|---|---|
| Common stock, $10 par, 100,000 shares authorized, 40,000 shares issued and outstanding | $ 400,000 |
| Additional paid-in capital from issuance of common stock | 640,000 |
| Retained earnings | 1,000,000 |
| Total equity | $2,040,000 |

Each of the 40,000 shares of common stock outstanding was issued at a price of $26. On January 2, year 2, 2,000 shares were reacquired for $30 per share. The cost method is used in accounting for this treasury stock. Which of the following correctly describes the effect of the acquisition of the treasury stock?

A. Common stock is reduced by $20,000.

B. Additional paid-in capital from issuance of common stock is reduced by $32,000.

C. The retained earnings account balance is reduced by $8,000.

D. Total equity is reduced by $60,000.

Answer (D) is correct. *(CIA, adapted)*
**REQUIRED:** The effect of the acquisition of the treasury stock under the cost method.
**DISCUSSION:** Using the cost method, the journal entry to record the acquisition of the treasury stock includes a debit to treasury stock for $60,000. The balance of the treasury stock account is classified as a contra equity item. Thus, the acquisition of the treasury stock reduces total equity by $60,000 (2,000 shares × $30 = $60,000).
Answer (A) is incorrect because the common stock account balance is not affected when treasury stock is acquired. Answer (B) is incorrect because additional paid-in capital is not affected when treasury stock is acquired and accounted for by the cost method. Answer (C) is incorrect because the retained earnings account is not affected by treasury stock acquisitions when the cost method is used.

**17.** The purchase of treasury stock with a firm's surplus cash

A. Increases a firm's assets.

B. Increases a firm's financial leverage.

C. Increases a firm's interest coverage ratio.

D. Dilutes a firm's earnings per share.

Answer (B) is correct. *(CMA, adapted)*
**REQUIRED:** The true statement about a purchase of treasury stock.
**DISCUSSION:** A purchase of treasury stock involves a decrease in assets (usually cash) and a corresponding decrease in equity. Thus, equity is reduced and the debt-to-equity ratio and financial leverage increase.
Answer (A) is incorrect because assets decrease when treasury stock is purchased. Answer (C) is incorrect because a firm's interest coverage ratio is unaffected. Earnings, interest expense, and taxes will all be the same regardless of the transaction. Answer (D) is incorrect because the purchase of treasury stock is antidilutive; the same earnings will be spread over fewer shares. Some firms purchase treasury stock for this reason.

Questions 18 and 19 are based on the following information. On January 4, Plant Co. was organized with 5,000 authorized shares of $50 par common stocks. During the year, Plant had the following capital transactions:

January 7 -- issued 2,000 shares at $60 per share
June 20 -- reacquired 500 shares at $65 per share
November 19 -- reissued 400 shares held in treasury at $70 per share
December 3 -- retired the 100 shares of treasury stock

These were the only transactions affecting Plant's treasury stock.

**18.** Under the cost method of accounting for treasury stock, what amount should Plant credit on treasury stock on December 31?

A. $1,000

B. $5,000

C. $6,500

D. $26,000

Answer (C) is correct. *(Publisher)*
**REQUIRED:** The credit to treasury stock for the retirement of treasury stock.
**DISCUSSION:** Plant Co. retired 100 shares of treasury stock on December 3. Under the cost method, treasury stock that is retired when reacquired at a price in excess of par reduces the treasury stock account by the pro rata share debit to treasury stock when acquired. Therefore, the credit to treasury stock at December 3 is $6,500.
Answer (A) is incorrect because $1,000 is the credit under the par value method. Answer (B) is incorrect because $5,000 is the debit to common stock on December 31. Answer (D) is incorrect because $26,000 is the credit to treasury stock on November 19.

**19.** Under the par-value method of accounting for treasury stock, what amount should Plant report as additional paid-in capital on its December 31 balance sheet?

A. $15,000

B. $20,500

C. $21,000

D. $23,000

Answer (D) is correct. *(Publisher)*
**REQUIRED:** The additional paid-in capital reported under the par-value method.
**DISCUSSION:** Under the par-value method, additional paid-in capital is credited for $20,000 (2,000 shares × $10 excess over par) for the initial sale of common stock. It is then debited for $5,000 (500 shares × $10 excess over par) for the purchase of treasury stock. Additional paid-in capital is then credited for $8,000 (400 shares × $20 excess over par) for the reissuance of treasury stock. Thus, ending additional paid-in capital is $23,000 ($20,000 − $5,000 + $8,000).
Answer (A) is incorrect because $15,000 excludes the $8,000 credit from the reissuance of treasury stock. Answer (B) is incorrect because $20,500 includes the $2,500 debit to retained earnings on the acquisition of treasury stock. Answer (C) is incorrect because $21,000 includes a $2,000 credit from the sale of treasury stock and a $1,000 debit from the retirement of treasury stock.

## 17.4 Dividends

**20.** In practice, dividends

A. Usually exhibit greater stability than earnings.

B. Fluctuate more widely than earnings.

C. Tend to be a lower percentage of earnings for mature firms.

D. Are usually set as a fixed percentage of earnings.

Answer (A) is correct. *(CMA, adapted)*
**REQUIRED:** The true statement about dividends and their relation to earnings.
**DISCUSSION:** Dividend policy determines the portion of net income distributed to shareholders. Corporations normally try to maintain a stable level of dividends, even though profits may fluctuate considerably, because many shareholders buy stock with the expectation of receiving a certain dividend every year. Thus, management tends not to raise dividends if the payout cannot be sustained. The desire for stability has led theorists to propound the information content or signaling hypothesis: A change in dividend policy is a signal to the market regarding management's forecast of future earnings. This stability often results in a stock that sells at a higher market price because shareholders perceive less risk in receiving their dividends.
Answer (B) is incorrect because most companies try to maintain stable dividends. Answer (C) is incorrect because mature firms have less need of earnings to reinvest for expansion; thus, they tend to pay a higher percentage of earnings as dividends. Answer (D) is incorrect because dividend payout ratios normally fluctuate with earnings to maintain stable dividends.

**21.** On December 1, Charles Company's board of directors declared a cash dividend of $1.00 per share on the 50,000 shares of common stock outstanding. The company also has 5,000 shares of treasury stock. Shareholders of record on December 15 are eligible for the dividend, which is to be paid on January 1. On December 1, the company should

    A. Make no accounting entry.

    B. Debit retained earnings for $50,000.

    C. Debit retained earnings for $55,000.

    D. Debit retained earnings for $50,000 and paid-in capital for $5,000.

Answer (B) is correct. *(CMA, adapted)*
    **REQUIRED:** The proper journal entry on the declaration date of a dividend.
    **DISCUSSION:** Dividends are recorded on their declaration date by a debit to retained earnings and a credit to dividends payable. The dividend is the amount payable to all shares outstanding. Treasury stock is not eligible for dividends because it is not outstanding. Thus, the December 1 entry is to debit retained earnings and credit dividends payable for $50,000 (50,000 × $1).
    Answer (A) is incorrect because a liability should be recorded. Answer (C) is incorrect because the treasury stock is not eligible for a dividend. Answer (D) is incorrect because paid-in capital is not affected by the declaration of a dividend.

**22.** Treating dividends as an active policy strategy assumes that

    A. Dividends provide information to the market.

    B. Dividends are irrelevant.

    C. Dividend payments should be made to common shareholders first.

    D. Dividends are costly, and the firm should retain earnings and issue stock dividends.

Answer (A) is correct. *(CMA, adapted)*
    **REQUIRED:** The assumption made when dividends are treated as an active policy strategy.
    **DISCUSSION:** Stock prices often move in the same direction as dividends. Moreover, companies dislike cutting dividends. They tend not to raise dividends unless anticipated future earnings will be sufficient to sustain the higher payout. Thus, some theorists have proposed the information content or signaling hypothesis. According to this view, a change in dividend policy is a signal to the market regarding management's forecast of future earnings. Consequently, the relation of stock price changes to changes in dividends reflects not an investor preference for dividends over capital gains but rather the effect of the information conveyed.
    Answer (B) is incorrect because an active dividend policy suggests management assumes that dividends are relevant to investors. Answer (C) is incorrect because preferred shareholders always receive their dividends ahead of common shareholders. Answer (D) is incorrect because an active dividend policy recognizes that investors want dividends.

**23.** At December 31, 20X1 and 20X2, Maui Co. had 3,000 shares of $100 par, 5% cumulative preferred stock outstanding. No dividends were in arrears as of December 31, 20X0. Maui did not declare a dividend during 20X1. During 20X2, Maui paid a cash dividend of $10,000 on its preferred stock. Maui should report dividends in arrears in its 20X2 financial statements as a(n)

    A. Accrued liability of $15,000.

    B. Disclosure of $15,000.

    C. Accrued liability of $20,000.

    D. Disclosure of $20,000.

Answer (D) is correct. *(CPA, adapted)*
    **REQUIRED:** The amount and means of reporting preferred dividends in arrears.
    **DISCUSSION:** Dividends in arrears on preferred stock are not an obligation of the company and are not recognized in the financial statements. However, the aggregate and per-share amounts of arrearages in cumulative preferred dividends should be disclosed on the face of the balance sheet or in the notes (APB 10). The aggregate amount in arrears is $20,000 [(3,000 shares × $100 par × 5% × 2 years) – $10,000 paid in 20X2].
    Answer (A) is incorrect because dividends in arrears do not meet recognition criteria. Answer (B) is incorrect because $15,000 is the arrearage for one year. Answer (C) is incorrect because dividends in arrears do not meet recognition criteria.

**24.** If a company uses the residual dividend policy, it will pay

    A. A fixed cash dividend each quarter and use the residual as retained earnings.

    B. A fixed stock dividend each quarter and retain all earnings as a residual.

    C. All earnings as dividends each year.

    D. Dividends only if earnings exceed the amount needed to support an optimal capital budget.

Answer (D) is correct. *(CIA, adapted)*
    **REQUIRED:** The definition of a residual dividend policy.
    **DISCUSSION:** Under the residual theory of dividends, the amount (residual) of earnings paid as dividends depends on the available investment opportunities and the debt-equity ratio at which cost of capital is minimized. The rational investor should prefer reinvestment of retained earnings when the return exceeds what the investor could earn on investments of equal risk. However, the firm may prefer to pay dividends when investment opportunities are poor and the use of internal equity financing would move the firm away from its ideal capital structure.
    Answer (A) is incorrect because the cash dividend would not be stable, but a residual. Answer (B) is incorrect because the residual theory concerns cash dividends. Answer (C) is incorrect because all earnings are not distributed as dividends.

**25.** Frasier Corp.'s outstanding capital stock at December 15 consisted of the following:

- 30,000 shares of 5% cumulative preferred stock, par value $10 per share, fully participating as to dividends. No dividends were in arrears.
- 200,000 shares of common stock, par value $1 per share

On December 15, Frasier declared dividends of $100,000. What was the amount of dividends payable to Frasier's common shareholders?

- A. $10,000
- B. $34,000
- C. $40,000
- D. $60,000

Answer (C) is correct. *(CPA, adapted)*
**REQUIRED:** The dividends to common shareholders.
**DISCUSSION:** The stated rate of dividends must be paid to preferred shareholders before any amount is paid to common shareholders. Given no dividends in arrears, this amount is $15,000 (30,000 shares × $10 par × 5%). The preferred stock will also participate equally in the cash dividend after a 5% return is paid on the common. The basic return to common shareholders is $10,000 (200,000 shares × $1 par × 5%). The remaining $75,000 ($100,000 − $15,000 − $10,000) will be shared in proportion to the par values of the shares outstanding. The aggregate par value of the preferred is $300,000 (30,000 shares × $10 par). The aggregate par value of the common is $200,000 (200,000 shares × $1 par). The distribution will therefore be in the ratio of 3:2, and $45,000 ($75,000 × 60%) is the participating share of the preferred shareholders. The balance of $30,000 ($75,000 − $45,000) will be paid to the common shareholders. The total of the dividends on the common stock is $40,000 ($10,000 + $30,000).
Answer (A) is incorrect because $10,000 is the basic return to common shareholders. Answer (B) is incorrect because $34,000 results from assuming that no basic return is paid to the common shareholders. Answer (D) is incorrect because $60,000 is paid to the preferred shareholders.

**26.** Brady Corporation has 6,000 shares of 5% cumulative, $100 par value preferred stock outstanding and 200,000 shares of common stock outstanding. Brady's board of directors last declared dividends for the year ended May 31, 2000, and there were no dividends in arrears. For the year ended May 31, 2002, Brady had net income of $1,750,000. The board of directors is declaring a dividend for common shareholders equivalent to 20% of net income. The total amount of dividends to be paid by Brady at May 31, 2002 is

- A. $350,000
- B. $380,000
- C. $206,000
- D. $410,000

Answer (D) is correct. *(CMA, adapted)*
**REQUIRED:** The total amount of dividends to be paid given cumulative preferred stock.
**DISCUSSION:** If a company has cumulative preferred stock, all preferred dividends for the current and any unpaid prior years must be paid before any dividends can be paid on common stock. The total preferred dividends that must be paid equal $60,000 (6,000 shares × $100 par × 5% × 2 years), and the common dividend is $350,000 ($1,750,000 × 20%), for a total of $410,000.
Answer (A) is incorrect because $350,000 is the common stock dividend. Answer (B) is incorrect because $380,000 omits the $30,000 of cumulative dividends for 2001. Answer (C) is incorrect because $206,000 is based on a flat rate of $1 per share of stock.

**27.** Residco Inc. expects net income of $800,000 for the next fiscal year. Its targeted and current capital structure is 40% debt and 60% common equity. The director of capital budgeting has determined that the optimal capital spending for next year is $1.2 million. If Residco follows a strict residual dividend policy, what is the expected dividend payout ratio for next year?

- A. 90.0%
- B. 66.7%
- C. 40.0%
- D. 10.0%

Answer (D) is correct. *(CMA, adapted)*
**REQUIRED:** The expected dividend payout ratio assuming a strict residual dividend policy.
**DISCUSSION:** Under the residual theory of dividends, the residual of earnings paid as dividends depends on the available investments and the debt-equity ratio at which cost of capital is minimized. The rational investor should prefer reinvestment of retained earnings when the return exceeds what the investor could earn on investments of equal risk. However, the firm may prefer to pay dividends when investment returns are poor and the internal equity financing would move the firm away from its ideal capital structure. If Residco wants to maintain its current structure, 60% of investments should be financed from equity. Hence, it needs $720,000 ($1,200,000 × 60%) of equity funds, leaving $80,000 of net income ($800,000 NI − $720,000) available for dividends. The dividend payout ratio is therefore 10% ($80,000 ÷ $800,000 NI).
Answer (A) is incorrect because 90% is the reinvestment ratio. Answer (B) is incorrect because 66.7% is the ratio between earnings and investment. Answer (C) is incorrect because 40% is the ratio of debt in the ideal capital structure.

**28.** A stock dividend

A. Increases the debt-to-equity ratio of a firm.

B. Decreases future earnings per share.

C. Decreases the size of the firm.

D. Increases shareholders' wealth.

Answer (B) is correct. *(CMA, adapted)*
**REQUIRED:** The true statement about a stock dividend.
**DISCUSSION:** A stock dividend is a transfer of equity from retained earnings to paid-in capital. The debit is to retained earnings, and the credits are to common stock and additional paid-in capital. More shares are outstanding following the stock dividend, but every shareholder maintains the same percentage of ownership. In effect, a stock dividend divides the pie (the corporation) into more pieces, but the pie is still the same size. A stock dividend has no effect except on the composition of the equity section of the balance sheet. Hence, a corporation will have a lower EPS and a lower carrying amount per share following a stock dividend, but every shareholder will be just as well off as previously.

**29.** A company declares and pays both a $200,000 cash dividend and a 10% stock dividend. The effect of the <List A> dividend is to <List B>.

| | List A | List B |
|---|---|---|
| A. | Cash | Increase retained earnings |
| B. | Cash | Decrease retained earnings and increase equity |
| C. | Stock | Decrease retained earnings |
| D. | Stock | Decrease retained earnings and decrease equity |

Answer (C) is correct. *(CIA, adapted)*
**REQUIRED:** The effect of a dividend.
**DISCUSSION:** A stock dividend results in a transfer from retained earnings to paid-in capital equal to the fair value of the stock.
Answer (A) is incorrect because cash dividends reduce retained earnings. Answer (B) is incorrect because cash dividends decrease both retained earnings and equity. Answer (D) is incorrect because stock dividends have no net effect on equity.

**30.** Which of the following types of dividends do not reduce equity in the corporation?

A. Cash dividends.

B. Property dividends.

C. Liquidating dividends.

D. Stock dividends and split-ups in the form of a dividend.

Answer (D) is correct. *(CIA, adapted)*
**REQUIRED:** The dividends that do not reduce shareholders' equity.
**DISCUSSION:** The issuance of a stock dividend results in a debit to retained earnings and credits to contributed capital for the fair value of the stock. A split-up effected in the form of a dividend requires capitalization of retained earnings equal to the amount established by the issuer's state of incorporation (usually par value). Consequently, neither a stock dividend nor a split-up effected in the form of a dividend has a net effect on equity.
Answer (A) is incorrect because cash dividends reduce equity. They involve an immediate or promised future nonreciprocal distribution of assets. Answer (B) is incorrect because property dividends reduce equity. They involve an immediate or promised future nonreciprocal distribution of assets. Answer (C) is incorrect because liquidating dividends reduce equity. They involve an immediate or promised future nonreciprocal distribution of assets.

Questions 31 through 33 are based on the following information. Excerpts from the statement of financial position for Markham Corporation as of April 30 are presented as follows:

| | | | |
|---|---|---|---|
| Cash | $ 725,000 | Accounts payable | $1,236,000 |
| Accounts receivable (net) | 1,640,000 | Accrued liabilities | 831,000 |
| Inventories | 2,945,000 | Total current liabilities | $2,067,000 |
| Total current assets | $5,310,000 | | |

The board of directors of Markham met on May 5 and declared a quarterly cash dividend in the amount of $800,000 ($.50 per share). The dividend was paid on May 28 to shareholders of record as of May 15. Assume that the only transactions that affected Markham during May were the dividend transactions and that the closing entries have been made.

**31.** Markham's total equity is

A. Increased by the dividend declaration and unchanged by the dividend payment.

B. Unchanged by the dividend declaration and decreased by the dividend payment.

C. Unchanged by either the dividend declaration or the dividend payment.

D. Decreased by the dividend declaration and unchanged by the dividend payment.

Answer (D) is correct. *(CMA, adapted)*
**REQUIRED:** The effect on a firm's total equity resulting from the declaration and payment of a dividend.
**DISCUSSION:** The declaration of a dividend results in an increase in current liabilities and a corresponding decrease in retained earnings (an equity account). Thus, the declaration of a dividend decreases equity. The subsequent payment of the dividend has no effect on equity because that transaction involves using cash (a current asset) to pay the previously recorded current liability.

**32.** If the dividend declared by Markham Corporation had been a 10% stock dividend instead of a cash dividend, Markham's total equity would have been

A. Decreased by the dividend declaration and increased by the dividend distribution.

B. Unchanged by the dividend declaration and increased by the dividend distribution.

C. Increased by the dividend declaration and unchanged by the dividend distribution.

D. Unchanged by either the dividend declaration or the dividend distribution.

Answer (D) is correct. *(CMA, adapted)*
**REQUIRED:** The effect on total equity of the declaration and distribution of a stock dividend.
**DISCUSSION:** The entry to record the declaration of a stock dividend involves a debit to one equity account (retained earnings) and a credit to one or more other equity accounts (common stock dividend distributable and possibly additional paid-in capital) for the fair value of the stock. Consequently, the declaration has no effect on total equity because the entry merely entails a transfer from retained earnings to permanent capital. The subsequent distribution of a stock dividend requires only a debit to common stock dividend distributable and a credit to common stock. Because both are equity accounts, the distribution has no effect on total equity.
Answer (A) is incorrect because the declaration of a stock dividend has no effect on total equity. Answer (B) is incorrect because the distribution of a stock dividend has no effect on total equity. Answer (C) is incorrect because the declaration of a stock dividend has no effect on total equity.

**33.** If the dividend declared by Markham had been a 10% stock dividend instead of a cash dividend, Markham's current liabilities would have been

A. Decreased by the dividend declaration and increased by the dividend distribution.

B. Unchanged by the dividend declaration and increased by the dividend distribution.

C. Unchanged by the dividend declaration and decreased by the dividend distribution.

D. Unchanged by either the dividend declaration or the dividend distribution.

Answer (D) is correct. *(CMA, adapted)*
**REQUIRED:** The effect of the declaration and distribution of a stock dividend on a firm's current liabilities.
**DISCUSSION:** The declaration and distribution of a stock dividend involves transferring some amount from retained earnings to permanent equity. No liability account is affected by either the declaration or the distribution because shareholders are not receiving anything that they did not already have. A stock dividend merely divides the corporate pie into more pieces.

**34.** Stock dividends and stock splits differ in that

A. Stock splits involve a bookkeeping transfer from retained earnings to the capital stock account.

B. Stock splits are paid in additional shares of common stock, whereas a stock dividend results in replacement of all outstanding shares with a new issue of shares.

C. In a stock split, a larger number of new shares replaces the outstanding shares.

D. A stock dividend results in a decline in the par value per share.

Answer (C) is correct. *(CIA, adapted)*
**REQUIRED:** The difference between stock dividends and stock splits.
**DISCUSSION:** A stock split does not involve any accounting entries. Instead, a larger number of new shares are issued to replace and retire all outstanding shares.
Answer (A) is incorrect because stock dividends involve a bookkeeping transfer. Stock splits do not involve a change in the capital accounts. Answer (B) is incorrect because stock dividends are paid in additional shares of common stock. In stock splits, all outstanding shares are replaced with a new issue of shares. Answer (D) is incorrect because, in a stock split, there is a large decline in the book value and in the market value per share. A stock dividend does not affect the par value of stock.

**35.** On May 28, a company announced that its directors had met on May 26 and declared a dividend of 25 cents per share, payable to shareholders of record on June 20, with payment to be made on July 5. The date on which the declared dividend becomes a liability of the company is

A. May 26.

B. May 28.

C. June 20.

D. July 5.

Answer (A) is correct. *(CIA, adapted)*
**REQUIRED:** The date on which the declared dividend becomes a liability.
**DISCUSSION:** The dividend becomes a liability of the company on the declaration date (May 26), which is the date the directors meet and formally vote to declare a dividend.
Answer (B) is incorrect because May 28 is the announcement date. The dividend becomes a liability as soon as it is declared. Answer (C) is incorrect because June 20 is the record date on which the list of shareholders owning the shares who will receive the dividend payments is determined. Answer (D) is incorrect because July 5 is the dividend payment date. The declared dividend is no longer a liability after the payment is made.

**36.** The policy decision that by itself is least likely to affect the value of the firm is the

A. Investment in a project with a large net present value.

B. Sale of a risky division that will now increase the credit rating of the entire company.

C. Distribution of stock dividends to shareholders.

D. Use of a more highly leveraged capital structure that resulted in a lower cost of capital.

Answer (C) is correct. *(CIA, adapted)*
**REQUIRED:** The policy decision that is least likely to affect the value of the firm.
**DISCUSSION:** A stock dividend does not significantly affect the value of the firm. It simply divides ownership interests into smaller pieces without changing any shareholder's proportionate share of ownership.
Answer (A) is incorrect because a positive NPV project should increase the value of the firm. Answer (B) is incorrect because the higher credit rating should reduce the cost of capital and therefore increase the value of the firm. Answer (D) is incorrect because the lower cost of capital should reduce the required rate of return and increase the value of the firm.

**37.** When a company desires to increase the market value per share of common stock, the company will

A. Sell treasury stock.

B. Implement a reverse stock split.

C. Sell preferred stock.

D. Split the stock.

Answer (B) is correct. *(CMA, adapted)*
**REQUIRED:** The transaction that increases the market value per share of common stock.
**DISCUSSION:** A reverse stock split decreases the number of shares outstanding, thereby increasing the market price per share. A reverse stock split may be desirable when a stock is selling at such a low price that management is concerned that investors will avoid the stock because it has an undesirable image.
Answer (A) is incorrect because a sale of treasury stock increases the supply of shares and could lead to a decline in market price. Answer (C) is incorrect because a sale of preferred stock will take dollars out of investors' hands, thereby reducing funds available to invest in common stock. Hence, market price per share of common stock will not increase. Answer (D) is incorrect because a stock split increases the shares issued and outstanding. The market price per share is likely to decline as a result.

Questions 38 and 39 are based on the following information. A company has 1,000 shares of $10 par value common stock and $5,000 of retained earnings. Two proposals are under consideration. The first is a stock split giving each shareholder two new shares for each share formerly held. The second is to declare and distribute a 50% split-up effected in the form of a dividend.

**38.** The stock split proposal will <List A> earnings per share by <List B> than will the proposal for a split-up effected in the form of a dividend.

|     | List A | List B |
|-----|--------|--------|
| A.  | Increase | More |
| B.  | Increase | Less |
| C.  | Decrease | More |
| D.  | Decrease | Less |

Answer (C) is correct. *(CIA, adapted)*
**REQUIRED:** The effect of a stock split and a split-up effected in the form of a dividend on earnings per share.
**DISCUSSION:** The stock split will double the number of shares outstanding to 2,000. The 50% split-up effected in the form of a dividend will increase the number of outstanding shares to 1,500. The higher number of shares in the stock split will result in a lower earnings per share than will result from the split-up effected in the form of a dividend.

**39.** Under the <List A>, the par value per outstanding share will <List B>.

|     | List A | List B |
|-----|--------|--------|
| A.  | Split-up effected in the form of a dividend | Increase |
| B.  | Stock split | Increase |
| C.  | Split-up effected in the form of a dividend | Decrease |
| D.  | Stock split | Decrease |

Answer (D) is correct. *(CIA, adapted)*
**REQUIRED:** The effect of a stock split and a split-up effected in the form of a dividend on par value.
**DISCUSSION:** A stock split results in a lower par value per share because the total number of shares increases but the total par value of outstanding stock does not change.
Answer (A) is incorrect because par value per share does not change following a split-up effected in the form of a dividend. Answer (B) is incorrect because par value per share decreases following a stock split. Answer (C) is incorrect because par value per share does not change following a split-up effected in the form of a dividend.

**40.** Natural Co. had 100,000 shares of common stock issued and outstanding at January 1. During the year, Natural took the following actions:

March 15   -- declared a 2-for-1 stock split when the fair value of the stock was $80 per share
December 15  -- declared a $.50 per share cash dividend

In Natural's statement of equity for the year, what amount should Natural report as dividends?

A. $50,000
B. $100,000
C. $850,000
D. $950,000

Answer (B) is correct. *(CPA, adapted)*
**REQUIRED:** The amount to be reported as dividends.
**DISCUSSION:** The 100,000 shares of common stock split 2-for-1, leaving 200,000 shares at year-end. The dividends declared equaled $100,000 (200,000 shares × $0.50).
Answer (A) is incorrect because $50,000 does not reflect the stock split. Answer (C) is incorrect because $850,000 equals the fair value of the stock on March 15 plus the dividend, assuming no stock split. Answer (D) is incorrect because $950,000 equals the fair value of the stock on March 15 plus the dividend on 200,000 shares.

## 17.5 Retained Earnings

**41.** Items reported as prior-period adjustments

A. Do not include the effect of a mistake in the application of accounting principles, as this is accounted for as a change in accounting principle rather than as a prior-period adjustment.

B. Do not affect the presentation of prior-period comparative financial statements.

C. Do not require further disclosure in the body of the financial statements.

D. Are reflected as adjustments of the opening balance of the retained earnings of the earliest period presented.

Answer (D) is correct. *(CMA, adapted)*
**REQUIRED:** The true statement about items reported as prior-period adjustments.
**DISCUSSION:** Prior-period adjustments are made for the correction of errors. According to SFAS 16, *Prior Period Adjustments*, the effects of errors on prior-period financial statements are reported as adjustments to beginning retained earnings for the earliest period presented in the retained earnings statement. Such errors do not affect the income statement for the current period.
Answer (A) is incorrect because accounting errors of any type are corrected by a prior-period adjustment. Answer (B) is incorrect because a prior-period adjustment will affect the presentation of prior-period comparative financial statements. Answer (C) is incorrect because prior-period adjustments should be fully disclosed in the notes or elsewhere in the financial statements.

**42.** An appropriation of retained earnings by the board of directors of a corporation for bonded indebtedness will result in

A. The establishment of a sinking fund to retire bonds when they mature.

B. A decrease in cash on the balance sheet with an equal increase in the investment and funds section of the balance sheet.

C. A decrease in the total amount of retained earnings presented on the balance sheet.

D. The disclosure that management does not intend to distribute assets, in the form of dividends, equal to the amount of the appropriation.

Answer (D) is correct. *(CMA, adapted)*
**REQUIRED:** The effect of an appropriation of retained earnings.
**DISCUSSION:** The appropriation of retained earnings is a transfer from one retained earnings account to another. The only practical effect is to decrease the amount of retained earnings available for dividends. An appropriation of retained earnings is purely for disclosure purposes.
Answer (A) is incorrect because the establishment of a sinking fund is entirely independent of appropriating retained earnings. Answer (B) is incorrect because cash is unaffected. Answer (C) is incorrect because the total retained earnings will not change; however, the total will appear as the sum of two retained earnings accounts instead of one.

**43.** Page Co. had retained earnings of $200,000 on January 1. On April 20, Page reacquired 2,000 shares of its common stock at $10 per share. On October 3, Page sold 500 of these shares of treasury stock for $12 per share. Page uses the cost method to record treasury stock. During the year, Page had paid cash dividends of $70,000. Also, Page had distributed property dividends of $20,000. Its net income for the year ended December 31 was $80,000. On December 31, how much should Page report as retained earnings?

A. $190,000

B. $191,000

C. $210,000

D. $211,000

Answer (A) is correct. *(Publisher)*
**REQUIRED:** The amount to be reported as retained earnings.
**DISCUSSION:** Retained earnings is increased by net income and can be decreased by net losses, certain treasury stock transactions, and dividends. Thus, retained earnings is $190,000 ($200,000 – $70,000 – $20,000 + $80,000). The $1,000 excess of proceeds over the cost of treasury stock does not affect retained earnings because Page uses the cost method to account for treasury stock. Under the cost method, the excess should be a credit to additional paid-in capital from treasury stock transactions.
Answer (B) is incorrect because $191,000 includes the $1,000 excess from the sale of treasury stock. Answer (C) is incorrect because $210,000 results from a failure to subtract $20,000 due to the distribution of the property dividends. Answer (D) is incorrect because $211,000 is the result of erroneously including the $1,000 excess from the sale of treasury stock and failing to subtract $20,000 in distributed property dividends.

## 17.6 Stock Options, Warrants, and Rights

**44.** When stock rights are issued without consideration and are allowed to lapse, the following occurs on the books of the issuing company:

A. Common stock at par value is increased.

B. Additional paid-in capital is credited.

C. Investment in stock warrants is debited.

D. None of the answers are correct.

**Answer (D) is correct.**  *(Publisher)*
**REQUIRED:** The effect on the issuing company when stock rights without consideration are allowed to lapse.
**DISCUSSION:** When rights are issued without consideration, such as in a dividend distribution, only a memorandum entry is made by the issuer. If the rights are exercised and stock is issued, the effect on the books of the issuing company is an increase in common stock at par value with any remainder credited to additional paid-in capital. However, if the rights are allowed to lapse, contributed capital is unaffected.

**45.** SFAS 123 (revised 2004), *Share-Based Payment*, normally requires entities to account for share-based employee compensation awards classified as equity in accordance with which of the following methods?

|    | Fair-Value Method | Intrinsic-Value Method |
|----|-------------------|------------------------|
| A. | Yes | Yes |
| B. | Yes | No |
| C. | No | Yes |
| D. | No | No |

**Answer (B) is correct.**  *(Publisher)*
**REQUIRED:** The method(s) prescribed for accounting for share-based employee compensations awards.
**DISCUSSION:** Entities must account for share-based payments classified as equity in accordance with the fair-value method except in the rare cases in which a nonpublic entity cannot reasonably estimate the fair value of the equity instruments at the grant date. In these cases, entities must account for such payments in accordance with the intrinsic-value method.
Answer (A) is incorrect because the pronouncement superseded by SFAS 123(R) permitted either method. However, an award classified as equity now must be measured at fair value except in rare cases. Answer (C) is incorrect because the pronouncement superseded by SFAS 123(R) permitted either method. However, an award classified as equity now must be measured at fair value except in rare cases. Answer (D) is incorrect because SFAS 123(R) prescribes the fair-value method except in rare cases.

**46.** The date on which an employer becomes contingently obligated to make share-based payments compensation to an employee who renders the requisite service is the

A. Grant date.

B. Service inception date.

C. Vesting date.

D. Date of completion of the requisite service period.

**Answer (A) is correct.**  *(Publisher)*
**REQUIRED:** The date on which an employer becomes contingently obligated to issue share-based payments to an employee who renders the requisite service.
**DISCUSSION:** SFAS 123(R) generally requires a public entity to measure the cost of employee services received in exchange for equity instruments at the fair value of the instruments on the grant date and to allocate that cost to the requisite service period. The grant date is the date at which (1) a mutual understanding of the key terms and conditions of a share-based payment award is reached by an employer and an employee, (2) the employer becomes contingently obligated to issue share-based payments to an employee who renders the requisite service, (3) any necessary approvals are obtained, and (4) the subsequent changes in the market price of the underlying stock begin to benefit or adversely affect the employee.
Answer (B) is incorrect because the service inception date is the date on which the requisite service period begins. The service inception date usually is the same as, but under certain conditions may precede, the grant date. Answer (C) is incorrect because the vesting date is the date on which an employee has earned the right to receive the share-based payments. Answer (D) is incorrect because the requisite service period is the period during which an employee is required to provide services in exchange for an award.

**47.** When bonds with detachable stock warrants are purchased, the price should be allocated between the warrants and the bonds based upon their relative fair values at issuance. The amount debited to investment in stock warrants relative to the total amount paid

A. Increases the premium on the investment in bonds.

B. Increases the discount on investment in bonds.

C. Increases either any premium on the bonds or any discount on the bonds.

D. Has no effect on the investment of bond premium or discount as the warrants are purchased separately.

**Answer (B) is correct.** *(Publisher)*
**REQUIRED:** The effect on the carrying amount of bonds of debiting investment in stock warrants.
**DISCUSSION:** The portion of the price allocated to the detachable stock warrants decreases the allocation to investment in bonds. Thus, amounts debited to investment in stock warrants increase the discount or decrease the premium recorded for the investment in bonds.

**48.** On January 2, year 1, Kine Co. granted Morgan, its president, fully vested share options to buy 1,000 shares of Kine's $10 par common stock. The options have an exercise price of $20 per share and are exercisable for 3 years following the grant date. Morgan exercised the options on December 31, year 1. The market price of the shares was $50 on January 2, year 1 and $70 on the following December 31. If the fair value of the options is not reasonably estimable at the grant date, by what net amount should equity increase as a result of the grant and exercise of the options?

A. $20,000

B. $30,000

C. $50,000

D. $70,000

**Answer (A) is correct.** *(CIA, adapted)*
**REQUIRED:** The amount equity increases as a result of the grant and exercise of share options.
**DISCUSSION:** In the rare case in which an entity cannot reasonably estimate the fair value of equity instruments at the grant date, the accounting is based on intrinsic value (fair value of the underlying shares – exercise price of an option). Remeasurement is required at each reporting date and on final settlement. The measurement date is January 2, year 1. At that date, the intrinsic value of the options is $30,000 [1,000 shares × ($50 market price – $20 option price)]. This $30,000 will be recorded as both compensation expense and options outstanding. The net effect on equity is $0. When the options are exercised, the $20,000 (1,000 shares × $20 exercise price) cash received and the $30,000 of options outstanding will be allocated to share capital as $10,000 common stock and $40,000 additional paid-in capital. Moreover, compensation expense will be debited and additional paid-in capital will be credited for $20,000 to reflect the final measure of intrinsic value. The net effect on equity will be a $20,000 increase.
Answer (B) is incorrect because $30,000 is the amount of the initial debit to compensation expense and credit to options outstanding. Answer (C) is incorrect because $50,000 is the final measure of intrinsic value. Answer (D) is incorrect because $70,000 is the market price of the shares issued on the settlement date.

**49.** Early in its fiscal year, Starr Co. purchased 1,000 shares of Pack Co. common stock for $54,000. In the same transaction, Starr acquired 2,000 detachable stock warrants. Two of the warrants are required to purchase one additional share of Pack Co. common stock. The market price of the stock without the warrants was $49 per share. The market price of the warrants was $3.50 per warrant. Starr sold 50% of the warrants several weeks later. If the proceeds received by Starr equaled $4,000, it recognized a realized gain of

A. $3,000

B. $625

C. $500

D. $0

**Answer (B) is correct.** *(Publisher)*
**REQUIRED:** The gain on sale of detachable warrants.
**DISCUSSION:** The recipient of stock rights must allocate the carrying amount of the shares owned between those shares and the rights based on their relative fair values at the time the rights are received. Thus, the amounts to be allocated to the common stock and warrants are $47,250 ({(1,000 × $49) ÷ [(1,000 × $49) + (2,000 × $3.50)]} × $54,000) and $6,750 ($54,000 – $47,250), respectively. The realized gain is therefore $625 [$4,000 – ($6,750 × 50%)].
Answer (A) is incorrect because $3,000 is the excess of the fair value of 2,000 rights over the sale price of 1,000 rights. Answer (C) is incorrect because $500 equals the excess of the sale price of 1,000 rights over their fair value. Answer (D) is incorrect because Starr should recognize a realized gain for the excess of the price over the carrying amount.

## 17.7 Earnings per Share (EPS)

Questions 50 through 56 are based on the following information.

Pubco is a public company that uses a calendar year and has a complex capital structure. In the computation of its basic and diluted earnings per share (BEPS and DEPS, respectively) in accordance with SFAS 128, *Earnings per Share,* Pubco uses income before extraordinary items as the control number. Pubco reported no cumulative effect of accounting changes or discontinued operations, but it had an extraordinary loss (net of tax) of $1,200,000 in the first quarter when its income before the extraordinary item was $1,000,000.

The average market price of Pubco's common stock for the first quarter was $25, the shares outstanding at the beginning of the period equaled 300,000, and 12,000 shares were issued on March 1.

At the beginning of the quarter, Pubco had outstanding $2,000,000 of 5% convertible bonds, with each $1,000 bond convertible into 10 shares of common stock. No bonds were converted.

At the beginning of the quarter, Pubco also had outstanding 120,000 shares of preferred stock paying a quarterly dividend of $.10 per share and convertible to common stock on a one-to-one basis. Holders of 60,000 shares of preferred stock exercised their conversion privilege on February 1.

Throughout the first quarter, warrants to buy 50,000 shares of Pubco's common stock for $28 per share were outstanding but unexercised.

Pubco's tax rate was 30%.

**50.** The weighted-average number of shares used to calculate BEPS amounts for the first quarter is

A. 444,000

B. 372,000

C. 344,000

D. 300,000

Answer (C) is correct. *(Publisher)*
**REQUIRED:** The weighted-average number of shares used to calculate BEPS amounts for the first quarter.
**DISCUSSION:** The number of shares outstanding at January 1 was 300,000, 12,000 shares were issued on March 1, and 60,000 shares of preferred stock were converted to 60,000 shares of common stock on February 1. Thus, the weighted-average number of shares used to calculate BEPS amounts for the first quarter is 344,000 {300,000 + [12,000 × (1 ÷ 3)] + [60,000 × (2 ÷ 3)]}.
Answer (A) is incorrect because 444,000 is the adjusted weighted-average number of shares used in the DEPS calculation. Answer (B) is incorrect because 372,000 is the total outstanding at March 31. Answer (D) is incorrect because 300,000 equals the shares outstanding at January 1.

**51.** The BEPS amount for the net income or loss available to common shareholders after the extraordinary item is

A. $2.89

B. $(0.46)

C. $(0.60)

D. $(3.49)

Answer (C) is correct. *(Publisher)*
**REQUIRED:** The BEPS amount for the net income or loss available to common shareholders after the extraordinary item.
**DISCUSSION:** The weighted-average of shares used in the BEPS denominator is 344,000. The numerator equals income before extraordinary item, minus preferred dividends, minus the extraordinary loss. Thus, it equals the control number minus the extraordinary loss, or $(206,000) [$994,000 − $1,200,000]. The BEPS amount for the net income or loss available to common shareholders after the extraordinary item is $(0.60) [$(206,000) ÷ 344,000 shares].
Answer (A) is incorrect because $2.89 is the BEPS amount for income available to common shareholders before the extraordinary item. Answer (B) is incorrect because $(0.46) uses the denominator of the DEPS calculation. Answer (D) is incorrect because $(3.49) is the BEPS amount for the extraordinary loss.

**52.** The difference between BEPS and DEPS for the extraordinary item is

A. $2.89

B. $2.10

C. $.79

D. $.60

Answer (C) is correct. *(Publisher)*
**REQUIRED:** The difference between BEPS and DEPS for the extraordinary item.
**DISCUSSION:** BEPS for the extraordinary loss is $(3.49) [$(1,200,000) ÷ 344,000]. DEPS for the extraordinary item is $(2.70) [$(1,200,000) ÷ 444,000 shares].
Answer (A) is incorrect because $2.89 is the difference between DEPS and BEPS for the extraordinary loss. Answer (B) is incorrect because $2.10 is the difference between DEPS for the extraordinary loss and the BEPS for the net loss available to common shareholders after the extraordinary loss. Answer (D) is incorrect because $.60 is the BEPS for the net loss available to common shareholders after the extraordinary loss.

**53.** The control number for determining whether potential common shares are dilutive or antidilutive is

A. $1,000,000

B. $994,000

C. $(206,000)

D. $(1,200,000)

Answer (B) is correct. *(Publisher)*
**REQUIRED:** The control number for determining whether potential common shares are dilutive or antidilutive.
**DISCUSSION:** If a company reports discontinued operations, extraordinary items, or accounting changes, it uses income from continuing operations (in Pubco's case, income before extraordinary item), adjusted for preferred dividends, as the control number for determining whether potential common shares are dilutive or antidilutive. Hence, the number of potential common shares used in calculating DEPS for income from continuing operations is also used in calculating the other DEPS amounts even if the effect is antidilutive with respect to the corresponding BEPS amounts. However, if the entity has a loss from continuing operations available to common shareholders, no potential common shares are included in the calculation of any DEPS amount (SFAS 128). The control number for Pubco is $994,000 {$1,000,000 income before extraordinary item − [$.10 per share dividend × (120,000 preferred shares − 60,000 preferred shares converted)]}.
Answer (A) is incorrect because $1,000,000 is unadjusted income from continuing operations. Answer (C) is incorrect because $(206,000) is the net loss available to common shareholders after subtracting the extraordinary loss. Answer (D) is incorrect because $(1,200,000) is the extraordinary loss.

**54.** The weighted-average number of shares used to calculate DEPS amounts for the first quarter is

A. 444,000

B. 438,000

C. 372,000

D. 344,000

Answer (A) is correct. *(Publisher)*
**REQUIRED:** The weighted-average number of shares used to calculate DEPS amounts for the first quarter.
**DISCUSSION:** The denominator of DEPS equals the weighted-average number of shares used in the BEPS calculation (344,000) plus dilutive potential common shares (assuming the control number is not a loss). The incremental shares from assumed conversion of warrants is zero because they are antidilutive. The $25 market price is less than the $28 exercise price. The assumed conversion of all the preferred shares at the beginning of the quarter results in 80,000 incremental shares {[120,000 shares × (3 ÷ 3)] − [60,000 shares × (2 ÷ 3)]}. The assumed conversion of all the bonds at the beginning of the quarter results in 20,000 incremental shares [($2,000,000 ÷ $1,000 per bond) × 10 common shares per bond]. Consequently, the weighted-average number of shares used to calculate DEPS amounts for the first quarter is 444,000 (344,000 + 0 + 80,000 + 20,000).
Answer (B) is incorrect because 438,000 assumes the hypothetical exercise of all the warrants at the beginning of the period at a price of $28 and the repurchase of shares using the proceeds at a price of $25. Answer (C) is incorrect because 372,000 is the total outstanding at March 31. Answer (D) is incorrect because 344,000 is the denominator of the BEPS fraction.

**55.** The effect of assumed conversions on the numerator of the DEPS fraction is

A. $31,000

B. $25,000

C. $23,500

D. $17,500

Answer (C) is correct. *(Publisher)*
**REQUIRED:** The effect of assumed conversions on the numerator of the DEPS fraction.
**DISCUSSION:** If all of the convertible preferred shares are assumed to be converted on January 1, $6,000 of dividends [$.10 × (120,000 − 60,000) preferred shares] will not be paid. Furthermore, if the bonds are assumed to be converted on January 1, interest of $17,500 {[5% × $2,000,000 ÷ 4] × (1.0 − .3 tax rate)} will not be paid. Accordingly, the effect of assumed conversions on the numerator of the DEPS fraction is an addition of $23,500 ($6,000 + $17,500) to the income available to common shareholders.
Answer (A) is incorrect because $31,000 disregards the tax shield provided by bond interest. Answer (B) is incorrect because $25,000 equals one quarter's bond interest payment. Answer (D) is incorrect because $17,500 is the effect of the assumed conversion of the bonds alone.

**56.** Refer to the information on the preceding page(s). The DEPS amount for the net income or loss available to common shareholders after the extraordinary item is

A. $2.29

B. $(0.41)

C. $(0.53)

D. $(2.70)

Answer (B) is correct. *(Publisher)*
**REQUIRED:** The DEPS amount for the net income or loss available to common shareholders.
**DISCUSSION:** The numerator equals the income available to common shareholders (the control number), plus the effect of the assumed conversions, minus the extraordinary loss. The denominator equals the weighted-average of shares outstanding plus the dilutive potential common shares. Hence, the DEPS amount for the net income or loss available to common shareholders after the extraordinary item is $(.41) [($994,000 + $23,500 − $1,200,000) ÷ 444,000].
Answer (A) is incorrect because $2.29 is the DEPS amount for income before the extraordinary item. Answer (C) is incorrect because $(0.53) is based on the BEPS denominator. Answer (D) is incorrect because $(2.70) is the DEPS for the extraordinary item.

---

Questions 57 through 60 are based on the following information.

Spark Automotive uses a calendar year for financial reporting. The company is authorized to issue 10 million shares of $10 par common stock. At no time has Spark issued any potential common stock. Listed at the right is a summary of Spark's common stock activities. A two-for-one stock split of one of Spark's common stock took place on March 31, 20X5.

- Number of common shares issued and outstanding at December 31, 20X2 = 2,000,000 shares.
- Shares issued as a result of a 10% stock dividend on September 30, 20X3 = 200,000 shares.
- Shares issued for cash on March 31, 20X4 = 2,000,000 shares.
- Number of common shares issued and outstanding at December 31, 20X4 = 4,200,000 shares.

---

**57.** The weighted-average number of common shares used in computing basic earnings per common share for 20X4 on the 20X4 comparative income statement was

A. 3,150,000

B. 3,700,000

C. 4,200,000

D. 7,400,000

Answer (B) is correct. *(Publisher)*
**REQUIRED:** The weighted-average number of shares used in computing basic EPS for 20X4 on the 20X4 income statement.
**DISCUSSION:** At the beginning of 20X4, 2.2 million shares were outstanding. This figure remained unchanged for 3 months until March 31 when an additional 2 million shares were issued. Thus, for the last 9 months of the year, 4.2 million shares were outstanding. Hence, the weighted-average number of shares outstanding throughout the year was 3,700,000 {[2,200,000 × (3 ÷ 12)] + [4,200,000 × (9 ÷ 12)]}.
Answer (A) is incorrect because 3,150,000 is the weight assigned to 4,200,000 shares for 9 months. Answer (C) is incorrect because 4,200,000 shares were not outstanding during the first 3 months of the year. Answer (D) is incorrect because the stock split did not occur until the following year.

**58.** The weighted-average number of common shares used in computing basic earnings per common share for 20X3 on the 20X4 comparative income statement was

A. 2,200,000

B. 2,100,000

C. 2,050,000

D. 4,200,000

Answer (A) is correct. *(Publisher)*
**REQUIRED:** The weighted-average number of shares used in computing basic earnings per common share for 20X3 on the 20X4 comparative income statement.
**DISCUSSION:** There were 2 million shares outstanding at the beginning of 20X3. Another 200,000 were issued as a result of a stock dividend on September 30. Because a stock dividend merely divides existing shares into more pieces, the dividend is assumed to have occurred at the beginning of the year. Thus, on the 20X3 income statement, the number of shares outstanding throughout the year would have been 2.2 million. No subsequent changes were made in those 2.2 million shares in 20X4 (no stock dividends or stock splits). Consequently, the comparative statements for 20X3 and 20X4 will report basic earnings per share using the same weighted-average number of common shares for 20X3 as the 20X3 income statement.
Answer (B) is incorrect because no weighting is required. Common stock outstanding during 20X3 did not change as a result of 20X4 transactions. Answer (C) is incorrect because no weighting is required. Common stock outstanding during 20X3 did not change as a result of 20X4 transactions. Answer (D) is incorrect because the stock split does not occur until 20X5.

**59.** The weighted-average number of common shares to be used in computing basic earnings per common share for 20X4 on the 20X5 comparative income statement is

A. 3,700,000

B. 4,200,000

C. 7,400,000

D. 8,400,000

Answer (C) is correct. *(Publisher)*
**REQUIRED:** The weighted-average number of common shares to be used in computing basic EPS for 20X4 on the 20X5 comparative income statement.
**DISCUSSION:** The number of shares used in computing the 20X4 basic EPS on the 20X4 income statement was 3.7 million. However, because of the stock split on March 31, 20X5, those shares were doubled. Thus, the basic EPS calculation for 20X4 on the 20X5 comparative income statement is 7.4 million shares (2 × 3,700,000 shares).
Answer (A) is incorrect because 3,700,000 is the number of shares used on the 20X4 income statement. Answer (B) is incorrect because the shares outstanding must be weighted. The full 4,200,000 shares were not outstanding during the first 3 months of 20X4. Answer (D) is incorrect because the shares outstanding must be weighted. The full 4,200,000 shares were not outstanding during the first 3 months of 20X4.

**60.** The weighted-average number of common shares to be used in computing basic earnings per common share for 20X5 on the 20X5 comparative income statement is

A. 4,200,000

B. 6,300,000

C. 7,350,000

D. 8,400,000

Answer (D) is correct. *(Publisher)*
**REQUIRED:** The weighted-average number of shares used in computing basic EPS for 20X5 on the 20X5 comparative income statement.
**DISCUSSION:** At the beginning of 20X5, 4.2 million shares were outstanding. However, the March 31 stock split increased that number to 8.4 million. Because a stock split is assumed to have occurred on the first day of the year, the number of shares outstanding throughout 20X5 is 8.4 million.
Answer (A) is incorrect because 4,200,000 does not consider the stock split. Answer (B) is incorrect because stock splits do not require a weighting of the shares outstanding; stock splits and stock dividends are assumed to have occurred on the first day of the fiscal year. Answer (C) is incorrect because stock splits do not require a weighting of the shares outstanding; stock splits and stock dividends are assumed to have occurred on the first day of the fiscal year.

Questions 61 through 63 are based on the following information.

Peters Corp.'s capital structure was as follows:

| | December 31 | |
| | Year 1 | Year 2 |
| --- | --- | --- |
| Outstanding shares of stock: | | |
| Common | 100,000 | 100,000 |
| Convertible preferred | 10,000 | 10,000 |
| 9% convertible bonds | $1,000,000 | $1,000,000 |

During year 2, Peters paid dividends of $3.00 per share on its preferred stock. The preferred shares are convertible into 20,000 shares of common stock, and the 9% bonds are convertible into 30,000 shares of common stock. Assume that the income tax rate is 30%.

**61.** If net income for year 2 is $350,000, Peters should report DEPS as

A. $3.20

B. $2.95

C. $2.92

D. $2.75

Answer (D) is correct. *(CPA, adapted)*
**REQUIRED:** The DEPS, given convertible preferred stock and convertible bonds outstanding and net income of $350,000.
**DISCUSSION:** Potential common stock is included in the calculation of DEPS if it is dilutive. When two or more issues of potential common stock are outstanding, each issue is considered separately in sequence, from the most to the least dilutive. This procedure is necessary because a convertible security may be dilutive on its own, but antidilutive when included with other potential common shares in the calculation of DEPS.
The incremental effect on EPS determines the degree of dilution. The lower the incremental effect, the more dilutive. The incremental effect of the convertible preferred stock is $1.50 [($3 preferred dividend × 10,000) ÷ 20,000 potential common shares]. The incremental effect of the convertible debt is $2.10 {[$1,000,000 × 9% × (1.0 – 30%)] ÷ 30,000 potential common shares}. Because the $1.50 incremental effect of the convertible preferred is lower, it is the more dilutive, and its incremental effect is compared with the BEPS amount, which equals $3.20 [($350,000 – $30,000) ÷ 100,000]. Because $1.50 is lower than $3.20, the convertible preferred is dilutive and is included in a trial calculation of DEPS. The result is $2.92 [($350,000 – $30,000 + $30,000) ÷ (100,000 + 20,000)]. However, the $2.10 incremental effect of the convertible debt is lower than the $2.92 trial calculation, so the convertible debt is also dilutive and should be included in the calculation of DEPS. Thus, the DEPS amount is $2.75 as indicated below.

$$\frac{\$350,000 - \$30,000 + \$30,000 + \$63,000}{100,000 + 20,000 + 30,000} = \$2.75$$

Answer (A) is incorrect because $3.20 equals BEPS. Answer (B) is incorrect because $2.95 excludes the convertible preferred stock. Answer (C) is incorrect because $2.92 excludes the convertible debt.

**62.** If net income for year 2 is $245,000, Peters should report DEPS as

A. $2.15

B. $2.14

C. $2.05

D. $2.04

Answer (D) is correct. *(Publisher)*
**REQUIRED:** The DEPS, given convertible preferred stock and convertible debt outstanding and net income of $245,000.
**DISCUSSION:** The incremental effect of the convertible preferred is $1.50 and of the convertible debt is $2.10. Given net income of $245,000, the BEPS amount equals $2.15 [($245,000 – $30,000) ÷ 100,000]. The $1.50 incremental effect of the convertible preferred stock is lower than BEPS, so it is dilutive and should be included in a trial calculation of DEPS. The result is $2.04 [($245,000 – $30,000 + $30,000) ÷ (100,000 + 20,000)]. Because the $2.10 incremental effect of the convertible debt is higher than $2.04, the convertible debt is antidilutive and should not be included in the DEPS calculation. Thus, DEPS should be reported as $2.04.
Answer (A) is incorrect because $2.15 equals BEPS. Answer (B) is incorrect because $2.14 excludes the convertible preferred stock. Answer (C) is incorrect because $2.05 includes the convertible debt.

**63.** If net income for year 2 is $170,000, Peters should report DEPS as

A. $1.40

B. $1.42

C. $1.55

D. $1.70

Answer (A) is correct. *(Publisher)*
**REQUIRED:** The DEPS, given convertible preferred stock and convertible debt outstanding and net income of $170,000.
**DISCUSSION:** Given net income of $170,000, the BEPS amount equals $1.40 [($170,000 – $30,000) ÷ 100,000]. This amount is lower than both the $2.10 incremental effect of the convertible debt and the $1.50 incremental effect of the convertible preferred. Thus, both convertible securities are antidilutive, and Peters should report that DEPS is equal to BEPS. This dual presentation can be presented in one line on the income statement.
Answer (B) is incorrect because $1.42 includes the convertible preferred stock. Answer (C) is incorrect because $1.55 includes the convertible debt. Answer (D) is incorrect because $1.70 results from not adjusting the $170,000 of net income for the $30,000 of preferred dividends when determining income available to common shareholders.

**64.** Which one of the following items most likely increases earnings per share (EPS) of a corporation?

A. Purchase of treasury stock.

B. Declaration of a stock split.

C. Declaration of a stock dividend.

D. A reduction in the amount of cash dividends paid to common shareholders.

Answer (A) is correct. *(CMA, adapted)*
**REQUIRED:** The item most likely to increase EPS.
**DISCUSSION:** A purchase of treasury stock increases EPS because fewer shares are outstanding. The numerator of the EPS fraction (income available to common shareholders) remains unchanged, but the denominator (weighted-average number of shares outstanding) decreases.
Answer (B) is incorrect because a stock split reduces EPS. More shares are outstanding after the split. Answer (C) is incorrect because a stock dividend increases the shares outstanding and thus decreases EPS. Answer (D) is incorrect because a change in cash dividends paid to common shareholders has no effect on EPS. Dividends on common shares are declared out of income available to common shareholders.

## 17.8 Revenue Recognition

**65.** A company that sprays chemicals in residences to eliminate or prevent infestation of insects requires that customers prepay for 3 months' service at the beginning of each new quarter. Select the term that appropriately describes this situation from the viewpoint of the exterminating company.

A. Deferred revenue.

B. Earned revenue.

C. Accrued revenue.

D. Prepaid expense.

Answer (A) is correct. *(CIA, adapted)*
**REQUIRED:** The classification of the collected fees.
**DISCUSSION:** Under the revenue recognition principle, revenue is recognized in the period in which it is earned; therefore, when it is received in advance of its being earned, the amount applicable to future periods is deferred. The amount unearned is considered a liability because it represents an obligation to perform a service in the future arising from a past transaction. Unearned revenue is revenue that has been received but not earned.
Answer (B) is incorrect because the revenue is not earned. The exterminator has not performed the related services for the customer. Answer (C) is incorrect because accrued revenue is revenue that has been earned but not received. Answer (D) is incorrect because the customer has a prepaid expense (expense paid but not incurred); the exterminator has unearned revenue (revenue received but not earned).

Questions 66 through 68 are based on the following information.  On May 28, Markal Company purchased a tooling machine from Arens and Associates for $1,000,000, payable as follows: 50% at the transaction closing date and 50% due June 28.  The cost of the machine to Arens is $800,000.  Markal paid Arens $500,000 at the transaction closing date and took possession of the machine.  On June 10, Arens determined that a change in the business environment has created a great deal of uncertainty regarding the collection of the balance due from Markal, and the amount is probably uncollectible.  Arens and Markal have a fiscal year end of May 31.

**66.** The revenue recognized by Arens and Associates on May 28 is

A. $200,000

B. $800,000

C. $1,000,000

D. $0

Answer (C) is correct.  *(CMA, adapted)*
**REQUIRED:** The revenue to be recognized on May 28.
**DISCUSSION:** Revenue is recognized when (1) realized or realizable and (2) earned.  On May 28, $500,000 of the sales price was realized while the remaining $500,000 was realizable in the form of a receivable.  The revenue was earned on May 28 since the title of the goods passed to the purchaser.  The cost-recovery method is not used because the receivable was not deemed uncollectible until June 10.
Answer (A) is incorrect because $200,000 is the apparent gross profit on the sale, not the revenue.  Answer (B) is incorrect because $800,000 was the original cost of the machine to Arens.  Answer (D) is incorrect because, at May 28, a sale appeared to have been consummated in the amount of $1,000,000.

**67.** The gross profit recognized by Arens and Associates on its financial statements dated and issued June 15 is

A. $1,000,000

B. $200,000

C. $0

D. $500,000

Answer (C) is correct.  *(CMA, adapted)*
**REQUIRED:** The gross profit recognized by Arens on its financial statements issued on June 15.
**DISCUSSION:** Gross profit is defined as the difference between selling price and the cost of goods sold.  The balance sheet presentation should be based on the net realizable value of the receivable.  Because that amount is assumed to be zero, the machine was actually sold for $500,000, not for $1,000,000.  Therefore, no gross profit is shown on the financial statements.
Answer (A) is incorrect because the last $500,000 is not considered collectible; thus the sale was not for $1,000,000.  Answer (B) is incorrect because $200,000 would have been the gross profit if the last $500,000 had been collectible.  Answer (D) is incorrect because $500,000 was the amount of cash collected, not the amount of gross profit.

**68.** The effect of the purchase on Markal Company's financial reporting on May 28 is a(n)

A. Increase in fixed assets of $500,000 and a decrease in cash of $500,000.

B. Increase in fixed assets of $1,000,000, a decrease in cash of $500,000, and an increase in liabilities of $500,000.

C. Increase in fixed assets of $500,000 and an increase in liabilities of $500,000.

D. Decrease in fixed assets of $1,000,000, a decrease in cash of $500,000, and an increase in liabilities of $500,000.

Answer (B) is correct.  *(CMA, adapted)*
**REQUIRED:** The effect of the May 28 machine purchase on Markal Company's financial reporting.
**DISCUSSION:** The purchase of the machine involves a debit to fixed assets of $1,000,000, a credit to cash of $500,000, and a credit to a current liability of $500,000.
Answer (A) is incorrect because the contract price of the machine was $1,000,000, and that amount should be recorded as a fixed asset; Markal is liable for the remaining $500,000 unless it declares bankruptcy.  Answer (C) is incorrect because the machine is valued at $1,000,000, and that amount should be debited to a fixed asset account.  Answer (D) is incorrect because there is an increase in fixed assets.

**69.** If sales are accounted for using the installment method, which of the following is (are) only recognized in proportion to the cash collected on the sales during the period?

    A. Sales.

    B. Sales and cost of sales.

    C. Sales and cost of sales and selling expenses.

    D. Sales and cost of sales and administrative expenses.

**Answer (B) is correct.** *(CIA, adapted)*
**REQUIRED:** The item(s) recognized only in proportion to cash collected under the installment method.
**DISCUSSION:** Under the installment method, the gross profit on sales (sales – cost of sales) is not recognized until cash is collected. The proportion of cash collected on the sales during the accounting period determines the proportion of the gross profit on those sales that is recognized during the period. Hence, both sales and cost of sales are deferred.
Answer (A) is incorrect because sales and cost of sales are recognized in proportion to cash collections. Answer (C) is incorrect because only the gross profit (sales – cost of sales) is deferred on sales for which cash has not yet been collected. Answer (D) is incorrect because only the gross profit (sales – cost of sales) is deferred on sales for which cash has not yet been collected.

**70.** On January 1, Dell, Inc. contracted with the City of Little to provide custom-built desks for the city schools. The contract made Dell the city's sole supplier, and required Dell to supply no less than 4,000 desks and no more than 5,500 desks per year for 2 years. In turn, Little agreed to pay a fixed price of $110 per desk. During the year, Dell produced 5,000 desks for Little. At December 31, 500 of these desks were segregated from the regular inventory and were accepted and awaiting pickup by Little. Little paid Dell $450,000 during the year. What amount should Dell recognize as contract revenue for the current year?

    A. $450,000

    B. $495,000

    C. $550,000

    D. $605,000

**Answer (C) is correct.** *(CPA, adapted)*
**REQUIRED:** The contract revenue for the year.
**DISCUSSION:** Dell has done what it was required to do under the contract, that is, produce desks for Little. Thus, it has substantially accomplished what it must do to be entitled to the benefits represented by the revenues. Dell should therefore recognize as earned an amount equaling $550,000 (5,000 desks produced for Little × $110 fixed price per desk).
Answer (A) is incorrect because $450,000 is the amount received. Answer (B) is incorrect because $495,000 is based on production of 4,500 desks. Answer (D) is incorrect because $605,000 is based on production of 5,500 desks.

**71.** On October 1, year 1, Acme Fuel Co. sold 100,000 gallons of heating oil to Karn Co. at $3 per gallon. Fifty thousand gallons were delivered on December 15, year 1, and the remaining 50,000 gallons were delivered on January 15, year 2. Payment terms were 50% due on October 1, year 1, 25% due on first delivery, and the remaining 25% due on second delivery. What amount of revenue should Acme recognize from this sale during year 1?

    A. $75,000

    B. $150,000

    C. $225,000

    D. $300,000

**Answer (B) is correct.** *(CPA, adapted)*
**REQUIRED:** The revenue to be recognized.
**DISCUSSION:** Revenue is recognized when it is realized or realizable and earned. Revenue is ordinarily earned upon delivery. Given that 50% of the heating oil was delivered in year 1, 50% of the price was earned in year 1. Thus, Acme should recognize $150,000 ($300,000 × 50%) of revenue from the sale.
Answer (A) is incorrect because $75,000 was the amount due on first delivery. Answer (C) is incorrect because $225,000 was the amount due in year 1. Answer (D) is incorrect because $300,000 is the total price, but this amount has not been earned because the last 50,000 gallons were not delivered in year 1.

**72.** Amar Farms produced 300,000 pounds of cotton during the current season. Amar sells all of its cotton to Brye Co., which has agreed to purchase Amar's entire production at the prevailing market price. Recent legislation assures that the market price will not fall below $.70 per pound during the next 2 years. Amar's costs of selling and distributing the cotton are immaterial and can be reasonably estimated. Amar reports its inventory at expected exit value. During the year, Amar sold and delivered 200,000 pounds to Brye at the market price of $.70. Amar sold the remaining 100,000 pounds during the following year at the market price of $.72. What amount of revenue should Amar recognize in the current year?

A. $140,000

B. $144,000

C. $210,000

D. $216,000

Answer (C) is correct. *(CPA, adapted)*
**REQUIRED:** The revenue recognized by an enterprise that reports its inventory at expected exit value.
**DISCUSSION:** According to SFAC 5, "If products or other assets are readily realizable because they are salable at reliably determinable prices without significant effort (for example, certain agricultural products, precious metals, and marketable securities), revenues and some gains or losses may be recognized at completion of production or when prices of the assets change." The cotton is readily realizable (convertible) because it consists of interchangeable (fungible) units and can be sold at a guaranteed price. Thus, Amar should recognize revenue at the completion of production in the current year based on the guaranteed price (300,000 lbs. × $.70 = $210,000).
Answer (A) is incorrect because $140,000 is the revenue on current year sales. Answer (B) is incorrect because $144,000 equals 200,000 pounds times $.72 per pound. Answer (D) is incorrect because $216,000 is based on the following year price. However, in the current year, the price had not yet changed.

**73.** The following information pertains to Eagle Co.'s current year sales:

Cash sales

| | |
|---|---|
| Gross | $80,000 |
| Returns and allowances | 4,000 |

Credit sales

| | |
|---|---|
| Gross | $120,000 |
| Discounts | 6,000 |

On January 1, customers owed Eagle $40,000. On December 31, customers owed Eagle $30,000. Under the cash basis of accounting, what amount of net revenue should Eagle report for the current year?

A. $76,000

B. $170,000

C. $190,000

D. $200,000

Answer (D) is correct. *(CPA, adapted)*
**REQUIRED:** The revenue under the cash basis of accounting.
**DISCUSSION:** Under the cash-basis of accounting, revenue is recognized when cash is received. Eagle had $76,000 ($80,000 – $4,000) in net cash sales and $114,000 ($120,000 – $6,000) in net credit sales. Given that accounts receivable decreased, cash collections thereon must have exceeded net credit sales by $10,000 ($40,000 – $30,000). Accordingly, net revenue is $200,000 ($76,000 + $114,000 + $10,000).
Answer (A) is incorrect because $76,000 equals net cash sales. Answer (B) is incorrect because $170,000 equals total gross sales minus ending accounts receivable. Answer (C) is incorrect because $190,000 does not reflect an adjustment for the change in receivables.

---

Questions 74 through 76 are based on the following information.

A company sells goods on an installment basis. The table to the right includes information about the level of installment sales, the cost of the goods sold on installment, and the cash receipts on installment sales for year 1 through year 3. All cash receipt amounts shown are net of any interest charges.

| | Year 1 | Year 2 | Year 3 |
|---|---|---|---|
| Installment sales | $10,000 | $5,000 | $20,000 |
| Cost of installment sales | 6,000 | 4,000 | 10,000 |
| Cash receipts on year 1 sales | 2,000 | 4,000 | 4,000 |
| Cash receipts on year 2 sales | | 1,000 | 2,000 |
| Cash receipts on year 3 sales | | | 4,000 |

---

**74.** The company has a rate of gross profit on year 2 installment sales of

- A. 20%
- B. 40%
- C. 50%
- D. 80%

Answer (A) is correct. *(CIA, adapted)*
**REQUIRED:** The rate of gross profit on year 2 installment sales.
**DISCUSSION:** The rate of gross profit on year 2 installment sales is 20% [($5,000 of year 2 installment sales − $4,000 cost of year 2 installment sales) ÷ $5,000 of year 2 installment sales].
Answer (B) is incorrect because 40% is the gross profit on year 1 installment sales. Answer (C) is incorrect because 50% is the gross profit on year 3 installment sales. Answer (D) is incorrect because 80% is the ratio of the cost of year 2 installment sales to year 2 installment sales.

**75.** The amount of gross profit the company will recognize in year 1 on year 1 installment sales is

- A. $800
- B. $2,000
- C. $3,200
- D. $4,000

Answer (A) is correct. *(CIA, adapted)*
**REQUIRED:** The amount of gross profit the company will recognize in year 1 on year 1 installment sales.
**DISCUSSION:** In year 1, the company had cash receipts of $2,000 from its year 1 installment sales. The gross profit realized is the gross profit on the portion of sales for which payment has been received. This amount equals the year 1 gross profit percentage multiplied by the cash receipts, or $800 {[($10,000 − $6,000) ÷ $10,000] × $2,000}.
Answer (B) is incorrect because $2,000 is the amount of cash receipts during year 1 on year 1 installment sales. Answer (C) is incorrect because $3,200 is the amount of the total gross profit on year 1 installment sales that is deferred to future periods. Answer (D) is incorrect because $4,000 is the total gross profit on year 1 installment sales.

**76.** The company's gross profit amount from year 3 sales to be deferred to future years would be

- A. $2,000
- B. $3,000
- C. $8,000
- D. $10,000

Answer (C) is correct. *(CIA, adapted)*
**REQUIRED:** The gross profit amount from year 3 sales to be deferred to future years.
**DISCUSSION:** The total gross profit on year 3 sales is $10,000 ($20,000 sales − $10,000 cost), and the amount realized is $2,000 {[($20,000 − $10,000) ÷ $20,000] × $4,000 of year 3 cash receipts}. Accordingly, the amount deferred is $8,000 ($10,000 − $2,000).
Answer (A) is incorrect because $2,000 is the realized gross profit on year 3 sales. Answer (B) is incorrect because $3,000 equals total receipts for year 2 and year 3 on year 2 sales. Answer (D) is incorrect because $10,000 is the total gross profit on year 3 sales.

**77.** A company sells inventory for $80,000 that had an inventory cost of $40,000. The terms of the sale involve payments receivable of $10,000 in the first year, $45,000 in the second year, and $25,000 in the third year. The buyer of the inventory is a new firm with no credit history. If the cost recovery method of revenue recognition is used, then the amount of gross profit the company will recognize in the second year is

- A. $0
- B. $5,000
- C. $15,000
- D. $45,000

Answer (C) is correct. *(CIA, adapted)*
**REQUIRED:** The gross profit in the second year under the cost recovery method.
**DISCUSSION:** The profit recognized in the second year equals the cumulative payments received minus the seller's cost, or $15,000 [($10,000 + $45,000) − $40,000].
Answer (A) is incorrect because, under the cost recovery method, profit is recognized in the second year when cash payments by the buyer exceed the seller's cost of merchandise. Answer (B) is incorrect because $5,000 is the profit to be recognized without consideration of the payment received in the first year. Answer (D) is incorrect because $45,000 is the payment received in the second year.

**78.** Which method of revenue recognition is required for sales of real estate that involve a contractual provision permitting the buyer to cancel the contract for a period of time after the completion of the sale transaction?

    A.  Deposit accounting method.

    B.  Installment method.

    C.  Cost recovery method.

    D.  Percentage-of-completion method.

Answer (A) is correct.  *(Publisher)*
    **REQUIRED:** The revenue recognition method for real estate transactions with a right-of-return privilege.
    **DISCUSSION:** SFAS 66 requires deposit accounting to be used in real estate transactions involving a right-of-return privilege.  A liability is recorded when cash is received, and no revenue is recognized until the period has expired during which the customer may cancel.
    Answer (B) is incorrect because installment accounting is used when full payment is not received and eventual collection is questionable.  Answer (C) is incorrect because the cost recovery method is used when collectibility is in considerable doubt and a reasonable estimate of the amount of loss cannot be determined.  Answer (D) is incorrect because the percentage-of-completion method is used to account for large construction projects, not sales of real estate.

**79.** The percentage-of-completion method of accounting for long-term construction contracts is an exception to the

    A.  Matching principle.

    B.  Going-concern assumption.

    C.  Economic-entity assumption.

    D.  Revenue recognition principle.

Answer (D) is correct.  *(CMA, adapted)*
    **REQUIRED:** The principle or assumption to which the percentage-of-completion method is an exception.
    **DISCUSSION:** The revenue recognition principle states that revenue should be recognized (recorded) when realized or realizable and earned.  Revenue is earned when the earning process is essentially complete.  In effect, revenue is recorded when the most important event in the earning of that revenue has occurred.  Thus, revenue is normally recorded at the time of the sale or, occasionally, at the time cash is collected.  However, sometimes neither the sales basis nor the cash basis is appropriate, such as when a construction contract extends over several accounting periods.  As a result, contractors ordinarily recognize revenue using the percentage-of-completion method so that some revenue is recognized each year over the life of the contract.  Hence, this method is an exception to the general principle of revenue recognition, primarily because it better matches revenues and expenses.
    Answer (A) is incorrect because the percentage-of-completion method attempts to match revenues and expenses with the appropriate periods.  Answer (B) is incorrect because the going-concern assumption is appropriate for a contractor using the percentage-of-completion method, as for any other type of company.  Answer (C) is incorrect because the economic-entity assumption is appropriate for a contractor using the percentage-of-completion method, as for any other type of company.

**80.** An organization has a long-term construction contract in process.  During the current period, the estimated total contract cost has increased sufficiently so that there is a current-period loss, even though the contract is still estimated to be profitable overall.  Under these circumstances, the [List A] method of revenue recognition would require a [List B] period adjustment of expected gross profit recognized on the contract.

| | List A | List B |
|---|---|---|
| A. | Percentage-of-completion | Prior |
| B. | Percentage-of-completion | Current |
| C. | Completed-contract | Prior |
| D. | Completed-contract | Current |

Answer (B) is correct.  *(CIA, adapted)*
    **REQUIRED:** The adjustment needed for a current-period loss if the contract is expected to be profitable overall.
    **DISCUSSION:** Under the percentage-of-completion method, a current-period loss on a profitable contract is treated as a change in accounting estimate.  Thus, a current-period adjustment is required.  Prior-period adjustments are made to correct errors, not to reflect changes in estimates.
    Answer (A) is incorrect because, under the percentage-of-completion method, a current-period loss on a profitable contract requires a current-period adjustment.  Answer (C) is incorrect because, under the completed-contract method, no profit is recognized until the contract is completed.  Cost estimate adjustments while construction is in progress do not result in profit or loss recognition prior to completion unless an overall loss is expected on the contract.  Answer (D) is incorrect because, under the completed-contract method, no profit is recognized until the contract is completed.  Cost estimate adjustments while construction is in progress do not result in profit or loss recognition prior to completion unless an overall loss is expected on the contract.

**81.** Jessica, a consultant, keeps her accounting records on a cash basis. During year 2, Jessica collected $200,000 in fees from clients. At December 31, year 1, Jessica had accounts receivable of $40,000. At December 31, year 2, Jessica had accounts receivable of $60,000 and unearned fees of $5,000. On an accrual basis, what was Jessica's service revenue for year 2?

    A. $175,000

    B. $180,000

    C. $215,000

    D. $225,000

Answer (C) is correct. *(CPA, adapted)*
    **REQUIRED:** The accrual-basis service revenue.
    **DISCUSSION:** Of the $200,000 in fees collected during year 2, $5,000 was unearned; therefore, $195,000 reflected collections of earned fees. Given that the ending balance in accounts receivable was $20,000 higher than the beginning balance ($60,000 – $40,000), and that $195,000 in fees were collected, service revenue on the accrual basis was $215,000 ($20,000 + $195,000).
    Answer (A) is incorrect because $175,000 equals $200,000 collections, minus $20,000 change in accounts receivable, minus $5,000 unearned fees. Answer (B) is incorrect because $180,000 equals $200,000 collections, minus $20,000 change in accounts receivable. Answer (D) is incorrect because $225,000 is the result of assuming that the unearned fees were added to the $200,000 of fees collected.

**82.** Dolce Co., which began operations on January 1, year 1, appropriately uses the installment method of accounting to record revenues. The following information is available for the years ended December 31, year 1 and year 2:

| | Year 1 | Year 2 |
|---|---|---|
| Sales | $1,000,000 | $2,000,000 |
| Gross profit realized on sales made in | | |
|   Year 1 | 150,000 | 90,000 |
|   Year 2 | -- | 200,000 |
| Gross profit percentages | 30% | 40% |

What amount of installment accounts receivable should Dolce report in its December 31, year 2 balance sheet?

    A. $1,100,000

    B. $1,300,000

    C. $1,700,000

    D. $1,900,000

Answer (C) is correct. *(CPA, adapted)*
    **REQUIRED:** The amount of installment accounts receivable.
    **DISCUSSION:** Gross profit realized equals the gross profit percentage times cash collected. Hence, cash collected on year 1 sales was $800,000 [($150,000 + $90,000) ÷ 30%], and cash collected on year 2 sales was $500,000 ($200,000 ÷ 40%). The remaining balance of installment receivables is therefore $1,700,000 ($1,000,000 + $2,000,000 – $800,000 – $500,000).
    Answer (A) is incorrect because $1,100,000 equals the total gross profit (both realized and unrealized) for year 1 and year 2. Answer (B) is incorrect because $1,300,000 is the total cash collected. Answer (D) is incorrect because $1,900,000 equals total sales minus total gross profit for year 1 and year 2.

**83.** Leon Co., which began operations on January 2, appropriately uses the installment sales method of accounting. The following information is available for the year:

| | |
|---|---|
| Installment sales | $1,800,000 |
| Realized gross profit on installment sales | 240,000 |
| Gross profit percentage on sales | 40% |

What amounts should Leon report as accounts receivable and deferred gross profit for the year ended December 31?

| | Accounts Receivable | Deferred Gross Profit |
|---|---|---|
| A. | $600,000 | $480,000 |
| B. | $600,000 | $360,000 |
| C. | $1,200,000 | $480,000 |
| D. | $1,200,000 | $720,000 |

Answer (C) is correct. *(CPA, adapted)*
    **REQUIRED:** The accounts receivable balance and deferred gross profit under the installment sales method.
    **DISCUSSION:** The installment method recognizes income on a sale when the related receivable is collected. The amount recognized each period is the gross profit percentage (gross profit ÷ selling price) on the sale multiplied by the cash collected. Given realized gross profit on installment sales of $240,000 and a gross profit percentage on sales of 40%, cash collections must have been $600,000 ($240,000 ÷ 40%). The accounts receivable at year-end is the difference between total installment sales and cash collected; therefore, accounts receivable must be $1,200,000 ($1,800,000 – $600,000) on December 31. Deferred gross profit on the year-end accounts receivable is $480,000 ($1,200,000 × 40%).
    Answer (A) is incorrect because $600,000 equals cash collections for the year. Answer (B) is incorrect because $600,000 equals cash collections for the year, and $360,000 is the difference between cash collections and realized gross profit. Answer (D) is incorrect because $720,000 is the total of realized and unrealized gross profit.

Questions 84 and 85 are based on the following information.

A company began work on a long-term construction contract in year 1. The contract price was $3,000,000. Year-end information related to the contract is as follows:

| | Year 1 | Year 2 | Year 3 |
|---|---|---|---|
| Estimated total cost | $2,000,000 | $2,000,000 | $2,000,000 |
| Cost incurred | 700,000 | 900,000 | 400,000 |
| Billings | 800,000 | 1,200,000 | 1,000,000 |
| Collections | 600,000 | 1,200,000 | 1,200,000 |

**84.** If the company uses the percentage-of-completion method of accounting for this contract, the gross profit to be recognized in year 1 is

A. $(100,000)

B. $100,000

C. $200,000

D. $350,000

Answer (D) is correct.  *(CIA, adapted)*
**REQUIRED:** The gross profit to be recognized.
**DISCUSSION:** The percentage-of-completion method recognizes income based on the ratio of the costs incurred to date to the estimated total costs. Billings and collections are irrelevant information when using the percentage-of-completion method. The percentage-of-completion at year-end is 35% ($700,000 ÷ $2,000,000). The gross profit for year 1 is the anticipated gross profit on the contract times the completion percentage. Thus, gross profit for year 1 is $350,000 [($3,000,000 – $2,000,000) × 35%].
Answer (A) is incorrect because $(100,000) is the difference between costs incurred and collections. Answer (B) is incorrect because $100,000 is the difference between billings and costs incurred. Answer (C) is incorrect because $200,000 is the difference between billings and collections.

**85.** If the company uses the completed-contract method of accounting for this contract, the gross profit to be recognized in year 3 is

A. $200,000

B. $600,000

C. $800,000

D. $1,000,000

Answer (D) is correct.  *(CIA, adapted)*
**REQUIRED:** The gross profit to be recognized in year 3 using the completed-contract method.
**DISCUSSION:** Under the completed-contract method, profit is recognized as being realized or realizable and earned only when the contract is complete. The total contract price and total contract costs are recognized as revenue and cost of goods sold, respectively, in the year of completion of the contract. The gross profit in year 3 is $1,000,000 ($3,000,000 revenue – $2,000,000 cost of goods sold).
Answer (A) is incorrect because $200,000 is the difference between collections and billings in year 3. Answer (B) is incorrect because $600,000 is the difference between billings and costs incurred in year 3. Answer (C) is incorrect because $800,000 is the difference between estimated total cost and collections.

**86.** A vendor sells specialty inks on consignment to a manufacturer of colored paper at a price of $200 per barrel. Payment is made to the vendor in the month the manufacturer uses the barrels in production. The vendor records revenues when the barrels are shipped and makes no adjusting entries to record unearned revenues until the December 31 closing of the books. At the end of July, the manufacturer had 40 barrels of ink on consignment. During August, the vendor consigned 50 barrels and received payment for 30 barrels. Another five barrels were returned to the vendor by the manufacturer for credit. At the end of August, what is the amount of unearned revenue contained in the vendor's accounts receivable from the manufacturer?

A. $3,000

B. $4,000

C. $11,000

D. $12,000

Answer (C) is correct.  *(CIA, adapted)*
**REQUIRED:** The amount of unearned revenue in the accounts receivable of a consignor.
**DISCUSSION:** Consignment does not meet the criteria for recognition of revenue. The barrels have not been sold, so revenue has not been realized or earned. However, 30 barrels have been paid for. Thus, the revenue is recognized for these barrels. The five barrels returned are not included in unearned revenue because they constitute a return of consigned goods. Accordingly, the amount of inappropriately recognized revenue is $11,000 [(40 consigned + 50 consigned – 30 paid for – 5 returns) × $200].
Answer (A) is incorrect because $3,000 does not include the 40 barrels consigned in July. Answer (B) is incorrect because $4,000 does not include the 40 barrels consigned in July or deduct the five barrels returned. Answer (D) is incorrect because $12,000 does not reflect the five barrels returned.

Questions 87 and 88 are based on the following information. Diamond Clover Construction, Inc. uses the percentage-of-completion method of accounting. In year 1, the company began work on job #4115, with a contract price of $5,000,000.

Other data are:

|  | Year 1 | Year 2 |
|---|---|---|
| Costs incurred during the year | $ 900,000 | $2,350,000 |
| Estimated costs to complete | 2,700,000 | 0 |
| Billings during the year | 1,000,000 | 4,000,000 |
| Collections during the year | 700,000 | 4,300,000 |

**87.** The amount of total gross profit to be recognized in year 1 is

A. $350,000

B. $700,000

C. $1,400,000

D. $766,667

Answer (A) is correct. *(CMA, adapted)*
**REQUIRED:** The amount of gross profit to be recognized in year 1 under the percentage-of-completion method of accounting.
**DISCUSSION:** By the end of year 1, the company had incurred costs of $900,000 and expected to incur additional costs of $2,700,000. Therefore, the total cost of completing the job was estimated to be the total of the two amounts, or $3,600,000. The $900,000 incurred in year 1 represents 25% of the total costs expected to be incurred. If 25% of the work has been completed, then the company should recognize 25% of the expected revenue. Because the total contract price is $5,000,000, the revenue associated with the 25% point is $1,250,000. Subtracting the $900,000 of costs incurred from the $1,250,000 of revenue produces a gross profit for year 1 of $350,000.
Answer (B) is incorrect because the $700,000 represents the cash collected for the year, which is irrelevant to the gross profit to be recognized. Answer (C) is incorrect because the $1,400,000 is the amount of gross profit that is expected over the life of the project. Answer (D) is incorrect because $766,667 is based on a percentage of completion greater than 25%.

**88.** If Diamond Clover Construction, Inc. were to use the completed-contract method of accounting, the total amount to be recognized as income in year 2 would be

A. $1,400,000

B. $1,750,000

C. $2,650,000

D. $700,000

Answer (B) is correct. *(CMA, adapted)*
**REQUIRED:** The total income to be recognized in year 2 if the company uses the completed-contract method of accounting.
**DISCUSSION:** Under the completed-contract method, no income is recognized until the year the project is completed. In this case, the costs incurred over 2 years ($900,000 + $2,350,000), or $3,250,000, are subtracted from the total contract price of $5,000,000 to arrive at income of $1,750,000. There would have been zero income in year 1 since the contract had not been completed during that year.
Answer (A) is incorrect because $1,400,000 was the estimated profit based on the costs incurred in year 1; ultimately those expectations proved erroneous since actual costs in year 2 were less than those estimated to complete the project at the end of year 1. Answer (C) is incorrect because the $2,650,000 overlooks the $900,000 of costs incurred during year 1. Answer (D) is incorrect because $700,000 was the cash collected during year 1, not the profit for any year.

**89.** ABC Manufacturing Company ships merchandise costing $40,000 on consignment to XYZ Stores. ABC pays $3,000 of freight costs to a transport company, and XYZ pays $2,000 for local advertising costs that are reimbursable from ABC. By the end of the period, three fourths of the consigned merchandise has been sold for $50,000 cash. XYZ notifies ABC of the sales, retains a 10% commission and the paid advertising costs, and remits the cash due ABC. Select the journal entry that appropriately records the notification of sale and the receipt of cash by ABC.

A.  
| | | |
|---|---|---|
| Cash | $40,000 | |
| Advertising expense | 2,000 | |
| Commission expense | 5,000 | |
| Freight expense | 3,000 | |
| Revenue from | | |
| consignment sales | | $50,000 |

B.  
| | | |
|---|---|---|
| Cash | $43,000 | |
| Advertising expense | 2,000 | |
| Commission expense | 5,000 | |
| Revenue from | | |
| consignment sales | | $50,000 |

C.  
| | | |
|---|---|---|
| Cash | $50,000 | |
| Revenue from | | |
| consignment sales | | $50,000 |

D.  
| | | |
|---|---|---|
| Cash | $45,000 | |
| Commission expense | 5,000 | |
| Revenue from | | |
| consignment sales | | $50,000 |

Answer (B) is correct.  *(CIA, adapted)*
**REQUIRED:** The journal entry to record the consignor's notification of sale and receipt of cash.
**DISCUSSION:** ABC debits the cash received $43,000 [$50,000 sales – $2,000 advertising – ($50,000 × .10) sales commission]. The advertising and commission expenses are debited for $2,000 and $5,000, respectively. Finally, $50,000 of gross revenue is credited.
Answer (A) is incorrect because the freight was paid earlier in the period and would have been recorded then by a credit to cash and a debit to inventory. Thus, the freight costs will be released to income via cost of goods sold. Answer (C) is incorrect because the 10% commission and the advertising costs are ignored in this answer. Answer (D) is incorrect because the reimbursable advertising costs are ignored in this answer.

**90.** Several of Fox, Inc.'s customers are having cash flow problems. Information pertaining to these customers for the years ended March 31, year 1 and year 2 follows:

| | 3/31/year 1 | 3/31/year 2 |
|---|---|---|
| Sales | $10,000 | $15,000 |
| Cost of sales | 8,000 | 9,000 |
| Cash collections | | |
| on year 1 sales | 7,000 | 3,000 |
| on year 2 sales | -- | 12,000 |

If the cost-recovery method is used, what amount would Fox report as gross profit from sales to these customers for the year ended March 31, year 2?

A. $2,000

B. $3,000

C. $5,000

D. $15,000

Answer (C) is correct.  *(CPA, adapted)*
**REQUIRED:** The gross profit from sales if the cost-recovery method is used.
**DISCUSSION:** The cost-recovery method recognizes profit only after collections exceed the cost of the item sold, that is, when the full cost has been recovered. Subsequent amounts collected are treated entirely as revenue (debit cash and deferred gross profit, credit the receivable and realized gross profit). The sum of collections in excess of costs to be recognized as gross profit is $5,000 {[$3,000 for year 2 collections on year 1 sales – ($8,000 cost – $7,000 in year 1 collections on year 1 sales)] + ($12,000 collections on year 2 sales – $9,000 cost)}.
Answer (A) is incorrect because $2,000 excludes the profit on year 2 sales. Answer (B) is incorrect because $3,000 excludes the profit on year 1 sales. Answer (D) is incorrect because $15,000 equals year 2 sales.

**91.** During the current year, Kam Co. began offering its goods to selected retailers on a consignment basis. The following information was derived from Kam's current year accounting records:

| | |
|---|---:|
| Beginning inventory | $122,000 |
| Purchases | 540,000 |
| Freight-in | 10,000 |
| Transportation to consignees | 5,000 |
| Freight-out | 35,000 |
| Ending inventory -- held by Kam | 145,000 |
| held by consignees | 20,000 |

In its current year income statement, what amount should Kam report as cost of goods sold?

A. $507,000

B. $512,000

C. $527,000

D. $547,000

Answer (B) is correct. *(CPA, adapted)*
**REQUIRED:** The total cost of goods sold.
**DISCUSSION:** Cost of goods sold is equal to the cost of goods available for sale minus the ending inventory. Cost of goods available for sale is equal to beginning inventory, plus purchases, plus additional costs (such as freight-in and transportation to consignees) that are necessary to prepare the inventory for sale. The cost of goods sold for Kam Co. is $512,000 [($122,000 beginning inventory + $540,000 purchases + $10,000 freight-in + $5,000 transportation to consignees) – ($145,000 Kam's ending inventory + $20,000 consignee ending inventory)]. Freight-out is a selling cost and is not included in cost of goods sold.
Answer (A) is incorrect because $507,000 does not include $5,000 for transportation to consignees. Answer (C) is incorrect because $527,000 does not include $5,000 for transportation to consignees or reflect the $20,000 of inventory held by consignees. Answer (D) is incorrect because $547,000 includes $35,000 of freight-out.

**92.** On December 31, year 1, Melanie Company sold on account and shipped merchandise with a list price of $150,000 to Desoto Company. The terms of the sale were n/30, FOB shipping point. The merchandise arrived at Desoto on January 5, year 2. Due to confusion about the shipping terms, the sale was not recorded until January year 2, and the merchandise, sold at a markup of 25% of cost, was included in Melanie's inventory on December 31, year 1. Melanie uses a periodic inventory system. As a result of the error, Melanie's income before income taxes for the year ended December 31, year 1 was

A. Understated by $30,000.

B. Understated by $150,000.

C. Understated by $37,500.

D. Overstated by $120,000.

Answer (A) is correct. *(Publisher)*
**REQUIRED:** The effect on income for year 1 because a sale was not recorded in the proper year.
**DISCUSSION:** The freight term was FOB shipping point, so title to the goods passed to the buyer in December. Thus, the $150,000 sale should have been recorded in December. At December 31, the inventory included the merchandise at its cost of $120,000 ($150,000 price ÷ 1.25). Because of the failure to record the sale, the seller reported inventory of $120,000 instead of an account receivable of $150,000. Assets were therefore understated by $30,000. Moreover, income was understated by $30,000 because of the failure to report the $150,000 sale and the $120,000 of cost of goods sold.
Answer (B) is incorrect because revenue, not net income, is understated by $150,000. The net effect of the revenue and cost errors misstates income. Answer (C) is incorrect because $37,500 is the markup on selling price, not cost. Answer (D) is incorrect because the omission of $150,000 of revenue and $120,000 of cost of goods sold understated income.

Questions 93 through 95 are based on the following information. The Katie Howell Construction Company uses the percentage-of-completion method of accounting. In year 1, the company began work on Job 21, which had a contract price of $10 million.

Other data are:

|  | Year 1 | Year 2 |
| --- | --- | --- |
| Costs incurred during the year | $1,800,000 | $4,700,000 |
| Estimated costs to complete | 5,400,000 | 0 |
| Billings during the year | 2,000,000 | 8,000,000 |
| Collections during the year | 1,400,000 | 8,600,000 |

**93.** Using the percentage-of-completion method, the total gross profit to be recognized in year 1 is

A. $700,000

B. $1,400,000

C. $2,800,000

D. $2,500,000

Answer (A) is correct. *(Publisher)*
**REQUIRED:** The gross profit to be recognized.
**DISCUSSION:** By the end of year 1, the company had incurred costs of $1.8 million and expected to incur additional costs of $5.4 million. Thus, the total cost of the job was estimated to be $7.2 million. The $1.8 million incurred in year 1 represents 25% of the total costs expected to be incurred. If 25% of the work has been completed, the company should recognize 25% of the expected revenue. Hence, gross profit for year 1 is $700,000 [(($10,000,000 contract price − $7,200,000 total estimated costs) × 25%].
Answer (B) is incorrect because the $1,400,000 equals the cash collected for the year. Answer (C) is incorrect because $2,800,000 is the total estimated gross profit for the project. Answer (D) is incorrect because $2,500,000 is the total revenue to be recognized during year 1.

**94.** Using the percentage-of-completion method, the total gross profit to be recognized in year 2 is

A. $2,100,000

B. $2,800,000

C. $3,500,000

D. $3,900,000

Answer (B) is correct. *(Publisher)*
**REQUIRED:** The gross profit to be recognized.
**DISCUSSION:** By the end of year 2, the company had incurred costs of $1.8 million in year 1 and $4.7 million in year 2. Consequently, the total cost of completing the job was $6.5 million. Given a total contract price of $10 million, the total gross profit over the life of the contract is $3.5 million. The gross profit recognized in year 1 was $700,000 {[($1,800,000 year 1 costs ÷ ($1,800,000 + $5,400,000 estimated costs to complete)] × [$10,000,000 contract price − ($1,800,000 + $5,400,000)]}. The gross profit recognized in year 2 is therefore $2,800,000 ($3,500,000 total − $700,000 recognized in year 1).
Answer (A) is incorrect because $2,100,000 is based on the total estimated gross profit at the end of year 1. Answer (C) is incorrect because $3,500,000 is the total gross profit over 2 years. Answer (D) is incorrect because $3,900,000 is the difference between collections and costs in year 2.

**95.** If Katie Howell Construction Company uses the completed-contract method, the income recognized in year 2 will be

A. $2,800,000

B. $3,500,000

C. $5,300,000

D. $1,400,000

Answer (B) is correct. *(Publisher)*
**REQUIRED:** The income recognized.
**DISCUSSION:** Under the completed-contract method, no income is recognized until the project is completed. In this case, the costs incurred over 2 years ($1,800,000 + $4,700,000), or $6.5 million, are subtracted from the total contract price of $10 million to arrive at income of $3.5 million. No income would have been reported in year 1 because the contract had not been completed by the end of that year.
Answer (A) is incorrect because $2,800,000 was the estimated gross profit at the end of year 1. Answer (C) is incorrect because $5,300,000 does not consider the $1,800,000 of costs incurred during year 1. Answer (D) is incorrect because $1,400,000 was the cash collected during year 1.

Questions 96 through 98 are based on the following information. Roebling Construction signed a $24 million contract on August 1, year 0 with the city of Candu to construct a bridge over the Vine River. Roebling's estimated cost of the bridge on that date was $18 million. The bridge was to be completed by April year 3. Roebling uses the percentage-of-completion method for income recognition. Roebling's fiscal year ends May 31.

Data regarding the bridge contract are presented in the schedule below.

|  | At May 31 ($000 omitted) | |
|  | year 1 | year 2 |
| --- | --- | --- |
| Actual costs to date | $ 6,000 | $15,000 |
| Estimated costs to complete | 12,000 | 5,000 |
| Progress billings to date | 5,000 | 14,000 |
| Cash collected to date | 4,000 | 12,000 |

**96.** The gross profit or loss recognized in the fiscal year ended May 31, year 1 from this bridge contract is

A. $6,000,000 gross profit.

B. $2,000,000 gross profit.

C. $3,000,000 gross profit.

D. $1,000,000 gross loss.

Answer (B) is correct. *(CMA, adapted)*
**REQUIRED:** The gross profit for the first year of a long-term construction contract.
**DISCUSSION:** Given that one-third of all costs have already been incurred ($6,000,000), the company should recognize revenue equal to one-third of the contract price, or $8,000,000. Revenues of $8,000,0000 minus costs of $6,000,000 equals a gross profit of $2,000,000.
Answer (A) is incorrect because $6,000,000 is the actual cost to date. Answer (C) is incorrect because $3,000,000 is the gross profit for both the year 1 and the year 2 fiscal years. Answer (D) is incorrect because $1,000,000 is the difference between the actual costs and the progress billings to date.

**97.** The gross profit or loss recognized in the fiscal year ended May 31, year 2 from the bridge contract is

A. $4,000,000 gross profit.

B. $1,000,000 gross profit.

C. $3,000,000 gross profit.

D. $1,000,000 gross loss.

Answer (B) is correct. *(CMA, adapted)*
**REQUIRED:** The amount of gross profit or loss recognized in the second year of a long-term construction contract.
**DISCUSSION:** Because the firm has already incurred 75% of its total expected costs ($15 ÷ $20), it should recognize 75% of the total contract price as revenue. Thus, revenue of $18,000,000 should be recognized. The total gross profit is $3,000,000 ($18,000,000 – $15,000,000 in costs). However, the $3,000,000 of gross profit is the total for both years. Given that $2,000,000 had already been recognized in year 1, only the excess $1,000,000 is recognized in year 2.
Answer (A) is incorrect because $4,000,000 is the difference between the total contract price and the sum of the actual costs to date and the estimated costs to complete. Answer (C) is incorrect because $3,000,000 is the gross profit for both the year 1 and the year 2 fiscal years. Answer (D) is incorrect because $1,000,000 is the difference between actual costs and progress billings to date.

**98.** Assume that the estimated costs to complete at May 31, year 2 were $10,000,000 rather than the $5,000,000 shown in the schedule. The gross loss recognized on the contract from its inception on August 1, year 0 through May 31, year 2 is

A. $3,000,000 gross loss.

B. $7,000,000 gross loss.

C. $600,000 gross loss.

D. $1,000,000 gross loss.

Answer (D) is correct. *(CMA, adapted)*
**REQUIRED:** The loss to be recorded for the total period of a long-term construction contract.
**DISCUSSION:** The conservatism principle should be followed, and the company should report the entire loss on the contract as soon as that loss becomes obvious. A loss of $1,000,000 should be recognized up through May 31, year 2 ($24,000,000 of revenue – $25,000,000 in costs).
Answer (A) is incorrect because $3,000,000 is 60% of the additional $5,000,000 of estimated costs. Answer (B) is incorrect because $7,000,000 is the difference between $10,000,000 of estimated costs to complete and the $3,000,000 profit calculated in prior questions. Answer (C) is incorrect because $600,000 is 60% ($15,000,000 actual costs ÷ $25,000,000 total costs) of the estimated loss of $1,000,000. However, the conservatism principle requires a loss to be recognized as soon as the loss becomes obvious.

# STUDY UNIT EIGHTEEN
# OTHER INCOME STATEMENT ITEMS

(15 pages of outline)

This study unit is the **eighth of ten** on **external financial reporting**. The relative weight assigned to this major topic in Part 2 of the exam is **25%** at **skill level B** (four skill types required). The ten study units are

Study Unit 11:  Overview of External Financial Reporting
Study Unit 12:  Overview of Financial Statements
Study Unit 13:  Cash and Receivables
Study Unit 14:  Inventories and Investments
Study Unit 15:  Long-Lived Assets
Study Unit 16:  Liabilities
Study Unit 17:  Equity and Revenue Recognition
Study Unit 18:  Other Income Statement Items
Study Unit 19:  Business Combinations and Derivatives
Study Unit 20:  SEC Requirements and the Annual Report

After studying the outlines and answering the multiple-choice questions in this study unit, you will have the skills necessary to address the following topics listed in the IMA's Learning Outcome Statements:

Part 2 – Section E.4. Recognition, measurement, valuation, and disclosure

For each of the subtopics listed, the candidate should be able to:

1.   define the subtopic and describe the characteristics of its components
2.   demonstrate an understanding of appropriate valuation techniques for the components of each subtopic
3.   demonstrate an understanding of the appropriate accounting conventions for the components of each subtopic
4.   compare and contrast valuation techniques and accounting methods
5.   show the correct financial statement presentation
6.   identify the appropriate disclosure requirements in the body of the financial statements and/or in the footnotes

Segment reporting

a.   define operating segment
b.   identify the disclosures required for a reportable operating segment
c.   determine if a segment is reportable given a set of data

Multinational considerations

a.   recognize the challenges inherent in translating foreign entities' financial statements to the parent's reporting currency
b.   define functional currency

    c.    distinguish between the monetary/nonmonetary method and the current rate method

    d.    translate a foreign entity's financial statements from the entity's functional currency to the reporting currency

    e.    remeasure a foreign entity's financial statement to the functional currency

    f.    describe the significance of a foreign currency transaction gain (loss) on the financial statements

    g.    define "highly inflationary economy" and identify which currency should be used as the reporting currency for a company in this environment

    h.    identify disclosure requirements for translation of foreign currency financial statements

**Part 2 – Sections E.1. Objectives of external financial reporting; and E.2. Financial accounting fundamentals**

NOTE:  Statements a. through e. are covered in Study Unit 11.

    f.    Special topics:  discontinued operations, extraordinary items, accounting changes, and early extinguishment of debt

For each special topic, the candidate should be able to:

    1.    Define and describe its characteristics
    2.    Demonstrate a basic understanding of the relevant accounting issues
    3.    Describe the impact on a firm's financial statements

## 18.1 SEGMENT REPORTING

1.    **SFAS 131**, *Disclosures about Segments of an Enterprise and Related Information*, applies to the interim financial reports and annual financial statements of **public business enterprises**.

2.    The **objective** of segment reporting is to provide information about the different types of business activities of the entity and the economic environments in which it operates. Ordinarily, information is to be reported on the basis that is **used internally for performance evaluation and resource allocation**.  This information is reported on an operating segment basis.

3.    SFAS 131 defines an **operating segment** as "a component of an enterprise

    a.    That engages in business activities from which it may earn revenues and incur expenses (including revenues and expenses relating to transactions with other components of the same enterprise),

    b.    Whose operating results are regularly reviewed by the enterprise's chief operating decision maker [CODM] to make decisions about resources to be allocated to the segment and assess its performance, and

    c.    For which discrete financial information is available."

4.    **Aggregation Criteria.**  Operating segments may be aggregated if doing so is consistent with the objective of SFAS 131; if they have similar economic characteristics; and if they have similar products and services, production processes, classes of customers, distribution methods, and regulatory environments.

5.    **Reportable segments** are those that have been identified in accordance with items 2. through 4. above and also meet any of the quantitative thresholds described below and on the next page.  However, SFAS 131 does not define how these quantitative thresholds are calculated.  Instead, the amounts of reported segment items are the measures that are reviewed by the enterprise's CODM.  Furthermore, if an operating segment does not meet any of the quantitative thresholds, management has the discretion to treat it as reportable if such information would be useful to readers of the financial statements.

    a.    **Revenue test.**  Reported revenue, including sales to external customers and intersegment sales or transfers, is at least 10% of the combined revenue of all operating segments.

b.   **Asset test.** Assets are at least 10% of the combined assets of all operating segments.

c.   **Profit (loss) test.** The absolute amount of reported profit or loss is at least 10% of the greater, in absolute amount, of either the combined reported profit of all operating segments that did not report a loss, or the combined reported loss of all operating segments that did report a loss.

6.   Information about operating segments not meeting the quantitative thresholds may be **combined** to produce a reportable segment only if the operating segments share a majority of the aggregation criteria.

7.   If the **total external revenue** of the operating segments is less than 75% of consolidated revenue, additional operating segments are identified as reportable until the 75% level is reached.

8.   Information about nonreportable activities and segments is combined and disclosed in an **"all other" category** as a reconciling item.

9.   As the number of reportable segments increases above 10, the enterprise may decide that it has reached a practical limit.

10.  **Disclosures** include the following:

a.   Such **general information** as the factors used to identify the reportable segments, including the basis of organization, and the types of revenue-generating products and services for each reportable segment.

b.   A **measure of profit or loss and total assets** for each reportable segment. Moreover, if the amounts are included in the measure of segment profit or loss reviewed by the CODM, other disclosures include the following: revenues from external customers, revenues from other operating segments, interest revenue, interest expense, depreciation, depletion, amortization, unusual items, equity in the net income of equity-based investees, income tax expense or benefit, extraordinary items, and other significant noncash items.

c.   The amount of investment in **equity-based investees** and total expenditures for additions to most **long-lived assets** for each reportable segment if they are included in segment assets reviewed by the CODM.

11.  If a majority of a segment's revenues are from interest and **net interest revenue** is the primary basis for assessing its performance and the resources allocated to it, net interest revenue may be reported given proper disclosure.

12.  **Measurement.** The general principle is that the information reported is measured in the same way as the internal information used to evaluate a segment's performance and to allocate assets to it.

a.   If the chief operating decision maker uses more than one measure of a segment's profit or loss or assets, the reported measures are those most consistent with the consolidated financial statements. Explanations of the measurements of segment profit or loss and segment assets should be given for each reportable segment.

13.  **Reconciliations** should be provided for the total reportable segments' revenues and consolidated revenues, the total of the reportable segments' measures of profit or loss and pretax consolidated operating income (but if the enterprise allocates other items, such as income taxes, the reconciliation may be to income after those items), the total reportable segments' assets and consolidated assets, and the total reportable segments' amounts for every other significant item of information disclosed and the consolidated amount. Significant reconciling items should be separately identified and described.

14. **Interim period information** is disclosed for each reportable segment in condensed financial statements. Disclosures include external revenues, intersegment revenues, a measure of segment profit or loss, total assets that have materially changed since the last annual report, differences from the last annual report in the basis of segmentation or of segment profit or loss, and a reconciliation of the total reportable segments' profit or loss and consolidated pretax income.

15. **Restatement of previously reported information** is required if changes in internal organization cause the composition of reportable segments to change. However, an enterprise must restate only items of disclosure that it can practicably restate.

    a. In these circumstances, if segment information for earlier periods, including interim periods, is not restated, segment information for the year of the change must be disclosed under the old basis and the new basis of segmentation if practicable.

16. Certain **enterprise-wide disclosures** must be provided only if they are not given in the reportable operating segment information.

    a. **Information about products and services.** Revenues from external customers for each product and service or each group of similar products and services are reported if practicable based on the financial information used to produce the general-purpose financial statements.

    b. The following information about **geographic areas** is also reported if practicable: external revenues attributed to the home country, external revenues attributed to all foreign countries, material external revenues attributed to an individual foreign country, the basis for attributing revenues from external customers, and certain information about assets.

    c. If 10% or more of revenue is derived from sales to any **single customer**, that fact, the amount of revenue from each such customer, and the segment(s) reporting the revenues must be disclosed. Single customers include entities under common control and each federal, state, local, or foreign government.

17. Stop and review! You have completed the outline for this subunit. Study multiple-choice questions 1 through 7 beginning on page 723.

## 18.2 FOREIGN CURRENCY ISSUES

1. Currently, accounting data for foreign operations are consolidated into domestic financial statements using a functional currency approach described in **SFAS 52**, *Foreign Currency Translation.*

    a. An entity's **functional currency** is the currency of the primary economic environment in which it operates. The functional currency is normally that of the environment in which the entity primarily expends and generates cash. For example, the functional currency of a British subsidiary is the pound.

        1) A **highly inflationary currency**, that is, one with a 3-year inflation rate of 100% or more, is not considered stable enough to be a functional currency. Instead, the financial statements of the foreign entity are remeasured as if the reporting currency were the functional currency.

        2) Indications that the subsidiary's currency is the functional currency include the following:

           a) Its cash flows are primarily in that foreign currency,

           b) They do not affect the parent's cash flows,

           c) Labor and materials are obtained in the local market of the foreign subsidiary,

        d)    Subsidiary financing is obtained from local foreign sources and from the subsidiary's operations, and

        e)    Few intercompany transactions occur between the foreign subsidiary and the parent.

    3)    However, sales prices that are responsive to exchange rate fluctuations and international competition suggest that the functional currency is the parent's currency.

  b.    The following are the steps in the **functional currency translation approach**:

    1)    The functional currency should be identified.

    2)    The financial statement amounts should be measured in the functional currency. For example, a Swiss company may prepare its statements in Swiss francs even though it conducts most of its business in euros (the euro is the functional currency).

        a)    If the subsidiary's financial statements are not maintained in the functional currency, they must be **remeasured** into that currency using the temporal rate method.

            i)    Remeasurement presents statements as if they had been originally prepared in the functional currency.

            ii)    The **current exchange rate** is used to remeasure all accounts except those specified in **SFAS 52**.

            iii)    **Historical rates** should be used for the specified accounts, which include common **nonmonetary** balance sheet items and related revenue, expense, gain, and loss accounts. Thus, historical rates are used for inventory; property, plant, and equipment; prepaid expenses; deferred charges and credits; cost of sales; intangible assets; amortization of intangible assets; and common stock.

        b)    **Gains and losses** arising from remeasurement of **monetary** assets and liabilities are recognized currently in income.

        c)    An entity may be in any form, including subsidiary, division, branch, or joint venture.

    3)    Once the financial statement elements have been measured in terms of the functional currency, a **current exchange rate** is used to **translate** assets and liabilities from the functional currency into the reporting currency of the parent.

        a)    In theory, revenues, expenses, gains, and losses are translated at the rate in effect when they were recognized, but they are so numerous that a **weighted-average rate** for the period may be used.

    4)    **Translation adjustments** for a foreign operation that is relatively self-contained and integrated within its environment do not affect cash flows of the reporting enterprise and should be excluded from net income. Thus, they are reported in **other comprehensive income**.

    5)    **FASB Interpretation No. 37**, *Accounting for Translation Adjustments upon Sale of Part of an Investment in a Foreign Entity*, clarifies SFAS 52. A pro rata portion of the accumulated translation adjustment attributable to an investment shall be recognized in measuring the gain or loss on the sale of all or part of a company's interest in a foreign entity.

     6)   Disclosures should include the following:

        a)   Aggregate transaction gain or loss included in net income

        b)   An analysis of changes in the accumulated amount of translation adjustments reported in equity

           i)   Beginning and ending amounts

           ii)   Aggregate periodic translation adjustment and gains (losses) from certain hedges and intercompany balances

           iii)   Periodic taxes allocated to translation adjustments

           iv)   Cumulative translation adjustments included in periodic net income resulting from sale or liquidation of an investment in a foreign entity

        c)   If necessary, significant rate changes and their effects after the date of the enterprise's or a foreign entity's financial statements (if consolidated, combined, or accounted for under the equity method)

2.    When a **foreign currency transaction** gives rise to a receivable or a payable that is fixed in terms of the amount of foreign currency to be received or paid, a change in the exchange rate between the functional currency and the currency in which the transaction is denominated results in a gain or loss that ordinarily should be included in determining net income in the period in which the exchange rate changes. The same treatment applies when the transaction is settled. **Transaction gains and losses** are reported in the aggregate in the income statement and should be disclosed.

    a.   EXAMPLE: Assume that inventory was purchased for 10,000 foreign currency units (FCUs) at a time when the FCU was worth $.25 U.S. The entry for the purchase is

| | | |
|---|---|---|
| Purchases | $2,500 | |
| Accounts payable | | $2,500 |

       1)   If the FCU strengthens compared with the dollar before the payment date, the company will have to pay more to obtain the 10,000 FCUs necessary to make payment to the supplier. If the price of the FCU rises to $.26, the entry for payment will be

| | | |
|---|---|---|
| Accounts payable | $2,500 | |
| Transaction loss | 100 | |
| Cash | | $2,600 |

       2)   If the dollar strengthens during the intervening period, a gain is recorded. If the FCU falls to $.22, the entry for payment is

| | | |
|---|---|---|
| Accounts payable | $2,500 | |
| Cash | | $2,200 |
| Transaction gain | | 300 |

    b.   Certain transaction gains and losses are excluded from the determination of net income and are reported in the same way as translation adjustments, that is, in **other comprehensive income**:

       1)   Transactions that are designated and effective as economic hedges of a net investment in a foreign entity

       2)   Long-term investments in foreign entities to be consolidated, combined, or accounted for by the equity method

    c.   The subject of **foreign currency hedging** is treated in Study Unit 19.

    d.   The previous examples recorded the sales or purchases at the exchange rate prevailing at the transaction date. Later adjustments were recorded directly to transaction gain or loss. This treatment is known as the **two-transaction approach** because the sale or purchase is viewed as a transaction separate from the financing arrangement.

3. **Tax Issues for Multinational Companies**

   a. A U.S. corporation that operates a business through a foreign subsidiary must report the income from that foreign operation on the company's U.S. income tax return. This foreign income will be taxed the same way as domestic income.

   b. A foreign subsidiary's income will not be taxed to the U.S. parent until it is distributed as a dividend to the parent.

   c. All U.S. companies doing business in foreign countries will be taxed by the foreign countries on their foreign income.

      1) Taxes may be levied on dividend income, undistributed income, or the value added to goods and services.

      2) Many countries lower taxes on foreign companies to increase incentives to foreign investors.

      3) The U.S. has entered into **tax treaties** with many foreign governments to avoid international double taxation and prevent tax evasion.

4. Stop and review! You have completed the outline for this subunit. Study multiple-choice questions 8 through 22 beginning on page 726.

## 18.3 DISCONTINUED OPERATIONS

1. According to **SFAS 144**, *Accounting for the Impairment or Disposal of Long-Lived Assets*, a **component of an entity** ("component") encompasses operations and cash flows that are clearly distinguishable for operating and financial reporting purposes from the rest of the entity.

   a. A component may be a reportable segment or an operating segment, a reporting unit, a subsidiary, or an asset group.

2. If a component has been disposed of or is classified as held for sale based on appropriate criteria, its operating results are reported in discontinued operations as described below, provided that

   a. Its operations and cash flows have been or will be eliminated from the entity's ongoing operations as a result of the disposal, and

   b. The entity will have no significant continuing involvement after the disposal.

3. When a component has been disposed of or is classified as held for sale, the income statements for current and prior periods must report its operating results in **discontinued operations** in the period(s) **when they occur**.

   a. **Operating results** include any loss for a writedown to fair value minus cost to sell of a long-lived asset held for sale or a gain arising from an increase in fair value minus cost to sell (but limited to the losses previously recognized).

   b. Discontinued operations, minus (plus) income tax (benefit), is reported separately in a caption before extraordinary items (if any). The following format may be used by a business enterprise:

      1) EXAMPLE: Shadow Corporation is a computer manufacturer that services various market segments with its diverse product groups. Each such group is a component of the entity. The Upscale Division's results are declining. Consequently, Shadow decided on July 15, 20X5 to commit to a plan to sell Upscale. The sale was consummated on December 1, 20X5. As a result, the operations and cash flows of Upscale were eliminated from the ongoing operations of Shadow. Moreover, the entity will have no continuing post-sale involvement in Upscale's operations. Shadow's income statement after the disposal of Upscale appears on the next page.

      a)   The **gain or loss on disposal** must be disclosed on the face of the financial statements or in the notes.

      b)   The caption "Income from continuing operations" should be revised if extraordinary items or the cumulative effects of accounting changes are reported. The EPS presentation may also require revision.

4.    **Amounts previously reported in discontinued operations** in a prior period may require adjustment in the current period. If such an adjustment is **directly related** to a prior-period disposal of a component, it is reported in the current income statement as a separate item in discontinued operations, and its nature and amount are disclosed. **Adjustments** may include the following:

    a.   Contingencies arising under the terms of the disposal transaction may be resolved, for example, by purchase price adjustments or indemnification of the purchaser.

    b.   Contingencies arising from and directly related to the **predisposal operations** of the component may be resolved. Examples are the seller's environmental and warranty obligations.

    c.   **Employee benefit plan obligations** for pensions and other postemployment benefits may be settled. Reporting in discontinued operations is required if the settlement is directly related to the disposal.

5.    If a long-lived asset (or disposal group) is held for sale but is not a component, a gain or loss on disposal is included in **income from continuing operations**.

*Shadow Corporation*
**INCOME STATEMENT**
*For the Year Ended 12/31/X3*

| | | |
|---|---:|---:|
| Revenue: | | |
| Net sales | $1,500,000 | |
| Other revenue | 40,000 | |
| Total revenue | | $1,540,000 |
| Expenses: | | |
| Cost of goods sold | $ 750,000 | |
| Selling expense | 75,000 | |
| Administrative expense | 90,000 | |
| Interest expense | 70,000 | |
| Total expenses | | (985,000) |
| Income from continuing operations before income taxes | | $ 555,000 |
| Income taxes | | (206,000) |
| Income from continuing operations | | $ 349,000 |
| Discontinued operations: | | |
| Loss from operations of component unit -- Upscale | | |
| Division (including gain on disposal of $200,000) | $ (340,000) | |
| Income tax benefit | 56,000 | |
| Loss on discontinued operations | | (284,000) |
| Net income | | $ 65,000 |

6.    Stop and review! You have completed the outline for this subunit. Study multiple-choice questions 23 through 28 beginning on page 731.

## 18.4 EXTRAORDINARY ITEMS

1. According to **APB 30**, a material transaction or event that is unusual in nature and infrequent in occurrence in the environment in which the entity operates should be reported as an extraordinary item.

   a. These criteria, however, do not apply when a pronouncement specifically defines certain gains and losses as extraordinary items.

   b. Extraordinary items should be displayed separately in the income statement, net of tax, after results of discontinued operations.

      1) The nature of the event or transaction and the principal items included in the determination of the gain or loss should be described.

      2) The basic EPS and diluted EPS amounts for an extraordinary item should be presented on the face of the income statement or in the related notes.

   c. A transaction or event is **unusual** if it has a high degree of abnormality and is of a type clearly unrelated to, or only incidentally related to, the ordinary and typical activities of the entity.

   d. A transaction or event is **infrequent** if it is not reasonably expected to recur in the foreseeable future; e.g., earthquakes are extraordinary in Florida, not Japan.

   e. If **only one criterion is met**, a material item should be reported, but not net of tax, as a separate component of income from continuing operations. The nature and financial effects of the event or transaction should be disclosed, and similar gains or losses that are not material should be aggregated.

2. APB 30 gives specific examples of items that are not extraordinary, subject to certain exceptions.

   a. The following are classes of items that are **not extraordinary**:

      1) Write-downs of receivables, inventories, and intangible assets

      2) Gains and losses from exchange or translation of foreign currencies, including those resulting from major devaluations and revaluations

      3) Gains and losses on disposal of a component of an entity

      4) Other gains and losses from sale or abandonment of property, plant, and equipment used in the business

      5) Effects of strikes, including those against competitors and major suppliers

      6) Adjustments of accruals on long-term contracts

   b. **Exceptions**. In rare cases, however, an event or transaction that is material, unusual, and infrequent may result in an extraordinary gain or loss that includes one or more of the gains or losses listed above. In those cases, gains and losses, for example, from writedowns or from sale or abandonment of property used in the business, should be included in the extraordinary item if they directly result from a major casualty, an expropriation, or a prohibition under a newly enacted law or regulation.

      1) Any portion of the losses that would have resulted from valuation of assets on a going-concern basis (such as the loss from writing down assets to fair value) is not included in the extraordinary item.

3. Extraordinary gains and losses should be recorded in the **interim financial statements** in the quarters in which they occur. They should not be prorated.

4. Any **insurance reimbursements** reduce the related loss.

| | | |
|---|---|---|
| Loss | $XXX | |
| Receivable from insurance company | XXX | |
|     Assets | | $XXX |
|     Liability (for repairs, etc.) | | XXX |

5.  Stop and review! You have completed the outline for this subunit. Study multiple-choice questions 29 through 32 beginning on page 734.

## 18.5 ACCOUNTING CHANGES AND ERROR CORRECTIONS

1.  **SFAS 154**, *Accounting Changes and Error Corrections*, applies to annual statements and other financial information of business enterprises and not-for-profit organizations. It defines an **accounting change** as a change in an accounting principle, an accounting estimate, or the reporting entity. An accounting change does **NOT** include a correction of an accounting error in previously issued financial statements.

2.  A **change in accounting principle** occurs when an entity (a) adopts a generally accepted principle different from the one previously used, (b) changes the **method** of applying a generally accepted principle, or (c) changes to a generally accepted principle when the principle previously used is no longer generally accepted.

    a.  A change in principle does not include the initial adoption of a principle because of an **event or transaction occurring for the first time** or that previously had an immaterial effect. It also does not include adoption or modification of a principle to account for an event or transaction that clearly **differs in substance** from a previously occurring event or transaction.

    b.  The **general presumption** in preparing financial statements is that a principle once adopted should be applied **consistently**. However, a change in principle is appropriate if the change is required by a new pronouncement, or the entity is able to justify it as **preferable**.

3.  **Retrospective application** is required for all direct effects and the related income tax effects of a change in principle. Exceptions are made when it is impracticable to determine the cumulative effect or the period-specific effects of the change. **Direct effects** are the changes in assets or liabilities necessary to make the change in principle. An example is an adjustment of an inventory balance to implement a change in the method of measurement. (However, a new pronouncement may prescribe a different transition method.)

    a.  Retrospective application should not include **indirect effects**. They are changes in current or future cash flows from a change in principle applied retrospectively.

        1)  An example is a required profit-sharing payment based on a reported amount (e.g., revenue).

        2)  Indirect effects actually incurred and recognized are reported in the period when the change in principle is made.

        3)  Indirect effects that would have been reported if the new principle had been used in a prior period are excluded from the retrospective application.

    b.  Retrospective application requires that carrying amounts of (1) assets, (2) liabilities, and (3) retained earnings at the beginning of the first period reported be adjusted for the **cumulative effect** of the new principle on all periods not reported. All periods reported must be individually adjusted for the **period-specific effects** of applying the new principle.

        1)  It may be **impracticable** to determine the **cumulative effect** of applying a new principle to any prior period (for example, when the change is from FIFO to LIFO). In that case, the new principle is applied as if the change had been made prospectively at the earliest date practicable.

2) It may be practicable to determine the cumulative effect of applying the new principle to all prior periods. However, determining the period-specific effects on all prior periods presented may be impracticable. In these circumstances, cumulative-effect adjustments should be made to the beginning balances for the first period to which the new principle can be applied.

3) Retrospective application is impracticable when

   a) The entity cannot apply the new principle after all reasonable efforts;

   b) Assumptions about management's intent in a prior period are required that cannot be independently substantiated; or

   c) Significant estimates are required, and it is not possible to obtain objective evidence (1) about circumstances existing when amounts would have been recognized, measured, or disclosed and (2) that would have been available when the prior statements were issued.

4. A **change in accounting estimate** results from new information and a reassessment of the current status and future benefits and obligations represented by assets and liabilities. The effects of a change in estimate should be accounted for **prospectively**. Thus, they should be recognized only in the period of change and any future periods affected.

   a. A **change in estimate inseparable from (effected by) a change in principle** is accounted for as a change in estimate. An example is a change in a method of **depreciation, amortization, or depletion** of long-lived, nonfinancial assets.

   b. When a change in estimate affects several future periods, **disclosures** include

      1) The effect on income from continuing operations,
      2) Net income (or other appropriate captions), and
      3) Related per-share amounts of the current period.

5. A **change in reporting entity** is retrospectively applied to interim and annual statements. It results when (a) consolidated or combined statements are presented in place of statements of individual entities, (b) consolidated statements include subsidiaries different from those previously included, or (c) combined statements include entities different from those previously included.

   a. A change in reporting entity does not result from a business combination or consolidation of a variable interest entity.

      1) **Interest cost** previously capitalized under **SFAS 58**, *Capitalization of Interest Cost in Financial Statements That Include Investments Accounted for by the Equity Method*, is not changed. According to SFAS 58, assets qualifying for interest capitalization may include an equity-method investment if the investee meets certain criteria.

   b. In the period of change, **disclosures** must include

      1) The nature of the change;
      2) The reasons for it; and
      3) The effect on (a) income before extraordinary items, (b) net income (or other appropriate captions), (c) comprehensive income, and (d) related per-share amounts for all periods presented.

6. For **all changes in principle**, the nature of, and reason for, the change should be disclosed when the change is made. If retrospective application is impracticable, disclosures of the reasons and the method used to report the change are required. Additional disclosures include

   a. The method of applying the change;

   b. The information adjusted;

   c. The effects on income from continuing operations, any other affected line items, and any affected per-share amounts;

  d. The cumulative-effect adjustment; and

  e. A description of indirect effects and any related per-share amounts.

7. An **accounting error** results from (a) a mathematical mistake, (b) a mistake in the application of GAAP, or (c) an oversight or misuse of facts existing when the statements were prepared. A change to a generally accepted accounting principle from one that is not is an error correction, not an accounting change.

  a. According to SFAS 154, an accounting error related to a prior period is reported as a **prior period adjustment** by restating the prior-period statements. Restatement requires the same adjustments as retrospective application of a new principle.

  b. When the statements are **restated**, the entity must disclose the restatement and the nature of the error.

  c. **Other required disclosures** include

   1) The effect of the correction on each line item and per-share amount affected for all prior statements presented,

   2) The cumulative effect on retained earnings, and

   3) The disclosures required by **APB 9**, *Reporting the Results of Operations*.

8. According to **SFAS 16**, *Prior Period Adjustments*, items of profit or loss related to **corrections of errors** in prior-period statements are prior-period adjustments. They are debited or credited (net of tax) to **retained earnings** and reported as adjustments in the statement of changes in equity or in the statement of retained earnings. They are not included in net income. Prior-period adjustments reported in **single-period statements** are adjustments of the opening balance of retained earnings.

  a. According to **APB 9**, *Reporting the Results of Operations*, if **comparative statements** are presented, corresponding adjustments should be made to the amounts of net income (and its components) and retained earnings balances (and other affected balances) for all periods reported.

9. **Error Analysis.** A correcting journal entry combines the reversal of the error with the correct entry. Thus, it requires a determination of the journal entry originally recorded, event or transaction that occurred, and correct journal entry.

  a. EXAMPLE: If the purchase of a fixed asset on account had been debited to purchases:

| Incorrect Entry | Correct Entry | Correcting Entry |
|---|---|---|
| Purchases | Fixed asset | Fixed asset |
|  Payables |  Payables |  Purchases |

   1) If cash had been incorrectly credited:

| Incorrect Entry | Correct Entry | Correcting Entry |
|---|---|---|
| Purchases | Fixed asset | Fixed Asset |
|  Cash |  Payables |  Cash |
| | |  Purchases |
| | |  Payables |

  b. Error analysis addresses whether an error affects prior-period statements, the timing of error detection, whether comparative statements are presented, and whether the error is counterbalancing.

   1) An error affecting **prior-period statements** may or may not affect net income. For example, misclassifying an item as a gain rather than a revenue does not affect income and is readily correctable. No prior-period adjustment to retained earnings is required.

2) An error that affects prior-period net income is **counterbalancing** if it self-corrects over two periods. For example, understating ending inventory for one period (and the beginning inventory of the next period) understates the net income and retained earnings of the first period but overstates the net income and retained earnings of the next period by the same amount (assuming no tax changes). However, despite the self-correction, the financial statements remain misstated. They are restated if **presented comparatively** in a later period.

   a) An example of a **non-counterbalancing** error is a misstatement of depreciation. Such an error does not self-correct over two periods. Thus, a prior-period adjustment will be necessary.

   b) In principle, a counterbalancing error requires no correcting entry if detection occurs two or more periods afterward (assuming no tax changes). Earlier detection necessitates a correcting entry.

10. Stop and review! You have completed the outline for this subunit. Study multiple-choice questions 33 through 51 beginning on page 735.

## 18.6 EARLY EXTINGUISHMENT OF DEBT

1. **APB 26**, *Early Extinguishment of Debt*, applies to all extinguishments, regardless of the means used, except troubled debt restructurings. It states that all extinguishments of debt before scheduled maturities are fundamentally alike and should be accounted for similarly. **SFAS 140**, *Accounting for Transfers and Servicing of Financial Assets and Extinguishments of Liabilities*, defines the transactions that extinguish liabilities.

   a. Gains or losses are **recognized** in income in the period of extinguishment. They are included in income from continuing operations unless a pronouncement specifically states otherwise, or the evidence clearly supports classification as extraordinary. The rationale for current recognition is that such gains or losses reflect a change in the value of the old debt caused by a change in the market rate of interest not recognized in the accounts.

   b. The **net carrying amount** is the amount due at maturity, adjusted for unamortized premium, discount, and cost of issuance.

   c. The reacquisition price is the amount paid on extinguishment, including a call premium and miscellaneous costs of reacquisition. If extinguishment is by a direct exchange of new securities (a **refunding**), the reacquisition price is equal to the total **present value** of the new securities. However, debt-equity swaps are rare because they are no longer tax-exempt.

2. The **gain or loss** is measured by the difference between the proceeds paid (including any call premium and miscellaneous costs of reacquisition) and the carrying amount of the debt.

   a. The carrying amount of the debt is equal to the face amount plus any unamortized premium or minus any unamortized discount.

   b. In addition, any **unamortized issue costs** are considered in effect a reduction of the carrying amount even though they are accounted for separately from the bond discount or premium.

3. An **in-substance defeasance** is an arrangement in which an entity places essentially risk-free assets in an irrevocable trust to provide cash flows approximating the interest and principal payments due on the debt to be extinguished.

   a. An in-substance defeasance does not meet the **criteria for derecognition** of debt stated in SFAS 140. The liability is still outstanding, and the debtor has not obtained a legal release from being the primary obligor. Under SFAS 140, a debtor derecognizes a liability only if it has been extinguished. One of the following must occur to extinguish a liability:

      1) The debtor pays the creditor and is relieved of its obligation with respect to the liability. Paying the creditor includes delivering cash, financial assets, goods or services, or reacquiring the outstanding debt securities.

      2) The debtor is legally released from being the primary obligor, either judicially or by the creditor.

         a) However, if the release is on the condition that the original debtor become secondarily liable as a guarantor, a guarantee obligation should be recognized at fair value. This amount reduces the gain or increases the loss on the extinguishment.

4. Stop and review! You have completed the outline for this subunit. Study multiple-choice questions 52 through 55 beginning on page 741.

## 18.7 CORE CONCEPTS

### Segment Reporting

- **Reportable segments** are those that provide information about the different types of business activities of the entity and the economic environment in which it operates.
- A business unit should be **treated as a reportable segment** if (a) its reported revenues are at least 10% of the combined revenues of all segments, (b) its assets are at least 10% of the combined assets of all operating segments, or (c) the absolute amount of reported profit or loss is at least 10% of the greater of combined segments that reported a loss or combined segments that did not report a loss.

### Foreign Currency Issues

- An entity's **functional currency** is the currency of the primary economic environment in which it operates.
- Financial statement amounts must be measured in the functional currency (i.e., the currency of the country where the subsidiary is doing business) then **translated** using a **current exchange rate** into the **domestic currency** of the parent.
- When the **exchange rate** between the functional and domestic currencies **changes** before a foreign-denominated receivable or payable is settled, a **gain or loss** must be included in net income in the period of the change.

### Discontinued Operations

- When a segment has been **disposed of** or is classified as **held for sale**, the results of its operations are **reported separately** in the income statement after results from continuing operations.
- The operating results of the disposed segment include any **loss for a writedown** or **gain for a writeup** to fair value of a long-lived asset.

### Extraordinary Items

- An extraordinary item is one that is **unusual in nature** and **infrequent in occurrence**.
- Extraordinary items are **reported separately** in the income statement, net of applicable taxes, after results of discontinued operations.

## Accounting Changes and Error Corrections

- ■  An **accounting change** is (a) a change in accounting principle, (b) a change in the application of a principle, or (c) a change to a generally accepted principle when the principle previously used is no longer generally accepted.
- ■  An accounting change is reported in the **balance sheet** by adjusting the **beginning balances** of assets and liabilities (of the earliest period presented) for the effect of the change **as if the change had been in effect** in earlier periods.  (Formerly, the cumulative effect of an accounting change was presented in the income statement.)
- ■  **Prior-period adjustments** are debited or credited, net of tax, to retained earnings and reported as adjustments in the statement of retained earnings.

## Early Extinguishment of Debt

- ■  **Gains or losses** on the extinguishment of debt before maturity are **recognized in income** in the period of the extinguishment.

## QUESTIONS

### 18.1  Segment Reporting

**1.**  SFAS 131, *Disclosures about Segments of an Enterprise and Related Information*, requires reporting of information about

- A.  Industry segments.
- B.  Operating segments.
- C.  For-profit and not-for-profit organizations.
- D.  Public and nonpublic enterprises.

Answer (B) is correct.  *(Publisher)*
**REQUIRED:**  The reporting required by SFAS 131.
**DISCUSSION:**  The objective of segment reporting is to provide information about the different types of business activities of the entity and the economic environments in which it operates.  This information is reported on an operating segment basis.  SFAS 131 defines an operating segment as "a component of an enterprise that engages in business activities from which it may earn revenues and incur expenses (including revenues and expenses relating to transactions with other components of the same enterprise), whose operating results are regularly reviewed by the enterprise's chief operating decision maker to make decisions about resources to be allocated to the segment and assess its performance, and for which discrete financial information is available."  A reportable segment is one that satisfies the foregoing definition and also meets one of three quantitative thresholds.
    Answer (A) is incorrect because SFAS 131 superseded SFAS 14, which required line-of-business information classified by industry segment.  Instead, SFAS 131 defines segments based on the entity's internal organization.  Answer (C) is incorrect because SFAS 131 applies to public business enterprises.  Answer (D) is incorrect because SFAS 131 applies to public business enterprises.

**2.**  Company M has identified four operating segments.  Which of the following segments meet(s) the quantitative threshold for reported profit or loss?

| Segment | Reported Profit (Loss) |
|---------|------------------------|
| S | $   90,000 |
| T | (100,000) |
| U | 910,000 |
| V | (420,000) |

- A.  Segment U only.
- B.  Segments U and V.
- C.  Segments T, U, and V.
- D.  Segments S, T, U, and V.

Answer (C) is correct.  *(Publisher)*
**REQUIRED:**  The segment(s) meeting the quantitative threshold for reported profit or loss.
**DISCUSSION:**  Under SFAS 131, information must be reported separately about an operating segment that reaches one of three quantitative thresholds.  Under the profit or loss test, if the absolute amount of the reported profit or loss equals at least 10% of the greater, in absolute amount, of (1) the combined profit of all operating segments not reporting a loss or (2) the combined loss of all operating segments reporting a loss, the segment meets the threshold.  Segments T, U, and V are reportable segments.  As shown below, the sum of the reported profits of S and U ($1,000,000) is greater than the sum of the losses of T and V ($520,000).  Consequently, the test criterion is $100,000 ($1,000,000 × 10%).

| Segment | Reported Profit | Reported Loss |
|---------|-----------------|---------------|
| S | $   90,000 | $            0 |
| T | 0 | 100,000 |
| U | 910,000 | 0 |
| V | 0 | 420,000 |
|   | $1,000,000 | $520,000 |

**3.** In accordance with SFAS 131, *Disclosures about Segments of an Enterprise and Related Information*, what ordinarily must be reported for each reportable segment?

    A. Segment cash flow.

    B. Interest revenue net of interest expense.

    C. A measure of profit or loss.

    D. External revenues from export sales if they are 10% or more of consolidated sales.

Answer (C) is correct. *(Publisher)*
    **REQUIRED:** The item ordinarily reported for each reportable segment.
    **DISCUSSION:** For each reportable segment, an enterprise must report a measure of profit or loss, certain items included in the determination of that profit or loss, total segment assets, and certain related items. Segment cash flow need not be reported.
    Answer (A) is incorrect because segment cash flow need not be reported. Answer (B) is incorrect because interest revenue and expense are reported separately unless a majority of revenues derive from interest and the chief operating decision maker relies primarily on net interest revenue for assessing segment performance and allocating resources. Answer (D) is incorrect because, if practicable, geographic information is reported for external revenues attributed to the home country and to all foreign countries in total. If external revenues attributed to a foreign country are material, they are disclosed separately.

**4.** For each of the following groups of customers, purchases amounted to 10% or more of the revenue of a publicly held company. For which of these groups must the company disclose information about major customers?

    A. Federal governmental agencies, 6%; state governmental agencies, 4%.

    B. French governmental agencies, 6%; German governmental agencies, 4%.

    C. Parent company, 6%; subsidiary of parent company, 4%.

    D. Federal governmental agencies, 6%; foreign governmental agencies, 4%.

Answer (C) is correct. *(Publisher)*
    **REQUIRED:** The set of circumstances requiring disclosure about major customers.
    **DISCUSSION:** For purposes of SFAS 131, a group of customers under common control must be regarded as a single customer in determining whether 10% or more of the revenue of an enterprise is derived from sales to any single customer. A parent and a subsidiary are under common control, and they should be regarded as a single customer. Major customer disclosure is required because total combined revenue is 10% (6% + 4%).

**5.** Correy Corp. and its divisions are engaged solely in manufacturing operations. The following data (consistent with prior years' data) pertain to the industries in which operations were conducted for the year ended December 31:

| Operating Segment | Total Revenue | Profit | Assets at 12/31 |
|---|---|---|---|
| A | $10,000,000 | $1,750,000 | $20,000,000 |
| B | 8,000,000 | 1,400,000 | 17,500,000 |
| C | 6,000,000 | 1,200,000 | 12,500,000 |
| D | 3,000,000 | 550,000 | 7,500,000 |
| E | 4,250,000 | 675,000 | 7,000,000 |
| F | 1,500,000 | 225,000 | 3,000,000 |
| | $32,750,000 | $5,800,000 | $67,500,000 |

In its segment information for the year, how many reportable operating segments does Correy have?

    A. Three.

    B. Four.

    C. Five.

    D. Six.

Answer (C) is correct. *(CPA, adapted)*
    **REQUIRED:** The number of reportable operating segments.
    **DISCUSSION:** Four operating segments (A, B, C, and E) have revenue equal to or greater than 10% of the $32,750,000 total revenue of all operating segments. These four segments also have profit equal to or greater than 10% of the $5,800,000 total profit of all operating segments that did not report a loss. Five segments (A, B, C, D, and E) have assets greater than 10% of the $67,500,000 total assets of all operating segments. Because an operating segment is reportable if it meets one or more of the three tests established by SFAS 131, Correy Corp. has five reportable operating segments for the year.

**6.** Terra Co.'s total revenues from its three operating segments were as follows:

| Segment | Sales to External Customers | Intersegment Sales | Total Revenues |
|---|---|---|---|
| Lion | $ 70,000 | $ 30,000 | $100,000 |
| Monk | 22,000 | 4,000 | 26,000 |
| Nevi | 8,000 | 16,000 | 24,000 |
| Combined | $100,000 | $ 50,000 | $150,000 |
| Elimination | – | (50,000) | (50,000) |
| Consolidated | $100,000 | $ – | $100,000 |

Which operating segment(s) is (are) deemed to be (a) reportable segment(s)?

A. None.

B. Lion only.

C. Lion and Monk only.

D. Lion, Monk, and Nevi.

Answer (D) is correct. *(CPA, adapted)*
**REQUIRED:** The reportable operating segments in conformity with the revenue test.
**DISCUSSION:** For the purpose of identifying reportable operating segments, SFAS 131 defines revenue to include sales to external customers and intersegment sales or transfers. In accordance with the revenue test, a reportable operating segment has revenue equal to 10% or more of the total combined revenue, internal and external, of all of the enterprise's operating segments. Given combined revenues of $150,000, Lion, Monk, and Nevi all qualify because their revenues are at least $15,000 ($150,000 × 10%).

**7.** Hyde Corp. has three manufacturing divisions, each of which has been determined to be a reportable operating segment. In the year just ended, Clay division had sales of $3,000,000, which was 25% of Hydes total sales, and had traceable operating costs of $1,900,000. Hyde incurred operating costs of $500,000 that were not directly traceable to any of the divisions. In addition, Hyde incurred interest expense of $300,000. The calculation of the measure of segment profit or loss reviewed by Hyde's chief operating decision maker does not include an allocation of interest expense incurred by Hyde. However, it does include traceable costs. It also includes nontraceable operating costs allocated based on the ratio of divisional sales to aggregate sales. In reporting segment information, what amount should be shown as Clay's profit for the year?

A. $875,000

B. $900,000

C. $975,000

D. $1,100,000

Answer (C) is correct. *(CPA, adapted)*
**REQUIRED:** The amount to be shown as profit for a reportable operating segment.
**DISCUSSION:** The amount of a segment item reported, such as profit or loss, is the measure reported to the chief operating decision maker for purposes of making resource allocation and performance evaluation decisions regarding the segment. However, SFAS 131 does not stipulate the specific items included in the calculation of that measure. Consequently, allocation of revenues, expenses, gains, and losses are included in the determination of reported segment profit or loss only if they are included in the measure of segment profit or loss reviewed by the chief operating decision maker. Given that this measure for Clay reflects traceable costs and an allocation of nontraceable operating costs, the profit is calculated by subtracting the $1,900,000 traceable costs and the $125,000 ($500,000 × 25%) of the allocated costs from the division's sales of $3,000,000. The profit for the division is $975,000.

| | |
|---|---|
| Sales | $ 3,000,000 |
| Traceable costs | (1,900,000) |
| Allocated costs (25%) | (125,000) |
| Profit | $ 975,000 |

Answer (A) is incorrect because no amount of interest expense should be included in the calculation. Answer (B) is incorrect because Clay's share of interest expense ($300,000 × 25% = $75,000) is excluded from the calculation of profit. Answer (D) is incorrect because the allocated nontraceable operating costs must also be subtracted.

## 18.2 Foreign Currency Issues

**8.** SFAS 52, *Foreign Currency Translation*, requires the application of the functional currency concept. Before the financial statements of a foreign subsidiary may be translated into the parent company's currency, the functional currency of the foreign subsidiary must be determined. All of the following factors indicate that a foreign subsidiary's functional currency is the foreign currency rather than the parent's currency except when

   A. Its cash flows are primarily in foreign currency and do not affect the parent's cash flows.

   B. Its sales prices are responsive to exchange rate changes and to international competition.

   C. Its labor, material, and other costs are obtained in the local market of the foreign subsidiary.

   D. Its financing is primarily obtained from local foreign sources and from the subsidiary's operations.

Answer (B) is correct. *(CMA, adapted)*
**REQUIRED:** The factor not indicating that a foreign subsidiary's functional currency is the foreign currency rather than the parent's currency.
**DISCUSSION:** SFAS 52 states that the functional currency is that of the primary economic environment in which an entity operates. Thus, it is usually the currency in which cash is generated and expended by the entity whose financial statements are being translated. Indications that the subsidiary's currency is the functional currency include the following: Its cash flows are primarily in that foreign currency, they do not affect the parent's cash flows, labor and materials are obtained in the local market of the foreign subsidiary, subsidiary financing is obtained from local foreign sources and from the subsidiary's operations, and few intercompany transactions take place between the foreign subsidiary and the parent. However, sales prices that are responsive to exchange rate fluctuations and international competition suggest that the functional currency is the parent's currency.

**9.** The economic effects of a change in foreign exchange rates on a relatively self-contained and integrated operation within a foreign country relate to the net investment by the reporting enterprise in that operation. Consequently, translation adjustments that arise from the consolidation of that operation

   A. Directly affect cash flows but should not be reflected in income.

   B. Directly affect cash flows and should be reflected in income.

   C. Do not directly affect cash flows and should not be reflected in income.

   D. Do not directly affect cash flows but should be reflected in income.

Answer (C) is correct. *(Publisher)*
**REQUIRED:** The true statement about translation adjustments arising from consolidation of a self-contained foreign operation with its U.S. parent/investor.
**DISCUSSION:** SFAS 52, *Foreign Currency Translation*, concludes that foreign currency translation adjustments for a foreign operation that is relatively self-contained and integrated within its environment do not affect cash flows of the reporting enterprise and should be excluded from net income. When an operation is relatively self-contained, the cash generated and expended by the entity is normally in the currency of the foreign country, and that currency is deemed to be the operation's functional currency.
Answer (A) is incorrect because, when an operation is relatively self-contained, the assumption is that translation adjustments do not affect cash flows. Answer (B) is incorrect because, when an operation is relatively self-contained, the assumption is that translation adjustments do not affect cash flows. Additionally, translation adjustments should be included in other comprehensive income, not recognized in income. Answer (D) is incorrect because translation adjustments should be included in other comprehensive income, not recognized in income.

**10.** If an entity's books of account are not maintained in its functional currency, SFAS 52, *Foreign Currency Translation*, requires remeasurement into the functional currency prior to the translation process. An item that should be remeasured by use of the current exchange rate is

   A. An investment in bonds to be held until maturity.

   B. A plant asset and the associated accumulated depreciation.

   C. A patent and the associated accumulated amortization.

   D. The revenue from a long-term construction contract.

Answer (A) is correct. *(CMA, adapted)*
**REQUIRED:** The item that should be remeasured into the functional currency using the current exchange rate.
**DISCUSSION:** The current rate should be used for all items except common nonmonetary balance sheet accounts and their related revenues, expenses, gains, and losses, which are remeasured at historical rates. Thus, most monetary items, such as an investment in bonds, are remeasured at the current exchange rate.
Answer (B) is incorrect because plant assets and marketable equity securities are not monetary assets. They should be remeasured at historical rates. Answer (C) is incorrect because a patent is remeasured at historical rates. Answer (D) is incorrect because the revenue from a long-term construction contract is one of the exceptions for which the current rate is not to be used.

**11.** SFAS 52 requires that, in a highly inflationary economy, the financial statements of a foreign entity be remeasured as if the functional currency were the reporting currency. For this requirement, a highly inflationary economy is one that has

A. An inflation rate of at least 33% in the most recent past year.

B. An inflation rate of at least 50% in the most recent past year.

C. An inflation rate of at least 100% in the most recent past year.

D. A cumulative inflation rate of at least 100% over a 3-year period.

Answer (D) is correct. *(CMA, adapted)*
   **REQUIRED:** The definition of a highly inflationary economy.
   **DISCUSSION:** SFAS 52 recognized that the currency in a highly inflationary economy is not stable enough to be a functional currency. Instead, the more stable currency of the parent corporation should be used as the functional currency. A highly inflationary economy has a cumulative inflation rate over a 3-year period of at least 100%.

**12.** SFAS 52 states that transaction gains and losses have direct cash flow effects when foreign-denominated monetary assets are settled in amounts greater or less than the functional currency equivalent of the original transactions. These transaction gains and losses should be reflected in income

A. At the date the transaction originated.

B. On a retroactive basis.

C. In the period the exchange rate changes.

D. Only at the year-end balance sheet date.

Answer (C) is correct. *(CMA, adapted)*
   **REQUIRED:** The time when foreign currency transaction gains and losses should be reflected in income.
   **DISCUSSION:** A foreign currency transaction is one whose terms are denominated in a currency other than the entity's functional currency. When a foreign currency transaction gives rise to a receivable or a payable that is fixed in terms of the amount of foreign currency to be received or paid, a change in the exchange rate between the functional currency and the currency in which the transaction is denominated results in a gain or loss that ordinarily should be included as a component of income from continuing operations in the period in which the exchange rate changes.
   Answer (A) is incorrect because the extent of any gain or loss cannot be known at the date of the original transaction. Answer (B) is incorrect because retroactive recognition is not permitted. Answer (D) is incorrect because gains and losses are to be recognized in the period of the rate change.

**13.** FASB 52, *Foreign Currency Translation*, defines foreign currency transactions as those denominated in other than an entity's functional currency. Transaction gains and losses are reported as

A. Extraordinary items.

B. Adjustments to the beginning balance of retained earnings.

C. A component of equity.

D. A component of income from continuing operations.

Answer (D) is correct. *(CMA, adapted)*
   **REQUIRED:** The proper treatment of foreign currency transaction gains (losses).
   **DISCUSSION:** When a foreign currency transaction gives rise to a receivable or a payable, a change in the exchange rate between the measurement currency and the currency in which the transaction is denominated is a foreign currency transaction gain (loss) that should be included as a component of income from continuing operations.
   Answer (A) is incorrect because transaction gains (losses) are not so unusual as to warrant extraordinary status. Answer (B) is incorrect because adjustments to retained earnings are made only for prior-period adjustments, and transaction gains (losses) do not meet the criteria for such treatment. Answer (C) is incorrect because foreign currency translation gains and losses (not transaction gains and losses) are reported in other comprehensive income, a component of equity.

**14.** On September 22, 20X1, Yumi Corp. purchased merchandise from an unaffiliated foreign company for 10,000 units of the foreign company's local currency. On that date, the spot rate was $.55. Yumi paid the bill in full on March 20, 20X2, when the spot rate was $.65. The spot rate was $.70 on December 31, 20X1. What amount should Yumi report as a foreign currency transaction loss in its income statement for the year ended December 31, 20X1?

    A.  $0

    B.  $500

    C.  $1,000

    D.  $1,500

Answer (D) is correct. *(CPA, adapted)*
    **REQUIRED:** The amount of foreign currency transaction loss to be reported in the income statement.
    **DISCUSSION:** The FASB requires that a receivable or payable denominated in a foreign currency be adjusted to its current exchange rate at each balance sheet date. The resulting gain or loss should ordinarily be reflected in current income. It is the difference between the spot rate on the date the transaction originates and the spot rate at year-end. Thus, the 20X1 transaction loss for Yumi Corp. is $1,500 [10,000 units × ($0.55 – $0.70)].
    Answer (A) is incorrect because a loss resulted when the spot rate increased. Answer (B) is incorrect because $500 results from using the spot rates at 12/31/X1 and 3/20/X2. Answer (C) is incorrect because $1,000 results from using the spot rates at 9/22/X1 and 3/20/X2.

**15.** SFAS 52, *Foreign Currency Translation*, requires the use of different methods to translate or remeasure foreign currency financial statements. When the foreign affiliate's functional currency is not the reporting currency of the parent (or investor), the

    A.  Current/noncurrent method should be used to translate the foreign affiliate's financial statements.

    B.  Monetary/nonmonetary method should be used to translate the foreign affiliate's financial statements.

    C.  Temporal method should be used to remeasure the foreign affiliate's financial statements.

    D.  Current exchange rate method should be used to translate the foreign affiliate's financial statements.

Answer (D) is correct. *(CMA, adapted)*
    **REQUIRED:** The method that should be used to translate or remeasure when the foreign affiliate's functional currency is not the reporting currency of the parent.
    **DISCUSSION:** SFAS 52 requires that the affiliate's statements first be remeasured into its functional currency. Then, a current exchange rate is used to translate the foreign entity's financial statements into U.S. dollars. This method applies the current exchange rate to all elements of the financial statements. The resulting adjustments are reported in other comprehensive income to be recognized in income upon the sale or liquidation of the foreign entity.
    Answer (A) is incorrect because SFAS 52 requires translation using a current exchange rate. Noncurrent (historical) rates are used in the remeasurement of certain items. Answer (B) is incorrect because consideration of whether items are monetary or nonmonetary is a factor in remeasurement, not translation. Thus, nonmonetary balance sheet items and related revenues and expenses are remeasured at historical exchange rates. Answer (C) is incorrect because, although the temporal method should be used for remeasurement, the question does not state whether the financial statements are presented in a currency other than the functional currency.

**16.** Unrealized foreign currency gains and losses included in the other comprehensive income section of a consolidated balance sheet represent

    A.  Foreign currency transaction gains and losses.

    B.  The amount resulting from translating foreign currency financial statements into the reporting currency.

    C.  Remeasurement gains and losses.

    D.  Accounting not in accordance with generally accepted accounting principles.

Answer (B) is correct. *(CMA, adapted)*
    **REQUIRED:** The meaning of unrealized foreign currency gains and losses reported as other comprehensive income.
    **DISCUSSION:** Unrealized foreign currency gains and losses in the other comprehensive income section of the balance sheet can arise from unrealized gains and losses on available-for-sale securities, from certain hedging transactions (cash flow hedges), and from translation of foreign currency financial statements. SFAS 52 requires that foreign currency translation adjustments resulting from translation of an entity's financial statements into the reporting currency be reported on the balance sheet in other comprehensive income. Accumulated currency translation gains or losses remain in that section until the foreign entity is sold or liquidated. At that time, translation gains or losses will be recognized in the income statement.
    Answer (A) is incorrect because transaction gains and losses (as opposed to translation gains and losses) are recognized in the income statement as they occur. Answer (C) is incorrect because remeasurement gains and losses are included in net income. Answer (D) is incorrect because SFAS 52 states the GAAP for reporting of translation adjustments.

**17.** When restating financial statements originally recorded in a foreign currency,

A. Income taxes are ignored in calculating and disclosing the results of foreign currency translations.

B. A component of annual net income, "Adjustment from Foreign Currency Translation," should be presented in the notes to the financial statements or in a separate schedule.

C. The aggregate transaction gain or loss included in net income should be disclosed in the financial statements or in the notes to the financial statements.

D. The financial statements should be adjusted for a rate change that occurs after the financial statement date but prior to statement issuance.

Answer (C) is correct. *(CMA, adapted)*
**REQUIRED:** The true statement about restating financial statements originally recorded in a foreign currency.
**DISCUSSION:** SFAS 52 adopts the functional currency translation approach. Translation adjustments resulting from translating the functional currency into U.S. dollars are not reported in the income statement but are accumulated in a separate shareholders' equity account to be recognized in income upon the sale or liquidation of the foreign entity. However, foreign currency transaction gains or losses are ordinarily recognized in the income statement of the period in which the exchange rate changes. Accordingly, the aggregate transaction gain or loss included in earnings shall be disclosed.

Answer (A) is incorrect because allocation of income tax expense is required, including those income taxes related to translation adjustments and those transaction gains and losses recorded in a separate component of equity. Answer (B) is incorrect because the adjustment for foreign currency translation is reported in other comprehensive income. Answer (D) is incorrect because an enterprise's financial statements are not adjusted for rate changes after their effective date or after the date of foreign currency statements of a foreign entity if they are consolidated, combined, or accounted for under the equity method in the enterprise's financial statements.

**18.** Prior to SFAS 52, there was significant disagreement among informed observers regarding the basic nature, information content, and meaning of results produced by various methods of translating amounts from foreign currencies into the reporting currency. SFAS 52 directs that organizations

A. Change the accounting model to recognize currently the effects of all changing prices in the primary statements.

B. Defer any recognition of changing currency prices until they are realized by an actual exchange of foreign currency into the reporting currency.

C. Recognize currently the effect of changing currency prices on the carrying amounts of designated foreign assets and liabilities.

D. Recognize currently the effect of changing currency prices on the carrying amounts of all foreign assets, liabilities, revenues, expenses, gains, and losses.

Answer (D) is correct. *(CMA, adapted)*
**REQUIRED:** The true statement about the requirements of SFAS 52.
**DISCUSSION:** The elements of the financial statements of separate entities within an enterprise must be consolidated if the performance, financial position, and cash flows of the enterprise are to be presented. If those statements are in different currencies, they must be translated into the reporting currency. According to SFAS 52, the functional currency translation approach is appropriate for use in accounting for and reporting the financial results and relationships of foreign subsidiaries in consolidated statements. It involves identifying the functional currency of the entity (the currency of the primary economic environment in which the entity operates), measuring all elements of the financial statements in the functional currency, and using a current exchange rate for translation from the functional currency to the reporting currency.

Answer (A) is incorrect because the primary financial statements are based on historical cost and nominal dollar accounting. They do not reflect changes in general or specific price levels, except for changes in foreign exchange rates. Answer (B) is incorrect because SFAS 52 ordinarily requires immediate recognition of changes in exchange rates. Answer (C) is incorrect because SFAS 52 also applies to revenues, expenses, gains, and losses.

**19.** The Brinjac Company owns a foreign subsidiary. Included among the subsidiary's liabilities for the year just ended are 400,000 local currency units (LCUs) of revenue received in advance, recorded when $.50 was the dollar equivalent per LCU, and a deferred tax liability for 187,500 LCUs, recognized when $.40 was the dollar equivalent per LCU. The rate of exchange in effect at year-end was $.35 per LCU. If the accounting is in accordance with SFAS 52 and SFAS 109 and the dollar is the functional currency, what total should be included for these two liabilities on Brinjac's consolidated balance sheet at year-end?

A. $205,625

B. $215,000

C. $265,625

D. $275,000

Answer (D) is correct.  *(C.J. Skender)*

**REQUIRED:** The total of two liability accounts of a foreign subsidiary in the consolidated statements.

**DISCUSSION:** When a foreign entity's functional currency is the U.S. dollar, the financial statements of the entity recorded in a foreign currency must be remeasured in terms of the U.S. dollar. In accordance with SFAS 52, revenue received in advance (deferred income) is considered a nonmonetary balance sheet item and is translated at the applicable historical rate (400,000 LCUs × $.50 per LCU = $200,000). Deferred charges and credits (except policy acquisition costs for life insurance companies) are also remeasured at historical exchange rates. Deferred taxes were formerly not subject to this rule, but SFAS 109 amended SFAS 52 to eliminate the exception. Consequently, the deferred tax liability (a deferred credit) should be remeasured at the historical rate (187,500 LCUs × $.40 per LCU) = $75,000). The total for these two liabilities is therefore $275,000 ($200,000 + $75,000).

Answer (A) is incorrect because $205,625 results from applying the year-end rate to the total liabilities. Answer (B) is incorrect because the historical, not current, rate should be used to remeasure the deferred income. Answer (C) is incorrect because the historical rate is used to remeasure nonmonetary balance sheet items, including deferred tax assets and liabilities.

**20.** Certain balance sheet accounts of a foreign subsidiary of Rowan, Inc., on December 31 have been translated into U.S. dollars as follows:

|  | Translated at | |
| --- | --- | --- |
|  | Current Rates | Historical Rates |
| Note receivable, long-term | $240,000 | $200,000 |
| Prepaid rent | 85,000 | 80,000 |
| Patent | 150,000 | 170,000 |
|  | $475,000 | $450,000 |

The subsidiary's functional currency is the currency of the country in which it is located. What total amount should be included in Rowan's December 31 consolidated balance sheet for the above accounts?

A. $450,000

B. $455,000

C. $475,000

D. $495,000

Answer (C) is correct.  *(CPA, adapted)*

**REQUIRED:** The total translated amount to be included in the consolidated balance sheet.

**DISCUSSION:** When the currency used to prepare a foreign entity's financial statements is its functional currency, SFAS 52 specifies that the current rate method be used to translate the foreign entity's financial statements into the reporting currency. The translation gains and losses arising from applying this method are included in other comprehensive income in the owners' equity section of the consolidated balance sheet. Thus, Rowan's listed assets translated at current rates should be included in the consolidated balance sheet at $475,000.

Answer (A) is incorrect because $450,000 reflects translation at historical rates. Answer (B) is incorrect because the note and patent are translated at historical rates. Answer (D) is incorrect because the patent is translated at historical rates.

**21.** A widely diversified U.S. corporation sold portions of three wholly owned foreign subsidiaries in the same year. The functional currency of each subsidiary was the currency of the country in which it was located. The percentage sold and the amount of the translation adjustment attributable to each subsidiary at the time of sale follow:

| | % Sold | Translation Adjustment |
|---|---|---|
| Sub A | 100% | $90,000 credit |
| Sub B | 50% | 40,000 debit |
| Sub C | 10% | 25,000 debit |

What total amount of the translation adjustment should be reported as part of the gain on sale of the three subsidiaries?

A. $90,000 credit.

B. $70,000 net credit.

C. $67,500 net credit.

D. $0

Answer (C) is correct. *(Publisher)*
**REQUIRED:** The total translation adjustment included in the gain on the sale of subsidiaries.
**DISCUSSION:** FASB Interpretation No. 37, *Accounting for Translation Adjustments upon Sale of Part of an Investment in a Foreign Entity*, clarifies SFAS 52. A pro rata portion of the accumulated translation adjustment attributable to an investment shall be recognized in measuring the gain or loss on the sale of all or part of a company's interest in a foreign entity. Here, the total amount to be reported is a $67,500 net credit [($90,000 × 100%) − ($40,000 × 50%) − ($25,000 × 10%)].
Answer (A) is incorrect because a $90,000 credit fails to consider Subs B and C. Answer (B) is incorrect because a $70,000 net credit fails to consider Sub C. Answer (D) is incorrect because a translation adjustment is recognized as part of the gain on the sale of the subsidiaries.

**22.** A U.S. company and a German company purchased the same stock on the German stock exchange and held the stock for 1 year. The value of the euro weakened against the dollar over this period. Comparing the returns of the two companies, the United States company's return will be

A. Lower.

B. Higher.

C. The same.

D. Indeterminate from the information provided.

Answer (A) is correct. *(CIA, adapted)*
**REQUIRED:** The effect of the exchange rate movement.
**DISCUSSION:** The returns on the stock are presumably paid in euros. Hence, the change in the value of the euro relative to the dollar does not affect the German company's return. However, the weakening of the euro reduces the number of dollars it will buy, and the U.S. company's return in dollars is correspondingly reduced.
Answer (B) is incorrect because the return to the U.S. company is adversely affected by the exchange rate movement. Answer (C) is incorrect because the return to the U.S. company was directly affected by the exchange rate movement, but the return to the German company was not. Answer (D) is incorrect because the return to the U.S. company was directly affected by the exchange rate movement, but the return to the German company was not.

## 18.3 Discontinued Operations

**23.** For the purpose of reporting discontinued operations, a component of an entity is

A. An operating segment or one level below an operating segment.

B. A set of operations and cash flows clearly distinguishable from the rest of the entity for operational and financial reporting purposes.

C. A separate major line of business or class of customer.

D. A significant disposal group.

Answer (B) is correct. *(Publisher)*
**REQUIRED:** The nature of a component of an entity.
**DISCUSSION:** According to SFAS 144, a component of an entity is a set of operations and cash flows clearly distinguishable from the rest of the entity for operational and financial reporting purposes. It may be, but is not limited to, a reportable segment or an operating segment, a reporting unit, a subsidiary, or an asset group. The results of operations of a component that has been disposed of or is classified as held for sale are reported in discontinued operations if (1) its operations and cash flows have been or will be eliminated from the ongoing operations of the entity as a result of the disposal, and (2) the entity will have no significant continuing post-disposal involvement in the component's operations.
Answer (A) is incorrect because the term "component of an entity" was intentionally broadly defined to improve the usefulness of information provided to users by requiring more frequent reporting of discontinued operations. Thus, a component of an entity is not restricted to a reporting unit, that is, an operating segment as defined in SFAS 131 or one level below an operating segment as defined in SFAS 142. Answer (C) is incorrect because, under the pronouncement superseded by SFAS 144, reporting of a discontinued operation was limited to a separate major line of business or class of customer. Answer (D) is incorrect because the criteria for the reporting of discontinued operations does not emphasize either the significance of a component or any quantitative threshold.

**24.** Good Fast Foods (GFF) operates entity-owned stores and has franchise agreements with entrepreneurs in the East, South, and West Regions. During the year, GFF committed to a plan to sell the entity-owned stores in the East and South Regions to its franchisees. These stores are classified as held for sale. In the East Region, GFF will receive future fees based on revenues from the stores and will continue to be significantly involved in post-sale operations. In the South Region, GFF will have no post-sale involvement in the operations of the stores, and their operations and cash flows will be eliminated from GFF's ongoing operations. Assuming that each store to be sold is a component of the entity, GFF is required to report the results of operations of which stores classified as held for sale in discontinued operations?

| | East Region | South Region |
|---|---|---|
| A. | Yes | Yes |
| B. | Yes | No |
| C. | No | Yes |
| D. | No | No |

Answer (C) is correct. *(Publisher)*
**REQUIRED:** The components of the entity, if any, for which the operating results must be reported in discontinued operations.
**DISCUSSION:** The results of operations of a component that has been disposed of or is classified as held for sale are reported in discontinued operations if (1) its operations and cash flows have been or will be eliminated from the ongoing operations of the entity as a result of the disposal and (2) the entity will have no significant continuing post-disposal involvement in the component's operations (SFAS 144). These criteria are met for the stores classified as held for sale in the South Region but not the East Region.

**25.** On May 31, 20X1, Foxco committed to a plan to sell a component of the entity. As a result, the component's operations and cash flows will be eliminated from the entity's operations, and the entity will have no significant continuing post-disposal involvement in the component's operations. For the period January 1 through May 31, 20X1, the component had revenues of $1,000,000 and expenses of $1,600,000. The assets of the component were sold on November 30, 20X1, at a loss for which no tax benefit is available. In its income statement for the year ended December 31, 20X1, how should Foxco report the component's operations from January 1 through May 31, 20X1?

A. $1,000,000 and $1,600,000 should be included with revenues and expenses, respectively, as part of continuing operations.

B. $600,000 should be reported as part of the loss on disposal of a component.

C. $600,000 should be reported as an extraordinary loss.

D. $600,000 should be included in the determination of income or loss from operations of a discontinued component.

Answer (D) is correct. *(Publisher)*
**REQUIRED:** The proper reporting of a loss related to operations of a discontinued component.
**DISCUSSION:** The results of operations of a component that has been disposed of or is classified as held for sale, together with any loss on a writedown to fair value minus cost to sell (or a gain from recoupment thereof), minus applicable income taxes (benefit), should be reported separately as a component of income (discontinued operations) before extraordinary items and the cumulative effect of accounting changes. These results should be reported in the period(s) when they occur. Thus, the operating results of the component from January 1, 20X1 through November 30, 20X1 and the loss on disposal are included in the determination of income or loss from operations of the discontinued component.
Answer (A) is incorrect because discontinued operations should not be reported as part of continuing operations. Answer (B) is incorrect because discontinued operations should be presented in two categories: income or loss from operations of the discontinued component and the applicable income taxes (benefit). The loss on disposal is included in the determination of income or loss from the discontinued component. Answer (C) is incorrect because income or loss from discontinued operations should be reported separately as a component of income before extraordinary items.

**26.** On January 1, 20X2, Janco agreed to sell an operating segment of the business. The sale was consummated on December 31, 20X2 and resulted in a gain on disposal of $800,000. The segment's operations resulted in losses before income tax of $450,000 in 20X2 and $250,000 in 20X1. Janco's income tax rate is 30% for both years, and the criteria for reporting a discontinued operation have been met. In a comparative statement of income for 20X2 and 20X1, under the caption discontinued operations, Janco should report a gain (loss) of

|   | 20X2 | 20X1 |
|---|------|------|
| A. | $245,000 | $(175,000) |
| B. | $245,000 | $0 |
| C. | $(315,000) | $(175,000) |
| D. | $(315,000) | $0 |

Answer (A) is correct. *(CPA, adapted)*

**REQUIRED:** The amounts reported in comparative statements for discontinued operations.

**DISCUSSION:** When a component (e.g., an operating segment) has been disposed of or is classified as held for sale, and the criteria for reporting a discontinued operation have been met, the income statement of a business enterprise for current and prior periods must report its operating results in discontinued operations. The gain from operations of the component for 20X2 equals the $450,000 operating loss for 20X2 plus the $800,000 gain on disposal. The pretax gain is therefore $350,000 ($800,000 – $450,000). The after-tax amount is $245,000 [$350,000 × (1 – 30%)]. Because 20X1 was prior to the time that the component was classified as held for sale, the $125,000 of operating losses would have been reported under income from continuing operations in the 20X1 income statement as originally issued. This loss is now attributable to discontinued operations, and the 20X1 financial statements presented for comparative purposes must be reclassified. In the reclassified 20X1 income statement, the $250,000 pretax loss should be shown as a $175,000 [$250,000 × (1 – 30%)] loss from discontinued operations.

Answer (B) is incorrect because the comparative statement of income for 20X2 and 20X1 should show a loss on discontinued operations for 20X1. Answer (C) is incorrect because an after-tax loss of $315,000 for 20X2 does not consider the gain on disposal. Answer (D) is incorrect because the comparative statement of income for 20X2 and 20X1 should show a loss on discontinued operations for 20X1, and an after-tax loss of $315,000 for 20X2 does not consider the gain on disposal.

**27.** A business enterprise disposed of a component of the entity during its fiscal year that ended on December 31, 20X1. The results of operations of this component were properly reported in discontinued operations. Which of the following adjustments recognized in 20X2 to amounts previously reported in discontinued operations in 20X1 most likely should be reported in continuing operations?

A. The resolution of a contingency involving adjustment of the purchase price as provided for in the terms of the disposal.

B. The resolution of a contingency involving an environmental liability directly related to the predisposal operations of the component.

C. The settlement of a pension benefit obligation to employees affected by the sale of the component at the time of the sale and at the discretion of the employer.

D. The settlement of a pension benefit obligation to employees affected by the sale of the component as a condition of the sale but more than 1 year after the disposal because of the occurrence of unexpected events.

Answer (C) is correct. *(Publisher)*

**REQUIRED:** The adjustment to amounts previously recognized in discontinued operations that most likely should be reported in discontinued operations.

**DISCUSSION:** According to SFAS 144, amounts previously reported in discontinued operations in a prior period may require adjustment in the current period. If such an adjustment is directly related to a prior-period disposal of a component, it is reported in the current income statement as a separate item in discontinued operations, and its nature and amount are disclosed. A settlement of an employee benefit plan obligation is directly related to the disposal given a demonstrated direct cause-and-effect relationship. Moreover, the settlement should occur no later than 1 year after the disposal unless delayed by events or circumstances not within the entity's control. However, if the timing of a settlement is at the discretion of the employer, the mere coincidence that settlement occurred at the time of sale does not, by itself, establish a cause-and-effect relationship. Thus, a discretionary settlement of a pension benefit obligation at the time of sale is the least likely to qualify for reporting in discontinued operations and the most likely to be reported in continuing operations.

Answer (A) is incorrect because the resolution of a contingency involving adjustment of the purchase price as provided for in the terms of the disposal meets the direct-relationship criterion for current reporting of an adjustment in discontinued operations. Answer (B) is incorrect because the resolution of a contingency involving an environmental liability directly related to the predisposal operations of the component meets the direct-relationship criterion for current reporting of an adjustment in discontinued operations. Answer (D) is incorrect because settlement of a pension benefit obligation as a condition of the disposal meets the direct-relationship criterion for current reporting of an adjustment in discontinued operations, even if the settlement occurred more than 1 year after the sale, provided that the delay was the result of events or circumstances beyond the entity's control.

**28.** During January 20X1, Karco agreed to sell a component unit. The sale was completed on January 31, 20X2 and resulted in a gain on disposal of $1,800,000. The component's operating losses were $1,200,000 for 20X1 and $100,000 for the period January 1 through January 31, 20X2. Disregarding income taxes, and assuming that the criteria for reporting a discontinued operation are met, what amount of net gain (loss) should be reported in Karco's comparative 20X2 and 20X1 income statements?

| | 20X2 | 20X1 |
|---|---|---|
| A. | $0 | $500,000 |
| B. | $500,000 | $0 |
| C. | $1,700,000 | $(1,200,000) |
| D. | $1,800,000 | $(1,300,000) |

Answer (C) is correct.  *(Publisher)*
**REQUIRED:** The amounts reported in comparative statements for discontinued operations.
**DISCUSSION:** The results of operations of a component classified as held for sale are reported separately in the income statement under discontinued operations in the periods when they occur. Thus, in its 20X1 income statement, Karco should recognize a $1,200,000 loss. For 20X2, a gain of $1,700,000 should be recognized ($1,800,000 – $100,000).
Answer (A) is incorrect because $500,000 is the net gain for 20X1 and 20X2. However, the results for 20X2 may not be anticipated, and the results for 20X1 should not be deferred. Answer (B) is incorrect because $500,000 is the net gain for 20X1 and 20X2. However, the results for 20X2 may not be anticipated, and the results for 20X1 should not be deferred. Answer (D) is incorrect because the operating loss for January 20X2 should be recognized in 20X2.

## 18.4 Extraordinary Items

**29.** When reporting extraordinary items,

A. Each item (net of tax) is presented on the face of the income statement separately as a component of net income for the period.

B. Each item is presented exclusive of any related income tax.

C. Each item is presented as an unusual item within income from continuing operations.

D. All extraordinary gains or losses that occur in a period are summarized as total gains and total losses, then offset to present the net extraordinary gain or loss.

Answer (A) is correct.  *(CMA, adapted)*
**REQUIRED:** The true statement about the reporting of extraordinary items.
**DISCUSSION:** Extraordinary items should be presented net of tax after discontinued operations. APB 30 states, "Descriptive captions and the amounts for individual extraordinary events or transactions should be presented, preferably on the face of the income statement, if practicable; otherwise, disclosure in related notes is acceptable."
Answer (B) is incorrect because extraordinary items are to be reported net of the related tax effect. Answer (C) is incorrect because extraordinary items are not reported in the continuing operations section of the income statement. Answer (D) is incorrect because each extraordinary item is to be reported separately.

**30.** Which one of the following material events would be classified as an extraordinary item on an income statement?

A. A write-down of inventories.

B. A loss due to the effects of a strike against a major supplier.

C. A gain or loss on the disposal of a portion of the business.

D. A gain or loss from a hurricane in a non-coastal area.

Answer (D) is correct.  *(CMA, adapted)*
**REQUIRED:** The event classified as an extraordinary item on the income statement.
**DISCUSSION:** APB 30 gives examples of certain transactions that ordinarily are not to be considered extraordinary items. These include write-downs of receivables and inventories, translation of foreign exchange, disposal of a component of an entity, disposal of productive assets, the effects of strikes, and the adjustments of accruals on long-term contracts. A gain or loss from a hurricane is normally an extraordinary item, particularly if the company is located in a non-coastal area.
Answer (A) is incorrect because APB 30 specifically excludes a write-down of inventories from the definition of extraordinary items. Answer (B) is incorrect because APB 30 specifically excludes a loss due to the effects of a strike against a major supplier from the definition of extraordinary items. Answer (C) is incorrect because APB 30 specifically excludes a gain or loss on the disposal of a portion of the business from the definition of extraordinary items.

**31.** On January 1, 2006, Hart, Inc. redeemed its 15-year bonds of $500,000 par value for 102. They were originally issued on January 1, 1994 at 98 with a maturity date of January 1, 2009. The bond issue costs relating to this transaction were $20,000. Hart amortizes discounts, premiums, and bond issue costs using the straight-line method. The results of using this method are not materially different from the results of using the effective interest method. What amount of loss should Hart recognize on the redemption of these bonds?

A. $16,000

B. $12,000

C. $10,000

D. $0

Answer (A) is correct. *(CPA, adapted)*
**REQUIRED:** The loss on the redemption of bonds.
**DISCUSSION:** The gain or loss on the retirement of debt is equal to the difference between the proceeds paid and the carrying amount of the debt. The carrying amount of the debt is equal to the face amount plus any unamortized premium or minus any unamortized discount. In addition, any unamortized issue costs are considered, in effect, a reduction of the carrying amount, even though they are accounted for separately from the bond discount or premium. The unamortized discount is $2,000 {3 ÷ 15 × [$500,000 × (1 − 98%)]}, and the unamortized bond issue costs equal $4,000 (3 ÷ 15 × $20,000)]. Hence, the effective carrying amount is $494,000 ($500,000 − $2,000 − $4,000), and the loss on this early extinguishment of debt is $16,000 [($500,000 redemption price × 102%) − $494,000].
Answer (B) is incorrect because $12,000 does not consider the issue costs. Answer (C) is incorrect because $10,000 does not consider the issue costs or the discount. Answer (D) is incorrect because a loss should be recognized.

**32.** Strand, Inc. incurred the following infrequent losses during the year:

● A $90,000 write-down of equipment leased to others

● A $50,000 adjustment of accruals on long-term contracts

● A $75,000 write-off of obsolete inventory

In its current year income statement, what amount should Strand report as total infrequent losses that are not considered extraordinary?

A. $215,000

B. $165,000

C. $140,000

D. $125,000

Answer (A) is correct. *(CPA, adapted)*
**REQUIRED:** The amount to be reported as total infrequent losses not considered extraordinary.
**DISCUSSION:** To be classified as an extraordinary item, a transaction must be both unusual in nature and infrequent in occurrence in the environment in which the business operates. APB 30 specifies six items that ordinarily are not considered extraordinary. These items include the write-down of equipment, the adjustment of accruals on long-term contracts, and the write-off of obsolete inventory. Thus, Strand should report $215,000 ($90,000 + $50,000 + $75,000) of total infrequent losses as a separate component of income from continuing operations.
Answer (B) is incorrect because $165,000 improperly excludes the adjustment of accruals. Answer (C) is incorrect because $140,000 improperly excludes the write-off of inventory. Answer (D) is incorrect because $125,000 improperly excludes the write-down of equipment.

## 18.5 Accounting Changes and Error Corrections

**33.** Jordan Company signed a new $136,800 3-year lease beginning March 1, 20X1 for a storage facility for finished goods inventory. Jordan recorded the first year's payment of $45,600 in the prepaid rent account. The balance in the prepaid rent account prior to this entry was $30,780. This prior balance relates to the previous lease for this facility that had expired February 28, 20X1. Jordan records adjustments only at May 31, the end of the fiscal year. At May 31, 20X1, the adjusting entry needed to reflect the correct balances in the prepaid rent and rent expense accounts is to debit

A. Prepaid rent for $11,400 and credit rent expense for $11,400.

B. Rent expense for $11,400 and credit prepaid rent for $11,400.

C. Prepaid rent for $42,180 and credit rent expense for $42,180.

D. Rent expense for $42,180 and credit prepaid rent for $42,180.

Answer (D) is correct. *(CMA, adapted)*
**REQUIRED:** The entry necessary to correct the prepaid rent and rent expense accounts.
**DISCUSSION:** The existing balance ($30,780) in prepaid rent at March 1, 20X1 reflects a prepayment for the first 9 months of the fiscal year that should now be expensed. The initial payment on the new lease is for the last 3 months of the current fiscal year and the first 9 months of the next. Accordingly, 25% (3 months ÷ 12 months) of this initial payment should be expensed. The entry is therefore to debit rent expense and credit prepaid rent for $42,180 [$30,780 + ($45,600 × 25%)].
Answer (A) is incorrect because prepaid rent should be credited for $42,180. Answer (B) is incorrect because the existing amount in prepaid rent also needs to be expensed. Answer (C) is incorrect because prepaid rent should be credited for $42,180.

**34.** An accounting change requiring the cumulative effect of the adjustment to be presented on the income statement is a change in the

A. Life of equipment from 10 to 7 years.

B. Depreciation method from straight-line to double-declining-balance.

C. Specific subsidiaries included in the group for which consolidated statements are presented.

D. None of the answers is correct.

Answer (B) is correct. *(CMA, adapted)*
REQUIRED: The accounting change that should be reported as a cumulative-effect-type change.
DISCUSSION: Per SFAS 154, *Accounting Changes and Error Corrections*, accounting changes are no longer reported as cumulative effects on the income statement.

**35.** Separate disclosure in the statement of retained earnings is required for

A. Repurchase and cancelation of long-term debt at an amount different from its carrying value.

B. An extraordinary loss.

C. Resale of treasury stock at an amount greater than the price at which it was purchased.

D. Discovery that estimated warranty expense for machines sold last year was recorded twice.

Answer (D) is correct. *(CMA, adapted)*
REQUIRED: The item that would be separately disclosed in the retained earnings statement.
DISCUSSION: The only items that appear on a retained earnings statement are dividends, net income, and prior-period adjustments. Prior-period adjustments are essentially defined as clerical errors. Thus, the discovery that estimated warranty expense had been recorded twice would result in a prior-period adjustment.
Answer (A) is incorrect because it would appear on the income statement. Answer (B) is incorrect because it would appear on the income statement. Answer (C) is incorrect because the resale of treasury stock at a price greater than cost would result in a credit to a paid-in capital account, not to retained earnings. Thus, this transaction would not appear on the retained earnings statement.

**36.** The failure to record an accrued expense at year-end will result in which of the following overstatement errors in the financial statements prepared at that date?

|   | Net Income | Working Capital | Cash |
|---|---|---|---|
| A. | No | No | Yes |
| B. | No | Yes | No |
| C. | Yes | No | No |
| D. | Yes | Yes | No |

Answer (D) is correct. *(CIA, adapted)*
REQUIRED: The overstatement errors resulting from the failure to record an accrued expense at year-end.
DISCUSSION: An accrued expense is an expense that has been incurred but not paid. The appropriate adjusting entry to record an accrued expense will increase an expense account and increase a liability account. The failure to record an accrued expense will result in an understatement of expenses leading to an overstatement of net income. The failure to record the increase in a liability account will result in an understatement of current liabilities leading to an overstatement of working capital. There will be no effect on cash.
Answer (A) is incorrect because the failure to record an accrued expense will result in an overstatement of net income and an overstatement of working capital and will have no effect on cash. Answer (B) is incorrect because the failure to record an accrued expense will result in an overstatement of net income. Answer (C) is incorrect because the failure to record an accrued expense will result in an overstatement of working capital.

**37.** If ending inventory is underestimated due to an error in the physical count of items on hand, the cost of goods sold for the period will be <List A>, and net earnings will be <List B>.

|   | List A | List B |
|---|---|---|
| A. | Underestimated | Underestimated |
| B. | Underestimated | Overestimated |
| C. | Overestimated | Underestimated |
| D. | Overestimated | Overestimated |

Answer (C) is correct. *(CIA, adapted)*
REQUIRED: The effect on cost of goods sold and net earnings when ending inventory is underestimated.
DISCUSSION: Cost of goods sold equals beginning inventory, plus purchases, minus ending inventory. If the ending inventory is underestimated, the cost of goods sold will be overestimated. If cost of goods sold is overestimated, net earnings will be underestimated.
Answer (A) is incorrect because the cost of goods sold will be overestimated. Answer (B) is incorrect because the cost of goods sold will be overestimated, and net earnings will be underestimated. Answer (D) is incorrect because net earnings will be underestimated.

**38.** A company had sales in both year 1 and year 2 of $100,000. Cost of sales for year 1 was $70,000. In computing cost of sales for year 1, an item of inventory purchased in that year for $50 was incorrectly written down to current replacement cost of $35. The item is currently selling in year 2 for $100, its normal selling price. As a result of this error,

A. Income for year 1 is overstated.

B. Cost of sales for year 2 will be overstated.

C. Income for year 2 will be overstated.

D. Income for year 2 will be unaffected.

Answer (C) is correct. *(Publisher)*
**REQUIRED:** The effect of an inventory understatement.
**DISCUSSION:** The effect of erroneously writing down inventory is to understate inventory at the end of year 1. The understatement of ending inventory causes cost of goods sold to be overstated in year 1. The overstatement of cost of goods sold in turn causes year 1 income to be understated. The understatement of year 2 beginning inventory causes cost of goods sold to be understated and income to be overstated in year 2.
Answer (A) is incorrect because year 1 income is understated as a result of the understatement of ending inventory. Answer (B) is incorrect because the understatement of year 1 ending inventory results in understated year 2 beginning inventory and understated year 2 cost of sales. Answer (D) is incorrect because the year 2 income will be overstated due to the understatement of beginning inventory.

**39.** If a company erroneously pays one of its liabilities twice during the year, what are the effects of this mistake?

A. Assets, liabilities, and equity will be understated.

B. Assets, net income, and equity will be unaffected.

C. Assets and liabilities will be understated.

D. Assets, net income, and equity will be understated, and liabilities will be overstated.

Answer (C) is correct. *(CIA, adapted)*
**REQUIRED:** The effects of paying a liability twice.
**DISCUSSION:** When a liability is paid, an entry debiting accounts payable and crediting cash is made. If a company erroneously pays a liability twice, the accounts payable and cash accounts will be understated by the amount of the liability. Hence, assets and liabilities will be understated.
Answer (A) is incorrect because the double payment of a liability does not affect expenses of the period, so it does not affect net income and equity. Answer (B) is incorrect because assets will be reduced. Answer (D) is incorrect because both assets and liabilities will be understated, whereas net income and equity will be unaffected.

**40.** Which of the following errors is not self-correcting over two accounting periods?

A. Failure to record accrued wages.

B. Failure to record depreciation.

C. Overstatement of inventory.

D. Failure to record prepaid expenses.

Answer (B) is correct. *(CIA, adapted)*
**REQUIRED:** The error that is not self-correcting over two accounting periods.
**DISCUSSION:** A failure to record depreciation must be corrected as it does not correct itself over two periods. It is a noncounterbalancing error.
Answer (A) is incorrect because a failure to record accrued wages will correct itself when the wages are paid in the following period and represents a counterbalancing error. Answer (C) is incorrect because the overstatement of inventory will correct itself over two periods and is therefore a counterbalancing error. Answer (D) is incorrect because a failure to record prepaid expenses will correct itself in the next period when the prepaid expense is consumed and is therefore a counterbalancing error.

**41.** When the Sonia Co. began business, it included such indirect costs of manufacturing as janitorial expenses, depreciation of machinery, and insurance on the factory as inventory costs. At the beginning of 20X6, the company began expensing all insurance costs when they are incurred. The company must justify and disclose the reason for the change. The most appropriate reason is that the new principle

A. Constitutes an improvement in financial reporting.

B. Has been and continues to be the treatment used for tax purposes.

C. Is easier to apply because no assumptions about allocation must be made.

D. Is one used by the company for insurance costs other than those on factory-related activities.

Answer (A) is correct. *(Publisher)*
**REQUIRED:** The most appropriate reason for making a change in accounting principle.
**DISCUSSION:** The presumption is that, once adopted, an accounting principle should not be changed in accounting for events and transactions of a similar type. This presumption in favor of continuity may be overcome if the enterprise justifies the use of an alternative acceptable principle. The new principle should be preferable because it constitutes an improvement in financial reporting. If the GAAP hierarchy is followed, preferability automatically is established if a pronouncement of the FASB (or other designated standard setter) (1) requires use of a new principle, (2) expresses a preference for a principle not being used, (3) interprets an existing principle, or (4) rejects a specific principle. FASB Interpretation No. 1, *Accounting Changes Related to the Cost of Inventory*, states that preferability should be determined on the basis of whether the new principle constitutes an improvement in financial reporting. Other bases are not sufficient justification.

Questions 42 through 44 are based on the following information. Loire Co. has used the FIFO method since it began operations in 20X3. Loire changed to the weighted-average method for inventory measurement at the beginning of 20X6. This change was justified. In its 20X6 financial statements, Loire included comparative statements for 20X5 and 20X4. The following shows year-end inventory balances under the FIFO and weighted-average methods:

| Year | FIFO | Weighted-Average |
|------|------|------------------|
| 20X3 | $90,000 | $108,000 |
| 20X4 | 156,000 | 142,000 |
| 20X5 | 166,000 | 150,000 |

**42.** What adjustment, before taxes, should Loire make retrospectively to the balance reported for retained earnings at the beginning of 20X4?

A. $18,000 increase.

B. $18,000 decrease.

C. $4,000 increase.

D. $0

Answer (A) is correct. *(CPA, adapted)*
**REQUIRED:** The pretax retrospective adjustment to retained earnings at the beginning of the first period reported.
**DISCUSSION:** Retrospective application requires that the carrying amounts of assets, liabilities, and retained earnings at the beginning of the first period reported be adjusted for the cumulative effect of the new principle on periods prior to the first period reported. The pretax cumulative-effect adjustment to retained earnings at the beginning of 20X4 equals the $18,000 increase ($108,000 – $90,000) in inventory. If the weighted-average method had been applied in 20X3, cost of goods sold would have been $18,000 lower. Pretax net income and ending retained earnings for 20X3 (beginning retained earnings for 20X4) would have been $18,000 greater.
Answer (B) is incorrect because beginning retained earnings for 20X4 is increased. Answer (C) is incorrect because $4,000 is equal to the difference at the end of 20X3 minus the difference at the end of 20X4. Answer (D) is incorrect because a cumulative-effect adjustment should be recorded.

**43.** What amount should Loire report as inventory in its financial statements for the year ended December 31, 20X4 presented for comparative purposes?

A. $90,000

B. $108,000

C. $142,000

D. $156,000

Answer (C) is correct. *(Publisher)*
**REQUIRED:** The amount to be reported as inventory at December 31, 20X4.
**DISCUSSION:** Retrospective application requires that all periods reported be individually adjusted for the period-specific effects of applying the new principle. Thus, the ending inventory for 20X4 following the retrospective adjustment should be reported as the weighted-average amount of $142,000.
Answer (A) is incorrect because $90,000 is the FIFO amount at December 31, 20X3. Answer (B) is incorrect because $108,000 is the weighted-average amount at December 31, 20X3. Answer (D) is incorrect because $156,000 is the FIFO amount at December 31, 20X4.

**44.** By what amount should cost of sales be retrospectively adjusted for the year ended December 31, 20X5?

A. $0

B. $2,000 increase.

C. $14,000 increase.

D. $16,000 increase.

Answer (B) is correct. *(Publisher)*
**REQUIRED:** The retrospective adjustment to cost of sales for the year ended December 31, 20X5.
**DISCUSSION:** Retrospective application requires that all periods reported be individually adjusted for the period-specific effects of applying the new principle. Cost of sales equals beginning inventory, plus purchases, minus ending inventory. Purchases are the same under FIFO and weighted average. Thus, the retrospective adjustment to cost of sales equals the change in beginning inventory resulting from the change from FIFO to weighted average minus the change in ending inventory. This adjustment equals an increase in cost of sales of $2,000 [($156,000 – $142,000) – ($166,000 – $150,000)].
Answer (A) is incorrect because period-specific adjustments are required. Answer (C) is incorrect because $14,000 is the difference between FIFO and weighted-average inventory amounts at the end of 20X4. Answer (D) is incorrect because $16,000 is the difference between FIFO and weighted-average inventory amounts at the end of 20X5.

**45.** JKC is a calendar-year firm that changed its method for measuring inventory from FIFO to LIFO on January 1, 20X6. Records of inventory purchases and sales were not available for certain earlier years of its existence. Thus, it was impracticable for JKC to determine the cumulative effect of applying the change in principle retrospectively. If records are available for recent years, JKC should retrospectively apply LIFO at the

A. End of the latest accounting period presented for which retrospective application is impracticable.

B. Beginning of the earliest accounting period presented for which retrospective application is practicable.

C. Beginning of the current accounting period.

D. Earliest date practicable.

Answer (D) is correct. *(CPA, adapted)*
**REQUIRED:** The proper accounting for a change in accounting principle.
**DISCUSSION:** When it is impracticable to determine the cumulative effect of applying a new accounting principle to any prior period, it should be applied prospectively at the earliest date practicable (SFAS 154). For example, if JKC has all the required information for applying LIFO beginning with January 1, 20X6, it will carry forward the 20X5 FIFO ending inventory balance. It will then begin using LIFO on January 1, 20X6.

**46.** How should the effect of a change in accounting estimate be accounted for?

A. By retrospectively applying the change to amounts reported in financial statements of prior periods.

B. By reporting pro forma amounts for prior periods.

C. As a prior-period adjustment to beginning retained earnings.

D. By prospectively applying the change to current and future periods.

Answer (D) is correct. *(CPA, adapted)*
**REQUIRED:** The accounting for the effect of a change in accounting estimate.
**DISCUSSION:** The effect of a change in accounting estimate is accounted for in the period of change, if the change affects that period only, or in the period of change and future periods, if the change affects both. For a change in accounting estimate, the entity may not (1) restate or retrospectively adjust prior-period statements or (2) report pro forma amounts for prior periods.

**47.** In early January 20X6, Off-Line Co. changed its method of accounting for demo costs from writing off the costs over 2 years to expensing the costs immediately. Off-Line made the change in recognition that an increasing number of demos placed with potential customers did not result in sales. Off-Line had deferred demo costs of $500,000 at December 31, 20X5, of which $300,000 were to be written off in 20X6 and the remainder in 20X7. Off-Line's income tax rate is 30%. In its 20X6 statement of retained earnings, what amount should Off-Line report as a retrospective adjustment of its January 1, 20X6 retained earnings?

A. $0

B. $210,000

C. $300,000

D. $500,000

Answer (A) is correct. *(CPA, adapted)*
**REQUIRED:** The retrospective adjustment of retained earnings at the beginning of the year in which an entity changed from capitalizing a cost to expensing it as incurred.
**DISCUSSION:** In general, the retrospective application method is used to account for a change in accounting principle. However, a change in accounting estimate inseparable from (effected by) a change in principle should be accounted for as a change in estimate. A change in estimate results from new information, such as the decreasing sales resulting from the demo placements. The effects of a change in estimate should be accounted for prospectively. Thus, the effects should be recognized in the period of change and any future periods affected. Accordingly, the write-off of the $500,000 in deferred demo costs should be reported in the 20X6 income statement. Retained earnings at the beginning of the year should not be retrospectively adjusted.
Answer (B) is incorrect because $210,000 is the after-tax effect of expensing $300,000 of the deferred costs in 20X6. Answer (C) is incorrect because $300,000 is the amount that had been scheduled to be expensed in 20X6. Answer (D) is incorrect because $500,000 is the pretax write-off to be recorded in the 20X6 income statement.

**48.** On January 1, 20X4, Colorado Corp. purchased a machine having an estimated useful life of 8 years and no salvage value. The machine was depreciated by the double-declining-balance (DDB) method for both financial statement and income tax reporting. On January 1, 20X6, Colorado justifiably changed to the straight-line method for both financial statement and income tax reporting. Accumulated depreciation at December 31, 20X5 was $525,000. If the straight-line method had been used, the accumulated depreciation at December 31, 20X5 would have been $300,000. The retroactive adjustment to the accumulated depreciation account on January 1, 20X6 as a result of the change in depreciation method is

A. $0

B. $225,000

C. $300,000

D. $525,000

Answer (A) is correct.  *(CPA, adapted)*
**REQUIRED:** The retroactive adjustment to accumulated depreciation at the beginning of the year in which a change in depreciation method was made.
**DISCUSSION:** A change in accounting estimate inseparable from (effected by) a change in accounting principle includes a change in depreciation, amortization, or depletion method. When a change in estimate and a change in principle are inseparable, the transaction should be accounted for as a change in estimate. The effects of a change in estimate should be accounted for prospectively. Thus, the effects should be recognized in the period of change and any future periods affected. The effects should not be recognized in prior periods. Consequently, the accumulated depreciation at January 1, 20X6 should carry forth the $525,000 balance determined in accordance with the DDB method as of December 31, 20X5.
Answer (B) is incorrect because $225,000 is the excess of the DDB over the straight-line amount. Answer (C) is incorrect because $300,000 is the balance under the straight-line method. Answer (D) is incorrect because $525,000 is the balance under the DDB method.

**49.** Volga Co. included a foreign subsidiary in its 20X6 consolidated financial statements. The subsidiary was acquired in 20X4 and was excluded from previous consolidations. The change was caused by the elimination of foreign currency controls. Including the subsidiary in the 20X6 consolidated financial statements results in an accounting change that should be reported

A. By note disclosure only.

B. Currently and prospectively.

C. Currently with note disclosure of pro forma effects of retrospective application.

D. By retrospective application to the financial statements of all prior periods presented.

Answer (D) is correct.  *(CPA, adapted)*
**REQUIRED:** The reporting of the change in the subsidiaries included in consolidated financial statements.
**DISCUSSION:** A change in the reporting entity requires retrospective application to all prior periods presented to report information for the new entity. The following are changes in the reporting entity: (1) presenting consolidated or combined statements in place of statements of individual entities, (2) changing the specific subsidiaries included in the group for which consolidated statements are presented, and (3) changing the entities included in combined statements.

**50.** Lore Co. changed from the cash basis of accounting to the accrual basis of accounting during 20X6. The cumulative effect of this change should be reported in Lore's 20X6 financial statements as a

A. Prior-period adjustment resulting from the correction of an error.

B. Prior-period adjustment resulting from the change in accounting principle.

C. Component of income before extraordinary items.

D. Component of income after extraordinary items.

Answer (A) is correct.  *(CPA, adapted)*
**REQUIRED:** The reporting of the cumulative effect of a change from the cash basis to the accrual basis.
**DISCUSSION:** A change from an accounting principle, e.g., the cash basis, that is not generally accepted to one that is generally accepted, e.g., the accrual basis, is the correction of an error. According to SFAS 154, it is treated as a prior-period adjustment. A change in an accounting principle, an accounting estimate, or the reporting entity is an accounting change. An error correction is not an accounting change.
Answer (B) is incorrect because a prior-period adjustment restates previously issued statements to correct an error. Answer (C) is incorrect because neither a prior-period adjustment nor an accounting change is effected by recognition of the cumulative effect in the current period's income. Answer (D) is incorrect because, prior to the effective date of SFAS 154, the cumulative effect of a change in principle was recognized in a component of income after extraordinary items.

**51.** In which of the following situations should a company report a prior-period adjustment?

A. A change in the estimated useful lives of fixed assets purchased in prior years.

B. The correction of a mathematical error in the calculation of prior years' depreciation.

C. A switch from the straight-line to double-declining-balance method of depreciation.

D. The scrapping of an asset prior to the end of its expected useful life.

Answer (B) is correct. *(CPA, adapted)*
**REQUIRED:** The basis for a prior-period adjustment.
**DISCUSSION:** Items of profit or loss related to corrections of errors in prior-period statements are accounted for as prior-period adjustments. Errors include mathematical mistakes, mistakes in applying accounting principles, and oversight or misuse of facts existing when the statements were prepared. A prior-period adjustment requires restatement of the prior-period statements presented (SFAS 16 and SFAS 154).
Answer (A) is incorrect because a change in the estimated useful lives of fixed assets is a change in estimate. It is accounted for prospectively. Answer (C) is incorrect because a switch from the straight-line to double-declining-balance method of depreciation is a change in estimate inseparable from a change in accounting principle. It is accounted for prospectively. Answer (D) is incorrect because the scrapping of an asset prior to the end of its expected useful life is accounted for prospectively. The gain or loss is recognized in earnings in the period of disposal.

## 18.6 Early Extinguishment of Debt

**52.** A liability may be derecognized in the financial statements in all of the following situations except

A. The debtor pays off the obligation with financial assets (other than cash) and is relieved of its obligation for the liability.

B. The debtor places purchased securities into an irrevocable trust and uses the principal and interest to pay off the liability as it matures.

C. The judicial system legally releases the debtor from being the primary obligor of the liability.

D. The debtor reacquires the outstanding debt from the creditor and holds the securities as treasury bonds.

Answer (B) is correct. *(Publisher)*
**REQUIRED:** The situation in which a liability cannot be derecognized in the financial statements.
**DISCUSSION:** SFAS 140, *Accounting for Transfers and Servicing of Financial Assets and Extinguishments of Liabilities*, does not allow the debtor to derecognize a liability unless the liability is considered extinguished. A liability is extinguished if either of the following conditions is met: (1) The debtor pays the creditor and is relieved of its obligation for the liability, or (2) the debtor is legally released from being the primary obligor of the liability, either judicially or by the creditor. Creating an irrevocable trust and using the proceeds (principal and interest) to pay off the debt securities as they mature is called "in-substance defeasance." In-substance defeasance does not meet the derecognition criteria. First, the debtor is not legally released as the primary obligor of the liability. Second, the debtor has not been relieved of its obligation for the liability because the creditor has not been paid. In many cases, the creditor is not even aware that the trust has been created.
Answer (A) is incorrect because paying the creditor includes the delivery of cash, other financial assets, goods, or services or the reacquisition of the outstanding debt securities whether the securities are canceled or held as so-called treasury bonds. Answer (C) is incorrect because a debtor may be legally released as the primary obligor of the liability either judicially or by the creditor. Answer (D) is incorrect because paying the creditor includes the delivery of cash, other financial assets, goods, or services or the reacquisition of the outstanding debt securities whether the securities are canceled or held as so-called treasury bonds.

**53.** An entity should not derecognize an existing liability under which of the following circumstances?

A. The entity exchanges convertible preferred stock for its outstanding debt securities. The debt securities are not canceled but are held as treasury bonds.

B. Because of financial difficulties being experienced by the entity, a creditor accepts a parcel of land as full satisfaction of an overdue loan. The value of the land is less than 50% of the loan balance.

C. The entity irrevocably places cash into a trust that will be used solely to satisfy scheduled principal and interest payments of a specific bond obligation. Because the trust investments will generate a higher return, the amount of cash is less than the carrying amount of the debt.

D. As part of the agreement to purchase a shopping center from the entity, the buyer assumes without recourse the mortgage for which the center serves as collateral.

Answer (C) is correct.  *(Publisher)*
  **REQUIRED:** The circumstances under which an existing liability should not be derecognized.
  **DISCUSSION:** The derecognition of a liability is permitted only if it has been extinguished. Extinguishment occurs when either (1) the debtor pays the creditor and is relieved of its obligation for the liability, or (2) the debtor is legally released from being the primary obligor under the liability, either judicially or by the creditor.

**54.** On December 1, 20X1, Catfish Company issued its 10%, $2 million face amount bonds for $2.3 million. Interest is payable on November 1 and May 1. On December 31, 20X3, the carrying amount of the bonds, inclusive of the unamortized premium, was $2.1 million. On July 1, 20X4, Catfish reacquired the bonds at 97, plus accrued interest. Catfish appropriately uses the straight-line method of amortization. The gain on Catfish's extinguishment of debt is

A. $48,000

B. $52,000

C. $112,000

D. $160,000

Answer (C) is correct.  *(Publisher)*
  **REQUIRED:** The gain on extinguishment of debt.
  **DISCUSSION:** The gain is the difference in carrying amount at the date of extinguishment and the price paid. As of December 31, 20X3, the bonds had been outstanding 25 months. Because $200,000 ($2.3 million – $2.1 million) had been amortized over those 25 months, the straight-line rate is apparently $8,000 per month ($200,000 ÷ 25 months). Thus, during the first half of 20X2, an additional $48,000 ($8,000 × 6 months) would be amortized, leaving a carrying amount of $2,052,000. Subtracting the $1,940,000 ($2 million × 97%) from the $2,052,000 carrying amount results in a gain of $112,000.
  Answer (A) is incorrect because $48,000 is the amortization for the final 6 months. Answer (B) is incorrect because $52,000 is the unamortized premium on July 1, 20X4; it would be the gain if the bonds had been purchased at their face amount. Answer (D) is incorrect because $160,000 is the result of including the amount to be amortized during the first half of the year into the gain.

**55.** On January 2, 20X4, Wright Corporation entered into an in-substance debt defeasance transaction by placing cash of $875,000 into an irrevocable trust. The trust assets are to be used solely for satisfying the interest and principal payments on Wright's 6%, $1,100,000, 30-year bond payable. Wright has not been legally released under the bond agreement, but the probability is remote that Wright will be required to place additional cash in the trust. On December 31, 20X3, the bond's carrying amount was $1,050,000; its fair value was $800,000. Disregarding income taxes, what amount of extraordinary gain (loss) should Wright report in its 20X4 income statement?

A. $(75,000)

B. $0

C. $175,000

D. $225,000

Answer (B) is correct.  *(Publisher)*
  **REQUIRED:** The amount of extraordinary gain (loss) to be recognized on an in-substance defeasance.
  **DISCUSSION:** SFAS 140 prohibits the recognition of a gain (loss) from an in-substance defeasance.

# STUDY UNIT NINETEEN
# BUSINESS COMBINATIONS AND DERIVATIVES

(26 pages of outline)

This study unit is the **ninth of ten** on **external financial reporting**. The relative weight assigned to this major topic in Part 2 of the exam is **25%** at **skill level B** (four skill types required). The ten study units are

Study Unit 11:  Overview of External Financial Reporting
Study Unit 12:  Overview of Financial Statements
Study Unit 13:  Cash and Receivables
Study Unit 14:  Inventories and Investments
Study Unit 15:  Long-Lived Assets
Study Unit 16:  Liabilities
Study Unit 17:  Equity and Revenue Recognition
Study Unit 18:  Other Income Statement Items
Study Unit 19:  Business Combinations and Derivatives
Study Unit 20:  SEC Requirements and the Annual Report

After studying the outlines and answering the multiple-choice questions in this study unit, you will have the skills necessary to address the following topics listed in the IMA's Learning Outcome Statements:

Part 2 – Sections E.1. Objectives of external financial reporting and E.2. Financial accounting fundamentals

f.    Special topics:  business combinations, consolidated financial statements, and accounting for derivatives

For each special topic, the candidate should be able to:

1.    Define and describe its characteristics
2.    Demonstrate a basic understanding of the relevant accounting issues
3.    Describe the impact on a firm's financial statements

## 19.1 BUSINESS COMBINATIONS

1.    **Legal Perspective**

a.    In a **merger**, only one of the combining companies survives. The assets and liabilities of the other combining companies are merged into the surviving company.

1)    A **vertical merger** is a union of two companies, one of which supplies inputs (e.g., raw materials) for the other.

2)    A **horizontal merger** is a union of two companies that engage in the same or similar activities.

3)    A **conglomerate merger** is a union of two unrelated companies.

b.    In a **consolidation**, a new company is organized to take over the combining companies.

c.    In an **acquisition**, one company exchanges cash, equity securities, or debt securities for the majority of the outstanding stock of another company, and both companies continue to operate separately.

2.   The **tax perspective** is to consider whether a business combination is a tax-free or a taxable event.

a.    Certain exchanges of stock are tax-free exchanges, which permit the owners of one company to exchange their stock for the stock of the purchaser without paying taxes.

b.    Inheritance-tax problems of owners force the sale of many closely held businesses.

3.   The **accounting perspective** is that a business combination must be treated as a purchase.

a.    **Purchase accounting**

1)    A **business combination** is an entity's acquisition of net assets constituting a business or of controlling equity interests of one or more other entities. The governing pronouncement is **SFAS 141**, *Business Combinations*, which applies when entities are merged or become subsidiaries, one entity's net assets or equity interests are transferred to another entity, or net assets or equity interests of the existing entities are transferred to a newly formed entity. SFAS 141 also applies regardless of the nature of the consideration given or whether the owners of a combining entity have a majority of the voting rights of the combined entity. However, combinations of not-for-profit organizations or of mutual enterprises are not currently subject to SFAS 141. Acquisitions of for-profit businesses by not-for-profit organizations are also not within its scope.

2)    An exchange of businesses qualifies as a business combination, but joint ventures, the acquisition of noncontrolling interests in a subsidiary (a minority interest), and exchange of equity interests (or transfers of net assets) between entities under common control are not business combinations.

3)    A business combination subject to SFAS 141 is accounted for using the purchase method.

b.    **Pooling accounting.** According to SFAS 141, the pooling method of accounting for business combinations is no longer permitted.

4.   The **financial perspective** is the most important, encompassing all the previous perspectives; the legal, tax, and accounting perspectives all have economic impact.

a.    Additional factors determining the terms of business combinations

1)    Earnings levels and growth rates
2)    Sales levels and growth rates
3)    Dividends
4)    Market values
5)    Carrying amounts
6)    Net current assets

b.    The exchanges of stock in business combinations involving public companies often result in a greater market value than the sum of the market values of the individual companies. The reason is that qualitative considerations not reflected in the historical financial data may operate to create a synergistic effect.

1)    For example, a firm needing stronger management expertise, a better distribution network, or an R&D capacity may seek a complementary merger partner.

5.   **Holding companies** are formed solely to own investments in the stock of other operating companies.

a.    The purchase method of business combination is pertinent.

b.    Holding-company pyramiding results in control of assets with a very small percentage of ownership. Thus, the potential profits (and losses) are high.

c. **Advantages**

1) Control can often be obtained with small percentages of total stock ownership if ownership is widely distributed.

2) Risk is isolated because investees are legally separate. If one investee has problems, it can be sold.

3) The stock may be purchased in public markets or directly from current shareholders, so the investment does not require the approval of shareholders or the investee's board of directors.

4) An alternative is to make a **tender offer** to the shareholders of the potential investee with or without the approval of the potential investee management.

   a) If the potential investee management does not cooperate, the potential investor can advertise the offer, e.g., in *The Wall Street Journal*.

   b) A tender offer asks shareholders to tender their shares for a specified price, provided that a certain number of shares is tendered.

5) If an antitrust violation occurs, it is easier to be forced to liquidate a stock investment than an internal operating division.

d. **Disadvantage**

1) If the entity meets the criteria of a **personal holding company (PHC)**, undistributed PHC income is subject to a 38.6% tax rate. A company is a PHC if five or fewer shareholders own 50% or more of the shares and 60% or more of the adjusted ordinary gross income is PHC income (essentially, passive income). However, certain organizations are exempt from treatment as PHCs, e.g., S corporations, banks, and insurance companies.

6. Stop and review! You have completed the outline for this subunit. Study multiple-choice questions 1 through 5 beginning on page 769.

## 19.2 ACCOUNTING FOR BUSINESS COMBINATIONS

1. **Applicability of Historical-Cost Accounting.** The customary principles relevant to initial recognition and measurement of assets, liabilities, and equity interests issued; cost allocation; and subsequent accounting also apply to business combinations.

   a. **Initial recognition** of assets, liabilities, and equity interests ordinarily results from exchange transactions. Assets surrendered are derecognized, and liabilities assumed or equity interests issued are recognized, at the acquisition date.

   b. **Initial measurement** of exchange transactions is at **fair value**, and the assumption is that the fair values exchanged are equal.

   1) Accordingly, the cost of an acquisition equals the fair value of the consideration given, and gain or loss is not recognized unless

      a) The carrying amount of noncash assets surrendered differs from their fair value, or

      b) The fair value of net assets acquired exceeds cost, and the excess is not fully allocated.

   2) If the consideration given is cash, an exchange transaction is measured based on the amount paid. Otherwise, the fair value of the more clearly evident of the consideration given or the asset (net assets) acquired is the basis for measurement.

    c.    **Cost allocation** to the elements of an asset (net asset) group is based on their fair values. The cost of the group acquired in a business combination may be greater than the sum of the fair values assigned to the acquired assets (tangible assets, financial assets, and separately recognized intangible assets), minus the liabilities assumed. This difference is recognized as **goodwill**. It is tested for impairment but not amortized.

    d.    **Post-acquisition accounting** for an asset is determined by its nature, not the method of acquisition or the basis for initial measurement.

2.    A business combination subject to SFAS 141 is accounted for using the **purchase method**. An acquisition of a **minority interest** is also accounted for in this way.

3.    The **acquiring entity** must be identified. Thus, when no equity interests are exchanged, the entity that distributes cash or other assets or incurs liabilities is the acquiring entity.

    a.    However, if a business combination is consummated through an **exchange of equity interests**, the determination is often more difficult because neither the issuer of equity interests nor the larger entity is necessarily the acquirer. Thus, all facts and circumstances should be considered, such as

        1)    Relative voting rights in the combined entity,
        2)    The presence of a large minority interest when other voting interests are fragmented,
        3)    The ability to determine the voting majority of the combined entity's governing body,
        4)    Domination of senior management of the combined entity, and
        5)    Which party paid a premium for the equity securities of the other combining party.

    b.    When **three or more entities** are involved, the initiator of the combination and whether one entity has significantly greater assets, revenues, and earnings than the other combining entities are additional factors to be considered.

    c.    If a **new entity** is created to issue equity securities to consummate the combination, one of the existing entities must be designated as the acquiring entity.

4.    **Issues in Determining the Cost of the Acquired Entity**

    a.    The **fair value of preferred shares** that are more nearly akin to debt often may be determined on the same basis as debt securities, that is, by comparison of their terms (e.g., dividend and redemption provisions) with those of comparable securities and by considering market factors. This determination differs from the usual practice of recording the fair value of the consideration received as the initial carrying amount of shares issued.

    b.    The **quoted market price of equity securities** issued in a business combination ordinarily is more clearly evident than the fair value of the acquired entity and therefore is the usual basis for estimating that fair value. The market price for a reasonable time before and after the announcement of the terms of the combination, as adjusted for such factors as the quantity traded and issue costs, should be considered.

        1)    If the quoted market price is not the fair value, the consideration received must be estimated. The extent of the adjustment to the quoted market price and the net assets received are considered. The net assets received include goodwill. The negotiations and all other facets of the combination should be evaluated, independent appraisals may be obtained, and the other consideration paid may be evidence of the total fair value received.

5. **Costs of the business combination** are accounted for as follows:

   a. **Direct costs** are treated as costs of the acquired entity. Examples are legal, accounting, consulting, and finders' fees.

   b. The fair value of securities issued is reduced by their **registration and issuance costs**.

   c. **Indirect and general expenses** are expensed as incurred. Examples are the time spent by combining entity executives negotiating the combination and other normal business expenses of the combination.

6. **Contingent Consideration.** An issuance of securities or the payment of other consideration may be contingent upon specified future events or transactions. A typical practice is to place part of the consideration in escrow, with its disposition determined by subsequent specified events.

   a. The **cost of the acquired entity** includes the determinable amount of contingent consideration at the acquisition date. Other contingent amounts are disclosed but not recorded as liabilities or outstanding securities until the contingency is resolved beyond a reasonable doubt.

   b. When resolution of a contingency based on **future earnings** levels results in the issuance or issuability of additional consideration, its fair value should be treated as an additional cost of the acquired entity.

   c. Resolution of a contingency based on **security prices** does not result in an adjustment of the cost of the acquired entity. The additional consideration currently distributable because of failure to achieve or maintain a security price is recorded at current fair value, but securities issued at the acquisition date are reduced to the lower current fair value.

      1) The reduction of the fair value of debt securities results in a discount that is amortized from the time of issuance of additional securities.

      2) The foregoing principles provide guidance applicable to other circumstances involving contingent consideration, for example, when the contingency involves both earnings and security prices.

      3) If the contingent consideration relates to future settlement of a contingency, any increase in the cost of the acquired assets may be amortizable over the useful lives of those assets, depending on their nature.

   d. The accounting for **interest and dividends** on securities held in escrow depends on the accounting for the securities, which is dependent on the resolution of the contingency. Pending that resolution, no interest expense or dividend distributable is recorded for payments into escrow.

      1) Later distributions from escrow to former shareholders are added to the cost of the acquired assets at the distribution date.

   e. **Imputed interest** on contingently issuable shares that reduces taxes also reduces the recorded contingent consideration based on earnings. Moreover, it increases the additional capital resulting from contingent consideration based on security prices.

   f. Contingent consideration is expensed if it is given as compensation for services or use of property or profit sharing.

7. **Purchase Price Allocation.** The general principles of historical-cost accounting apply. Thus, the cost of the acquired entity is determined at the acquisition date. It is allocated to the assets acquired and liabilities assumed in accordance with their fair values at the acquisition date. However, before this step, the noncash purchase consideration should be reviewed to determine that it has been properly valued, and all of the assets acquired (possibly including intangible assets not on the acquired entity's balance sheet) and liabilities assumed should be identified.

a.   Estimated fair values may be based on independent appraisals, actuarial valuations, or other sources of relevant information but not on the tax bases of assets or liabilities.

b.   SFAS 141 provides the following guidance for assigning amounts to the assets (excluding goodwill) acquired and liabilities assumed by the acquiring entity:

1) **Marketable securities** at fair values.

2) **Receivables** at present values based on current interest rates, minus allowances for uncollectibility and collection costs.

3) **Finished goods and merchandise** at estimated selling prices minus disposal costs and a reasonable profit allowance for the selling effort of the acquiring entity.

4) **Work-in-process** inventory at estimated selling prices minus costs to complete, disposal costs, and a reasonable profit allowance for the completing and selling effort of the acquiring entity.

5) **Raw materials** at current replacement costs.

6) **Plant and equipment to be used** at current replacement costs for similar capacity unless expected use indicates a lower value to the acquirer.

7) **Plant and equipment to be sold** at fair values minus costs to sell.

8) **Intangible assets** meeting the recognition criteria below and on the following page at estimated fair values.

9) **Other assets**, such as land, natural resources, and nonmarketable securities, at appraised values.

10) A liability for the **projected benefit obligation in excess of plan assets** or an asset for the **excess of plan assets over the PBO** of a single-employer defined-benefit pension plan. After the employer is acquired, the amount is determined in accordance with the provisions in SFAS 87 for the calculation of such liability or asset.

11) A liability for the **accumulated postretirement benefit obligation in excess of the fair value of plan assets** or an asset for the **fair value of the plan assets in excess of the APBO** of a single-employer defined-benefit postretirement plan. After the employer is acquired, the amount is determined in accordance with the provisions in SFAS 106 for the calculation of such liability or asset.

12) Amounts for **pre-acquisition contingencies** as determined on the following page.

13) **Other liabilities, accruals, and commitments** at present values of amounts to be paid based on current interest rates.

c.   **Pre-acquisition goodwill and deferred tax amounts** on the acquired entity's balance sheet are not recognized. However, the acquiring entity should recognize deferred tax amounts for differences between assigned values and tax bases of assets acquired and liabilities assumed.

d.   An **intangible asset distinct from goodwill** is recognized if it arises from contractual or other legal rights even if it is not transferable or separable. If this criterion is not met, it may still be recognized if it is separable.

1) Examples of intangible assets meeting the **contractual-legal criterion** include trade names and trademarks, Internet domain names, noncompetition agreements, order or production backlogs, artistic works, licensing agreements, service or supply contracts, leases, broadcast rights, franchises, patents, computer software, and trade secrets.

2) The **separability criterion** may be met even if the intangible asset is not individually separable if it can be sold, transferred, licensed, rented, or exchanged along with a related item.

    a)   Examples of intangible assets meeting the separability criterion include customer lists, noncontractual customer relationships, unpatented technology, and databases.

  3)   An assembled workforce is an example of an item not recognizable as an intangible asset distinct from goodwill.

  4)   The criteria for recognition of intangible assets stated in this section apply only to those acquired in a business combination.

e.   A **pre-acquisition contingency** is a contingent asset, liability, or impairment of an asset of the acquired entity that existed prior to consummation of the business combination. It is included in the allocation of the purchase price unless it consists of (1) possible income tax effects (accounted for under SFAS 109) of temporary differences and carryforwards or (2) tax uncertainties concerning the acquisition (e.g., whether the tax basis of an asset will be accepted by the tax authorities).

  1)   A pre-acquisition contingency is included in the purchase price allocation at fair value unless the fair value is not determinable during the **allocation period**. This period ends when the acquiring entity no longer is waiting for information it has arranged to obtain and that is available or obtainable. The period for identifying assets and liabilities and measuring fair values ordinarily is not more than 1 year after the combination is consummated.

  2)   If its fair value is not determinable during the allocation period, a pre-acquisition contingency is included in the allocation based on an amount determined according to the following:

    a)   Based on information available before the allocation period ends, it is probable that an asset existed, a liability was incurred, or an asset was impaired when the combination was consummated, and

    b)   The amount is capable of reasonable estimation. (SFAS 5 and FASB Interpretation No. 14 are pertinent to applying the foregoing criteria.)

  3)   After the allocation period, an adjustment for a pre-acquisition contingency (other than a loss carryforward, which is accounted for under SFAS 109) is included in net income when determined.

f.   Amounts assigned to assets used in a particular R&D project and having no alternative future use are expensed at the acquisition date.

g.   **Goodwill** includes acquired intangible assets that do not satisfy either the contractual-legal or the separability criterion.

h.   The total amount assigned to assets acquired and liabilities assumed may exceed the cost of the acquired entity. This **excess over cost**, also known as **negative goodwill**, is allocated proportionately to reduce the amounts assignable to certain acquired assets.

  1)   Before the excess over cost is allocated, the acquiring entity should

    a)   Reevaluate whether all assets and liabilities have been identified and

    b)   Remeasure the consideration paid, assets acquired, and liabilities assumed.

  2)   The acquired assets to which the excess over cost is **NOT** allocated are

    a)   Financial assets (excluding equity-method investments)
    b)   Assets to be disposed of by sale
    c)   Deferred tax assets
    d)   Prepaid assets of postretirement benefit plans, including pension plans
    e)   Other current assets

3) The excess over cost may not be fully allocated because a partial allocation has reduced to zero the amounts assignable to specified types of acquired assets. The **remaining excess over cost** is treated as an **extraordinary gain** in accordance with APB 30 when the combination is completed.

   a) An extraordinary gain recognized during the allocation period may require subsequent adjustment because of changes in the purchase price allocation. Such an adjustment is an extraordinary item.

   b) However, recognition of the excess over cost is delayed when the combination involves **contingent consideration** that potentially will increase the cost of the acquired entity (a contingency based on **earnings**). Thus, reduction of the amounts otherwise assignable to the acquired assets or recognition of an extraordinary gain must await resolution of such a contingency. Pending resolution of a contingency based on earnings, the lesser of the excess over cost or the maximum contingent consideration is recognized as if it were a **liability**.

      i) Upon resolution of the contingency, the amount by which the fair value of the contingent consideration issued or issuable is greater than the "as-if" liability is an additional cost of the acquired entity. If the "as-if" liability is greater than the fair value of the contingent consideration issued or issuable, the difference is allocated as an excess over cost.

      ii) The result of this method of accounting is that the excess over cost is reduced or eliminated by an amount equal to the post-resolution fair value of the contingent consideration. Any remaining excess over cost is then allocated either to reduce the amounts assigned to certain acquired assets or recognized as an extraordinary gain.

8. **Subsequent accounting** for goodwill and other intangible assets acquired in a business combination is prescribed by **SFAS 142**, *Goodwill and Other Intangible Assets* (see Study Unit 15).

9. The **acquisition date** may for the sake of convenience be specified as the end of an accounting period between the initiation and the consummation of the combination. For accounting purposes, this date is appropriate if a written agreement transfers control on that date, subject only to restrictions needed to protect the owners of the acquired entity.

   a. Specifying an acquisition date that is not the date of consummation of the combination necessitates adjustment of the cost of the acquired entity and net income otherwise reported. This adjustment compensates for recognizing income prior to transfer of consideration.

      1) Accordingly, **imputed interest** at an appropriate current rate is recognized on the consideration transferred (assets surrendered, liabilities assumed or incurred, or preferred shares issued). The effect is to reduce the cost of the acquired entity and net income.

   b. For the period of the business combination, the acquiring entity recognizes the acquired entity's income after the acquisition date. However, these revenues and expenses are based on the acquiring entity's cost incurred.

10. **Documentation.** Under SFAS 142, assets and liabilities must be assigned to reporting units. Hence, the determination of the purchase price of the acquired entity and related factors (e.g., reasons for the acquisition) should be documented at the acquisition date.

11. **Disclosures** regarding a material combination include

    a.   The primary reasons for the acquisition

    b.   Description of the acquired entity and the percentage of voting interests acquired

    c.   The period for which the operating results of the acquired entity are included in income

    d.   Cost of the acquired entity and the equity interests issued or issuable, their value, and the basis therefor

    e.   Assignment of the price of the acquired entity to major condensed balance sheet captions

    f.   Contingencies and their accounting treatment

    g.   Purchased R&D assets acquired and written off and the line item where writeoffs are aggregated

    h.   Information about price allocations not yet finalized

    i.   If material, information for the period of the combination about amortizable intangible assets, nonamortizable intangible assets, and goodwill

    j.   Information about business combinations during the period that are material in the aggregate

    k.   If the combined entity is a public business enterprise, supplemental pro forma information about operations as of the beginning of the period and for a comparable prior period

    l.   Information about an extraordinary gain as required by APB 30

    m.   Interim information of a public business enterprise, such as that in 11.a.–d. and supplemental pro forma information

12. Stop and review!  You have completed the outline for this subunit.  Study multiple-choice questions 6 through 16 beginning on page 770.

## 19.3 CONSOLIDATED FINANCIAL STATEMENTS

1.   **SFAS 94**, *Consolidation of All Majority-Owned Subsidiaries*, requires consolidation of all companies in which a parent has a controlling financial interest through direct or indirect ownership of a majority voting interest (over 50% of the outstanding voting shares).

    a.   However, consolidation is not required if control does not rest with the majority owner. For example, the subsidiary may be in bankruptcy or in legal reorganization or be subject to foreign exchange restrictions or other government-imposed restrictions that preclude exercise of control.

    b.   If the conditions dictating consolidation are met, subsidiaries should be reported on a consolidated basis with the parent.

2.   Consolidation is an **accounting process** for a business combination when the combined entities remain legally separate.  It should not be confused with a business combination effected as a consolidation, that is, one in which a new company is formed to account for the assets and liabilities of the combining companies.

3.   Consolidated statements are intended to present the results of operations, financial position, and cash flows of a parent and its subsidiaries as if they were a **single economic entity**.

    a.   When consolidated financial statements are prepared, the normal procedure is to start with the output of the formal accounting systems of the parent and the subsidiary(ies).  On a worksheet only, the informal adjusting and eliminating entries are then prepared.

        1)   These consolidating adjusting entries must be cumulative because previous worksheet entries were not recorded in the accounts of either the parent or the subsidiary.

2)   The working papers may be based on balances after year-end closing or on trial balances before closing. Thus, the latter include revenue and expense accounts.

b.   The following are the two main approaches to valuing a business combination:

1)   Under the **entity theory**, goodwill is established as if 100% of the subsidiary were purchased, regardless of the parent's actual ownership percentage in the subsidiary.

2)   Under the **proprietary theory**, the goodwill amount is the difference between the amount actually paid for a percentage of a subsidiary and the value of that percentage of the subsidiary.

c.   The basis of consolidation is a significant accounting policy that should be disclosed in the financial statements (APB 22). Normally, the disclosure is made either as the first note to the financial statements or in a separate summary preceding the notes.

4.   The guidance provided by authoritative pronouncements regarding consolidations is not extensive. However, **ARB 51**, *Consolidated Financial Statements*, gives the following description of the general consolidation procedures:

a.   **Parent-subsidiary balances and transactions**, such as open account balances (receivables and payables), the parent's investment in the subsidiary, sales and purchases, interest, holdings of securities, and dividends, should be eliminated in full even if a minority interest exists.

1)   Elimination means debits are credited and credits are debited.

2)   Retained earnings or deficits of a purchased subsidiary at the date of acquisition are excluded from consolidated retained earnings in the entry eliminating the parent's investment account and the subsidiary's equity accounts.

3)   Shares of the parent held by a subsidiary should not be treated as outstanding in the consolidated balance sheet. They are eliminated.

b.   **Profits and losses** on transactions within the consolidated entity are completely eliminated, but the procedure varies with the direction of the sale.

1)   **Parent to subsidiary (downstream):** The entire profit or loss not realized by sale outside of the consolidated entity is subtracted from the parent's income. The minority interest is unaffected by the elimination.

2)   **Subsidiary to parent (upstream):** The entire profit or loss not realized by sale outside of the consolidated entity is subtracted from the subsidiary's income. In the upstream case, the effect is to allocate the elimination of the unrealized profit or loss between the parent (or consolidated entity) and the minority interest. The upstream case is relevant only if the subsidiary has a minority interest. However, if the asset is sold to someone outside the group, the original unrealized profit or loss will be realized and will no longer need to be eliminated.

c.   The amount of the **minority interest** recognized at the date of the combination equals a proportionate share of the subsidiary's carrying amount.

1)   Subsequently, the minority interest is adjusted for its share of the subsidiary's income and dividends. On consolidating worksheets, an adjustment to minority interest is also needed for unrealized profits and losses on upstream sales of inventory and fixed assets and purchases of combining entity debt.

d.   In the **income statement**, the minority interest's adjusted share of the subsidiary's income is usually treated as a deduction in arriving at consolidated income. The parent's investment in subsidiary account and its proportionate share of the subsidiary's equity accounts, which include retained earnings, are eliminated in a consolidation. The remainder of the subsidiary's equity is reported separately as the minority interest.

e. The **parent's net income** reported in its separate income statement equals the consolidated net income because the parent should account for the investment using the equity method. **Consolidated net income** is also equal to the parent's net income, plus subsidiary net income, minus minority interest net income, minus adjustments for profit or loss on transactions within the consolidated entity (the latter adjustments involve certain inventory, fixed assets, and debt).

1) **ARB 51** states that, when a subsidiary is purchased during the year, the preferred method of presenting the results of operations is to include the subsidiary's operations in the consolidated income statement as though it had been acquired at the beginning of the year and to deduct from the total earnings the pre-acquisition earnings. The minority interest income for the entire year is also deducted.

f. In the consolidated balance sheet, the **equity section** should reflect the parent's equity section. Placement of the minority interest is in dispute, although SFAC 6 indicates a preference for treating it as part of equity.

5. **Consolidating journal entries**, which appear only on a worksheet, are used in preparation of the consolidated financial statements.

a. **Basic elimination entry.** This entry eliminates investment account and subsidiary equity accounts attributable to the parent.

| | | |
|---|---|---|
| Common stock (sub) | $XXX | |
| Additional paid-in capital (sub) | XXX | |
| Retained earnings (sub) | XXX | |
| Dividends (sub) | | $XXX |
| Investment (parent) | | XXX |
| Minority interest | | XXX |

The above entries to the subsidiary's accounts effectively allocate the subsidiary's net assets between the parent's "investment in investee" account and the minority interest.

b. **Elimination of directly offsetting interentity accounts.** They are reciprocal and do not affect consolidated net income or minority interest. The purpose is to eliminate inter-company sales and loans.

| | | |
|---|---|---|
| Sales | $XXX | |
| Cost of sales | | $XXX |
| Payables | $XXX | |
| Receivables | | $XXX |
| Interest income | $XXX | |
| Interest expense | | $XXX |

c. **Elimination of unrealized profit or loss from inventory.** If ending inventory of a combining entity includes purchased goods from another combining entity that were sold at a profit, unrealized profit exists from a consolidated perspective because the goods have not been sold outside the consolidated group.

| | | |
|---|---|---|
| Cost of sales | $XXX | |
| Inventory | | $XXX |

This entry writes the inventory down to cost and decreases consolidated net income. Part of this reduction of income should be allocated to the minority interest if the sale is upstream (sale by a combining entity with a minority interest).

d.  **Elimination of unrealized profit or loss in fixed asset purchase/sale transactions**

1)  In the period of the purchase/sale, any gain (loss) recognized on the sale of a **fixed asset** between combining entities is eliminated.

    | | | |
    |---|---|---|
    | Gain on sale | $XXX | |
    |     Fixed asset | | $XXX |

2)  Any **depreciation** taken by the purchaser is eliminated to the extent it represents an amount different from what would have been taken if the seller had retained and depreciated the fixed asset.

    | | | |
    |---|---|---|
    | Accumulated depreciation | $XXX | |
    |     Depreciation expense | | $XXX |

3)  In subsequent periods, the previously reported gain currently included in retained earnings is eliminated.  The next step is to eliminate the excess depreciation taken in the period and in all prior periods (i.e., a cumulative adjustment).

    | | | |
    |---|---|---|
    | Retained earnings | $XXX | |
    |     Fixed asset | | $XXX |
    | Accumulated depreciation | XXX | |
    |     Depreciation expense | | XXX |
    |     Retained earnings | | XXX |

4)  If the seller has a **minority interest**, minority interest and minority interest income are adjusted as appropriate.  All adjustments for unrealized profit or loss elimination flow through to consolidated totals unless explicitly adjusted to minority interest.

e.  **Elimination of interentity debt transactions**

1)  The debt issued by one combining entity of a consolidated group may be purchased by another combining entity of the group from a third party so that the debt accounts are not reciprocal.  Thus, the purchase price is not equal to the carrying amount of the debt on the books of the issuer, another combining entity.

2)  The gain on **extinguishment of debt** from a consolidated perspective must be recognized in the period the debt is purchased by a combining entity.  There are five issues to resolve.

    a)  Maturity or face amount of the debt
    b)  Interest receivable/payable at period-end
    c)  Interest income/expense based on the maturity amount and stated rate
    d)  Discount or premium on the books of the issuer (debtor)
    e)  Discount or premium on the books of the purchaser (creditor)

3)  The maturity amount, interest receivable/payable, and interest income/expense are direct eliminations and should be so handled.

4)  The **premium or discount** on the debtor's and creditor's books and any related amortization should be eliminated and recognized as a gain or loss on extinguishment in the period of purchase.  Retained earnings is adjusted in each subsequent period.

    a)  The **"investment in debt"** account of the investor/creditor is debited (credited) to reduce the balance to zero (after the maturity amount is eliminated).  Any amortization of that balance that was an adjustment of interest income during the period must also be eliminated.

        i)  If the purchase was at a premium (discount), amortization requires a debit (credit) to interest income.  Thus, the elimination entry is to credit (debit) interest income.

ii) The balance of the journal entry recognizes gain or loss in the period of debt acquisition and adjusts retained earnings in all remaining periods.

b) The premium or discount on the books of the debtor is debited or credited. Any related amortization of premium or discount that was an adjustment of interest expense during the period is eliminated.

i) If the purchase was at a premium (discount), amortization results in a credit (debit) to interest expense that must be reversed.

ii) The balance of the journal entry recognizes gain or loss in the period of debt acquisition and adjusts retained earnings in all remaining periods.

c) The cumulative adjustments to **retained earnings** decrease over the life of the debt because amortization of the gain or loss flows into retained earnings.

f. All **upstream profit or loss items** require an adjustment to minority interest.

1) Adjustments are made to retained earnings and current minority interest income.

2) In the preceding journal entries, adjustments to retained earnings can individually be made pro rata to retained earnings and minority interest; e.g., if minority interest is 10%, 10% of every entry to retained earnings would be made to minority interest instead of retained earnings.

a) Alternatively, one summary entry can be made to retained earnings to adjust minority interest (which was established with the first elimination entry).

3) All entries to **nominal accounts** involving upstream transactions (those from combining entities with minority interests) require an adjustment to minority interest income.

a) The entry to establish minority interest net income is to debit a contra consolidated net income account and credit minority interest income.

| | | |
|---|---|---|
| Consolidated net income | $XXX | |
| Minority interest income | | $XXX |

b) The amount is the minority interest percentage times the subsidiary's/ combining entity's net income adjusted for any upstream transactions.

c) For example, if inventory, which includes $1,000 of gross profit sold upstream by a 10% minority interest combining entity, has not been resold out of the consolidated group, the previous minority interest entry is reduced by $100 ($1,000 × 10%) in the period of the sale.

6. **FASB Interpretation No. 46 (revised December 2003), *Consolidation of Variable Interest Entities*,** is a response to accounting scandals involving abuse of off-balance-sheet arrangements.

a. A **variable interest entity (VIE)** is an off-balance-sheet arrangement that may take any legal form (e.g., corporation, partnership, limited liability company, or trust). Moreover, a VIE either has insufficient equity or its equity investors lack one of the specified characteristics of financial control.

1) The **primary beneficiary (PB)** consolidates a VIE. An enterprise determines whether it is the PB when it becomes involved with the VIE. The PB is an entity with variable interests that absorb a majority of expected losses or receive a majority of expected residual returns.

       a)    Variable interests are ownership, contractual, or monetary interests that vary with changes in the **fair value of the VIE's net assets** (excluding variable interests). Examples are equity investments in a VIE that are at risk, subordinated debt or subordinated beneficial interests issued by the VIE, and guarantees of the VIE's assets or liabilities.

    b.    An entity must be consolidated as a VIE if, **by design**, any of three conditions exist.

       1)    The VIE is not properly capitalized; i.e., its equity at risk is insufficient to finance its operations without additional subordinated financial support from any parties.

       2)    As a group, the holders of equity at risk lack any one of the following characteristics of a controlling financial interest:

           a)    The ability, based on voting or similar rights, to make decisions significantly affecting the VIE's success,

           b)    An obligation to absorb expected losses, or

           c)    The right to receive expected residual returns.

       3)    Equity investors as a group lack characteristic 2)a) if

           a)    Voting rights of some investors are disproportional to their obligations to absorb expected losses or their rights to receive expected returns of the VIE, and

           b)    Substantially all of the VIE's activities involve or are performed for an investor with disproportionately few voting rights.

    c.    The PB's **initial measurement** of the VIE's assets, liabilities, and noncontrolling interests is at **fair value** on the date the enterprise becomes the PB (the first date it consolidates the VIE).

       1)    However, initial measurement is at the carrying amount if the PB and VIE are **under common control**.

       2)    Transfers of assets or liabilities to the VIE by the PB made shortly before, at, or after the date when the enterprise became the PB are measured as if they had not been transferred. Thus, these transfers do not result in gain or loss.

       3)    A loss from initial measurement is an **extraordinary item** if the VIE is not a business or **goodwill** if it is a business. A **gain** is **allocated** to reduce assets as described in **SFAS 141**, *Business Combinations*.

           a)    A gain is the excess of

               i)    The sum of the fair values of the consolidated assets of the VIE and the reported amounts of assets transferred by the PB over

              ii)    The sum of the consideration given (measured at fair value), the reported amounts of interests in the VIE previously held, and the fair values of the VIE's liabilities and noncontrolling interests.

           b)    A loss is recognized for any excess of ii) over i).

       4)    **Subsequent accounting** follows the principles that apply to ordinary consolidations.

7.    According to ARB 51, **combined financial statements** (as opposed to consolidated statements) may be more meaningful than the separate statements of commonly controlled entities.

    a.    For example, they are useful when one individual owns a controlling interest in several entities with related operations.

    b.    They are also used to present the financial position, results of operations, and cash flows of a group of unconsolidated subsidiaries and to combine the statements of entities under common management.

    c.    Combined statements are prepared in much the same manner as consolidated statements.

        1)    Interentity ownership and the related portion of equity must be eliminated.

        2)    According to ARB 51, when combined statements are prepared for a group of related entities, e.g., a group of unconsolidated subsidiaries or a group of commonly controlled entities, such matters as minority interests, foreign operations, different fiscal periods, and income taxes should be treated in the same manner as in consolidated statements.

8.    Stop and review! You have completed the outline for this subunit. Study multiple-choice questions 17 through 31 beginning on page 774.

## 19.4 DERIVATIVES AND HEDGING

1.    **SFAS 133**, *Accounting for Derivative Instruments and Hedging Activities*, as amended by **SFAS 138**, *Accounting for Certain Derivative Instruments and Certain Hedging Activities*, applies to all entities, including not-for-profit organizations and defined benefit pension plans. The standards it establishes for derivative instruments, including those embedded in other contracts, and hedging activities are based on four principles:

    a.    Derivatives should be recognized as **assets or liabilities** in the statement of financial position.

    b.    **Fair value** is the only relevant measure for derivatives. Moreover, the carrying amount of a hedged item should reflect any changes in its fair value while the hedge is in effect that are attributable to the hedged risk.

        1)    Derivatives usually have no value at inception but result in positive or negative fair value as the price of the underlying item changes.

    c.    Only items that are assets and liabilities should be recognized as such.

    d.    Designated hedged items should receive special accounting treatment only if they meet **qualifying criteria**, for example, the likelihood of effectiveness of the hedge in producing offsetting fair value or cash flow changes during the term of the hedge for the risk being hedged.

2.    A derivative is **defined informally** as an investment transaction in which the buyer purchases the right to a potential gain with a commitment for a potential loss. It is a wager on whether the value of something will go up or down. The purpose of the transaction is either to speculate (incur risk) or to hedge (avoid risk).

    a.    Thus, a derivative is an executory contract that results in cash flow between two **counterparties** based on the change in some other indicator of value. Examples of these indicators include prices of financial instruments, such as common shares or government bonds; currency exchange rates; interest rates; commodity prices; or indexes, such as the S&P 500 or the Dow Jones Industrial Average.

3.    Derivative instruments (derivatives) should be contrasted with **financial instruments**, which include cash, accounts receivable, notes receivable, bonds, preferred shares, common shares, etc. The following are examples of derivative instruments:

    a.    A **call option** is the right to purchase something (e.g., a commodity, foreign currency, etc.) at an exercise (strike) price. The purchaser pays a premium for the opportunity to benefit from the appreciation in the underlying item. An **American call option** is a right to purchase during the term of the option. A **European call option** permits purchase at a given date.

b.   A **forward contract** is an agreement negotiated between two parties for the purchase and sale of a stated amount of a commodity, foreign currency, or financial instrument at a stated price, with delivery or settlement at a stated future date.  Unlike futures contracts, forward contracts are usually specifically negotiated agreements and are not traded on regulated exchanges.  Thus, the parties are subject to default risk (i.e., that the other party will not perform).

c.   A **futures contract** is a forward-based agreement to make or receive delivery or make a cash settlement that involves a specified quantity of a commodity, foreign currency, or financial instrument during a specified time interval.  Futures contracts are usually standardized and exchange traded.  They are therefore less risky than forward contracts.  Another reason for their lesser risk is that they are "marked to market" daily; that is, money must be paid to cover any losses as they occur.  Furthermore, unlike forward contracts, futures contracts very rarely result in actual delivery.  The parties customarily make a **net settlement** in cash on the expiration date.

d.   An **interest rate swap** is an exchange of one party's interest payments based on a **fixed rate** for another party's interest payments based on a **variable rate**.  The maturity amount may or may not be swapped.  Moreover, most interest rate swaps permit **net settlement** because they do not require delivery of interest-bearing assets with a principal equal to the contracted amount.  Thus, an interest rate swap is appropriate when one counterparty prefers the payment pattern of the other.  For example, if a firm with fixed-rate debt has revenues that vary with interest rates, it may prefer floating rate debt so that its debt service burden will correlate directly with its revenues.

e.   A **put option** is the right to sell something at an exercise (strike) price.  The gain is the excess of the exercise price over the market price of the underlying item.  An **American put option** is the right to sell during the term of the option.  A **European put option** is the right to sell at a given date.

4.   **Hedging** is not defined in SFAS 133.  However, *The CPA Letter* (October 2000) defines a hedge as "a defensive strategy designed to protect an entity against the risk of adverse price or interest-rate movements on certain of its assets, liabilities, or anticipated transactions.  A hedge is used to avoid or reduce risks by creating a relationship by which losses on certain positions are expected to be counterbalanced in whole or in part by gains on separate positions in another market."

a.   Thus, the purchase or sale of a derivative or other instrument is a hedge if it is expected to neutralize the risk of a recognized asset or liability, an unrecognized firm commitment, a forecasted transaction, etc.  For example, if a flour company buys and uses 1 million bushels of wheat each month, it may wish to guard against increases in wheat costs when it has committed to sell at a price related to the current cost of wheat.  If so, the company will purchase wheat futures contracts that will result in gains if the price of wheat increases (offsetting the actual increased costs).

5.   SFAS 133 formally defines a **derivative** as a financial instrument or other contract with certain characteristics.  It states that a derivative, including one embedded in another contract, has at least one **underlying** (interest rate, exchange rate, price index, etc.) and at least one **notional amount** (number of units specified in the contract) or payment provision, or both.  The terms of a derivative also permit or require net settlement or provide for the equivalent.  Moreover, no **initial net investment** or one smaller than that necessary for contracts with similar responses to the market is required.

a.   **Net settlement** means that the derivative can be readily settled with only a net delivery of assets.  Thus, neither party need deliver an asset associated with its underlying or an asset that has a principal, stated amount, etc., equal to the notional amount (possibly adjusted for discount or premium).  If one party must deliver such an asset, the net settlement criterion is still met if a **market mechanism** exists to facilitate net settlement, or the asset is readily convertible to cash or is a derivative.

6.　The following are not within the **scope** of SFAS 133:

    a.　"Regular-way" security trades (contracts lacking a provision for net settlement or a market mechanism to facilitate net settlement)

    b.　Normal purchases and sales (contracts providing for purchase or sale of nonfinancial assets – even if readily convertible to cash – that will be delivered in quantities expected to be used or sold over a reasonable period in the normal course of business)

    c.　Traditional life, property, and casualty insurance contracts

    d.　Certain guarantee contracts and certain contracts that are not exchange traded

    e.　Derivatives that impede recognition of a sale (for example, a call option that permits a transferor to repurchase financial assets that are not readily available)

7.　From the **issuer's** perspective, the following are NOT deemed to be derivatives for purposes of SFAS 133:

    a.　Contracts issued or held that are indexed to the entity's own shares and classified in equity in its balance sheet

    b.　Contracts issued that are related to stock-based compensation (SFAS 123)

    c.　Contracts issued as contingent consideration in a business combination by an entity accounting for the transaction using the purchase method

8.　**Gains and losses** from changes in the fair value of a derivative, whether or not it is designated and qualifies as a hedging instrument, are **included in earnings** in the period of change. Exceptions are certain gains and losses on a derivative designated as a cash flow hedge or as a hedge of a net investment in a foreign operation.

9.　**Types of Hedges.** Hedge accounting ordinarily is limited to derivatives. Provided that the hedging derivatives (and the hedged items) meet the complex criteria in SFAS 133, for example, formal documentation of the hedging relationship and the entity's risk management objective and strategy (as well as many other criteria beyond the scope of this outline), such derivatives may qualify and be designated as hedges of

    a.　**Changes in the fair value** of a recognized asset or liability (or part thereof) or of an unrecognized firm commitment that are attributable to a specified risk (fair value hedge).

        1)　A **firm commitment** is an agreement with an unrelated party that is binding on both parties and is usually legally enforceable. It specifies all significant terms, and its performance is probable because it contains a sufficiently large disincentive for nonperformance.

    b.　The **variable cash flows** of a recognized asset or liability or of a forecasted transaction that are attributable to a specified risk (cash flow hedge).

        1)　A **forecasted transaction** is expected, although no firm commitment exists. It does not confer current rights to future benefits or impose a current obligation for future sacrifices because no transaction or event has occurred. When such a transaction or event occurs, it will be at the prevailing market price.

    c.　Certain foreign currency exposures.

10.　An exception to the rule limiting hedging instruments to derivatives is permitted for a **nonderivative financial instrument** that is designated as a fair value hedge of the foreign currency exposure of an unrecognized firm commitment. The same exception applies to hedges of the foreign currency exposure of a net investment in a foreign operation. The nonderivative hedging instrument in these cases is one that may result in foreign currency transaction gain or loss accounted for under SFAS 52.

11. **Accounting for Hedging Gain or Loss**

a. **Fair value hedges** reduce risk when a recognized asset or liability or a firm commitment has fixed cash flows. For example, fixed rate investments and debt and firm commitments to purchase or sell assets or incur liabilities may be subject to fair value hedging.

   1) The gain or loss on the **hedged item** attributable to the risk being hedged is an adjustment to the carrying amount of the item and is recognized currently in **earnings**.

      a) When the hedged item is a **previously unrecognized firm commitment**, the recognition of gain or loss on the firm commitment includes debiting an asset or crediting a liability, respectively. Accordingly, the phrase "asset and liability" used in SFAS 133 includes a firm commitment.

   2) The loss or gain on the **hedging instrument** (normally, a derivative) is also recognized currently in **earnings**.

   3) SFAS 133 (as amended) permits a **fair value hedge** of certain types of **foreign currency exposures**. They include an unrecognized firm commitment and a recognized asset or liability (including an available-for-sale security) for which a foreign currency transaction gain or loss is recognized in earnings under SFAS 52.

      a) Accordingly, the gain or loss on the hedging derivative (or hedging nonderivative) instrument in a fair value hedge of a **foreign-currency-denominated firm commitment**. The offsetting loss or gain on the hedged firm commitment attributable to the hedged risk is also recognized in earnings in the same period.

      b) Similarly, in a fair value hedge of a **recognized asset or liability** (one for which a foreign currency transaction gain or loss is recognized), the gain or loss on the hedging derivative instrument (a nonderivative may not be used in this case) is recognized in earnings. The offsetting loss or gain on the hedged recognized asset or liability attributable to the hedged risk also is recognized in earnings in the same period.

b. **Cash-flow hedges** reduce risk when a recognized asset or liability (for example, all or certain interest payments on variable rate debt) or a forecasted transaction (for example, an anticipated issue of debt, purchase, or sale) has **variable cash flows**.

   1) Because the gain or loss on the hedged item will not occur until a future period, the **effective** portion of the loss or gain on the designated hedging instrument is reported in **other comprehensive income (OCI)**. It will be recognized in earnings (**reclassified** from OCI) when the gain or loss on the intended transaction is recognized in earnings. The ineffective portion is recognized in earnings immediately.

      a) The **effectiveness** of a hedge is the percentage of gain or loss on the hedged item that is offset by the hedging instrument's loss or gain. Hedges should be highly effective.

   2) A nonderivative instrument may not be the hedging instrument in a **foreign currency cash flow hedge**. However, according to SFAS 138, a derivative instrument may be designated as a hedge of "the foreign currency exposure to variability in the functional-currency-equivalent cash flows associated with a forecasted transaction, a recognized asset or liability, an unrecognized firm commitment, or a forecasted intercompany transaction" (e.g., a forecasted sale to a foreign subsidiary).

        a)    Thus, the **effective portion** of the gain or loss on the hedging derivative instrument in a foreign currency cash flow hedge is recognized as a component of OCI. The **ineffective portion** is recognized in earnings in the period in which the gain or loss is recognized. The gain or loss recognized as a component of OCI is reclassified into **earnings** in the same period(s) during which the hedged item affects earnings.

    c.    Gains and losses on a derivative designated as a hedge of a foreign currency exposure of a **net investment in a foreign operation** are reported as part of the **cumulative translation adjustment in OCI** to the extent the hedge is effective. If the hedging instrument is a nonderivative financial instrument, the foreign currency transaction gain or loss determined under SFAS 52 is treated in the same manner.

12.  **Embedded Derivatives**

    a.    A common example of an embedded derivative is the conversion feature of convertible debt. It represents a call option on the issuer's stock. Embedded derivatives must be **accounted for separately** from the related **host contract** if the following conditions are met:

        1)    The economic characteristics and risks of the embedded derivative instrument are **not clearly and closely related** to the economic characteristics of the host.

        2)    The hybrid instrument is **not remeasured at fair value** under otherwise applicable GAAP, with changes in fair value reported in earnings as they occur.

        3)    A freestanding instrument with the same terms as the embedded derivative would be subject to the requirements of SFAS 133.

    b.    If an embedded derivative is accounted for separately, the **host contract** is accounted for based on the accounting standards that are applicable to instruments of its type. The **separated derivative** should be accounted for under SFAS 133.

        1)    If separating the two instruments is impossible, the entire contract must be measured at fair value, with gains and losses recognized in earnings. It may not be designated as a hedging instrument because nonderivatives usually do not qualify as hedging instruments.

13.  The accounting for changes in fair value of a derivative depends on the reasons for holding it. The accounting also depends on whether the entity has elected to **designate** it as part of a hedging relationship and whether it meets the **qualifying criteria** for the particular type of accounting.

    a.    All or part of a derivative may be designated as a hedging instrument. The proportion must be expressed as a **percentage of the entire derivative**.

    b.    SFAS 133 establishes qualifying criteria that are numerous and complex and, accordingly, are not reproduced here. They relate to effectiveness, the degree of formal documentation needed regarding the hedging relationship, requirements for particular hedging instruments and hedged items, etc.

        1)    A reporting entity that elects hedge accounting must, among other things, formally determine at the **hedge's inception** the methods (consistent with the entity's risk management strategy) for determining the **effectiveness and ineffectiveness** of the hedge. Thus, an entity must specify whether all of the gain or loss on the hedging instrument will be included in the assessment of effectiveness. For example, an entity may exclude all or part of the time value from the assessment of effectiveness.

14.   A **not-for-profit organization** or other entity not reporting earnings separately recognizes the change in fair value of all derivatives as a **change in net assets** (unless a derivative hedges a foreign currency exposure of a net investment in a foreign operation). In a **fair value hedge**, the change in fair value of the hedged item attributable to the risk being hedged is recognized as a change in net assets. These entities may **NOT** use cash flow hedge accounting.

15.   The following are among the **disclosures** required for derivatives and hedging:

   a.   Objectives for holding or issuing derivatives.

   b.   Context for understanding the objectives.

   c.   Strategies for achieving the objectives.

   d.   Risk management policies.

   e.   Details about fair value hedges, cash flow hedges, and hedges of a net investment in a foreign operation.

   f.   Display within OCI of a separate classification for net gain or loss on derivatives designated and qualifying as cash flow hedges to the extent they are reported in comprehensive income.

16.   **Examples of Hedging Transactions**

   a.   **Fair value hedge.** A company wishes to hedge the fair value of its investment in an inventory of Commodity A by selling futures contracts on August 1, 20X2 for delivery on February 1, 20X3, the date on which it intends to sell the inventory. The following information is available about spot and futures prices and the company's estimates of changes in the fair value of the inventory (changes in spot rates adjusted for its transportation costs, storage costs, etc.):

|  | Spot Rate | Futures Rate for February 1 Delivery | Change in Fair Value of Inventory |
|---|---|---|---|
| August 1, 20X2 | $.51 | $.53 | |
| December 31, 20X2 | .49 | .51 | $(21,000) |
| February 1, 20X3 | .52 | .52 | 32,000 |

The company sold futures contracts for 1 million pounds of Commodity A at $.53 per pound, its inventory had an average cost of $.38 per pound, and it sold the entire inventory of Commodity A on February 1, 20X3 at the spot rate of $.52 per pound. The company also bought offsetting February 20X3 futures contracts on February 1, 20X3 for 1 million pounds of Commodity A at $.52 per pound. This transaction closed out its futures position. The following journal entries should be made (ignoring the margin deposit with the broker):

August 1, 20X2

The fair value of the futures contracts is zero at the inception date. Thus, no entry is made to record their fair value.

December 31, 20X2

| Loss | $21,000 | |
| Inventory -- Commodity A | | $21,000 |

(The company estimates a loss of $21,000.)

| Receivable from/liability to broker | $20,000 | |
| Gain on the hedge | | $20,000 |

[The gain on the futures contract is $.02 per pound ($.53 futures rate at August 1, 20X2 − $.51 futures rate at December 31, 20X2 for February 1, 20X3 delivery) times 1,000,000 pounds, or a $20,000 gain.]

February 1, 20X3

| | | |
|---|---|---|
| Inventory -- Commodity A | $32,000 | |
| Gain | | $32,000 |

(The company estimates a loss of $32,000.)

| | | |
|---|---|---|
| Loss on the hedge | $10,000 | |
| Receivable from/liability to broker | | $10,000 |

[The loss on the futures contracts is $.01 per pound ($.52 rate at February 1, 20X3 – $.51 futures rate at December 31, 20X2 for February 1, 20X3 delivery) times 1,000,000 pounds, or a $10,000 loss.]

| | | |
|---|---|---|
| Cash | $10,000 | |
| Receivable from/liability to broker | | $10,000 |

(This entry records settlement of the futures contracts.)

| | | |
|---|---|---|
| Accounts receivable | $520,000 | |
| Cost of goods sold | 391,000 | |
| Sales | | $520,000 |
| Inventory -- Commodity A | | 391,000 |

[The revenue from the sale equaled the spot rate ($.52) times 1,000,000 pounds, or $520,000. The inventory equaled the average cost ($.38) times 1,000,000 pounds, minus the fair value loss on December 31, 20X2 ($21,000), plus the fair value gain on February 1, 20X3 ($32,000), or $391,000.]

b. **Cash flow hedge.** At January 2, 20X2, a company determines that it will need to purchase 100,000 pounds of Commodity B in June 20X2. The purchase is expected to be at the spot rate. To hedge this forecasted transaction, the company agrees to purchase futures contracts for 100,000 pounds of Commodity B at the June 20X2 futures price of $3.05 per pound. Hedge effectiveness will be determined by comparing the total change in the fair value of the futures contracts with the changes in the cash flows of the anticipated purchase. In June, the company buys 100,000 pounds of Commodity B at the spot rate of $3.20 per pound. Ignoring the margin deposit for the futures contracts, the following are the journal entries for this transaction:

January 20X2

Because the margin deposit is ignored in this problem, no journal entry is made. The futures contract is not recorded because, at its inception, its fair value is zero.

June 20X2

| | | |
|---|---|---|
| Commodity B inventory | $320,000 | |
| Cash | | $320,000 |

[The quantity purchased (100,000 pounds) times the spot rate ($3.20 per pound) equals $320,000.]

| | | |
|---|---|---|
| Futures contracts | $15,000 | |
| Other comprehensive income | | $15,000 |

[The gain, which will subsequently be reclassified into earnings when the inventory is sold, equals the difference between the spot rate and the futures contract rate ($3.20 – $3.05 = $.15) times 100,000 pounds, or $15,000.]

| | | |
|---|---|---|
| Cash | $15,000 | |
| Futures contracts | | $15,000 |

(This entry records the net cash settlement. In practice, futures contracts are settled daily.)

c. **Hedge of a net investment in a foreign operation.** Parent, Inc., a U.S. company, has a net investment in its Xenadian subsidiary, Subco, of 100 million foreign currency units (FCU), the subsidiary's functional currency. At November 1, 20X2, Parent sells a forward exchange contract for the delivery of 100 million FCU on February 1, 20X3. This contract is designated as a hedge of the net investment in Subco. The contract rate equals the forward rate at November 1, 20X2 of $1.15 per FCU. On that date, the spot rate is $1.17 per FCU. Parent records the premium on the forward contract [($1.17 – $1.15) × 100,000,000 FCU = $2,000,000] as a translation adjustment. Moreover, Parent records the change in fair value of the forward contract at fair value in its statement of financial position, with the effective portion of the hedge (100% in this case) recorded in other comprehensive income (OCI). In accordance with SFAS 52, Parent also translates its net investment in Subco into U.S. dollars, and it reports the effects of changes in exchange rates as a cumulative translation adjustment in OCI.

The following table provides information about exchange rates, the forward contract's changes in fair value, and the translation adjustments (change in spot rates × the notional amount). Measuring the fair value of a foreign currency forward contract requires discounting the estimated future cash flows. This estimate of cash flows is based on the changes in the forward rate, not in the spot rate.

| | Gain (Loss) – Forward Contract's Change in Fair Value (Discounted) | Gain (Loss) – Cumulative Translation Adjustment | Spot Rates per FCU | Forward Rates per FCU for 2/1 Delivery |
|---|---|---|---|---|
| November 1, 20X2 | | | $1.17 | $1.15 |
| December 31, 20X2 | $3,920,000 | $(4,000,000) | 1.13 | 1.11 |
| February 1, 20X3 | 2,080,000 | (4,000,000) | 1.09 | 1.09 |
| | $6,000,000 | $ 8,000,000 | | |

The following are the basic journal entries:

November 1, 20X2

No entry is made because the forward rate and the contract rate were the same.

December 31, 20X2

| | | |
|---|---|---|
| Receivable -- forward contract | $3,920,000 | |
| OCI | | $3,920,000 |

[The change in fair value of the contract (discounted future cash flows based on changes in the forward rate) is recorded in OCI in the same manner as a translation adjustment. Parent determined that the estimated change in cash flows equaled the change in forward rates ($1.15 – $1.11 = $0.04) times 100,000,000 FCU, or $4,000,000. It then determined that the present value of that change was $3,920,000 (given).]

| | | |
|---|---|---|
| OCI | $4,000,000 | |
| Net investment -- Subco | | $4,000,000 |

[The translation adjustment in accordance with SFAS 52 is the change in spot rates ($1.17 – $1.13 = $.04) times 100,000,000 FCU, or a loss of $4,000,000.]

February 1, 20X3

| Receivable -- forward contract | $2,080,000 | |
| OCI | | $2,080,000 |

[The total change in fair value of the contract is the change in forward rates ($1.15 − $1.09 = $.06) times 100,000,000 FCU, or a gain of $6,000,000. Of this amount, $3,920,000 (discounted) was recognized at December 31, 20X2. Thus, to record the fair value of the contract on the settlement date requires an additional credit to OCI of $2,080,000 ($6,000,000 gain − $3,920,000).]

| OCI | $4,000,000 | |
| Net investment -- Subco | | $4,000,000 |

[The translation adjustment is the change in spot rates ($1.13 − $1.09) times 100,000,000 FCU, or a loss of $4,000,000.]

| Cash | $6,000,000 | |
| Receivable -- forward contract | | $6,000,000 |

(This entry reflects the net cash settlement of the foreign currency forward contract.)

d.   **Fair value hedge using an interest-rate swap.** Major Manufacturer borrowed $1 million on December 31, 20X2 for 3 years at 8% fixed interest. The debt is not prepayable, and interest is due semiannually. On the same date, Major entered into an interest-rate swap by which it receives 8% fixed interest on $1 million and pays variable interest on the same amount in accordance with an agreed index of standard interest rates. Payments on the debt and settlement of the swap are on the same dates, with no premium/discount resulting from the swap. Major designates the swap as a fair value hedge, and the risk hedged is stated to be the change in market interest rates. Furthermore, the hedge is assumed to be completely effective because all of the criteria in SFAS 133 are met; i.e., the swap's fair value at its inception is zero, the notional amount of the swap equals the principal amount of the debt, the expiration date of the swap equals the maturity date of the debt, etc. Given that the hedge is completely effective, changes in its fair value are used to measure the changes in the fair value of the debt. The following are illustrative data at the inception date and the first two reset dates:

| | Fair Value of the Debt | Fair Value of the Interest Rate Swap Based on Dealer Quotes (After Settlement) | Index Variable Rate (Rate Changed on Indicated Date) |
| --- | --- | --- | --- |
| December 31, 20X2 | $1,000,000 | $        0 | 6.5% |
| June 30, 20X3 | 970,000 | (30,000) | 7.5% |
| December 31, 20X3 | 1,010,000 | 10,000 | 6.0% |

Under the shortcut method described in SFAS 133, the variable rate paid on the swap is combined with the difference between the fixed rates paid and received (in this case, zero). The result is multiplied by the principal of the debt to determine the annual interest expense. The following are illustrative journal entries:

December 31, 20X2

| Cash | $1,000,000 | |
| Debt | | $1,000,000 |

(The swap's fair value at its inception is given as zero. Thus, no entry is made.)

June 30, 20X3

| | | |
|---|---|---|
| Interest expense | $40,000 | |
| Interest payable | | $40,000 |

| | | |
|---|---|---|
| Interest payable | $40,000 | |
| Cash | | $40,000 |

(The interest on the debt is $1,000,000 times the 8% fixed rate for 6 months.)

| | | |
|---|---|---|
| Cash | $7,500 | |
| Interest expense | | $7,500 |

[The semiannual interest expense equals the 6.5% variable rate for the first 6 months of 20X3 times $1,000,000 times 6 divided by 12 months, or $32,500. Accordingly, Major receives a net settlement of $7,500 ($40,000 paid on the debt – $32,500 semiannual interest expense).]

| | | |
|---|---|---|
| Debt | $30,000 | |
| Gain from hedge | | $30,000 |

(The increase in interest rates at June 30, 20X3 reduced the debt's fair value.)

| | | |
|---|---|---|
| Loss from hedge | $30,000 | |
| Interest rate swap contract | | $30,000 |

(The swap's fair value decreased.)

December 31, 20X3

(The entries to accrue and pay the $40,000 interest on the debt are the same.)

| | | |
|---|---|---|
| Cash | $2,500 | |
| Interest expense | | $2,500 |

[The semiannual interest expense equals the 7.5% variable rate for the last 6 months of 20X3 times $1,000,000 times 6 divided by 12 months, or $37,500. Accordingly, Major receives a net settlement of $2,500 ($40,000 paid on the debt – $37,500 semiannual interest expense).]

| | | |
|---|---|---|
| Loss from hedge | $40,000 | |
| Debt | | $40,000 |

(The decrease in interest rates at December 31, 20X3 increased the debt's fair value.)

| | | |
|---|---|---|
| Interest rate from swap contract | $40,000 | |
| Gain from hedge | | $40,000 |

(The swap's fair value increased.)

e. **Embedded derivative used as a cash flow hedge of a forecasted transaction.** Aviatrix Co. bought a one-year crude oil knock-in note on January 1, 20X2 for $20,000,000. Such a note combines an interest-bearing instrument with a series of options. This note had a 1% coupon rate and provided for investor gains if specified oil prices rose. The contingency was not separable from the note. In effect, part of the normal coupon rate purchased an option tied to changes in oil prices. This embedded option should be accounted for separately because it is not clearly and closely related to the economic characteristics of the host contract (a fixed rate note); the option is indexed to the price of oil and is not related to interest rates. Moreover, the host contract is not remeasured at fair value, and the option qualifies as a derivative instrument.

Aviatrix appropriately designated the option as a hedge of fuel purchases it expects to make on January 1, 20X3, and it has ascertained that the option should be highly effective as a hedge because the intrinsic value of the option is closely correlated with the expected cash outflows for fuel purchases. Under SFAS 133, an entity that elects hedge accounting must determine at the outset the methods for assessing the effectiveness and ineffectiveness of the hedge. Aviatrix has decided to assess hedge effectiveness based on the option's intrinsic value; hence, the change in time value is excluded from the assessment of hedge effectiveness (paragraph 63 of SFAS 133).

The note had a fair value on January 1, 20X2 of $18,800,000, and the option had a fair value of $1,200,000 (but a $0 intrinsic value). If the option's maturity value (an intrinsic, not a time, value) was $1,500,000, the journal entries made by Aviatrix in accordance with SFAS 133 are as follows:

January 1, 20X2

| | | |
|---|---|---|
| Investment in knock-in note | $18,800,000 | |
| Option | 1,200,000 | |
| Cash | | $20,000,000 |

(To record the note's purchase.)

December 31, 20X2

| | | |
|---|---|---|
| Investment in knock-in note | $1,200,000 | |
| Interest outcome | | $1,200,000 |

(To amortize the discount on the note.)

| | | |
|---|---|---|
| Interest receivable | $200,000 | |
| Interest income | | $200,000 |

[This entry accrues annual interest at the nominal rate of 1% ($20,000,000 × 1%).]

| | | |
|---|---|---|
| Option | $1,500,000 | |
| Other comprehensive income | | $1,500,000 |

[To record the change in the intrinsic value of the option ($1,500,000 − $0 = $1,500,000). The credit is to OCI because the option is a cash flow hedge of a forecasted transaction. This gain will be reclassified into earnings when the fuel purchases are recorded.]

| | | |
|---|---|---|
| Loss from hedge | $1,200,000 | |
| Option | | $1,200,000 |

[To record the extent of ineffectiveness of the hedge, that is, the change in the time value. Because the effectiveness of the option is assessed based only on intrinsic value, the change in time value ($1,200,000 − $0 = $1,200,000 loss) is debited to a loss. The ineffective portion of the gain or loss on a derivative designated as a cash flow hedge is reported in earnings.]

January 1, 20X3

| | | |
|---|---|---|
| Cash | $21,700,000 | |
| Investment in knock-in note | | $20,000,000 |
| Option | | 1,500,000 |
| Interest receivable | | 200,000 |

17. Stop and review! You have completed the outline for this subunit. Study multiple-choice questions 32 through 44 beginning on page 779.

## 19.5  CORE CONCEPTS

<u>Business Combinations</u>

- A **business combination** takes place anytime an entity acquires the net assets or a controlling equity interest in another company.
- All such combinations are accounted for as **purchases**.  (Formerly, combinations could, under certain circumstances, be accounted for as poolings-of-interests, in which the existing valuations of assets and liabilities were simply carried over to the new entity.)

<u>Accounting for Business Combinations</u>

- In general, the **cost of the acquired entity** is allocated to the assets acquired and liabilities assumed in accordance with their **fair values** at the acquisition date.
- Specifically, the FASB has provided guidance for the **valuation of individual assets** (work-in-process is booked at estimated selling price minus costs to complete, raw materials are booked at current replacement costs, etc.).
- Any **excess paid** by the acquiring entity over the assessed value of the acquired entity's net assets is recorded as an intangible asset named **goodwill**.

<u>Consolidated Financial Statements</u>

- **Consolidated statements** are intended to present the results of operations, financial position, and cash flows of a parent and its subsidiaries **as if they were a single economic entity**.
- **Profits and losses** on transactions within the consolidated entity are **completely eliminated**, but the procedure varies depending on whether the transaction was **downstream** (parent to subsidiary) or **upstream** (subsidiary to parent).
- **Interentity debt transactions** are also eliminated.

<u>Derivatives and Hedging</u>

- A **derivative** is an **investment transaction** in which the buyer purchases the right to a potential gain with a commitment for a potential loss.  Examples include call options, forward contracts, futures contracts, interest rate swaps, and put options.
- Derivatives should be **contrasted with financial instruments**, such as cash, accounts receivable, and equity securities.
- Derivatives should be recognized as **assets or liabilities** in the balance sheet.  **Fair value** is the only relevant measure for derivatives.
- **Hedging** is the purchase or sale of a derivative or other instrument in order to **neutralize the risk** of another transaction.  Types include fair-value hedges and cash-flow hedges.

## QUESTIONS

### 19.1 Business Combinations

**1.** A business combination may be legally structured as a merger, a consolidation, or an acquisition. Which of the following describes a business combination that is legally structured as a merger?

   A. The surviving company is one of the two combining companies.

   B. The surviving company is neither of the two combining companies.

   C. An investor-investee relationship is established.

   D. A parent-subsidiary relationship is established.

**Answer (A) is correct.** *(Publisher)*
**REQUIRED:** The characteristic of a business combination legally structured as a merger.
**DISCUSSION:** In a business combination legally structured as a merger, the assets and liabilities of one of the combining companies are transferred to the books of the other combining company (the surviving company). The surviving company continues to exist as a separate legal entity. The nonsurviving company ceases to exist as a separate entity. Its stock is canceled, and its books are closed.
Answer (B) is incorrect because it describes a consolidation, in which a new firm is formed to account for the assets and liabilities of the combining companies. Answer (C) is incorrect because it describes an acquisition. A parent-subsidiary relationship exists when the investor holds more than 50% of the outstanding stock of the investee. Answer (D) is incorrect because it describes an acquisition. A parent-subsidiary relationship exists when the investor holds more than 50% of the outstanding stock of the investee.

**2.** A horizontal merger is a merger between

   A. Two or more firms from different and unrelated markets.

   B. Two or more firms at different stages of the production process.

   C. A producer and its supplier.

   D. Two or more firms in the same market.

**Answer (D) is correct.** *(CMA, adapted)*
**REQUIRED:** The example of a horizontal merger.
**DISCUSSION:** A horizontal merger is one between competitors in the same market. From the viewpoint of the Justice Department, it is the most closely scrutinized type of merger because it has the greatest tendency to reduce competition.
Answer (A) is incorrect because a merger between firms in different and unrelated markets is a conglomerate merger. Answer (B) is incorrect because a merger between two or more firms at different stages of the production process is a vertical merger. Answer (C) is incorrect because a merger between a producer and a supplier is a vertical merger.

**3.** Which type of acquisition does not require shareholders to have a formal vote to approve?

   A. Merger.

   B. Acquisition of stock.

   C. Acquisition of all of the firm's assets.

   D. Consolidation.

**Answer (B) is correct.** *(Publisher)*
**REQUIRED:** The type of acquisition that does not require a formal vote by shareholders for approval.
**DISCUSSION:** Purchasing the stock of another company is advantageous when management and the board of directors of the purchased company are hostile to the combination because the acquisition does not require a formal vote by the shareholders. Thus, the management and the board of directors cannot influence shareholders. Also, after the acquisition, both companies continue to operate separately.
Answer (A) is incorrect because a merger is not an acquisition. In a merger, only one of the combining companies survives. Answer (C) is incorrect because an acquisition of all of the firm's assets requires a vote from the shareholders. Answer (D) is incorrect because a consolidation is different from an acquisition since, in a consolidation, a new company is formed and neither of the merging companies survives.

**4.** The acquisition of a retail shoe store by a shoe manufacturer is an example of

   A. Vertical integration.

   B. A conglomerate.

   C. Market extension.

   D. Horizontal integration.

**Answer (A) is correct.** *(CMA, adapted)*
**REQUIRED:** The type of transaction represented.
**DISCUSSION:** The acquisition of a shoe retailer by a shoe manufacturer is an example of vertical integration. Vertical integration is typified by a merger or acquisition involving companies that are in the same industry but at different levels in the supply chain. In other words, one of the companies supplies inputs for the other.
Answer (B) is incorrect because a conglomerate is a company made up of subsidiaries in unrelated industries. Answer (C) is incorrect because market extension involves expanding into new market areas. Answer (D) is incorrect because horizontal integration involves a merger between competing firms in the same industry.

**5.** Which of the following is a combination involving the absorption of one firm by another?

    A. Merger.

    B. Consolidation.

    C. Proxy fight.

    D. Acquisition.

Answer (A) is correct.    *(Publisher)*
    **REQUIRED:** The combination involving the absorption of one firm by another.
    **DISCUSSION:** A merger is a business combination in which an acquiring firm absorbs another firm. The acquiring firm remains in business as a combination of the two merged firms. Thus, the acquiring firm maintains its name and identity. However, approval of the merger is required by votes of the shareholders of each firm.
    Answer (B) is incorrect because a consolidation merges two companies and forms a new company in which neither of the two merging firms survives. It is similar to a merger, but one firm is not absorbed by another. Answer (C) is incorrect because a proxy fight is an attempt by dissident shareholders to gain control of the corporation by electing directors. Answer (D) is incorrect because both companies continue to operate separately after an acquisition.

## 19.2 Accounting for Business Combinations

**6.** In a business combination that does not create negative goodwill, the acquiring entity records the assets of the acquired entity at the

    A. Original cost.

    B. Original cost minus accumulated depreciation.

    C. Fair market value.

    D. Carrying amount.

Answer (C) is correct.    *(CMA, adapted)*
    **REQUIRED:** The accounting for a business combination not resulting in negative goodwill.
    **DISCUSSION:** Under SFAS 141, *Business Combinations*, a business combination initiated after June 30, 2001 is accounted for as a purchase regardless of the form of consideration given. Under purchase accounting, assets acquired and liabilities assumed should be recorded at their fair values.
    Answer (A) is incorrect because assets are recorded at their fair value. Answer (B) is incorrect because assets are recorded at their fair value. Answer (D) is incorrect because the carrying amount was the method used to record assets in a pooling of interests. A business combination initiated after June 30, 2001 is accounted for as a purchase regardless of the form of consideration given. Assets acquired and liabilities assumed should be recorded at their fair values.

**7.** In a business combination, the sum of the amounts assigned by the acquiring entity to assets acquired and liabilities assumed exceeds the cost of the acquired entity. The excess should be reported as a

    A. Deferred credit.

    B. Reduction of the amounts assigned to current assets and a deferred credit for any unallocated portion.

    C. Reduction of the amounts assigned to certain acquired assets and an extraordinary gain for any unallocated portion.

    D. Pro rata reduction of the amounts assigned to all acquired assets and an extraordinary gain for any unallocated portion.

Answer (C) is correct.    *(CPA, adapted)*
    **REQUIRED:** The accounting for the excess of the fair value of acquired net assets over cost.
    **DISCUSSION:** In a business combination, any excess of the fair value assigned to the net assets acquired over the cost of the purchase must be allocated proportionately to reduce the amounts otherwise assignable to all of the acquired assets except (a) financial assets (excluding equity-method investments), (b) assets to be disposed of by sale, (c) deferred tax assets, (d) prepaid assets relating to post-retirement benefit plans, and (e) other current assets. Any remainder after the amounts otherwise assignable to those assets have been reduced to zero is reported as an extraordinary gain (SFAS 141).
    Answer (A) is incorrect because a deferred credit is never recognized for the excess of the fair value of acquired net assets over cost. Answer (B) is incorrect because a deferred credit is never recognized for the excess of the fair value of acquired net assets over cost. Answer (D) is incorrect because the amounts assigned to certain acquired assets (most financial assets, assets to be disposed of by sale, etc.) are not reduced.

**8.** For the past several years, Mozza Company has invested in the common stock of Chedd Company. As of July 1, 20X1, Mozza owned approximately 13% of the total of Chedd's outstanding voting common stock. Recently, managements of the two companies have discussed a possible combination of the two entities. However, no public announcement has been made, and no notice to owners has been given. The resulting business combination would be accounted for as a

A. Pooling of interests.

B. Purchase.

C. Part purchase, part pooling.

D. Joint venture.

Answer (B) is correct. *(Publisher)*
REQUIRED: The accounting for a business combination, given 13% ownership of one combining entity by the other.
DISCUSSION: A business combination is an entity's acquisition of (1) net assets constituting a business or (2) controlling equity interests of one or more other entities. A business combination initiated after June 30, 20X1 must be accounted for using the purchase method. A business combination is initiated at the earlier of the date the major terms (including the ratio of exchange) are announced publicly or formally made known to owners of any combining entity or the date owners of a combining entity are notified in writing of an exchange offer. Thus, no combination was initiated before July 1, 20X1, and any subsequent combination of these entities must be accounted for using the purchase method.
Answer (A) is incorrect because the pooling-of-interests method may not be used to account for a business combination initiated after June 30, 20X1. Answer (C) is incorrect because accounting for a business combination as part purchase and part pooling is not allowed. Answer (D) is incorrect because a joint venture does not meet the definition of a business combination.

**9.** To effect a business combination initiated on July 1, 20X1, Proper Co. acquired all the outstanding common shares of Scapula Co. for cash equal to the carrying amount of Scapula's net assets. The carrying amounts of Scapula's assets and liabilities approximated their fair values, except that the carrying amount of its building was more than fair value. In preparing Proper's December 31, 20X1 consolidated income statement, what is the effect of recording the assets acquired and liabilities assumed at fair value and should goodwill amortization be recognized?

|   | Depreciation Expense | Goodwill Amortization |
|---|---|---|
| A. | Lower | Yes |
| B. | Higher | Yes |
| C. | Lower | No |
| D. | Higher | No |

Answer (C) is correct. *(CPA, adapted)*
REQUIRED: The adjustments made in preparing the consolidated income statement.
DISCUSSION: A business combination initiated after June 30, 20X1 is accounted for as a purchase regardless of the form of consideration given. Under purchase accounting, assets acquired and liabilities assumed should be recorded at their fair values. The differences between fair values and carrying amounts will affect net income when related expenses are incurred. The effect of recording the building at fair value in the consolidated balance sheet instead of its higher carrying amount on Scapula's books will be to decrease future depreciation. If the building is to be used, fair value is its current replacement cost for similar capacity unless expected use indicates a lower value to the acquirer. If the building is to be sold, it should be reported at fair value minus cost to sell. The excess of the cost over fair value of the net assets acquired will be recognized as goodwill, but, under SFAS 142, this amount will be tested for impairment but not amortized.

**10.** Zuider Corp. acquired 100% of the outstanding common stock of Zee Corp. in a business combination initiated in September 20X1. The cost of the acquisition exceeded the fair value of the acquired net assets. The general guidelines for assigning amounts to the inventories acquired provide for

A. Raw materials to be valued at original cost.

B. Work-in-process to be valued at the estimated selling prices of finished goods, minus both costs to complete and costs of disposal.

C. Finished goods to be valued at replacement cost.

D. Finished goods to be valued at estimated selling prices, minus both costs of disposal and a reasonable profit allowance.

Answer (D) is correct. *(CPA, adapted)*
REQUIRED: The proper accounting for inventories when the cost of the acquisition exceeds the fair value of the net assets acquired.
DISCUSSION: Finished goods and merchandise should be assigned amounts equal to estimated selling prices minus the sum of (1) costs of disposal and (2) a reasonable profit allowance for the selling effort of the acquiring entity.
Answer (A) is incorrect because raw materials should be valued at current replacement cost. Answer (B) is incorrect because work-in-process should be valued at estimated selling prices of finished goods minus the sum of (1) costs to complete, (2) costs of disposal, and (3) a reasonable profit allowance for the completing and selling effort of the acquiring entity based on profit for similar finished goods. Answer (C) is incorrect because finished goods are valued at estimated selling prices minus the sum of (1) costs of disposal and (2) a reasonable profit allowance.

**11.** Dire Co., in a business combination initiated and completed in October 20X1, purchased Wall Co. at a cost that resulted in recognition of goodwill having an expected 10-year benefit period. However, Dire plans to make additional expenditures to maintain goodwill for a total of 40 years. What costs should be capitalized and over how many years should they be amortized?

| Costs Capitalized | Amortization Period |
|---|---|
| A. Acquisition costs only | 0 years |
| B. Acquisition costs only | 40 years |
| C. Acquisition and maintenance costs | 10 years |
| D. Acquisition and maintenance costs | 40 years |

**Answer (A) is correct.** *(CPA, adapted)*
**REQUIRED:** The costs to be capitalized and the amortization period.
**DISCUSSION:** SFAS 141 requires that goodwill (the excess of the cost of the acquired entity over the fair value of the acquired net assets) from a business combination be capitalized. Subsequent accounting for goodwill is governed by SFAS 142, which provides that goodwill be tested for impairment but not amortized. This rule applies regardless of when the goodwill was initially recognized. Furthermore, the cost of developing, maintaining, or restoring intangible assets that (1) are not specifically identifiable, (2) have indeterminate lives, or (3) are inherent in a continuing business and related to an enterprise as a whole should be expensed as incurred.
Answer (B) is incorrect because the goodwill acquired externally is not amortized. Answer (C) is incorrect because the goodwill acquired externally is not amortized and the costs of maintaining goodwill should be expensed as incurred. Answer (D) is incorrect because the goodwill acquired externally is not amortized and the costs of maintaining goodwill should be expensed as incurred.

**12.** Costs incurred in completing a business combination initiated on July 1, 20X1 are listed below.

| | |
|---|---|
| Direct acquisition costs | $240,000 |
| Indirect acquisition expenses | 120,000 |
| Cost to register and issue equity securities | 80,000 |

The amount charged to expenses of business combination account should be

A. $80,000

B. $120,000

C. $200,000

D. $240,000

**Answer (B) is correct.** *(CMA, adapted)*
**REQUIRED:** The treatment of the costs of a business combination.
**DISCUSSION:** Three types of costs may be incurred in effecting a business combination: direct costs of acquisition, costs of registering and issuing equity securities, and indirect and general expenses. Direct costs, such as finders' and consultants' fees, should be included in the determination of the cost of the acquired entity. Costs of registering and issuing equity securities should be treated as a reduction of their otherwise determinable fair value. Indirect and general expenses related to a combination should be expensed as incurred. Thus, only the $120,000 in indirect acquisition expenses should be charged to the expenses of the business combination.
Answer (A) is incorrect because $80,000 equals the cost to register and issue equity securities, which reduces their otherwise determinable fair value. Answer (C) is incorrect because $200,000 includes the cost to register and issue equity securities. Answer (D) is incorrect because $240,000 equals direct acquisition costs, which are included in the cost of the acquired entity.

**13.** On July 1, 20X2, Pushway Corporation issued 200,000 shares of $5 par value common stock in exchange for all of Stroker Company's common stock. This stock had a fair value that was $200,000 in excess of the equity of Stroker Company on the date of exchange. This difference was solely attributed to the excess of the fair value of Stroker Company's equipment over its carrying amount. The equipment has an estimated remaining life of 10 years. Pushway Corporation and Stroker Company reported depreciation expense for the year of the combination of $400,000 and $100,000 respectively before consolidation and before any adjustment for the exchange. For financial reporting purposes, both companies use a calendar year and the straight-line depreciation method, with depreciation calculated on a monthly basis beginning with the month of acquisition. Consolidated depreciation expense reported for the year of the combination was

A. $400,000

B. $500,000

C. $510,000

D. $460,000

**Answer (D) is correct.** *(CMA, adapted)*
**REQUIRED:** The consolidated depreciation expense.
**DISCUSSION:** Under the purchase method, depreciation expense consists of amounts recorded by the companies, plus depreciation on amounts assigned to depreciable assets in excess of their carrying amounts on the subsidiary's balance sheet. The entire excess of the cost of the acquisition over the carrying amount of the net assets acquired is assigned to the equipment. Allocating this $200,000 amount over 10 years results in additional depreciation on the consolidated worksheet (appearing on neither company's individual books) of $20,000 per year. Because the combination occurred at midyear, only one-half year's extra depreciation should be recorded, or $10,000. Thus, the consolidated depreciation expense is $460,000 ($400,000 + $50,000 Stroker depreciation for 6 months + $10,000).
Answer (A) is incorrect because $400,000 equals Pushway's depreciation for the year of the combination. Answer (B) is incorrect because $500,000 assumes a pooling of interests, which is no longer permitted under SFAS 141. Answer (C) is incorrect because $510,000 includes Pushway's depreciation, Stroker's depreciation, and 6 months of the extra depreciation.

**14.** Poe, Inc. acquired 100% of Shaw Co. in a business combination on September 30, 20X2. During 20X2, Poe declared quarterly dividends of $25,000, and Shaw declared quarterly dividends of $10,000. What amount should be reported as dividends declared in the December 31, 20X2 consolidated statement of retained earnings?

A. $100,000

B. $110,000

C. $120,000

D. $140,000

Answer (A) is correct. *(CPA, adapted)*
**REQUIRED:** The dividends declared by the parent and subsidiary to be reported in the consolidated statements.
**DISCUSSION:** Under the purchase method, no part of the equity of the acquired entity is carried forward after the combination. Thus, only the $100,000 of dividends declared by Poe will be included in the statement of retained earnings.

**15.** On January 1, 20X2, Pane Corp. exchanged 150,000 shares of its $20 par value common stock for all of Sky Corp.'s common stock in a business combination initiated in November 20X1. At that date, the fair value of Pane's common stock issued was equal to the carrying amount of Sky's net assets. Both corporations continued to operate as separate businesses, maintaining accounting records with years ending June 30. Information from separate company operations follows:

|  | Pane | Sky |
|---|---|---|
| Retained earnings -- 12/31/X1 | $3,200,000 | $925,000 |
| Net income -- 6 months ended 6/30/X2 | 800,000 | 275,000 |
| Dividends paid -- 3/25/X2 | 750,000 | -- |

What amount of retained earnings should Pane report in its June 30, 20X2 consolidated balance sheet?

A. $5,200,000

B. $4,450,000

C. $3,525,000

D. $3,250,000

Answer (D) is correct. *(CPA, adapted)*
**REQUIRED:** The retained earnings at the date of a business combination.
**DISCUSSION:** The purchase method must be used to account for a business combination initiated after June 30, 20X1. It accounts for a business combination on the basis of the values exchanged. Hence, the cost of the acquired entity is allocated to the assets acquired and liabilities assumed based on their fair values, with possible adjustments for goodwill or the excess of fair value over cost. Accordingly, only the cost of the acquired entity is included in a consolidated balance sheet prepared using the purchase method. The equity, including retained earnings of the acquired entity, is excluded. Pane's separate retained earnings is therefore equal to the amount in the consolidated balance sheet, i.e., $3,250,000 ($3,200,000 beginning RE + $800,000 NI – $750,000 dividends).
Answer (A) is incorrect because $5,200,000 includes Sky's retained earnings at 6/30/X2 and does not deduct the dividends paid. Answer (B) is incorrect because $4,450,000 equals the consolidated retained earnings if the combination had been accounted for as a pooling, a method not applicable to a combination initiated after June 30, 20X1. Answer (C) is incorrect because $3,525,000 double counts Sky's net income through 6/30/X2. The income statement of the acquiring entity for the period in which a business combination occurs includes the income of the acquired entity after the acquisition date, with revenues and expenses based on the cost to the acquiring entity.

**16.** On December 31, 20X1, Saxe Corporation was merged into Poe Corporation in a business combination initiated in July 20X1. On December 31, Poe issued 200,000 shares of its $10 par common stock, with a market price of $18 a share, for all of Saxe's common stock. The equity section of each company's balance sheet immediately before the combination was as presented below:

|  | Poe | Saxe |
|---|---|---|
| Common stock | $3,000,000 | $1,500,000 |
| Additional paid-in capital | 1,300,000 | 150,000 |
| Retained earnings | 2,500,000 | 850,000 |
|  | $6,800,000 | $2,500,000 |

In the December 31, 20X1 consolidated balance sheet, additional paid-in capital should be reported at

A. $950,000

B. $1,300,000

C. $1,450,000

D. $2,900,000

Answer (D) is correct. *(CPA, adapted)*
**REQUIRED:** The additional paid-in capital to be reported in the consolidated balance sheet.
**DISCUSSION:** A business combination initiated after June 30, 20X1 is accounted for using the purchase method. To effect the acquisition, the 200,000 shares were issued for $3,600,000 (200,000 shares × $18 market price per share). Of this amount, $2,000,000 (200,000 shares × $10 par) should be allocated to the common stock of Poe, with the remaining $1,600,000 ($3,600,000 – $2,000,000) allocated to additional paid-in capital. The additional paid-in capital recorded on Poe's (the parent company's) books is $2,900,000 ($1,300,000 + $1,600,000). This balance is also reported on the 20X1 consolidated balance sheet.
Answer (A) is incorrect because $950,000 is the additional paid-in capital reported under the pooling-of-interests method, which may not be applied to combinations initiated after June 30, 20X1. Answer (B) is incorrect because $1,300,000 is the amount reported by Poe immediately before the combination.
Answer (C) is incorrect because $1,450,000 is the sum of the amounts reported by Poe and Saxe immediately before the combination.

## 19.3 Consolidated Financial Statements

**17.** When issuing consolidated financial statements,

- A. The notes must show how the gross consolidated income tax return expense is allocated to the entities comprising the consolidation.
- B. The consolidation policy must be disclosed either in the body of the financial statements or in a note to the financial statements.
- C. Parent company statements and consolidated statements should not be presented in the same set of statements in a comparative format.
- D. The consolidation policy must be presented in the notes to the financial statements as the first item in the accounting policies note.

Answer (B) is correct. *(CMA, adapted)*
   **REQUIRED:** The true statement about the issuance of consolidated financial statements.
   **DISCUSSION:** A description of all significant accounting policies should be included as an integral part of the financial statements. An example of a required disclosure is the basis of consolidation. This disclosure is normally made in the first note to the financial statements or in a separate summary preceding the notes (APB 22).
   Answer (A) is incorrect because the provisions requiring taxes to be allocated among entities relates only to financial accounting income tax expense, not the tax return income tax expense. Answer (C) is incorrect because there are no prohibitions against reporting parent company and consolidated statements in a comparative format. Answer (D) is incorrect because consolidation policies may be shown on the face of the financial statements.

**18.** When preparing consolidated financial statements, the entity being accounted for is the

- A. Legal entity.
- B. Parent.
- C. Minority interest.
- D. Economic entity.

Answer (D) is correct. *(CMA, adapted)*
   **REQUIRED:** The entity being accounted for when consolidated financial statements are prepared.
   **DISCUSSION:** The preparation of consolidated financial statements is based upon the concept of economic entity, not legal entity. Each of the organizations in a consolidated group is a separate legal entity, but consolidated statements are prepared because all of the organizations are under common economic control.
   Answer (A) is incorrect because each corporation is a separate legal entity. However, there is no legal entity representing the entire group. Answer (B) is incorrect because consolidated financial statements are for the parent company and all of its subsidiaries. Answer (C) is incorrect because the financial statements represent the holdings of the consolidated group, not the minority interest. The minority interest has equity only in certain subsidiaries.

**19.** Panco, Inc. owns 90% of the voting stock of Spany Corporation. After consolidated financial statements have been prepared, the entries to eliminate intercompany payables and receivables will

- A. Be reflected only in the accounts of Panco.
- B. Be reflected only in the accounts of Spany.
- C. Be reflected in the accounts of both Panco and Spany.
- D. Not be reflected in the accounts of either company.

Answer (D) is correct. *(CMA, adapted)*
   **REQUIRED:** The accounts affected by elimination entries.
   **DISCUSSION:** Elimination entries appear only in the working papers used to consolidate a parent and its subsidiaries. They never appear on the books of either the parent or the subsidiary. Thus, Panco and Spany are separate entities, and their individual company books should present intercompany payables and receivables without adjustment for the effect of elimination entries.

**20.** In the preparation of consolidated financial statements, the investment in subsidiary account should not be eliminated against the

- A. Retained earnings of the subsidiary.
- B. Par value of capital stock of the subsidiary.
- C. Paid-in capital above par value of the subsidiary.
- D. Interentity accounts receivable.

Answer (D) is correct. *(CMA, adapted)*
   **REQUIRED:** The account against which the investment in subsidiary account is not eliminated.
   **DISCUSSION:** Interentity accounts receivables must be eliminated (credited) in the consolidation working papers, but the offsetting debit is to interentity payables. In the preparation of consolidated financial statements, the investment in subsidiary account has to be eliminated (credited) in the working papers against the accounts of the subsidiaries. In addition to this elimination entry, other entries eliminate interentity receivables, payables, sales, and purchases.

**21.** In the process of preparing consolidated financial statements, which one of the following items does not need to be eliminated?

A. Profit in beginning inventory acquired from a parent.

B. Profit on sale of a fixed asset to a subsidiary.

C. Dividends receivable from a subsidiary.

D. Profit on inventory sold to a nonaffiliate.

Answer (D) is correct. *(CMA, adapted)*
  **REQUIRED:** The item that is not eliminated in the preparation of consolidated financial statements.
  **DISCUSSION:** Profits must be eliminated whenever the assets sold are still within the consolidated group. For example, if the parent sells equipment to a subsidiary at a profit, the profit must be eliminated before the consolidated statements are prepared or the assets will not be recorded (on the consolidated balance sheet) at historical cost to the group. If the subsidiary subsequently sells the assets to someone outside the group, the original profit will be realized (through sale to the outsider) and no longer will need to be eliminated.
  Answer (A) is incorrect because profits in inventory, or any other assets still within the group, must be eliminated.
  Answer (B) is incorrect because profits in inventory, or any other assets still within the group, must be eliminated. Answer (C) is incorrect because dividends receivable/payable from/to another entity within the group must be eliminated. Otherwise, the consolidated entity would report an asset receivable from itself.

**22.** Palmer, Inc. purchased 75% of the outstanding shares of Weller, Inc. for $3,900,000. At that time, Weller had $7,200,000 of total recorded liabilities, and total recorded assets of $10,500,000, while the fair value of all Weller's assets was $11,800,000. The amount of goodwill purchased by Palmer, Inc. is

A. $1,425,000

B. $1,300,000

C. $700,000

D. $450,000

Answer (D) is correct. *(CMA, adapted)*
  **REQUIRED:** The amount of goodwill purchased.
  **DISCUSSION:** The fair value of the subsidiary's net assets was $4,600,000 ($11,800,000 – $7,200,000). Palmer acquired 75% of these net assets, or $3,450,000. Subtracting the $3,450,000 fair value of net assets from the purchase price of $3,900,000 results in goodwill of $450,000.
  Answer (A) is incorrect because $1,425,000 assumes the recorded amount of the assets was their fair value. Answer (B) is incorrect because $1,300,000 is the excess of the fair value over the carrying amount of the assets. Answer (C) is incorrect because $700,000 equals the fair value of the net assets minus the cost of 75% of the outstanding shares.

**23.** If a parent purchases a 90% interest in a subsidiary accounted for by the entity theory, and if the investment cost exceeds the carrying amount of the subsidiary's net assets, the minority interest will

A. Be the same amount as if the parent had used the proprietary theory in preparing consolidated financial statements.

B. Be less in amount than if the parent had used the proprietary theory in preparing consolidated financial statements.

C. Be more in amount than if the parent had used the proprietary theory in preparing consolidated financial statements.

D. Not be separately disclosed in the consolidated financial statements.

Answer (C) is correct. *(CMA, adapted)*
  **REQUIRED:** The true statement about the minority interest under the entity theory if a subsidiary is purchased at an amount in excess of the carrying amount of its net assets.
  **DISCUSSION:** The issue is whether goodwill is recognized only on the portion of the subsidiary bought by the parent (proprietary theory), or whether goodwill should be recognized in total for the subsidiary, i.e., on the portion of assets bought by the parent plus the portion retained by the minority shareholders (the entity theory). For example, if a subsidiary's net assets are $100,000 and the parent pays $99,000 for a 90% interest, goodwill is $9,000 under the proprietary theory. In other words, equity of $90,000 in identifiable assets was acquired for $99,000. Hence, goodwill must be $9,000. However, if $9,000 of goodwill is attributable to the $90,000 of assets acquired by the parent, the entity theory argues that $1,000 of goodwill should be attributable to the $10,000 (10%) of net assets owned by the minority shareholders. Because the consolidated assets are greater under the entity theory ($10,000 of goodwill versus $9,000 under the proprietary theory), the minority interest is also greater.
  Answer (A) is incorrect because the entity theory results in greater assets and a larger minority interest than the proprietary theory. Answer (B) is incorrect because the entity theory results in greater assets and a larger minority interest than the proprietary theory. Answer (D) is incorrect because the minority interest is always separately disclosed in the consolidated balance sheet.

---

Questions 24 through 26 are based on the following information.

On January 2, 20X2, Pare Co. purchased 75% of Kidd Co.'s outstanding common stock. Selected balance sheet data at December 31, 20X2, is as follows:

|  | Pare | Kidd |
|---|---|---|
| Total assets | $420,000 | $180,000 |
| Liabilities | $120,000 | $ 60,000 |
| Common stock | 100,000 | 50,000 |
| Retained earnings | 200,000 | 70,000 |
|  | $420,000 | $180,000 |

During 20X2, Pare and Kidd paid cash dividends of $25,000 and $5,000, respectively, to their shareholders. There were no other intercompany transactions.

---

**24.** In its December 31, 20X2, consolidated statement of retained earnings, what amount should Pare report as dividends paid?

A. $5,000

B. $25,000

C. $26,250

D. $30,000

**Answer (B) is correct.** *(CPA, adapted)*
**REQUIRED:** The amount reported as dividends paid.
**DISCUSSION:** In consolidated statements, the amount of dividends paid equals the parent's dividends paid. The subsidiary's dividends paid to the parent ($5,000 × 75% = $3,750) are eliminated as an intercompany transaction. The remaining $1,250 of the subsidiary's dividends reduces the amount reported as the minority interest.
Answer (A) is incorrect because $5,000 is the subsidiary's dividends paid. Answer (C) is incorrect because $26,250 includes the minority interest. Answer (D) is incorrect because $30,000 includes the subsidiary's dividends paid.

**25.** In Pare's December 31, 20X2 consolidated balance sheet, what amount should be reported as minority interest in net assets?

A. $0

B. $30,000

C. $45,000

D. $105,000

**Answer (B) is correct.** *(CPA, adapted)*
**REQUIRED:** The minority interest in net assets.
**DISCUSSION:** Given that 25% of the stock is held by minority interests, $30,000 equals the minority interest in net assets [($180,000 – $60,000) × 25%].

**26.** In its December 31, 20X1 consolidated balance sheet, what amount should Pare report as common stock?

A. $50,000

B. $100,000

C. $137,500

D. $150,000

**Answer (B) is correct.** *(CPA, adapted)*
**REQUIRED:** The amount reported as common stock.
**DISCUSSION:** In consolidated statements, the parent's common stock equals the consolidated common stock.

**27.** Sun, Inc. is a wholly owned subsidiary of Patton, Inc. On June 1, 20X2, Patton declared and paid a $1 per share cash dividend to shareholders of record on May 15, 20X2. On May 1, 20X2, Sun bought 10,000 shares of Patton's common stock for $700,000 on the open market, when the carrying amount per share was $30. What amount of gain should Patton report from this transaction in its consolidated income statement for the year ended December 31, 20X2?

A. $0

B. $390,000

C. $400,000

D. $410,000

Answer (A) is correct. *(CPA, adapted)*
**REQUIRED:** The amount of gain to be reported from the purchase of parent's stock by a subsidiary.
**DISCUSSION:** Subsidiary stockholdings in a parent are normally treated as treasury stock on the consolidated balance sheet. Gains and losses on treasury stock are not recognized. Thus, no gain is recognized in the consolidated income statement when a subsidiary purchases the parent's stock on the open market.
Answer (B) is incorrect because $390,000 equals the $700,000 paid, minus the $300,000 carrying amount, minus the $10,000 dividend. Answer (C) is incorrect because $400,000 equals the $700,000 paid minus the $300,000 carrying amount. Answer (D) is incorrect because $410,000 equals the $700,000 paid, minus the $300,000 carrying amount, plus the $10,000 dividend.

**28.** Clark Co. had the following transactions with affiliated parties during 20X1:

- Sales of $50,000 to Dean, Inc., with $20,000 gross profit. Dean had $15,000 of this inventory on hand at year-end. Clark owns a 15% interest in Dean and does not exert significant influence.

- Purchases of raw materials totaling $240,000 from Kent Corp., a wholly owned subsidiary. Kent's gross profit on the sale was $48,000. Clark had $60,000 of this inventory remaining on December 31, 20X1.

Before eliminating entries, Clark had consolidated current assets of $320,000. What amount should Clark report in its December 31, 20X1 consolidated balance sheet for current assets?

A. $320,000

B. $314,000

C. $308,000

D. $302,000

Answer (C) is correct. *(CPA, adapted)*
**REQUIRED:** The amount reported on the consolidated balance sheet for current assets.
**DISCUSSION:** When a parent buys inventory from a subsidiary (an upstream transaction), the inventory on the consolidated balance sheet must be adjusted to the price paid by the subsidiary until the inventory is sold to an outside party. Hence, the gross profit made by Kent, which was included in the $60,000 of inventory held by Clark, must be reduced by the pro rata share of profit made on the sale by Kent, reducing the inventory to Kent's original cost. The reduction is $12,000 [($60,000 EI ÷ $240,000 purchases) × $48,000 gross profit]. Thus, current assets equal $308,000 ($320,000 – $12,000). Because Kent is wholly owned, no allocation of the reduction in gross profit to a minority interest is necessary. The transaction with Dean requires no elimination. Dean is not consolidated.
Answer (A) is incorrect because $320,000 does not eliminate intercompany transactions. Answer (B) is incorrect because $314,000 does not involve eliminating the effect of the transactions with Kent but does involve deducting the gross profit included in the inventory held by Dean. Answer (D) is incorrect because $302,000 treats the sales to Dean as occurring between a parent and a consolidated subsidiary.

**29.** According to FASB Interpretation No. 46 (revised December 2003), *Consolidation of Variable Interest Entities*,

A. A not-for-profit organization may not be treated as a variable interest entity.

B. A variable interest entity has an equity investment of more than 10% of its total assets.

C. A variable interest entity is consolidated by its primary beneficiary when it becomes involved with the entity.

D. Corporations may not be organized as variable interest entities.

Answer (C) is correct. *(Publisher)*
**REQUIRED:** The true statement about VIEs.
**DISCUSSION:** In essence, a variable interest entity (VIE) is any legal structure with insufficient equity investment or whose equity investors lack one of the essential characteristics of financial control. When an enterprise becomes involved with a VIE, it must determine whether it is the primary beneficiary (PB) and therefore must consolidate the VIE. A PB holds a variable interest(s) that will absorb a majority of the VIE's expected losses or receive a majority of its expected residual returns (or both).
Answer (A) is incorrect because this Interpretation applies to NPOs if they are used to avoid the requirements of the pronouncement. Answer (B) is incorrect because an entity qualifies as a VIE if the equity at risk does not suffice to finance entity activities without additional subordinated financial support (other variable interests that will absorb expected losses). An equity investment of less than 10% of total assets is usually considered to be insufficient. But a greater investment also may not suffice if, for example, assets or entity activities are high risk. Answer (D) is incorrect because a VIE may take any form.

**30.** According to FASB Interpretation No. 46 (revised 12/03), *Consolidation of Variable Interest Entities*, which of the following must be treated as VIEs?

I.   An enterprise is controlled by its equity investors but has sustained large operating losses.

II.  A development stage enterprise has minority owners with veto rights.

III. An entity's investors have voting rights that are not proportional to their obligations to absorb expected losses, and substantially all of its activities involve an investor with disproportionately fewer voting rights.

IV.  The right of an entity's investors to receive expected residual returns is capped.

    A.   I and II only.

    B.   II and III only.

    C.   III and IV only.

    D.   I, II, III and IV.

**31.** Selected data for two subsidiaries of Dunn Corp. taken from December 31, 20X4 preclosing trial balances are as follows:

|  | Banks Co. Debit | Lamm Co. Credit |
|---|---|---|
| Shipments to Banks | -- | $150,000 |
| Shipments from Lamm | $200,000 | -- |
| Interentity inventory profit on total shipments | -- | 50,000 |

Additional data relating to the December 31, 20X4 inventory are as follows:

|  | Banks Co. Debit | Lamm Co. Credit |
|---|---|---|
| Inventory acquired from outside parties | $175,000 | $250,000 |
| Inventory acquired from Lamm | 60,000 | -- |

At December 31, 20X4, the inventory reported on the combined balance sheet of the two subsidiaries should be

    A.   $425,000

    B.   $435,000

    C.   $470,000

    D.   $485,000

Answer (C) is correct.   *(Publisher)*
    **REQUIRED:** The variable interest entities.
    **DISCUSSION:** An entity is a VIE if, by design, the equity at risk does not suffice to finance entity activities without additional subordinated financial support. An entity is also a VIE if at least one of the essential characteristics of a controlling financial interest is not present; that is, the holders of equity at risk do not have (1) decision-making ability based on voting or similar rights, (2) an obligation to absorb the VIE's expected losses, or (3) the right to receive the expected residual returns. Item (1) is satisfied if (a) some investors' votes are disproportionate to their obligations to absorb expected losses or to receive expected residual returns and (b) substantially all of the VIE's activities involve or are performed for an investor with disproportionately few voting rights. Item (3) is satisfied if the investors' return is capped by the entity's governing documents or by arrangements with the entity or other holders of variable interests. However, an enterprise controlled by its equity investors that was not initially a VIE does not change its status by reason of operating losses, regardless of the amount. Moreover, veto rights of minority shareholders are not a basis for classification of the entity as a VIE if the shareholders as a whole control the enterprise, and the equity at risk is sufficient to finance the entity's activities.

Answer (C) is correct.   *(CPA, adapted)*
    **REQUIRED:** The inventory to be reported on the combined balance sheet of two subsidiaries.
    **DISCUSSION:** When combined financial statements are prepared for unconsolidated subsidiaries, interentity profits should be eliminated. The $60,000 of ending inventory acquired by Banks from Lamm is equal to 30% ($60,000 inventory remaining ÷ $200,000 shipments) of the total received from Lamm. Accordingly, $15,000 ($50,000 inventory profit on total shipments × 30%) should be eliminated. Given that $425,000 ($175,000 + $250,000) of the ending inventory held by Banks and Lamm was obtained from outside parties, the combined balance sheet of the two subsidiaries should report inventory of $470,000 ($425,000 + $60,000 – $15,000).
    Answer (A) is incorrect because $425,000 is the total inventory acquired from outside parties. Answer (B) is incorrect because $435,000 excludes the profit on inventory acquired from Lamm and subsequently sold. Answer (D) is incorrect because $485,000 does not exclude the interentity inventory profit.

## 19.4 Derivatives and Hedging

**32.** To the extent the hedge is effective, a loss arising from the decrease in fair value of a derivative is included in current earnings if the derivative qualifies and is designated as a

|     | Fair-value Hedge | Cash-flow Hedge |
| --- | --- | --- |
| A.  | Yes | No  |
| B.  | No  | Yes |
| C.  | Yes | Yes |
| D.  | No  | No  |

Answer (A) is correct. *(Publisher)*
**REQUIRED:** The treatment of a loss arising from a decrease in fair value of a derivative qualified and designated as either a fair-value or a cash-flow hedge.
**DISCUSSION:** A fair-value hedge includes a hedge of an exposure to changes in the fair value of a recognized asset or liability or of an unrecognized firm commitment. Changes in both (1) the fair value of a derivative that qualifies and is designated as a fair-value hedge and (2) the fair value of the hedged item attributable to the hedged risk are included in earnings in the period of change. Thus, the net effect on earnings is limited to the ineffective portion, i.e., the difference between the changes in fair value. A cash-flow hedge includes a hedge of an exposure to variability in the cash flows of a recognized asset or liability or a forecasted transaction. Changes in the fair value of a derivative that qualifies and is designated as a cash-flow hedge are recognized as a component of other comprehensive income to the extent the hedge is effective. The ineffective portion of the hedge is recognized in current earnings. The changes accumulated in other comprehensive income are reclassified to earnings in the period(s) the hedged transaction affects earnings. For example, accumulated amounts related to a forecasted purchase of equipment are reclassified as the equipment is depreciated.

**33.** Herbert Corporation was a party to the following transactions during November and December 20X1. Which of these transactions most likely resulted in an investment in a derivative subject to the accounting prescribed by SFAS 133, *Accounting for Derivative Instruments and Hedging Activities*?

A. Purchased 1,000 shares of common stock of a public corporation based on the assumption that the stock would increase in value.

B. Purchased a term life insurance policy on the company's chief executive officer to protect the company from the effects of an untimely demise of this officer.

C. Agreed to cosign the note of its 100%-owned subsidiary to protect the lender from the possibility that the subsidiary might default on the loan.

D. Based on its forecasted need to purchase 300,000 bushels of wheat in 3 months, entered into a 3-month forward contract to purchase 300,000 bushels of wheat to protect itself from changes in wheat prices during the period.

Answer (D) is correct. *(Publisher)*
**REQUIRED:** The transaction resulting in an investment in a derivative instrument.
**DISCUSSION:** SFAS 133 defines a derivative as a financial instrument or other contract that (1) has (a) one or more underlyings and (b) one or more notional amounts or payment provisions, or both; (2) requires either no initial net investment or an immaterial net investment; and (3) requires or permits net settlement. An underlying may be a specified interest rate, security price, commodity price, foreign exchange rate, index of prices or rates, or other variable. A notional amount is a number of currency units, shares, bushels, pounds, or other units specified. Settlement of a derivative is based on the interaction of the notional amount and the underlying. The purchase of the forward contract as a hedge of a forecasted need to purchase wheat meets the criteria prescribed by SFAS 133.
Answer (A) is incorrect because it involves a net investment equal to the fair value of the stock. Answer (B) is incorrect because it is based on an identifiable event, not an underlying. Answer (C) is incorrect because it is based on an identifiable event, not an underlying.

**34.** Garcia Corporation has entered into a binding agreement with Hernandez Company to purchase 400,000 pounds of Colombian coffee at $2.53 per pound for delivery in 90 days. This contract is accounted for as a

A. Financial instrument.

B. Firm commitment.

C. Forecasted transaction.

D. Fair value hedge.

Answer (B) is correct. *(Publisher)*
**REQUIRED:** The type of transaction defined.
**DISCUSSION:** A firm commitment is an agreement with an unrelated party, binding on both parties and usually legally enforceable, that specifies all significant terms and includes a disincentive for nonperformance.
Answer (A) is incorrect because a financial instrument does not involve the delivery of a product. Answer (C) is incorrect because a forecasted transaction is a transaction that is expected to occur for which no firm commitment exists. Answer (D) is incorrect because the purchase commitment is an exposure to risk, not a hedge of an exposure to risk.

Questions 35 and 36 are based on the following information. As part of its risk management strategy, a copper mining company sells futures contracts to hedge changes in fair value of its inventory. On March 12, the commodity exchange spot price was $0.81 per lb., and the futures price for mid-June was $0.83 per lb. On that date, the company, which has a March 31 fiscal year-end, sold 200 futures contracts on the commodity exchange at $0.83 per lb. for delivery in June. Each contract was for 25,000 lbs. The company designated these contracts as a fair-value hedge of 5 million lbs. of current inventory for which a mid-June sale is expected. The average cost of this inventory was $0.58 per lb. The company documented (1) the hedging relationship between the futures contracts and its inventory, (2) its objectives and strategy for undertaking the hedge, and (3) its conclusion that the hedging relationship will be highly effective. On March 31, the mid-June commodity exchange futures price was $0.85 per lb.

**35.** In the March 31 statement of financial position, the company should record the value of the futures contracts as a(n)

    A. $100,000 asset.

    B. $100,000 liability.

    C. $4,250,000 liability.

    D. $4,250,000 asset.

Answer (B) is correct. *(Publisher)*
    **REQUIRED:** The amount at which the futures contracts should be recorded on March 31.
    **DISCUSSION:** SFAS 133 requires that derivative instruments be recorded as assets and liabilities and measured at fair value. At the inception of the futures contracts, their fair value was $0 because the contracts were entered into at the futures price at that date. On March 31, the fair value of the futures contracts is equal to the change in the futures price between the inception price and the March 31 price. Given that the futures contracts created an obligation to deliver 5 million lbs. (25,000 lbs. × 200 contracts) of copper at $0.83 per lb. and that the price had risen to $0.85 per lb. at the date of the financial statements, the company should record a loss and a liability of $100,000 [5 million lbs. × ($0.83 – $0.85)].
    Answer (A) is incorrect because the futures contracts should be recorded as a liability. Answer (C) is incorrect because $4,250,000 is the value of the inventory at the futures price on March 31. Answer (D) is incorrect because $4,250,000 is the value of the inventory at the futures price on March 31.

**36.** If, on March 31, the company concluded that the hedge was 100% effective, it should record the value of the hedged copper inventory in the March 31 statement of financial position at

    A. $4,350,000

    B. $4,250,000

    C. $3,000,000

    D. $2,900,000

Answer (C) is correct. *(Publisher)*
    **REQUIRED:** The amount at which the hedged inventory should be recorded on March 31.
    **DISCUSSION:** On March 31, the company recognized a loss and liability for the futures contracts of $100,000 [5 million lbs. × ($0.83 contract price – $0.85 futures price)]. If the hedge was completely effective, the loss on the hedging derivatives must have been offset by a $100,000 gain on the hedged item. For a fair-value hedge, changes in the fair value of the hedged item attributable to the hedged risk are reflected as adjustments to the carrying amount of the hedged recognized asset or liability or the previously unrecognized firm commitment. The adjustments to the carrying amount are accounted for in the same manner as other components of the carrying amount of the asset or liability. Thus, the inventory should be recorded at $3,000,000 [(5 million lbs. × $0.58) original cost + $100,000 gain in fair value].
    Answer (A) is incorrect because $4,350,000 equals the value of the inventory at the futures price on March 31 plus $100,000. Answer (B) is incorrect because $4,250,000 equals the value of the inventory at the futures price on March 31. Answer (D) is incorrect because $2,900,000 is the original cost of the inventory.

**37.** On October 1, 20X1, Bordeaux, Inc., a calendar-year-end firm, invested in a derivative designed to hedge the risk of changes in fair value of certain assets, currently valued at $1.5 million. The derivative is structured to result in an effective hedge. However, some ineffectiveness may result. On December 31, 20X1, the fair value of the hedged assets has decreased by $350,000; the fair value of the derivative has increased by $325,000. Bordeaux should recognize a net effect on 20X1 earnings of

A. $0

B. $25,000

C. $325,000

D. $350,000

Answer (B) is correct. *(Publisher)*
**REQUIRED:** The net effect on earnings of a partially effective hedge of changes in fair value of a recognized asset.
**DISCUSSION:** A hedge of an exposure to changes in the fair value of a recognized asset or liability is classified as a fair value hedge. Gains and losses arising from changes in fair value of a derivative classified as a fair value hedge are included in the determination of earnings in the period of change. They are offset by losses or gains on the hedged item attributable to the risk being hedged. Thus, earnings of the period of change are affected only by the net gain or loss attributable to the ineffective aspect of the hedge. The ineffective portion is equal to $25,000 ($350,000 – $325,000).
Answer (A) is incorrect because the effect on earnings is equal to the ineffective portion of the hedge. Answer (C) is incorrect because it is the gross effect of the increase in fair value of the derivative. Answer (D) is incorrect because it is the gross effect of the decrease in fair value of the hedged assets.

**38.** At the beginning of period 1, Forecast Corporation enters into a qualifying cash flow hedge of a transaction it expects to occur at the beginning of period 4. Forecast assesses hedge effectiveness by comparing the change in present value (PV) of the expected cash flows associated with the forecasted transaction with all of the hedging derivative's gain or loss (change in fair value). The change in those cash flows that occurs for any reason has been designated as the hedged risk. The following information about the periodic changes in the hedging relationship is available:

| Period | Change in Fair Value of the Derivative | Change in PV of Expected Cash Flows from the Forecasted Transaction |
|---|---|---|
| 1 | $ 50,000 | $(48,000) |
| 2 | 47,000 | (51,000) |
| 3 | (81,000) | 80,000 |

Given that the hedge is effective to the extent it offsets the change in the present value of the expected cash flows on the forecasted transaction, Forecast should

A. Recognize a loss of $2,000 in earnings for period 1.

B. Report a balance in other comprehensive income (OCI) of $16,000 at the end of period 3.

C. Recognize a gain of $47,000 in earnings for period 2.

D. Record other comprehensive income of $97,000 for period 2.

Answer (B) is correct. *(Publisher)*
**REQUIRED:** The appropriate accounting for a cash flow hedge of a forecasted transaction.
**DISCUSSION:** The effective portion of a cash flow hedge of a forecasted transaction is included in OCI until periods in which the forecasted transaction affects earnings. At the end of period 3, the net change in the hedging derivative's fair value is $16,000 ($50,000 + $47,000 – $81,000), and the change in the PV of the expected cash flows on the forecasted transaction is – $19,000 ($80,000 – $48,000 – $51,000). Thus, the hedge is effective at the end of period 3 to the extent it offsets $16,000 of the net $19,000 decrease in the cash flows of the forecasted transaction that are expected to occur in period 4.
Answer (A) is incorrect because Forecast should recognize earnings for period 1 of $2,000. The increase in fair value of the derivative exceeds the decrease in PV of the cash flows by $2,000. The derivative is adjusted to fair value by a $50,000 debit, OCI is credited for $48,000, and earnings is credited for $2,000. Answer (C) is incorrect because the entry for period 2 is to debit the derivative for $47,000, debit earnings for $2,000, and credit OCI for $49,000 ($50,000 + $47,000 – $48,000 credit in period 1). At the end of period 2, OCI should have a credit balance of $97,000 (the extent of the hedge's effectiveness). Answer (D) is incorrect because the entry for period 2 is to debit the derivative for $47,000, debit earnings for $2,000, and credit OCI for $49,000 ($50,000 + $47,000 – $48,000 credit in period 1). At the end of period 2, OCI should have a credit balance of $97,000 (the extent of the hedge's effectiveness).

Questions 39 through 41 are based on the following information.

On November 15, 20X1, Hector Corp., a calendar-year-end U.S. company, signed a legally binding contract to purchase equipment from Diego Corp., a foreign company. The negotiated price is FC1,000,000. The scheduled delivery date is February 15, 20X2. Terms require payment by Hector Corp. upon delivery. The terms also impose a 10% penalty on Diego Corp. if the equipment is not delivered by February 15, 20X2.

To hedge its commitment to pay FC1,000,000, Hector entered into a forward-exchange contract on November 15, 20X1 to receive FC1,000,000 on February 15, 20X2 at an exchange rate of FC1.00 = U.S.$0.36. Additional exchange rate information:

| Date | Spot Rates | Forward Rates for February 15, 20X2 |
|---|---|---|
| 11/15/X1 | 1 FC = $0.35 U.S. | 1 FC = $0.36 U.S. |
| 12/31/X1 | 1 FC = $0.36 U.S. | 1 FC = $0.38 U.S. |
| 02/15/X2 | 1 FC = $0.39 U.S. | 1 FC = $0.39 U.S. |

Quotes obtained from dealers indicate the following incremental changes in the fair values of the forward-exchange contract based on the changes in forward rates discounted on a net-present-value basis:

| Date | Gain/(Loss) |
|---|---|
| 11/15/X1 | $    0 |
| 12/31/X1 | $19,600 |
| 02/15/X2 | $10,400 |

Hector formally documented its objective and strategy for entering into this hedge. Hector also decided to assess hedge effectiveness based on an assessment of the difference between changes in value of the forward-exchange contract and the U.S.-dollar equivalent of the firm commitment. Because both changes are based on changes in forward rates, Hector further determined that the hedge is 100% effective.

**39.** What are the amounts reported for the forward contract receivable and the firm commitment liability at December 31, 20X1 and February 15, 20X2 (prior to the settlement of the contract)?

| | 12/31/X1 | 02/15/X2 |
|---|---|---|
| A. | $10,000 | $40,000 |
| B. | $19,600 | $30,000 |
| C. | $19,600 | $10,400 |
| D. | $20,000 | $30,000 |

Answer (B) is correct.   *(Publisher)*
**REQUIRED:** The amounts to be recorded for a forward contract receivable and a firm commitment at 12/31/X1 and 02/15/X2 (prior to the settlement of the contract).
**DISCUSSION:** This hedge is a foreign currency fair value hedge because it hedges a foreign currency exposure of an unrecognized firm commitment whose cash flows are fixed. Thus, unlike a foreign currency cash flow hedge, it does not hedge the foreign currency exposure to variability in the functional-currency-equivalent cash flows associated with an unrecognized firm commitment. SFAS 133 requires recognition of the forward contract receivable as an asset at fair value, with the changes in fair value recognized in earnings. SFAS 133 further requires recognition of the changes in the fair value of the firm commitment that are attributable to the changes in exchange rates. These changes in fair value are recognized in earnings and as entries to a liability. Fair values should reflect changes in the forward exchange rates on a net-present-value basis. Thus, the forward contract receivable should be debited and a gain credited for $19,600 at 12/31/X1. A loss should be debited and a firm commitment liability should be credited in the same amount at the same date. (NOTE: Under current GAAP, no asset or liability is recognized for a firm commitment when the contract is signed.) At 2/15/X2, a further $10,400 forward contract gain and firm commitment loss should be recorded. Because the changes in value of both the forward contract and the U.S.-dollar equivalent of the firm commitment are based on changes in forward rates, the hedge is completely effective; the changes in fair values ($19,600 and $10,400) of the forward contract receivable (gains) and the firm commitment (losses) offset each other in the income statement.
Answer (A) is incorrect because the balance sheet amounts should be based on the discounted changes in forward rates, not the undiscounted changes in spot rates. Answer (C) is incorrect because $19,600 and $10,400 are the respective income statement effects. Answer (D) is incorrect because $20,000 is the undiscounted change in the forward rates at 12/31/X1.

**40.** As a result of this hedging transaction, at what amount should Hector recognize the equipment on February 15, 20X2?

A. $350,000

B. $360,000

C. $390,000

D. $420,000

Answer (B) is correct. *(Publisher)*
**REQUIRED:** The amount at which the equipment should be recognized as a result of the hedging transaction.
**DISCUSSION:** The equipment should be recorded at $360,000. This amount equals $390,000 (FC1,000,000 × $0.39 spot rate at 2/15/X2) minus the $30,000 balance in the firm commitment liability account. The entry is to debit equipment for $360,000, debit the firm commitment liability for $30,000, and credit a payable for $390,000. On the same date, Hector will debit the payable for $390,000, credit the forward contract receivable for $30,000, and credit cash for $360,000. The latter entry reflects settlement of the payable and of the forward contract.
Answer (A) is incorrect because $350,000 is the amount that would have been recognized if the equipment had been delivered on 11/15/X1. Answer (C) is incorrect because $390,000 is the amount that would have been recognized if the firm commitment had not been hedged. Answer (D) is incorrect because $420,000 equals $390,000 plus the $30,000 balance in the firm commitment liability account.

**41.** The contract signed by Hector Corp. to purchase the equipment from Diego Corp. meets the definition of a

| | Firm Commitment | Forecasted Transaction |
|---|---|---|
| A. | Yes | Yes |
| B. | No | No |
| C. | Yes | No |
| D. | No | Yes |

Answer (C) is correct. *(Publisher)*
**REQUIRED:** The type of contract described.
**DISCUSSION:** SFAS 133 defines a firm commitment as an agreement between unrelated parties, binding on both and usually legally enforceable, that specifies all significant terms and includes a disincentive for nonperformance. SFAS 133 defines a forecasted transaction as a transaction that is expected to occur for which there is no firm commitment.

**42.** According to SFAS 133, *Accounting for Derivative Instruments and Hedging Activities*, as amended by SFAS 138, *Accounting for Certain Derivative Instruments and Certain Hedging Activities*, the effective portion of a loss associated with a change in fair value of a derivative instrument shall be reported as a component of other comprehensive income only if the derivative is appropriately designated as a

A. Cash flow hedge of the foreign currency exposure of a forecasted transaction.

B. Fair value hedge of the foreign currency exposure of an unrecognized firm commitment.

C. Fair value hedge of the foreign currency exposure of a recognized asset or liability for which a foreign currency transaction gain or loss is recognized in earnings.

D. Speculation in a foreign currency.

Answer (A) is correct. *(Publisher)*
**REQUIRED:** The derivative for which the effective portion of a loss associated with its change in fair value is reported as a component of other comprehensive income.
**DISCUSSION:** The hedge of the foreign currency exposure of a forecasted transaction is designated as a cash flow hedge. The effective portion of gains and losses associated with changes in fair value of a derivative instrument designated and qualifying as a cash flow hedging instrument is reported as a component of other comprehensive income.
Answer (B) is incorrect because a hedge of the foreign currency exposure of either an unrecognized firm commitment or of a recognized asset or liability for which a foreign currency transaction gain or loss is recognized in earnings may be a cash flow hedge (if cash flows are variable) or a fair value hedge. The effective portion of gains and losses arising from changes in fair value of a derivative classified as a fair value hedge is included in earnings of the period of change. It is offset by losses and gains on the hedged item that are attributable to the risk being hedged. Answer (C) is incorrect because a hedge of the foreign currency exposure of either an unrecognized firm commitment or of a recognized asset or liability for which a foreign currency transaction gain or loss is recognized in earnings may be a cash flow hedge (if cash flows are variable) or a fair value hedge. The effective portion of gains and losses arising from changes in fair value of a derivative classified as a fair value hedge is included in earnings of the period of change. It is offset by losses and gains on the hedged item that are attributable to the risk being hedged. Answer (D) is incorrect because gains and losses associated with changes in fair value of a derivative used as a speculation in a foreign currency are included in earnings of the period of change.

**43.** The effective portion of a gain arising from an increase in the fair value of a derivative is included in earnings in the period of change if the derivative is appropriately designated and qualifies as a hedge of

- A. A foreign currency exposure of a net investment in a foreign operation.
- B. A foreign currency exposure of a forecasted transaction.
- C. A foreign currency exposure of an available-for-sale security.
- D. The variable cash flows of a forecasted transaction.

Answer (C) is correct. *(Publisher)*
**REQUIRED:** The derivative for which the effective portion of a gain is included in earnings in the period in which a change in fair value occurs.
**DISCUSSION:** A fair value hedge includes a hedge of an exposure to changes in the fair value of a recognized asset or liability or an unrecognized firm commitment. Such a hedge minimizes the risk associated with fixed cash flows. A foreign currency fair value hedge includes a hedge of a foreign currency exposure of an unrecognized firm commitment. It also includes a hedge of a foreign currency exposure of a recognized asset or liability (including an available-for-sale security) for which a foreign currency transaction gain or loss is recognized in earnings under SFAS 52. Gains and losses arising from changes in fair value of a derivative classified as either a fair value or a foreign fair value hedge are included in the determination of earnings in the period of change. They are offset by losses or gains on the hedged item attributable to the risk being hedged. Thus, earnings of the period of change are affected only by the net gain or loss attributable to the ineffective aspect of the hedge.
Answer (A) is incorrect because the effective portion of gains and losses on this hedge is reported as a component of the cumulative translation adjustment in other comprehensive income. Answer (B) is incorrect because the effective portion of gains and losses on these hedges is included in other comprehensive income until periods in which the forecasted transaction affects earnings. Answer (D) is incorrect because the effective portion of gains and losses on these hedges is included in other comprehensive income until periods in which the forecasted transaction affects earnings.

**44.** On October 1, 20X1, Weeks Co., a calendar-year-end U.S. company, forecasts that, near the end of March 20X2, Sullivan Corp., a foreign entity, will purchase 50,000 gallons of Weeks's primary product for FC500,000. Sullivan has not firmly committed to the purchase. However, based on Sullivan's purchasing pattern, Weeks believes that the sale is probable. Weeks's risk-management policy includes avoiding foreign currency exposure through the use of foreign currency forward contracts. Thus, on October 1, Weeks enters into a 6-month foreign currency forward contract to sell FC500,000 to a dealer on March 31. Weeks designates the contract as a hedge and determines that hedge effectiveness will be based on changes in forward rates. The following information is available:

| | Value of FC500,000 Based on Spot Rates | Value of FC500,000 Based on Forward Rates for 03/31/X3 | Incremental Discounted Changes in Value of Forward Contract Based on Changes in Forward Rates |
|---|---|---|---|
| 10/02/X1 | $570,000 | $500,000 | $      0 |
| 12/31/X1 | $540,000 | $490,000 | $  9,800 |
| 03/31/X2 | $475,000 | $475,000 | $15,200 |

At what amounts should Weeks record the forward contract on December 31, 20X1 and March 31, 20X2?

| | 12/31/X1 | 03/31/X2 |
|---|---|---|
| A. | $9,800 | $25,000 |
| B. | $10,000 | $25,000 |
| C. | $540,000 | $475,000 |
| D. | $490,000 | $475,000 |

Answer (A) is correct. *(Publisher)*
**REQUIRED:** The amounts at which the forward contract should be recognized.
**DISCUSSION:** Weeks should record the forward contract as a receivable at fair value. Fair value is based on changes in forward rates discounted on a net present value basis. Thus, the receivable should be recorded at $9,800 on December 31, 20X1 and $25,000 ($9,800 + $15,200) on March 31, 20X2. Because a hedge of the foreign currency exposure of a forecasted transaction is a cash flow hedge, Weeks should also credit these amounts to other comprehensive income. On March 31, the sale should be recorded at $500,000 ($475,000 value based on the spot rate at March 31 + $25,000 balance in other comprehensive income). The amount of cash received also is equal to $500,000 ($475,000 + $25,000 balance in the forward contract receivable).
Answer (B) is incorrect because the change in forward rates should be adjusted for the time value of money. Answer (C) is incorrect because $540,000 and $475,000 reflect the value of FC500,000 at spot rates. Answer (D) is incorrect because $490,000 and $475,000 reflect the value of FC500,000 at forward rates.

# STUDY UNIT TWENTY
# SEC REQUIREMENTS AND THE ANNUAL REPORT

(19 pages of outline)

This study unit is the **last of ten** on **external financial reporting**. The relative weight assigned to this major topic in Part 2 of the exam is **25%** at **skill level B** (four skill types required). The ten study units are

Study Unit 11: Overview of External Financial Reporting
Study Unit 12: Overview of Financial Statements
Study Unit 13: Cash and Receivables
Study Unit 14: Inventories and Investments
Study Unit 15: Long-Lived Assets
Study Unit 16: Liabilities
Study Unit 17: Equity and Revenue Recognition
Study Unit 18: Other Income Statement Items
Study Unit 19: Business Combinations and Derivatives
Study Unit 20: SEC Requirements and the Annual Report

On July 30, 2002, President George W. Bush signed into law the **Corporate and Criminal Fraud Accountability Act of 2002**, commonly known as **Sarbanes-Oxley** after the Maryland Senator and Ohio Representative who sponsored the legislation. This law required some of the most far-reaching changes in financial reporting by public companies since the securities legislation of the 1930s. New **reporting requirements** were placed on both the **management** of publicly held companies **and the accounting firms** that audit their financial statements. These changes are covered in this study unit.

After studying the outlines and answering the multiple-choice questions in this study unit, you will have the skills necessary to address the following topics listed in the IMA's Learning Outcome Statements:

Part 2 – Section E.5. The SEC and its reporting requirements

The candidate should be able to:

a. identify the two major Acts establishing the SEC and its powers (Securities Act of 1933 and the Securities Exchange Act of 1934); and demonstrate knowledge of the major provisions of each

b. describe the general reporting requirements of public companies

c. define the integrated disclosure system, standardized financial statements, and Management Discussion and Analysis

d. identify other disclosures regarding business operations

e. identify and describe the SEC disclosure requirements, including the registration with SEC (initial filing), the annual report to SEC or Form 10-K, the quarterly report or Form 10-Q, disclosure of material events or Form 8-K, and proxy solicitations

f. identify and explain the major provisions of the Sarbanes-Oxley Act of 2002

g. identify the functions and responsibilities of the Public Company Accounting Oversight Board (PCAOB)

Part 2 – Section E.6. The annual report

The candidate should be able to:

a.    identify audit services related to the annual report

b.    identify the basic components of the annual report, including management's statement of responsibility for the financial statements and the independent auditor's report

c.    demonstrate an awareness of the Audit Committee's level of responsibility for the integrity of the financial information presented in the annual reports

d.    identify the Audit Committee's functions to include (a) nominating the public accounting firm that will conduct the annual external audit, (b) participating in the process of setting the scope of internal and external audits, and (c) inviting direct audit communications on major problems encountered during the course of internal and external audits

e.    identify and describe the other sections in the annual report, including the letter to shareholders, management discussion and analysis, and the statement on social responsibility

## 20.1  THE SEC AND ITS REPORTING STANDARDS

1.    The **Securities and Exchange Commission (SEC)** was created by the **Securities Exchange Act of 1934** to regulate the trading of securities and otherwise to enforce securities legislation.

    a.    The basic purposes of the securities laws are to

        1)    Prevent fraud and misrepresentation

        2)    Require full and fair disclosure so investors can evaluate investments on their own

    b.    Under the **Securities Act of 1933**, disclosure is made before the initial issuance of securities by registering with the SEC **(initial filing)** and providing a **prospectus** to potential investors.

    c.    Under the **Securities Exchange Act of 1934**, disclosures regarding subsequent trading of securities are made by filing periodic reports that are available to the public for review.

    d.    The SEC requires **registration statements** and reports to comply with certain accounting standards and policies.

        1)    **Regulation S-X** governs the reporting of financial statements, including notes and schedules.

        2)    **Regulation S-K** provides disclosure standards, including many of a nonfinancial nature.  Regulation S-K also covers certain aspects of corporate annual reports to shareholders.

        3)    **Regulation S-B** applies to small business issuers.  It reduces the disclosure requirements for a small business when it files a registration statement under the 1933 act or reports under the 1934 act.

        4)    **Financial Reporting Releases (FRRs)** announce accounting and auditing matters of general interest.

            a)    They provide explanations and clarifications of changes in accounting or auditing procedures used in reports filed with the SEC.

            b)    FRRs and **Accounting and Auditing Enforcement Releases (AAERs)** replace what used to be called Accounting Series Releases.

        5)    AAERs disclose enforcement actions involving accountants.

6) **Staff Accounting Bulletins (SABs)** are promulgated as interpretations to be followed by the SEC staff in administering disclosure requirements.

   a) Because they are merely the views of the staff, SABs are not legally required to be followed by registrants, but a company should have a good reason not to comply.

2. **Integrated Disclosure System**

   a. The integrated disclosure system

      1) Standardizes the financial statements

      2) Uses a basic information package (BIP) common to most of the filings

      3) Allows incorporation by reference from the annual shareholders' report to the annual SEC report (Form 10-K)

   b. **Standardized financial statements** are required.

      1) Annual statements must be audited and include

         a) Balance sheets for the 2 most recent fiscal year-ends

         b) Statements of income, cash flows, and changes in equity for the 3 most recent fiscal years

      2) They are required in the annual shareholders' report as well as in forms filed with the SEC.

      3) The accountant certifying the financial statements must be independent of the management of the filing company. The accountant is not required to be a CPA, but (s)he must be registered with a state.

   c. The **basic information package (BIP)** includes the following:

      1) Standardized financial statements

      2) Selected financial information

         a) Columnar format for the preceding 5 fiscal years

         b) Presentation of financial trends through comparison of key information from year to year

      3) **Management's discussion and analysis** of financial condition and results of operations

         a) This information addresses such matters as liquidity (including cash flow trends), capital resources, results of operations (including trends in sales and expenses), effects of tax legislation, and the impact of changing prices. Management must also discuss the firm's outlook and the significant effects of known trends, events, and uncertainties.

            i) The statement of cash flows should be used to discuss liquidity and the components of cash flow (operating, financing, and investing). Moreover, management must discuss transactions or events with long-term liquidity effects.

            ii) Management should discuss discontinued operations, extraordinary items, and items that are unusual or infrequent with material implications for financial condition or results of operations.

            iii) Management's discussion and analysis information should be updated by disclosures in interim statements.

            iv) Management must disclose certain information about segments: need for cash, contribution to revenues or profits, and restriction on funds flows among segments.

         b) Forward-looking information (a forecast) is encouraged but not required.

    4) Market price of securities and dividends

        a) Principal market in which security is traded
        b) High and low sales prices for each quarter in the last 2 years
        c) Most recent number of shareholders
        d) Frequency and amount of dividends in the last 2 years
        e) Any restrictions on the payment of dividends

    5) Description of business

        a) Fundamental developments for past 5 years, e.g., organization, reorganizations, bankruptcies, and major dispositions or acquisitions of assets

        b) Financial information of industry segments, and also foreign and domestic operations

        c) Narrative description including

            i) Principal products or services for each industry segment and principal markets for them

            ii) Total revenues of each class of products equaling 10% or more of consolidated revenue (15% if consolidated revenue is not in excess of $50,000,000)

            iii) Other information material to the business on the basis of industry segments

    6) Locations and descriptions of physical properties

    7) Pending litigation, e.g., principal parties, allegations, and relief sought

    8) Management

        a) General data for each director and officer

        b) Financial transactions with the company involving amounts in excess of $60,000

        c) Remuneration for the five highest paid directors and officers whose compensation exceeds $50,000 (including personal benefits)

    9) Security holdings of directors, officers, and those owning 5% or more of the security

    10) Matters submitted to shareholders for approval

    11) Description of certain business relationships, such as those with related parties

**3. Registration (initial filing under the Securities Act of 1933)**

  a. The issuer must register new issuances of securities with the SEC.

    1) **Form S-1** is used for the **registration statement** for companies that have never registered securities.

        a) Incorporation by reference is usually not allowed, and all material must be included.

    2) **Form S-2** is a shorter form for companies that have been reporting to the SEC (Form 10-K, etc.) for at least 3 years and have done so on a timely basis.

        a) Form S-2 allows BIP to be incorporated by reference from the latest annual shareholders' report.

    3) **Form S-3** is another short form for companies that meet the requirements for Form S-2 and have at least $50,000,000 of stock held by nonaffiliates (or at least $100,000,000 with an annual trading volume of 3,000,000 or more shares).

        a) Form S-3 allows most information to be incorporated by reference from other filings with the SEC.

    4)    Other forms

         a)    **Form S-4** is a simplified form for business combinations.

             i)    **Form F-4** is to be used by foreign registrants in business combinations.

             ii)    **Form N-14** is to be used by investment companies to register securities in business combinations.

         b)    **Form S-8** is for securities offered to employees under a stock option or other employee benefit plan.

         c)    **Form S-11** is used by real estate investment trusts and real estate companies.

         d)    **Form SB-1** is used by certain small business issuers to register up to $10 million of securities provided that no more than $10 million has been registered in the preceding 12 months. A small business issuer has revenues and public market float of less than $25 million.

         e)    **Form SB-2** is also for small business issuers. It has no limit on the dollar amount of securities that may be sold.

    5)    Initial and other filings become public information. They can be accessed at <u>sec.gov/edgar.shtml</u>, in the SEC's **EDGAR** (electronic data gathering, analysis, and retrieval) database.

    6)    Securities may not be offered to the public until the registration is effective.

         a)    The registration statement is examined by the Division of Corporation Finance.

         b)    Registration becomes effective 20 days after filing unless an amendment is filed or the SEC issues a stop order.

         c)    A preliminary prospectus is allowed that contains the same information as a regular prospectus (prices are omitted) but is clearly marked in red. Thus, it is called a **red herring prospectus**.

b.    **Registration forms requirements** (especially Form S-1)

    1)    Basic information package
    2)    Plan of distribution, name of underwriter, use of broker, and commissions
    3)    Use of proceeds and details of offerings other than cash
    4)    Description of the capital structure of the registrant
    5)    Risk factors
    6)    Signatures of

         a)    Issuer
         b)    Principal executive, financial, and accounting officers
         c)    Majority of board of directors

c.    The **prospectus** is **Part I** of the registration statement.

    1)    Its purpose is to provide investors with information to make an informed investment decision. It must be given to persons to whom the securities are offered or sold.

    2)    It usually may be presented in a more condensed or summarized form than Form S-1.

    3)    **Part II** of the registration statement is available on the SEC's website but is not required to be given to all investors. It contains agreements relevant to the securities, the articles of incorporation, major contracts, legal opinions, and agreements with underwriters.

4.   **Form 10** is used to register securities under the 1934 act.

   a.   Securities must be registered if they are traded in one of the ways listed below.

      1)   On a national securities exchange
      2)   Over the counter if the issuer has assets in excess of $10,000,000 and 500 or more shareholders

   b.   An issuer may voluntarily register its securities.

   c.   An issuer may deregister its securities if its shareholders decrease to fewer than 300 or if its shareholders are fewer than 500 and it had less than $10,000,000 in assets for each of the three most recent fiscal year-ends.

   d.   Banks must also register their securities, but they file with the appropriate banking authority, not with the SEC.

   e.   The required contents of Form 10 are

      1)   Basic information package
      2)   Other information required for Form S-1

5.   **Form 10-K** is the annual report to the SEC.

   a.   It is filed within 90 days (60 days for most entities by 2006) of the corporation's year-end.

   b.   It is certified by an independent accountant and signed by the following:

      1)   Principal executive, financial, and accounting officers
      2)   Majority of the board of directors

   c.   **Form 10-K** is presented with the basic information package.

      1)   Information contained in the annual report to shareholders may be incorporated by reference.

      2)   Information contained in proxy statements may also be incorporated by reference into Form 10-K.  A proxy statement is a published source readily available to the shareholders and investing public.

   d.   **Form 10-KSB** is filed by small businesses.

6.   **Form 10-Q** is the quarterly report to the SEC.

   a.   It must be filed for each of the first three quarters of the year within 45 days (30 days beginning in 2006) after the end of each quarter.

   b.   Financial statements need not be audited by an independent accountant, but they must be prepared in accordance with **APB 28**, *Interim Financial Reporting*.  However, an SEC registrant must obtain a **review** by an independent auditor of interim financial information that will be included in a quarterly report to the SEC.

   c.   Also required are changes during the quarter, for example,

      1)   Legal proceedings
      2)   Increase, decrease, or change in securities or indebtedness
      3)   Matters submitted to shareholders for a vote
      4)   Exhibits and reports on Form 8-K
      5)   Other material events not reported on Form 8-K

   d.   **SEC Staff Accounting Bulletin No. 74** encourages a public company to disclose in its registration statement and in Form 10-Q the anticipated effect of recently issued accounting standards on financial statements when they are adopted in a future period.

   e.   **Form 10-QSB** is filed by small businesses.

7. **Form 8-K** is a current report to disclose material events.

    a. In certain cases, it must be filed within 15 calendar days after the material event occurs. However, a change in independent accountants or the resignation of a director must be reported within 5 business days.

    b. Material events

        1) Change in control (15 calendar days)

        2) Acquisition or disposition of a significant amount of assets not in the ordinary course of business (15 calendar days)

        3) Bankruptcy or receivership (15 calendar days)

        4) Resignation of directors (5 business days)

        5) A change in the registrant's certifying accountant (5 business days). The reporting requirements are

            a) Date.

            b) Disclosure of any disagreements in the prior 2 years.

            c) Disclosure of certain reportable events, e.g., the former accountants' concerns about internal control or the reliability of management's representations.

            d) Disclosure of prior consultations with the new accountants.

            e) Whether a disagreement or reportable event was discussed with the audit committee.

            f) Whether the company authorized the former accountants to respond fully to the new accountants' inquiries about disagreements.

            g) Whether the former accountants were dismissed, resigned, or refused to seek reemployment.

            h) Disclosure of any qualification of reports in the prior 2 years.

            i) Letter from the former accountant indicating agreement (or disagreement) with the above. The letter must be submitted within 10 business days.

            j) Whether the decision to change was recommended or approved by the audit committee or the board of directors.

        6) Other events. Reporting of "other events" is optional, so no mandatory time for filing is established. Nevertheless, registrants are encouraged to file promptly and with due regard for the accuracy, completeness, and currency of the information.

        7) Form 8-K may be a vehicle for making **Regulation FD** disclosures. This regulation seeks to prevent selective disclosure. It requires public disclosure of material nonpublic information that the issuer has disclosed to certain market professionals or to shareholders likely to trade on the information.

        8) Under the **Sarbanes-Oxley Act of 2002**, issuers must make real time disclosure on a rapid and current basis of material changes in financial condition or operations.

8. **Shareholder Proposal Rules**

    a. Minority shareholders are permitted to submit proposals in management's proxy statement to be voted upon at a meeting of shareholders.

    b. However, the SEC has placed limitations on this right of shareholders because of abuses. For example, without these restrictions, an owner of one share of stock can submit a proposal supporting his/her favorite political cause. Although the proposal may be certain to be defeated, the shareholder may receive much free publicity.

c.    To submit a proposal, a shareholder or group of shareholders must have owned at least 1% of the voting shares or $1,000 in market value of voting securities, whichever is less, for at least 1 year and must continue to own them through the date of the meeting.

d.    A shareholder may submit only one proposal per meeting to an issuer.

e.    Persons engaged in proxy contests (persons who deliver written proxy materials to holders of more than 25% of a class of voting securities) are ineligible to use the shareholder proposal process.

f.    Proposals may be rejected if

1)    They are not a proper subject for shareholder voting under state law.

2)    They relate to operations that account for less than 5% of an issuer's total assets or less than 5% of its net earnings and gross sales for the current year, and are not otherwise significant to the business.

g.    To be resubmitted to shareholders in a proxy statement, proposals that have been previously voted down must be approved by at least 5% of the shareholders if submitted once before, 8% if submitted twice before, and 10% if submitted three times before.

9.    **Shelf Registration.** SEC Rule 415 (under the Securities Act of 1933) allows corporations to file registration statements covering a stipulated amount of securities that may be issued over the 2-year effective period of the statement. The securities are placed on the shelf and issued at an opportune moment without the necessity of filing a new registration statement, observing a 20-day waiting period, or preparing a new prospectus. The issuer is required only to provide updating amendments or to refer investors to quarterly and annual statements filed with the SEC. It is most advantageous to large corporations that frequently offer securities to the public.

10.    **Proxy Solicitations**

a.    A proxy is a written grant of authority by a shareholder allowing the holder of the proxy to vote for the shareholder at a meeting. A proxy is revoked by signing a later proxy, by personally voting the shares, or upon death.

b.    Under Section 14(a) of the 1934 act, a formal proxy statement must be sent before or with any proxy solicitation.

1)    A proxy solicitation is a request by any person (usually management or someone trying to gain control of the corporation) for a shareholder's proxy to vote at a corporate meeting.

c.    The **proxy statement** must

1)    Include meeting information (date, time, and place), how the proxy will be voted, a statement of whether it is revocable, facts about the solicitor of the proxy and its interests, and whether a statute allows an appraisal remedy (an ability of a dissenting shareholder to obtain payment for shares when an extraordinary corporate transaction occurs)

2)    Contain disclosure of all material facts regarding matters to be voted upon at the meeting

3)    Include an annual **shareholders' report** if the solicitation is on behalf of the current management at a meeting at which directors are to be elected

a)    Shareholders receive a **proxy form** for recording their votes on each proposal to be acted on at the meeting.

b)    Management solicitations must state the compensation and share ownership of directors and officers.

4)    Be filed with the SEC

     5)    Contain representations by the audit committee about its oversight function, for example, whether the members discussed the financial statements with management and the outside auditors

  d.    Management must mail proxy materials of insurgents, if so requested, and the insurgents pay the expenses.

  e.    A solicitation of proxies that contains a false or misleading statement is unlawful.

11.  In **"Staff Accounting Bulletin No. 99:** *Materiality*," the SEC emphasizes that any misstatement in a financial statement, even if it involves a seemingly immaterial amount, may be material if it is intentional. SAB 99 warns that numerical thresholds alone are unacceptable. Management should weigh qualitative issues as well, including whether the misstatement masks a change in earnings or concerns a vital business segment.

  a.    Financial executives worry that SAB 99 will increase the burden of the financial-reporting process, adding to the cost of audits, and will encourage shareholder lawsuits.

  b.    The SAB also specifies that the materiality of a misstatement depends on where it appears in the financial statement. Registrants and their auditors must consider not only the size of the misstatement but also the significance of the segment information to the financial statement taken as a whole.

  c.    Moreover, the **volatility of stock** must be considered. When management expects a market reaction to certain misstatements, it should be part of the materiality determination. For example, a one-cent differential in earnings may be material if management has reason to believe it will cause a sharp swing in a stock's price. The SEC's position is that companies know the items to which the market is particularly sensitive. The objective of the SEC is to stop management from using materiality judgments to manage earnings.

  d.    Another purpose of SAB 99 is to address the **netting out of misstatements**. For example, if a misstatement of an individual amount causes financial statements as a whole to be materially misstated, it cannot be offset by other misstatements.

  e.    Furthermore, the SEC warns of the materiality potential of misstatements from **prior reporting periods**. Thus, immaterial misstatements may recur for several years, with the cumulative effect becoming material in the current year.

  f.    In summary, the SEC guidelines on materiality state that qualitative factors may require that quantitatively small amounts be regarded as material misstatements. In addition, SAB 99 lists what it describes as a less than exhaustive list of considerations. They include whether a misstatement

     1)    Arises from an item capable of precise measurement or whether it arises from an estimate, and, if so, the degree of imprecision inherent in the estimate

     2)    Masks a change in earnings or other trends

     3)    Hides a failure to meet analysts' consensus expectations for the enterprise

     4)    Changes a loss into income or vice versa

     5)    Concerns a segment or other portion of the business that has been identified as playing a significant role in operations or profitability

     6)    Affects compliance with regulatory requirements

     7)    Affects compliance with loan covenants or other contractual requirements

     8)    Increases management's compensation, for example, by satisfying requirements for the award of bonuses or other forms of incentive compensation

     9)    Involves the concealment of an unlawful transaction

12.  Stop and review! You have completed the outline for this subunit. Study multiple-choice questions 1 through 16 beginning on page 804.

## 20.2 THE ANNUAL REPORT

1. The **SEC has authority to regulate external financial reporting** by publicly traded companies. Nevertheless, its traditional role has been to promote disclosure rather than to exercise its power to establish accounting standards. Thus, it **usually allows the accounting profession (through the FASB) to promulgate GAAP**.

   a. To promote disclosure, the SEC has adopted a system that integrates the information required to be presented in annual reports to shareholders and in SEC filings (Form 10-K is the annual report to the SEC).

2. Certain information must be included in both Form 10-K and the annual report to the shareholders.

   a. Information about the market for the company's common stock, such as where it is principally traded, high and low sales prices, frequency and amount of dividends, and number of shares

   b. Selected financial data summarized for the past 5 years, with an emphasis on financial trends, including net sales or operating revenues, income from continuing operations, total assets, long-term obligations, redeemable preferred stock, and cash dividends per share

   c. **Management's discussion and analysis (MD&A)** of financial condition and results of operations

      1) This discussion must address liquidity, capital resources, results of operations, and the effects of inflation and changing prices.

      2) Forward-looking information (a forecast) is encouraged but not required.

         a) The SEC's safe harbor rule protects a company that issues an erroneous forecast if it is prepared on a reasonable basis and in good faith.

      3) The MD&A need not be audited.

      4) SEC Regulation S-K provides guidelines for MD&A disclosures.

   d. Financial statements and supplementary data

      1) Standardized consolidated financial statements are required. They must be audited and include

         a) Balance sheets for the two most recent fiscal year-ends and

         b) Statements of income, cash flows, and changes in shareholders' equity for the three most recent fiscal years.

      2) The accountant certifying the financial statements must be independent of the management of the filing company. The accountant is not required to be a CPA, but (s)he must be registered with a state.

   e. Changes in accountants and disagreements about accounting and financial disclosures

3.    Other matters are required to be included in Form 10-K but not in the annual report. However, companies often include these items in their annual reports.

   a.    A history and description of the business encompassing important recent developments, such as reorganizations, bankruptcies, and major dispositions or acquisitions of assets; information on industry segments and foreign operations; and principal products and services

   b.    Locations and descriptions of physical properties

   c.    Pending litigation, e.g., principal parties, allegations, and relief sought

   d.    Matters submitted to shareholders for approval

   e.    Information about officers and directors, for example, transactions with the company and executive compensation

   f.    Ownership of the company's securities

   g.    Description of certain other business relationships, such as those with related parties

   h.    Exhibits, supporting schedules, and other reports

4.    The **Corporate and Criminal Fraud Accountability Act of 2002**, commonly known as **Sarbanes-Oxley**, is federal legislation that requires an important addition to the reporting of all publicly held companies:

   a.    Under Section 404 of the Act, the annual report must include a **report** from the chief executive officer (CEO) and chief financial officer (CFO) on the company's **system of internal control over financial reporting**.  In this report, the CEO and CFO must:

      1)    Acknowledge **management's responsibility** for establishing and maintaining the system, and affirm that the system has been **functioning effectively**.

      2)    Identify the **internal control standard** that was used in assessing the system's effectiveness.  Very often the standard used is the *Internal Control – Integrated Framework* issued in 1992 by the Committee of Sponsoring Organizations of the Treadway Commission (COSO).

      3)    State whether **significant changes** in controls were made after their evaluation, including any corrective actions.

      4)    State that the **external auditor** has issued an **attestation report** on management's assessment.

5.    A company may include a **social responsibility report** that describes the entity's actions regarding workplace safety, workforce diversity, commitments to employees and communities, human resource development, ethical behavior, environmental protection, and other qualitative factors that may affect the user's evaluation of its performance.  Such a report may be significant for financial analysis of the company because a consistent, proven record of social responsibility may have material financial benefits.

6.    **Audit Report.**  The financial statements of a publicly traded company are accompanied by the report of the independent external auditors.  Their audit is conducted in accordance with generally accepted auditing standards (or the standards of the PCAOB) and is intended to provide assurance to creditors, investors, and other users of financial statements.

7.    The content of the **letter to shareholders** is at the discretion of management.  The typical letter emphasizes accomplishments and plans and is drafted in nontechnical language.  Of course, it may also describe the reasons for any difficulties and how such obstacles will be overcome.  The letter may include summary financial information and discussion of the firm's strategic direction, mission, and values.

8.    Stop and review!  You have completed the outline for this subunit.  Study multiple-choice questions 17 through 22 beginning on page 809.

## 20.3 AUDIT REPORTS

1. **The Attestation Function.** External auditors (CPAs) are independent public accountants. Their primary function is to **attest** to the **fair presentation of financial statements**. Thus, the independent accountants perform an audit in accordance with **generally accepted auditing standards** (or other applicable standards) as a basis for **expressing an opinion** on those statements. This opinion provides **assurance** to third parties, such as creditors and investors, that the financial statements are fairly presented in accordance with generally accepted accounting principles.

   a. The auditor's standard report must contain certain crucial pieces of information. It must refer to:

      1) The **statements** that were audited and the time periods covered by them

      2) The fact that the statements are the **responsibility** of the company's management and that the auditor's responsibility only extends to expressing an opinion on the statements

      3) The **relevant standards** governing the conduct of the audit, usually auditing standards generally accepted in the U.S.

      4) The fact that an audit is designed to obtain only **reasonable assurance** about whether the financial statements are free from **material misstatement**

      5) The fact that an audit does not involve scrutinizing every single document and transaction, but only includes examining on a **test basis** evidence that supports the amounts and disclosures in the financial statements

      6) The fact that part of an audit is assessing the appropriateness of the **accounting principles** management has chosen to apply in its recordkeeping practices

      7) The auditor's **belief** that his or her audit provides a **reasonable** basis for the opinion that is being expressed

      8) The opinion itself, that is, the auditor's professional assessment that the customer's financial statements **present fairly, in all material respects,** the financial position, results of operations, and cash flows for the periods covered by the audit

2. An independent accountant can issue **one of five basic types** of audit reports.

   a. The **standard unqualified** opinion states that the financial statements present fairly, in all material respects, the financial position, results of operations, and cash flows of the entity in conformity with GAAP.

   b. An **unqualified opinion with an explanatory paragraph or modified wording** is used in circumstances where the auditor wishes to draw the reader's attention to a matter, but the financial statements taken as a whole are still fairly presented. Unless otherwise required, an explanatory paragraph may precede or follow the opinion paragraph in the auditor's report. The most common instances of the addition of an explanatory paragraph or the use of modified wording are as follows:

      1) Lack of consistent application of GAAP;

      2) The auditor has substantial doubt about the entity as a going concern;

      3) The statements contain a departure from GAAP necessary to prevent them from being misleading;

      4) The auditor wishes to emphasize a matter; matters often resulting in auditor emphasis include significant related party transactions and the occurrence of important events after the balance sheet date;

      5) The opinion is based in part on the report of another auditor; and

      6) The auditor changes the opinion on a prior period when reporting on current statements in comparative form.

    c.  A **qualified** opinion can be expressed in two circumstances:

        1)  The first case is when the auditor has been prevented by the client from gathering sufficient evidence to form an opinion, or when the auditor has been unable to conduct a complete audit; this results in a **qualification of both the scope and the opinion** in the audit report.

        2)  The second case is when the financial statements are fairly presented except for the effects of a material departure from GAAP; this results in a **qualification of the opinion only**.

        3)  A qualified opinion states that, **except for** the effects of the matter(s) to which the qualification relates, the financial statements present fairly, in all material respects, the financial position, results of operation, and cash flows of the entity in conformity with GAAP.

    d.  An auditor expresses an **adverse** opinion when he or she has concluded that the financial statements, taken as a whole, are so materially misstated or misleading that they do not present fairly, in all material respects, the financial position, results of operations, or cash flows of the entity in conformity with GAAP.

    e.  An auditor issues a **disclaimer** of opinion when (s)he is unable to express an opinion on the financial statements. A disclaimer is issued when the audit has been subject to a severe scope limitation or when the auditor is not independent of the client.

3.  The **Sarbanes-Oxley Act**, mentioned above in connection with the annual report of publicly held companies, also places **new reporting requirements on auditors**. The Act was a response to numerous financial reporting scandals involving large public companies. The auditing changes brought about by Sarbanes-Oxley can be summarized as follows:

    a.  The **Public Company Accounting Oversight Board (PCAOB)** was created. The PCAOB is a private sector, nonprofit corporation that registers public accounting firms within its jurisdiction; adopts standards concerning audit reports; inspects and investigates accounting firms; conducts disciplinary proceedings; imposes sanctions; and enforces compliance with its rules, the Act, professional standards, and securities laws relevant to audit reports and the obligations of accountants.

    b.  Public accounting firms must **register** with the PCAOB and must adopt **quality control** standards. Firms are subject to **inspection** every three years, one year for large firms.

    c.  **Auditing Standard Number 1**, issued by the PCAOB, requires the independent auditor's report to make reference to "the standards of the Public Company Accounting Oversight Board (United States)," rather than to "generally accepted auditing standards" as was the case previously.

        1)  This requirement reflects the Board's **authority to set standards** for audits of publicly held companies. The Board adopted, on an interim basis, U.S. generally accepted auditing standards as they existed on April 6, 2003.

    d.  **Auditing Standard Number 2** requires the independent auditor to **attest to** whether **management's assessment** of its system of internal control over financial reporting (required under Section 404 of the Act; see item 4. under subunit 20.2) is sound.

        1)  The evaluation is not to be the subject of a separate engagement but **must be in conjunction with the audit** of the financial statements.

        2)  The auditor's report also must describe any **material weaknesses** in the controls.

        3)  This **opinion on internal controls** can be expressed in a separate report or incorporated into the main audit report.

           a)  See page 799 for an example of a **combined** internal control and audit report.

    e.   Auditors must retain their **audit working papers** for at least **seven years**. Under Title VIII of the Act, it is a **crime** for auditors to fail to maintain all audit or review working papers for **five years**.

    f.   **Second partner review** and approval of audit reports is required. Furthermore, the lead audit partner and the reviewing partner must **rotate** off the audit every five years

4.   **Other Audit Report Concepts**

    a.   If only **single-year financial statements** are presented, the report is adjusted to refer only to those statements.

    b.   Statements prepared in accordance with GAAP and audited in accordance with GAAS (or the standards of the PCAOB) may be disseminated outside the U.S. Thus, the standard report refers to the **country of origin** of the accounting and auditing standards.

    c.   Financial statements that disclose segment data (see **SFAS 131**, *Disclosures about Segments of an Enterprise and Related Information*) require special audit procedures. However, the auditor need not refer to segment information in the report unless the audit reveals a material misstatement or omission or unless the audit was subject to a scope limitation.

    d.   If a qualified opinion or disclaimer of opinion is expressed, **negative assurance** is inappropriate. Thus, a statement that "nothing has come to our attention indicating the financial statements are not fairly presented" should not be included.

    e.   Audit reports are usually dated as of the last day of fieldwork.

    f.   Auditors have a responsibility to determine that other data appearing in documents containing audited financial statements do not conflict with the data in the audited statements.

    g.   Auditors are responsible for **subsequent events**, those occurring after year-end and prior to the issuance of the financial statements.

    h.   Auditors also may have a responsibility for taking action after issuance of the financial statements if information comes to their attention that would have affected their audit report had it been known at the date of the report.

    i.   Instead of the standard report, a longer, more analytical report may be issued.

    j.   **Other engagements** may address

        1)   Financial statements prepared on a comprehensive basis of accounting other than GAAP

        2)   Specific elements, accounts, or items of statements

        3)   Compliance with contractual or regulatory provisions

        4)   Information on prescribed forms

        5)   Internal control

        6)   The application of accounting principles

        7)   Financial statements prepared for use in other countries

        8)   Information accompanying the basic financial statements in auditor-submitted documents

        9)   Condensed financial statements and selected financial data

        10)  Required supplementary information

        11)  Application of agreed-upon procedures to specified elements, accounts, or items of a financial statement

Example of a Combined Report on the Financial Statements and on Internal Control

<u>Report of Independent Registered Public Accounting Firm</u>

To:                    <----------- Addressed to the Board of Directors and/or Stockholders

[Introductory paragraph]

We have audited the accompanying balance sheets of W Company as of December 31, year 3 and year 2, and the related statements of income, stockholders' equity and comprehensive income, and cash flows for each of the years in the three-year period ended December 31, year 3. We also have audited management's assessment, included in the accompanying [title of management's report], that W Company maintained effective internal control over financial reporting as of December 31, year 3, based on Internal Control – Integrated Framework issued by the Committee of Sponsoring Organizations of the Treadway Commission (COSO). W Company's management is responsible for these financial statements, for maintaining effective internal control over financial reporting, and for its assessment of the effectiveness of internal control over financial reporting. Our responsibility is to express an opinion on these financial statements, an opinion on management's assessment, and an opinion on the effectiveness of the company's internal control over financial reporting based on our audits.

[Scope paragraph]

We conducted our audits in accordance with the standards of the Public Company Accounting Oversight Board (United States). Those standards require that we plan and perform the audits to obtain reasonable assurance about whether the financial statements are free of material misstatement and whether effective internal control over financial reporting was maintained in all material respects. Our audit of financial statements included examining, on a test basis, evidence supporting the amounts and disclosures in the financial statements, assessing the accounting principles used and significant estimates made by management, and evaluating the overall financial statement presentation. Our audit of internal control over financial reporting included obtaining an understanding of internal control over financial reporting, evaluating management's assessment, testing and evaluating the design and operating effectiveness of internal control, and performing such other procedures as we considered necessary in the circumstances. We believe that our audits provide a reasonable basis for our opinions.

[Definition paragraph]

A company's internal control over financial reporting is a process designed to provide reasonable assurance regarding the reliability of financial reporting and the preparation of financial statements for external purposes in accordance with generally accepted accounting principles. A company's internal control over financial reporting includes those policies and procedures that (1) pertain to the maintenance of records that, in reasonable detail, accurately and fairly reflect the transactions and dispositions of the assets of the company; (2) provide reasonable assurance that transactions are recorded as necessary to permit preparation of financial statements in accordance with generally accepted accounting principles, and that receipts and expenditures of the company are being made only in accordance with authorizations of management and directors of the company; and (3) provide reasonable assurance regarding prevention or timely detection of unauthorized acquisition, use, or disposition of the company's assets that could have a material effect on the financial statements.

[Inherent limitations paragraph]

Because of its inherent limitations, internal control over financial reporting may not prevent or detect misstatements. Also, projections of any evaluation of effectiveness to future periods are subject to the risk that controls may become inadequate because of changes in conditions or that the degree of compliance with the policies or procedures may deteriorate.

[Opinion paragraph]

In our opinion, the financial statements referred to above present fairly, in all material respects, the financial position of W Company as of December 31, year 3 and year 2, and the results of its operations and its cash flows for each of the years in the three-year period ended December 31, year 3 in conformity with accounting principles generally accepted in the United States of America. Also in our opinion, management's assessment that W Company maintained effective internal control over financial reporting as of December 31, year 3, is fairly stated, in all material respects, based on criteria established in Internal Control – Integrated Framework issued by the Committee of Sponsoring Organizations of the Treadway Commission (COSO). Furthermore, in our opinion, W Company maintained, in all material respects, effective internal control over financial reporting as of December 31, year 3, based on criteria established in Internal Control – Integrated Framework issued by the Committee of Sponsoring Organizations of the Treadway Commission (COSO).

Signature              <---------- May be signed, typed, or printed
City and State or Country  <---------- Location of audit
Date                   <---------- Date of completion of field work

      k.    Auditors may be requested to provide special **letters to underwriters** that are issuing securities of a client.

      l.    Accountants may undertake limited reviews of **interim statements** based on inquiry, analytical, and certain other procedures.

5.    Stop and review!  You have completed the outline for this subunit.  Study multiple-choice questions 23 through 29 beginning on page 810.

## 20.4 THE AUDIT COMMITTEE

1.    The audit committee is a subcommittee of **outside directors** who are independent of management.  Its purpose is to help keep external and internal auditors independent of management and to assure that the directors are exercising due care.

    a.    The **role of an audit committee** or an equivalent body in strengthening the position of both internal and external auditing is now widely recognized.  The following are some of its characteristics and responsibilities:

        1)    The appropriate governing authority should develop and approve a written **charter** describing the audit committee's duties and responsibilities.

        2)    The audit committee should review the **independence** of the independent public accountant.

        3)    Reports to shareholders or other stakeholders should include a letter from the chair of the audit committee describing its responsibilities and activities.

        4)    The audit committee should monitor compliance with **codes of conduct**.

        5)    The audit committee should have necessary resources available.

        6)    The audit committee should oversee the **regulatory reporting** process.

        7)    The audit committee should monitor instances in which management seeks second opinions on **significant accounting issues**.

    b.    Many **stock exchanges** require a listed organization to have an audit committee.

    c.    An audit committee composed of nonmanagement directors promotes the independence of internal as well as external auditors, especially when it selects the external audit firm and the chief audit executive.  Thus, a strong audit committee insulates the auditors from influences that may compromise their independence and objectivity.

        1)    An audit committee may also serve as a mediator of disputes between the auditors and management.

    d.    The **functions of the audit committee** are to

        1)    Select an external auditor and review the audit fee and the engagement letter

        2)    Review the external auditor's overall audit plan

        3)    Review preliminary annual and interim financial statements

        4)    Review results of engagements performed by external auditors

        5)    Approve the charter of the internal audit activity

        6)    Review and approve the internal audit activity's plans and resource requirements and receive a summary of its work schedule, staffing plan, and financial budget

        7)    Directly communicate with the chief audit executive, who should regularly attend and participate in meetings

        8)    Review evaluations of risk management, control, and governance processes reported by the internal auditors

        9)    As an entity able to ensure that engagement results are given due consideration, receive distributions of final engagement communications by the internal auditors

10) Review policies on unethical and illegal procedures

11) Review financial statements to be transmitted to regulatory agencies

12) Review observations of organizational personnel

13) Participate in the selection of accounting policies

14) Review the impact of new or proposed legislation or governmental regulations

15) Review the organizations' insurance program

16) Review the external auditor's management letter

e.  **External auditors** have recognized the importance of **reporting to audit committees**. Among the matters that may be communicated are internal control-related matters, significant accounting policies, management judgments and accounting estimates, significant audit adjustments, disagreements with management, and difficulties encountered during the audit.

1) One of the factors encompassed by the **control environment** component of internal control is participation by the board, audit committee, or other governing authority. The control consciousness of the entity is improved if the audit committee is independent, composed of experienced and respected people, extensively involved in scrutinizing entity activities, willing to raise and pursue difficult questions with management, and in close communication with the internal and external auditors.

2) **Fraud** involving senior management or fraud that materially misstates the financial statements should be reported directly to the audit committee.

a) The auditors also should be assured that the audit committee is adequately informed about other illegal acts coming to their attention.

2. The **Sarbanes-Oxley Act** contains provisions that impose new responsibilities on public companies and their auditors. The act applies to **issuers** of publicly traded securities subject to federal securities laws.

a.  The act requires that each member of the **audit committee**, including at least one who is a **financial expert**, be an **independent** member of the issuer's **board of directors**. An independent director is not affiliated with, and receives no compensation (other than for service on the board) from, the issuer.

1) The audit committee must be directly responsible for **appointing, compensating, and overseeing** the work of the public accounting firm employed by the issuer. In addition, this audit firm must **report directly** to the audit committee, not to management.

2) Another function of the audit committee is to implement procedures for the receipt, retention, and treatment of **complaints about accounting and auditing matters**.

3) The audit committee also must be appropriately funded by the issuer and may hire independent counsel or other advisors.

b.  The **chief executive officer (CEO)** and **chief financial officer (CFO)** of the issuer must **certify** that the issuer's **financial statements and disclosures** "fairly present, in all material respects, the operation and financial condition of the issuer." This statement must accompany the audit report. A CEO or CFO will be liable only if (s)he **knowingly and intentionally** violates this part of the act. The maximum penalty for a violation is a fine of $500,000 and imprisonment for 5 years.

1) It is also illegal for an officer or director to exert **improper influence on the conduct of an audit** with the intent to make financial statements materially misleading.

2) Moreover, if an issuer materially **restates its financial statements** as a result of material noncompliance with reporting requirements, the CEO and CFO must return to the issuer any amounts received within 12 months after the issuance or filing in the form of incentive-or-equity-based compensation and profits from sale of the issuer's securities.

3) The SEC also may **freeze extraordinary payments** to directors, officers, and others during an investigation of securities law violations, and it may prohibit anyone convicted of **securities fraud** from serving as an officer or director of a publicly traded firm.

4) Directors, officers, and 10% owners must report **transactions with the issuer** by the end of the second business day.

5) **Personal loans** to executives or directors are generally prohibited.

c. **SEC regulations** promulgated under the act prohibit auditors of public companies from performing certain **nonaudit services**:

1) Appraisal and other valuation services

2) Designing and implementing financial information systems

3) Internal auditing or actuarial functions unless the firm reasonably concludes it will not examine such work during the financial statement audit

a) The Federal Reserve, Federal Deposit Insurance Corporation, Comptroller of the Currency, and Office of Thrift Supervision prohibit public companies and depository institutions with $500,000,000 or more in assets from outsourcing internal auditing to external auditors.

4) Management services

5) Human resource services

6) Bookkeeping if the firm also conducts an audit

7) Expert services not pertaining to the audit

8) Investment banking or advisory services

9) Broker-dealer services

d. Audit firms may continue to provide conventional tax planning and other nonaudit services not listed above to audit clients if preapproved by the audit committee.

e. Still another provision of the act prohibits the **conflict of interest** that arises when the CEO, CFO, controller, chief accounting officer, or the equivalent was employed by the company's public accounting firm within one year preceding the audit.

f. **Audit reports** to **audit committees** must include

1) All critical accounting policies and practices to be used

2) All material alternative treatments of financial information within GAAP discussed with management

3) Ramifications of the use of alternative disclosures and treatments

4) The treatments preferred by the external auditors

3. Under the act, disclosures in periodic reports required to be prepared in accordance with GAAP must include all material **correcting adjustments** identified by the external auditors.

a. Disclosures in annual and quarterly reports must include all material **off-balance sheet transactions** and other relationships with unconsolidated entities having material current or future effects on financial condition.

b. A presentation of **pro forma financial information** must not contain an untrue statement or omit a material fact necessary to make it not misleading.

4. Stop and review! You have completed the outline for this subunit. Study multiple-choice questions 30 through 36 beginning on page 813.

## 20.5 CORE CONCEPTS

<u>The SEC and Its Reporting Standards</u>

- The **Securities and Exchange Commission** was created by an Act of Congress to **regulate the trading of securities** and otherwise to enforce securities legislation.
- The **integrated disclosure system** regularizes the information that must be submitted by publicly traded companies.
- **Audited financial statements** along with management's discussion and analysis are inherent parts of the **basic information package**.
- **Form 10** is filed by companies that wish to register securities.
- **Form 10-K** is the annual report to the SEC. It must be certified by an independent accountant and filed within 90 days (60 days for most entities by 2006).
- **Form 10-Q** is the quarterly report. It need not be accompanied by an independent accountant's report, but it must be filed within 45 days (30 days beginning in 2006) of the end of each of the company's first three quarters.
- **Form 8-K** is a current report to disclose material events such as a change in control, bankruptcy or receivership, or the resignation of directors.

<u>The Annual Report</u>

- The SEC generally delegates the authority to **promulgate external reporting standards** (through the FASB) to the accounting profession.
- The **Sarbanes-Oxley Act of 2002** requires public companies to include a statement in the annual reports affirming **management's responsibility** for internal control over financial reporting.
- The financial statements of a publicly traded company are accompanied by the **report of the independent external auditors**.

<u>Audit Reports</u>

- The primary function of **external auditors** (independent public accountants) is to **attest** to the fair presentation of financial statements in all material respects in conformity with U.S. GAAP.
- The **standard audit reports** are the unqualified opinion, the unqualified opinion with explanatory language, the qualified opinion, the adverse opinion, and the disclaimer of opinion.
- The **unqualified opinion** asserts the auditors' conclusion that the financial statements are free of material misstatement. The other opinions are departures to varying degrees from this "clean" audit opinion.
- The **Sarbanes-Oxley Act** created the **Public Company Accounting Oversight Board** to register and monitor accounting firms that perform audits of publicly held companies.
- The Act also requires auditors to **attest to** whether **management's assessment** of its system of **internal control** over financial reporting is sound.

<u>The Audit Committee</u>

- The purpose of an audit committee (a subcommittee of outside directors) is to **help keep external and internal auditors independent of management** and to assure that the directors are exercising due care.
- The **Sarbanes-Oxley Act** requires **each member** of the audit committee, including at least one who is a financial expert, to be an **independent member** of the issuer's board of directors (an independent member is not affiliated with, and receives no compensation from, the issuer).

## QUESTIONS

### 20.1 The SEC and Its Reporting Standards

**1.** The act that gives the SEC the ultimate power to suspend trading of a security, delist a security, and prevent brokers and dealers from working in the securities market is the

- A. Securities Investor Protection Act of 1970.
- B. Securities Act of 1933.
- C. Securities Exchange Act of 1934.
- D. Investment Company Act of 1940.

Answer (C) is correct. *(CMA, adapted)*
**REQUIRED:** The statute providing the SEC ultimate regulatory authority in the trading of securities.
**DISCUSSION:** The Securities Exchange Act of 1934 generally regulates the trading markets in securities. It requires the registration of brokers, dealers, and securities exchanges.
Answer (A) is incorrect because the Securities Investor Protection Act of 1970 created the Securities Investor Protection Corporation (SIPC) to intercede when brokers or dealers encounter financial difficulty endangering their customers. Answer (B) is incorrect because the Securities Act of 1933 requires registration of securities involved in initial public offerings but does not apply to subsequent trading. Answer (D) is incorrect because the Investment Company Act of 1940 deals narrowly with the registration of investment companies.

**2.** Requirements not imposed by the Securities Exchange Act of 1934 and its amendments are

- A. Proxy solicitation requirements.
- B. Prospectus requirements.
- C. Insider trading requirements.
- D. Tender offer requirements.

Answer (B) is correct. *(CMA, adapted)*
**REQUIRED:** The requirements not imposed by the Securities Exchange Act of 1934.
**DISCUSSION:** Prospectus requirements are imposed by the Securities Act of 1933. Prospectuses are used to sell securities, and the Securities Act of 1933 regulates the initial sale of securities.

**3.** The SEC has issued Regulation S-K to govern disclosures in filings with the SEC of nonfinancial statement matters. It concerns descriptions of the company's securities, business, properties, and legal proceedings; information about its directors and officers; management's discussion and analysis of financial condition and results of operations; and

- A. The form and content of the required financial statements.
- B. The requirements for filing interim financial statements.
- C. Unofficial interpretations and practices regarding securities laws disclosure requirements.
- D. Guidelines for voluntary financial projections.

Answer (D) is correct. *(CMA, adapted)*
**REQUIRED:** The item included under the disclosure requirements of Regulation S-K.
**DISCUSSION:** In addition to those items mentioned in the body of the question, Regulation S-K also provides guidelines for the filing of projections of future economic performance (financial projections). The SEC encourages but does not require the filing of management's projections as a supplement to the historical financial statements.
Answer (A) is incorrect because financial statement disclosures are specified in Regulation S-X, not S-K. Answer (B) is incorrect because financial statement disclosures are specified in Regulation S-X, not S-K. Answer (C) is incorrect because unofficial interpretations and practices, if codified at all, are made public through the issuance of Staff Accounting Bulletins (SABs).

**4.** Regulation S-X disclosure requirements of the Securities and Exchange Commission (SEC) concern

- A. Summary information, risk factors, and the ratio of earnings to fixed charges.
- B. The requirements for filing interim financial statements and pro forma financial information.
- C. Information concerning recent sales of unregistered securities.
- D. Management's discussion and analysis of the financial condition and the results of operations.

Answer (B) is correct. *(CMA, adapted)*
**REQUIRED:** The concern of Regulation S-X disclosure requirements.
**DISCUSSION:** Regulation S-X governs the reporting of financial statements, including footnotes and schedules. Both interim and annual statements are covered by Regulation S-X.
Answer (A) is incorrect because Regulation S-X requires more than summary information. Answer (C) is incorrect because Regulation S-X concerns financial statement reporting, not securities. Answer (D) is incorrect because the MD&A is part of the corporate annual report. Disclosure standards for annual reports are covered by Regulation S-K.

**5.** An external auditor's involvement with Form 10-Q that is being prepared for filing with the SEC most likely will consist of

A. An audit of the financial statements included in Form 10-Q.

B. A compilation report on the financial statements included in Form 10-Q.

C. A comfort letter that covers stub-period financial data.

D. A review of the interim financial statements included in Form 10-Q.

Answer (D) is correct. *(CMA, adapted)*
**REQUIRED:** The external auditor's most likely involvement with Form 10-Q.
**DISCUSSION:** Form 10-Q is the quarterly report to the SEC. It must be filed for each of the first three quarters of the year within 45 days (30 days in 2006) after the end of the quarter. It need not contain audited financial statements, but it should be prepared in accordance with APB 28, *Interim Financial Reporting.* A review by an accountant based on inquiries and analytical procedures permits an expression of limited assurance that no material modifications need to be made to interim information for it to be in conformity with GAAP. A review helps satisfy the SEC requirement of "accurate, representative, and meaningful" quarterly information. Thus, an SEC registrant must obtain a review by an independent auditor of its interim financial information that is to be included in a quarterly report to the SEC.
Answer (A) is incorrect because audited statements are not required in quarterly reports. Answer (B) is incorrect because a compilation provides no assurance and would thus not satisfy the SEC requirement of "accurate, representative, and meaningful" quarterly information. Answer (C) is incorrect because comfort letters are addressed to underwriters, not the SEC.

**6.** Form 10-K is filed with the SEC to update the information a company supplied when filing a registration statement under the Securities Exchange Act of 1934. Form 10-K is a report that is currently filed

A. Annually within 90 days of the end of a company's fiscal year.

B. Semiannually within 30 days of the end of a company's second and fourth fiscal quarters.

C. Quarterly within 45 days of the end of each quarter.

D. Monthly within 2 weeks of the end of each month.

Answer (A) is correct. *(CMA, adapted)*
**REQUIRED:** The true statement about filing Form 10-K.
**DISCUSSION:** Form 10-K is the annual report to the SEC. It must be filed within 90 days (60 days in 2006) after the corporation's year-end. It must contain audited financial statements and be signed by the principal executive, financial, and accounting officers and by a majority of the board. The content is essentially that required in the Basic Information Package.
Answer (B) is incorrect because Form 10-K is an annual report. Answer (C) is incorrect because Form 10-Q is filed quarterly within 45 days (30 days in 2006) of the end of each quarter except for the fourth quarter. Answer (D) is incorrect because no monthly reports are required.

**7.** SEC Form S-3 is an optional, short-form registration statement that relies on the incorporation by reference of periodic reports required by the Securities Exchange Act of 1934. Form S-3 offers substantial savings in filing costs over other forms since minimal disclosures are required in the prospectus. The SEC permits the use of Form S-3 only by those firms that have filed periodic reports with the SEC for at least 3 years and if the registrant

A. Has less than $150 million of voting stock held by nonaffiliates.

B. Is widely followed and actively traded.

C. Is seeking more than $150 million in funds.

D. Has not had to file Form 8-K during the most recent 2-year period.

Answer (B) is correct. *(CMA, adapted)*
**REQUIRED:** The requirement for use of Form S-3.
**DISCUSSION:** Form S-1 is used for a first registration. Form S-2 is used by companies that have filed timely reports for 3 years. Incorporation by reference from the annual shareholders' report of Basic Information Package disclosures is allowed in Form S-2. If a company meets the requirements for use of Form S-2 and at least $50,000,000 in value of its stock is held by nonaffiliates (or at least $100,000,000 is outstanding and annual trading volume is at least 3,000,000 shares), Form S-3 may be used. It allows most information to be incorporated by reference to other SEC filings.
Answer (A) is incorrect because the language of the requirement is that a company may use Form S-3 if nonaffiliates hold "at least $50,000,000" of the company's stock (not "less than $150,000,000"). Answer (C) is incorrect because it is not a requirement for use of Form S-3. Answer (D) is incorrect because it is not a requirement for use of Form S-3.

**8.** In an effort to consolidate the registration process, the SEC has adopted a three-tier system of new security forms. However, these three forms do not cover all circumstances. Under which one of the following circumstances would a registrant use Form S-4?

A. Registering securities in connection with mergers and related business-combination transactions.

B. Registering securities in which the registrant does not qualify for Form S-1.

C. Registering securities when the registrant has not had to file Form 8-K during the most recent 2-year period.

D. Registering securities of real estate investment trusts.

Answer (A) is correct. *(CMA, adapted)*
**REQUIRED:** The circumstance under which a registrant would use Form S-4.
**DISCUSSION:** Form S-4 is a simplified form for business combinations, such as mergers. It is part of the integrated disclosure system established to simplify reporting requirements under the Securities Act of 1933 and the Securities Exchange Act of 1934. Thus, Form S-4 may incorporate much information by reference to other reports already filed with the SEC. The integrated disclosure system permits many companies to use the required annual report to shareholders (if prepared in conformity with Regulations S-X and S-K) as the basis for the annual report to the SEC on Form 10-K. Some may even use this report as the basis for registration statements.
Answer (B) is incorrect because Form S-1 may be used by any registrant. Answer (C) is incorrect because the filing of Form 8-K to report certain material events has no effect on the subsequent filing of the S forms. Answer (D) is incorrect because Form S-11 is used by REITs and real estate companies.

**9.** The SEC has adopted a three-tier system of forms in an effort to consolidate the registration process. However, these three forms do not cover all circumstances. A registrant would use Form S-8 when registering securities

A. When the registrant does not qualify for Form S-1.

B. To be offered to employees under any stock option or other employee benefit plan.

C. Of real estate investment trusts.

D. When the registrant has not had to file Form 8-K during the most recent 2-year period.

Answer (B) is correct. *(CMA, adapted)*
**REQUIRED:** The situation that would require a company to use Form S-8.
**DISCUSSION:** SEC Form S-8 is used when securities are to be offered to employees under any stock option or other employee benefit plan. It has become more commonly used in recent years because of the adoption of employee stock ownership plans (ESOPs).
Answer (A) is incorrect because Form S-1 is a long form than includes all possible required information. It can be used by any company. Forms S-2 and S-3 may be used as a substitute by companies that have been timely reporting to the SEC for 3 years. Answer (C) is incorrect because Form S-11 is used by REITs and real estate companies. Answer (D) is incorrect because the filing of Form 8-K to report certain material events has no effect on the subsequent filing of the S forms.

**10.** Form 8-K ordinarily must be submitted to the SEC after the occurrence of a significant event. All of the following events would be reported by Form 8-K except

A. The acquisition of a major company.

B. The resignation of several directors.

C. A change in the registrant's certifying accountant.

D. A change from the percentage-of-completion method of accounting to the completed-contract method for a company in the construction business.

Answer (D) is correct. *(CMA, adapted)*
**REQUIRED:** The event not reported on Form 8-K.
**DISCUSSION:** Form 8-K is a current report to disclose material events. It must be filed within 15 days after the material event takes place. However, a change in independent accountants or the resignation of a director must be reported within 5 business days. Material events that must be reported include a change in control; acquisition or disposition of a significant amount of assets not in the ordinary course of business; bankruptcy or receivership; resignation of directors; and the resignation or dismissal of the firm's independent accountants. Reposting of other material events that are deemed by the registrant to be of importance to security holders is optional. A change in accounting principle does not require reporting on Form 8-K.

**11.** Shareholders may ask or allow others to enter their votes at a shareholders meeting that they are unable to attend. The document furnished to shareholders to provide background information for their vote is a

A. Registration statement.

B. Proxy statement.

C. 10-K report.

D. Prospectus.

Answer (B) is correct. *(CMA, adapted)*
**REQUIRED:** The document furnished to shareholders on behalf of a person seeking permission to vote their shares.
**DISCUSSION:** Under the Securities Exchange Act of 1934, Section 14 seeks to ensure that proxy solicitations are accompanied by adequate disclosure of information about the agenda items for which authority to vote is being sought. One requirement is that the proxy statement be filed with the SEC at least 10 days prior to mailing proxy materials to shareholders. The proxy statement must identify the party making the solicitation and details about the matters to be voted on such as mergers, authorizations to issue new stock, or election of directors.
     Answer (A) is incorrect because a registration statement is the document submitted to the SEC when a new issue of securities is being registered prior to sale. Answer (C) is incorrect because public companies must submit an annual 10-K report to the SEC. Answer (D) is incorrect because a prospectus is sent to potential investors to provide them with information about the investment potential of a new issue of securities. The prospectus is very similar to the registration statement.

**12.** Shelf registration is a registration with the Securities and Exchange Commission (SEC) in which the security issuer

A. Registers the issue price range for a specified period of time.

B. Registers a new issue with the SEC, then files an amendment to its initial filing, and then sells the security on a piecemeal basis.

C. Puts a new security out for bid to all of the underwriters associated with a particular market.

D. Announces its intention to issue a new security but delays its issuance until a detailed financial analysis is available.

Answer (B) is correct. *(CMA, adapted)*
**REQUIRED:** The action of a security issuer pursuant to a shelf registration.
**DISCUSSION:** Shelf registration under SEC Rule 415 allows corporations to file registration statements covering a stipulated amount of securities that may be issued on a piecemeal basis over the two-year effective period of the statement. The securities are essentially placed on the shelf and issued at an opportune moment without the necessity of filing a new registration statement, observing a 20-day waiting period, or preparing a new prospectus. The issuer is only required to provide updating amendments or to refer investors to quarterly and annual statements filed with the SEC. Shelf registration is most advantageous to large corporations that frequently offer securities to the public.
     Answer (A) is incorrect because shelf registration does not stipulate the price that will be charged for securities. Answer (C) is incorrect because shelf registration has nothing to do with the bidding by underwriters. Answer (D) is incorrect because the detailed financial analysis is required as a part of a shelf registration.

**13.** A red herring prospectus is a

A. Misleading or false prospectus.

B. Prospectus that has not been filed with the Securities and Exchange Commission.

C. Prospectus that has been disapproved by the Securities and Exchange Commission.

D. Preliminary prospectus filed with the Securities and Exchange Commission but not approved and, accordingly, subject to change.

Answer (D) is correct. *(CMA, adapted)*
**REQUIRED:** The definition of a red herring prospectus.
**DISCUSSION:** A red herring prospectus is a preliminary prospectus filed with the SEC. The red herring prospectus contains the same information as a regular prospectus, but prices are omitted and the information is subject to change. The prospectus is clearly marked in red to indicate that it is preliminary.
     Answer (A) is incorrect because a red herring prospectus is not misleading or false; it is simply subject to change. Answer (B) is incorrect because a red herring prospectus has been filed with the SEC. Answer (C) is incorrect because a red herring prospectus is filed with the SEC, but is neither approved nor disapproved.

**14.** Form 8-K must be filed within

A. 90 days after the end of the fiscal year covered by the report.

B. 45 days after the end of each of the first three quarters of each fiscal year.

C. 90 days after the end of an employee stock purchase plan's fiscal year.

D. 15 calendar days or, in certain cases, 5 business days after the occurrence of a significant event.

Answer (D) is correct.   *(CMA, adapted)*
**REQUIRED:** The time when Form 8-K must be filed with the SEC.
**DISCUSSION:** Form 8-K is a current report used to disclose material events. For specified events, it must be filed within 15 calendar days after the material event occurs. However, a change in independent accounts or the resignation of a director must be reported within 5 business days. Other material events that must be reported on Form 8-K are a change in control, bankruptcy or receivership, and the acquisition or disposition of a significant amount of assets not in the ordinary course of business.

**15.** Form 10-Q is filed with the SEC to keep both investors and experts apprised of a company's operations and financial position. Form 10-Q is a report that is currently filed within

A. 90 days after the end of an employee stock purchase plan's fiscal year.

B. 15 days after the occurrence of a significant event.

C. 90 days after the end of the fiscal year covered by the report.

D. 45 days after the end of each of the first three quarters of each fiscal year.

Answer (D) is correct.   *(CMA, adapted)*
**REQUIRED:** The time when Form 10-Q must be filed.
**DISCUSSION:** Form 10-Q is a quarterly report to the SEC. It must be filed for each of the first three quarters of the year within 45 days (30 days in 2006) after the end of each quarter. Quarterly financial statements need not be audited, but they must be prepared in accordance with APB 28, *Interim Financial Reporting*. Moreover, an SEC registrant must obtain a review by an independent auditor of its interim financial information that is to be included in a quarterly report to the SEC.
Answer (A) is incorrect because Form 10-Q is the regular quarterly financial report; it is not a specific report for employee stock purchase plans. Answer (B) is incorrect because Form 10-Q is a quarterly financial report. It is not related to specific events. Answer (C) is incorrect because Form 10-Q is a quarterly report, not an annual report.

**16.** Under the SEC's *Staff Accounting Bulletin No. 99: Materiality*, which of the following is not one of the factors that may render material a quantitatively small misstatement of a financial statement item?

A. A misstatement hides a failure to meet analyst's consensus expectations for the enterprise.

B. A misstatement conceals an unlawful transaction.

C. A misstatement affects compliance with regulatory requirements.

D. A misstatement overstates liquidity ratios.

Answer (D) is correct.   *(Publisher)*
**REQUIRED:** The item not a factor that may render a quantitatively small misstatement material.
**DISCUSSION:** SAB 99 lists nine factors that will render material an otherwise quantitatively small misstatement of a financial statement item. These factors include whether a misstatement

1. Arises from an item capable of precise measurement or whether it arises from an estimate and, if so, the degree of imprecision inherent in the estimate.

2. Masks a change in earnings or other trends.

3. Hides a failure to meet analyst's consensus expectations for the enterprise.

4. Changes a loss into income or vice versa.

5. Concerns a segment or other portion of the business that has been identified as playing a significant role in operations or profitability.

6. Affects compliance with regulatory requirements.

7. Affects compliance with loan covenants or other contractual requirements.

8. Increases management's compensation, for example, by satisfying requirements for the award of bonuses or other forms of incentive compensation.

9. Involves the concealment of an unlawful transaction.

SAB 99 has no specific provision regarding the overstatement of liquidity ratios. However, overstatement could be a factor if they affected a loan covenant or other contractual requirement.
Answer (A) is incorrect because a misstatement that hides a failure to meet analyst's consensus expectations for the enterprise is a factor listed in SAB 99. Answer (B) is incorrect because a misstatement that conceals an unlawful transaction is a factor listed in SAB 99. Answer (C) is incorrect because a misstatement that affects compliance with regulatory requirements is a factor listed in SAB 99.

## 20.2 The Annual Report

**17.** Regarding financial accounting for public companies, the role of the Securities and Exchange Commission (SEC) as currently practiced is to

A. Make rules and regulations regarding filings with the SEC but not to regulate annual or quarterly reports to shareholders.

B. Regulate financial disclosures for corporate, state, and municipal reporting.

C. Make rules and regulations pertaining more to disclosure of financial information than to the establishment of accounting recognition and measurement principles.

D. Develop and promulgate most generally accepted accounting principles.

Answer (C) is correct. *(CMA, adapted)*
**REQUIRED:** The role of the SEC as it applies to financial accounting for public companies.
**DISCUSSION:** The SEC has authority to regulate external financial reporting. Nevertheless, its traditional role has been to promote disclosure rather than to exercise its power to establish accounting recognition and measurement principles. Its objective is to allow the accounting profession (through the FASB) to establish principles and then to ensure that corporations abide by those principles. This approach allows investors to evaluate investments for themselves.
Answer (A) is incorrect because the SEC regulates both quarterly and annual reporting. Answer (B) is incorrect because the SEC has no jurisdiction over state and municipal reporting. Answer (D) is incorrect because the SEC has allowed the accounting profession to develop and promulgate GAAP.

**18.** Many firms include 5 or 10 years of financial data in their annual reports. This information

A. Is the forecast of future business.

B. Highlights trends in the financial statements.

C. Highlights inventory valuation methods used by the firm.

D. Is required by generally accepted accounting principles.

Answer (B) is correct. *(CMA, adapted)*
**REQUIRED:** The true statement about financial data in annual reports.
**DISCUSSION:** The information required by the SEC to be reported in Part II of Form 10-K and in the annual report includes a 5-year summary of selected financial data. If trends are relevant, management's discussion and analysis should emphasize the summary. Favorable and unfavorable trends and significant events and uncertainties should be identified.
Answer (A) is incorrect because the required data are for prior periods. Answer (C) is incorrect because the required data include net sales or operating revenues, income from continuing operations, total assets, long-term obligations, redeemable preferred stock, and cash dividends per share. Answer (D) is incorrect because the data are required by the SEC.

**19.** The content of the Management's Discussion and Analysis (MD&A) section of an annual report is

A. Mandated by pronouncements of the Financial Accounting Standards Board.

B. Mandated by regulations of the Securities and Exchange Commission.

C. Reviewed by independent auditors.

D. Mandated by regulations of the Internal Revenue Service.

Answer (B) is correct. *(CMA, adapted)*
**REQUIRED:** The true statement about the MD&A section of the annual financial report.
**DISCUSSION:** The content of the MD&A section is mandated by regulations of the SEC. The MD&A, standard financial statements, summarized financial data for at least 5 years, and other matters must be included in annual reports to shareholders and in Form 10-K filed with the SEC. Forward-looking information in the form of forecasts is encouraged in the MD&A but not required.
Answer (A) is incorrect because the MD&A is required by the SEC. Answer (C) is incorrect because auditors are expected to read (not review or audit) the contents of the MD&A to be certain it contains no material inconsistencies with the financial statements. Answer (D) is incorrect because the MD&A is required by the SEC.

**20.** The responsibility for the proper preparation of a company's financial statements rests with its

A. Management.

B. Audit committee.

C. Internal auditors.

D. External auditors.

Answer (A) is correct. *(CMA, adapted)*
**REQUIRED:** The persons ultimately responsible for the proper preparation of a company's financial statements.
**DISCUSSION:** Management has the responsibility to adopt sound accounting policies and to establish and maintain internal controls that will record, process, summarize, and report transactions, events, and conditions consistent with the assertions in the financial statements. The fairness of the representations made therein is the responsibility of management alone because the transactions and the related assets, liabilities, and equity reflected are within management's direct knowledge and control.

**21.** The Management's Discussion and Analysis (MD&A) section of an annual report

A. Includes the company president's letter.

B. Covers three financial aspects of a firm's business: liquidity, capital resources, and results of operations.

C. Is a technical analysis of past results and a defense of those results by management.

D. Covers marketing and product line issues.

Answer (B) is correct.  *(CMA, adapted)*
**REQUIRED:** The content of the MD&A section of the annual report.
**DISCUSSION:** The MD&A section is included in SEC filings. It addresses in a nonquantified manner the prospects of a company. The SEC examines it with care to determine that management has disclosed material information affecting the company's future results. Disclosures about commitments and events that may affect operations or liquidity are mandatory. Thus, the MD&A section pertains to liquidity, capital resources, and results of operations.
Answer (A) is incorrect because the MD&A section may be separate from the president's letter. Answer (C) is incorrect because a technical analysis and a defense are not required in the MD&A section; it is more forward-looking. Answer (D) is incorrect because the MD&A section does not have to include marketing and product line issues.

**22.** The Securities and Exchange Commission continues to encourage management to provide forward-looking information to users of financial statements and has a safe harbor rule that

A. Protects a company that may present an erroneous forecast as long as the forecast is prepared on a reasonable basis and in good faith.

B. Allows injured users of the forecasted information to sue the company for damages but protects management from personal liability.

C. Delays disclosure of such forward-looking information until all major uncertainties have been resolved.

D. Bars competition from using the information to gain a competitive advantage.

Answer (A) is correct.  *(CMA, adapted)*
**REQUIRED:** The true statement about the SEC's safe harbor rule applicable to forward-looking information.
**DISCUSSION:** The SEC does not require forecasts but encourages companies to issue projections of future economic performance. To encourage the publication of such information in SEC filings, the safe harbor rule was established to protect a company that prepares a forecast on a reasonable basis and in good faith.
Answer (B) is incorrect because both the company and management are protected if the forecast is made in good faith. Answer (C) is incorrect because the objective is to encourage forecasts, not to delay them. Answer (D) is incorrect because anyone may use the forecast information.

## 20.3 Audit Reports

**23.** When two or more auditing firms participate in an audit, one firm should be the principal auditor. If the principal auditor refers to another auditor in a report on an audit that would otherwise result in an unqualified opinion, the audit report issued should contain a(n)

A. Unqualified opinion.

B. Qualified opinion.

C. Except for opinion.

D. Disclaimer of opinion.

Answer (A) is correct.  *(CMA, adapted)*
**REQUIRED:** The audit opinion expressed when the principal auditor refers to the work of another auditor.
**DISCUSSION:** The principal auditor must decide whether to accept responsibility for the work of the other auditors. If the principal auditor does not accept responsibility, the introductory and opinion paragraphs of the report should state the division of responsibility. However, the nature of the opinion expressed is not affected. If the statements are fairly presented in accordance with GAAP, an unqualified opinion is indicated. Referring to the work of another auditor does not preclude an unqualified opinion.

**24.** An auditor may express an unqualified opinion with an explanatory paragraph in all the following circumstances except a(n)

A. Substantial doubt about an entity's going-concern status accounted for in conformity with generally accepted accounting principles.

B. Opinion based in part on the report of another auditor.

C. Scope limitation resulting from inadequate client records.

D. Lack of consistency in the application of accounting principles that has a material effect on comparability.

Answer (C) is correct. *(CMA, adapted)*
**REQUIRED:** The situation in which an unqualified opinion with an explanatory paragraph is not justified.
**DISCUSSION:** Inclusion of an explanatory paragraph does not preclude expression of an unqualified opinion. However, restrictions on the scope of the audit, whether imposed by the client or circumstances, such as the timing of the work, the inability to obtain sufficient competent evidence, or an inadequacy of the accounting records, may require a qualified opinion or a disclaimer of an opinion.
Answer (A) is incorrect because an auditor may express an unqualified opinion with an explanatory paragraph when (s)he has substantial doubt about an entity's going-concern status. Answer (B) is incorrect because an auditor may express an unqualified opinion with an explanatory paragraph when the opinion is based in part on the report of another auditor. Answer (D) is incorrect because an auditor may express an unqualified opinion with an explanatory paragraph when accounting principles have not been consistently observed in the current period in relation to the preceding period, but the auditor concurs with the change.

**25.** An external auditor discovers that a payroll supervisor of the firm being audited has misappropriated $10,000. The firm's total assets and before-tax net income are $14 million and $3 million, respectively. Assuming there are no other issues that will affect the report, the external auditor's report would most likely contain a(n)

A. Disclaimer of opinion.

B. Adverse opinion.

C. Scope qualification.

D. Unqualified opinion.

Answer (D) is correct. *(CMA, adapted)*
**REQUIRED:** The opinion an auditor should render if a misappropriation is discovered.
**DISCUSSION:** An unqualified opinion will probably be rendered because $10,000 is not a material amount in this case. Also, the amount is known and will be disclosed as either a loss or as a receivable from a bonding company, etc.
Answer (A) is incorrect because a disclaimer of opinion is issued only when the auditor does not have an adequate basis for expressing an opinion on financial statements or if a material uncertainty exists. Answer (B) is incorrect because adverse opinions are issued when financial statements are materially misstated. Answer (C) is incorrect because a scope qualification refers to a restriction in necessary auditing procedures.

**26.** If the financial statements contain a departure from an official pronouncement of the Financial Accounting Standards Board that has a material effect on the financial statements, the auditor must express a(n)

A. Adverse opinion.

B. Qualified opinion.

C. Disclaimer of opinion.

D. An adverse opinion or a qualified opinion.

Answer (D) is correct. *(CMA, adapted)*
**REQUIRED:** The type of opinion an auditor must express when financial statements contain a material departure from an official pronouncement of the FASB.
**DISCUSSION:** A qualified opinion states that the financial statements are fairly presented except for the effects of a certain matter. A qualified opinion is expressed when the statements contain a material, unjustified departure from GAAP, but only if an adverse opinion is not appropriate. An adverse opinion is expressed when the financial statements, taken as a whole, are not presented fairly in accordance with GAAP.
Answer (A) is incorrect because a departure from GAAP may justify a qualified opinion, depending on the circumstances. Answer (B) is incorrect because a departure from GAAP may justify an adverse opinion, depending on the circumstances. Answer (C) is incorrect because a disclaimer states that the auditor does not express an opinion. A disclaimer is not appropriate given a material departure from GAAP.

**27.**   A firm wants to obtain an unqualified opinion from its external auditor.  Which one of the following situations would most likely lead to a firm's external auditor's issuance of a qualified opinion, assuming the amounts involved are material?

A.   The client agreed to disclose illegal kickbacks in the financial statements.

B.   The client's financial statements reflected the use of an accounting principle that had substantial authoritative support but was not an officially established principle, and the external auditor agreed with the client's presentation.

C.   The client changed the method of accounting for machinery depreciation from the units-of-production method to the sum-of-the-years'-digits method without providing reasonable justification.

D.   The external auditor was unable to determine with certainty the fairness of the allowance for doubtful accounts using normal procedures because of the large volume of customer accounts; consequently, extended procedures were employed by the external auditor.

Answer (C) is correct.   *(CMA, adapted)*
   **REQUIRED:**  The situation most likely to require a qualified opinion.
   **DISCUSSION:**  The opinion may be qualified as the result of an accounting change when the new principle is not generally accepted, the method of accounting for the change is not in conformity with GAAP, or management has not provided reasonable justification for the change.
   Answer (A) is incorrect because financial statements are fairly presented when illegal kickbacks are properly disclosed in the financial statements.  Answer (B) is incorrect because principles with substantial authoritative support are GAAP even though they are not officially established [category (a) in the hierarchy].  Answer (D) is incorrect because the auditor can be satisfied with the allowance for doubtful accounts using extended (other than normal) audit procedures.

**28.**   If the financial statements taken as a whole are not presented fairly in conformity with generally accepted accounting principles, the auditor must express a(n)

A.   Unqualified opinion.

B.   Qualified opinion.

C.   Except for opinion.

D.   Adverse opinion.

Answer (D) is correct.   *(CMA, adapted)*
   **REQUIRED:**  The opinion an external auditor must express if the financial statements as a whole are not presented fairly in conformity with GAAP.
   **DISCUSSION:**  An auditor must express an adverse opinion when the financial statements taken as a whole are not presented fairly in conformity with GAAP.  An adverse opinion states that the financial statements do not present fairly the financial position or the results of operations or cash flows in conformity with GAAP.
   Answer (A) is incorrect because an unqualified opinion can be expressed only when statements are fairly presented in accordance with GAAP.  Answer (B) is incorrect because a qualified (except for) opinion is expressed when, except for the matter to which the qualification relates, the financial statements are presented fairly, in all material respects, in conformity with GAAP.  Possible bases for a qualified opinion are a scope limitation not sufficient for a disclaimer, a lack of sufficient competent evidence, or a material departure from GAAP that the auditor concludes is not a basis for an adverse opinion.
   Answer (C) is incorrect because a qualified (except for) opinion is expressed when, except for the matter to which the qualification relates, the financial statements are presented fairly, in all material respects, in conformity with GAAP.  Possible bases for a qualified opinion are a scope limitation not sufficient for a disclaimer, a lack of sufficient competent evidence, or a material departure from GAAP that the auditor concludes is not a basis for an adverse opinion.

**29.** When an auditor for some reason is not independent of the client, the report issued should be a(n)

    A. Unqualified report.

    B. Unqualified report with explanatory language.

    C. Qualified report.

    D. Disclaimer.

Answer (D) is correct. *(CMA, adapted)*
    **REQUIRED:** The appropriate report when an auditor lacks independence.
    **DISCUSSION:** A disclaimer of opinion states that the auditor does not express an opinion. It is appropriate when the auditor has not performed an audit sufficient in scope to permit formation of an opinion or when the auditor is not independent of the client. A disclaimer is not appropriate when the financial statements contain material departures from GAAP.
    Answer (A) is incorrect because an auditor must be independent to express an unqualified opinion. Answer (B) is incorrect because an auditor must be independent to express an unqualified opinion. Answer (C) is incorrect because a qualified opinion states that the financial statements are fairly presented except for the effects of a certain matter. It cannot be expressed when the auditor lacks independence.

## 20.4 The Audit Committee

**30.** Audit committees have been identified as a major factor in promoting both the internal and external auditor's independence. Which of the following is the most important limitation on the effectiveness of audit committees?

    A. Audit committees may be composed of independent directors. However, those directors may have close personal and professional friendships with management.

    B. Audit committee members are compensated by the organization and thus favor a shareholder's view.

    C. Audit committees devote most of their efforts to external audit concerns and do not pay much attention to internal auditing and the overall control environment.

    D. Audit committee members do not normally have degrees in the accounting or auditing fields.

Answer (A) is correct. *(CIA, adapted)*
    **REQUIRED:** The most important limitation on the effectiveness of audit committees.
    **DISCUSSION:** The audit committee is a subcommittee made up of outside directors who are independent of corporate management. Its purpose is to help keep external and internal auditors independent of management and to assure that the directors are exercising due care. However, if independence is impaired by personal and professional friendships, the effectiveness of the audit committee may be limited.
    Answer (B) is incorrect because the compensation audit committee members receive is usually minimal. They should be independent and therefore not limited to a shareholder's perspective. Answer (C) is incorrect because, although audit committees are concerned with external audits, they also devote attention to the internal auditing function. Answer (D) is incorrect because audit committee members do not need degrees in accounting or auditing to understand audit reports.

**31.** The Sarbanes-Oxley Act has strengthened auditor independence by requiring that management

    A. Engage auditors to report in accordance with the Foreign Corrupt Practices Act.

    B. Report the nature of disagreements with former auditors.

    C. Select auditors through audit committees.

    D. Hire a different CPA firm from the one that performs the audit to perform the company's tax work.

Answer (C) is correct. *(CPA, adapted)*
    **REQUIRED:** The Sarbanes-Oxley requirement that strengthened auditor independence.
    **DISCUSSION:** The Sarbanes-Oxley Act requires that the audit committee of a public company hire and pay the external auditors. Such affiliation inhibits management from changing auditors to gain acceptance of a questionable accounting method. Also, a potential successor auditor must inquire of the predecessor auditor before accepting an engagement.
    Answer (A) is incorrect because the SEC does not require an audit report in accordance with the FCPA. Answer (B) is incorrect because reporting the nature of disagreements with auditors has been a long-time SEC requirement. Answer (D) is incorrect because the Sarbanes-Oxley Act does not restrict who may perform a company's tax work. Other types of engagements, such as the outsourcing of the internal audit function and certain consulting services, are limited.

**32.** An auditor is least likely to initiate a discussion with a client's audit committee concerning

A. The methods used to account for significant unusual transactions.

B. The maximum dollar amount of misstatements that could exist without causing the financial statements to be materially misstated.

C. Indications of fraud and illegal acts committed by a corporate officer that were discovered by the auditor.

D. Disagreements with management as to accounting principles that were resolved during the current year's audit.

Answer (B) is correct.  *(CPA, adapted)*
  **REQUIRED:**  The item least likely to be discussed with the audit committee.
  **DISCUSSION:**  The auditor is responsible for determining the levels of materiality appropriate in the audit of a client's financial statements.  This decision is made in relation to the acceptable level of audit risk but need not be communicated to the audit committee.

**33.** Which of the following statements is true about an auditor's required communication with an entity's audit committee?

A. Any matters communicated to the audit committee are also required to be communicated to the entity's management.

B. The auditor is required to inform the audit committee about misstatements discovered by the auditor and not subsequently corrected by management.

C. Disagreements with management about the application of accounting principles are required to be communicated in writing to the audit committee.

D. Weaknesses in internal control previously reported to the audit committee are required to be communicated to the audit committee after each subsequent audit until the weaknesses are corrected.

Answer (B) is correct.  *(CPA, adapted)*
  **REQUIRED:**  The true statement about an auditor's required communication with an audit committee.
  **DISCUSSION:**  The matters to be discussed with the audit committee include the auditors' responsibility under generally accepted auditing standards, significant accounting policies, sensitive accounting estimates, audit adjustments, including not only adjustments having a significant effect on financial reports but also uncorrected misstatements pertaining to the latest period presented that were determined by management to be immaterial, the quality of the accounting principles used by management, auditor disagreements with management, whether or not satisfactorily resolved, management's consultations with other accountants, and any serious difficulties the auditors may have had with management during the audit.
  Answer (A) is incorrect because the requirement is that certain information be communicated to the audit committee, not management.  Answer (C) is incorrect because communication with the entity's audit committee may be oral or written.  Answer (D) is incorrect because communication of recurring matters ordinarily need not be repeated.

**34.** Which of the following statements is true concerning an auditor's required communication with an entity's audit committee?

A. This communication is required to occur before the auditor's report on the financial statements is issued.

B. This communication should include management changes in the application of significant accounting policies.

C. Any significant matter communicated to the audit committee should also be communicated to management.

D. Audit adjustments proposed by the auditor, whether or not recorded by management, need not be communicated to the audit committee.

Answer (B) is correct.  *(CPA, adapted)*
  **REQUIRED:**  The true statement concerning an auditor's required communication with the audit committee.
  **DISCUSSION:**  The auditor should communicate to the audit committee, among other things, management's selection of and changes in significant accounting policies or their application.  The auditor should also determine that the committee is informed about the methods used to account for significant unusual transactions and the effects of significant accounting policies in controversial or emerging areas.  Moreover, in an SEC engagement, the auditor should discuss the quality of the auditee's accounting principles as applied in its financial reports.
  Answer (A) is incorrect because the communication typically comes near the end of the audit, after the auditor has identified the items that should be communicated.  Answer (C) is incorrect because the communication is required to be made only to the audit committee.  Answer (D) is incorrect because audit adjustments, whether or not recorded, should be communicated to the audit committee.

**35.** The Sarbanes-Oxley Act of 2002 requires management of publicly-traded corporations to do all of the following except

    A. Establish and document internal control procedures and to include in their annual reports a report on the company's internal control over financial reporting.

    B. Provide a report to include a statement of management's responsibility for internal control and of management's assessment of the effectiveness of internal control as of the end of the company's most recent fiscal year.

    C. Provide an identification of the framework used to evaluate the effectiveness of internal control (such as the COSO report), and a statement that the external auditor has issued an attestation report on management's assessment.

    D. Provide a statement that the board approves the choice of accounting methods and policies.

Answer (D) is correct. *(Publisher)*
    **REQUIRED:** The false statement with regard to management's responsibilities under the Sarbanes-Oxley Act of 2002.
    **DISCUSSION:** The Sarbanes-Oxley Act of 2002 imposes many requirements on management, boards of directors, and auditors. Section 404 applies to internal controls and reports thereon. Section 404 requires management to establish and document internal control procedures and to include in their annual reports a report on the company's internal control over financial reporting. The report is to include a statement of management's responsibility for internal control, management's assessment of the effectiveness of internal control as of the end of the most recent fiscal year, identification of the framework used to evaluate the effectiveness of internal control (such as the COSO report), and a statement that the external auditor has issued an attestation report on management's assessment. Because of this requirement, there are two audit opinions: one on the internal controls and one on the financial statements. Section 301 does address activities of the board, but it does not require the board to approve the choice of accounting methods and policies. Rather, it may assist in the choices of methods and policies.

**36.** The Sarbanes-Oxley Act limits the nonaudit services that an audit firm can provide to public company audit clients. Which of the following services is still an allowable service that an auditor may provide to a public client?

    A. Internal audit outsourcing.

    B. Legal services.

    C. Management consulting services.

    D. Tax compliance services.

Answer (D) is correct. *(Publisher)*
    **REQUIRED:** The type of service that an audit firm may provide to an audit client.
    **DISCUSSION:** The Sarbanes-Oxley Act prohibits audit firms from providing consulting, legal, and internal auditing services to public audit clients. Audit firms may provide conventional tax planning and compliance services to public audit clients.

---

Use Gleim's **CMA Test Prep** for interactive testing with **over 2,000 additional multiple-choice questions!**

# APPENDIX A: TAXES ON THE CMA EXAM

This appendix provides a background and overview of taxes as tested on the CMA exam. The intended emphasis is on a user's point of view rather than a preparer's point of view.

Obviously, taxes are a major expense of doing business, and each business attempts to minimize taxes. Thus, financial managers and management accountants must be knowledgeable about taxes.

Below is a reprint of the IMA's Learning Outcome Statements that apply to Appendix A. After studying the outlines and answering the multiple-choice questions, you will have the skills necessary to address the topics covered in the following:

## Part 3 – Section C.2. Financial instruments

The candidate should be able to:

- recognize how income taxes impact financing decisions

## Part 3 – Section C.3. Cost of capital

The candidate should be able to:

- recognize how income taxes impact capital structures and capital investment decisions

## Part 3 – Section D.2. Relevant data concepts

The candidate should be able to:

- demonstrate an understanding of the impact of income taxes on the relevant revenue and cost data employed in the decision process

## Part 3 – Section D.4. Marginal analysis

The candidate should be able to:

- demonstrate an understanding of the impact of income taxes on marginal analysis decisions

## TAXATION

1. **Two Principles of Taxation**

    a. Benefits received. Individuals should pay a tax based on the benefits received from the services (e.g., paying for the use of a public park or swimming pool).

    b. Ability to pay. Consumers should pay taxes based on their ability to pay them (e.g., taxes on income and wealth).

2. **Three Classifications of Taxes by Rate Structure**

    a. **Progressive**. As the taxable base increases, the tax rate increases. An example is the U.S. income tax. As a taxpayer's income increases, the tax rate also increases.

    1) Forcing taxpayers into higher tax brackets as they earn more is a contractionary automatic stabilizer.

    b. **Proportional**. Under a "strict" definition, this classification refers to taxes for which the rate remains unchanged throughout the entire range of the taxable base. Examples are sales, property, and excise taxes).

   c.   **Regressive**. Under a "strict" definition, this classification refers to taxes for which the rate decreases as the taxable base increases. An example is the Social Security Tax, which is only paid by those below a specified income level.

       1)   Under an "impact" definition, however, all flat-rate taxes (which are defined "strictly" as proportional) are regressive. This is because as taxpayers' incomes decrease, such taxes as sales, property, and excise taxes represent an increasing percentage of their incomes.

3.    Taxes also may be classified as either direct or indirect.

   a.   **Direct taxes** are imposed upon the taxpayer and paid directly to the government, e.g., the personal income tax.

   b.   **Indirect taxes** are levied against others and thus only indirectly on the individual taxpayer, e.g., sales taxes and Social Security taxes paid by employers.

4.   **Incidence of Taxation** -- the parties who actually bear a particular tax. For example, the person who actually bears the burden of an indirect tax may not be the same one who pays the tax to the government.

   a.   The incidence of taxation becomes important when a government wants to change the tax structure. Because taxation is a form of fiscal policy, the government needs to know who will actually bear the incidence of taxation, not just who will pay the tax.

   b.   EXAMPLE: Taxes such as the corporate income tax, the corporate property tax, and the excise tax are often shifted to the consumer in the form of higher prices.

   c.   EXAMPLE: Taxes such as windfall profits taxes are not shifted to the consumer via higher prices. This type of one-time-only tax levied on part of the output produced does not increase the equilibrium price of the taxed good.

5.    In recent years, some authorities have supported a **value-added tax**, a tax based on consumption.

   a.   Many major industrial nations have already adopted a value-added tax.

   b.   The tax is levied on the value added to goods by each business unit in the production and distribution chain.

       1)   The amount of value added is measured by the difference between a firm's sales and its purchases.

       2)   Each firm in the chain collects the tax on its sales, takes a credit for taxes paid on purchases, and remits the difference to the government.

       3)   The consumer ultimately bears the incidence of the tax through higher prices.

   c.   A value-added tax encourages consumer saving because taxes are paid on consumption only, not on savings.

       1)   Because the value-added tax is based on consumption, people in the lower income groups would spend a greater proportion of their income on taxes.

       2)   The value-added tax is thus regressive.

   d.   Only those businesses that make a profit have to pay income taxes. Under the value-added tax, however, all businesses have to pay taxes, regardless of income.

6.   **Taxes** as a business expense (federal, state, local, and foreign) are an important consideration because they are frequently 25% to 50% of all costs.

   a.   They include income, use, excise, property, legal document, payroll, and others.

   b.   Thus, governmental services (national defense, fire, police, etc.) are an important and costly factor of production.

   c.   Tax planning is very important in investment and financing decisions.

       1)   Investment tax credits have at times provided direct reduction of taxes when assets were purchased for use in the business.

      a)    The net effect is to decrease the cost of the asset.

      b)    The amount of the credit and limitations on the tax credit on used equipment affect investment decisions.

      c)    Investment tax credit is currently available for solar and geothermal property (business energy credit), for rehabilitation of historic structures, and for certain reforestation property.

  2)    Accelerated depreciation is permitted on many types of business assets.

      a)    Accordingly, in the early periods of an asset's life, depreciation is higher, taxable income is lower, and the rate of return on investment is higher.

  3)    Corporate capital gains are taxed at regular rates, and the capital gains of individuals are generally taxed at a maximum rate of 15% (5% for low-income taxpayers).

  4)    Special loss carryforward and carryback rules permit businesses to deduct net operating losses incurred in one period against income earned in other periods.

  5)    A dividends-received deduction makes tax-free 70% to 100% of dividends received by one company from investments in the stock of another company.

      a)    This deduction prevents or reduces double taxation.

      b)    It also encourages one company to invest in the stock of another company.

  6)    Interest is a tax-deductible expense of the debtor company.

      a)    But dividends on common or preferred stock are not deductible by the issuer.

  d.    Federal tax policy is fiscal policy that affects the overall economy, which in turn affects production and the finished-goods markets in which the company deals.

  e.    Government monetary policy determines the availability and cost of capital, which affects financing (and in turn, investing) decisions.

    1)    Monetary policy also affects overall economic activity.

7.    **Stop and review!**  You have completed the outline for this subunit.  Study multiple-choice questions 1 through 3 on page 821.

# FUNDAMENTALS OF CORPORATE TAXATION

1.    A C corporation is subject to tax liability imposed on its income (S corporations are taxed as partnerships).

2.    **Gross income** means all income from whatever source derived (unless excluded by statute).

  a.    Income is considered realized when certain transactions occur.

    1)    Mere increases in value (appreciation) do not create income.

      a)    EXAMPLE:  Land owned by a corporation increases in value from $5,000 to $20,000 per acre.  There is no income until the land is sold or exchanged.

    2)    Transactions are normally in the form of a sale, an exchange, or the rendering of services.

    3)    Taxation of realized income may be excluded or deferred, for example, upon exchange of like-kind property.

    4)    The term "recognized" is used when income is realized and also taxed.

    5)    Nonresident aliens (including foreign corporations) are generally subject to federal income tax on U.S.-source income.

3.  **Deductions** are those expenses and other statutorily prescribed items that are subtracted from gross income to determine taxable income.

    a.  Deductions should be distinguished from **exclusions**.  Exclusions are never included in gross income (e.g., interest on tax-exempt bonds).

4.  **Taxable income** is gross income minus deductions.

    a.  Taxable income is analogous to net income.
    b.  The tax rates are applied to taxable income to determine the tax liability.

5.  **Credits** are subtracted from the tax liability.

    a.  Credits directly reduce taxes, while deductions reduce taxable income upon which the taxes are computed.

6.  **Book Income vs. Taxable Income**

    a.  CMA candidates are required to understand the difference between book income and taxable income.  Problems may begin with book income, list numerous transactions, and require the adjustments necessary to arrive at taxable income.
    b.  The following adjustments are necessary to adjust book income to taxable income:

        1)  Add to book income

            a)  Federal income tax
            b)  Excess of capital losses over capital gains
            c)  Taxable income not reported on books
            d)  Expenses reported on books but not deducted on tax return (e.g., charitable contributions in excess of limit)

        2)  Subtract from book income

            a)  Income reported on books but not included on tax return (e.g., interest income from tax-exempt municipal bonds)
            b)  Deductions on tax return but not reported on books (e.g., dividends-received deduction)

    c.  These adjustments are the fundamental differences between net income for financial accounting purposes (book income) and taxable income.  The discussion of income and deductions that follows will concentrate on these differences and assume that candidates can already compute book (i.e., accrual accounting) income.
    d.  According to generally accepted accounting principles (SFAS 109), accounting for income taxes (interperiod tax allocation) is based on the asset and liability method.

7.  **Temporary Differences**

    a.  Depreciation expense arises from using different methods for tax and book purposes.
    b.  To account for bad debt expense, the direct write-off method is used for tax purposes, and the allowance method (estimating expenses) is used for book purposes.
    c.  For tax purposes, warranty expense is deductible only when paid, even if reserves based on estimates are used for book purposes.
    d.  Charitable contributions exceeding 10% of corporate taxable income before charitable contributions and special deductions are deductible during the 5 succeeding tax years.
    e.  Capital losses in excess of capital gains are not deductible in the current year. Instead, a net capital loss must be carried back 3 years (as a short-term capital loss) and applied towards any capital gains.  Any loss remaining can be carried forward for 5 years.  Capital losses can be used only to offset capital gains (i.e., ordinary income is unaffected).

f.   Prepaid rent income is included in taxable income when received.  Prepaid rent expense is deductible in computing taxable income for the period to which it is attributable.

g.   Amortization of organizational costs and business start-up costs can be elected for a period of not less than 60 months for tax purposes.

8.   **Permanent Differences**

a.   Life insurance premiums paid on key persons are not deductible if the corporation is the beneficiary.  Proceeds from the policy are not taxed.

b.   'Seventy percent of dividends received from taxable domestic corporations are deductible by a distributee corporation that owns less than 20% of the stock of the distributing corporation.  The percentage deductible is 80 if the distributee owns 20% to 80% of the distributing corporation.  A 100% dividend-received deduction is permitted for dividends received among members of an affiliated group of corporations (80% ownership).

c.   Federal income tax expense is not deductible in computing taxable income.

d.   Tax-exempt interest is included in book income.  Expense attributable to earning it is not deductible for tax purposes.

e.   Business gifts exceeding $25 are generally not deductible for income tax purposes.

f.   Compensation in excess of $1 million paid to the chief executive officer and certain other employees is not deductible in computing taxable income.  Premiums, tax-free benefits, and compensation based on performance goals are excluded from the $1 million limit.

9.   **Nonrecognition Transactions**.  Certain types of transactions result in deferral or nonrecognition of gains.  Examples are like-kind exchanges, involuntary conversions, and tax-free reorganizations.

a.   **Like-kind exchanges**.  Sec. 1031 defers recognizing gain or loss to the extent that property productively used in a trade or business or held for the production of income (investment) is exchanged for property of like-kind.

b.   **Involuntary conversions**.  A taxpayer may elect to defer recognition of gain, but not losses, if property is involuntarily converted (e.g., by fire, loss, or government condemnation for public use) into money or property that is not similar or related in use.  Nonrecognition of gain is contingent on the involuntarily converted property being reinvested in qualified replacement property.

c.   **Tax-free reorganization**.  A nontaxable reorganization of one or more corporations is considered a mere change in form of investment rather than a disposition of assets.  For this reason, a general rule of nonrecognition of gain or loss applies to qualifying reorganizations.  However, gain is recognized to the extent of receipt of cash or other nonqualifying payment.

10.   **Taxation on Multinational Corporations**

a.   Multinational corporations frequently derive income from several countries.  The government of each country in which a corporation does business may enact statutes imposing one or more types of tax on the corporation.

b.   To avoid double taxation, most countries have adopted treaties to coordinate or synchronize the effects of their taxing statutes.

11.   Stop and review!  You have completed the outline for this subunit.  Study multiple-choice questions 4 through 9 beginning on page 822.

## QUESTIONS

### Taxation

**1.** A regressive tax is a tax in which

A. Individuals with higher incomes pay a higher percentage of their income in tax.

B. The burden for payment falls disproportionately on lower-income persons.

C. The individual pays a constant percentage in taxes, regardless of income level.

D. Individuals with lower incomes pay a lower percentage of their income in tax.

**Answer (B) is correct.** *(Publisher)*
**REQUIRED:** The statement that describes a regressive tax.
**DISCUSSION:** With a regressive tax, the percentage paid in taxes decreases as income increases. For example, excise taxes and payroll taxes are both regressive taxes. An excise tax is regressive because its burden falls disproportionally on lower-income persons. As personal income increases, the percentage of income paid declines because an excise tax is a flat amount per quality of the good or service purchased.
Answer (A) is incorrect because a tax in which individuals with higher incomes pay a higher percentage of their income is a progressive tax. For example, income taxes are progressive. Answer (C) is incorrect because a proportional tax is a tax in which the individual pays a constant percentage in taxes, regardless of income level. A sales tax is a proportional tax. Answer (D) is incorrect because a tax in which individuals with lower incomes pay a lower percentage of their income is a progressive tax. For example, income taxes are progressive.

**2.** Two examples of indirect taxes are

A. Taxes on business and rental property and personal income taxes.

B. Sales taxes and Social Security taxes paid by employees.

C. Sales taxes and Social Security taxes paid by employers.

D. Social Security taxes paid by employees and personal income taxes.

**Answer (C) is correct.** *(CMA, adapted)*
**REQUIRED:** The two forms of indirect taxes.
**DISCUSSION:** Indirect taxes are those levied against someone other than individual taxpayers and thus only indirectly affect the individual. Sales taxes are levied against businesses and are then passed along to the individual purchaser. Social Security taxes are levied against both the employer and the employee. Those levied against the employee are direct taxes; those levied against the employer are indirect.
Answer (A) is incorrect because personal income taxes and Social Security taxes levied against the employee are direct taxes. Answer (B) is incorrect because personal income taxes and Social Security taxes levied against the employee are direct taxes. Answer (D) is incorrect because personal income taxes and Social Security taxes levied against the employee are direct taxes.

**3.** When a fixed plant asset with a 5-year estimated useful life is sold during the second year, how would the use of an accelerated depreciation method instead of the straight-line method affect the gain or loss on the sale of the fixed plant asset?

| | Gain | Loss |
|---|---|---|
| A. | Increase | Increase |
| B. | Increase | Decrease |
| C. | Decrease | Increase |
| D. | Decrease | Decrease |

**Answer (B) is correct.** *(CMA, adapted)*
**REQUIRED:** The effect of using an accelerated depreciation method instead of straight-line.
**DISCUSSION:** An accelerated method reduces the book value of the asset more rapidly in the early years of the useful life than does the straight-line method. Hence, the effect of an early sale is to increase the gain or decrease the loss that would have been recognized under the straight-line method.

## Fundamentals of Corporate Taxation

Questions 4 and 5 are based on the following information. The Hando Communications Corporation (HCC) has just finished its first year of operations. For the year, HCC had $80,000 of income, including $11,000 of interest earned on a tax-exempt bond. HCC also has a $10,000 depreciation deduction, and an $8,000 tax credit. Assume that HCC has a 30% tax rate.

**4.** What is HCC's net tax liability?

A. $17,700

B. $15,300

C. $9,700

D. $2,000

Answer (C) is correct. *(Publisher)*
**REQUIRED:** The net tax liability.
**DISCUSSION:** The first step in calculating HCC's net tax liability is to subtract the exclusion for tax-exempt interest from income, for a gross income amount of $69,000 ($80,000 – $11,000). Next, the deprecation deduction is subtracted from gross income, for a taxable income of $59,000 ($69,000 – $10,000). Then, the taxable income is multiplied by the tax rate, for a gross tax liability of $17,700 ($59,000 × 30%). Finally, net tax liability is computed by subtracting the tax credits from the gross tax liability. Therefore, HCC's net tax liability is $9,700 ($17,700 – $8,000).
Answer (A) is incorrect because $17,700 is the gross tax liability. Answer (B) is incorrect because $15,300 is the net tax liability found when incorrectly treating the tax credit as a direct reduction in taxable income. Answer (D) is incorrect because $2,000 is the net tax liability found when incorrectly treating the exclusion as a credit.

**5.** Which item reduces HCC's gross tax liability by the largest amount?

A. Gross income.

B. The tax-exempt interest exclusion.

C. The depreciation deduction.

D. The tax credit.

Answer (D) is correct. *(Publisher)*
**REQUIRED:** The item that decreases HCC's gross tax liability by the largest amount.
**DISCUSSION:** Credits directly reduce taxes, whereas exclusions and deductions reduce income prior to the computation of the gross tax liability. Thus, the credit reduces the gross tax liability on a dollar-for-dollar basis, or $8,000. An exclusion or deduction reduces gross tax liability by the amount of the exclusion or deduction multiplied by the tax rate. Accordingly, the exclusion will reduce HCC's gross tax liability by $3,300 ($11,000 × 30%), and the deduction will reduce HCC's gross tax liability by $3,000 ($10,000 × 30%). Gross income does not reduce the gross tax liability; rather, it increases the gross tax liability by $20,700 ($69,000 × 30%).

**6.** None of the following items are deductible in calculating taxable income except

A. Estimated liabilities for product warranties expected to be incurred in the future.

B. Dividends on common stock declared but not payable until next year.

C. Bonus accrued but not paid by the end of the year to a cash-basis 90% shareholder.

D. Vacation pay accrued on an employee-by-employee basis.

Answer (D) is correct. *(CMA, adapted)*
**REQUIRED:** The item that is deductible in the calculation of taxable income.
**DISCUSSION:** Sec. 162(a) states that a deduction is allowed for the ordinary and necessary expenses incurred during the year in any trade or business. A corporation may therefore deduct a reasonable amount for compensation. Accrued vacation pay is a form of compensation that results in an allowable deduction for federal income tax purposes.
Answer (A) is incorrect because warranty expenses are not deductible until paid. Answer (B) is incorrect because dividends on common stock are never deductible by a corporation; they are distributions of after-tax income. Answer (C) is incorrect because amounts accrued by an accrual-basis taxpayer to be paid to a related cash-basis taxpayer in a subsequent period are not deductible until the latter taxpayer includes the items in income. This rule effectively puts related taxpayers on the cash basis.

**7.** All of the following are adjustments/preference items to corporate taxable income in calculating alternative minimum taxable income except

    A. Accelerated depreciation over straight-line on most real property placed into service prior to 1987.

    B. Mining exploration and development costs.

    C. A charitable contribution of appreciated property.

    D. Sales commission earned in the current year but paid in the following year.

Answer (D) is correct. *(CMA, adapted)*
    **REQUIRED:** The item that is not an adjustment or preference item in calculating the alternative minimum tax (AMT).
    **DISCUSSION:** Taxable income is adjusted to arrive at alternative minimum taxable income. Some of the common adjustments include gains or losses from long-term contracts, gains on installment sales of real property, mining exploration and development costs, charitable contributions of appreciated property, accelerated depreciation, the accumulated current earnings adjustment, and tax-exempt interest on private activity bonds issued after August 7, 1986. A sales commission accrued in the current year but paid in the following year is not an example of an AMT adjustment.
    Answer (A) is incorrect because accelerated depreciation over straight-line on most real property placed into service prior to 1987 is an adjustment. Answer (B) is incorrect because mining exploration and development costs are adjustments to taxable income for purposes of computing alternative minimum taxable income. Answer (C) is incorrect because a charitable contribution of appreciated property is an adjustment to taxable income for purposes of computing alternative minimum taxable income.

**8.** Which one of the following factors might cause a firm to increase the debt in its financial structure?

    A. An increase in the corporate income tax rate.

    B. Increased economic uncertainty.

    C. An increase in the federal funds rate.

    D. An increase in the price-earnings ratio.

Answer (A) is correct. *(CMA, adapted)*
    **REQUIRED:** The factor that might encourage a firm to increase the debt in its financial structure.
    **DISCUSSION:** An increase in the corporate income tax rate might encourage a company to borrow because interest on debt is tax deductible, whereas dividends are not. Accordingly, an increase in the tax rate means that the after-tax cost of debt capital will decrease. Given equal interest rates, a firm with a high tax rate will have a lower after-tax cost of debt capital than a firm with a low tax rate.
    Answer (B) is incorrect because increased uncertainty encourages equity financing. Dividends do not have to be paid in bad years, but interest on debt is a fixed charge. Answer (C) is incorrect because an increase in interest rates discourages debt financing. Answer (D) is incorrect because an increase in the price-earnings ratio means that the return to shareholders (equity investors) is declining; therefore, equity capital is a more attractive financing alternative.

**9.** The deferral or nonrecognition of gains is not allowed for tax purposes when the transaction is a(n)

    A. Reorganization that is a change in the form of investment.

    B. Exchange of property that is used in a business for like-kind property.

    C. Reorganization that is considered a disposition of assets.

    D. Involuntary conversion of property into qualified replacement property.

Answer (C) is correct. *(Publisher)*
    **REQUIRED:** The statement that does not allow for the deferral or nonrecognition of gain.
    **DISCUSSION:** Like-kind exchanges, involuntary conversions, and tax-free reorganizations are examples of transactions that result in the deferral or nonrecognition of gain. A reorganization is nontaxable when it is considered a mere change in investment, not a disposition of assets.
    Answer (A) is incorrect because a reorganization that is a mere change in the form of investment is nontaxable. Answer (B) is incorrect because a like-kind exchange allows for the deferral of gain. Answer (D) is incorrect because an involuntary conversion allows for the deferral of gain.

---

Use Gleim's **CMA Test Prep** for interactive testing with **over 2,000 additional multiple-choice questions!**

# APPENDIX B
# IMA MEMBERSHIP AND EXAMINATION FORMS

You must apply and become an IMA member in order to participate in the IMA Certification programs. The cost is $185 per year for Regular or International membership. Recent graduates have discounted fees of $61 their first year out of school and $122 the second year out of school. Full-time faculty dues (in the U.S., Canada, and Mexico) are $93 and dues for full-time students are $37 per year (must carry at least 6 equivalent hours per semester and reside in the U.S., Canada, or Mexico).

The IMA offers four member interest groups at $75 per year: the Controllers Council, the Cost Management Group, the Small-Business Council, and the Sarbanes-Oxley Knowledge Network. Everyone except students and associates must pay a $15 IMA registration fee.

The following two pages can be photocopied and used to apply for IMA membership, or call the IMA at (800) 638-4427 ext. 510 and ask for a CMA "kit." You may also e-mail the IMA at info@imanet.org to request an information kit or apply online on the IMA's website at www.imanet.org.

Completion of the registration form on the two pages following the IMA membership application is required in order to take any of the examination parts.

NOTE: The ICMA application has been replaced by the IMA Certification Program. You can apply for admission into the Certification Program by checking the appropriate box on either the IMA Membership Application or the Exam Registration Form. The fee is $125 and is waived for students.

# INSTITUTE OF MANAGEMENT ACCOUNTANTS®

IMAWEBAPP

## ＋　＋　＋　MEMBERSHIP APPLICATION　＋　＋　＋

☐ **New Application**

☐ **Renewal**

☐ **Certification**
(IMA membership required)

**PERSONAL INFORMATION** *(please print)*

☐ Mr. ☐ Ms. ☐ Mrs. ☐ Miss ☐ Dr.　Last/Family Name/Surname: _____

First/Given Name: _____　Middle Initial: _____ Suffix: _____

Date of Birth (month/day/year): ____ /____ /____

### Please indicate your contact preference:

☐ **BUSINESS MAILING ADDRESS:**
*(See reverse side to enter SIC, job title, and responsibility codes)*

Title: _____

Company Name: _____

Street/P.O. Box: _____

_____

City: _____

State/Province: _____

Zip Code/Postal Code: _____

Country: _____

Business Phone: *(Include Country/Area/City Codes)* _____

☐ **HOME MAILING ADDRESS:**

Street/P.O. Box: _____

City: _____

State/Province: _____

Zip Code/Postal Code: _____

Country: _____

Phone: *(Include Country/Area/City Codes)* _____

*If you are applying for Student Membership, please note your school information under "Business Mailing Address."*

E-mail Address: _____　Fax: _____

## EDUCATION HISTORY

| | Name of Institution | Degree | Major | Date Received/Expected |
|---|---|---|---|---|
| Undergraduate: | | | | |
| Graduate: | | | | |

Professional Designations Earned: ☐ U.S. CPA ☐ CFA ☐ CIA ☐ Other: _____

## CHAPTER AFFILIATION
See a list of Regular/Student Chapter options by visiting our website www.imanet.org, or call (800) 638-4427.

Chapter Name: _____　Chapter Number: _____

☐ Member-At-Large (Check here if no chapter affiliation is desired)

☐ International Member-At-Large

## A. MEMBERSHIP INFORMATION *(All payments must be in U.S. Dollars)*

☐ **Regular Membership** .................................... $185.00
*(You must reside in the U.S., Canada, or Mexico)*

☐ **International Membership** ......................... $185.00
*(Available to professionals residing outside the U.S., Canada, or Mexico)*

☐ **Student Membership** ................................ $ 37.00
*(You must be taking 6 or more hours per semester and reside in the U.S., Canada, or Mexico)*

Expected Graduation Date (Year) _____

☐ **Associate Membership**
*(You must apply within 2 years of completing full-time studies and reside in the U.S., Canada, or Mexico)*

Select One: ☐ 1st year after graduation ............ $ 61.00

☐ 2nd year after graduation ............ $122.00

☐ **Academic Membership** ............................. $ 93.00
*(You must be a full-time faculty member and reside in the U.S., Canada, or Mexico)*

## B. OPTIONAL SERVICES
*(IMA membership required. All payments must be in U.S. Dollars)*

☐ **Member Interest Groups** ......................... $ 75.00 each
☐ Controllers Council ☐ Cost Management Group ☐ Small Business Council

☐ **CPE Offerings**
☐ IMA Knowledge Exchange (Unlimited CPE) ........... $245.00
☐ IMA Advantage (Unlimited CPE) ........... $245.00
☐ IMA Knowledge Exchange/Advantage Combo ........... $369.00
☐ IMA CPEdge ........................................ $179.00

☐ **Certification** ☐ CMA ☐ CFM
☐ Entrance Fee *(One-time payment)* ................... $125.00
*(Except for students in the U.S., Canada, and Mexico)*

☐ **Exam Waiver Fee** *(See www.imanet.org for more information)* ......... $115.00

**INSTITUTE OF MANAGEMENT ACCOUNTANTS, INC.**
· 10 Paragon Drive, Montvale, NJ 07645-1760 · (800) 638-4427 or (201) 573-9000 · fax (201) 474-1600 · ima@imanet.org · www.imanet.org

## C. REGISTRATION FEES

☐ **Membership Registration Fee** . . . . . . . . . . . . . . . . . . . . . . . . . . . . . . . . . . . . $15.00
*(All new members except Students and Associates)*

☐ **Reinstatement Fee** . . . . . . . . . . . . . . . . . . . . . . . . . . . . . . . . . . . . . . . . . . . $15.00
*(If your membership has lapsed for 90 days, a $15.00 reinstatement fee applies)*

> **TOTAL DUE (add sections A, B, and C)** . . . . . . . . . . . . . . . . . . . . . . $ _____

## APPLICANT STATEMENT

☐ Check here if you have ever been convicted of a felony. Please enclose a confidential letter with a brief explanation of circumstances to the attention of President & CEO.

**I affirm that the statements on this application are correct, and I agree to abide by the Statement of Ethical Professional Practice.**

Signature: _____ Date: _____

IMA occasionally makes available its members' addresses (excluding telephone and e-mail) to vendors who provide products and services to the management accounting and finance community. If you prefer not to be included in these lists, please check this box. ☐

### PREFERRED METHOD OF PAYMENT
*(All payments must be in U.S. Dollars)*

☐ **Wire Payments** . . . . . . . . . . . . . . . . . . . . . . . . . . . . . . . . . . . . . . . . . . . . . . . . . .
All wire transfers must be made with bank fees prepaid. Please notify IMA by e-mail (dhuckins@imanet.org) that you are paying by wire transfer. Include your name, amount sent, and wire transfer receipt number.

☐ **Check Payments**
My check for $ _____ , payable to IMA, is enclosed.
No checks drawn on foreign banks will be accepted unless they are payable through U.S. correspondent banks and in U.S. dollars.

☐ **Credit Card Payments**
Charge my credit card: ☐ AMEX ☐ Discover ☐ MasterCard ☐ VISA

Card Number: _____ Exp.: _____

Cardholder Name: _____

Signature: _____

---

## CMA/CFM CERTIFICATION PROGRAMS

IMA membership required. If you are applying to the certification programs for the first time, please check the program(s) you wish to enter and enclose the Entrance Fee ($125.00) required of new certification applicants only. (Students in the U.S., Canada, and Mexico are exempt.)

☐ Applying as a **Student** *(U.S., Canada, and Mexico only)* — Upon graduation, arrange for an official copy of your transcript to be sent.

☐ Applying as **Faculty** *(U.S., Canada, and Mexico only)* — Please provide a letter on school stationery affirming full-time teaching status.

☐ Certified Management Accountant

☐ Certified Financial Manager

*Please complete the Additional Educational Information below:*

## ADDITIONAL EDUCATIONAL INFORMATION

Check the appropriate box and make arrangements for supporting documents to be forwarded to the IMA certification department. Only one form of credentials is required.

☐ **Later** — By selecting this option, many applicants choose to provide their educational credentials after completing the exams.

If you would like to have your credentials reviewed prior to taking the exams to ensure that they are acceptable, please select one of the options below. Please note that the educational requirement must be fulfilled prior to certification.

☐ **College Graduate** — Submit official transcript (translated into English) showing university degree conferred and official university seal, or arrange to have proof of degree sent directly from university.

☐ **GMAT or GRE Scores** — Provide copy of scores.

☐ **U.S. CPA Exam, U.S. CFA Exam, or other acceptable certification or license** — Arrange to have proof sent directly from your certifying organization. Acceptable designations are listed at www.imanet.org.

---

### *Strategic Finance* Magazine
Subscription rates per year:
Members: . . . . . . . . . . . . $ 48 (Included in dues, nondeductible)
Student Members: . . . . $ 25 (Included in dues, nondeductible)

### *Management Accounting Quarterly*
Subscription rates per year:
Members: . . . . . . . . . . . . $ 10 (Included in dues, nondeductible)

---

### SIC CODE – STANDARD INDUSTRY CLASSIFICATIONS
*(Please Circle One)*

01 Education
02 Healthcare
03 Media and Entertainment
16 Construction, Mining, Agriculture
21 Manufacturing
41 Transportation, Communication, Utilities
51 Wholesale/Retail Trades
61 Finance
63 Insurance
81 Business Services
82 Real Estate
86 High Tech
90 Nonprofit
93 Government
96 Pharmaceuticals & Biotechnology
99 Other _____

### JOB TITLE CODE
*(Please Circle One)*

05 Executive Officer
11 Corporate Officer
15 Vice President
31 Controller
33 Chief Financial Officer
35 Director/Manager
41 Supervisor
47 Accountant
51 Analyst
55 Programmer
57 Administrative
59 Consultant
65 Academic
99 Other _____

### RESPONSIBILITY CODE
*(Please Circle One)*

01 General Management
05 Corporate Management
10 Public Accounting
15 General Accounting
20 Personnel Accounting
25 Cost Accounting
30 Government Accounting
33 Environmental Accounting
35 Finance
40 Risk Management
45 Budget and Planning
50 Taxation
55 Internal Auditing
60 Education
65 Information Systems
70 Student
75 Retired
80 Other _____

---

## MEMBER PROFILE

1. **Do you have international responsibilities?**
   ☐ Yes   ☐ No

2. **Does your company have international locations?**
   ☐ Yes   ☐ No

3. **Who will pay your IMA dues?**
   ☐ Me   ☐ My Company

4. **What are you looking for most from your IMA Membership?**
   ☐ Career assistance    ☐ Professional networking
   ☐ Certification        ☐ Industry news
   ☐ Education            ☐ Leadership training
   ☐ CPE                 ☐ Research
   ☐ Other (please specify) _____

5. **Are you a member of any other association?**
   ☐ AAA  ☐ AFP  ☐ AICPA  ☐ ASWA
   ☐ CFA Institute (AIMR)  ☐ FEI  ☐ IIA
   ☐ Other (please specify) _____

6. **Is your organization:**
   ☐ Public sector
   ☐ Private sector
   ☐ Nonprofit

8. **How did you learn about IMA?**
   ☐ Chapter meeting          ☐ Marketing piece
   ☐ IMA educational program  ☐ Company recommended
   ☐ IMA website              ☐ Industry associate
   ☐ Industry publication     ☐ Professor
   ☐ Other _____
   ☐ Other website _____

9. **How many employees are in your company or organization?**
   ☐ Under 50  ☐ 51-100  ☐ 101-200  ☐ 201-500
   ☐ 501-1,000  ☐ 1,001-10,000  ☐ Over 10,000

10. **What is your company's current annual revenue?**
   ☐ Under $1 million        ☐ $500 million - $1 billion
   ☐ $1 - $10 million        ☐ $1 billion - $5 billion
   ☐ $10 - $100 million      ☐ $5 billion - $10 billion
   ☐ $100 - $500 million     ☐ Over $10 billion

---

*Please send your completed application and payment (made out to IMA) to:*

**INSTITUTE OF MANAGEMENT ACCOUNTANTS, INC.**

Rev. 0506

· 10 Paragon Drive, Montvale, NJ 07645-1760 · (800) 638-4427 or (201) 573-9000 · fax (201) 474-1600 · ima@imanet.org · www.imanet.org ·

827

| OFFICE USE ONLY | BATCH NUMBER | PAYMENT BY CHECK #_____<br>☐ PERSONAL<br>☐ COMPANY | AMOUNT |
|---|---|---|---|

**Institute of Certified Management Accountants**
10 Paragon Drive • Montvale, New Jersey 07645-1759
(201) 573-9000 • (800) 638-4427 • FAX: (201) 474-1600
*Endorsed by the Institute of Management Accountants*

CMALSKIT

# REVISED CMA EXAMINATION REGISTRATION FORM

**PERSONAL INFORMATION** *TYPE OR PRINT CLEARLY*

☐ Mr. ☐ Ms. ☐ Miss ☐ Mrs. ☐ Dr. ☐ CMA ☐ CFM ☐ Certification Candidate   Social Security Number _____

☐ IMA #_____ or ☐ FMA #_____

Last Name/Family Name/Surname          First Name          Middle Initial          Suffix

Preferred Mailing Address

City          State/Province/Country          Zip Code/Postal Code

Daytime Telephone (include area code or country/city code)          Please Specify ☐ Home  ☐ Business

E-mail:          Fax Number: (Include Area/Country/City Codes)

☐ Please check box if this is a new address.

☐ Please check box if you are applying to the ICMA program, complete side two and pay the $125 entrance fee.

**PLACE A CHECK MARK IN THE BOX(ES) BELOW FOR THE PART(S) YOU WISH TO TAKE AT THIS TIME**

☐ **PART 1**<br>Business<br>Analysis     ☐ **PART 2**<br>Management<br>Accounting<br>and Reporting     ☐ **PART 3**<br>Strategic<br>Management     ☐ **PART 4**<br>Business<br>Applications*     ☐ **PART 2 CFM**<br>Corporate<br>Financial<br>Management**

| TOTAL PARTS _____ |

*Parts 1, 2, and 3 must be passed before registering for Part 4.*
**You must complete Parts 1, 2, 3 and 4 before registering for Part 2 CFM.*

X $130 Domestic Fee (U.S., Mexico and Canada) ........................ $ _____

X $165 International Fee (outside U.S. and Canada, excluding Japan) ........... $ _____

X $235 Per-Part Fee Japan Only .................................... $ _____

Less: Student/Faculty Discount (50% students, 100% faculty) (U.S., Mexican and Canadian students/faculty only) ...... $ _____

Plus: $115 Part I Waiver Fee if applicable (Revised CMA program only) ........... $ _____

Plus: $125 Entrance Fee if applicable (New certification applicants only; U.S., Mexican and Canadian students are exempt) ...... $ _____

**AMOUNT DUE** ........................................................ $ _____

**NOTES:** (1) Examination fees are not refundable.
(2) You are required to take all the parts you register for within the same 120 day authorization period.
(3) Faculty retakes are 50%.

**PLEASE COMPLETE BOTH SIDES**          **NOTE: PAYMENT IN FULL MUST ACCOMPANY REGISTRATION FORM - FEES SUBJECT TO CHANGE**

1/06

## CERTIFICATION PROGRAM APPLICATION

If you are applying for admission to the certification program, please complete the following.

Check the programs you wish to enter: ☐CMA ☐CFM

☐ **Applying as a Student** (U.S., Mexico and Canada) – Upon graduation, arrange for an official copy of your transcript to be sent.

☐ **Applying as Faculty** (U.S., Mexico and Canada) – Please provide a letter on school stationery affirming full-time teaching status.

☐ **Waiver for Part I** – Arrange to have proof of certification sent directly from your certifying organization. Include the waiver fee with this application.

## ADDITIONAL EDUCATIONAL INFORMATION

*Check one of the following and make arrangements for supporting documents to be forwarded to the IMA certification department.*

☐ **Later** - By selecting this option, many applicants choose to provide their educational credentials after completing the exams. If you would like to have your credentials reviewed prior to taking the exams to ensure that they are acceptable, please select one of the options below. Please note that the educational requirement must be fulfilled prior to certification.

☐ **College Graduate** - Submit official transcript showing university degree conferred and official university seal or arrange to have proof of degree sent directly from university. Applicants with degrees conferred outside the U.S. must have their degree evaluated by an independent agency unless the school appears on the IMA list of acceptable universities (www.imanet.org, Certification, General Requirements).

Name on transcript (if different from front of application)

☐ **GMAT or GRE Scores** - Provide copy of scores.

☐ **Professional Certification** – Arrange to have proof of certification sent directly from the certifying organization. See listing of acceptable certifications at www.imanet.org, Certification, General Requirements.

## CONFIDENTIALITY STATEMENT & PAYMENT INFORMATION

I hereby attest that I will not divulge the content of this examination, nor will I remove any examination materials, notes, or other unauthorized materials from the examination room. I understand that failure to comply with this attestation may result in invalidation of my grades and disqualification from future examinations. For those already certified by the Institute of Certified Management Accountants, failure to comply with the statement will be considered a violation of the Standards of Ethical Conduct for Practitioners of Management Accounting and Financial Management and could result in revocation of the certification.

I affirm that the statements on this application are correct and agree to abide by the Standards of Ethical Conduct.

Signature of Applicant: _____ Date: _____

☐ Check Enclosed (Make check payable in U.S. currency to Institute of Management Accountants, Inc.)
☐ Charge my credit card: ☐VISA ☐MasterCard ☐American Express ☐Discover

Credit Card Number: _____ Expiration Date: ____/____ MM/YY

**PLEASE COMPLETE BOTH SIDES** NOTE: PAYMENT IN FULL MUST ACCOMPANY REGISTRATION FORM - FEES SUBJECT TO CHANGE

**IMA** INSTITUTE OF MANAGEMENT ACCOUNTANTS *Advancing the Profession™*
10 Paragon Drive • Montvale, New Jersey 07645-1760 • www.imanet.org
(201) 573-9000 • (800) 638-4427 • Fax (201) 474-1600

1/06

# APPENDIX C
# ICMA CONTENT SPECIFICATION OUTLINES

The following pages consist of a reprint of the ICMA's Content Specification Outlines (CSOs) for Part 2, effective July 1, 2004.  Please use these CSOs as reference material only.  The ICMA's CSOs have been carefully analyzed and have been incorporated into 20 study units to provide systematic and rational coverage of exam topics.

We believe we provide comprehensive coverage of the subject matter tested on the revised CMA exam.  If, after taking the exam, you feel that certain topics, concepts, etc., tested were not covered or were inadequately covered, please call, fax, or e-mail us.  We do not want information about CMA questions, only information/feedback about our *CMA Review* system's coverage.

## Content Specification Outlines for the
## Certified Management Accountant (CMA)
## Examinations

The content specification outlines presented below represent the body of knowledge that will be covered on the CMA examinations.  The outlines may be changed in the future when new subject matter becomes part of the common body of knowledge.

Candidates for the CMA designation are required to take Parts 1, 2, 3, and 4.  Part 4, Business Applications, may only be taken <u>after</u> successful completion of Parts 1, 2, and 3.

Candidates are responsible for being informed on the most recent developments in the areas covered in the outlines.  This includes understanding of public pronouncements issued by accounting organizations as well as being up-to-date on recent developments reported in current accounting, financial and business periodicals.

The content specification outlines serve several purposes.  The outlines are intended to:

- Establish the foundation from which each examination will be developed.
- Provide a basis for consistent coverage on each examination.
- Communicate to interested parties more detail as to the content of each examination part.
- Assist candidates in their preparation for each examination.
- Provide information to those who offer courses designed to aid candidates in preparing for the examinations.

Important additional information about the content specification outlines and the examinations is listed below.

1. The coverage percentage given for each major topic within each examination part represents the relative weight given to that topic in an examination part.  The number of questions presented in each major topic area approximates this percentage.

2. Each examination will sample from the subject areas contained within each major topic area to meet the relative weight specifications.  No relative weights have been assigned to the subject areas within each major topic.  No inference should be made from the order in which the subject areas are listed or from the number of subject areas as to the relative weight or importance of any of the subjects.

3.    Each major topic within each examination part has been assigned a coverage level designating the depth and breadth of topic coverage, ranging from an introductory knowledge of a subject area (Level A) to a thorough understanding of and ability to apply the essentials of a subject area (Level C). Detailed explanations of the coverage levels and the skills expected of candidates are presented below.

4.    The topics for Parts 1, 2, and 3 have been selected to minimize the overlapping of subject areas among the examination parts. The topics within an examination part and the subject areas within topics may be combined in individual questions. Questions within Parts 1, 2, and 3 will only cover subject areas outlined in the respective content specifications. The exception is Part 4, Business Applications, which may include any of the subject areas tested in Parts 1, 2, and 3.

5.    With regard to Federal income taxation issues, candidates will be expected to understand the impact of income taxes when reporting and analyzing financial results. In addition, the tax code provisions that impact decisions (e.g., depreciation, interest, etc.) will be tested.

6.    Candidates for the CMA designation are expected to have a minimum level of business knowledge that transcends all examination parts. This minimum level would include knowledge of basic financial statements, time value of money concepts, and elementary statistics.

7.    Parts 1, 2, and 3 are 100% objective and consist of carefully constructed multiple-choice questions that test all levels of cognitive skills. Parts 1 and 3 are three-hour exams and contain 110 questions each. Part 2 is a four-hour exam and has 140 questions. A small number of the questions on each exam are being validated for future use and will not count in the final score.

8.    Part 4, Business Applications, consists of several essay questions and problems that are delivered in a computer-based format. Both written and quantitative responses will be required. Candidates will be expected to present written answers that are responsive to the question asked, presented in a logical manner, and demonstrate an appropriate understanding of the subject matter. It should be noted that candidates are expected to have working knowledge in the use of word processing and electronic spreadsheets.

9.    Ethical issues and considerations will be tested on Part 4, Business Applications. At least one question in this part will be devoted to an ethical situation presented in a business-oriented context. Candidates will be expected to evaluate the issues involved and make recommendations for the resolution of the situation.

In order to more clearly define the topical knowledge required by a candidate, varying levels of coverage for the treatment of major topics of the content specification outlines have been identified and defined. The cognitive skills that a successful candidate should possess and that should be tested on the examinations can be defined as follows:

*Knowledge:*    Ability to remember previously learned material such as specific facts, criteria, techniques, principles, and procedures (i.e., identify, define, list).

*Comprehension:*    Ability to grasp and interpret the meaning of material (i.e., classify, explain, distinguish between).

*Application:*    Ability to use learned material in new and concrete situations (i.e., demonstrate, predict, solve, modify, relate).

*Analysis:*    Ability to break down material into its component parts so that its organizational structure can be understood; ability to recognize causal relationships, discriminate between behaviors, and identify elements that are relevant to the validation of a judgment (i.e., differentiate, estimate, order).

**Synthesis:** Ability to put parts together to form a new whole or proposed set of operations; ability to relate ideas and formulate hypotheses (i.e., combine, formulate, revise).

**Evaluation:** Ability to judge the value of material for a given purpose on the basis of consistency, logical accuracy, and comparison to standards; ability to appraise judgments involved in the selection of a course of action (i.e., criticize, justify, conclude).

The three levels of coverage can be defined as follows:

**Level A:** Requiring the skill levels of knowledge and comprehension.

**Level B:** Requiring the skill levels of knowledge, comprehension, application, and analysis.

**Level C:** Requiring all six skill levels, knowledge, comprehension, application, analysis, synthesis, and evaluation.

The levels of coverage as they apply to each of the major topics of the Content Specification Outlines are shown on the following pages with each topic listing. The levels represent the manner in which topic areas are to be treated and represent ceilings, i.e., a topic area designated as Level C may contain requirements at the "A," "B," or "C" level, but a topic designated as Level B will not contain requirements at the "C" level.

# Part 2 – Management Accounting and Reporting

A. **Budget Preparation (15% - Level C)**

1. *Budgeting concepts*

   a. Operations and performance goals
   b. Characteristics of a successful budget process
   c. Resource allocation
   d. Other budgeting concepts

2. *Budget systems*

   a. Annual business plans (master budgets)
   b. Project budgeting
   c. Activity-based budgeting
   d. Zero-based budgeting
   e. Continuous (rolling) budgets
   f. Kaizen budgeting
   g. Flexible budgeting

3. *Annual profit plan and supporting schedules*

   a. Operational budgets
   b. Financial budgets
   c. Capital budgets
   d. Pro forma financial statements

B. **Cost Management (25% - Level C)**

1. *Terminology*

   a. Product versus period cost
   b. Manufacturing versus non-manufacturing
   c. Direct versus indirect
   d. Fixed versus variable

2. **Measurement concepts**

    a. Cost behavior and cost objects
    b. Actual/normal/standard costs
    c. Absorption (full) and variable (direct) costing
    d. Joint product and by-product costing

3. **Accumulation systems**

    a. Job order costing
    b. Process costing
    c. Activity-based costing
    d. Life-cycle costing
    e. Other costing methods

4. **Overhead costs**

    a. Fixed and variable overhead expenses
    b. Plant-wide versus departmental overhead
    c. Determination of allocation base
    d. Allocation of service department costs

C. **Information Management (15% - Level A)**

1. **Nature and purpose of an information system**

    a. Business information systems
    b. Transaction processing systems
    c. Management information systems

2. **Systems development and design**

    a. Systems development life cycle
    b. Cost benefit analysis

3. **Technology of information systems**

    a. Data communications, networks, and client/server systems
    b. Database management systems
    c. Decision support systems
    d. Artificial intelligence and expert systems
    e. Spreadsheets
    f. Internet and intranet

4. **Electronic commerce**

    a. Electronic data interchange
    b. Business-to-business
    c. Other e-commerce technologies

5. **Integrated enterprise-wide data model**

    a. Enterprise resource planning (ERP) systems
    b. Data warehousing and data mining

D. **Performance Measurement (20% - Level C)**

1. **Cost and variance measures**

    a. Comparison of actual to planned results
    b. Use of flexible budgets to analyze performance
    c. Management by exception
    d. Use of standard cost systems
    e. Analysis of variation from standard cost expectations

2. **Responsibility centers and reporting segments**

    a.   Types of responsibility centers
    b.   Transfer pricing models
    c.   Reporting of organizational segments

3. **Financial measures**

    a.   Product profitability analysis
    b.   Business unit profitability analysis
    c.   Customer profitability analysis
    d.   Return on investment
    e.   Residual income
    f.   Economic value added
    g.   Market value added
    h.   Investment base issues
    i.   Cash flow return on investment
    j.   Effect of international operations

4. **Balanced scorecard**

    a.   Critical success factors
    b.   Financial measures
    c.   Customer satisfaction measures
    d.   Internal business process measures
    e.   Innovation and learning measures
    f.   Effective use of a balanced scorecard

5. **Quality considerations**

    a.   Total quality management concepts and techniques
    b.   Techniques to analyze quality problems
    c.   Relationship between quality and productivity
    d.   Cost of quality analysis
    e.   Cost of design quality

E. **External Financial Reporting (25% - Level B)**

1. **Objectives of external financial reporting**

    a.   Information on resources and obligations
    b.   Comprehensive income information
    c.   Cash flow information

2. **Financial accounting fundamentals**

    a.   Accounting assumptions and conventions
    b.   Recognition and measurement concepts
    c.   Financial statement elements
    d.   Special topics

3. **Financial statements and statement users**

    a.   Statement of Cash Flow
    b.   Statement of Financial Position (balance sheet)
    c.   Statement of Earnings (income statement)
    d.   Users of financial statements
    e.   Needs of external users

4.  **Recognition, measurement, valuation, and disclosure**

    a.  Cash and marketable securities
    b.  Accounts receivable
    c.  Inventory
    d.  Investments
    e.  Property, plant, and equipment
    f.  Intangibles
    g.  Current liabilities
    h.  Long-term liabilities and bonds payable
    i.  Equity transactions and earnings per share
    j.  Revenues
    k.  Expenses
    l.  Comprehensive income
    m.  Segment reporting
    n.  Multinational considerations

5.  **The SEC and its reporting requirements**

    a.  Acts establishing the SEC and its power
    b.  SEC reporting requirements for public companies
    c.  SEC disclosure requirements for public companies
    d.  Provisions of Sarbanes-Oxley legislation

6.  **The annual report**

    a.  Audit services related to financial reporting
    b.  Management's responsibility for financial statements
    c.  Role of the audit committee/Board of directors
    d.  Independent auditor's report
    e.  Other components of the annual report

# APPENDIX D
# ICMA SUGGESTED READING LIST

The ICMA suggested reading list for that follows is reproduced to give you an overview of the scope of Part 2. You will not have the time to study these texts. Our *CMA Review* system is complete and thorough and is designed to maximize your study time. For all four parts, candidates are expected to stay up-to-date by reading articles from journals, newspapers, and professional publications.

## Part 2 – Management Accounting and Reporting

### Budget Preparation
Blocher, Edward J., Chen, Kung, H., Cokins, Gary, and Lin, Thomas W., *Cost Management: A Strategic Emphasis*, 3rd edition, Irwin/McGraw Hill, New York, NY 2005, or

Horngren, Charles T., Foster, George, and Datar, Srikant M., *Cost Accounting*, 12th edition, Prentice-Hall Inc., Upper Saddle River, NJ, 2006.

### Cost Management
Blocher, Edward J., Chen, Kung, H., Cokins, Gary, and Lin, Thomas W., *Cost Management: A Strategic Emphasis*, 3rd edition, Irwin/McGraw Hill, New York, NY 2005, or

Horngren, Charles T., Foster, George, and Datar, Srikant M., *Cost Accounting*, 12th edition, Prentice-Hall Inc., Upper Saddle River, NJ, 2006.

### Information Management
Moscove, Stephen A., Simkin, Mark G., and Bagranoff, Nancy A., *Core Concepts of Accounting Information Systems*, 9th edition, John Wiley & Sons Inc., New York, NY, 2004, or

Bodnar, George H., Hopwood, William S., *Accounting Information Systems*, 9th edition, Prentice Hall, Upper Saddle River, NJ, 2004.

O'Brien, James A., *Introduction to Information Systems*, 12th edition, Irwin/McGraw-Hill Publishers, Barr Ridge, IL, 2005.

### Performance Management
Blocher, Edward J., Chen, Kung, H., Cokins, Gary, and Lin, Thomas W., *Cost Management: A Strategic Emphasis*, 3rd edition, Irwin/McGraw Hill, New York, NY 2005 or

Horngren, Charles T., Foster, George, and Datar, Srikant M., *Cost Accounting*, 12th edition, Prentice-Hall Inc., Upper Saddle River, NJ, 2006.

Evans, James R., Lindsay, William M., *The Management and Control of Quality*, 6th edition, South-Western, Cincinnati, OH, 2005.

### External Financial Reporting
Kieso, Donald E., Warfield, Terry D., and Weygandt, Jerry J., *Intermediate Accounting*, 12th edition, John Wiley & Sons, New York, NY, 2006, or

Nikolai, Loren A., and Bazley, John D., *Intermediate Accounting*, 9th edition, South-Western Publishing Company, Boston, MA, 2003, or

Spiceland, J. David, Sepe, James F., Tomassini, Lawrence A., *Intermediate Accounting*, 3rd edition, McGraw-Hill/Irwin, New York, NY, 2004.

Larsen, E. John, *Modern Advanced Accounting*, 10th edition, McGraw-Hill\Irwin Book Co., New York, NY, 2006.

Afterman, Allan B., *SEC Regulation of Public Companies*, Prentice-Hall Inc., Upper Saddle River, NJ, 1995.

*IAS 2006, Interpretation and Application of International Accounting and Financial Reporting Standards*, Epstein, Barry J. Mirza, Abbas Ali, John Wiley & Sons, New York, NY, 2006.

Arens, Alvin A., Elders, Randal J., and Beasley, Mark, *Auditing and Assurance Services: An Integrated Approach*, 11th edition, Prentice-Hall Inc., Upper Saddle River, NJ, 2006.

# APPENDIX E
# TYPES AND LEVELS OF EXAM QUESTIONS

The following is an excerpt reprinted from the ICMA's Resource Guide for the Revised CMA exam, July 2004.

## TYPES OF EXAM QUESTIONS

All items within the CMA parts 1, 2, and 3 are of the 4-option multiple-choice type, with one and only one correct answer for each question. There are, however, a number of variations on this type of item used in the CMA exams. In the examples below, the term "stem" refers to all the information that precedes the answer options or alternatives.

### Closed Stem Item

This item type is characterized by a stem that is a complete sentence which concludes with a question mark. The options may be complete or incomplete sentences.

Example:

Which one of the following would have the effect of increasing the working capital of a firm?

a.  Cash payment of payroll taxes payable.
b.  Cash collection of accounts receivable.
c.  The purchase of a new plant, financed by a 20-year mortgage.
d.  Refinancing a short-term note with a 2-year note.

Key = d

### Sentence Completion Item

This type of item is characterized by a stem that is an incomplete sentence. The options represent conclusions to that sentence.

Example:

If a product's elasticity coefficient is 2.0, this means the demand is

a.  perfectly elastic.
b.  elastic.
c.  inelastic.
d.  perfectly inelastic.

Key = b

## Except Format

This type of item is employed when you are required to select the option that does not "fit." In this case, three of the options will fit or be defined by the stem, and one option (the correct option) will not fit. A variation on this type of question is to use the word **not** instead of **except** in the stem, in the form of "Which one of the following is **not**...".

Example:

All of the following are considered tangible assets **except**

a. real estate.
b. copyrights.
c. prepaid taxes.
d. accounts receivable.

Key = b

## Most/Least/Best Format

This type of item requires you to select an option which is either better or worse than the others. In all cases, the correct answer represents the collective judgment of a group of experts within the field.

Example #1:

Which one of the following **best** describes a production budget?

a. It is based on required direct labor hours.
b. It includes required material purchases.
c. It is based on desired ending inventory and sales forecasts.
d. It is an aggregate of the monetary details of the operating budget.

Key = c

Example #2:

Which one of the following is **least** likely to help an organization overcome communication problems between the Accounting Department and other departments?

a. Job rotation.
b. Cross-functional teams.
c. Written policies and procedures.
d. Performance appraisals.

Key = d

All items within the CMA part 4 are written-response questions, which will be delivered via computer at Prometric Testing Centers in the same manner as the other exam parts. For essay questions that require a purely written answer, you will have a box in which to type your response. For problems that require quantitative responses, a form resembling a spreadsheet will be available along with a free-form area to present your calculations.

## QUESTION LEVELS

In addition to the variety of item formats previously described, the CMA exams present test items at varying cognitive levels. These levels range from questions that require a recall of material to questions that require a sophisticated understanding such that you must apply your knowledge to a novel situation, or judge the value of information as it may apply to a particular scenario. A description of each of these levels, along with sample questions, appear below. The cognitive level required for each major topic area of the CMA exams is shown in the Topic/Resource outline.

### Level A

This cognitive level represents the "lowest" or most basic level, and includes items that require the recall of facts and the recognition of principles. This level includes the categories of knowledge and comprehension.

> **Knowledge:** This is the lowest level of learning. Items in this category are those that require the recall of ideas, material, or phenomena related to the topic of interest. In these questions, you will be asked to define, identify, and select information.
>
> Example:
>
> A market situation where a small number of sellers comprise an entire industry is known as
>
> a.   a natural monopoly.
> b.   monopolistic competition.
> c.   an oligopoly.
> d.   pure competition.
>
> Key = c

To correctly respond to the item above, you must recall the textbook definition of an oligopoly.

> **Comprehension:** Items in this category require you to grasp the meaning of the material presented in some novel way. A question testing for comprehension describes some principle or fact in words different from those used in textbooks, and often uses a situation as a way to present the idea. In order to answer the item correctly, you must recognize the principle demonstrated in the problem; memory alone will not be sufficient for identifying the correct answer.
>
> Example:
>
> Social legislation, such as the Occupational Safety and Health Act (OSHA) and the Environmental Protection Act (EPA), is frequently criticized for being inefficient because the agencies
>
> a.   use flexible rather than rigid standards.
> b.   rely heavily on the free market to allocate resources.
> c.   rarely consider the marginal benefits relative to the marginal costs.
> d.   enforce their policies too leniently.
>
> Key = c

In order to answer this item correctly, you must know something about the issues or principles in connection with OSHA and the EPA. Other questions dealing with this level of testing are those that ask you to identify an option which best explains, illustrates, or provides an example of the concept in question.

## Level B

This cognitive level includes items that test for the application of material to novel situations and the ability to analyze or break down information into its component parts. Items that require application or analysis are included in this level.

**Application:** Items in this category measure understanding of ideas or content to a point where you can apply that understanding to an entirely new situation. The objective of these items is to test whether you can use the knowledge in an appropriate manner in a real-life situation.

Example:

The balance sheet for Miller Industries shows the following.

| | |
|---|---|
| Cash | $ 8,000,000 |
| Accounts Receivable | 13,500,000 |
| Inventory | 7,800,000 |
| Prepaid Expenses | 245,000 |
| Property, Plant, & Equipment | 4,700,000 |

Based on this information, what are the Total Current Assets for this firm?

a. $21,500,000
b. $29,300,000
c. $29,545,000
d. $34,245,000

Key = c

Rather than rely on memory or comprehension alone, the situation presented in this item requires you to draw on your knowledge of the calculation of Total Current Assets and apply that knowledge to the particular data presented in the problem. Other items dealing with this level of testing might ask you to identify a specific situation requiring a certain course of action, or the most appropriate procedure or steps to apply to a particular problem.

**Analysis:** Analysis involves the ability to break down material into its component parts so that its organizational structure can be understood. It involves the ability to recognize parts, as well as the relationships between those parts, and to recognize the principles involved. Items in this category ask you to differentiate, discriminate, distinguish, infer, and determine the relevancy of data.

Example:

A firm is considering the implementation of a lock-box collection system at a cost of $80,000 per year. Annual sales are $90 million, and the lock-box system will reduce collection time by 3 days. The firm currently is in debt for $3,000,000. If the firm can invest the funds designated for the lock-box at 8%, should it use the lock-box system? Assume a 360-day year.

a. Yes, it will produce a savings of $140,000 per year.
b. Yes, it will produce a savings of $60,000 per year.
c. No, it will produce a loss of $20,000 per year.
d. No, it will produce a loss of $60,000 per year.

Key = c

In this item, you are presented with a novel situation, and asked to identify the data that are relevant to the problem at hand, which in this case involves the determination of the savings or loss of implementing a lock-box type of collection system. You are required to apply principles to determine savings or loss, and then to make an analysis of the outcomes of the alternative courses of action.

## Level C

This cognitive level is considered the "highest" or most challenging level, and includes items that require you to evaluate information.

> **<u>Evaluation</u>:** Items in this category are those that require the ability to judge the value of material for a given purpose, based on definite criteria. These questions include those that ask you to appraise, conclude, support, compare, contrast, interpret, and summarize information.
>
> Example:
>
> A home services organization has been using the straight-line depreciation method for calculating the depreciation expenses of its equipment. Based on recently acquired information, the firm's assistant controller has altered the estimated useful lives of the equipment. The corresponding changes in depreciation result in a change from a small profit for the year to a loss. The assistant controller is asked by the controller to reduce by half the total depreciation expense for the current year. Believing he is faced with an ethical conflict, the assistant controller reports the problem to the Board of Directors. In accordance with **Statements on Management Accounting Number 1C (SMA 1C) (revised)**, "Standards of Ethical Conduct for Members," which one of the following is the correct evaluation of the assistant controller's action?
>
> a. The assistant controller's action was appropriate as an immediate step.
> b. The assistant controller's action would have been appropriate only if other alternatives had first been tried.
> c. The assistant controller's action was not appropriate under any circumstances.
> d. Not enough information has been given to evaluate the assistant controller's action.
>
> Key = b

The situation presented in this item requires you to evaluate the course of action that the assistant controller has taken. Option b is the correct option. While the assistant controller's action is appropriate, the situation may be resolved by less drastic means first. You are asked to make a judgment on the appropriateness of the actions to the situation described, and answer the question on the basis of this information.

# INDEX

**CPE EQE EA CIA CMA/CFM CPA**

## COMPLETE GLEIM CPA SYSTEM

All 4 sections, including Gleim Online, books*, *Test Prep CD-Rom*, audio cds, plus bonus book bag.

☐ $989.95

Also available by exam section @ $274.95 (does not include book bag).

*Fifth book: *CPA Review: A System for Success*

$_____

## COMPLETE GLEIM CMA/CFM SYSTEM for the UNCHANGED EXAM

Includes: Gleim Online, books, *Test Prep CD-Rom*, audio cds, plus bonus book bag.

☐ CMA ~~$681.95~~ $340.98     ☐ CFM ~~$681.95~~ $340.98     ☐ CMA/CFM ~~$855.95~~ $427.98

Also available by exam part @ $198.95 (does not include book bag).

$_____

## COMPLETE GLEIM CMA SYSTEM for the "REORGANIZED" EXAM

Includes: Gleim Online, books, *Test Prep CD-Rom*, audio cds, plus bonus book bag.

☐ CMA $739.95     ☐ CMA/CFM $913.95

Also available by exam part @ $213.95 (does not include book bag).

$_____

## COMPLETE GLEIM CIA SYSTEM

Includes: Gleim Online, books, *Test Prep CD-Rom*, audio cds, plus bonus book bag.

☐ $824.95

Also available by exam part @ $224.95 (does not include book bag).

$_____

## GLEIM EA REVIEW SYSTEM

Includes: Gleim Online, books, and *Test Prep CD-Rom*.
Also available by exam part @ $185.95 (does not include book bag).

☐ $529.95

$_____

## "THE GLEIM SERIES" EXAM QUESTIONS AND EXPLANATIONS

Includes: 5 books and *Test Prep CD-Rom*.
Also available by part @ $29.95.

☐ $112.25

## GLEIM Paper and Pencil CPE

$200 each   ☐ Financial Acctg   ☐ Auditing   ☐ Federal Tax

**Visit** gleim.com/CPE for Online CPE courses and course catalog.

$_____

Contact
**GLEIM PUBLICATIONS**
for further assistance:

**gleim.com**
**(800) 874-5346**
**sales@gleim.com**

**SUBTOTAL** $_____

Complete your
order on the
next page

# GLEIM PUBLICATIONS, INC.

## P. O. Box 12848    Gainesville, FL 32604

TOLL FREE:    (888) 874-5346

LOCAL:    (352) 375-0772

FAX:    (888) 375-6940 (toll free)

INTERNET    gleim.com

E-MAIL:    sales@gleim.com

Customer service is available (Eastern Time):

8:00 a.m. - 7:00 p.m., Mon. - Fri.

9:00 a.m. - 2:00 p.m., Saturday

Please have your credit card ready,

or save time by ordering online!

| | |
|---|---|
| **SUBTOTAL** (from previous page) | $_____ |
| Add applicable sales tax for shipments within Florida. | _____ |
| Shipping (nonrefundable) | 25.00 |
| **TOTAL** | $_____ |

Fax or write for prices/instructions on shipments outside the 48 contiguous states, or simply order online.

NAME   (please print) _____

ADDRESS _____ Apt. _____

(street address required for UPS)

CITY _____ STATE _____ ZIP _____

_____ MC/VISA/DISC _____ Check/M.O.    Daytime Telephone (____) _____

Credit Card No. _____ - _____ - _____ - _____

Exp. _____ / _____    Signature _____

Month / Year

E-mail address _____

1. We process and ship orders daily, within one business day over 98.8% of the time. Call by 3:00 pm for same day service.

2. Please PHOTOCOPY this order form for others.

3. No CODs. Orders from individuals must be prepaid.

4. Gleim Publications, Inc. guarantees the immediate refund of all resalable texts and unopened software and audios if returned within 30 days. Applies only to items purchased direct from Gleim Publications, Inc. Our shipping charge is nonrefundable.

5. Components of specially priced package deals are nonrefundable.

Prices subject to change without notice.

07/26/06

For updates and other important information, visit our website.

GLEIM
KNOWLEDGE
TRANSFER
SYSTEMS

## gleim.com

Please forward your suggestions, corrections, and comments concerning typographical errors, etc., to **Irvin N. Gleim • c/o Gleim Publications, Inc. • P.O. Box 12848 • University Station • Gainesville, Florida • 32604.** Please include your name and address so we can properly thank you for your interest.

1. _____

2. _____

3. _____

4. _____

5. _____

6. _____

7. _____

8. _____

9. _____

10. _____

11. _____

12. _____

13. _____

14. _____

15. _____

16. _____

17. _____

18. _____

Remember, for superior service:  <u>Mail</u>, <u>e-mail</u>, or <u>fax</u> questions about our books or software.
<u>Telephone</u> questions about orders, prices, shipments, or payments.

Name: _____

Address: _____

City/State/Zip: _____

Telephone:  Home: _____  Work: _____  Fax: _____

E-mail: _____